RAND McNALLY

Volume 1: Guide
137th Edition

Commercial
Atlas & Marketing Guide
2006

The First Place to Look for Up-to-Date Business Planning Data!

Population, Economic, and Geographic Data for more than 120,000 U.S. places — complete with large-scale, detailed maps.

Rand McNally 2006 Commercial Atlas & Marketing Guide
Copyright ©2006 by Rand McNally & Company
All Rights Reserved
Published in the USA. Printed in Canada.

How to Order the Commercial Atlas & Marketing Guide

To order the Rand McNally 2006 Commercial Atlas & Marketing Guide, please contact Rand McNally at 1-800-678-7263.

The information in this Atlas was collected directly from the sources cited or from other sources considered reliable. The Atlas is published for general reference and not as a substitute for independent verification by users of this information when circumstances warrant. While care and diligence have been used in its preparation, the Publisher does not guarantee the accuracy of the information.

Contents | Volume 1

Volume 2 Contents on next page

Contents | Volume 2

Preface

Through the *Commercial Atlas & Marketing Guide*, Rand McNally brings together the most current economic and geographic information. With maps, tables and charts, this *Atlas* combines maximum demographic coverage of the United States with an authoritative interpretation of business data.

The *Commercial Atlas & Marketing Guide* is organized into two volumes. Volume 1 includes an Introduction to the Atlas, Economic Data section, Population Data section and Map section. Volume 2 includes Statistics by State and a State Index that includes references to the state maps in Volume 1.

The Introduction to the Atlas includes a Table of Contents and a Glossary of Terms that provides definitions of terms and concepts used throughout the atlas.

The Economic section describes business activity for states, counties, cities, Trading Areas, Metropolitan Statistical Areas (MSAs), and the latest Core Based Statistical Areas (CBSAs) announced by the Office of Management and Budget (OMB) in 2003.

The Population section provides 2000 Census figures and current population estimates for states, counties, Metropolitan Statistical Areas, Core Based Statistical Areas, and Ranally Metro Areas (RMAs). In addition, projected population figures for Metropolitan Statistical Areas, Core Based Statistical Areas, and counties are presented.

The Maps section includes maps of Minor Civil Divisions, and maps of the fifty states and the District of Columbia. The state map pages also include detailed inset maps for important cities.

The State Statistics section includes a list of Principal Places ranked by population, and a Business Data table that includes all the counties in each state. The State Index is arranged alphabetically by state. This section provides location information and statistics for virtually all inhabited places in the United States. In fact, over 120,000 places (including townships and counties) are described in the State Index. Of these, more than 41,000 have populations that are not available through the U.S. Census Bureau and are provided exclusively by Rand McNally.

Once again, Rand McNally is proud to present the *Commercial Atlas and Marketing Guide,* the oldest annually published reference atlas in existence. This edition of the *Commercial Atlas & Marketing Guide* continues to represent Rand McNally's unique background in research, mapmaking, and publishing.

Glossary of Terms

Annexation Population: Population of a place following annexation (expansion of boundary) since the 2000 Census. In the State Index, this population figure is preceded by the symbol Ⓐ.

Apparel Store Sales*: Sales for establishments engaged primarily in selling new clothing and related articles. It includes men's and women's clothing stores, family and children's clothing stores, shoe stores and other clothing and clothing accessories stores. Not included are apparel and accessories sales made in department or general merchandise stores, or custom tailoring.

Bank: In the State Index, places with one or more full-service banks are indicated with a Ⓢ symbol. The source of this information is Thomson Financial Publishing.

Basic Trading Area: An area surrounding at least one Basic Trading Center. Each Basic Trading Area is named after one or more cities which are its Basic Trading Centers. All Basic Trading Area boundaries follow county lines and are drawn to include the county or counties whose residents make the bulk of their shopping goods purchases in the area's Basic Trading Center or its suburbs. Some Basic Trading Areas have two or more Basic Trading Centers, generally because residents may conveniently shop at either one.

Basic Trading Center: A city which serves as a center for shopping goods purchases for the surrounding area. Shopping goods are those retail items a shopper ordinarily travels some distance to purchase and for which he or she compares qualities, styles and prices before buying. Most sales of shopping goods are made through general merchandise or apparel stores. Basic Trading Centers also serve their surroundings with various specialized services, such as medical care, entertainment, higher education and a daily newspaper.

Census Designated Place (CDP): A geographic entity defined by the U.S. Census Bureau that serves as the statistical counterpart of an incorporated place for the purpose of presenting census data. CDPs are defined for areas with concentrations of population, housing and commercial structures that are identifiable by name, but are not located within incorporated places. A CDP may contain one or more unincorporated places within its established boundaries. Census designated places are specifically identified in the State Indexes. CDPs with the designation "Census Area Only" are those that Rand McNally has determined to be not locally recognized.

Census Population: Official U.S. Census Bureau population resulting from the 2000 Population and Housing Census of the United States. *See also: Final Census Population, Revised Census Population, and Special Census Population.*

Combined Statistical Area (CSA): A geographic area consisting of two or more adjacent Core Based Statistical Areas (CBSAs) with a high degree of employment interchange. *See also: Core Based Statistical Area.*

Consolidated Metropolitan Statistical Area (CMSA): Contains two or more Primary Metropolitan Statistical Areas (PMSAs) that are considered as a single unit for statistical purposes due to their economic and social integration. To qualify as a CMSA, the metropolitan area as a whole must have a population of at least one million.

Core Based Statistical Area (CBSA): A metropolitan area consisting of the county or counties associated with an urban core having a population of at least 10,000, plus adjacent counties having a high degree of social and economic integration with the core as measured through commuting ties. Counties or county equivalents form the building blocks for CBSAs for the entire U.S. CBSA definitions were announced by the Office of Management and Budget (OMB) effective June 6, 2003, and were updated November, 2004. CBSAs are more current definitions of metropolitan areas than the older Metropolitan Statistical Areas (MSAs) as defined and revised by the OMB through June 30, 1999. The *Commercial Atlas and Marketing Guide* provides data on both CBSAs and MSAs. *See also: Metropolitan Core Based Statistical Area; Micropolitan Core Based Statistical Area; Combined Statistical Area; Metropolitan Statistical Area.*

County: The primary political subdivision of every state except Alaska and Louisiana. The total number of counties in each state is specified in the Counties: Population/Income/Sales table on pages 52-73, and also in the State Statistics section for each state in Volume 2.

Most places in the U.S. are included within a county. Areas not included in any county are Alaska, the District of Columbia and certain independent cities.

A number of counties do not function as political entities (in Connecticut and Rhode Island, for example). Although there are no county officials or functions, the name and boundaries of each county are well known locally.

In Louisiana, county-level subdivisions are called parishes. In Alaska, the *Commercial Atlas & Marketing Guide* recognizes Alaska's census areas and boroughs as county equivalents.

County Subdivision: This term is used by the U.S. Census Bureau as a generic name for primary divisions of counties and statistically equivalent areas. There are two main categories of County Subdivisions:

- Those that are delineated by the Census Bureau in cooperation with state and local governments for data presentation purposes. The census-only divisions are called "Census County Divisions" (CCDs) or "Census Subareas" in Alaska.

- Those that have an intrinsic governmental or administrative function. These are referred to as "Minor Civil Divisions" (MCDs). They include an impressive and diverse mixture of legal entities with different governmental and administrative functions, the most important of which are townships.

There is enormous variability in terms of the importance, function and local recognition of townships. In some states, mostly located in New England, townships are of such importance that they essentially function as incorporated places. At the other extreme, there are states in which the townships have virtually no governmental significance and may be almost unknown to local residents.

Many MCD states include MCDs other than townships, including boroughs, gores and precincts. In addition, MCD states may contain incorporated places that are independent of any MCD and "unorganized territories" that are not part of an MCD or an independent incorporated place.

The *Commercial Atlas* contains township data for a subset of MCD states that can be broadly grouped into two main categories.

Northeastern Group (9 states: CT, ME, MA, NH, NJ, NY, PA, RI, VT). In these states, counties are divided into townships or "towns". Other types of MCDs, as well as unorganized territories, may also occur. In these states, townships are important administratively and are well known locally. In the six New England states (CT, ME, MA, NH, RI, VT) the "towns" are much more important in local life than the counties themselves. Moreover, these "towns" and townships possess most or all of the powers exercised by incorporated places.

In most states outside of the Northeast, a "town" is a built-up community, usually smaller than a city but larger than a village. In many Northeastern states, however, a "town" is a fairly large area (15 square miles or even larger), containing a central village having the same name as the "town" and possibly other villages, smaller localities and farms. Only rarely do the villages within the "town" have a separate corporate status. Such "towns" come closer to the townships found in the Midwest than the incorporated places known as "towns" in other states.

Because of this, the Census Bureau does not consider these "towns" to be incorporated places. The *Commercial Atlas* follows this practice. "Towns" in New England and New York are listed in the State Indexes but are not identified as incorporated places.

In Pennsylvania and New Jersey, townships have much the same character as "towns" in New England and New York. Both these states also have incorporated cities and numerous incorporated boroughs that are similar to villages in other states.

The State Indexes for the Northeastern states include entries for the "towns" and townships with active governments as recognized by the U.S. Census of Governments. The indexes also indicate the "town" or township in which each indexed place is located. Each of these indexes has a head note describing the Minor Civil Divisions in the state.

Great Lakes Group (5 states: IL, IN, MI, OH, WI). In these states, as in most of the Midwest, most counties are divided

---

* Estimates for economic activity in this edition of the *Atlas* are based on data from the U.S. Census Bureau's 1997 Economic Census and utilize the North American Industry Classification System (NAICS); estimates from editions of the *Atlas* before 2001 are based on census data using the 1987 Standard Industrial Classification (SIC) system. Trade statistics are not directly comparable between systems. Consult U.S. Census Bureau documentation for further information.

into townships. However, these divisions are considerably less significant administratively and are less well known than in the Northeast. Though they may possess legal status, they are usually not thought of locally as "incorporated". One exception is Wisconsin, where townships do retain much local importance and are officially called "towns" just as in New England.

The relationship between townships and incorporated places is variable among and even within these states. Larger places are generally independent of any township, while smaller places often remain within the township for governmental purposes.

For the five Great Lake states, the State Indexes list the townships with active governments as recognized by the U.S. Census of Governments. For Michigan, Ohio and Wisconsin, location by township is provided for each place. Each of these indexes has a head note describing the Minor Civil Divisions in the state.

The remaining states represent a mixture of conditions. Some are CCD-only states where townships and other MCDs do not exist. These include many of the Western, Southwestern and Southeastern states. In other cases MCDs may exist but have little local significance governmentally or do not figure prominently in local knowledge. The *Commercial Atlas* does not include township data for such states.

Cross-References and Alternate Names: Cities and towns that are known by more than one name (e.g. places whose post office name differs from their corporate name, or the name used by a railroad serving them) are shown in the State Indexes under all such names.

Disincorporated Place: A place that has lost its corporate status and no longer functions as a legal municipality.

Disposable Income (DI): Represents an estimate of a household's purchasing power or after-tax income. The proportion of household income left after taxes is estimated from special studies conducted by the Census Bureau to simulate household taxes. Four types of taxes are deducted: Federal individual income taxes, State individual income taxes, FICA (Social Security) and Federal retirement payroll taxes, and property taxes for owner-occupied housing.

Duplicated Name: A place name representing two or more places located in the same state. All such places are distinguished in the State Indexes by indicating the county in which each place is located.

Estimated Population: Population estimates as of 7/1/05 are available for all counties, all populated places with a population of more than 20,000 people and selected places with fewer than 20,000 people. The source of these population estimates is Devonshire Associates Ltd. and Scan/US, Inc. In the State Index, these population figures are preceded by the symbol ◆. *See also: Rand McNally Population Estimates for Unincorporated Places.*

Final Census Population: 2000 Census population of a place. In the State Indexes, this population figure is preceded by the symbol ©.

FIPS (Federal Information Processing Standards) Place Code: County and state codes established by the federal government for the purpose of standardizing the coding of statistical information made available through various reference sources.

Food Store Sales*: Sales for establishments selling food and beverages primarily for home consumption. Not included are sales for establishments primarily selling items prepared on premises, such as bakeries.

Furniture, Home Furnishings and Appliance Store Sales*: Sales for establishments selling furniture and home furnishings, plus electronics and appliances. Not included are sales from custom manufacturing.

General Merchandise Store Sales*: Sales from department stores, general merchandise stores, warehouse clubs, and superstores.

Health, Drug and Personal Care Sales*: Total sales for establishments primarily engaged in the sale of prescription and nonprescription drugs, cosmetics and toiletries, optical goods, food (health) supplements, and other health and personal care products.

Household: A household consists of all persons occupying a single housing unit (a house, apartment, room or group of rooms) whether related or not. Persons residing in institutions, college dormitories or military barracks are living in group quarters rather than within households and are not included in household counts.

Incorporated Place: A place which has met the various legal requirements for its respective state for incorporation as a municipality. The rules for incorporation vary widely from state to state; some states have only a few incorporated places, while others have a great many. The *Commercial Atlas and Marketing Guide* follows the same standards in determining which places are incorporated as are used by the U.S. Census Bureau. Incorporated places are specifically identified in the State Indexes.

Generally speaking, incorporated places are the only localities that have official legal boundaries.

Places incorporated since 2000 have the year of incorporation specified by a date after the incorporation symbol.

Census populations are available for all incorporated places. For places incorporated since the 2000 Census, population figures are estimates, usually for the date of incorporation. Though the Census was taken as of April 1, 2000, usually it did not report separately any place incorporated after January 1, 2000.

See also: Unincorporated Place.

Independent City: These cities are administered independently of any adjoining county, and have the status of separate counties. The term is commonly used to refer to Baltimore, MD; St. Louis, MO; Carson City, NV; and 39 cities in Virginia. In the cases of Baltimore and St. Louis, there is also a Baltimore County, MD and a St. Louis County, MO (each separate from the city).

All of the larger cities in Virginia are independent cities. Users of statistics may find it difficult to treat cities as separate units in this one state, preferring to combine the cities with an adjoining county. A list of such combinations is given in a footnote to the County Business Data table for Virginia, which is located in Volume 2 of the *Commercial Atlas & Marketing Guide.*

In the State Index, the name of each independent city is followed by "Independent City".

Major Trading Area: An area consisting of two or more Basic Trading Areas. A Major Trading Area's boundaries follow the boundaries of its Basic Trading Areas. Each Major Trading Area is named after one or more cities which are its Major Trading Centers.

Major Trading Center: A city within a Major Trading Area that serves as one of the trading area's primary centers of wholesaling, distribution, banking, and specialized services such as advertising.

Map Key: Index to the location of a place on the appropriate state map.

Market Ability Index (MAI): A measure of a market's potential, expressed as a percentage of the U.S. total. It is calculated by multiplying .5 times the percent of the total Disposable Income, .3 times the percent of Total Retail Sales, and .2 times the percent of Total Population. The sum of these weighted percents is the Market Ability Index.

Median Household Income: This figure divides the Disposable Income distribution into two equal parts with one-half of the households above it, the other half below it.

Metropolitan Area: A large urban center that includes the central city, its suburbs, and the satellite communities whose economic and social life is tied to the city.

Metropolitan Core Based Statistical Area: A Core Based Statistical Area (CBSA) associated with at least one urban core having a population of at least 50,000. The Metropolitan Core Based Statistical Area comprises the central county or counties containing the core, plus adjacent counties having a high degree of social and economic integration with the core as measured through commuting ties. *See also: Core Based Statistical Area; Micropolitan Core Based Statistical Area.*

Metropolitan Statistical Area (MSA): A metropolitan area as defined and revised by the Office of Management and Budget (OMB) through June 30, 1999. An area qualifies for recognition as a Metropolitan Statistical Area in one of two ways: the area has (1) a city of at least 50,000 population, or (2) an urbanized area of at least 50,000 with a total metropolitan population of at least 100,000. MSAs are defined in terms of entire counties, except in the six New England states (Connecticut, Maine, Massachusetts, New Hampshire, Rhode Island and Vermont), where they are defined in terms of cities and towns. In addition to the county containing the main city, an MSA may include counties having strong economic and social ties to the central county. *See also: Core Based Statistical Area.*

Micropolitan Core Based Statistical Area: A Core Based Statistical Area (CBSA) associated with at least one urban core having a population of at least 10,000 but less than 50,000. The Micropolitan Core Based Statistical Area comprises the central county or counties containing the core, plus adjacent counties having a high degree of social and economic integration with the core as measured through commuting ties. *See also: Core Based Statistical Area; Metropolitan Core Based Statistical Area.*

Military Installation: All important Army, Navy, Marine Corps, and Air Force bases and other establishments are shown on the Major Military Installations map on pages 34-35. The map also includes Coast Guard stations, but excludes recruiting stations.

Minor Civil Division: *See County Subdivision.*

New England City and Town Area (NECTA): A metropolitan area in New England conceptually similar to a Core Based Statistical Area but based on cities and towns rather than counties. NECTAs are defined using the same criteria as Metropolitan and Micropolitan Core Based Statistical Areas. *See also: Core Based Statistical Area; Metropolitan Core Based Statistical Area; Micropolitan Core Based Statistical Area.*

New England County Metropolitan Area (NECMA): A NECMA provides county-based data for metropolitan areas in Connecticut, Maine, Massachusetts, New Hampshire, Rhode Island and Vermont. Because MSAs for these states are

---

* Estimates for economic activity in this edition of the *Atlas* are based on data from the U.S. Census Bureau's 1997 Economic Census and utilize the North American Industry Classification System (NAICS); estimates from editions of the *Atlas* before 2001 are based on census data using the 1987 Standard Industrial Classification (SIC) system. Trade statistics are not directly comparable between systems. Consult U.S. Census Bureau documentation for further information.

defined in terms of cities and towns rather than by county, the NECMA offers data consistent with those for MSAs throughout the rest of the country.

Passenger Car Registrations: The total number of non-commercial automobiles registered.

Per Capita Income: Average income per person; arrived at by dividing the Disposable Income by the total population.

Place incorporated in recent years: A place that has been incorporated in recent years is shown in the State Index with the year of incorporation noted.

Place indicated as "pop included with" another place: Any place listed in the State Index with the "pop included with" designation is within the generally accepted limits of another place, and the population is included in the figure for that place.

Place listed as "rural": Any place listed in the State Index with the "rural" designation is an open-country locality with a locally recognized name, although no concentrated area of settlement exists and the population is scattered over a wide area. Populations are not available for these places.

Population: The total number of people living in an area. Populations for all counties, townships, and many places are provided by the U.S. Census Bureau. Annual population estimates for important places are provided by Devonshire Associates Ltd. and Scan/US, Inc. Populations are estimated by Rand McNally for unincorporated places that are not provided by the U.S. Census Bureau. Population includes people living in group quarters such as colleges, plus permanently assigned armed forces, but generally excludes tourists and transients unless otherwise stated. *See also: Final Census Population, Estimated Population, Rand McNally Population Estimates for Unincorporated Places, Revised Census Population, and Special Census Population.*

Population Change: The increase or decrease in population, determined by comparing the population of a place at one point in time to the population of the place at a second point in time. The amount of change is expressed as a percentage (gain or loss) from the earlier population.

Population Projection: The projected total number of people that will be living in an area at the beginning of the stated year.

Post Office: A facility maintained by the U.S. Postal Service for the purpose of processing and distributing mail. In the State Index, all places that have a Post Office, Branch Post Office, Community Post Office, or Postal Station are identified with a special symbol **P**. If a place does not have its own post office, it may or may not be recognized as a place (an acceptable "last line") according to the Postal Service. If a place is not an acceptable last line, then the index entry indicates the name of the post office to which its mail should be addressed. For example, the index entry for Tinyplace, AL shows "mail Someplace **Z**12345". In this example, Someplace is an acceptable last line on an envelope, while Tinyplace is not. For places indicated as "pop included with" another place, if no mailing point is stated, the mailing point is the same as that for the incorporated place in which it is included.

Previous Census Population: 1990 Census population of a place. In the State Indexes, this population figure is preceded by the symbol Ⓟ.

Primary Metropolitan Statistical Area (PMSA): Any metropolitan area which is a component of a Consolidated Metropolitan Statistical Area.

Principal Business Center: A city of significant economic importance within its region or state based on a number of criteria, including population, total retail sales volume, shopping goods volume, volume of wholesaling, the number of headquarters of major corporations, banking activity and hospital facilities. Another important factor is circulation statistics for locally published daily newspapers, the extent of the area in which they circulate and the degree to which they undergo competition locally with newspapers from other cities. Principal Business Centers include, but are not limited to, Basic Trading Centers and Major Trading Centers. *See also: Ranally City Ratings.*

Projected Population Change: The increase or decrease in population, determined by comparing the Projected Population to the Estimated Population. The amount of change is expressed as a percentage (gain or loss) from the Estimated Population.

Processing and Distribution Center: A large U.S. Postal Service facility for processing and distributing mail to/from all of the smaller post offices in one or more ZIP Code Service Areas. Processing and Distribution Centers are usually located in "hub" cities that serve as the natural centers of local transportation.

Ranally City Ratings: The Ranally City Ratings classify Principal Business Centers by assigning each a rating which reflects the city's relative business and economic importance. Special thanks to Editorial Consultant, Richard L. Forstall, for his major contributions in the development of the Ranally City Rating System.

The Ranally City Rating utilizes a number of criteria, including population, total retail sales volume, shopping goods volume, volume of wholesaling, the number of headquarters of major corporations, banking activity and hospital facilities. Another important factor is circulation statistics for locally published daily newspapers, the extent of the area in which they circulate and the degree to which they undergo competition locally with newspapers from other cities. All of these variables are used to determine the extent to which the city is a shopping focus for the surrounding area and the degree of business competition from neighboring cities.

Because the Ranally City Rating employs a much more comprehensive set of criteria than systems based solely on population, it provides a more reliable and broad-based indicator of a city's relative economic importance. Used alone, population may give a misleading impression of a city's actual importance. For example, many smaller cities within metropolitan areas are important business centers for surrounding suburbs, despite having relatively modest populations. Likewise, urban centers in different parts of the country may have nearly the same population totals but still vary greatly in their relative importance.

The meaning of the city ratings are as follows:

Each city rating includes a number and one or more letters. The **number** indicates the city's general level of importance and is the most significant item in the rating. Within each general level, the **number of capital letters** used distinguishes the more important cities (for which two or more letters are used) from the less important cities, which have only one capital letter. Finally, a **lower-case letter** is used to identify certain special groups of suburbs.

The specific letter, **A, B, C,** or **S,** indicates the city's status as a trading center for its immediate area. A city rated **A** is a **primary** Basic Trading Center—the most important center of shopping for a wide surrounding area.

A **B** city is a **secondary** Basic Trading Center—the second (or third) most important center for its area. Both **A** and **B** cities are mentioned in the titles of Basic Trading Areas. For example, in the Minneapolis-St. Paul Basic Trading Area, Minneapolis is a primary center and is rated **A**, and St. Paul is a secondary center and is rated **B**.

Cities designated **C** do not qualify as Basic Trading Centers, but are within the trading area of a larger city. Cities designated **S** are actually within the Ranally Metro Area of a larger city—they are suburbs or satellite cities.

The specific city ratings are described below. All of the Principal Business Centers appear in a table on pages 74-87.

Rating 1—National Business Centers. Each of these cities is an independent center of large-scale financial and wholesaling activity, as well as a very large retailing center. Each has a large tributary territory in which its dominant importance is overwhelming. Firms with nationwide distribution are almost certain to have important branches or outlets in every one of these cities. Each city rated **1** has at least $850 million annual sales of general merchandise and apparel stores in its urban area (including immediate suburbs) and has daily newspapers whose total circulation is over 300,000.

1-AAAA. New York City is the only city with this rating, in recognition of its unique business importance and nationwide economic influence.

1-AAA. Los Angeles and Chicago have been recognized with this special rating, as the only cities besides New York whose economic importance and influence operate over a large part of the U.S.

1-AA—Major national business centers. These cities are distinguished from the **1-A**s, the next lower category, by a greater volume of retailing, financial activity, newspaper circulation, etc. They account for most of the headquarters of firms that do a nationwide range of business. Their annual urban area shopping goods volume ranges from $1.5 to $4.5 billion, and their Sunday newspaper circulation ranges upward from 500,000. In over-all business importance these cities are comparable with the leading cities of many foreign countries.

1-A—Other national business centers. These cities are only slightly less important than the **1-AA**s. They include many of the cities most often selected as branch headquarters by major firms, but they are less likely to be headquarters for national firms.

Rating 2—Regional Business Centers. The business importance of these cities operates on a regional rather than a national scale. A regional center is likely to be the largest city within a radius of 100 to 150 miles. It is an important wholesaling center and the headquarters of many businesses of regional scope; it has branch offices or assembly plants of some of the larger national concerns, but only rarely has headquarters of such firms. The **2**s are divided into two general groups: **2-AA** and **2-A**. The smallest **2-AA** cities have annual general merchandise and apparel stores sales volume in their urban area of at least $280 million, and dailies with a total circulation of at least 100,000. Most **2-AA** cities have morning dailies. The **2-A** cities generally have at least $185 million general merchandise and apparel store sales volume and 50,000 daily newspaper circulation.

2-AA—Major regional business centers. The largest of these cities are only slightly less important than the **1-A** centers. It is worth noting that major regional centers in the North and on the West Coast are rated **1**, while many of those in the South are rated **2**. Though they are of great importance for their immediate area, the overall importance of most Southern cities is still not comparable to that of major cities in the North and West with their large concentrations of manufacturing and other activities of long standing. Many of the **2-AA** cities are growing rapidly and some of them will probably qualify for a **1** rating before long.

2-BB, 2-CC. Fort Worth, St. Paul, Oakland, San Jose and similar cities, within the metropolitan areas of larger cities, are rated **2-BB**. Newark, NJ is the only **2-CC** city.

2-A, 2-B, 2-C—Other regional business centers. The **2-A** cities are regional centers of somewhat lesser importance than the **2-AA**s. Several are major industrial centers of a size great enough to qualify for this rating, in spite of the lack of a large tributary area.

The **2-B** cities are mainly secondary central cities of large metropolitan areas. Like Newark, St. Paul, and Oakland mentioned above, their close relationship to a large metropolis should not obscure their major importance in many respects.

2-S These cities are key business centers in major metropolitan areas, though not large enough to be recognized as central cities. Typically, their retailing volume is very high but serves only a limited section of the metropolitan area. Such activities as wholesaling may also be important. These centers represent the choice of many businesses as the best locations for supplying consumer products to the suburban sections of the chief metropolitan areas.

Rating 3—Significant Local Business Centers. The cities rated **3** are those whose business importance is significant, but is typically local rather than regional. They are usually the largest place within a radius of fifty miles or so, but a larger center rated **2** or **1** is usually not far away, and a **3** city will have close connections with this larger center, especially for wholesaling, finance, and similar activities that do not directly involve the consumer. Cities rated **3** serve their immediate areas as the main source for shopping goods, are important as general retailing centers, but are usually not important for wholesaling. The **3** cities have daily newspapers, but their circulation is limited to the immediate area.

3-AA, 3-BB, 3-CC—Major local business centers. Approximately the upper quarter of the **3**s are of sufficient importance to be rated as a separate group. They show some tendency to move up into **2** status, but so far have not developed a large enough tributary area to do so, often because of proximity to a larger center. Generally the **3-AA** centers have

* Estimates for economic activity in this edition of the *Atlas* are based on data from the U.S. Census Bureau's 1997 Economic Census and utilize the North American Industry Classification System (NAICS); estimates from editions of the *Atlas* before 2001 are based on census data using the 1987 Standard Industrial Classification (SIC) system. Trade statistics are not directly comparable between systems. Consult U.S. Census Bureau documentation for further information.

at least $100 million annual urban-area general merchandise and apparel stores and a daily of at least 25,000 circulation. Most of these cities are Basic Trading Centers, but there are also some **3-BB**s (secondary Basic Trading Centers) and **3-CC**s.

3-SS. This is an additional group of suburban shopping centers of significance comparable to that of the **3-AA** cities.

3-A, 3-B, 3-C—Other significant local business centers. These cities usually have a well-defined but limited tributary area, outside of which they have relatively little influence. Nearly all have $35 to $100 million annual volume in general merchandise and apparel store sales, a daily with 10,000 circulation and at least one general hospital.

3-S. These are suburban shopping centers of importance comparable to those of the **3-A** cities outside of metropolitan areas. Typically they supply shopping goods to their own population and to a few adjoining suburbs. Many have a daily newspaper and most have a general hospital. However, most suburbs with over $100 million in shopping goods sales are rated **3** even if they lack these other characteristics.

Rating 4—Other Local Business Centers. The cities rated **4** are local business centers which are of some importance, but do not qualify for a **3** rating in one respect or another. Some are isolated centers in hilly or mountainous areas in the West or South, whose local importance is unquestioned, but whose tributary area is simply too small to support a larger business center. Some are established centers for declining mining or agricultural districts. Others are centers of small tributary areas in prosperous farming or industrial regions, in each case with larger centers (rated **3** or even **2**) close by. Most **4**s have a daily newspaper with 7,000 or more circulation, as well as at least $14 million in annual general merchandise and apparel stores, and a general hospital.

4-A. These are small Basic Trading Centers. Most of them are in relatively isolated areas, especially in the West, and a few have very small populations. But in each case they are clearly the chief local shopping focus for their area.

4-B, 4-C. These cities (not suburbs) are within the Basic Trading Areas of larger cities. Many are found in well-developed agricultural or industrial areas, which are able to support local trading centers spaced quite close together.

4-S. These suburban centers are of moderate retailing importance, though some have sizable populations.

Special Groups of Suburbs. A lower-case letter at the end of the Ranally City Rating is used to identify two special categories of suburban business centers. The letter **m** concluding the rating identifies suburbs where a major portion of total retail volume and shopping-goods sales are accounted for by a large mall or planned shopping center (or, in a few cases, two or more such centers). Such suburbs may have only a small "downtown" in the traditional sense; although their sales volume may be larger than that of some Basic Trading Centers, they generally lack a daily newspaper or a hospital and do not have a wide range of other professional and business services. The letter **r** concluding the rating identifies suburbs which are of modest importance as shopping-goods centers, but which have substantial non-shopping-goods retailing (for example, automobile dealers). Many of these suburbs are also important employment centers, with numerous workers commuting in from other suburbs or from the area's main city.

Collectively the rated cities include about 45 percent of the nation's population, but about 60 percent of the total retail sales and about 70 percent of shopping-goods sales. Counting activity in immediate suburban areas, the rated cities account for almost 90 percent of all shopping-goods sales. Over 90 percent of U.S. daily newspaper circulation originates in the rated cities.

Business centers below the level of the rated cities are mostly small in size and very local in importance—such as numerous county-seat towns of the Midwest and South. One group of exceptions are business and shopping centers located in unincorporated suburban communities. Details of the business activity for these places appear only in limited form in the Economic Census and it is not possible to rate them on a comparable basis with that of other business centers.

See also: Principal Business Center.

Ranally Manufacturing Unit (RMU): Each Ranally Manufacturing Unit represents one millionth of the U.S. total value added by manufacture, according to the 1997 Census of Manufactures.

Ranally Metro Area (RMA): Rand McNally's definition of a metropolitan area. Like Metropolitan Statistical Areas (MSAs) and Core Based Statistical Areas (CBSAs), RMAs include one or more central cities, satellite communities and suburbs. Unlike MSAs and CBSAs, RMAs are not restricted to following county boundaries. For this reason, RMAs provide a better portrayal of the extent of urban and suburban development than MSAs or CBSAs. While MSAs and CBSAs are useful for making general comparisons between major urban centers or for summarizing the importance of a given area for business purposes the RMA offers a more precise look at areas of concentrated population.

There are two basic criteria that determine inclusion within an RMA. In general, an area must have 1) at least 70 people per square mile and 2) at least 20% of the labor force must commute to the central urban area of the RMA. These requirements provide general guidelines for drawing consistent boundaries for RMAs across the nation.

In general the population threshold for RMAs is 50,000. Selected areas of less than 50,000 are also defined as RMAs because they either have populations close to 50,000, include a central city of an official MSA, or are of special significance to the state. *See also: Metropolitan Statistical Area.*

Ranally Population Unit (RPU): Each Ranally Population Unit represents one millionth of the U.S. total population.

Ranally Sales Units (RSU): Each Ranally Sales Unit represents one millionth of the U.S. total volume for a sales category. RSUs are presented for Total Retail Sales, General Merchandise Store Sales and Apparel Store Sales. The value appearing in the RSU column is computed by dividing the area's dollar sales value by the U.S. total dollar sales value and multiplying the result by one million.

Rand McNally & Co. Designated Place (RMC Place): A place that has not met the legal requirements of its state for incorporation as a municipality, and is not defined as a Census Designated Place. These are unincorporated places not reported by the U.S. Census Bureau. These places are identified by Rand McNally by consulting a variety of map and statistical sources. Populations for these places are Rand McNally estimates that refer to the central or built-up sections of these places. *See also: Incorporated Place; Census Designated Place; Rand McNally Population Estimates for Unincorporated Places.*

Rand McNally Population Estimates for Unincorporated Places: Population estimates for unincorporated places that are not reported separately by the U.S. Census Bureau. Rand McNally secures these estimates by contacting local authorities and consulting a variety of map and statistical sources. In the State Index these population figures are preceded by the symbol ●.

Retail Trade Sales*: Net sales for establishments engaged in retail trade. Receipts from repairs and other services are included, but retail sales by non-retailers such as service establishments and wholesalers are not. Sales and other taxes collected from customers and credit charges are not included. Total retail sales are all-encompassing, including (among others) general merchandise and apparel store sales.

Revised Census Population: Official revision of final 2000 Census figures. In the State Indexes, this population figure is preceded by the symbol Ⓡ.

Shopping Goods Sales*: Retail items that the shopper ordinarily travels some distance to purchase, and for which he or she compares qualities, styles and prices from store to store before buying. Shopping goods represent the best category of distinguishing the towns to which the buying public travels. Such towns are natural centers for other activities such as entertainment, education and medical care. Most sales of shopping goods are made through general merchandise or apparel stores.

Special Census Population: Official Census population figure taken at a time other than the normal Census. In the State Indexes, this population figure is preceded by the symbol Ⓢ.

Township and "Town": Commonly used generic term for minor civil divisions (MCDs) in the U.S. Townships and "towns" are indexed in the State Index for Connecticut, Illinois, Indiana, Maine, Massachusetts, Michigan, New Hampshire, New Jersey, New York, Ohio, Pennsylvania, Rhode Island, Vermont, and Wisconsin. Maps displaying townships (and other selected MCDs) for these states appear on pages 255-271 of the *Commercial Atlas*. The information on the township or "town" is given in a separate entry in the State Index. These entries are specifically identified as MCDs in the index. *See also: County Subdivision.*

Unincorporated Place: *See Rand McNally Designated Place.*

Value Added By Manufacture: The value added to raw materials during the manufacturing process.

ZIP Code: Numerical codes assigned by the U.S. Postal Service to speed the distribution of mail. The *Commercial Atlas & Marketing Guide* specifies the correct ZIP Code for cities, towns and rural areas where there are residents to receive mail; all ZIP Codes shown in the Index are preceded by a "**Z**" symbol.

For places where the name of the town is not recognized by the U.S. Postal Service as an acceptable "last line" on an envelope, the place name that should instead be shown is given immediately before the ZIP code. For example, an index entry for Tinyplace, AL shows "mail Someplace **Z** 12345". In this example, Someplace is an acceptable last line on an envelope, while Tinyplace is not.

Some ZIP Codes are assigned to individual companies or entities (Unique ZIP Codes) while others are used exclusively for mail box deliveries. In the *Commercial Atlas & Marketing Guide*, no distinction is made between delivery, unique or post office box ZIP Codes. All are reported in the same manner.

Many large cities have each been assigned multiple ZIP Code areas. Index entries for these major multi-zoned cities specify ZIP information as one or more ranges. Megaburg, CA, for example, might show ZIP Codes of **Z** 55055-99, **Z** 55150-99, and **Z** 55250.

USPS definitions of city boundaries do not necessarily correspond to legal corporate boundaries. The ZIP Codes listed in this atlas for a given city include ZIPs for which the USPS considers that city name to be an acceptable last line.

The mail delivery area of numerous other communities is also subdivided by ZIP Code, usually into just a few zones. ZIP information for these minor multi-zoned cities is also presented in the index as a range, although generally singular and shorter than those of major multi-zoned cities.

ZIP Code Service Area: An area surrounding an U.S. Postal Service Processing and Distribution Center. These areas are defined by the first three digits, or prefix, of the five-digit ZIP Code. As the ZIP Code system has evolved, ZIP Code Service Areas have become widely recognized as a useful and practical means for delineating marketing units. The three-digit Zip Code prefixes that define the Service Areas are conveniently available as

* Estimates for economic activity in this edition of the *Atlas* are based on data from the U.S. Census Bureau's 1997 Economic Census and utilize the North American Industry Classification System (NAICS); estimates from editions of the *Atlas* before 2001 are based on census data using the 1987 Standard Industrial Classification (SIC) system. Trade statistics are not directly comparable between systems. Consult U.S. Census Bureau documentation for further information.

part of mailing addresses, and no further coding or allocation to county or sales area is required.

Each ZIP Code Service Area surrounds a large post office, many of which operate as Processing and Distribution Centers serving between 40 and 75 other post offices in the area. The Processing and Distribution Center is usually located at the natural center of local transportation patterns. As a result, Service Areas generally represent economically homogeneous units of value to the marketer in defining prospective customers, establishing market potential, measuring market penetration and maximizing corporate resources. Service Areas are shown on the ZIP Code Service Areas map (pages 18-19) and are listed in the table called ZIP Code Service Areas: Population/Sales on pages 20-21.

The ZIP Code system assigns over 40,000 different five-digit codes to individual post offices, individual branch offices (in medium-sized cities) and individual postal delivery areas (in large cities). Because many Processing and Distribution Centers require more than one three-digit prefix, the number of prefixes exceeds the number of Service Areas. The extra prefixes are necessary either to handle individually zoned cities within a Service Area or because the area has a large number of separate post offices. In most cases, however, within any given Service Area, the prefixes are consecutive. Thus, in northern Illinois, ZIP Code prefixes 600 and 602 are used for post offices in the northern portion of the Chicago metropolitan area, 601, 603, and 605 for Chicago's western suburbs, and 604 for the southern suburbs. Consequently, Chicago's three-digit ZIP Code Service Area comprises prefixes 606-608 inclusive. The prefix 606 is used for Chicago proper and several bordering suburbs; 607 and 608 for several other adjacent suburbs. Some further subdivision of the Chicago metropolitan area by ZIP Codes is theoretically possible, but there is no advantage in doing so. The areas served by the north and west suburban prefixes could be distinguished from one another, but the current boundaries separating them simply reflect postal convenience and have little or no marketing significance.

Likewise, it would be possible to distinguish Chicago and suburbs such as Evanston and Oak Park from their surroundings, but the areas served by these post offices do not necessarily correspond to the corporate limits of these cities. For example, the Evanston Post Office (ZIP Code delivery areas 60201-04 and 60208-09) serves a sizable portion of the neighboring village of Skokie, so the Skokie residents of that area have ZIP Codes beginning with 602 instead of the Skokie Post Office's 600. The area served by the Chicago Post Office includes Norridge and several other suburban communities that have codes beginning 606.

Besides the combinations reflected in the Postal Service's official list, a few additional combinations of three-digit areas have been made for purposes of the ZIP Code Service Areas table. For example, the Brockton MA Service Area (023-024) has been treated along with Boston (017-024), because by itself it comprises neither a coherent independent area nor a useful subdivision of the greater Boston metropolitan area. There are also a few areas listed in the table under a name that differs from the one used by the Postal Service. For example, 208-209 appears as Rockville, MD, not Suburban Maryland.

This classification has been made primarily from the point of view of the business user interested in retail distribution through existing trading centers. Of course, there are other important marketing considerations relative to smaller areas. One example is the setting up of sales territories or territories for branch offices, where a center is chosen not so much because local people shop there

as because it is a convenient place from which to cover the surrounding district.

ZIP Code Service Areas in principal do not cross state lines. With minor exceptions, if a Processing and Distribution Center services territory in another state, that portion of its area is given its own three-digit prefix. Many users will want to ignore state lines and combine these separate areas. *See also: ZIP Code, ZIP Code Service Area Classification Codes.*

ZIP Code Service Area Classification Codes:

Codes developed by Rand McNally to indicate the degree to which ZIP Code Service Areas conform to city trading areas as defined on the Rand McNally Trading Areas Map *(see pages 22-23)*. Because ZIP Code Service Areas were developed to provide postal service, they usually include with each city the territory conveniently served from it by rail and other ground transportation. In many cases, these areas conform very closely to those of the city's trading area as defined by Rand McNally. However, there are also many ZIP Code Service Areas that differ significantly from what would generally be considered the trading area of the city. To aid users of ZIP Code Service Areas, Rand McNally has classified the Service Areas according to the degree to which they represent realistic trading areas.

Service Areas are classified by a letter (**A, B, C, D, M, W,** or **X**) followed in some cases by a number to indicate a subcategory of the main group. The classifications are as follows:

A—Accurate as a trading area. All of the Service Area is essentially served for retailing from one trading center, and its boundaries match quite closely the boundaries of the center's trading area. Some Service Areas encompass two or even three cities so close to one another that most shoppers can readily visit any one of them. Such Areas are classified as **A**, provided the Processing and Distribution Center city is also the most important of the multiple trading centers.

Service Areas classed as **A** sometimes have a trading area extending across a state line. The designation is still **A** if essentially all of the center's trading territory within the home state is within the Service Area.

A2—Cross-line area. The Service Area is served from a Processing and Distribution Center outside the state, but it conforms fairly closely to the portion of the corresponding trading area that is within the state. Most users will want to combine such areas with the portion across the state line. To aid in making these combinations, the ZIP prefix for the parent Service Area is given in parentheses after the **A2** classification.

B—Fairly accurate as a trading area. These in turn divide into:

B1—Fairly accurate, but larger than the actual trading area. The Processing and Distribution Center city is the most important trading center in the Area, but the Service Area is somewhat larger than the trading territory, and includes counties or districts whose residents would rarely if ever visit the Processing and Distribution Center city for shopping. For most marketing purposes, however, the Area is a fairly accurate approximation of the trading area.

B2—Fairly accurate, but smaller than the actual trading area. Many of these Areas center on large cities, whose actual trading areas are significantly more extensive than the Postal Service arrangements recognize. The outlying portions of their trading areas are often separate Service Areas for postal purposes and are classified as **W1** or **W2** (see below).

C—Multicentered Service Area. These Service Areas have two or more trading centers, too far apart to be treated as adjacent centers of a single trading area. Thus, they are not single units for shopping.

The **C** Service Areas are good examples of situations which may provide quite satisfactory units for sales territories and related purposes, so long as it is recognized that they do not represent the trading area for any single city. In several cases a **C** Area is closely related to a city across a state line and has that city's ZIP prefix specified.

C1. The Service Area has two trading centers, and the Processing and Distribution Center city is the most important.

C2. The Service Area has two trading centers, but the Processing and Distribution Center city is *not* the most important. It would be misleading to treat these Service Areas as comprising the shopping area of the city named, when in fact there is a more important shopping focus elsewhere in the Service Area.

C3. The Service Area has three or more trading centers, which are relatively independent of one another. The Processing and Distribution Center city may or may not be the most important of these trading centers.

D—Fairly accurate as a trading area, but the Processing and Distribution Center is not the trading center. The Processing and Distribution Center city is a fairly important trading center, but is not the most important in the Area, as comparison with the Rand McNally Trading Areas Map will show. These Areas form satisfactory units if the presence of the more important trading center is recognized. In some cases the ZIP prefix of a nearby city across a state line is specified.

M—Metropolitan Service Area. The Service Area is a well-defined central or outlying portion of a major metropolitan area. Because sections of all metropolitan areas are not readily distinguishable in ZIP Code terms, some *Atlas* users will want to combine these into one Area with their main city (whose ZIP prefix is specified following the classification).

W—Weak Service Area. The Service Area represents a somewhat accurate trading area, but is centered on a relatively small town that does not qualify as a Rand McNally Basic Trading Center. Many of these centers are in fairly remote regions in the Appalachians or the West. For mail distribution purposes they may still be the convenient centers for serving their surroundings. However, residents of these areas would often not be satisfied with the limited range of goods available in the stores of such small communities, and they would go further afield for their shopping to larger cities. For marketing purposes, most of the **W** Areas could logically be combined with the neighboring Service Area with whose trading center they are most closely associated. The ZIP Codes for these stronger areas are specified following the **W** classifications.

W1. The Service Area, usually with a rather small population, does represent fairly closely the trading area of the designated Processing and Distribution Center city.

W2. The Service Area is considerably larger than the territory served for trading purposes by the designated center. An example is Jasper, AL (355). This small city northwest of Birmingham is a significant shopping center for Walker County, its immediate vicinity, but not for the several additional counties or portions of counties to the west which are also included in 355. Residents of these counties would probably travel past Jasper to Birmingham more often than to any other city. Thus, Area 355 decidedly exaggerates the area realistically served for shopping by Jasper. However, such an area could be served by a salesman from Jasper quite readily, if it were desired to recognize it separately from a larger Birmingham area.

X—Unsatisfactory as a Trading Area. This small group of Areas defies treatment as marketing units. Sometimes this is because the Processing and Distribution Center city selected is very limited in importance. Or it is because the shape of the area does not conform at all closely to actual trading patterns.

See also: ZIP Code Service Area, Basic Trading Area.

---

* Estimates for economic activity in this edition of the *Atlas* are based on data from the U.S. Census Bureau's 1997 Economic Census and utilize the North American Industry Classification System (NAICS); estimates from editions of the *Atlas* before 2001 are based on census data using the 1987 Standard Industrial Classification (SIC) system. Trade statistics are not directly comparable between systems. Consult U.S. Census Bureau documentation for further information.

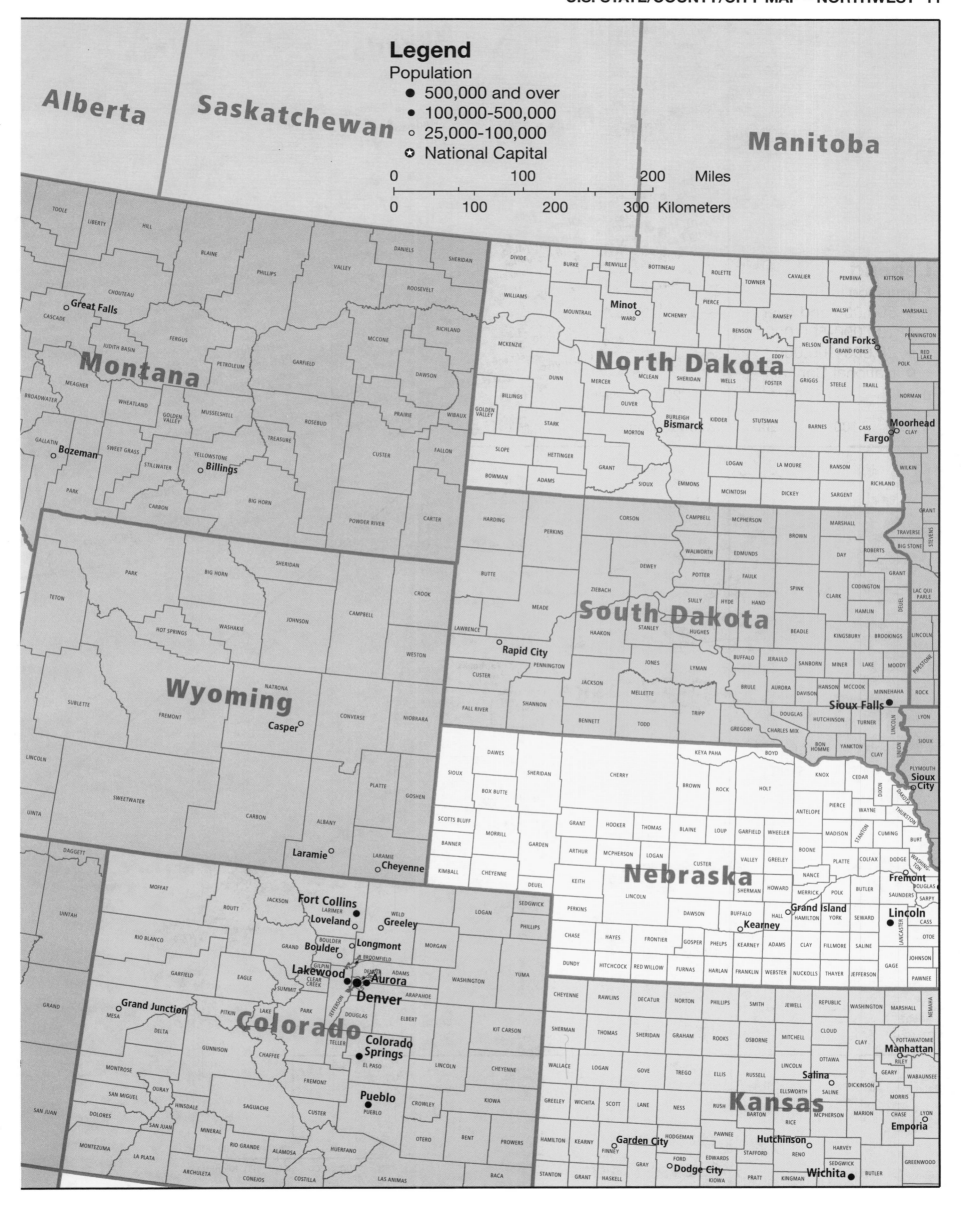

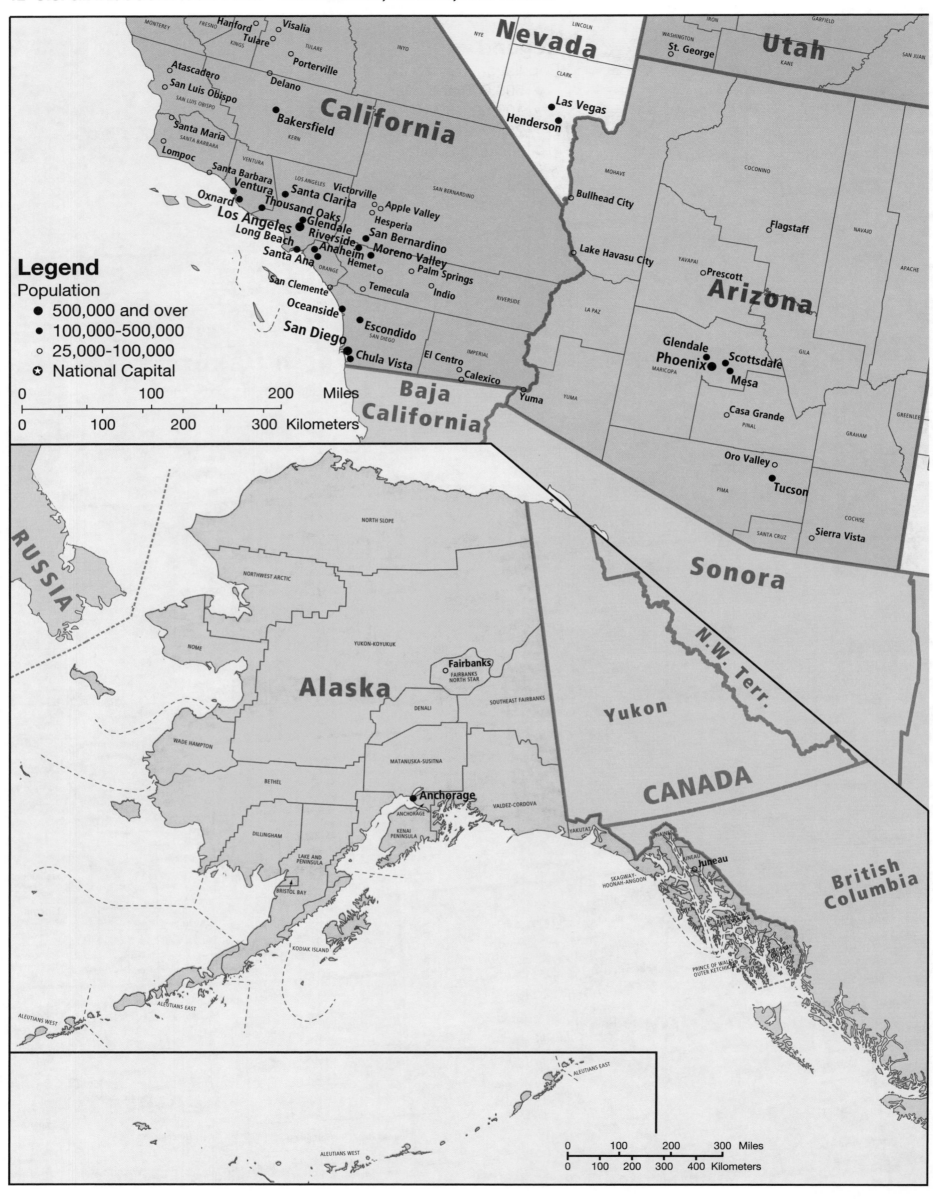

Legend
Population
● 500,000 and over
● 100,000-500,000
○ 25,000-100,000
✪ National Capital

0   100   200   Miles
0 100 200 300 Kilometers

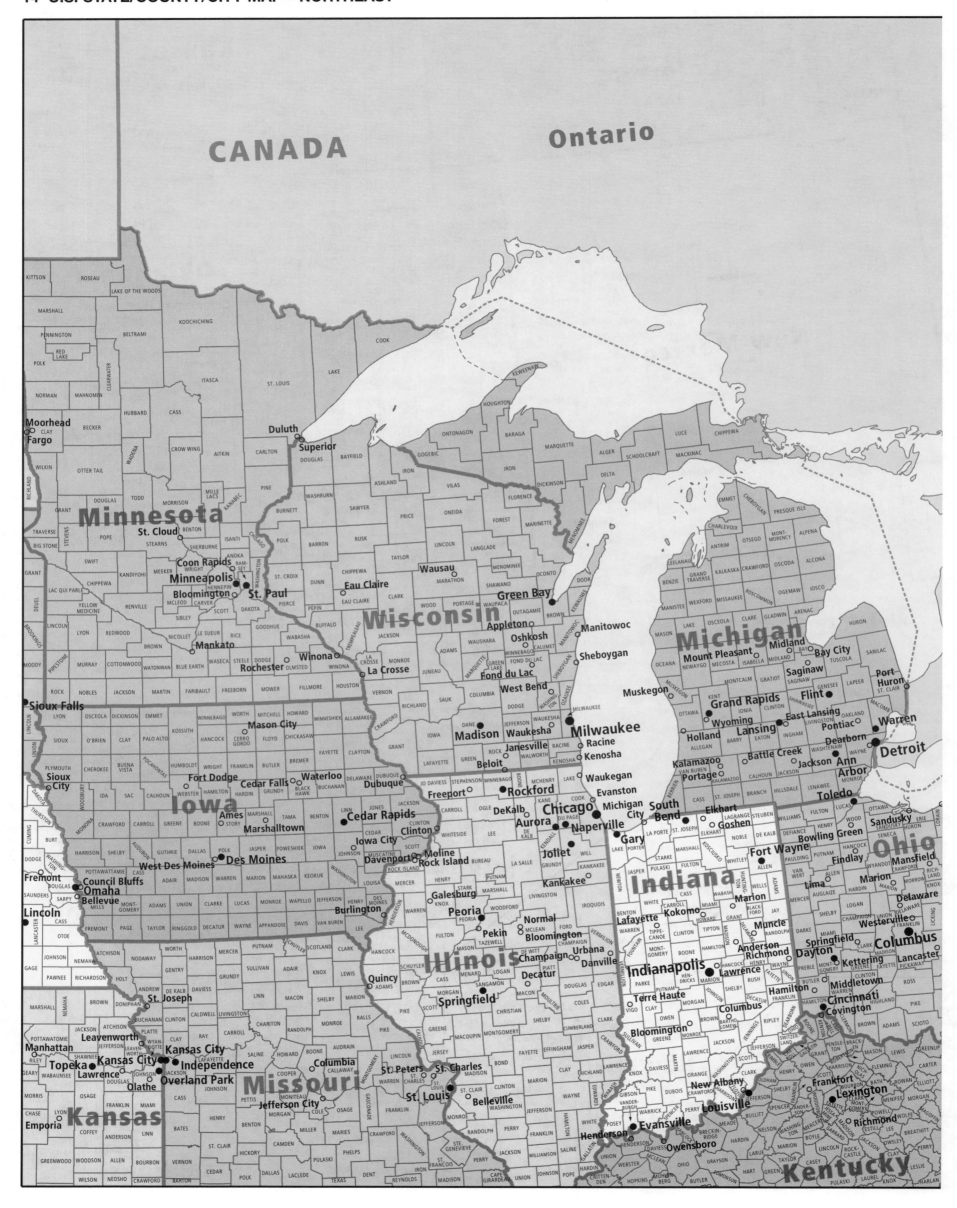

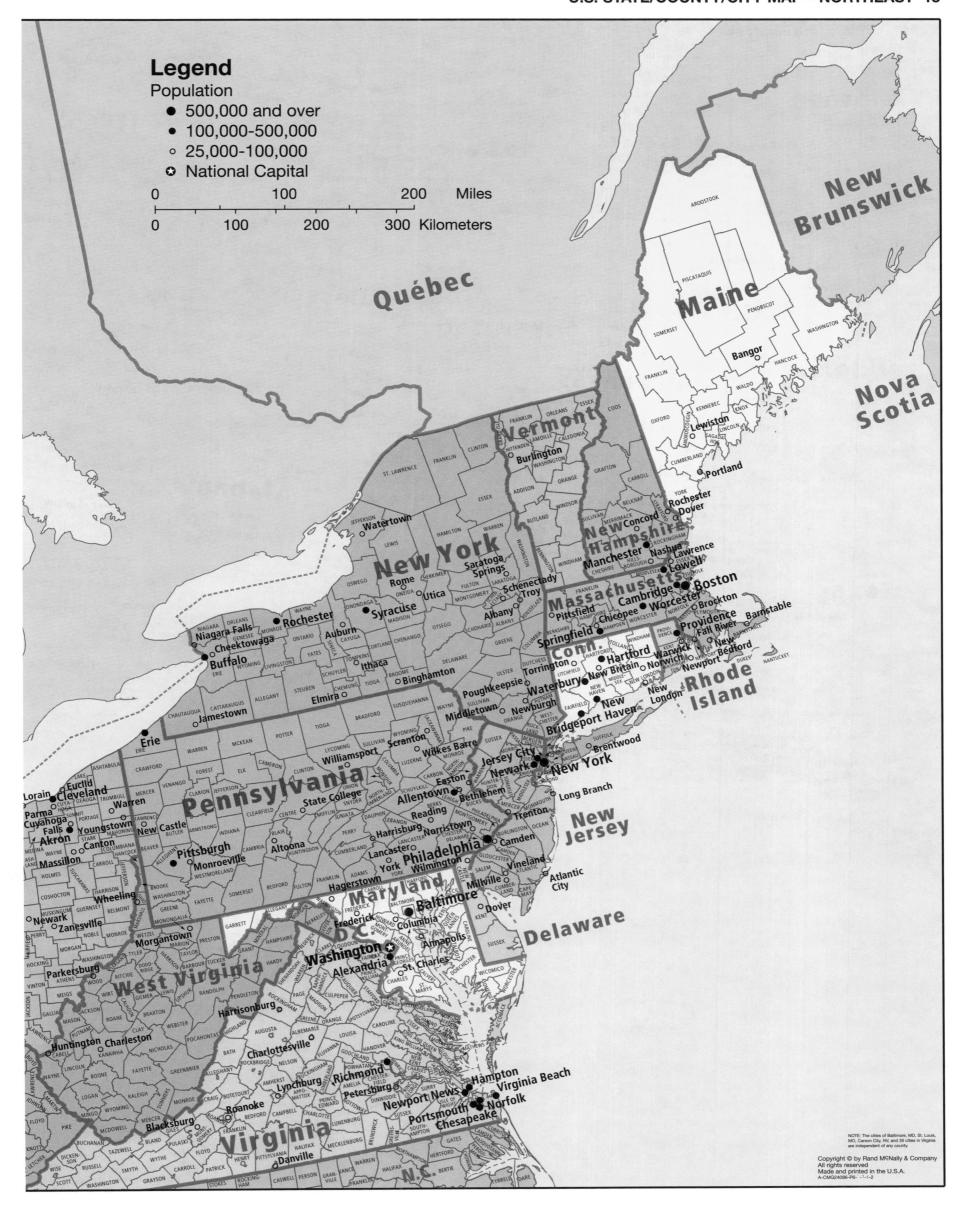

Legend
Population
- ● 500,000 and over
- ● 100,000-500,000
- ○ 25,000-100,000
- ☆ National Capital

| 0 | 100 | 200 | Miles |
| 0 | 100 | 200 | 300 | Kilometers |

Québec

New Brunswick

Nova Scotia

Maine
AROOSTOOK
PISCATAQUIS
SOMERSET
FRANKLIN
PENOBSCOT
WASHINGTON
OXFORD
KENNEBEC
WALDO
HANCOCK
KNOX
LINCOLN
ANDROSCOGGIN
SAGADAHOC
CUMBERLAND
YORK

Bangor

Vermont

New Hampshire

Lewiston
Portland
Rochester
Dover
Concord
Manchester
Nashua
Lawrence
Lowell

Watertown
New York
Burlington
Rome
Saratoga Springs
Schenectady
Troy
Albany
Syracuse
Utica
Auburn
Rochester
Niagara Falls
Cheektowaga
Buffalo
Ithaca
Binghamton
Elmira
Jamestown
Erie

Massachusetts
Pittsfield
Springfield
Chicopee
Cambridge
Worcester
Boston
Brockton
Providence
Fall River
Barnstable
Hartford
New Britain
Torrington
Waterbury
Conn.
New Haven
Bridgeport
Norwich
New London
Warwick
Newport
New Bedford
Rhode Island
Nantucket
Poughkeepsie
Newburgh
Middletown

Pennsylvania
Scranton
Wilkes Barre
Williamsport
State College
Easton
Allentown
Bethlehem
Reading
Harrisburg
Norristown
Lancaster
York
Philadelphia
Camden
Trenton
Jersey City
Newark
New York
Brentwood
Long Branch
Long Island

New Jersey
Vineland
Atlantic City
Wilmington
Milville

Lorain
Euclid
Cleveland
Parma
Cuyahoga Falls
Akron
Canton
Massillon
Youngstown
Warren
New Castle
Pittsburgh
Monroeville
Altoona
Wheeling
Newark
Zanesville
Morgantown
Parkersburg

Maryland
Hagerstown
Frederick
Columbia
Baltimore
Annapolis
Washington D.C.
Alexandria
St. Charles
Dover
Delaware

West Virginia
Huntington
Charleston
Harrisonburg
Charlottesville
Blacksburg
Roanoke
Lynchburg
Danville

Virginia
Richmond
Petersburg
Newport News
Hampton
Virginia Beach
Portsmouth
Norfolk
Chesapeake

N.C.

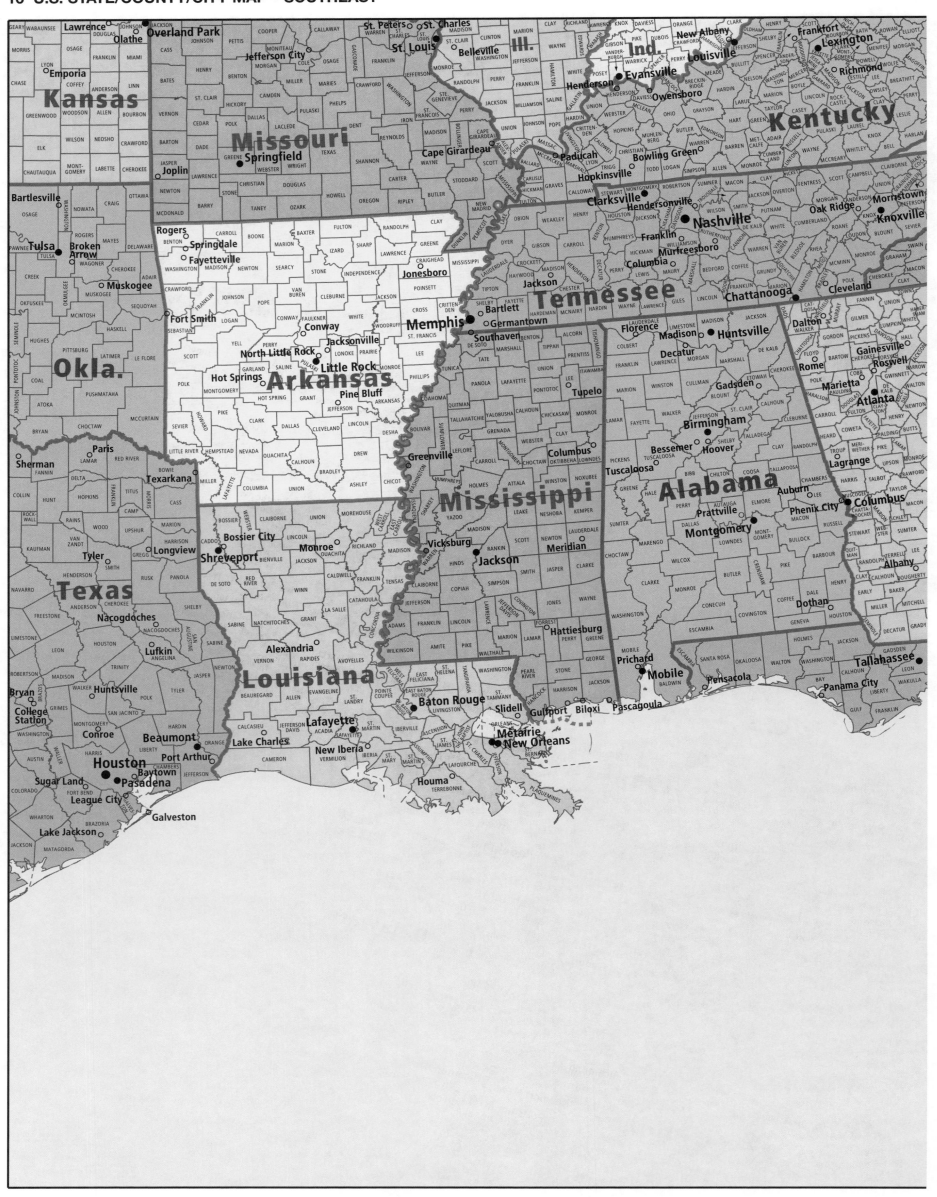

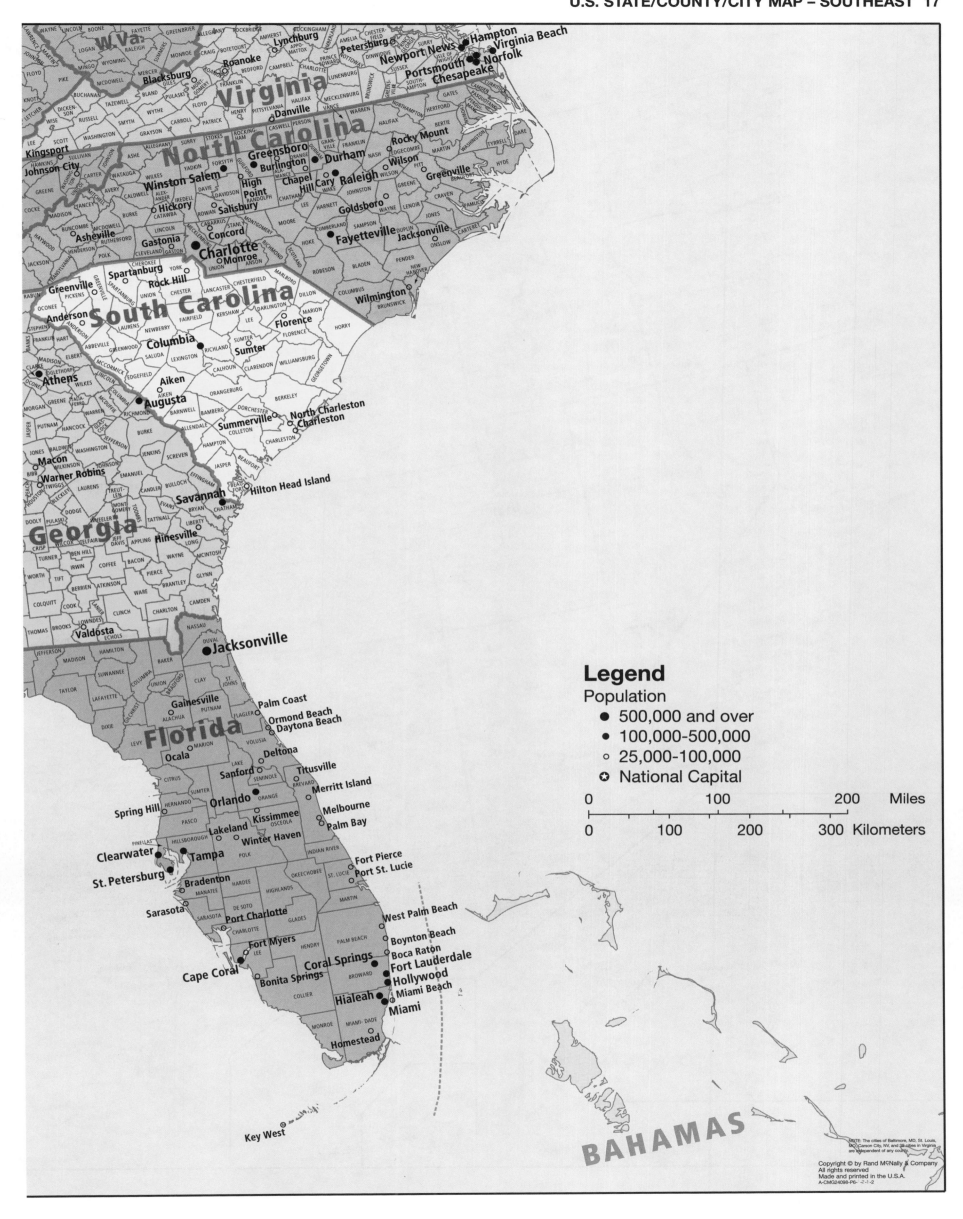

Legend

Population

- ● 500,000 and over
- ● 100,000-500,000
- ○ 25,000-100,000
- ⊗ National Capital

0	100	200	Miles

0	100	200	300	Kilometers

NOTE: The cities of Baltimore, MD, St. Louis, MO, Carson City, NV, and 39 cities in Virginia are independent of any county.

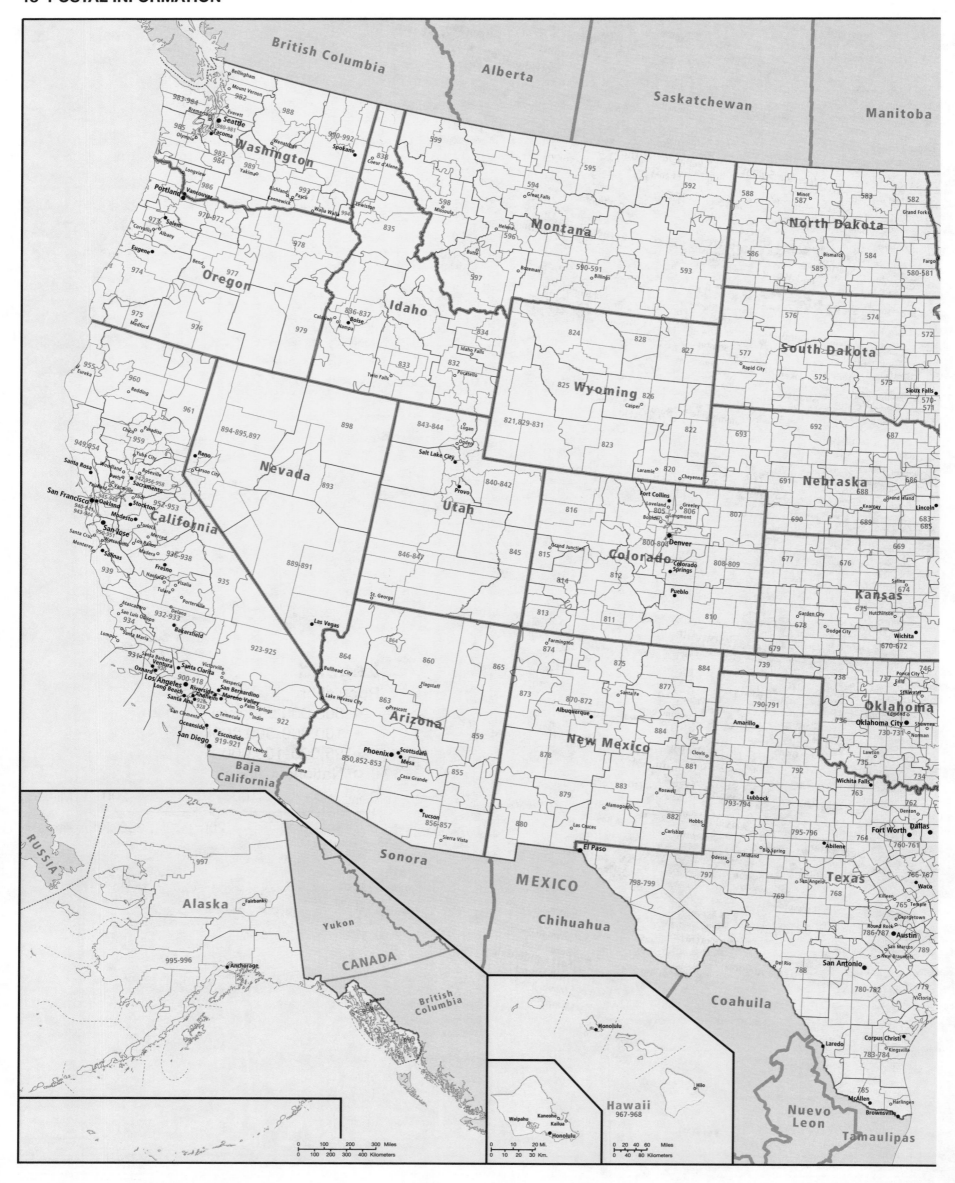

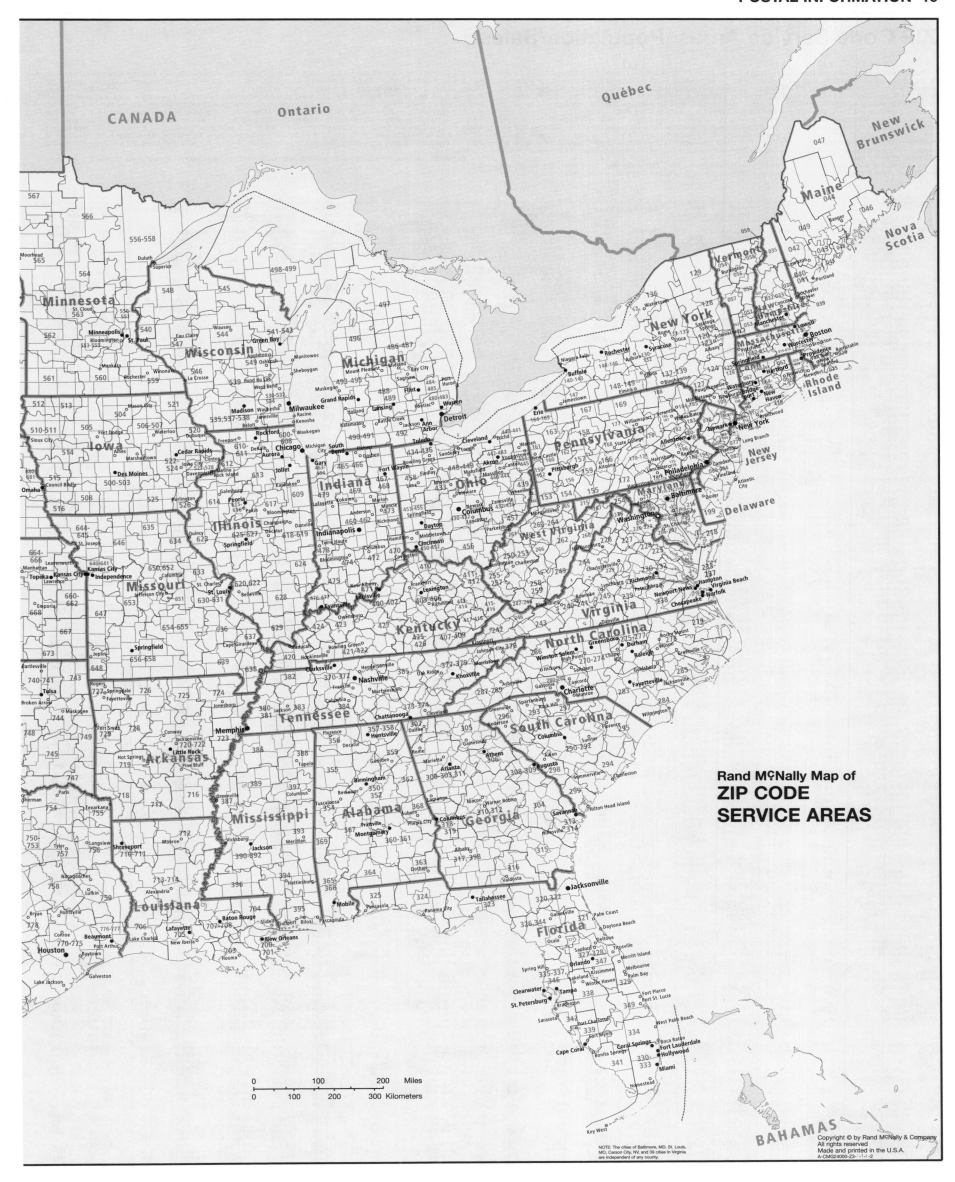

Rand McNally Map of
**ZIP CODE
SERVICE AREAS**

NOTE: The cities of Baltimore, MD, St. Louis, MO, Carson City, NV, and 39 cities in Virginia are independent of any county.

ZIP Code Service Areas: Population/Sales

This table provides current marketing information for areas identified by 3-digit ZIP Codes. Each Service Area is served by a Postal Service Processing and Distribution Center usually located in its principal city or the principal city of an adjacent area. The Processing and Distribution Centers and the area served by each one appear on the map on pages 18-19. ZIP Code Service Areas have received increasing attention as marketing units because of the great convenience they afford in alloting sales prospects, inquiries, etc., since the ZIP Codes for these areas are already available as part of the mailing address and no further coding or allocation to county or sales area is required.

Since the ZIP Areas were set up originally to provide postal service, they usually include with each city the territory conveniently served from it by rail and other ground transportation. In many cases the boundaries of the ZIP Area conform very closely to those of the city's trading area as defined on the Rand McNally Trading Area Map (see pages 22-23). However, many ZIP Areas differ significantly from what would generally be considered the trading area of the city. To aid users of ZIP Areas, Rand McNally has classified the Service Areas according to the degree to which they represent realistic trading areas for the principal cities named.

Areas classified **A** conform closely to the actual trading areas of the cities. Those classified **B** are reasonably similar, but are either somewhat larger (**B1**) or somewhat smaller (**B2**) than the city's actual trading area. Areas denoted **C** contain more than one distinct center and do not constitute single areas for retail sales purposes, though they might be satisfactory units for sales territories or branch offices. In Areas denoted **D**, the main trading center is not the town designated by the Post Office. Areas denoted **M** constitute convenient portions of large metropolitan areas rather than independent trading areas. Areas denoted **W**, many of them in thinly populated regions, center on towns which have only a weak status as regional trading centers; often, these ZIP Areas are larger than the trading area served from their center. Finally, the Areas classified **X** either have very small towns as centers or consist of essentially unrelated territory, and cannot be considered meaningful marketing units. Rand McNally recommends combining the **X** Areas with the adjoining Area with which each is most closely related; the ZIP Code of this related Area is stated in parentheses following the **X** classification. Many users will also want to combine some of the **M** and **W** areas with adjoining areas, to treat whole metropolitan areas as units or to eliminate disproportionately small areas. Suggested combinations for all of the **M** and **W** areas are specified following the classification.

A further discussion of the classification and a detailed explanation of the categories appear in the Introduction on pages 5-9.

ZIP Code	Sectional Center or Principal City	Classification	Population Estimate 7/1/05	Households Estimate 7/1/05	Auto Registrations 2004	Total Retail Sales 2004 Sales ($1,000)	Total Retail Sales Ranally Sales Units	Shopping Goods Sales** 2004 Sales ($1,000)	Shopping Goods Sales** Ranally Sales Units
010-011	Springfield, MA	B2	631,841	241,491	416,980	6,659,613	1,891	995,275	1,436
012	Pittsfield, MA	A	130,794	56,583	90,249	1,605,558	456	275,790	398
013	Greenfield, MA	W1(010)	84,517	34,869	60,027	658,432	187	61,126	88
014	Fitchburg, MA	W1(015)	212,607	77,164	146,263	2,659,764	755	335,506	484
015-016	Worcester, MA	B2	554,177	204,910	371,465	6,404,545	1,819	917,445	1,324
017-024	Boston, MA	B2	4,035,787	1,495,163	2,585,963	54,182,313	15,385	8,740,578	12,617
025	Buzzards Bay, MA	X(026)	118,143	47,873	87,472	1,859,960	528	183,635	265
026	Hyannis, MA	B2	161,620	70,550	120,735	2,598,016	738	392,596	567
027	Providence, RI (MA Part)	C3(028)	532,906	202,870	378,968	6,777,867	1,925	1,601,808	2,312
028-029	Providence, RI (RI Part)	A	1,097,162	413,543	778,207	11,215,085	3,185	1,672,155	2,413
030-031	Manchester, NH	B2	529,421	195,292	441,224	10,961,389	3,113	2,459,988	3,551
032-033	Concord, NH	W2(030)	250,715	95,630	191,441	3,754,633	1,066	540,726	780
034	Keene, NH	B2	85,260	32,355	65,447	1,610,941	457	201,103	290
035	Littleton, NH (NH Part)	W2(042)	46,309	19,745	35,609	950,942	270	50,064	72
036	Bellows Falls, VT (NH Part)	W1(034)	13,236	5,309	10,727	122,744	35	11,921	17
037	White River Jct., VT (NH Part)	D	76,635	30,047	56,468	1,487,432	422	249,811	361
038	Portsmouth, NH	B1	318,606	125,939	264,299	6,250,236	1,775	1,079,191	1,558
039	Portsmouth, NH (ME Part)	A2(038)	51,957	20,415	41,282	432,512	123	99,938	144
040-041	Portland, ME	B2	446,756	179,290	363,056	7,435,761	2,111	1,084,917	1,566
042	Auburn, ME	D	177,591	72,661	135,228	2,382,950	677	299,589	432
043	Augusta, ME	A	80,696	33,793	63,953	1,288,231	366	170,463	246
044	Bangor, ME	B2	171,788	70,300	131,235	2,386,908	678	376,988	544
045	Bath, ME	W2(040)	50,478	21,503	41,873	668,699	190	27,469	40
046	Ellsworth, ME	W2(044)	72,904	32,256	60,523	971,993	276	123,852	179
047	Houlton, ME	D	73,218	31,391	56,944	730,345	207	120,317	174
048	Rockland, ME	W1(044)	42,072	18,091	33,529	582,826	165	65,883	95
049	Waterville, ME	B1	159,588	65,068	121,662	1,996,487	567	242,836	350
050	White River Junction, VT (VT Part)	D1(037)	62,901	24,722	49,018	529,820	150	16,250	23
051	Bellows Falls, VT (VT Part)	W1(034)	29,905	12,473	24,016	296,918	84	25,296	37
052	Bennington, VT	W1(057)	33,446	13,457	25,254	737,067	209	131,879	190
053	Brattleboro, VT	W1(034)	37,652	15,557	29,889	479,145	136	25,245	36
054	Burlington, VT	B2	229,559	86,546	170,988	3,658,067	1,039	472,939	683
056	Montpelier, VT	W1(054)	85,666	33,742	63,660	1,016,285	289	78,192	113
057	Rutland, VT	B2	84,081	32,592	61,323	1,187,972	337	135,419	195
058	St. Johnsbury, VT	W1(054)	58,664	22,410	42,283	614,105	174	60,153	87
059	Littleton, NH (VT Part)	X(054)	3,664	1,394	2,675	1,951	1	0	0
060-061	Hartford, CT	M	959,686	376,437	658,318	12,276,392	3,486	2,033,811	2,936
062	Willimantic, CT	M(060)	162,161	57,043	109,857	1,095,437	311	117,346	169
063	New London, CT	A	262,808	104,045	223,274	3,402,850	966	629,410	908
064-066	New Haven, CT	C1	1,234,877	460,140	853,147	16,170,518	4,591	2,349,540	3,391
067	Waterbury, CT	A	331,550	126,036	231,373	4,192,292	1,190	583,296	842
068-069	Stamford, CT	M(100)	583,780	213,221	418,932	14,486,974	4,114	1,565,104	2,259
070-076, 079	Newark, NJ	M(100)	3,912,888	1,386,052	2,296,616	48,734,687	13,838	7,429,475	10,723
077	Monmouth, NJ	M(100)	619,841	228,061	451,921	8,869,152	2,518	1,521,737	2,196
078	Dover, NJ	M(100)	370,037	130,630	258,339	5,416,816	1,538	912,125	1,316
080-084	South Jersey, NJ	M(189)	1,855,282	695,537	1,261,162	23,462,382	6,662	3,630,696	5,241
085-086	Trenton, NJ	A	566,683	191,510	370,516	6,156,101	1,748	890,332	1,285
087	Lakewood, NJ	M(100)	457,275	177,383	319,677	5,753,740	1,634	716,190	1,034
088-089	New Brunswick, NJ	M(100)	999,900	349,158	694,417	14,824,679	4,209	2,147,611	3,100
100-104	New York, NY	M	3,442,121	1,381,669	740,048	38,729,658	10,997	13,495,116	19,477
105-108	White Plains, NY	M(100)	1,043,862	368,017	667,428	13,614,943	3,866	2,561,446	3,697
109	Suffern, NY	M(100)	523,854	166,650	342,813	6,000,042	1,704	1,469,481	2,121
110-116	Brooklyn-Queens-Nassau, NY	M(100)	5,646,922	1,948,555	1,992,176	39,182,882	11,127	7,274,600	10,498
117-118	Hicksville, NY	M(100)	1,652,592	537,657	1,203,162	22,958,345	6,519	3,894,428	5,621
119	Riverhead, NY	M(100)	245,799	92,349	190,829	3,473,414	986	682,019	984
120-123	Albany, NY	B2	907,782	361,988	619,052	9,906,366	2,812	1,592,026	2,298
124	Kingston, NY	B1	157,562	63,557	108,265	1,691,389	480	222,609	321
125-126	Poughkeepsie, NY	C1	536,491	186,726	356,528	5,134,386	1,458	859,897	1,241
127	Monticello, NY	X(100)	99,482	37,612	64,522	747,227	212	47,833	69
128	Glens Falls, NY	B1	224,286	87,638	152,388	2,581,615	733	513,620	741
129	Plattsburgh, NY	B1	162,942	60,819	103,669	1,594,554	453	221,909	320
130-132	Syracuse, NY	A	796,770	312,450	560,919	8,489,306	2,411	1,366,608	1,973
133-135	Utica, NY	A	400,929	158,016	258,768	3,684,167	1,046	624,435	901
136	Watertown, NY	B2	234,843	85,942	140,920	2,409,643	684	376,971	544
137-139	Binghamton, NY	C1	356,716	145,006	241,748	3,635,864	1,033	630,408	910
140-143	Buffalo, NY	A	1,294,886	531,125	879,453	13,173,094	3,741	2,110,204	3,047
144-146	Rochester, NY	A	1,097,022	424,330	800,269	12,099,681	3,435	1,918,912	2,770
147	Jamestown, NY	C3	184,460	73,767	120,151	1,641,645	466	320,853	463
148-149	Elmira, NY	C1	335,863	131,453	217,882	3,108,040	883	514,498	743
150-152	Pittsburgh, PA	M	1,539,552	639,603	1,014,306	19,450,401	5,523	3,188,404	4,601
153	Washington, PA	W2(150)	180,648	71,790	125,309	1,911,795	543	240,882	348
154	Uniontown, PA	W1(150)	151,790	63,128	105,152	1,476,088	419	299,580	432
155	Somerset, PA	W2(159)	89,790	35,730	65,674	1,220,278	346	126,547	183
156	Greensburg, PA	M(150)	307,699	122,077	227,773	3,511,394	997	508,181	733
157	Indiana, PA	A	115,748	45,627	80,414	1,122,052	319	203,417	294
158	Du Bois, PA	B1	92,428	38,302	65,635	1,022,093	290	144,584	209
159	Johnstown, PA	B2	149,224	61,478	99,920	1,497,776	425	233,576	337
160	Butler, PA	W1(150)	196,826	75,706	141,017	2,113,541	600	355,125	513
161	New Castle, PA	C1	230,887	92,925	158,558	2,795,789	794	562,303	812
162	Kittanning, PA	W2(150)	89,942	36,180	63,003	988,545	281	130,788	189
163	Oil City, PA	C3	152,729	63,180	104,849	2,241,744	637	299,134	432
164-165	Erie, PA	A	314,385	122,550	217,955	3,485,715	990	596,583	861
166	Altoona, PA	B2	210,164	83,305	144,658	2,366,619	672	429,821	620
167	Bradford, PA	B2	50,268	20,338	32,605	431,385	122	25,845	37
168	State College, PA	C1	182,562	69,263	122,383	2,053,992	583	407,370	588
169	Wellsboro, PA	A2(148)	66,854	26,043	47,124	517,646	147	58,742	85
170-171	Harrisburg, PA	A	740,530	298,895	546,466	10,289,815	2,922	1,403,118	2,025
172	Chambersburg, PA	B1	189,278	73,683	143,094	2,014,021	572	239,059	345
173-174	York, PA	A	478,869	181,379	337,868	4,617,165	1,311	815,276	1,177
175-176	Lancaster, PA	A	462,062	172,718	322,356	6,636,263	1,885	989,144	1,427
177	Williamsport, PA	A	172,317	69,803	118,079	1,962,440	557	358,834	518
178	Sunbury, PA	C1	228,488	87,660	153,241	2,381,956	676	349,642	505
179	Pottsville, PA	A	123,342	48,413	89,183	1,405,299	399	169,845	245
180-181	Lehigh Valley (Bethlehem), PA	A	664,281	248,917	488,478	7,851,352	2,230	1,135,387	1,639
182	Hazleton, PA	B1	128,764	51,988	92,045	1,269,786	361	213,720	308
183	East Stroudsburg, PA	A	172,603	57,475	111,641	1,957,641	556	499,165	720
184-185	Scranton, PA	A	309,281	123,102	202,740	3,402,809	966	578,492	835
186-187	Wilkes-Barre, PA	A	305,823	122,429	214,252	3,687,712	1,047	605,298	874
188	Montrose, PA	X(137)	75,568	30,507	54,113	788,658	224	90,993	131
189-194	Philadelphia, PA	M	3,842,374	1,429,402	2,228,284	49,267,669	13,990	7,260,302	10,479
195-196	Reading, PA	A	406,324	152,445	284,691	4,617,274	1,311	886,333	1,279
197-198	Wilmington, DE	M(189)	519,286	186,199	364,213	8,179,817	2,322	1,370,286	1,977
199	Dover, DE	A	319,323	120,448	220,891	4,109,141	1,167	910,412	1,314
200, 202-205	Washington, D.C.	M	548,946	245,671	227,261	3,571,555	1,013	649,935	938
201, 220-223	Northern Virginia, VA	M(200)	2,070,129	771,544	1,584,902	27,499,548	7,808	5,991,531	8,647
206-207	Waldorf, MD	M(200)	1,282,530	453,563	895,329	12,249,118	3,478	2,137,955	3,086
208-209	Rockville, MD	M(200)	957,634	348,861	694,978	11,559,220	3,282	1,974,695	2,850
210-212, 214	Baltimore, MD	A	2,419,495	916,894	1,634,444	27,251,516	7,738	5,179,045	7,475
215	Cumberland, MD (MD Part)	A	102,851	40,702	72,516	1,086,147	308	198,337	286
216	Easton, MD	X(210)	162,185	65,946	124,005	2,032,276	577	365,745	528
217	Frederick, MD	C2	456,583	163,494	334,843	5,181,567	1,471	948,885	1,370
218	Salisbury, MD	A	166,661	65,084	115,680	2,221,124	631	582,563	841
219	Northeastern Maryland, MD	X(189)	97,330	34,969	69,373	840,390	239	141,361	204
224-225	Fredericksburg, VA	B1	372,841	127,857	276,451	3,677,112	1,044	796,254	1,149
226	Winchester, VA	A	165,225	62,111	129,199	2,304,355	654	514,251	742
227	Culpeper, VA	W2(200)	74,088	25,209	55,285	733,622	208	73,029	105
228	Harrisonburg, VA	A	150,141	55,095	117,985	1,918,847	545	295,580	427
229	Charlottesville, VA	B2	229,701	91,703	182,355	2,135,673	606	428,097	618
230-232	Richmond, VA	M	1,034,738	388,678	772,452	12,429,137	3,530	2,711,989	3,914
233-237	Norfolk, VA	B2	1,552,552	565,524	1,082,019	16,709,675	4,745	3,694,074	5,331
238	Petersburg, VA	M(230)	318,009	114,002	228,573	2,608,217	741	604,239	872
239	Farmville, VA	W2(230)	101,513	38,344	72,568	708,872	201	67,255	97
240-241	Roanoke, VA	C1	556,560	231,116	462,838	6,309,081	1,791	1,316,481	1,900
242	Bristol, VA	A	191,783	79,966	147,533	2,236,730	635	411,160	593
243	Pulaski, VA	W2(240)	153,313	64,518	125,091	1,473,207	418	210,878	304
244	Staunton, VA	B1	137,353	54,779	112,176	1,364,089	387	125,997	182
245	Lynchburg, VA	C1	361,520	147,152	287,281	4,082,376	1,159	783,896	1,131
246	Bluefield, WV (VA Part)	A2(247)	70,070	28,967	54,546	788,828	224	188,921	273
247-248	Bluefield, WV (WV Part)	B1	101,926	43,076	71,906	1,003,127	285	239,878	346
249	Lewisburg, WV	X(258)	52,882	21,520	42,107	427,367	121	101,870	147
250-253	Charleston, WV	B2	324,606	135,411	233,786	3,998,800	1,136	769,873	1,111
254	Martinsburg, WV	A	158,597	58,393	119,652	1,148,455	326	213,422	308
255-257	Huntington, WV	B1	265,168	107,954	185,156	2,773,883	788	541,087	780
258-259	Beckley, WV	B2	135,501	53,974	93,716	1,513,875	430	359,011	518
260	Wheeling, WV	C1	135,997	55,775	98,787	1,044,761	297	174,126	251
261	Parkersburg, WV	A	131,646	53,504	97,570	1,736,234	493	477,594	689
262	Buckhannon, WV	W2(263)	83,321	32,409	59,395	711,164	202	123,416	178
263-264	Clarksburg, WV	B2	142,325	55,607	101,310	1,441,828	409	341,749	494
265	Morgantown, WV	C1	162,690	64,143	117,160	1,621,059	460	408,663	590
266	Gassaway, WV	X(250)	32,810	13,026	24,003	361,286	103	70,516	102
267	Cumberland, MD (WV Part)	A2(215)	52,262	20,442	41,253	356,161	101	89,945	130
268	Petersburg, WV	W2(228)	34,105	13,718	28,544	192,139	55	20,239	29
270-274	Greensboro, NC	C1	1,691,311	659,469	1,315,086	20,914,147	5,940	3,604,848	5,202
275-277	Raleigh, NC	C1	1,563,682	595,682	1,161,851	21,257,198	6,036	4,008,167	5,785
278	Rocky Mount, NC	C1	516,153	205,035	364,926	6,002,010	1,704	1,076,809	1,554
279	Elizabeth City, NC	W1(233)	188,740	71,464	131,132	2,320,360	659	412,288	595
280-282	Charlotte, NC (NC Part)	A	1,802,715	695,143	1,375,974	22,963,497	6,521	4,367,345	6,303
283	Fayetteville, NC	A	783,999	287,274	537,489	7,851,189	2,229	1,687,097	2,435
284	Wilmington, NC	A	402,794	165,099	299,694	5,615,063	1,594	973,847	1,406
285	Kinston, NC	C3	440,282	167,021	305,601	4,827,933	1,371	931,191	1,344
286	Hickory, NC	C1	608,481	241,646	489,015	7,790,649	2,212	1,447,522	2,089
287-289	Asheville, NC	A	644,898	268,406	508,035	8,254,939	2,343	1,591,383	2,298
290-292	Columbia, SC	C3	1,044,626	390,948	737,806	11,367,096	3,228	2,676,711	3,864
293	Spartanburg, SC	A	373,142	140,345	265,930	4,405,107	1,251	957,104	1,381
294	Charleston, SC	A	656,327	235,850	421,823	7,251,218	2,059	1,802,547	2,602
295	Florence, SC	C3	574,762	223,738	383,013	7,728,859	2,195	1,831,470	2,643
296	Greenville, SC	C1	889,497	338,824	658,585	10,639,532	3,021	2,081,573	3,004
297	Charlotte, NC (SC Part)	A2(280)	299,788	113,781	217,211	2,912,096	827	495,717	715
298	Augusta, GA (SC Part)	A2(308)	209,207	77,743	143,027	1,555,869	442	338,648	489
299	Savannah, GA (SC Part)	A2(313)	183,921	67,593	118,919	2,388,313	678	544,996	787
300-303, 311	Atlanta, GA	B1	4,853,525	1,736,271	3,383,964	64,653,854	18,359	12,054,902	17,398
304	Swainsboro, GA	X(313)	212,424	75,149	134,891	1,834,750	521	384,341	555
305	Gainesville, GA	B1	551,822	198,826	411,040	6,402,248	1,818	1,475,474	2,130
306	Athens, GA	B1	346,831	131,886	260,457	3,542,469	1,006	726,124	1,048
307	Chattanooga, TN (GA Part)	C1(373)	344,908	123,653	241,859	3,513,722	998	691,633	998
308-309	Augusta, GA (GA Part)	B2	361,137	132,604	237,710	4,212,350	1,197	955,922	1,380
310, 312	Macon, GA	A	673,318	245,283	453,033	6,839,165	1,942	1,463,285	2,112
313-314	Savannah, GA (GA Part)	B2	396,582	147,796	259,428	4,416,348	1,254	1,140,053	1,646
315	Waycross, GA	C2	307,461	113,001	203,587	3,230,516	917	663,191	957
316	Valdosta, GA	A	173,586	62,625	113,911	1,786,448	507	326,720	472
317, 398	Albany, GA	A	487,762	176,869	304,112	5,077,852	1,442	1,017,532	1,469
318-319	Columbus, GA	A	260,457	98,977	172,100	2,771,951	787	633,640	915
320, 322	Jacksonville, FL	A	1,392,650	523,531	963,384	17,191,016	4,881	3,288,181	4,746
321	Daytona Beach, FL	B1	508,175	210,858	356,682	5,321,542	1,511	991,711	1,431
323	Tallahassee, FL	B2	387,121	156,905	271,745	4,127,377	1,172	897,786	1,296
324	Panama City, FL	B1	316,583	122,504	210,763	3,367,913	956	774,696	1,118
325	Pensacola, FL	C1	626,807	245,516	439,215	7,413,695	2,105	1,767,453	2,551
326, 344	Gainesville, FL	C1	713,638	296,501	495,278	7,596,998	2,157	1,441,435	2,080
327-328, 347	Orlando, FL	C3	2,153,531	795,061	1,423,885	28,301,367	8,037	6,067,293	8,758
329	Melbourne, FL	C1	583,575	245,903	432,142	6,884,067	1,955	1,470,030	2,122
330-333	Miami, FL	A	4,201,972	1,484,555	2,524,978	51,351,010	14,581	10,081,857	14,551
334	West Palm Beach, FL	A	1,381,921	540,720	906,885	19,094,818	5,422	4,280,063	6,178
335-337, 346	Tampa, FL	A	2,640,274	1,076,747	1,819,314	35,206,130	9,996	5,893,346	8,507
338	Lakeland, FL	A	639,408	249,001	408,829	7,289,231	2,070	1,399,642	2,020
339	Fort Myers, FL	A	638,443	265,687	440,674	8,548,810	2,427	1,912,113	2,760
341	Naples, FL	A	353,252	148,208	245,770	4,987,601	1,416	961,066	1,387
342	Sarasota, FL	A	714,270	310,277	510,150	9,056,891	2,572	1,658,956	2,394
349	Fort Pierce, FL	A	382,989	150,707	241,598	4,397,213	1,249	737,829	1,065
350-352	Birmingham, AL	B2	1,212,877	468,618	904,317	14,550,457	4,131	3,224,884	4,655
354	Tuscaloosa, AL	B2	200,257	80,977	145,671	2,324,471	660	515,957	745
355	Jasper, AL	W2(350)	158,965	65,936	126,907	1,449,964	412	274,954	397
356	Decatur, AL	C2	355,699	141,031	278,840	4,106,584	1,166	1,006,864	1,453
357-358	Huntsville, AL	B2	372,188	146,451	290,288	4,476,391	1,271	1,218,256	1,758
359	Gadsden, AL	A	272,561	105,418	204,072	2,875,373	816	691,491	998
360-361	Montgomery, AL	A	485,895	182,247	325,880	5,324,859	1,512	1,272,103	1,836
362	Anniston, AL	A	178,497	70,787	138,001	1,577,769	448	364,870	527
363	Dothan, AL	A	222,515	87,109	160,373	2,845,312	808	678,181	979
364	Evergreen, AL	X(365)	105,606	43,452	79,362	988,377	281	182,574	264
365-366	Mobile, AL	B2	606,730	208,779	400,613	6,341,882	1,801	1,630,399	2,354
367	Selma, AL	B1	122,385	46,823	77,647	902,735	256	211,841	306
368	Opelika, AL	C1	222,308	91,002	168,264	1,816,916	516	457,867	661
369	Meridian, MS (AL Part)	A2(393)	21,606	8,962	15,955	122,347	35	7,987	12
370-372	Nashville, TN	B2	1,713,384	660,125	1,300,195	23,605,710	6,703	5,370,898	7,752
373-374	Chattanooga, TN (TN Part)	C1	719,933	281,486	576,338	8,204,098	2,330	1,903,157	2,747
376	Johnson City, TN	C2	398,292	165,971	329,805	4,310,267	1,224	1,079,484	1,558
377-379	Knoxville, TN	A	1,180,189	478,770	963,598	16,210,957	4,603	3,531,887	5,097
375, 380-381	Memphis, TN (TN Part)	A	1,132,204	429,196	763,880	13,550,769	3,847	3,217,404	4,644
382	McKenzie, TN	X(380)	114,772	48,044	91,145	1,077,115	306	315,159	455
383	Jackson, TN	A	280,679	114,632	218,078	3,040,831	863	738,705	1,066
384	Columbia, TN	W2(370)	175,681	68,189	137,642	1,534,152	436	346,305	500
385	Cookeville, TN	B1	216,942	86,863	173,400	2,054,161	583	520,582	751
386	Memphis, TN (MS Part)	A2(380)	372,548	132,382	255,943	3,467,684	985	811,479	1,171
387	Greenville, MS	B2	134,897	46,292	74,471	1,436,524	408	331,261	478
388	Tupelo, MS	B2	254,496	95,668	188,386	2,885,707	819	976,472	1,409
389	Grenada, MS	W2(387)	115,094	43,910	74,928	1,010,437	287	246,931	356
390-392	Jackson, MS	B1	784,852	280,598	527,075	8,963,820	2,545	2,299,506	3,319
393	Meridian, MS (MS Part)	B1	207,869	77,542	143,858	1,969,140	559	531,943	768
394	Hattiesburg, MS	C1	354,428	125,551	241,869	3,558,419	1,010	1,071,030	1,546
395	Gulfport, MS	A	381,374	146,546	282,550	4,296,455	1,220	1,231,668	1,778
396	McComb, MS	B1	130,056	47,892	89,557	1,235,071	351	321,873	465
397	Columbus, MS	A	168,905	64,964	123,019	1,637,952	465	431,264	622
400-402	Louisville, KY (KY Part)	B2	1,061,975	405,860	762,056	11,560,966	3,282	2,404,284	3,471
403-406	Lexington, KY	B2	812,934	321,681	613,405	9,230,909	2,621	1,995,576	2,880
407-409	London, KY	C3	216,932	82,828	140,954	1,957,007	555	579,714	837
410	Cincinnati, OH (KY Part)	A2(450)	463,309	175,451	332,100	5,413,792	1,537	1,105,314	1,595
411-412	Ashland, KY	B1	190,135	73,479	134,158	1,723,707	489	399,182	576
413-414	Campton, KY	X(403)	62,985	24,039	41,624	347,786	98	46,047	67
415-416	Pikeville, KY	B2	109,525	45,402	77,551	1,142,042	324	290,465	419
417-418	Hazard, KY	W2(403)	75,513	29,915	51,776	602,518	171	148,378	214
420	Paducah, KY	A	219,627	90,160	168,608	2,649,772	752	757,833	1,094
421-422	Bowling Green, KY	C1	346,698	130,470	245,879	3,313,563	941	676,273	976
423	Owensboro, KY	A	166,891	67,272	129,793	1,561,987	444	402,943	582
424	Evansville, IN (KY Part)	C2(476)	136,268	53,759	100,907	1,308,178	371	281,053	406
425-426	Somerset, KY	A	137,531	52,674	96,744	1,214,701	344	254,183	367
427	Elizabethtown, KY	X(400)	170,305	65,553	126,330	1,754,699	498	479,298	692
430-432	Columbus, OH	A	1,836,314	698,537	1,382,559	26,288,908	7,465	4,429,465	6,393
433	Marion, OH	C1	181,384	69,752	138,076	1,654,336	470	319,970	462
434-436	Toledo, OH	A	815,323	322,838	618,665	10,446,801	2,966	1,916,704	2,766
437-438	Zanesville, OH	B1	258,210	98,526	195,225	2,371,738	674	384,851	555
439	Steubenville, OH	C3	181,941	76,337	140,002	2,075,516	589	512,370	740
440-441	Cleveland, OH	M	2,130,195	853,620	1,496,206	27,695,376	7,864	4,273,809	6,168
442-443	Akron, OH	M(440)	835,644	320,078	622,859	10,408,300	2,956	1,475,731	2,130
444-445	Youngstown, OH	A	529,519	211,461	393,481	5,947,957	1,689	954,733	1,378
446-447	Canton, OH	B1	645,642	245,027	482,288	7,801,397	2,215	1,313,919	1,897
448-449	Mansfield, OH	C3	441,616	175,031	340,383	4,426,243	1,257	876,595	1,265
450-452	Cincinnati, OH	A	1,681,732	659,886	1,285,193	20,973,691	5,955	3,896,292	5,623
453-455	Dayton, OH	B2	1,080,634	434,672	849,707	12,965,008	3,682	2,565,097	3,703
456	Chillicothe, OH	C3	343,366	134,543	259,020	3,033,982	862	676,527	976
457	Athens, OH	C2	156,123	60,021	119,014	1,311,970	373	185,033	267
458	Lima, OH	C1	369,508	141,972	284,916	4,616,008	1,311	945,041	1,364
460-462	Indianapolis, IN	A	1,840,734	691,891	1,348,487	25,347,054	7,197	5,455,599	7,874
463-464	Gary, IN	M(600)	782,719	282,494	536,709	8,953,891	2,543	1,775,877	2,563
465-466	South Bend, IN	C1	612,966	217,618	417,049	7,995,062	2,270	1,620,076	2,338
467-468	Fort Wayne, IN	A	624,141	225,602	451,624	7,584,498	2,153	1,637,666	2,363
469	Kokomo, IN	C3	317,052	124,772	233,776	3,555,464	1,010	700,867	1,012
470	Cincinnati, OH (IN Part)	A2(450)	114,929	41,952	89,730	948,096	269	81,715	118
471	Louisville, KY (IN Part)	A2(400)	276,096	108,615	212,683	2,908,954	826	553,136	798
472	Columbus, IN	C1	201,725	77,399	153,201	2,327,888	661	573,840	828
473	Muncie, IN	C3	323,621	129,062	244,277	3,548,272	1,008	786,373	1,135
474	Bloomington, IN	A	249,978	99,348	192,204	2,445,381	694	551,433	796
475	Washington, IN	X(476)	159,211	60,526	117,096	2,049,851	582	317,957	459
476-477	Evansville, IN (IN Part)	B2	301,304	119,784	222,061	4,349,360	1,235	956,472	1,381
478	Terre Haute, IN	A	182,883	70,139	130,326	3,540,180	1,005	680,708	982
479	Lafayette, IN	B1	284,497	110,637	210,369	3,310,360	940	730,972	1,055
480-483	Detroit, MI	A	4,788,081	1,844,051	3,373,041	66,949,085	19,010	13,998,443	20,205
484-485	Flint, MI	B1	682,153	254,667	498,941	8,099,761	2,300	1,750,180	2,526
486-487	Saginaw, MI	A	638,600	262,094	479,677	8,340,222	2,368	1,823,733	2,632
488-489	Lansing, MI	B1	780,164	307,532	585,920	9,338,046	2,652	2,620,900	3,783
490-491	Kalamazoo, MI	C3	863,332	342,941	641,070	9,201,749	2,613	2,478,123	3,577
492	Jackson, MI	C1	360,347	136,141	262,608	3,909,777	1,110	918,315	1,325
493-495	Grand Rapids, MI	C3	1,281,469	480,313	947,536	16,162,862	4,589	3,958,216	5,713
496	Traverse City, MI	A	268,465	107,661	203,988	3,689,455	1,048	821,297	1,185
497	Gaylord, MI	C3	236,502	97,248	176,637	3,222,813	915	620,949	896

Source: Devonshire Associates Ltd. and Scan/US, Inc. 2005.

** Estimates for Retail Sales, including Shopping Goods Sales, are based on data from the U.S. Census Bureau's 1997 Economic Census and utilize the North American Industry Classification System (NAICS). Shopping Goods include sales data for general merchandise and apparel stores.

ZIP Codes Service Areas: Population/Sales, *Continued*

ZIP Code	Sectional Center or Principal City	Classification	Population Estimate 7/1/05	Households Estimate 7/1/05	Auto Registrations 2004	Total Retail Sales 2004 Sales ($1,000)	Total Retail Sales Ranally Sales Units	Shopping Goods Sales** 2004 Sales ($1,000)	Shopping Goods Sales** Ranally Sales Units
498-499	Iron Mountain, MI	C3	265,319	112,077	200,127	2,859,806	812	576,484	832
500-503	Des Moines, IA	A	841,009	325,236	693,299	9,529,183	2,706	1,637,095	2,363
504	Mason City, IA	A	108,027	44,366	91,569	1,218,216	346	239,915	346
505	Fort Dodge, IA	A	127,189	51,888	105,323	1,398,006	397	236,121	341
506-507	Waterloo, IA	B2	241,771	95,644	206,497	2,798,474	795	481,665	695
508	Creston, IA	W2(500)	33,667	14,381	30,854	284,431	81	36,853	53
510-511	Sioux City, IA	B2	174,424	66,307	133,987	2,183,335	620	367,889	531
512	Sheldon, IA	W2(510)	43,165	15,678	33,756	526,864	150	42,523	61
513	Spencer, IA	W2(510)	47,535	20,334	41,016	669,663	190	108,703	157
514	Carroll, IA	W2(500)	47,731	19,058	39,328	543,248	154	87,817	127
515	Omaha, NE (IA Part)	A2(680)	146,110	57,089	117,068	1,885,749	535	218,752	316
516	Shenandoah, IA	W2(680)	24,625	9,969	20,462	201,941	57	32,407	47
520	Dubuque, IA	B2	139,386	53,658	108,237	1,792,956	509	300,446	434
521	Decorah, IA	W1(506)	59,899	23,224	48,814	561,439	159	63,696	92
522-524	Cedar Rapids, IA	C1	432,594	174,040	353,757	5,454,994	1,549	1,006,697	1,453
525	Ottumwa, IA	A	112,270	45,372	92,426	1,286,237	365	280,918	405
526	Burlington, IA	A	107,438	43,274	88,011	1,367,927	388	275,434	398
527-528	Rock Island, IL (IA Part)	A2(612)	264,816	103,996	205,719	3,631,210	1,031	710,729	1,026
530-532, 534	Milwaukee, WI	B1	2,213,567	860,175	1,606,740	24,147,899	6,856	4,460,090	6,439
535, 537-538	Madison, WI	C1	841,249	345,112	649,778	12,868,559	3,654	1,983,528	2,863
539	Portage, WI	W2(535)	190,739	75,470	146,602	2,215,394	629	430,053	621
540	St. Paul, MN (WI Part)	A2(553)	136,406	52,053	112,977	1,307,249	371	293,235	423
541-543	Green Bay, WI	C3	547,895	221,185	422,730	6,237,403	1,771	1,546,691	2,232
544	Wausau, WI	C3	384,964	155,192	304,120	4,963,916	1,410	1,083,674	1,564
545	Rhinelander, WI	W1(544)	94,791	40,805	76,274	1,211,322	344	204,833	296
546	La Crosse, WI	A	235,893	93,172	179,049	2,701,448	767	531,745	767
547	Eau Claire, WI	B1	251,225	99,859	202,464	3,534,749	1,004	796,817	1,150
548	Spooner, WI	X(556)	183,611	76,373	146,180	1,994,637	566	389,962	563
549	Oshkosh, WI	C2	463,200	185,732	353,409	6,302,587	1,790	1,211,395	1,748
550-551	St. Paul, MN	M(553)	1,364,306	526,667	1,100,500	18,167,472	5,159	3,226,357	4,656
553-555	Minneapolis, MN	M	1,906,713	772,978	1,518,805	34,021,453	9,661	6,287,230	9,075
556-558	Duluth, MN	A	298,042	129,739	245,785	3,376,894	959	698,193	1,008
559	Rochester, MN	C1	317,334	132,490	262,470	3,548,229	1,008	778,630	1,124
560	Mankato, MN	A	255,806	105,397	212,506	2,704,933	768	509,797	736
561	Windom, MN	D	91,954	39,588	79,285	848,009	241	67,569	98
562	Willmar, MN	B1	146,889	62,680	124,150	1,666,827	473	250,923	362
563	St. Cloud, MN	B1	302,293	119,912	245,035	4,140,864	1,176	859,593	1,241
564	Brainerd, MN	A	139,645	59,946	117,845	1,626,776	462	290,685	420
565	Detroit Lakes, MN	X(580)	165,743	68,213	136,302	1,814,643	515	295,706	427
566	Bemidji, MN	B1	91,193	37,025	72,169	1,028,555	292	196,771	284
567	Thief River Falls, MN	W2(582)	68,871	29,352	58,046	635,177	180	62,339	90
570-571	Sioux Falls, SD	B1	304,492	120,446	261,569	11,891,052	3,377	918,227	1,326
572	Watertown, SD	A	71,023	28,981	64,280	1,123,864	319	76,997	111
573	Mitchell, SD	C2	80,605	32,908	71,620	1,287,037	365	115,201	166
574	Aberdeen, SD	B2	58,062	24,955	52,344	1,322,912	376	73,740	106
575	Pierre, SD	W2(573)	54,656	20,516	44,312	597,707	170	74,100	107
576	Mobridge, SD	W2(574)	22,310	8,124	17,391	160,799	46	12,301	18
577	Rapid City, SD	A	179,721	68,951	150,821	3,072,228	872	617,915	892
580-581	Fargo, ND	B2	168,699	69,917	145,529	3,022,412	859	458,566	661
582	Grand Forks, ND	B2	95,216	37,456	77,039	1,748,424	496	361,348	522
583	Devils Lake, ND	W2(582)	50,363	19,365	40,706	467,942	133	51,380	74
584	Jamestown, ND	W2(580)	47,475	20,061	45,144	544,179	155	64,913	94
585	Bismarck, ND	A	124,820	48,764	108,162	1,706,409	485	298,855	431
586	Dickinson, ND	A	38,773	15,660	35,302	548,689	156	64,717	93
587	Minot, ND	A	79,157	32,169	72,354	1,141,304	324	179,727	259
588	Williston, ND	A	23,612	9,487	20,640	321,916	91	59,538	86
590-591	Billings, MT	B2	199,292	79,271	162,399	2,617,846	743	522,127	754
592	Wolf Point, MT	W2(590)	33,725	14,122	30,748	304,788	87	17,877	26
593	Miles City, MT	W1(590)	34,174	14,328	32,380	350,686	100	46,872	68
594	Great Falls, MT	B1	128,277	51,780	107,124	1,426,515	405	298,821	431
595	Havre, MT	W1(594)	30,123	12,026	25,646	256,098	73	35,239	51
596	Helena, MT	A	70,815	27,686	59,268	811,366	230	151,922	219
597	Butte, MT	C1	143,636	57,739	123,019	1,861,042	528	269,801	389
598	Missoula, MT	A	182,022	72,254	153,127	2,202,875	626	463,703	669
599	Kalispell, MT	B1	105,728	40,748	90,413	1,184,933	336	276,437	399
600-608	Chicago, IL	M	8,645,212	2,993,575	5,218,717	102,609,725	29,137	17,720,168	25,575
609	Kankakee, IL	A	164,546	62,246	111,629	1,725,748	490	335,468	484
610-611	Rockford, IL	C1	538,697	205,646	384,164	6,107,021	1,734	1,171,314	1,690
612	Rock Island, IL (IL Part)	A	215,486	86,959	157,322	2,481,545	705	379,033	547
613	La Salle, IL	A	151,746	61,431	111,129	2,158,933	613	414,558	598
614	Galesburg, IL	C1	148,572	60,323	109,430	1,500,058	426	326,641	471
615-616	Peoria, IL	B2	365,646	147,402	262,045	4,711,469	1,338	858,361	1,239
617	Bloomington, IL	A	226,683	87,219	162,195	2,929,108	832	539,869	779
618-619	Champaign, IL	C1	383,742	154,735	268,521	4,483,367	1,273	1,083,984	1,565
620, 622	St. Louis, MO (IL Part)	M(630)	755,602	294,898	555,468	7,928,590	2,252	1,560,454	2,252
623	Quincy, IL	B1	112,323	45,507	84,170	1,213,034	344	230,610	333
624	Effingham, IL	W2(625)	149,946	59,903	114,317	1,754,618	498	241,535	349
625-627	Springfield, IL	C1	487,810	201,079	356,195	5,973,954	1,697	1,198,177	1,729
628	Centralia, IL	D	215,794	89,341	160,969	2,248,748	639	414,843	599
629	Carbondale, IL	B1	225,650	94,344	161,259	2,083,221	592	486,097	702
630-631	St. Louis, MO (MO Part)	M	1,659,204	670,266	1,260,952	21,536,085	6,115	3,927,734	5,669
633	St. Charles, MO	M(630)	441,636	163,665	363,654	3,957,511	1,124	752,879	1,087
634	Hannibal, MO	A	68,296	28,122	56,352	573,227	163	88,669	128
635	Kirksville, MO	A	61,638	26,451	52,519	529,017	150	88,046	127
636	Flat River, MO	X(630)	130,846	50,050	97,893	1,011,336	287	232,648	336
637	Cape Girardeau, MO	B2	121,547	49,521	96,735	1,681,457	477	409,719	591
638	Sikeston, MO	W2(637)	125,521	53,628	91,178	1,420,533	403	211,017	305
639	Poplar Bluff, MO	A	82,092	35,529	65,275	764,480	217	158,325	229
640-641	Kansas City, MO	B2	1,111,422	449,932	863,940	14,629,023	4,154	2,615,832	3,776
644-645	St. Joseph, MO	A	184,117	74,240	145,045	2,052,122	583	439,460	634
646	Chillicothe, MO	W2(640)	74,274	31,841	63,695	526,870	150	87,491	126
647	Harrisonville, MO	X(640)	119,881	48,909	100,769	1,036,045	294	188,974	273
648	Joplin, MO	B2	184,765	73,596	142,790	1,983,165	563	498,334	719
650, 652	Columbia, MO	A	394,469	161,213	320,460	4,401,072	1,250	825,573	1,192
651	Jefferson City, MO	A	64,539	27,129	52,061	1,295,605	368	306,954	443
653	Sedalia, MO	A	101,958	41,586	80,272	847,633	241	186,455	269
654-655	Rolla, MO	B1	201,865	78,920	155,106	1,858,084	528	331,157	478
656-658	Springfield, MO	B1	664,648	275,715	539,632	7,725,106	2,193	1,450,854	2,094
660-662	Kansas City, KS	A2(640)	954,223	363,799	728,030	12,149,254	3,449	2,543,266	3,671
664-666	Topeka, KS	C1	351,435	140,154	274,575	4,014,864	1,140	951,803	1,374
667	Fort Scott, KS	D	118,647	49,427	99,649	1,076,775	306	277,619	401
668	Emporia, KS	B2	62,896	24,950	50,612	556,422	158	99,477	144
669	Concordia, KS	W2(674)	26,351	12,131	25,537	196,393	56	21,076	30
670-672	Wichita, KS	A	673,702	257,058	525,614	7,129,372	2,024	1,657,579	2,392
673	Independence, KS	D	62,523	26,619	52,157	561,705	159	114,287	165
674	Salina, KS	B2	134,727	55,054	113,333	1,767,958	502	365,058	527
675	Hutchinson, KS	C1	121,873	50,116	99,590	1,259,431	358	232,049	335
676	Hays, KS	A	58,081	25,038	51,256	718,234	204	131,027	189
677	Colby, KS	W2(676)	31,784	14,062	30,713	394,156	112	61,901	89
678	Dodge City, KS	C2	120,272	42,891	85,685	1,344,645	382	254,981	368
679	Liberal, KS (KS Part)	B1	29,884	10,152	18,867	388,241	110	97,688	141
680-681	Omaha, NE (NE Part)	B2	727,404	276,541	540,393	10,525,497	2,988	1,775,577	2,563
683-685	Lincoln, NE	B1	402,603	156,587	329,146	4,565,012	1,297	888,035	1,282
686	Columbus, NE	W1(680)	72,369	28,632	60,804	755,234	214	74,056	107
687	Norfolk, NE	A	133,300	51,639	106,425	1,436,909	408	224,339	324
688	Grand Island, NE	A	158,371	60,395	125,990	2,052,514	583	521,687	753
689	Hastings, NE	A	74,388	30,302	63,588	737,062	209	83,331	120
690	McCook, NE	A	26,097	11,040	23,931	352,636	100	68,504	99
691	North Platte, NE	B1	78,308	33,340	70,002	1,749,342	497	164,005	237
692	Valentine, NE	W1(691)	9,204	3,941	8,291	115,042	33	10,971	16
693	Alliance, NE	D	70,155	28,858	58,632	835,324	237	183,494	265
700-701	New Orleans, LA	B2	1,107,197	414,341	662,702	12,737,777	3,617	3,127,084	4,514
703	Thibodaux, LA	C2	265,714	96,440	160,122	2,969,985	843	713,846	1,030
704	Hammond, LA	B1	386,532	141,906	254,438	4,096,082	1,163	830,410	1,199
705	Lafayette, LA	A	596,491	223,395	363,030	7,027,594	1,996	1,693,058	2,444
706	Lake Charles, LA	A	250,325	97,146	166,255	2,727,994	775	817,949	1,181
707-708	Baton Rouge, LA	A	700,231	246,238	454,497	8,513,515	2,417	1,904,064	2,748
710-711	Shreveport, LA	B2	489,853	191,638	337,027	5,180,860	1,471	1,167,334	1,685
712	Monroe, LA	B2	326,646	124,616	203,339	3,494,384	992	996,330	1,438
713-714	Alexandria, LA	B1	386,939	147,148	242,957	3,519,950	1,000	838,565	1,210
716	Pine Bluff, AR	A	178,023	68,276	123,014	1,791,068	509	475,554	686
717	Camden, AR	D	113,909	47,607	82,790	1,121,817	319	323,537	467
718	Texarkana, TX (AR Part)	A2(755)	128,190	50,429	90,256	929,860	264	240,833	348
719	Hot Springs National Park, AR	B1	164,340	68,233	121,758	1,825,530	518	533,214	770
720-722	Little Rock, AR	B2	845,423	340,021	652,708	11,313,784	3,212	2,842,325	4,103
723	Memphis, TN (AR Part)	A2(380)	180,775	71,163	110,044	1,885,373	535	456,274	659
724	Jonesboro, AR	B1	207,063	84,392	152,725	2,232,066	634	700,139	1,011
725	Batesville, AR	W1(720)	102,590	42,410	79,654	972,754	276	321,353	464
726	Harrison, AR	A	135,253	56,815	107,653	1,357,767	386	410,721	593
727	Fayetteville, AR	A	372,343	139,121	265,684	4,280,736	1,216	1,520,812	2,195
728	Russellville, AR	A	116,733	45,020	86,669	1,149,025	326	284,416	410
729	Fort Smith, AR (AR Part)	B2	215,799	83,276	152,897	2,572,771	731	832,172	1,201
730-731	Oklahoma City, OK	B2	1,212,824	465,486	868,310	14,225,627	4,040	2,953,603	4,263
734	Ardmore, OK	A	87,378	33,771	61,731	827,019	235	200,854	290
735	Lawton, OK	B1	198,375	75,243	135,232	1,708,740	485	557,077	804
736	Clinton, OK	W2(730)	54,019	21,515	40,715	604,262	172	129,330	187
737	Enid, OK	A	102,246	40,125	76,655	1,000,761	284	244,507	353
738	Woodward, OK	W1(730)	30,106	12,041	24,381	335,832	95	99,514	144
739	Liberal, KS (OK Part)	A2(679)	27,745	10,598	21,124	203,102	58	41,641	60
740-741	Tulsa, OK	B2	948,485	347,506	677,682	11,447,094	3,250	2,850,888	4,115
743	Vinita, OK	X(740)	126,656	48,831	92,779	819,750	233	193,941	280
744	Muskogee, OK	B1	220,445	83,823	150,422	1,797,868	511	516,991	746
745	McAlester, OK	B1	88,888	34,028	60,597	701,826	199	206,330	298
746	Ponca City, OK	A	58,509	23,117	42,361	531,488	151	159,316	230
747	Durant, OK	X(750)	83,947	32,938	57,939	584,290	166	144,257	208
748	Shawnee, OK	C1	191,086	71,541	134,267	1,294,035	367	379,587	548
749	Fort Smith, AR (OK part)	A2(729)	111,119	40,452	74,406	719,089	204	174,857	252
750-753	Dallas, TX	M	3,808,269	1,287,285	2,460,154	51,194,748	14,536	10,968,652	15,832
754	Greenville, TX	X(750)	320,865	115,984	216,179	3,064,158	870	609,683	880
755	Texarkana, TX (TX Part)	A	124,647	48,363	84,501	1,489,074	423	369,887	534
756	Longview, TX	A	319,754	120,143	214,335	3,618,898	1,028	752,943	1,087
757	Tyler, TX	A	322,418	116,583	209,528	4,078,095	1,158	997,930	1,440
758	Palestine, TX	W2(757)	121,596	39,309	68,487	874,812	248	138,079	199
759	Lufkin, TX	B1	247,736	93,684	162,465	2,564,955	728	544,749	786
760-761	Fort Worth, TX	M(750)	1,916,384	652,933	1,258,186	24,777,844	7,036	4,065,194	5,867
762	Denton, TX	X(760)	338,590	114,214	226,122	3,826,526	1,087	827,053	1,194
763	Wichita Falls, TX	B2	170,634	66,594	118,200	1,852,469	526	394,079	569
764	Stephenville, TX	W2(760)	134,888	51,160	94,308	1,125,237	320	183,245	264
765	Temple, TX	A	420,405	147,174	264,861	3,432,665	975	599,619	865
766-767	Waco, TX	A	323,846	117,197	206,887	3,244,947	922	694,876	1,003
768	Brownwood, TX	B1	87,083	34,091	61,277	886,977	252	162,848	235
769	San Angelo, TX	B2	123,208	47,828	82,475	1,369,513	389	315,011	455
770-775	Houston, TX	B2	5,477,751	1,811,554	3,357,906	64,674,841	18,366	14,555,852	21,009
776-777	Beaumont, TX	B1	408,731	156,284	263,659	4,811,893	1,367	1,014,658	1,464
778	Bryan, TX	B1	256,477	98,147	175,055	2,899,408	823	624,436	901
779	Victoria, TX	A	163,651	59,971	106,059	1,772,973	503	364,755	526
780-782	San Antonio, TX	C1	2,223,537	748,090	1,299,042	25,596,010	7,269	5,264,191	7,598
783-784	Corpus Christi, TX	A	520,666	181,639	325,652	5,388,347	1,530	1,155,770	1,668
785	McAllen, TX	C3	1,136,538	297,136	514,469	8,977,154	2,549	2,561,179	3,697
733, 786-787	Austin, TX	A	1,524,959	554,314	1,046,087	30,942,425	8,786	3,693,163	5,330
788	Uvalde, TX	C3	171,667	52,282	87,084	1,335,819	379	337,579	487
789	La Grange, TX	W2(770)	68,531	24,735	45,771	660,528	188	78,867	114
790-791	Amarillo, TX	B1	422,590	156,466	284,109	4,636,989	1,317	822,050	1,187
792	Childress, TX	W2(793)	35,938	13,954	25,145	222,101	63	24,184	35
793-794	Lubbock, TX	B2	369,919	141,375	259,921	4,560,725	1,295	856,295	1,235
795-796	Abilene, TX	A	213,504	81,633	144,736	2,342,814	666	486,757	702
797	Midland, TX	C3	348,389	125,877	217,784	4,032,769	1,145	943,730	1,362
798-799	El Paso, TX	A	743,586	227,600	406,101	6,863,997	1,949	1,978,892	2,856
800-804	Denver, CO	B2	2,595,616	1,075,611	2,174,938	34,847,999	9,895	6,628,611	9,568
805	Longmont, CO	X(800)	430,800	177,784	387,304	5,390,448	1,531	1,043,122	1,506
806	Brighton, CO	X(800)	217,149	81,645	178,358	2,132,732	606	393,828	568
807	Fort Morgan, CO	X(800)	68,111	27,133	57,197	640,316	182	86,975	126
808-809	Colorado Springs, CO	B1	593,637	229,276	467,973	7,443,459	2,113	1,469,728	2,121
810	Pueblo, CO	B2	227,008	94,256	184,487	2,330,851	662	590,611	852
811	Alamosa, CO	W2(810)	71,217	30,070	62,571	582,505	165	71,849	104
812	Salida, CO	W2(800)	83,981	34,420	72,228	688,368	195	97,374	141
813	Durango, CO	A	62,533	26,944	56,174	889,355	253	116,661	168
814	Montrose, CO	W2(815)	79,993	33,561	70,932	788,541	224	107,049	154
815	Grand Junction, CO	B2	125,778	53,981	111,231	1,603,360	455	433,862	626
816	Glenwood Springs, CO	W2(815)	138,029	56,611	120,820	2,132,043	605	384,905	556
820	Cheyenne, WY	A	117,539	47,506	101,574	1,801,906	512	364,339	526
821, 829-831	Rock Springs, WY	B1	97,829	38,500	88,091	1,451,326	412	255,570	369
822	Wheatland, WY	W2(826)	22,912	9,896	22,589	207,072	59	19,828	29
823	Rawlins, WY	W1(826)	15,818	6,462	14,517	204,833	58	14,245	21
824	Worland, WY	W2(590)	49,584	20,593	45,257	531,221	151	96,391	139
825	Riverton, WY	B1	34,872	13,536	29,186	433,042	123	87,362	126
826	Casper, WY	B2	83,748	33,029	71,187	1,065,074	302	240,944	348
827	Gillette, WY	W1(826)	50,798	18,128	45,101	474,391	135	105,058	152
828	Sheridan, WY	W1(590)	34,429	14,331	30,118	417,148	118	76,549	110
832	Pocatello, ID	B1	163,556	58,518	134,629	1,616,059	459	223,473	323
833	Twin Falls, ID	A	170,352	62,536	139,757	2,066,120	587	410,031	592
834	Idaho Falls, ID	B2	170,595	58,237	134,466	1,878,926	534	436,823	630
835	Lewiston, ID (ID Part)	B2	66,518	27,683	61,528	739,972	210	124,131	179
836-837	Boise, ID (ID Part)	A	611,121	228,244	512,803	7,743,157	2,198	1,576,680	2,275
838	Spokane, WA (ID Part)	A2(990)	229,181	88,564	197,036	3,269,672	928	437,670	632
840-842	Salt Lake City, UT	B2	1,610,967	514,725	1,133,358	21,708,238	6,164	4,392,542	6,340
843-844	Ogden, UT	C1	321,962	109,077	232,182	3,928,461	1,115	1,028,696	1,485
845	Price, UT	X(840)	51,972	19,655	41,282	479,293	136	93,532	135
846-847	Provo, UT	C2	437,983	139,876	307,451	4,619,297	1,312	812,918	1,173
850, 852-853	Phoenix, AZ	B1	3,993,259	1,433,160	2,523,963	46,148,420	13,104	8,195,662	11,830
855	Globe, AZ	X(850)	88,632	34,240	61,836	569,653	162	128,478	185
856-857	Tucson, AZ	B1	1,102,253	425,621	728,272	9,904,755	2,813	2,050,802	2,960
859	Show Low, AZ	X(850)	67,523	22,443	41,570	540,799	154	107,077	155
860	Flagstaff, AZ	A	169,232	53,598	93,822	1,509,761	429	375,456	542
863	Prescott, AZ	B1	192,749	81,397	148,892	1,802,792	512	392,319	566
864	Kingman, AZ	A2(889)	177,413	71,755	126,487	1,770,000	503	281,647	407
865	Gallup, NM (AZ Part)	A2(873)	63,696	17,557	23,509	136,591	39	12,224	18
870-872	Albuquerque, NM	B2	835,013	318,837	639,178	9,941,402	2,823	2,260,622	3,263
873	Gallup, NM (NM Part)	A	69,323	21,260	34,525	749,971	213	200,042	289
874	Farmington, NM	A	128,003	38,252	73,511	1,436,673	408	429,862	620
875	Santa Fe, NM	A	226,513	88,312	168,879	2,564,596	728	649,434	937
877	Las Vegas, NM	W2(870)	41,234	16,390	30,029	361,251	103	59,820	86
878	Socorro, NM	X(870)	18,827	7,592	13,475	76,043	22	4,873	7
879	Truth or Consequences, NM	W1(880)	18,327	7,745	13,491	114,276	32	8,851	13
880	Las Cruces, NM	B1	247,402	87,687	162,391	1,951,554	554	437,781	632
881	Clovis, NM	A	66,026	24,608	44,530	594,111	169	158,960	229
882	Roswell, NM	C3	168,677	61,354	109,818	1,451,608	412	348,512	503
883	Carrizozo, NM	X(798)	78,854	31,013	57,670	633,003	180	155,927	225
884	Tucumcari, NM	W2(790)	16,915	7,498	13,652	174,410	50	15,350	22
889-891	Las Vegas, NV	A	1,739,939	635,709	1,103,229	20,566,835	5,840	4,273,123	6,168
893	Ely, NV	W1(894)	9,542	3,863	7,530	46,648	13	1,994	3
894-895, 897	Reno, NV (NV Part)	B2	593,794	226,875	445,783	7,175,980	2,037	1,089,603	1,573
898	Elko, NV	W2(894)	48,193	17,961	34,985	471,345	134	60,274	87
900-918	Los Angeles, CA	M	10,826,057	3,424,350	6,504,787	104,682,625	29,726	21,672,241	31,280
919-921	San Diego, CA	A	2,978,557	1,026,599	1,979,390	33,969,015	9,645	6,687,169	9,652
922	Palm Springs, CA	C1	717,535	244,035	440,503	7,051,317	2,002	1,524,333	2,200
923-925	San Bernardino, CA	M(900)	2,441,696	759,983	1,562,045	19,222,367	5,458	3,710,631	5,356
926-928	Santa Ana, CA	M(900)	2,979,594	962,663	1,989,974	39,679,677	11,267	8,110,702	11,707
930	Oxnard, CA	M(900)	679,639	214,973	453,545	7,097,679	2,015	1,043,658	1,506
931	Santa Barbara, CA	B2	184,950	68,563	132,939	2,682,126	762	412,360	595
932-933	Bakersfield, CA	C1	1,168,464	348,397	637,030	8,885,701	2,524	1,653,671	2,387
934	San Luis Obispo, CA	C2	460,751	168,367	360,021	4,823,113	1,370	807,441	1,165
935	Mojave, CA	X(900)	472,167	151,344	311,575	3,930,800	1,116	773,376	1,116
936-938	Fresno, CA	A	1,086,728	329,438	630,633	8,570,188	2,433	1,516,162	2,189
939	Salinas, CA	A	389,805	122,422	252,922	4,227,451	1,200	797,362	1,151
940-941, 943-944	San Francisco, CA	M	1,740,407	691,446	1,169,506	31,847,943	9,043	7,944,747	11,467
942, 956-958	Sacramento, CA	B2	2,202,618	786,270	1,576,639	23,476,981	6,667	4,244,980	6,127
945-948	Oakland, CA	M(940)	2,932,913	1,015,016	2,020,171	33,025,483	9,378	5,888,262	8,498
949, 954	North Bay, CA	M(940)	870,933	336,101	662,322	11,736,658	3,333	1,929,035	2,785
950-951	San Jose, CA	M(940)	1,688,690	543,531	1,194,012	24,842,068	7,054	4,914,308	7,093
952-953	Stockton, CA	C3	1,512,916	466,214	955,181	12,198,559	3,464	2,234,225	3,225
955	Eureka, CA	A	160,132	64,137	110,740	1,484,479	422	221,833	320
959	Marysville, CA	C2	497,661	184,924	345,310	4,475,817	1,271	778,447	1,124
960	Redding, CA	A	302,354	115,254	211,895	2,747,224	780	458,642	662
961	Reno, NV (CA Part)	A2(894)	130,725	48,478	94,356	1,050,940	298	138,623	200
967-968	Honolulu, HI	B1	1,274,014	429,453	768,403	14,244,399	4,045	4,481,614	6,468
970-972	Portland, OR (OR Part)	A	1,837,212	724,593	1,347,231	26,471,261	7,517	6,238,747	9,004
973	Salem, OR	A	568,537	215,803	421,511	5,774,041	1,640	1,514,926	2,187
974	Eugene, OR	C3	534,773	226,391	451,534	6,246,528	1,774	1,368,450	1,975
975	Medford, OR	A	275,513	114,892	227,950	4,227,596	1,200	894,801	1,291
976	Klamath Falls, OR	A	69,954	28,732	56,391	767,409	218	171,115	247
977	Bend, OR	A	190,436	77,937	165,949	2,516,319	715	595,964	860
978	Pendleton, OR	B1	143,301	56,447	116,986	1,797,617	510	268,495	388
979	Boise, ID (OR Part)	A2(836)	32,154	11,205	22,460	412,787	117	126,443	182
980-981	Seattle, WA	B2	2,029,287	842,725	1,586,792	31,513,940	8,949	6,713,148	9,689
982	Everett, WA	C1	821,580	315,253	660,902	9,156,650	2,600	1,779,324	2,568
983-984	Tacoma, WA	C1	1,078,684	409,015	829,581	11,061,226	3,140	2,582,010	3,726
985	Olympia, WA	A	439,912	171,065	338,685	4,813,802	1,367	1,243,207	1,794
986	Portland, OR (WA Part)	A2(970)	541,938	199,554	418,476	4,708,538	1,337	1,098,747	1,586
988	Wenatchee, WA	A	202,149	75,272	149,027	2,217,370	630	448,913	644
989	Yakima, WA	A	266,001	92,105	197,174	2,371,541	673	578,315	835
990-992	Spokane, WA (WA Part)	A	562,267	229,347	456,591	6,018,567	1,709	1,364,390	1,970
993	Pasco, WA	C2	313,152	107,682	216,787	3,201,435	909	737,627	1,065
994	Lewiston, ID (WA Part)	A2(835)	20,656	8,715	17,157	208,570	59	90,069	130
995-996	Anchorage, AK	A	468,376	163,126	313,952	6,391,371	1,815	1,586,883	2,290
997	Fairbanks, AK	B1	120,576	41,368	71,672	1,416,246	402	368,008	531
998	Juneau, AK	B2	49,185	19,600	32,651	523,723	149	153,150	221
999	Ketchikan, AK	W1(998)	20,629	9,021	14,019	273,823	78	35,259	51
	United States Total		296,460,358	110,228,421	203,446,969	3,521,709,000	1,000,000	692,842,000	1,000,000

Source: Devonshire Associates Ltd. and Scan/US, Inc. 2005.

** Estimates for Retail Sales, including Shopping Goods Sales, are based on data from the U.S. Census Bureau's 1997 Economic Census and utilize the North American Industry Classification System (NAICS). Shopping Goods include sales data for general merchandise and apparel stores.

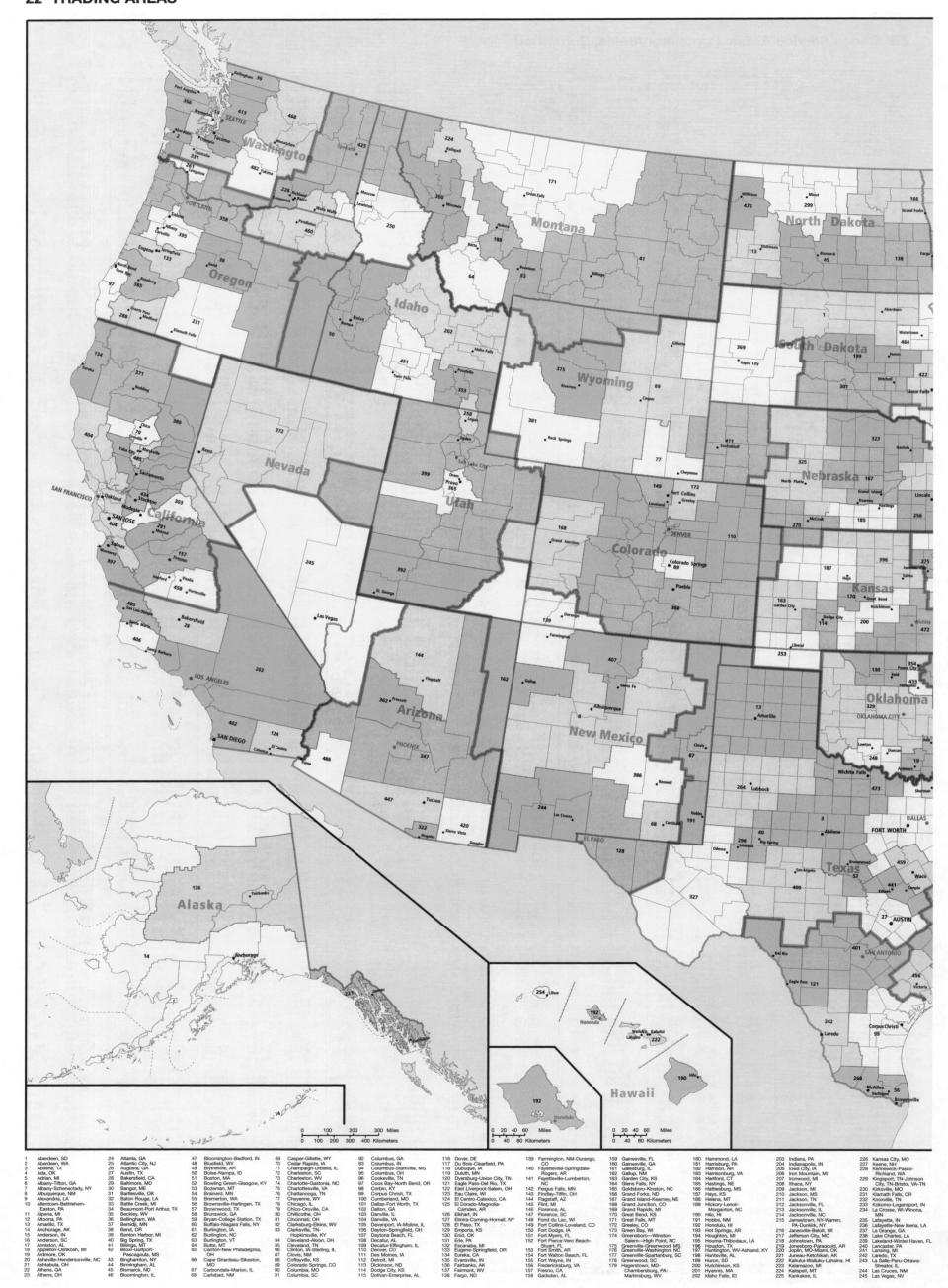

Rand McNally Map of
TRADING AREAS

THE 487 BASIC TRADING AREAS are indicated on this map by separate colors, and by numbers keyed to the alphabetical list at the foot of the page.

THE 47 MAJOR TRADING AREAS, each comprised of two or more Basic Trading Areas, are bounded by wide red lines. The names of the Major Trading Centers appear in red.

The Trading Area boundaries have been drawn on a county-line basis because most statistics relevant to marketing are published in terms of whole counties. The boundaries have been determined after an intensive study of such factors as physiography, population distribution, newspaper circulation, economic activities, highway facilities, railroad service, suburban transportation, and field reports of experienced sales analysts.

NOTE: The cities of Baltimore, MD, St. Louis, MO, Carson City, NV, and 39 cities in Virginia are independent of any county.

Major Trading Areas: Population/Income/Sales

This table gives the 2000 Census population, 2005 estimates of population and households, and 2004 estimates of income, purchasing power, retail sales (total and by various store groups) and passenger car registrations for the 47 Major Trading Areas as defined by Rand McNally. The Major Trading Areas are combinations of Basic Trading Areas as shown on the map on pages 22-23. Statistics for Total Retail Sales, General Merchandise, Apparel Store, Food Store Sales, and Health and Drug Store Sales in this edition are estimates based on data from the U.S. Census Bureau, and utilize the 1997 North American Industry Classification System (NAICS). A detailed explanation of Retail Trade, and Major and Basic Trading Areas, can be found in the Introduction on pages 5-9.

MTA No.	Major Trading Area	MTA Abbrev.	Number of Basic Areas	Number of Counties	Population: Estimate 7/1/05	Population: Census 4/1/00	Population: % Change 4/1/90-4/1/00	Per Capita Income 2004	Households Estimate 7/1/05	Disposable Income 2004 ($1,000)	Market Ability Index 2004	Total Retail Sales: 2004 Sales ($1,000)	Total Retail Sales: Ranally Sales Units	General Merchandise: 2004 Sales ($1,000)	General Merchandise: Ranally Sales Units	Apparel Store: 2004 Sales ($1,000)	Apparel Store: Ranally Sales Units	Food Store Sales 2004 ($1,000)	Health & Drug Store 2004 ($1,000)	Passenger Car Registrations 2004
01	Atlanta	ATL	14	156	9,530,091	8,731,699	25.8	18,733	3,469,151	178,525,880	3.1671	114,119,876	32,399	17,210,351	34,227	5,856,160	30,820	15,829,225	5,422,169	6,633,522
03	Birmingham	BIR	10	55	3,630,909	3,555,114	9.6	17,044	1,415,813	61,885,250	1.1303	40,736,724	11,572	7,723,552	15,360	1,766,062	9,296	4,995,718	2,163,202	2,695,898
05	Boston-Providence	BOS-	14	47	10,310,385	10,009,759	5.9	21,880	3,937,160	225,590,300	3.8458	139,584,246	39,636	13,930,158	27,703	8,489,789	44,688	23,419,312	9,541,402	7,233,986
07	Buffalo-Rochester	BUF-	4	19	2,779,477	2,792,296	0.5	20,051	1,110,197	55,732,230	.9203	29,153,777	8,279	3,148,711	6,260	1,494,341	7,864	5,307,528	1,940,401	1,936,087
09	Charlotte-Greensboro-Greenville-Raleigh	C-G-G-R	23	134	12,386,785	11,613,265	19.1	17,988	4,764,812	222,809,180	4.0551	150,581,027	42,759	22,242,851	44,231	7,406,393	38,982	19,909,752	8,500,946	9,110,291
11	Chicago	CHI	18	84	13,650,267	13,220,193	9.5	20,114	4,900,559	274,567,640	4.6838	161,515,442	45,866	21,468,813	42,696	7,976,770	41,986	20,947,677	12,716,913	8,771,255
13	Cincinnati-Dayton	CIN-	9	71	4,929,648	4,888,525	3.6	18,298	1,957,144	90,203,000	1.5989	56,642,176	16,084	8,795,225	17,490	2,309,250	12,155	7,794,686	3,706,843	3,712,183
15	Cleveland	CLEV	10	25	5,070,528	5,084,468	2.8	18,773	1,998,092	95,190,710	1.7008	62,363,929	17,708	7,187,397	14,295	2,933,328	15,438	9,077,326	5,630,505	3,667,298
17	Columbus	COL	6	29	2,510,899	2,392,826	11.5	18,699	956,666	46,950,990	.8579	32,923,089	9,348	4,329,140	8,611	1,523,327	8,018	4,168,122	1,526,252	1,886,312
19	Dallas-Fort Worth	DAL-	22	210	12,710,951	11,688,918	20.6	18,052	4,522,341	229,459,770	4.2483	164,003,145	46,576	23,631,555	46,996	7,303,983	38,442	20,245,893	7,068,503	8,388,945
21	Denver	DEN	12	105	5,308,552	4,907,635	26.5	22,104	2,162,029	117,342,220	1.9654	68,920,503	19,571	10,484,466	20,850	2,663,060	14,022	9,209,849	2,443,558	4,472,643
23	Des Moines-Quad Cities	DES-	13	102	3,179,055	3,157,069	5.0	18,079	1,254,645	57,473,220	1.0824	43,233,380	12,274	5,384,590	10,706	1,184,754	6,235	4,937,134	1,848,243	2,564,731
25	Detroit	DET	18	84	10,886,268	10,658,459	6.6	20,236	4,218,240	220,299,290	3.8575	141,764,027	40,253	25,561,534	50,834	5,883,085	30,963	16,266,564	9,198,235	7,924,463
27	El Paso-Albuquerque	ELP-	8	37	2,674,109	2,533,752	19.9	14,761	943,102	39,473,530	.7531	26,901,232	7,640	5,306,349	10,552	1,240,529	6,529	3,030,770	1,308,967	1,782,885
29	Honolulu	HON	4	5	1,273,900	1,211,537	9.3	19,757	429,411	25,168,690	.4259	14,229,466	4,040	2,783,330	5,535	1,694,358	8,919	2,349,624	1,173,546	768,349
31	Houston	HOU	6	46	6,903,029	6,307,777	21.5	17,381	2,352,353	119,980,020	2.1931	80,346,919	22,817	13,745,519	27,339	4,322,732	22,751	11,750,662	3,767,830	4,292,817
33	Indianapolis	IND	11	54	3,447,904	3,333,121	10.5	18,393	1,322,952	63,417,110	1.1623	44,425,433	12,617	7,907,614	15,727	1,620,947	8,534	4,220,738	2,700,050	2,545,265
35	Jacksonville	JAX	7	49	2,939,996	2,740,381	20.5	17,883	1,127,308	52,576,700	.9383	33,221,988	9,431	5,173,652	10,285	1,546,033	8,140	4,789,562	1,691,493	2,019,183
37	Kansas City	K.C.	9	71	3,331,082	3,202,863	9.9	19,173	1,324,846	63,866,420	1.1169	39,530,548	11,222	6,633,602	13,195	1,366,998	7,194	4,841,129	2,054,734	2,600,186
39	Knoxville	KNOX	3	38	2,016,606	1,944,407	12.9	16,074	823,581	32,414,350	.6306	25,011,705	7,100	4,450,083	8,844	1,183,564	6,230	3,164,909	1,513,979	1,623,824
41	Little Rock	L.R.	9	61	2,485,933	2,3[illegible]5,905	16.3	16,244	984,956	40,382,180	.7644	28,866,918	8,197	7,380,268	14,676	942,961	4,964	2,794,293	1,216,501	1,845,067
43	Los Angeles-San Diego	L.A.-	7	16	24,289,857	22,223,875	16.1	18,328	7,920,801	445,193,330	7.6435	250,652,951	71,173	31,808,203	63,257	18,432,195	97,011	39,301,137	13,715,561	15,316,253
45	Louisville-Lexington-Evansville	L-L-E	9	117	4,026,756	3,905,399	9.8	16,833	1,571,891	67,780,430	1.2344	43,785,452	12,432	7,756,265	15,424	1,742,683	9,175	4,799,021	2,818,001	2,961,784
47	Memphis-Jackson	MEM-	11	94	3,808,610	3,761,294	8.5	15,499	1,430,192	59,029,320	1.1221	41,265,450	11,715	8,394,486	16,697	1,926,087	10,133	4,379,016	2,591,080	2,609,797
49	Miami-Fort Lauderdale	MIA-	5	13	7,101,808	6,436,114	25.3	19,089	2,655,249	135,564,640	2.4255	90,160,124	25,601	11,053,631	21,985	7,349,810	38,685	12,522,610	6,472,502	4,463,724
51	Milwaukee	MILW	16	66	5,076,485	4,941,046	8.8	19,753	2,027,659	100,275,490	1.7431	62,060,948	17,620	10,048,976	19,982	1,666,942	8,771	7,659,913	2,868,026	3,832,551
53	Minneapolis-St. Paul	MPLS-	23	211	6,875,191	6,621,619	10.6	20,723	2,778,749	142,473,550	2.5554	100,073,682	28,415	14,739,562	29,317	3,002,834	15,804	11,845,035	4,253,135	5,639,201
55	Nashville	NASH	3	43	2,296,458	2,165,007	22.5	18,865	888,148	43,322,160	.7784	28,981,169	8,231	5,272,642	10,486	1,341,098	7,058	3,530,213	1,634,546	1,750,940
57	New Orleans-Baton Rouge	N.O.-	13	67	5,508,234	5,399,308	9.6	15,977	2,031,774	88,004,800	1.6599	61,428,072	17,445	12,130,864	24,123	2,938,986	15,470	7,753,114	3,899,016	3,578,756
59	New York	N.Y.	20	94	29,052,361	28,198,690	6.8	22,492	10,645,817	653,454,200	10.4526	330,186,497	93,758	30,534,035	60,722	29,932,541	157,536	53,055,374	25,582,954	16,181,135
61	Oklahoma City	O.C.	8	50	2,076,512	2,029,571	8.1	16,002	796,768	33,228,120	.6154	21,849,473	6,202	4,467,115	8,885	682,317	3,589	2,374,786	1,232,428	1,480,855
63	Omaha	OMA	7	90	1,835,795	1,794,352	8.1	17,940	713,986	32,934,470	.6100	23,450,370	6,653	3,317,813	6,599	734,383	3,865	2,879,126	1,316,632	1,455,336
65	Philadelphia	PHIL	11	37	9,803,153	9,510,948	6.5	20,841	3,667,296	204,304,910	3.4922	123,839,560	35,161	12,077,583	24,020	7,178,127	37,781	19,724,211	8,540,208	6,350,479
67	Phoenix	PHOE	7	13	5,604,136	4,906,177	39.8	18,289	2,047,107	102,494,190	1.7830	60,324,362	17,130	8,917,531	17,734	2,300,452	12,107	8,266,337	3,074,256	3,589,764
69	Pittsburgh	PGH	12	42	3,995,931	4,048,998	-1.3	17,032	1,623,879	68,056,700	1.2463	45,240,359	12,850	5,792,145	11,516	1,839,942	9,684	7,109,296	3,242,665	2,765,908
71	Portland	POR	9	35	4,026,000	3,738,321	22.2	19,560	1,590,966	78,749,170	1.3879	50,720,462	14,401	9,667,124	19,223	2,197,653	11,569	7,196,714	1,760,388	3,096,318
73	Richmond-Norfolk	RICH-	7	97	4,403,013	4,242,383	10.5	17,746	1,675,325	78,137,550	1.3997	49,775,960	14,137	7,886,691	15,686	2,419,117	12,731	6,774,346	2,746,400	3,277,129
75	St. Louis	ST.L.	12	103	5,155,780	5,018,297	7.6	18,508	2,074,242	95,422,660	1.6778	58,761,949	16,693	9,415,208	18,726	1,900,109	9,997	7,452,459	3,546,279	3,985,958
77	Salt Lake City	S.L.C.	8	65	3,609,794	3,319,967	29.0	16,885	1,219,153	60,950,050	1.1576	45,201,309	12,832	7,590,409	15,096	1,640,167	8,633	6,512,530	1,172,223	2,697,429
79	San Antonio	SANT	6	40	4,093,193	3,716,676	24.4	13,179	1,293,473	53,943,830	1.0995	41,615,927	11,816	6,835,356	13,593	2,537,208	13,353	6,733,467	1,662,647	2,253,105
81	San Francisco-Oakland-San Jose	SF-O-SJ	13	58	14,697,003	13,782,432	15.9	21,923	5,103,375	322,203,130	5.2453	170,622,430	48,445	21,681,886	43,117	11,186,777	58,879	30,814,033	9,472,438	9,989,896
83	Seattle	SEAT	11	48	5,530,961	5,231,647	19.5	21,540	2,151,052	119,135,780	2.0038	69,862,112	19,842	12,089,581	24,042	3,403,943	17,916	10,160,665	2,707,287	4,217,798
85	Spokane-Billings	SPOK-	11	87	2,282,631	2,178,445	16.9	16,630	897,484	37,959,400	.7114	26,704,020	7,578	4,446,606	8,840	802,132	4,222	4,107,606	967,366	1,872,824
87	Tampa-St. Petersburg-Orlando	T-SP-O	7	20	7,421,933	6,660,705	22.9	19,405	2,961,535	144,022,750	2.5534	94,004,890	26,697	13,029,058	25,910	4,718,407	24,834	13,258,964	5,763,603	5,070,033
89	Tulsa	TUL	4	20	1,264,732	1,224,694	11.7	16,077	469,124	20,333,340	.3776	13,549,300	3,847	2,966,938	5,900	416,460	2,193	1,467,882	808,514	902,767
91	Washington-Baltimore	WASH-	9	67	9,462,394	8,799,742	13.1	24,396	3,549,659	230,842,630	3.5511	106,399,278	30,212	14,099,211	28,042	6,523,820	34,339	17,554,100	5,809,434	6,678,906
93	Wichita	WICH	8	66	1,205,263	1,206,230	7.3	17,341	468,359	20,900,210	.3749	13,117,342	3,725	2,347,319	4,666	474,385	2,495	1,868,572	612,135	953,133
	United States Total		**487**	**3,141**	**296,460,358**	**281,421,906**	**13.2**	**19,402**	**110,228,421**	**5,752,025,490**	**100.0000**	**3,521,709,000**	**1,000,000**	**502,845,000**	**1,000,000**	**189,997,000**	**1,000,000**	**498,151,000**	**205,404,000**	**203,446,969**

Source: Devonshire Associates Ltd. and Scan/US, Inc. 2005.

Basic Trading Areas: Population/Income/Sales

This table gives the 2000 Census population, 2005 estimates of population and households, and 2004 estimates of income, purchasing power, retail sales (total and by various store groups) and passenger car registrations for the 487 Basic Trading Areas (BTAs) as defined by Rand McNally. The Basic Trading Areas are shown on the map on pages 22-23. Statistics for Total Retail Sales, General Merchandise, Apparel Store, Food Store Sales, and Health and Drug Store Sales in this edition are estimates based on data from the U.S. Census Bureau, and utilize the 1997 North American Industry Classification System (NAICS). A detailed explanation of Retail Trade, and Major and Basic Trading Areas, can be found in the Introduction on pages 5-9.

BTA No.	Basic Trading Area	Population: Estimate 7/1/05	Population: Census 4/1/00	Population: % Change 4/1/90-4/1/00	Per Capita Income 2004	Households Estimate 7/1/05	Disposable Income 2004 ($1,000)	Market Ability Index 2004	Total Retail Sales: 2004 Sales ($1,000)	Total Retail Sales: Ranally Sales Units	General Merchandise: 2004 Sales ($1,000)	General Merchandise: Ranally Sales Units	Apparel Store: 2004 Sales ($1,000)	Apparel Store: Ranally Sales Units	Food Store Sales 2004 ($1,000)	Health & Drug Store 2004 ($1,000)	Passenger Car Registrations 2004
001	Aberdeen, SD	82,618	86,789	-2.4	15,241	34,091	1,259,190	.0298	1,551,460	439	75,756	151	9,940	53	68,078	9,283	71,340
002	Aberdeen, WA	91,408	88,178	6.2	16,067	37,154	1,468,690	.0249	703,169	200	112,043	223	11,365	60	176,709	60,734	68,065
003	Abilene, TX	253,019	261,706	3.4	15,019	97,788	3,800,080	.0740	2,812,191	799	471,561	939	77,661	408	314,599	117,107	173,205
004	Ada, OK	55,209	55,053	4.5	12,658	21,148	698,840	.0139	479,750	136	141,217	281	14,694	77	52,781	27,194	38,365
005	Adrian, MI	102,302	98,890	8.1	19,568	38,178	2,001,830	.0349	1,245,869	354	245,964	489	16,924	89	129,296	80,319	75,249
006	Albany-Tifton, GA	364,731	355,474	9.4	13,423	131,272	4,895,760	.0988	3,720,776	1,058	588,757	1,169	139,167	733	570,776	182,198	225,765
007	Albany-Schenectady, NY	1,074,584	1,047,324	1.8	21,157	427,852	22,735,140	.3704	11,780,905	3,345	1,347,080	2,678	605,280	3,185	1,680,931	760,190	733,359
008	Albuquerque, NM	892,110	831,850	20.8	17,641	342,539	15,737,310	.2858	10,417,900	2,958	1,974,211	3,928	353,250	1,859	930,024	542,181	680,871
009	Alexandria, LA	266,472	270,223	-3.5	13,903	100,928	3,704,890	.0713	2,495,615	709	560,044	1,114	81,655	429	295,182	166,553	168,050
010	Allentown-Bethlehem-Easton, PA	785,814	740,395	7.8	20,371	296,297	16,007,810	.2729	9,467,904	2,689	950,519	1,890	391,866	2,061	1,653,435	659,754	570,635
011	Alpena, MI	66,891	67,759	6.8	16,942	29,599	1,133,290	.0207	739,606	209	114,570	228	21,732	115	103,608	46,737	54,358
012	Altoona, PA	222,622	224,714	0.9	15,925	89,369	3,545,220	.0710	2,956,920	840	414,012	823	75,324	397	410,313	188,148	158,036
013	Amarillo, TX	412,704	410,323	7.9	16,045	155,431	6,622,030	.1245	4,615,113	1,309	609,272	1,211	168,579	887	478,737	185,887	282,743
014	Anchorage, AK	491,194	456,392	17.3	20,611	169,566	10,123,860	.1768	6,549,614	1,860	1,362,226	2,710	267,240	1,407	1,034,958	91,189	320,171
015	Anderson, IN	177,091	181,866	1.7	18,008	71,717	3,189,070	.0557	1,877,546	533	294,526	586	41,146	217	207,880	134,334	133,880
016	Anderson, SC	363,254	347,350	13.8	16,475	141,517	5,984,490	.1076	3,651,810	1,037	568,864	1,131	130,705	688	582,656	246,903	273,999
017	Anniston, AL	164,105	163,006	0.7	15,419	65,275	2,530,270	.0461	1,530,472	434	318,549	634	43,157	228	221,692	75,489	126,056
018	Appleton-Oshkosh, WI	472,380	452,355	13.3	20,235	188,222	9,558,720	.1670	6,109,153	1,734	874,835	1,741	202,420	1,065	741,667	244,086	363,697
019	Ardmore, OK	93,427	90,772	8.1	13,774	35,903	1,286,890	.0254	929,280	263	198,053	393	27,663	145	114,117	59,395	65,586
020	Asheville-Hendersonville, NC	639,822	608,250	19.3	17,257	265,541	11,041,240	.2102	8,343,944	2,369	1,294,300	2,576	339,533	1,786	1,119,396	459,923	502,758
021	Ashtabula, OH	103,185	102,728	2.9	16,748	40,666	1,728,100	.0294	873,011	248	125,687	250	26,267	138	150,692	75,500	77,941
022	Athens, GA	227,069	207,668	25.1	16,285	87,477	3,697,730	.0688	2,506,223	711	394,398	784	186,134	981	325,202	114,235	174,420
023	Athens, OH	134,037	130,742	5.6	12,777	50,310	1,712,590	.0320	952,248	270	119,551	238	27,286	144	214,785	72,769	99,396
024	Atlanta, GA	4,987,395	4,407,446	37.9	21,370	1,787,523	106,580,590	1.8305	66,611,144	18,913	8,993,756	17,888	3,492,322	18,382	9,226,379	2,901,230	3,500,015
025	Atlantic City, NJ	362,796	354,878	11.1	23,372	151,746	8,479,390	.1383	4,710,388	1,337	446,396	888	343,199	1,807	1,046,330	313,014	244,256
026	Augusta, GA	607,787	590,218	13.1	16,308	224,672	9,912,090	.1779	5,976,011	1,696	1,052,755	2,095	263,524	1,387	852,100	311,065	406,498
027	Austin, TX	1,540,187	1,325,029	47.3	21,057	557,904	32,431,970	.6491	30,916,727	8,780	2,572,743	5,117	1,114,421	5,867	3,161,090	1,520,882	1,051,214
028	Bakersfield, CA	743,729	661,645	21.7	14,153	234,348	10,526,210	.1907	5,759,480	1,635	787,831	1,567	234,327	1,233	863,026	390,768	437,779
029	Baltimore, MD	2,713,502	2,606,003	7.2	22,492	1,021,896	61,032,770	.9700	30,112,122	8,549	3,874,694	7,706	1,740,410	9,161	5,325,612	1,770,976	1,855,614
030	Bangor, ME	334,702	323,784	2.2	16,796	140,353	5,621,660	.1094	4,445,459	1,262	516,651	1,028	92,890	490	970,271	193,739	263,455
031	Bartlesville, OK	49,163	48,996	1.9	17,800	19,855	875,090	.0145	417,857	119	150,301	299	15,166	80	31,628	23,568	36,538
032	Baton Rouge, LA	727,726	705,760	13.2	16,566	255,901	12,055,390	.2274	8,602,382	2,443	1,577,670	3,137	358,974	1,888	1,048,954	433,016	470,235
033	Battle Creek, MI	246,176	240,527	5.7	18,393	95,731	4,527,980	.0779	2,573,841	731	579,363	1,152	60,518	318	314,813	158,364	179,190
034	Beaumont-Port Arthur, TX	461,862	467,106	8.1	16,388	176,951	7,569,190	.1415	5,231,734	1,485	892,016	1,774	219,577	1,155	705,561	306,240	299,258
035	Beckley, WV	166,064	166,963	-0.1	13,594	66,470	2,257,510	.0448	1,651,289	469	352,972	702	31,526	167	171,539	130,489	119,448
036	Bellingham, WA	182,534	166,814	30.5	18,455	71,812	3,368,700	.0612	2,303,589	654	435,895	867	99,789	525	459,114	114,322	139,293
037	Bemidji, MN	70,127	66,449	15.3	15,146	27,342	1,062,150	.0218	924,859	262	149,796	298	43,097	227	163,258	33,413	54,059
038	Bend, OR	179,911	153,558	49.5	19,377	73,228	3,486,070	.0630	2,422,181	687	524,909	1,043	69,054	363	362,563	61,782	156,080
039	Benton Harbor, MI	162,940	162,453	0.7	18,150	65,840	2,957,340	.0504	1,604,788	456	295,720	588	32,671	172	224,588	119,269	117,237
040	Big Spring, TX	34,502	35,762	3.4	13,455	12,181	464,240	.0093	340,080	97	56,768	113	9,442	50	43,483	14,924	20,427
041	Billings, MT	316,282	312,138	7.5	16,490	127,558	5,215,530	.1000	3,902,903	1,106	618,233	1,226	114,210	598	505,885	122,425	269,519
042	Biloxi-Gulfport-Pascagoula, MS	407,743	396,754	16.8	17,232	154,982	7,026,180	.1263	4,424,006	1,257	1,121,303	2,230	153,372	809	458,514	205,329	300,118
043	Binghamton, NY	343,614	345,959	-3.0	18,245	139,308	6,269,320	.1054	3,260,291	925	413,616	823	105,540	555	551,152	262,152	234,081
044	Birmingham, AL	1,350,969	1,319,776	10.0	17,906	524,748	24,190,620	.4341	15,556,714	4,419	2,703,051	5,375	722,703	3,804	1,971,925	820,452	1,012,286
045	Bismarck, ND	130,504	129,398	4.6	17,360	51,474	2,265,530	.0436	1,772,923	504	262,568	521	37,636	198	192,785	110,136	114,434
046	Bloomington, IL	246,431	238,092	10.3	20,105	94,203	4,954,460	.0867	3,168,996	900	444,394	884	146,233	769	349,194	193,671	172,854
047	Bloomington-Bedford, IN	244,430	240,734	10.5	15,733	96,881	3,845,700	.0705	2,406,055	683	465,433	925	80,421	423	320,281	133,333	186,581
048	Bluefield, WV	162,049	168,756	-8.3	12,818	67,613	2,077,130	.0437	1,732,347	491	371,301	739	41,611	219	232,421	163,698	120,327
049	Blytheville, AR	66,761	72,026	-9.3	13,365	27,798	892,280	.0174	601,803	171	113,687	226	14,276	75	86,938	37,796	44,013
050	Boise-Nampa, ID	658,683	584,008	40.2	17,727	246,305	11,676,470	.2167	8,319,699	2,362	1,458,755	2,902	249,021	1,311	1,163,617	277,829	548,863
051	Boston, MA	4,457,319	4,391,344	6.2	24,540	1,656,326	109,383,350	1.7852	62,649,565	17,791	5,876,246	11,687	4,707,924	24,780	9,933,443	4,633,205	2,943,223
052	Bowling Green-Glasgow, KY	263,545	254,561	14.3	15,179	101,873	4,000,360	.0753	2,670,022	758	438,564	872	92,785	488	305,037	167,202	194,183
053	Bozeman, MT	92,504	83,525	28.5	17,355	36,141	1,605,380	.0311	1,283,125	364	122,390	244	37,452	197	185,342	32,917	78,377
054	Brainerd, MN	105,262	97,550	24.3	17,854	45,560	1,879,390	.0346	1,317,269	374	252,159	501	11,392	60	167,054	37,889	88,824
055	Bremerton, WA	241,196	231,969	22.3	20,793	92,982	5,015,170	.0800	2,360,051	670	567,682	1,129	73,505	387	316,380	119,693	184,355
056	Brownsville-Harlingen, TX	400,052	355,309	27.9	8,444	103,273	3,377,920	.0813	2,926,540	831	689,711	1,371	196,699	1,035	504,194	126,956	169,159
057	Brownwood, TX	62,421	63,037	9.3	14,513	24,183	905,890	.0177	664,737	189	105,290	209	20,914	110	68,668	36,727	43,791
058	Brunswick, GA	83,246	78,415	10.2	18,137	33,487	1,509,820	.0275	1,033,505	293	157,242	313	86,466	455	143,834	54,238	58,883
059	Bryan-College Station, TX	189,774	184,885	22.4	14,501	74,942	2,751,960	.0544	2,068,824	588	381,083	758	100,897	531	275,095	53,217	133,863
060	Buffalo-Niagara Falls, NY	1,197,505	1,213,535	-1.5	20,107	492,614	24,077,740	.3953	12,353,272	3,507	1,256,197	2,499	727,095	3,827	2,222,088	995,772	814,516
061	Burlington, IA	131,283	136,489	-0.8	17,578	53,955	2,307,630	.0422	1,548,283	440	243,737	485	37,212	195	238,528	73,967	108,434
062	Burlington, NC	140,105	130,800	20.9	18,162	54,708	2,544,520	.0467	1,771,538	503	233,033	463	113,462	597	219,919	99,591	106,644
063	Burlington, VT	421,831	406,799	10.2	18,568	160,078	7,832,680	.1454	5,738,847	1,630	408,933	813	229,060	1,205	972,645	341,851	311,955
064	Butte, MT	63,690	67,256	3.1	15,434	27,290	982,990	.0189	711,254	201	83,595	167	35,038	185	129,545	35,937	55,898
065	Canton-New Philadelphia, OH	536,591	534,503	4.1	17,662	208,678	9,477,350	.1749	6,615,439	1,879	872,502	1,736	332,641	1,751	1,030,975	596,349	414,191
066	Cape Girardeau-Sikeston, MO	191,420	189,401	4.2	15,912	78,783	3,045,890	.0600	2,404,399	682	449,721	895	54,767	289	221,074	111,315	145,381
067	Carbondale-Marion, IL	214,074	214,191	2.2	14,704	87,909	3,147,680	.0598	2,115,996	603	460,617	916	69,098	363	266,175	107,265	151,465
068	Carlsbad, NM	51,414	51,658	6.3	14,760	19,363	758,860	.0137	428,156	122	75,227	150	14,770	78	75,411	26,416	35,068
069	Casper-Gillette, WY	153,748	146,211	8.2	17,639	59,312	2,712,030	.0495	1,831,035	521	332,357	662	33,279	176	225,824	43,218	133,223
070	Cedar Rapids, IA	298,199	289,492	11.1	20,107	119,136	5,995,930	.1040	3,729,472	1,060	544,504	1,083	173,618	913	445,762	193,454	247,566
071	Champaign-Urbana, IL	236,507	230,197	3.5	18,456	94,723	4,364,900	.0781	2,839,284	806	531,562	1,057	133,549	704	357,713	203,102	163,570
072	Charleston, SC	722,391	680,311	9.0	16,510	261,739	11,926,800	.2191	7,829,953	2,223	1,419,650	2,823	497,490	2,620	1,203,201	383,699	466,341
073	Charleston, WV	482,696	486,731	1.1	15,992	197,861	7,719,290	.1458	5,418,246	1,539	844,933	1,679	174,684	920	655,577	433,529	348,156
074	Charlotte-Gastonia, NC	2,289,481	2,078,083	24.4	19,708	880,535	45,120,960	.7833	27,782,013	7,887	3,938,694	7,833	1,247,930	6,567	3,643,748	1,645,246	1,725,265
075	Charlottesville, VA	241,840	228,045	19.9	19,183	95,105	4,639,230	.0804	2,780,809	790	336,568	670	139,081	733	462,242	160,097	191,309

Source: Devonshire Associates Ltd. and Scan/US, Inc. 2005.
... Represents a change of less than 0.1%.

Basic Trading Areas: Population/Income/Sales, *Continued*

BTA No.	Basic Trading Area	Population Estimate 7/1/05	Population Census 4/1/00	Population % Change 4/1/90-4/1/00	Per Capita Income 2004	Households Estimate 7/1/05	Disposable Income 2004 ($1,000)	Market Ability Index 2004	Total Retail Sales 2004 Sales ($1,000)	Total Retail Sales Ranally Sales Units	General Merchandise 2004 Sales ($1,000)	General Merchandise Ranally Sales Units	Apparel Store 2004 Sales ($1,000)	Apparel Store Ranally Sales Units	Food Store Sales 2004 ($1,000)	Health & Drug Store Sales 2004 ($1,000)	Passenger Car Registrations 2004
076	Chattanooga, TN	587,991	568,186	11.2	16,797	225,124	9,876,370	.1794	6,311,875	1,793	1,054,078	2,095	338,736	1,782	834,133	418,002	458,494
077	Cheyenne, WY	117,446	113,621	9.3	17,209	47,470	2,021,130	.0408	1,800,017	511	333,173	663	30,847	163	182,784	32,412	101,491
078	Chicago, IL	9,471,425	9,098,316	11.2	20,848	3,293,572	197,462,610	3.3057	111,549,447	31,675	13,109,705	26,071	6,321,481	33,269	14,695,301	9,643,813	5,787,518
079	Chico-Oroville, CA	243,364	229,624	11.0	15,777	94,138	3,839,510	.0692	2,276,212	646	360,281	717	82,839	436	451,298	164,597	173,490
080	Chillicothe, OH	103,543	101,040	8.0	15,839	38,858	1,640,060	.0295	974,583	277	216,611	431	26,641	140	176,035	60,916	77,071
081	Cincinnati, OH	2,237,847	2,170,768	9.1	20,213	869,029	45,232,900	.7742	27,029,279	7,673	3,816,548	7,588	1,250,377	6,582	3,842,283	1,530,064	1,691,966
082	Clarksburg-Elkins, WV	190,635	190,767	0.1	13,822	74,176	2,634,880	.0524	1,968,975	560	385,379	766	62,442	329	237,799	122,417	134,825
083	Clarksville, TN-Hopkinsville, KY	271,405	265,119	20.3	16,397	103,285	4,450,200	.0793	2,616,112	742	634,295	1,261	105,621	556	242,201	107,379	198,311
084	Cleveland-Akron, OH	2,996,876	2,993,610	3.4	19,707	1,179,095	59,060,840	1.0437	38,519,634	10,938	3,888,086	7,733	1,848,283	9,727	5,615,422	3,881,264	2,129,760
085	Cleveland, TN	107,706	104,015	19.1	16,825	43,070	1,812,120	.0323	1,084,301	308	205,247	409	35,902	189	124,984	73,840	87,343
086	Clinton, IA-Sterling, IL	145,559	147,772	-0.1	18,019	58,490	2,622,870	.0460	1,571,265	447	246,222	490	21,221	112	218,581	90,214	112,725
087	Clovis, NM	75,526	75,318	6.0	13,080	27,788	987,850	.0192	651,878	185	132,230	263	27,642	146	77,202	30,624	50,553
088	Coffeyville, KS	59,506	61,512	-3.1	14,878	24,826	885,310	.0152	405,440	116	79,078	157	9,867	52	64,780	31,553	48,323
089	Colorado Springs, CO	592,836	537,484	31.3	20,800	227,594	12,331,020	.2094	7,302,778	2,074	1,264,886	2,515	200,312	1,055	759,294	276,150	465,450
090	Columbia, MO	224,745	216,756	13.8	17,952	93,923	4,034,650	.0731	2,682,880	762	434,004	863	72,618	382	303,743	132,916	181,338
091	Columbia, SC	709,560	668,081	17.5	18,423	268,913	13,072,530	.2358	8,737,460	2,480	1,755,498	3,491	454,435	2,391	1,111,451	465,571	523,368
092	Columbus, GA	359,471	364,510	6.5	15,355	137,394	5,519,720	.1031	3,618,999	1,027	682,248	1,356	196,741	1,035	508,485	243,609	238,430
093	Columbus, IN	158,678	155,281	11.6	18,370	61,139	2,914,900	.0504	1,685,109	479	314,592	626	108,732	573	189,568	102,197	123,203
094	Columbus-Starkville, MS	168,775	174,971	5.1	13,877	65,796	2,342,160	.0461	1,670,801	474	357,052	709	69,886	367	218,885	86,743	124,011
095	Columbus, OH	1,800,250	1,692,240	14.5	20,017	684,574	36,034,970	.6559	25,967,451	7,373	3,104,585	6,173	1,286,880	6,773	3,082,931	1,081,021	1,354,988
096	Cookeville, TN	144,189	138,089	17.4	14,178	57,654	2,044,380	.0396	1,417,394	404	261,079	519	54,548	288	200,254	72,240	115,326
097	Coos Bay-North Bend, OR	85,530	83,916	5.4	16,521	37,809	1,413,070	.0252	840,347	239	192,056	382	16,101	85	145,221	43,623	70,511
098	Corbin, KY	150,728	144,931	13.1	10,430	55,684	1,572,080	.0360	1,417,249	402	349,838	695	46,699	246	134,002	83,073	97,300
099	Corpus Christi, TX	553,024	548,161	9.6	14,336	190,389	7,928,190	.1543	5,633,447	1,599	931,843	1,853	251,961	1,326	933,491	234,971	340,631
100	Cumberland, MD	164,231	163,356	4.2	15,085	64,723	2,477,440	.0452	1,477,446	420	247,179	493	46,495	244	219,149	131,208	121,350
101	Dallas-Fort Worth, TX	6,286,526	5,571,828	28.7	19,607	2,131,664	123,262,480	2.1888	81,400,114	23,116	11,835,472	23,534	4,216,842	22,193	10,348,334	3,385,064	4,092,738
102	Dalton, GA	132,298	120,031	21.7	15,991	45,801	2,115,570	.0426	1,795,168	510	251,728	500	59,924	315	241,492	65,992	88,319
103	Danville, IL	108,750	110,292	-3.5	16,796	43,563	1,826,540	.0324	1,074,709	305	183,899	366	23,355	123	162,885	70,929	77,161
104	Danville, VA	167,713	171,012	7.9	15,264	69,083	2,560,050	.0468	1,559,147	444	282,652	562	43,726	230	276,539	94,764	134,140
105	Davenport, IA-Moline, IL	428,993	429,924	2.4	18,885	170,606	8,101,390	.1470	5,600,031	1,591	829,756	1,650	216,571	1,140	670,968	367,628	319,966
106	Dayton-Springfield, OH	1,214,625	1,219,933	1.0	19,681	486,637	23,905,500	.4106	14,179,865	4,027	2,168,856	4,313	542,518	2,854	2,002,112	786,711	955,640
107	Daytona Beach, FL	554,014	493,175	23.5	18,262	220,945	10,117,500	.1771	6,075,367	1,725	882,131	1,754	253,960	1,337	957,383	421,164	395,442
108	Decatur, AL	148,289	145,867	10.9	17,603	57,646	2,610,310	.0471	1,685,295	479	261,428	520	65,151	343	156,749	93,514	114,108
109	Decatur-Effingham, IL	241,807	248,778	0.5	18,119	100,063	4,381,380	.0821	3,244,839	921	481,197	957	96,155	506	391,304	173,855	182,853
110	Denver, CO	2,928,236	2,712,488	30.8	24,731	1,209,302	72,417,260	1.1616	39,288,689	11,154	5,360,874	10,659	1,970,195	10,371	5,772,212	1,502,084	2,461,212
111	Des Moines, IA	838,103	804,543	10.4	18,953	325,405	15,884,810	.2766	9,613,270	2,729	1,299,063	2,581	318,881	1,678	1,314,885	447,771	694,122
112	Detroit, MI	5,047,892	4,965,944	5.5	22,019	1,938,628	111,149,710	1.9018	69,845,843	19,833	11,179,770	22,233	3,344,275	17,601	8,138,147	5,158,404	3,576,809
113	Dickinson, ND	34,063	35,772	-5.9	14,960	13,638	509,590	.0109	498,051	141	54,294	109	10,110	53	55,093	26,125	30,522
114	Dodge City, KS	43,759	42,837	14.4	14,993	14,985	656,070	.0132	525,818	151	89,752	178	13,257	69	53,532	14,329	29,699
115	Dothan-Enterprise, AL	229,971	223,605	6.4	15,961	90,182	3,670,460	.0720	2,873,593	817	576,903	1,148	102,585	540	257,187	124,690	166,407
116	Dover, DE	346,913	313,107	24.6	17,771	131,319	6,164,830	.1145	4,397,249	1,249	635,324	1,263	287,130	1,511	558,544	227,414	241,470
117	Du Bois-Clearfield, PA	128,774	129,314	4.1	15,253	51,877	1,964,250	.0371	1,325,519	377	171,752	341	41,923	221	200,639	78,375	90,267
118	Dubuque, IA	181,507	179,707	1.8	17,091	70,402	3,102,080	.0573	2,129,151	604	296,086	589	51,360	271	269,052	107,765	138,784
119	Duluth, MN	414,992	413,956	3.3	17,948	179,375	7,448,400	.1322	4,614,909	1,310	787,149	1,567	105,793	557	657,169	225,872	338,270
120	Dyersburg-Union City, TN	118,617	120,330	5.6	15,628	48,350	1,853,790	.0347	1,236,186	351	305,317	607	67,479	355	137,295	64,332	88,406
121	Eagle Pass-Del Rio, TX	124,528	117,380	16.4	8,991	36,808	1,119,590	.0261	930,315	264	193,715	385	82,731	436	212,765	19,887	60,045
122	East Liverpool-Salem, OH	111,181	112,075	3.5	16,097	43,951	1,789,730	.0318	1,025,022	291	106,839	212	21,773	115	166,091	77,945	85,435
123	Eau Claire, WI	203,593	195,408	8.2	17,579	80,918	3,578,890	.0728	3,278,561	931	671,232	1,336	111,192	585	325,543	156,173	163,303
124	El Centro-Calexico, CA	153,484	142,361	30.2	11,514	43,593	1,767,170	.0381	1,451,398	412	276,417	550	94,280	496	260,442	69,041	75,806
125	El Dorado-Magnolia-Camden, AR	101,418	105,766	-2.8	15,070	42,305	1,528,410	.0288	1,018,261	289	254,901	508	50,089	264	123,757	56,491	73,852
126	Elkhart, IN	281,107	268,804	14.3	17,953	101,947	5,046,730	.0906	3,267,298	927	480,609	956	44,880	236	353,773	164,593	188,327
127	Elmira-Corning-Hornell, NY	313,425	313,154	-0.6	17,511	125,020	5,488,510	.0958	3,169,263	901	409,023	813	107,807	567	528,189	187,727	213,663
128	El Paso, TX	787,979	748,239	15.1	11,912	244,429	9,386,270	.1956	7,133,690	2,026	1,572,330	3,126	477,091	2,511	836,941	322,157	438,613
129	Emporia, KS	47,270	47,830	3.6	15,448	18,415	730,240	.0135	464,217	132	76,551	152	20,324	107	66,224	21,176	36,745
130	Enid, OK	83,166	85,696	-0.4	15,907	33,404	1,322,920	.0245	847,810	242	201,690	401	18,822	99	114,928	41,934	62,999
131	Erie, PA	279,281	280,843	1.9	17,187	109,682	4,799,900	.0894	3,381,763	960	451,424	898	142,791	752	538,747	194,570	194,833
132	Escanaba, MI	46,964	47,423	2.9	17,471	20,211	820,510	.0142	462,698	132	58,750	116	16,681	87	67,844	27,051	36,561
133	Eugene-Springfield, OR	335,284	322,959	14.2	18,570	141,340	6,226,310	.1146	4,441,395	1,261	819,155	1,629	129,203	680	689,971	164,173	285,037
134	Eureka, CA	156,777	154,025	8.0	15,766	62,735	2,471,690	.0446	1,478,294	420	167,017	332	54,141	285	323,803	121,982	108,098
135	Evansville, IN	528,454	523,510	3.7	17,492	210,608	9,243,510	.1742	6,811,770	1,934	1,059,432	2,106	256,280	1,350	777,652	360,159	395,388
136	Fairbanks, AK	100,347	97,458	5.8	19,115	35,756	1,918,100	.0342	1,262,843	359	289,006	574	37,260	196	110,162	14,926	66,579
137	Fairmont, WV	56,491	56,598	-1.1	14,717	22,825	831,350	.0155	522,818	148	120,843	240	8,107	43	78,585	38,941	41,144
138	Fargo, ND	319,634	316,537	6.2	17,471	131,357	5,584,480	.1102	4,708,675	1,337	591,835	1,178	130,761	688	470,224	222,675	272,696
139	Farmington, NM-Durango, CO	228,199	208,285	28.0	14,889	79,906	3,397,680	.0665	2,521,641	716	478,516	950	70,699	372	323,127	72,297	160,240
140	Fayetteville-Springdale-Rogers, AR	375,486	325,364	46.2	16,951	140,320	6,364,840	.1171	4,278,192	1,215	1,400,444	2,785	119,036	626	355,034	128,449	268,185
141	Fayetteville-Lumberton, NC	687,400	663,154	16.1	15,287	251,475	10,507,960	.1975	7,012,602	1,992	1,166,265	2,319	333,083	1,754	912,533	415,699	475,393
142	Fergus Falls, MN	133,752	131,271	9.2	17,666	57,623	2,362,830	.0425	1,514,068	431	265,565	528	28,137	148	203,268	62,251	115,630
143	Findlay-Tiffin, OH	154,500	152,886	3.6	18,911	60,947	2,921,820	.0520	1,904,339	541	316,137	628	51,744	272	211,818	100,238	120,915
144	Flagstaff, AZ	124,093	116,320	20.4	16,494	43,459	2,046,830	.0374	1,313,802	373	283,592	564	32,136	169	229,169	28,901	79,415
145	Flint, MI	518,966	507,828	1.5	18,353	195,121	9,515,320	.1706	6,209,260	1,763	1,227,490	2,441	200,377	1,054	697,969	451,498	371,273
146	Florence, AL	188,407	191,015	10.4	16,086	76,744	3,030,690	.0559	1,963,294	558	453,029	900	82,345	434	224,673	102,402	150,757
147	Florence, SC	264,887	259,343	8.4	14,231	96,923	3,769,690	.0761	2,987,525	848	471,860	938	144,907	762	426,508	188,033	165,271
148	Fond du Lac, WI	98,664	97,296	8.0	19,585	38,452	1,932,370	.0330	1,116,093	317	218,023	434	23,248	122	144,958	55,570	73,815
149	Fort Collins-Loveland, CO	275,364	251,494	35.1	24,187	119,115	6,660,320	.1075	3,647,791	1,036	666,158	1,325	150,251	791	477,472	113,594	258,940
150	Fort Dodge, IA	122,812	128,475	-2.5	16,961	50,734	2,083,070	.0368	1,223,275	346	173,899	345	21,503	113	176,851	53,921	104,211
151	Fort Myers, FL	732,816	629,301	31.3	20,577	304,441	15,078,960	.2605	9,394,173	2,668	1,514,369	3,012	553,792	2,914	1,277,479	602,707	504,261
152	Fort Pierce-Vero Beach-Stuart, FL	492,151	432,373	26.7	20,718	204,927	10,196,500	.1729	5,998,264	1,703	824,350	1,640	304,263	1,602	872,650	509,295	328,908
153	Fort Smith, AR	338,038	326,881	15.8	14,631	129,462	4,945,790	.0956	3,499,086	993	1,017,948	2,024	81,973	431	393,997	151,320	238,640
154	Fort Walton Beach, FL	232,296	211,099	23.1	19,769	91,733	4,592,330	.0829	3,209,331	911	582,960	1,159	245,723	1,293	401,168	159,280	165,894
155	Fort Wayne, IN	735,411	715,480	10.6	18,025	269,848	13,255,650	.2408	8,910,923	2,532	1,547,927	3,078	323,332	1,702	994,595	454,770	542,008
156	Fredericksburg, VA	199,471	165,316	32.6	19,305	68,983	3,850,870	.0689	2,580,420	733	540,218	1,074	79,790	421	281,698	110,980	148,012
157	Fresno, CA	1,023,612	922,516	22.1	13,455	310,660	13,772,950	.2578	8,098,841	2,300	1,107,057	2,201	341,667	1,798	1,458,744	503,267	595,488
158	Gadsden, AL	195,230	191,899	10.3	15,098	76,494	2,947,510	.0535	1,722,810	490	375,648	747	62,582	329	283,113	108,877	148,922
159	Gainesville, FL	334,617	320,199	22.9	15,776	132,477	5,278,990	.0967	3,310,278	940	486,775	967	155,279	817	585,320	146,805	231,195
160	Gainesville, GA	292,844	246,560	44.7	16,915	99,694	4,953,330	.0885	3,013,479	855	523,129	1,041	167,874	883	342,936	152,142	207,497
161	Galesburg, IL	71,510	74,571	-1.3	17,397	29,066	1,244,090	.0222	768,771	218	157,392	313	13,990	74	107,617	43,869	51,464
162	Gallup, NM	138,972	144,221	17.9	9,136	41,884	1,269,670	.0284	934,870	266	165,459	329	56,888	299	139,364	25,290	65,818
163	Garden City, KS	69,712	73,686	13.3	16,168	25,529	1,127,080	.0212	788,263	224	120,839	240	31,725	167	112,290	22,705	50,908
164	Glens Falls, NY	128,724	124,345	4.9	19,074	50,295	2,455,280	.0420	1,402,324	398	126,801	252	106,760	562	207,045	81,573	86,734
165	Goldsboro-Kinston, NC	244,504	241,014	10.9	14,835	92,843	3,627,250	.0695	2,517,618	715	413,903	823	102,090	537	362,338	142,862	170,512
166	Grand Forks, ND	195,212	203,087	-5.1	16,698	79,940	3,259,720	.0639	2,636,491	748	396,529	788	63,860	334	300,373	108,893	161,527
167	Grand Island-Kearney, NE	150,900	149,977	6.0	16,003	58,695	2,414,860	.0479	1,972,797	560	421,962	839	67,272	355	158,164	76,730	122,652
168	Grand Junction, CO	273,685	246,119	31.6	18,805	115,314	5,146,620	.0922	3,382,092	961	609,849	1,212	71,201	376	493,629	105,351	240,589
169	Grand Rapids, MI	1,138,129	1,079,340	17.8	19,525	424,070	22,221,650	.3916	14,267,079	4,051	2,949,000	5,865	496,524	2,613	1,306,641	675,384	843,498
170	Great Bend, KS	37,059	38,989	-4.4	15,832	15,550	586,700	.0113	418,370	119	63,784	126	8,850	46	68,866	25,834	30,852
171	Great Falls, MT	159,876	164,305	2.0	15,269	64,385	2,441,170	.0465	1,694,094	482	289,853	575	43,962	233	237,261	71,389	134,067
172	Greeley, CO	230,756	180,936	37.3	18,917	88,114	4,365,170	.0702	1,958,366	556	298,091	593	26,630	140	250,995	54,456	192,281
173	Green Bay, WI	372,022	355,786	14.6	19,625	149,424	7,300,800	.1277	4,586,120	1,302	1,060,153	2,109	120,673	635	503,524	141,475	285,163
174	Greensboro—Winston-Salem—High Point, NC	1,523,567	1,454,066	17.1	18,430	599,732	28,079,470	.5138	19,591,533	5,564	2,575,167	5,121	917,038	4,830	2,335,426	1,209,902	1,197,738
175	Greenville-Greenwood, MS	197,071	209,666	-2.0	10,946	69,686	2,157,090	.0486	1,934,020	550	348,906	694	82,482	433	233,366	99,730	111,405
176	Greenville-Washington, NC	254,611	247,820	13.2	15,542	104,242	3,957,040	.0788	3,188,631	906	370,359	737	162,902	857	440,964	176,532	183,520
177	Greenville-Spartanburg, SC	954,817	914,473	16.0	17,420	360,224	16,633,040	.3080	11,608,581	3,296	1,649,723	3,280	612,953	3,225	1,456,124	719,810	700,497
178	Greenwood, SC	78,681	76,229	11.4	15,570	29,529	1,225,060	.0228	805,078	229	157,841	313	45,118	237	119,158	48,154	52,079
179	Hagerstown, MD-Chambersburg, PA-Martinsburg, WV	397,477	366,345	11.8	18,449	152,793	7,333,160	.1262	4,183,896	1,188	615,567	1,225	142,883	752	626,376	233,815	290,912
180	Hammond, LA	114,856	111,113	16.2	13,752	42,872	1,579,500	.0318	1,216,116	345	228,707	454	36,183	191	135,884	62,990	71,592
181	Harrisburg, PA	713,808	698,708	6.7	20,053	287,681	14,314,040	.2585	10,072,616	2,860	1,016,670	2,021	363,308	1,913	1,370,179	528,090	526,065
182	Harrison, AR	95,028	92,314	24.0	14,051	38,840	1,335,250	.0258	918,555	261	265,786	528	22,432	119	95,494	35,668	75,129
183	Harrisonburg, VA	156,739	152,235	18.1	15,431	58,184	2,418,690	.0473	1,856,766	528	264,570	526	48,990	257	258,598	88,973	123,823
184	Hartford, CT	1,197,175	1,148,618	2.2	26,530	463,800	31,761,140	.4830	14,817,105	4,207	1,281,098	2,548	1,120,244	5,896	2,339,379	1,185,681	828,784
185	Hastings, NE	71,500	73,440	0.8	16,624	29,021	1,188,620	.0211	702,278	200	71,627	143	11,708	61	130,288	39,674	61,087
186	Hattiesburg, MS	189,935	182,113	12.5	12,915	66,405	2,453,070	.0522	2,124,755	603	579,967	1,153	77,314	406	173,485	152,664	126,368
187	Hays, KS	56,974	60,018	-1.5	16,627	24,556	947,310	.0191	808,113	228	110,853	220	35,426	185	119,536	30,621	51,320
188	Helena, MT	73,395	70,150	19.4	17,633	28,608	1,294,210	.0232	818,169	232	139,897	278	12,686	67	136,419	25,168	61,491
189	Hickory-Lenoir-Morganton, NC	356,039	341,851	16.9	17,856	140,143	6,357,350	.1156	4,259,162	1,209	596,263	1,186	159,755	841	500,673	277,190	284,177
190	Hilo, HI	163,051	148,677	23.6	17,202	58,374	2,804,870	.0492	1,623,949	461	332,411	661	97,410	513	375,296	104,587	103,422
191	Hobbs, NM	56,128	55,511	-0.5	12,940	19,605	726,310	.0144	504,459	143	93,373	186	17,430	92	62,107	25,056	35,313
192	Honolulu, HI	910,475	876,156	4.8	20,281	302,181	18,465,370	.3063	9,903,032	2,812	1,988,367	3,954	1,320,832	6,952	1,401,658	865,911	537,678
193	Hot Springs, AR	143,943	138,969	18.3	15,832	59,404	2,278,970	.0434	1,626,719	462	406,885	810	48,303	254	170,004	85,564	105,835
194	Houghton, MI	46,273	47,063	4.4	14,116	18,513	653,210	.0127	454,560	128	79,652	159	17,809	94	80,245	17,881	32,809
195	Houma-Thibodaux, LA	272,512	271,365	2.9	15,324	99,077	4,175,910	.0812	3,110,555	883	694,637	1,381	100,989	532	490,424	183,927	164,168
196	Houston, TX	5,637,714	5,045,022	24.4	17,738	1,868,675	100,001,080	1.8144	66,309,150	18,831	11,021,054	21,919	3,744,318	19,707	9,828,795	3,097,352	3,459,368
197	Huntington, WV-Ashland, KY	367,760	368,924	1.4	14,414	147,149	5,300,810	.1036	3,827,725	1,089	738,603	1,470	173,942	916	464,383	393,709	263,625
198	Huntsville, AL	538,878	509,873	15.9	19,104	209,885	10,294,510	.1835	6,760,035	1,919	1,425,901	2,835	329,273	1,733	786,453	292,592	416,253
199	Huron, SD	51,308	53,386	0.4	17,152	21,705	880,020	.0183	864,013	246	61,781	124	21,023	111	30,890	17,427	46,238
200	Hutchinson, KS	124,712	128,235	2.5	16,980	50,571	2,117,630	.0374	1,251,577	356	204,146	406	30,936	163	155,083	50,744	101,036
201	Hyannis, MA	258,481	246,737	20.8	23,927	109,972	6,184,660	.1061	4,092,655	1,162	210,110	418	306,758	1,614	881,986	288,730	191,940
202	Idaho Falls, ID	240,545	223,017	17.2	16,169	83,854	3,889,460	.0730	2,716,647	771	482,439	960	83,246	440	400,135	85,926	194,207
203	Indiana, PA	89,103	89,605	-0.4	14,272	34,918	1,271,710	.0253	971,024	276	165,326	329	26,432	139	139,506	52,438	61,421
204	Indianapolis, IN	1,674,207	1,552,963	17.5	20,022	626,301	33,521,520	.6069	23,789,320	6,757	4,253,860	8,460	941,407	4,955	2,094,327	1,529,018	1,226,564
205	Iowa City, IA	138,810	131,676	13.8	18,747	56,490	2,602,250	.0477	1,844,207	523	258,207	514	60,711	320	308,144	84,401	110,018
206	Iron Mountain, MI	44,684	45,698	2.5	16,929	19,583	756,450	.0141	529,586	150	88,004	175	14,223	75	79,951	31,252	34,767
207	Ironwood, MI	31,171	32,049	-3.1	15,148	14,123	472,180	.0090	319,803	91	38,934	78	9,960	53	53,534	12,199	23,804
208	Ithaca, NY	100,996	96,501	2.6	18,164	38,542	1,834,480	.0295	790,679	225	80,341	160	35,530	187	182,026	55,756	62,907
209	Jackson, MI	212,484	204,949	6.1	18,757	81,036	3,985,660	.0687	2,307,889	655	577,760	1,149	60,896	320	249,943	123,784	151,990
210	Jackson, MS	696,998	677,489	10.1	15,324	248,211	10,680,920	.2084	8,018,241	2,276	1,670,360	3,323	323,027	1,700	820,151	508,831	470,176
211	Jackson, TN	291,594	287,020	12.4	16,359	118,801	4,770,090	.0876	3,100,444	880	602,073	1,198	133,330	702	337,411	189,866	225,792
212	Jacksonville, FL	1,499,671	1,358,825	21.9	19,591	567,630	29,379,840	.5100	18,022,608	5,118	2,596,659	5,163	853,750	4,495	2,501,411	874,665	1,040,845
213	Jacksonville, IL	69,667	70,609	-0.3	16,843	27,590	1,173,370	.0201	599,334	171	93,590	187	16,566	88	92,345	44,265	50,700
214	Jacksonville, NC	149,754	150,355	0.3	14,047	51,435	2,103,590	.0423	1,637,736	465	298,217	593	55,104	290	193,779	64,913	95,703
215	Jamestown, NY-Warren, PA-Dunkirk, NY	179,257	183,613	-1.8	17,440	73,207	3,126,330	.0568	2,066,905	587	248,263	493	52,857	278	280,616	108,676	119,166
216	Janesville-Beloit, WI	256,303	246,066	14.7	19,506	98,597	4,999,390	.0861	2,976,482	846	542,058	1,078	50,430	265	403,987	154,700	190,134
217	Jefferson City, MO	168,831	163,616	15.7	18,614	67,029	3,142,640	.0567	2,108,879	599	335,048	666	30,786	162	253,802	82,330	136,650
218	Johnstown, PA	226,882	232,621	-3.6	14,855	92,161	3,370,270	.0632	2,182,504	620	243,454	484	60,578	319	351,510	159,540	153,825
219	Jonesboro-Paragould, AR	186,287	181,062	13.6	15,128	74,786	2,818,240	.0548	2,082,829	592	586,331	1,165	94,138	496	186,955	94,103	135,185
220	Joplin, MO-Miami, OK	255,703	247,343	15.0	14,961	102,128	3,825,650	.0715	2,462,729	698	517,406	1,029	56,377	296	262,847	115,889	198,830
221	Juneau-Ketchikan, AK	70,479	73,082	5.9	24,842	28,891	1,750,860	.0269	813,021	232	136,787	271	56,874	299	202,130	23,926	47,062
222	Kahului-Wailuku-Lahaina, HI	138,920	128,241	27.6	19,701	47,270	2,736,840	.0496	1,931,368	548	318,270	633	219,781	1,157	383,189	147,602	87,040
223	Kalamazoo, MI	385,760	377,288	7.1	19,143	154,090	7,384,460	.1306	4,739,492	1,346	1,323,775	2,632	149,922	789	474,318	242,852	289,982
224	Kalispell, MT	82,627	74,471	25.8	15,631	31,183	1,291,570	.0256	1,031,483	293	243,893	485	21,762	115	138,613	27,548	70,547
225	Kankakee, IL	138,116	135,167	6.4	18,073	51,627	2,496,200	.0436	1,472,491	418	270,595	539	43,932	232	154,937	111,292	92,426
226	Kansas City, MO	2,167,409	2,049,447	11.4	20,731	856,333	44,933,300	.7703	27,391,794	7,778	4,273,904	8,501	1,022,085	5,381	3,201,695	1,461,735	1,680,003
227	Keene, NH	122,399	118,041	5.7	18,684	47,983	2,286,950	.0461	2,107,800	599	180,379	358	45,489	240	302,780	83,266	93,937

Source: Devonshire Associates Ltd. and Scan/US, Inc. 2005.
... Represents a change of less than 0.1%

Continued on next page

Basic Trading Areas: Population/Income/Sales, *Continued*

BTA No.	Basic Trading Area	Population: Estimate 7/1/05	Population: Census 4/1/00	Population: % Change 4/1/90-4/1/00	Per Capita Income 2004	House-holds Estimate 7/1/05	Disposable Income 2004 ($1,000)	Market Ability Index 2004	Total Retail Sales: 2004 Sales ($1,000)	Total Retail Sales: Ranally Sales Units	General Merchandise: 2004 Sales ($1,000)	General Merchandise: Ranally Sales Units	Apparel Store: 2004 Sales ($1,000)	Apparel Store: Ranally Sales Units	Food Store Sales 2004 ($1,000)	Health & Drug Store 2004 ($1,000)	Passenger Car Regis-trations 2004
228	Kennewick-Pasco-Richland, WA	221,935	191,822	27.9	18,028	76,668	4,000,970	.0714	2,544,894	723	540,447	1,075	69,057	364	403,609	106,339	157,375
229	Kingsport, TN-Johnson City, TN-Bristol, VA-TN	719,024	707,899	8.5	15,356	299,138	11,041,330	.2117	7,898,611	2,242	1,433,154	2,848	305,144	1,605	1,089,546	535,429	582,844
230	Kirksville, MO	56,604	57,351	3.2	14,446	24,366	817,690	.0151	481,813	138	72,590	144	12,600	65	69,697	32,580	48,271
231	Klamath Falls, OR	82,541	80,646	8.2	15,263	33,841	1,259,860	.0234	816,777	232	158,037	315	14,003	74	155,739	32,397	66,431
232	Knoxville, TN	1,180,810	1,118,107	17.9	17,001	476,095	20,075,180	.3926	16,276,508	4,621	2,770,974	5,507	847,538	4,462	1,883,970	902,427	956,872
233	Kokomo-Logansport, IN	191,481	192,308	4.0	18,783	75,731	3,596,500	.0635	2,261,315	642	429,157	853	62,261	328	227,937	168,934	142,167
234	La Crosse, WI-Winona, MN	325,038	320,367	8.3	17,184	129,611	5,585,380	.1006	3,546,197	1,008	583,935	1,161	66,067	348	437,857	106,200	251,384
235	Lafayette, IN	279,277	275,303	11.2	17,518	107,597	4,892,410	.0884	3,173,654	901	630,152	1,253	98,216	516	312,121	172,855	203,980
236	Lafayette-New Iberia, LA	556,799	548,154	10.4	14,522	208,834	8,085,570	.1632	6,506,024	1,847	1,225,662	2,436	270,713	1,425	792,529	463,680	339,952
237	La Grange, GA	72,690	69,791	8.8	15,877	27,361	1,154,120	.0218	808,809	229	126,745	252	38,237	201	127,900	32,257	49,334
238	Lake Charles, LA	282,285	283,429	9.3	16,268	108,313	4,592,320	.0857	3,131,549	889	810,893	1,612	114,805	604	361,245	165,923	183,799
239	Lakeland-Winter Haven, FL	526,208	483,924	19.4	17,926	205,086	9,432,930	.1709	6,270,722	1,781	1,004,624	1,998	225,818	1,189	1,044,350	328,355	342,035
240	Lancaster, PA	490,254	470,658	11.3	19,871	183,207	9,741,670	.1767	6,915,084	1,964	618,456	1,230	403,743	2,125	1,058,381	357,146	343,004
241	Lansing, MI	526,431	509,246	4.0	20,552	212,291	10,819,060	.1841	6,396,962	1,816	1,454,586	2,892	232,402	1,222	753,680	360,257	396,774
242	Laredo, TX	248,500	216,446	41.6	9,288	66,488	2,308,040	.0584	2,536,913	720	511,538	1,017	298,412	1,570	397,925	105,133	109,561
243	La Salle-Peru-Ottawa-Streator, IL	153,795	153,098	3.2	19,041	60,937	2,928,350	.0543	2,158,334	613	354,723	705	60,957	321	281,199	117,282	111,396
244	Las Cruces, NM	260,578	249,902	26.7	12,646	93,903	3,295,340	.0639	2,065,010	586	389,093	773	56,997	301	266,676	95,733	173,031
245	Las Vegas, NV	1,923,403	1,568,418	82.8	18,753	708,473	36,068,680	.6336	22,348,533	6,346	3,153,840	6,272	1,408,481	7,413	3,398,982	969,385	1,231,875
246	Laurel, MS	83,422	83,107	5.0	12,970	30,551	1,081,970	.0211	710,758	201	160,440	319	24,387	129	73,434	47,889	58,511
247	Lawrence, KS	103,269	99,962	22.2	17,848	42,198	1,843,120	.0326	1,126,641	320	164,334	327	62,103	327	202,198	54,513	81,312
248	Lawton-Duncan, OK	172,775	180,897	1.7	14,958	65,251	2,584,410	.0463	1,436,171	408	408,941	813	41,362	217	145,990	77,981	118,568
249	Lebanon-Claremont, NH	186,138	179,619	7.2	19,273	74,853	3,587,500	.0664	2,663,281	757	265,212	527	68,222	359	535,596	109,000	143,382
250	Lewiston-Moscow, ID	123,183	123,481	12.2	16,340	50,615	2,012,870	.0369	1,304,148	370	267,059	531	25,858	136	273,388	64,459	109,443
251	Lewiston-Auburn, ME	227,833	221,126	-0.3	16,849	94,077	3,838,740	.0760	3,203,829	909	313,006	623	37,310	197	537,853	151,606	173,236
252	Lexington, KY	967,536	927,633	13.7	16,693	380,953	16,150,740	.2938	10,336,709	2,935	1,715,888	3,411	469,303	2,471	1,191,006	709,701	718,255
253	Liberal, KS	61,807	62,064	15.0	15,600	22,029	964,180	.0176	598,472	170	108,570	215	30,679	162	89,617	22,293	42,990
254	Lihue, HI	61,454	58,463	14.2	18,902	21,586	1,161,610	.0208	771,118	219	144,281	287	56,335	297	189,482	55,446	40,209
255	Lima, OH	248,923	251,414	0.7	17,801	95,355	4,431,130	.0798	2,875,241	816	543,672	1,081	82,249	433	307,899	197,152	189,196
256	Lincoln, NE	362,085	346,818	12.1	17,881	139,820	6,474,460	.1168	4,230,857	1,202	727,688	1,446	134,788	709	575,941	271,963	293,585
257	Little Rock, AR	994,284	963,155	13.0	17,672	404,789	17,571,370	.3292	12,863,723	3,651	2,869,482	5,707	431,646	2,272	1,177,480	495,173	770,329
258	Logan, UT	110,700	102,720	29.3	14,281	35,019	1,580,900	.0307	1,111,610	315	220,568	439	32,728	172	166,167	29,823	80,399
259	Logan, WV	36,230	37,710	-12.4	12,845	14,772	465,380	.0105	476,546	135	73,984	147	13,947	73	68,700	53,166	24,434
260	Longview-Marshall, TX	323,015	314,446	7.4	15,533	121,433	5,017,370	.0963	3,627,187	1,031	633,874	1,261	119,778	631	497,963	178,120	216,398
261	Longview, WA	100,229	96,772	13.3	18,700	40,133	1,874,290	.0318	1,027,395	292	230,528	458	18,571	98	178,953	42,801	79,814
262	Los Angeles, CA	17,816,585	16,391,590	12.7	18,175	5,663,905	323,821,500	5.5434	179,224,358	50,891	22,613,435	44,971	13,727,785	72,252	28,036,291	9,976,538	11,084,238
263	Louisville, KY	1,540,990	1,486,048	9.8	18,187	592,185	28,025,350	.4900	16,677,914	4,736	2,907,089	5,782	638,993	3,361	1,771,674	1,077,657	1,123,671
264	Lubbock, TX	416,750	409,227	4.2	14,783	158,081	6,160,650	.1242	4,984,659	1,417	722,563	1,437	217,752	1,147	750,918	162,150	289,485
265	Lufkin-Nacogdoches, TX	164,371	162,058	12.5	14,487	62,209	2,381,300	.0473	1,817,270	516	340,080	677	77,791	411	292,858	65,764	108,241
266	Lynchburg, VA	161,985	161,946	4.8	16,502	65,102	2,673,090	.0541	2,347,466	667	352,509	701	75,247	396	290,601	173,919	124,591
267	McAlester, OK	54,531	54,645	7.3	13,348	21,130	727,900	.0143	499,309	142	147,310	293	14,645	77	34,401	20,521	37,370
268	McAllen, TX	736,382	623,060	46.9	8,055	193,832	5,931,840	.1527	6,039,893	1,715	1,230,197	2,447	443,127	2,333	954,444	256,666	345,270
269	McComb-Brookhaven, MS	115,344	114,119	6.4	12,108	42,427	1,396,620	.0299	1,174,134	334	265,238	528	51,399	270	109,907	66,433	80,235
270	McCook, NE	32,439	33,749	-7.8	15,625	13,953	506,860	.0101	415,757	117	62,067	124	7,474	40	51,557	17,802	29,641
271	Macon-Warner Robins, GA	695,423	662,942	12.5	15,229	253,255	10,590,390	.1991	7,050,029	1,999	1,198,306	2,384	298,796	1,573	1,041,179	385,610	465,238
272	Madison, WI	726,250	682,098	15.0	21,201	302,694	15,397,030	.2808	11,486,212	3,261	1,395,417	2,774	296,744	1,561	1,103,700	434,367	571,066
273	Madisonville, KY	46,972	46,519	0.9	15,190	18,717	713,510	.0134	477,177	135	107,466	214	29,207	154	53,531	42,327	34,411
274	Manchester-Nashua-Concord, NH	662,179	617,057	14.1	21,658	250,857	14,341,310	.2750	12,399,986	3,521	1,655,745	3,292	548,490	2,887	1,729,670	449,086	529,294
275	Manhattan-Junction City, KS	115,459	117,821	-4.1	14,800	43,965	1,708,790	.0328	1,183,565	336	222,382	443	43,784	230	174,996	36,564	88,066
276	Manitowoc, WI	81,467	82,887	3.1	20,138	34,006	1,640,590	.0259	725,976	206	159,448	317	10,470	55	114,801	16,936	64,155
277	Mankato-Fairmont, MN	251,967	250,632	2.2	18,893	104,362	4,760,530	.0809	2,611,319	741	398,564	791	69,894	369	422,812	123,883	211,174
278	Mansfield, OH	227,742	228,341	3.1	17,693	90,488	4,029,380	.0712	2,434,621	691	439,817	875	69,621	366	299,196	159,318	175,726
279	Marinette, WI-Menominee, MI	68,351	68,710	5.0	16,857	29,178	1,152,190	.0199	611,730	173	137,453	273	14,350	76	92,483	30,335	54,470
280	Marion, IN	105,076	108,363	-0.8	16,867	41,232	1,772,310	.0318	1,089,446	309	145,136	289	41,516	219	116,665	70,124	76,692
281	Marion, OH	101,237	97,845	6.3	16,898	36,968	1,710,660	.0295	913,569	259	186,504	371	24,254	127	135,425	50,797	72,874
282	Marquette, MI	74,205	74,496	-6.7	17,155	30,418	1,272,950	.0233	842,307	239	179,747	358	26,797	141	106,231	44,254	55,848
283	Marshalltown, IA	56,962	57,414	3.1	17,034	22,069	970,300	.0166	501,218	142	79,356	157	22,595	119	79,852	30,038	45,978
284	Martinsville, VA	90,453	92,753	2.4	15,228	38,592	1,377,400	.0253	847,530	241	170,302	339	36,265	191	123,957	60,179	75,715
285	Mason City, IA	113,217	116,657	-1.8	17,139	46,396	1,940,390	.0357	1,304,875	370	236,249	470	25,068	131	174,908	37,047	95,653
286	Mattoon, IL	62,105	64,449	3.4	16,469	25,645	1,022,800	.0199	799,065	227	211,607	421	9,500	50	72,770	48,915	46,185
287	Meadville, PA	89,827	90,366	4.9	15,924	35,359	1,430,410	.0255	822,751	234	91,572	182	23,839	125	128,960	55,416	59,651
288	Medford-Grants Pass, OR	277,029	256,995	22.9	17,390	115,530	4,817,610	.0966	4,228,438	1,200	788,921	1,568	105,096	553	475,444	126,305	229,248
289	Melbourne-Titusville, FL	523,567	476,230	19.4	20,941	216,202	10,963,820	.1797	5,760,123	1,636	986,272	1,961	242,067	1,274	880,605	408,228	391,524
290	Memphis, TN	1,602,474	1,553,276	11.2	16,860	599,903	27,018,260	.4967	18,048,366	5,124	3,270,360	6,505	974,867	5,129	1,831,697	1,236,130	1,071,569
291	Merced, CA	261,826	227,684	18.2	13,262	77,333	3,472,270	.0617	1,632,568	464	294,476	585	46,347	244	301,837	87,054	139,545
292	Meridian, MS	207,160	209,027	4.5	13,224	78,505	2,739,540	.0542	1,912,147	542	451,487	898	52,203	274	233,895	119,736	144,260
293	Miami-Fort Lauderdale, FL	4,263,821	3,955,969	21.0	17,472	1,513,860	74,498,140	1.3803	52,245,087	14,835	5,958,257	11,850	4,219,589	22,209	7,023,286	3,864,975	2,568,242
294	Michigan City-La Porte, IN	109,651	110,106	2.8	17,627	40,827	1,932,830	.0353	1,302,656	370	234,559	466	121,147	638	131,313	81,814	74,175
295	Middlesboro-Harlan, KY	116,772	118,401	-2.3	11,114	48,348	1,297,840	.0263	836,586	237	245,955	489	30,882	163	191,392	76,123	84,108
296	Midland, TX	125,274	120,755	8.2	17,217	45,049	2,156,790	.0421	1,750,270	497	319,844	636	87,217	459	195,252	58,570	79,711
297	Milwaukee, WI	1,883,428	1,849,490	5.6	20,341	733,954	38,310,410	.6424	21,388,701	6,073	3,245,867	6,454	678,073	3,568	2,947,747	1,402,237	1,367,022
298	Minneapolis-St. Paul, MN	3,484,888	3,293,598	15.9	23,505	1,387,468	81,913,370	1.4064	53,913,058	15,309	8,002,170	15,913	1,976,799	10,404	6,682,849	2,417,308	2,795,857
299	Minot, ND	111,406	118,459	-3.4	14,830	44,656	1,652,200	.0343	1,459,499	413	166,199	331	29,432	155	166,048	65,132	99,860
300	Missoula, MT	185,786	175,320	25.9	15,695	73,835	2,915,860	.0569	2,236,622	635	414,943	825	48,917	257	341,839	67,131	156,735
301	Mitchell, SD	82,871	84,187	0.1	13,300	31,762	1,102,220	.0256	1,227,271	350	93,624	187	12,048	64	86,215	19,152	69,944
302	Mobile, AL	678,203	663,075	11.6	14,954	237,639	10,141,590	.1941	7,047,689	2,001	1,408,056	2,800	384,444	2,024	914,332	423,806	452,829
303	Modesto, CA	577,893	501,498	19.7	15,854	183,047	9,162,040	.1642	5,353,669	1,520	818,246	1,627	195,916	1,031	1,001,627	356,060	374,374
304	Monroe, LA	324,899	331,088	2.1	13,980	124,769	4,542,150	.0899	3,349,592	951	797,218	1,585	117,129	618	418,276	164,369	203,698
305	Montgomery, AL	490,161	484,647	10.0	15,922	185,849	7,804,420	.1474	5,460,450	1,552	1,051,929	2,092	225,054	1,185	675,967	345,879	332,678
306	Morgantown, WV	114,517	111,200	6.4	14,021	44,304	1,605,690	.0313	1,129,188	321	210,194	418	69,160	364	118,140	79,368	82,027
307	Mount Pleasant, MI	139,419	136,888	15.5	15,550	54,227	2,167,970	.0398	1,350,532	383	334,774	665	34,453	181	155,367	65,150	103,289
308	Mount Vernon-Centralia, IL	120,930	122,656	2.8	16,864	49,511	2,039,420	.0389	1,523,993	433	238,618	475	37,151	195	140,922	84,930	90,725
309	Muncie, IN	179,838	182,024	-0.2	15,882	71,061	2,856,220	.0528	1,859,752	528	390,988	777	62,178	328	198,833	105,169	134,531
310	Muskegon, MI	233,048	225,347	8.9	16,875	89,891	3,932,770	.0721	2,600,291	738	631,031	1,255	65,488	345	287,608	180,788	167,709
311	Muskogee, OK	169,642	164,258	10.8	12,616	63,584	2,140,200	.0421	1,409,035	400	343,952	683	32,080	170	211,088	73,685	112,941
312	Myrtle Beach, SC	219,791	196,629	36.5	18,431	91,467	4,050,980	.0826	3,819,977	1,085	609,030	1,211	439,072	2,311	501,810	168,795	159,066
313	Naples, FL	306,973	251,377	65.3	24,916	127,885	7,648,670	.1250	4,435,456	1,259	409,669	815	470,567	2,477	683,833	249,092	211,428
314	Nashville, TN	1,880,864	1,761,799	23.3	19,580	727,209	36,827,580	.6595	24,947,663	7,085	4,377,267	8,706	1,180,929	6,214	3,087,757	1,454,927	1,437,303
315	Natchez, MS	69,590	72,775	-0.6	11,975	27,374	833,370	.0174	648,378	184	189,245	376	20,589	108	77,774	30,591	46,805
316	New Bern, NC	176,348	174,134	12.4	17,654	71,306	3,113,320	.0569	2,102,734	597	339,264	675	70,432	371	298,530	95,391	129,488
317	New Castle, PA	92,801	94,643	-1.7	16,282	37,654	1,510,980	.0272	913,512	259	109,326	217	14,722	77	148,663	61,782	64,483
318	New Haven-Waterbury-Meriden, CT	1,045,311	1,006,201	2.9	24,655	394,498	25,772,390	.4113	13,699,003	3,890	1,233,545	2,453	711,441	3,745	2,089,903	961,671	727,566
319	New London-Norwich, CT	382,531	368,179	3.0	24,805	148,781	9,488,830	.1457	4,397,998	1,249	553,351	1,100	184,265	970	680,113	306,305	310,573
320	New Orleans, LA	1,425,798	1,430,273	4.6	16,588	530,095	23,651,810	.4393	16,156,734	4,590	2,896,445	5,761	968,298	5,097	2,220,043	1,217,530	878,754
321	New York, NY	20,227,583	19,620,902	8.7	23,150	7,237,265	468,274,500	7.3846	228,887,923	64,993	19,940,540	39,656	24,647,180	129,722	36,451,669	18,440,575	10,063,875
322	Nogales, AZ	41,238	38,381	29.3	12,214	13,732	503,690	.0110	449,398	128	116,411	231	48,089	253	84,199	13,345	24,630
323	Norfolk, NE	109,032	112,342	-0.2	15,054	43,295	1,641,320	.0328	1,310,583	371	172,949	345	31,054	163	152,050	60,223	90,125
324	Norfolk-Virginia Beach-Newport News-Hampton, VA	1,877,341	1,784,356	9.1	17,599	689,496	33,038,490	.5870	20,360,061	5,782	3,184,125	6,333	1,176,186	6,189	2,771,885	969,559	1,320,732
325	North Platte, NE	84,776	86,263	7.5	16,526	34,475	1,401,040	.0260	933,449	262	156,126	311	17,810	94	117,971	46,155	73,174
326	Ocala, FL	294,555	258,916	32.9	16,944	121,424	4,991,010	.0921	3,382,818	961	535,220	1,064	94,712	498	427,647	197,001	196,457
327	Odessa, TX	208,131	209,080	-2.0	13,709	76,119	2,853,370	.0565	2,080,715	591	430,968	858	58,634	309	279,921	98,293	130,080
328	Oil City-Franklin, PA	102,076	104,276	-1.5	15,418	41,328	1,573,760	.0301	1,118,863	318	127,020	253	33,942	178	204,767	70,257	70,486
329	Oklahoma City, OK	1,489,279	1,434,827	9.9	16,615	569,953	24,744,190	.4551	16,358,368	4,643	3,009,325	5,986	525,253	2,764	1,791,710	928,574	1,065,836
330	Olean, NY-Bradford, PA	236,087	238,984	-0.1	16,498	93,156	3,894,960	.0660	1,910,118	543	202,806	402	46,491	244	374,116	176,524	155,223
331	Olympia-Centralia, WA	355,702	325,360	25.7	19,597	138,243	6,970,520	.1201	4,163,577	1,183	997,127	1,983	123,140	648	707,589	162,500	276,741
332	Omaha, NE	1,025,063	991,763	9.5	18,835	394,727	19,307,310	.3553	13,884,648	3,941	1,705,393	3,391	464,278	2,443	1,693,155	804,086	785,072
333	Oneonta, NY	109,869	109,731	1.8	17,647	45,680	1,938,880	.0333	1,064,983	302	106,653	212	21,117	111	147,752	55,147	78,484
334	Opelika-Auburn, AL	156,925	151,675	22.3	15,516	63,601	2,434,780	.0439	1,423,173	404	279,810	556	61,675	324	238,923	54,261	119,486
335	Orangeburg, SC	121,708	123,425	7.8	13,674	46,443	1,664,260	.0322	1,123,743	319	143,684	286	46,816	246	187,043	86,272	80,562
336	Orlando, FL	1,962,360	1,697,906	35.1	19,404	727,715	38,077,680	.6881	26,381,919	7,493	3,879,618	7,715	1,791,694	9,430	3,442,106	1,422,749	1,283,983
337	Ottumwa, IA	122,541	124,054	0.9	15,546	49,380	1,905,030	.0359	1,307,767	371	250,906	499	30,361	160	189,891	55,457	101,817
338	Owensboro, KY	166,433	164,630	4.8	16,791	67,124	2,794,600	.0488	1,560,350	443	359,246	715	43,344	229	175,921	121,698	129,480
339	Paducah-Murray-Mayfield, KY	232,357	232,585	7.1	16,364	95,425	3,802,390	.0715	2,676,995	761	605,051	1,204	128,865	679	239,549	157,480	178,596
340	Panama City, FL	213,753	201,086	17.5	17,282	84,234	3,694,160	.0665	2,352,999	668	511,060	1,017	92,261	486	361,959	131,868	144,804
341	Paris, TX	95,868	95,149	6.4	14,172	38,403	1,358,600	.0261	918,044	260	176,174	351	35,316	185	104,455	56,112	67,148
342	Parkersburg, WV-Marietta, OH	180,185	182,549	1.4	16,481	73,262	2,969,660	.0570	2,229,418	633	461,402	919	65,706	346	249,574	136,186	137,415
343	Pensacola, FL	437,128	412,153	19.7	18,438	170,330	8,059,970	.1392	4,649,972	1,321	829,735	1,650	185,536	977	639,256	315,918	302,050
344	Peoria, IL	458,026	461,289	1.2	19,497	184,177	8,930,050	.1556	5,523,957	1,569	824,858	1,640	148,257	781	809,746	397,362	333,463
345	Petoskey, MI	113,564	107,276	24.9	18,522	46,852	2,103,460	.0416	1,844,020	524	299,603	596	70,187	370	246,313	81,828	86,652
346	Philadelphia, PA-Wilmington, DE-Trenton, NJ	6,352,452	6,184,346	4.8	21,666	2,325,184	137,633,870	2.3185	81,443,677	23,124	7,335,285	14,589	4,996,061	26,295	13,057,245	6,075,839	3,927,841
347	Phoenix, AZ	4,021,099	3,462,432	44.0	18,905	1,441,419	76,020,430	1.3239	45,989,908	13,059	6,361,779	12,652	1,761,242	9,269	5,874,377	2,333,314	2,540,902
348	Pine Bluff, AR	150,336	154,005	0.7	13,729	56,128	2,064,000	.0411	1,525,711	435	340,440	676	71,591	377	178,098	130,573	103,028
349	Pittsburg-Parsons, KS	90,416	92,459	1.7	14,748	37,415	1,333,420	.0260	981,922	278	232,652	462	24,628	129	157,404	50,990	74,833
350	Pittsburgh, PA	2,440,332	2,471,759	-1.4	18,246	997,936	44,525,390	.7986	28,997,740	8,235	3,325,886	6,613	1,333,452	7,017	4,664,699	2,122,847	1,659,473
351	Pittsfield, MA	131,527	134,953	-3.2	20,937	56,899	2,753,800	.0465	1,607,360	456	145,868	290	131,236	691	316,206	119,866	90,832
352	Plattsburgh, NY	121,724	118,745	-3.6	17,573	46,495	2,139,110	.0383	1,352,150	383	155,287	309	66,305	349	231,516	78,971	80,222
353	Pocatello, ID	100,283	100,943	12.6	16,048	37,667	1,609,390	.0307	1,161,715	330	166,105	331	20,963	110	183,097	55,398	84,453
354	Ponca City, OK	46,817	48,080	0.0	15,098	18,589	706,850	.0137	517,974	147	146,203	291	12,736	67	49,501	34,730	33,170
355	Poplar Bluff, MO	153,182	154,045	3.9	13,719	66,833	2,101,530	.0413	1,501,166	427	253,838	505	26,776	140	200,341	101,541	120,672
356	Port Angeles, WA	97,026	90,478	18.1	18,908	42,004	1,834,600	.0299	864,091	245	165,826	329	24,667	130	219,163	40,665	78,342
357	Portland-Brunswick, ME	553,890	521,184	10.5	20,389	222,582	11,293,290	.2085	8,546,336	2,426	697,181	1,387	515,688	2,714	1,610,710	336,978	450,336
358	Portland, OR	2,298,591	2,114,640	25.1	20,900	898,004	48,041,570	.8305	30,280,222	8,598	5,525,647	10,989	1,619,766	8,526	4,132,236	1,032,496	1,710,100
359	Portsmouth, OH	89,929	93,287	-0.1	13,695	37,319	1,231,570	.0227	694,601	197	106,850	213	25,534	134	121,716	56,798	69,036
360	Pottsville, PA	146,247	150,336	-1.5	15,643	57,934	2,287,810	.0429	1,543,237	438	139,705	278	32,868	173	283,819	206,102	107,089
361	Poughkeepsie-Kingston, NY	481,801	457,899	7.8	21,670	172,588	10,440,630	.1638	4,748,809	1,349	512,063	1,019	275,396	1,449	893,733	287,127	317,036
362	Prescott, AZ	194,839	167,517	55.5	18,019	82,257	3,510,890	.0580	1,685,447	479	326,787	650	48,378	255	346,624	66,184	150,405
363	Presque Isle, ME	72,859	73,938	-15.0	14,864	31,228	1,082,960	.0205	724,335	206	106,383	212	13,715	72	157,651	46,843	56,711
364	Providence-Pawtucket, RI-New Bedford-Fall River, MA	1,650,151	1,582,997	4.8	19,333	622,197	31,902,970	.5441	18,250,551	5,182	2,098,849	4,175	1,181,391	6,218	3,176,311	1,757,969	1,171,154
365	Provo-Orem, UT	418,644	376,774	39.9	15,051	121,920	6,301,210	.1208	4,442,435	1,261	895,851	1,781	147,868	778	683,989	85,494	284,554
366	Pueblo, CO	326,297	312,828	17.6	15,385	133,585	5,020,210	.0920	3,082,039	876	672,592	1,338	41,492	220	461,648	134,183	265,749
367	Quincy, IL-Hannibal, MO	182,626	184,825	4.3	15,828	73,166	2,890,660	.0531	1,837,827	521	303,071	603	32,699	171	275,062	108,985	140,017
368	Raleigh-Durham, NC	1,669,882	1,475,053	35.4	20,829	634,365	34,781,270	.6014	21,891,807	6,218	2,904,720	5,776	1,088,707	5,730	2,996,869	1,027,790	1,242,786
369	Rapid City, SD	203,466	196,855	8.6	15,654	78,479	3,184,960	.0699	3,327,094	945	537,338	1,069	91,481	482	227,881	96,885	174,067
370	Reading, PA	393,253	373,638	11.0	19,745	147,995	7,764,710	.1320	4,459,882	1,266	520,167	1,034	360,634	1,898	665,140	278,677	275,607
371	Redding, CA	302,565	276,618	9.2	15,777	115,306	4,773,620	.0849	2,706,009	769	398,441	792	58,578	309	527,344	150,949	211,883
372	Reno, NV	656,705	589,751	34.3	20,415	251,287	13,406,880	.2270	7,774,921	2,205	968,411	1,926	194,597	1,024	1,216,486	417,060	493,007
373	Richmond, IN	101,572	104,034	-0.9	16,610	40,600	1,687,110	.0321	1,250,951	355	237,764	473	30,299	160	168,321	79,326	75,104
374	Richmond-Petersburg, VA	1,321,384	1,256,479	15.2	18,814	491,018	24,860,520	.4357	15,326,987	4,353	2,546,176	5,063	753,583	3,966	2,112,220	955,249	972,690
375	Riverton, WY	48,383	48,975	4.5	15,634	19,557	756,430	.0146	565,284	160	100,314	200	7,566	39	73,032	11,381	42,193
376	Roanoke, VA	668,036	664,313	9.0	17,371	276,705	11,604,600	.2140	8,005,133	2,272	1,142,378	2,273	291,373	1,534	988,678	405,457	555,065
377	Roanoke Rapids, NC	77,352	79,456	4.1	12,801	30,638	990,220	.0199	713,560	203	113,500	225	29,776	157	105,183	46,987	52,686
378	Rochester-Austin-Albert Lea, MN	269,584	255,927	9.8	21,596	113,950	5,821,870	.0967	3,263,960	927	659,106	1,311	86,530	455	382,963	130,367	224,572

Source: Devonshire Associates Ltd. and Scan/US, Inc. 2005.
... Represents a change of less than 0.1%.

Basic Trading Areas: Population/Income/Sales, *Continued*

BTA No.	Basic Trading Area	Population: Estimate 7/1/05	Population: Census 4/1/00	Population: % Change 4/1/90-4/1/00	Per Capita Income 2004	Households Estimate 7/1/05	Disposable Income 2004 ($1,000)	Market Ability Index 2004	Total Retail Sales: 2004 Sales ($1,000)	Total Retail Sales: Ranally Sales Units	General Merchandise: 2004 Sales ($1,000)	General Merchandise: Ranally Sales Units	Apparel Store: 2004 Sales ($1,000)	Apparel Store: Ranally Sales Units	Food Store Sales 2004 ($1,000)	Health & Drug Store 2004 ($1,000)	Passenger Car Registrations 2004
379	Rochester, NY	1,166,628	1,156,164	3.3	21,115	451,220	24,633,200	.4022	12,823,482	3,642	1,441,445	2,866	667,898	3,515	2,430,708	659,430	847,182
380	Rockford, IL	474,815	456,277	10.7	19,622	179,110	9,316,910	.1581	5,299,833	1,505	823,838	1,639	175,076	921	839,644	329,585	336,426
381	Rock Springs, WY	60,078	59,027	3.6	19,593	23,244	1,177,130	.0207	751,259	213	105,976	211	16,345	85	109,193	15,339	53,434
382	Rocky Mount-Wilson, NC	222,187	216,840	8.8	16,042	86,172	3,564,410	.0673	2,503,366	711	312,887	622	132,371	696	291,292	160,648	155,795
383	Rolla, MO	111,962	104,820	6.7	14,049	42,003	1,572,910	.0289	893,753	255	158,283	315	15,007	78	102,773	29,336	81,864
384	Rome, GA	136,042	128,692	11.8	15,209	49,700	2,069,080	.0380	1,273,119	361	294,317	586	51,970	273	162,349	93,396	93,390
385	Roseburg, OR	103,471	100,399	6.1	16,693	43,031	1,727,220	.0299	926,696	263	187,051	372	23,687	125	170,593	49,089	87,114
386	Roswell, NM	82,038	80,793	15.3	14,050	30,926	1,152,650	.0220	753,143	214	181,122	360	30,278	159	102,244	46,982	55,641
387	Russellville, AR	101,113	98,389	20.2	14,591	38,922	1,475,310	.0286	1,053,842	299	238,051	473	23,752	125	113,474	39,158	74,884
388	Rutland-Bennington, VT	100,821	100,394	2.5	17,682	40,172	1,782,760	.0366	1,682,789	478	117,658	234	131,291	691	251,401	101,903	75,039
389	Sacramento, CA	2,299,077	2,001,001	20.8	20,636	831,044	47,443,570	.7741	24,263,552	6,890	2,937,881	5,843	1,251,753	6,588	4,412,900	1,107,258	1,649,094
390	Saginaw-Bay City, MI	641,126	638,851	3.8	17,981	262,121	11,528,020	.2169	8,633,664	2,452	1,570,882	3,124	461,989	2,432	924,384	474,255	482,229
391	St. Cloud, MN	323,343	287,947	18.1	19,049	122,115	6,159,410	.1120	4,291,565	1,219	680,403	1,352	77,786	409	576,519	125,722	258,014
392	St. George, UT	164,799	140,919	69.2	14,543	56,814	2,396,690	.0504	2,181,495	619	296,092	588	65,350	344	300,948	42,584	115,747
393	St. Joseph, MO	194,734	196,619	2.7	16,266	79,348	3,167,470	.0580	2,027,425	575	377,622	751	31,615	166	282,251	78,347	154,307
394	St. Louis, MO	2,950,290	2,873,395	4.8	20,428	1,165,588	60,267,140	1.0137	34,156,428	9,700	5,222,561	10,388	1,226,588	6,457	4,663,483	2,371,127	2,253,011
395	Salem-Albany-Corvallis, OR	563,414	528,436	20.1	17,577	208,050	9,903,170	.1729	5,737,011	1,629	1,240,820	2,467	202,171	1,065	885,993	207,722	411,983
396	Salina, KS	139,323	144,345	0.7	16,910	58,823	2,355,990	.0443	1,695,541	482	295,215	588	55,356	291	225,472	75,789	121,162
397	Salinas-Monterey, CA	421,269	401,762	13.0	18,324	130,913	7,719,290	.1321	4,297,922	1,220	496,897	988	304,946	1,605	763,460	273,308	273,730
398	Salisbury, MD	195,857	186,608	14.5	17,966	77,429	3,518,680	.0663	2,644,490	752	546,036	1,086	180,893	952	409,715	161,449	136,365
399	Salt Lake City-Ogden, UT	1,745,772	1,629,189	24.6	17,669	575,034	30,846,720	.5832	23,200,821	6,588	3,735,905	7,430	965,449	5,082	3,315,483	514,375	1,249,440
400	San Angelo, TX	158,554	161,869	3.9	15,433	61,941	2,446,900	.0462	1,674,837	475	296,087	589	56,373	296	225,242	50,437	108,200
401	San Antonio, TX	2,030,707	1,856,320	21.3	16,388	702,683	33,278,250	.6267	23,548,820	6,687	3,278,352	6,520	1,264,277	6,653	3,730,649	919,034	1,228,439
402	San Diego, CA	2,990,693	2,813,833	12.6	19,889	1,027,661	59,482,050	1.0104	34,231,355	9,720	4,237,412	8,427	2,478,722	13,046	5,315,838	1,790,799	1,982,651
403	Sandusky, OH	138,823	139,038	4.5	19,504	55,200	2,707,600	.0460	1,539,869	437	254,488	506	61,689	325	217,420	120,663	106,082
404	San Francisco-Oakland-San Jose, CA	7,328,480	7,237,170	12.7	26,695	2,618,622	195,635,140	3.0685	102,536,538	29,114	12,681,685	25,219	8,230,659	43,320	18,391,552	5,637,818	5,120,873
405	San Luis Obispo, CA	257,381	246,681	13.6	21,248	102,969	5,468,890	.0887	2,798,082	795	240,208	478	153,387	807	552,099	196,306	233,271
406	Santa Barbara-Santa Maria, CA	404,582	399,347	8.0	19,919	139,852	8,058,830	.1386	4,839,745	1,374	499,060	992	335,212	1,764	874,460	322,723	270,633
407	Santa Fe, NM	232,819	218,804	25.4	19,224	90,152	4,475,750	.0772	2,646,821	752	470,393	936	180,556	950	356,982	177,911	173,603
408	Sarasota-Bradenton, FL	694,757	622,168	21.2	21,995	300,900	15,280,990	.2559	8,941,038	2,539	1,080,597	2,149	545,809	2,873	1,335,020	557,917	495,980
409	Sault Ste. Marie, MI	56,933	57,510	12.7	15,377	21,993	875,470	.0163	563,124	159	76,621	153	24,209	128	91,755	23,774	37,641
410	Savannah, GA	801,719	754,491	19.7	16,108	293,207	12,914,230	.2424	8,926,771	2,535	1,565,078	3,112	525,159	2,762	1,232,385	394,332	519,293
411	Scottsbluff, NE	98,257	101,597	-0.4	15,774	40,943	1,549,940	.0370	1,984,062	564	202,857	403	23,462	124	175,886	58,504	84,014
412	Scranton—Wilkes-Barre—Hazleton, PA	662,440	672,498	-0.9	16,528	266,829	10,948,950	.2086	8,059,762	2,288	1,033,998	2,056	379,530	1,997	1,416,048	565,286	454,403
413	Seattle-Tacoma, WA	3,412,043	3,232,492	19.3	23,292	1,360,708	79,474,750	1.3141	46,149,238	13,105	7,114,750	14,150	2,594,170	13,654	6,108,870	1,923,554	2,677,870
414	Sedalia, MO	96,230	92,562	16.1	15,174	38,808	1,460,180	.0271	935,497	265	167,198	332	19,294	101	122,639	45,098	76,341
415	Selma, AL	68,961	71,409	-4.1	10,752	26,677	741,440	.0153	508,579	145	98,485	196	23,614	124	83,663	39,900	42,744
416	Sharon, PA	119,699	120,293	-0.6	16,717	47,949	2,001,010	.0409	1,811,143	514	258,804	515	176,771	930	225,340	118,242	80,797
417	Sheboygan, WI	114,016	112,646	8.4	20,368	45,505	2,322,260	.0378	1,160,993	330	251,599	500	16,223	85	172,267	56,215	83,247
418	Sherman-Denison, TX	187,973	178,371	17.4	16,128	69,824	3,031,620	.0568	2,085,345	592	483,511	961	41,671	220	238,556	84,883	128,472
419	Shreveport, LA	631,864	605,690	3.8	15,279	246,340	9,654,170	.1816	6,479,773	1,840	1,215,974	2,419	256,262	1,350	822,643	300,000	429,052
420	Sierra Vista-Douglas, AZ	124,122	117,755	20.6	15,174	47,040	1,883,480	.0325	904,859	257	174,929	348	27,736	146	191,816	20,681	82,188
421	Sioux City, IA	339,804	344,417	4.7	16,288	129,027	5,534,570	.1548	9,846,199	2,796	496,484	987	126,691	667	488,411	155,214	263,769
422	Sioux Falls, SD	262,741	244,947	17.9	19,134	104,269	5,027,340	.1084	5,510,408	1,564	748,001	1,487	84,358	443	357,610	210,821	227,854
423	Somerset, KY	129,741	124,982	12.1	11,391	49,322	1,477,890	.0314	1,157,266	328	213,690	425	37,206	197	150,648	98,703	90,500
424	South Bend-Mishawaka, IN	356,427	354,754	7.2	16,287	126,150	5,805,280	.1136	4,593,806	1,305	830,667	1,652	172,099	906	509,642	307,554	248,748
425	Spokane, WA	781,918	741,519	21.0	17,040	313,269	13,323,590	.2461	9,121,772	2,588	1,422,172	2,829	331,805	1,747	1,365,162	334,708	642,066
426	Springfield, IL	271,777	267,461	5.0	20,120	111,671	5,468,150	.0943	3,336,913	948	591,972	1,177	93,591	494	419,112	210,973	194,744
427	Springfield-Holyoke, MA	689,619	680,014	1.0	19,551	266,392	13,482,560	.2241	7,089,078	2,013	700,829	1,393	347,601	1,830	1,358,554	569,374	458,778
428	Springfield, MO	703,187	660,151	23.9	16,147	291,870	11,354,140	.2176	8,392,109	2,383	1,317,914	2,621	305,085	1,606	873,085	345,375	570,979
429	State College, PA	141,710	135,758	9.7	16,078	52,454	2,278,390	.0430	1,600,239	454	218,370	434	91,218	480	222,490	77,825	92,574
430	Staunton-Waynesboro, VA	116,101	111,524	11.2	17,428	45,329	2,023,400	.0368	1,329,635	378	208,549	415	42,735	225	210,466	87,272	94,196
431	Steubenville, OH-Weirton, WV	126,448	132,008	-7.4	16,713	53,884	2,113,340	.0358	1,048,619	298	175,680	350	33,988	179	207,784	110,680	98,165
432	Stevens Point-Marshfield-Wisconsin Rapids, WI	216,858	214,617	6.6	18,175	87,283	3,941,380	.0706	2,548,561	724	510,730	1,015	40,644	214	272,317	31,052	171,232
433	Stillwater, OK	81,308	79,601	9.7	14,219	31,390	1,156,120	.0222	780,809	221	214,376	427	27,142	143	71,358	42,101	58,961
434	Stockton, CA	721,404	604,152	17.9	15,758	219,608	11,368,050	.1939	5,457,823	1,549	686,448	1,365	250,800	1,320	956,108	365,394	467,147
435	Stroudsburg, PA	164,314	138,687	44.9	17,826	54,370	2,929,020	.0519	1,798,093	511	250,720	499	181,531	955	350,567	123,096	105,625
436	Sumter, SC	160,177	157,267	5.2	13,575	56,446	2,174,460	.0411	1,343,798	382	193,213	384	67,161	354	198,791	70,328	98,331
437	Sunbury-Shamokin, PA	191,525	191,962	2.5	15,903	73,754	3,045,820	.0558	1,919,354	545	228,428	455	40,725	214	306,203	109,260	126,642
438	Syracuse, NY	789,248	780,716	-1.3	19,481	308,792	15,375,120	.2582	8,358,186	2,373	877,667	1,745	421,993	2,222	1,560,698	606,071	553,635
439	Tallahassee, FL	517,426	502,539	19.9	17,179	204,525	8,888,990	.1589	5,475,969	1,554	923,662	1,836	237,021	1,248	825,531	356,878	353,804
440	Tampa-St. Petersburg-Clearwater, FL	2,866,472	2,628,386	16.8	19,243	1,169,263	55,158,820	.9896	37,192,903	10,562	4,660,597	9,269	1,564,347	8,233	5,171,853	2,428,189	1,964,612
441	Temple-Killeen, TX	376,847	354,952	21.7	15,817	132,077	5,960,420	.1041	3,167,946	900	469,762	934	94,973	499	459,270	70,896	238,114
442	Terre Haute, IN	241,389	245,348	3.5	15,567	94,265	3,757,790	.0834	4,043,421	1,149	603,270	1,201	122,442	644	285,151	142,656	176,145
443	Texarkana, TX-AR	271,871	270,420	5.6	14,444	105,706	3,926,860	.0749	2,602,727	741	565,624	1,125	104,881	551	320,848	99,258	186,254
444	Toledo, OH	789,895	789,378	0.9	18,735	312,559	14,798,930	.2666	9,924,692	2,819	1,455,325	2,895	364,194	1,917	1,391,915	586,752	597,330
445	Topeka, KS	260,592	258,820	5.3	18,666	106,236	4,864,250	.0851	2,956,757	840	601,551	1,198	86,789	457	370,877	190,422	209,749
446	Traverse City, MI	263,829	247,138	20.8	18,196	105,551	4,800,760	.0915	3,742,284	1,063	681,213	1,356	145,002	764	481,091	190,698	200,379
447	Tucson, AZ	921,681	843,746	26.5	17,523	359,359	16,151,030	.2750	8,503,748	2,415	1,331,237	2,647	348,394	1,834	1,318,403	534,417	611,509
448	Tulsa, OK	986,421	949,928	13.6	16,659	360,859	16,432,740	.3058	11,316,967	3,212	2,393,607	4,761	359,347	1,891	1,160,386	679,708	704,965
449	Tupelo-Corinth, MS	329,667	323,239	10.8	14,683	123,905	4,840,550	.0934	3,425,863	973	952,623	1,896	155,627	820	319,270	188,407	244,041
450	Tuscaloosa, AL	255,938	254,017	6.8	15,883	102,313	4,065,020	.0754	2,675,483	759	458,630	913	109,598	576	334,296	159,407	185,687
451	Twin Falls, ID	170,368	162,397	18.7	15,550	62,540	2,649,210	.0521	2,066,888	586	334,695	665	75,543	396	299,096	80,794	139,766
452	Tyler, TX	334,958	313,226	16.1	14,961	116,461	5,011,170	.1001	3,985,728	1,132	745,932	1,484	223,448	1,176	505,395	180,567	207,560
453	Utica-Rome, NY	297,654	299,896	-5.3	17,783	117,853	5,293,320	.0902	2,830,331	804	431,672	859	107,101	564	423,720	275,720	188,438
454	Valdosta, GA	172,471	166,053	19.3	13,347	62,233	2,302,000	.0468	1,787,791	506	236,878	470	91,510	482	219,923	64,951	113,481
455	Vicksburg, MS	59,903	61,475	3.8	15,045	21,863	901,270	.0176	669,201	190	133,375	265	32,321	170	82,332	28,919	39,319
456	Victoria, TX	167,023	165,277	10.2	16,071	61,263	2,684,170	.0498	1,788,392	508	300,395	599	65,345	343	287,109	79,333	108,288
457	Vincennes-Washington, IN	94,865	94,897	1.2	14,585	36,428	1,383,580	.0268	988,864	281	142,736	284	32,328	171	99,655	62,104	66,418
458	Visalia-Porterville-Hanford, CA	550,154	497,482	20.3	12,543	158,065	6,900,690	.1274	3,561,319	1,011	526,627	1,048	143,296	754	752,315	200,807	290,220
459	Waco, TX	317,109	303,669	12.4	14,759	115,163	4,680,120	.0895	3,221,951	915	514,023	1,023	179,358	943	543,152	131,572	203,135
460	Walla Walla, WA-Pendleton, OR	181,435	174,458	15.1	15,847	67,932	2,875,260	.0548	2,055,554	584	304,124	605	61,384	323	390,544	79,345	137,306
461	Washington, DC	5,213,005	4,769,729	15.8	27,288	1,942,500	142,252,060	2.0846	58,284,414	16,548	7,238,545	14,396	4,066,996	21,406	9,663,285	3,013,600	3,669,463
462	Waterloo-Cedar Falls, IA	261,265	266,449	2.1	16,929	102,555	4,422,900	.0818	3,014,369	855	430,121	856	78,961	416	361,302	151,365	221,688
463	Watertown, NY	302,902	301,747	1.9	15,471	111,302	4,686,330	.0857	2,879,152	818	303,468	603	103,304	543	443,452	246,398	184,121
464	Watertown, SD	74,291	75,962	1.9	16,008	30,581	1,189,240	.0247	1,083,963	308	58,240	118	26,273	138	95,545	19,959	65,633
465	Waterville-Augusta, ME	172,813	168,002	1.4	17,054	71,467	2,947,150	.0586	2,503,580	711	292,105	580	43,793	231	433,623	115,415	132,482
466	Wausau-Rhinelander, WI	249,582	244,048	10.9	18,558	102,008	4,631,850	.0870	3,515,581	997	663,305	1,318	72,092	380	390,332	74,416	197,181
467	Waycross, GA	118,812	113,264	14.4	12,818	42,722	1,522,900	.0319	1,238,838	352	261,375	519	29,747	157	151,584	62,088	76,171
468	Wenatchee, WA	223,554	213,481	28.2	15,340	81,982	3,429,210	.0647	2,319,397	660	400,048	796	46,315	244	428,324	89,891	162,505
469	West Palm Beach-Boca Raton, FL	1,306,047	1,167,094	30.7	21,548	504,136	28,142,370	.4868	18,087,143	5,136	2,346,986	4,668	1,801,600	9,483	2,665,361	1,246,433	850,885
470	West Plains, MO	77,929	77,090	14.8	12,939	33,261	1,008,310	.0196	662,706	190	168,942	335	16,935	89	82,302	38,580	65,585
471	Wheeling, WV	205,250	211,493	-3.8	15,152	83,447	3,109,860	.0588	2,104,676	598	343,272	682	79,873	421	346,893	157,871	151,756
472	Wichita, KS	671,917	656,056	9.8	18,076	256,316	12,145,250	.2108	7,031,189	1,995	1,354,161	2,693	268,156	1,412	1,044,177	369,821	525,166
473	Wichita Falls, TX	216,825	222,462	6.3	15,952	84,431	3,458,730	.0630	2,169,074	616	383,293	761	58,261	305	329,782	117,006	151,654
474	Williamson, WV-Pikeville, KY	172,448	175,453	-5.5	11,673	70,294	2,012,910	.0430	1,632,277	464	321,178	639	55,111	290	235,955	158,679	119,551
475	Williamsport, PA	161,301	164,514	1.6	16,210	65,573	2,614,740	.0504	1,978,317	562	272,300	542	87,209	459	315,636	142,996	110,145
476	Williston, ND	24,647	25,498	-7.3	14,320	9,723	352,950	.0075	323,415	92	51,200	102	8,286	43	42,843	17,119	20,898
477	Willmar-Marshall, MN	122,713	126,335	2.1	18,506	52,486	2,270,880	.0398	1,362,279	387	186,698	372	24,565	130	189,825	54,516	104,185
478	Wilmington, NC	360,467	329,281	31.9	18,086	148,476	6,519,270	.1266	5,356,858	1,521	716,915	1,425	215,553	1,135	702,358	300,707	268,312
479	Winchester, VA	180,272	162,105	17.9	18,415	68,046	3,319,730	.0622	2,478,916	704	435,833	866	78,281	413	307,426	138,335	142,058
480	Worcester-Fitchburg-Leominster, MA	790,475	750,963	5.8	21,359	291,974	16,883,400	.2793	9,300,431	2,641	871,592	1,733	449,285	2,365	1,474,657	686,325	535,226
481	Worthington, MN	94,504	96,475	-0.1	17,578	40,231	1,661,170	.0295	1,025,862	291	87,759	174	23,961	127	154,537	46,818	80,563
482	Yakima, WA	265,478	255,943	18.7	14,243	91,954	3,781,320	.0710	2,373,523	674	508,190	1,010	69,619	366	397,266	65,888	196,815
483	York-Hanover, PA	502,894	473,043	13.2	19,844	190,449	9,979,640	.1616	4,799,517	1,362	646,482	1,286	172,030	906	840,243	223,846	355,786
484	Youngstown-Warren, OH	467,323	482,671	-2.0	17,475	187,024	8,166,390	.1480	5,340,675	1,516	698,179	1,388	229,652	1,209	704,483	351,238	342,882
485	Yuba City-Marysville, CA	153,877	139,149	13.5	14,540	50,617	2,237,430	.0399	1,184,765	337	238,417	474	31,237	165	256,559	86,882	92,947
486	Yuma, AZ	177,064	160,026	49.7	13,429	59,841	2,377,840	.0452	1,477,200	419	322,796	642	34,478	181	221,749	77,415	100,715
487	Zanesville-Cambridge, OH	191,647	188,410	5.7	15,044	72,694	2,883,050	.0540	1,885,820	536	240,486	479	92,559	488	309,372	124,563	144,568
	United States Total	**296,460,358**	**281,421,906**	**13.2**	**19,402**	**110,228,421**	**5,752,025,490**	**100.0000**	**3,521,709,000**	**1,000,000**	**502,845,000**	**1,000,000**	**189,997,000**	**1,000,000**	**498,151,000**	**205,404,000**	**203,446,969**

Source: Devonshire Associates Ltd. and Scan/US, Inc. 2005.

... Represents a change of less than 0.1%.

150 Largest Basic Trading Areas: Population/Income/Sales

This table lists the 150 largest Basic Trading Areas (BTAs), as defined by Rand McNally, ranked by July 1, 2005 estimated population. The data shown are consistent with the data in the BTA table which appears on pages 24-27. The Basic Trading Areas are shown on the map which appears on pages 22-23. Statistics for Total Retail Sales, General Merchandise, Apparel Store, Food Store Sales, and Health and Drug Store Sales in this edition are estimates based on data from the U.S. Census Bureau, and utilize the 1997 North American Industry Classification System (NAICS). A detailed explanation of Retail Trade and Trading Areas can be found in the Introduction on pages 5-9.

BTA Rank	Basic Trading Area	Population: Estimate 7/1/05	Population: Census 4/1/00	Population: % Change 4/1/90-4/1/00	Per Capita Income 2004	House-holds Estimate 7/1/05	Disposable Income 2004 ($1,000)	Market Ability Index 2004	Total Retail Sales: 2004 Sales ($1,000)	Total Retail Sales: Ranally Sales Units	General Merchandise: 2004 Sales ($1,000)	General Merchandise: Ranally Sales Units	Apparel Store: 2004 Sales ($1,000)	Apparel Store: Ranally Sales Units	Food Store Sales 2004 ($1,000)	Health & Drug Store 2004 ($1,000)	Passenger Car Regis-trations 2004
1	New York, NY	20,227,583	19,620,902	8.7	23,150	7,237,265	468,274,500	7.3846	228,887,923	64,993	19,940,540	39,656	24,647,180	129,722	36,451,669	18,440,575	10,063,875
2	Los Angeles, CA	17,816,585	16,391,590	12.7	18,175	5,663,905	323,821,500	5.5434	179,224,358	50,891	22,613,435	44,971	13,727,785	72,252	28,036,291	9,976,538	11,084,238
3	Chicago, IL	9,471,425	9,098,316	11.2	20,848	3,293,572	197,462,610	3.3057	111,549,447	31,675	13,109,705	26,071	6,321,481	33,269	14,695,301	9,643,813	5,787,518
4	San Francisco-Oakland-San Jose, CA	7,328,480	7,237,170	12.7	26,695	2,618,622	195,635,140	3.0685	102,536,538	29,114	12,681,685	25,219	8,230,659	43,320	18,391,552	5,637,818	5,120,873
5	Philadelphia, PA-Wilmington, DE-Trenton, NJ	6,352,452	6,184,346	4.8	21,666	2,325,184	137,633,870	2.3185	81,443,677	23,124	7,335,285	14,589	4,996,061	26,295	13,057,245	6,075,839	3,927,841
6	Dallas-Fort Worth, TX	6,286,526	5,571,828	28.7	19,607	2,131,664	123,262,480	2.1888	81,400,114	23,116	11,835,472	23,534	4,216,842	22,193	10,348,334	3,385,064	4,092,738
7	Houston, TX	5,637,714	5,045,022	24.4	17,738	1,868,675	100,001,080	1.8144	66,309,150	18,831	11,021,054	21,919	3,744,318	19,707	9,828,795	3,097,352	3,459,368
8	Washington, DC	5,213,005	4,769,729	15.8	27,288	1,942,500	142,252,060	2.0846	58,284,414	16,548	7,238,545	14,396	4,066,996	21,406	9,663,285	3,013,600	3,669,463
9	Detroit, MI	5,047,892	4,965,944	5.5	22,019	1,938,628	111,149,710	1.9018	69,845,843	19,833	11,179,770	22,233	3,344,275	17,601	8,138,147	5,158,404	3,576,809
10	Atlanta, GA	4,987,395	4,407,446	37.9	21,370	1,787,523	106,580,590	1.8305	66,611,144	18,913	8,993,756	17,888	3,492,322	18,382	9,226,379	2,901,230	3,500,015
11	Boston, MA	4,457,319	4,391,344	6.2	24,540	1,656,326	109,383,350	1.7852	62,649,565	17,791	5,876,246	11,687	4,707,924	24,780	9,933,443	4,633,205	2,943,223
12	Miami-Fort Lauderdale, FL	4,263,821	3,955,969	21.0	17,472	1,513,860	74,498,140	1.3803	52,245,087	14,835	5,958,257	11,850	4,219,589	22,209	7,023,286	3,864,975	2,568,242
13	Phoenix, AZ	4,021,099	3,462,432	44.0	18,905	1,441,419	76,020,430	1.3239	45,989,908	13,059	6,361,779	12,652	1,761,242	9,269	5,874,377	2,333,314	2,540,902
14	Minneapolis-St. Paul, MN	3,484,888	3,293,598	15.9	23,505	1,387,468	81,913,370	1.4064	53,913,058	15,309	8,002,170	15,913	1,976,799	10,404	6,682,849	2,417,308	2,795,857
15	Seattle-Tacoma, WA	3,412,043	3,232,492	19.3	23,292	1,360,708	79,474,750	1.3141	46,149,238	13,105	7,114,750	14,150	2,594,170	13,654	6,108,870	1,923,554	2,677,870
16	Cleveland-Akron, OH	2,996,876	2,993,610	3.4	19,707	1,179,095	59,060,840	1.0437	38,519,634	10,938	3,888,086	7,733	1,848,283	9,727	5,615,422	3,881,264	2,129,760
17	San Diego, CA	2,990,693	2,813,833	12.6	19,889	1,027,661	59,482,050	1.0104	34,231,355	9,720	4,237,412	8,427	2,478,722	13,046	5,315,838	1,790,799	1,982,651
18	St. Louis, MO	2,950,290	2,873,395	4.8	20,428	1,165,588	60,267,140	1.0137	34,156,428	9,700	5,222,561	10,388	1,226,588	6,457	4,663,483	2,371,127	2,253,011
19	Denver, CO	2,928,236	2,712,488	30.8	24,731	1,209,302	72,417,260	1.1616	39,288,689	11,154	5,360,874	10,659	1,970,195	10,371	5,772,212	1,502,084	2,461,212
20	Tampa-St. Petersburg-Clearwater, FL	2,866,472	2,628,386	16.8	19,243	1,169,263	55,158,820	.9896	37,192,903	10,562	4,660,597	9,269	1,564,347	8,233	5,171,853	2,428,189	1,964,612
21	Baltimore, MD	2,713,502	2,606,003	7.2	22,492	1,021,896	61,032,770	.9700	30,112,122	8,549	3,874,694	7,706	1,740,410	9,161	5,325,612	1,770,976	1,855,614
22	Pittsburgh, PA	2,440,332	2,471,759	-1.4	18,246	997,936	44,525,390	.7986	28,997,740	8,235	3,325,886	6,613	1,333,452	7,017	4,664,699	2,122,847	1,659,473
23	Sacramento, CA	2,299,077	2,001,001	20.8	20,636	831,044	47,443,570	.7741	24,263,552	6,890	2,937,881	5,843	1,251,753	6,588	4,412,900	1,107,258	1,649,094
24	Portland, OR	2,298,591	2,114,640	25.1	20,900	898,004	48,041,570	.8305	30,280,222	8,598	5,525,647	10,989	1,619,766	8,526	4,132,236	1,032,496	1,710,100
25	Charlotte-Gastonia, NC	2,289,481	2,078,083	24.4	19,708	880,535	45,120,960	.7833	27,782,013	7,887	3,938,694	7,833	1,247,930	6,567	3,643,748	1,645,246	1,725,265
26	Cincinnati, OH	2,237,847	2,170,768	9.1	20,213	869,029	45,232,900	.7742	27,029,279	7,673	3,816,548	7,588	1,250,377	6,582	3,842,283	1,530,064	1,691,966
27	Kansas City, MO	2,167,409	2,049,447	11.4	20,731	856,333	44,933,300	.7703	27,391,794	7,778	4,273,904	8,501	1,022,085	5,381	3,201,695	1,461,735	1,680,003
28	San Antonio, TX	2,030,707	1,856,320	21.3	16,388	702,683	33,278,250	.6267	23,548,820	6,687	3,278,352	6,520	1,264,277	6,653	3,730,649	919,034	1,228,439
29	Orlando, FL	1,962,360	1,697,906	35.1	19,404	727,715	38,077,680	.6881	26,381,919	7,493	3,879,618	7,715	1,791,694	9,430	3,442,106	1,422,749	1,283,983
30	Las Vegas, NV	1,923,403	1,568,418	82.8	18,753	708,473	36,068,680	.6336	22,348,533	6,346	3,153,840	6,272	1,408,481	7,413	3,398,982	969,385	1,231,875
31	Milwaukee, WI	1,883,428	1,849,490	5.6	20,341	733,954	38,310,410	.6424	21,388,701	6,073	3,245,867	6,454	678,073	3,568	2,947,747	1,402,237	1,367,022
32	Nashville, TN	1,880,864	1,761,799	23.3	19,580	727,209	36,827,580	.6595	24,947,663	7,085	4,377,267	8,706	1,180,929	6,214	3,087,757	1,454,927	1,437,303
33	Norfolk-Virginia Beach-Newport News-Hampton, VA	1,877,341	1,784,356	9.1	17,599	689,496	33,038,490	.5870	20,360,061	5,782	3,184,125	6,333	1,176,186	6,189	2,771,885	969,559	1,320,732
34	Columbus, OH	1,800,250	1,692,240	14.5	20,017	684,574	36,034,970	.6559	25,967,451	7,373	3,104,585	6,173	1,286,880	6,773	3,082,931	1,081,021	1,354,988
35	Salt Lake City-Ogden, UT	1,745,772	1,629,189	24.6	17,669	575,034	30,846,720	.5832	23,200,821	6,588	3,735,905	7,430	965,449	5,082	3,315,483	514,375	1,249,440
36	Indianapolis, IN	1,674,207	1,552,963	17.5	20,022	626,301	33,521,520	.6069	23,789,320	6,757	4,253,860	8,460	941,407	4,955	2,094,327	1,529,018	1,226,564
37	Raleigh-Durham, NC	1,669,882	1,475,053	35.4	20,829	634,365	34,781,270	.6014	21,891,807	6,218	2,904,720	5,776	1,088,707	5,730	2,996,869	1,027,790	1,242,786
38	Providence-Pawtucket, RI-New Bedford-Fall River, MA	1,650,151	1,582,997	4.8	19,333	622,197	31,902,970	.5441	18,250,551	5,182	2,098,849	4,175	1,181,391	6,218	3,176,311	1,757,969	1,171,154
39	Memphis, TN	1,602,474	1,553,276	11.2	16,860	599,903	27,018,260	.4967	18,048,366	5,124	3,270,360	6,505	974,867	5,129	1,831,697	1,236,130	1,071,569
40	Louisville, KY	1,540,990	1,486,048	9.8	18,187	592,185	28,025,350	.4900	16,677,914	4,736	2,907,089	5,782	638,993	3,361	1,771,674	1,077,657	1,123,671
41	Austin, TX	1,540,187	1,325,029	47.3	21,057	557,904	32,431,970	.6491	30,916,727	8,780	2,572,743	5,117	1,114,421	5,867	3,161,090	1,520,882	1,051,214
42	Greensboro—Winston-Salem—High Point, NC	1,523,567	1,454,066	17.1	18,430	599,732	28,079,470	.5138	19,591,533	5,564	2,575,167	5,121	917,038	4,830	2,335,426	1,209,902	1,197,738
43	Jacksonville, FL	1,499,671	1,358,825	21.9	19,591	567,630	29,379,840	.5100	18,022,608	5,118	2,596,659	5,163	853,750	4,495	2,501,411	874,665	1,040,845
44	Oklahoma City, OK	1,489,279	1,434,827	9.9	16,615	569,953	24,744,190	.4551	16,358,368	4,643	3,009,325	5,986	525,253	2,764	1,791,710	928,574	1,065,836
45	New Orleans, LA	1,425,798	1,430,273	4.6	16,588	530,095	23,651,810	.4393	16,156,734	4,590	2,896,445	5,761	968,298	5,097	2,220,043	1,217,530	878,754
46	Birmingham, AL	1,350,969	1,319,776	10.0	17,906	524,748	24,190,620	.4341	15,556,714	4,419	2,703,051	5,375	722,703	3,804	1,971,925	820,452	1,012,286
47	Richmond-Petersburg, VA	1,321,384	1,256,479	15.2	18,814	491,018	24,860,520	.4357	15,326,987	4,353	2,546,176	5,063	753,583	3,966	2,112,220	955,249	972,690
48	West Palm Beach-Boca Raton, FL	1,306,047	1,167,094	30.7	21,548	504,136	28,142,370	.4868	18,087,143	5,136	2,346,986	4,668	1,801,600	9,483	2,665,361	1,246,433	850,885
49	Dayton-Springfield, OH	1,214,625	1,219,933	1.0	19,681	486,637	23,905,500	.4106	14,179,865	4,027	2,168,856	4,313	542,518	2,854	2,002,112	786,711	955,640
50	Buffalo-Niagara Falls, NY	1,197,505	1,213,535	-1.5	20,107	492,614	24,077,740	.3953	12,353,272	3,507	1,256,197	2,499	727,095	3,827	2,222,088	995,772	814,516
51	Hartford, CT	1,197,175	1,148,618	2.2	26,530	463,800	31,761,140	.4830	14,817,105	4,207	1,281,098	2,548	1,120,244	5,896	2,339,379	1,185,681	828,784
52	Knoxville, TN	1,180,810	1,118,107	17.9	17,001	476,095	20,075,180	.3926	16,276,508	4,621	2,770,974	5,507	847,538	4,462	1,883,970	902,427	956,872
53	Rochester, NY	1,166,628	1,156,164	3.3	21,115	451,220	24,633,200	.4022	12,823,482	3,642	1,441,445	2,866	667,898	3,515	2,430,708	659,430	847,182
54	Grand Rapids, MI	1,138,129	1,079,340	17.8	19,525	424,070	22,221,650	.3916	14,267,079	4,051	2,949,000	5,865	496,524	2,613	1,306,641	675,384	843,498
55	Albany-Schenectady, NY	1,074,584	1,047,324	1.8	21,157	427,852	22,735,140	.3704	11,780,905	3,345	1,347,080	2,678	605,280	3,185	1,680,931	760,190	733,359
56	New Haven-Waterbury-Meriden, CT	1,045,311	1,006,201	2.9	24,655	394,498	25,772,390	.4113	13,699,003	3,890	1,233,545	2,453	711,441	3,745	2,089,903	961,671	727,566
57	Omaha, NE	1,025,063	991,763	9.5	18,835	394,727	19,307,310	.3553	13,884,648	3,941	1,705,393	3,391	464,278	2,443	1,693,155	804,086	785,072
58	Fresno, CA	1,023,612	922,516	22.1	13,455	310,660	13,772,950	.2578	8,098,841	2,300	1,107,057	2,201	341,667	1,798	1,458,744	503,267	595,488
59	Little Rock, AR	994,284	963,155	13.0	17,672	404,789	17,571,370	.3292	12,863,723	3,651	2,869,482	5,707	431,646	2,272	1,177,480	495,173	770,329
60	Tulsa, OK	986,421	949,928	13.6	16,659	360,859	16,432,740	.3058	11,316,967	3,212	2,393,607	4,761	359,347	1,891	1,160,386	679,708	704,965
61	Lexington, KY	967,536	927,633	13.7	16,693	380,953	16,150,740	.2938	10,336,709	2,935	1,715,888	3,411	469,303	2,471	1,191,006	709,701	718,255
62	Greenville-Spartanburg, SC	954,817	914,473	16.0	17,420	360,224	16,633,040	.3080	11,608,581	3,296	1,649,723	3,280	612,953	3,225	1,456,124	719,810	700,497
63	Tucson, AZ	921,681	843,746	26.5	17,523	359,359	16,151,030	.2750	8,503,748	2,415	1,331,237	2,647	348,394	1,834	1,318,403	534,417	611,509
64	Honolulu, HI	910,475	876,156	4.8	20,281	302,181	18,465,370	.3063	9,903,032	2,812	1,988,367	3,954	1,320,832	6,952	1,401,658	865,911	537,678
65	Albuquerque, NM	892,110	831,850	20.8	17,641	342,539	15,737,310	.2858	10,417,900	2,958	1,974,211	3,928	353,250	1,859	930,024	542,181	680,871
66	Des Moines, IA	838,103	804,543	10.4	18,953	325,405	15,884,810	.2766	9,613,270	2,729	1,299,063	2,581	318,881	1,678	1,314,885	447,771	694,122
67	Savannah, GA	801,719	754,491	19.7	16,108	293,207	12,914,230	.2424	8,926,771	2,535	1,565,078	3,112	525,159	2,762	1,232,385	394,332	519,293
68	Worcester-Fitchburg-Leominster, MA	790,475	750,963	5.8	21,359	291,974	16,883,400	.2793	9,300,431	2,641	871,592	1,733	449,285	2,365	1,474,657	686,325	535,226
69	Toledo, OH	789,895	789,378	0.9	18,735	312,559	14,798,930	.2666	9,924,692	2,819	1,455,325	2,895	364,194	1,917	1,391,915	586,752	597,330
70	Syracuse, NY	789,248	780,716	-1.3	19,481	308,792	15,375,120	.2582	8,358,186	2,373	877,667	1,745	421,993	2,222	1,560,698	606,071	553,635
71	El Paso, TX	787,979	748,239	15.1	11,912	244,429	9,386,270	.1956	7,133,690	2,026	1,572,330	3,126	477,091	2,511	836,941	322,157	438,613
72	Allentown-Bethlehem-Easton, PA	785,814	740,395	7.8	20,371	296,297	16,007,810	.2729	9,467,904	2,689	950,519	1,890	391,866	2,061	1,653,435	659,754	570,635
73	Spokane, WA	781,918	741,519	21.0	17,040	313,269	13,323,590	.2461	9,121,772	2,588	1,422,172	2,829	331,805	1,747	1,365,162	334,708	642,066
74	Bakersfield, CA	743,729	661,645	21.7	14,153	234,348	10,526,210	.1907	5,759,480	1,635	787,831	1,567	234,327	1,233	863,026	390,768	437,779
75	McAllen, TX	736,382	623,060	46.9	8,055	193,832	5,931,840	.1527	6,039,893	1,715	1,230,197	2,447	443,127	2,333	954,444	256,666	345,270
76	Fort Wayne, IN	735,411	715,480	10.6	18,025	269,848	13,255,650	.2408	8,910,923	2,532	1,547,927	3,078	323,332	1,702	994,595	454,770	542,008
77	Fort Myers, FL	732,816	629,301	31.3	20,577	304,441	15,078,960	.2605	9,394,173	2,668	1,514,369	3,012	553,792	2,914	1,277,479	602,707	504,261
78	Baton Rouge, LA	727,726	705,760	13.2	16,566	255,901	12,055,390	.2274	8,602,382	2,443	1,577,670	3,137	358,974	1,888	1,048,954	433,016	470,235
79	Madison, WI	726,250	682,098	15.0	21,201	302,694	15,397,030	.2808	11,486,212	3,261	1,395,417	2,774	296,744	1,561	1,103,700	434,367	571,066
80	Charleston, SC	722,391	680,311	9.0	16,510	261,739	11,926,800	.2191	7,829,953	2,223	1,419,650	2,823	497,490	2,620	1,203,201	383,699	466,341
81	Stockton, CA	721,404	604,152	17.9	15,758	219,608	11,368,050	.1939	5,457,823	1,549	686,448	1,365	250,800	1,320	956,108	365,394	467,147
82	Kingsport, TN-Johnson City, TN-Bristol, VA-TN	719,024	707,899	8.5	15,356	299,138	11,041,330	.2117	7,898,611	2,242	1,433,154	2,848	305,144	1,605	1,089,546	535,429	582,844
83	Harrisburg, PA	713,808	698,708	6.7	20,053	287,681	14,314,040	.2585	10,072,616	2,860	1,016,670	2,021	363,308	1,913	1,370,179	528,090	526,065
84	Columbia, SC	709,560	668,081	17.5	18,423	268,913	13,072,530	.2358	8,737,460	2,480	1,755,498	3,491	454,435	2,391	1,111,451	465,571	523,368
85	Springfield, MO	703,187	660,151	23.9	16,147	291,870	11,354,140	.2176	8,392,109	2,383	1,317,914	2,621	305,085	1,606	873,085	345,375	570,979
86	Jackson, MS	696,998	677,489	10.1	15,324	248,211	10,680,920	.2084	8,018,241	2,276	1,670,360	3,323	323,027	1,700	820,151	508,831	470,176
87	Macon-Warner Robins, GA	695,423	662,942	12.5	15,229	253,255	10,590,390	.1991	7,050,029	1,999	1,198,306	2,384	298,796	1,573	1,041,179	385,610	465,238
88	Sarasota-Bradenton, FL	694,757	622,168	21.2	21,995	300,900	15,280,990	.2559	8,941,038	2,539	1,080,597	2,149	545,809	2,873	1,335,020	557,917	495,980
89	Springfield-Holyoke, MA	689,619	680,014	1.0	19,551	266,392	13,482,560	.2241	7,089,078	2,013	700,829	1,393	347,601	1,830	1,358,554	569,374	458,778
90	Fayetteville-Lumberton, NC	687,400	663,154	16.1	15,287	251,475	10,507,960	.1975	7,012,602	1,992	1,166,265	2,319	333,083	1,754	912,533	415,699	475,393
91	Mobile, AL	678,203	663,075	11.6	14,954	237,639	10,141,590	.1941	7,047,689	2,001	1,408,056	2,800	384,444	2,024	914,332	423,806	452,829
92	Wichita, KS	671,917	656,056	9.8	18,076	256,316	12,145,250	.2108	7,031,189	1,995	1,354,161	2,693	268,156	1,412	1,044,177	369,821	525,166
93	Roanoke, VA	668,036	664,313	9.0	17,371	276,705	11,604,600	.2140	8,005,133	2,272	1,142,378	2,273	291,373	1,534	988,678	405,457	555,065
94	Scranton—Wilkes-Barre—Hazleton, PA	662,440	672,498	-0.9	16,528	266,829	10,948,950	.2086	8,059,762	2,288	1,033,998	2,056	379,530	1,997	1,416,048	565,286	454,403
95	Manchester-Nashua-Concord, NH	662,179	617,057	14.1	21,658	250,857	14,341,310	.2750	12,399,986	3,521	1,655,745	3,292	548,490	2,887	1,729,670	449,086	529,294
96	Boise-Nampa, ID	658,683	584,008	40.2	17,727	246,305	11,676,470	.2167	8,319,699	2,362	1,458,755	2,902	249,021	1,311	1,163,617	277,829	548,863
97	Reno, NV	656,705	589,751	34.3	20,415	251,287	13,406,880	.2270	7,774,921	2,205	968,411	1,926	194,597	1,024	1,216,486	417,060	493,007
98	Saginaw-Bay City, MI	641,126	638,851	3.8	17,981	262,121	11,528,020	.2169	8,633,664	2,452	1,570,882	3,124	461,989	2,432	924,384	474,255	482,229
99	Asheville-Hendersonville, NC	639,822	608,250	19.3	17,257	265,541	11,041,240	.2102	8,343,944	2,369	1,294,300	2,576	339,533	1,786	1,119,396	459,923	502,758
100	Shreveport, LA	631,864	605,690	3.8	15,279	246,340	9,654,170	.1816	6,479,773	1,840	1,215,974	2,419	256,262	1,350	822,643	300,000	429,052
101	Augusta, GA	607,787	590,218	13.1	16,308	224,672	9,912,090	.1779	5,976,011	1,696	1,052,755	2,095	263,524	1,387	852,100	311,065	406,498
102	Colorado Springs, CO	592,836	537,484	31.3	20,800	227,594	12,331,020	.2094	7,302,778	2,074	1,264,886	2,515	200,312	1,055	759,294	276,150	465,450
103	Chattanooga, TN	587,991	568,186	11.2	16,797	225,124	9,876,370	.1794	6,311,875	1,793	1,054,078	2,095	338,736	1,782	834,133	418,002	458,494
104	Modesto, CA	577,893	501,498	19.7	15,854	183,047	9,162,040	.1642	5,353,669	1,520	818,246	1,627	195,916	1,031	1,001,627	356,060	374,374
105	Salem-Albany-Corvallis, OR	563,414	528,436	20.1	17,577	208,050	9,903,170	.1729	5,737,011	1,629	1,240,820	2,467	202,171	1,065	885,993	207,722	411,983
106	Lafayette-New Iberia, LA	556,799	548,154	10.4	14,522	208,834	8,085,570	.1632	6,506,024	1,847	1,225,662	2,436	270,713	1,425	792,529	463,680	339,952
107	Daytona Beach, FL	554,014	493,175	23.5	18,262	220,945	10,117,500	.1771	6,075,367	1,725	882,131	1,754	253,960	1,337	957,383	421,164	395,442
108	Portland-Brunswick, ME	553,890	521,184	10.5	20,389	222,582	11,293,290	.2085	8,546,336	2,426	697,181	1,387	515,688	2,714	1,610,710	336,978	450,336
109	Corpus Christi, TX	553,024	548,161	9.6	14,336	190,389	7,928,190	.1543	5,633,447	1,599	931,843	1,853	251,961	1,326	933,491	234,971	340,631
110	Visalia-Porterville-Hanford, CA	550,154	497,482	20.3	12,543	158,065	6,900,690	.1274	3,561,319	1,011	526,627	1,048	143,296	754	752,315	200,807	290,220
111	Huntsville, AL	538,878	509,873	15.9	19,104	209,885	10,294,510	.1835	6,760,035	1,919	1,425,901	2,835	329,273	1,733	786,453	292,592	416,253
112	Canton-New Philadelphia, OH	536,591	534,503	4.1	17,662	208,678	9,477,350	.1749	6,615,439	1,879	872,502	1,736	332,641	1,751	1,030,975	596,349	414,191
113	Evansville, IN	528,454	523,510	3.7	17,492	210,608	9,243,510	.1742	6,811,770	1,934	1,059,432	2,106	256,280	1,350	777,652	360,159	395,388
114	Lansing, MI	526,431	509,246	4.0	20,552	212,291	10,819,060	.1841	6,396,962	1,816	1,454,586	2,892	232,402	1,222	753,680	360,257	396,774
115	Lakeland-Winter Haven, FL	526,208	483,924	19.4	17,926	205,086	9,432,930	.1709	6,270,722	1,781	1,004,624	1,998	225,818	1,189	1,044,350	328,355	342,035
116	Melbourne-Titusville, FL	523,567	476,230	19.4	20,941	216,202	10,963,820	.1797	5,760,123	1,636	986,272	1,961	242,067	1,274	880,605	408,228	391,524
117	Flint, MI	518,966	507,828	1.5	18,335	195,121	9,515,320	.1706	6,209,260	1,763	1,227,490	2,441	200,377	1,054	697,969	451,498	371,273
118	Tallahassee, FL	517,426	502,539	19.9	17,179	204,525	8,888,990	.1589	5,475,969	1,554	923,662	1,836	237,021	1,248	825,531	356,878	353,804
119	York-Hanover, PA	502,894	473,043	13.2	19,844	190,449	9,979,640	.1616	4,799,517	1,362	646,482	1,286	172,030	906	840,243	223,846	355,786
120	Fort Pierce-Vero Beach-Stuart, FL	492,151	432,373	26.7	20,718	204,927	10,196,500	.1729	5,998,264	1,703	824,350	1,640	304,263	1,602	872,650	509,295	328,908
121	Anchorage, AK	491,194	456,392	17.3	20,611	169,566	10,123,860	.1768	6,549,614	1,860	1,362,226	2,710	267,240	1,407	1,034,958	91,189	320,171
122	Lancaster, PA	490,254	470,658	11.3	19,871	183,207	9,741,670	.1767	6,915,084	1,964	618,456	1,230	403,743	2,125	1,058,381	357,146	343,004
123	Montgomery, AL	490,161	484,647	10.0	15,922	185,849	7,804,420	.1474	5,460,450	1,552	1,051,929	2,092	225,054	1,185	675,967	345,879	332,678
124	Charleston, WV	482,696	486,731	1.1	15,992	197,861	7,719,290	.1458	5,418,246	1,539	844,933	1,679	174,684	920	655,577	433,529	348,156
125	Poughkeepsie-Kingston, NY	481,801	457,899	7.8	21,670	172,588	10,440,630	.1638	4,748,809	1,349	512,063	1,019	275,396	1,449	893,733	287,127	317,036
126	Rockford, IL	474,815	456,277	10.7	19,622	179,110	9,316,910	.1581	5,299,833	1,505	823,838	1,639	175,076	921	839,644	329,585	336,426
127	Appleton-Oshkosh, WI	472,380	452,355	13.3	20,235	188,222	9,558,720	.1670	6,109,153	1,734	874,835	1,741	202,420	1,065	741,667	244,086	363,697
128	Youngstown-Warren, OH	467,323	482,671	-2.0	17,475	187,024	8,166,390	.1480	5,340,675	1,516	698,179	1,388	229,652	1,209	704,483	351,238	342,882
129	Beaumont-Port Arthur, TX	461,862	467,106	8.1	16,388	176,951	7,569,190	.1415	5,231,734	1,485	892,016	1,774	219,577	1,155	705,561	306,240	299,258
130	Peoria, IL	458,026	461,289	1.2	19,497	184,177	8,930,050	.1556	5,523,957	1,569	824,858	1,640	148,257	781	809,746	397,362	333,463
131	Pensacola, FL	437,128	412,153	19.7	18,438	170,330	8,059,970	.1392	4,649,972	1,321	829,735	1,650	185,536	977	639,256	315,918	302,050
132	Davenport, IA-Moline, IL	428,993	429,924	2.4	18,885	170,606	8,101,390	.1470	5,600,031	1,591	829,756	1,650	216,571	1,140	670,968	367,628	319,966
133	Burlington, VT	421,831	406,799	10.2	18,568	160,078	7,832,680	.1454	5,738,847	1,630	408,933	813	229,060	1,205	972,645	341,851	311,955
134	Salinas-Monterey, CA	421,269	401,762	13.0	18,324	130,913	7,719,290	.1321	4,297,922	1,220	496,897	988	304,946	1,605	763,460	273,308	273,730
135	Provo-Orem, UT	418,644	376,774	39.9	15,051	121,920	6,301,210	.1208	4,442,435	1,261	895,851	1,781	147,868	778	683,989	85,494	284,554
136	Lubbock, TX	416,750	409,227	4.2	14,783	158,081	6,160,650	.1242	4,984,659	1,417	722,563	1,437	217,752	1,147	750,918	162,150	289,485
137	Duluth, MN	414,992	413,956	3.3	17,948	179,375	7,448,400	.1322	4,614,909	1,310	787,149	1,567	105,793	557	657,169	225,872	338,270
138	Amarillo, TX	412,704	410,323	7.9	16,045	155,431	6,622,030	.1245	4,615,113	1,309	609,272	1,211	168,579	887	478,737	185,887	282,743
139	Biloxi-Gulfport-Pascagoula, MS	407,743	396,754	16.8	17,232	154,982	7,026,180	.1263	4,424,006	1,257	1,121,303	2,230	153,372	809	458,514	205,329	300,118
140	Santa Barbara-Santa Maria, CA	404,582	399,347	8.0	19,919	139,852	8,058,830	.1386	4,839,745	1,374	499,060	992	335,212	1,764	874,460	322,723	270,633
141	Brownsville-Harlingen, TX	400,052	355,309	27.9	8,444	103,273	3,377,920	.0813	2,926,540	831	689,711	1,371	196,699	1,035	504,194	126,956	169,159
142	Hagerstown, MD-Chambersburg, PA-Martinsburg, WV	397,477	366,345	11.8	18,449	152,793	7,333,160	.1262	4,183,896	1,188	615,567	1,225	142,883	752	626,376	233,815	290,912
143	Reading, PA	393,253	373,638	11.0	19,745	147,995	7,764,710	.1320	4,459,882	1,266	520,167	1,034	360,634	1,898	665,140	278,677	275,607
144	Kalamazoo, MI	385,760	377,288	7.1	19,143	154,090	7,384,460	.1306	4,739,492	1,346	1,323,775	2,632	149,922	789	474,318	242,852	289,982
145	New London-Norwich, CT	382,531	368,179	3.0	24,805	148,781	9,488,830	.1457	4,397,998	1,249	553,351	1,100	184,265	970	680,113	306,305	310,573
146	Temple-Killeen, TX	376,847	354,952	21.7	15,817	132,077	5,960,420	.1041	3,167,946	900	469,762	934	94,973	499	459,270	70,896	238,114
147	Fayetteville-Springdale-Rogers, AR	375,486	325,364	46.2	16,951	140,320	6,364,840	.1171	4,278,192	1,215	1,400,444	2,785	119,036	626	355,034	128,449	268,185
148	Green Bay, WI	372,022	355,786	14.6	19,625	149,424	7,300,800	.1277	4,586,120	1,302	1,060,153	2,109	120,673	635	503,524	141,475	285,163
149	Huntington, WV-Ashland, KY	367,760	368,924	1.4	14,414	147,149	5,300,810	.1036	3,827,725	1,089	738,603	1,470	173,942	916	464,383	393,709	263,625
150	Albany-Tifton, GA	364,731	355,474	9.4	13,423	131,272	4,895,760	.0988	3,720,776	1,058	588,757	1,169	139,167	733	570,776	182,198	225,765

Source: Devonshire Associates Ltd. and Scan/US, Inc. 2005.

Business/Manufactures, by State

State	State Abbreviation†	FIPS State Code‡	Bank Deposits, 12/31/03‡‡: Number of Banks	Bank Deposits, 12/31/03‡‡: Total Deposits ($1,000)	Total Wholesale Trade, 1997*: Establishments	Total Wholesale Trade, 1997*: Sales ($1,000)	Manufactures, 1997*: Number of Establishments	Manufactures, 1997*: Establishments With 20 or More Employees	Manufactures, 1997*: Total Employees	Manufactures, 1997*: Value Added by Manufacture: Total ($1,000)	Manufactures, 1997*: Value Added by Manufacture: Ranally Mfg. Units	Automobile Registrations: Automobiles Registered 2004††	Automobile Registrations: Automobiles Registered 2000**
Alabama	AL	01	162	60,300,000	6,315	40,986,328	5,444	2,089	352,618	29,221,522	15,998	3,315,864	3,114,091
Alaska	AK	02	7	5,700,000	784	2,989,820	488	102	10,770	1,159,253	635	433,812	370,973
Arizona	AZ	04	50	56,000,000	6,689	45,899,068	4,917	1,370	193,616	26,898,948	14,726	3,748,432	3,272,230
Arkansas	AR	05	170	37,700,000	3,619	27,515,382	3,316	1,248	230,153	19,346,813	10,592	2,025,125	1,785,861
California	CA	06	318	614,700,000	57,841	548,864,451	49,418	15,266	1,809,667	195,872,810	107,234	23,599,626	20,372,623
Colorado	CO	08	180	61,100,000	7,383	60,310,393	5,480	1,264	173,069	20,673,048	11,318	3,945,196	3,137,147
Connecticut	CT	09	63	69,600,000	5,283	76,167,938	5,844	1,926	252,330	27,295,212	14,943	2,494,437	2,267,536
Delaware	DE	10	34	96,800,000	906	12,585,529	675	232	41,084	5,389,453	2,951	585,608	533,235
District of Columbia	DC	11	5	15,600,000	348	3,918,622	200	35	2,858	170,849	94	227,253	217,821
Florida	FL	12	304	268,200,000	31,214	187,079,940	15,992	3,628	433,149	40,213,354	22,016	11,690,979	10,229,301
Georgia	GA	13	345	124,900,000	13,978	163,782,649	9,083	3,301	533,830	55,550,096	30,412	6,175,644	5,481,753
Hawaii	HI	15	8	21,200,000	1,872	7,147,462	921	159	15,109	1,262,448	691	768,349	684,415
Idaho	ID	16	18	12,600,000	1,980	10,127,777	1,647	419	66,184	6,393,062	3,500	1,180,207	944,739
Illinois	IL	17	769	281,800,000	21,951	275,968,383	17,953	6,572	887,350	95,287,251	52,167	8,218,278	7,260,999
Indiana	IN	18	206	80,300,000	8,896	66,350,132	9,303	3,946	625,692	67,210,944	36,796	4,558,595	4,173,377
Iowa	IA	19	422	52,100,000	5,399	35,453,705	3,749	1,413	235,880	28,673,277	15,698	2,409,872	2,099,301
Kansas	KS	20	380	44,900,000	5,085	42,209,864	3,309	1,151	193,742	17,650,640	9,663	2,155,359	1,915,734
Kentucky	KY	21	243	56,100,000	5,051	37,242,872	4,218	1,712	288,405	38,337,622	20,989	3,019,571	2,705,637
Louisiana	LA	22	170	52,600,000	6,390	46,972,265	3,545	1,170	165,777	29,066,923	15,913	2,844,586	2,559,794
Maine	ME	23	40	16,100,000	1,726	7,305,592	1,812	513	82,288	6,530,588	3,575	1,050,735	880,559
Maryland	MD	24	122	77,900,000	6,283	54,906,650	3,996	1,213	163,992	18,721,618	10,249	3,941,293	3,426,815
Massachusetts	MA	25	209	172,400,000	9,993	112,792,386	9,554	3,313	417,135	44,337,768	24,274	4,257,803	3,760,685
Michigan	MI	26	178	137,100,000	13,936	159,432,288	16,045	5,753	833,429	93,809,468	51,358	7,369,528	6,525,706
Minnesota	MN	27	486	97,400,000	9,348	99,444,542	8,091	2,728	382,530	36,629,931	20,054	4,172,823	3,395,174
Mississippi	MS	28	103	32,900,000	3,173	18,445,224	3,008	1,282	227,800	17,088,506	9,355	2,001,366	1,757,459
Missouri	MO	29	377	91,600,000	9,522	91,411,852	7,497	2,498	371,448	43,186,072	23,643	4,547,989	3,814,641
Montana	MT	30	80	11,300,000	1,574	7,596,802	1,160	179	19,611	1,732,158	948	784,244	688,762
Nebraska	NE	31	270	31,500,000	3,157	38,015,440	1,960	612	106,690	10,822,657	5,925	1,386,698	1,237,634
Nevada	NV	32	37	31,900,000	2,253	12,806,893	1,615	408	37,849	3,298,077	1,806	1,591,636	1,353,743
New Hampshire	NH	33	31	29,700,000	2,033	11,371,112	2,328	757	98,934	11,320,082	6,197	1,065,097	856,901
New Jersey	NJ	34	146	196,300,000	17,812	227,309,002	11,812	3,828	409,788	50,101,691	27,429	5,652,559	4,944,083
New Mexico	NM	35	60	16,700,000	2,182	7,397,572	1,593	293	39,664	13,440,222	7,358	1,360,948	1,236,492
New York	NY	36	206	580,700,000	37,499	319,697,562	23,908	6,689	785,891	76,999,763	42,155	9,761,897	8,615,553
North Carolina	NC	37	104	147,000,000	12,284	98,080,086	11,306	4,621	773,548	78,638,044	43,052	6,488,469	5,674,382
North Dakota	ND	38	104	11,000,000	1,604	8,618,382	704	188	21,956	1,802,403	987	544,730	477,318
Ohio	OH	39	304	211,000,000	17,322	160,415,587	17,974	6,897	984,201	112,491,355	61,585	8,606,795	7,651,217
Oklahoma	OK	40	278	44,300,000	5,191	32,132,263	4,087	1,191	164,060	17,233,699	9,435	2,518,182	2,360,076
Oregon	OR	41	38	37,300,000	5,943	53,679,098	5,768	1,675	213,111	25,077,180	13,729	2,810,031	2,411,395
Pennsylvania	PA	42	270	208,000,000	17,138	159,354,185	17,128	6,357	826,521	86,212,087	47,198	8,202,103	7,364,754
Rhode Island	RI	44	15	17,800,000	1,590	7,602,702	2,535	704	75,599	5,484,173	3,002	778,185	682,914
South Carolina	SC	45	97	44,900,000	5,035	34,179,799	4,450	1,873	346,142	33,657,787	18,427	2,946,040	2,671,612
South Dakota	SD	46	94	15,700,000	1,402	7,874,169	888	292	46,539	3,880,867	2,125	662,201	555,129
Tennessee	TN	47	208	86,700,000	8,234	82,626,370	7,407	2,906	483,823	44,355,170	24,283	4,556,048	3,978,403
Texas	TX	48	698	297,300,000	33,346	323,111,661	21,808	6,788	959,665	129,390,041	70,837	14,286,277	12,791,932
Utah	UT	49	64	85,000,000	3,277	21,271,857	2,860	861	119,140	11,343,518	6,210	1,714,107	1,393,778
Vermont	VT	50	19	8,800,000	941	4,731,383	1,226	340	42,533	4,044,564	2,214	469,160	413,235
Virginia	VA	51	141	129,700,000	7,868	61,046,705	5,986	2,042	370,595	43,563,006	23,849	5,690,714	4,902,369
Washington	WA	53	100	81,500,000	10,039	75,397,750	7,801	2,159	328,511	30,434,838	16,662	4,870,945	4,261,854
West Virginia	WV	54	74	22,300,000	1,956	10,290,356	1,505	517	72,813	9,310,976	5,097	1,313,962	1,139,393
Wisconsin	WI	55	311	95,900,000	8,025	57,192,863	9,936	3,905	562,479	54,947,083	30,082	4,200,034	3,629,972
Wyoming	WY	56	46	7,800,000	800	2,547,065	503	90	8,448	1,031,057	564	447,577	385,272
United States Total			**9,164**	**5,087,900,000**	**453,470**	**4,059,657,778**	**363,753**	**120,475**	**16,888,016**	**1,826,589,974**	**1,000,000**	**203,446,969**	**178,365,779**

† U.S. Postal Service standard abbreviations for state names.
‡ Federal Information Processing Standards (FIPS) codes for states, as published by the National Bureau of Standards, U.S. Department of Commerce.
‡‡ Source: Statistical Abstract of the United States: 2004-2005.
* Source: U.S. Bureau of the Census.
†† Source: Devonshire Associates Ltd. and Scan/US, Inc, 2005.
** Data compiled by Devonshire Associates Ltd. and Scan/US, Inc. 2001.

Retail Sales, by State

State	FIPS State Code†	Retail Sales: 2004‡* Sales ($1,000)	Retail Sales: Ranally Sales Units	Retail Sales: 1997* Sales ($1,000)	Retail Sales: Ranally Sales Units	Retail Sales: 1992** Sales ($1,000)	Retail Sales: Ranally Sales Units	Shopping Goods††: 2004‡* Sales ($1,000)	Shopping Goods††: Ranally Sales Units	Shopping Goods††: 1997* Sales ($1,000)	Shopping Goods††: Ranally Sales Units	General Merchandise Stores 2004‡* Sales ($1,000)	Apparel & Accessories Stores 2004‡* Sales ($1,000)	Health & Drug Stores 2004‡* Sales ($1,000)	Food Stores 2004‡* Sales ($1,000)	Furniture, Home Furnishing & Appliance Stores 2004‡* Sales ($1,000)	Automotive Dealers 2004‡* Sales ($1,000)
Alabama	01	49,659,109	14,104	36,623,327	14,882	27,733,562	14,636	11,728,165	16,928	7,605,392	16,291	9,510,896	2,217,269	2,667,555	6,284,132	1,909,323	12,390,372
Alaska	02	8,625,478	2,451	6,251,372	2,540	4,981,919	2,629	2,149,392	3,102	1,533,403	3,285	1,788,019	361,373	130,041	1,347,251	309,868	1,749,378
Arizona	04	62,317,372	17,696	43,960,933	17,864	29,365,954	15,498	11,533,551	16,647	7,574,645	16,225	9,195,407	2,338,144	3,153,968	8,643,505	3,097,199	16,365,708
Arkansas	05	31,411,949	8,922	21,643,695	8,795	15,925,313	8,404	8,938,784	12,902	4,819,230	10,323	7,926,811	1,011,973	1,346,983	3,121,449	1,150,024	8,158,233
California	06	391,314,575	111,113	263,118,346	106,921	224,593,152	118,524	77,398,164	111,711	51,304,332	109,895	49,374,886	28,023,277	21,811,974	65,552,847	29,148,395	96,703,349
Colorado	08	59,432,099	16,876	40,536,034	16,472	28,532,646	15,058	11,417,507	16,479	7,056,296	15,115	8,937,511	2,479,995	2,201,196	8,336,296	4,027,032	15,142,948
Connecticut	09	51,563,168	14,641	34,938,893	14,198	27,753,739	14,647	7,272,130	10,496	5,655,183	12,114	4,065,735	3,206,395	3,245,949	7,378,023	2,789,636	12,185,842
Delaware	10	12,276,075	3,486	8,236,970	3,347	6,491,936	3,426	2,278,700	3,289	1,569,710	3,362	1,630,847	647,854	697,069	1,795,320	1,019,627	3,147,802
District of Columbia	11	3,540,123	1,005	2,788,831	1,133	3,586,625	1,893	645,744	932	558,663	1,197	143,774	501,970	520,795	938,614	253,694	104,318
Florida	12	219,912,395	62,448	151,191,241	61,438	118,741,770	62,665	43,585,257	62,908	28,992,896	62,104	29,779,347	13,805,910	14,157,189	30,948,673	13,278,405	62,198,379
Georgia	13	108,200,674	30,717	72,212,484	29,344	49,940,017	26,355	21,516,335	31,055	13,464,419	28,841	16,112,097	5,404,238	5,026,149	14,835,054	6,100,017	28,167,382
Hawaii	15	14,229,466	4,040	11,317,752	4,599	11,250,217	5,937	4,477,687	6,463	4,025,448	8,623	2,783,330	1,694,358	1,173,546	2,349,624	510,835	2,513,767
Idaho	16	17,342,549	4,922	11,649,609	4,734	7,726,843	4,078	3,209,555	4,632	1,892,114	4,053	2,744,471	465,084	614,814	2,557,218	853,488	4,527,420
Illinois	17	149,785,179	42,539	108,002,177	43,888	85,765,697	45,262	26,946,092	38,892	20,204,186	43,278	19,542,758	7,403,334	11,972,529	19,947,099	9,438,855	37,272,424
Indiana	18	78,806,901	22,383	57,241,650	23,261	42,373,476	22,362	16,409,612	23,684	10,998,165	23,559	13,563,530	2,846,082	4,764,374	8,038,084	3,481,165	19,896,843
Iowa	19	35,315,827	10,025	26,723,822	10,859	19,959,786	10,534	6,125,115	8,841	4,539,020	9,723	5,012,123	1,112,992	1,707,580	4,662,985	1,760,275	9,381,506
Kansas	20	31,558,250	8,962	22,571,918	9,172	17,566,800	9,271	6,807,554	9,825	4,390,088	9,404	5,494,837	1,312,717	1,568,954	4,371,187	1,843,961	7,922,719
Kentucky	21	43,754,896	12,421	33,332,675	13,545	25,267,776	13,335	9,812,958	14,163	6,735,095	14,427	8,002,399	1,810,560	2,999,020	5,105,732	1,766,153	10,812,666
Louisiana	22	50,236,004	14,266	35,807,894	14,551	27,806,373	14,674	12,078,906	17,434	7,519,239	16,107	9,803,298	2,275,608	3,103,259	6,474,003	2,115,409	12,154,720
Maine	23	18,856,922	5,353	12,737,087	5,176	10,286,757	5,429	2,609,962	3,767	2,093,023	4,483	1,912,403	697,559	812,148	3,627,151	550,130	4,254,966
Maryland	24	62,355,917	17,705	46,428,206	18,866	37,624,742	19,856	11,518,487	16,625	8,597,434	18,416	7,932,159	3,586,329	3,325,328	10,994,151	3,799,567	17,358,346
Massachusetts	25	83,318,628	23,659	58,578,048	23,804	47,663,248	25,154	13,491,928	19,473	10,206,959	21,864	7,440,687	6,051,241	6,542,819	13,661,875	4,845,749	19,527,517
Michigan	26	131,655,124	37,381	93,706,078	38,078	71,523,046	37,745	29,546,211	42,645	19,499,555	41,769	24,038,233	5,507,978	8,587,582	15,029,183	7,011,890	35,881,637
Minnesota	27	73,548,970	20,883	48,097,982	19,545	35,622,218	18,799	13,548,304	19,555	8,264,490	17,703	11,103,652	2,444,651	3,233,862	9,441,980	4,511,391	18,002,341
Mississippi	28	30,449,639	8,646	20,774,508	8,442	14,780,984	7,800	8,246,849	11,903	4,492,439	9,623	7,094,418	1,152,431	1,768,487	3,145,066	1,109,061	7,298,579
Missouri	29	67,777,368	19,246	51,269,881	20,834	37,918,234	20,011	12,793,567	18,465	9,888,877	21,182	10,713,022	2,080,546	3,921,735	8,113,431	2,736,271	17,206,044
Montana	30	11,022,426	3,127	7,779,112	3,161	6,246,712	3,297	2,081,755	3,005	1,390,384	2,978	1,781,479	300,276	373,333	1,606,684	414,106	2,919,984
Nebraska	31	23,147,225	6,567	16,529,333	6,717	11,521,818	6,080	3,993,571	5,764	2,819,227	6,039	3,290,557	703,014	1,239,022	2,777,602	1,368,211	5,261,315
Nevada	32	28,240,763	8,017	18,220,790	7,404	11,546,436	6,093	5,421,022	7,824	3,512,726	7,524	3,855,163	1,565,859	1,312,355	4,246,589	1,398,235	6,614,908
New Hampshire	33	25,111,964	7,132	15,812,027	6,425	11,099,193	5,857	4,588,781	6,623	2,875,100	6,159	3,600,853	987,927	920,553	3,939,668	1,447,467	6,464,054
New Jersey	34	113,098,864	32,114	79,914,892	32,474	63,109,174	33,305	17,233,056	24,873	13,967,808	29,920	9,425,753	7,807,303	7,598,965	20,203,086	8,254,854	28,655,525
New Mexico	35	20,126,775	5,715	14,984,454	6,089	11,279,262	5,952	4,731,683	6,829	2,788,711	5,974	3,935,122	796,560	1,031,154	2,175,450	899,238	4,883,765
New York	36	193,660,204	54,990	139,303,944	56,607	118,885,698	62,740	40,662,216	58,689	29,089,261	62,311	19,962,926	20,699,290	16,761,435	30,771,689	11,933,232	39,393,121
North Carolina	37	107,693,075	30,583	72,356,763	29,403	49,564,327	26,157	20,084,838	28,989	12,198,301	26,129	15,111,629	4,973,209	6,043,252	14,001,045	5,599,268	29,044,845
North Dakota	38	9,512,875	2,700	6,702,134	2,723	4,696,871	2,479	1,540,609	2,224	1,148,405	2,460	1,290,581	250,028	477,987	956,600	437,720	2,379,616
Ohio	39	141,869,295	40,284	102,938,830	41,830	79,030,973	41,708	24,705,849	35,659	19,350,352	41,449	18,429,412	6,276,437	9,854,297	19,867,867	7,461,388	36,165,114
Oklahoma	40	36,779,875	10,439	27,065,555	10,998	21,212,771	11,195	8,847,261	12,769	5,629,926	12,060	7,733,198	1,114,063	2,095,771	4,057,057	1,709,583	9,871,218
Oregon	41	48,170,766	13,677	33,396,849	13,571	24,170,222	12,756	11,169,704	16,122	7,128,228	15,269	9,043,205	2,126,499	1,597,000	6,806,775	2,738,389	11,397,970
Pennsylvania	42	150,200,264	42,651	109,948,462	44,678	87,787,842	46,329	23,385,687	33,753	18,566,576	39,771	15,579,866	7,805,821	10,453,945	23,829,978	6,515,017	36,923,403
Rhode Island	44	11,203,327	3,181	7,505,754	3,050	6,734,282	3,554	1,670,690	2,411	1,209,085	2,590	947,014	723,676	1,212,306	2,021,832	533,522	2,638,503
South Carolina	45	48,201,831	13,686	33,634,264	13,668	24,743,214	13,058	10,719,367	15,472	6,332,483	13,565	7,911,617	2,807,751	2,713,093	6,821,670	2,142,963	11,808,596
South Dakota	46	19,685,031	5,591	11,707,133	4,757	5,108,398	2,696	1,892,613	2,732	1,210,935	2,594	1,631,533	261,080	371,687	862,978	313,766	2,546,982
Tennessee	47	73,585,974	20,895	50,813,221	20,648	37,508,350	19,795	17,012,518	24,555	10,389,135	22,254	13,197,164	3,815,354	4,471,274	8,624,391	3,274,167	19,396,018
Texas	48	277,178,962	78,714	182,516,112	74,167	130,686,364	68,968	56,376,563	81,370	35,237,668	75,481	42,317,101	14,059,461	12,056,216	37,556,608	16,205,388	74,322,004
Utah	49	30,709,350	8,720	19,964,601	8,113	12,373,482	6,530	6,322,210	9,125	3,435,212	7,358	5,112,456	1,209,753	666,059	4,439,600	1,940,865	7,633,886
Vermont	50	8,515,041	2,419	5,898,646	2,397	4,734,763	2,499	945,528	1,365	726,043	1,555	555,792	389,736	497,331	1,392,833	317,113	2,107,494
Virginia	51	89,195,181	25,329	62,569,924	25,426	48,048,593	25,357	18,632,692	26,893	12,311,328	26,372	13,870,118	4,762,573	4,663,419	12,155,350	5,797,573	21,777,232
Washington	53	75,211,170	21,358	52,472,866	21,323	40,909,824	21,590	16,619,898	23,988	9,966,496	21,349	13,095,191	3,524,707	3,198,774	11,031,248	4,130,890	17,463,017
West Virginia	54	18,336,092	5,208	14,057,933	5,713	11,194,130	5,908	3,933,752	5,678	2,773,789	5,942	3,305,329	628,422	1,532,224	2,208,983	567,728	4,615,536
Wisconsin	55	67,422,874	19,144	50,520,463	20,529	38,350,527	20,239	12,920,693	18,649	8,489,600	18,185	11,096,962	1,823,731	3,068,802	8,263,929	3,262,956	15,901,114
Wyoming	56	6,585,140	1,869	4,530,537	1,841	3,554,153	1,876	1,262,927	1,823	815,025	1,746	1,118,329	144,598	138,844	831,556	244,941	1,529,574
United States Total		**3,521,709,000**	**1,000,000**	**2,460,886,012**	**1,000,000**	**1,894,880,209**	**1,000,000**	**692,842,000**	**1,000,000**	**466,842,105**	**1,000,000**	**502,845,000**	**189,997,000**	**205,404,000**	**498,151,000**	**198,326,000**	**882,040,000**

† Federal Information Processing Standards (FIPS) codes for states, as published by the National Bureau of Standards, U.S. Department of Commerce.
‡ Source: Devonshire Associates Ltd. and Scan/US, Inc, 2005.
* Data based on 1997 NAICS classification system; not directly comparable with 1987 SIC system data.
** Data based on 1992 SIC classification system; not directly comparable with NAICS data.
†† Shopping Goods figures are the combination of Apparel and General Merchandise sales.

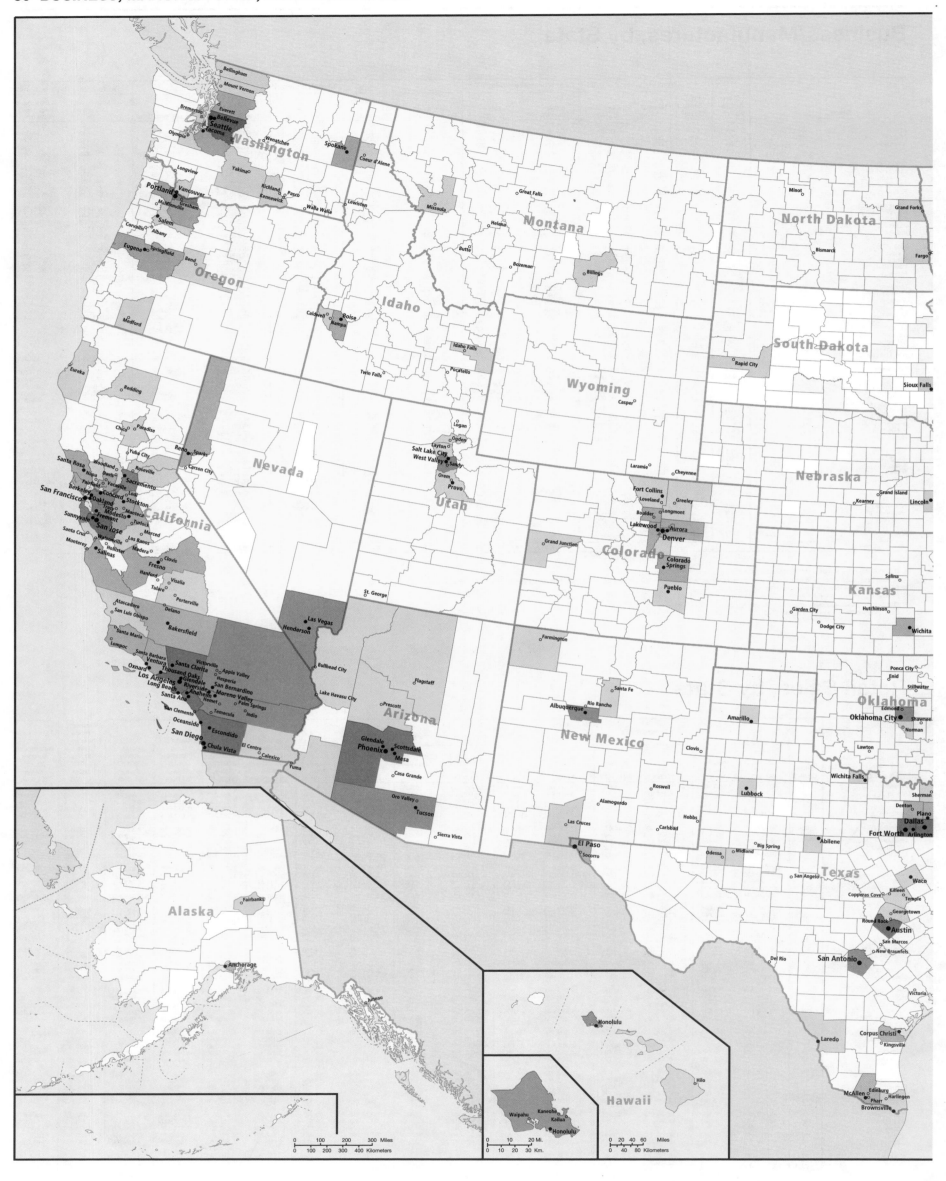

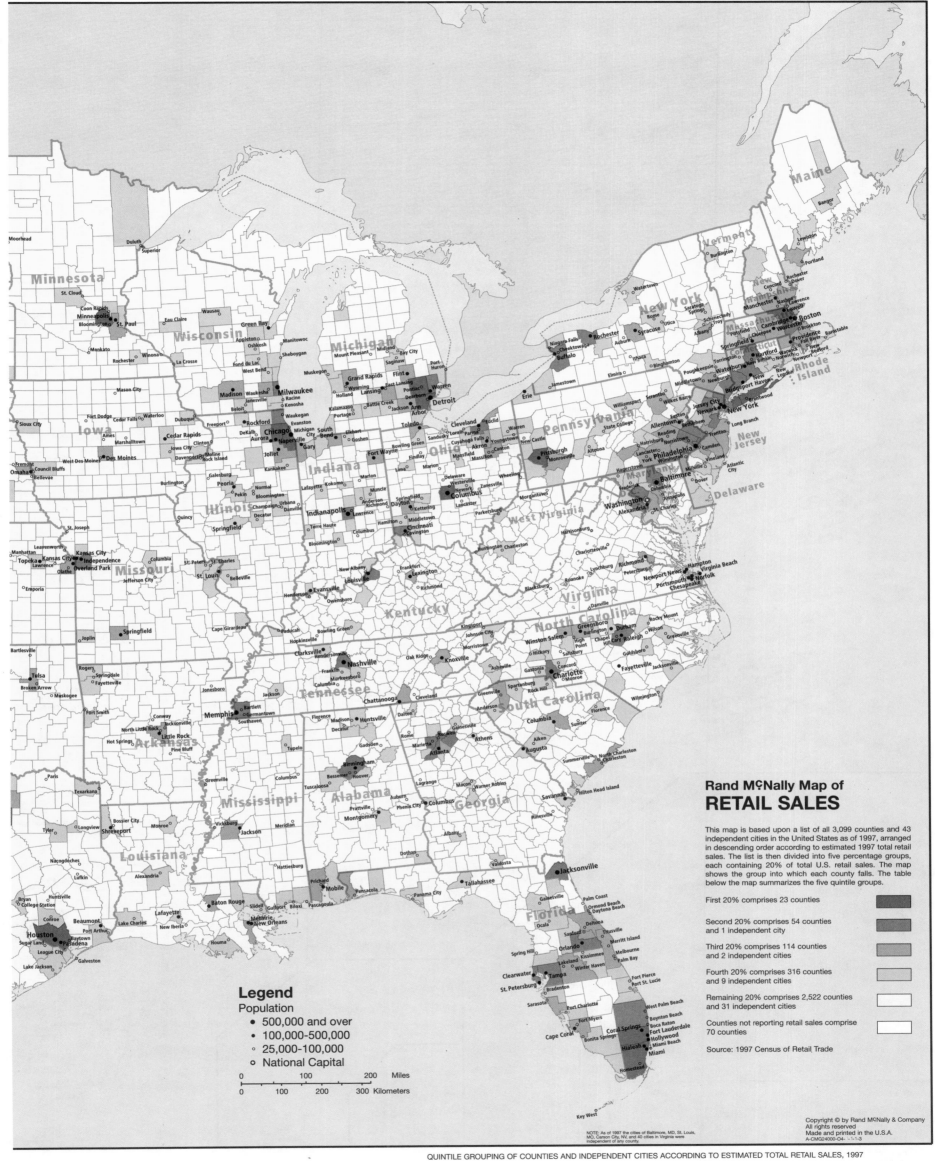

Rand McNally Map of
RETAIL SALES

This map is based upon a list of all 3,099 counties and 43 independent cities in the United States as of 1997, arranged in descending order according to estimated 1997 total retail sales. The list is then divided into five percentage groups, each containing 20% of total U.S. retail sales. The map shows the group into which each county falls. The table below the map summarizes the five quintile groups.

First 20% comprises 23 counties

Second 20% comprises 54 counties and 1 independent city

Third 20% comprises 114 counties and 2 independent cities

Fourth 20% comprises 316 counties and 9 independent cities

Remaining 20% comprises 2,522 counties and 31 independent cities

Counties not reporting retail sales comprise 70 counties

Source: 1997 Census of Retail Trade

NOTE: As of 1997 the cities of Baltimore, MD, St. Louis, MO, Carson City, NV, and 40 cities in Virginia were independent of any county.

Legend
Population
- ● 500,000 and over
- ● 100,000-500,000
- ○ 25,000-100,000
- ⊚ National Capital

```
0        100        200  Miles
0   100   200   300  Kilometers
```

QUINTILE GROUPING OF COUNTIES AND INDEPENDENT CITIES ACCORDING TO ESTIMATED TOTAL RETAIL SALES, 1997

Group	Range in retail sales of counties and independent cities in each group — Largest	Smallest	Total retail sales of each group	Retail sales of each group plus all preceding groups	% of total U.S. value added contained in each group	% of total U.S. retail sales contained in each group plus all preceding groups	Number of counties & indep. cities in each group	% of the total number of counties & indep. cities in each group	Numbers of counties & indep. cities in each group plus all preceding groups	% of the total number of counties & indep. cities in each group plus all preceding groups
1	$69,534,164 to	12,825,281	500,716,144	500,716,144	20.4	20.4	23	0.7	23	0.7
2	12,662,922 to	6,497,655	487,653,772	988,369,916	19.9	40.3	55	1.8	78	2.5
3	6,491,770 to	2,759,547	485,382,377	1,473,752,293	19.8	60.1	116	3.7	194	6.2
4	2,754,452 to	891,209	490,501,062	1,964,253,355	19.9	80.0	325	10.3	519	16.5
5	890,734 to	332	490,866,097	2,455,119,452	20.0	100.0	2,553	81.3	3,072	97.8
*Counties reporting no retail sales							70	2.2	3,142	100.0
			Dollar figures are in thousands							

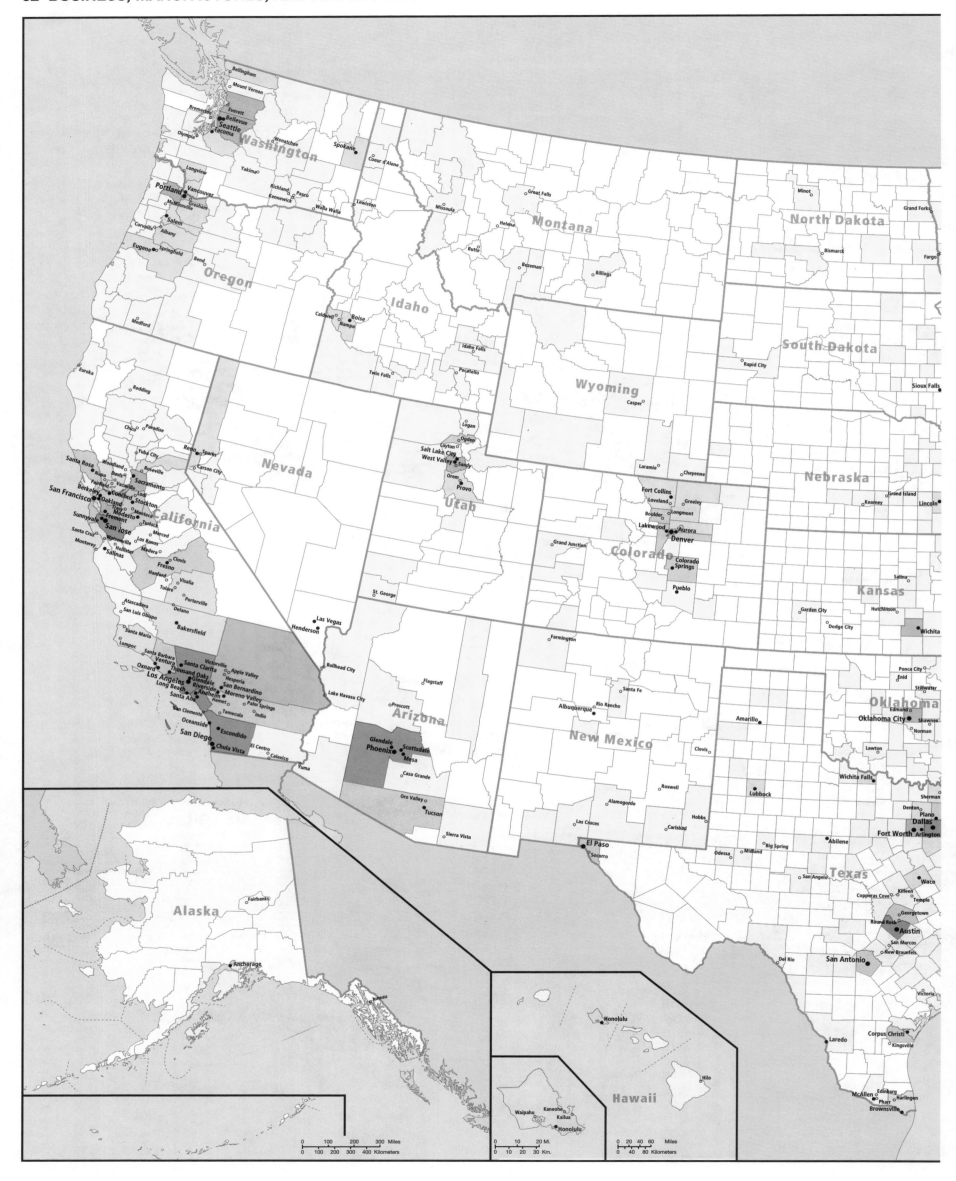

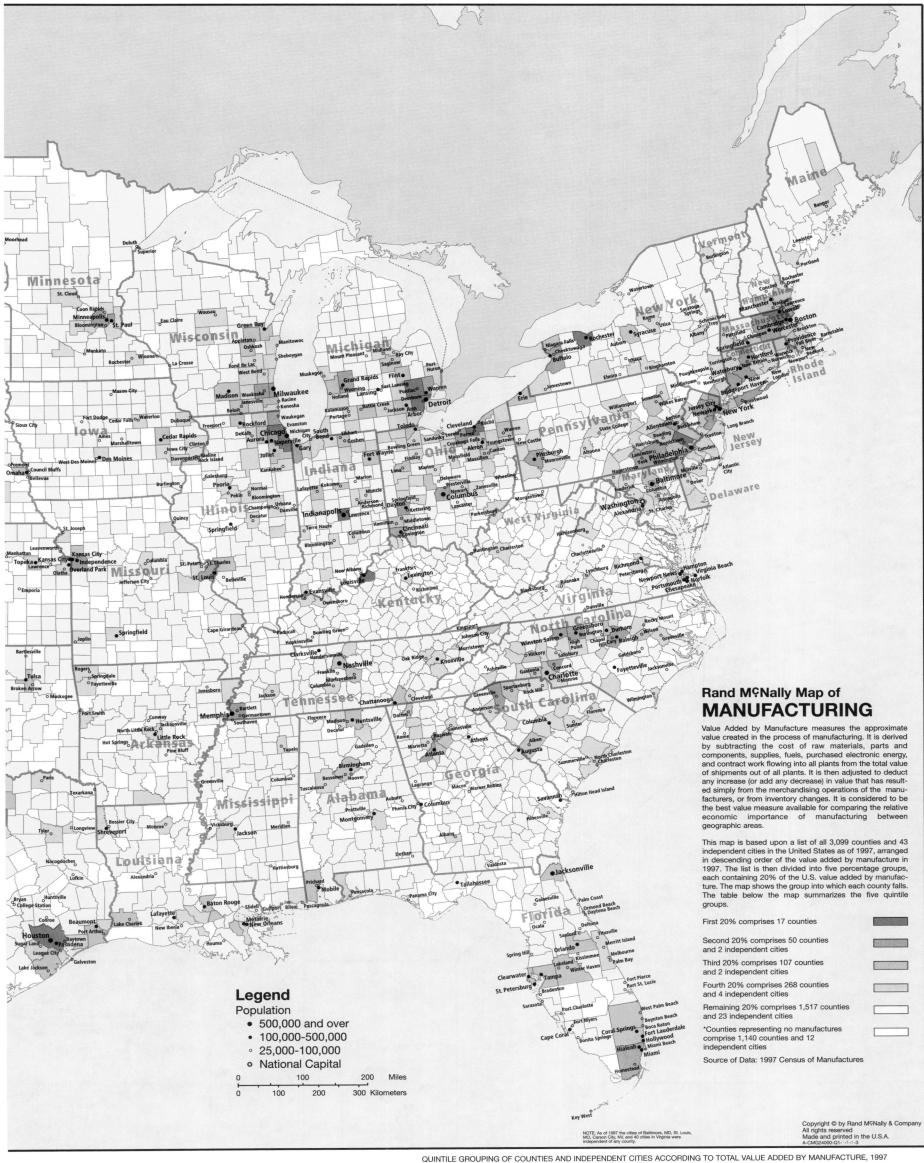

Rand McNally Map of
MANUFACTURING

Value Added by Manufacture measures the approximate value created in the process of manufacturing. It is derived by subtracting the cost of raw materials, parts and components, supplies, fuels, purchased electronic energy, and contract work flowing into all plants from the total value of shipments out of all plants. It is then adjusted to deduct any increase (or add any decrease) in value that has resulted simply from the merchandising operations of the manufacturers, or from inventory changes. It is considered to be the best value measure available for comparing the relative economic importance of manufacturing between geographic areas.

This map is based upon a list of all 3,099 counties and 43 independent cities in the United States as of 1997, arranged in descending order of the value added by manufacture in 1997. The list is then divided into five percentage groups, each containing 20% of the U.S. value added by manufacture. The map shows the group into which each county falls. The table below the map summarizes the five quintile groups.

First 20% comprises 17 counties

Second 20% comprises 50 counties
and 2 independent cities

Third 20% comprises 107 counties
and 2 independent cities

Fourth 20% comprises 268 counties
and 4 independent cities

Remaining 20% comprises 1,517 counties
and 23 independent cities

*Counties representing no manufactures
comprise 1,140 counties and 12
independent cities

Source of Data: 1997 Census of Manufactures

Legend
Population
- 500,000 and over
- 100,000-500,000
- ○ 25,000-100,000
- ⊙ National Capital

0   100   200 Miles

0   100   200   300 Kilometers

NOTE: As of 1997 the cities of Baltimore, MD, St. Louis, MO, Carson City, NV, and 40 cities in Virginia were independent of any county.

QUINTILE GROUPING OF COUNTIES AND INDEPENDENT CITIES ACCORDING TO TOTAL VALUE ADDED BY MANUFACTURE, 1997

Group	Range in value added of counties and independent cities in each group — Largest	Range in value added of counties and independent cities in each group — Smallest	Total value added of each group	Value added of each group plus all preceding groups	% of total U.S. value added contained in each group	% of total U.S. value added contained in each group plus all preceding groups	Number of counties & indep. cities in each group	% of the total number of counties & indep. cities in each group	Numbers of counties & indep. cities in each group plus all preceding groups	% of the total number of counties & indep. cities in each group plus all preceding groups
1	$53,692,011 to	10,999,196	359,926,496	359,926,496	20.5	20.5	17	0.5	17	0.5
2	10,459,875 to	4,578,744	343,781,647	703,708,143	19.6	40.1	52	1.7	69	2.2
3	4,452,897 to	2,319,323	350,580,035	1,054,288,178	19.9	60.0	109	3.5	178	5.7
4	2,317,378 to	765,725	351,313,142	1,405,601,320	20.0	80.0	272	8.7	450	14.3
5	765,645 to	5,372	350,723,151	1,756,324,471	20.0	100.0	1,540	49.0	1,990	63.4
*Counties reporting no manufactures							1,152	36.6	3,142	100.0

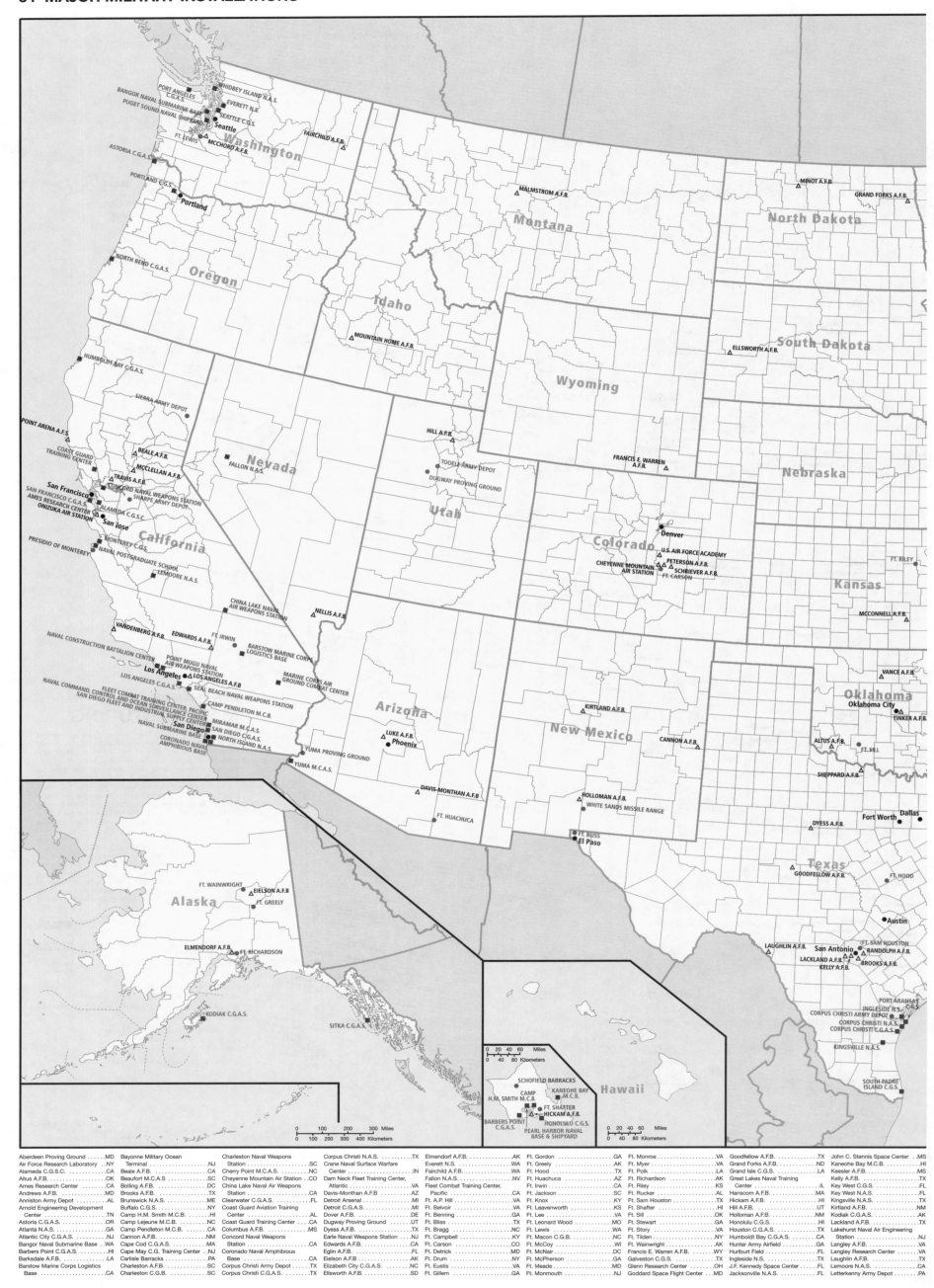

Aberdeen Proving Ground ......MD	Bayonne Military Ocean Terminal ......NJ	Charleston Naval Weapons Station ......SC
Air Force Research Laboratory ..NY	Beale A.F.B. ......CA	Cherry Point M.C.A.S. ......NC
Alameda C.G.S.C. ......CA	Beaufort M.C.A.S ......SC	Cheyenne Mountain Air Station ..CO
Altus A.F.B. ......OK	Bolling A.F.B. ......DC	China Lake Naval Air Weapons Station ......CA
Ames Research Center ......CA	Brooks A.F.B. ......TX	Clearwater C.G.A.S. ......FL
Andrews A.F.B. ......MD	Brunswick N.A.S. ......ME	Coast Guard Aviation Training Center ......AL
Anniston Army Depot ......AL	Buffalo C.G.S. ......NY	Coast Guard Training Center ...CA
Arnold Engineering Development Center ......TN	Cape Cod C.G.A.S. ......MA	Columbus A.F.B. ......MS
Astoria C.G.A.S. ......OR	Cape May C.G. Training Center ...NJ	Concord Naval Weapons Station ......CA
Atlanta N.A.S. ......GA	Carlisle Barracks ......PA	Corpus Christi Army Depot ...TX
Atlantic City C.G.A.S. ......NJ	Charleston A.F.B. ......SC	Corpus Christi C.G.A.S. ......TX
Bangor Naval Submarine Base .WA	Charleston C.G.B. ......SC	
Barksdale A.F.B. ......LA		
Barstow Marine Corps Logistics Base ......CA		

Corpus Christi N.A.S. ......TX	Elmendorf A.F.B. ......AK	Ft. Gordon ......GA
Crane Naval Surface Warfare Center ......IN	Everett N.S. ......WA	Ft. Greely ......AK
Dam Neck Fleet Training Center, Atlantic ......VA	Fairchild A.F.B. ......WA	Ft. Hood ......TX
Davis-Monthan A.F.B ......AZ	Fallon N.A.S. ......NV	Ft. Huachuca ......AZ
Detroit Arsenal ......MI	Fleet Combat Training Center, Pacific ......CA	Ft. Irwin ......CA
Detroit C.G.A.S. ......MI	Ft. Benning ......GA	Ft. Jackson ......SC
Dover A.F.B. ......DE	Ft. Bliss ......TX	Ft. Knox ......KY
Dugway Proving Ground ......UT	Ft. Bragg ......NC	Ft. Leavenworth ......KS
Dyess A.F.B. ......TX	Ft. Campbell ......KY	Ft. Lee ......VA
Edwards A.F.B. ......CA	Ft. Carson ......CO	Ft. Leonard Wood ......MO
Eglin A.F.B. ......FL	Ft. Detrick ......MD	Ft. Lewis ......WA
Eielson A.F.B. ......AK	Ft. Drum ......NY	Ft. McCoy ......WI
Elizabeth City C.G.A.S. ......NC	Ft. Eustis ......VA	Ft. McNair ......DC
Ellsworth A.F.B. ......SD	Ft. Gillem ......GA	Ft. McPherson ......GA
		Ft. Meade ......MD
		Ft. Monmouth ......NJ

Ft. Monroe ......VA	Goodfellow A.F.B. ......TX	John C. Stennis Space Center ..MS
Ft. Myer ......VA	Grand Forks A.F.B. ......ND	Kaneohe Bay M.C.B. ......HI
Ft. Polk ......LA	Grand Isle C.G.S. ......LA	Keesler A.F.B. ......MS
Ft. Richardson ......AK	Great Lakes Naval Training Center IL	Kelly A.F.B. ......TX
Ft. Riley ......KS	Hanscom A.F.B. ......MA	Key West C.G.S. ......FL
Ft. Rucker ......AL	Hickam A.F.B. ......HI	Key West N.A.S. ......FL
Ft. Sam Houston ......TX	Hill A.F.B. ......UT	Kingsville N.A.S. ......TX
Ft. Shafter ......HI	Holloman A.F.B. ......NM	Kirtland A.F.B. ......NM
Ft. Sill ......OK	Houston C.G.S. ......TX	Kodiak C.G.A.S. ......AK
Ft. Stewart ......GA	Hunter Army Airfield ......GA	Lackland A.F.B. ......TX
Ft. Story ......VA	Hurlburt Field ......FL	Lakehurst Naval Air Engineering Station ......NJ
Ft. Tilden ......NY	Ingleside N.S. ......TX	Langley A.F.B. ......VA
Ft. Wainwright ......AK	J.F. Kennedy Space Center .FL	Langley Research Center ......VA
Francis E. Warren A.F.B. ......WY	Jacksonville N.A.S. ......FL	Laughlin A.F.B. ......TX
Glenn Research Center ......OH		Lemoore N.A.S. ......CA
Goddard Space Flight Center .MD		Letterkenny Army Depot ......PA

This map, in a state/county outline format, shows major military installations in the U.S. All branches of the U.S. military are included: Army, Navy, Air Force, Marine Corps, Coast Guard, and the National Aeronautics and Space Administration (NASA). The legend in the lower right portion of the map indicates the symbol used for each type of military installation.

The table below the map lists the official name of each installation and the state in which it is located.

Rand McNally Map of MAJOR MILITARY INSTALLATIONS

△ **Air Force**
  A.F.B. *Air Force Base*
  A.F.S. *Air Force Station*
● **Army**
  Ft. *Fort*
■ **Navy, Marine Corps, Coast Guard**
  N.A.S. *Naval Air Station*
  N.S. *Naval Station*
  N.T.C. *Naval Training Center*
  M.C.A.S. *Marine Corps Air Station*
  M.C.B. *Marine Corps Base*
  C.G.A.S. *Coast Guard Air Station*
  C.G.B. *Coast Guard Base*
  C.G.S. *Coast Guard Station*
  C.G.S.C. *Coast Guard Support Center*
◇ **National Aeronautics and Space Administration (NASA)**

| 0 | | 100 | | 200 | Miles |
| 0 | 100 | 200 | 300 | Kilometers |

Installation	State		Installation	State		Installation	State		Installation	State
Little Creek Naval Amphibious Base	VA		Mayport N.S.	FL		National Naval Medical Center	MD		Naval Submarine Base	CA
Little Rock A.F.B.	AR		McChord A.F.B.	WA		Naval Air Warfare Center	MD		Naval Submarine Base	GA
Los Angeles A.F.B.	CA		McClellan A.F.B.	CA		Naval Command, Control and Ocean Surveillance Center	CA		Naval Surface Warfare Center	VA
Los Angeles C.G.A.S.	CA		McConnell A.F.B.	KS		Naval Command, Control and Ocean Surveillance Center	SC		Naval Undersea Warfare Center	FL
Luke A.F.B.	AZ		McGuire A.F.B.	NJ		Naval Construction Battalion Center	CA		Naval Undersea Warfare Center	RI
Lyndon B. Johnson Space Center	TX		Memphis Naval Support Activity	TN		Naval Construction Battalion Center	MS		Naval Computer and Telecommunications Center	ME
MacDill A.F.B.	FL		Meridian N.A.S.	MS		Naval Education and Training Center	RI		New London Submarine Base	CT
Malmstrom A.F.B.	MT		Milwaukee C.G.S.	WI		Naval Postgraduate School	CA		New Orleans C.G.S.	LA
Marine Corps Air Ground Combat Center	CA		Minot A.F.B.	ND		Naval Research Laboratory	DC		New River M.C.A.S.	NC
Marine Corps Logistics Base	GA		Miramar M.C.A.S.	CA					Norfolk Fleet and Industrial Supply Center	VA
Marshall Space Flight Center	AL		Mobile C.G.B.	AL					Norfolk Naval Shipyard	VA
Maxwell A.F.B.	AL		Monterey C.G.S.	CA					North Bend C.G.A.S.	OR
Mayport C.G.B.	FL		Moody A.F.B.	GA					North Island N.A.S.	CA
			Mountain Home A.F.B.	ID						

Installation	State		Installation	State		Installation	State		Installation	State		Installation	State
Oceana N.A.S.	VA		Port Angeles C.G.A.S.	WA		San Francisco C.G.A.S.	CA		South Padre Island C.G.S.	TX		Vance A.F.B.	OK
Offutt A.F.B.	NE		Port Aransas C.G.S.	TX		Sault Ste. Marie C.G.S.	MI		South Portland C.G.S.	ME		Vandenberg A.F.B.	CA
Onizuka Air Station	CA		Portland C.G.S.	OR		Savannah C.G.A.S.	GA		Southwest Harbor C.G.S.	ME		Walter Reed Army Medical Center	DC
Opa Locka C.G.A.S.	FL		Portsmouth Naval Shipyard	NH		Schofield Barracks	HI		St. Petersburg C.G.S.	FL		Watervliet Arsenal	NY
Parris Island Marine Corps Recruiting Depot	SC		Presidio of Monterey	CA		Schriever A.F.B.	CO		Sunny Point Military Ocean Terminal	NC		Whidbey Island N.A.S.	WA
Patrick A.F.B.	FL		Puget Sound Naval Shipyard	WA		Scott A.F.B.	IL		Tinker A.F.B.	OK		White Sands Missile Range	NM
Pearl Harbor Naval Base & Shipyard	HI		Quantico M.C.B.	VA		Seal Beach Naval Weapons Station	CA		Tobyhanna Army Depot	PA		Whiteman A.F.B.	MO
Pensacola N.A.S.	FL		Randolph A.F.B.	TX		Seattle C.G.S.	WA		Tooele Army Depot	UT		Whiting Field N.A.S.	FL
Peterson A.F.B.	CO		Red River Army Depot	TX		Seneca Army Depot	NY		Traverse City C.G.A.S.	MI		Woods Hole C.G.S.	MA
Point Arena A.F.S.	CA		Redstone Arsenal	AL		Seymour Johnson A.F.B.	NC		Travis A.F.B.	CA		Wright-Patterson A.F.B.	OH
Point Mugu Naval Air Weapons Station	CA		Robins A.F.B.	GA		Sharpe Army Depot	CA		Tyndall A.F.B.	FL		Yorktown Naval Weapons Station	VA
Pope A.F.B.	NC		Rock Island Arsenal	IL		Shaw A.F.B	SC		U.S. Air Force Academy	CO		Yuma M.C.A.S.	AZ
			San Diego C.G.A.S.	CA		Sheppard A.F.B.	TX		U.S. Coast Guard Academy	CT		Yuma Proving Ground	AZ
			San Diego Fleet and Industrial Supply Center	CA		Sierra Army Depot	CA		U.S. Military Academy	NY			
						Sitka C.G.A.S.	AK		U.S. Naval Academy	MD			

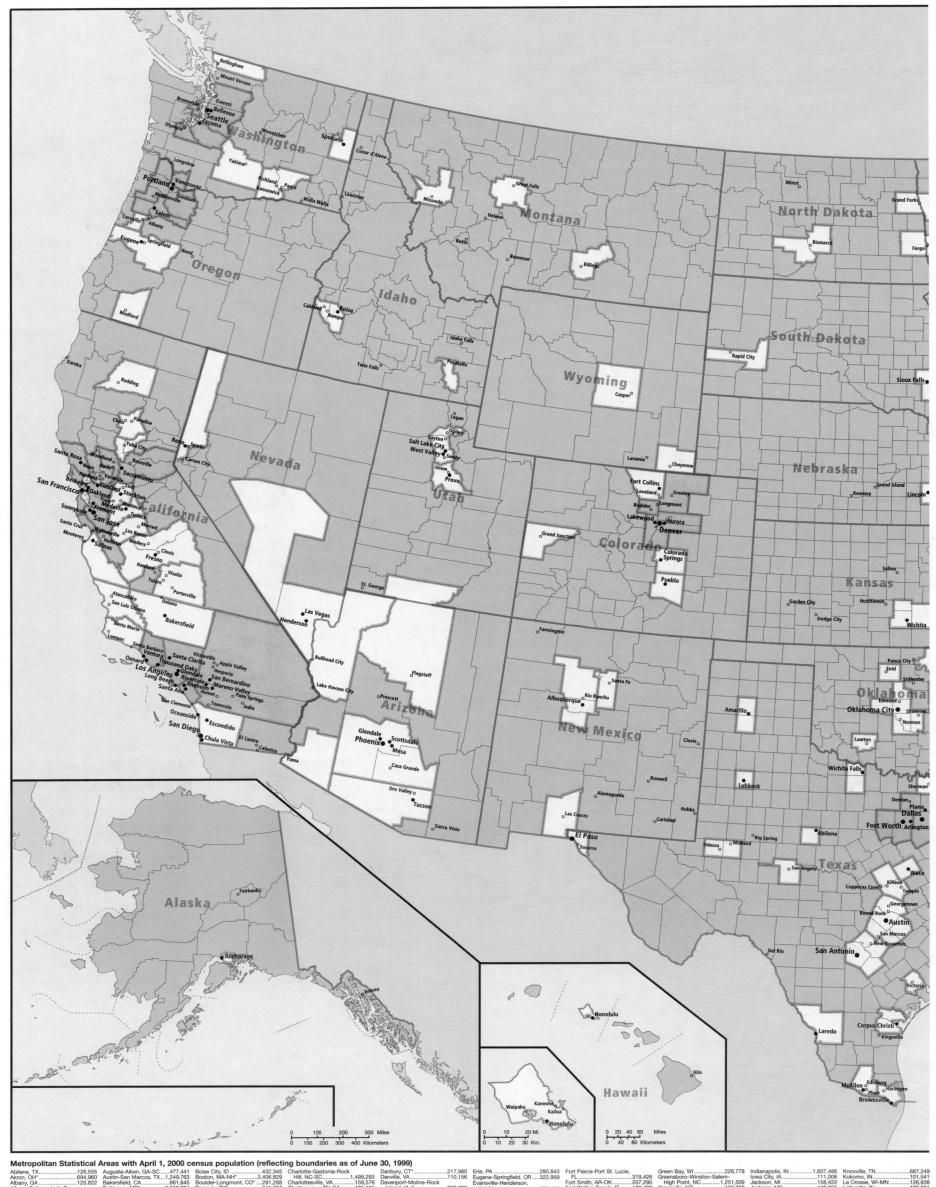

Metropolitan Statistical Areas with April 1, 2000 census population (reflecting boundaries as of June 30, 1999)

Abilene, TX..........126,555	Augusta-Aiken, GA-SC....477,441	Charlotte-Gastonia-Rock	Danbury, CT.........217,980	Erie, PA.........280,843	Fort Pierce-Port St. Lucie,
Akron, OH*.........694,960	Austin-San Marcos, TX...1,249,763	Hill, NC-SC........1,499,293	Danville, VA.........110,156	Eugene-Springfield, OR....322,959	FL.........319,426
Albany, GA.........120,822	Baltimore, MD*.........2,552,994	Charlottesville, VA.........159,576	Davenport-Moline-Rock	Evansville-Henderson,	Fort Smith, AR-OK.........207,290
Albany-Schenectady-Troy,	Bakersfield, CA.........661,645	Chattanooga, TN-GA.........465,161	Island, IA-IL.........359,062	IN-KY.........296,195	Fort Walton Beach, FL....170,498
NY.........875,583	Boulder-Longmont, CO*....291,288	Cheyenne, WY.........81,607	Dayton-Springfield, OH....950,558		Fort Wayne, IN.........502,141
Albuquerque, NM.........712,738	Barnstable-Yarmouth,	Chico-Paradise, CA.........203,171	Daytona Beach, FL.........493,175	Fargo-Moorhead,	Fort Worth-Arlington,
Alexandria, LA.........126,337	MA.........162,582	Chicago, IL*.........8,272,768	Decatur, AL.........145,867	ND-MN.........174,367	TX*.........1,702,625
Allentown-Bethlehem-	Baton Rouge, LA.........602,894	Brockton, MA*.........255,459	Decatur, IL.........114,706	Fayetteville, NC.........302,963	Fresno, CA.........922,516
Easton, PA.........637,958	Beaumont-Port Arthur,	Cincinnati, OH-KY-IN*...1,646,395	Denver, CO*.........2,109,282	Fayetteville-Springdale-	Gadsden, AL.........103,459
Altoona, PA.........129,144	TX.........385,090	Clarksville-Hopkinsville,	Des Moines, IA.........456,022	Rogers, AR.........311,121	Gainesville, FL.........217,955
Amarillo, TX.........217,858	Bellingham, WA.........166,814	TN-KY.........207,033	Detroit, MI*.........4,441,551	Fitchburg-Leominster,	Galveston-Texas City,
Anchorage, AK.........260,283	Benton Harbor, MI.........162,453	Cleveland-Lorain-Elyria,	Dothan, AL.........137,916	MA*.........142,284	TX*.........250,158
Ann Arbor, MI*.........578,736	Bergen-Passaic, NJ*.....1,373,167	OH*.........2,250,871	Dover, DE.........126,697	Flagstaff, AZ-UT.........122,366	Grand Forks, ND-MN.........97,478
Anniston, AL.........112,249	Billings, MT.........129,352	Colorado Springs, CO....516,929	Dubuque, IA.........89,143	Flint, MI*.........436,141	Grand Junction, CO.........116,255
Appleton-Oshkosh-Neenah,	Biloxi-Gulfport-Pascagoula,	Columbia, MO.........135,454	Duluth-Superior, MN-WI...243,815	Florence, AL.........142,950	Grand Rapids-Muskegon-
WI.........358,365	MS.........363,988	Columbia, SC.........536,691	Dutchess County, NY*.....280,150	Florence, SC.........125,761	Holland, MI.........1,088,514
Asheville, NC.........225,965	Binghamton, NY.........252,320	Columbus, GA-AL.........274,624	Eau Claire, WI.........148,337	Fort Collins-Loveland,	Great Falls, MT.........80,357
Athens, GA.........153,444	Birmingham, AL.........921,106	Columbus, OH*.........1,540,157	El Paso, TX.........679,622	CO.........251,494	Greeley, CO*.........180,936
Atlanta, GA.........4,112,198	Bismarck, ND.........94,719	Champaign-Urbana, IL....179,669	Elkhart-Goshen, IN.........182,791	Fort Lauderdale, FL*...1,623,018	
Atlantic-Cape May, NJ*....354,878	Bloomington, IN.........120,563	Charleston-North	Elmira, NY.........91,070	Fort Myers-Cape Coral,	
Auburn-Opelika, AL.........115,092	Bloomington-Normal, IL....150,433	Charleston, SC.........549,033	Enid, OK.........57,813	FL.........440,888	

Green Bay, WI.........226,778	Indianapolis, IN.........1,607,486	Knoxville, TN.........687,249	
Greensboro-Winston-Salem-	Iowa City, IA.........111,006	Kokomo, IN.........101,541	
High Point, NC.........1,251,509	Jackson, MI.........158,422	La Crosse, WI-MN.........126,838	
Greenville, NC.........133,798	Jackson, MS.........440,801	Lafayette, IN.........182,821	
Greenville-Spartanburg-	Jackson, TN.........107,377	Lafayette, LA.........385,647	
Anderson, SC.........962,441	Jacksonville, FL.........1,100,491	Lake Charles, LA.........183,577	
Hagerstown, MD*.........131,923	Jacksonville, NC.........150,355	Lakeland-Winter Haven,	
Hamilton-Middletown,	Jamestown, NY.........139,750	FL.........483,924	
OH*.........332,807	Janesville-Beloit, WI.........152,307	Lancaster, PA.........470,658	
Harrisburg-Lebanon-	Jersey City, NJ*.........608,975	Lansing-East Lansing,	
Carlisle, PA.........629,401	Johnson City-Kingsport-	MI.........447,728	
Hartford, CT.........1,183,110	Bristol, TN-VA.........480,091	Laredo, TX.........193,117	
Hattiesburg, MS.........111,674	Johnstown, PA.........232,621	Las Cruces, NM.........174,682	
Hickory-Morganton-	Jonesboro, AR.........82,148	Las Vegas, NV-AZ.........1,563,282	
Lenoir, NC.........341,851	Joplin, MO.........157,322	Lawrence, KS.........99,962	
Honolulu, HI.........876,156	Kalamazoo-Battle Creek,	Lawrence, MA-NH*.........396,230	
Houma, LA.........194,477	MI.........452,851	Lawton, OK.........114,996	
Houston, TX*.........4,177,646	Kankakee, IL*.........103,833	Lewiston-Auburn, ME.........90,830	
Huntington-Ashland,	Kansas City, MO-KS.....1,776,062	Lexington, KY.........479,198	
WV-KY-OH.........315,538	Kenosha, WI*.........149,577	Lima, OH.........155,084	
Huntsville, AL.........342,376	Killeen-Temple, TX.........312,952	Lincoln, NE.........250,291	

* Primary Metropolitan Statistical Area

This map shows the official **Metropolitan Statistical Areas** (MSAs) as defined and published by the Office of Management and Budget (OMB) on December 31, 1992, and as revised through June 30, 1999. The general "metropolitan area" concept is that of a geographic area consisting of a large population nucleus together with adjacent communities and areas having a high degree of economic and social integration with that nucleus. The major purpose of defining these areas is to enable all Federal statistical agencies to use common definitions when studying metropolitan characteristics. The Federal government makes available various types of data for each of these MSAs; they are also used by many state and local agencies.

OMB follows specific rules in determining MSA status. An area qualifies for recognition as a Metropolitan Statistical Area in one of two ways: the area has **(1)** a city of at least 50,000 population, or **(2)** an urbanized area of at least 50,000 with a total metropolian population of at least 100,000. (Urbanized areas are defined by the Census Bureau and include the continuously built-up territory in and around each large city.) MSAs are defined in terms of entire counties, except in the six New England states where they are defined in terms of cities and towns (townships). In addition to including the county containing the main city, an MSA may also include additional counties having strong economic and social ties to the central county. If a metropolitan area has more than one million population and meets certain other requirements, it is designated a **Consolidated Metropolitan Statistical Area** (CMSA) and consists of several component areas which are termed **Primary Metropolitan Statistical Areas** (PMSAs). Federal statistics are issued both for the CMSAs and their constituent PMSAs.

New England County Metropolitan Areas (NECMAs) have also been defined in order to provide a uniform set of county-based metropolitan areas, as a convenience for users whose data are not available on a subcounty basis. Generally, each NECMA includes those counties that have more than half of their populations included in the corresponding MSA or CMSA; however, some NECMAs include more than one MSA located in the same county. Names of NECMAs are based on those of the associated MSAs and PMSAs. NECMAs are not shown on this map.

All metropolitan area boundaries are outlined on this map in red. MSAs are untinted while CMSAs and their component PMSAs are identified by the presence of a red tint. The alphabetical list below the map includes all MSAs and PMSAs with their 2000 census population. The table at the right margin of the map lists each CMSA and its component PMSAs, along with their 2000 census populations.

Metropolitan Statistical Areas as defined by OMB differ from **Ranally Metro Areas** in that MSA boundaries, except for the six New England states, are based solely upon county boundaries. Although RMAs offer the most precise look at areas of concentrated population, the use of MSAs is sometimes more convenient for the compilation of detailed statistics or for making general comparisons. Statistical information on MSAs, PMSAs and CMSAs is presented in the Population, Income and Sales Data tables for Metropolitan Statistical Areas found on pages 40-44.

Rand McNally Map of
METROPOLITAN STATISTICAL AREAS
Legend
Population
500,000 and over
100,000-500,000
25,000-100,000
National Capital
MSA, PMSA boundary
CMSA area
0 100 200 Miles
0 100 200 300 Kilometers
NOTE: As of 2000 the cities of Baltimore, MD, St. Louis, MO, Carson City, NV, and 40 cities in Virginia were independent of any county.

Consolidated Metropolitan Statistical Areas (CMSAs) and their component Primary Metropolitan Statistical Areas (PMSAs), with 2000 census population

Boston-Worcester-Lawrence, MA-NH-ME-CT **CMSA**	5,819,100
Boston, MA-NH **PMSA**	3,406,829
Brockton, MA **PMSA**	255,459
Fitchburg-Leominster, MA **PMSA**	142,284
Lawrence, MA-NH **PMSA**	396,230
Lowell, MA-NH **PMSA**	301,686
Manchester, NH **PMSA**	198,378
Nashua, NH **PMSA**	190,949
New Bedford, MA **PMSA**	175,198
Portsmouth-Rochester, NH-ME **PMSA**	240,698
Worcester, MA-CT **PMSA**	511,389
Chicago-Gary-Kenosha, IL-IN-WI **CMSA**	9,157,540
Chicago, IL **PMSA**	8,272,768
Gary, IN **PMSA**	631,362
Kankakee, IL **PMSA**	103,833
Kenosha, WI **PMSA**	149,577
Cincinnati-Hamilton, OH-KY-IN **CMSA**	1,979,202
Cincinnati, OH-KY-IN **PMSA**	1,646,395
Hamilton-Middletown, OH **PMSA**	332,807
Cleveland-Akron, OH **CMSA**	2,945,831
Akron, OH **PMSA**	694,960
Cleveland-Lorain-Elyria, OH **PMSA**	2,250,871
Dallas-Fort Worth, TX **CMSA**	5,221,801
Dallas, TX **PMSA**	3,519,176
Fort Worth-Arlington, TX **PMSA**	1,702,625
Denver-Boulder-Greeley, CO **CMSA**	2,581,506
Boulder-Longmont, CO **PMSA**	291,288
Denver, CO **PMSA**	2,109,282
Greeley, CO **PMSA**	180,936
Detroit-Ann Arbor-Flint, MI **CMSA**	5,456,428
Ann Arbor, MI **PMSA**	578,736
Detroit, MI **PMSA**	4,441,551
Flint, MI **PMSA**	436,141
Houston-Galveston-Brazoria, TX **CMSA**	4,669,571
Brazoria, TX **PMSA**	241,767
Galveston-Texas City, TX **PMSA**	250,158
Houston, TX **PMSA**	4,177,646
Los Angeles-Riverside-Orange County, CA **CMSA**	16,373,645
Los Angeles-Long Beach, CA **PMSA**	9,519,338
Orange County, CA **PMSA**	2,846,289
Riverside-San Bernardino, CA **PMSA**	3,254,821
Ventura, CA **PMSA**	753,197
Miami-Fort Lauderdale, FL **CMSA**	3,876,380
Fort Lauderdale, FL **PMSA**	1,623,018
Miami, FL **PMSA**	2,253,362
Milwaukee-Racine, WI **CMSA**	1,689,572
Milwaukee-Waukesha, WI **PMSA**	1,500,741
Racine, WI **PMSA**	188,831
New York-Northern New Jersey-Long Island, NY-NJ-CT-PA **CMSA**	21,199,865
Bergen-Passaic, NJ **PMSA**	1,373,167
Bridgeport, CT **PMSA**	459,479
Danbury, CT **PMSA**	217,980
Dutchess County, NY **PMSA**	280,150
Jersey City, NJ **PMSA**	608,975
Middlesex-Somerset-Hunterdon, NJ **PMSA**	1,169,641
Monmouth-Ocean, NJ **PMSA**	1,126,217
Nassau-Suffolk, NY **PMSA**	2,753,913
New Haven-Meriden, CT **PMSA**	542,149
New York, NY **PMSA**	9,314,235
Newark, NJ **PMSA**	2,032,989
Newburgh, NY-PA **PMSA**	387,669
Stamford-Norwalk, CT **PMSA**	353,556
Trenton, NJ **PMSA**	350,761
Waterbury, CT **PMSA**	228,984
Philadelphia-Wilmington-Atlantic City, PA-NJ-DE-MD **CMSA**	6,188,463
Atlantic-Cape May, NJ **PMSA**	354,878
Philadelphia, PA-NJ **PMSA**	5,100,931
Vineland-Millville-Bridgeton, NJ **PMSA**	146,438
Wilmington-Newark, DE-MD **PMSA**	586,216
Portland-Salem, OR-WA **CMSA**	2,265,223
Portland-Vancouver, OR-WA **PMSA**	1,918,009
Salem, OR **PMSA**	347,214
Sacramento-Yolo, CA **CMSA**	1,796,857
Sacramento, CA **PMSA**	1,628,197
Yolo, CA **PMSA**	168,660
San Francisco-Oakland-San Jose, CA **CMSA**	7,039,362
Oakland, CA **PMSA**	2,392,557
San Francisco, CA **PMSA**	1,731,183
San Jose, CA **PMSA**	1,682,585
Santa Cruz-Watsonville, CA **PMSA**	255,602
Santa Rosa, CA **PMSA**	458,614
Vallejo-Fairfield-Napa, CA **PMSA**	518,821
Seattle-Tacoma-Bremerton, WA **CMSA**	3,554,760
Bremerton, WA **PMSA**	231,969
Olympia, WA **PMSA**	207,355
Seattle-Bellevue-Everett, WA **PMSA**	2,414,616
Tacoma, WA **PMSA**	700,820
Washington-Baltimore, DC-MD-VA-WV **CMSA**	7,608,070
Baltimore, MD **PMSA**	2,552,994
Hagerstown, MD **PMSA**	131,923
Washington, DC-MD-VA-WV **PMSA**	4,923,153

Little Rock-North Little Rock, AR 583,845
Longview-Marshall, TX 208,780
Los Angeles-Long Beach, CA* 9,519,338
Louisville, KY-IN 1,025,598
Lowell, MA-NH* 301,686
Lubbock, TX 242,628
Lynchburg, VA 214,911
Macon, GA 322,549
Madison, WI 426,526
Manchester, NH* 198,378
Mansfield, OH 175,818
McAllen-Edinburg-Mission, TX 569,463
Medford-Ashland, OR 181,269
Melbourne-Titusville-Palm Bay, FL 476,230
Memphis, TN-AR-MS 1,135,614
Merced, CA 210,554
Miami, FL* 2,253,362
Middlesex-Somerset-Hunterdon, NJ* 1,169,641
Milwaukee-Waukesha, WI* 1,500,741
Minneapolis-St. Paul, MN-WI 2,968,806
Missoula, MT 95,802
Mobile, AL 540,258
Modesto, CA 446,997
Monmouth-Ocean, NJ* 1,126,217
Monroe, LA 147,250
Montgomery, AL 333,055
Muncie, IN 118,769
Myrtle Beach, SC 196,629
Naples, FL 251,377
Nashua, NH* 190,949
Nashville, TN 1,231,311
Nassau-Suffolk, NY* 2,753,913
Newark, NJ* 2,032,989
New Bedford, MA* 175,198
Newburgh, NY-PA* 387,669
New Haven-Meriden, CT* 542,149
New London-Norwich, CT-RI 293,566
New Orleans, LA 1,337,726
New York, NY* 9,314,235
Norfolk-Virginia Beach-Newport News, VA-NC 1,569,541
Oakland, CA* 2,392,557
Ocala, FL 258,916
Odessa-Midland, TX 237,132
Oklahoma City, OK 1,083,346
Olympia, WA* 207,355
Omaha, NE-IA 716,998
Orange County, CA* 2,846,289
Orlando, FL 1,644,561
Owensboro, KY 91,545
Panama City, FL 148,217
Parkersburg-Marietta, WV-OH 151,237
Pensacola, FL 412,153
Peoria-Pekin, IL 347,387
Philadelphia, PA-NJ* 5,100,931
Phoenix-Mesa, AZ 3,251,876
Pine Bluff, AR 84,278
Pittsburgh, PA 2,358,695
Pittsfield, MA 84,699
Pocatello, ID 75,565
Portland, ME 243,537
Portland-Vancouver, OR-WA* 1,918,009
Portsmouth-Rochester, NH-ME* 240,698
Providence-Fall River-Warwick, RI-MA 1,188,613
Provo-Orem, UT 368,536
Pueblo, CO 141,472
Punta Gorda, FL 141,627
Racine, WI* 188,831
Raleigh-Durham-Chapel Hill, NC 1,187,941
Rapid City, SD 88,565
Reading, PA 373,638
Redding, CA 163,256
Reno, NV 339,486
Richland-Kennewick-Pasco, WA 191,822
Richmond-Petersburg, VA 996,512
Riverside-San Bernardino, CA* 3,254,821
Roanoke, VA 235,932
Rochester, MN 124,277
Rochester, NY 1,098,201
Rockford, IL 371,236
Rocky Mount, NC 143,026
Sacramento, CA* 1,628,197
Saginaw-Bay City-Midland, MI 403,070
St. Cloud, MN 167,392
St. Joseph, MO 102,490
St. Louis, MO-IL 2,603,607
Salem, OR* 347,214
Salinas, CA 401,762
Salt Lake City-Ogden, UT 1,333,914
San Angelo, TX 104,010
San Antonio, TX 1,592,383
San Diego, CA 2,813,833
San Francisco, CA* 1,731,183
San Jose, CA* 1,682,585
San Luis Obispo-Atascadero-Paso Robles, CA 246,681
Santa Barbara-Santa Maria-Lompoc, CA 399,347
Santa Cruz-Watsonville, CA* 255,602
Santa Fe, NM 147,635
Santa Rosa, CA* 458,614
Sarasota-Bradenton, FL 589,959
Savannah, GA 293,000
Scranton–Wilkes-Barre–Hazleton, PA 624,776
Seattle-Bellevue-Everett, WA* 2,414,616
Sharon, PA 120,293
Sheboygan, WI 112,646
Sherman-Denison,TX 110,595
Shreveport-Bossier City, LA 392,302
Sioux City, IA-NE 124,130
Sioux Falls, SD 172,412
South Bend, IN 265,559
Spokane, WA 417,939
Springfield, IL 201,437
Springfield, MA 591,932
Springfield, MO 325,721
Stamford-Norwalk, CT* 353,556
State College, PA 135,758
Steubenville-Weirton, OH-WV 132,008
Stockton-Lodi, CA 563,598
Sumter, SC 104,646
Syracuse, NY 732,117
Tacoma, WA* 700,820
Tallahassee, FL 284,539
Tampa-St. Petersburg-Clearwater, FL 2,395,997
Terre Haute, IN 149,192
Texarkana,TX-AR 129,749
Toledo, OH 618,203
Topeka, KS 169,871
Trenton, NJ* 350,761
Tucson, AZ 843,746
Tulsa, OK 803,235
Tuscaloosa, AL 164,875
Tyler, TX 174,706
Utica-Rome, NY 299,896
Vallejo-Fairfield-Napa, CA* 518,821
Ventura, CA* 753,197
Victoria, TX 84,088
Vineland-Millville-Bridgeton, NJ* 146,438
Visalia-Tulare-Porterville, CA 368,021
Waco, TX 213,517
Washington, DC-MD-VA-WV* 4,923,153
Waterbury, CT* 228,984
Waterloo-Cedar Falls, IA 128,012
Wausau, WI 125,834
West Palm Beach-Boca Raton, FL 1,131,184
Wheeling, WV-OH 153,172
Wichita Falls, TX 140,518
Wichita, KS 545,220
Williamsport, PA 120,044
Wilmington, NC 233,450
Wilmington-Newark, DE-MD* 586,216
Worcester, MA-CT* 511,389
Yakima, WA 222,581
Yolo, CA* 168,660
York, PA 381,751
Youngstown-Warren, OH 594,746
Yuba City, CA 139,149
Yuma, AZ 160,026

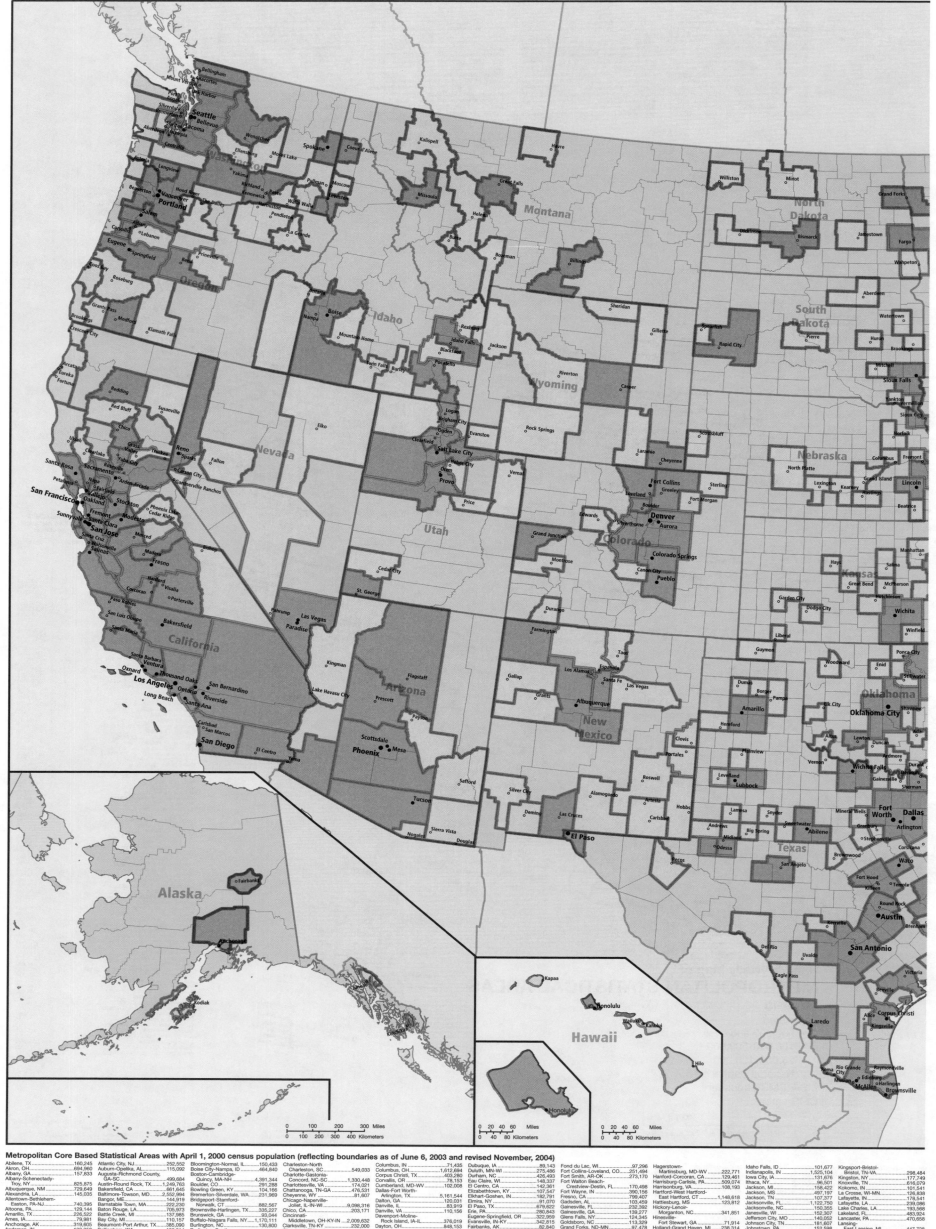

Metropolitan Core Based Statistical Areas with April 1, 2000 census population (reflecting boundaries as of June 6, 2003 and revised November, 2004)

This map shows Core Based Statistical Areas (CBSAs) as announced by the Office of Management and Budget (OMB) effective June 6, 2003 and revised November, 2004. A CBSA is a metropolitan area consisting of the county or counties associated with an urban core having a population of at least 10,000, plus adjacent counties having a high degree of social and economic integration with the core as measured through commuting ties. CBSAs are more current definitions of metropolitan areas than the older Metropolitan Statistical Areas (MSAs) as defined and revised by the OMB through June 30, 1999.

The term CBSA refers collectively to Metropolitan CBSAs and Micropolitan CBSAs. Metropolitan CBSAs are associated with at least one urban core having a population of at least 50,000, while Micropolitan CBSAs are associated with at least one urban core having a population of at least 10,000 but less than 50,000.

Combined Statistical Areas (CSAs) consist of two or more adjacent CBSAs with a high degree of employment interchange.

Counties or county equivalents form the building blocks for CBSAs for the entire U.S. The largest city in each CBSA is designated the principal city. Other cities may also be principal cities if specific population and employment criteria are met. The title of each CBSA consists of the names of up to three of its principal cities, plus the name of each state into which the CBSA extends.

This map shows both Micropolitan and Metropolitan CBSAs in different colors. CSA boundaries are also shown.

Rand McNally Map of
CORE BASED STATISTICAL AREAS

Legend

Population
- • 500,000 and over
- • 100,000-500,000
- ○ Less than 100,000
- ⊚ National Capital

Metropolitan CBSA
Micropolitan CBSA
CSA

0   100   200   Miles
0 100 200 300 Kilometers

Metropolitan Statistical Areas (MSAs): Population/Income/Sales#

This table provides population and marketing information for each of the 331 MSAs and PMSAs. Included are all of the data items given for Basic Trading Areas in the table starting on page 24. Data are from Devonshire Associates Ltd. and Scan/US, Inc. 2005. Also included are codes for MSAs published in the FIPS series of the National Bureau of Standards. A map showing the MSAs, with a detailed explanation of how they are determined, appears on pages 36-37. For information on the Ranally Metro Areas (RMAs), whose boundaries differ from those of the MSAs, see the table on pages 126-127.

MSA FIPS Code	Metropolitan Statistical Area	Population: Estimate 7/1/05	Population: Census 4/1/00	Population: % Change 4/1/90-4/1/00	Per Capita Income 2004	House-holds Estimate 7/1/05	Disposable Income 2004 ($1,000)	Market Ability Index 2004	Total Retail Sales: 2004 Sales ($1,000)	Total Retail Sales: Ranally Sales Units	General Merchandise: 2004 Sales ($1,000)	General Merchandise: Ranally Sales Units	Apparel Store: 2004 Sales ($1,000)	Apparel Store: Ranally Sales Units	Food Store Sales 2004 ($1,000)	Health & Drug Store 2004 ($1,000)
0040	Abilene, TX	123,775	126,555	5.8	16,487	48,220	2,040,720	.0405	1,697,028	482	377,627	751	62,994	332	188,548	70,018
0080	Akron, OH (PMSA)	704,396	694,960	5.7	19,435	272,491	13,689,650	.2478	9,538,485	2,709	920,437	1,830	401,349	2,112	1,321,069	843,663
0120	Albany, GA	126,968	120,822	7.3	14,968	45,539	1,900,410	.0388	1,614,035	459	342,705	681	77,818	410	239,377	66,674
0160	Albany-Schenectady-Troy, NY	900,791	875,583	1.6	21,591	358,455	19,449,370	.3176	10,308,913	2,927	1,204,857	2,396	592,503	3,118	1,364,827	663,496
0200	Albuquerque, NM	772,209	712,738	21.0	18,422	298,024	14,225,380	.2575	9,597,929	2,726	1,906,111	3,791	340,445	1,791	802,412	511,305
0220	Alexandria, LA	127,099	126,337	-4.0	14,480	48,457	1,840,400	.0385	1,634,018	464	396,986	789	70,943	373	181,022	112,390
0240	Allentown-Bethlehem-Easton, PA	672,335	637,958	7.2	19,306	253,826	12,980,260	.2270	8,072,675	2,293	826,404	1,643	344,846	1,814	1,380,468	582,180
0280	Altoona, PA	126,465	129,144	-1.1	16,251	51,843	2,055,160	.0421	1,839,118	522	340,485	677	66,222	349	262,688	130,976
0320	Amarillo, TX	228,556	217,858	16.2	16,571	85,000	3,787,490	.0746	3,077,351	873	453,978	903	129,647	683	251,297	125,590
0380	Anchorage, AK	278,263	260,283	15.0	23,461	103,824	6,528,250	.1139	4,510,522	1,281	1,086,418	2,161	230,765	1,215	522,594	52,268
0440	Ann Arbor, MI (PMSA)	633,040	578,736	18.1	24,094	243,947	15,252,770	.2514	8,932,166	2,537	1,549,143	3,081	327,587	1,724	947,477	458,502
0450	Anniston, AL	112,624	112,249	-3.3	16,048	45,425	1,807,370	.0339	1,246,973	354	279,922	557	40,491	213	167,833	58,882
0460	Appleton-Oshkosh-Neenah, WI	376,237	358,365	13.7	20,797	149,305	7,824,600	.1368	5,095,443	1,446	746,975	1,486	193,307	1,017	567,911	213,205
0480	Asheville, NC	237,670	225,965	17.8	18,136	99,311	4,310,360	.0816	3,297,080	937	541,867	1,078	179,865	946	376,099	203,890
0500	Athens, GA	162,302	153,444	21.5	16,093	64,178	2,611,940	.0498	1,903,483	540	343,136	682	88,722	468	243,636	85,267
0520	Atlanta, GA	4,657,401	4,112,198	38.9	21,747	1,661,826	101,285,150	1.7416	64,204,134	18,229	8,644,892	17,194	3,419,869	18,001	8,840,483	2,720,352
0560	Atlantic-Cape May, NJ (PMSA)	362,796	354,878	11.1	23,372	151,746	8,479,390	.1383	4,710,388	1,337	446,396	888	343,199	1,807	1,046,330	313,014
0580	Auburn-Opelika, AL	121,616	115,092	32.1	15,690	49,426	1,908,140	.0345	1,142,527	324	219,487	436	59,149	311	192,903	39,194
0600	Augusta-Aiken, GA-SC	494,516	477,441	15.0	17,247	182,862	8,529,020	.1524	5,278,220	1,499	982,041	1,954	250,758	1,320	711,597	246,835
0640	Austin-San Marcos, TX	1,453,856	1,249,763	47.7	21,294	525,442	30,958,890	.6241	30,159,309	8,564	2,441,369	4,855	1,101,729	5,800	3,038,880	1,493,719
0680	Bakersfield, CA	743,729	661,645	21.7	14,153	234,348	10,526,210	.1907	5,759,480	1,635	787,831	1,567	234,327	1,233	863,026	390,768
0720	Baltimore, MD (PMSA)	2,658,807	2,552,994	7.2	22,490	997,379	59,797,030	.9484	29,277,161	8,312	3,797,673	7,552	1,701,986	8,959	5,186,939	1,711,640
0730	Bangor, ME	92,604	90,864	-0.8	17,777	38,025	1,646,240	.0351	1,721,151	488	253,676	504	47,114	248	288,904	80,099
0740	Barnstable-Yarmouth, MA	169,973	162,582	20.5	23,866	72,560	4,056,583	.0683	2,527,453	718	174,375	347	168,993	889	554,918	190,536
0760	Baton Rouge, LA	627,014	602,894	14.1	17,163	222,147	10,761,580	.2029	7,857,816	2,232	1,504,974	2,993	352,913	1,857	906,884	395,165
0840	Beaumont-Port Arthur, TX	380,783	385,090	6.6	16,794	144,982	6,394,940	.1213	4,697,396	1,333	797,667	1,586	210,488	1,108	605,208	276,284
0860	Bellingham, WA	182,534	166,814	30.5	18,455	71,812	3,368,700	.0612	2,303,589	654	435,895	867	99,789	525	459,114	114,322
0870	Benton Harbor, MI	162,940	162,453	0.7	18,150	65,840	2,957,340	.0504	1,604,788	456	295,720	588	32,671	172	224,588	119,269
0875	Bergen-Passaic, NJ (PMSA)	1,410,908	1,373,167	7.4	26,454	497,988	37,324,830	.5956	20,662,302	5,867	1,801,247	3,582	1,681,158	8,848	3,591,953	1,403,095
0880	Billings, MT	135,784	129,352	14.0	17,833	54,868	2,421,380	.0489	2,199,002	624	431,695	858	77,026	405	224,767	63,476
0920	Biloxi-Gulfport-Pascagoula, MS	371,758	363,988	16.5	17,633	143,559	6,555,210	.1178	4,197,560	1,192	1,071,270	2,130	152,026	801	423,274	185,769
0960	Binghamton, NY	249,856	252,320	-4.6	18,851	102,035	4,710,130	.0798	2,593,351	736	366,506	729	103,385	544	454,988	206,715
1000	Birmingham, AL	952,851	921,106	9.6	19,050	368,193	18,152,200	.3241	11,979,568	3,402	1,973,330	3,924	623,491	3,282	1,471,521	601,380
1010	Bismarck, ND	98,303	94,719	13.0	18,296	38,484	1,798,600	.0350	1,489,757	423	258,853	515	35,852	188	152,830	93,133
1020	Bloomington, IN	120,813	120,563	10.6	15,717	48,736	1,898,800	.0369	1,437,695	408	308,733	614	60,281	317	182,489	64,917
1040	Bloomington-Normal, IL	160,498	150,433	16.5	21,223	62,003	3,406,260	.0592	2,197,078	624	332,254	661	135,942	715	218,032	143,217
1080	Boise City, ID	504,057	432,345	46.1	18,751	188,844	9,451,660	.1759	7,007,764	1,990	1,276,182	2,538	230,777	1,214	916,023	230,300
1120	Boston, MA-NH (PMSA)	3,452,176	3,406,829	5.5	25,382	1,296,664	87,624,672	1.3994	47,507,067	13,491	4,239,209	8,431	4,248,638	22,358	7,462,025	3,825,518
1125	Boulder-Longmont, CO (PMSA)[1]	282,452	291,288	29.3	25,153	111,722	7,104,400	.1167	4,216,806	1,197	418,126	832	137,945	726	786,632	154,369
1145	Brazoria, TX (PMSA)	276,715	241,767	26.1	19,374	92,366	5,361,020	.0852	2,345,214	666	569,951	1,133	62,344	328	318,997	90,787
1150	Bremerton, WA (PMSA)	241,196	231,969	22.3	20,793	92,982	5,015,170	.0800	2,360,051	670	567,682	1,129	73,505	387	316,380	119,693
1160	Bridgeport, CT (PMSA)	471,392	459,479	3.6	21,964	172,115	10,353,506	.1909	8,123,648	2,308	592,196	1,178	466,036	2,454	946,621	402,815
1200	Brockton, MA (PMSA)	268,337	255,459	8.1	20,247	91,748	5,433,115	.1026	4,375,568	1,243	335,431	666	86,137	454	582,223	221,438
1240	Brownsville-Harlingen-San Benito, TX	379,998	335,227	28.9	8,453	97,445	3,212,080	.0778	2,844,598	808	682,514	1,357	195,900	1,031	495,642	117,593
1260	Bryan-College Station, TX	156,700	152,415	25.1	14,404	62,130	2,257,060	.0460	1,859,016	528	361,493	719	99,437	523	226,349	46,272
1280	Buffalo-Niagara Falls, NY	1,154,526	1,170,111	-1.6	20,193	477,362	23,313,710	.3832	12,048,915	3,421	1,230,258	2,447	724,512	3,813	2,155,690	978,261
1305	Burlington, VT	174,694	169,391	11.8	20,568	66,606	3,593,134	.0700	3,177,523	901	307,137	611	138,077	728	483,213	174,562
1320	Canton-Massillon, OH	407,131	406,934	3.3	18,072	158,114	7,357,550	.1373	5,385,396	1,529	695,727	1,384	280,842	1,478	801,334	503,254
1350	Casper, WY	69,348	66,533	8.7	17,101	27,462	1,185,920	.0231	956,827	272	208,531	415	22,617	119	100,078	22,464
1360	Cedar Rapids, IA	198,432	191,701	13.6	21,505	81,755	4,267,200	.0754	2,921,835	830	477,656	950	121,799	641	351,974	165,571
1400	Champaign-Urbana, IL	186,135	179,669	3.8	18,227	74,726	3,392,710	.0615	2,285,663	649	514,212	1,023	90,197	475	295,686	174,833
1440	Charleston-North Charleston, SC	586,872	549,033	8.3	17,044	210,746	10,002,730	.1828	6,608,271	1,877	1,199,377	2,385	418,395	2,203	993,263	297,458
1480	Charleston, WV	247,085	251,662	0.5	18,814	104,891	4,648,630	.0875	3,568,375	1,014	587,692	1,168	143,534	756	371,118	285,524
1520	Charlotte-Gastonia-Rock Hill, NC-SC	1,686,002	1,499,293	29.0	21,005	648,683	35,414,250	.6081	21,907,722	6,220	3,117,357	6,200	1,045,991	5,504	2,725,308	1,238,736
1540	Charlottesville, VA	168,000	159,576	21.7	20,363	67,520	3,421,060	.0609	2,322,178	660	325,831	649	136,443	719	378,284	122,449
1560	Chattanooga, TN-GA	479,572	465,161	9.6	17,548	184,389	8,415,440	.1546	5,760,291	1,636	961,302	1,912	330,468	1,739	727,043	373,586
1580	Cheyenne, WY	86,122	81,607	11.6	17,927	33,481	1,543,880	.0305	1,326,732	377	210,135	418	24,046	127	135,941	26,824
1600	Chicago, IL (PMSA)	8,619,113	8,272,768	11.6	21,095	2,984,840	181,820,540	3.0339	102,348,553	29,062	11,736,404	23,340	5,964,334	31,390	13,488,123	8,936,424
1620	Chico-Paradise, CA	215,649	203,171	11.6	16,053	84,743	3,461,920	.0631	2,162,007	614	337,895	672	81,188	427	421,916	159,025
1640	Cincinnati, OH-KY-IN (PMSA)	1,688,541	1,646,395	7.9	20,542	661,875	34,685,280	.6008	21,779,620	6,183	3,117,466	6,198	1,144,705	6,027	2,992,762	1,254,371
1660	Clarksville-Hopkinsville, TN-KY	212,517	207,033	22.2	16,708	79,785	3,550,650	.0642	2,226,683	632	588,104	1,169	101,389	534	165,019	78,683
1680	Cleveland-Lorain-Elyria, OH (PMSA)	2,239,726	2,250,871	2.2	19,873	892,883	44,511,170	.7797	28,379,441	8,058	2,952,752	5,873	1,438,587	7,571	4,208,298	3,036,617
1720	Colorado Springs, CO	570,479	516,929	30.2	20,654	218,133	11,782,890	.2021	7,180,198	2,039	1,264,761	2,515	198,849	1,047	725,989	271,165
1740	Columbia, MO	143,667	135,454	20.5	19,229	61,157	2,762,520	.0501	1,920,330	545	319,106	635	60,113	316	197,448	85,118
1760	Columbia, SC	573,167	536,691	18.4	19,044	218,427	10,915,360	.1999	7,794,655	2,213	1,593,880	3,169	430,539	2,266	942,757	402,030
1800	Columbus, GA-AL	270,357	274,624	5.3	16,217	104,336	4,384,360	.0811	2,907,245	825	546,877	1,087	178,721	940	406,938	204,320
1840	Columbus, OH	1,639,166	1,540,157	14.5	20,212	624,436	33,131,310	.6061	24,357,956	6,916	2,930,602	5,828	1,119,931	5,895	2,814,809	992,965
1880	Corpus Christi, TX	383,948	380,783	8.8	15,361	133,326	5,897,640	.1143	4,352,658	1,236	742,324	1,476	206,792	1,089	708,266	183,922
1890	Corvallis, OR	79,778	78,153	10.4	20,737	33,621	1,654,350	.0250	619,285	176	82,101	163	24,988	132	143,655	30,072
1900	Cumberland, MD-WV	100,474	102,008	0.4	15,057	39,878	1,512,830	.0284	1,005,621	286	234,621	467	42,851	225	142,375	89,912
1920	Dallas, TX (PMSA)	3,984,198	3,519,176	31.5	20,413	1,343,196	81,327,990	1.4200	52,155,059	14,810	8,148,528	16,203	2,913,107	15,333	6,769,241	2,168,854
1930	Danbury, CT (PMSA)	230,641	217,980	12.6	26,875	81,560	6,198,532	.1055	4,221,369	1,199	407,517	810	301,892	1,589	671,564	224,856
1950	Danville, VA	107,753	110,156	1.3	15,396	45,230	1,658,970	.0314	1,135,480	323	211,467	420	34,975	184	189,329	64,305
1960	Davenport-Moline-Rock Island, IA-IL	357,408	359,062	2.3	19,094	143,678	6,824,320	.1256	4,956,018	1,408	732,417	1,457	204,976	1,079	583,387	337,804
2000	Dayton-Springfield, OH	942,462	950,558	-0.1	19,838	381,183	18,696,450	.3254	11,656,512	3,310	1,897,994	3,774	486,276	2,558	1,587,983	649,452
2020	Daytona Beach, FL	554,014	493,175	23.5	18,262	220,945	10,117,500	.1771	6,075,367	1,725	882,131	1,754	253,960	1,337	957,383	421,164
2030	Decatur, AL	148,289	145,867	10.9	17,603	57,646	2,610,310	.0471	1,685,295	479	261,428	520	65,151	343	156,749	93,514
2040	Decatur, IL	109,127	114,706	-2.1	19,482	47,005	2,125,990	.0396	1,612,803	458	305,716	608	54,606	287	210,392	109,435
2080	Denver, CO (PMSA)[1]	2,271,459	2,109,282	30.0	24,810	938,966	56,355,400	.9073	31,014,716	8,807	4,643,809	9,235	1,491,361	7,850	4,280,226	1,191,900
2120	Des Moines, IA	490,399	456,022	16.1	20,198	188,322	9,904,880	.1714	6,129,021	1,740	839,842	1,670	242,908	1,278	793,960	295,568
2160	Detroit, MI (PMSA)	4,472,407	4,441,551	4.1	21,721	1,715,343	97,145,860	1.6723	61,752,046	17,534	9,851,389	19,591	3,029,987	15,947	7,262,506	4,742,686
2180	Dothan, AL	142,862	137,916	5.3	16,411	55,748	2,344,450	.0476	2,054,807	584	426,635	848	83,896	442	170,538	88,065
2190	Dover, DE	139,558	126,697	14.1	17,806	51,903	2,484,910	.0451	1,653,667	470	366,822	729	47,176	248	190,185	71,144
2200	Dubuque, IA	91,167	89,143	3.2	17,393	34,683	1,585,710	.0307	1,266,703	360	217,773	433	34,204	180	145,758	78,435
2240	Duluth-Superior, MN-WI	241,789	243,815	1.6	18,068	104,762	4,368,760	.0791	2,907,556	826	564,340	1,123	79,379	418	380,421	159,176
2281	Dutchess County, NY (PMSA)	297,806	280,150	8.0	22,445	102,228	6,684,180	.1041	3,035,458	862	364,401	725	207,370	1,091	575,075	167,837
2290	Eau Claire, WI	154,337	148,337	7.8	17,947	62,324	2,769,920	.0573	2,672,277	759	569,895	1,134	105,458	555	270,575	99,099
2320	El Paso, TX	720,147	679,622	14.9	11,701	218,789	8,426,220	.1787	6,673,517	1,895	1,498,168	2,979	459,278	2,417	781,502	305,744
2330	Elkhart-Goshen, IN	192,614	182,791	17.0	18,129	69,511	3,491,820	.0667	2,737,857	777	461,665	918	39,013	205	272,318	127,424
2335	Elmira, NY	90,031	91,070	-4.3	18,393	35,794	1,655,900	.0303	1,148,737	326	193,665	385	58,842	310	156,337	77,465
2340	Enid, OK	56,753	57,813	1.9	16,418	22,797	931,760	.0174	639,603	182	159,589	317	17,110	90	89,321	29,742
2360	Erie, PA	279,281	280,843	1.9	17,187	109,682	4,799,900	.0894	3,381,763	960	451,424	898	142,791	752	538,747	194,570
2400	Eugene-Springfield, OR	335,284	322,959	14.2	18,570	141,340	6,226,310	.1146	4,441,395	1,261	819,155	1,629	129,203	680	689,971	164,173
2440	Evansville-Henderson, IN-KY	301,479	296,195	6.2	18,090	119,894	5,453,700	.1056	4,438,263	1,260	778,136	1,548	211,259	1,112	450,872	245,222
2520	Fargo-Moorhead, ND-MN	181,535	174,367	13.7	18,396	74,974	3,339,550	.0688	3,234,323	919	465,786	927	100,188	527	280,838	149,962
2560	Fayetteville, NC	306,556	302,963	10.3	16,580	112,683	5,082,570	.0957	3,616,858	1,027	706,497	1,405	191,060	1,006	419,738	163,935
2580	Fayetteville-Springdale-Rogers, AR	360,974	311,121	47.5	17,092	134,714	6,169,910	.1138	4,202,271	1,193	1,382,455	2,749	118,782	625	351,016	124,291
2600	Fitchburg-Leominster, MA (PMSA)	145,300	142,284	3.0	18,857	54,369	2,739,989	.0497	1,908,385	541	170,635	340	102,451	539	313,402	107,709
2620	Flagstaff, AZ-UT	130,122	122,366	20.2	16,512	46,023	2,148,530	.0390	1,348,718	383	283,782	564	32,539	171	240,612	30,678
2640	Flint, MI (PMSA)	445,626	436,141	1.3	18,240	166,917	8,128,190	.1460	5,313,381	1,509	1,042,068	2,072	191,549	1,008	611,856	393,603
2650	Florence, AL	140,981	142,950	8.9	17,079	58,420	2,407,870	.0448	1,680,401	477	414,962	825	79,419	418	163,649	72,908
2655	Florence, SC	130,435	125,761	10.0	15,344	47,128	2,001,340	.0424	1,899,095	539	331,941	660	101,088	532	222,876	102,627
2670	Fort Collins-Loveland, CO	275,364	251,494	35.1	24,187	119,115	6,660,320	.1075	3,647,791	1,036	666,158	1,325	150,251	791	477,472	113,594
2680	Fort Lauderdale, FL (PMSA)	1,794,053	1,623,018	29.3	20,451	696,396	36,689,620	.6613	25,980,621	7,377	2,886,091	5,740	1,594,217	8,391	3,363,389	1,693,187
2700	Fort Myers-Cape Coral, FL	523,512	440,888	31.6	21,374	219,465	11,189,420	.1957	7,409,505	2,104	1,087,208	2,162	462,470	2,434	956,522	481,928
2710	Fort Pierce-Port St. Lucie, FL	367,537	319,426	27.2	20,044	148,535	7,366,920	.1250	4,250,091	1,207	569,115	1,132	144,124	759	627,822	360,130
2720	Fort Smith, AR-OK	216,321	207,290	17.8	15,455	83,001	3,343,190	.0661	2,634,140	748	745,703	1,483	68,821	362	276,524	111,088
2750	Fort Walton Beach, FL	182,186	170,498	18.6	20,670	71,945	3,765,750	.0679	2,690,307	764	517,655	1,029	221,038	1,163	309,568	131,402
2760	Fort Wayne, IN	519,862	502,141	10.1	17,648	187,695	9,174,710	.1697	6,438,496	1,829	1,202,048	2,390	228,385	1,203	669,795	352,604
2800	Fort Worth-Arlington, TX (PMSA)	1,924,870	1,702,625	25.1	18,850	655,408	36,282,860	.6569	24,855,874	7,059	2,915,762	5,798	1,130,353	5,949	3,138,495	1,036,459
2840	Fresno, CA	1,023,612	922,516	22.1	13,455	310,660	13,772,950	.2578	8,098,841	2,300	1,107,057	2,201	341,667	1,798	1,458,744	503,267
2880	Gadsden, AL	103,021	103,459	3.6	15,806	41,635	1,628,300	.0296	998,934	284	210,213	418	44,852	236	175,131	60,568
2900	Gainesville, FL	223,316	217,955	20.0	17,330	95,536	3,869,970	.0712	2,640,469	750	375,796	747	147,304	775	463,403	110,924
2920	Galveston-Texas City, TX (PMSA)	277,119	250,158	15.1	20,343	108,269	5,637,460	.0889	2,484,736	706	458,480	912	150,792	794	482,952	159,029
2960	Gary, IN (PMSA)	645,927	631,362	4.4	18,131	231,992	11,711,290	.2085	7,414,460	2,106	1,138,119	2,263	262,852	1,383	958,556	582,985
2975	Glens Falls, NY	128,724	124,345	4.9	19,074	50,295	2,455,280	.0420	1,402,324	398	126,801	252	106,760	562	207,045	81,573
2980	Goldsboro, NC	113,461	113,329	8.3	15,801	43,498	1,792,770	.0345	1,320,622	375	253,513	504	59,248	312	168,453	67,902
2985	Grand Forks, ND-MN	94,524	97,478	-5.5	16,316	37,199	1,542,210	.0336	1,617,709	459	315,509	628	47,227	248	149,096	61,226
2995	Grand Junction, CO	129,419	116,255	24.8	18,268	55,438	2,364,210	.0430	1,607,761	457	399,198	794	34,875	184	198,421	41,576
3000	Grand Rapids-Muskegon-Holland, MI	1,144,317	1,088,514	16.1	19,772	428,897	22,625,540	.4000	14,799,151	4,202	3,176,156	6,317	520,071	2,738	1,291,001	738,655
3040	Great Falls, MT	79,409	80,357	3.4	16,614	32,956	1,319,290	.0256	1,027,263	292	244,590	486	25,008	132	107,838	48,119
3060	Greeley, CO (PMSA)[1]	230,756	180,936	37.3	18,917	88,114	4,365,170	.0702	1,958,366	556	298,091	593	26,630	140	250,995	54,456
3080	Green Bay, WI	238,847	226,778	16.5	20,437	95,295	4,881,200	.0880	3,453,490	981	921,590	1,833	93,558	492	323,144	107,664
3120	Greensboro—Winston-Salem—High Point, NC	1,322,689	1,251,509	19.2	19,046	518,301	25,192,450	.4552	17,241,148	4,896	2,220,660	4,415	857,366	4,514	2,013,241	1,034,100
3150	Greenville, NC	141,666	133,798	24.0	16,773	59,080	2,376,140	.0479	2,073,721	589	230,337	458	132,141	695	247,586	103,215
3160	Greenville-Spartanburg-Anderson, SC	1,011,759	962,441	15.9	17,565	382,174	17,771,980	.3329	12,935,864	3,673	1,862,457	3,703	695,042	3,658	1,615,194	801,432
3180	Hagerstown, MD (PMSA)	140,320	131,923	8.7	18,615	53,417	2,612,090	.0465	1,685,288	479	306,637	610	46,962	247	244,511	83,377
3200	Hamilton-Middletown, OH (PMSA)	349,225	332,807	14.2	20,901	132,118	7,298,990	.1152	3,315,271	941	441,690	878	68,628	361	546,611	174,591
3240	Harrisburg-Lebanon-Carlisle, PA	644,200	629,401	7.0	20,516	260,218	13,216,590	.2389	9,452,727	2,684	945,453	1,880	342,116	1,801	1,274,186	498,443
3280	Hartford, CT	1,227,673	1,183,110	2.2	26,184	473,622	32,144,998	.4835	14,232,627	4,044	1,296,944	2,578	976,829	5,144	2,229,698	1,212,028
3285	Hattiesburg, MS	118,728	111,674	13.1	13,729	41,652	1,630,060	.0362	1,637,922	465	499,599	994	68,535	360	103,705	120,344
3290	Hickory-Morganton-Lenoir, NC	356,039	341,851	16.9	17,856	140,143	6,357,350	.1156	4,259,162	1,209	596,263	1,186	159,755	841	500,673	277,190
3320	Honolulu, HI	910,475	876,156	4.8	20,281	302,181	18,465,370	.3063	9,903,032	2,812	1,988,367	3,954	1,320,832	6,952	1,401,658	865,911
3350	Houma, LA	198,122	194,477	6.4	15,783	70,892	3,127,010	.0614	2,446,990	695	530,216	1,054	84,487	445	374,137	119,175
3360	Houston, TX (PMSA)	4,689,135	4,177,646	25.8	17,810	1,532,154	83,514,340	1.5344	57,776,090	16,406	9,476,893	18,847	3,420,696	18,004	8,393,316	2,702,292
3400	Huntington-Ashland, WV-KY-OH	313,378	315,538	1.0	14,791	126,421	4,635,180	.0898	3,324,885	946	677,704	1,349	163,806	863	378,401	355,801
3440	Huntsville, AL	367,395	342,376	16.8	20,622	142,882	7,576,500	.1297	4,590,366	1,303	1,044,405	2,077	226,391	1,192	539,630	193,264
3480	Indianapolis, IN	1,724,043	1,607,486	16.4	20,046	649,692	34,559,880	.6243	24,378,934	6,924	4,368,601	8,688	966,234	5,086	2,147,629	1,582,166
3500	Iowa City, IA	117,205	111,006	15.5	19,117	48,430	2,240,610	.0413	1,638,902	465	237,604	473	56,364	297	277,736	76,779
3520	Jackson, MI	164,674	158,422	5.8	18,936	62,458	3,118,220	.0547	1,930,675	548	510,788	1,016	53,668	282	204,847	103,303
3560	Jackson, MS	461,453	440,801	11.5	17,283	164,958	7,975,300	.1543	6,318,893	1,795	1,362,861	2,711	284,801	1,499	566,855	368,876
3580	Jackson, TN	110,724	107,377	18.3	17,951	44,163	1,987,600	.0400	1,786,027	507	377,370	750	113,990	600	160,349	98,608
3600	Jacksonville, FL	1,224,737	1,100,491	21.4	20,764	470,038	25,430,140	.4361	15,548,123	4,415	2,163,127	4,301	792,713	4,173	2,167,951	746,799
3605	Jacksonville, NC	149,754	150,355	0.3	14,047	51,435	2,103,590	.0423	1,637,736	465	298,217	593	55,104	290	193,779	64,913
3610	Jamestown, NY	136,986	139,750	-1.5	17,230	55,411	2,360,230	.0399	1,194,716	339	183,712	365	31,959	168	221,135	87,985
3620	Janesville-Beloit, WI	156,477	152,307	9.2	19,832	61,510	3,103,240	.0553	2,090,244	594	382,774	761	34,271	180	272,604	109,715
3640	Jersey City, NJ (PMSA)	607,051	608,975	10.1	19,048	220,754	11,563,320	.1812	4,658,618	1,323	361,795	719	554,459	2,918	870,328	384,860
3660	Johnson City-Kingsport-Bristol, TN-VA	489,628	480,091	10.1	16,293	205,493	7,977,390	.1512	5,729,468	1,627	1,115,462	2,217	248,987	1,309	691,688	350,663
3680	Johnstown, PA	226,882	232,621	-3.6	14,855	92,161	3,370,270	.0632	2,182,504	620	243,454	484	60,578	319	351,510	159,540
3700	Jonesboro, AR	86,335	82,148	19.1	15,939	34,155	1,376,100	.0286	1,267,386	360	361,786	719	80,295	423	87,497	49,672

Source: Devonshire Associates Ltd. and Scan/US, Inc. 2005.

Estimates for Total Retail Sales, General Merchandise Sales, Apparel Store Sales, Food Store Sales and Health and Drug Store Sales are based on data from the U.S. Census Bureau's 1997 Economic Census and utilize the North American Industry Classification System (NAICS).

[1] Census population includes a portion of Broomfield county.

Metropolitan Statistical Areas (MSAs): Population/Income/Sales#, *Continued*

MSA FIPS Code	Metropolitan Statistical Area	Population Estimate 7/1/05	Population Census 4/1/00	Population % Change 4/1/90-4/1/00	Per Capita Income 2004	Households Estimate 7/1/05	Disposable Income 2004 ($1,000)	Market Ability Index 2004	Total Retail Sales 2004 Sales ($1,000)	Total Retail Sales Ranally Sales Units	General Merchandise 2004 Sales ($1,000)	General Merchandise Ranally Sales Units	Apparel Store 2004 Sales ($1,000)	Apparel Store Ranally Sales Units	Food Store Sales 2004 ($1,000)	Health & Drug Store 2004 ($1,000)
3710	Joplin, MO	166,062	157,322	16.6	15,603	66,337	2,591,010	.0495	1,857,785	527	443,839	883	51,226	269	147,141	84,259
3720	Kalamazoo-Battle Creek, MI	462,127	452,851	5.4	19,050	185,915	8,803,730	.1559	5,653,871	1,605	1,631,035	3,243	176,597	929	497,676	318,660
3740	Kankakee, IL (PMSA)	107,719	103,833	7.9	18,016	39,461	1,940,650	.0349	1,262,073	358	246,649	491	43,039	227	124,092	101,960
3760	Kansas City, MO-KS	1,889,911	1,776,062	12.2	21,485	744,584	40,605,020	.6954	25,222,364	7,162	3,845,162	7,647	985,915	5,190	2,874,928	1,328,445
3800	Kenosha, WI (PMSA)	160,165	149,577	16.7	19,412	59,894	3,109,160	.0487	1,281,385	364	195,888	390	91,653	482	198,533	80,426
3810	Killeen-Temple, TX	331,158	312,952	22.6	15,943	116,071	5,279,650	.0926	2,869,387	815	436,379	867	92,081	484	409,654	53,731
3840	Knoxville, TN	728,734	687,249	17.3	18,458	297,259	13,450,740	.2703	12,241,599	3,476	1,948,737	3,875	719,740	3,789	1,270,074	639,245
3850	Kokomo, IN	101,209	101,541	4.7	20,481	41,291	2,072,820	.0371	1,434,777	407	358,512	713	38,011	200	127,415	109,168
3870	La Crosse, WI-MN	129,409	126,838	9.0	17,892	51,810	2,315,440	.0439	1,765,347	501	349,252	695	38,034	200	206,997	49,530
3880	Lafayette, LA	393,730	385,647	11.8	15,144	149,594	5,962,500	.1209	4,993,804	1,418	1,014,572	2,017	218,948	1,152	557,241	361,121
3920	Lafayette, IN	186,643	182,821	13.2	17,200	71,907	3,210,280	.0595	2,233,764	634	530,960	1,056	87,111	458	198,275	124,716
3960	Lake Charles, LA	183,193	183,577	9.2	17,610	72,541	3,226,040	.0603	2,332,523	662	599,640	1,192	99,182	522	259,216	130,276
3980	Lakeland-Winter Haven, FL	526,208	483,924	19.4	17,926	205,086	9,432,930	.1709	6,270,722	1,781	1,004,624	1,998	225,818	1,189	1,044,350	328,355
4000	Lancaster, PA	490,254	470,658	11.3	19,871	183,207	9,741,670	.1767	6,915,084	1,964	618,456	1,230	403,743	2,125	1,058,381	357,146
4040	Lansing-East Lansing, MI	461,446	447,728	3.5	21,034	189,983	9,705,850	.1657	5,885,672	1,671	1,344,212	2,673	230,071	1,210	671,101	332,191
4080	Laredo, TX	224,381	193,117	44.9	9,241	58,794	2,073,610	.0538	2,426,335	689	508,362	1,011	297,333	1,565	374,549	102,163
4100	Las Cruces, NM	187,285	174,682	28.9	12,484	63,506	2,338,100	.0450	1,409,430	400	290,364	577	45,270	238	147,833	81,908
4120	Las Vegas, NV-AZ	1,918,279	1,563,282	83.3	18,761	706,472	35,989,540	.6324	22,330,283	6,341	3,153,624	6,272	1,408,481	7,413	3,397,026	964,794
4150	Lawrence, KS	103,269	99,962	22.2	17,848	42,198	1,843,120	.0326	1,126,641	320	164,334	327	62,103	327	202,198	54,513
4160	Lawrence, MA-NH (PMSA)	416,134	396,230	12.2	22,590	148,052	9,400,346	.1517	4,930,957	1,402	857,237	1,703	258,092	1,358	883,529	316,440
4200	Lawton, OK	109,018	114,996	3.1	15,172	39,373	1,654,020	.0287	814,320	231	282,458	562	24,492	129	71,642	32,806
4240	Lewiston-Auburn, ME	93,061	90,830	-3.0	17,526	38,322	1,630,954	.0350	1,705,356	485	210,714	420	21,395	112	213,422	65,119
4280	Lexington, KY	507,373	479,198	18.0	19,329	203,505	9,806,860	.1775	6,817,904	1,936	1,077,408	2,142	367,739	1,935	687,458	415,723
4320	Lima, OH	153,334	155,084	0.5	17,669	58,822	2,709,200	.0520	2,124,967	603	453,361	902	66,927	352	180,618	130,278
4360	Lincoln, NE	266,575	250,291	17.2	18,286	101,357	4,874,460	.0883	3,277,448	931	625,758	1,244	120,834	636	456,411	225,440
4400	Little Rock-North Little Rock, AR	612,049	583,845	13.8	19,375	248,420	11,858,670	.2224	9,167,590	2,603	1,874,491	3,728	337,843	1,778	740,411	311,574
4420	Longview-Marshall, TX	216,141	208,780	7.7	15,884	80,449	3,433,170	.0688	2,861,417	813	553,696	1,102	101,271	533	351,721	122,556
4480	Los Angeles-Long Beach, CA (PMSA)	10,076,928	9,519,338	7.4	16,791	3,192,402	169,200,500	2.9617	95,230,986	27,041	11,726,649	23,321	7,977,490	41,987	15,007,662	5,683,828
4520	Louisville, KY-IN	1,055,433	1,025,598	8.1	19,246	412,458	20,312,520	.3556	12,636,394	3,588	2,198,239	4,372	514,793	2,710	1,341,926	835,632
4560	Lowell, MA-NH (PMSA)	303,949	301,686	7.5	20,625	103,776	6,269,096	.0992	2,827,700	802	202,177	402	99,102	522	510,187	224,627
4600	Lubbock, TX	255,027	242,628	9.0	16,025	101,319	4,086,700	.0845	3,724,640	1,058	576,586	1,147	183,780	967	535,172	115,234
4640	Lynchburg, VA	218,478	214,911	10.8	17,306	87,421	3,780,940	.0691	2,532,433	719	376,469	749	77,678	409	304,274	189,651
4680	Macon, GA	343,865	322,549	10.9	17,260	129,275	5,935,190	.1115	4,299,136	1,220	745,854	1,482	221,174	1,164	562,561	203,738
4720	Madison, WI	463,177	426,526	16.2	22,795	196,124	10,558,140	.1825	6,977,606	1,981	914,396	1,818	244,878	1,289	756,141	323,059
4760	Manchester, NH (PMSA)	213,149	198,378	14.2	21,959	79,991	4,680,545	.0845	3,448,314	978	541,870	1,077	145,271	764	478,253	147,488
4800	Mansfield, OH	173,148	175,818	1.0	17,905	70,355	3,100,160	.0556	1,989,041	564	386,585	769	59,166	311	228,379	127,729
4880	McAllen-Edinburg-Mission, TX	675,597	569,463	48.5	8,316	179,247	5,618,500	.1432	5,723,037	1,625	1,172,978	2,333	428,765	2,257	870,770	248,513
4890	Medford-Ashland, OR	196,043	181,269	23.8	18,053	81,232	3,539,120	.0732	3,428,121	973	602,138	1,197	88,759	467	352,409	91,518
4900	Melbourne-Titusville-Palm Bay, FL	523,567	476,230	19.4	20,941	216,202	10,963,820	.1797	5,760,123	1,636	986,272	1,961	242,067	1,274	880,605	408,228
4920	Memphis, TN-AR-MS	1,188,935	1,135,614	12.7	18,374	447,194	21,845,960	.3937	14,505,139	4,118	2,535,346	5,043	866,405	4,560	1,405,128	1,036,338
4940	Merced, CA	243,619	210,554	18.0	12,985	70,306	3,163,490	.0572	1,559,661	443	279,329	555	41,746	220	281,012	82,724
5000	Miami, FL (PMSA)	2,391,206	2,253,362	16.3	15,028	782,688	35,933,990	.6861	24,937,816	7,081	2,984,280	5,935	2,500,650	13,162	3,337,422	2,044,796
5015	Middlesex-Somerset-Hunterdon, NJ (PMSA)	1,254,329	1,169,641	14.7	29,321	439,191	36,777,750	.5590	18,175,229	5,161	1,505,044	2,994	1,121,242	5,900	2,953,420	975,370
5080	Milwaukee-Waukesha, WI (PMSA)	1,521,473	1,500,741	4.8	20,533	597,839	31,239,920	.5262	17,833,569	5,063	2,618,965	5,208	605,954	3,189	2,459,679	1,231,828
5120	Minneapolis-St. Paul, MN-WI	3,154,675	2,968,806	16.9	24,093	1,251,827	76,004,390	1.3070	50,893,048	14,452	7,484,790	14,884	1,876,788	9,878	6,162,603	2,302,183
5140	Missoula, MT	100,118	95,802	21.8	17,414	41,813	1,743,480	.0355	1,600,814	455	351,579	699	41,311	217	176,081	45,603
5160	Mobile, AL	558,139	540,258	13.3	15,224	191,163	8,497,060	.1626	5,993,132	1,702	1,221,428	2,429	352,485	1,855	737,702	358,432
5170	Modesto, CA	519,823	446,997	20.6	15,585	161,250	8,101,680	.1473	4,910,210	1,394	756,250	1,504	190,893	1,005	890,064	318,684
5190	Monmouth-Ocean, NJ (PMSA)	1,213,007	1,126,217	14.2	26,287	453,624	31,886,460	.4923	15,656,156	4,446	1,406,895	2,798	983,110	5,175	3,042,376	997,766
5200	Monroe, LA	147,371	147,250	3.6	15,667	56,614	2,308,890	.0457	1,843,979	524	521,548	1,037	98,193	517	182,315	88,264
5240	Montgomery, AL	343,079	333,055	13.9	17,363	126,886	5,956,800	.1117	4,318,168	1,226	866,507	1,724	198,796	1,047	479,908	274,303
5280	Muncie, IN	117,847	118,769	-0.7	15,782	46,441	1,859,920	.0361	1,411,758	401	345,291	687	57,863	305	130,438	71,255
5330	Myrtle Beach, SC	219,791	196,629	36.5	18,431	91,467	4,050,980	.0826	3,819,977	1,085	609,030	1,211	439,072	2,311	501,810	168,795
5345	Naples, FL	306,973	251,377	65.3	24,916	127,885	7,648,670	.1250	4,435,456	1,259	409,669	815	470,567	2,477	683,833	249,092
5350	Nashua, NH (PMSA)	202,556	190,949	13.5	23,852	74,403	4,831,386	.0966	4,822,362	1,369	743,237	1,479	202,029	1,063	584,187	145,065
5360	Nashville, TN	1,324,828	1,231,311	25.0	20,939	510,191	27,740,880	.5019	20,127,372	5,716	3,353,344	6,668	1,044,827	5,498	2,326,601	1,180,599
5380	Nassau-Suffolk, NY (PMSA)	2,842,538	2,753,913	5.5	26,972	934,263	76,669,060	1.2211	42,600,443	12,097	4,137,605	8,229	3,648,276	19,201	6,184,752	2,937,674
5400	New Bedford, MA (PMSA)	175,529	175,198	-0.3	19,251	67,054	3,379,038	.0551	1,631,214	464	258,484	513	78,247	412	304,040	129,878
5480	New Haven-Meriden, CT (PMSA)	560,471	542,149	2.3	25,013	208,851	14,019,262	.2219	7,289,069	2,070	577,222	1,148	471,228	2,481	1,135,348	508,832
5520	New London-Norwich, CT-RI	302,259	293,566	1.0	25,399	119,810	7,677,150	.1234	4,279,410	1,216	539,455	1,073	210,793	1,109	646,576	282,265
5560	New Orleans, LA	1,329,657	1,337,726	4.1	16,844	494,477	22,397,090	.4147	15,301,973	4,347	2,688,387	5,347	940,553	4,950	2,125,707	1,165,355
5600	New York, NY (PMSA)	9,499,149	9,314,235	9.0	19,586	3,492,463	186,052,060	2.9271	78,543,603	22,302	7,481,382	14,877	13,218,413	69,572	12,199,167	8,872,091
5640	Newark, NJ (PMSA)	2,095,245	2,032,989	6.1	25,419	739,306	53,259,010	.8289	26,350,323	7,482	1,623,331	3,229	1,856,413	9,770	4,910,221	1,850,721
5660	Newburgh, NY-PA (PMSA)	433,484	387,669	15.5	20,736	143,640	8,988,760	.1445	4,362,928	1,239	716,896	1,426	432,075	2,274	579,285	254,214
5720	Norfolk-Virginia Beach-Newport News, VA-NC	1,650,742	1,569,541	8.8	17,958	602,650	29,644,350	.5210	17,865,597	5,073	2,872,048	5,712	1,052,683	5,541	2,296,955	817,388
5775	Oakland, CA (PMSA)	2,497,921	2,392,557	14.9	24,937	865,288	62,290,960	.9545	28,700,509	8,149	3,388,368	6,738	1,577,698	8,304	5,522,794	1,487,100
5790	Ocala, FL	294,555	258,916	32.9	16,944	121,424	4,991,010	.0921	3,382,818	961	535,220	1,064	94,712	498	427,647	197,001
5800	Odessa-Midland, TX	245,163	237,132	5.1	15,705	88,662	3,850,290	.0776	3,237,694	919	682,910	1,358	136,921	721	394,557	127,203
5880	Oklahoma City, OK	1,142,506	1,083,346	13.0	17,418	437,517	19,900,220	.3654	13,542,593	3,845	2,453,982	4,881	448,693	2,361	1,416,033	771,990
5910	Olympia, WA (PMSA)	229,500	207,355	28.6	21,189	90,231	4,862,910	.0830	2,958,276	840	761,569	1,515	83,210	438	469,563	106,737
5920	Omaha, NE-IA	756,323	716,998	12.1	19,499	287,638	14,747,300	.2730	11,005,219	3,124	1,417,220	2,819	405,125	2,132	1,290,290	622,424
5945	Orange County, CA (PMSA)	3,020,648	2,846,289	18.1	23,420	988,370	70,743,570	1.1619	40,282,551	11,438	5,068,317	10,079	3,229,084	16,995	5,793,345	2,111,368
5960	Orlando, FL	1,900,560	1,644,561	34.3	19,478	701,773	37,018,160	.6726	26,135,598	7,423	3,848,482	7,653	1,791,331	9,428	3,390,238	1,412,260
5990	Owensboro, KY	92,957	91,545	5.0	18,768	38,701	1,744,600	.0304	1,052,628	299	245,961	489	38,546	203	107,853	76,423
6015	Panama City, FL	159,012	148,217	16.7	18,470	63,684	2,936,920	.0537	2,053,327	583	456,342	908	90,167	475	304,639	103,824
6020	Parkersburg-Marietta, WV-OH	149,251	151,237	1.4	17,025	61,162	2,541,050	.0499	2,082,739	591	445,571	886	64,980	342	221,037	123,698
6080	Pensacola, FL	437,128	412,153	19.7	18,438	170,330	8,059,970	.1392	4,649,972	1,321	829,735	1,650	185,536	977	639,256	315,918
6120	Peoria-Pekin, IL	346,545	347,387	2.4	20,359	139,322	7,055,270	.1236	4,569,647	1,298	676,296	1,344	125,674	662	660,389	319,108
6160	Philadelphia, PA-NJ (PMSA)	5,210,435	5,100,931	3.6	21,642	1,928,013	112,763,060	1.8967	66,353,040	18,840	5,657,668	11,252	4,171,829	21,957	10,601,780	4,949,698
6200	Phoenix-Mesa, AZ	3,801,803	3,251,876	45.3	19,272	1,365,972	73,268,000	1.2707	44,288,930	12,576	6,083,481	12,098	1,737,542	9,145	5,560,900	2,306,866
6240	Pine Bluff, AR	82,043	84,278	-1.4	14,092	29,791	1,156,190	.0238	967,724	275	204,175	406	61,309	323	122,491	108,319
6280	Pittsburgh, PA	2,329,028	2,358,695	-1.5	18,398	953,217	42,850,160	.7685	28,055,533	7,967	3,252,438	6,467	1,323,802	6,966	4,509,281	2,003,571
6320	Pittsfield, MA	81,228	84,699	-4.5	20,578	35,953	1,671,538	.0284	984,059	280	81,759	162	85,758	452	210,364	72,551
6340	Pocatello, ID	75,502	75,565	14.4	16,358	28,449	1,235,080	.0240	957,307	272	163,293	325	20,513	108	154,005	47,217
6400	Portland, ME	254,021	243,537	10.1	21,148	103,276	5,372,020	.1060	4,945,418	1,407	426,387	849	253,532	1,334	877,014	207,103
6440	Portland-Vancouver, OR-WA (PMSA)	2,099,630	1,918,009	26.6	21,192	812,973	44,495,920	.7688	28,227,950	8,015	5,153,465	10,249	1,511,846	7,958	3,698,130	926,589
6450	Portsmouth-Rochester, NH-ME (PMSA)	258,660	240,698	7.8	23,383	102,736	6,048,294	.1119	4,874,936	1,383	517,102	1,031	255,124	1,342	735,204	195,976
6480	Providence-Fall River-Warwick, RI-MA	1,241,359	1,188,613	4.8	18,787	465,655	23,321,729	.4004	13,384,443	3,799	1,469,736	2,919	904,070	4,755	2,254,684	1,377,419
6520	Provo-Orem, UT	409,622	368,536	39.8	15,081	119,096	6,177,510	.1186	4,378,818	1,243	892,140	1,774	147,868	778	679,220	84,277
6560	Pueblo, CO	153,579	141,472	15.0	16,245	63,299	2,494,870	.0468	1,726,230	490	451,637	898	33,545	177	213,548	71,466
6580	Punta Gorda, FL	159,967	141,627	27.6	20,390	70,158	3,261,650	.0531	1,641,420	466	381,639	759	88,332	465	248,328	115,633
6600	Racine, WI (PMSA)	194,975	188,831	7.9	19,876	73,303	3,875,310	.0640	2,014,987	572	340,901	678	46,824	246	298,620	135,936
6640	Raleigh-Durham-Chapel Hill, NC	1,360,180	1,187,941	38.9	22,041	521,946	29,979,320	.5134	18,916,873	5,372	2,503,225	4,978	1,006,058	5,294	2,505,533	848,678
6660	Rapid City, SD	93,346	88,565	8.9	17,313	36,862	1,616,070	.0387	2,156,687	612	458,899	913	84,210	443	161,146	78,277
6680	Reading, PA	393,253	373,638	11.0	19,745	147,995	7,764,710	.1320	4,459,882	1,266	520,167	1,034	360,634	1,898	665,140	278,677
6690	Redding, CA	183,315	163,256	11.0	16,233	68,490	2,975,750	.0525	1,677,238	476	289,803	576	48,662	256	305,136	97,029
6720	Reno, NV	390,302	339,486	33.3	20,811	151,394	8,122,740	.1409	5,166,455	1,467	834,750	1,660	170,959	900	705,819	218,418
6740	Richland-Kennewick-Pasco, WA	221,935	191,822	27.9	18,028	76,668	4,000,970	.0714	2,544,894	723	540,447	1,075	69,057	364	403,609	106,339
6760	Richmond-Petersburg, VA	1,053,657	996,512	15.1	19,761	389,531	20,821,320	.3643	13,186,716	3,744	2,317,775	4,610	706,378	3,719	1,769,512	827,046
6780	Riverside-San Bernardino, CA (PMSA)	3,886,808	3,254,821	25.7	16,596	1,212,880	64,505,060	1.1101	33,712,896	9,573	4,782,057	9,510	1,947,213	10,249	5,672,476	1,586,227
6800	Roanoke, VA	235,526	235,932	5.1	19,252	100,134	4,534,390	.0879	3,839,383	1,090	584,992	1,164	173,475	913	442,158	181,022
6820	Rochester, MN	135,319	124,277	16.7	24,235	57,362	3,279,440	.0552	2,060,541	585	513,789	1,022	68,601	361	189,607	77,452
6840	Rochester, NY	1,106,020	1,098,201	3.4	21,353	429,111	23,617,250	.3845	12,264,371	3,483	1,401,369	2,787	575,969	3,031	2,347,424	626,020
6880	Rockford, IL	391,588	371,236	12.6	19,727	145,971	7,725,050	.1315	4,457,927	1,265	690,627	1,374	156,446	823	718,191	263,398
6895	Rocky Mount, NC	145,779	143,026	7.3	16,141	56,140	2,352,980	.0427	1,454,070	413	185,504	369	84,602	445	164,321	97,894
6920	Sacramento, CA (PMSA)	1,891,938	1,628,197	21.5	21,069	684,467	39,861,950	.6485	20,478,151	5,815	2,694,438	5,358	1,147,650	6,040	3,574,860	904,570
6960	Saginaw-Bay City-Midland, MI	403,186	403,070	0.9	18,795	162,786	7,577,940	.1445	6,048,370	1,718	1,255,896	2,498	399,771	2,104	538,935	335,740
6980	St. Cloud, MN	183,879	167,392	12.4	18,514	70,216	3,404,300	.0663	2,845,390	808	567,554	1,128	69,903	368	340,212	89,390
7000	St. Joseph, MO	101,951	102,490	4.9	17,370	41,496	1,770,910	.0328	1,234,798	350	309,560	615	22,399	118	146,996	50,747
7040	St. Louis, MO-IL	2,672,574	2,603,607	4.5	20,958	1,058,488	56,011,440	.9377	31,775,486	9,023	4,883,008	9,712	1,197,116	6,302	4,351,956	2,236,203
7080	Salem, OR (PMSA)	374,986	347,214	24.9	16,813	131,258	6,304,480	.1141	3,997,943	1,135	850,280	1,691	145,165	764	577,419	135,511
7120	Salinas, CA	421,269	401,762	13.0	18,324	130,913	7,719,290	.1321	4,297,922	1,220	496,897	988	304,946	1,605	763,460	273,308
7160	Salt Lake City-Ogden, UT	1,426,891	1,333,914	24.4	17,943	468,349	25,602,800	.4908	20,210,119	5,739	3,404,248	6,770	845,948	4,452	2,719,564	447,921
7200	San Angelo, TX	103,625	104,010	5.6	15,895	40,080	1,647,170	.0317	1,216,496	345	260,149	517	51,673	272	166,583	40,858
7240	San Antonio, TX	1,745,135	1,592,383	20.2	16,688	605,290	29,122,710	.5469	20,676,442	5,871	2,951,205	5,869	1,191,906	6,274	3,059,804	830,072
7320	San Diego, CA	2,990,693	2,813,833	12.6	19,889	1,027,661	59,482,050	1.0104	34,231,355	9,720	4,237,412	8,427	2,478,722	13,046	5,315,838	1,790,799
7360	San Francisco, CA (PMSA)	1,669,327	1,731,183	8.0	30,643	667,243	51,153,900	.8069	29,312,056	8,323	3,664,351	7,288	3,463,886	18,231	5,083,572	1,701,395
7400	San Jose, CA (PMSA)	1,669,973	1,682,585	12.4	29,371	557,576	49,048,290	.7777	28,016,175	7,955	3,571,238	7,102	2,391,823	12,589	4,358,548	1,477,292
7460	San Luis Obispo-Atascadero-Paso Robles, CA	257,381	246,681	13.6	21,248	102,969	5,468,890	.0887	2,798,082	795	240,208	478	153,387	807	552,099	196,306
7480	Santa Barbara-Santa Maria-Lompoc, CA	404,582	399,347	8.0	19,919	139,852	8,058,830	.1386	4,839,745	1,374	499,060	992	335,212	1,764	874,460	322,723
7485	Santa Cruz-Watsonville, CA (PMSA)	248,347	255,602	11.3	23,192	87,640	5,759,610	.0926	3,020,791	858	310,796	618	162,723	856	605,097	265,080
7490	Santa Fe, NM	160,279	147,635	26.1	21,710	61,910	3,479,620	.0586	2,051,904	583	419,737	835	159,723	840	240,122	126,594
7500	Santa Rosa, CA (PMSA)	470,813	458,614	18.1	24,088	175,179	11,340,910	.1822	6,084,888	1,728	691,543	1,375	280,632	1,477	1,212,686	357,793
7510	Sarasota-Bradenton, FL	659,642	589,959	20.5	22,508	289,874	14,847,510	.2476	8,683,476	2,466	1,053,100	2,094	544,300	2,865	1,298,388	549,755
7520	Savannah, GA	312,351	293,000	13.5	17,889	118,298	5,587,730	.1023	3,839,729	1,091	752,694	1,497	218,315	1,149	491,346	146,081
7560	Scranton—Wilkes-Barre—Hazleton, PA	612,464	624,776	-2.1	16,616	247,987	10,176,730	.1934	7,459,598	2,118	981,413	1,951	370,102	1,947	1,296,555	521,290
7600	Seattle-Bellevue-Everett, WA (PMSA)	2,517,924	2,414,616	18.8	24,683	1,027,123	62,148,740	1.0211	36,512,076	10,368	5,326,255	10,593	2,234,950	11,763	4,806,692	1,509,870
7610	Sharon, PA	119,699	120,293	-0.6	16,717	47,949	2,001,010	.0409	1,811,143	514	258,804	515	176,771	930	225,340	118,242
7620	Sheboygan, WI	114,016	112,646	8.4	20,368	45,505	2,322,260	.0378	1,160,993	330	251,599	500	16,223	85	172,267	56,215
7640	Sherman-Denison, TX	117,502	110,595	16.4	17,315	43,814	2,034,550	.0385	1,514,081	430	384,275	764	35,926	189	174,651	59,560
7680	Shreveport-Bossier City, LA	420,461	392,302	4.2	16,334	164,674	6,867,670	.1289	4,791,525	1,360	892,594	1,775	204,576	1,077	578,291	212,094
7720	Sioux City, IA-NE	123,592	124,130	7.9	16,416	45,525	2,028,940	.0395	1,588,439	451	257,847	513	64,447	339	217,424	61,215
7760	Sioux Falls, SD	191,365	172,412	23.8	20,041	75,857	3,835,180	.0863	4,701,875	1,335	694,172	1,381	68,081	358	317,442	191,030
7800	South Bend, IN	266,795	265,559	7.5	15,977	92,598	4,262,660	.0870	3,750,271	1,065	723,593	1,439	153,610	808	377,992	263,481
7840	Spokane, WA	439,273	417,939	15.7	18,223	180,505	8,004,860	.1437	5,223,271	1,483	985,255	1,959	248,626	1,309	753,870	200,787
7880	Springfield, IL	206,549	201,437	6.3	21,276	86,148	4,394,610	.0744	2,609,732	741	485,355	965	82,539	435	316,127	169,767
7920	Springfield, MO	350,755	325,721	23.2	17,441	146,533	6,117,630	.1189	4,945,824	1,405	752,850	1,498	110,452	582	416,294	218,716
8000	Springfield, MA	601,031	591,932	0.7	19,303	230,127	11,601,550	.1949	6,305,655	1,793	549,251	1,090	328,187	1,725	1,226,270	537,359
8040	Stamford-Norwalk, CT (PMSA)	366,016	353,556	7.2	41,147	136,357	15,060,424	.2254	8,174,385	2,321	278,841	554	582,245	3,064	878,019	324,756
8050	State College, PA	141,710	135,758	9.7	16,078	52,454	2,278,390	.0430	1,600,239	454	218,370	434	91,218	480	222,490	77,825
8080	Steubenville-Weirton, OH-WV	126,448	132,008	-7.4	16,713	53,884	2,113,340	.0358	1,048,619	298	175,680	350	33,988	179	207,784	110,680
8120	Stockton-Lodi, CA	674,080	563,598	17.3	15,489	201,595	10,441,010	.1808	5,234,961	1,486	683,333	1,359	247,667	1,304	900,861	341,266
8140	Sumter, SC	106,517	104,646	2.0	14,511	37,845	1,545,670	.0291	1,000,202	284	156,992	312	57,119	301	121,933	48,459
8160	Syracuse, NY	740,003	732,117	-1.4	19,682	290,321	14,564,740	.2429	7,780,798	2,209	820,305	1,631	412,184	2,170	1,430,926	573,891
8200	Tacoma, WA (PMSA)	765,698	700,820	19.6	19,356	283,473	14,820,820	.2482	7,947,017	2,257	1,476,200	2,936	288,392	1,518	1,044,483	335,167
8240	Tallahassee, FL	289,597	284,539	21.8	19,742	121,933	5,717,320	.1001	3,620,838	1,028	682,241	1,357	184,911	973	530,264	239,955
8280	Tampa-St. Petersburg-Clearwater, FL	2,613,412	2,395,997	15.9	19,546	1,065,621	51,081,900	.9188	35,052,229	9,954	4,364,151	8,679	1,494,823	7,868	4,733,677	2,309,521
8320	Terre Haute, IN	146,116	149,192	1.1	15,406	57,161	2,251,110	.0583	3,391,310	964	545,333	1,085	114,465	602	197,087	99,484
8360	Texarkana, TX-AR	132,846	129,749	8.0	15,232	50,436	2,023,530	.0405	1,629,014	463	328,077	652	84,528	445	161,075	45,071
8400	Toledo, OH	618,775	618,203	0.7	18,518	244,572	11,458,640	.2113	8,206,394	2,330	1,249,737	2,486	332,651	1,751	1,125,745	484,420
8440	Topeka, KS	172,022	169,871	5.5	19,403	71,180	3,337,700	.0609	2,376,520	675	545,020	1,084	78,894	415	274,053	169,017
8480	Trenton, NJ (PMSA)	369,496	350,761	7.7	24,296	124,536	8,977,430	.1416	4,534,000	1,287	431,841	859	361,412	1,902	714,006	472,475
8520	Tucson, AZ	921,681	843,746	26.5	17,523	359,359	16,151,030	.2750	8,503,748	2,415	1,331,237	2,647	348,394	1,834	1,318,403	534,417
8560	Tulsa, OK	835,699	803,235	13.3	17,153	303,696	14,334,910	.2692	10,357,386	2,940	2,139,732	4,256	346,953	1,826	1,020,393	633,111

Source: Devonshire Associates Ltd. and Scan/US, Inc. 2005.

Estimates for Total Retail Sales, General Merchandise Sales, Apparel Store Sales, Food Store Sales and Health and Drug Store Sales are based on data from the U.S. Census Bureau's 1997 Economic Census and utilize the North American Industry Classification System (NAICS).

Continued on next page

Metropolitan Statistical Areas (MSAs): Population/Income/Sales[#], *Continued*

MSA FIPS Code	Metropolitan Statistical Area	Population Estimate 7/1/05	Population Census 4/1/00	% Change 4/1/90-4/1/00	Per Capita Income 2004	House-holds Estimate 7/1/05	Disposable Income 2004 ($1,000)	Market Ability Index 2004	Total Retail Sales 2004 Sales ($1,000)	Total Retail Sales Ranally Sales Units	General Merchandise 2004 Sales ($1,000)	General Merchandise Ranally Sales Units	Apparel Store 2004 Sales ($1,000)	Apparel Store Ranally Sales Units	Food Store Sales 2004 ($1,000)	Health & Drug Store Sales 2004 ($1,000)
8600	Tuscaloosa, AL	167,273	164,875	9.5	17,430	67,678	2,915,500	.0544	2,086,587	592	386,453	769	96,797	509	235,724	121,137
8640	Tyler, TX	189,133	174,706	15.5	16,668	68,560	3,152,460	.0649	2,900,030	823	492,616	980	195,885	1,031	351,168	135,119
8680	Utica-Rome, NY	297,654	299,896	-5.3	17,783	117,853	5,293,320	.0902	2,830,331	804	431,672	859	107,101	564	423,720	275,720
8720	Vallejo-Fairfield-Napa, CA (PMSA)	558,215	518,821	15.0	22,050	189,213	12,308,720	.1919	5,545,671	1,574	846,555	1,683	329,352	1,733	1,135,394	230,523
8735	Ventura, CA (PMSA)	813,570	753,197	12.6	23,388	262,514	19,028,060	.3036	9,778,861	2,777	1,019,623	2,028	564,619	2,972	1,522,187	578,898
8750	Victoria, TX	86,168	84,088	13.1	17,025	30,781	1,467,050	.0289	1,213,957	345	245,245	488	55,150	290	155,184	57,549
8760	Vineland-Millville-Bridgeton, NJ (PMSA)	151,331	146,438	6.1	17,001	50,414	2,572,830	.0457	1,545,886	439	141,137	281	57,136	301	329,106	128,153
8780	Visalia-Tulare-Porterville, CA	404,818	368,021	18.0	12,914	120,917	5,227,730	.0963	2,765,611	785	418,656	833	108,161	569	563,264	158,385
8800	Waco, TX	222,879	213,517	12.9	15,287	81,749	3,407,130	.0644	2,317,504	658	441,422	878	85,844	452	368,221	97,552
8840	Washington, DC-MD-VA-WV (PMSA)	5,407,889	4,923,153	16.6	26,922	2,009,841	145,592,220	2.1487	60,848,183	17,278	7,783,305	15,479	4,188,047	22,044	9,881,573	3,123,583
8880	Waterbury, CT (PMSA)	236,173	228,984	3.3	22,487	88,673	5,310,862	.0855	2,755,791	783	327,016	650	119,929	631	519,243	208,083
8920	Waterloo-Cedar Falls, IA	125,273	128,012	3.4	16,930	49,292	2,120,890	.0423	1,814,899	515	309,770	616	58,825	310	210,206	103,938
8940	Wausau, WI	128,048	125,834	9.0	19,994	51,263	2,560,230	.0472	1,913,179	543	394,943	785	40,798	215	199,109	39,650
8960	West Palm Beach-Boca Raton, FL	1,267,148	1,131,184	31.0	21,809	491,239	27,635,140	.4766	17,715,284	5,030	2,295,344	4,565	1,788,194	9,412	2,598,542	1,224,457
9000	Wheeling, WV-OH	148,237	153,172	-3.8	15,196	60,369	2,252,640	.0444	1,740,262	494	300,060	597	74,593	393	271,061	120,770
9040	Wichita, KS[2]	530,928	512,351	12.8	18,410	199,308	9,774,570	.1713	5,929,099	1,683	1,206,862	2,400	242,570	1,277	843,599	299,169
9080	Wichita Falls, TX	135,207	140,518	7.8	16,477	52,390	2,227,870	.0421	1,597,223	454	323,859	644	48,793	256	228,918	78,797
9140	Williamsport, PA	117,787	120,044	1.1	16,584	47,746	1,953,340	.0380	1,538,724	437	234,178	466	69,595	366	245,666	120,115
9160	Wilmington-Newark, DE-MD (PMSA)	621,190	586,216	14.2	21,444	222,221	13,320,550	.2345	9,010,751	2,558	1,104,639	2,197	405,684	2,135	1,412,354	525,513
9200	Wilmington, NC	260,741	233,450	36.3	19,520	110,120	5,089,570	.1004	4,532,400	1,287	630,092	1,253	190,657	1,004	544,694	240,204
9240	Worcester, MA-CT (PMSA)	538,836	511,389	6.9	21,458	199,998	11,562,194	.1922	6,487,555	1,844	667,599	1,328	319,795	1,684	983,866	494,022
9260	Yakima, WA	229,468	222,581	17.9	13,955	77,113	3,202,190	.0607	2,041,424	580	479,903	954	65,560	345	329,172	58,849
9270	Yolo, CA (PMSA)	189,696	168,660	19.5	17,604	65,586	3,339,440	.0553	1,581,386	449	108,998	217	28,406	150	369,339	83,914
9280	York, PA	403,361	381,751	12.4	20,209	154,303	8,151,520	.1339	4,206,302	1,194	585,240	1,164	159,393	839	714,134	198,492
9320	Youngstown-Warren, OH	578,504	594,746	-1.0	17,210	230,975	9,956,120	.1798	6,365,697	1,807	805,018	1,600	251,425	1,324	870,574	429,184
9340	Yuba City, CA	153,877	139,149	13.5	14,540	50,617	2,237,430	.0399	1,184,765	337	238,417	474	31,237	165	256,559	86,882
9360	Yuma, AZ	177,064	160,026	49.7	13,429	59,841	2,377,840	.0452	1,477,200	419	322,796	642	34,478	181	221,749	77,415
	MSA Total	239,593,150	225,948,810	13.9	20,240	88,274,983	4,849,464,495	83.4490	2,950,352,715	837,774	416,591,500	828,465	172,178,921	906,213	412,859,034	175,573,661

Source: Devonshire Associates Ltd. and Scan/US, Inc. 2005.
[#] Estimates for Total Retail Sales, General Merchandise Sales, Apparel Store Sales, Food Store Sales and Health and Drug Store Sales are based on data from the U.S. Census Bureau's 1997 Economic Census and utilize the North American Industry Classification System (NAICS).

[2] Data excludes Harvey county, Kansas (7/1/05 estimated population 34,021) which fails to meet published standards for MSA inclusion, but has been included with the Wichita MSA as the result of Congressional action.

Consolidated Metropolitan Statistical Areas (CMSAs): Population/Income/Sales#

CMSAs are MSAs of one million or more population that meet certain requirements officially established by the Office of Management and Budget (OMB). Each CMSA constitutes a comprehensive definition of one of the nation's large metropolitan complexes. Within each CMSA, the Bureau defines component portions termed PMSAs. Data for PMSAs are included in the table on page 37. Both CMSAs and PMSAs appear on the map on pages 36-37.

CMSA FIPS Code	Consolidated Metropolitan Statistical Area	Population Estimate 7/1/05	Population Census 4/1/00	Population % Change 4/1/90-4/1/00	Per Capita Income 2004	House-holds Estimate 7/1/05	Disposable Income 2004 ($1,000)	Market Ability Index 2004	Total Retail Sales 2004 Sales ($1,000)	Total Retail Sales Ranally Sales Units	General Merchandise 2004 Sales ($1,000)	General Merchandise Ranally Sales Units	Apparel Store 2004 Sales ($1,000)	Apparel Store Ranally Sales Units	Food Store Sales 2004 ($1,000)	Health & Drug Store 2004 ($1,000)
07	Boston-Worcester-Lawrence, MA-NH-ME-CT	5,974,626	5,819,100	6.7	23,762	2,218,791	141,968,675	2.3429	82,814,058	23,517	8,532,981	16,970	5,794,886	30,496	12,836,915	5,808,162
14	Chicago-Gary-Kenosha, IL-IN-WI	9,532,924	9,157,540	11.1	20,831	3,316,187	198,581,640	3.3260	112,306,471	31,890	13,317,060	26,484	6,361,877	33,482	14,769,303	9,701,795
21	Cincinnati-Hamilton, OH-KY-IN	2,037,766	1,979,202	8.9	20,603	793,993	41,984,270	.7160	25,094,891	7,124	3,559,156	7,076	1,213,333	6,388	3,539,372	1,428,962
28	Cleveland-Akron, OH	2,944,122	2,945,831	3.0	19,768	1,165,374	58,200,820	1.0275	37,917,926	10,767	3,873,189	7,703	1,839,936	9,683	5,529,367	3,880,280
31	Dallas-Fort Worth, TX	5,909,068	5,221,801	29.3	19,903	1,998,604	117,610,850	2.0769	77,010,933	21,869	11,064,290	22,001	4,043,460	21,282	9,907,736	3,205,313
34	Denver-Boulder-Greeley, CO[1]	2,784,667	2,581,506	30.4	24,357	1,138,802	67,824,970	1.0942	37,189,888	10,560	5,360,025	10,660	1,655,936	8,716	5,317,852	1,400,724
35	Detroit-Ann Arbor-Flint, MI	5,551,073	5,456,428	5.2	21,712	2,126,207	120,526,820	2.0697	75,997,592	21,580	12,442,600	24,744	3,549,123	18,679	8,821,838	5,594,790
42	Houston-Galveston-Brazoria, TX	5,242,969	4,669,571	25.2	18,027	1,732,789	94,512,820	1.7085	62,606,040	17,778	10,505,324	20,892	3,633,832	19,126	9,195,264	2,952,108
49	Los Angeles-Riverside-Orange County, CA	17,797,954	16,373,645	12.7	18,175	5,656,166	323,477,190	5.5373	179,005,294	50,829	22,596,646	44,938	13,718,406	72,203	27,995,671	9,960,320
56	Miami-Fort Lauderdale, FL	4,185,259	3,876,380	21.4	17,352	1,479,084	72,623,610	1.3474	50,918,437	14,458	5,870,371	11,675	4,094,867	21,553	6,700,811	3,737,983
63	Milwaukee-Racine, WI	1,716,448	1,689,572	5.1	20,458	671,142	35,115,230	.5902	19,848,556	5,635	2,959,865	5,886	652,778	3,435	2,758,299	1,367,764
70	New York-Northern NJ-Long Island, NY-NJ-CT-PA	21,887,706	21,199,865	8.4	23,261	7,835,549	509,125,445	8.0246	249,143,322	70,747	22,013,230	43,778	26,005,258	136,870	39,771,377	19,985,445
77	Philadelphia-Wilmington-Atlantic City, PA-NJ-DE-MD	6,345,752	6,188,463	5.0	21,611	2,352,394	137,135,830	2.3152	81,620,065	23,174	7,349,840	14,618	4,977,848	26,200	13,389,569	5,916,378
79	Portland-Salem, OR-WA	2,474,616	2,265,223	26.3	20,529	944,231	50,800,400	.8829	32,225,893	9,150	6,003,745	11,940	1,657,012	8,722	4,275,550	1,062,099
82	Sacramento-Yolo, CA	2,081,634	1,796,857	21.3	20,754	750,053	43,201,390	.7038	22,059,537	6,264	2,803,436	5,575	1,176,056	6,190	3,944,199	988,483
84	San Francisco-Oakland-San Jose, CA	7,114,596	7,039,362	12.6	26,973	2,542,139	191,902,390	3.0058	100,680,090	28,587	12,472,850	24,804	8,206,114	43,190	17,918,091	5,519,182
91	Seattle-Tacoma-Bremerton, WA	3,754,318	3,554,760	19.7	23,133	1,493,809	86,847,640	1.4323	49,777,419	14,135	8,131,706	16,173	2,680,058	14,106	6,637,117	2,071,467
97	Washington-Baltimore, DC-MD-VA-WV	8,207,016	7,608,070	13.1	25,344	3,060,637	208,001,340	3.1436	91,810,633	26,069	11,887,615	23,641	5,936,996	31,250	15,313,023	4,918,600
CMSA Total		**115,542,514**	**109,423,176**	**12.5**	**21,632**	**41,275,951**	**2,499,441,331**	**41.3448**	**1,388,027,046**	**394,133**	**170,743,929**	**339,558**	**97,197,777**	**511,571**	**208,621,355**	**89,499,856**

Source: Devonshire Associates Ltd. and Scan/US, Inc. 2005.
Estimates for Total Retail Sales, General Merchandise Sales, Apparel Store Sales, Food Store Sales and Health and Drug Store Sales are based on data from the U.S. Census Bureau's 1997 Economic Census and utilize the North American Industry Classification System (NAICS).

[1] Census population includes a portion of Broomfield county.

New England County Metropolitan Areas (NECMAs): Population/Income/Sales#

NECMA FIPS Code	New England County Metropolitan Area	Population Estimate 7/1/05	Population Census 4/1/00	Population % Change 4/1/90-4/1/00	Per Capita Income 2004	House-holds Estimate 7/1/05	Disposable Income 2004 ($1,000)	Market Ability Index 2004	Total Retail Sales 2004 Sales ($1,000)	Total Retail Sales Ranally Sales Units	General Merchandise 2004 Sales ($1,000)	General Merchandise Ranally Sales Units	Apparel Store 2004 Sales ($1,000)	Apparel Store Ranally Sales Units	Food Store Sales 2004 ($1,000)	Health & Drug Store 2004 ($1,000)
0733	Bangor, ME	149,585	144,919	-1.1	16,697	61,196	2,497,590	.0514	2,300,599	653	323,935	644	49,968	263	436,404	94,177
0743	Barnstable-Yarmouth, MA	232,312	222,230	19.1	23,822	99,127	5,534,160	.0937	3,512,843	997	198,575	395	245,378	1,291	737,688	261,847
1123	Boston-Worcester-Lawrence-Lowell-Brockton, MA-NH	6,204,190	6,057,826	6.5	23,615	2,308,128	146,514,600	2.4344	87,147,841	24,747	9,096,763	18,092	5,959,964	31,370	13,578,137	6,143,531
1303	Burlington, VT	206,121	198,889	12.3	20,067	77,913	4,136,190	.0789	3,407,950	968	302,836	602	168,595	888	548,209	184,224
3283	Hartford, CT	1,197,175	1,148,618	2.2	26,530	463,800	31,761,140	.4830	14,817,105	4,207	1,281,098	2,548	1,120,244	5,896	2,339,379	1,185,681
4243	Lewiston-Auburn, ME	107,666	103,793	-1.4	17,403	44,083	1,873,750	.0392	1,842,778	523	214,005	426	21,774	115	236,464	73,545
5483	New Haven-Bridgeport-Stamford-Danbury-Waterbury, CT	1,762,900	1,706,575	4.6	27,088	649,526	47,753,040	.7871	29,707,011	8,435	2,086,492	4,149	1,840,561	9,688	3,942,044	1,573,072
5523	New London-Norwich, CT	267,325	259,088	1.6	25,951	105,718	6,937,430	.1077	3,447,478	979	454,153	903	177,940	937	489,257	222,901
6323	Pittsfield, MA	131,527	134,953	-3.2	20,937	56,899	2,753,800	.0465	1,607,360	456	145,868	290	131,236	691	316,206	119,866
6403	Portland, ME	275,908	265,612	9.2	20,813	111,595	5,742,570	.1178	5,779,560	1,641	532,872	1,060	378,464	1,992	970,747	230,718
6483	Providence-Warwick-Pawtucket, RI	1,011,599	962,886	5.1	18,452	377,042	18,666,410	.3177	10,238,162	2,907	920,087	1,830	654,149	3,443	1,862,209	1,110,704
8003	Springfield, MA	617,467	608,479	0.9	19,371	236,204	11,960,690	.2014	6,549,226	1,860	654,872	1,302	337,410	1,776	1,255,145	537,042
NECMA Total		**12,163,775**	**11,813,868**	**5.4**	**23,523**	**4,591,231**	**286,131,370**	**4.7588**	**170,357,914**	**48,373**	**16,211,557**	**32,241**	**11,085,683**	**58,350**	**26,711,888**	**11,737,308**

Source: Devonshire Associates Ltd. and Scan/US, Inc. 2005.
Estimates for Total Retail Sales, General Merchandise Sales, Apparel Store Sales, Food Store Sales and Health and Drug Store Sales are based on data from the U.S. Census Bureau's 1997 Economic Census and utilize the North American Industry Classification System (NAICS).

Metropolitan Statistical Areas (MSAs): State Totals for Population/Income/Sales#

State	Population Estimate 7/1/05	Population Census 4/1/00	Population % Change 4/1/90-4/1/00	Per Capita Income 2004	House-holds Estimate 7/1/05	Disposable Income 2004 ($1,000)	Market Ability Index 2004	Total Retail Sales 2004 Sales ($1,000)	Total Retail Sales Ranally Sales Units	General Merchandise 2004 Sales ($1,000)	General Merchandise Ranally Sales Units	Apparel Store 2004 Sales ($1,000)	Apparel Store Ranally Sales Units	Food Store Sales 2004 ($1,000)	Health & Drug Store 2004 ($1,000)
Alabama	3,206,685	3,108,959	11.2	17,626	1,225,521	56,520,040	1.0323	38,105,017	10,820	7,410,945	14,738	1,877,390	9,882	4,584,139	1,981,156
Alaska	278,263	260,283	15.0	23,461	103,824	6,528,250	.1139	4,510,522	1,281	1,086,418	2,161	230,765	1,215	522,594	52,268
Arizona	5,207,416	4,527,000	41.4	18,562	1,901,142	96,657,920	1.6804	57,384,186	16,294	8,281,555	16,469	2,185,042	11,500	7,665,989	3,020,875
Arkansas	1,411,360	1,321,019	19.1	17,529	550,904	24,739,180	.4714	18,922,417	5,373	4,730,723	9,407	686,166	3,612	1,624,237	734,286
California	35,230,631	32,750,394	13.7	19,847	11,652,679	699,218,200	11.7023	381,264,798	108,259	48,245,081	95,943	27,698,393	145,782	63,304,399	21,189,152
Colorado	3,913,508	3,607,656	29.8	23,285	1,594,787	91,127,260	1.4936	51,351,868	14,582	8,141,779	16,192	2,073,457	10,915	6,933,281	1,898,525
Connecticut	3,372,438	3,256,900	3.5	26,759	1,271,862	90,241,652	1.4259	48,586,132	13,802	3,961,608	7,876	3,116,125	16,405	6,911,519	3,128,757
Delaware	663,422	626,962	13.4	20,726	239,157	13,749,920	.2480	9,824,909	2,790	1,373,022	2,730	410,062	2,158	1,465,818	557,817
District of Columbia	548,902	572,059	-5.7	26,120	245,648	14,337,490	.1918	3,540,123	1,005	143,774	286	501,970	2,642	938,614	520,795
Florida	16,398,330	14,837,497	23.4	19,390	6,350,757	317,958,310	5.6498	208,933,564	59,331	28,312,221	56,303	13,317,234	70,095	28,963,227	13,444,331
Georgia	6,286,014	5,666,664	30.2	20,492	2,273,070	128,811,680	2.2545	83,440,468	23,691	12,184,112	24,230	4,410,806	23,217	11,301,438	3,638,903
Hawaii	910,475	876,156	4.8	20,281	302,181	18,465,370	.3063	9,903,032	2,812	1,988,367	3,954	1,320,832	6,952	1,401,658	865,911
Idaho	579,559	507,910	40.4	18,439	217,293	10,686,740	.1999	7,965,071	2,262	1,439,475	2,863	251,289	1,322	1,070,029	277,518
Illinois	10,938,021	10,541,708	10.1	20,787	3,900,135	227,372,460	3.8251	130,398,197	37,027	16,526,031	32,868	6,957,909	36,621	17,377,887	10,853,117
Indiana	4,566,255	4,389,903	10.8	18,515	1,711,341	84,546,440	1.5688	61,735,552	17,534	11,230,713	22,335	2,270,761	11,952	5,970,878	3,768,059
Iowa	1,374,023	1,326,133	10.5	19,310	539,031	26,532,150	.4861	19,107,401	5,425	2,881,685	5,731	731,749	3,852	2,368,143	994,760
Kansas[1]	1,574,120	1,488,194	14.3	20,658	602,662	32,518,560	.5577	19,812,937	5,626	3,511,775	6,984	965,182	5,080	2,644,709	1,043,753
Kentucky	2,045,056	1,973,102	10.9	19,123	798,594	39,108,360	.6897	24,857,324	7,057	4,242,462	8,437	1,151,832	6,064	2,752,571	1,620,459
Louisiana	3,426,647	3,370,210	6.7	16,486	1,279,396	56,491,180	1.0733	41,202,628	11,702	8,148,916	16,204	2,069,796	10,893	5,164,814	2,583,840
Maine	485,788	466,606	5.3	20,056	197,685	9,742,792	.1922	8,773,595	2,494	896,161	1,784	427,937	2,252	1,405,735	369,873
Maryland	5,235,998	4,911,040	10.6	23,918	1,929,273	125,234,920	1.9305	57,396,873	16,296	7,137,227	14,194	3,335,767	17,558	10,152,513	3,009,819
Massachusetts	6,218,544	6,101,425	5.4	23,235	2,329,766	144,489,531	2.3533	79,577,090	22,602	7,212,180	14,339	5,858,805	30,832	12,921,015	6,291,597
Michigan	8,349,763	8,169,466	6.1	20,996	3,222,086	175,315,440	3.0409	111,920,120	31,780	20,656,406	41,079	4,961,973	26,114	12,249,987	7,542,608
Minnesota	3,659,835	3,463,360	15.0	23,384	1,463,916	85,580,440	1.4861	58,132,464	16,508	8,957,142	17,813	2,092,369	11,013	7,023,863	2,627,709
Mississippi	1,086,942	1,023,662	17.1	17,418	397,816	18,932,820	.3539	13,612,338	3,866	3,237,443	6,439	521,567	2,745	1,246,220	776,280
Missouri	3,943,727	3,794,801	8.7	20,413	1,588,263	80,504,260	1.3915	49,977,236	14,190	7,744,195	15,401	1,631,642	8,589	5,784,086	3,042,304
Montana	315,311	305,511	13.2	17,393	129,637	5,484,150	.1100	4,827,078	1,371	1,027,863	2,043	143,345	754	508,685	157,198
Nebraska	954,896	899,838	14.3	19,208	361,346	18,341,880	.3349	13,035,037	3,701	1,909,452	3,798	486,562	2,560	1,637,966	777,569
Nevada	2,125,806	1,747,736	72.4	19,427	785,355	41,298,060	.7212	25,696,232	7,297	3,727,926	7,414	1,546,946	8,142	3,767,078	1,109,936
New Hampshire	792,116	739,699	12.3	23,154	298,440	18,340,820	.3512	16,228,427	4,607	2,755,842	5,482	683,504	3,595	2,381,373	581,730
New Jersey	8,781,525	8,414,350	8.9	25,405	3,158,187	223,094,560	3.4949	113,098,864	32,114	9,425,753	18,747	7,807,303	41,090	20,203,086	7,598,965
New Mexico	1,119,773	1,035,055	23.0	17,899	423,440	20,043,100	.3611	13,059,263	3,709	2,616,212	5,203	545,438	2,869	1,190,368	719,807
New York	17,821,611	17,473,058	5.8	21,033	6,570,626	374,839,720	5.9928	179,860,918	51,071	18,592,719	36,975	20,213,513	106,387	28,261,152	15,793,762
North Carolina	5,916,205	5,437,056	24.3	19,724	2,298,475	116,692,690	2.0820	78,481,100	22,286	11,018,583	21,912	3,895,195	20,500	9,591,291	4,233,204
North Dakota	290,968	283,966	10.3	18,051	117,031	5,252,370	.1124	5,522,404	1,568	905,752	1,802	174,863	919	462,550	270,985
Ohio	9,311,374	9,213,776	4.4	19,491	3,668,549	181,491,860	3.2353	120,855,498	34,314	15,576,005	30,976	5,562,713	29,277	16,509,647	8,550,416
Oklahoma	2,184,596	2,098,362	12.2	17,095	818,601	37,344,620	.6905	25,645,854	7,281	5,074,246	10,093	839,030	4,415	2,655,924	1,482,222
Oregon	2,684,622	2,502,366	21.7	20,234	1,057,642	54,320,190	.9699	37,189,143	10,559	6,784,741	13,492	1,790,871	9,427	4,897,221	1,147,490
Pennsylvania	10,505,749	10,391,529	3.1	19,306	4,068,578	202,823,500	3.5858	130,776,342	37,133	13,492,598	26,831	7,240,303	38,105	20,640,236	9,126,432
Rhode Island	1,033,642	986,351	5.1	18,594	385,944	19,219,226	.3245	10,298,647	2,923	892,279	1,771	646,517	3,399	1,869,919	1,130,026
South Carolina	2,989,986	2,806,962	15.9	17,725	1,123,820	52,996,270	.9804	37,350,310	10,606	6,267,197	12,462	2,268,313	11,940	4,936,015	2,005,132
South Dakota	284,711	260,977	18.3	19,147	112,719	5,451,250	.1250	6,858,562	1,947	1,153,071	2,294	152,290	801	478,588	269,306
Tennessee	4,045,245	3,862,144	16.7	18,993	1,584,321	76,832,300	1.4289	57,304,927	16,272	9,933,918	19,754	3,319,841	17,472	6,195,159	3,452,798
Texas	19,616,791	17,691,880	24.9	17,531	6,627,912	343,896,380	6.4300	248,565,345	70,583	38,212,067	75,989	13,123,694	69,076	32,938,146	10,881,487
Utah	1,842,542	1,708,496	27.4	17,303	590,009	31,882,010	.6110	24,623,853	6,992	4,296,578	8,544	994,219	5,232	3,410,227	533,975
Vermont	174,694	169,391	11.8	20,568	66,606	3,593,134	.0700	3,177,523	901	307,137	611	138,077	728	483,213	174,562
Virginia	5,955,628	5,528,068	15.8	22,476	2,222,205	133,860,970	2.1903	73,413,583	20,848	11,610,458	23,092	4,333,681	22,812	9,832,105	3,677,808
Washington	5,228,627	4,899,154	21.4	21,674	2,042,689	113,324,350	1.8951	65,416,150	18,576	11,295,603	22,465	3,272,179	17,223	9,147,246	2,752,136
West Virginia	773,158	765,568	2.3	17,378	315,070	13,436,060	.2448	8,896,259	2,527	1,620,512	3,222	375,375	1,976	981,683	782,801
Wisconsin	3,776,382	3,640,308	9.3	20,513	1,498,049	77,463,860	1.3342	47,651,976	13,530	7,994,904	15,900	1,521,666	8,006	5,894,775	2,480,157
Wyoming	155,470	148,140	10.2	17,558	60,943	2,729,800	.0536	2,283,559	649	418,665	833	46,663	246	236,019	49,287
MSA Total	**239,593,150**	**225,948,810**	**13.9**	**20,240**	**88,274,983**	**4,849,464,495**	**83.4490**	**2,950,352,715**	**837,774**	**416,591,500**	**828,465**	**172,178,921**	**906,213**	**412,859,034**	**175,573,661**

Source: Devonshire Associates Ltd. and Scan/US, Inc. 2005.
Estimates for Total Retail Sales, General Merchandise Sales, Apparel Store Sales, Food Store Sales and Health and Drug Store Sales are based on data from the U.S. Census Bureau's 1997 Economic Census and utilize the North American Industry Classification System (NAICS).

[1] Data for Kansas excludes Harvey county, Kansas (7/1/05 estimated population 34,021) which fails to meet published standards for MSA inclusion, but has been included with the Wichita MSA as the result of Congressional action.

150 Largest Metropolitan Statistical Areas (MSAs): Population/Income/Sales#

This table lists the 150 largest Metropolitan Statistical Areas (MSAs) and Primary Metropolitan Statistical Areas (PMSAs), ranked by July 1, 2005 estimated population. The data shown are consistent with the data on the MSA Table which appears on pages 40-42. A map showing the MSAs, with a detailed explanation of how they are determined, appears on pages 36-37. An explanation of MSAs may also be found in the Introduction on pages 5-9.

MSA Rank	Metropolitan Statistical Area	Population			Per Capita Income 2004	House-holds Estimate 7/1/05	Disposable Income 2004 ($1,000)	Market Ability Index 2004	Total Retail Sales		General Merchandise		Apparel Store		Food Store Sales 2004 ($1,000)	Health & Drug Store 2004 ($1,000)
		Estimate 7/1/05	Census 4/1/00	% Change 4/1/90-4/1/00					2004 Sales ($1,000)	Ranally Sales Units	2004 Sales ($1,000)	Ranally Sales Units	2004 Sales ($1,000)	Ranally Sales Units		
1	Los Angeles-Long Beach, CA (PMSA)	10,076,928	9,519,338	7.4	16,791	3,192,402	169,200,500	2.9617	95,230,986	27,041	11,726,649	23,321	7,977,490	41,987	15,007,662	5,683,828
2	New York, NY (PMSA)	9,499,149	9,314,235	9.0	19,586	3,492,463	186,052,060	2.9271	78,543,603	22,302	7,481,382	14,877	13,218,413	69,572	12,199,167	8,872,091
3	Chicago, IL (PMSA)	8,619,113	8,272,768	11.6	21,095	2,984,840	181,820,540	3.0339	102,348,553	29,062	11,736,404	23,340	5,964,334	31,390	13,488,123	8,936,424
4	Washington, DC-MD-VA-WV (PMSA)	5,407,889	4,923,153	16.6	26,922	2,009,841	145,592,220	2.1487	60,848,183	17,278	7,783,305	15,479	4,188,047	22,044	9,881,573	3,123,583
5	Philadelphia, PA-NJ (PMSA)	5,210,435	5,100,931	3.6	21,642	1,928,013	112,763,060	1.8967	66,353,040	18,840	5,657,668	11,252	4,171,829	21,957	10,601,780	4,949,698
6	Houston, TX (PMSA)	4,689,135	4,177,646	25.8	17,810	1,532,154	83,514,340	1.5344	57,776,090	16,406	9,476,893	18,847	3,420,696	18,004	8,393,316	2,702,292
7	Atlanta, GA	4,657,401	4,112,198	38.9	21,747	1,661,826	101,285,150	1.7416	64,204,134	18,229	8,644,892	17,194	3,419,869	18,001	8,840,483	2,720,352
8	Detroit, MI (PMSA)	4,472,407	4,441,551	4.1	21,721	1,715,343	97,145,860	1.6723	61,752,046	17,534	9,851,389	19,591	3,029,987	15,947	7,262,506	4,742,686
9	Dallas, TX (PMSA)	3,984,198	3,519,176	31.5	20,413	1,343,196	81,327,990	1.4200	52,155,059	14,810	8,148,528	16,203	2,913,107	15,333	6,769,241	2,168,854
10	Riverside-San Bernardino, CA (PMSA)	3,886,808	3,254,821	25.7	16,596	1,212,880	64,505,060	1.1101	33,712,896	9,573	4,782,057	9,510	1,947,213	10,249	5,672,476	1,586,227
11	Phoenix-Mesa, AZ	3,801,803	3,251,876	45.3	19,272	1,365,972	73,268,000	1.2707	44,288,930	12,576	6,083,481	12,098	1,737,542	9,145	5,560,900	2,306,866
12	Boston, MA-NH (PMSA)	3,452,176	3,406,829	5.5	25,382	1,296,664	87,624,672	1.3994	47,507,067	13,491	4,239,209	8,431	4,248,638	22,358	7,462,025	3,825,518
13	Minneapolis-St. Paul, MN-WI	3,154,675	2,968,806	16.9	24,093	1,251,827	76,004,390	1.3070	50,893,048	14,452	7,484,790	14,884	1,876,788	9,878	6,162,603	2,302,183
14	Orange County, CA (PMSA)	3,020,648	2,846,289	18.1	23,420	988,370	70,743,570	1.1619	40,282,551	11,438	5,068,317	10,079	3,229,084	16,995	5,793,345	2,111,368
15	San Diego, CA	2,990,693	2,813,833	12.6	19,889	1,027,661	59,482,050	1.0104	34,231,355	9,720	4,237,412	8,427	2,478,722	13,046	5,315,838	1,790,799
16	Nassau-Suffolk, NY (PMSA)	2,842,538	2,753,913	5.5	26,972	934,263	76,669,060	1.2211	42,600,443	12,097	4,137,605	8,229	3,648,276	19,201	6,184,752	2,937,674
17	St. Louis, MO-IL	2,672,574	2,603,607	4.5	20,958	1,058,488	56,011,440	.9377	31,775,486	9,023	4,883,008	9,712	1,197,116	6,302	4,351,956	2,236,203
18	Baltimore, MD (PMSA)	2,658,807	2,552,994	7.2	22,490	997,379	59,797,030	.9484	29,277,161	8,312	3,797,673	7,552	1,701,986	8,959	5,186,939	1,711,640
19	Tampa-St. Petersburg-Clearwater, FL	2,613,412	2,395,997	15.9	19,546	1,065,621	51,081,900	.9188	35,052,229	9,954	4,364,151	8,679	1,494,823	7,868	4,733,677	2,309,521
20	Seattle-Bellevue-Everett, WA (PMSA)	2,517,924	2,414,616	18.8	24,683	1,027,123	62,148,740	1.0211	36,512,076	10,368	5,326,255	10,593	2,234,950	11,763	4,806,692	1,509,870
21	Oakland, CA (PMSA)	2,497,921	2,392,557	14.9	24,937	865,288	62,290,960	.9545	28,700,509	8,149	3,388,368	6,738	1,577,698	8,304	5,522,794	1,487,100
22	Miami, FL (PMSA)	2,391,206	2,253,362	16.3	15,028	782,688	35,933,990	.6861	24,937,816	7,081	2,984,280	5,935	2,500,650	13,162	3,337,422	2,044,796
23	Pittsburgh, PA	2,329,028	2,358,695	-1.5	18,398	953,217	42,850,160	.7685	28,055,533	7,967	3,252,438	6,467	1,323,802	6,966	4,509,281	2,003,571
24	Denver, CO (PMSA)[1]	2,271,459	2,109,282	30.0	24,810	938,966	56,355,400	.9073	31,014,716	8,807	4,643,809	9,235	1,491,361	7,850	4,280,226	1,191,900
25	Cleveland-Lorain-Elyria, OH (PMSA)	2,239,726	2,250,871	2.2	19,873	892,883	44,511,170	.7797	28,379,441	8,058	2,952,752	5,873	1,438,587	7,571	4,208,298	3,036,617
26	Portland-Vancouver, OR-WA (PMSA)	2,099,630	1,918,009	26.6	21,192	812,973	44,495,920	.7688	28,227,950	8,015	5,153,465	10,249	1,511,846	7,958	3,698,130	926,589
27	Newark, NJ (PMSA)	2,095,245	2,032,989	6.1	25,419	739,306	53,259,010	.8289	26,350,323	7,482	1,623,331	3,229	1,856,413	9,770	4,910,221	1,850,721
28	Fort Worth-Arlington, TX (PMSA)	1,924,870	1,702,625	25.1	18,850	655,408	36,282,860	.6569	24,855,874	7,059	2,915,762	5,798	1,130,353	5,949	3,138,495	1,036,459
29	Las Vegas, NV-AZ	1,918,279	1,563,282	83.3	18,761	706,472	35,989,540	.6324	22,330,283	6,341	3,153,624	6,272	1,408,481	7,413	3,397,026	964,794
30	Orlando, FL	1,900,560	1,644,561	34.3	19,478	701,773	37,018,160	.6726	26,135,598	7,423	3,848,482	7,653	1,791,331	9,428	3,390,238	1,412,260
31	Sacramento, CA (PMSA)	1,891,938	1,628,197	21.5	21,069	684,467	39,861,950	.6485	20,478,151	5,815	2,694,438	5,358	1,147,650	6,040	3,574,860	904,570
32	Kansas City, MO-KS	1,889,911	1,776,062	12.2	21,485	744,584	40,605,020	.6954	25,222,364	7,162	3,845,162	7,647	985,915	5,190	2,874,928	1,328,445
33	Fort Lauderdale, FL (PMSA)	1,794,053	1,623,018	29.3	20,451	696,396	36,689,620	.6613	25,980,621	7,377	2,886,091	5,740	1,594,217	8,391	3,363,389	1,693,187
34	San Antonio, TX	1,745,135	1,592,383	20.2	16,688	605,290	29,122,710	.5469	20,676,442	5,871	2,951,205	5,869	1,191,906	6,274	3,059,804	830,072
35	Indianapolis, IN	1,724,043	1,607,486	16.4	20,046	649,692	34,559,880	.6243	24,378,934	6,924	4,368,601	8,688	966,234	5,086	2,147,629	1,582,166
36	Cincinnati, OH-KY-IN (PMSA)	1,688,541	1,646,395	7.9	20,542	661,875	34,685,280	.6008	21,779,620	6,183	3,117,466	6,198	1,144,705	6,027	2,992,762	1,254,371
37	Charlotte-Gastonia-Rock Hill, NC-SC	1,686,002	1,499,293	29.0	21,005	648,683	35,414,250	.6081	21,907,722	6,220	3,117,357	6,200	1,045,991	5,504	2,725,308	1,238,736
38	San Jose, CA (PMSA)	1,669,973	1,682,585	12.4	29,371	557,576	49,048,290	.7777	28,016,175	7,955	3,571,238	7,102	2,391,823	12,589	4,358,548	1,477,292
39	San Francisco, CA (PMSA)	1,669,327	1,731,183	8.0	30,643	667,243	51,153,900	.8069	29,312,056	8,323	3,664,351	7,288	3,463,886	18,231	5,083,572	1,701,395
40	Norfolk-Virginia Beach-Newport News, VA-NC	1,650,742	1,569,541	8.8	17,958	602,650	29,644,350	.5210	17,865,597	5,073	2,872,048	5,712	1,052,683	5,541	2,296,955	817,388
41	Columbus, OH	1,639,166	1,540,157	14.5	20,212	624,436	33,131,310	.6061	24,357,956	6,916	2,930,602	5,828	1,119,931	5,895	2,814,809	992,965
42	Milwaukee-Waukesha, WI (PMSA)	1,521,473	1,500,741	4.8	20,533	597,839	31,239,920	.5262	17,833,569	5,063	2,618,965	5,208	605,954	3,189	2,459,679	1,231,828
43	Austin-San Marcos, TX	1,453,856	1,249,763	47.7	21,294	525,442	30,958,890	.6241	30,159,309	8,564	2,441,369	4,855	1,101,729	5,800	3,038,880	1,493,719
44	Salt Lake City-Ogden, UT	1,426,891	1,333,914	24.4	17,943	468,349	25,602,800	.4908	20,210,119	5,739	3,404,248	6,770	845,948	4,452	2,719,564	447,921
45	Bergen-Passaic, NJ (PMSA)	1,410,908	1,373,167	7.4	26,454	497,988	37,324,830	.5956	20,662,302	5,867	1,801,247	3,582	1,681,158	8,848	3,591,953	1,403,095
46	Raleigh-Durham-Chapel Hill, NC	1,360,180	1,187,941	38.9	22,041	521,946	29,979,320	.5134	18,916,873	5,372	2,503,225	4,978	1,006,058	5,294	2,505,533	848,678
47	New Orleans, LA	1,329,657	1,337,726	4.1	16,844	494,477	22,397,090	.4147	15,301,973	4,347	2,688,387	5,347	940,553	4,950	2,125,707	1,165,355
48	Nashville, TN	1,324,828	1,231,311	25.0	20,939	510,191	27,740,880	.5019	20,127,372	5,716	3,353,344	6,668	1,044,827	5,498	2,326,601	1,180,599
49	Greensboro—Winston-Salem—High Point, NC	1,322,689	1,251,509	19.2	19,046	518,301	25,192,450	.4552	17,241,148	4,896	2,220,660	4,415	857,366	4,514	2,013,241	1,034,100
50	West Palm Beach-Boca Raton, FL	1,267,148	1,131,184	31.0	21,809	491,239	27,635,140	.4766	17,715,284	5,030	2,295,344	4,565	1,788,194	9,412	2,598,542	1,224,457
51	Middlesex-Somerset-Hunterdon, NJ (PMSA)	1,254,329	1,169,641	14.7	29,321	439,191	36,777,750	.5590	18,175,229	5,161	1,505,044	2,994	1,121,242	5,900	2,953,420	975,370
52	Providence-Fall River-Warwick, RI-MA	1,241,359	1,188,613	4.8	18,787	465,655	23,321,729	.4004	13,384,443	3,799	1,469,736	2,919	904,070	4,755	2,254,684	1,377,419
53	Hartford, CT	1,227,673	1,183,110	2.2	26,184	473,622	32,144,998	.4835	14,232,627	4,044	1,296,944	2,578	976,829	5,144	2,229,698	1,212,028
54	Jacksonville, FL	1,224,737	1,100,491	21.4	20,764	470,038	25,430,140	.4361	15,548,123	4,415	2,163,127	4,301	792,713	4,173	2,167,951	746,799
55	Monmouth-Ocean, NJ (PMSA)	1,213,007	1,126,217	14.2	26,287	453,624	31,886,460	.4923	15,656,156	4,446	1,406,895	2,798	983,110	5,175	3,042,376	997,766
56	Memphis, TN-AR-MS	1,188,935	1,135,614	12.7	18,374	447,194	21,845,960	.3937	14,505,139	4,118	2,535,346	5,043	866,405	4,560	1,405,128	1,036,338
57	Buffalo-Niagara Falls, NY	1,154,526	1,170,111	-1.6	20,193	477,362	23,313,710	.3832	12,048,915	3,421	1,230,258	2,447	724,512	3,813	2,155,690	978,261
58	Grand Rapids-Muskegon-Holland, MI	1,144,317	1,088,514	16.1	19,772	428,897	22,625,540	.4000	14,799,151	4,202	3,176,156	6,317	520,071	2,738	1,291,001	738,655
59	Oklahoma City, OK	1,142,506	1,083,346	13.0	17,418	437,517	19,900,220	.3654	13,542,593	3,845	2,453,982	4,881	448,693	2,361	1,416,033	771,990
60	Rochester, NY	1,106,020	1,098,201	3.4	21,353	429,111	23,617,250	.3845	12,264,371	3,483	1,401,369	2,787	575,969	3,031	2,347,424	626,020
61	Louisville, KY-IN	1,055,433	1,025,598	8.1	19,246	412,458	20,312,520	.3556	12,636,394	3,588	2,198,239	4,372	514,793	2,710	1,341,926	835,632
62	Richmond-Petersburg, VA	1,053,657	996,512	15.1	19,761	389,531	20,821,320	.3643	13,186,716	3,744	2,317,775	4,610	706,378	3,719	1,769,512	827,046
63	Fresno, CA	1,023,612	922,516	22.1	13,455	310,660	13,772,950	.2578	8,098,841	2,300	1,107,057	2,201	341,667	1,798	1,458,744	503,267
64	Greenville-Spartanburg-Anderson, SC	1,011,759	962,441	15.9	17,565	382,174	17,771,980	.3329	12,935,864	3,673	1,862,457	3,703	695,042	3,658	1,615,194	801,432
65	Birmingham, AL	952,851	921,106	9.6	19,050	368,193	18,152,200	.3241	11,979,568	3,402	1,973,330	3,924	623,491	3,282	1,471,521	601,380
66	Dayton-Springfield, OH	942,462	950,558	-0.1	19,838	381,183	18,696,450	.3254	11,656,512	3,310	1,897,994	3,774	486,276	2,558	1,587,983	649,452
67	Tucson, AZ	921,681	843,746	26.5	17,523	359,359	16,151,030	.2750	8,503,748	2,415	1,331,237	2,647	348,394	1,834	1,318,403	534,417
68	Honolulu, HI	910,475	876,156	4.8	20,281	302,181	18,465,370	.3063	9,903,032	2,812	1,988,367	3,954	1,320,832	6,952	1,401,658	865,911
69	Albany-Schenectady-Troy, NY	900,791	875,583	1.6	21,591	358,455	19,449,370	.3176	10,308,913	2,927	1,204,857	2,396	592,503	3,118	1,364,827	663,496
70	Tulsa, OK	835,699	803,235	13.3	17,153	303,696	14,334,910	.2692	10,357,386	2,940	2,139,732	4,256	346,953	1,826	1,020,393	633,111
71	Ventura, CA (PMSA)	813,570	753,197	12.6	23,388	262,514	19,028,060	.3036	9,778,861	2,777	1,019,623	2,028	564,619	2,972	1,522,187	578,898
72	Albuquerque, NM	772,209	712,738	21.0	18,422	298,024	14,225,380	.2575	9,597,929	2,726	1,906,111	3,791	340,445	1,791	802,412	511,305
73	Tacoma, WA (PMSA)	765,698	700,820	19.6	19,356	283,473	14,820,820	.2482	7,947,017	2,257	1,476,200	2,936	288,392	1,518	1,044,483	335,167
74	Omaha, NE-IA	756,323	716,998	12.1	19,499	287,638	14,747,300	.2730	11,005,219	3,124	1,417,220	2,819	405,125	2,132	1,290,290	622,424
75	Bakersfield, CA	743,729	661,645	21.7	14,153	234,348	10,526,210	.1907	5,759,480	1,635	787,831	1,567	234,327	1,233	863,026	390,768
76	Syracuse, NY	740,003	732,117	-1.4	19,682	290,321	14,564,740	.2429	7,780,798	2,209	820,305	1,631	412,184	2,170	1,430,926	573,891
77	Knoxville, TN	728,734	687,249	17.3	18,458	297,259	13,450,740	.2703	12,241,599	3,476	1,948,737	3,875	719,740	3,789	1,270,074	639,245
78	El Paso, TX	720,147	679,622	14.9	11,701	218,789	8,426,220	.1787	6,673,517	1,895	1,498,168	2,979	459,278	2,417	781,502	305,744
79	Akron, OH (PMSA)	704,396	694,960	5.7	19,435	272,491	13,689,650	.2478	9,538,485	2,709	920,437	1,830	401,349	2,112	1,321,069	843,663
80	McAllen-Edinburg-Mission, TX	675,597	569,463	48.5	8,316	179,247	5,618,500	.1432	5,723,037	1,625	1,172,978	2,333	428,765	2,257	870,770	248,513
81	Stockton-Lodi, CA	674,080	563,598	17.3	15,489	201,595	10,441,010	.1808	5,234,961	1,486	683,333	1,359	247,667	1,304	900,861	341,266
82	Allentown-Bethlehem-Easton, PA	672,335	637,958	7.2	19,306	253,826	12,980,260	.2270	8,072,675	2,293	826,404	1,643	344,846	1,814	1,380,468	582,180
83	Sarasota-Bradenton, FL	659,642	589,959	20.5	22,508	289,874	14,847,510	.2476	8,683,476	2,466	1,053,100	2,094	544,300	2,865	1,298,388	549,755
84	Gary, IN (PMSA)	645,927	631,362	4.4	18,131	231,992	11,711,290	.2085	7,414,460	2,106	1,138,119	2,263	262,852	1,383	958,556	582,985
85	Harrisburg-Lebanon-Carlisle, PA	644,200	629,401	7.0	20,516	260,218	13,216,590	.2389	9,452,727	2,684	945,453	1,880	342,116	1,801	1,274,186	498,443
86	Ann Arbor, MI (PMSA)	633,040	578,736	18.1	24,094	243,947	15,252,770	.2514	8,932,166	2,537	1,549,143	3,081	327,587	1,724	947,477	458,502
87	Baton Rouge, LA	627,014	602,894	14.1	17,163	222,147	10,761,580	.2029	7,857,816	2,232	1,504,974	2,993	352,913	1,857	906,884	395,165
88	Wilmington-Newark, DE-MD (PMSA)	621,190	586,216	14.2	21,444	222,221	13,320,550	.2345	9,010,751	2,558	1,104,639	2,197	405,684	2,135	1,412,354	525,513
89	Toledo, OH	618,775	618,203	0.7	18,518	244,572	11,458,640	.2113	8,206,394	2,330	1,249,737	2,486	332,651	1,751	1,125,745	484,420
90	Scranton—Wilkes-Barre—Hazleton, PA	612,464	624,776	-2.1	16,616	247,987	10,176,730	.1934	7,459,598	2,118	981,413	1,951	370,102	1,947	1,296,555	521,290
91	Little Rock-North Little Rock, AR	612,049	583,845	13.8	19,375	248,420	11,858,670	.2224	9,167,590	2,603	1,874,491	3,728	337,843	1,778	740,411	311,574
92	Jersey City, NJ (PMSA)	607,051	608,975	10.1	19,048	220,754	11,563,320	.1812	4,658,618	1,323	361,795	719	554,459	2,918	870,328	384,860
93	Springfield, MA	601,031	591,932	0.7	19,303	230,127	11,601,550	.1949	6,305,655	1,793	549,251	1,090	328,187	1,725	1,226,270	537,359
94	Charleston-North Charleston, SC	586,872	549,033	8.3	17,044	210,746	10,002,730	.1828	6,608,271	1,877	1,199,377	2,385	418,395	2,203	993,263	297,458
95	Youngstown-Warren, OH	578,504	594,746	-1.0	17,210	230,975	9,956,120	.1798	6,365,697	1,807	805,018	1,600	251,425	1,324	870,574	429,184
96	Columbia, SC	573,167	536,691	18.4	19,044	218,427	10,915,360	.1999	7,794,655	2,213	1,593,880	3,169	430,539	2,266	942,757	402,030
97	Colorado Springs, CO	570,479	516,929	30.2	20,654	218,133	11,782,890	.2021	7,180,198	2,039	1,264,761	2,515	198,849	1,047	725,989	271,165
98	New Haven-Meriden, CT (PMSA)	560,471	542,149	2.3	25,013	208,851	14,019,262	.2219	7,289,069	2,070	577,222	1,148	471,228	2,481	1,135,348	508,832
99	Vallejo-Fairfield-Napa, CA (PMSA)	558,215	518,821	15.0	22,050	189,213	12,308,720	.1919	5,545,671	1,574	846,555	1,683	329,352	1,733	1,135,394	230,523
100	Mobile, AL	558,139	540,258	13.3	15,224	191,163	8,497,060	.1626	5,993,132	1,702	1,221,428	2,429	352,485	1,855	737,702	358,432
101	Daytona Beach, FL	554,014	493,175	23.5	18,262	220,945	10,117,500	.1771	6,075,367	1,725	882,131	1,754	253,960	1,337	957,383	421,164
102	Worcester, MA-CT (PMSA)	538,836	511,389	6.9	21,458	199,998	11,562,194	.1922	6,487,555	1,844	667,599	1,328	319,795	1,684	983,866	494,022
103	Wichita, KS[2]	530,928	512,351	12.8	18,410	199,308	9,774,570	.1713	5,929,099	1,683	1,206,862	2,400	242,570	1,277	843,599	299,169
104	Lakeland-Winter Haven, FL	526,208	483,924	19.4	17,926	205,086	9,432,930	.1709	6,270,722	1,781	1,004,624	1,998	225,818	1,189	1,044,350	328,355
105	Melbourne-Titusville-Palm Bay, FL	523,567	476,230	19.4	20,941	216,202	10,963,820	.1797	5,760,123	1,636	986,272	1,961	242,067	1,274	880,605	408,228
106	Fort Myers-Cape Coral, FL	523,512	440,888	31.6	21,374	219,465	11,189,420	.1957	7,409,505	2,104	1,087,208	2,162	462,470	2,434	956,522	481,928
107	Fort Wayne, IN	519,862	502,141	10.1	17,648	187,695	9,174,710	.1697	6,438,496	1,829	1,202,048	2,390	228,385	1,203	669,795	352,604
108	Modesto, CA	519,823	446,997	20.6	15,585	161,250	8,101,680	.1473	4,910,210	1,394	756,250	1,504	190,893	1,005	890,064	318,684
109	Lexington, KY	507,373	479,198	18.0	19,329	203,505	9,806,860	.1775	6,817,904	1,936	1,077,408	2,142	367,739	1,935	687,458	415,723
110	Boise City, ID	504,057	432,345	46.1	18,751	188,844	9,451,660	.1759	7,007,764	1,990	1,276,182	2,538	230,777	1,214	916,023	230,300
111	Augusta-Aiken, GA-SC	494,516	477,441	15.0	17,247	182,862	8,529,020	.1524	5,278,220	1,499	982,041	1,954	250,758	1,320	711,597	246,835
112	Des Moines, IA	490,399	456,022	16.1	20,198	188,322	9,904,880	.1714	6,129,021	1,740	839,842	1,670	242,908	1,278	793,960	295,568
113	Lancaster, PA	490,254	470,658	11.3	19,871	183,207	9,741,670	.1767	6,915,084	1,964	618,456	1,230	403,743	2,125	1,058,381	357,146
114	Johnson City-Kingsport-Bristol, TN-VA	489,628	480,091	10.1	16,293	205,493	7,977,390	.1512	5,729,468	1,627	1,115,462	2,217	248,987	1,309	691,688	350,663
115	Chattanooga, TN-GA	479,572	465,161	9.6	17,548	184,389	8,415,440	.1546	5,760,291	1,636	961,302	1,912	330,468	1,739	727,043	373,586
116	Bridgeport, CT (PMSA)	471,392	459,479	3.6	21,964	172,115	10,353,506	.1909	8,123,648	2,308	592,196	1,178	466,036	2,454	946,621	402,815
117	Santa Rosa, CA (PMSA)	470,813	458,614	18.1	24,088	175,179	11,340,910	.1822	6,084,888	1,728	691,543	1,375	280,632	1,477	1,212,686	357,793
118	Madison, WI	463,177	426,526	16.2	22,795	196,124	10,558,140	.1825	6,977,606	1,981	914,396	1,818	244,878	1,289	756,141	323,059
119	Kalamazoo-Battle Creek, MI	462,127	452,851	5.4	19,050	185,915	8,803,730	.1559	5,653,871	1,605	1,631,035	3,243	176,597	929	497,676	318,660
120	Jackson, MS	461,453	440,801	11.5	17,283	164,958	7,975,300	.1543	6,318,893	1,795	1,362,861	2,711	284,801	1,499	566,855	368,876
121	Lansing-East Lansing, MI	461,446	447,728	3.5	21,034	189,983	9,705,850	.1657	5,885,672	1,671	1,344,212	2,673	230,071	1,210	671,101	332,191
122	Flint, MI (PMSA)	445,626	436,141	1.3	18,240	166,917	8,128,190	.1460	5,313,381	1,509	1,042,068	2,072	191,549	1,008	611,856	393,603
123	Spokane, WA	439,273	417,939	15.7	18,223	180,505	8,004,860	.1437	5,223,271	1,483	985,255	1,959	248,626	1,309	753,870	200,787
124	Pensacola, FL	437,128	412,153	19.7	18,438	170,330	8,059,970	.1392	4,649,972	1,321	829,735	1,650	185,536	977	639,256	315,918
125	Newburgh, NY-PA (PMSA)	433,484	387,669	15.5	20,736	143,640	8,988,760	.1445	4,362,928	1,239	716,896	1,426	432,075	2,274	579,285	254,214
126	Salinas, CA	421,269	401,762	13.0	18,324	130,913	7,719,290	.1321	4,297,922	1,220	496,897	988	304,946	1,605	763,460	273,308
127	Shreveport-Bossier City, LA	420,461	392,302	4.2	16,334	164,674	6,867,670	.1289	4,791,525	1,360	892,594	1,775	204,576	1,077	578,291	212,094
128	Lawrence, MA-NH (PMSA)	416,134	396,230	12.2	22,590	148,052	9,400,346	.1517	4,930,957	1,402	857,237	1,703	258,092	1,358	883,529	316,440
129	Provo-Orem, UT	409,622	368,536	39.8	15,081	119,096	6,177,510	.1186	4,378,818	1,243	892,140	1,774	147,868	778	679,220	84,277
130	Canton-Massillon, OH	407,131	406,934	3.3	18,072	158,114	7,357,550	.1373	5,385,396	1,529	695,727	1,384	280,842	1,478	801,334	503,254
131	Visalia-Tulare-Porterville, CA	404,818	368,021	18.0	12,914	120,917	5,227,730	.0963	2,765,611	785	418,656	833	108,161	569	563,264	158,385
132	Santa Barbara-Santa Maria-Lompoc, CA	404,582	399,347	8.0	19,919	139,852	8,058,830	.1386	4,839,745	1,374	499,060	992	335,212	1,764	874,460	322,723
133	York, PA	403,361	381,751	12.4	20,209	154,303	8,151,520	.1339	4,206,302	1,194	585,240	1,164	159,393	839	714,134	198,492
134	Saginaw-Bay City-Midland, MI	403,186	403,070	0.9	18,795	162,786	7,577,940	.1445	6,048,370	1,718	1,255,896	2,498	399,771	2,104	538,935	335,740
135	Lafayette, LA	393,730	385,647	11.8	15,144	149,594	5,962,500	.1209	4,993,804	1,418	1,014,572	2,017	218,948	1,152	557,241	361,121
136	Reading, PA	393,253	373,638	11.0	19,745	147,995	7,764,710	.1320	4,459,882	1,266	520,167	1,034	360,634	1,898	665,140	278,677
137	Rockford, IL	391,588	371,236	12.6	19,727	145,971	7,725,050	.1315	4,457,927	1,265	690,627	1,374	156,446	823	718,191	263,398
138	Reno, NV	390,302	339,486	33.3	20,811	151,394	8,122,740	.1409	5,166,455	1,467	834,750	1,660	170,959	900	705,819	218,418
139	Corpus Christi, TX	383,948	380,783	8.8	15,361	133,326	5,897,640	.1143	4,352,658	1,236	742,324	1,476	206,792	1,089	708,266	183,922
140	Beaumont-Port Arthur, TX	380,783	385,090	6.6	16,794	144,982	6,394,940	.1213	4,697,396	1,333	797,667	1,586	210,488	1,108	605,208	276,284
141	Brownsville-Harlingen-San Benito, TX	379,998	335,227	28.9	8,453	97,445	3,212,080	.0778	2,844,598	808	682,514	1,357	195,900	1,031	495,642	117,593
142	Appleton-Oshkosh-Neenah, WI	376,237	358,365	13.7	20,797	149,305	7,824,600	.1368	5,095,443	1,446	746,975	1,486	193,307	1,017	567,911	213,205
143	Salem, OR (PMSA)	374,986	347,214	24.9	16,813	131,258	6,304,480	.1141	3,997,943	1,135	850,280	1,691	145,165	764	577,419	135,511
144	Biloxi-Gulfport-Pascagoula, MS	371,758	363,988	16.5	17,633	143,559	6,555,210	.1178	4,197,560	1,192	1,071,270	2,130	152,026	801	423,274	185,769
145	Trenton, NJ (PMSA)	369,496	350,761	7.7	24,296	124,536	8,977,430	.1416	4,534,000	1,287	431,841	859	361,412	1,902	714,006	472,475
146	Fort Pierce-Port St. Lucie, FL	367,537	319,426	27.2	20,044	148,535	7,366,920	.1250	4,250,091	1,207	569,115	1,132	144,124	759	627,822	360,130
147	Huntsville, AL	367,395	342,376	16.8	20,622	142,882	7,576,500	.1297	4,590,366	1,303	1,044,405	2,077	226,391	1,192	539,630	193,264
148	Stamford-Norwalk, CT (PMSA)	366,016	353,556	7.2	41,147	136,357	15,060,424	.2254	8,174,385	2,321	278,841	554	582,245	3,064	878,019	324,756
149	Atlantic-Cape May, NJ (PMSA)	362,796	354,878	11.1	23,372	151,746	8,479,390	.1383	4,710,388	1,337	446,396	888	343,199	1,807	1,046,330	313,014
150	Fayetteville-Springdale-Rogers, AR	360,974	311,121	47.5	17,092	134,714	6,169,910	.1138	4,202,271	1,193	1,382,455	2,749	118,782	625	351,016	124,291

Source: Devonshire Associates Ltd. and Scan/US, Inc. 2005.

Estimates for Total Retail Sales, General Merchandise Sales, Apparel Store Sales, Food Store Sales and Health and Drug Store Sales are based on data from the U.S. Census Bureau's 1997 Economic Census and utilize the North American Industry Classification System (NAICS).

[1] Census population includes a portion of Broomfield county.

[2] Data excludes Harvey county, Kansas (7/1/05 estimated population 34,021) which fails to meet published standards for MSA inclusion, but has been included with the Wichita MSA as the result of Congressional action.

Core Based Statistical Areas (CBSAs): Population/Income/Sales#†

This table provides population and marketing information for each Metropolitan CBSA and for all Micropolitan CBSAs as a group. Included are all of the data items given for Basic Trading Areas in the table starting on page 24. Data are from Devonshire Associates Ltd. and Scan/US, Inc. 2005. Also included are CBSA FIPS codes. A map showing the CBSAs, with a detailed explanation of how they are determined, appears on pages 38-39. For information on the Ranally Metro Areas (RMAs), whose boundaries differ from those of the CBSAs, see the table on pages 126-127.

CBSA FIPS Code	Core Based Statistical Area	Population: Estimate 7/1/05	Population: Census 4/1/00	Population: % Change 4/1/90-4/1/00	Per Capita Income 2004	Households Estimate 7/1/05	Disposable Income 2004 ($1,000)	Market Ability Index 2004	Total Retail Sales: 2004 Sales ($1,000)	Total Retail Sales: Ranally Sales Units	General Merchandise: 2004 Sales ($1,000)	General Merchandise: Ranally Sales Units	Apparel Store: 2004 Sales ($1,000)	Apparel Store: Ranally Sales Units	Food Store Sales 2004 ($1,000)	Health & Drug Store 2004 ($1,000)
10180	Abilene, TX	156,762	160,245	8.3	15,786	59,528	2,474,680	.0490	1,988,461	565	394,718	785	64,045	337	204,605	75,226
10420	Akron, OH	704,396	694,960	5.7	19,435	272,491	13,689,650	.2478	9,538,485	2,709	920,437	1,830	401,349	2,112	1,321,069	843,663
10500	Albany, GA	164,365	157,833	7.7	14,638	59,256	2,406,000	.0474	1,806,947	514	350,512	696	80,467	424	276,901	78,891
10580	Albany-Schenectady-Troy, NY	851,730	825,875	2.0	21,852	338,233	18,611,750	.3030	9,840,485	2,794	1,158,361	2,304	575,198	3,027	1,285,764	628,243
10740	Albuquerque, NM	788,925	729,649	21.7	18,329	304,262	14,460,280	.2616	9,706,280	2,757	1,906,387	3,792	340,863	1,793	815,878	515,259
10780	Alexandria, LA	145,923	145,035	-2.7	14,463	55,686	2,110,500	.0426	1,696,150	482	399,893	795	70,943	373	184,972	114,976
10900	Allentown-Bethlehem-Easton, PA-NJ	785,814	740,395	7.8	20,371	296,297	16,007,810	.2729	9,467,904	2,689	950,519	1,890	391,866	2,061	1,653,435	659,754
11020	Altoona, PA	126,465	129,144	-1.1	16,251	51,843	2,055,160	.0421	1,839,118	522	340,485	677	66,222	349	262,688	130,976
11100	Amarillo, TX	237,137	226,522	15.5	16,644	88,278	3,946,920	.0769	3,112,801	883	454,088	903	129,742	683	252,486	125,940
11180	Ames, IA	80,417	79,981	7.7	17,793	30,803	1,430,830	.0255	892,888	254	173,052	344	38,747	204	132,989	33,762
11260	Anchorage, AK	352,186	319,605	20.1	21,974	124,883	7,738,950	.1359	5,269,302	1,496	1,171,178	2,330	247,318	1,302	652,337	67,815
11300	Anderson, IN	129,750	133,358	2.1	17,933	52,189	2,326,790	.0407	1,374,189	390	235,435	468	34,190	180	160,766	98,307
11340	Anderson, SC	175,558	165,740	14.1	17,283	68,265	3,034,240	.0560	2,090,904	594	326,516	649	101,958	537	310,355	140,498
11460	Ann Arbor, MI	347,941	322,895	14.1	23,471	138,498	8,166,530	.1404	5,391,343	1,531	894,465	1,779	250,305	1,317	593,151	281,683
11500	Anniston-Oxford, AL	112,624	112,249	-3.3	16,048	45,425	1,807,370	.0339	1,246,973	354	279,922	557	40,491	213	167,833	58,882
11540	Appleton, WI	216,505	201,602	15.3	21,269	84,091	4,604,790	.0807	3,065,349	870	475,477	946	121,212	638	368,631	91,753
11700	Asheville, NC	391,007	369,171	19.9	18,204	163,266	7,117,980	.1357	5,573,344	1,583	807,062	1,606	258,605	1,360	648,317	319,272
12020	Athens-Clarke County, GA	176,112	166,079	22.1	16,023	69,105	2,821,920	.0530	1,951,797	554	343,703	683	88,722	468	246,883	89,318
12060	Atlanta-Sandy Springs-Marietta, GA	4,809,992	4,247,981	38.4	21,568	1,716,371	103,742,350	1.7807	65,071,961	18,475	8,692,216	17,287	3,504,410	18,445	8,986,048	2,785,761
12100	Atlantic City, NJ	261,127	252,552	12.6	23,217	106,895	6,062,550	.0989	3,352,942	952	390,047	776	238,389	1,255	677,404	206,415
12220	Auburn-Opelika, AL	121,616	115,092	32.1	15,690	49,426	1,908,140	.0345	1,142,527	324	219,487	436	59,149	311	192,903	39,194
12260	Augusta-Richmond County, GA-SC	517,953	499,684	14.7	16,980	190,824	8,795,000	.1578	5,455,921	1,549	991,510	1,973	252,791	1,331	744,963	258,910
12420	Austin-Round Rock, TX	1,453,856	1,249,763	47.7	21,294	525,442	30,958,890	.6241	30,159,309	8,564	2,441,369	4,855	1,101,729	5,800	3,038,880	1,493,719
12540	Bakersfield, CA	743,729	661,645	21.7	14,153	234,348	10,526,210	.1907	5,759,480	1,635	787,831	1,567	234,327	1,233	863,026	390,768
12580	Baltimore-Towson, MD	2,658,807	2,552,994	7.2	22,490	997,379	59,797,030	.9484	29,277,161	8,312	3,797,673	7,552	1,701,986	8,959	5,186,939	1,711,640
12620	Bangor, ME	149,585	144,919	-1.1	16,697	61,196	2,497,590	.0514	2,300,599	653	323,935	644	49,968	263	436,404	94,177
12700	Barnstable Town, MA	232,312	222,230	19.1	23,822	99,127	5,534,160	.0937	3,512,843	997	198,575	395	245,378	1,291	737,688	261,847
12940	Baton Rouge, LA	727,551	705,973	13.2	16,621	256,285	12,092,610	.2275	8,586,477	2,438	1,578,219	3,138	359,252	1,890	1,044,785	428,807
12980	Battle Creek, MI	139,305	137,985	1.5	18,350	56,104	2,556,210	.0448	1,546,564	439	425,650	846	40,673	214	155,361	106,743
13020	Bay City, MI	109,101	110,157	-1.4	18,772	45,419	2,048,080	.0391	1,641,352	466	360,529	717	52,994	279	163,796	79,616
13140	Beaumont-Port Arthur, TX	380,783	385,090	6.6	16,794	144,982	6,394,940	.1213	4,697,396	1,333	797,667	1,586	210,488	1,108	605,208	276,284
13380	Bellingham, WA	182,534	166,814	30.5	18,455	71,812	3,368,700	.0612	2,303,589	654	435,895	867	99,789	525	459,114	114,322
13460	Bend, OR	138,176	115,367	53.9	20,225	56,974	2,794,630	.0517	2,124,592	603	522,176	1,038	63,805	336	282,969	50,914
13740	Billings, MT	145,703	138,904	14.3	17,714	58,917	2,581,000	.0513	2,245,140	637	431,695	858	78,066	410	232,172	65,432
13780	Binghamton, NY	249,856	252,320	-4.6	18,851	102,035	4,710,130	.0798	2,593,351	736	366,506	729	103,385	544	454,988	206,715
13820	Birmingham-Hoover, AL	1,086,137	1,052,238	10.0	18,515	419,291	20,109,880	.3619	13,359,508	3,794	2,267,574	4,509	666,826	3,510	1,639,893	689,336
13900	Bismarck, ND	98,303	94,719	13.0	18,296	38,484	1,798,600	.0350	1,489,757	423	258,853	515	35,852	188	152,830	93,133
13980	Blacksburg-Christiansburg-Radford, VA	150,162	151,272	7.5	15,151	60,052	2,275,080	.0440	1,650,595	468	314,900	627	44,022	231	199,857	89,637
14020	Bloomington, IN	177,866	175,506	12.0	15,650	70,725	2,783,650	.0514	1,775,770	504	374,192	744	61,234	322	231,775	90,134
14060	Bloomington-Normal, IL	160,498	150,433	16.5	21,223	62,003	3,406,260	.0592	2,197,078	624	332,254	661	135,942	715	218,032	143,217
14260	Boise City-Nampa, ID	539,170	464,840	45.4	18,472	201,602	9,959,580	.1837	7,131,256	2,025	1,277,037	2,540	231,216	1,217	954,572	234,231
14460	Boston-Cambridge-Quincy, MA-NH	4,457,319	4,391,344	6.2	24,540	1,656,326	109,383,350	1.7852	62,649,565	17,791	5,876,246	11,687	4,707,924	24,780	9,933,443	4,633,205
14500	Boulder, CO	282,452	269,814	29.1	25,153	111,722	7,104,400	.1167	4,216,806	1,197	418,126	832	137,945	726	786,632	154,369
14540	Bowling Green, KY	109,420	104,166	19.7	16,591	42,020	1,815,410	.0347	1,359,846	386	254,703	507	75,781	399	121,013	57,155
14740	Bremerton-Silverdale, WA	241,196	231,969	22.3	20,793	92,982	5,015,170	.0800	2,360,051	670	567,682	1,129	73,505	387	316,380	119,693
14860	Bridgeport-Stamford-Norwalk, CT	909,263	882,567	6.6	30,162	329,595	27,424,940	.4586	18,649,061	5,295	997,741	1,984	1,190,445	6,266	2,268,628	792,292
15180	Brownsville-Harlingen, TX	379,998	335,227	28.9	8,453	97,445	3,212,080	.0778	2,844,598	808	682,514	1,357	195,900	1,031	495,642	117,593
15260	Brunswick, GA	99,197	93,044	13.2	17,280	39,030	1,714,160	.0307	1,076,935	305	158,504	316	86,705	456	153,566	56,304
15380	Buffalo-Niagara Falls, NY	1,154,526	1,170,111	-1.6	20,193	477,362	23,313,710	.3832	12,048,915	3,421	1,230,258	2,447	724,512	3,813	2,155,690	978,261
15500	Burlington, NC	140,105	130,800	20.9	18,162	54,708	2,544,520	.0467	1,771,538	503	233,033	463	113,462	597	219,919	99,591
15540	Burlington-South Burlington, VT	206,121	198,889	12.3	20,067	77,913	4,136,190	.0789	3,407,950	968	302,836	602	168,595	888	548,209	184,224
15940	Canton-Massillon, OH	407,131	406,934	3.3	18,072	158,114	7,357,550	.1373	5,385,396	1,529	695,727	1,384	280,842	1,478	801,334	503,254
15980	Cape Coral-Fort Myers, FL	523,512	440,888	31.6	21,374	219,465	11,189,420	.1957	7,409,505	2,104	1,087,208	2,162	462,470	2,434	956,522	481,928
16180	Carson City, NV	57,139	52,457	29.7	18,725	21,471	1,069,920	.0212	948,543	269	50,822	101	1,398	7	156,413	109,780
16220	Casper, WY	69,348	66,533	8.7	17,101	27,462	1,185,920	.0231	956,827	272	208,531	415	22,617	119	100,078	22,464
16300	Cedar Rapids, IA	245,799	237,230	12.6	20,637	99,116	5,072,600	.0887	3,287,794	934	507,680	1,010	124,600	656	389,200	176,332
16580	Champaign-Urbana, IL	216,661	210,275	3.7	18,477	87,025	4,003,190	.0713	2,572,213	730	526,795	1,048	93,708	494	332,375	191,208
16620	Charleston, WV	305,915	309,635	0.6	17,483	127,586	5,348,220	.1000	3,857,895	1,096	607,111	1,207	144,158	759	448,368	314,145
16700	Charleston-North Charleston, SC	586,872	549,033	8.3	17,044	210,746	10,002,730	.1828	6,608,271	1,877	1,199,377	2,385	418,395	2,203	993,263	297,458
16740	Charlotte-Gastonia-Concord, NC-SC	1,505,429	1,330,448	29.8	21,307	578,871	32,075,610	.5518	20,128,261	5,715	2,893,237	5,754	990,108	5,210	2,441,442	1,099,655
16820	Charlottesville, VA	183,141	174,021	20.9	20,072	73,476	3,675,990	.0646	2,375,158	675	326,262	650	137,040	722	395,245	125,071
16860	Chattanooga, TN-GA	492,047	476,531	10.0	17,464	189,045	8,592,880	.1577	5,842,511	1,659	971,155	1,932	331,462	1,744	734,748	378,230
16940	Cheyenne, WY	86,122	81,607	11.6	17,927	33,481	1,543,880	.0305	1,326,732	377	210,135	418	24,046	127	135,941	26,824
16980	Chicago-Naperville-Joliet, IL-IN-WI	9,471,425	9,098,316	11.2	20,848	3,293,572	197,462,610	3.3057	111,549,447	31,675	13,109,705	26,071	6,321,481	33,269	14,695,301	9,643,813
17020	Chico, CA	215,649	203,171	11.6	16,053	84,743	3,461,920	.0631	2,162,007	614	337,895	672	81,188	427	421,916	159,025
17140	Cincinnati-Middletown, OH-KY-IN	2,069,601	2,009,632	8.9	20,544	805,228	42,517,790	.7239	25,217,656	7,159	3,561,073	7,080	1,214,527	6,394	3,568,727	1,435,529
17300	Clarksville, TN-KY	238,672	232,000	22.6	16,646	90,066	3,972,870	.0708	2,361,653	670	601,490	1,196	102,298	538	189,993	84,957
17420	Cleveland, TN	107,706	104,015	19.1	16,825	43,070	1,812,120	.0323	1,084,301	308	205,247	409	35,902	189	124,984	73,840
17460	Cleveland-Elyria-Mentor, OH	2,136,541	2,148,143	2.2	20,024	852,217	42,783,070	.7503	27,506,430	7,810	2,827,065	5,623	1,412,321	7,433	4,057,606	2,961,118
17660	Coeur d'Alene, ID	122,971	108,685	55.7	17,137	47,174	2,107,400	.0397	1,540,992	438	232,236	462	50,041	263	243,800	60,243
17780	College Station-Bryan, TX	189,774	184,885	22.4	14,501	74,942	2,751,960	.0544	2,068,824	588	381,083	758	100,897	531	275,095	53,217
17820	Colorado Springs, CO	592,836	537,484	31.3	20,800	227,594	12,331,020	.2094	7,302,778	2,074	1,264,886	2,515	200,312	1,055	759,294	276,150
17860	Columbia, MO	153,576	145,666	19.4	18,995	65,205	2,917,130	.0524	1,953,687	554	320,161	637	60,685	319	206,860	87,182
17900	Columbia, SC	687,420	647,158	18.0	18,560	261,102	12,758,230	.2295	8,500,202	2,413	1,702,017	3,385	446,397	2,349	1,075,119	456,952
17980	Columbus, GA-AL	277,462	281,768	5.7	16,147	107,040	4,480,090	.0828	2,949,179	837	551,358	1,096	179,298	943	412,531	207,758
18020	Columbus, IN	72,772	71,435	12.2	19,023	27,728	1,384,350	.0240	833,936	237	166,855	332	58,441	308	99,350	55,949
18140	Columbus, OH	1,719,360	1,612,694	14.8	20,173	652,918	34,684,830	.6301	24,952,201	7,085	2,989,934	5,946	1,127,376	5,934	2,921,109	1,023,296
18580	Corpus Christi, TX	408,295	403,280	9.7	15,343	142,915	6,264,520	.1205	4,509,115	1,280	773,638	1,538	212,548	1,119	753,998	185,691
18700	Corvallis, OR	79,778	78,153	10.4	20,737	33,621	1,654,350	.0250	619,285	176	82,101	163	24,988	132	143,655	30,072
19060	Cumberland, MD-WV	100,474	102,008	0.4	15,057	39,878	1,512,830	.0284	1,005,621	286	234,621	467	42,851	225	142,375	89,912
19100	Dallas-Fort Worth-Arlington, TX	5,844,700	5,161,544	29.4	19,933	1,972,103	116,503,670	2.0633	77,051,908	21,881	11,147,019	22,166	4,034,977	21,237	9,765,406	3,161,786
19140	Dalton, GA	132,298	120,031	21.7	15,991	45,801	2,115,570	.0426	1,795,168	510	251,728	500	59,924	315	241,492	65,992
19180	Danville, IL	82,252	83,919	-4.9	16,564	33,259	1,362,390	.0249	879,347	250	181,418	361	21,925	115	127,479	60,189
19260	Danville, VA	107,753	110,156	1.3	15,396	45,230	1,658,970	.0314	1,135,480	323	211,467	420	34,975	184	189,329	64,305
19340	Davenport-Moline-Rock Island, IA-IL	374,314	376,019	2.1	19,080	150,259	7,141,890	.1304	5,066,064	1,439	744,429	1,481	206,063	1,085	594,908	341,552
19380	Dayton, OH	843,320	848,153	0.5	19,913	340,224	16,792,740	.2918	10,437,674	2,964	1,677,421	3,335	455,065	2,394	1,387,244	518,273
19460	Decatur, AL	148,289	145,867	10.9	17,603	57,646	2,610,310	.0471	1,685,295	479	261,428	520	65,151	343	156,749	93,514
19500	Decatur, IL	109,127	114,706	-2.1	19,482	47,005	2,125,990	.0396	1,612,803	458	305,716	608	54,606	287	210,392	109,435
19660	Deltona-Daytona Beach-Ormond Beach, FL	483,444	443,343	19.6	17,897	192,195	8,652,230	.1564	5,702,643	1,619	826,756	1,644	245,601	1,293	886,271	390,946
19740	Denver-Aurora, CO	2,371,414	2,179,240	30.7	24,951	980,328	59,168,450	.9423	31,455,018	8,931	4,690,236	9,327	1,493,830	7,863	4,358,133	1,208,969
19780	Des Moines, IA	516,976	481,394	15.6	20,050	198,486	10,365,480	.1788	6,317,987	1,794	847,802	1,686	244,194	1,285	820,372	306,407
19820	Detroit-Warren-Livonia, MI	4,501,430	4,452,557	4.8	21,935	1,722,915	98,740,090	1.6927	62,291,351	17,687	9,917,465	19,723	3,024,962	15,921	7,300,349	4,729,277
20020	Dothan, AL	135,324	130,861	8.7	16,092	53,798	2,177,650	.0453	2,018,512	574	406,585	809	82,670	435	169,112	89,001
20100	Dover, DE	139,558	126,697	14.1	17,806	51,903	2,484,910	.0451	1,653,667	470	366,822	729	47,176	248	190,185	71,144
20220	Dubuque, IA	91,167	89,143	3.2	17,393	34,683	1,585,710	.0307	1,266,703	360	217,773	433	34,204	180	145,758	78,435
20260	Duluth, MN-WI	275,790	275,486	2.3	18,103	118,369	4,992,590	.0892	3,190,048	906	604,263	1,202	80,298	423	423,117	174,302
20500	Durham, NC	458,673	426,493	23.8	20,325	184,337	9,322,540	.1562	5,192,795	1,475	524,011	1,042	292,911	1,542	865,702	306,608
20740	Eau Claire, WI	154,337	148,337	7.8	17,947	62,324	2,769,920	.0573	2,672,277	759	569,895	1,134	105,458	555	270,575	99,099
20940	El Centro, CA	153,484	142,361	30.2	11,514	43,593	1,767,170	.0381	1,451,398	412	276,417	550	94,280	496	260,442	69,041
21060	Elizabethtown, KY	109,851	107,547	6.6	17,307	41,683	1,901,140	.0342	1,209,968	343	289,385	575	64,576	340	92,099	63,407
21140	Elkhart-Goshen, IN	192,614	182,791	17.0	18,129	69,511	3,491,820	.0667	2,737,857	777	461,665	918	39,013	205	272,318	127,424
21300	Elmira, NY	90,031	91,070	-4.3	18,393	35,794	1,655,900	.0303	1,148,737	326	193,665	385	58,842	310	156,337	77,465
21340	El Paso, TX	720,147	679,622	14.9	11,701	218,789	8,426,220	.1787	6,673,517	1,895	1,498,168	2,979	459,278	2,417	781,502	305,744
21500	Erie, PA	279,281	280,843	1.9	17,187	109,682	4,799,900	.0894	3,381,763	960	451,424	898	142,791	752	538,747	194,570
21660	Eugene-Springfield, OR	335,284	322,959	14.2	18,570	141,340	6,226,310	.1146	4,441,395	1,261	819,155	1,629	129,203	680	689,971	164,173
21780	Evansville, IN-KY	348,860	342,815	5.5	17,876	138,511	6,236,290	.1189	4,823,000	1,369	829,036	1,649	216,952	1,142	510,448	262,823
21820	Fairbanks, AK	86,784	82,840	6.6	19,495	30,453	1,691,880	.0308	1,207,437	343	283,785	564	37,121	195	97,724	14,793
22020	Fargo, ND-MN	181,535	174,367	13.7	18,396	74,974	3,339,550	.0688	3,234,323	919	465,786	927	100,188	527	280,838	149,962
22140	Farmington, NM	127,992	113,801	24.2	12,484	38,249	1,597,810	.0348	1,437,477	408	384,722	765	44,763	236	142,782	43,540
22180	Fayetteville, NC	346,350	336,609	13.2	16,132	125,340	5,587,260	.1036	3,714,741	1,055	713,751	1,419	191,617	1,009	452,306	171,353
22220	Fayetteville-Springdale-Rogers, AR-MO	397,806	347,045	44.9	16,726	149,079	6,653,550	.1222	4,405,775	1,251	1,403,194	2,790	119,274	627	405,447	133,061
22380	Flagstaff, AZ	124,093	116,320	20.4	16,494	43,459	2,046,830	.0374	1,313,802	373	283,592	564	32,136	169	229,169	28,901
22420	Flint, MI	445,626	436,141	1.3	18,240	166,917	8,128,190	.1460	5,313,381	1,509	1,042,068	2,072	191,549	1,008	611,856	393,603
22500	Florence, SC	198,594	193,155	9.6	14,994	72,801	2,977,760	.0601	2,442,587	693	394,167	784	124,809	657	330,441	142,985
22520	Florence-Muscle Shoals, AL	140,981	142,950	8.9	17,079	58,420	2,407,870	.0448	1,680,401	477	414,962	825	79,419	418	163,649	72,908
22540	Fond du Lac, WI	98,664	97,296	8.0	19,585	38,452	1,932,370	.0330	1,116,093	317	218,023	434	23,248	122	144,958	55,570
22660	Fort Collins-Loveland, CO	275,364	251,494	35.1	24,187	119,115	6,660,320	.1075	3,647,791	1,036	666,158	1,325	150,251	791	477,472	113,594
22900	Fort Smith, AR-OK	283,847	273,170	16.7	14,892	107,994	4,227,100	.0825	3,122,450	886	886,926	1,764	72,713	382	355,347	130,349
23020	Fort Walton Beach-Crestview-Destin, FL	182,186	170,498	18.6	20,670	71,945	3,765,750	.0679	2,690,307	764	517,655	1,029	221,038	1,163	309,568	131,402
23060	Fort Wayne, IN	406,015	390,156	10.1	17,706	146,486	7,188,940	.1338	5,151,663	1,463	1,039,579	2,067	209,959	1,106	509,086	298,637
23420	Fresno, CA	881,918	799,407	19.8	13,549	271,021	11,949,320	.2266	7,423,260	2,108	1,040,968	2,070	331,031	1,742	1,229,784	460,666
23460	Gadsden, AL	103,021	103,459	3.6	15,806	41,635	1,628,300	.0296	998,934	284	210,213	418	44,852	236	175,131	60,568
23540	Gainesville, FL	239,650	232,392	21.5	17,004	100,805	4,075,010	.0745	2,685,515	763	377,162	750	147,304	775	475,219	114,482
23580	Gainesville, GA	166,966	139,277	45.9	17,131	54,415	2,860,320	.0508	1,727,114	490	350,946	698	46,007	242	181,228	89,952
24020	Glens Falls, NY	128,724	124,345	4.9	19,074	50,295	2,455,280	.0420	1,402,324	398	126,801	252	106,760	562	207,045	81,573
24140	Goldsboro, NC	113,461	113,329	8.3	15,801	43,498	1,792,770	.0345	1,320,622	375	253,513	504	59,248	312	168,453	67,902
24220	Grand Forks, ND-MN	94,524	97,478	-5.5	16,316	37,199	1,542,210	.0336	1,617,709	459	315,509	628	47,227	248	149,096	61,226
24300	Grand Junction, CO	129,419	116,255	24.8	18,268	55,438	2,364,210	.0430	1,607,761	457	399,198	794	34,875	184	198,421	41,576
24340	Grand Rapids-Wyoming, MI	775,198	740,482	14.6	19,460	291,002	15,085,200	.2681	9,934,388	2,821	1,928,255	3,835	361,397	1,901	843,769	490,057
24500	Great Falls, MT	79,409	80,357	3.4	16,614	32,956	1,319,290	.0256	1,027,263	292	244,590	486	25,008	132	107,838	48,119
24540	Greeley, CO	230,756	180,926	37.3	18,917	88,114	4,365,170	.0702	1,958,366	556	298,091	593	26,630	140	250,995	54,456
24580	Green Bay, WI	297,520	282,599	16.0	20,091	118,666	5,977,450	.1049	3,844,510	1,092	936,201	1,862	94,715	498	391,704	118,209
24660	Greensboro-High Point, NC	673,134	643,430	19.1	19,161	266,769	12,897,820	.2351	9,113,147	2,588	1,138,679	2,264	437,889	2,305	1,067,469	560,145
24780	Greenville, NC	162,183	152,772	23.9	16,244	65,842	2,634,510	.0521	2,137,584	607	232,861	463	132,141	695	263,853	105,711
24860	Greenville, SC	588,729	559,940	18.6	17,811	221,455	10,486,140	.1943	7,439,633	2,113	997,813	1,984	380,205	2,000	908,811	428,288
25060	Gulfport-Biloxi, MS	251,585	246,190	18.4	17,188	98,383	4,324,290	.0799	2,977,668	846	753,574	1,499	122,948	648	281,258	142,502
25180	Hagerstown-Martinsburg, MD-WV	247,661	222,771	15.6	18,177	93,073	4,501,670	.0771	2,493,335	708	433,638	863	105,692	556	348,912	142,018
25260	Hanford-Corcoran, CA	145,336	129,461	27.6	11,511	37,148	1,672,960	.0311	795,708	226	107,971	215	35,135	185	189,051	42,422
25420	Harrisburg-Carlisle, PA	519,424	509,074	7.3	20,915	211,439	10,863,640	.1957	7,773,012	2,207	747,981	1,487	312,581	1,646	1,055,813	423,900
25500	Harrisonburg, VA	111,801	108,193	22.7	15,353	40,251	1,716,460	.0359	1,579,559	449	238,249	473	39,794	209	200,739	65,039
25540	Hartford-West Hartford-East Hartford, CT	1,197,175	1,148,618	2.2	26,530	463,800	31,761,140	.4830	14,817,105	4,207	1,281,098	2,548	1,120,244	5,896	2,339,379	1,185,681
25620	Hattiesburg, MS	130,975	123,812	13.0	13,608	46,033	1,782,350	.0387	1,679,651	477	505,524	1,006	68,958	362	111,892	124,740
25860	Hickory-Lenoir-Morganton, NC	356,039	341,851	16.9	17,856	140,143	6,357,350	.1156	4,259,162	1,209	596,263	1,186	159,755	841	500,673	277,190
25980	Hinesville-Fort Stewart, GA	69,723	71,914	22.0	13,676	23,838	953,520	.0165	416,086	118	98,854	196	18,650	98	56,176	12,094
26100	Holland-Grand Haven, MI	255,839	238,314	26.9	21,326	91,969	5,455,970	.0912	3,108,964	883	819,109	1,629	101,983	537	267,200	119,978
26180	Honolulu, HI	910,475	876,156	4.8	20,281	302,181	18,465,370	.3063	9,903,032	2,812	1,988,367	3,954	1,320,832	6,952	1,401,658	865,911
26300	Hot Springs, AR	93,078	88,068	20.0	16,116	38,546	1,500,060	.0304	1,299,442	369	345,207	687	43,650	230	117,473	68,521
26380	Houma-Bayou Cane-Thibodaux, LA	198,122	194,477	6.4	15,783	70,892	3,127,010	.0614	2,446,990	695	530,216	1,054	84,487	445	374,137	119,175
26420	Houston-Sugar Land-Baytown, TX	5,293,972	4,715,407	25.2	18,002	1,750,735	95,302,000	1.7217	62,946,069	17,875	10,532,152	20,945	3,653,061	19,227	9,249,211	2,965,555
26580	Huntington-Ashland, WV-KY-OH	285,791	288,649	0.2	14,989	115,864	4,283,820	.0827	3,072,624	874	650,794	1,295	154,964	816	338,679	335,447

Source: Devonshire Associates Ltd. and Scan/US, Inc. 2005.

Estimates for Total Retail Sales, General Merchandise Sales, Apparel Store Sales, Food Store Sales and Health and Drug Store Sales are based on data from the U.S. Census Bureau's 1997 Economic Census, and utilize the North American Industry Classification System (NAICS).

† CBSA totals are for Metropolitan Core Based Statistical Areas. A U.S. total for Micropolitan Core Based Statistical Areas is also provided.

Continued on next page

Core Based Statistical Areas (CBSAs): Population/Income/Sales[#†], *Continued*

CBSA FIPS Code	Core Based Statistical Area	Population: Estimate 7/1/05	Population: Census 4/1/00	Population: % Change 4/1/90-4/1/00	Per Capita Income 2004	House-holds Estimate 7/1/05	Disposable Income 2004 ($1,000)	Market Ability Index 2004	Total Retail Sales: 2004 Sales ($1,000)	Total Retail Sales: Ranally Sales Units	General Merchandise: 2004 Sales ($1,000)	General Merchandise: Ranally Sales Units	Apparel Store: 2004 Sales ($1,000)	Apparel Store: Ranally Sales Units	Food Store Sales 2004 ($1,000)	Health & Drug Store 2004 ($1,000)
26620	Huntsville, AL	367,395	342,376	16.8	20,622	142,882	7,576,500	.1297	4,590,366	1,303	1,044,405	2,077	226,391	1,192	539,630	193,264
26820	Idaho Falls, ID	111,058	101,677	14.6	16,676	38,397	1,852,050	.0359	1,445,979	410	343,398	683	35,077	185	190,347	53,358
26900	Indianapolis, IN	1,646,860	1,525,104	17.8	20,092	616,038	33,089,180	.5977	23,361,123	6,636	4,189,056	8,331	939,876	4,947	2,042,869	1,503,273
26980	Iowa City, IA	138,810	131,676	13.8	18,747	56,490	2,602,250	.0477	1,844,207	523	258,207	514	60,711	320	308,144	84,401
27060	Ithaca, NY	100,996	96,501	2.6	18,164	38,542	1,834,480	.0295	790,679	225	80,341	160	35,530	187	182,026	55,756
27100	Jackson, MI	164,674	158,422	5.8	18,936	62,458	3,118,220	.0547	1,930,675	548	510,788	1,016	53,668	282	204,847	103,303
27140	Jackson, MS	518,326	497,197	11.2	16,706	184,703	8,658,910	.1674	6,704,402	1,904	1,451,620	2,888	290,291	1,528	621,694	408,231
27180	Jackson, TN	110,724	107,377	18.3	17,951	44,163	1,987,600	.0400	1,786,027	507	377,370	750	113,990	600	160,349	98,608
27260	Jacksonville, FL	1,248,873	1,122,750	21.4	20,664	477,545	25,806,650	.4424	15,714,417	4,462	2,187,393	4,349	793,699	4,178	2,209,549	758,340
27340	Jacksonville, NC	149,754	150,355	0.3	14,047	51,435	2,103,590	.0423	1,637,736	465	298,217	593	55,104	290	193,779	64,913
27500	Janesville, WI	156,477	152,307	9.2	19,832	61,510	3,103,240	.0553	2,090,244	594	382,774	761	34,271	180	272,604	109,715
27620	Jefferson City, MO	144,091	140,052	16.0	19,188	56,886	2,764,890	.0495	1,842,648	523	320,673	637	28,178	148	209,591	73,506
27740	Johnson City, TN	188,570	181,607	13.2	15,788	77,624	2,977,050	.0567	2,124,380	603	406,387	808	139,426	733	233,294	135,754
27780	Johnstown, PA	147,675	152,598	-6.4	14,830	60,359	2,190,070	.0418	1,496,756	425	197,260	392	36,268	191	280,379	106,411
27860	Jonesboro, AR	111,567	107,762	15.1	15,389	44,417	1,716,960	.0345	1,411,898	401	387,250	770	80,807	426	116,205	62,072
27900	Joplin, MO	166,062	157,322	16.6	15,603	66,337	2,591,010	.0495	1,857,785	527	443,839	883	51,226	269	147,141	84,259
28020	Kalamazoo-Portage, MI	322,822	314,866	7.3	19,353	129,811	6,247,520	.1111	4,107,307	1,166	1,205,385	2,397	135,925	715	342,315	211,917
28100	Kankakee-Bradley, IL	107,719	103,833	7.9	18,016	39,461	1,940,650	.0349	1,262,073	358	246,649	491	43,039	227	124,092	101,960
28140	Kansas City, MO-KS	1,952,760	1,836,038	12.2	21,306	768,988	41,605,740	.7120	25,651,310	7,284	3,955,017	7,867	988,727	5,204	2,937,196	1,347,170
28420	Kennewick-Richland-Pasco, WA	221,935	191,822	27.9	18,028	76,668	4,000,970	.0714	2,544,894	723	540,447	1,075	69,057	364	403,609	106,339
28660	Killeen-Temple-Fort Hood, TX	351,367	330,714	23.0	15,871	122,755	5,576,370	.0978	3,019,409	858	444,708	884	93,408	491	426,421	61,779
28700	Kingsport-Bristol-Bristol, TN-VA	301,058	298,484	8.3	16,609	127,869	5,000,340	.0945	3,605,089	1,024	709,075	1,409	109,561	576	458,394	214,908
28740	Kingston, NY	183,995	177,749	7.5	20,416	70,360	3,756,450	.0597	1,713,351	487	147,662	294	68,026	358	318,658	119,290
28940	Knoxville, TN	650,649	616,079	15.2	18,522	264,396	12,051,140	.2416	10,922,212	3,101	1,801,409	3,582	458,772	2,415	1,112,616	599,485
29020	Kokomo, IN	101,209	101,541	4.7	20,481	41,291	2,072,820	.0371	1,434,777	407	358,512	713	38,011	200	127,415	109,168
29100	La Crosse, WI-MN	129,409	126,838	9.0	17,892	51,810	2,315,440	.0439	1,765,347	501	349,252	695	38,034	200	206,997	49,530
29140	Lafayette, IN	182,561	178,541	12.4	17,405	70,815	3,177,400	.0589	2,221,462	631	507,140	1,009	85,447	449	186,859	116,183
29180	Lafayette, LA	245,465	239,086	14.5	17,275	94,908	4,240,450	.0860	3,821,453	1,085	751,349	1,494	180,198	949	359,936	270,949
29340	Lake Charles, LA	192,666	193,568	9.1	17,568	76,213	3,384,810	.0627	2,372,772	673	605,359	1,203	99,182	522	273,964	130,819
29460	Lakeland, FL	526,208	483,924	19.4	17,926	205,086	9,432,930	.1709	6,270,722	1,781	1,004,624	1,998	225,818	1,189	1,044,350	328,355
29540	Lancaster, PA	490,254	470,658	11.3	19,871	183,207	9,741,670	.1767	6,915,084	1,964	618,456	1,230	403,743	2,125	1,058,381	357,146
29620	Lansing-East Lansing, MI	461,446	447,728	3.5	21,034	189,983	9,705,850	.1657	5,885,672	1,671	1,344,212	2,673	230,071	1,210	671,101	332,191
29700	Laredo, TX	224,381	193,117	44.9	9,241	58,794	2,073,610	.0538	2,426,335	689	508,362	1,011	297,333	1,565	374,549	102,163
29740	Las Cruces, NM	187,285	174,682	28.9	12,484	63,506	2,338,100	.0450	1,409,430	400	290,364	577	45,270	238	147,833	81,908
29820	Las Vegas-Paradise, NV	1,697,755	1,375,765	85.5	19,197	620,452	32,591,720	.5707	20,294,277	5,763	2,891,887	5,751	1,375,438	7,239	3,018,726	841,646
29940	Lawrence, KS	103,269	99,962	22.2	17,848	42,198	1,843,120	.0326	1,126,641	320	164,334	327	62,103	327	202,198	54,513
30020	Lawton, OK	109,018	114,996	3.1	15,172	39,373	1,654,020	.0287	814,320	231	282,458	562	24,492	129	71,642	32,806
30140	Lebanon, PA	124,776	120,327	5.8	18,857	48,779	2,352,950	.0432	1,679,715	477	197,472	393	29,535	155	218,373	74,543
30300	Lewiston, ID-WA	58,492	57,961	12.9	17,470	24,431	1,021,880	.0193	754,895	214	199,766	397	12,381	65	125,041	30,949
30340	Lewiston-Auburn, ME	107,666	103,793	-1.4	17,403	44,083	1,873,750	.0392	1,842,778	523	214,005	426	21,774	115	236,464	73,545
30460	Lexington-Fayette, KY	430,696	408,326	17.2	20,119	175,319	8,665,210	.1563	6,097,113	1,731	896,211	1,782	331,891	1,746	606,627	370,562
30620	Lima, OH	106,543	108,473	-1.2	16,950	40,979	1,805,860	.0372	1,684,654	478	408,689	813	47,477	250	125,580	104,889
30700	Lincoln, NE	283,022	266,787	16.5	18,291	107,517	5,176,890	.0930	3,392,611	964	644,531	1,281	121,281	638	461,409	231,826
30780	Little Rock-North Little Rock, AR	639,802	610,518	14.1	19,246	259,036	12,313,800	.2292	9,286,474	2,637	1,910,532	3,800	338,114	1,779	763,297	316,058
30860	Logan, UT-ID	110,700	102,720	29.3	14,281	35,019	1,580,900	.0307	1,111,610	315	220,568	439	32,728	172	166,167	29,823
30980	Longview, TX	201,588	194,042	7.8	15,713	74,563	3,167,470	.0632	2,583,776	734	523,833	1,042	87,112	459	336,470	113,047
31020	Longview, WA	96,590	92,948	13.2	18,627	38,508	1,799,210	.0308	1,018,200	289	228,810	455	18,571	98	178,499	42,485
31100	Los Angeles-Long Beach-Santa Ana, CA	13,097,576	12,365,627	9.7	18,320	4,180,772	239,944,070	4.1236	135,513,537	38,479	16,794,966	33,400	11,206,574	58,982	20,801,007	7,795,195
31140	Louisville, KY-IN	1,207,123	1,161,975	10.0	19,057	466,718	23,003,710	.3980	13,660,496	3,879	2,273,288	4,522	531,866	2,799	1,444,039	887,014
31180	Lubbock, TX	261,585	249,700	8.6	15,925	103,779	4,165,810	.0862	3,788,689	1,076	577,169	1,148	184,433	970	555,329	117,783
31340	Lynchburg, VA	232,242	228,616	10.9	17,275	92,908	4,012,030	.0729	2,637,010	749	379,697	755	79,202	417	332,038	199,165
31420	Macon, GA	229,720	222,368	7.6	16,446	86,247	3,778,000	.0724	2,823,536	802	546,488	1,087	141,137	743	381,045	159,170
31460	Madera, CA	141,694	123,109	39.8	12,870	39,639	1,823,630	.0312	675,580	192	66,089	131	10,636	56	228,960	42,601
31540	Madison, WI	541,809	501,774	16.1	22,329	227,338	12,098,280	.2182	8,967,520	2,546	1,048,681	2,085	255,440	1,344	848,118	350,067
31700	Manchester-Nashua, NH	403,350	380,841	13.3	22,648	151,152	9,135,020	.1760	8,150,622	2,314	1,197,089	2,381	345,041	1,816	1,015,559	278,338
31900	Mansfield, OH	127,690	128,852	2.2	17,821	51,202	2,275,620	.0425	1,656,330	470	368,119	732	53,257	280	172,943	81,571
32580	McAllen-Edinburg-Mission, TX	675,597	569,463	48.5	8,316	179,247	5,618,500	.1432	5,723,037	1,625	1,172,978	2,333	428,765	2,257	870,770	248,513
32780	Medford, OR	196,043	181,269	23.8	18,053	81,232	3,539,120	.0732	3,428,121	973	602,138	1,197	88,759	467	352,409	91,518
32820	Memphis, TN-MS-AR	1,261,492	1,205,204	12.9	18,088	472,473	22,817,440	.4114	15,010,204	4,262	2,643,359	5,258	872,386	4,591	1,444,738	1,063,617
32900	Merced, CA	243,619	210,554	18.0	12,985	70,306	3,163,490	.0572	1,559,661	443	279,329	555	41,746	220	281,012	82,724
33100	Miami-Fort Lauderdale-Miami Beach, FL	5,452,407	5,007,564	23.5	18,388	1,970,323	100,258,750	1.8240	68,633,721	19,488	8,165,715	16,240	5,883,062	30,965	9,299,353	4,962,440
33140	Michigan City-La Porte, IN	109,651	110,106	2.8	17,627	40,827	1,932,830	.0353	1,302,656	370	234,559	466	121,147	638	131,313	81,814
33260	Midland, TX	120,852	116,009	8.8	17,296	43,353	2,090,260	.0408	1,702,551	483	319,844	636	87,217	459	191,235	56,316
33340	Milwaukee-Waukesha-West Allis, WI	1,521,473	1,500,741	4.8	20,533	597,839	31,239,920	.5262	17,833,569	5,063	2,618,965	5,208	605,954	3,189	2,459,679	1,231,828
33460	Minneapolis-St. Paul-Bloomington, MN-WI	3,154,675	2,968,806	16.9	24,093	1,251,827	76,004,390	1.3070	50,893,048	14,452	7,484,790	14,884	1,876,788	9,878	6,162,603	2,302,183
33540	Missoula, MT	100,118	95,802	21.8	17,414	41,813	1,743,480	.0355	1,600,814	455	351,579	699	41,311	217	176,081	45,603
33660	Mobile, AL	399,727	399,843	5.6	13,702	130,235	5,477,160	.1077	3,885,168	1,103	857,409	1,705	158,982	837	475,635	231,633
33700	Modesto, CA	519,823	446,997	20.6	15,585	161,250	8,101,680	.1473	4,910,210	1,394	756,250	1,504	190,893	1,005	890,064	318,684
33740	Monroe, LA	170,239	170,053	4.4	15,561	65,756	2,649,170	.0514	1,986,223	564	543,119	1,080	98,563	519	218,532	93,613
33780	Monroe, MI	153,774	145,945	9.2	22,697	59,699	3,490,180	.0557	1,755,648	499	342,638	681	65,382	344	187,187	109,909
33860	Montgomery, AL	356,454	346,528	13.6	17,113	131,702	6,099,830	.1142	4,362,627	1,239	873,591	1,738	198,796	1,047	486,039	276,503
34060	Morgantown, WV	114,517	111,200	6.4	14,021	44,304	1,605,690	.0313	1,129,188	321	210,194	418	69,160	364	118,140	79,368
34100	Morristown, TN	130,096	123,081	22.4	15,618	51,517	2,031,780	.0388	1,454,393	413	273,253	542	46,011	242	166,301	88,819
34580	Mount Vernon-Anacortes, WA	113,129	102,979	29.4	18,878	42,775	2,135,630	.0395	1,562,875	444	309,228	615	69,381	365	201,334	68,712
34620	Muncie, IN	117,847	118,769	-0.7	15,782	46,441	1,859,920	.0361	1,411,758	401	345,291	687	57,863	305	130,438	71,255
34740	Muskegon-Norton Shores, MI	175,106	170,200	7.1	17,302	67,837	3,029,740	.0553	2,018,064	573	535,830	1,066	55,245	291	188,469	141,432
34820	Myrtle Beach-Conway-North Myrtle Beach, SC	219,791	196,629	36.5	18,431	91,467	4,050,980	.0826	3,819,977	1,085	609,030	1,211	439,072	2,311	501,810	168,795
34900	Napa, CA	136,414	124,279	12.2	22,695	48,973	3,095,930	.0489	1,498,422	425	93,230	185	135,315	712	377,458	80,638
34940	Naples-Marco Island, FL	306,973	251,377	65.3	24,916	127,885	7,648,670	.1250	4,435,456	1,259	409,669	815	470,567	2,477	683,833	249,092
34980	Nashville-Davidson—Murfreesboro, TN	1,409,811	1,311,789	25.1	20,569	541,913	28,998,860	.5225	20,587,302	5,846	3,432,129	6,825	1,054,711	5,551	2,416,395	1,215,471
35300	New Haven-Milford, CT	853,637	824,008	2.5	23,814	319,931	20,328,100	.3285	11,057,950	3,140	1,088,751	2,165	650,116	3,422	1,673,415	780,780
35380	New Orleans-Metairie-Kenner, LA	1,308,631	1,316,510	4.1	16,870	487,345	22,076,390	.4096	15,192,435	4,316	2,684,592	5,339	940,553	4,950	2,086,751	1,160,187
35620	New York-Northern New Jersey-Long Island, NY-NJ-PA	18,864,705	18,323,002	8.8	22,872	6,753,723	431,479,210	6.7737	205,505,417	58,354	18,259,896	36,314	23,021,887	121,168	33,518,468	17,353,182
35660	Niles-Benton Harbor, MI	162,940	162,453	0.7	18,150	65,840	2,957,340	.0504	1,604,788	456	295,720	588	32,671	172	224,588	119,269
35980	Norwich-New London, CT	267,325	259,088	1.6	25,951	105,718	6,937,430	.1077	3,447,478	979	454,153	903	177,940	937	489,257	222,901
36100	Ocala, FL	294,555	258,916	32.9	16,944	121,424	4,991,010	.0921	3,382,818	961	535,220	1,064	94,712	498	427,647	197,001
36140	Ocean City, NJ	101,669	102,326	7.6	23,772	44,851	2,416,840	.0394	1,357,446	385	56,349	112	104,810	552	368,926	106,599
36220	Odessa, TX	124,311	121,123	1.8	14,158	45,309	1,760,030	.0368	1,535,143	436	363,065	722	49,705	262	203,323	70,887
36260	Ogden-Clearfield, UT	504,508	442,656	25.8	17,915	163,118	9,038,400	.1597	5,551,935	1,577	1,085,440	2,159	165,317	870	826,730	126,827
36420	Oklahoma City, OK	1,155,595	1,095,421	12.8	17,415	442,750	20,125,060	.3679	13,499,265	3,832	2,372,974	4,719	448,005	2,358	1,424,293	745,883
36500	Olympia, WA	229,500	207,355	28.6	21,189	90,231	4,862,910	.0830	2,958,276	840	761,569	1,515	83,210	438	469,563	106,737
36540	Omaha-Council Bluffs, NE-IA	807,305	767,041	11.8	19,390	306,915	15,653,930	.2878	11,414,520	3,240	1,424,659	2,833	408,037	2,148	1,344,280	640,405
36740	Orlando-Kissimmee, FL	1,900,560	1,644,561	34.3	19,478	701,773	37,018,160	.6726	26,135,598	7,423	3,848,482	7,653	1,791,331	9,428	3,390,238	1,412,260
36780	Oshkosh-Neenah, WI	159,732	156,763	11.7	20,158	65,214	3,219,810	.0561	2,030,094	576	271,497	540	72,095	379	199,281	121,453
36980	Owensboro, KY	111,282	109,875	5.0	18,297	45,880	2,036,130	.0350	1,151,487	327	250,306	498	38,546	203	123,435	84,334
37100	Oxnard-Thousand Oaks-Ventura, CA	813,570	753,197	12.6	23,388	262,514	19,028,060	.3036	9,778,861	2,777	1,019,623	2,028	564,619	2,972	1,522,187	578,898
37340	Palm Bay-Melbourne-Titusville, FL	523,567	476,230	19.4	20,941	216,202	10,963,820	.1797	5,760,123	1,636	986,272	1,961	242,067	1,274	880,605	408,228
37460	Panama City-Lynn Haven, FL	159,012	148,217	16.7	18,470	63,684	2,936,920	.0537	2,053,327	583	456,342	908	90,167	475	304,639	103,824
37620	Parkersburg-Marietta-Vienna, WV-OH	162,350	164,624	1.7	16,888	66,196	2,741,800	.0532	2,155,591	612	454,802	905	65,706	346	232,638	126,167
37700	Pascagoula, MS	156,158	150,564	14.1	17,302	56,599	2,701,890	.0464	1,446,338	411	367,729	731	30,424	161	177,256	62,826
37860	Pensacola-Ferry Pass-Brent, FL	437,128	412,153	19.7	18,438	170,330	8,059,970	.1392	4,649,972	1,321	829,735	1,650	185,536	977	639,256	315,918
37900	Peoria, IL	365,630	366,899	2.3	20,319	147,233	7,429,080	.1291	4,676,451	1,328	677,301	1,346	126,009	664	672,669	327,676
37980	Philadelphia-Camden-Wilmington, PA-NJ-DE-MD	5,831,625	5,687,147	4.6	21,621	2,150,234	126,083,610	2.1312	75,363,791	21,398	6,762,307	13,449	4,577,513	24,092	12,014,134	5,475,211
38060	Phoenix-Mesa-Scottsdale, AZ	3,801,803	3,251,876	45.3	19,272	1,365,972	73,268,000	1.2707	44,288,930	12,576	6,083,481	12,098	1,737,542	9,145	5,560,900	2,306,866
38220	Pine Bluff, AR	105,209	107,341	0.4	13,810	37,558	1,452,970	.0285	1,031,905	294	210,973	419	61,541	324	132,629	114,497
38300	Pittsburgh, PA	2,400,344	2,431,087	-1.5	18,315	982,565	43,962,330	.7882	28,664,871	8,140	3,316,295	6,594	1,332,924	7,014	4,615,707	2,088,178
38340	Pittsfield, MA	131,527	134,953	-3.2	20,937	56,899	2,753,800	.0465	1,607,360	456	145,868	290	131,236	691	316,206	119,866
38540	Pocatello, ID	82,761	83,103	13.7	16,175	31,124	1,338,700	.0258	1,005,022	286	163,727	326	20,963	110	161,952	48,759
38860	Portland-South Portland-Biddeford, ME	518,365	487,568	10.5	20,470	207,575	10,610,940	.1961	8,073,922	2,292	685,482	1,364	507,672	2,672	1,504,442	316,414
38900	Portland-Vancouver-Beaverton, OR-WA	2,110,156	1,927,881	26.5	21,174	816,926	44,680,070	.7713	28,248,512	8,021	5,153,465	10,249	1,511,846	7,958	3,705,264	927,293
38940	Port St. Lucie-Fort Pierce, FL	367,537	319,426	27.2	20,044	148,535	7,366,920	.1250	4,250,091	1,207	569,115	1,132	144,124	759	627,822	360,130
39100	Poughkeepsie-Newburgh-Middletown, NY	675,333	621,517	9.6	21,765	227,263	14,698,670	.2342	7,144,415	2,029	1,014,586	2,018	633,609	3,334	1,115,141	412,872
39140	Prescott, AZ	194,839	167,517	55.5	18,019	82,257	3,510,890	.0580	1,685,447	479	326,787	650	48,378	255	346,624	66,184
39300	Providence-New Bedford-Fall River, RI-MA	1,650,151	1,582,997	4.8	19,333	622,197	31,902,970	.5441	18,250,551	5,182	2,098,849	4,175	1,181,391	6,218	3,176,311	1,757,969
39340	Provo-Orem, UT	418,644	376,774	39.9	15,051	121,920	6,301,210	.1208	4,442,435	1,261	895,851	1,781	147,868	778	683,989	85,494
39380	Pueblo, CO	153,579	141,472	15.0	16,245	63,299	2,494,870	.0468	1,726,230	490	451,637	898	33,545	177	213,548	71,466
39460	Punta Gorda, FL	159,967	141,627	27.6	20,390	70,158	3,261,650	.0531	1,641,420	466	381,639	759	88,332	465	248,328	115,633
39540	Racine, WI	194,975	188,831	7.9	19,876	73,303	3,875,310	.0640	2,014,987	572	340,901	678	46,824	246	298,620	135,936
39580	Raleigh-Cary, NC	939,136	797,071	47.3	22,686	352,158	21,305,610	.3685	14,089,312	4,001	2,030,616	4,038	724,476	3,812	1,711,878	562,537
39660	Rapid City, SD	118,072	112,818	9.3	17,100	46,194	2,018,980	.0457	2,375,395	674	464,014	923	85,732	451	171,370	80,493
39740	Reading, PA	393,253	373,638	11.0	19,745	147,995	7,764,710	.1320	4,459,882	1,266	520,167	1,034	360,634	1,898	665,140	278,677
39820	Redding, CA	183,315	163,256	11.0	16,233	68,490	2,975,750	.0525	1,677,238	476	289,803	576	48,662	256	305,136	97,029
39900	Reno-Sparks, NV	393,925	342,885	33.3	20,837	152,950	8,208,150	.1420	5,176,296	1,470	834,750	1,660	171,290	902	706,590	218,418
40060	Richmond, VA	1,160,991	1,096,957	15.6	19,465	429,120	22,598,170	.3920	13,781,951	3,912	2,325,635	4,626	711,099	3,745	1,856,016	856,663
40140	Riverside-San Bernardino-Ontario, CA	3,886,808	3,254,821	25.7	16,596	1,212,880	64,505,060	1.1101	33,712,896	9,573	4,782,057	9,510	1,947,213	10,249	5,672,476	1,586,227
40220	Roanoke, VA	290,770	288,309	7.4	18,980	122,594	5,518,700	.1039	4,274,744	1,213	639,504	1,272	182,004	958	498,915	192,407
40340	Rochester, MN	177,491	163,618	15.3	23,279	74,200	4,131,820	.0678	2,325,506	660	521,908	1,039	70,143	369	243,382	90,830
40380	Rochester, NY	1,046,284	1,037,831	3.5	21,442	405,908	22,434,410	.3661	11,789,930	3,348	1,338,730	2,662	557,077	2,932	2,275,968	603,771
40420	Rockford, IL	337,385	320,204	12.9	19,770	126,099	6,670,200	.1156	4,101,173	1,164	657,662	1,308	154,269	812	683,652	252,244
40580	Rocky Mount, NC	145,779	143,026	7.3	16,141	56,140	2,352,980	.0427	1,454,070	413	185,504	369	84,602	445	164,321	97,894
40660	Rome, GA	95,112	90,565	11.5	15,664	34,940	1,489,880	.0279	1,005,428	285	246,219	490	47,928	252	95,400	71,700
40900	Sacramento—Arden-Arcade—Roseville, CA	2,081,634	1,796,857	21.3	20,754	750,053	43,201,390	.7038	22,059,537	6,264	2,803,436	5,575	1,176,056	6,190	3,944,199	988,483
40980	Saginaw-Saginaw Township North, MI	208,826	210,039	-0.9	18,088	83,826	3,777,280	.0745	3,243,013	921	628,319	1,250	299,025	1,574	277,335	166,225
41060	St. Cloud, MN	183,879	167,392	12.4	18,514	70,216	3,404,300	.0663	2,845,390	808	567,554	1,128	69,903	368	340,212	89,390
41100	St. George, UT	112,063	90,354	86.1	14,745	38,015	1,652,320	.0358	1,634,619	464	208,871	415	56,203	296	210,035	29,423
41140	St. Joseph, MO-KS	122,298	122,336	5.6	16,655	48,471	2,036,880	.0376	1,361,916	386	311,120	618	22,442	118	166,889	54,578
41180	St. Louis, MO-IL	2,769,054	2,698,687	4.6	20,781	1,095,739	57,542,920	.9635	32,488,202	9,227	4,945,403	9,837	1,203,617	6,337	4,460,102	2,272,744
41420	Salem, OR	374,986	347,214	24.9	16,813	131,258	6,304,480	.1141	3,997,943	1,135	850,280	1,691	145,165	764	577,419	135,511
41500	Salinas, CA	421,269	401,762	13.0	18,324	130,913	7,719,290	.1321	4,297,922	1,220	496,897	988	304,946	1,605	763,460	273,308
41540	Salisbury, MD	115,401	109,391	11.9	17,074	43,697	1,970,340	.0372	1,441,635	410	325,222	647	59,258	312	182,801	84,041
41620	Salt Lake City, UT	1,016,096	968,858	26.1	18,104	335,646	18,395,070	.3602	15,467,351	4,392	2,375,916	4,725	759,475	3,997	2,103,917	340,947
41660	San Angelo, TX	105,375	105,781	5.7	15,928	40,768	1,678,450	.0321	1,218,006	345	260,149	517	51,673	272	166,583	40,858
41700	San Antonio, TX	1,879,915	1,711,703	21.6	16,589	648,985	31,186,610	.5849	21,956,787	6,235	3,052,042	6,070	1,201,202	6,322	3,314,254	854,794
41740	San Diego-Carlsbad-San Marcos, CA	2,990,693	2,813,833	12.6	19,889	1,027,661	59,482,050	1.0104	34,231,355	9,720	4,237,412	8,427	2,478,722	13,046	5,315,838	1,790,799
41780	Sandusky, OH	78,323	79,551	3.6	20,617	32,271	1,614,780	.0275	965,059	274	200,248	398	52,598	277	121,844	78,924
41860	San Francisco-Oakland-Fremont, CA	4,167,248	4,123,740	11.9	27,223	1,532,531	113,444,860	1.7614	58,012,565	16,472	7,052,719	14,026	5,041,584	26,535	10,606,366	3,188,494
41940	San Jose-Sunnyvale-Santa Clara, CA	1,727,639	1,735,819	13.1	29,104	575,043	50,281,040	.7963	28,482,536	8,087	3,631,347	7,222	2,399,605	12,630	4,478,947	1,503,449
42020	San Luis Obispo-Paso Robles, CA	257,381	246,681	13.6	21,248	102,969	5,468,890	.0887	2,798,082	795	240,208	478	153,387	807	552,099	196,306
42060	Santa Barbara-Santa Maria, CA	404,582	399,347	8.0	19,919	139,852	8,058,830	.1386	4,839,745	1,374	499,060	992	335,212	1,764	874,460	322,723
42100	Santa Cruz-Watsonville, CA	248,347	255,602	11.3	23,192	87,640	5,759,610	.0926	3,020,791	858	310,796	618	162,723	856	605,097	265,080
42140	Santa Fe, NM	141,278	129,292	30.7	19,564	53,845	2,763,920	.0503	1,960,868	557	417,468	830	156,790	825	196,529	123,851
42220	Santa Rosa-Petaluma, CA	470,813	458,614	18.1	24,088	175,179	11,340,910	.1822	6,084,888	1,728	691,543	1,375	280,632	1,477	1,212,686	357,793
42260	Sarasota-Bradenton-Venice, FL	659,642	589,959	20.5	22,508	289,874	14,847,510	.2476	8,683,476	2,466	1,053,100	2,094	544,300	2,865	1,298,388	549,755

Source: Devonshire Associates Ltd. and Scan/US, Inc. 2005.

[#] Estimates for Total Retail Sales, General Merchandise Sales, Apparel Store Sales, Food Store Sales and Health and Drug Store Sales are based on data from the U.S. Census Bureau's 1997 Economic Census, and utilize the North American Industry Classification System (NAICS).

[†] CBSA totals are for Metropolitan Core Based Statistical Areas. A U.S. total for Micropolitan Core Based Statistical Areas is also provided.

Core Based Statistical Areas (CBSAs): Population/Income/Sales#†, *Continued*

CBSA FIPS Code	Core Based Statistical Area	Population Estimate 7/1/05	Population Census 4/1/00	% Change 4/1/90-4/1/00	Per Capita Income 2004	House-holds Estimate 7/1/05	Disposable Income 2004 ($1,000)	Market Ability Index 2004	Total Retail Sales 2004 Sales ($1,000)	Total Retail Sales Ranally Sales Units	General Merchandise 2004 Sales ($1,000)	General Merchandise Ranally Sales Units	Apparel Store 2004 Sales ($1,000)	Apparel Store Ranally Sales Units	Food Store Sales 2004 ($1,000)	Health & Drug Store Sales 2004 ($1,000)
42340	Savannah, GA	312,351	293,000	13.5	17,889	118,298	5,587,730	.1023	3,839,729	1,091	752,694	1,497	218,315	1,149	491,346	146,081
42540	Scranton—Wilkes-Barre, PA	547,294	560,625	-2.5	16,680	222,408	9,128,760	.1743	6,804,099	1,932	906,799	1,803	348,582	1,834	1,192,943	478,962
42660	Seattle-Tacoma-Bellevue, WA	3,202,012	3,043,878	18.9	23,536	1,279,990	75,362,930	1.2459	43,999,118	12,494	6,760,818	13,446	2,516,203	13,243	5,748,586	1,817,459
43100	Sheboygan, WI	114,016	112,646	8.4	20,368	45,505	2,322,260	.0378	1,160,993	330	251,599	500	16,223	85	172,267	56,215
43300	Sherman-Denison, TX	117,502	110,595	16.4	17,315	43,814	2,034,550	.0385	1,514,081	430	384,275	764	35,926	189	174,651	59,560
43340	Shreveport-Bossier City, LA	405,822	375,965	4.5	16,278	157,589	6,605,850	.1235	4,540,878	1,289	845,493	1,681	195,105	1,027	532,795	204,266
43580	Sioux City, IA-NE-SD	143,077	143,053	8.9	16,738	53,157	2,394,870	.0933	7,373,880	2,094	257,847	513	64,447	339	238,693	64,411
43620	Sioux Falls, SD	205,714	187,093	21.9	19,827	81,620	4,078,590	.0906	4,838,639	1,373	694,172	1,381	68,330	359	319,705	194,689
43780	South Bend-Mishawaka, IN-MI	318,467	316,663	6.8	16,509	113,467	5,257,570	.1011	3,986,552	1,132	732,085	1,456	156,473	823	421,491	279,547
43900	Spartanburg, SC	264,032	253,791	11.9	17,007	98,341	4,490,450	.0847	3,268,756	928	533,561	1,061	138,696	730	398,905	232,753
44060	Spokane, WA	439,273	417,939	15.7	18,223	180,505	8,004,860	.1437	5,223,271	1,483	985,255	1,959	248,626	1,309	753,870	200,787
44100	Springfield, IL	206,549	201,437	6.3	21,276	86,148	4,394,610	.0744	2,609,732	741	485,355	965	82,539	435	316,127	169,767
44140	Springfield, MA	689,619	680,014	1.0	19,551	266,392	13,482,560	.2241	7,089,078	2,013	700,829	1,393	347,601	1,830	1,358,554	569,374
44180	Springfield, MO	396,026	368,374	23.3	16,984	163,919	6,726,150	.1303	5,297,481	1,505	817,599	1,627	113,442	598	486,608	236,576
44220	Springfield, OH	141,771	144,742	-1.9	19,206	57,550	2,722,860	.0463	1,530,971	435	237,291	472	35,580	187	246,663	151,117
44300	State College, PA	141,710	135,758	9.7	16,078	52,454	2,278,390	.0430	1,600,239	454	218,370	434	91,218	480	222,490	77,825
44700	Stockton, CA	674,080	563,598	17.3	15,489	201,595	10,441,010	.1808	5,234,961	1,486	683,333	1,359	247,667	1,304	900,861	341,266
44940	Sumter, SC	106,517	104,646	2.0	14,511	37,845	1,545,670	.0291	1,000,202	284	156,992	312	57,119	301	121,933	48,459
45060	Syracuse, NY	657,851	650,154	-1.5	19,867	259,096	13,069,470	.2187	7,121,442	2,022	727,272	1,446	391,145	2,059	1,319,427	506,269
45220	Tallahassee, FL	332,381	320,304	23.6	19,244	136,829	6,396,380	.1102	3,771,080	1,070	687,992	1,368	185,765	978	577,012	250,701
45300	Tampa-St. Petersburg-Clearwater, FL	2,613,412	2,395,997	15.9	19,546	1,065,621	51,081,900	.9188	35,052,229	9,954	4,364,151	8,679	1,494,823	7,868	4,733,677	2,309,521
45460	Terre Haute, IN	168,071	170,943	2.6	15,174	64,969	2,550,300	.0635	3,522,605	1,001	563,297	1,121	116,709	614	211,768	105,240
45500	Texarkana, TX-Texarkana, AR	132,846	129,749	8.0	15,232	50,436	2,023,530	.0405	1,629,014	463	328,077	652	84,528	445	161,075	45,071
45780	Toledo, OH	660,207	659,188	0.8	18,686	261,574	12,336,350	.2261	8,715,587	2,475	1,279,575	2,545	339,161	1,785	1,205,392	508,701
45820	Topeka, KS	228,099	224,551	6.8	19,083	92,667	4,352,770	.0760	2,665,840	757	566,757	1,128	82,380	434	320,664	178,089
45940	Trenton-Ewing, NJ	369,496	350,761	7.7	24,296	124,536	8,977,430	.1416	4,534,000	1,287	431,841	859	361,412	1,902	714,006	472,475
46060	Tucson, AZ	921,681	843,746	26.5	17,523	359,359	16,151,030	.2750	8,503,748	2,415	1,331,237	2,647	348,394	1,834	1,318,403	534,417
46140	Tulsa, OK	892,708	859,532	12.9	16,921	325,055	15,105,360	.2830	10,740,382	3,049	2,251,087	4,477	353,338	1,860	1,078,609	649,765
46220	Tuscaloosa, AL	195,477	192,034	9.0	16,512	78,114	3,227,670	.0600	2,196,777	623	399,495	795	97,660	513	266,861	129,619
46340	Tyler, TX	189,133	174,706	15.5	16,668	68,560	3,152,460	.0649	2,900,030	823	492,616	980	195,885	1,031	351,168	135,119
46540	Utica-Rome, NY	297,654	299,896	-5.3	17,783	117,853	5,293,320	.0902	2,830,331	804	431,672	859	107,101	564	423,720	275,720
46660	Valdosta, GA	124,076	119,560	20.5	13,736	44,744	1,704,290	.0358	1,490,393	422	219,013	435	84,546	445	167,827	46,162
46700	Vallejo-Fairfield, CA	421,801	394,542	15.9	21,842	140,240	9,212,790	.1430	4,047,249	1,149	753,325	1,498	194,037	1,021	757,937	149,885
46940	Vero Beach, FL	124,614	112,947	25.2	22,707	56,392	2,829,580	.0479	1,748,173	496	255,235	508	160,139	843	244,829	149,165
47020	Victoria, TX	113,679	111,663	12.3	16,814	41,082	1,911,430	.0362	1,405,413	399	266,161	530	60,857	320	208,414	60,390
47220	Vineland-Millville-Bridgeton, NJ	151,331	146,438	6.1	17,001	50,414	2,572,830	.0457	1,545,886	439	141,137	281	57,136	301	329,106	128,153
47260	Virginia Beach-Norfolk-Newport News, VA-NC	1,657,806	1,576,370	8.8	17,951	605,358	29,759,360	.5226	17,878,284	5,077	2,872,048	5,712	1,052,924	5,542	2,298,054	818,082
47300	Visalia-Porterville, CA	404,818	368,021	18.0	12,914	120,917	5,227,730	.0963	2,765,611	785	418,656	833	108,161	569	563,264	158,385
47380	Waco, TX	222,879	213,517	12.9	15,287	81,749	3,407,130	.0644	2,317,504	658	441,422	878	85,844	452	368,221	97,552
47580	Warner Robins, GA	126,391	110,765	24.2	19,243	47,127	2,432,130	.0413	1,360,434	386	209,754	417	65,940	347	171,168	43,838
47900	Washington-Arlington-Alexandria, DC-VA-MD-WV	5,255,607	4,796,183	16.3	27,193	1,956,365	142,915,930	2.1044	59,584,175	16,919	7,598,428	15,111	4,119,320	21,682	9,723,739	3,048,892
47940	Waterloo-Cedar Falls, IA	161,128	163,706	3.2	17,211	63,320	2,773,120	.0527	2,085,410	591	329,929	656	62,452	329	247,531	118,328
48140	Wausau, WI	128,048	125,834	9.0	19,994	51,263	2,560,230	.0472	1,913,179	543	394,943	785	40,798	215	199,109	39,650
48260	Weirton-Steubenville, WV-OH	126,448	132,008	-7.4	16,713	53,884	2,113,340	.0358	1,048,619	298	175,680	350	33,988	179	207,784	110,680
48300	Wenatchee, WA	103,338	99,219	26.5	16,906	39,072	1,747,020	.0334	1,321,595	376	259,869	517	31,312	165	239,518	48,149
48540	Wheeling, WV-OH	148,237	153,172	-3.8	15,196	60,369	2,252,640	.0444	1,740,262	494	300,060	597	74,593	393	271,061	120,770
48620	Wichita, KS	589,782	571,166	11.7	18,371	222,302	10,834,610	.1881	6,353,689	1,803	1,285,957	2,557	258,667	1,362	930,859	314,872
48660	Wichita Falls, TX	146,648	151,524	7.9	16,505	56,755	2,420,430	.0452	1,679,367	477	324,785	646	49,352	259	235,393	80,012
48700	Williamsport, PA	117,787	120,044	1.1	16,584	47,746	1,953,340	.0380	1,538,724	437	234,178	466	69,595	366	245,666	120,115
48900	Wilmington, NC	305,944	274,532	37.2	19,028	127,137	5,821,440	.1120	4,785,890	1,359	638,298	1,269	198,342	1,044	613,090	254,604
49020	Winchester, VA-WV	114,788	102,997	22.4	17,745	42,966	2,036,860	.0396	1,668,427	473	393,152	782	63,306	334	168,609	108,592
49180	Winston-Salem, NC	447,369	421,961	16.7	18,954	173,506	8,479,430	.1546	5,943,063	1,688	810,281	1,611	293,126	1,544	669,754	340,918
49340	Worcester, MA	790,475	750,963	5.8	21,359	291,974	16,883,400	.2793	9,300,431	2,641	871,592	1,733	449,285	2,365	1,474,657	686,325
49420	Yakima, WA	229,468	222,581	17.9	13,955	77,113	3,202,190	.0607	2,041,424	580	479,903	954	65,560	345	329,172	58,849
49620	York-Hanover, PA	403,361	381,751	12.4	20,209	154,303	8,151,520	.1339	4,206,302	1,194	585,240	1,164	159,393	839	714,134	198,492
49660	Youngstown-Warren-Boardman, OH-PA	587,022	602,964	-1.7	17,320	234,973	10,167,400	.1889	7,151,818	2,030	956,983	1,903	406,424	2,139	929,823	469,480
49700	Yuba City, CA	153,877	139,149	13.5	14,540	50,617	2,237,430	.0399	1,184,765	337	238,417	474	31,237	165	256,559	86,882
49740	Yuma, AZ	177,064	160,026	49.7	13,429	59,841	2,377,840	.0452	1,477,200	419	322,796	642	34,478	181	221,749	77,415
	Micropolitan Statistical Area Total	30,246,680	29,477,802	10.0	16,313	11,662,263	493,428,880	9.1417	329,980,240	93,709	56,369,705	112,093	12,298,414	64,731	47,654,976	17,467,665
	CBSA Total	276,916,224	262,057,742	13.6	19,716	102,549,379	5,459,558,560	94.7259	3,355,809,775	952,895	483,593,619	961,717	186,545,843	981,835	470,691,106	195,984,550

Source: Devonshire Associates Ltd. and Scan/US, Inc. 2005.
Estimates for Total Retail Sales, General Merchandise Sales, Apparel Store Sales, Food Store Sales and Health and Drug Store Sales are based on data from the U.S. Census Bureau's 1997 Economic Census, and utilize the North American Industry Classification System (NAICS).

† CBSA totals are for Metropolitan Core Based Statistical Areas. A U.S. total for Micropolitan Core Based Statistical Areas is also provided.

Combined Statistical Areas (CSAs): Population/Income/Sales[#]

CSAs are groups of two or more adjacent CBSAs with a high degree of employment interchange.

CSA FIPS Code	Combined Statistical Area	Population			Per Capita Income 2004	House-holds Estimate 7/1/05	Disposable Income 2004 ($1,000)	Market Ability Index 2004	Total Retail Sales		General Merchandise		Apparel Store		Food Store Sales 2004 ($1,000)	Health & Drug Store 2004 ($1,000)
		Estimate 7/1/05	Census 4/1/00	% Change 4/1/90-4/1/00					2004 Sales ($1,000)	Ranally Sales Units	2004 Sales ($1,000)	Ranally Sales Units	2004 Sales ($1,000)	Ranally Sales Units		
102	Albany-Corvallis-Lebanon, OR	188,428	181,222	11.8	19,098	76,792	3,598,690	.0588	1,739,068	494	390,540	776	57,006	301	308,573	72,212
104	Albany-Schenectady-Amsterdam, NY	1,148,794	1,118,095	1.9	21,077	456,848	24,213,200	.3966	12,761,509	3,623	1,444,514	2,872	702,155	3,695	1,798,555	811,961
112	Ames-Boone, IA	106,698	106,205	6.8	17,992	41,268	1,919,660	.0336	1,134,029	322	214,449	426	41,739	220	164,563	46,941
118	Appleton-Oshkosh-Neenah, WI	376,237	358,365	13.7	20,797	149,305	7,824,600	.1368	5,095,443	1,446	746,975	1,486	193,307	1,017	567,911	213,205
120	Asheville-Brevard, NC	420,538	398,505	19.5	18,326	176,058	7,706,690	.1449	5,816,310	1,652	867,404	1,726	267,858	1,409	696,718	329,663
122	Atlanta-Sandy Springs-Gainesville, GA-AL	5,142,784	4,548,344	37.1	21,214	1,833,715	109,098,960	1.8773	68,305,574	19,393	9,313,034	18,522	3,602,186	18,959	9,435,771	2,951,947
132	Baton Rouge-Pierre Part, LA	750,528	729,361	12.8	16,567	264,889	12,433,970	.2329	8,686,737	2,466	1,603,667	3,189	359,252	1,890	1,064,036	433,143
138	Beckley-Oak Hill, WV	126,490	126,799	1.6	13,504	49,862	1,708,180	.0355	1,428,489	406	315,329	627	30,465	161	142,336	104,104
140	Bend-Prineville, OR	159,725	134,549	51.1	19,785	65,570	3,160,230	.0575	2,265,580	643	522,779	1,039	65,757	346	320,941	57,652
142	Birmingham-Hoover-Cullman, AL	1,165,267	1,129,721	10.3	18,331	450,006	21,360,440	.3852	14,188,077	4,029	2,399,875	4,772	687,319	3,618	1,760,172	731,599
148	Boston-Worcester-Manchester, MA-NH	5,862,486	5,715,698	6.9	23,829	2,179,554	139,697,250	2.3223	83,640,880	23,752	8,375,171	16,656	5,628,970	29,628	12,991,625	5,744,801
154	Brownsville-Harlingen-Raymondville, TX	400,052	355,309	27.9	8,444	103,273	3,377,920	.0813	2,926,540	831	689,711	1,371	196,699	1,035	504,194	126,956
160	Buffalo-Niagara-Cattaraugus, NY	1,237,664	1,254,066	-1.5	19,963	510,114	24,707,010	.4080	12,881,795	3,658	1,355,566	2,696	754,601	3,971	2,294,311	1,041,297
164	Cape Girardeau-Sikeston-Jackson, MO-IL	133,531	130,734	6.9	16,462	54,477	2,198,180	.0435	1,797,261	510	389,898	775	51,446	271	172,629	94,076
172	Charlotte-Gastonia-Salisbury, NC-SC	2,107,174	1,897,034	26.3	20,205	809,419	42,575,370	.7344	26,089,612	7,407	3,724,996	7,408	1,194,765	6,287	3,349,060	1,522,977
174	Chattanooga-Cleveland-Athens, TN-GA	651,300	629,561	11.8	17,189	252,300	11,195,040	.2044	7,407,819	2,104	1,265,128	2,517	378,570	1,992	932,400	481,910
176	Chicago-Naperville-Michigan City, IL-IN-WI	9,688,795	9,312,255	11.1	20,780	3,373,860	201,336,090	3.3759	114,114,176	32,403	13,590,913	27,028	6,485,666	34,134	14,950,706	9,827,587
178	Cincinnati-Middletown-Wilmington, OH-KY-IN	2,112,096	2,050,175	9.0	20,497	821,487	43,292,170	.7389	25,855,772	7,340	3,627,215	7,212	1,221,617	6,431	3,663,476	1,455,228
180	Claremont-Lebanon, NH-VT	215,748	207,845	7.3	18,958	85,655	4,090,180	.0745	2,871,696	816	270,770	538	68,496	360	570,827	120,624
184	Cleveland-Akron-Elyria, OH	2,944,122	2,945,831	3.0	19,768	1,165,374	58,200,820	1.0275	37,917,926	10,767	3,873,189	7,703	1,839,936	9,683	5,529,367	3,880,280
188	Clovis-Portales, NM	63,702	63,062	7.0	13,044	23,497	830,920	.0165	582,188	165	131,867	262	26,953	142	68,651	28,345
192	Columbia-Newberry, SC	724,958	683,266	17.5	18,368	274,969	13,315,780	.2393	8,783,575	2,493	1,756,890	3,494	455,542	2,397	1,121,050	473,027
194	Columbus-Auburn-Opelika, GA-AL	422,147	420,965	11.2	15,726	165,394	6,638,780	.1217	4,172,599	1,184	780,510	1,551	238,627	1,255	621,322	252,240
198	Columbus-Marion-Chillicothe, OH	1,947,508	1,835,189	13.7	19,787	738,766	38,535,920	.6999	27,415,290	7,784	3,444,664	6,850	1,331,449	7,007	3,301,838	1,155,828
200	Columbus-West Point, MS	81,355	83,565	3.9	14,645	30,568	1,191,450	.0247	1,034,030	294	237,503	472	46,392	244	120,506	56,002
202	Corbin-London, KY	94,979	88,580	15.4	11,524	34,510	1,094,500	.0246	1,015,090	288	269,003	535	20,227	107	68,121	49,644
204	Corpus Christi-Kingsville, TX	439,490	435,243	9.2	15,153	153,842	6,659,730	.1288	4,828,713	1,371	849,839	1,690	227,319	1,197	798,534	198,851
206	Dallas-Fort Worth, TX	6,079,128	5,377,361	29.2	19,785	2,057,085	120,275,970	2.1311	79,301,664	22,520	11,518,330	22,903	4,122,080	21,696	10,087,475	3,269,500
212	Dayton-Springfield-Greenville, OH	1,077,865	1,085,094	0.4	19,731	434,118	21,267,560	.3668	12,822,676	3,642	2,029,342	4,035	510,202	2,684	1,779,806	704,795
214	Deltona-Daytona Beach-Palm Coast, FL	554,014	493,175	23.5	18,262	220,945	10,117,500	.1771	6,075,367	1,725	882,131	1,754	253,960	1,337	957,383	421,164
216	Denver-Aurora-Boulder, CO	2,653,866	2,449,054	30.6	24,972	1,092,050	66,272,850	1.0590	35,671,824	10,128	5,108,361	10,159	1,631,775	8,589	5,144,765	1,363,338
218	Des Moines-Newton-Pella, IA	587,776	550,659	14.4	19,855	225,604	11,670,020	.2013	7,076,529	2,009	923,886	1,837	256,134	1,348	927,588	348,098
220	Detroit-Warren-Flint, MI	5,448,771	5,357,538	5.1	21,753	2,088,029	118,524,990	2.0348	74,751,724	21,226	12,196,636	24,255	3,532,199	18,590	8,692,543	5,514,472
222	Dothan-Enterprise-Ozark, AL	229,971	223,605	6.4	15,961	90,182	3,670,460	.0720	2,873,593	817	576,903	1,148	102,585	540	257,187	124,690
232	Eau Claire-Menomonie, WI	196,150	188,195	8.5	17,614	77,998	3,455,000	.0702	3,160,001	897	660,709	1,315	109,914	578	320,332	154,200
242	Fairmont-Clarksburg, WV	148,005	148,742	-0.0	14,706	58,773	2,176,570	.0429	1,650,416	469	349,391	695	58,820	310	194,480	108,319
244	Fargo-Wahpeton, ND-MN	205,820	199,503	11.5	18,192	84,394	3,744,250	.0756	3,435,787	976	470,802	937	103,920	546	313,892	160,908
248	Findlay-Tiffin, OH	131,788	129,978	3.8	19,022	51,866	2,506,920	.0456	1,752,018	498	309,133	614	50,039	263	187,930	82,832
252	Fond du Lac-Beaver Dam, WI	186,879	183,193	9.9	19,138	71,258	3,576,480	.0599	1,896,956	539	381,579	759	38,337	201	222,878	69,864
256	Fort Polk South-De Ridder, LA	82,559	85,517	-7.1	14,976	30,765	1,236,400	.0214	593,529	169	145,241	289	16,392	86	53,458	19,403
258	Fort Wayne-Huntington-Auburn, IN	567,257	548,416	11.0	17,623	204,640	9,996,680	.1830	6,787,867	1,928	1,249,774	2,485	233,382	1,229	716,704	367,026
260	Fresno-Madera, CA	1,023,612	922,516	22.1	13,455	310,660	13,772,950	.2578	8,098,841	2,300	1,107,057	2,201	341,667	1,798	1,458,744	503,267
266	Grand Rapids-Muskegon-Holland, MI	1,319,894	1,254,661	15.8	19,514	492,502	25,755,800	.4502	16,107,560	4,574	3,376,877	6,716	532,432	2,802	1,482,242	820,268
268	Greensboro—Winston-Salem—High Point, NC	1,489,023	1,414,656	18.1	18,722	584,338	27,878,220	.5056	19,101,592	5,424	2,526,683	5,023	921,848	4,854	2,287,656	1,170,576
273	Greenville-Spartanburg-Anderson, SC	1,181,206	1,128,104	15.5	17,400	448,438	20,553,570	.3795	14,216,582	4,037	2,098,642	4,173	731,285	3,848	1,832,375	894,535
274	Gulfport-Biloxi-Pascagoula, MS	407,743	396,754	16.8	17,232	154,982	7,026,180	.1263	4,424,006	1,257	1,121,303	2,230	153,372	809	458,514	205,329
276	Harrisburg-Carlisle-Lebanon, PA	644,200	629,401	7.0	20,516	260,218	13,216,590	.2389	9,452,727	2,684	945,453	1,880	342,116	1,801	1,274,186	498,443
278	Hartford-West Hartford-Willimantic, CT	1,312,381	1,257,709	2.6	26,145	506,863	34,312,540	.5210	15,767,625	4,477	1,380,295	2,745	1,126,569	5,929	2,530,235	1,269,084
288	Houston-Baytown-Huntsville, TX	5,394,905	4,815,122	24.9	17,909	1,783,800	96,619,650	1.7475	63,831,362	18,127	10,687,155	21,254	3,691,407	19,429	9,387,712	3,005,943
290	Huntsville-Decatur, AL	515,684	488,243	15.0	19,754	200,528	10,186,810	.1768	6,275,661	1,782	1,305,833	2,597	291,541	1,535	696,379	286,778
292	Idaho Falls-Blackfoot, ID	154,711	143,412	13.5	15,845	52,339	2,451,330	.0467	1,761,927	500	374,708	745	35,595	188	249,414	62,023
294	Indianapolis-Anderson-Columbus, IN	1,963,161	1,843,588	15.6	19,782	740,938	38,836,210	.6971	26,656,765	7,572	4,748,371	9,444	1,045,242	5,503	2,427,132	1,727,919
296	Ithaca-Cortland, NY	150,241	145,100	1.4	17,604	57,013	2,644,860	.0448	1,368,066	389	137,704	274	45,340	239	311,798	87,937
297	Jackson-Humboldt, TN	158,577	155,529	13.4	17,361	64,205	2,752,980	.0528	2,124,776	603	440,397	875	119,811	631	203,163	116,389
298	Jackson-Yazoo City, MS	546,547	525,346	11.2	16,355	193,626	8,938,700	.1739	6,955,313	1,975	1,482,393	2,949	294,912	1,552	649,848	419,425
304	Johnson City-Kingsport-Bristol (Tri-Cities), TN-VA	489,628	480,091	10.1	16,293	205,493	7,977,390	.1512	5,729,468	1,627	1,115,462	2,217	248,987	1,309	691,688	350,663
312	Kansas City-Overland Park-Kansas City, MO-KS	2,021,011	1,901,070	12.1	21,106	794,124	42,655,340	.7298	26,130,635	7,420	4,083,987	8,123	996,473	5,245	2,994,057	1,367,582
314	Knoxville-Sevierville-La Follette, TN	821,927	779,013	16.6	18,083	335,358	14,862,560	.2948	12,947,469	3,676	2,072,633	4,121	728,356	3,835	1,408,793	696,870
316	Kokomo-Peru, IN	137,399	137,623	2.8	19,518	54,910	2,681,820	.0474	1,732,477	492	365,717	727	42,012	221	169,515	135,686
318	Lafayette-Acadiana, LA	521,932	512,720	10.7	14,820	195,754	7,735,160	.1561	6,305,317	1,790	1,198,345	2,382	267,718	1,409	751,658	437,718
320	Lafayette-Frankfort, IN	216,614	212,407	11.9	17,301	83,104	3,747,680	.0683	2,476,530	703	534,902	1,064	88,326	464	220,060	136,615
324	Lake Charles-Jennings, LA	223,358	225,003	8.1	16,998	87,852	3,796,540	.0711	2,698,853	766	687,698	1,367	103,388	544	305,522	149,530
330	Lansing-East Lansing-Owosso, MI	534,786	519,415	3.4	20,743	218,187	11,092,980	.1903	6,781,551	1,925	1,529,635	3,042	238,899	1,256	757,214	390,086
332	Las Vegas-Paradise-Pahrump, NV	1,735,504	1,408,250	85.5	19,116	633,961	33,175,320	.5803	20,529,777	5,830	2,893,176	5,754	1,375,987	7,242	3,061,259	891,517
336	Lexington-Fayette—Frankfort—Richmond, KY	634,845	602,773	17.4	18,880	254,373	11,985,820	.2156	8,037,046	2,282	1,328,934	2,642	406,467	2,139	826,956	503,805
338	Lima-Van Wert-Wapakoneta, OH	182,374	184,743	-0.0	17,846	70,584	3,254,640	.0611	2,406,651	683	494,790	984	72,942	384	224,573	145,456
340	Little Rock-North Little Rock-Pine Bluff, AR	815,978	785,024	12.7	18,167	322,889	14,823,800	.2781	11,072,814	3,145	2,357,292	4,688	433,723	2,282	956,918	468,323
346	Longview-Marshall, TX	263,835	256,152	7.8	15,726	98,022	4,149,040	.0808	3,156,067	897	610,654	1,215	108,601	572	405,847	139,137
348	Los Angeles-Long Beach-Riverside, CA	17,797,954	16,373,645	12.7	18,175	5,656,166	323,477,190	5.5373	179,005,294	50,829	22,596,646	44,938	13,718,406	72,203	27,995,671	9,960,320
350	Louisville-Elizabethtown-Scottsburg, KY-IN	1,340,908	1,292,482	9.7	18,855	517,863	25,282,710	.4390	15,092,082	4,285	2,612,921	5,197	597,306	3,144	1,557,335	966,940
352	Lubbock-Levelland, TX	284,511	272,416	7.2	15,738	111,853	4,477,570	.0924	4,011,866	1,139	606,569	1,206	189,281	996	586,991	125,816
354	Lumberton-Laurinburg, NC	163,450	159,337	14.7	12,452	58,235	2,035,300	.0422	1,581,077	449	229,065	455	70,665	372	213,182	82,248
356	Macon-Warner Robins-Fort Valley, GA	381,000	356,801	12.6	17,251	142,199	6,572,520	.1205	4,412,888	1,253	767,552	1,526	221,446	1,166	588,731	212,015
358	Madison-Baraboo, WI	599,114	556,999	16.2	22,091	251,494	13,234,990	.2397	9,872,686	2,803	1,197,324	2,381	273,772	1,440	957,387	384,148
360	Mansfield-Bucyrus, OH	173,148	175,818	1.0	17,905	70,355	3,100,160	.0556	1,989,041	564	386,585	769	59,166	311	228,379	127,729
372	Midland-Odessa, TX	245,163	237,132	5.1	15,705	88,662	3,850,290	.0776	3,237,694	919	682,910	1,358	136,921	721	394,557	127,203
376	Milwaukee-Racine-Waukesha, WI	1,716,448	1,689,572	5.1	20,458	671,142	35,115,230	.5902	19,848,556	5,635	2,959,865	5,886	652,778	3,435	2,758,299	1,367,764
378	Minneapolis-St. Paul-St. Cloud, MN-WI	3,482,271	3,271,888	16.4	23,653	1,377,882	82,367,700	1.4204	55,102,662	15,647	8,244,423	16,394	1,991,312	10,481	6,754,177	2,450,363
380	Mobile-Daphne-Fairhope, AL	558,139	540,258	13.3	15,224	191,163	8,497,060	.1626	5,993,132	1,702	1,221,428	2,429	352,485	1,855	737,702	358,432
384	Monroe-Bastrop, LA	200,434	201,074	3.2	15,091	77,335	3,024,690	.0591	2,266,301	644	596,702	1,187	103,839	547	256,421	108,052
388	Montgomery-Alexander City, AL	408,053	400,205	12.7	16,927	152,803	6,907,300	.1277	4,709,594	1,338	950,404	1,891	210,690	1,109	540,017	299,120
392	Morristown-Newport, TN	165,061	156,646	20.7	15,032	65,683	2,481,180	.0471	1,688,029	479	345,869	686	53,914	284	208,901	103,698
396	Myrtle Beach-Conway-Georgetown, SC	280,520	252,426	32.6	17,970	114,457	5,040,980	.1012	4,511,628	1,281	762,646	1,516	501,537	2,640	609,839	218,948
400	Nashville-Davidson—Murfreesboro—Columbia, TN	1,485,190	1,381,287	25.2	20,516	571,171	30,470,010	.5465	21,305,769	6,050	3,566,750	7,093	1,088,378	5,728	2,525,588	1,251,840
406	New Orleans-Metairie-Bogalusa, LA	1,352,374	1,360,436	4.0	16,712	504,110	22,600,880	.4197	15,501,959	4,404	2,734,891	5,439	949,391	4,997	2,136,401	1,183,619
408	New York-Newark-Bridgeport, NY-NJ-CT-PA	22,048,103	21,361,797	8.4	23,227	7,899,975	512,109,090	8.0791	251,245,248	71,342	22,085,271	43,922	25,986,820	136,773	40,024,803	20,111,782
416	Oklahoma City-Shawnee, OK	1,223,461	1,160,942	12.7	17,234	467,266	21,085,380	.3854	14,034,161	3,984	2,514,238	5,000	473,522	2,492	1,484,472	794,533
420	Omaha-Council Bluffs-Fremont, NE-IA	843,112	803,201	11.5	19,311	321,534	16,281,040	.3019	12,149,838	3,449	1,545,575	3,073	423,692	2,230	1,409,273	690,874
422	Orlando-The Villages, FL	1,962,360	1,697,906	35.1	19,404	727,715	38,077,680	.6881	26,381,919	7,493	3,879,618	7,715	1,791,694	9,430	3,442,106	1,422,749
424	Paducah-Mayfield, KY-IL	134,919	135,793	6.0	16,654	55,934	2,246,880	.0443	1,832,814	521	470,595	936	98,144	517	149,568	109,101
426	Peoria-Canton, IL	402,994	405,149	2.1	19,930	161,962	8,031,700	.1394	4,978,333	1,414	727,389	1,446	133,277	702	730,050	353,717
428	Philadelphia-Camden-Vineland, PA-NJ-DE-MD	5,982,956	5,833,585	4.7	21,504	2,200,648	128,656,440	2.1769	76,909,677	21,837	6,903,444	13,730	4,634,649	24,393	12,343,239	5,603,364
430	Pittsburgh-New Castle, PA	2,493,145	2,525,730	-1.5	18,239	1,020,219	45,473,310	.8154	29,578,383	8,399	3,425,621	6,811	1,347,647	7,091	4,764,369	2,149,961
438	Portland-Lewiston-South Portland, ME	626,031	591,361	8.2	19,943	251,658	12,484,690	.2353	9,916,700	2,815	899,486	1,790	529,446	2,787	1,740,906	389,959
450	Raleigh-Durham-Cary, NC	1,501,912	1,314,589	37.9	21,401	572,614	32,142,870	.5510	19,996,135	5,679	2,675,835	5,321	1,028,680	5,413	2,692,081	919,285
464	Rochester-Batavia-Seneca Falls, NY	1,141,819	1,131,543	3.2	21,214	441,953	24,222,220	.3955	12,658,650	3,595	1,431,782	2,847	665,375	3,502	2,389,644	646,160
466	Rockford-Freeport-Rochelle, IL	439,376	420,215	11.2	19,732	165,752	8,669,610	.1475	4,991,627	1,417	788,280	1,568	172,171	906	806,521	303,967
472	Sacramento—Arden-Arcade—Truckee, CA-NV	2,226,161	1,930,149	21.6	20,933	808,924	46,599,860	.7542	23,366,041	6,635	2,838,580	5,645	1,231,066	6,479	4,287,803	1,087,738
474	Saginaw-Bay City-Saginaw Township North, MI	317,927	320,196	-1.1	18,323	129,245	5,825,360	.1136	4,884,365	1,387	988,848	1,967	352,019	1,853	441,131	245,841
476	St. Louis-St. Charles-Farmington, MO-IL	2,830,590	2,754,328	4.7	20,626	1,118,018	58,383,280	.9801	33,086,271	9,397	5,114,204	10,173	1,222,377	6,436	4,530,943	2,327,751
480	Salisbury-Ocean Pines, MD	165,220	155,934	17.4	18,041	64,457	2,980,810	.0559	2,215,406	630	415,118	826	166,934	879	325,250	134,090
482	Salt Lake City-Ogden-Clearfield, UT	1,584,748	1,469,474	26.0	17,990	519,325	28,509,380	.5381	21,559,221	6,122	3,514,638	6,990	935,761	4,925	3,026,185	476,361
488	San Jose-San Francisco-Oakland, CA	7,172,262	7,092,596	12.8	26,928	2,559,606	193,135,140	3.0244	101,146,451	28,719	12,532,960	24,924	8,213,897	43,231	18,038,490	5,545,339
492	Santa Fe-Espanola, NM	181,875	170,482	27.9	18,273	69,122	3,323,380	.0606	2,283,445	649	428,904	853	159,469	839	257,170	163,287
496	Savannah-Hinesville-Fort Stewart, GA	382,074	364,914	15.1	17,120	142,136	6,541,250	.1188	4,255,815	1,209	851,548	1,693	236,965	1,247	547,523	158,175
500	Seattle-Tacoma-Olympia, WA	3,808,481	3,604,165	19.8	23,054	1,514,412	87,801,390	1.4472	50,121,249	14,233	8,192,077	16,293	2,684,839	14,131	6,716,819	2,085,686
508	Shreveport-Bossier City-Minden, LA	446,519	417,796	4.0	16,172	174,576	7,220,980	.1350	4,946,520	1,404	918,765	1,827	207,407	1,092	597,174	220,752
512	Sioux City-Vermillion, IA-NE-SD	156,102	156,590	8.3	16,384	58,136	2,557,620	.0967	7,508,165	2,132	262,928	523	64,712	340	253,539	66,747
526	Sunbury-Lewisburg-Selinsgrove, PA	173,421	173,726	2.4	15,647	66,491	2,713,580	.0501	1,737,020	493	224,129	446	38,055	200	265,402	105,654
532	Syracuse-Auburn, NY	740,003	732,117	-1.4	19,682	290,321	14,564,740	.2429	7,780,798	2,209	820,305	1,631	412,184	2,170	1,430,926	573,891
534	Toledo-Fremont, OH	721,803	720,980	0.7	18,692	285,694	13,491,960	.2456	9,338,601	2,652	1,381,742	2,748	353,126	1,859	1,304,081	542,424
538	Tulsa-Bartlesville, OK	941,871	908,528	12.3	16,967	344,910	15,980,450	.2975	11,158,239	3,168	2,401,388	4,776	368,504	1,940	1,110,236	673,333
540	Tyler-Jacksonville, TX	237,448	221,365	15.1	15,909	85,600	3,777,570	.0769	3,290,630	934	573,865	1,142	203,719	1,072	415,206	149,765
542	Union City-Martin, TN-KY	73,415	75,097	4.4	15,852	30,573	1,163,810	.0210	689,706	196	176,598	352	35,214	185	68,769	34,429
548	Washington-Baltimore-Northern Virginia, DC-MD-VA-WV	8,167,341	7,572,647	13.1	25,425	3,044,708	207,655,670	3.1382	91,848,608	26,078	12,003,788	23,872	5,919,697	31,160	15,325,656	4,945,536
554	Wausau-Merrill, WI	158,465	155,475	9.2	19,562	63,574	3,099,940	.0565	2,213,364	628	438,851	872	45,284	239	235,030	52,326
556	Wichita-Winfield, KS	625,277	607,457	10.8	18,240	236,571	11,404,830	.1983	6,691,897	1,899	1,333,225	2,651	266,923	1,405	992,637	344,531
558	Williamsport-Lock Haven, PA	154,932	157,958	1.3	16,247	62,909	2,517,240	.0489	1,947,627	553	270,365	538	87,209	459	309,440	140,197
564	York-Hanover-Gettysburg, PA	502,894	473,043	13.2	19,844	190,449	9,979,640	.1616	4,799,517	1,362	646,482	1,286	172,030	906	840,243	223,846
566	Youngstown-Warren-East Liverpool, OH-PA	698,203	715,039	-1.0	17,126	278,924	11,957,130	.2207	8,176,840	2,321	1,063,822	2,115	428,197	2,254	1,095,914	547,426
CSA Total		**183,624,479**	**174,094,288**	**12.7**	**20,730**	**67,382,624**	**3,806,539,540**	**64.6312**	**2,248,602,727**	**638,497**	**305,462,522**	**607,463**	**134,241,065**	**706,540**	**318,640,245**	**135,520,445**

Source: Devonshire Associates Ltd. and Scan/US, Inc. 2005.
[#] Estimates for Total Retail Sales, General Merchandise Sales, Apparel Store Sales, Food Store Sales and Health and Drug Store Sales are based on data from the U.S. Census Bureau's 1997 Economic Census, and utilize the North American Industry Classification System (NAICS).

Core Based Statistical Areas (CBSAs): State Totals for Population/Income/Sales[#†]

State	Population Estimate 7/1/05	Population Census 4/1/00	% Change 4/1/90-4/1/00	Per Capita Income 2004	Households Estimate 7/1/05	Disposable Income 2004 ($1,000)	Market Ability Index 2004	Total Retail Sales 2004 Sales ($1,000)	Total Retail Sales Ranally Sales Units	General Merchandise 2004 Sales ($1,000)	General Merchandise Ranally Sales Units	Apparel Store 2004 Sales ($1,000)	Apparel Store Ranally Sales Units	Food Store Sales 2004 ($1,000)	Health & Drug Store 2004 ($1,000)
Alabama	3,215,600	3,133,253	10.2	17,336	1,228,993	55,746,220	1.0210	37,495,347	10,647	7,341,246	14,600	1,726,859	9,089	4,526,286	1,953,932
Alaska	438,970	402,445	17.1	21,484	155,336	9,430,830	.1667	6,476,739	1,839	1,454,962	2,894	284,439	1,497	750,061	82,609
Arizona	5,219,480	4,539,485	41.1	18,652	1,910,888	97,354,590	1.6863	57,269,127	16,262	8,347,894	16,601	2,200,927	11,584	7,676,846	3,013,783
Arkansas	1,613,233	1,516,451	18.8	17,228	630,695	27,792,980	.5270	20,738,727	5,890	5,184,810	10,311	731,517	3,850	1,828,625	838,029
California	35,587,117	33,075,450	13.9	19,779	11,750,887	703,891,080	11.7901	383,978,265	109,029	48,689,579	96,828	27,835,590	146,504	63,874,291	21,326,772
Colorado	4,035,820	3,676,685	30.4	23,412	1,645,610	94,488,440	1.5359	51,914,750	14,741	8,188,331	16,284	2,077,390	10,936	7,044,494	1,920,579
Connecticut	3,227,400	3,114,281	3.4	26,787	1,219,044	86,451,610	1.3778	47,971,594	13,621	3,821,743	7,600	3,138,746	16,521	6,770,680	2,981,654
Delaware	663,422	626,962	13.4	20,726	239,157	13,749,920	.2480	9,824,909	2,790	1,373,022	2,730	410,062	2,158	1,465,818	557,817
District of Columbia	548,902	572,059	-5.7	26,120	245,648	14,337,490	.1918	3,540,123	1,005	143,774	286	501,970	2,642	938,614	520,795
Florida	16,535,628	14,973,073	23.4	19,387	6,406,071	320,583,230	5.6967	210,670,596	59,823	28,543,464	56,763	13,470,854	70,904	29,237,107	13,589,123
Georgia	7,219,972	6,526,455	29.2	19,870	2,603,792	143,458,840	2.5190	92,165,113	26,166	13,589,411	27,024	4,830,270	25,423	12,412,075	4,077,567
Hawaii	910,475	876,156	4.8	20,281	302,181	18,465,370	.3063	9,903,032	2,812	1,988,367	3,954	1,320,832	6,952	1,401,658	865,911
Idaho	906,127	807,044	35.8	17,760	337,802	16,093,140	.3011	11,748,677	3,336	2,130,208	4,237	347,883	1,830	1,658,593	417,300
Illinois	11,104,863	10,713,406	9.9	20,731	3,968,416	230,213,110	3.8746	131,997,186	37,482	16,740,872	33,296	6,988,575	36,784	17,812,427	10,966,014
Indiana	4,869,076	4,686,372	10.7	18,431	1,825,089	89,742,980	1.6567	64,320,526	18,269	11,627,280	23,123	2,450,967	12,900	6,269,769	3,949,503
Iowa	1,616,647	1,563,592	10.0	19,035	630,930	30,772,930	.5581	21,308,670	6,050	3,136,740	6,238	784,167	4,129	2,659,601	1,085,988
Kansas	1,733,414	1,644,292	13.7	20,377	664,152	35,322,340	.6020	20,889,065	5,931	3,710,803	7,381	986,979	5,195	2,825,848	1,083,353
Kentucky	2,361,789	2,272,494	11.4	18,972	917,735	44,808,620	.7852	27,741,580	7,874	4,712,702	9,374	1,264,505	6,656	2,996,376	1,751,098
Louisiana	3,394,419	3,340,667	6.8	16,582	1,264,674	56,286,790	1.0647	40,643,378	11,542	7,938,240	15,784	2,028,283	10,675	5,075,872	2,522,793
Maine	775,616	736,280	6.2	19,317	312,854	14,982,280	.2867	12,217,299	3,468	1,223,422	2,434	579,414	3,050	2,177,309	484,136
Maryland	5,351,399	5,020,431	10.7	23,770	1,972,970	127,205,260	1.9677	58,838,507	16,706	7,462,449	14,841	3,395,025	17,870	10,335,314	3,093,860
Massachusetts	6,435,592	6,324,590	5.4	23,206	2,420,407	149,341,150	2.4371	82,738,815	23,494	7,429,152	14,775	5,989,862	31,527	13,517,577	6,515,936
Michigan	8,275,700	8,099,288	6.1	20,965	3,193,147	173,501,310	3.0038	110,008,791	31,237	20,258,924	40,289	4,898,714	25,780	12,074,823	7,401,268
Minnesota	3,736,008	3,534,372	14.9	23,302	1,494,361	87,056,650	1.5088	58,679,922	16,663	9,005,183	17,909	2,094,829	11,026	7,120,335	2,656,212
Mississippi	1,264,604	1,194,552	16.6	16,773	458,644	21,211,170	.3957	14,771,087	4,196	3,490,172	6,943	534,808	2,815	1,384,097	866,869
Missouri	4,228,355	4,069,962	9.2	20,140	1,698,860	85,159,240	1.4742	52,666,045	14,953	8,168,249	16,244	1,664,780	8,763	6,185,746	3,149,446
Montana	325,230	315,063	13.4	17,353	133,686	5,643,770	.1124	4,873,216	1,384	1,027,863	2,043	144,385	759	516,091	159,154
Nebraska	997,542	942,503	13.9	19,164	377,698	19,117,350	.3469	13,306,249	3,778	1,932,408	3,843	488,312	2,569	1,673,437	789,468
Nevada	2,148,819	1,771,107	70.4	19,485	794,873	41,869,790	.7339	26,419,116	7,502	3,777,460	7,512	1,548,126	8,148	3,881,729	1,169,845
New Hampshire	822,056	770,433	12.3	23,045	310,139	18,943,970	.3616	16,618,307	4,719	2,712,884	5,395	694,317	3,655	2,473,008	578,683
New Jersey	8,781,525	8,414,350	8.9	25,405	3,158,187	223,094,560	3.4949	113,098,864	32,114	9,425,753	18,747	7,807,303	41,090	20,203,086	7,598,965
New Mexico	1,245,480	1,147,424	24.0	16,990	459,862	21,160,110	.3917	14,514,055	4,122	2,998,941	5,964	587,687	3,092	1,303,022	764,558
New York	17,778,667	17,415,517	5.9	21,068	6,549,467	374,554,690	5.9849	179,568,008	50,989	18,434,842	36,662	20,227,874	106,463	28,278,682	15,755,700
North Carolina	5,970,031	5,485,424	24.3	19,604	2,320,285	117,034,750	2.0960	79,344,974	22,532	11,090,378	22,054	3,924,733	20,655	9,712,823	4,220,841
North Dakota	290,968	283,966	10.3	18,051	117,031	5,252,370	.1124	5,522,404	1,568	905,752	1,802	174,863	919	462,550	270,985
Ohio	9,247,337	9,140,806	4.6	19,585	3,641,282	181,111,310	3.2252	120,565,069	34,233	15,586,477	30,996	5,560,237	29,264	16,436,105	8,478,898
Oklahoma	2,247,335	2,157,030	12.3	16,920	840,395	38,026,020	.7013	25,720,859	7,301	5,063,639	10,071	831,077	4,374	2,690,737	1,454,285
Oregon	2,822,798	2,617,733	22.9	20,233	1,114,616	57,114,820	1.0216	39,313,735	11,162	7,306,917	14,530	1,854,676	9,763	5,180,190	1,198,404
Pennsylvania	10,432,688	10,319,747	3.0	19,334	4,040,545	201,707,500	3.5650	130,044,432	36,925	13,435,648	26,718	7,203,596	37,912	20,571,920	9,115,583
Rhode Island	1,097,105	1,048,319	4.5	18,950	413,521	20,790,140	.3502	11,203,327	3,181	947,014	1,884	723,676	3,809	2,021,832	1,212,306
South Carolina	3,188,958	3,001,853	15.8	17,578	1,198,055	56,054,410	1.0298	38,462,778	10,922	6,432,994	12,793	2,233,708	11,757	5,178,820	2,100,519
South Dakota	337,251	312,495	17.1	18,879	133,048	6,367,010	.1886	12,975,087	3,683	1,158,186	2,304	154,062	810	508,764	276,992
Tennessee	4,315,548	4,122,288	16.8	18,751	1,687,498	80,920,090	1.4982	59,127,606	16,788	10,362,232	20,606	3,152,488	16,591	6,436,545	3,617,539
Texas	19,890,111	17,944,548	24.9	17,490	6,718,651	347,875,800	6.5051	251,131,382	71,312	38,491,458	76,545	13,146,184	69,192	33,297,316	10,895,545
Utah	2,149,752	1,970,033	30.6	17,121	689,957	36,806,740	.7043	28,129,066	7,987	4,784,653	9,515	1,161,345	6,112	3,971,802	608,790
Vermont	206,121	198,889	12.3	20,067	77,913	4,136,190	.0789	3,407,950	968	302,836	602	168,595	888	548,209	184,224
Virginia	6,448,140	6,007,063	15.8	22,000	2,413,345	141,859,560	2.3396	78,887,330	22,400	12,557,731	24,975	4,485,896	23,613	10,510,814	3,959,410
Washington	5,491,184	5,153,165	21.5	21,476	2,145,078	117,931,360	1.9841	69,087,757	19,619	12,139,822	24,144	3,386,346	17,824	9,707,299	2,898,573
West Virginia	997,449	983,274	3.4	16,590	401,612	16,547,380	.3012	10,557,530	2,999	1,866,541	3,713	446,406	2,350	1,214,820	912,708
Wisconsin	4,012,351	3,868,673	9.4	20,445	1,591,086	82,032,620	1.4198	51,149,002	14,523	8,361,823	16,630	1,556,632	8,189	6,200,270	2,573,279
Wyoming	155,470	148,140	10.2	17,558	60,943	2,729,800	.0536	2,283,559	649	418,665	833	46,663	246	236,019	49,287
Micropolitan Statistical Area Total	30,246,680	29,477,802	10.0	16,313	11,662,263	493,428,880	9.1417	329,980,240	93,709	56,369,705	112,093	12,298,414	64,731	47,654,976	17,467,665
CBSA Total	276,916,224	262,057,742	13.6	19,716	102,549,379	5,459,558,560	94.7259	3,355,809,775	952,895	483,593,619	961,717	186,545,843	981,835	470,691,106	195,984,550

Source: Devonshire Associates Ltd. and Scan/US, Inc. 2005.
Estimates for Total Retail Sales, General Merchandise Sales, Apparel Store Sales, Food Store Sales and Health and Drug Store Sales are based on data from the U.S. Census Bureau's 1997 Economic Census, and utilize the North American Industry Classification System (NAICS).

† State totals are for Metropolitan Core Based Statistical Areas. A U.S. total for Micropolitan Core Based Statistical Areas is also provided.

150 Largest Core Based Statistical Areas (CBSAs): Population/Income/Sales#

This table lists the 150 largest Core Based Statistical Areas (CBSAs) ranked by July 1, 2005 estimated population. The data shown are consistent with the data in the CBSA Table which appears on pages 45-47. A map showing the CBSAs, with a detailed explanation of how they are determined, appears on pages 38-39. An explanation of CBSAs may also be found in the Introduction on pages 5-9.

CBSA Rank	Core Based Statistical Area	Population Estimate 7/1/05	Population Census 4/1/00	Population % Change 4/1/90-4/1/00	Per Capita Income 2004	Households Estimate 7/1/05	Disposable Income 2004 ($1,000)	Market Ability Index 2004	Total Retail Sales 2004 Sales ($1,000)	Total Retail Sales Ranally Sales Units	General Merchandise 2004 Sales ($1,000)	General Merchandise Ranally Sales Units	Apparel Store 2004 Sales ($1,000)	Apparel Store Ranally Sales Units	Food Store Sales 2004 ($1,000)	Health & Drug Store 2004 ($1,000)
1	New York-Northern New Jersey-Long Island, NY-NJ-PA	18,864,705	18,323,002	8.8	22,872	6,753,723	431,479,210	6.7737	205,505,417	58,354	18,259,896	36,314	23,021,887	121,168	33,518,468	17,353,182
2	Los Angeles-Long Beach-Santa Ana, CA	13,097,576	12,365,627	9.7	18,320	4,180,772	239,944,070	4.1236	135,513,537	38,479	16,794,966	33,400	11,206,574	58,982	20,801,007	7,795,195
3	Chicago-Naperville-Joliet, IL-IN-WI	9,471,425	9,098,316	11.2	20,848	3,293,572	197,462,610	3.3057	111,549,447	31,675	13,109,705	26,071	6,321,481	33,269	14,695,301	9,643,813
4	Dallas-Fort Worth-Arlington, TX	5,844,700	5,161,544	29.4	19,933	1,972,103	116,503,670	2.0633	77,051,908	21,881	11,147,019	22,166	4,034,977	21,237	9,765,406	3,161,786
5	Philadelphia-Camden-Wilmington, PA-NJ-DE-MD	5,831,625	5,687,147	4.6	21,621	2,150,234	126,083,610	2.1312	75,363,791	21,398	6,762,307	13,449	4,577,513	24,092	12,014,134	5,475,211
6	Miami-Fort Lauderdale-Miami Beach, FL	5,452,407	5,007,564	23.5	18,388	1,970,323	100,258,750	1.8240	68,633,721	19,488	8,165,715	16,240	5,883,062	30,965	9,299,353	4,962,440
7	Houston-Sugar Land-Baytown, TX	5,293,972	4,715,407	25.2	18,002	1,750,735	95,302,000	1.7217	62,946,069	17,875	10,532,152	20,945	3,653,061	19,227	9,249,211	2,965,555
8	Washington-Arlington-Alexandria, DC-VA-MD-WV	5,255,607	4,796,183	16.3	27,193	1,956,365	142,915,930	2.1044	59,584,175	16,919	7,598,428	15,111	4,119,320	21,682	9,723,739	3,048,892
9	Atlanta-Sandy Springs-Marietta, GA	4,809,992	4,247,981	38.4	21,568	1,716,371	103,742,350	1.7807	65,071,961	18,475	8,692,216	17,287	3,504,410	18,445	8,986,048	2,785,761
10	Detroit-Warren-Livonia, MI	4,501,430	4,452,557	4.8	21,935	1,722,915	98,740,090	1.6927	62,291,351	17,687	9,917,465	19,723	3,024,962	15,921	7,300,349	4,729,277
11	Boston-Cambridge-Quincy, MA-NH	4,457,319	4,391,344	6.2	24,540	1,656,326	109,383,350	1.7852	62,649,565	17,791	5,876,246	11,687	4,707,924	24,780	9,933,443	4,633,205
12	San Francisco-Oakland-Fremont, CA	4,167,248	4,123,740	11.9	27,223	1,532,531	113,444,860	1.7614	58,012,565	16,472	7,052,719	14,026	5,041,584	26,535	10,606,366	3,188,494
13	Riverside-San Bernardino-Ontario, CA	3,886,808	3,254,821	25.7	16,596	1,212,880	64,505,060	1.1101	33,712,896	9,573	4,782,057	9,510	1,947,213	10,249	5,672,476	1,586,227
14	Phoenix-Mesa-Scottsdale, AZ	3,801,803	3,251,876	45.3	19,272	1,365,972	73,268,000	1.2707	44,288,930	12,576	6,083,481	12,098	1,737,542	9,145	5,560,900	2,306,866
15	Seattle-Tacoma-Bellevue, WA	3,202,012	3,043,878	18.9	23,536	1,279,990	75,362,930	1.2459	43,999,118	12,494	6,760,818	13,446	2,516,203	13,243	5,748,586	1,817,459
16	Minneapolis-St. Paul-Bloomington, MN-WI	3,154,675	2,968,806	16.9	24,093	1,251,827	76,004,390	1.3070	50,893,048	14,452	7,484,790	14,884	1,876,788	9,878	6,162,603	2,302,183
17	San Diego-Carlsbad-San Marcos, CA	2,990,693	2,813,833	12.6	19,889	1,027,661	59,482,050	1.0104	34,231,355	9,720	4,237,412	8,427	2,478,722	13,046	5,315,838	1,790,799
18	St. Louis, MO-IL	2,769,054	2,698,687	4.6	20,781	1,095,739	57,542,920	.9635	32,488,202	9,227	4,945,403	9,837	1,203,617	6,337	4,460,102	2,272,744
19	Baltimore-Towson, MD	2,658,807	2,552,994	7.2	22,490	997,379	59,797,030	.9484	29,277,161	8,312	3,797,673	7,552	1,701,986	8,959	5,186,939	1,711,640
20	Tampa-St. Petersburg-Clearwater, FL	2,613,412	2,395,997	15.9	19,546	1,065,621	51,081,900	.9188	35,052,229	9,954	4,364,151	8,679	1,494,823	7,868	4,733,677	2,309,521
21	Pittsburgh, PA	2,400,344	2,431,087	-1.5	18,315	982,565	43,962,330	.7882	28,664,871	8,140	3,316,295	6,594	1,332,924	7,014	4,615,707	2,088,178
22	Denver-Aurora, CO	2,371,414	2,179,240	30.7	24,951	980,328	59,168,450	.9423	31,455,018	8,931	4,690,236	9,327	1,493,830	7,863	4,358,133	1,208,969
23	Cleveland-Elyria-Mentor, OH	2,136,541	2,148,143	2.2	20,024	852,217	42,783,070	.7503	27,506,430	7,810	2,827,065	5,623	1,412,321	7,433	4,057,606	2,961,118
24	Portland-Vancouver-Beaverton, OR-WA	2,110,156	1,927,881	26.5	21,174	816,926	44,680,070	.7713	28,248,512	8,021	5,153,465	10,249	1,511,846	7,958	3,705,264	927,293
25	Sacramento—Arden-Arcade—Roseville, CA	2,081,634	1,796,857	21.3	20,754	750,053	43,201,390	.7038	22,059,537	6,264	2,803,436	5,575	1,176,056	6,190	3,944,199	988,483
26	Cincinnati-Middletown, OH-KY-IN	2,069,601	2,009,632	8.9	20,544	805,228	42,517,790	.7239	25,217,656	7,159	3,561,073	7,080	1,214,527	6,394	3,568,727	1,435,529
27	Kansas City, MO-KS	1,952,760	1,836,038	12.2	21,306	768,988	41,605,740	.7120	25,651,310	7,284	3,955,017	7,867	988,727	5,204	2,937,196	1,347,170
28	Orlando-Kissimmee, FL	1,900,560	1,644,561	34.3	19,478	701,773	37,018,160	.6726	26,135,598	7,423	3,848,482	7,653	1,791,331	9,428	3,390,238	1,412,260
29	San Antonio, TX	1,879,915	1,711,703	21.6	16,589	648,985	31,186,610	.5849	21,956,787	6,235	3,052,042	6,070	1,201,202	6,322	3,314,254	854,794
30	San Jose-Sunnyvale-Santa Clara, CA	1,727,639	1,735,819	13.1	29,104	575,043	50,281,040	.7963	28,482,536	8,087	3,631,347	7,222	2,399,605	12,630	4,478,947	1,503,449
31	Columbus, OH	1,719,360	1,612,694	14.8	20,173	652,918	34,684,830	.6301	24,952,201	7,085	2,989,934	5,946	1,127,376	5,934	2,921,109	1,023,296
32	Las Vegas-Paradise, NV	1,697,755	1,375,765	85.5	19,197	620,452	32,591,720	.5707	20,294,277	5,763	2,891,887	5,751	1,375,438	7,239	3,018,726	841,646
33	Virginia Beach-Norfolk-Newport News, VA-NC	1,657,806	1,576,370	8.8	17,951	605,358	29,759,360	.5226	17,878,284	5,077	2,872,048	5,712	1,052,924	5,542	2,298,054	818,082
34	Providence-New Bedford-Fall River, RI-MA	1,650,151	1,582,997	4.8	19,333	622,197	31,902,970	.5441	18,250,551	5,182	2,098,849	4,175	1,181,391	6,218	3,176,311	1,757,969
35	Indianapolis, IN	1,646,860	1,525,104	17.8	20,092	616,038	33,089,180	.5977	23,361,123	6,636	4,189,056	8,331	939,876	4,947	2,042,869	1,503,273
36	Milwaukee-Waukesha-West Allis, WI	1,521,473	1,500,741	4.8	20,533	597,839	31,239,920	.5262	17,833,569	5,063	2,618,965	5,208	605,954	3,189	2,459,679	1,231,828
37	Charlotte-Gastonia-Concord, NC-SC	1,505,429	1,330,448	29.8	21,307	578,871	32,075,610	.5518	20,128,261	5,715	2,893,237	5,754	990,108	5,210	2,441,442	1,099,655
38	Austin-Round Rock, TX	1,453,856	1,249,763	47.7	21,294	525,442	30,958,890	.6241	30,159,309	8,564	2,441,369	4,855	1,101,729	5,800	3,038,880	1,493,719
39	Nashville-Davidson—Murfreesboro, TN	1,409,811	1,311,789	25.1	20,569	541,913	28,998,860	.5225	20,587,302	5,846	3,432,129	6,825	1,054,711	5,551	2,416,395	1,215,471
40	New Orleans-Metairie-Kenner, LA	1,308,631	1,316,510	4.1	16,870	487,345	22,076,390	.4096	15,192,435	4,316	2,684,592	5,339	940,553	4,950	2,086,751	1,160,187
41	Memphis, TN-MS-AR	1,261,492	1,205,204	12.9	18,088	472,473	22,817,440	.4114	15,010,204	4,262	2,643,359	5,258	872,386	4,591	1,444,738	1,063,617
42	Jacksonville, FL	1,248,873	1,122,750	21.4	20,664	477,545	25,806,650	.4424	15,714,417	4,462	2,187,393	4,349	793,699	4,178	2,209,549	758,340
43	Louisville, KY-IN	1,207,123	1,161,975	10.0	19,057	466,718	23,003,710	.3980	13,660,496	3,879	2,273,288	4,522	531,866	2,799	1,444,039	887,014
44	Hartford-West Hartford-East Hartford, CT	1,197,175	1,148,618	2.2	26,530	463,800	31,761,140	.4830	14,817,105	4,207	1,281,098	2,548	1,120,244	5,896	2,339,379	1,185,681
45	Richmond, VA	1,160,991	1,096,957	15.6	19,465	429,120	22,598,170	.3920	13,781,951	3,912	2,325,635	4,626	711,099	3,745	1,856,016	856,663
46	Oklahoma City, OK	1,155,595	1,095,421	12.8	17,415	442,750	20,125,060	.3679	13,499,265	3,832	2,372,974	4,719	448,005	2,358	1,424,293	745,883
47	Buffalo-Niagara Falls, NY	1,154,526	1,170,111	-1.6	20,193	477,362	23,313,710	.3832	12,048,915	3,421	1,230,258	2,447	724,512	3,813	2,155,690	978,261
48	Birmingham-Hoover, AL	1,086,137	1,052,238	10.0	18,515	419,291	20,109,880	.3619	13,359,508	3,794	2,267,574	4,509	666,826	3,510	1,639,893	689,336
49	Rochester, NY	1,046,284	1,037,831	3.5	21,442	405,908	22,434,410	.3661	11,789,930	3,348	1,338,730	2,662	557,077	2,932	2,275,968	603,771
50	Salt Lake City, UT	1,016,096	968,858	26.1	18,104	335,646	18,395,070	.3602	15,467,351	4,392	2,375,916	4,725	759,475	3,997	2,103,917	340,947
51	Raleigh-Cary, NC	939,136	797,071	47.3	22,686	352,158	21,305,610	.3685	14,089,312	4,001	2,030,616	4,038	724,476	3,812	1,711,878	562,537
52	Tucson, AZ	921,681	843,746	26.5	17,523	359,359	16,151,030	.2750	8,503,748	2,415	1,331,237	2,647	348,394	1,834	1,318,403	534,417
53	Honolulu, HI	910,475	876,156	4.8	20,281	302,181	18,465,370	.3063	9,903,032	2,812	1,988,367	3,954	1,320,832	6,952	1,401,658	865,911
54	Bridgeport-Stamford-Norwalk, CT	909,263	882,567	6.6	30,162	329,595	27,424,940	.4586	18,649,061	5,295	997,741	1,984	1,190,445	6,266	2,268,628	792,292
55	Tulsa, OK	892,708	859,532	12.9	16,921	325,055	15,105,360	.2830	10,740,382	3,049	2,251,087	4,477	353,338	1,860	1,078,609	649,765
56	Fresno, CA	881,918	799,407	19.8	13,549	271,021	11,949,320	.2266	7,423,260	2,108	1,040,968	2,070	331,031	1,742	1,229,784	460,666
57	New Haven-Milford, CT	853,637	824,008	2.5	23,814	319,931	20,328,100	.3285	11,057,950	3,140	1,088,751	2,165	650,116	3,422	1,673,415	780,780
58	Albany-Schenectady-Troy, NY	851,730	825,875	2.0	21,852	338,233	18,611,750	.3030	9,840,485	2,794	1,158,361	2,304	575,198	3,027	1,285,764	628,243
59	Dayton, OH	843,320	848,153	0.5	19,913	340,224	16,792,740	.2918	10,437,674	2,964	1,677,421	3,335	455,065	2,394	1,387,244	518,273
60	Oxnard-Thousand Oaks-Ventura, CA	813,570	753,197	12.6	23,388	262,514	19,028,060	.3036	9,778,861	2,777	1,019,623	2,028	564,619	2,972	1,522,187	578,898
61	Omaha-Council Bluffs, NE-IA	807,305	767,041	11.8	19,390	306,915	15,653,930	.2878	11,414,520	3,240	1,424,659	2,833	408,037	2,148	1,344,280	640,405
62	Worcester, MA	790,475	750,963	5.8	21,359	291,974	16,883,400	.2793	9,300,431	2,641	871,592	1,733	449,285	2,365	1,474,657	686,325
63	Albuquerque, NM	788,925	729,649	21.7	18,329	304,262	14,460,280	.2616	9,706,280	2,757	1,906,387	3,792	340,863	1,793	815,878	515,259
64	Allentown-Bethlehem-Easton, PA-NJ	785,814	740,395	7.8	20,371	296,297	16,007,810	.2729	9,467,904	2,689	950,519	1,890	391,866	2,061	1,653,435	659,754
65	Grand Rapids-Wyoming, MI	775,198	740,482	14.6	19,460	291,002	15,085,200	.2681	9,934,388	2,821	1,928,255	3,835	361,397	1,901	843,769	490,057
66	Bakersfield, CA	743,729	661,645	21.7	14,153	234,348	10,526,210	.1907	5,759,480	1,635	787,831	1,567	234,327	1,233	863,026	390,768
67	Baton Rouge, LA	727,551	705,973	13.2	16,621	256,285	12,092,610	.2275	8,586,477	2,438	1,578,219	3,138	359,252	1,890	1,044,785	428,807
68	El Paso, TX	720,147	679,622	14.9	11,701	218,789	8,426,220	.1787	6,673,517	1,895	1,498,168	2,979	459,278	2,417	781,502	305,744
69	Akron, OH	704,396	694,960	5.7	19,435	272,491	13,689,650	.2478	9,538,485	2,709	920,437	1,830	401,349	2,112	1,321,069	843,663
70	Springfield, MA	689,619	680,014	1.0	19,551	266,392	13,482,560	.2241	7,089,078	2,013	700,829	1,393	347,601	1,830	1,358,554	569,374
71	Columbia, SC	687,420	647,158	18.0	18,560	261,102	12,758,230	.2295	8,500,202	2,413	1,702,017	3,385	446,397	2,349	1,075,119	456,952
72	McAllen-Edinburg-Mission, TX	675,597	569,463	48.5	8,316	179,247	5,618,500	.1432	5,723,037	1,625	1,172,978	2,333	428,765	2,257	870,770	248,513
73	Poughkeepsie-Newburgh-Middletown, NY	675,333	621,517	9.6	21,765	227,263	14,698,670	.2342	7,144,415	2,029	1,014,586	2,018	633,609	3,334	1,115,141	412,872
74	Stockton, CA	674,080	563,598	17.3	15,489	201,595	10,441,010	.1808	5,234,961	1,486	683,333	1,359	247,667	1,304	900,861	341,266
75	Greensboro-High Point, NC	673,134	643,430	19.1	19,161	266,769	12,897,820	.2351	9,113,147	2,588	1,138,679	2,264	437,889	2,305	1,067,469	560,145
76	Toledo, OH	660,207	659,188	0.8	18,686	261,574	12,336,350	.2261	8,715,587	2,475	1,279,575	2,545	339,161	1,785	1,205,392	508,701
77	Sarasota-Bradenton-Venice, FL	659,642	589,959	20.5	22,508	289,874	14,847,510	.2476	8,683,476	2,466	1,053,100	2,094	544,300	2,865	1,298,388	549,755
78	Syracuse, NY	657,851	650,154	-1.5	19,867	259,096	13,069,470	.2187	7,121,442	2,022	727,272	1,446	391,145	2,059	1,319,427	506,269
79	Knoxville, TN	650,649	616,079	15.2	18,522	264,396	12,051,140	.2416	10,922,212	3,101	1,801,409	3,582	458,772	2,415	1,112,616	599,485
80	Little Rock-North Little Rock, AR	639,802	610,518	14.1	19,246	259,036	12,313,800	.2292	9,286,474	2,637	1,910,532	3,800	338,114	1,779	763,297	316,058
81	Colorado Springs, CO	592,836	537,484	31.3	20,800	227,594	12,331,020	.2094	7,302,778	2,074	1,264,886	2,515	200,312	1,055	759,294	276,150
82	Wichita, KS	589,782	571,166	11.7	18,371	222,302	10,834,610	.1881	6,353,689	1,803	1,285,957	2,557	258,667	1,362	930,859	314,872
83	Greenville, SC	588,729	559,940	18.6	17,811	221,455	10,486,140	.1943	7,439,633	2,113	997,813	1,984	380,205	2,000	908,811	428,288
84	Youngstown-Warren-Boardman, OH-PA	587,022	602,964	-1.7	17,320	234,973	10,167,400	.1889	7,151,818	2,030	956,983	1,903	406,424	2,139	929,823	469,480
85	Charleston-North Charleston, SC	586,872	549,033	8.3	17,044	210,746	10,002,730	.1828	6,608,271	1,877	1,199,377	2,385	418,395	2,203	993,263	297,458
86	Scranton—Wilkes-Barre, PA	547,294	560,625	-2.5	16,680	222,408	9,128,760	.1743	6,804,099	1,932	906,799	1,803	348,582	1,834	1,192,943	478,962
87	Madison, WI	541,809	501,774	16.1	22,329	227,338	12,098,280	.2182	8,967,520	2,546	1,048,681	2,085	255,440	1,344	848,118	350,067
88	Boise City-Nampa, ID	539,170	464,840	45.4	18,472	201,602	9,959,580	.1837	7,131,256	2,025	1,277,037	2,540	231,216	1,217	954,572	234,231
89	Lakeland, FL	526,208	483,924	19.4	17,926	205,086	9,432,930	.1709	6,270,722	1,781	1,004,624	1,998	225,818	1,189	1,044,350	328,355
90	Palm Bay-Melbourne-Titusville, FL	523,567	476,230	19.4	20,941	216,202	10,963,820	.1797	5,760,123	1,636	986,272	1,961	242,067	1,274	880,605	408,228
91	Cape Coral-Fort Myers, FL	523,512	440,888	31.6	21,374	219,465	11,189,420	.1957	7,409,505	2,104	1,087,208	2,162	462,470	2,434	956,522	481,928
92	Modesto, CA	519,823	446,997	20.6	15,585	161,250	8,101,680	.1473	4,910,210	1,394	756,250	1,504	190,893	1,005	890,064	318,684
93	Harrisburg-Carlisle, PA	519,424	509,074	7.3	20,915	211,439	10,863,640	.1957	7,773,012	2,207	747,981	1,487	312,581	1,646	1,055,813	423,900
94	Portland-South Portland-Biddeford, ME	518,365	487,568	10.5	20,470	207,575	10,610,940	.1961	8,073,922	2,292	685,482	1,364	507,672	2,672	1,504,442	316,414
95	Jackson, MS	518,326	497,197	11.2	16,706	184,703	8,658,910	.1674	6,704,402	1,904	1,451,620	2,888	290,291	1,528	621,694	408,231
96	Augusta-Richmond County, GA-SC	517,953	499,684	14.7	16,980	190,824	8,795,000	.1578	5,455,921	1,549	991,510	1,973	252,791	1,331	744,963	258,910
97	Des Moines, IA	516,976	481,394	15.6	20,050	198,486	10,365,480	.1788	6,317,987	1,794	847,802	1,686	244,194	1,285	820,372	306,407
98	Ogden-Clearfield, UT	504,508	442,656	25.8	17,915	163,118	9,038,400	.1597	5,551,935	1,577	1,085,440	2,159	165,317	870	826,730	126,827
99	Chattanooga, TN-GA	492,047	476,531	10.0	17,464	189,045	8,592,880	.1577	5,842,511	1,659	971,155	1,932	331,462	1,744	734,748	378,230
100	Lancaster, PA	490,254	470,658	11.3	19,871	183,207	9,741,670	.1767	6,915,084	1,964	618,456	1,230	403,743	2,125	1,058,381	357,146
101	Deltona-Daytona Beach-Ormond Beach, FL	483,444	443,343	19.6	17,897	192,195	8,652,230	.1564	5,702,643	1,619	826,756	1,644	245,601	1,293	886,271	390,946
102	Santa Rosa-Petaluma, CA	470,813	458,614	18.1	24,088	175,179	11,340,910	.1822	6,084,888	1,728	691,543	1,375	280,632	1,477	1,212,686	357,793
103	Lansing-East Lansing, MI	461,446	447,728	3.5	21,034	189,983	9,705,850	.1657	5,885,672	1,671	1,344,212	2,673	230,071	1,210	671,101	332,191
104	Durham, NC	458,673	426,493	23.8	20,325	184,337	9,322,540	.1562	5,192,795	1,475	524,011	1,042	292,911	1,542	865,702	306,608
105	Winston-Salem, NC	447,369	421,961	16.7	18,954	173,506	8,479,430	.1546	5,943,063	1,688	810,281	1,611	293,126	1,544	669,754	340,918
106	Flint, MI	445,626	436,141	1.3	18,240	166,917	8,128,190	.1460	5,313,381	1,509	1,042,068	2,072	191,549	1,008	611,856	393,603
107	Spokane, WA	439,273	417,939	15.7	18,223	180,505	8,004,860	.1437	5,223,271	1,483	985,255	1,959	248,626	1,309	753,870	200,787
108	Pensacola-Ferry Pass-Brent, FL	437,128	412,153	19.7	18,438	170,330	8,059,970	.1392	4,649,972	1,321	829,735	1,650	185,536	977	639,256	315,918
109	Lexington-Fayette, KY	430,696	408,326	17.2	20,119	175,319	8,665,210	.1563	6,097,113	1,731	896,211	1,782	331,891	1,746	606,627	370,562
110	Vallejo-Fairfield, CA	421,801	394,542	15.9	21,842	140,240	9,212,790	.1430	4,047,249	1,149	753,325	1,498	194,037	1,021	757,937	149,885
111	Salinas, CA	421,269	401,762	13.0	18,324	130,913	7,719,290	.1321	4,297,922	1,220	496,897	988	304,946	1,605	763,460	273,308
112	Provo-Orem, UT	418,644	376,774	39.9	15,051	121,920	6,301,210	.1208	4,442,435	1,261	895,851	1,781	147,868	778	683,989	85,494
113	Corpus Christi, TX	408,295	403,280	9.7	15,343	142,915	6,264,520	.1205	4,509,115	1,280	773,638	1,538	212,548	1,119	753,998	185,691
114	Canton-Massillon, OH	407,131	406,934	3.3	18,072	158,114	7,357,550	.1373	5,385,396	1,529	695,727	1,384	280,842	1,478	801,334	503,254
115	Fort Wayne, IN	406,015	390,156	10.1	17,706	146,486	7,188,940	.1338	5,151,663	1,463	1,039,579	2,067	209,959	1,106	509,086	298,637
116	Shreveport-Bossier City, LA	405,822	375,965	4.5	16,278	157,589	6,605,850	.1235	4,540,878	1,289	845,493	1,681	195,105	1,027	532,795	204,266
117	Visalia-Porterville, CA	404,818	368,021	18.0	12,914	120,917	5,227,730	.0963	2,765,611	785	418,656	833	108,161	569	563,264	158,385
118	Santa Barbara-Santa Maria, CA	404,582	399,347	8.0	19,919	139,852	8,058,830	.1386	4,839,745	1,374	499,060	992	335,212	1,764	874,460	322,723
119	York-Hanover, PA	403,361	381,751	12.4	20,209	154,303	8,151,520	.1339	4,206,302	1,194	585,240	1,164	159,393	839	714,134	198,492
120	Manchester-Nashua, NH	403,350	380,841	13.3	22,648	151,152	9,135,020	.1760	8,150,622	2,314	1,197,089	2,381	345,041	1,816	1,015,559	278,338
121	Mobile, AL	399,727	399,843	5.6	13,702	130,235	5,477,160	.1077	3,885,168	1,103	857,409	1,705	158,982	837	475,635	231,633
122	Fayetteville-Springdale-Rogers, AR-MO	397,806	347,045	44.9	16,726	149,079	6,653,550	.1222	4,405,775	1,251	1,403,194	2,790	119,274	627	405,447	133,061
123	Springfield, MO	396,026	368,374	23.3	16,984	163,919	6,726,150	.1303	5,297,481	1,505	817,599	1,627	113,442	598	486,608	236,576
124	Reno-Sparks, NV	393,925	342,885	33.3	20,837	152,950	8,208,150	.1420	5,176,296	1,470	834,750	1,660	171,290	902	706,590	218,418
125	Reading, PA	393,253	373,638	11.0	19,745	147,995	7,764,710	.1320	4,459,882	1,266	520,167	1,034	360,634	1,898	665,140	278,677
126	Asheville, NC	391,007	369,171	19.9	18,204	163,266	7,117,980	.1357	5,573,344	1,583	807,062	1,606	258,605	1,360	648,317	319,272
127	Beaumont-Port Arthur, TX	380,783	385,090	6.6	16,794	144,982	6,394,940	.1213	4,697,396	1,333	797,667	1,586	210,488	1,108	605,208	276,284
128	Brownsville-Harlingen, TX	379,998	335,227	28.9	8,453	97,445	3,212,080	.0778	2,844,598	808	682,514	1,357	195,900	1,031	495,642	117,593
129	Salem, OR	374,986	347,214	24.9	16,813	131,258	6,304,480	.1141	3,997,943	1,135	850,280	1,691	145,165	764	577,419	135,511
130	Davenport-Moline-Rock Island, IA-IL	374,314	376,019	2.1	19,080	150,259	7,141,890	.1304	5,066,064	1,439	744,429	1,481	206,063	1,085	594,908	341,552
131	Trenton-Ewing, NJ	369,496	350,761	7.7	24,296	124,536	8,977,430	.1416	4,534,000	1,287	431,841	859	361,412	1,902	714,006	472,475
132	Port St. Lucie-Fort Pierce, FL	367,537	319,426	27.2	20,044	148,535	7,366,920	.1250	4,250,091	1,207	569,115	1,132	144,124	759	627,822	360,130
133	Huntsville, AL	367,395	342,376	16.8	20,622	142,882	7,576,500	.1297	4,590,366	1,303	1,044,405	2,077	226,391	1,192	539,630	193,264
134	Peoria, IL	365,630	366,899	2.3	20,319	147,233	7,429,080	.1291	4,676,451	1,328	677,301	1,346	126,009	664	672,669	327,676
135	Montgomery, AL	356,454	346,528	13.6	17,113	131,702	6,099,830	.1142	4,362,627	1,239	873,591	1,738	198,796	1,047	486,039	276,503
136	Hickory-Lenoir-Morganton, NC	356,039	341,851	16.9	17,856	140,143	6,357,350	.1156	4,259,162	1,209	596,263	1,186	159,755	841	500,673	277,190
137	Anchorage, AK	352,186	319,605	20.1	21,974	124,883	7,738,950	.1359	5,269,302	1,496	1,171,178	2,330	247,318	1,302	652,337	67,815
138	Killeen-Temple-Fort Hood, TX	351,367	330,714	23.0	15,871	122,755	5,576,370	.0978	3,019,409	858	444,708	884	93,408	491	426,421	61,779
139	Evansville, IN-KY	348,860	342,815	5.5	17,876	138,511	6,236,290	.1189	4,823,000	1,369	829,036	1,649	216,952	1,142	510,448	262,823
140	Ann Arbor, MI	347,941	322,895	14.1	23,471	138,498	8,166,530	.1404	5,391,343	1,531	894,465	1,779	250,305	1,317	593,151	281,683
141	Fayetteville, NC	346,350	336,609	13.2	16,132	125,340	5,587,260	.1036	3,714,741	1,055	713,751	1,419	191,617	1,009	452,306	171,353
142	Rockford, IL	337,385	320,204	12.9	19,770	126,099	6,670,200	.1156	4,101,173	1,164	657,662	1,308	154,269	812	683,652	252,244
143	Eugene-Springfield, OR	335,284	322,959	14.2	18,570	141,340	6,226,310	.1146	4,441,395	1,261	819,155	1,629	129,203	680	689,971	164,173
144	Tallahassee, FL	332,381	320,304	23.6	19,244	136,829	6,396,380	.1102	3,771,080	1,070	687,992	1,368	185,765	978	577,012	250,701
145	Kalamazoo-Portage, MI	322,822	314,866	7.3	19,353	129,811	6,247,520	.1111	4,107,307	1,166	1,205,385	2,397	135,925	715	342,315	211,917
146	South Bend-Mishawaka, IN-MI	318,467	316,663	6.8	16,509	113,467	5,257,570	.1011	3,986,552	1,132	732,085	1,456	156,473	823	421,491	279,547
147	Savannah, GA	312,351	293,000	13.5	17,889	118,298	5,587,730	.1023	3,839,729	1,091	752,694	1,497	218,315	1,149	491,346	146,081
148	Naples-Marco Island, FL	306,973	251,377	65.3	24,916	127,885	7,648,670	.1250	4,435,456	1,259	409,669	815	470,567	2,477	683,833	249,092
149	Wilmington, NC	305,944	274,532	37.2	19,028	127,137	5,821,440	.1120	4,785,890	1,359	638,298	1,269	198,342	1,044	613,090	254,604
150	Charleston, WV	305,915	309,635	0.6	17,483	127,586	5,348,220	.1000	3,857,895	1,096	607,111	1,207	144,158	759	448,368	314,145

Source: Devonshire Associates Ltd. and Scan/US, Inc. 2005.

Estimates for Total Retail Sales, General Merchandise Sales, Apparel Store Sales, Food Store Sales and Health and Drug Store Sales are based on data from the U.S. Census Bureau's 1997 Economic Census and utilize the North American Industry Classification System (NAICS).

150 Largest Counties: Population/Income/Sales[#]

The table lists the 150 largest counties, ranked by July 1, 2005 estimated population. The data shown are consistent with the data in the County Table on pages 52-73.

County Rank	County or County Equivalent	Population: Estimate 7/1/05	Population: Census 4/1/00	Per Capita Income 2004	Households Estimate 7/1/05	Median Household Income 2004	Disposable Income 2004 ($1,000)	Market Ability Index 2004	Total Retail Sales: 2004 Sales ($1,000)	Total Retail Sales: Ranally Sales Units	General Merchandise: 2004 Sales ($1,000)	General Merchandise: Ranally Sales Units	Apparel Store: 2004 Sales ($1,000)	Apparel Store: Ranally Sales Units	Food Store Sales 2004 ($1,000)	Health & Drug Store 2004 ($1,000)	Passenger Car Registrations 2004	County or County Equivalent
1	Los Angeles, CA	10,076,928	9,519,338	16,791	3,192,402	39,739	169,200,500	2.9617	95,230,986	27,041	11,726,649	23,321	7,977,490	41,987	15,007,662	5,683,828	5,997,792	Los Angeles, CA
2	Cook, IL	5,332,321	5,376,741	19,020	1,886,418	42,611	101,421,380	1.7279	57,112,166	16,217	6,691,173	13,307	4,085,212	21,501	8,603,726	5,892,431	2,978,549	Cook, IL
3	Harris, TX	3,713,507	3,400,578	17,676	1,258,645	40,526	65,639,600	1.2294	47,930,192	13,610	7,461,373	14,838	2,977,973	15,674	7,117,190	2,349,763	2,297,170	Harris, TX
4	Maricopa, AZ	3,582,040	3,072,149	19,534	1,290,757	42,913	69,970,650	1.2197	43,410,524	12,327	5,973,166	11,879	1,699,770	8,946	5,354,760	2,255,113	2,282,542	Maricopa, AZ
5	Orange, CA	3,020,648	2,846,289	23,420	988,370	54,079	70,743,570	1.1619	40,282,551	11,438	5,068,317	10,079	3,229,084	16,995	5,793,345	2,111,368	2,025,430	Orange, CA
6	San Diego, CA	2,990,693	2,813,833	19,889	1,027,661	43,667	59,482,050	1.0104	34,231,355	9,720	4,237,412	8,427	2,478,722	13,046	5,315,838	1,790,799	1,982,651	San Diego, CA
7	Kings, NY	2,480,420	2,465,326	14,611	872,191	31,137	36,242,150	.5758	10,970,708	3,115	847,248	1,685	1,264,957	6,658	2,092,774	1,620,360	559,335	Kings, NY
8	Miami-Dade, FL	2,391,206	2,253,362	15,028	782,688	34,461	35,933,990	.6861	24,937,816	7,081	2,984,280	5,935	2,500,650	13,162	3,337,422	2,044,796	1,348,550	Miami-Dade, FL
9	Dallas, TX	2,319,427	2,218,899	17,628	772,468	40,691	40,885,960	.8073	34,683,969	9,849	5,131,277	10,204	2,013,339	10,597	3,983,118	1,304,871	1,433,930	Dallas, TX
10	Queens, NY	2,225,143	2,229,379	18,665	773,138	40,171	41,531,430	.6132	11,981,875	3,402	898,792	1,787	1,043,787	5,494	2,418,562	1,713,694	829,192	Queens, NY
11	Wayne, MI	2,008,158	2,061,162	17,599	746,956	38,349	35,340,730	.6260	21,515,241	6,109	3,238,824	6,441	950,938	5,005	3,072,231	1,890,405	1,252,417	Wayne, MI
12	San Bernardino, CA	1,957,135	1,709,434	15,531	577,153	39,791	30,395,760	.5334	16,102,044	4,572	2,355,210	4,684	942,871	4,963	2,773,850	764,307	1,219,682	San Bernardino, CA
13	Riverside, CA	1,929,673	1,545,387	17,676	635,727	40,822	34,109,300	.5767	17,610,853	5,001	2,426,846	4,826	1,004,342	5,286	2,898,626	821,920	1,269,979	Riverside, CA
14	Broward, FL	1,794,053	1,623,018	20,451	696,396	39,618	36,689,620	.6613	25,980,621	7,377	2,886,091	5,740	1,594,217	8,391	3,363,389	1,693,187	1,165,011	Broward, FL
15	King, WA	1,776,888	1,737,034	25,356	740,874	49,031	45,055,510	.7566	28,773,498	8,170	4,043,337	8,041	1,871,552	9,850	3,667,624	1,227,647	1,373,484	King, WA
16	Clark, NV	1,697,755	1,375,765	19,197	620,452	43,184	32,591,720	.5707	20,294,277	5,763	2,891,887	5,751	1,375,438	7,239	3,018,726	841,646	1,074,001	Clark, NV
17	Santa Clara, CA	1,669,973	1,682,585	29,371	557,576	65,828	49,048,290	.7777	28,016,175	7,955	3,571,238	7,102	2,391,823	12,589	4,358,548	1,477,292	1,194,252	Santa Clara, CA
18	Tarrant, TX	1,626,962	1,446,219	19,074	558,390	43,459	31,032,520	.5681	22,136,303	6,286	2,479,052	4,930	1,063,464	5,597	2,745,265	937,248	1,077,111	Tarrant, TX
19	New York, NY	1,588,044	1,537,195	26,832	730,318	43,660	42,609,670	.7445	31,346,074	8,901	3,426,024	6,813	8,658,940	45,574	3,042,648	3,214,471	216,437	New York, NY
20	Bexar, TX	1,512,995	1,392,931	16,421	525,519	36,844	24,844,960	.4782	18,807,064	5,340	2,686,228	5,342	1,143,594	6,019	2,849,856	754,871	895,728	Bexar, TX
21	Suffolk, NY	1,498,863	1,419,369	26,283	501,523	58,944	39,394,130	.6151	20,136,013	5,718	2,044,905	4,067	1,428,479	7,518	3,233,887	1,319,179	1,106,624	Suffolk, NY
22	Middlesex, MA	1,469,958	1,465,396	27,014	545,938	55,510	39,709,890	.6359	22,486,458	6,385	1,802,975	3,586	1,637,580	8,619	3,275,576	1,592,989	961,744	Middlesex, MA
23	Alameda, CA	1,466,375	1,443,741	24,082	514,750	51,403	35,313,910	.5542	17,409,448	4,943	1,745,449	3,471	860,637	4,530	3,306,808	946,660	994,504	Alameda, CA
24	Philadelphia, PA	1,456,998	1,517,550	14,450	567,762	29,655	21,053,750	.3663	9,981,344	2,834	794,491	1,580	1,203,647	6,335	2,107,907	1,457,217	612,457	Philadelphia, PA
25	Sacramento, CA	1,395,768	1,223,499	19,326	494,021	41,674	26,974,040	.4525	14,542,941	4,130	2,167,858	4,311	944,882	4,973	2,469,951	612,794	963,855	Sacramento, CA
26	Bronx, NY	1,385,071	1,332,650	12,499	480,811	26,842	17,312,080	.2806	4,302,652	1,222	316,644	630	493,247	2,596	1,052,902	712,213	265,303	Bronx, NY
27	Cuyahoga, OH	1,344,252	1,393,978	19,182	557,717	36,978	25,785,490	.4635	17,454,772	4,956	1,677,803	3,337	1,093,042	5,753	2,709,994	2,056,841	905,392	Cuyahoga, OH
28	Nassau, NY	1,343,675	1,334,544	27,741	432,740	64,264	37,274,930	.6060	22,464,430	6,379	2,092,700	4,162	2,219,797	11,683	2,950,865	1,618,495	892,018	Nassau, NY
29	Palm Beach, FL	1,267,148	1,131,184	21,809	491,239	41,984	27,635,140	.4766	17,715,284	5,030	2,295,344	4,565	1,788,194	9,412	2,598,542	1,224,457	830,286	Palm Beach, FL
30	Allegheny, PA	1,249,911	1,281,666	19,001	518,543	36,324	23,749,790	.4335	16,756,392	4,758	1,758,024	3,496	932,020	4,905	2,767,469	1,152,625	811,277	Allegheny, PA
31	Oakland, MI	1,214,978	1,194,156	27,460	479,227	56,419	33,363,780	.5710	23,357,225	6,632	3,487,459	6,935	1,522,696	8,014	2,287,508	1,628,633	927,628	Oakland, MI
32	Hennepin, MN	1,123,455	1,116,200	24,488	476,779	47,667	27,511,100	.5292	25,156,032	7,143	3,489,342	6,939	1,225,659	6,451	2,481,545	1,181,332	878,753	Hennepin, MN
33	Hillsborough, FL	1,118,988	998,948	19,508	424,109	38,855	21,829,310	.3981	15,595,099	4,428	1,867,205	3,713	747,996	3,937	1,769,962	969,158	772,722	Hillsborough, FL
34	Franklin, OH	1,100,544	1,068,978	19,441	425,624	40,555	21,395,270	.4219	18,973,154	5,387	2,325,256	4,624	971,342	5,112	1,977,266	772,272	816,702	Franklin, OH
35	Contra Costa, CA	1,031,546	948,816	26,152	350,538	57,990	26,977,050	.4003	11,291,061	3,206	1,642,920	3,267	717,061	3,774	2,215,986	540,440	701,952	Contra Costa, CA
36	Fairfax, VA	1,016,742	969,749	31,192	367,922	70,784	31,713,770	.4513	12,565,689	3,568	1,817,553	3,615	1,007,026	5,300	1,974,501	569,883	769,581	Fairfax, VA
37	St. Louis, MO	1,015,417	1,016,315	23,155	402,919	46,326	23,511,940	.4117	16,296,065	4,627	2,295,446	4,565	727,471	3,829	2,128,216	1,178,575	787,231	St. Louis, MO
38	Orange, FL	1,006,134	896,344	19,195	370,292	38,988	19,312,580	.3714	15,927,297	4,523	2,095,813	4,168	1,199,561	6,314	1,749,029	705,351	660,462	Orange, FL
39	Westchester, NY	951,137	923,459	27,386	336,611	58,055	26,047,630	.4013	12,998,481	3,691	1,345,677	2,676	1,180,669	6,214	2,165,138	960,620	600,726	Westchester, NY
40	Montgomery, MD	947,578	873,341	29,807	345,603	63,924	28,244,410	.4080	11,570,405	3,285	1,109,503	2,206	863,462	4,545	2,006,126	502,992	690,047	Montgomery, MD
41	DuPage, IL	937,264	904,161	27,711	335,462	61,183	25,972,140	.4309	16,653,697	4,729	1,959,526	3,897	960,105	5,053	1,622,279	1,066,411	653,602	DuPage, IL
42	Erie, NY	936,770	950,265	20,218	387,148	36,596	18,940,050	.3141	10,128,257	2,876	1,001,036	1,991	563,691	2,967	1,816,172	800,999	638,494	Erie, NY
43	Salt Lake, UT	930,006	898,387	17,953	307,564	44,586	16,696,420	.3331	14,700,927	4,174	2,318,808	4,611	680,631	3,582	1,899,566	323,003	643,149	Salt Lake, UT
44	Milwaukee, WI	927,823	940,164	17,202	369,437	36,173	15,960,420	.2778	8,974,974	2,548	1,369,742	2,724	368,054	1,937	1,235,264	828,625	620,735	Milwaukee, WI
45	Pinellas, FL	927,210	921,482	20,988	410,580	35,413	19,460,670	.3551	14,493,954	4,116	1,497,829	2,979	558,149	2,938	2,071,010	953,452	632,008	Pinellas, FL
46	Pima, AZ	921,681	843,746	17,523	359,359	35,369	16,151,030	.2750	8,503,748	2,415	1,331,237	2,647	348,394	1,834	1,318,403	534,417	611,509	Pima, AZ
47	Shelby, TN	912,260	897,472	18,368	348,231	37,820	16,756,180	.3085	11,890,926	3,376	2,029,744	4,037	833,803	4,389	1,136,381	872,261	613,625	Shelby, TN
48	Honolulu, HI	910,475	876,156	20,281	302,181	47,743	18,465,370	.3063	9,903,032	2,812	1,988,367	3,954	1,320,832	6,952	1,401,658	865,911	537,678	Honolulu, HI
49	Fairfield, CT	909,263	882,567	30,162	329,595	58,781	27,424,940	.4586	18,649,061	5,295	997,741	1,984	1,190,445	6,266	2,268,628	792,292	627,514	Fairfield, CT
50	Bergen, NJ	906,873	884,118	29,952	334,596	58,828	27,162,500	.4224	14,689,636	4,171	1,122,047	2,231	1,120,494	5,897	2,609,949	1,027,825	613,623	Bergen, NJ
51	Travis, TX	882,137	812,280	21,969	344,485	44,208	19,380,040	.4426	25,198,059	7,155	1,838,931	3,657	740,524	3,898	2,214,813	1,244,357	652,744	Travis, TX
52	Fresno, CA	881,918	799,407	13,549	271,021	33,341	11,949,320	.2266	7,423,260	2,108	1,040,968	2,070	331,031	1,742	1,229,784	460,666	521,285	Fresno, CA
53	Hartford, CT	881,552	857,183	25,818	346,129	46,551	22,759,710	.3583	11,858,586	3,367	1,151,316	2,290	890,392	4,686	1,770,165	895,073	603,057	Hartford, CT
54	Marion, IN	865,538	860,454	17,907	335,684	38,333	15,499,200	.3179	14,652,331	4,161	2,255,055	4,485	729,320	3,839	1,210,661	1,164,055	623,175	Marion, IN
55	Prince George's, MD	863,468	801,515	23,369	311,846	50,649	20,178,000	.3011	7,918,222	2,248	853,439	1,697	410,577	2,161	1,545,056	399,087	583,954	Prince George's, MD
56	New Haven, CT	853,637	824,008	23,814	319,931	44,926	20,328,100	.3285	11,057,950	3,140	1,088,751	2,165	650,116	3,422	1,673,415	780,780	584,714	New Haven, CT
57	Duval, FL	838,841	778,879	19,976	326,098	38,349	16,756,550	.3047	12,030,540	3,416	1,689,674	3,360	549,599	2,893	1,602,761	578,821	600,348	Duval, FL
58	Macomb, MI	829,028	788,149	23,354	327,622	48,147	19,361,480	.3280	12,178,708	3,458	2,153,508	4,283	389,754	2,051	1,370,284	953,554	625,033	Macomb, MI
59	Fulton, GA	822,956	816,006	21,647	322,701	44,163	17,814,710	.3252	13,481,892	3,828	1,797,457	3,575	1,154,709	6,078	1,841,428	559,764	517,018	Fulton, GA
60	Ventura, CA	813,570	753,197	23,388	262,514	54,638	19,028,060	.3036	9,778,861	2,777	1,019,623	2,028	564,619	2,972	1,522,187	578,898	557,088	Ventura, CA
61	Hamilton, OH	809,794	845,303	19,942	335,551	38,570	16,149,060	.2995	12,266,060	3,483	1,547,940	3,078	874,702	4,604	1,737,505	790,611	623,286	Hamilton, OH
62	Middlesex, NJ	800,915	750,162	26,500	274,736	56,224	21,224,180	.3235	9,983,512	2,835	972,789	1,935	677,432	3,565	1,540,211	591,887	537,098	Middlesex, NJ
63	Essex, NJ	800,056	793,633	20,002	276,836	41,584	16,002,500	.2461	6,228,174	1,769	427,748	851	678,474	3,571	1,452,794	617,675	398,283	Essex, NJ
64	Baltimore, MD	791,384	754,292	22,904	306,509	46,397	18,125,720	.3024	10,751,602	3,053	1,484,595	2,952	675,157	3,554	1,811,939	615,778	566,832	Baltimore, MD
65	Worcester, MA	790,475	750,963	21,359	291,974	44,299	16,883,400	.2793	9,300,431	2,641	871,592	1,733	449,285	2,365	1,474,657	686,325	535,226	Worcester, MA
66	Mecklenburg, NC	787,867	695,454	23,125	311,927	47,386	18,219,660	.3172	12,410,603	3,524	1,733,721	3,448	688,385	3,623	1,397,245	621,767	612,023	Mecklenburg, NC
67	Montgomery, PA	785,423	750,097	25,705	288,624	55,699	20,189,250	.3371	12,752,083	3,621	1,386,418	2,757	1,131,124	5,953	1,961,407	903,981	518,141	Montgomery, PA
68	Pierce, WA	765,698	700,820	19,356	283,473	42,060	14,820,820	.2482	7,947,017	2,257	1,476,200	2,936	288,392	1,518	1,044,483	335,167	586,648	Pierce, WA
69	Essex, MA	744,047	723,419	23,094	276,526	47,431	17,183,050	.2703	8,299,350	2,357	721,897	1,436	584,293	3,075	1,294,880	777,045	487,433	Essex, MA
70	Kern, CA	743,729	661,645	14,153	234,348	33,848	10,526,210	.1907	5,759,480	1,635	787,831	1,567	234,327	1,233	863,026	390,768	437,779	Kern, CA
71	Monroe, NY	738,925	735,343	21,936	290,346	41,738	16,209,150	.2640	8,593,168	2,440	939,333	1,868	423,910	2,231	1,726,847	409,234	552,051	Monroe, NY
72	Wake, NC	737,573	627,846	24,201	279,880	50,939	17,849,910	.3106	12,410,844	3,524	1,838,820	3,657	624,028	3,284	1,461,740	489,136	573,971	Wake, NC
73	San Francisco, CA	734,587	776,733	29,289	317,359	50,717	21,515,350	.3346	11,511,398	3,269	1,090,215	2,168	2,270,361	11,949	1,932,648	783,829	404,999	San Francisco, CA
74	Gwinnett, GA	725,943	588,448	22,639	236,177	54,986	16,434,850	.2904	11,566,248	3,284	1,268,188	2,522	582,022	3,063	1,255,903	389,066	491,136	Gwinnett, GA
75	El Paso, TX	720,147	679,622	11,701	218,789	30,082	8,426,220	.1787	6,673,517	1,895	1,498,168	2,979	459,278	2,417	781,502	305,744	391,428	El Paso, TX
76	Lake, IL	704,726	644,356	24,587	229,248	60,326	17,327,020	.3181	14,075,214	3,997	936,293	1,862	503,323	2,649	1,135,337	803,943	464,361	Lake, IL
77	Jefferson, KY	701,817	693,604	19,001	277,510	37,153	13,335,190	.2434	9,403,155	2,670	1,637,657	3,257	454,412	2,392	1,032,431	625,704	493,749	Jefferson, KY
78	San Mateo, CA	689,423	707,161	30,314	247,340	63,279	20,899,240	.3436	13,548,512	3,847	2,148,421	4,273	829,558	4,366	2,333,520	690,844	515,151	San Mateo, CA
79	Multnomah, OR	688,787	660,486	20,245	286,135	38,576	13,944,220	.2615	11,016,058	3,128	1,750,833	3,482	731,462	3,850	1,432,122	356,373	460,028	Multnomah, OR
80	Oklahoma, OK	687,070	660,448	17,050	271,354	33,692	11,714,620	.2318	9,815,970	2,787	1,539,214	3,061	345,467	1,818	1,031,109	537,882	491,025	Oklahoma, OK
81	DeKalb, GA	679,804	665,865	21,118	253,114	45,091	14,355,870	.2377	7,869,939	2,235	867,680	1,726	462,678	2,435	1,238,177	409,724	435,344	DeKalb, GA
82	Cobb, GA	677,675	607,751	23,239	233,556	53,174	15,748,450	.2926	12,908,015	3,665	1,935,940	3,850	653,279	3,438	1,736,796	583,517	489,094	Cobb, GA
83	Hidalgo, TX	675,597	569,463	8,316	179,247	24,020	5,618,500	.1432	5,723,037	1,625	1,172,978	2,333	428,765	2,257	870,770	248,513	322,531	Hidalgo, TX
84	San Joaquin, CA	674,080	563,598	15,489	201,595	39,475	10,441,010	.1808	5,234,961	1,486	683,333	1,359	247,667	1,304	900,861	341,266	430,326	San Joaquin, CA
85	Suffolk, MA	673,720	689,807	18,288	253,047	36,881	12,321,110	.2121	6,987,026	1,984	408,689	813	1,202,732	6,330	1,482,739	853,610	313,981	Suffolk, MA
86	Jackson, MO	665,173	654,880	19,289	273,954	37,299	12,830,360	.2330	8,997,248	2,555	1,327,520	2,640	302,007	1,590	955,431	528,017	505,505	Jackson, MO
87	Collin, TX	660,783	491,675	29,477	236,366	64,239	19,477,740	.2816	7,954,314	2,259	1,215,534	2,417	493,002	2,595	1,122,993	303,737	479,877	Collin, TX
88	Snohomish, WA	659,426	606,024	23,485	255,643	48,830	15,486,600	.2411	7,278,603	2,067	1,241,281	2,469	356,259	1,875	1,036,480	254,645	553,617	Snohomish, WA
89	Jefferson, AL	655,970	662,047	18,230	260,997	35,314	11,958,100	.2318	9,810,475	2,786	1,578,467	3,139	592,521	3,119	1,133,924	490,536	488,759	Jefferson, AL
90	Norfolk, MA	655,077	650,308	28,528	247,518	57,628	18,687,860	.2878	9,528,471	2,706	935,197	1,860	660,720	3,478	1,347,103	720,147	464,869	Norfolk, MA
91	Providence, RI	653,201	621,602	16,192	237,843	35,316	10,576,640	.1849	5,740,257	1,630	350,084	696	422,619	2,224	1,150,284	659,724	443,235	Providence, RI
92	Monmouth, NJ	644,487	615,301	29,638	238,052	58,476	19,101,530	.2872	9,123,567	2,591	864,002	1,718	697,011	3,669	1,716,845	583,879	472,932	Monmouth, NJ
93	Will, IL	640,443	502,266	22,223	199,257	57,634	14,232,730	.2092	4,966,459	1,410	614,968	1,223	110,865	584	705,123	472,662	410,357	Will, IL
94	Bucks, PA	622,393	597,635	24,908	226,010	54,755	15,502,700	.2671	10,608,647	3,012	906,388	1,803	427,256	2,249	1,629,157	600,178	452,286	Bucks, PA
95	Baltimore, MD*	617,204	651,154	14,301	240,250	28,904	8,826,780	.1515	3,887,601	1,104	195,612	389	271,094	1,427	766,785	536,954	305,028	Baltimore, MD
96	Hudson, NJ	607,051	608,975	19,048	220,754	38,221	11,563,320	.1812	4,658,618	1,323	361,795	719	554,459	2,918	870,328	384,860	269,178	Hudson, NJ
97	Kent, MI	599,621	574,335	19,937	227,397	42,574	11,954,940	.2179	8,625,979	2,449	1,727,533	3,436	349,036	1,837	652,528	408,445	451,431	Kent, MI
98	Bernalillo, NM	598,254	556,678	19,004	239,638	36,968	11,369,390	.2126	8,620,223	2,448	1,740,137	3,461	317,923	1,673	638,809	468,309	481,415	Bernalillo, NM
99	Tulsa, OK	574,848	563,299	17,228	210,356	36,646	9,903,560	.2024	9,098,051	2,583	1,842,757	3,665	330,944	1,742	841,269	553,409	409,916	Tulsa, OK
100	Davidson, TN	570,911	569,891	19,575	231,320	37,471	11,175,760	.2364	11,824,729	3,358	1,697,954	3,377	706,536	3,719	1,165,989	802,806	412,285	Davidson, TN
101	El Paso, CO	570,479	516,929	20,654	218,133	43,569	11,782,890	.2021	7,180,198	2,039	1,264,761	2,515	198,849	1,047	725,989	271,165	443,682	El Paso, CO
102	Ocean, NJ	568,520	510,916	22,488	215,572	42,885	12,784,930	.2051	6,532,589	1,855	542,894	1,080	286,099	1,506	1,325,531	413,887	396,538	Ocean, NJ
103	Denton, TX	558,392	432,976	23,061	185,789	53,874	12,876,850	.1968	5,542,632	1,574	1,160,247	2,307	279,879	1,473	907,692	355,892	372,045	Denton, TX
104	Denver, CO	558,088	554,636	21,096	252,189	37,304	11,773,190	.2076	7,942,001	2,255	917,312	1,824	422,490	2,224	952,255	320,196	453,155	Denver, CO
105	Delaware, PA	556,280	550,864	20,552	198,206	45,910	11,432,720	.1901	6,249,010	1,774	564,538	1,123	356,062	1,874	1,351,257	580,140	345,349	Delaware, PA
106	Bristol, MA	553,046	534,678	20,094	208,676	40,703	11,112,830	.1939	7,047,223	2,001	1,151,836	2,291	457,714	2,409	1,154,479	545,663	392,969	Bristol, MA
107	Summit, OH	549,026	542,899	19,289	212,381	40,137	10,590,380	.1979	8,074,226	2,293	824,382	1,639	318,103	1,674	1,104,975	747,813	396,561	Summit, OH
108	District of Columbia, DC	548,902	572,059	26,120	245,648	37,484	14,337,490	.1918	3,540,123	1,005	143,774	286	501,970	2,642	938,614	520,795	227,253	District of Columbia, DC
109	Montgomery, OH	547,810	559,062	19,352	224,247	37,774	10,601,050	.1900	7,146,156	2,029	1,152,638	2,292	260,529	1,371	987,131	369,266	427,932	Montgomery, OH
110	Union, NJ	534,259	522,541	25,356	192,874	50,679	13,546,510	.2137	7,027,513	1,995	323,058	642	358,739	1,888	1,285,743	507,211	352,870	Union, NJ
111	Arapahoe, CO	531,667	487,967	25,588	222,336	50,686	13,604,070	.2357	9,574,512	2,719	1,446,704	2,877	395,689	2,083	1,211,842	377,756	427,483	Arapahoe, CO
112	Jefferson, CO[1]	529,190	527,056	27,285	219,599	53,090	14,439,070	.2207	6,983,811	1,983	1,310,735	2,607	293,348	1,544	1,126,018	320,757	468,788	Jefferson, CO
113	Polk, FL	526,208	483,924	17,926	205,086	34,382	9,432,930	.1709	6,270,722	1,781	1,004,624	1,998	225,818	1,189	1,044,350	328,355	342,035	Polk, FL
114	New Castle, DE	523,864	500,265	21,504	187,254	48,371	11,265,010	.2029	8,171,242	2,320	1,006,201	2,001	362,885	1,910	1,275,633	486,673	366,791	New Castle, DE
115	Brevard, FL	523,567	476,230	20,941	216,202	38,037	10,963,820	.1797	5,760,123	1,636	986,272	1,961	242,067	1,274	880,605	408,228	391,524	Brevard, FL
116	Lee, FL	523,512	440,888	21,374	219,465	38,521	11,189,420	.1957	7,409,505	2,104	1,087,208	2,162	462,470	2,434	956,522	481,928	368,844	Lee, FL
117	Stanislaus, CA	519,823	446,997	15,585	161,250	37,782	8,101,680	.1473	4,910,210	1,394	756,250	1,504	190,893	1,005	890,064	318,684	331,624	Stanislaus, CA
118	Camden, NJ	518,146	508,932	21,721	184,104	44,199	11,254,830	.1868	6,338,456	1,800	467,956	931	387,219	2,038	1,099,932	454,604	327,805	Camden, NJ
119	Anne Arundel, MD	517,299	489,656	26,194	189,075	56,214	13,550,250	.2087	6,572,851	1,866	1,020,879	2,030	407,431	2,144	1,062,988	226,222	401,489	Anne Arundel, MD
120	Johnson, KS	507,661	451,086	26,178	194,514	57,165	13,289,780	.2203	8,283,596	2,352	1,332,072	2,649	551,071	2,900	926,652	396,910	399,613	Johnson, KS
121	Passaic, NJ	504,035	489,049	20,162	163,392	45,024	10,162,330	.1732	5,972,666	1,696	679,201	1,351	560,664	2,951	982,004	375,269	263,915	Passaic, NJ
122	Ramsey, MN	502,508	511,035	20,542	199,968	42,303	10,322,350	.1863	7,360,441	2,090	1,095,851	2,179	300,991	1,584	1,096,491	432,245	386,496	Ramsey, MN
123	Washington, OR	500,313	445,342	23,091	192,236	47,739	11,552,810	.2039	8,188,900	2,325	1,697,503	3,376	468,873	2,468	930,500	181,498	378,697	Washington, OR
124	Plymouth, MA	495,811	472,822	23,542	174,310	51,046	11,672,490	.1935	6,880,574	1,954	491,693	978	273,323	1,439	1,075,696	389,070	360,031	Plymouth, MA
125	Morris, NJ	492,011	470,212	33,152	173,146	68,182	16,311,390	.2625	10,268,969	2,916	699,821	1,392	744,571	3,919	1,554,501	572,965	343,694	Morris, NJ
126	Lancaster, PA	490,254	470,658	19,871	183,207	42,188	9,741,670	.1767	6,915,084	1,964	618,456	1,230	403,743	2,125	1,058,381	357,146	343,004	Lancaster, PA
127	Kane, IL	490,051	404,119	21,633	155,267	55,242	10,601,320	.1629	4,424,098	1,256	797,153	1,585	186,418	981	697,748	343,810	311,207	Kane, IL
128	Lake, IN	489,391	484,564	16,975	174,312	39,520	8,307,540	.1552	5,866,120	1,666	807,115	1,605	240,957	1,268	781,761	463,041	326,903	Lake, IN
129	Douglas, NE	483,981	463,585	18,981	185,006	41,092	9,186,290	.1794	7,852,521	2,230	901,902	1,794	329,346	1,733	954,433	462,063	349,593	Douglas, NE
130	Volusia, FL	483,444	443,343	17,897	192,195	33,831	8,652,230	.1564	5,702,643	1,619	826,756	1,644	245,601	1,293	886,271	390,946	346,315	Volusia, FL
131	Chester, PA	471,979	433,501	26,126	166,783	58,937	12,331,100	.2238	9,955,995	2,827	297,766	592	204,567	1,077	806,704	334,670	336,851	Chester, PA
132	Sonoma, CA	470,813	458,614	24,088	175,179	48,834	11,340,910	.1822	6,084,888	1,728	691,543	1,375	280,632	1,477	1,212,686	357,793	370,462	Sonoma, CA
133	Richmond, NY	470,056	443,728	24,609	170,972	50,531	11,567,790	.1582	3,040,329	863	268,197	533	320,240	1,686	724,948	313,667	258,235	Richmond, NY
134	Sedgwick, KS	468,918	452,869	18,305	176,145	40,290	8,583,550	.1524	5,421,507	1,539	1,154,687	2,296	237,989	1,253	762,179	287,054	356,030	Sedgwick, KS
135	Dane, WI	463,177	426,526	22,795	196,124	45,190	10,558,140	.1825	6,977,606	1,981	914,396	1,818	244,878	1,289	756,141	323,059	360,324	Dane, WI
136	Hampden, MA	463,031	456,228	18,878	178,576	37,310	8,741,300	.1520	5,260,320	1,494	575,750	1,145	275,936	1,452	918,013	446,287	305,489	Hampden, MA
137	Onondaga, NY	462,726	458,336	20,646	185,938	38,491	9,553,310	.1615	5,544,935	1,575	585,852	1,165	368,834	1,941	1,003,122	379,355	341,702	Onondaga, NY
138	Fort Bend, TX	459,581	354,452	20,499	125,540	58,325	9,421,150	.1504	4,403,988	1,251	908,063	1,806	193,800	1,020	501,094	171,263	264,251	Fort Bend, TX
139	Burlington, NJ	458,701	423,394	27,501	170,181	53,526	12,614,840	.1970	6,626,422	1,882	671,042	1,334	236,039	1,242	1,073,853	398,827	327,639	Burlington, NJ
140	Orleans, LA**	456,285	484,674	13,448	174,662	26,719	6,136,230	.1143	3,541,633	1,006	389,671	775	339,037	1,784	628,347	314,738	233,169	Orleans, LA
141	Lucas, OH	452,909	455,054	17,874	179,516	36,154	8,095,090	.1564	6,508,999	1,848	1,048,213	2,085	297,542	1,566	837,264	399,591	327,278	Lucas, OH
142	Virginia Beach, VA*	447,757	425,257	19,490	160,377	44,630	8,726,910	.1461	4,702,261	1,335	626,959	1,247	309,382	1,628	678,813	207,923	365,791	Virginia Beach, VA
143	Jefferson, LA**	447,509	455,466	18,072	167,439	36,380	8,087,470	.1679	7,918,924	2,249	1,636,023	3,254	486,294	2,559	845,888	546,126	303,717	Jefferson, LA
144	Genesee, MI	445,626	436,141	18,240	166,917	39,688	8,128,190	.1460	5,313,381	1,509	1,042,068	2,072	191,549	1,008	611,856	393,603	314,173	Genesee, MI
145	Guilford, NC	442,093	421,048	20,198	176,286	40,413	8,929,590	.1676	7,062,888	2,006	831,891	1,654	366,030	1,927	737,610	382,138	350,559	Guilford, NC
146	Spokane, WA	439,273	417,939	18,223	180,505	35,565	8,004,860	.1437	5,223,271	1,483	985,255	1,959	248,626	1,309	753,870	200,787	357,490	Spokane, WA
147	Solano, CA	421,801	394,542	21,842	140,240	49,727	9,212,790	.1430	4,047,249	1,149	753,325	1,498	194,037	1,021	757,937	149,885	322,260	Solano, CA
148	Monterey, CA	421,269	401,762	18,324	130,913	44,335	7,719,290	.1321	4,297,922	1,220	496,897	988	304,946	1,605	763,460	273,308	273,730	Monterey, CA
149	Pasco, FL	415,912	344,765	17,341	169,524	32,040	7,212,230	.1195	3,379,762	960	704,347	1,401	115,966	610	586,851	253,052	296,790	Pasco, FL
150	Utah, UT	409,622	368,536	15,081	119,096	42,310	6,177,510	.1186	4,378,818	1,243	892,140	1,774	147,868	778	679,220	84,277	277,886	Utah, UT

* Independent City ** Parish
Source: Devonshire Associates Ltd. and Scan/US, Inc. 2005.
[1] Census population includes a portion of Bloomfield county.

[#] Estimates for Total Retail Sales, General Merchandise Sales, Apparel Store Sales, Food Store Sales and Health and Drug Store Sales are based on data from the U.S. Census Bureau's 1997 Economic Census and utilize the North American Industry Classification System (NAICS).

Counties: Population/Income/Sales

This table presents 2000 Census populations, 2005 estimates of population and households, and 2004 estimates of income, purchasing power, retail sales (total and by various store groups) and passenger car registrations. All data except 2000 Census populations are from Devonshire Associates Ltd. and Scan/US, Inc. State and County Codes are from the Federal Information Processing Standards (FIPS) of the National Bureau of Standards. Statistics for Total Retail Sales, General Merchandise Sales, Apparel Store Sales, Food Store Sales, and Health and Drug Store Sales in this edition are estimates based on data from the U.S. Census Bureau, and utilize the 1997 North American Industry Classification System (NAICS).

County or County Equivalent	FIPS County Code	Population Estimate 7/1/05	Population Census 4/1/00	Per Capita Income 2004	House-holds Estimate 7/1/05	Median Household Income 2004	Disposable Income 2004 ($1,000)	Market Ability Index 2004	Total Retail Sales 2004 Sales ($1,000)	Total Retail Sales Ranally Sales Units	General Merchandise 2004 Sales ($1,000)	General Merchandise Ranally Sales Units	Apparel Store 2004 Sales ($1,000)	Apparel Store Ranally Sales Units	Food Store Sales 2004 ($1,000)	Health & Drug Store 2004 ($1,000)	Passenger Car Regis-trations 2004	County or County Equivalent
Alabama (AL; Code 01; 67 Counties)																		
Autauga*	.001	47,987	43,671	18,247	16,900	39,537	875,620	.0159	595,741	169	166,236	331	9,787	52	52,877	69,569	33,384	Autauga
Baldwin**	.003	158,412	140,415	19,064	60,928	37,711	3,019,900	.0549	2,107,963	599	364,019	724	193,503	1,018	262,067	126,798	115,170	Baldwin
Barbour**	.005	28,584	29,038	11,550	10,364	24,620	330,150	.0068	230,367	65	49,187	98	6,288	33	40,997	13,587	18,199	Barbour
Bibb*	.007	21,699	20,826	13,521	7,419	31,089	293,400	.0051	123,397	35	20,082	40	...	...	27,373	10,549	14,564	Bibb
Blount*	.009	56,200	51,024	15,236	19,418	33,681	856,280	.0138	305,134	87	73,819	147	3,367	18	31,605	14,856	40,947	Blount
Bullock	.011	11,135	11,714	9,269	3,897	20,428	103,210	.0021	52,522	15	10,773	21	...	...	8,360	4,391	6,123	Bullock
Butler	.013	20,400	21,399	12,995	8,434	24,372	265,090	.0054	203,174	58	41,318	82	4,474	24	46,355	9,110	14,680	Butler
Calhoun*	.015	112,624	112,249	16,048	45,425	30,609	1,807,370	.0339	1,246,973	354	279,922	557	40,491	213	167,833	58,882	85,776	Calhoun
Chambers**	.017	35,309	36,583	14,915	14,175	28,666	526,640	.0094	280,646	80	60,322	120	2,526	13	46,020	15,067	25,151	Chambers
Cherokee	.019	24,686	23,988	15,097	9,717	29,420	372,690	.0064	175,458	50	29,229	58	2,695	14	34,603	9,076	20,347	Cherokee
Chilton*	.021	41,805	39,593	15,177	15,438	31,448	634,470	.0114	359,088	102	91,151	181	5,545	29	48,225	20,796	31,155	Chilton
Choctaw	.023	15,018	15,922	13,276	6,354	23,830	199,380	.0034	80,380	23	3,885	8	1,535	8	17,279	7,669	11,747	Choctaw
Clarke	.025	27,198	27,867	13,527	10,519	26,868	367,900	.0076	295,762	84	73,939	147	8,530	45	54,263	18,671	18,692	Clarke
Clay	.027	14,184	14,254	14,162	5,695	27,157	200,880	.0032	61,540	17	7,078	14	...	...	12,453	7,257	11,493	Clay
Cleburne	.029	14,929	14,123	14,382	5,616	29,282	214,710	.0037	92,977	26	7,920	16	...	...	8,013	2,336	11,907	Cleburne
Coffee**	.031	45,144	43,615	16,349	17,580	32,186	738,060	.0143	566,554	161	116,933	233	15,802	83	37,904	19,446	33,291	Coffee
Colbert*	.033	54,455	54,984	16,569	22,518	30,843	902,250	.0174	686,759	195	133,930	266	7,904	42	70,363	29,661	44,011	Colbert
Conecuh	.035	13,271	14,089	12,733	5,725	22,396	168,980	.0028	53,627	15	6,693	13	...	...	10,391	4,535	10,163	Conecuh
Coosa**	.037	11,373	12,202	15,285	4,641	28,836	173,840	.0025	24,237	7	1,507	3	...	...	5,703	2,085	9,311	Coosa
Covington	.039	36,551	37,631	14,026	15,364	25,569	512,670	.0101	368,415	105	55,285	110	12,630	66	58,433	28,248	28,304	Covington
Crenshaw	.041	13,659	13,665	13,437	5,543	25,425	183,530	.0032	76,658	22	6,585	13	...	...	17,366	5,445	10,165	Crenshaw
Cullman**	.043	79,130	77,483	15,804	30,715	31,192	1,250,560	.0233	828,569	235	132,301	263	20,493	108	120,279	42,263	61,845	Cullman
Dale**	.045	49,503	49,129	15,247	18,804	30,993	754,750	.0124	288,526	82	53,386	106	4,113	22	50,171	16,243	36,287	Dale
Dallas**	.047	44,339	46,365	11,769	17,559	22,762	521,840	.0109	400,612	114	88,475	176	22,778	120	52,672	29,439	28,326	Dallas
DeKalb**	.049	67,523	64,452	14,018	25,142	28,892	946,520	.0175	548,418	156	136,206	271	15,036	79	73,379	39,232	49,909	DeKalb
Elmore*	.051	73,325	65,874	16,412	23,722	38,646	1,203,440	.0193	453,995	129	67,845	135	3,949	21	85,834	34,634	48,972	Elmore
Escambia	.053	38,227	38,440	13,201	14,147	27,457	504,650	.0105	412,756	117	64,244	128	8,347	44	57,713	19,478	25,945	Escambia
Etowah*	.055	103,021	103,459	15,806	41,635	30,232	1,628,300	.0296	998,934	284	210,213	418	44,852	236	175,131	60,568	78,666	Etowah
Fayette	.057	18,182	18,495	14,721	7,466	27,432	267,650	.0048	151,541	43	25,186	50	2,802	15	21,414	10,973	14,716	Fayette
Franklin	.059	30,561	31,223	13,723	12,160	26,436	419,400	.0076	217,506	62	30,285	60	2,259	12	44,819	16,340	23,371	Franklin
Geneva*	.061	25,405	25,764	13,626	10,378	25,713	346,180	.0059	135,851	39	28,041	56	1,138	6	31,734	7,998	19,262	Geneva
Greene*	.063	9,862	9,974	10,184	3,924	19,638	100,430	.0019	40,480	11	8,643	17	...	...	6,176	1,841	6,397	Greene
Hale*	.065	18,342	17,185	11,544	6,512	25,364	211,740	.0037	69,710	20	4,399	9	...	...	24,961	6,641	11,019	Hale
Henry*	.067	16,560	16,310	14,600	6,476	29,317	241,770	.0042	116,381	33	5,294	11	1,749	9	17,012	9,181	12,014	Henry
Houston*	.069	93,359	88,787	17,028	36,944	32,897	1,589,700	.0352	1,766,280	502	373,249	742	79,783	420	120,367	71,822	65,553	Houston
Jackson**	.071	53,881	53,926	16,070	21,664	30,727	865,870	.0151	456,638	130	83,679	166	17,665	93	68,390	22,543	44,306	Jackson
Jefferson*	.073	655,970	662,047	18,230	260,997	35,314	11,958,100	.2318	9,810,475	2,786	1,578,467	3,139	592,521	3,119	1,133,924	490,536	488,759	Jefferson
Lamar	.075	14,719	15,904	15,393	6,402	26,878	226,570	.0037	89,748	25	6,226	12	...	...	26,809	7,224	12,380	Lamar
Lauderdale*	.077	86,526	87,966	17,401	35,902	32,235	1,505,620	.0274	993,642	282	281,032	559	71,515	376	93,287	43,247	70,928	Lauderdale
Lawrence*	.079	34,317	34,803	15,707	13,588	30,601	539,010	.0085	171,423	49	28,351	56	5,308	28	26,937	15,882	27,979	Lawrence
Lee*	.081	121,616	115,092	15,690	49,426	30,371	1,908,140	.0345	1,142,527	324	219,487	436	59,149	311	192,903	39,194	94,335	Lee
Limestone*	.083	69,788	65,676	16,848	25,168	35,638	1,175,800	.0204	645,273	183	142,317	283	19,541	103	72,668	38,832	51,251	Limestone
Lowndes*	.085	13,375	13,473	10,694	4,816	22,790	143,030	.0025	44,459	13	7,084	14	...	...	6,131	2,200	8,262	Lowndes
Macon**	.087	23,069	24,105	10,861	8,928	21,035	250,550	.0044	80,893	23	9,664	19	...	...	15,889	5,289	14,429	Macon
Madison*	.089	297,607	276,700	21,507	117,714	41,734	6,400,700	.1093	3,945,093	1,120	902,088	1,794	206,849	1,089	466,962	154,432	231,503	Madison
Marengo	.091	21,976	22,539	13,714	8,687	26,021	301,380	.0057	184,987	53	27,438	55	5,766	30	27,746	8,441	14,731	Marengo
Marion	.093	29,666	31,214	15,207	12,750	27,168	451,120	.0079	227,195	65	49,512	98	2,760	15	38,957	11,334	24,051	Marion
Marshall**	.095	85,329	82,231	15,570	32,651	31,204	1,328,540	.0294	1,415,810	402	224,818	447	76,405	402	138,297	62,800	62,948	Marshall
Mobile*	.097	399,727	399,843	13,702	130,235	32,433	5,477,160	.1077	3,885,168	1,103	857,409	1,705	158,982	837	475,635	231,633	252,896	Mobile
Monroe	.099	23,551	24,324	14,511	9,384	27,780	341,750	.0065	222,305	63	34,466	69	14,040	74	40,104	15,645	16,853	Monroe
Montgomery*	.101	221,767	223,510	17,486	86,264	34,885	3,877,740	.0765	3,268,432	928	632,426	1,258	185,059	974	341,198	170,099	147,637	Montgomery
Morgan*	.103	113,972	111,064	18,174	44,058	35,869	2,071,300	.0386	1,513,872	430	233,077	464	59,843	315	129,812	77,632	86,129	Morgan
Perry	.105	11,552	11,861	9,871	4,313	20,019	114,030	.0021	44,399	13	4,348	9	...	...	15,749	5,389	6,741	Perry
Pickens	.107	20,303	20,949	13,216	8,046	25,989	268,320	.0049	142,178	40	6,510	13	3,371	18	18,274	10,374	14,476	Pickens
Pike**	.109	28,893	29,605	13,482	11,981	24,929	389,540	.0080	316,162	90	54,712	109	8,005	42	43,524	16,894	20,722	Pike
Randolph	.111	22,368	22,380	13,739	8,539	27,158	307,310	.0053	128,981	37	23,628	47	1,484	8	33,392	7,014	16,880	Randolph
Russell*	.113	48,555	49,756	14,737	20,419	27,004	715,540	.0123	328,259	93	106,176	211	6,474	34	92,851	19,511	35,319	Russell
St. Clair*	.115	70,917	64,742	16,636	25,257	35,616	1,179,800	.0184	397,836	113	64,434	128	4,999	26	78,381	20,885	51,975	St. Clair
Shelby*	.117	169,764	143,293	24,493	62,521	50,664	4,158,020	.0601	1,466,123	416	256,610	510	22,604	119	227,611	75,103	127,210	Shelby
Sumter	.119	13,859	14,798	9,926	5,672	18,440	137,570	.0029	85,377	24	14,787	29	...	...	13,562	5,433	8,698	Sumter
Talladega**	.121	80,037	80,321	15,179	30,805	30,369	1,214,890	.0215	650,933	185	143,182	285	20,079	106	98,105	40,705	57,879	Talladega
Tallapoosa**	.123	40,226	41,475	15,752	16,460	30,160	633,630	.0110	322,730	92	75,306	150	11,666	61	48,275	20,533	30,899	Tallapoosa
Tuscaloosa*	.125	167,273	164,875	17,430	67,678	33,492	2,915,500	.0544	2,086,587	592	386,453	769	96,797	509	235,724	121,137	124,348	Tuscaloosa
Walker*	.127	69,782	70,713	14,758	28,241	28,032	1,029,810	.0213	897,454	255	183,012	364	36,832	194	92,773	56,611	54,227	Walker
Washington	.129	17,817	18,097	14,663	6,701	30,090	261,250	.0041	70,108	20	7,286	14	...	...	14,159	7,045	13,110	Washington
Wilcox	.131	13,070	13,183	8,077	4,805	16,388	105,570	.0023	63,568	18	5,662	11	...	...	15,242	5,072	7,677	Wilcox
Winston	.133	24,400	24,843	14,619	10,086	27,066	356,700	.0060	143,541	41	33,669	67	...	...	20,713	14,196	19,464	Winston
Alabama Total		**4,537,634**	**4,447,100**	**16,604**	**1,747,412**	**33,067**	**75,343,810**	**1.3846**	**49,659,109**	**14,104**	**9,510,896**	**18,914**	**2,217,269**	**11,671**	**6,284,132**	**2,667,555**	**3,315,864**	**Alabama**
Alaska (AK; Code 02; 16 Boroughs, 11 Census Areas)																		
Aleutians East	.013	2,690	2,697	10,517	530	43,094	28,290	.0005	9,866	3	1,059	2	...	...	4,663	...	711	Aleutians East
Aleutians West	.016	5,460	5,465	17,053	1,353	55,803	93,110	.0015	38,532	11	3,870	8	...	...	14,557	...	2,524	Aleutians West
Anchorage*	.020	278,263	260,283	23,461	103,824	50,900	6,528,250	.1139	4,510,522	1,281	1,086,418	2,161	230,765	1,215	522,594	52,268	204,694	Anchorage
Bethel	.050	17,248	16,006	10,772	4,410	34,461	185,800	.0036	100,417	29	37,885	75	...	...	34,483	...	4,726	Bethel
Bristol Bay	.060	1,044	1,258	27,088	483	46,953	28,280	.0004	14,008	4	3,047	6	...	...	5,529	...	833	Bristol Bay
Denali	.068	1,874	1,893	26,051	802	49,453	48,820	.0006	5,321	2	...	...	...	...	1,533	...	1,700	Denali
Dillingham	.070	4,882	4,922	15,877	1,575	40,020	77,510	.0013	32,983	9	2,550	5	...	...	18,526	...	1,915	Dillingham
Fairbanks North Star*	.090	86,784	82,840	19,495	30,453	45,009	1,691,880	.0308	1,207,437	343	283,785	564	37,121	195	97,724	14,793	58,103	Fairbanks North Star
Haines	.100	2,231	2,392	21,847	1,028	37,922	48,740	.0007	19,981	6	1,173	2	...	...	9,554	...	1,763	Haines
Juneau**	.110	31,260	30,711	26,710	11,972	56,604	834,950	.0123	342,867	97	116,565	232	21,689	114	39,607	9,140	20,864	Juneau
Kenai Peninsula	.122	52,237	49,691	19,025	18,722	42,787	993,820	.0177	653,718	186	78,096	155	15,480	81	135,387	19,025	36,091	Kenai Peninsula
Ketchikan Gateway**	.130	12,871	14,070	25,608	5,672	47,300	329,600	.0056	223,442	63	9,530	19	22,405	118	71,118	6,157	8,949	Ketchikan Gateway
Kodiak Island**	.150	12,962	13,913	22,668	4,735	50,211	293,820	.0044	119,398	34	5,656	11	1,434	8	47,694	1,939	8,593	Kodiak Island
Lake and Peninsula	.164	1,452	1,823	17,259	585	34,832	25,060	.0004	4,263	1	2,317	5	...	...	...	...	688	Lake and Peninsula
Matanuska-Susitna*	.170	73,923	59,322	16,378	21,059	46,521	1,210,700	.0220	758,780	215	84,760	169	16,553	87	129,742	15,548	44,894	Matanuska-Susitna
Nome	.180	9,174	9,196	14,124	2,689	38,585	129,570	.0023	65,464	19	1,921	4	...	...	36,949	...	2,692	Nome
North Slope	.185	7,080	7,385	22,530	2,256	57,416	159,510	.0024	61,078	17	20,799	41	...	...	17,908	...	2,013	North Slope
Northwest Arctic	.188	7,522	7,208	12,487	1,793	42,399	93,930	.0017	44,034	13	19,942	40	...	...	16,954	...	1,456	Northwest Arctic
Prince of Wales-Outer Ketchikan	.201	5,545	6,146	20,159	2,351	38,311	111,780	.0016	27,009	8	2,022	4	...	...	12,180	...	3,527	Prince of Wales-Outer Ketchikan
Sitka	.220	8,879	8,835	22,587	3,446	46,937	200,550	.0032	101,295	29	3,253	6	8,901	47	33,871	7,232	5,387	Sitka
Skagway-Hoonah-Angoon	.232	2,973	3,436	23,545	1,483	38,210	70,000	.0011	30,053	9	2,068	4	...	...	8,425	...	2,028	Skagway-Hoonah-Angoon
Southeast Fairbanks	.240	5,487	6,174	17,831	2,151	36,472	97,840	.0015	30,750	9	...	...	...	...	5,070	...	4,254	Southeast Fairbanks
Valdez-Cordova	.261	9,821	10,195	22,297	3,946	44,954	218,980	.0034	99,876	28	3,565	7	2,100	11	30,651	1,442	6,893	Valdez-Cordova
Wade Hampton	.270	7,436	7,028	7,696	1,606	28,924	57,230	.0013	36,675	10	10,341	21	...	...	18,378	...	1,448	Wade Hampton
Wrangell-Petersburg	.280	6,054	6,684	23,221	2,670	42,457	140,580	.0022	63,058	18	2,024	4	2,055	11	26,295	1,199	4,155	Wrangell-Petersburg
Yakutat	.282	666	808	22,012	269	43,986	14,660	.0002	5,316	2	...	...	...	...	1,080	...	389	Yakutat
Yukon-Koyukuk	.290	6,202	6,551	12,828	2,350	27,167	79,560	.0013	19,335	5	3,675	7	...	...	5,835	...	2,522	Yukon-Koyukuk
Alaska Total		**662,020**	**626,932**	**20,834**	**234,213**	**47,658**	**13,792,820**	**.2379**	**8,625,478**	**2,451**	**1,788,019**	**3,555**	**361,373**	**1,902**	**1,347,251**	**130,041**	**433,812**	**Alaska**
Arizona (AZ; Code 04; 15 Counties)																		
Apache	.001	67,835	69,423	8,661	20,125	22,186	587,530	.0113	192,504	55	17,428	35	5,198	27	41,401	6,435	30,523	Apache
Cochise**	.003	124,122	117,755	15,174	47,040	31,114	1,883,480	.0325	904,859	257	174,929	348	27,736	146	191,816	20,681	82,188	Cochise
Coconino*	.005	124,093	116,320	16,494	43,459	36,525	2,046,830	.0374	1,313,802	373	283,592	564	32,136	169	229,169	28,901	79,415	Coconino
Gila**	.007	51,287	51,335	15,604	21,174	29,757	800,270	.0134	351,036	100	72,655	144	3,777	20	80,604	10,216	37,206	Gila
Graham**	.009	32,757	33,489	11,688	10,491	28,574	382,880	.0076	237,810	68	50,080	100	4,954	26	45,239	3,381	18,990	Graham
Greenlee**	.011	6,942	8,547	21,582	3,148	36,727	149,820	.0020	28,455	8	1,390	3	1,215	6	12,122	...	6,543	Greenlee
La Paz	.012	19,709	19,715	14,079	8,595	25,392	277,490	.0062	286,409	81	3,424	7	...	...	23,587	...	14,969	La Paz
Maricopa*	.013	3,582,040	3,072,149	19,534	1,290,757	42,913	69,970,650	1.2197	43,410,524	12,327	5,973,166	11,879	1,699,770	8,946	5,354,760	2,255,113	2,282,542	Maricopa
Mohave**	.015	182,775	155,032	15,397	72,511	30,463	2,814,220	.0521	1,800,506	511	260,449	518	32,494	171	335,768	73,276	128,145	Mohave
Navajo	.017	108,601	97,470	10,515	32,039	27,784	1,141,970	.0240	797,267	226	150,749	300	12,901	68	151,924	12,114	52,427	Navajo
Pima*	.019	921,681	843,746	17,523	359,359	35,369	16,151,030	.2750	8,503,748	2,415	1,331,237	2,647	348,394	1,834	1,318,403	534,417	611,509	Pima
Pinal*	.021	219,763	179,727	15,004	75,215	34,354	3,297,350	.0510	878,406	249	110,315	219	37,772	199	206,141	51,753	128,225	Pinal
Santa Cruz**	.023	41,238	38,381	12,214	13,732	29,095	503,690	.0110	449,398	128	116,411	231	48,089	253	84,199	13,345	24,630	Santa Cruz
Yavapai*	.025	194,839	167,517	18,019	82,257	33,197	3,510,890	.0580	1,685,447	479	326,787	650	48,378	255	346,624	66,184	150,405	Yavapai
Yuma*	.027	177,064	160,026	13,429	59,841	30,728	2,377,840	.0452	1,477,200	419	322,796	642	34,478	181	221,749	77,415	100,715	Yuma
Arizona Total		**5,854,746**	**5,130,632**	**18,087**	**2,139,743**	**38,899**	**105,895,940**	**1.8464**	**62,317,372**	**17,696**	**9,195,407**	**18,287**	**2,338,144**	**12,305**	**8,643,505**	**3,153,968**	**3,748,432**	**Arizona**
Arkansas (AR; Code 05; 75 Counties)																		
Arkansas	.001	19,811	20,749	16,061	8,489	29,231	318,180	.0066	287,889	82	84,577	168	7,191	38	29,765	17,484	14,652	Arkansas
Ashley	.003	23,444	24,209	16,268	9,652	30,779	381,380	.0064	178,652	51	42,247	84	7,409	39	35,665	10,299	17,151	Ashley
Baxter**	.005	39,577	38,386	16,242	17,776	27,996	642,820	.0121	453,400	129	116,913	232	8,620	45	71,018	12,866	31,828	Baxter
Benton*	.007	183,859	153,406	17,767	66,780	37,824	3,266,680	.0570	1,899,047	539	548,160	1,090	29,047	153	129,978	64,805	129,103	Benton
Boone**	.009	35,283	33,948	14,892	14,196	28,698	525,440	.0113	514,647	146	156,408	311	13,665	72	26,184	16,278	27,437	Boone
Bradley	.011	12,321	12,600	12,116	4,794	24,050	149,280	.0028	76,005	22	7,053	14	2,208	12	12,309	3,196	8,203	Bradley
Calhoun**	.013	5,517	5,744	15,202	2,374	27,192	83,870	.0012	16,702	5	1,551	3	...	...	2,975	3,010	4,339	Calhoun
Carroll	.015	27,143	25,357	13,312	10,360	27,040	361,320	.0072	265,454	75	74,675	148	7,528	40	40,835	10,928	20,335	Carroll
Chicot	.017	13,038	14,117	11,618	5,298	22,090	151,480	.0032	112,706	32	12,059	24	2,893	15	17,879	6,213	8,144	Chicot
Clark**	.019	22,973	23,546	14,463	9,347	27,272	332,250	.0064	234,811	67	47,487	94	5,200	27	22,425	21,639	16,344	Clark
Clay	.021	16,521	17,609	14,348	7,489	24,720	237,040	.0043	136,404	39	18,985	38	1,193	6	17,012	8,415	13,359	Clay
Cleburne	.023	25,192	24,046	16,384	10,530	30,405	412,740	.0071	208,556	59	56,257	112	1,498	8	31,911	11,463	19,885	Cleburne
Cleveland*	.025	8,871	8,571	15,220	3,359	32,290	135,020	.0019	12,934	4	2,214	4	...	...	1,036	...	6,542	Cleveland
Columbia**	.027	24,407	25,603	14,342	10,128	26,826	350,050	.0064	198,176	56	57,114	114	13,313	70	28,209	7,508	18,085	Columbia
Conway	.029	20,660	20,336	15,157	8,103	30,236	313,150	.0061	229,124	65	71,313	142	2,644	14	28,939	6,750	15,623	Conway
Craighead*	.031	86,335	82,148	15,939	34,155	31,300	1,376,100	.0286	1,267,386	360	361,786	719	80,295	423	87,497	49,672	61,412	Craighead
Crawford*	.033	57,169	53,247	14,702	20,617	31,440	840,490	.0145	394,625	112	99,263	197	2,131	11	57,195	15,841	39,557	Crawford
Crittenden*	.035	51,287	50,866	14,275	19,584	29,297	732,110	.0154	655,502	186	130,155	259	11,178	59	42,259	34,860	30,673	Crittenden
Cross	.037	18,969	19,526	14,637	7,674	27,956	277,650	.0050	151,108	43	30,530	61	4,991	26	21,251	3,905	12,839	Cross
Dallas	.039	8,445	9,210	13,871	3,547	25,589	117,140	.0023	82,632	23	15,004	30	2,194	12	10,348	4,732	5,837	Dallas
Desha	.041	14,313	15,341	12,844	6,033	24,229	183,840	.0043	201,085	57	39,864	79	2,163	11	20,907	8,412	9,085	Desha
Drew	.043	18,493	18,723	15,028	7,743	27,797	277,910	.0055	216,716	62	82,551	164	5,680	30	12,253	4,469	14,242	Drew
Faulkner*	.045	96,723	86,014	17,268	35,692	36,079	1,670,170	.0288	914,232	260	257,513	512	35,130	185	51,460	42,764	67,654	Faulkner
Franklin*	.047	18,132	17,771	14,672	6,994	29,746	266,040	.0045	113,370	32	22,588	45	...	...	21,164	8,002	13,640	Franklin
Fulton	.049	11,665	11,642	13,496	4,928	24,979	157,430	.0024	30,536	9	3,173	6	...	...	7,607	5,801	9,858	Fulton
Garland*	.051	93,078	88,068	16,116	38,546	30,468	1,500,060	.0304	1,299,442	369	345,207	687	43,650	230	117,473	68,521	65,357	Garland

Source: Devonshire Associates Ltd. and Scan/US, Inc. 2005. ...Data less than 1,000. (d) Data not available.
* Component of a Metropolitan Core Based Statistical Area.
** Component of a Micropolitan Core Based Statistical Area.

Counties: Population/Income/Sales, *Continued*

County or County Equivalent	FIPS County Code	Population Estimate 7/1/05	Population Census 4/1/00	Per Capita Income 2004	House-holds Estimate 7/1/05	Median Household Income 2004	Disposable Income 2004 ($1,000)	Market Ability Index 2004	Total Retail Sales 2004 Sales ($1,000)	Total Retail Sales Ranally Sales Units	General Merchandise 2004 Sales ($1,000)	General Merchandise Ranally Sales Units	Apparel Store 2004 Sales ($1,000)	Apparel Store Ranally Sales Units	Food Store Sales 2004 ($1,000)	Health & Drug Store 2004 ($1,000)	Passenger Car Regis-trations 2004	County or County Equivalent
Grant*	.053	17,241	16,464	17,281	6,524	35,272	297,940	.0045	92,421	26	32,528	65	...	...	15,711	2,124	13,130	Grant
Greene**	.055	39,110	37,331	15,296	15,669	30,132	598,210	.0111	382,477	109	122,304	243	10,156	53	38,537	17,137	29,250	Greene
Hempstead**	.057	23,287	23,587	13,904	9,102	27,471	323,790	.0059	179,096	51	48,099	96	7,342	39	25,950	6,355	16,271	Hempstead
Hot Spring	.059	30,777	30,353	15,639	12,340	30,486	481,310	.0080	203,864	58	52,450	104	3,245	17	28,582	6,919	23,725	Hot Spring
Howard	.061	14,604	14,300	13,792	5,594	28,024	201,420	.0039	132,522	38	39,984	80	1,403	7	29,545	7,716	10,280	Howard
Independence**	.063	34,597	34,233	15,767	13,862	30,614	545,480	.0107	424,787	121	155,314	309	21,803	115	34,590	18,153	26,184	Independence
Izard	.065	13,352	13,249	13,384	5,570	25,076	178,700	.0033	99,888	28	5,508	11	...	...	12,353	7,678	10,324	Izard
Jackson	.067	16,885	18,418	13,272	7,065	24,544	224,090	.0046	180,882	51	33,116	66	4,337	23	27,065	7,306	11,905	Jackson
Jefferson*	.069	82,043	84,278	14,092	29,791	30,397	1,156,190	.0238	967,724	275	204,175	406	61,309	323	122,491	108,319	57,243	Jefferson
Johnson	.071	23,881	22,781	13,159	9,011	26,864	314,240	.0061	208,714	59	50,243	100	3,870	20	25,845	5,983	17,035	Johnson
Lafayette	.073	8,248	8,559	13,377	3,524	24,251	110,330	.0018	30,943	9	3,691	7	...	...	7,402	3,124	5,983	Lafayette
Lawrence	.075	17,378	17,774	13,901	7,186	25,936	241,580	.0046	160,363	46	29,362	58	2,643	14	15,385	8,173	13,040	Lawrence
Lee	.077	11,498	12,580	9,952	4,358	20,671	114,430	.0022	51,875	15	6,575	13	1,029	5	8,420	4,476	6,842	Lee
Lincoln*	.079	14,295	14,492	11,316	4,408	28,516	161,760	.0028	51,247	15	4,584	9	...	...	9,103	5,313	7,713	Lincoln
Little River	.081	13,264	13,628	15,274	5,543	28,375	202,600	.0035	93,625	27	19,079	38	...	...	17,522	4,999	10,189	Little River
Logan	.083	23,032	22,486	13,489	8,789	27,450	310,690	.0057	164,361	47	39,143	78	5,151	27	21,977	10,216	16,877	Logan
Lonoke*	.085	59,112	52,828	18,031	21,669	38,020	1,065,850	.0168	418,905	119	121,071	241	3,086	16	38,660	15,550	42,750	Lonoke
Madison*	.087	14,512	14,243	13,432	5,606	26,833	194,930	.0033	75,921	22	17,989	36	...	...	4,018	4,159	11,865	Madison
Marion	.089	16,248	16,140	14,782	7,155	26,033	240,180	.0037	62,276	18	15,625	31	...	...	17,960	3,322	13,779	Marion
Miller*	.091	42,971	40,443	14,585	16,457	29,904	626,720	.0111	319,758	91	70,442	140	9,720	51	62,574	9,054	28,354	Miller
Mississippi**	.093	47,179	51,979	14,126	19,531	26,542	666,440	.0127	437,559	124	96,943	193	13,343	70	54,980	21,657	30,774	Mississippi
Monroe	.095	9,342	10,254	12,792	4,194	21,874	119,500	.0027	122,787	35	15,001	30	1,439	8	17,202	8,054	6,356	Monroe
Montgomery	.097	9,181	9,245	15,154	3,898	28,114	139,130	.0021	29,070	8	1,933	4	...	...	7,882	2,903	7,717	Montgomery
Nevada**	.099	9,503	9,955	14,949	4,260	25,772	142,060	.0023	50,260	14	4,504	9	...	...	7,238	4,572	7,624	Nevada
Newton**	.101	8,568	8,608	12,942	3,553	24,151	110,890	.0018	26,776	8	1,617	3	...	...	...	1,690	6,798	Newton
Ouachita**	.103	27,020	28,790	15,654	11,663	28,120	422,970	.0077	253,195	72	52,633	105	13,887	73	34,829	10,426	19,906	Ouachita
Perry*	.105	10,512	10,209	14,953	4,092	30,025	157,190	.0023	26,464	8	3,513	7	...	...	7,175	2,360	8,222	Perry
Phillips**	.107	23,555	26,445	11,733	9,762	21,701	276,380	.0059	229,040	65	62,712	125	5,069	27	30,032	8,559	13,534	Phillips
Pike	.109	10,907	11,303	14,529	4,620	26,461	158,470	.0029	94,344	27	7,294	15	...	...	16,068	7,221	9,036	Pike
Poinsett*	.111	25,232	25,614	13,509	10,262	25,879	340,860	.0059	144,513	41	25,464	51	...	...	28,708	12,399	17,580	Poinsett
Polk	.113	20,178	20,229	12,907	8,240	24,671	260,430	.0050	166,861	47	78,687	156	3,396	18	10,706	6,478	15,406	Polk
Pope**	.115	55,567	54,469	15,591	21,723	30,820	866,330	.0176	743,964	211	166,620	331	19,356	102	70,408	25,159	41,821	Pope
Prairie	.117	9,216	9,539	15,506	3,936	28,189	142,900	.0024	57,175	16	5,517	11	...	...	7,653	2,441	7,181	Prairie
Pulaski*	.119	366,433	361,474	19,824	155,185	36,326	7,264,050	.1436	6,547,525	1,859	1,323,778	2,633	283,778	1,494	592,308	217,425	302,562	Pulaski
Randolph	.121	18,232	18,195	14,342	7,514	26,962	261,490	.0046	128,091	36	47,415	94	...	...	16,828	6,722	13,903	Randolph
St. Francis**	.123	27,991	29,329	11,875	10,328	25,240	332,390	.0078	353,808	100	84,155	167	6,982	37	47,691	14,815	15,787	St. Francis
Saline*	.125	89,781	83,529	20,701	35,874	40,062	1,858,600	.0332	1,286,927	365	172,130	342	15,848	83	57,983	35,834	71,159	Saline
Scott	.127	10,981	10,996	13,439	4,439	25,556	147,570	.0024	45,415	13	13,192	26	...	...	5,967	4,276	8,140	Scott
Searcy	.129	7,786	8,261	12,512	3,576	21,023	97,420	.0018	49,402	14	17,461	35	...	...	9,796	3,450	6,780	Searcy
Sebastian*	.131	118,532	115,071	16,696	47,166	32,581	1,978,990	.0418	1,947,562	553	607,956	1,209	64,909	342	160,795	80,674	83,647	Sebastian
Sevier	.133	15,999	15,757	13,422	5,799	28,859	214,740	.0040	118,789	34	34,833	69	...	...	17,559	6,064	11,393	Sevier
Sharp	.135	17,654	17,119	13,033	7,304	24,516	230,080	.0045	159,084	45	64,735	129	...	...	14,803	4,620	13,153	Sharp
Stone	.137	11,647	11,499	12,208	4,927	22,206	142,190	.0027	84,494	24	10,833	22	...	...	13,840	2,850	9,696	Stone
Union**	.139	44,474	45,629	15,099	18,140	28,905	671,520	.0135	550,188	156	143,603	286	22,342	118	57,744	35,547	31,522	Union
Van Buren	.141	16,590	16,192	14,274	6,970	26,286	236,810	.0040	99,646	28	30,830	61	1,244	7	9,235	4,669	12,967	Van Buren
Washington*	.143	177,115	157,715	16,392	67,934	33,088	2,903,230	.0568	2,303,224	654	834,295	1,659	89,735	472	221,038	59,486	127,217	Washington
White**	.145	70,967	67,165	14,895	26,295	30,980	1,057,030	.0204	754,435	214	235,787	469	34,068	179	60,992	37,768	49,552	White
Woodruff	.147	8,071	8,741	12,694	3,578	21,948	102,450	.0018	47,399	13	6,254	12	...	...	14,805	6,072	5,741	Woodruff
Yell**	.149	21,665	21,139	13,604	8,188	28,013	294,740	.0049	101,163	29	21,188	42	...	...	17,221	8,016	16,028	Yell
Arkansas Total		**2,759,439**	**2,673,400**	**16,035**	**1,096,362**	**31,326**	**44,246,930**	**.8382**	**31,411,949**	**8,922**	**7,926,811**	**15,763**	**1,011,973**	**5,326**	**3,121,449**	**1,346,983**	**2,025,125**	**Arkansas**

California (CA; Code 06; 58 Counties)

County or County Equivalent	FIPS County Code	Population Estimate 7/1/05	Population Census 4/1/00	Per Capita Income 2004	House-holds Estimate 7/1/05	Median Household Income 2004	Disposable Income 2004 ($1,000)	Market Ability Index 2004	Total Retail Sales 2004 Sales ($1,000)	Total Retail Sales Ranally Sales Units	General Merchandise 2004 Sales ($1,000)	General Merchandise Ranally Sales Units	Apparel Store 2004 Sales ($1,000)	Apparel Store Ranally Sales Units	Food Store Sales 2004 ($1,000)	Health & Drug Store 2004 ($1,000)	Passenger Car Regis-trations 2004	County or County Equivalent
Alameda*	.001	1,466,375	1,443,741	24,082	514,750	51,403	35,313,910	.5542	17,409,448	4,943	1,745,449	3,471	860,637	4,530	3,306,808	946,660	994,504	Alameda
Alpine	.003	1,173	1,208	24,297	539	40,327	28,500	.0004	4,242	1	...	...	...	...	...	...	1,042	Alpine
Amador	.005	38,762	35,100	18,889	13,726	40,112	732,160	.0151	719,811	204	73,177	146	7,590	40	98,749	16,012	27,246	Amador
Butte*	.007	215,649	203,171	16,053	84,743	30,865	3,461,920	.0631	2,162,007	614	337,895	672	81,188	427	421,916	159,025	155,608	Butte
Calaveras	.009	47,324	40,554	19,589	18,013	38,664	927,040	.0131	222,862	63	3,116	6	3,133	16	55,247	24,129	36,821	Calaveras
Colusa	.011	20,353	18,804	13,557	6,169	33,612	275,920	.0050	144,630	41	3,821	8	1,956	10	21,149	9,203	11,342	Colusa
Contra Costa*	.013	1,031,546	948,816	26,152	350,538	57,990	26,977,050	.4003	11,291,061	3,206	1,642,920	3,267	717,061	3,774	2,215,986	540,440	701,952	Contra Costa
Del Norte**	.015	28,063	27,507	12,655	9,413	28,343	355,130	.0062	146,663	42	34,661	69	3,516	19	43,363	9,785	15,891	Del Norte
El Dorado*	.017	176,979	156,299	23,464	65,828	47,600	4,152,690	.0599	1,398,145	397	50,772	101	87,213	459	374,785	82,591	135,173	El Dorado
Fresno*	.019	881,918	799,407	13,549	271,021	33,341	11,949,320	.2266	7,423,260	2,108	1,040,968	2,070	331,031	1,742	1,229,784	460,666	521,285	Fresno
Glenn	.021	27,715	26,453	13,624	9,395	30,473	377,590	.0061	114,205	32	22,386	45	1,651	9	29,383	5,572	17,882	Glenn
Humboldt**	.023	128,714	126,518	16,444	53,322	30,075	2,116,560	.0384	1,331,631	378	132,356	263	50,625	266	280,440	112,197	92,207	Humboldt
Imperial*	.025	153,484	142,361	11,514	43,593	31,028	1,767,170	.0381	1,451,398	412	276,417	550	94,280	496	260,442	69,041	75,806	Imperial
Inyo**	.027	18,631	17,945	18,480	7,739	33,253	344,310	.0061	219,064	62	16,788	33	9,379	49	40,620	16,218	14,267	Inyo
Kern*	.029	743,729	661,645	14,153	234,348	33,848	10,526,210	.1907	5,759,480	1,635	787,831	1,567	234,327	1,233	863,026	390,768	437,779	Kern
Kings*	.031	145,336	129,461	11,511	37,148	33,898	1,672,960	.0311	795,708	226	107,971	215	35,135	185	189,051	42,422	65,005	Kings
Lake**	.033	66,477	58,309	13,954	24,521	28,521	927,650	.0162	424,928	121	60,596	120	4,857	26	123,895	31,167	43,828	Lake
Lassen**	.035	34,769	33,828	13,203	9,990	34,759	459,040	.0076	151,175	43	18,661	37	8,748	46	36,562	5,586	19,826	Lassen
Los Angeles*	.037	10,076,928	9,519,338	16,791	3,192,402	39,739	169,200,500	2.9617	95,230,986	27,041	11,726,649	23,321	7,977,490	41,987	15,007,662	5,683,828	5,997,792	Los Angeles
Madera*	.039	141,694	123,109	12,870	39,639	34,748	1,823,630	.0312	675,580	192	66,089	131	10,636	56	228,960	42,601	74,203	Madera
Marin*	.041	245,317	247,289	35,625	102,544	63,710	8,739,310	.1287	4,252,146	1,207	425,715	847	363,967	1,916	817,403	226,721	187,616	Marin
Mariposa	.043	18,207	17,130	16,959	7,027	32,866	308,780	.0045	72,907	21	15,147	30	4,602	24	20,825	4,331	14,123	Mariposa
Mendocino**	.045	89,741	86,265	17,521	34,495	34,292	1,572,350	.0279	965,158	274	88,130	175	11,905	63	229,167	61,312	61,719	Mendocino
Merced*	.047	243,619	210,554	12,985	70,306	34,062	3,163,490	.0572	1,559,661	443	279,329	555	41,746	220	281,012	82,724	125,422	Merced
Modoc	.049	9,483	9,449	14,332	3,765	27,126	135,910	.0021	37,073	11	...	...	1,074	6	10,411	2,963	7,129	Modoc
Mono	.051	12,819	12,853	23,639	5,460	41,733	303,030	.0045	121,332	34	6,350	13	6,309	33	42,178	7,457	10,188	Mono
Monterey*	.053	421,269	401,762	18,324	130,913	44,335	7,719,290	.1321	4,297,922	1,220	496,897	988	304,946	1,605	763,460	273,308	273,730	Monterey
Napa*	.055	136,414	124,279	22,695	48,973	47,323	3,095,930	.0489	1,498,422	425	93,230	185	135,315	712	377,458	80,638	93,687	Napa
Nevada**	.057	98,587	92,033	22,992	40,026	42,512	2,266,750	.0349	1,005,939	286	35,143	70	53,410	281	254,747	78,124	80,732	Nevada
Orange*	.059	3,020,648	2,846,289	23,420	988,370	54,079	70,743,570	1.1619	40,282,551	11,438	5,068,317	10,079	3,229,084	16,995	5,793,345	2,111,368	2,025,430	Orange
Placer*	.061	319,191	248,399	27,367	124,618	52,462	8,735,220	.1361	4,537,065	1,288	475,807	946	115,555	608	730,125	209,184	272,391	Placer
Plumas	.063	21,450	20,824	20,455	9,548	34,809	438,760	.0068	175,401	50	3,643	7	3,993	21	56,381	8,610	18,167	Plumas
Riverside*	.065	1,929,673	1,545,387	17,676	635,727	40,822	34,109,300	.5767	17,610,853	5,001	2,426,846	4,826	1,004,342	5,286	2,898,626	821,920	1,269,979	Riverside
Sacramento*	.067	1,395,768	1,223,499	19,326	494,021	41,674	26,974,040	.4525	14,542,941	4,130	2,167,858	4,311	944,882	4,973	2,469,951	612,794	963,855	Sacramento
San Benito*	.069	57,666	53,234	21,377	17,467	52,868	1,232,750	.0186	466,361	132	60,109	120	7,782	41	120,399	26,157	37,332	San Benito
San Bernardino*	.071	1,957,135	1,709,434	15,531	577,153	39,791	30,395,760	.5334	16,102,044	4,572	2,355,210	4,684	942,871	4,963	2,773,850	764,307	1,219,682	San Bernardino
San Diego*	.073	2,990,693	2,813,833	19,889	1,027,661	43,667	59,482,050	1.0104	34,231,355	9,720	4,237,412	8,427	2,478,722	13,046	5,315,838	1,790,799	1,982,651	San Diego
San Francisco*	.075	734,587	776,733	29,289	317,359	50,717	21,515,350	.3346	11,511,398	3,269	1,090,215	2,168	2,270,361	11,949	1,932,648	783,829	404,999	San Francisco
San Joaquin*	.077	674,080	563,598	15,489	201,595	39,475	10,441,010	.1808	5,234,961	1,486	683,333	1,359	247,667	1,304	900,861	341,266	430,326	San Joaquin
San Luis Obispo*	.079	257,381	246,681	21,248	102,969	39,996	5,468,890	.0887	2,798,082	795	240,208	478	153,387	807	552,099	196,306	233,271	San Luis Obispo
San Mateo*	.081	689,423	707,161	30,314	247,340	63,279	20,899,240	.3436	13,548,512	3,847	2,148,421	4,273	829,558	4,366	2,333,520	690,844	515,151	San Mateo
Santa Barbara*	.083	404,582	399,347	19,919	139,852	43,041	8,058,830	.1386	4,839,745	1,374	499,060	992	335,212	1,764	874,460	322,723	270,633	Santa Barbara
Santa Clara*	.085	1,669,973	1,682,585	29,371	557,576	65,828	49,048,290	.7777	28,016,175	7,955	3,571,238	7,102	2,391,823	12,589	4,358,548	1,477,292	1,194,252	Santa Clara
Santa Cruz*	.087	248,347	255,602	23,192	87,640	49,511	5,759,610	.0926	3,020,791	858	310,796	618	162,723	856	605,097	265,080	193,111	Santa Cruz
Shasta*	.089	183,315	163,256	16,233	68,490	32,714	2,975,750	.0525	1,677,238	476	289,803	576	48,662	256	305,136	97,029	125,198	Shasta
Sierra	.091	3,522	3,555	19,747	1,532	34,164	69,550	.0009	7,059	2	...	...	...	...	1,112	1,241	2,989	Sierra
Siskiyou	.093	44,782	44,301	16,018	19,124	28,338	717,300	.0122	347,310	99	38,679	77	1,503	8	84,386	26,152	35,075	Siskiyou
Solano*	.095	421,801	394,542	21,842	140,240	49,727	9,212,790	.1430	4,047,249	1,149	753,325	1,498	194,037	1,021	757,937	149,885	322,260	Solano
Sonoma*	.097	470,813	458,614	24,088	175,179	48,834	11,340,910	.1822	6,084,888	1,728	691,543	1,375	280,632	1,477	1,212,686	357,793	370,462	Sonoma
Stanislaus*	.099	519,823	446,997	15,585	161,250	37,782	8,101,680	.1473	4,910,210	1,394	756,250	1,504	190,893	1,005	890,064	318,684	331,624	Stanislaus
Sutter*	.101	88,233	78,930	15,894	29,088	36,225	1,402,360	.0257	892,901	254	219,838	437	30,307	160	183,868	44,583	54,045	Sutter
Tehama**	.103	60,649	56,039	14,463	22,010	30,270	877,140	.0170	621,929	177	68,442	136	6,972	37	116,880	20,376	40,715	Tehama
Trinity	.105	13,819	13,022	14,721	5,682	27,063	203,430	.0032	59,533	17	1,518	3	1,440	8	20,942	7,391	10,895	Trinity
Tulare*	.107	404,818	368,021	12,914	120,917	32,438	5,227,730	.0963	2,765,611	785	418,656	833	108,161	569	563,264	158,385	225,215	Tulare
Tuolumne**	.109	58,070	54,501	18,260	21,797	36,311	1,060,360	.0169	443,459	126	61,996	123	5,023	26	111,562	37,376	42,750	Tuolumne
Ventura*	.111	813,570	753,197	23,388	262,514	54,638	19,028,060	.3036	9,778,861	2,777	1,019,623	2,028	564,619	2,972	1,522,187	578,898	557,088	Ventura
Yolo*	.113	189,696	168,660	17,604	65,586	38,436	3,339,440	.0553	1,581,386	449	108,998	217	28,406	150	369,339	83,914	117,373	Yolo
Yuba*	.115	65,644	60,219	12,721	21,529	29,215	835,070	.0142	291,865	83	18,579	37	...	...	72,692	42,299	38,902	Yuba
California Total		**36,430,227**	**33,871,648**	**19,720**	**12,074,180**	**44,218**	**718,388,340**	**12.0352**	**391,314,575**	**111,113**	**49,374,886**	**98,190**	**28,023,277**	**147,492**	**65,552,847**	**21,811,974**	**23,599,626**	**California**

Colorado (CO; Code 08; 64 Counties)

County or County Equivalent	FIPS County Code	Population Estimate 7/1/05	Population Census 4/1/00	Per Capita Income 2004	House-holds Estimate 7/1/05	Median Household Income 2004	Disposable Income 2004 ($1,000)	Market Ability Index 2004	Total Retail Sales 2004 Sales ($1,000)	Total Retail Sales Ranally Sales Units	General Merchandise 2004 Sales ($1,000)	General Merchandise Ranally Sales Units	Apparel Store 2004 Sales ($1,000)	Apparel Store Ranally Sales Units	Food Store Sales 2004 ($1,000)	Health & Drug Store 2004 ($1,000)	Passenger Car Regis-trations 2004	County or County Equivalent
Adams*[1]	.001	399,121	363,857	20,423	151,495	43,231	8,151,190	.1350	4,365,352	1,240	545,236	1,084	67,851	357	665,067	106,013	327,624	Adams
Alamosa	.003	15,125	14,966	14,378	6,111	28,723	217,470	.0048	225,338	64	61,536	122	3,328	18	31,750	5,256	12,341	Alamosa
Arapahoe*	.005	531,667	487,967	25,588	222,336	50,686	13,604,070	.2357	9,574,512	2,719	1,446,704	2,877	395,689	2,083	1,211,842	377,756	427,483	Arapahoe
Archuleta	.007	12,228	9,898	19,784	5,339	36,149	241,920	.0036	84,715	24	...	...	...	...	16,467	3,864	11,358	Archuleta
Baca	.009	3,948	4,517	17,396	2,069	26,554	68,680	.0010	18,579	5	1,510	3	...	...	4,829	...	4,591	Baca
Bent	.011	5,474	5,998	13,370	2,151	27,279	73,190	.0011	13,785	4	...	...	...	...	5,069	...	4,556	Bent
Boulder*[1]	.013	282,452	291,288	25,153	111,722	51,544	7,104,400	.1167	4,216,806	1,197	418,126	832	137,945	726	786,632	154,369	221,721	Boulder
Broomfield*[2]	.014	44,052	(d)	31,400	18,953	59,463	1,383,230	.0174	283,136	80	45,927	91	...	...	56,649	10,761	41,139	Broomfield
Chaffee	.015	17,225	16,242	18,828	7,907	33,072	324,320	.0056	194,584	55	27,192	54	1,249	7	39,528	7,291	16,588	Chaffee
Cheyenne	.017	1,952	2,231	21,542	959	35,073	42,050	.0006	16,618	5	...	...	...	...	1,374	...	2,215	Cheyenne
Clear Creek*	.019	9,627	9,322	26,788	4,411	47,346	257,890	.0033	49,860	14	...	...	1,338	7	12,710	3,918	9,831	Clear Creek
Conejos	.021	8,365	8,400	12,446	3,473	24,067	104,110	.0017	31,001	9	...	...	...	...	8,348	3,695	7,403	Conejos
Costilla	.023	3,504	3,663	11,173	1,624	19,531	39,150	.0006	5,859	2	...	...	...	...	1,418	...	2,872	Costilla
Crowley	.025	5,427	5,518	8,782	1,491	25,704	47,660	.0009	19,786	6	...	...	...	...	...	3,145	3,169	Crowley
Custer	.027	3,988	3,503	19,865	1,888	33,571	79,220	.0012	23,481	7	...	...	...	...	5,803	1,316	4,408	Custer
Delta	.029	30,319	27,834	15,752	12,214	31,500	477,570	.0080	214,910	61	8,806	18	1,364	7	53,806	10,927	26,870	Delta
Denver*	.031	558,088	554,636	21,096	252,189	37,304	11,773,190	.2076	7,942,001	2,255	917,312	1,824	422,490	2,224	952,255	320,196	453,155	Denver
Dolores	.033	1,787	1,844	18,970	882	31,160	33,900	.0005	6,233	2	...	...	...	...	3,664	...	1,848	Dolores
Douglas*	.035	253,393	175,766	33,102	93,347	73,029	8,387,880	.1083	2,149,040	610	423,822	843	311,984	1,642	325,042	67,177	214,843	Douglas
Eagle**	.037	47,310	41,659	27,415	18,078	57,592	1,297,010	.0203	688,142	195	37,912	75	93,612	493	150,500	14,770	39,350	Eagle
Elbert*	.039	23,618	19,872	25,666	8,463	56,732	606,180	.0074	63,156	18	...	...	...	...	4,022	2,179	22,887	Elbert
El Paso*	.041	570,479	516,929	20,654	218,133	43,569	11,782,890	.2021	7,180,198	2,039	1,264,761	2,515	198,849	1,047	725,989	271,165	443,682	El Paso
Fremont**	.043	48,435	46,145	14,912	17,759	33,185	722,240	.0120	283,543	81	51,693	103	...	...	53,817	20,895	37,069	Fremont
Garfield	.045	50,094	43,791	21,874	20,186	43,253	1,095,760	.0202	852,431	242	116,350	231	20,104	106	100,711	25,978	42,573	Garfield
Gilpin*	.047	4,945	4,757	27,842	2,347	46,965	137,680	.0016	4,869	1	...	...	...	...	1,700	...	5,429	Gilpin
Grand	.049	13,363	12,442	26,340	6,363	44,260	351,980	.0051	135,116	38	...	...	2,418	13	34,241	5,303	14,240	Grand
Gunnison	.051	13,914	13,956	21,207	6,642	36,130	295,080	.0050	178,897	51	10,245	20	5,117	27	34,833	4,347	13,660	Gunnison
Hinsdale	.053	769	790	22,289	383	35,642	17,140	.0003	7,363	2	1,102	2	...	...	1,630	...	831	Hinsdale
Huerfano	.055	7,874	7,862	13,738	3,483	25,424	108,170	.0019	48,270	14	...	...	...	...	11,723	2,111	6,636	Huerfano
Jackson	.057	1,429	1,577	19,713	734	30,894	28,170	.0004	9,135	3	...	...	...	...	2,029	...	1,639	Jackson
Jefferson*[1]	.059	529,190	527,056	27,285	219,599	53,090	14,439,070	.2207	6,983,811	1,983	1,310,735	2,607	293,348	1,544	1,126,018	320,757	468,788	Jefferson
Kiowa	.061	1,370	1,622	18,555	706	28,780	25,420	.0004	5,733	2	...	...	...	...	...	...	1,636	Kiowa
Kit Carson	.063	7,743	8,011	16,837	3,279	31,818	130,370	.0026	116,613	33	...	...	2,085	11	7,809	4,343	7,151	Kit Carson
Lake**	.065	7,603	7,812	20,141	3,376	36,250	153,130	.0021	33,526	10	...	...	...	...	14,453	1,334	7,516	Lake
La Plata**	.067	47,411	43,941	20,475	20,510	37,950	970,760	.0169	616,228	175	45,805	91	22,275	117	95,164	17,971	43,785	La Plata
Larimer*	.069	275,364	251,494	24,187	119,115	45,005	6,660,320	.1075	3,647,791	1,036	666,158	1,325	150,251	791	477,472	113,594	258,940	Larimer
Las Animas	.071	15,674	15,207	14,611	6,785	26,935	229,010	.0043	142,613	40	17,531	35	...	...	31,965	3,153	13,242	Las Animas
Lincoln	.073	5,750	6,087	14,983	2,210	31,037	86,150	.0018	82,074	23	...	...	...	...	6,185	3,352	4,878	Lincoln
Logan**	.075	21,116	20,504	15,220	8,224	31,655	321,390	.0063	242,983	69	56,554	112	5,776	30	19,699	10,137	16,765	Logan
Mesa*	.077	129,419	116,255	18,268	55,438	34,381	2,364,210	.0430	1,607,761	457	399,198	794	34,875	184	198,421	41,576	114,706	Mesa
Mineral	.079	920	831	18,424	406	33,257	16,950	.0003	5,202	1	...	...	...	...	1,213	...	861	Mineral
Moffat	.081	13,569	13,184	19,824	5,560	38,956	268,990	.0046	152,981	43	12,613	25	...	...	28,218	3,423	12,297	Moffat
Montezuma	.083	24,860	23,830	16,121	10,357	31,196	400,780	.0079	321,327	91	46,988	93	1,491	8	51,196	4,592	21,394	Montezuma

Source: Devonshire Associates Ltd. and Scan/US, Inc. 2005.
* Component of a Metropolitan Core Based Statistical Area.
** Component of a Micropolitan Core Based Statistical Area.

...Data less than 1,000. (d) Data not available.
[1] Census population includes a portion of Broomfield county.
[2] Created on November 15, 2001 from parts of Adams, Boulder, Jefferson and Weld counties.

Continued on next page

Counties: Population/Income/Sales, *Continued*

County or County Equivalent	FIPS County Code	Population: Estimate 7/1/05	Population: Census 4/1/00	Per Capita Income 2004	House-holds Estimate 7/1/05	Median Household Income 2004	Disposable Income 2004 ($1,000)	Market Ability Index 2004	Total Retail Sales: 2004 Sales ($1,000)	Total Retail Sales: Ranally Sales Units	General Merchandise: 2004 Sales ($1,000)	General Merchandise: Ranally Sales Units	Apparel Store: 2004 Sales ($1,000)	Apparel Store: Ranally Sales Units	Food Store Sales 2004 ($1,000)	Health & Drug Store 2004 ($1,000)	Passenger Car Regis-trations 2004	County or County Equivalent
Montrose**	.085	37,456	33,432	17,526	15,627	33,891	656,460	.0124	488,546	139	81,653	162	6,643	35	78,391	13,085	32,510	Montrose
Morgan**	.087	28,394	27,171	15,490	10,663	33,060	439,820	.0075	210,641	60	18,301	36	1,972	10	38,570	12,426	22,611	Morgan
Otero	.089	19,380	20,311	15,239	8,378	28,393	295,340	.0055	193,191	55	53,568	107	...	...	28,410	7,920	16,433	Otero
Ouray	.091	4,150	3,742	23,325	1,946	39,887	96,800	.0013	16,600	5	...	...	1,453	8	3,490	1,506	4,274	Ouray
Park*	.093	17,713	14,523	24,167	7,188	47,043	428,070	.0053	39,282	11	...	...	...	...	2,827	...	17,126	Park
Phillips	.095	4,522	4,480	16,559	1,906	31,455	74,880	.0013	44,384	13	...	...	...	...	7,533	5,373	3,882	Phillips
Pitkin	.097	14,924	14,872	35,221	7,728	54,512	525,640	.0089	389,879	111	...	...	102,352	539	49,858	31,227	15,030	Pitkin
Prowers	.099	13,904	14,483	14,878	5,739	29,008	206,860	.0041	161,018	46	29,178	58	1,256	7	27,196	5,586	11,386	Prowers
Pueblo*	.101	153,579	141,472	16,245	63,299	32,134	2,494,870	.0468	1,726,230	490	451,637	898	33,545	177	213,548	71,466	122,460	Pueblo
Rio Blanco	.103	5,997	5,986	18,851	2,518	35,893	113,050	.0017	31,259	9	...	...	...	...	10,746	4,018	5,634	Rio Blanco
Rio Grande	.105	12,217	12,413	16,659	5,352	30,955	203,520	.0038	139,008	39	1,339	3	1,424	7	29,871	5,913	11,109	Rio Grande
Routt	.107	21,335	19,690	27,959	9,810	49,262	596,500	.0089	265,641	75	26,424	53	16,640	88	60,697	5,829	20,857	Routt
Saguache	.109	7,113	5,917	12,421	2,871	24,865	88,350	.0016	39,401	11	1,073	2	...	...	5,012	1,821	5,577	Saguache
San Juan	.111	575	558	17,635	288	27,996	10,140	.0002	7,053	2	...	...	1,612	8	1,578	...	540	San Juan
San Miguel	.113	7,477	6,594	25,890	3,462	44,950	193,580	.0028	68,151	19	...	...	4,948	26	20,210	2,681	6,688	San Miguel
Sedgwick	.115	2,588	2,747	15,958	1,214	27,222	41,300	.0008	26,366	7	...	...	...	...	2,770	1,870	2,593	Sedgwick
Summit**	.117	25,865	23,548	28,038	11,197	52,222	725,200	.0124	510,979	145	32,494	65	99,077	521	86,967	11,477	24,190	Summit
Teller*	.119	22,357	20,555	24,517	9,461	46,482	548,130	.0073	122,580	35	...	...	1,464	8	33,306	4,985	21,768	Teller
Washington	.121	4,688	4,926	17,788	2,150	31,109	83,390	.0013	27,855	8	1,202	2	...	...	5,276	2,836	5,320	Washington
Weld*[1]	.123	230,756	180,936	18,917	88,114	40,448	4,365,170	.0702	1,958,366	556	298,091	593	26,630	140	250,995	54,456	192,281	Weld
Yuma	.125	9,827	9,841	16,372	4,067	31,716	160,890	.0031	120,311	34	...	...	1,540	8	16,108	6,587	8,957	Yuma
Colorado Total		**4,694,778**	**4,301,261**	**22,848**	**1,921,675**	**44,634**	**107,267,900**	**1.7555**	**59,432,099**	**16,876**	**8,937,511**	**17,770**	**2,479,995**	**13,056**	**8,336,296**	**2,201,196**	**3,945,196**	**Colorado**

Connecticut (CT; Code 09; 8 Counties)

County or County Equivalent	FIPS County Code	Population: Estimate 7/1/05	Population: Census 4/1/00	Per Capita Income 2004	House-holds Estimate 7/1/05	Median Household Income 2004	Disposable Income 2004 ($1,000)	Market Ability Index 2004	Total Retail Sales: 2004 Sales ($1,000)	Total Retail Sales: Ranally Sales Units	General Merchandise: 2004 Sales ($1,000)	General Merchandise: Ranally Sales Units	Apparel Store: 2004 Sales ($1,000)	Apparel Store: Ranally Sales Units	Food Store Sales 2004 ($1,000)	Health & Drug Store 2004 ($1,000)	Passenger Car Regis-trations 2004	County or County Equivalent
Fairfield*	.001	909,263	882,567	30,162	329,595	58,781	27,424,940	.4586	18,649,061	5,295	997,741	1,984	1,190,445	6,266	2,268,628	792,292	627,514	Fairfield
Hartford*	.003	881,552	857,183	25,818	346,129	46,551	22,759,710	.3583	11,858,586	3,367	1,151,316	2,290	890,392	4,686	1,770,165	895,073	603,057	Hartford
Litchfield**	.005	191,674	182,193	28,404	74,567	51,538	5,444,290	.0828	2,641,054	750	144,795	288	61,324	323	416,487	180,891	142,852	Litchfield
Middlesex*	.007	165,752	155,071	29,966	64,904	54,178	4,966,970	.0707	1,921,418	546	95,267	189	196,218	1,033	365,992	193,006	121,634	Middlesex
New Haven*	.009	853,637	824,008	23,814	319,931	44,926	20,328,100	.3285	11,057,950	3,140	1,088,751	2,165	650,116	3,422	1,673,415	780,780	584,714	New Haven
New London*	.011	267,325	259,088	25,951	105,718	46,303	6,937,430	.1077	3,447,478	979	454,153	903	177,940	937	489,257	222,901	232,196	New London
Tolland*	.013	149,871	136,364	26,920	52,767	54,015	4,034,460	.0540	1,037,102	294	34,515	69	33,634	177	203,221	97,602	104,093	Tolland
Windham**	.015	115,206	109,091	22,146	43,063	41,849	2,551,400	.0380	950,520	270	99,197	197	6,325	33	190,856	83,404	78,377	Windham
Connecticut Total		**3,534,280**	**3,405,565**	**26,723**	**1,336,674**	**49,554**	**94,447,300**	**1.4986**	**51,563,168**	**14,641**	**4,065,735**	**8,085**	**3,206,395**	**16,877**	**7,378,023**	**3,245,949**	**2,494,437**	**Connecticut**

Delaware (DE; Code 10; 3 Counties)

County or County Equivalent	FIPS County Code	Population: Estimate 7/1/05	Population: Census 4/1/00	Per Capita Income 2004	House-holds Estimate 7/1/05	Median Household Income 2004	Disposable Income 2004 ($1,000)	Market Ability Index 2004	Total Retail Sales: 2004 Sales ($1,000)	Total Retail Sales: Ranally Sales Units	General Merchandise: 2004 Sales ($1,000)	General Merchandise: Ranally Sales Units	Apparel Store: 2004 Sales ($1,000)	Apparel Store: Ranally Sales Units	Food Store Sales 2004 ($1,000)	Health & Drug Store 2004 ($1,000)	Passenger Car Regis-trations 2004	County or County Equivalent
Kent*	.001	139,558	126,697	17,806	51,903	38,246	2,484,910	.0451	1,653,667	470	366,822	729	47,176	248	190,185	71,144	94,564	Kent
New Castle*	.003	523,864	500,265	21,504	187,254	48,371	11,265,010	.2029	8,171,242	2,320	1,006,201	2,001	362,885	1,910	1,275,633	486,673	366,791	New Castle
Sussex**	.005	175,747	156,638	17,826	67,743	36,882	3,132,780	.0600	2,451,166	696	257,825	513	237,792	1,252	329,503	139,252	124,253	Sussex
Delaware Total		**839,169**	**783,600**	**20,118**	**306,900**	**43,889**	**16,882,700**	**.3080**	**12,276,075**	**3,486**	**1,630,847**	**3,243**	**647,854**	**3,410**	**1,795,320**	**697,069**	**585,608**	**Delaware**

District of Columbia (DC; Code 11; 1 District)

County or County Equivalent	FIPS County Code	Population: Estimate 7/1/05	Population: Census 4/1/00	Per Capita Income 2004	House-holds Estimate 7/1/05	Median Household Income 2004	Disposable Income 2004 ($1,000)	Market Ability Index 2004	Total Retail Sales: 2004 Sales ($1,000)	Total Retail Sales: Ranally Sales Units	General Merchandise: 2004 Sales ($1,000)	General Merchandise: Ranally Sales Units	Apparel Store: 2004 Sales ($1,000)	Apparel Store: Ranally Sales Units	Food Store Sales 2004 ($1,000)	Health & Drug Store 2004 ($1,000)	Passenger Car Regis-trations 2004	County or County Equivalent
District of Columbia*	.001	548,902	572,059	26,120	245,648	37,484	14,337,490	.1918	3,540,123	1,005	143,774	286	501,970	2,642	938,614	520,795	227,253	District of Columbia
District of Columbia Total		**548,902**	**572,059**	**26,120**	**245,648**	**37,484**	**14,337,490**	**.1918**	**3,540,123**	**1,005**	**143,774**	**286**	**501,970**	**2,642**	**938,614**	**520,795**	**227,253**	**District of Columbia**

Florida (FL; Code 12; 67 Counties)

County or County Equivalent	FIPS County Code	Population: Estimate 7/1/05	Population: Census 4/1/00	Per Capita Income 2004	House-holds Estimate 7/1/05	Median Household Income 2004	Disposable Income 2004 ($1,000)	Market Ability Index 2004	Total Retail Sales: 2004 Sales ($1,000)	Total Retail Sales: Ranally Sales Units	General Merchandise: 2004 Sales ($1,000)	General Merchandise: Ranally Sales Units	Apparel Store: 2004 Sales ($1,000)	Apparel Store: Ranally Sales Units	Food Store Sales 2004 ($1,000)	Health & Drug Store 2004 ($1,000)	Passenger Car Regis-trations 2004	County or County Equivalent
Alachua*	.001	223,316	217,955	17,330	95,536	30,541	3,869,970	.0712	2,640,469	750	375,796	747	147,304	775	463,403	110,924	166,378	Alachua
Baker*	.003	24,136	22,259	15,600	7,507	37,061	376,510	.0063	166,294	47	24,266	48	...	...	41,598	11,541	14,200	Baker
Bay*	.005	159,012	148,217	18,470	63,684	34,281	2,936,920	.0537	2,053,327	583	456,342	908	90,167	475	304,639	103,824	109,010	Bay
Bradford	.007	27,952	26,088	13,324	8,658	31,889	372,420	.0068	197,350	56	26,372	52	4,181	22	32,689	7,676	15,325	Bradford
Brevard*	.009	523,567	476,230	20,941	216,202	38,037	10,963,820	.1797	5,760,123	1,636	986,272	1,961	242,067	1,274	880,605	408,228	391,524	Brevard
Broward*	.011	1,794,053	1,623,018	20,451	696,396	39,618	36,689,620	.6613	25,980,621	7,377	2,886,091	5,740	1,594,217	8,391	3,363,389	1,693,187	1,165,011	Broward
Calhoun	.013	13,051	13,017	11,968	4,514	25,995	156,190	.0030	88,475	25	2,426	5	...	...	19,459	2,422	7,552	Calhoun
Charlotte*	.015	159,967	141,627	20,390	70,158	34,848	3,261,650	.0531	1,641,420	466	381,639	759	88,332	465	248,328	115,633	110,577	Charlotte
Citrus**	.017	131,797	118,085	17,178	56,816	30,186	2,264,060	.0382	1,125,067	319	160,301	319	37,484	197	230,676	66,865	92,121	Citrus
Clay*	.019	166,915	140,814	21,413	59,270	45,294	3,574,220	.0562	1,627,352	462	301,851	600	78,384	413	213,849	85,533	116,856	Clay
Collier*	.021	306,973	251,377	24,916	127,885	45,095	7,648,670	.1250	4,435,456	1,259	409,669	815	470,567	2,477	683,833	249,092	211,428	Collier
Columbia**	.023	62,510	56,513	13,783	21,785	29,819	861,550	.0196	922,350	262	203,669	405	34,339	181	89,193	41,739	37,233	Columbia
DeSoto**	.027	35,115	32,209	12,345	11,026	29,747	433,480	.0083	257,562	73	27,497	55	1,509	8	36,632	8,161	17,025	DeSoto
Dixie	.029	14,447	13,827	12,208	5,266	25,162	176,370	.0030	54,007	15	2,163	4	...	...	15,281	3,126	9,173	Dixie
Duval*	.031	838,841	778,879	19,976	326,098	38,349	16,756,550	.3047	12,030,540	3,416	1,689,674	3,360	549,599	2,893	1,602,761	578,821	600,348	Duval
Escambia*	.033	295,558	294,410	18,536	121,450	33,796	5,478,370	.0990	3,685,910	1,047	658,837	1,310	171,723	904	458,614	245,360	209,024	Escambia
Flagler**	.035	70,570	49,832	20,763	28,750	37,910	1,465,270	.0207	372,724	106	55,375	110	8,359	44	71,111	30,219	49,127	Flagler
Franklin	.037	10,215	11,057	15,136	4,391	26,485	154,610	.0029	103,518	29	2,716	5	...	...	23,372	9,994	7,021	Franklin
Gadsden*	.039	45,844	45,087	14,040	16,035	30,124	643,640	.0107	230,575	65	18,460	37	2,816	15	48,712	15,058	26,872	Gadsden
Gilchrist*	.041	16,334	14,437	12,553	5,269	29,877	205,040	.0033	45,046	13	1,365	3	...	...	11,816	3,558	9,577	Gilchrist
Glades	.043	11,231	10,576	13,554	3,850	29,799	152,230	.0024	37,933	11	1,858	4	...	...	13,839	...	6,491	Glades
Gulf	.045	13,588	13,332	15,608	5,413	29,599	212,080	.0034	77,781	22	2,094	4	...	...	27,286	5,376	9,320	Gulf
Hamilton	.047	14,356	13,327	9,795	4,206	25,160	140,610	.0028	66,754	19	2,542	5	...	...	12,185	3,628	6,832	Hamilton
Hardee**	.049	27,971	26,938	11,359	8,210	29,017	317,730	.0061	167,355	48	19,398	39	4,065	21	42,622	5,927	13,718	Hardee
Hendry**	.051	38,106	36,210	12,483	10,968	32,001	475,660	.0093	305,315	87	43,664	87	2,707	14	58,791	5,146	18,349	Hendry
Hernando*	.053	151,302	130,802	17,050	61,408	31,609	2,579,690	.0461	1,583,415	450	294,770	586	72,712	383	305,853	133,859	99,175	Hernando
Highlands**	.055	93,292	87,366	16,026	38,616	29,115	1,495,130	.0265	848,253	241	116,747	232	27,976	147	164,879	45,876	58,078	Highlands
Hillsborough*	.057	1,118,988	998,948	19,508	424,109	38,855	21,829,310	.3981	15,595,099	4,428	1,867,205	3,713	747,996	3,937	1,769,962	969,158	772,722	Hillsborough
Holmes	.059	19,226	18,564	13,014	7,001	26,465	250,210	.0040	60,143	17	2,272	5	...	...	9,328	2,050	11,992	Holmes
Indian River*	.061	124,614	112,947	22,707	56,392	37,367	2,829,580	.0479	1,748,173	496	255,235	508	160,139	843	244,829	149,165	90,089	Indian River
Jackson	.063	47,155	46,755	14,011	17,213	28,735	660,700	.0130	475,777	135	67,967	135	21,597	114	59,554	22,240	29,683	Jackson
Jefferson*	.065	14,917	12,902	13,751	4,887	31,627	205,120	.0033	54,123	15	1,981	4	...	...	14,368	4,374	8,566	Jefferson
Lafayette	.067	7,682	7,022	11,140	2,185	29,440	85,580	.0014	19,812	6	6,202	12	...	...	2,225	...	3,989	Lafayette
Lake*	.069	269,070	210,528	18,529	105,804	35,179	4,985,480	.0834	2,569,367	730	380,587	757	59,098	311	431,629	196,512	173,906	Lake
Lee*	.071	523,512	440,888	21,374	219,465	38,521	11,189,420	.1957	7,409,505	2,104	1,087,208	2,162	462,470	2,434	956,522	481,928	368,844	Lee
Leon*	.073	243,753	239,452	20,815	105,898	35,661	5,073,680	.0894	3,390,263	963	663,781	1,320	182,095	958	481,552	224,898	184,315	Leon
Levy	.075	37,537	34,450	13,430	14,300	26,303	504,120	.0098	341,305	97	79,504	158	3,211	17	57,035	18,581	24,422	Levy
Liberty	.077	7,548	7,021	11,065	2,222	28,264	83,520	.0014	16,562	5	...	...	...	...	2,713	1,758	3,882	Liberty
Madison	.079	18,873	18,733	12,251	6,740	25,687	231,210	.0041	93,493	27	2,518	5	...	...	25,085	9,285	11,458	Madison
Manatee*	.081	300,298	264,002	21,967	134,245	37,133	6,596,530	.1063	3,365,517	956	491,181	977	221,151	1,164	568,077	217,775	235,104	Manatee
Marion*	.083	294,555	258,916	16,944	121,424	30,771	4,991,010	.0921	3,382,818	961	535,220	1,064	94,712	498	427,647	197,001	196,457	Marion
Martin*	.085	140,204	126,731	23,176	59,914	40,046	3,249,320	.0566	2,217,187	630	276,590	550	99,533	524	301,746	193,694	95,612	Martin
Miami-Dade*	.086	2,391,206	2,253,362	15,028	782,688	34,461	35,933,990	.6861	24,937,816	7,081	2,984,280	5,935	2,500,650	13,162	3,337,422	2,044,796	1,348,550	Miami-Dade
Monroe**	.087	78,562	79,589	23,861	34,776	40,122	1,874,530	.0329	1,326,649	377	87,886	175	124,721	656	322,475	126,992	54,681	Monroe
Nassau*	.089	63,967	57,663	22,153	24,803	42,665	1,417,070	.0207	482,409	137	54,720	109	18,114	95	108,646	17,609	46,280	Nassau
Okaloosa*	.091	182,186	170,498	20,670	71,945	38,981	3,765,750	.0679	2,690,307	764	517,655	1,029	221,038	1,163	309,568	131,402	131,170	Okaloosa
Okeechobee**	.093	38,899	35,910	13,040	12,897	29,204	507,230	.0102	371,860	106	51,642	103	13,406	71	66,819	21,976	20,599	Okeechobee
Orange*	.095	1,006,134	896,344	19,195	370,292	38,988	19,312,580	.3714	15,927,297	4,523	2,095,813	4,168	1,199,561	6,314	1,749,029	705,351	660,462	Orange
Osceola*	.097	226,787	172,493	17,394	81,062	36,254	3,944,720	.0673	2,083,409	592	403,977	803	122,035	642	334,464	149,183	143,135	Osceola
Palm Beach*	.099	1,267,148	1,131,184	21,809	491,239	41,984	27,635,140	.4766	17,715,284	5,030	2,295,344	4,565	1,788,194	9,412	2,598,542	1,224,457	830,286	Palm Beach
Pasco*	.101	415,912	344,765	17,341	169,524	32,040	7,212,230	.1195	3,379,762	960	704,347	1,401	115,966	610	586,851	253,052	296,790	Pasco
Pinellas*	.103	927,210	921,482	20,988	410,580	35,413	19,460,670	.3551	14,493,954	4,116	1,497,829	2,979	558,149	2,938	2,071,010	953,452	632,008	Pinellas
Polk*	.105	526,208	483,924	17,926	205,086	34,382	9,432,930	.1709	6,270,722	1,781	1,004,624	1,998	225,818	1,189	1,044,350	328,355	342,035	Polk
Putnam**	.107	72,555	70,423	14,271	28,196	27,355	1,035,410	.0183	513,911	146	81,225	162	15,767	83	85,453	38,093	47,141	Putnam
St. Johns*	.109	155,014	123,135	23,755	59,867	45,932	3,682,300	.0545	1,407,822	400	116,882	232	146,616	772	242,695	64,836	106,771	St. Johns
St. Lucie*	.111	227,333	192,695	18,113	88,621	35,128	4,117,600	.0684	2,032,904	577	292,525	582	44,591	235	326,076	166,436	143,207	St. Lucie
Santa Rosa*	.113	141,570	117,743	18,236	48,880	39,359	2,581,600	.0402	964,063	274	170,898	340	13,813	73	180,642	70,559	93,026	Santa Rosa
Sarasota*	.115	359,344	325,957	22,961	155,629	39,708	8,250,980	.1413	5,317,959	1,510	561,919	1,117	323,149	1,701	730,311	331,980	243,851	Sarasota
Seminole*	.117	398,569	365,196	22,017	144,615	45,192	8,775,380	.1505	5,555,525	1,578	968,105	1,925	410,636	2,161	875,117	361,214	266,218	Seminole
Sumter**	.119	61,800	53,345	17,144	25,942	30,642	1,059,520	.0155	246,320	70	31,136	62	...	...	51,867	10,489	40,262	Sumter
Suwannee	.121	37,877	34,844	14,046	13,783	29,103	532,010	.0097	300,946	85	26,266	52	3,900	21	52,481	16,835	23,732	Suwannee
Taylor	.123	19,327	19,256	14,454	7,242	28,856	279,350	.0049	137,705	39	15,213	30	1,277	7	21,114	12,176	12,071	Taylor
Union	.125	15,031	13,442	10,051	3,448	32,444	151,070	.0026	32,101	9	1,575	3	...	...	5,097	2,940	6,320	Union
Volusia*	.127	483,444	443,343	17,897	192,195	33,831	8,652,230	.1564	5,702,643	1,619	826,756	1,644	245,601	1,293	886,271	390,946	346,315	Volusia
Wakulla*	.129	27,867	22,863	17,007	10,009	35,385	473,940	.0068	96,120	27	3,770	7	...	...	32,380	6,372	18,477	Wakulla
Walton	.131	50,110	40,601	16,495	19,788	31,390	826,580	.0150	519,023	147	65,305	130	24,685	130	91,600	27,878	34,724	Walton
Washington	.133	21,927	20,973	13,451	8,136	27,078	294,950	.0054	161,748	46	50,353	100	...	...	20,705	20,617	14,482	Washington
Florida Total		**17,633,938**	**15,982,378**	**19,147**	**6,822,409**	**37,061**	**337,636,610**	**5.9979**	**219,912,395**	**62,448**	**29,779,347**	**59,221**	**13,805,910**	**72,667**	**30,948,673**	**14,157,189**	**11,690,979**	**Florida**

Georgia (GA; Code 13; 159 Counties)

County or County Equivalent	FIPS County Code	Population: Estimate 7/1/05	Population: Census 4/1/00	Per Capita Income 2004	House-holds Estimate 7/1/05	Median Household Income 2004	Disposable Income 2004 ($1,000)	Market Ability Index 2004	Total Retail Sales: 2004 Sales ($1,000)	Total Retail Sales: Ranally Sales Units	General Merchandise: 2004 Sales ($1,000)	General Merchandise: Ranally Sales Units	Apparel Store: 2004 Sales ($1,000)	Apparel Store: Ranally Sales Units	Food Store Sales 2004 ($1,000)	Health & Drug Store 2004 ($1,000)	Passenger Car Regis-trations 2004	County or County Equivalent
Appling	.001	18,178	17,419	13,161	6,603	28,928	239,240	.0045	139,311	40	3,906	8	2,251	12	23,053	9,610	12,521	Appling
Atkinson**	.003	8,225	7,609	10,688	2,735	25,711	87,910	.0015	24,481	7	7,203	14	...	...	3,628	2,735	5,027	Atkinson
Bacon	.005	10,350	10,103	12,002	3,832	25,953	124,220	.0023	57,364	16	3,736	7	...	...	11,974	7,515	6,815	Bacon
Baker*	.007	4,458	4,074	12,445	1,532	28,682	55,480	.0008	5,486	2	...	...	...	...	1,927	...	2,738	Baker
Baldwin**	.009	45,160	44,700	14,203	15,176	33,915	641,430	.0129	500,547	142	135,549	270	21,149	111	79,992	23,603	28,020	Baldwin
Banks	.011	16,075	14,422	16,578	5,789	36,007	266,490	.0042	89,571	25	4,097	8	24,530	129	4,948	2,068	13,108	Banks
Barrow*	.013	58,111	46,144	18,527	20,434	41,609	1,076,650	.0183	586,053	166	88,019	175	8,685	46	99,830	50,047	42,465	Barrow
Bartow*	.015	90,793	76,019	18,226	32,239	40,762	1,654,800	.0283	916,819	260	181,937	362	19,961	105	96,431	36,898	66,022	Bartow
Ben Hill**	.017	16,997	17,484	12,782	6,607	26,398	217,260	.0046	180,602	51	30,686	61	4,407	23	30,732	9,299	10,911	Ben Hill
Berrien	.019	16,729	16,235	13,642	6,307	28,914	228,210	.0039	89,054	25	2,986	6	...	...	15,367	4,852	11,553	Berrien
Bibb*	.021	155,253	153,887	16,111	59,904	33,304	2,501,350	.0545	2,610,511	741	522,558	1,039	140,865	741	321,107	145,169	100,515	Bibb
Bleckley	.023	12,076	11,666	14,709	4,410	31,962	177,620	.0030	72,999	21	4,986	10	...	...	13,816	10,840	8,494	Bleckley
Brantley*	.025	15,951	14,629	12,810	5,543	29,530	204,340	.0032	43,430	12	1,262	3	...	...	9,733	2,065	10,880	Brantley
Brooks*	.027	16,171	16,450	12,292	6,099	26,839	198,780	.0034	68,146	19	3,681	7	...	...	12,044	5,287	11,175	Brooks
Bryan*	.029	27,955	23,417	19,022	9,505	44,921	531,760	.0075	121,793	35	9,831	20	...	...	14,912	6,510	19,758	Bryan
Bulloch**	.031	60,709	55,983	13,455	22,807	28,269	816,830	.0173	711,418	202	180,907	360	36,391	192	89,161	38,279	44,663	Bulloch
Burke*	.033	23,437	22,243	11,349	7,962	26,098	265,980	.0054	177,701	50	9,468	19	2,033	11	33,366	12,076	14,275	Burke
Butts*	.035	23,687	19,522	14,782	7,417	37,664	350,150	.0059	152,718	43	3,054	6	1,013	5	22,044	11,474	15,591	Butts
Calhoun	.037	6,034	6,320	9,720	1,937	24,179	58,650	.0013	45,146	13	3,651	7	...	...	6,718	3,013	3,196	Calhoun
Camden**	.039	44,789	43,664	17,916	16,554	38,163	802,440	.0137	439,317	125	85,577	170	5,520	29	45,316	10,613	31,490	Camden
Candler	.043	10,374	9,577	9,976	3,366	24,033	103,490	.0024	93,131	26	2,947	6	...	...	13,699	8,862	5,872	Candler
Carroll*	.045	106,138	87,268	16,865	38,835	36,467	1,789,980	.0297	813,977	231	145,818	290	31,763	167	144,363	53,938	77,488	Carroll
Catoosa*	.047	61,327	53,282	17,135	22,223	37,258	1,050,840	.0177	520,006	148	133,348	265	8,235	43	32,986	29,022	45,585	Catoosa
Charlton	.049	11,029	10,282	10,481	3,376	26,883	115,590	.0021	45,101	13	3,785	8	...	...	5,009	5,417	5,973	Charlton
Chatham*	.051	238,192	232,048	17,841	93,802	36,090	4,249,510	.0825	3,458,152	982	677,815	1,348	214,968	1,131	439,108	131,323	153,672	Chatham
Chattahoochee*	.053	13,213	14,882	9,616	2,840	35,131	127,060	.0020	4,326	1	...	...	...	...	...	...	7,581	Chattahoochee
Chattooga**	.055	27,124	25,470	12,958	9,484	29,747	351,480	.0063	164,500	47	31,931	63	2,750	14	35,292	14,876	18,051	Chattooga
Cherokee*	.057	182,558	141,903	24,954	65,215	55,193	4,555,530	.0675	1,834,622	521	183,419	365	13,603	72	355,905	57,032	141,801	Cherokee
Clarke*	.059	104,888	101,489	14,436	43,662	27,469	1,514,150	.0329	1,489,893	423	326,418	649	86,042	453	209,073	64,315	81,169	Clarke
Clay	.061	3,378	3,357	10,521	1,330	21,055	35,540	.0006	13,263	4	...	...	...	...	4,730	...	2,177	Clay
Clayton*	.063	241,082	236,517	17,378	82,641	40,155	4,189,490	.0843	3,717,053	1,055	734,677	1,461	145,792	767	352,643	141,664	191,970	Clayton
Clinch	.065	7,054	6,878	11,501	2,491	25,740	81,130	.0014	29,472	8	3,422	7	...	...	5,544	5,388	4,184	Clinch
Cobb*	.067	677,675	607,751	23,239	233,556	53,174	15,748,450	.2926	12,908,015	3,665	1,935,940	3,850	653,279	3,438	1,736,796	583,517	489,094	Cobb
Coffee**	.069	39,992	37,413	12,738	13,786	29,638	509,410	.0117	533,719	152	124,436	247	13,396	71	51,362	18,138	24,333	Coffee
Colquitt**	.071	43,916	42,053	12,185	15,345	27,910	535,110	.0121	525,906	149	72,061	143	20,143	106	84,985	19,639	26,154	Colquitt

Source: Devonshire Associates Ltd. and Scan/US, Inc. 2005.
* Component of a Metropolitan Core Based Statistical Area.
** Component of a Micropolitan Core Based Statistical Area.

...Data less than 1,000. (d) Data not available.
[1] Census population includes a portion of Broomfield county.

Counties: Population/Income/Sales, *Continued*

County or County Equivalent	FIPS County Code	Population: Estimate 7/1/05	Population: Census 4/1/00	Per Capita Income 2004	House-holds Estimate 7/1/05	Median Household Income 2004	Disposable Income 2004 ($1,000)	Market Ability Index 2004	Total Retail Sales: 2004 Sales ($1,000)	Total Retail Sales: Ranally Sales Units	General Merchandise: 2004 Sales ($1,000)	General Merchandise: Ranally Sales Units	Apparel Store: 2004 Sales ($1,000)	Apparel Store: Ranally Sales Units	Food Store Sales 2004 ($1,000)	Health & Drug Store 2004 ($1,000)	Passenger Car Regis-trations 2004	County or County Equivalent
Columbia*	.073	102,278	89,288	22,361	35,466	50,592	2,286,990	.0362	1,109,196	315	176,328	351	14,189	75	205,107	35,615	75,424	Columbia
Cook	.075	16,387	15,771	12,233	5,956	26,709	200,460	.0042	154,391	44	4,254	8	5,905	31	27,556	5,815	11,021	Cook
Coweta*	.077	109,445	89,215	21,136	37,940	48,407	2,313,240	.0354	923,716	262	102,008	203	33,956	179	229,162	53,381	78,070	Coweta
Crawford*	.079	12,802	12,495	17,520	4,970	35,478	224,290	.0029	15,982	5	...	...	...	...	10,323	...	10,213	Crawford
Crisp**	.081	22,085	21,996	12,139	8,349	25,933	268,080	.0061	271,906	77	46,670	93	13,809	73	36,065	8,703	13,423	Crisp
Dade*	.083	16,361	15,154	14,440	5,651	33,099	236,250	.0046	165,777	47	5,172	10	...	...	28,866	8,313	11,606	Dade
Dawson*	.085	20,058	15,999	20,240	7,315	43,763	405,970	.0066	200,956	57	...	...	82,143	432	33,224	11,039	16,351	Dawson
Decatur**	.087	28,502	28,240	12,864	10,534	27,717	366,640	.0071	233,877	66	21,905	44	8,403	44	36,203	8,933	18,885	Decatur
DeKalb*	.089	679,804	665,865	21,118	253,114	45,091	14,355,870	.2377	7,869,939	2,235	867,680	1,726	462,678	2,435	1,238,177	409,724	435,344	DeKalb
Dodge	.091	19,612	19,171	12,060	7,031	27,448	236,520	.0047	152,974	43	35,202	70	3,662	19	25,220	13,873	12,856	Dodge
Dooly	.093	11,706	11,525	11,113	3,859	26,822	130,090	.0025	68,364	19	2,481	5	...	...	5,915	3,403	6,777	Dooly
Dougherty*	.095	95,460	96,065	13,986	35,656	30,004	1,335,070	.0309	1,513,059	430	341,974	680	76,914	405	203,265	63,017	56,314	Dougherty
Douglas*	.097	108,297	92,174	21,502	40,419	45,453	2,328,580	.0421	1,708,674	485	148,479	295	28,302	149	233,455	50,004	83,009	Douglas
Early	.099	12,148	12,354	12,107	4,667	25,080	147,070	.0027	71,300	20	4,426	9	1,818	10	18,621	6,709	7,769	Early
Echols*	.101	4,131	3,754	10,027	1,290	25,684	41,420	.0006	...	...	...	...	...	...	...	...	2,535	Echols
Effingham*	.103	46,204	37,535	17,454	14,991	42,389	806,460	.0123	259,784	74	65,047	129	3,347	18	37,327	8,247	31,465	Effingham
Elbert	.105	20,869	20,511	13,355	7,989	27,865	278,700	.0052	163,937	47	25,510	51	3,107	16	34,218	12,498	15,404	Elbert
Emanuel	.107	22,014	21,837	10,893	7,971	23,771	239,800	.0051	173,940	49	26,777	53	7,408	39	34,768	8,804	13,608	Emanuel
Evans	.109	11,740	10,495	10,063	3,804	25,071	118,140	.0027	98,976	28	4,397	9	...	...	11,270	6,365	6,393	Evans
Fannin	.111	22,120	19,798	18,357	11,089	28,961	406,050	.0067	195,206	55	20,821	41	4,936	26	34,953	15,400	21,377	Fannin
Fayette*	.113	103,541	91,263	27,143	34,946	63,572	2,810,460	.0417	1,209,934	344	150,832	300	74,276	391	198,038	53,625	79,366	Fayette
Floyd*	.115	95,112	90,565	15,664	34,940	33,992	1,489,880	.0279	1,005,428	285	246,219	490	47,928	252	95,400	71,700	65,484	Floyd
Forsyth*	.117	140,241	98,407	25,665	46,255	61,063	3,599,290	.0514	1,253,576	356	190,039	378	13,680	72	204,426	38,713	101,280	Forsyth
Franklin	.119	21,827	20,285	13,971	7,893	30,825	304,950	.0066	291,548	83	8,019	16	1,777	9	34,294	13,961	16,355	Franklin
Fulton*	.121	822,956	816,006	21,647	322,701	44,163	17,814,710	.3252	13,481,892	3,828	1,797,457	3,575	1,154,709	6,078	1,841,428	559,764	517,018	Fulton
Gilmer	.123	27,505	23,456	16,429	10,844	33,008	451,870	.0075	197,488	56	52,072	104	1,611	8	31,756	17,783	21,927	Gilmer
Glascock	.125	2,616	2,556	13,723	996	28,790	35,900	.0005	4,087	1	...	...	...	...	...	...	2,014	Glascock
Glynn*	.127	72,136	67,568	18,683	29,035	37,054	1,347,690	.0242	898,413	255	144,823	288	49,608	261	127,767	47,480	50,962	Glynn
Gordon**	.129	50,284	44,104	16,726	18,251	36,310	841,060	.0151	517,378	147	102,900	205	51,397	271	52,036	23,812	36,263	Gordon
Grady	.131	24,428	23,659	12,525	8,846	27,863	305,970	.0058	176,575	50	24,679	49	3,020	16	30,083	10,858	15,618	Grady
Greene	.133	15,970	14,406	15,148	5,905	34,200	241,920	.0040	97,389	28	5,418	11	...	...	30,394	8,625	10,915	Greene
Gwinnett*	.135	725,943	588,448	22,639	236,177	54,986	16,434,850	.2904	11,566,248	3,284	1,268,188	2,522	582,022	3,063	1,255,903	389,066	491,136	Gwinnett
Habersham**	.137	40,178	35,902	15,735	14,565	34,460	632,220	.0115	390,085	111	81,235	162	6,082	32	71,617	25,400	29,384	Habersham
Hall*	.139	166,966	139,277	17,131	54,415	41,619	2,860,320	.0508	1,727,114	490	350,946	698	46,007	242	181,228	89,952	111,081	Hall
Hancock**	.141	9,935	10,076	9,210	3,324	22,539	91,500	.0017	21,857	6	2,616	5	...	...	6,252	3,390	5,338	Hancock
Haralson*	.143	28,594	25,690	13,948	10,372	30,730	398,840	.0073	219,097	62	25,191	50	...	...	41,509	17,519	20,608	Haralson
Harris*	.145	27,412	23,695	19,995	9,801	44,018	548,100	.0071	53,335	15	2,159	4	...	...	3,033	3,823	21,277	Harris
Hart	.147	23,536	22,997	15,334	9,074	31,488	360,910	.0060	149,114	42	36,825	73	5,093	27	31,898	11,190	18,238	Hart
Heard*	.149	11,272	11,012	15,263	4,206	32,984	172,050	.0024	21,924	6	2,161	4	...	...	2,003	2,132	8,490	Heard
Henry*	.151	169,496	119,341	23,341	59,750	52,177	3,956,230	.0567	1,275,282	362	212,149	422	74,667	393	179,091	60,116	131,037	Henry
Houston*	.153	126,391	110,765	19,243	47,127	41,687	2,432,130	.0413	1,360,434	386	209,754	417	65,940	347	171,168	43,838	93,353	Houston
Irwin**	.155	10,193	9,931	12,846	3,617	29,295	130,940	.0022	49,388	14	3,618	7	...	...	3,337	4,894	6,511	Irwin
Jackson	.157	50,957	41,589	17,187	18,372	38,051	875,810	.0158	554,426	157	50,695	101	97,412	513	78,319	24,916	38,391	Jackson
Jasper*	.159	13,413	11,426	17,016	4,784	37,777	228,240	.0031	25,382	7	2,933	6	...	...	4,500	4,010	9,928	Jasper
Jeff Davis	.161	12,914	12,684	12,359	4,839	26,363	159,610	.0037	167,903	48	28,034	56	3,481	18	20,338	6,878	8,619	Jeff Davis
Jefferson	.163	16,800	17,266	11,733	6,247	25,149	197,110	.0039	120,796	34	6,860	14	1,394	7	24,267	11,184	10,790	Jefferson
Jenkins	.165	8,803	8,575	10,573	3,143	23,267	93,070	.0018	49,733	14	3,292	7	...	...	5,157	8,134	5,635	Jenkins
Johnson**	.167	9,792	8,560	9,348	3,090	23,347	91,540	.0018	36,753	10	4,138	8	...	...	8,903	4,485	5,631	Johnson
Jones*	.169	26,799	23,639	18,360	9,578	40,456	492,040	.0067	73,210	21	1,589	3	...	...	26,814	5,114	20,756	Jones
Lamar*	.171	16,682	15,912	16,379	6,104	35,662	273,240	.0043	90,302	26	4,586	9	...	...	23,274	5,923	11,777	Lamar
Lanier*	.173	7,538	7,241	12,422	2,645	28,606	93,640	.0016	32,625	9	2,960	6	...	...	7,792	2,474	4,910	Lanier
Laurens**	.175	47,465	44,874	13,818	17,060	30,932	655,850	.0143	637,745	181	111,043	221	26,026	137	105,700	29,268	30,978	Laurens
Lee*	.177	31,508	24,757	17,943	9,883	44,445	565,340	.0079	100,976	29	...	...	...	...	36,111	3,657	20,482	Lee
Liberty*	.179	58,683	61,610	13,963	20,197	32,278	819,410	.0145	405,038	115	98,110	195	18,650	98	55,883	11,639	36,954	Liberty
Lincoln	.181	8,590	8,348	14,675	3,267	31,070	126,060	.0019	23,292	7	2,694	5	...	...	4,763	3,640	6,335	Lincoln
Long*	.183	11,040	10,304	12,148	3,641	29,453	134,110	.0020	11,049	3	...	...	...	...	...	...	6,841	Long
Lowndes*	.185	96,236	92,115	14,241	34,710	31,773	1,370,450	.0302	1,389,172	394	212,371	422	83,699	441	147,950	38,369	63,076	Lowndes
Lumpkin	.187	24,892	21,016	16,376	8,789	36,550	407,640	.0072	226,807	64	80,811	161	...	...	11,389	10,297	18,808	Lumpkin
McDuffie*	.189	21,591	21,231	14,445	8,011	30,913	311,880	.0075	393,287	112	91,652	182	6,720	35	32,666	11,510	15,029	McDuffie
McIntosh*	.191	11,110	10,847	14,593	4,452	28,878	162,130	.0033	135,092	38	12,419	25	36,858	194	16,066	6,758	7,921	McIntosh
Macon	.193	13,912	14,074	10,211	4,793	23,626	142,060	.0027	61,462	17	4,925	10	...	...	14,691	9,304	8,278	Macon
Madison*	.195	28,081	25,730	15,937	10,267	34,534	447,540	.0068	119,750	34	7,242	14	2,007	11	19,872	11,798	21,224	Madison
Marion*	.197	7,105	7,144	13,474	2,704	28,591	95,730	.0017	41,933	12	4,481	9	...	...	5,593	3,438	5,229	Marion
Meriwether*	.199	22,899	22,534	14,788	8,788	31,034	338,620	.0057	136,595	39	7,004	14	...	...	15,728	11,611	16,402	Meriwether
Miller	.201	6,207	6,383	13,245	2,467	26,144	82,210	.0016	52,315	15	6,147	12	...	...	14,286	2,722	4,621	Miller
Mitchell	.205	23,797	23,932	11,190	8,196	26,098	266,290	.0052	149,701	43	18,099	36	2,192	12	27,496	13,038	14,108	Mitchell
Monroe*	.207	24,333	21,757	16,974	7,954	41,257	413,040	.0061	97,770	28	21,396	43	...	...	15,848	7,307	16,788	Monroe
Montgomery**	.209	9,100	8,270	12,088	2,992	29,819	110,000	.0017	18,004	5	1,298	3	...	...	1,461	2,279	5,483	Montgomery
Morgan	.211	17,633	15,457	16,407	6,038	37,934	289,300	.0052	171,280	49	58,745	117	1,694	9	22,055	7,650	12,794	Morgan
Murray*	.213	41,502	36,506	15,081	14,054	35,354	625,910	.0104	259,341	74	11,783	23	...	...	78,113	13,719	27,203	Murray
Muscogee*	.215	181,177	186,291	16,523	71,276	33,575	2,993,660	.0597	2,521,325	716	438,386	872	172,186	906	310,807	180,834	116,839	Muscogee
Newton*	.217	85,695	62,001	18,723	30,509	41,705	1,604,500	.0242	521,906	148	82,889	165	23,369	123	116,151	16,920	62,558	Newton
Oconee*	.219	29,333	26,225	22,168	10,249	49,986	650,250	.0101	293,841	83	9,476	19	...	...	14,690	9,154	22,895	Oconee
Oglethorpe*	.221	13,810	12,635	15,205	4,927	33,623	209,980	.0032	48,314	14	...	...	...	...	3,248	4,051	10,741	Oglethorpe
Paulding*	.223	111,558	81,678	21,735	40,243	47,898	2,424,760	.0349	735,133	209	157,966	314	6,810	36	115,871	18,754	86,185	Paulding
Peach**	.225	24,889	23,668	14,560	8,825	32,543	362,390	.0068	228,918	65	11,310	22	14,369	76	36,518	9,008	16,194	Peach
Pickens*	.227	29,406	22,983	17,250	10,369	39,382	507,240	.0096	378,932	108	18,462	37	1,632	9	34,612	17,970	21,792	Pickens
Pierce**	.229	16,694	15,636	13,108	6,102	28,779	218,820	.0041	125,062	36	5,071	10	...	...	13,506	8,849	11,409	Pierce
Pike*	.231	15,986	13,688	18,147	5,559	42,029	290,090	.0038	20,854	6	1,648	3	...	...	3,284	1,702	12,755	Pike
Polk**	.233	40,930	38,127	14,151	14,760	31,211	579,200	.0101	267,691	76	48,098	96	4,042	21	66,949	21,696	27,906	Polk
Pulaski	.235	9,861	9,588	13,671	3,514	30,595	134,810	.0025	78,785	22	2,984	6	...	...	25,335	6,673	6,683	Pulaski
Putnam	.237	20,017	18,812	17,614	7,983	36,088	352,580	.0057	152,705	43	5,320	11	...	...	26,341	17,657	16,140	Putnam
Quitman**	.239	2,412	2,598	13,769	1,053	25,417	33,210	.0005	8,471	2	...	...	...	...	4,603	...	1,833	Quitman
Rabun	.241	16,342	15,050	17,224	6,846	32,517	281,470	.0049	162,980	46	4,301	9	1,117	6	29,380	17,777	13,743	Rabun
Randolph	.243	7,128	7,791	10,894	2,830	21,392	77,650	.0015	37,594	11	2,909	6	...	...	8,538	2,677	4,377	Randolph
Richmond*	.245	196,018	199,775	15,117	74,145	31,842	2,963,280	.0598	2,445,404	694	472,611	940	173,679	914	246,328	124,478	119,796	Richmond
Rockdale*	.247	78,002	70,111	21,709	27,299	49,589	1,693,330	.0317	1,370,530	389	206,533	411	49,558	261	177,044	74,795	56,561	Rockdale
Schley**	.249	4,070	3,766	13,585	1,449	30,522	55,290	.0009	12,170	3	1,407	3	...	...	2,390	...	2,527	Schley
Screven	.251	15,277	15,374	13,476	5,813	27,699	205,880	.0037	107,213	30	3,767	7	...	...	18,426	10,110	10,462	Screven
Seminole	.253	9,135	9,369	13,034	3,565	26,383	119,070	.0024	84,390	24	4,125	8	...	...	12,983	9,289	6,299	Seminole
Spalding*	.255	61,851	58,417	16,062	22,887	34,660	993,480	.0193	765,667	217	129,712	258	37,190	196	140,278	37,207	41,629	Spalding
Stephens**	.257	25,083	25,435	14,458	10,156	28,723	362,650	.0069	237,634	67	43,080	86	1,297	7	42,802	12,920	19,770	Stephens
Stewart	.259	4,915	5,252	12,018	1,944	24,087	59,070	.0010	23,511	7	4,755	9	...	...	4,688	4,160	3,107	Stewart
Sumter**	.261	33,187	33,200	13,423	11,998	29,783	445,460	.0093	372,224	106	69,806	139	11,155	59	40,839	16,155	20,286	Sumter
Talbot	.263	6,583	6,498	12,961	2,636	25,664	85,320	.0013	12,548	4	1,574	3	...	...	1,266	1,533	4,497	Talbot
Taliaferro	.265	1,864	2,077	13,718	867	22,961	25,570	.0004	4,261	1	...	...	...	...	...	...	1,445	Taliaferro
Tattnall	.267	22,737	22,305	10,599	6,943	27,554	240,990	.0048	135,931	39	15,768	31	6,671	35	22,315	13,392	12,151	Tattnall
Taylor	.269	9,046	8,815	11,166	3,293	24,228	101,010	.0020	61,362	17	8,592	17	1,073	6	11,159	3,705	5,645	Taylor
Telfair	.271	13,167	11,794	9,866	4,078	25,305	129,900	.0026	69,329	20	5,374	11	1,477	8	20,777	7,384	7,030	Telfair
Terrell*	.273	10,948	10,970	11,976	4,028	26,056	131,110	.0025	67,672	19	2,925	6	1,340	7	14,945	4,167	6,471	Terrell
Thomas**	.275	44,448	42,737	13,973	16,528	30,229	621,060	.0136	612,783	174	120,152	239	23,186	122	67,139	37,443	28,289	Thomas
Tift**	.277	40,386	38,407	13,964	14,118	31,606	563,930	.0125	577,148	164	97,189	193	24,721	130	66,129	24,596	24,806	Tift
Toombs**	.279	26,767	26,067	12,305	9,840	26,508	329,360	.0076	349,901	99	79,783	159	8,619	45	39,761	21,611	16,408	Toombs
Towns	.281	10,366	9,319	16,749	4,540	30,573	173,620	.0028	70,523	20	13,153	26	...	...	11,182	11,874	8,935	Towns
Treutlen	.283	6,997	6,854	10,949	2,516	24,481	76,610	.0013	20,496	6	1,476	3	...	...	3,819	4,224	4,522	Treutlen
Troup**	.285	61,418	58,779	15,990	23,155	33,937	982,070	.0194	786,885	223	124,584	248	38,217	201	125,897	30,125	40,844	Troup
Turner	.287	9,542	9,504	11,178	3,410	25,239	106,660	.0022	73,802	21	3,468	7	...	...	9,850	6,897	5,557	Turner
Twiggs*	.289	10,533	10,590	13,983	3,841	30,537	147,280	.0022	26,063	7	...	...	...	...	6,953	...	7,201	Twiggs
Union	.291	20,344	17,289	15,857	8,321	30,897	322,590	.0057	178,543	51	10,172	20	1,292	7	34,174	16,375	17,468	Union
Upson**	.293	28,169	27,597	14,497	10,839	30,248	408,380	.0069	171,276	49	36,866	73	6,984	37	29,629	9,345	19,696	Upson
Walker*	.295	63,750	61,053	15,266	24,541	31,455	973,200	.0159	367,294	104	35,019	70	9,840	52	63,997	23,045	47,131	Walker
Walton*	.297	74,809	60,687	19,165	26,297	43,444	1,433,710	.0206	366,166	104	42,686	85	3,936	21	90,880	17,220	56,011	Walton
Ware**	.299	35,825	35,483	13,011	13,459	27,596	466,110	.0106	479,263	136	126,869	252	15,329	81	65,010	25,521	22,734	Ware
Warren	.301	6,154	6,336	13,209	2,408	26,702	81,290	.0012	14,482	4	1,382	3	...	...	4,841	1,681	4,273	Warren
Washington	.303	20,879	21,176	12,768	7,393	28,765	266,580	.0053	179,542	51	25,153	50	4,030	21	25,430	11,203	13,239	Washington
Wayne**	.305	28,389	26,565	13,038	9,355	31,380	370,130	.0076	290,697	83	34,419	68	9,172	48	52,908	16,049	17,088	Wayne
Webster	.307	2,258	2,390	13,787	910	27,153	31,130	.0005	10,530	3	4,031	8	...	...	1,171	...	1,736	Webster
Wheeler	.309	6,736	6,179	8,722	1,995	23,133	58,750	.0011	21,125	6	...	...	...	...	3,748	2,484	3,394	Wheeler
White	.311	24,675	19,944	15,428	8,821	34,471	380,690	.0082	378,946	108	5,293	11	8,678	46	40,529	13,386	18,765	White
Whitfield*	.313	90,796	83,525	16,407	31,747	37,122	1,489,660	.0322	1,535,827	436	239,945	477	59,513	313	163,379	52,273	61,116	Whitfield
Wilcox	.315	8,759	8,577	10,731	2,760	26,792	93,990	.0016	21,475	6	2,099	4	...	...	3,356	2,262	5,213	Wilcox
Wilkes	.317	10,694	10,687	13,803	4,273	27,418	147,610	.0027	83,355	24	7,290	14	2,475	13	23,478	8,183	7,735	Wilkes
Wilkinson	.319	10,221	10,220	14,841	3,825	31,512	151,690	.0022	27,113	8	1,125	2	...	...	5,196	1,835	7,646	Wilkinson
Worth*	.321	21,991	21,967	14,506	8,157	31,106	319,000	.0053	119,753	34	4,730	9	1,309	7	20,652	7,902	15,300	Worth
Georgia Total		**8,969,042**	**8,186,453**	**18,691**	**3,242,705**	**40,467**	**167,638,820**	**2.9839**	**108,200,674**	**30,717**	**16,112,097**	**32,042**	**5,404,238**	**28,443**	**14,835,054**	**5,026,149**	**6,175,644**	**Georgia**

Hawaii (HI; Code 15; 5 Counties)

County or County Equivalent	FIPS County Code	Population: Estimate 7/1/05	Population: Census 4/1/00	Per Capita Income 2004	House-holds Estimate 7/1/05	Median Household Income 2004	Disposable Income 2004 ($1,000)	Market Ability Index 2004	Total Retail Sales: 2004 Sales ($1,000)	Total Retail Sales: Ranally Sales Units	General Merchandise: 2004 Sales ($1,000)	General Merchandise: Ranally Sales Units	Apparel Store: 2004 Sales ($1,000)	Apparel Store: Ranally Sales Units	Food Store Sales 2004 ($1,000)	Health & Drug Store 2004 ($1,000)	Passenger Car Regis-trations 2004	County or County Equivalent
Hawaii**	.001	163,051	148,677	17,202	58,374	37,210	2,804,870	.0492	1,623,949	461	332,411	661	97,410	513	375,296	104,587	103,422	Hawaii
Honolulu*	.003	910,475	876,156	20,281	302,181	47,743	18,465,370	.3063	9,903,032	2,812	1,988,367	3,954	1,320,832	6,952	1,401,658	865,911	537,678	Honolulu
Kalawao	.005	118	147	5,424	112	4,999	...	...	...	...	...	...	...	...	...	...	139	Kalawao
Kauai**	.007	61,454	58,463	18,902	21,586	41,867	1,161,610	.0208	771,118	219	144,281	287	56,335	297	189,482	55,446	40,209	Kauai
Maui**	.009	138,802	128,094	19,713	47,158	45,456	2,736,200	.0496	1,931,368	548	318,270	633	219,781	1,157	383,189	147,602	86,901	Maui
Hawaii Total		**1,273,900**	**1,211,537**	**19,757**	**429,411**	**45,936**	**25,168,690**	**.4259**	**14,229,466**	**4,040**	**2,783,330**	**5,535**	**1,694,358**	**8,919**	**2,349,624**	**1,173,546**	**768,349**	**Hawaii**

Idaho (ID; Code 16; 44 Counties)

County or County Equivalent	FIPS County Code	Population: Estimate 7/1/05	Population: Census 4/1/00	Per Capita Income 2004	House-holds Estimate 7/1/05	Median Household Income 2004	Disposable Income 2004 ($1,000)	Market Ability Index 2004	Total Retail Sales: 2004 Sales ($1,000)	Total Retail Sales: Ranally Sales Units	General Merchandise: 2004 Sales ($1,000)	General Merchandise: Ranally Sales Units	Apparel Store: 2004 Sales ($1,000)	Apparel Store: Ranally Sales Units	Food Store Sales 2004 ($1,000)	Health & Drug Store 2004 ($1,000)	Passenger Car Regis-trations 2004	County or County Equivalent
Ada*	.001	339,342	300,904	20,802	132,529	43,032	7,058,890	.1304	5,413,754	1,537	1,080,480	2,149	207,148	1,090	691,656	160,996	301,825	Ada
Adams	.003	3,472	3,476	15,922	1,607	27,838	55,280	.0009	24,221	7	...	...	...	...	6,792	1,437	3,726	Adams
Bannock*	.005	75,502	75,565	16,358	28,449	34,985	1,235,080	.0240	957,307	272	163,293	325	20,513	108	154,005	47,217	62,923	Bannock
Bear Lake	.007	6,270	6,411	15,006	2,430	31,167	94,090	.0017	53,670	15	1,973	4	...	...	11,740	2,114	5,747	Bear Lake
Benewah	.009	8,929	9,171	15,210	3,656	30,176	135,810	.0024	68,284	19	...	...	...	...	26,011	1,986	8,524	Benewah
Bingham**	.011	43,653	41,735	13,728	13,942	34,535	599,280	.0108	315,948	90	31,310	62	...	...	59,068	8,665	33,430	Bingham
Blaine	.013	21,809	18,991	23,009	8,760	46,230	501,810	.0087	338,978	96	11,724	23	28,960	152	76,518	16,410	19,003	Blaine
Boise*	.015	7,566	6,670	16,922	2,816	36,457	128,030	.0017	10,082	3	...	...	...	...	4,038	...	6,471	Boise
Bonner	.017	40,662	36,835	14,153	14,683	31,556	575,470	.0152	878,215	249	57,109	114	13,685	72	71,435	15,673	32,776	Bonner
Bonneville*	.019	90,159	82,522	17,366	31,949	39,435	1,565,660	.0313	1,359,992	386	339,851	676	34,722	183	162,811	52,669	70,657	Bonneville
Boundary	.021	10,340	9,871	13,916	3,886	30,308	143,890	.0027	85,654	24	...	...	...	...	26,638	...	9,139	Boundary
Butte	.023	2,832	2,899	14,047	1,086	29,792	39,780	.0006	11,140	3	...	...	...	...	...	...	2,584	Butte
Camas	.025	1,072	991	17,556	448	33,634	18,820	.0003	4,358	1	...	...	...	...	...	...	1,049	Camas
Canyon*	.027	164,715	131,441	14,527	56,315	34,337	2,392,770	.0455	1,594,010	453	195,702	389	23,628	124	224,367	69,304	122,864	Canyon
Caribou	.029	7,121	7,304	16,297	2,623	35,442	116,050	.0022	85,588	24	...	...	...	...	8,514	4,503	6,042	Caribou
Cassia**	.031	21,629	21,416	13,280	7,241	31,981	287,230	.0059	229,988	65	39,248	78	4,464	23	40,262	10,494	16,251	Cassia
Clark	.033	838	1,022	16,050	347	30,665	13,450	.0002	5,333	2	2,658	5	...	...	...	...	712	Clark
Clearwater	.035	8,154	8,930	17,015	3,604	31,045	138,740	.0023	64,623	18	...	...	...	...	23,257	4,566	8,087	Clearwater
Custer	.037	3,978	4,342	17,592	1,805	31,270	69,980	.0010	18,136	5	...	...	...	...	4,429	...	4,168	Custer
Elmore**	.039	28,526	29,130	14,211	9,823	33,096	405,380	.0081	315,431	90	64,373	128	...	...	31,774	6,523	21,178	Elmore
Franklin*	.041	12,259	11,329	13,146	3,761	34,506	161,160	.0029	78,884	22	1,993	4	...	...	19,036	3,725	9,428	Franklin

Source: Devonshire Associates Ltd. and Scan/US, Inc. 2005. ...Data less than 1,000. (d) Data not available.
* Component of a Metropolitan Core Based Statistical Area.
** Component of a Micropolitan Core Based Statistical Area.

Continued on next page

Counties: Population/Income/Sales, *Continued*

County or County Equivalent	FIPS County Code	Population Estimate 7/1/05	Population Census 4/1/00	Per Capita Income 2004	House-holds Estimate 7/1/05	Median Household Income 2004	Disposable Income 2004 ($1,000)	Market Ability Index 2004	Total Retail Sales 2004 Sales ($1,000)	Total Retail Sales Ranally Sales Units	General Merchandise 2004 Sales ($1,000)	General Merchandise Ranally Sales Units	Apparel Store 2004 Sales ($1,000)	Apparel Store Ranally Sales Units	Food Store Sales 2004 ($1,000)	Health & Drug Store 2004 ($1,000)	Passenger Car Regis-trations 2004	County or County Equivalent
Fremont**	.043	12,398	11,819	13,083	4,090	31,794	162,200	.0028	70,624	20	4,011	8	...	...	13,959	5,368	9,538	Fremont
Gem*	.045	16,167	15,181	15,250	6,040	32,723	246,540	.0038	69,686	20	...	...	...	...	21,556	3,383	13,985	Gem
Gooding	.047	14,420	14,155	14,132	5,357	30,746	203,790	.0034	79,441	23	...	...	1,112	6	16,108	4,845	12,332	Gooding
Idaho	.049	15,462	15,511	14,111	6,237	28,150	218,180	.0038	101,845	29	...	...	...	...	32,983	9,567	14,144	Idaho
Jefferson*	.051	20,899	19,155	13,704	6,448	35,656	286,390	.0046	85,988	24	3,546	7	...	...	27,536	...	16,297	Jefferson
Jerome**	.053	19,248	18,342	13,992	6,586	32,888	269,320	.0051	173,115	49	...	...	...	...	30,520	1,930	15,181	Jerome
Kootenai*	.055	122,971	108,685	17,137	47,174	35,860	2,107,400	.0397	1,540,992	438	232,236	462	50,041	263	243,800	60,243	105,675	Kootenai
Latah**	.057	34,968	34,935	15,372	13,799	30,541	537,540	.0099	341,219	97	66,411	132	12,208	64	82,858	18,134	30,220	Latah
Lemhi	.059	7,765	7,806	15,815	3,423	28,958	122,800	.0022	74,330	21	...	...	1,932	10	20,278	5,145	8,134	Lemhi
Lewis	.061	3,750	3,747	15,491	1,562	30,207	58,090	.0010	28,566	8	...	...	...	...	5,109	...	3,523	Lewis
Lincoln	.063	4,467	4,044	13,318	1,523	31,333	59,490	.0010	21,674	6	...	...	...	...	4,642	...	3,546	Lincoln
Madison**	.065	31,407	27,467	11,625	9,324	31,575	365,110	.0077	277,649	79	45,531	91	4,952	26	34,671	2,425	22,703	Madison
Minidoka**	.067	18,848	20,174	14,195	7,074	30,627	267,550	.0050	159,900	45	27,969	56	1,409	7	20,910	2,015	16,041	Minidoka
Nez Perce*	.069	37,908	37,410	17,786	15,744	34,498	674,250	.0131	546,544	155	111,818	222	10,339	54	88,885	16,985	34,438	Nez Perce
Oneida	.071	4,131	4,125	14,657	1,490	32,558	60,550	.0010	17,435	5	...	...	...	...	...	...	3,612	Oneida
Owyhee*	.073	11,380	10,644	11,718	3,902	27,615	133,350	.0023	43,724	12	...	...	...	...	12,956	...	9,082	Owyhee
Payette**	.075	22,047	20,578	14,222	7,947	31,758	313,560	.0051	109,775	31	...	...	...	...	25,504	...	17,507	Payette
Power*	.077	7,259	7,538	14,275	2,675	31,161	103,620	.0018	47,715	14	...	...	...	...	7,947	1,541	6,129	Power
Shoshone	.079	12,506	13,771	16,002	5,880	27,292	200,120	.0057	365,405	104	3,354	7	...	...	69,213	17,371	11,990	Shoshone
Teton**	.081	7,686	5,999	18,573	2,914	39,328	142,750	.0022	49,056	14	...	...	...	...	2,961	3,083	7,010	Teton
Twin Falls**	.083	68,875	64,284	15,117	25,551	32,790	1,041,200	.0227	1,059,434	301	254,153	505	39,032	205	109,757	45,066	56,363	Twin Falls
Valley	.085	7,846	7,651	19,104	3,443	35,021	149,890	.0027	96,632	27	...	...	1,623	9	26,507	5,656	7,754	Valley
Washington	.087	10,034	9,977	13,832	3,817	29,625	138,790	.0025	68,207	19	...	...	...	...	14,527	2,445	8,419	Washington
Idaho Total		**1,411,270**	**1,293,953**	**16,722**	**523,760**	**36,108**	**23,599,130**	**.4479**	**17,342,549**	**4,922**	**2,744,471**	**5,460**	**465,084**	**2,448**	**2,557,218**	**614,814**	**1,180,207**	**Idaho**

Illinois (IL; Code 17; 102 Counties)

County or County Equivalent	FIPS County Code	Population Estimate 7/1/05	Population Census 4/1/00	Per Capita Income 2004	House-holds Estimate 7/1/05	Median Household Income 2004	Disposable Income 2004 ($1,000)	Market Ability Index 2004	Total Retail Sales 2004 Sales ($1,000)	Total Retail Sales Ranally Sales Units	General Merchandise 2004 Sales ($1,000)	General Merchandise Ranally Sales Units	Apparel Store 2004 Sales ($1,000)	Apparel Store Ranally Sales Units	Food Store Sales 2004 ($1,000)	Health & Drug Store 2004 ($1,000)	Passenger Car Regis-trations 2004	County or County Equivalent
Adams**	.001	66,862	68,277	16,852	27,088	32,950	1,126,780	.0221	914,472	260	177,021	352	26,562	140	136,646	56,646	48,292	Adams
Alexander**	.003	9,087	9,590	13,223	3,805	25,247	120,160	.0020	35,110	10	1,930	4	...	...	7,613	...	5,648	Alexander
Bond*	.005	18,049	17,633	16,119	6,395	36,219	290,940	.0049	135,766	39	9,436	19	2,224	12	24,838	9,042	12,017	Bond
Boone*	.007	49,590	41,786	19,716	16,246	48,095	977,730	.0146	328,221	93	56,301	112	2,344	12	57,457	7,844	32,468	Boone
Brown	.009	6,793	6,950	13,321	2,137	33,832	90,490	.0015	25,688	7	4,297	9	...	...	4,018	1,219	4,108	Brown
Bureau**	.011	35,168	35,503	19,042	14,024	37,795	669,670	.0107	294,333	84	33,833	67	9,885	52	35,710	8,026	26,482	Bureau
Calhoun*	.013	5,139	5,084	16,669	2,073	32,695	85,660	.0014	40,898	12	...	...	...	...	4,457	...	4,168	Calhoun
Carroll	.015	16,220	16,674	18,647	6,847	35,314	302,450	.0048	122,388	35	10,692	21	1,325	7	22,550	1,716	12,794	Carroll
Cass	.017	13,901	13,695	15,947	5,271	33,492	221,680	.0036	80,624	23	15,883	32	...	...	17,512	5,531	9,700	Cass
Champaign*	.019	186,135	179,669	18,227	74,726	35,908	3,392,710	.0615	2,285,663	649	514,212	1,023	90,197	475	295,686	174,833	126,145	Champaign
Christian**	.021	35,006	35,372	17,459	13,998	34,975	611,170	.0110	390,587	111	57,474	114	6,558	35	58,851	22,054	25,545	Christian
Clark	.023	16,873	17,008	17,945	7,095	34,045	302,780	.0049	132,808	38	15,516	31	1,524	8	14,036	8,514	13,637	Clark
Clay	.025	14,093	14,560	15,556	5,948	29,475	219,230	.0038	112,042	32	15,751	31	...	...	14,821	3,556	10,929	Clay
Clinton*	.027	36,286	35,535	19,111	13,243	41,374	693,460	.0109	286,038	81	21,897	44	6,401	34	42,588	14,139	25,731	Clinton
Coles**	.029	51,199	53,196	16,179	21,161	30,276	828,350	.0170	745,498	212	210,015	418	8,698	46	64,322	47,368	37,113	Coles
Cook*	.031	5,332,321	5,376,741	19,020	1,886,418	42,611	101,421,380	1.7279	57,112,166	16,217	6,691,173	13,307	4,085,212	21,501	8,603,726	5,892,431	2,978,549	Cook
Crawford	.033	19,836	20,452	15,800	7,900	31,615	313,400	.0055	166,204	47	13,339	27	2,545	13	27,763	11,425	14,648	Crawford
Cumberland**	.035	10,906	11,253	17,830	4,484	34,646	194,450	.0029	53,567	15	1,592	3	...	...	8,448	1,547	9,072	Cumberland
DeKalb*	.037	96,267	88,969	18,958	33,996	41,660	1,825,010	.0302	925,962	263	130,732	260	25,140	132	95,693	48,350	66,576	DeKalb
De Witt	.039	16,524	16,798	20,285	6,838	39,004	335,190	.0056	183,523	52	13,145	26	...	...	23,632	7,925	13,222	De Witt
Douglas	.041	19,846	19,922	18,226	7,698	37,119	361,710	.0068	267,071	76	4,767	9	39,841	210	25,338	11,894	14,013	Douglas
DuPage*	.043	937,264	904,161	27,711	335,462	61,183	25,972,140	.4309	16,653,697	4,729	1,959,526	3,897	960,105	5,053	1,622,279	1,066,411	653,602	DuPage
Edgar	.045	19,157	19,704	17,244	7,935	33,084	330,340	.0055	153,342	44	10,764	21	...	...	20,498	9,792	15,039	Edgar
Edwards	.047	6,747	6,971	17,088	2,988	30,498	115,290	.0018	43,483	12	1,106	2	...	...	10,121	1,070	5,726	Edwards
Effingham**	.049	34,652	34,264	17,857	13,287	36,628	618,780	.0143	772,360	219	91,243	181	29,407	155	66,098	24,655	25,037	Effingham
Fayette	.051	21,437	21,802	14,936	8,302	30,704	320,190	.0060	204,476	58	25,984	52	1,278	7	28,122	7,357	15,784	Fayette
Ford*	.053	14,102	14,241	18,212	5,654	35,928	256,830	.0045	155,141	44	10,846	22	1,817	10	21,946	10,244	10,577	Ford
Franklin	.055	39,352	39,018	14,425	16,434	27,466	567,660	.0112	422,028	120	60,908	121	15,198	80	56,833	34,149	28,243	Franklin
Fulton**	.057	37,364	38,250	16,128	14,729	32,412	602,620	.0103	301,882	86	50,088	100	7,268	38	57,381	26,041	27,063	Fulton
Gallatin	.059	6,081	6,445	14,843	2,817	25,405	90,260	.0014	24,430	7	...	...	...	...	2,185	...	5,249	Gallatin
Greene	.061	14,612	14,761	15,099	5,810	30,522	220,630	.0037	94,081	27	...	...	...	...	15,408	7,796	10,830	Greene
Grundy*	.063	40,846	37,535	22,566	15,401	47,503	921,720	.0146	450,744	128	46,638	93	5,380	28	46,061	29,932	30,064	Grundy
Hamilton**	.065	8,191	8,621	15,844	3,530	28,823	129,780	.0021	45,381	13	2,347	5	...	...	5,078	...	6,722	Hamilton
Hancock	.067	19,150	20,121	18,885	8,200	35,094	361,650	.0056	134,818	38	1,304	3	1,593	8	14,112	10,462	16,198	Hancock
Hardin	.069	4,711	4,800	14,046	2,004	26,497	66,170	.0010	11,184	3	...	...	...	...	1,082	1,065	3,551	Hardin
Henderson**	.071	7,935	8,213	18,602	3,386	34,735	147,610	.0021	30,253	9	...	...	...	...	9,614	1,770	6,738	Henderson
Henry*	.073	50,536	51,020	18,708	20,031	37,528	945,420	.0161	530,885	151	83,978	167	9,240	49	53,228	20,858	38,723	Henry
Iroquois	.075	30,397	31,334	18,276	12,166	36,171	555,550	.0087	210,419	60	23,946	48	...	...	30,845	9,332	23,610	Iroquois
Jackson**	.077	57,629	59,612	13,279	24,911	22,683	765,240	.0164	692,207	197	181,101	360	34,833	183	84,589	31,856	41,399	Jackson
Jasper	.079	9,969	10,117	17,145	4,038	34,485	170,920	.0030	95,112	27	3,726	7	1,533	8	4,194	...	8,429	Jasper
Jefferson**	.081	40,445	40,045	15,825	15,771	32,634	640,050	.0145	727,793	207	125,406	249	21,908	115	53,034	42,409	28,026	Jefferson
Jersey*	.083	22,415	21,668	18,773	8,419	39,681	420,800	.0071	228,180	65	68,669	137	7,170	38	20,746	9,156	17,111	Jersey
Jo Daviess	.085	22,759	22,289	19,968	9,543	37,895	454,460	.0074	222,504	63	1,721	3	7,374	39	45,482	9,910	18,379	Jo Daviess
Johnson	.087	13,198	12,878	13,180	4,336	31,947	173,950	.0030	69,349	20	1,134	2	...	...	9,613	...	8,271	Johnson
Kane*	.089	490,051	404,119	21,633	155,267	55,242	10,601,320	.1629	4,424,098	1,256	797,153	1,585	186,418	981	697,748	343,810	311,207	Kane
Kankakee*	.091	107,719	103,833	18,016	39,461	39,119	1,940,650	.0349	1,262,073	358	246,649	491	43,039	227	124,092	101,960	68,816	Kankakee
Kendall*	.093	74,879	54,544	25,224	25,937	58,433	1,888,760	.0274	695,480	197	104,745	208	5,403	28	106,389	43,958	54,258	Kendall
Knox**	.095	53,551	55,836	17,497	22,014	33,818	936,980	.0172	640,293	182	132,209	263	13,240	70	92,594	37,626	38,528	Knox
Lake*	.097	704,726	644,356	24,587	229,248	60,326	17,327,020	.3181	14,075,214	3,997	936,293	1,862	503,323	2,649	1,135,337	803,943	464,361	Lake
La Salle**	.099	112,478	111,509	18,906	44,397	37,984	2,126,530	.0418	1,841,291	523	320,309	637	50,070	264	243,182	107,431	79,872	La Salle
Lawrence	.101	16,147	15,452	14,450	6,382	29,570	233,320	.0038	84,627	24	17,612	35	...	...	13,496	5,683	11,792	Lawrence
Lee**	.103	35,439	36,062	18,265	13,358	38,715	647,300	.0106	308,205	88	35,558	71	2,904	15	33,124	25,617	25,287	Lee
Livingston**	.105	38,958	39,678	17,938	14,375	38,464	698,810	.0124	439,071	125	53,946	107	5,296	28	65,000	19,190	26,282	Livingston
Logan**	.107	30,451	31,183	16,886	10,987	37,281	514,200	.0095	349,323	99	45,049	90	4,160	22	42,530	23,337	20,213	Logan
McDonough**	.109	32,343	32,913	15,381	12,851	30,824	497,460	.0095	347,054	99	88,134	175	12,539	66	59,272	29,731	23,810	McDonough
McHenry*	.111	302,316	260,077	25,240	103,854	58,842	7,630,460	.1127	3,044,734	865	455,176	905	82,490	434	475,767	234,926	232,180	McHenry
McLean*	.113	160,498	150,433	21,223	62,003	43,734	3,406,260	.0592	2,197,078	624	332,254	661	135,942	715	218,032	143,217	113,137	McLean
Macon*	.115	109,127	114,706	19,482	47,005	36,008	2,125,990	.0396	1,612,803	458	305,716	608	54,606	287	210,392	109,435	81,912	Macon
Macoupin*	.117	49,088	49,019	17,411	19,635	34,726	854,650	.0141	396,333	113	31,003	62	3,760	20	51,816	25,727	38,022	Macoupin
Madison*	.119	263,396	258,941	20,406	108,986	39,312	5,374,970	.0889	2,866,370	814	458,898	913	51,247	270	512,125	197,447	213,570	Madison
Marion**	.121	40,297	41,691	17,571	16,834	33,470	708,040	.0122	393,173	112	77,444	154	9,923	52	52,496	26,741	29,792	Marion
Marshall*	.123	12,965	13,180	20,288	5,354	38,860	263,030	.0038	71,286	20	1,005	2	...	...	9,804	6,300	10,504	Marshall
Mason	.125	15,822	16,038	17,290	6,324	34,367	273,560	.0046	141,132	40	7,562	15	1,310	7	16,699	10,177	12,107	Mason
Massac**	.127	15,190	15,161	15,873	6,333	30,341	241,110	.0039	94,009	27	1,024	2	...	...	17,250	11,013	11,076	Massac
Menard*	.129	12,738	12,486	21,610	5,089	43,038	275,270	.0041	95,917	27	...	...	...	...	12,561	2,668	10,099	Menard
Mercer*	.131	16,906	16,957	18,784	6,581	37,910	317,570	.0048	110,046	31	12,012	24	1,087	6	11,521	3,748	13,489	Mercer
Monroe*	.133	31,030	27,619	23,438	11,408	50,301	727,280	.0110	306,286	87	30,432	61	1,492	8	43,759	13,759	24,011	Monroe
Montgomery	.135	30,222	30,652	15,299	11,525	32,079	462,370	.0089	336,595	96	49,143	98	4,494	24	44,134	19,151	20,939	Montgomery
Morgan**	.137	35,707	36,616	17,676	14,247	35,408	631,140	.0113	397,825	113	75,769	151	15,336	81	53,468	29,264	25,617	Morgan
Moultrie	.139	14,456	14,287	18,067	5,504	37,543	261,180	.0038	60,558	17	...	...	1,974	10	11,061	8,588	10,244	Moultrie
Ogle**	.141	54,203	51,032	19,461	19,872	42,026	1,054,850	.0159	356,754	101	32,965	66	2,177	11	34,539	11,154	38,961	Ogle
Peoria*	.143	181,293	183,433	19,516	74,347	37,777	3,538,100	.0640	2,465,664	700	464,828	924	82,481	434	366,469	216,756	125,468	Peoria
Perry	.145	22,506	23,094	15,597	8,729	31,884	351,020	.0059	156,760	45	19,708	39	1,580	8	26,811	8,976	15,754	Perry
Piatt*	.147	16,424	16,365	21,533	6,645	42,109	353,650	.0053	131,409	37	1,737	3	1,694	9	14,743	6,131	12,835	Piatt
Pike	.149	16,771	17,384	15,442	6,878	30,114	258,970	.0046	143,466	41	18,899	38	...	...	19,180	1,058	12,879	Pike
Pope	.151	4,244	4,413	15,384	1,797	28,910	65,290	.0009	10,590	3	...	...	...	...	1,009	...	3,329	Pope
Pulaski	.153	6,877	7,348	13,244	2,945	24,633	91,080	.0015	25,759	7	1,372	3	...	...	7,180	1,523	4,882	Pulaski
Putnam**	.155	6,149	6,086	21,491	2,516	41,161	132,150	.0018	22,711	6	...	...	1,001	5	2,307	1,825	5,042	Putnam
Randolph	.157	33,022	33,893	16,348	12,140	35,379	539,850	.0097	323,126	92	49,156	98	1,335	7	33,375	14,774	22,955	Randolph
Richland	.159	15,777	16,149	16,314	6,868	30,317	257,380	.0054	247,621	70	33,130	66	4,012	21	39,465	10,935	12,639	Richland
Rock Island*	.161	146,919	149,374	18,887	60,272	36,430	2,774,860	.0504	1,925,162	547	240,771	479	81,930	431	267,809	173,986	102,946	Rock Island
St. Clair*	.163	260,165	256,082	17,583	98,300	36,773	4,574,590	.0821	2,911,800	827	633,874	1,261	147,653	777	406,600	205,630	171,208	St. Clair
Saline**	.165	25,795	26,733	15,280	11,272	27,787	394,140	.0080	327,448	93	45,195	90	3,592	19	90,052	27,729	19,319	Saline
Sangamon*	.167	193,811	188,951	21,254	81,059	40,645	4,119,340	.0703	2,513,815	714	484,638	964	81,825	431	303,566	167,100	138,161	Sangamon
Schuyler	.169	6,867	7,189	18,542	3,040	33,202	127,330	.0021	57,438	16	1,772	4	1,132	6	3,726	3,738	5,939	Schuyler
Scott**	.171	5,447	5,537	18,344	2,262	35,119	99,920	.0015	26,804	8	1,110	2	...	...	5,957	1,674	4,553	Scott
Shelby	.173	22,296	22,893	18,286	9,111	35,463	407,710	.0062	139,867	40	4,798	10	2,781	15	17,151	8,396	17,879	Shelby
Stark*	.175	6,120	6,332	18,101	2,557	34,613	110,780	.0017	35,518	10	...	...	...	...	2,475	2,269	4,795	Stark
Stephenson**	.177	47,788	48,979	19,766	19,781	37,886	944,560	.0160	533,700	152	97,653	194	15,725	83	88,330	40,570	35,764	Stephenson
Tazewell*	.179	128,302	128,485	21,228	51,509	41,931	2,723,540	.0474	1,769,971	503	206,328	410	41,565	219	256,462	88,557	95,905	Tazewell
Union	.181	18,216	18,293	15,200	7,427	30,011	276,890	.0050	160,708	46	27,457	55	2,139	11	37,456	3,333	12,936	Union
Vermilion*	.183	82,252	83,919	16,564	33,259	32,483	1,362,390	.0249	879,347	250	181,418	361	21,925	115	127,479	60,189	56,472	Vermilion
Wabash	.185	12,548	12,937	17,149	5,227	32,786	215,190	.0036	99,685	28	14,543	29	...	...	9,788	7,532	9,635	Wabash
Warren**	.187	17,959	18,735	17,101	7,052	34,550	307,110	.0050	128,478	36	25,183	50	...	...	15,023	6,243	12,936	Warren
Washington	.189	15,158	15,148	19,109	5,998	38,108	289,660	.0053	204,563	58	6,975	14	1,865	10	15,234	7,392	12,147	Washington
Wayne	.191	16,839	17,151	16,146	7,378	29,396	271,890	.0048	153,084	43	26,445	53	2,807	15	15,080	7,700	14,038	Wayne
White	.193	14,973	15,371	15,905	6,690	28,429	238,140	.0042	135,841	39	17,196	34	1,310	7	20,688	5,685	12,160	White
Whiteside**	.195	59,513	60,653	19,079	23,723	37,755	1,135,430	.0199	706,473	201	145,592	290	8,608	45	81,595	45,447	43,351	Whiteside
Will*	.197	640,443	502,266	22,223	199,257	57,634	14,232,730	.2092	4,966,459	1,410	614,968	1,223	110,865	584	705,123	472,662	410,357	Will
Williamson**	.199	63,173	61,296	16,034	26,072	31,022	1,012,920	.0183	614,944	175	170,309	339	15,007	79	50,871	28,671	44,862	Williamson
Winnebago*	.201	287,795	278,418	19,780	109,853	41,377	5,692,470	.1010	3,772,953	1,071	601,361	1,196	151,925	800	626,195	244,400	203,946	Winnebago
Woodford*	.203	36,950	35,469	21,478	13,466	47,232	793,630	.0122	334,012	95	5,140	10	1,627	9	37,459	13,795	27,872	Woodford
Illinois Total		**12,788,145**	**12,419,293**	**20,249**	**4,644,806**	**43,819**	**258,945,250**	**4.3899**	**149,785,179**	**42,539**	**19,542,758**	**38,872**	**7,403,334**	**38,968**	**19,947,099**	**11,972,529**	**8,218,278**	**Illinois**

Indiana (IN; Code 18; 92 Counties)

County or County Equivalent	FIPS County Code	Population Estimate 7/1/05	Population Census 4/1/00	Per Capita Income 2004	House-holds Estimate 7/1/05	Median Household Income 2004	Disposable Income 2004 ($1,000)	Market Ability Index 2004	Total Retail Sales 2004 Sales ($1,000)	Total Retail Sales Ranally Sales Units	General Merchandise 2004 Sales ($1,000)	General Merchandise Ranally Sales Units	Apparel Store 2004 Sales ($1,000)	Apparel Store Ranally Sales Units	Food Store Sales 2004 ($1,000)	Health & Drug Store 2004 ($1,000)	Passenger Car Regis-trations 2004	County or County Equivalent
Adams**	.001	33,818	33,625	16,062	11,760	38,010	543,190	.0110	471,214	134	54,944	109	4,826	25	51,311	13,993	22,046	Adams
Allen*	.003	345,326	331,849	17,501	123,848	40,451	6,043,530	.1148	4,575,451	1,299	981,138	1,951	201,693	1,062	412,460	260,863	250,100	Allen
Bartholomew*	.005	72,772	71,435	19,023	27,728	40,763	1,384,350	.0240	833,936	237	166,855	332	58,441	308	99,350	55,949	54,655	Bartholomew
Benton*	.007	9,138	9,421	17,105	3,446	37,346	156,310	.0029	103,994	30	...	...	...	...	9,912	7,735	6,827	Benton
Blackford	.009	13,816	14,048	16,479	5,655	33,309	227,680	.0040	123,997	35	1,196	2	...	...	23,220	13,565	10,914	Blackford
Boone*	.011	51,660	46,107	20,010	18,731	45,589	1,033,730	.0157	381,333	108	33,701	67	16,475	87	58,643	20,484	39,101	Boone
Brown*	.013	15,508	14,957	19,661	6,182	40,811	304,900	.0042	55,049	16	...	...	3,780	20	7,728	2,567	13,790	Brown
Carroll*	.015	20,833	20,165	18,293	7,751	40,481	381,090	.0059	138,771	39	3,412	7	...	...	11,873	4,164	15,888	Carroll
Cass**	.017	40,189	40,930	17,425	15,571	36,993	700,310	.0125	435,531	124	63,001	125	18,397	97	47,240	26,050	29,277	Cass
Clark*	.019	101,296	96,472	18,749	41,759	37,444	1,899,160	.0366	1,551,827	441	261,731	520	41,849	220	139,731	72,289	76,833	Clark
Clay*	.021	27,038	26,556	16,117	10,294	35,232	435,780	.0078	255,540	73	25,771	51	1,182	6	26,608	23,169	20,873	Clay
Clinton**	.023	34,053	33,866	16,747	12,289	38,213	570,280	.0094	255,068	72	27,762	55	2,879	15	33,201	20,432	23,738	Clinton
Crawford	.025	11,365	10,743	14,125	4,260	31,104	160,530	.0026	52,249	15	1,923	4	...	...	14,289	1,580	8,985	Crawford
Daviess**	.027	30,227	29,820	14,104	10,779	32,873	426,330	.0088	362,005	103	19,401	39	4,852	26	32,474	23,414	19,491	Daviess
Dearborn*	.029	49,138	46,109	19,504	17,686	44,836	958,370	.0160	516,225	147	55,572	111	8,114	43	51,321	13,207	38,286	Dearborn
Decatur**	.031	24,895	24,555	17,667	9,605	37,640	439,820	.0084	342,467	97	46,151	92	4,377	23	39,701	16,843	19,091	Decatur
De Kalb**	.033	41,636	40,285	18,508	15,267	41,341	770,590	.0129	400,845	114	39,601	79	6,283	33	62,167	20,031	31,967	De Kalb
Delaware*	.035	117,847	118,769	15,782	46,441	33,128	1,859,920	.0361	1,411,758	401	345,291	687	57,863	305	130,438	71,255	86,529	Delaware
Dubois**	.037	40,787	39,674	18,532	15,104	41,184	755,850	.0166	852,583	242	102,555	204	26,328	139	57,953	17,656	30,879	Dubois
Elkhart*	.039	192,614	182,791	18,129	69,511	41,355	3,491,820	.0667	2,737,857	777	461,665	918	39,013	205	272,318	127,424	127,951	Elkhart
Fayette**	.041	24,685	25,588	18,086	10,095	36,527	446,460	.0076	242,842	69	35,669	71	7,543	40	32,080	30,034	19,107	Fayette
Floyd*	.043	71,650	70,823	19,417	27,929	41,308	1,391,230	.0209	465,640	132	82,104	163	6,228	33	56,093	54,651	54,127	Floyd
Fountain	.045	17,607	17,954	17,214	6,934	35,949	303,090	.0052	155,920	44	2,481	5	1,429	8	27,388	10,734	13,495	Fountain
Franklin*	.047	23,182	22,151	17,221	8,053	40,903	399,220	.0059	97,290	28	...	...	...	...	22,258	4,919	17,964	Franklin
Fulton	.049	20,511	20,511	17,240	8,039	36,203	353,600	.0062	210,300	60	18,514	37	4,103	22	45,961	13,565	15,360	Fulton

Source: Devonshire Associates Ltd. and Scan/US, Inc. 2005. ...Data less than 1,000. (d) Data not available.
* Component of a Metropolitan Core Based Statistical Area.
** Component of a Micropolitan Core Based Statistical Area.

Counties: Population/Income/Sales, *Continued*

County or County Equivalent	FIPS County Code	Population: Estimate 7/1/05	Population: Census 4/1/00	Per Capita Income 2004	Households Estimate 7/1/05	Median Household Income 2004	Disposable Income 2004 ($1,000)	Market Ability Index 2004	Total Retail Sales: 2004 Sales ($1,000)	Total Retail Sales: Ranally Sales Units	General Merchandise: 2004 Sales ($1,000)	General Merchandise: Ranally Sales Units	Apparel Store: 2004 Sales ($1,000)	Apparel Store: Ranally Sales Units	Food Store Sales 2004 ($1,000)	Health & Drug Store 2004 ($1,000)	Passenger Car Registrations 2004	County or County Equivalent
Gibson*	.051	33,333	32,500	17,095	13,141	35,564	569,830	.0099	313,154	89	50,315	100	5,306	28	46,139	10,327	25,840	Gibson
Grant**	.053	71,191	73,403	16,532	28,224	34,543	1,176,910	.0213	733,149	208	100,120	199	16,116	85	76,941	46,692	51,611	Grant
Greene*	.055	33,439	33,157	15,906	13,579	32,612	531,890	.0089	232,597	66	52,517	104	...	...	30,078	18,875	27,191	Greene
Hamilton*	.057	244,530	182,740	26,187	83,039	64,061	6,403,550	.0982	3,062,562	870	595,582	1,184	50,925	268	270,684	106,855	168,866	Hamilton
Hancock*	.059	62,264	55,391	23,758	23,850	50,896	1,479,250	.0215	519,916	148	55,393	110	6,524	34	55,228	22,980	50,692	Hancock
Harrison*	.061	36,550	34,325	18,068	13,406	40,536	660,390	.0114	372,562	106	94,338	188	9,266	49	37,742	30,815	29,467	Harrison
Hendricks*	.063	127,940	104,093	22,489	46,771	50,672	2,877,210	.0476	1,640,976	466	538,372	1,071	30,889	163	157,375	49,808	100,330	Hendricks
Henry**	.065	47,341	48,508	18,214	19,528	36,588	862,280	.0150	503,357	143	59,091	118	6,956	37	47,114	36,026	38,905	Henry
Howard*	.067	84,735	84,964	20,410	34,912	41,016	1,729,400	.0316	1,274,854	362	354,288	705	38,011	200	109,780	96,552	62,425	Howard
Huntington**	.069	38,393	38,075	17,503	14,182	39,084	671,990	.0120	414,773	118	67,924	135	7,317	39	47,231	19,943	28,042	Huntington
Jackson**	.071	41,918	41,335	17,636	16,380	36,946	739,280	.0143	592,412	168	115,385	229	45,411	239	54,722	32,347	31,975	Jackson
Jasper*	.073	31,839	30,043	17,898	11,460	41,159	569,840	.0107	422,979	120	38,794	77	2,027	11	35,713	34,027	23,635	Jasper
Jay	.075	21,628	21,806	15,900	8,327	34,129	343,880	.0057	144,198	41	26,685	53	1,359	7	16,516	10,170	16,326	Jay
Jefferson**	.077	32,343	31,705	16,729	12,314	36,215	541,050	.0099	354,958	101	90,332	180	13,339	70	36,051	13,890	23,237	Jefferson
Jennings**	.079	28,480	27,554	17,078	10,849	36,739	486,370	.0079	203,712	58	31,947	64	1,100	6	27,769	11,334	22,783	Jennings
Johnson*	.081	128,689	115,209	21,367	47,097	48,118	2,749,660	.0471	1,703,334	484	545,430	1,085	83,469	439	107,550	69,884	96,111	Johnson
Knox**	.083	38,079	39,256	14,364	15,019	30,532	546,980	.0113	469,022	133	104,555	208	26,246	138	40,706	30,175	26,755	Knox
Kosciusko**	.085	76,065	74,057	18,478	28,312	41,017	1,405,550	.0239	766,854	218	114,285	227	21,092	111	93,526	43,773	55,211	Kosciusko
LaGrange	.087	36,821	34,909	15,209	11,567	39,895	560,000	.0098	293,160	83	10,452	21	3,005	16	37,956	21,103	19,063	LaGrange
Lake*	.089	489,391	484,564	16,975	174,312	39,520	8,307,540	.1552	5,866,120	1,666	807,115	1,605	240,957	1,268	781,761	463,041	326,903	Lake
LaPorte*	.091	109,651	110,106	17,627	40,827	39,103	1,932,830	.0353	1,302,656	370	234,559	466	121,147	638	131,313	81,814	74,175	LaPorte
Lawrence**	.093	46,645	45,922	16,676	18,428	35,374	777,830	.0137	449,135	128	86,040	171	18,033	95	58,226	29,408	35,900	Lawrence
Madison*	.095	129,750	133,358	17,933	52,189	36,685	2,326,790	.0407	1,374,189	390	235,435	468	34,190	180	160,766	98,307	94,975	Madison
Marion*	.097	865,538	860,454	17,907	335,684	38,333	15,499,200	.3179	14,652,331	4,161	2,255,055	4,485	729,320	3,839	1,210,661	1,164,055	623,175	Marion
Marshall**	.099	47,011	45,128	17,257	16,738	39,832	811,270	.0144	491,997	140	72,912	145	13,249	70	58,477	23,229	33,064	Marshall
Martin	.101	10,412	10,369	16,995	4,248	34,508	176,950	.0029	73,209	21	1,168	2	...	...	12,979	2,832	8,380	Martin
Miami**	.103	36,190	36,082	16,828	13,619	36,974	609,000	.0103	297,700	85	7,205	14	4,001	21	42,101	26,518	26,707	Miami
Monroe*	.105	120,813	120,563	15,717	48,736	32,380	1,898,800	.0369	1,437,695	408	308,733	614	60,281	317	182,489	64,917	91,175	Monroe
Montgomery**	.107	37,958	37,629	18,105	14,606	38,849	687,240	.0118	380,448	108	65,988	131	4,680	25	49,264	23,030	27,451	Montgomery
Morgan*	.109	70,108	66,689	19,677	25,906	44,094	1,379,520	.0217	590,082	168	59,803	119	7,437	39	76,298	30,688	56,586	Morgan
Newton*	.111	14,381	14,566	17,508	5,386	38,559	251,780	.0039	82,070	23	...	...	...	...	14,376	9,951	10,842	Newton
Noble**	.113	47,395	46,275	17,343	16,945	39,893	821,970	.0133	349,371	99	47,726	95	4,997	26	46,910	14,423	33,649	Noble
Ohio*	.115	5,809	5,623	18,310	2,255	38,937	106,360	.0015	26,745	8	...	...	...	...	4,532	2,022	4,866	Ohio
Orange	.117	19,919	19,306	14,269	7,728	30,585	284,220	.0054	181,150	51	5,202	10	1,155	6	30,281	13,791	14,828	Orange
Owen*	.119	23,614	21,786	14,947	8,410	34,854	352,960	.0056	105,478	30	12,942	26	...	...	19,207	6,341	17,487	Owen
Parke	.121	17,452	17,241	14,954	6,366	34,320	260,970	.0040	68,461	19	...	...	...	...	11,086	7,684	12,873	Parke
Perry	.123	18,981	18,899	15,841	7,209	34,807	300,680	.0054	174,572	50	26,352	52	4,644	24	24,858	16,295	14,282	Perry
Pike**	.125	13,037	12,837	16,230	5,308	33,050	211,590	.0032	57,013	16	...	...	...	...	5,175	6,067	11,039	Pike
Porter*	.127	156,536	146,798	21,744	57,680	48,830	3,403,750	.0533	1,548,340	440	331,004	658	21,895	115	176,794	119,944	115,214	Porter
Posey*	.129	26,837	27,061	19,185	10,235	41,556	514,880	.0082	221,061	63	7,964	16	1,154	6	19,752	12,486	21,313	Posey
Pulaski	.131	13,893	13,755	15,430	5,250	33,623	214,370	.0036	93,306	26	...	...	1,851	10	11,182	7,198	10,702	Pulaski
Putnam*	.133	37,059	36,019	14,873	12,353	36,912	551,190	.0099	301,329	86	55,484	110	4,051	21	48,278	16,847	25,482	Putnam
Randolph	.135	26,547	27,401	16,000	10,638	33,148	424,740	.0070	179,798	51	17,817	35	2,406	13	28,659	10,180	20,762	Randolph
Ripley	.137	27,851	26,523	17,542	10,364	38,780	488,560	.0085	282,103	80	13,490	27	1,901	10	43,014	19,656	21,410	Ripley
Rush	.139	17,960	18,261	16,560	6,840	35,866	297,420	.0050	140,779	40	19,058	38	...	...	19,485	11,470	13,676	Rush
St. Joseph*	.141	266,795	265,559	15,977	92,598	38,171	4,262,660	.0870	3,750,271	1,065	723,593	1,439	153,610	808	377,992	263,481	183,425	St. Joseph
Scott**	.143	23,934	22,960	15,788	9,462	32,940	377,860	.0068	221,618	63	50,247	100	...	...	21,198	16,519	19,081	Scott
Shelby*	.145	43,564	43,445	18,616	16,425	40,765	810,970	.0139	454,210	129	49,830	99	7,005	37	50,425	19,104	33,454	Shelby
Spencer	.147	20,210	20,391	18,817	7,871	40,105	380,300	.0059	142,988	41	...	...	...	...	22,374	3,888	16,729	Spencer
Starke	.149	22,110	23,556	17,085	8,775	35,454	377,750	.0060	141,238	40	15,648	31	1,137	6	27,212	7,280	16,899	Starke
Steuben**	.151	33,890	33,214	19,366	13,139	41,101	656,330	.0134	635,917	181	95,320	190	55,366	291	79,091	13,592	25,419	Steuben
Sullivan*	.153	21,955	21,751	13,627	7,808	31,651	299,190	.0052	131,295	37	17,964	36	2,244	12	14,681	5,756	15,490	Sullivan
Switzerland	.155	9,665	9,065	17,004	3,838	35,632	164,340	.0023	24,428	7	...	...	...	...	4,447	2,523	7,834	Switzerland
Tippecanoe*	.157	152,590	148,955	17,301	59,618	36,493	2,640,000	.0501	1,978,697	562	503,198	1,001	84,232	443	165,074	104,284	110,920	Tippecanoe
Tipton*	.159	16,474	16,577	20,846	6,379	44,663	343,420	.0055	159,923	45	4,224	8	...	...	17,635	12,616	13,056	Tipton
Union	.161	7,200	7,349	17,297	2,918	35,455	124,540	.0019	41,736	12	...	...	...	...	9,464	2,452	6,036	Union
Vanderburgh*	.163	173,036	171,922	17,447	70,876	35,469	3,019,030	.0673	3,447,991	979	679,251	1,351	194,714	1,025	317,270	166,072	120,204	Vanderburgh
Vermillion*	.165	16,339	16,788	16,415	6,598	33,666	268,200	.0046	142,682	41	18,402	37	1,175	6	13,072	5,508	12,956	Vermillion
Vigo*	.167	102,739	105,848	15,059	40,269	31,801	1,547,130	.0459	2,993,089	850	501,160	997	112,107	590	157,408	70,807	70,629	Vigo
Wabash**	.169	33,885	34,960	17,571	13,008	37,850	595,400	.0105	356,297	101	45,017	90	25,401	134	39,723	23,432	25,081	Wabash
Warren	.171	8,891	8,419	18,115	3,370	39,303	161,060	.0023	39,442	11	...	...	...	...	8,018	...	7,194	Warren
Warrick*	.173	56,136	52,383	20,056	20,709	44,900	1,125,870	.0160	282,561	80	15,965	32	...	...	61,245	21,798	44,600	Warrick
Washington*	.175	27,951	27,223	15,923	10,584	35,042	445,070	.0077	227,894	65	2,155	4	1,946	10	23,094	13,089	21,695	Washington
Wayne**	.177	69,687	71,097	16,016	27,587	33,502	1,116,110	.0226	966,372	274	202,095	402	21,986	116	126,776	46,840	49,961	Wayne
Wells*	.179	28,181	27,600	18,512	10,518	41,000	521,690	.0085	241,702	69	15,640	31	4,360	23	43,751	18,771	21,551	Wells
White	.181	24,705	25,267	18,518	9,887	38,139	457,490	.0083	316,677	90	29,262	58	5,211	27	42,797	13,210	19,156	White
Whitley*	.183	32,508	30,707	19,187	12,120	42,388	623,720	.0105	334,510	95	42,801	85	3,906	21	52,875	19,003	24,570	Whitley
Indiana Total		**6,270,352**	**6,080,485**	**18,110**	**2,359,291**	**39,519**	**113,552,990**	**2.0815**	**78,806,901**	**22,383**	**13,563,530**	**26,973**	**2,846,082**	**14,983**	**8,038,084**	**4,764,374**	**4,558,595**	**Indiana**

Iowa (IA; Code 19; 99 Counties)

County or County Equivalent	FIPS County Code	Population: Estimate 7/1/05	Population: Census 4/1/00	Per Capita Income 2004	Households Estimate 7/1/05	Median Household Income 2004	Disposable Income 2004 ($1,000)	Market Ability Index 2004	Total Retail Sales: 2004 Sales ($1,000)	Total Retail Sales: Ranally Sales Units	General Merchandise: 2004 Sales ($1,000)	General Merchandise: Ranally Sales Units	Apparel Store: 2004 Sales ($1,000)	Apparel Store: Ranally Sales Units	Food Store Sales 2004 ($1,000)	Health & Drug Store 2004 ($1,000)	Passenger Car Registrations 2004	County or County Equivalent
Adair	.001	7,823	8,243	17,659	3,372	33,455	138,150	.0024	74,286	21	2,194	4	...	...	10,755	4,320	7,177	Adair
Adams	.003	4,325	4,482	14,775	1,793	29,599	63,900	.0010	18,606	5	...	...	...	...	2,530	...	4,079	Adams
Allamakee	.005	14,567	14,675	15,585	5,735	32,413	227,020	.0041	134,447	38	6,316	13	3,578	19	23,869	6,577	12,044	Allamakee
Appanoose	.007	13,552	13,721	13,771	5,598	27,279	186,630	.0034	106,666	30	28,525	57	3,466	18	19,625	4,092	11,431	Appanoose
Audubon	.009	6,281	6,830	16,383	2,704	31,204	102,900	.0019	64,295	18	1,972	4	...	...	5,710	1,232	5,654	Audubon
Benton*	.011	26,911	25,308	17,852	9,926	39,870	480,410	.0077	198,146	56	8,911	18	2,281	12	18,987	5,284	22,891	Benton
Black Hawk*	.013	125,273	128,012	16,930	49,292	35,428	2,120,890	.0423	1,814,899	515	309,770	616	58,825	310	210,206	103,938	107,035	Black Hawk
Boone**	.015	26,281	26,224	18,600	10,465	38,262	488,830	.0081	241,141	68	41,397	82	2,992	16	31,574	13,180	22,419	Boone
Bremer*	.017	23,518	23,325	17,894	8,969	38,412	420,840	.0068	177,321	50	20,159	40	2,858	15	28,386	8,863	19,735	Bremer
Buchanan	.019	20,777	21,093	16,876	7,931	36,083	350,640	.0064	227,437	65	30,143	60	4,550	24	18,784	3,759	16,628	Buchanan
Buena Vista**	.021	20,184	20,411	14,561	7,216	33,433	293,890	.0059	228,587	65	34,841	69	7,720	41	27,064	8,239	14,377	Buena Vista
Butler	.023	14,884	15,305	16,767	6,000	34,053	249,560	.0039	80,635	23	3,282	7	...	...	8,308	2,736	13,646	Butler
Calhoun	.025	10,407	11,115	15,943	4,313	31,609	165,920	.0028	80,782	23	...	...	...	...	7,417	2,457	9,056	Calhoun
Carroll	.027	20,827	21,421	17,103	8,322	35,104	356,210	.0071	303,686	86	47,878	95	10,497	55	47,959	11,958	16,751	Carroll
Cass	.029	14,155	14,684	16,208	5,901	31,831	229,420	.0043	158,047	45	16,147	32	4,461	23	27,191	10,454	11,942	Cass
Cedar	.031	18,275	18,187	18,867	7,142	39,571	344,790	.0052	111,354	32	14,637	29	...	...	14,489	...	16,348	Cedar
Cerro Gordo**	.033	44,653	46,447	17,607	18,867	34,330	786,210	.0166	789,180	224	202,959	404	18,200	96	87,006	16,573	36,515	Cerro Gordo
Cherokee	.035	12,250	13,035	17,318	5,210	33,399	212,140	.0038	132,637	38	13,390	27	2,077	11	20,423	11,448	10,869	Cherokee
Chickasaw	.037	12,463	13,095	17,850	5,095	35,704	222,460	.0036	91,709	26	6,565	13	1,169	6	14,326	5,376	11,213	Chickasaw
Clarke	.039	9,228	9,133	15,522	3,595	32,758	143,240	.0025	75,462	21	7,992	16	...	...	18,523	1,267	7,755	Clarke
Clay**	.041	16,737	17,372	17,697	7,195	33,721	296,200	.0062	296,843	84	40,569	81	18,482	97	36,093	11,853	14,255	Clay
Clayton	.043	18,164	18,678	16,232	7,483	32,279	294,840	.0052	166,395	47	1,805	4	1,426	8	13,691	6,517	16,016	Clayton
Clinton**	.045	49,623	50,149	17,325	19,830	35,453	859,730	.0155	547,988	156	68,473	136	9,465	50	79,924	35,370	39,446	Clinton
Crawford	.047	16,870	16,942	14,618	6,274	32,184	246,600	.0045	141,416	40	19,337	38	2,507	13	27,122	6,215	13,227	Crawford
Dallas*	.049	50,179	40,750	19,241	17,850	45,130	965,490	.0145	319,554	91	9,322	19	1,917	10	33,689	8,068	39,161	Dallas
Davis	.051	8,594	8,541	14,387	3,204	31,839	123,640	.0021	55,088	16	6,130	12	...	...	5,173	4,758	6,962	Davis
Decatur	.053	8,535	8,689	12,368	3,254	26,633	105,560	.0018	38,008	11	1,604	3	...	...	8,543	3,376	6,635	Decatur
Delaware	.055	18,001	18,404	16,162	6,743	35,475	290,930	.0050	148,180	42	21,158	42	1,613	8	21,770	9,188	14,938	Delaware
Des Moines**	.057	40,609	42,351	17,827	16,908	35,281	723,920	.0148	672,146	191	151,494	301	20,420	107	118,444	31,742	33,289	Des Moines
Dickinson**	.059	16,443	16,424	20,039	7,294	36,922	329,500	.0062	263,603	75	35,802	71	7,163	38	34,869	10,905	14,695	Dickinson
Dubuque*	.061	91,167	89,143	17,393	34,683	37,482	1,585,710	.0307	1,266,703	360	217,773	433	34,204	180	145,758	78,435	67,321	Dubuque
Emmet	.063	10,581	11,027	15,912	4,345	31,845	168,370	.0030	91,696	26	5,290	11	1,120	6	18,052	6,139	8,991	Emmet
Fayette	.065	21,084	22,008	15,442	8,603	31,045	325,580	.0061	214,721	61	19,719	39	3,153	17	25,343	11,344	17,620	Fayette
Floyd	.067	16,410	16,900	16,200	6,583	33,012	265,850	.0047	149,315	42	20,154	40	2,993	16	28,791	...	13,817	Floyd
Franklin	.069	10,700	10,704	16,213	4,173	34,083	173,480	.0029	74,543	21	3,409	7	...	...	12,499	3,555	9,015	Franklin
Fremont	.071	7,708	8,010	17,867	3,119	36,055	137,720	.0020	37,144	11	...	...	...	...	4,117	6,077	6,755	Fremont
Greene	.073	9,847	10,366	16,353	4,078	32,525	161,030	.0025	55,213	16	5,700	11	...	...	9,695	4,596	8,368	Greene
Grundy*	.075	12,337	12,369	18,756	5,059	37,330	231,390	.0036	93,190	26	...	...	...	...	8,939	5,527	10,782	Grundy
Guthrie*	.077	11,570	11,353	16,931	4,627	34,840	195,890	.0032	79,376	23	...	...	...	...	6,786	4,793	10,205	Guthrie
Hamilton	.079	16,250	16,438	18,096	6,591	36,429	294,060	.0046	115,388	33	9,866	20	1,526	8	19,248	6,920	13,321	Hamilton
Hancock	.081	11,732	12,100	17,727	4,734	35,820	207,970	.0032	70,458	20	3,718	7	1,011	5	10,576	3,760	10,532	Hancock
Hardin	.083	17,900	18,812	17,036	7,430	33,639	304,950	.0055	192,190	55	26,858	53	1,396	7	29,480	8,467	15,255	Hardin
Harrison*	.085	15,710	15,666	17,230	6,168	35,981	270,690	.0052	211,825	60	2,252	4	1,094	6	13,880	9,851	13,588	Harrison
Henry	.087	20,212	20,336	16,658	7,495	36,765	336,690	.0062	224,469	64	26,440	53	2,583	14	22,389	6,203	15,630	Henry
Howard	.089	9,754	9,932	16,317	3,912	33,197	159,160	.0026	67,232	19	3,465	7	...	...	12,502	5,197	8,512	Howard
Humboldt	.091	9,931	10,381	18,918	4,285	35,817	187,870	.0031	93,032	26	7,485	15	2,002	11	22,368	1,574	9,024	Humboldt
Ida	.093	7,345	7,837	17,016	3,084	33,251	124,980	.0021	57,337	16	5,255	10	1,427	8	8,576	3,452	6,453	Ida
Iowa	.095	16,124	15,671	17,837	6,135	38,307	287,610	.0051	182,144	52	1,029	2	46,599	245	20,303	7,171	13,419	Iowa
Jackson	.097	20,203	20,296	16,100	8,090	32,954	325,260	.0058	194,415	55	21,465	43	1,822	10	34,512	7,682	17,134	Jackson
Jasper**	.099	38,018	37,213	18,247	14,570	38,874	693,720	.0120	405,303	115	43,655	87	6,207	33	59,506	27,465	30,742	Jasper
Jefferson	.101	15,888	16,181	16,392	6,666	32,147	260,430	.0059	301,604	86	79,499	158	2,248	12	48,742	10,763	13,046	Jefferson
Johnson*	.103	117,205	111,006	19,117	48,430	37,935	2,240,610	.0413	1,638,902	465	237,604	473	56,364	297	277,736	76,779	93,223	Johnson
Jones*	.105	20,456	20,221	15,887	7,435	35,840	324,990	.0056	167,812	48	21,113	42	...	...	18,240	5,476	16,267	Jones
Keokuk	.107	11,318	11,400	15,481	4,416	32,435	175,210	.0033	114,015	32	...	...	...	...	4,373	...	9,764	Keokuk
Kossuth	.109	16,036	17,163	16,663	6,728	32,631	267,210	.0050	187,482	53	18,515	37	3,591	19	28,536	4,993	14,327	Kossuth
Lee**	.111	35,939	38,052	17,388	14,841	34,695	624,900	.0116	434,025	123	61,843	123	12,414	65	68,713	19,741	29,907	Lee
Linn*	.113	198,432	191,701	21,505	81,755	42,720	4,267,200	.0754	2,921,835	830	477,656	950	121,799	641	351,974	165,571	163,703	Linn
Louisa**	.115	12,312	12,183	16,137	4,430	36,623	198,680	.0030	52,530	15	...	...	...	...	6,906	...	9,912	Louisa
Lucas	.117	9,606	9,422	13,915	3,712	30,000	133,670	.0025	76,122	22	9,428	19	...	...	12,295	1,177	8,004	Lucas
Lyon	.119	11,711	11,763	16,088	4,397	35,215	188,410	.0030	71,783	20	1,257	2	1,623	9	11,001	5,040	10,085	Lyon
Madison*	.121	15,007	14,019	17,639	5,537	40,445	264,710	.0042	109,591	31	7,089	14	...	...	19,626	6,046	12,807	Madison
Mahaska**	.123	21,924	22,335	17,392	8,861	35,379	381,300	.0068	235,990	67	36,200	72	8,228	43	39,053	10,089	18,218	Mahaska
Marion**	.125	32,782	32,052	18,633	12,548	39,904	610,820	.0105	353,238	100	32,430	64	5,733	30	47,709	14,226	27,147	Marion
Marshall**	.127	39,206	39,311	17,232	15,234	36,240	675,600	.0118	384,582	109	73,089	145	21,684	114	61,163	23,609	31,051	Marshall
Mills*	.129	15,093	14,547	17,186	5,315	39,977	259,390	.0038	65,815	19	1,004	2	...	...	13,217	4,003	11,895	Mills
Mitchell	.131	10,855	10,874	15,551	4,205	33,065	168,810	.0029	84,979	24	...	...	1,135	6	10,933	5,437	9,154	Mitchell
Monona	.133	9,679	10,020	16,424	4,120	31,628	158,970	.0030	116,663	33	8,888	18	...	...	12,776	9,685	8,434	Monona
Monroe	.135	7,770	8,016	15,968	3,101	32,874	124,070	.0022	72,081	20	5,123	10	...	...	12,279	3,713	7,017	Monroe
Montgomery	.137	11,050	11,771	16,348	4,669	31,606	180,650	.0031	94,012	27	11,124	22	1,333	7	21,226	7,665	9,040	Montgomery
Muscatine**	.139	42,367	41,722	17,958	15,917	39,074	760,820	.0136	481,437	137	84,592	168	10,493	55	69,154	25,315	32,547	Muscatine
O'Brien	.141	14,435	15,102	16,851	5,887	33,947	243,250	.0046	180,269	51	8,940	18	3,930	21	22,643	9,276	12,104	O'Brien
Osceola	.143	6,686	7,003	15,936	2,651	32,867	106,550	.0017	42,306	12	...	...	...	...	4,832	4,705	5,699	Osceola
Page	.145	15,994	16,976	16,497	6,448	33,517	263,860	.0048	163,104	46	29,458	59	2,921	15	26,631	7,738	12,726	Page
Palo Alto	.147	9,482	10,147	16,489	4,057	31,494	156,350	.0027	81,853	23	4,735	9	...	...	9,842	3,660	8,436	Palo Alto
Plymouth	.149	24,707	24,849	18,345	9,456	39,368	453,250	.0077	248,977	71	27,813	55	3,230	17	30,926	8,156	20,678	Plymouth
Pocahontas	.151	8,037	8,662	16,507	3,404	31,841	132,670	.0021	42,916	12	...	...	...	...	7,422	...	7,111	Pocahontas
Polk*	.153	397,152	374,601	20,326	154,982	43,130	8,072,550	.1430	5,406,360	1,535	796,696	1,584	239,220	1,259	708,435	270,374	331,172	Polk
Pottawattamie*	.155	88,801	87,704	18,032	34,845	37,810	1,601,300	.0316	1,368,063	388	151,563	301	39,848	210	141,312	77,960	69,247	Pottawattamie
Poweshiek	.157	19,018	18,815	17,056	7,364	35,978	324,380	.0062	251,326	71	24,615	49	1,524	8	33,546	7,994	14,959	Poweshiek
Ringgold	.159	5,276	5,469	14,111	2,201	27,589	74,450	.0014	44,242	13	...	...	...	...	5,701	...	4,875	Ringgold
Sac	.161	10,523	11,529	17,468	4,806	31,291	183,820	.0031	94,371	27	...	...	...	...	10,184	...	10,046	Sac
Scott*	.163	159,953	158,668	19,406	63,375	40,371	3,104,040	.0591	2,499,972	710	407,668	811	113,806	599	262,350	142,960	122,349	Scott
Shelby	.165	12,642	13,173	17,125	4,970	35,667	216,490	.0039	139,426	40	8,398	17	1,197	6	21,071	6,748	10,711	Shelby
Sioux	.167	32,252	31,589	15,366	10,747	37,668	495,600	.0102	430,918	122	29,354	58	4,058	21	47,625	12,999	23,095	Sioux
Story*	.169	80,417	79,981	17,793	30,803	38,306	1,430,830	.0255	892,888	254	173,052	344	38,747	204	132,989	33,762	63,249	Story
Tama	.171	17,756	18,103	16,597	6,835	35,474	294,700	.0048	116,636	33	6,267	12	...	...	18,689	6,430	14,927	Tama
Taylor	.173	6,624	6,958	14,988	2,751	29,762	99,280	.0016	31,671	9	...	...	...	...	4,786	...	6,280	Taylor
Union	.175	11,732	12,309	16,446	5,198	30,798	192,950	.0037	138,835	39	28,253	56	1,852	10	28,052	4,295	10,531	Union

Source: Devonshire Associates Ltd. and Scan/US, Inc. 2005. ...Data less than 1,000. (d) Data not available.
* Component of a Metropolitan Core Based Statistical Area.
** Component of a Micropolitan Core Based Statistical Area.

Continued on next page

Counties: Population/Income/Sales, *Continued*

County or County Equivalent	FIPS County Code	Population Estimate 7/1/05	Population Census 4/1/00	Per Capita Income 2004	Households Estimate 7/1/05	Median Household Income 2004	Disposable Income 2004 ($1,000)	Market Ability Index 2004	Total Retail Sales 2004 Sales ($1,000)	Total Retail Sales Ranally Sales Units	General Merchandise 2004 Sales ($1,000)	General Merchandise Ranally Sales Units	Apparel Store 2004 Sales ($1,000)	Apparel Store Ranally Sales Units	Food Store Sales 2004 ($1,000)	Health & Drug Store 2004 ($1,000)	Passenger Car Registrations 2004	County or County Equivalent
Van Buren	177	7,701	7,809	14,692	3,118	30,040	113,140	.0017	24,864	7	...	...	...	...	2,543	...	6,755	Van Buren
Wapello**	179	35,794	36,051	15,103	14,416	31,012	540,610	.0105	397,459	113	94,802	189	14,750	78	58,103	20,882	28,624	Wapello
Warren*	181	43,068	40,671	20,127	15,490	46,238	866,840	.0139	403,107	114	33,824	67	1,771	9	51,836	17,126	34,855	Warren
Washington*	183	21,605	20,670	16,739	8,060	36,655	361,640	.0064	205,304	58	20,603	41	4,347	23	30,408	7,623	16,795	Washington
Wayne	185	6,607	6,730	14,297	2,759	28,070	94,460	.0016	38,771	11	1,638	3	...	...	5,158	1,468	6,042	Wayne
Webster**	187	39,183	40,235	16,281	15,636	33,613	637,930	.0130	560,513	159	127,904	254	12,344	65	71,056	29,049	31,354	Webster
Winnebago	189	11,267	11,723	18,266	4,687	36,052	205,800	.0034	99,380	28	5,463	11	...	...	18,593	6,253	9,619	Winnebago
Winneshiek	191	21,175	21,310	16,169	7,694	36,341	342,380	.0065	247,225	70	37,018	74	6,522	34	34,509	4,624	16,517	Winneshiek
Woodbury*	193	102,793	103,877	16,611	38,329	36,492	1,707,520	.0343	1,468,006	417	239,810	477	63,995	337	184,847	53,550	74,312	Woodbury
Worth**	195	7,600	7,909	17,404	3,147	34,408	132,270	.0020	37,021	11	...	...	...	...	6,509	...	7,001	Worth
Wright	197	13,486	14,334	17,875	5,720	34,524	241,060	.0035	61,307	17	4,123	8	...	...	10,961	4,607	11,582	Wright
Iowa Total		**2,951,374**	**2,926,324**	**18,031**	**1,163,398**	**37,459**	**53,214,860**	**.9627**	**35,315,827**	**10,025**	**5,012,123**	**9,964**	**1,112,992**	**5,859**	**4,662,985**	**1,707,580**	**2,409,872**	**Iowa**

Kansas (KS; Code 20; 105 Counties)

County or County Equivalent	FIPS County Code	Population Estimate 7/1/05	Population Census 4/1/00	Per Capita Income 2004	Households Estimate 7/1/05	Median Household Income 2004	Disposable Income 2004 ($1,000)	Market Ability Index 2004	Total Retail Sales 2004 Sales ($1,000)	Total Retail Sales Ranally Sales Units	General Merchandise 2004 Sales ($1,000)	General Merchandise Ranally Sales Units	Apparel Store 2004 Sales ($1,000)	Apparel Store Ranally Sales Units	Food Store Sales 2004 ($1,000)	Health & Drug Store 2004 ($1,000)	Passenger Car Registrations 2004	County or County Equivalent
Allen	001	13,664	14,385	15,222	5,704	30,206	208,000	.0041	165,505	47	31,193	62	4,001	21	27,456	13,363	11,632	Allen
Anderson	003	8,295	8,110	14,978	3,224	31,517	124,240	.0023	75,343	21	2,049	4	...	...	7,572	3,228	6,801	Anderson
Atchison**	005	16,813	16,774	14,826	6,243	32,769	249,270	.0045	145,824	41	28,863	57	2,639	14	27,787	11,625	12,283	Atchison
Barber	007	4,892	5,307	17,484	2,200	31,864	85,530	.0015	54,014	15	3,492	7	...	...	8,214	5,117	4,534	Barber
Barton**	009	27,140	28,205	15,504	11,306	30,672	420,790	.0085	348,262	99	58,569	116	8,615	45	50,733	20,002	22,098	Barton
Bourbon	011	15,011	15,379	15,046	6,238	30,054	225,850	.0041	136,433	39	32,584	65	1,631	9	22,083	8,174	12,494	Bourbon
Brown	013	10,274	10,724	15,503	4,318	30,314	159,280	.0030	108,709	31	15,935	32	...	...	18,047	6,083	8,336	Brown
Butler*	015	62,010	59,482	19,207	23,163	42,318	1,191,020	.0189	507,592	144	52,175	104	4,581	24	81,420	12,114	50,860	Butler
Chase**	017	2,944	3,030	16,073	1,232	30,681	47,320	.0007	9,997	3	...	...	...	...	1,676	...	2,657	Chase
Chautauqua	019	4,104	4,359	14,773	1,821	28,101	60,630	.0009	15,939	5	...	...	...	...	3,791	3,675	3,992	Chautauqua
Cherokee	021	21,484	22,605	14,945	9,014	29,517	321,080	.0053	121,109	34	14,042	28	...	...	18,548	9,293	18,434	Cherokee
Cheyenne	023	2,884	3,165	16,359	1,331	29,308	47,180	.0008	17,523	5	...	...	...	...	4,623	...	2,765	Cheyenne
Clark	025	2,309	2,390	16,739	982	32,299	38,650	.0006	9,330	3	...	...	...	...	2,094	1,109	2,053	Clark
Clay	027	8,399	8,822	16,683	3,580	32,045	140,120	.0027	101,836	29	11,982	24	1,492	8	13,996	5,359	7,508	Clay
Cloud	029	9,665	10,268	15,574	4,077	30,442	150,520	.0028	94,647	27	14,399	29	1,969	10	12,961	5,582	8,378	Cloud
Coffey	031	8,814	8,865	17,806	3,591	35,638	156,940	.0026	74,251	21	...	...	...	...	7,894	4,592	8,196	Coffey
Comanche	033	1,887	1,967	15,437	844	28,327	29,130	.0005	11,756	3	...	...	...	...	2,829	...	1,752	Comanche
Cowley**	035	35,495	36,291	16,065	14,269	32,923	570,220	.0102	338,208	96	47,268	94	8,255	43	61,778	29,659	28,094	Cowley
Crawford**	037	38,321	38,242	14,321	15,890	28,466	548,790	.0107	395,428	112	140,485	279	8,476	45	54,024	11,603	30,917	Crawford
Decatur	039	3,215	3,472	15,894	1,470	28,590	51,100	.0008	12,749	4	...	...	...	...	3,883	1,142	3,088	Decatur
Dickinson	041	19,123	19,344	17,279	7,904	34,517	330,430	.0057	177,025	50	8,382	17	...	...	30,097	8,703	16,597	Dickinson
Doniphan*	043	8,113	8,249	14,892	3,173	31,148	120,820	.0021	55,331	16	...	...	...	...	8,116	1,055	6,614	Doniphan
Douglas*	045	103,269	99,962	17,848	42,198	35,969	1,843,120	.0326	1,126,641	320	164,334	327	62,103	327	202,198	54,513	81,312	Douglas
Edwards	047	3,181	3,449	16,055	1,433	29,576	51,070	.0007	10,701	3	...	...	...	...	5,160	...	2,878	Edwards
Elk	049	3,100	3,261	14,865	1,430	26,402	46,080	.0007	5,571	2	...	...	...	...	...	...	3,023	Elk
Ellis**	051	27,084	27,507	16,163	11,292	31,976	437,770	.0098	487,255	138	83,320	166	27,933	147	70,193	15,073	22,114	Ellis
Ellsworth	053	6,295	6,525	16,321	2,491	34,003	102,740	.0016	37,232	11	6,000	12	...	...	7,109	1,511	5,307	Ellsworth
Finney**	055	38,083	40,523	15,318	13,148	36,268	583,350	.0122	537,035	152	103,388	206	30,356	160	70,954	12,226	24,814	Finney
Ford**	057	33,216	32,458	14,663	11,074	36,091	487,050	.0104	459,917	131	89,752	178	13,009	68	42,413	11,443	21,224	Ford
Franklin*	059	26,406	24,784	16,877	9,929	36,770	445,650	.0079	265,412	75	97,875	195	2,156	11	26,203	11,191	21,110	Franklin
Geary**	061	25,042	27,947	15,664	10,513	30,882	392,270	.0073	256,847	73	58,195	116	1,957	10	43,880	3,101	18,510	Geary
Gove	063	2,769	3,068	17,815	1,252	32,372	49,330	.0009	29,902	8	...	...	...	...	5,094	1,817	2,977	Gove
Graham	065	2,738	2,946	16,687	1,251	30,153	45,690	.0008	28,924	8	...	...	...	...	5,038	1,898	2,762	Graham
Grant	067	7,668	7,909	16,930	2,805	38,018	129,820	.0023	80,488	23	10,731	21	...	...	17,134	3,974	5,580	Grant
Gray	069	6,062	5,904	16,044	2,123	37,541	97,260	.0016	40,651	12	...	...	...	...	3,899	1,755	4,500	Gray
Greeley	071	1,341	1,534	17,912	601	32,869	24,020	.0004	12,091	3	...	...	...	...	1,435	1,335	1,380	Greeley
Greenwood	073	7,475	7,673	15,160	3,221	29,220	113,320	.0019	45,838	13	4,403	9	...	...	6,397	3,570	6,848	Greenwood
Hamilton	075	2,709	2,670	14,895	1,057	31,191	40,350	.0007	20,013	6	...	...	...	...	3,138	1,251	2,206	Hamilton
Harper	077	6,157	6,536	15,253	2,715	28,482	93,910	.0016	40,523	12	2,746	5	...	...	6,245	3,762	5,596	Harper
Harvey*	079	34,021	32,869	17,941	13,026	38,512	610,360	.0100	278,951	79	56,535	112	14,616	77	61,034	12,407	26,398	Harvey
Haskell	081	4,163	4,307	16,212	1,520	36,346	67,490	.0010	14,216	4	...	...	...	...	1,365	...	3,168	Haskell
Hodgeman	083	2,172	2,085	15,244	806	33,577	33,110	.0006	15,920	5	...	...	...	...	5,127	...	1,922	Hodgeman
Jackson*	085	13,312	12,657	16,848	4,880	37,559	224,280	.0038	113,077	32	20,085	40	...	...	18,778	1,935	11,568	Jackson
Jefferson*	087	19,009	18,426	19,373	7,197	41,875	368,260	.0051	68,688	20	...	...	2,609	14	12,940	2,317	17,255	Jefferson
Jewell	089	3,251	3,791	18,136	1,670	28,973	58,960	.0008	10,879	3	...	...	...	...	2,508	...	3,589	Jewell
Johnson*	091	507,661	451,086	26,178	194,514	57,165	13,289,780	.2203	8,283,596	2,352	1,332,072	2,649	551,071	2,900	926,652	396,910	399,613	Johnson
Kearny	093	4,452	4,531	16,393	1,610	37,008	72,980	.0010	9,065	3	...	...	...	...	4,673	...	3,467	Kearny
Kingman	095	8,300	8,673	17,672	3,362	35,720	146,680	.0023	53,894	15	5,317	11	...	...	13,733	3,842	7,516	Kingman
Kiowa	097	3,044	3,278	16,583	1,351	30,870	50,480	.0008	23,741	7	...	...	2,131	11	3,363	4,671	2,709	Kiowa
Labette**	099	22,059	22,835	14,769	9,128	29,632	325,790	.0059	188,034	53	27,134	54	3,893	20	33,682	15,934	18,353	Labette
Lane	101	1,847	2,155	19,811	889	33,816	36,590	.0005	9,829	3	...	...	...	...	2,355	...	1,977	Lane
Leavenworth*	103	74,179	68,691	18,157	25,018	44,364	1,346,840	.0213	537,569	153	86,375	172	8,374	44	78,213	27,629	52,551	Leavenworth
Lincoln	105	3,473	3,578	15,301	1,498	29,446	53,140	.0008	18,047	5	...	...	...	...	3,795	1,143	3,307	Lincoln
Linn*	107	9,844	9,570	16,477	3,907	34,525	162,200	.0024	41,474	12	...	...	...	...	12,948	2,579	8,796	Linn
Logan	109	2,764	3,046	16,664	1,227	31,198	46,060	.0009	40,361	11	...	...	...	...	3,584	...	2,715	Logan
Lyon**	111	35,512	35,935	14,811	13,592	31,818	525,980	.0102	379,968	108	75,527	150	19,351	102	56,654	16,560	25,892	Lyon
McPherson**	113	29,232	29,554	18,426	11,537	38,033	538,640	.0090	275,411	78	34,161	68	3,976	21	24,163	7,915	24,053	McPherson
Marion	115	13,168	13,361	15,683	5,195	33,111	206,520	.0037	124,592	35	4,631	9	...	...	11,862	7,150	11,082	Marion
Marshall	117	10,244	10,965	16,279	4,403	31,172	166,760	.0031	115,300	33	27,669	55	2,080	11	16,491	2,426	9,261	Marshall
Meade	119	4,620	4,631	15,699	1,716	34,770	72,530	.0012	24,525	7	...	...	...	...	4,718	1,201	3,603	Meade
Miami*	121	29,658	28,351	19,552	11,010	43,566	579,860	.0098	319,657	91	33,661	67	2,960	16	119,478	16,398	25,348	Miami
Mitchell	123	6,545	6,932	16,651	2,783	31,996	108,980	.0023	107,936	31	6,564	13	...	...	12,145	4,658	5,812	Mitchell
Montgomery**	125	34,303	36,252	15,373	14,698	30,074	527,330	.0098	337,385	96	73,527	146	9,551	50	50,971	20,446	27,832	Montgomery
Morris	127	5,892	6,104	16,285	2,545	30,938	95,950	.0017	51,661	15	...	...	1,789	9	7,753	1,568	5,314	Morris
Morton	129	3,259	3,496	17,732	1,344	35,283	57,790	.0008	14,665	4	...	...	...	...	4,924	1,472	2,860	Morton
Nemaha	131	10,377	10,717	15,185	3,969	32,639	157,570	.0029	100,214	28	5,790	12	...	...	21,173	7,352	8,458	Nemaha
Neosho	133	16,372	16,997	15,321	6,693	30,930	250,840	.0053	232,956	66	33,841	67	8,257	43	42,241	10,090	13,931	Neosho
Ness	135	2,972	3,454	19,361	1,498	31,571	57,540	.0009	18,980	5	...	...	...	...	1,848	...	3,518	Ness
Norton	137	5,759	5,953	13,877	2,225	29,738	79,920	.0014	38,855	11	4,343	9	...	...	8,300	3,085	4,366	Norton
Osage*	139	16,950	16,712	17,363	6,724	36,054	294,300	.0044	81,894	23	...	...	...	...	13,588	4,798	15,404	Osage
Osborne	141	3,982	4,452	16,065	1,899	27,653	63,970	.0012	47,578	14	...	...	...	...	9,839	4,095	3,940	Osborne
Ottawa**	143	6,160	6,163	17,343	2,420	36,101	106,830	.0015	19,329	5	...	...	...	...	6,991	1,276	5,600	Ottawa
Pawnee	145	6,538	7,233	16,918	2,711	33,590	110,610	.0019	52,750	15	4,620	9	...	...	12,739	4,913	5,376	Pawnee
Phillips	147	5,446	6,001	18,076	2,468	32,795	98,440	.0016	41,050	12	6,277	12	...	...	9,500	1,772	5,387	Phillips
Pottawatomie**	149	18,976	18,209	17,388	7,169	37,551	329,960	.0055	156,115	44	1,037	2	3,071	16	62,011	8,535	16,075	Pottawatomie
Pratt	151	9,398	9,647	17,487	4,010	33,797	164,340	.0031	118,448	34	31,379	62	3,969	21	18,286	4,149	7,886	Pratt
Rawlins	153	2,750	2,966	16,905	1,248	30,647	46,490	.0007	15,167	4	...	...	...	...	4,333	...	2,651	Rawlins
Reno**	155	63,269	64,790	16,578	25,449	33,807	1,048,860	.0198	749,381	213	134,233	267	20,854	110	85,864	28,698	49,529	Reno
Republic	157	5,022	5,835	17,802	2,522	29,396	89,400	.0015	42,201	12	2,020	4	...	...	7,017	3,217	5,301	Republic
Rice	159	10,259	10,761	15,928	3,975	33,680	163,410	.0025	48,613	14	3,325	7	...	...	10,947	3,710	8,063	Rice
Riley**	161	63,042	62,843	13,427	22,703	30,921	846,440	.0173	668,767	190	151,168	301	37,265	196	55,109	19,568	45,973	Riley
Rooks	163	5,259	5,685	15,602	2,315	29,148	82,050	.0015	49,073	14	1,091	2	...	...	7,302	2,574	4,867	Rooks
Rush	165	3,381	3,551	16,356	1,533	29,779	55,300	.0009	17,358	5	...	...	...	...	5,394	...	3,378	Rush
Russell	167	6,688	7,370	16,086	3,117	28,489	107,580	.0018	49,805	14	5,188	10	...	...	8,394	3,688	6,409	Russell
Saline**	169	53,845	53,597	17,474	21,814	35,493	940,880	.0202	981,628	279	238,252	474	49,840	262	99,467	34,455	42,925	Saline
Scott	171	4,678	5,120	19,959	2,053	37,261	93,370	.0017	67,216	19	4,172	8	...	...	9,488	1,412	4,316	Scott
Sedgwick*	173	468,918	452,869	18,305	176,145	40,290	8,583,550	.1524	5,421,507	1,539	1,154,687	2,296	237,989	1,253	762,179	287,054	356,030	Sedgwick
Seward**	175	23,536	22,510	13,546	7,455	35,093	318,830	.0072	336,422	96	68,385	136	26,364	139	48,616	8,110	13,287	Seward
Shawnee*	177	172,022	169,871	19,403	71,180	38,725	3,337,700	.0609	2,376,520	675	545,020	1,084	78,894	415	274,053	169,017	130,392	Shawnee
Sheridan	179	2,595	2,813	17,067	1,145	31,716	44,290	.0008	23,588	7	...	...	...	...	3,733	1,644	2,618	Sheridan
Sherman	181	6,059	6,760	17,721	2,797	31,566	107,370	.0025	137,058	39	25,418	51	3,911	21	12,195	4,947	6,172	Sherman
Smith	183	4,069	4,536	15,778	1,935	27,394	64,200	.0011	29,331	8	1,941	4	...	...	7,349	2,151	4,244	Smith
Stafford	185	4,442	4,789	16,141	1,972	30,176	71,700	.0010	13,526	4	...	...	...	...	4,471	...	4,166	Stafford
Stanton	187	2,377	2,406	16,984	876	37,421	40,370	.0007	18,713	5	1,348	3	...	...	...	...	1,883	Stanton
Stevens	189	5,258	5,463	18,239	2,012	39,665	95,900	.0016	49,824	14	1,158	2	1,273	7	8,363	3,718	4,183	Stevens
Sumner*	191	24,833	25,946	18,108	9,968	37,083	449,680	.0068	145,639	41	22,560	45	1,482	8	26,227	3,297	21,671	Sumner
Thomas	193	7,804	8,180	17,518	3,208	35,124	136,710	.0027	110,143	31	24,327	48	6,327	33	18,424	3,865	6,726	Thomas
Trego	195	2,989	3,319	16,015	1,368	29,060	47,870	.0008	19,888	6	...	...	...	...	4,321	2,507	3,023	Trego
Wabaunsee*	197	6,806	6,885	18,841	2,686	39,175	128,230	.0018	25,662	7	...	...	...	...	1,306	...	6,534	Wabaunsee
Wallace	199	1,541	1,749	17,171	674	32,029	26,460	.0004	8,196	2	...	...	...	...	2,352	...	1,679	Wallace
Washington	201	5,980	6,483	15,251	2,652	28,233	91,200	.0014	23,742	7	...	...	...	...	4,795	...	5,563	Washington
Wichita	203	2,394	2,531	16,182	970	32,535	38,740	.0007	19,597	6	...	...	...	...	1,552	1,127	2,117	Wichita
Wilson	205	10,039	10,332	14,608	4,197	28,768	146,650	.0022	26,513	8	1,625	3	...	...	5,602	5,207	8,627	Wilson
Woodson	207	3,548	3,788	13,636	1,622	24,565	48,380	.0008	14,860	4	...	...	...	...	4,313	1,017	3,514	Woodson
Wyandotte*	209	156,403	157,882	15,004	59,434	32,455	2,346,690	.0415	1,239,856	352	143,451	285	19,209	101	200,516	80,117	101,392	Wyandotte
Kansas Total		**2,746,171**	**2,688,418**	**18,697**	**1,071,344**	**38,728**	**51,345,670**	**.9007**	**31,558,250**	**8,962**	**5,494,837**	**10,928**	**1,312,717**	**6,907**	**4,371,187**	**1,568,954**	**2,155,359**	**Kansas**

Kentucky (KY; Code 21; 120 Counties)

County or County Equivalent	FIPS County Code	Population Estimate 7/1/05	Population Census 4/1/00	Per Capita Income 2004	Households Estimate 7/1/05	Median Household Income 2004	Disposable Income 2004 ($1,000)	Market Ability Index 2004	Total Retail Sales 2004 Sales ($1,000)	Total Retail Sales Ranally Sales Units	General Merchandise 2004 Sales ($1,000)	General Merchandise Ranally Sales Units	Apparel Store 2004 Sales ($1,000)	Apparel Store Ranally Sales Units	Food Store Sales 2004 ($1,000)	Health & Drug Store 2004 ($1,000)	Passenger Car Registrations 2004	County or County Equivalent
Adair	001	17,625	17,244	11,247	6,555	23,412	198,230	.0038	99,045	28	19,589	39	...	...	10,999	12,119	12,142	Adair
Allen	003	18,589	17,800	14,303	6,912	30,102	265,880	.0043	83,519	24	5,106	10	...	...	13,653	10,671	13,133	Allen
Anderson**	005	20,199	19,111	20,682	7,757	41,474	417,750	.0059	102,997	29	15,847	32	...	...	11,302	10,818	16,945	Anderson
Ballard**	007	8,209	8,286	16,740	3,382	31,631	137,420	.0023	60,779	17	2,147	4	...	...	10,554	4,021	6,504	Ballard
Barren**	009	39,743	38,033	14,615	15,145	30,196	580,830	.0118	475,459	135	115,253	229	10,311	54	47,874	25,046	29,114	Barren
Bath**	011	11,651	11,085	12,301	4,488	25,000	143,320	.0025	51,288	15	1,509	3	...	...	7,990	4,916	8,458	Bath
Bell**	013	29,756	30,060	9,864	11,990	18,693	293,520	.0076	353,293	100	114,488	228	16,019	84	84,061	22,931	18,714	Bell
Boone*	015	103,836	85,991	22,966	37,771	50,442	2,384,710	.0473	2,297,575	652	521,144	1,036	99,678	525	127,548	79,841	77,188	Boone
Bourbon*	017	19,637	19,360	17,102	7,821	33,043	335,830	.0055	147,220	42	16,254	32	...	...	27,946	12,923	14,765	Bourbon
Boyd*	019	49,908	49,752	15,883	19,506	31,624	792,680	.0179	896,730	255	201,470	401	62,816	331	93,734	57,627	34,555	Boyd
Boyle**	021	27,990	27,697	16,496	10,749	33,349	461,720	.0091	377,663	107	99,297	197	18,919	100	30,544	16,996	19,361	Boyle
Bracken*	023	8,653	8,279	15,521	3,182	32,896	134,300	.0020	25,475	7	1,305	3	...	...	7,097	1,648	6,737	Bracken
Breathitt	025	15,664	16,100	9,834	6,265	18,863	154,040	.0033	111,578	32	24,263	48	2,223	12	15,182	10,848	9,971	Breathitt
Breckinridge	027	19,300	18,648	14,217	7,308	29,254	274,390	.0047	117,217	33	20,962	42	...	...	17,066	11,778	14,531	Breckinridge
Bullitt*	029	67,211	61,236	19,950	24,828	41,300	1,340,860	.0192	348,996	99	9,417	19	...	...	39,716	19,257	53,467	Bullitt
Butler	031	13,298	13,010	13,782	5,062	28,249	183,270	.0029	50,080	14	1,590	3	...	...	12,010	6,966	10,170	Butler
Caldwell	033	12,787	13,060	14,854	5,386	27,374	189,940	.0038	152,398	43	28,638	57	1,830	10	20,831	13,548	10,619	Caldwell
Calloway**	035	34,741	34,177	14,944	13,946	28,867	519,180	.0109	469,990	133	91,949	183	18,741	99	29,469	22,378	26,641	Calloway
Campbell*	037	87,132	88,616	19,938	34,166	39,877	1,737,270	.0281	839,385	238	105,261	209	25,274	133	180,994	60,966	61,284	Campbell
Carlisle	039	5,332	5,351	15,146	2,199	28,328	80,760	.0013	27,566	8	1,292	3	...	...	8,710	1,897	4,335	Carlisle
Carroll	041	10,323	10,155	16,642	3,878	34,875	171,800	.0036	164,947	47	4,599	9	5,790	30	21,400	9,901	7,029	Carroll
Carter	043	27,587	26,889	12,736	10,557	25,693	351,360	.0071	252,261	72	26,909	54	8,842	47	39,722	20,354	19,837	Carter
Casey	045	16,277	15,447	10,758	6,278	21,415	175,110	.0032	64,296	18	3,361	7	3,576	19	9,576	10,035	11,279	Casey
Christian*	047	70,255	72,265	13,817	25,226	30,281	970,720	.0183	595,466	169	119,315	237	23,697	125	52,076	36,016	44,509	Christian
Clark*	049	34,351	33,144	19,794	13,962	38,020	679,950	.0120	447,042	127	87,953	175	6,879	36	87,461	18,971	26,665	Clark
Clay	051	24,085	24,556	7,586	8,647	16,090	182,720	.0043	123,837	35	31,383	62	3,494	18	21,809	15,048	14,149	Clay
Clinton	053	9,568	9,634	10,593	4,033	19,235	101,350	.0020	56,162	16	2,310	5	...	...	13,726	8,702	7,533	Clinton
Crittenden	055	8,916	9,384	15,637	3,829	28,448	139,420	.0021	34,212	10	3,604	7	...	...	12,499	3,565	7,281	Crittenden
Cumberland	057	7,206	7,147	11,112	2,881	21,542	80,070	.0015	41,708	12	2,562	5	...	...	7,610	5,653	5,344	Cumberland
Daviess*	059	92,957	91,545	18,768	38,701	35,143	1,744,600	.0304	1,052,628	299	245,961	489	38,546	203	107,853	76,423	72,881	Daviess
Edmonson*	061	12,050	11,644	12,415	4,690	25,072	149,600	.0023	24,948	7	1,782	4	...	...	6,915	2,461	9,270	Edmonson
Elliott	063	6,960	6,748	10,256	2,664	20,808	71,380	.0012	13,944	4	...	...	...	...	3,556	3,055	4,852	Elliott
Estill	065	15,201	15,307	11,873	6,073	22,945	180,480	.0032	75,178	21	3,792	8	1,036	5	17,030	9,623	11,208	Estill
Fayette*	067	270,888	260,512	20,723	115,680	37,628	5,613,600	.1043	4,364,965	1,239	636,290	1,265	295,484	1,555	407,334	290,770	219,713	Fayette

Source: Devonshire Associates Ltd. and Scan/US, Inc. 2005. ...Data less than 1,000. (d) Data not available.
* Component of a Metropolitan Core Based Statistical Area.
** Component of a Micropolitan Core Based Statistical Area.

Counties: Population/Income/Sales, *Continued*

County or County Equivalent	FIPS County Code	Population Estimate 7/1/05	Population Census 4/1/00	Per Capita Income 2004	House-holds Estimate 7/1/05	Median Household Income 2004	Disposable Income 2004 ($1,000)	Market Ability Index 2004	Total Retail Sales 2004 Sales ($1,000)	Total Retail Sales Ranally Sales Units	General Merchandise 2004 Sales ($1,000)	General Merchandise Ranally Sales Units	Apparel Store 2004 Sales ($1,000)	Apparel Store Ranally Sales Units	Food Store Sales 2004 ($1,000)	Health & Drug Store 2004 ($1,000)	Passenger Car Regis-trations 2004	County or County Equivalent
Fleming	.069	14,724	13,792	12,608	5,306	27,313	185,640	.0038	145,093	41	4,020	8	...	...	12,129	8,708	10,192	Fleming
Floyd	.071	42,157	42,441	10,854	17,009	20,737	457,580	.0094	306,548	87	79,712	159	6,647	35	51,066	35,457	28,478	Floyd
Franklin**	.073	48,023	47,687	20,495	20,151	37,687	984,240	.0171	618,759	176	129,424	257	20,339	107	58,497	39,340	36,024	Franklin
Fulton**	.075	7,307	7,752	13,071	3,112	23,881	95,510	.0020	76,845	22	23,400	47	1,203	6	17,780	9,864	4,938	Fulton
Gallatin*	.077	8,122	7,870	15,948	2,894	34,828	129,530	.0019	25,613	7	1,882	4	...	...	4,659	1,164	5,664	Gallatin
Garrard	.079	16,590	14,792	14,678	5,701	32,669	243,500	.0036	41,817	12	1,310	3	...	...	10,095	6,316	11,313	Garrard
Grant*	.081	25,032	22,384	16,426	8,676	36,815	411,180	.0074	251,375	71	35,795	71	22,004	116	26,641	15,504	17,721	Grant
Graves**	.083	37,598	37,028	14,885	14,685	29,938	559,630	.0102	327,061	93	69,622	138	5,559	29	25,667	19,523	27,319	Graves
Grayson	.085	25,035	24,053	12,820	9,296	26,708	320,960	.0059	161,034	46	39,438	78	...	...	23,095	14,043	18,453	Grayson
Green	.087	11,931	11,518	12,116	4,528	25,062	144,560	.0024	42,365	12	2,479	5	...	...	7,368	6,636	8,852	Green
Greenup*	.089	37,186	36,891	15,477	14,380	30,921	575,520	.0086	128,544	37	6,404	13	...	...	24,347	19,678	27,660	Greenup
Hancock*	.091	8,450	8,392	17,111	3,178	35,245	144,590	.0022	41,208	12	2,376	5	...	...	10,210	3,176	6,869	Hancock
Hardin*	.093	96,438	94,174	17,383	36,142	35,813	1,676,340	.0309	1,155,873	328	288,129	573	64,576	340	79,097	52,997	71,563	Hardin
Harlan	.095	31,613	33,202	9,978	13,180	18,271	315,420	.0064	182,064	52	45,302	90	5,500	29	38,853	15,890	21,439	Harlan
Harrison	.097	18,398	17,983	16,973	6,999	34,893	312,270	.0051	138,181	39	25,942	52	2,029	11	27,388	14,330	13,897	Harrison
Hart	.099	18,189	17,445	11,664	6,684	24,963	212,160	.0038	84,542	24	3,804	8	5,534	29	15,987	11,390	12,718	Hart
Henderson*	.101	45,470	44,829	17,460	18,074	34,504	793,920	.0141	486,650	138	74,957	149	14,643	77	52,604	44,865	32,701	Henderson
Henry*	.103	15,830	15,060	17,563	6,039	35,895	278,030	.0043	93,366	27	8,397	17	...	...	8,974	8,030	12,076	Henry
Hickman	.105	5,147	5,262	16,598	2,182	30,358	85,430	.0012	17,701	5	...	...	...	...	6,919	2,318	4,100	Hickman
Hopkins**	.107	46,972	46,519	15,190	18,717	29,723	713,510	.0134	477,177	135	107,466	214	29,207	154	53,531	42,327	34,411	Hopkins
Jackson	.109	13,664	13,495	10,028	5,321	19,951	137,020	.0025	44,367	13	6,030	12	...	...	7,268	7,575	9,833	Jackson
Jefferson*	.111	701,817	693,604	19,001	277,510	37,153	13,335,190	.2434	9,403,155	2,670	1,637,657	3,257	454,412	2,392	1,032,431	625,704	493,749	Jefferson
Jessamine*	.113	42,965	39,041	17,888	15,742	37,555	768,560	.0150	635,001	180	73,570	146	10,833	57	53,343	17,561	30,943	Jessamine
Johnson	.115	23,704	23,445	11,738	8,946	24,143	278,240	.0061	241,269	69	62,443	124	8,497	45	34,948	8,824	15,840	Johnson
Kenton*	.117	152,794	151,464	20,861	60,136	41,091	3,187,390	.0478	1,152,402	327	115,197	229	31,079	164	261,812	128,446	108,592	Kenton
Knott	.119	17,716	17,649	10,062	6,821	20,234	178,250	.0032	53,033	15	1,491	3	...	...	16,741	6,944	11,869	Knott
Knox	.121	31,664	31,795	9,312	12,527	18,294	294,860	.0071	278,323	79	49,452	98	22,978	121	44,072	18,382	20,764	Knox
Larue*	.123	13,413	13,373	16,760	5,541	31,543	224,800	.0033	54,096	15	1,256	2	...	...	13,002	10,410	11,306	Larue
Laurel**	.125	57,008	52,715	12,283	20,658	26,181	700,240	.0151	603,144	171	159,858	318	13,632	72	44,153	21,540	38,226	Laurel
Lawrence	.127	16,075	15,569	9,979	5,985	20,665	160,410	.0033	92,045	26	12,560	25	1,884	10	22,822	14,182	10,900	Lawrence
Lee	.129	7,858	7,916	9,300	3,015	18,587	73,080	.0014	30,238	9	2,747	5	...	...	6,419	6,097	5,249	Lee
Leslie	.131	12,024	12,401	9,760	4,991	17,913	117,360	.0022	43,943	12	3,604	7	1,020	5	12,729	12,103	8,623	Leslie
Letcher	.133	24,549	25,277	10,958	10,114	20,460	269,020	.0051	127,333	36	29,853	59	7,153	38	28,899	22,007	17,930	Letcher
Lewis**	.135	13,510	14,092	11,424	5,452	21,795	154,340	.0025	27,516	8	...	...	...	...	7,132	5,063	9,997	Lewis
Lincoln**	.137	25,234	23,361	12,760	9,806	25,694	321,980	.0053	92,770	26	13,023	26	...	...	17,317	2,187	18,750	Lincoln
Livingston**	.139	9,709	9,804	16,204	4,024	30,567	157,320	.0023	31,350	9	...	...	...	...	9,095	5,306	8,404	Livingston
Logan	.141	27,005	26,573	15,371	10,307	31,480	415,100	.0070	183,247	52	30,890	61	1,334	7	25,743	15,214	19,992	Logan
Lyon	.143	8,156	8,080	14,212	2,917	30,979	115,910	.0020	51,359	15	...	...	10,286	54	5,903	3,399	5,728	Lyon
McCracken**	.145	64,213	65,514	17,931	27,510	32,641	1,151,400	.0256	1,319,616	375	397,508	791	91,698	483	87,002	69,239	48,780	McCracken
McCreary	.147	17,152	17,080	9,163	6,389	18,823	157,160	.0032	83,371	24	3,803	8	...	...	15,890	19,037	10,772	McCreary
McLean*	.149	9,875	9,938	14,880	4,001	28,694	146,940	.0024	57,651	16	1,969	4	...	...	5,372	4,734	7,819	McLean
Madison**	.151	76,677	70,872	14,889	28,186	31,584	1,141,650	.0212	720,790	205	181,197	360	35,848	189	80,831	45,161	53,936	Madison
Magoffin	.153	13,367	13,332	9,467	5,136	18,961	126,550	.0025	55,971	16	1,393	3	1,045	6	10,328	11,618	8,870	Magoffin
Marion	.155	18,754	18,212	12,961	6,498	29,258	243,070	.0043	105,430	30	26,230	52	1,959	10	24,767	7,718	12,451	Marion
Marshall	.157	30,902	30,125	17,783	12,621	33,810	549,520	.0088	232,761	66	36,614	73	...	...	25,472	14,070	25,099	Marshall
Martin	.159	12,456	12,578	9,225	4,890	17,969	114,910	.0024	70,272	20	4,152	8	...	...	15,981	16,585	8,470	Martin
Mason**	.161	16,851	16,800	14,536	6,653	29,016	244,950	.0061	336,000	95	80,484	160	20,131	106	58,033	10,437	11,890	Mason
Meade*	.163	28,244	26,349	15,419	9,596	35,144	435,500	.0070	149,232	42	3,474	7	...	...	15,691	11,487	20,002	Meade
Menifee**	.165	6,736	6,556	10,785	2,530	22,087	72,650	.0012	11,878	3	...	...	...	...	3,273	1,488	4,723	Menifee
Mercer	.167	21,579	20,817	17,183	8,554	33,878	370,790	.0061	165,480	47	40,478	80	1,843	10	22,562	6,889	16,658	Mercer
Metcalfe**	.169	10,066	10,037	12,055	4,024	23,456	121,350	.0022	48,867	14	1,135	2	1,123	6	12,423	6,518	8,018	Metcalfe
Monroe	.171	11,716	11,756	11,637	4,740	22,114	136,340	.0028	101,905	29	2,789	6	1,423	7	22,459	11,919	8,745	Monroe
Montgomery**	.173	24,092	22,554	15,116	9,345	30,266	364,180	.0080	373,612	106	98,749	196	17,774	94	39,802	22,772	17,516	Montgomery
Morgan	.175	14,508	13,948	9,442	4,836	21,843	136,990	.0029	85,030	24	8,266	16	...	...	12,174	14,321	9,052	Morgan
Muhlenberg**	.177	31,670	31,839	13,622	12,291	27,130	431,410	.0081	261,539	74	83,813	167	3,334	18	30,435	15,179	24,017	Muhlenberg
Nelson*	.179	40,940	37,477	18,011	15,554	36,459	737,370	.0117	291,943	83	44,521	89	6,989	37	33,080	15,620	32,048	Nelson
Nicholas	.181	7,094	6,813	13,816	2,664	28,458	98,010	.0015	20,154	6	2,829	6	...	...	6,430	2,319	5,021	Nicholas
Ohio	.183	23,481	22,916	13,929	8,953	28,391	327,060	.0057	147,324	42	25,127	50	1,464	8	22,051	22,185	17,894	Ohio
Oldham*	.185	52,975	46,178	24,688	17,564	57,448	1,307,830	.0173	272,597	77	62,744	125	1,214	6	15,015	16,396	39,241	Oldham
Owen	.187	11,437	10,547	14,410	4,057	31,593	164,810	.0027	62,294	18	1,120	2	...	...	8,508	4,147	8,266	Owen
Owsley	.189	4,637	4,858	8,324	1,901	15,472	38,600	.0009	26,800	8	...	...	...	...	18,981	1,710	3,128	Owsley
Pendleton*	.191	15,401	14,390	15,502	5,100	36,394	238,740	.0034	36,045	10	...	...	...	...	5,960	2,493	10,606	Pendleton
Perry	.193	29,906	29,390	10,814	11,553	21,465	323,410	.0081	380,363	108	87,142	173	18,757	99	47,673	26,711	19,550	Perry
Pike	.195	66,804	68,736	12,698	28,121	23,342	848,270	.0190	834,444	237	166,209	331	37,643	198	100,873	81,476	48,724	Pike
Powell	.197	13,460	13,237	12,193	5,123	25,005	164,120	.0028	54,452	15	3,270	6	...	...	10,560	9,867	9,249	Powell
Pulaski**	.199	59,052	56,217	12,734	22,167	26,225	751,950	.0168	741,272	210	155,022	308	30,793	162	72,479	40,211	41,623	Pulaski
Robertson	.201	2,356	2,266	13,302	848	28,616	31,340	.0005	3,271	1	...	...	...	...	...	...	1,709	Robertson
Rockcastle**	.203	16,771	16,582	11,736	6,597	23,211	196,820	.0034	60,607	17	5,403	11	...	...	18,634	8,748	12,726	Rockcastle
Rowan	.205	22,409	22,094	12,285	7,997	26,505	275,290	.0061	253,762	72	51,145	102	12,603	66	42,719	20,913	14,991	Rowan
Russell	.207	16,798	16,315	11,364	6,804	21,610	190,900	.0041	152,450	43	25,280	50	1,874	10	28,256	14,640	12,690	Russell
Scott*	.209	38,974	33,061	18,735	12,937	44,305	730,160	.0119	344,985	98	53,099	106	15,469	81	21,760	19,901	25,281	Scott
Shelby*	.211	37,573	33,337	19,422	13,406	42,082	729,730	.0125	430,223	122	64,956	129	7,816	41	24,295	12,514	27,575	Shelby
Simpson	.213	16,934	16,405	17,761	6,749	34,663	300,760	.0061	269,231	76	22,228	44	...	...	28,526	19,359	12,806	Simpson
Spencer*	.215	15,869	11,766	19,228	5,401	43,236	305,130	.0040	32,742	9	1,528	3	...	...	13,243	4,920	12,251	Spencer
Taylor**	.217	23,726	22,927	13,151	8,956	26,889	312,010	.0072	337,897	96	83,210	165	11,448	60	32,873	13,575	16,235	Taylor
Todd	.219	11,850	11,971	13,968	4,511	28,503	165,520	.0028	66,192	19	2,252	4	...	...	17,511	6,638	8,426	Todd
Trigg*	.221	13,027	12,597	16,439	5,206	31,920	214,150	.0034	73,750	21	4,882	10	...	...	14,915	3,947	10,573	Trigg
Trimble*	.223	9,217	8,125	14,996	3,142	34,245	138,220	.0020	20,320	6	...	...	...	...	4,933	2,241	6,473	Trimble
Union	.225	15,724	15,637	15,238	5,607	33,093	239,610	.0042	119,543	34	22,355	44	...	...	22,927	9,992	11,159	Union
Warren*	.227	97,370	92,522	17,108	37,330	34,434	1,665,810	.0324	1,334,897	379	252,920	503	75,781	399	114,098	54,694	70,058	Warren
Washington	.229	11,491	10,916	14,262	4,045	31,552	163,880	.0028	66,148	19	1,602	3	...	...	10,444	8,087	8,084	Washington
Wayne	.231	20,462	19,923	9,910	7,684	20,070	202,770	.0041	115,877	33	26,223	52	...	...	24,448	14,780	14,136	Wayne
Webster*	.233	14,048	14,120	15,145	5,476	30,400	212,760	.0034	71,584	20	...	...	...	...	13,438	7,274	11,002	Webster
Whitley**	.235	37,971	35,865	10,383	13,852	21,817	394,260	.0095	411,946	117	109,145	217	6,594	35	23,968	28,103	24,161	Whitley
Wolfe	.237	6,875	7,065	10,134	2,864	18,725	69,670	.0014	38,227	11	4,981	10	...	...	10,644	5,604	5,345	Wolfe
Woodford*	.239	23,881	23,208	22,491	9,177	45,313	537,110	.0076	157,902	45	29,045	58	2,353	12	8,782	10,436	18,455	Woodford
Kentucky Total		**4,164,333**	**4,041,769**	**16,518**	**1,617,409**	**32,636**	**68,788,080**	**1.2521**	**43,754,896**	**12,421**	**8,002,399**	**15,915**	**1,810,560**	**9,533**	**5,105,732**	**2,999,020**	**3,019,571**	**Kentucky**

Louisiana (LA; Code 22; 64 Parishes)

County or County Equivalent	FIPS County Code	Population Estimate 7/1/05	Population Census 4/1/00	Per Capita Income 2004	House-holds Estimate 7/1/05	Median Household Income 2004	Disposable Income 2004 ($1,000)	Market Ability Index 2004	Total Retail Sales 2004 Sales ($1,000)	Total Retail Sales Ranally Sales Units	General Merchandise 2004 Sales ($1,000)	General Merchandise Ranally Sales Units	Apparel Store 2004 Sales ($1,000)	Apparel Store Ranally Sales Units	Food Store Sales 2004 ($1,000)	Health & Drug Store 2004 ($1,000)	Passenger Car Regis-trations 2004	County or County Equivalent
Acadia**	.001	59,013	58,861	12,529	21,625	25,982	739,380	.0141	437,899	124	82,523	164	9,776	51	76,058	30,853	34,759	Acadia
Allen	.003	25,214	25,440	11,472	8,193	26,780	289,250	.0054	141,770	40	26,105	52	1,834	10	27,021	8,688	13,417	Allen
Ascension*	.005	88,503	76,627	19,088	30,827	41,378	1,689,320	.0278	833,291	237	143,351	285	66,631	351	111,530	47,041	56,609	Ascension
Assumption**	.007	22,977	23,388	14,857	8,604	29,781	341,360	.0054	100,261	28	25,449	51	...	...	19,251	4,335	14,386	Assumption
Avoyelles	.009	41,876	41,481	11,312	15,392	22,910	473,690	.0093	280,625	80	62,044	123	2,870	15	51,642	23,952	24,642	Avoyelles
Beauregard**	.011	33,713	32,986	15,025	12,268	31,299	506,530	.0092	290,927	83	97,090	193	9,583	50	28,702	7,704	21,670	Beauregard
Bienville	.013	14,968	15,752	12,666	6,199	22,888	189,590	.0032	69,203	20	4,397	9	13,052	69	10,542	4,047	10,063	Bienville
Bossier*	.015	103,854	98,310	18,637	39,482	36,946	1,935,490	.0345	1,248,408	354	287,279	571	46,593	245	131,076	35,433	70,131	Bossier
Caddo*	.017	275,910	252,161	15,647	108,205	30,593	4,317,050	.0829	3,137,475	891	532,043	1,058	145,681	767	382,836	160,175	193,365	Caddo
Calcasieu*	.019	183,193	183,577	17,610	72,541	33,704	3,226,040	.0603	2,332,523	662	599,640	1,192	99,182	522	259,216	130,276	122,874	Calcasieu
Caldwell	.021	10,642	10,560	12,991	3,955	26,442	138,250	.0025	67,805	19	1,135	2	...	...	18,446	7,882	6,704	Caldwell
Cameron*	.023	9,473	9,991	16,760	3,672	32,669	158,770	.0024	40,249	11	5,720	11	...	...	14,748	...	6,389	Cameron
Catahoula	.025	10,428	10,920	11,716	4,143	22,088	122,170	.0027	105,473	30	12,165	24	...	...	27,418	10,710	7,122	Catahoula
Claiborne	.027	16,301	16,851	12,630	6,318	24,808	205,880	.0036	80,597	23	14,606	29	1,134	6	18,719	4,579	10,308	Claiborne
Concordia**	.029	19,369	20,247	11,971	7,707	22,635	231,870	.0048	175,754	50	22,128	44	...	...	37,197	8,327	12,215	Concordia
De Soto*	.031	26,058	25,494	13,559	9,902	27,374	353,310	.0061	154,996	44	26,171	52	2,830	15	18,884	8,658	16,820	De Soto
East Baton Rouge*	.033	409,249	412,852	16,897	146,790	35,699	6,915,280	.1413	6,284,861	1,785	1,217,006	2,420	282,585	1,487	660,348	315,942	273,338	East Baton Rouge
East Carroll	.035	8,712	9,421	8,726	2,856	20,000	76,020	.0016	43,700	12	7,728	15	...	...	4,413	1,881	3,803	East Carroll
East Feliciana*	.037	20,787	21,360	13,279	6,819	32,335	276,030	.0044	68,646	19	1,305	3	...	...	15,101	7,661	11,939	East Feliciana
Evangeline	.039	34,867	35,434	10,050	13,080	20,486	350,410	.0071	200,707	57	27,317	54	2,995	16	40,872	25,962	20,126	Evangeline
Franklin	.041	20,507	21,263	11,558	7,847	22,670	237,010	.0052	205,397	58	66,472	132	2,950	16	18,632	6,893	12,696	Franklin
Grant*	.043	18,824	18,698	14,349	7,229	28,390	270,100	.0041	62,132	18	2,907	6	...	...	3,950	2,586	12,930	Grant
Iberia**	.045	74,008	73,266	13,699	25,828	30,079	1,013,830	.0215	901,906	256	123,277	245	41,020	216	118,223	47,735	42,197	Iberia
Iberville*	.047	32,225	33,320	12,479	10,868	27,967	402,120	.0078	245,682	70	32,770	65	4,569	24	44,905	17,506	17,697	Iberville
Jackson**	.049	15,103	15,397	14,771	6,136	27,798	223,090	.0037	82,415	23	18,053	36	1,095	6	8,094	6,789	10,395	Jackson
Jefferson*	.051	447,509	455,466	18,072	167,439	36,380	8,087,470	.1679	7,918,924	2,249	1,636,023	3,254	486,294	2,559	845,888	546,126	303,717	Jefferson
Jefferson Davis**	.053	30,692	31,435	13,415	11,639	26,791	411,730	.0084	326,081	93	82,339	164	4,206	22	31,557	18,711	19,449	Jefferson Davis
Lafayette*	.055	194,974	190,503	18,206	77,134	35,001	3,549,630	.0742	3,540,911	1,005	717,188	1,426	179,311	944	304,285	255,810	129,004	Lafayette
Lafourche*	.057	91,749	89,974	15,788	33,020	33,223	1,448,490	.0262	869,813	247	172,589	343	19,352	102	188,051	42,594	55,977	Lafourche
La Salle	.059	13,958	14,282	13,993	5,364	27,477	195,320	.0035	105,442	30	22,443	45	...	...	18,755	8,543	9,426	La Salle
Lincoln**	.061	41,641	42,509	13,087	15,607	26,625	544,950	.0116	477,228	136	110,381	220	17,501	92	48,757	13,236	26,621	Lincoln
Livingston*	.063	107,626	91,814	16,590	36,578	36,764	1,785,480	.0277	575,772	163	122,215	243	3,697	19	110,726	31,353	69,135	Livingston
Madison**	.065	12,480	13,728	9,607	4,450	20,423	119,890	.0029	114,618	33	10,603	21	...	...	16,105	6,814	6,043	Madison
Morehouse**	.067	30,195	31,021	12,436	11,579	24,775	375,520	.0077	280,078	80	53,584	107	5,276	28	37,889	14,439	18,498	Morehouse
Natchitoches**	.069	38,168	39,080	12,797	14,788	25,151	488,430	.0095	319,885	91	77,924	155	8,162	43	34,861	18,622	23,911	Natchitoches
Orleans*	.071	456,285	484,674	13,448	174,662	26,719	6,136,230	.1143	3,541,633	1,006	389,671	775	339,037	1,784	628,347	314,738	233,169	Orleans
Ouachita*	.073	147,371	147,250	15,667	56,614	31,143	2,308,890	.0457	1,843,979	524	521,548	1,037	98,193	517	182,315	88,264	92,321	Ouachita
Plaquemines*	.075	28,584	26,757	15,803	9,491	35,676	451,710	.0069	123,045	35	5,739	11	...	...	40,405	8,710	15,977	Plaquemines
Pointe Coupee*	.077	22,197	22,763	15,183	8,690	29,857	337,010	.0072	320,851	91	31,668	63	...	...	55,783	5,334	14,765	Pointe Coupee
Rapides*	.079	127,099	126,337	14,480	48,457	28,829	1,840,400	.0385	1,634,018	464	396,986	789	70,943	373	181,022	112,390	78,416	Rapides
Red River	.081	9,543	9,622	11,167	3,486	23,745	106,570	.0022	76,106	22	6,950	14	...	...	6,494	1,821	5,608	Red River
Richland	.083	20,197	20,981	11,623	7,583	23,282	234,750	.0055	250,989	71	22,784	45	...	...	23,175	10,416	12,053	Richland
Sabine	.085	23,316	23,459	13,739	9,412	25,911	320,350	.0060	198,285	56	43,024	86	3,901	21	39,563	11,474	16,058	Sabine
St. Bernard*	.087	64,622	67,229	17,751	25,362	34,307	1,147,100	.0185	488,158	139	140,526	279	16,348	86	114,126	47,267	41,748	St. Bernard
St. Charles*	.089	49,807	48,072	19,028	17,120	41,745	947,710	.0136	234,997	67	23,107	46	1,433	8	45,750	15,910	32,317	St. Charles
St. Helena*	.091	10,124	10,525	12,373	3,925	24,105	125,260	.0019	18,764	5	4,748	9	...	...	5,415	1,125	6,472	St. Helena
St. James	.093	21,026	21,216	15,253	7,132	33,786	320,700	.0051	109,539	31	3,795	8	...	...	38,956	5,168	12,585	St. James
St. John The Baptist*	.095	45,754	43,044	16,458	15,298	37,220	753,010	.0125	334,009	95	73,283	146	8,563	45	61,198	27,237	27,089	St. John The Baptist
St. Landry**	.097	89,252	87,700	11,010	33,061	22,473	982,670	.0208	734,451	209	180,700	359	28,974	152	121,247	59,320	50,399	St. Landry
St. Martin*	.099	50,491	48,583	13,682	17,774	29,743	690,820	.0118	280,543	80	34,161	68	...	...	55,652	15,139	29,832	St. Martin
St. Mary**	.101	51,413	53,500	13,762	19,581	27,361	707,540	.0144	563,305	160	138,973	276	16,502	87	97,036	60,416	30,249	St. Mary
St. Tammany*	.103	216,070	191,268	21,073	77,973	43,846	4,553,160	.0759	2,551,667	725	416,244	828	88,352	465	351,036	200,198	148,064	St. Tammany
Tangipahoa**	.105	104,732	100,588	13,885	38,947	28,403	1,454,240	.0299	1,197,352	340	223,958	445	35,870	189	130,469	61,865	65,120	Tangipahoa
Tensas	.107	6,061	6,618	10,340	2,394	19,854	62,670	.0013	38,789	11	1,409	3	...	...	6,288	...	3,457	Tensas
Terrebonne*	.109	106,373	104,503	15,780	37,872	33,537	1,678,520	.0352	1,577,177	448	357,627	711	65,136	343	186,085	76,581	63,556	Terrebonne
Union*	.111	22,868	22,803	14,880	9,142	28,197	340,280	.0057	142,244	40	21,571	43	...	...	36,217	5,349	15,937	Union
Vermilion**	.113	54,194	53,807	14,002	20,332	28,561	758,830	.0137	409,607	116	60,496	120	7,749	41	76,193	28,862	33,635	Vermilion
Vernon**	.115	48,846	52,531	14,942	18,497	30,004	729,870	.0122	302,601	86	48,151	96	6,810	36	24,756	11,699	33,141	Vernon
Washington**	.117	43,743	43,926	11,990	16,765	23,701	524,490	.0101	309,524	88	50,298	100	8,838	47	49,650	23,431	27,077	Washington
Webster**	.119	40,697	41,831	15,115	16,987	27,610	615,130	.0115	405,642	115	73,271	146	12,302	65	64,379	16,486	29,021	Webster
West Baton Rouge*	.121	21,636	21,601	17,170	7,952	35,370	371,500	.0061	163,892	47	22,401	45	...	...	24,280	...	13,715	West Baton Rouge
West Carroll	.123	11,994	12,314	12,116	4,554	24,163	145,320	.0027	77,867	22	35,973	72	...	...	11,714	...	7,913	West Carroll
West Feliciana*	.125	15,204	15,111	12,537	3,836	37,540	190,610	.0033	74,718	21	2,755	5	...	...	16,695	2,017	7,021	West Feliciana
Winn	.127	15,869	16,894	12,320	5,989	24,928	195,510	.0037	110,797	31	27,512	55	...	...	15,058	7,383	9,495	Winn
Louisiana Total		**4,510,134**	**4,468,976**	**15,680**	**1,682,972**	**31,811**	**70,719,600**	**1.3467**	**50,236,004**	**14,266**	**9,803,298**	**19,494**	**2,275,608**	**11,979**	**6,474,003**	**3,103,259**	**2,844,586**	**Louisiana**

Source: Devonshire Associates Ltd. and Scan/US, Inc. 2005. ...Data less than 1,000. (d) Data not available.
* Component of a Metropolitan Core Based Statistical Area.
** Component of a Micropolitan Core Based Statistical Area.

Continued on next page

Counties: Population/Income/Sales, *Continued*

County or County Equivalent	FIPS County Code	Population: Estimate 7/1/05	Population: Census 4/1/00	Per Capita Income 2004	Households Estimate 7/1/05	Median Household Income 2004	Disposable Income 2004 ($1,000)	Market Ability Index 2004	Total Retail Sales: 2004 Sales ($1,000)	Total Retail Sales: Ranally Sales Units	General Merchandise: 2004 Sales ($1,000)	General Merchandise: Ranally Sales Units	Apparel Store: 2004 Sales ($1,000)	Apparel Store: Ranally Sales Units	Food Store Sales 2004 ($1,000)	Health & Drug Store 2004 ($1,000)	Passenger Car Registrations 2004	County or County Equivalent
Maine (ME; Code 23; 16 Counties)																		
Androscoggin*	.001	107,666	103,793	17,403	44,083	34,251	1,873,750	.0392	1,842,778	523	214,005	426	21,774	115	236,464	73,545	78,667	Androscoggin
Aroostook	.003	72,859	73,938	14,864	31,228	27,787	1,082,960	.0205	724,335	206	106,383	212	13,715	72	157,651	46,843	56,711	Aroostook
Cumberland*	.005	275,908	265,612	20,813	111,595	41,105	5,742,570	.1178	5,779,560	1,641	532,872	1,060	378,464	1,992	970,747	230,718	231,982	Cumberland
Franklin	.007	29,764	29,467	15,488	12,255	30,214	460,980	.0088	329,164	93	37,396	74	5,323	28	102,220	15,039	23,758	Franklin
Hancock	.009	53,648	51,791	18,542	23,414	34,041	994,740	.0187	754,168	214	68,243	136	22,957	121	191,452	39,443	44,958	Hancock
Kennebec**	.011	121,139	117,114	17,937	50,348	34,789	2,172,820	.0439	1,975,460	561	221,991	441	40,599	214	334,644	83,107	92,563	Kennebec
Knox**	.013	41,375	39,618	18,763	17,764	35,155	776,300	.0145	577,174	164	50,088	100	15,146	80	139,158	31,338	32,918	Knox
Lincoln	.015	35,525	33,616	19,208	15,007	36,223	682,350	.0124	472,414	134	11,699	23	8,016	42	106,268	20,564	29,986	Lincoln
Oxford	.017	56,888	54,755	16,560	23,517	32,161	942,070	.0160	465,271	132	48,682	97	4,377	23	116,211	30,590	45,326	Oxford
Penobscot*	.019	149,585	144,919	16,697	61,196	32,725	2,497,590	.0514	2,300,599	653	323,935	644	49,968	263	436,404	94,177	112,713	Penobscot
Piscataquis	.021	17,564	17,235	14,365	7,442	27,055	252,300	.0046	143,841	41	18,745	37	...	...	38,967	10,026	14,326	Piscataquis
Sagadahoc*	.023	37,650	35,214	19,732	15,011	39,635	742,920	.0116	300,980	85	7,814	16	...	...	89,359	16,145	29,637	Sagadahoc
Somerset	.025	51,674	50,888	14,985	21,119	29,675	774,330	.0147	528,120	150	70,115	139	3,193	17	98,979	32,308	39,919	Somerset
Waldo	.027	39,306	36,280	16,394	15,907	32,342	644,380	.0111	333,816	95	23,014	46	2,188	12	77,270	10,010	31,397	Waldo
Washington	.029	33,224	33,941	13,736	14,630	25,115	456,350	.0091	335,860	95	32,626	65	2,043	11	87,020	8,745	27,143	Washington
York*	.031	204,807	186,742	20,143	80,969	40,728	4,125,450	.0667	1,993,381	566	144,796	288	128,884	678	444,337	69,551	158,731	York
Maine Total		**1,328,582**	**1,274,923**	**18,231**	**545,485**	**35,551**	**24,221,860**	**.4610**	**18,856,922**	**5,353**	**1,912,403**	**3,804**	**697,559**	**3,673**	**3,627,151**	**812,148**	**1,050,735**	**Maine**
Maryland (MD; Code 24; 23 Counties, 1 Independent City)																		
Allegany*	.001	73,274	74,930	14,770	28,820	29,710	1,082,250	.0208	762,885	217	149,172	297	40,145	211	108,844	70,291	50,730	Allegany
Anne Arundel*	.003	517,299	489,656	26,194	189,075	56,214	13,550,250	.2087	6,572,851	1,866	1,020,879	2,030	407,431	2,144	1,062,988	226,222	401,489	Anne Arundel
Baltimore*	.005	791,384	754,292	22,904	306,509	46,397	18,125,720	.3024	10,751,602	3,053	1,484,595	2,952	675,157	3,554	1,811,939	615,778	566,832	Baltimore
Calvert*	.009	90,186	74,563	24,299	29,095	58,934	2,191,440	.0301	586,256	166	72,202	144	15,116	80	146,077	27,295	73,082	Calvert
Caroline	.011	31,608	29,772	17,310	11,673	36,827	547,140	.0094	292,416	83	10,678	21	2,162	11	38,857	17,018	22,653	Caroline
Carroll*	.013	171,167	150,897	24,023	59,049	54,572	4,112,000	.0615	1,673,099	475	284,958	567	31,477	166	379,790	91,166	128,657	Carroll
Cecil*	.015	97,326	85,951	21,120	34,967	45,871	2,055,540	.0316	839,509	238	98,438	196	42,799	225	136,721	38,841	69,370	Cecil
Charles*	.017	139,740	120,546	24,873	48,174	56,743	3,475,800	.0545	1,748,629	497	334,174	665	108,372	570	259,359	54,113	102,182	Charles
Dorchester**	.019	30,637	30,674	17,556	12,972	32,846	537,870	.0104	429,084	122	130,918	260	13,959	73	84,464	27,359	21,927	Dorchester
Frederick*	.021	225,299	195,277	24,849	79,972	55,113	5,598,360	.0895	3,008,517	854	415,988	827	106,347	560	518,879	122,184	167,308	Frederick
Garrett	.023	30,309	29,846	15,669	12,171	30,793	474,920	.0090	326,461	93	7,872	16	2,877	15	55,204	24,130	22,346	Garrett
Harford*	.025	240,719	218,590	24,439	88,197	52,186	5,882,920	.0911	2,786,591	791	371,861	740	90,347	476	501,314	120,385	173,542	Harford
Howard*	.027	274,373	247,842	29,636	96,906	65,646	8,131,190	.1158	3,128,344	888	409,034	813	164,949	868	584,924	106,375	199,416	Howard
Kent	.029	19,647	19,197	21,568	8,922	37,038	423,740	.0065	173,667	49	12,360	25	8,917	47	48,150	26,469	16,135	Kent
Montgomery*	.031	947,578	873,341	29,807	345,603	63,924	28,244,410	.4080	11,570,405	3,285	1,109,503	2,206	863,462	4,545	2,006,126	502,992	690,047	Montgomery
Prince George's*	.033	863,468	801,515	23,369	311,846	50,649	20,178,000	.3011	7,918,222	2,248	853,439	1,697	410,577	2,161	1,545,056	399,087	583,954	Prince George's
Queen Anne's*	.035	46,661	40,563	25,035	17,393	52,412	1,168,170	.0174	477,074	135	30,734	61	61,529	324	79,198	14,761	36,239	Queen Anne's
St. Mary's**	.037	96,819	86,211	22,839	34,471	49,991	2,211,210	.0331	860,717	244	153,326	305	26,206	138	199,189	53,576	70,285	St. Mary's
Somerset*	.039	25,960	24,747	11,817	8,373	28,857	306,760	.0052	90,566	26	6,023	12	2,058	11	26,021	11,551	14,374	Somerset
Talbot**	.041	35,048	33,812	23,168	15,595	40,963	812,000	.0151	661,293	188	64,660	129	29,507	155	90,523	32,868	28,276	Talbot
Washington*	.043	140,320	131,923	18,615	53,417	38,556	2,612,090	.0465	1,685,288	479	306,637	610	46,962	247	244,511	83,377	97,357	Washington
Wicomico*	.045	89,441	84,644	18,600	35,324	37,092	1,663,580	.0320	1,351,068	384	319,199	635	57,200	301	156,780	72,490	63,541	Wicomico
Worcester**	.047	49,819	46,543	20,283	20,760	38,292	1,010,470	.0187	773,772	220	89,896	179	107,676	567	142,450	50,049	36,523	Worcester
INDEPENDENT CITY																		
Baltimore*	.510	617,204	651,154	14,301	240,250	28,904	8,826,780	.1515	3,887,601	1,104	195,612	389	271,094	1,427	766,785	536,954	305,028	Baltimore
Maryland Total		**5,645,286**	**5,296,486**	**23,599**	**2,089,534**	**49,172**	**133,222,610**	**2.0699**	**62,355,917**	**17,705**	**7,932,159**	**15,776**	**3,586,329**	**18,876**	**10,994,151**	**3,325,328**	**3,941,293**	**Maryland**
Massachusetts (MA; Code 25; 14 Counties)																		
Barnstable*	.001	232,312	222,230	23,822	99,127	42,550	5,534,160	.0937	3,512,843	997	198,575	395	245,378	1,291	737,688	261,847	171,667	Barnstable
Berkshire*	.003	131,527	134,953	20,937	56,899	36,863	2,753,800	.0465	1,607,360	456	145,868	290	131,236	691	316,206	119,866	90,832	Berkshire
Bristol*	.005	553,046	534,678	20,094	208,676	40,703	11,112,830	.1939	7,047,223	2,001	1,151,836	2,291	457,714	2,409	1,154,479	545,663	392,969	Bristol
Dukes	.007	15,901	14,987	23,611	6,780	42,217	375,440	.0068	287,153	82	10,690	21	22,541	119	83,247	13,474	12,653	Dukes
Essex*	.009	744,047	723,419	23,094	276,526	47,431	17,183,050	.2703	8,299,350	2,357	721,897	1,436	584,293	3,075	1,294,880	777,045	487,433	Essex
Franklin*	.011	72,152	71,535	21,093	30,188	38,407	1,521,870	.0227	539,852	153	45,957	91	10,191	54	103,409	32,333	51,910	Franklin
Hampden*	.013	463,031	456,228	18,878	178,576	37,310	8,741,300	.1520	5,260,320	1,494	575,750	1,145	275,936	1,452	918,013	446,287	305,489	Hampden
Hampshire*	.015	154,436	152,251	20,846	57,628	42,537	3,219,390	.0494	1,288,906	366	79,123	157	61,474	324	337,132	90,755	101,379	Hampshire
Middlesex*	.017	1,469,958	1,465,396	27,014	545,938	55,510	39,709,890	.6359	22,486,458	6,385	1,802,975	3,586	1,637,580	8,619	3,275,576	1,592,989	961,744	Middlesex
Nantucket	.019	10,268	9,520	26,788	4,065	52,275	275,060	.0056	292,660	83	...	...	38,839	204	61,052	13,409	7,620	Nantucket
Norfolk*	.021	655,077	650,308	28,528	247,518	57,628	18,687,860	.2878	9,528,471	2,706	935,197	1,860	660,720	3,478	1,347,103	720,147	464,869	Norfolk
Plymouth*	.023	495,811	472,822	23,542	174,310	51,046	11,672,490	.1935	6,880,574	1,954	491,693	978	273,323	1,439	1,075,696	389,070	360,031	Plymouth
Suffolk*	.025	673,720	689,807	18,288	253,047	36,881	12,321,110	.2121	6,987,026	1,984	408,689	813	1,202,732	6,330	1,482,739	853,610	313,981	Suffolk
Worcester*	.027	790,475	750,963	21,359	291,974	44,299	16,883,400	.2793	9,300,431	2,641	871,592	1,733	449,285	2,365	1,474,657	686,325	535,226	Worcester
Massachusetts Total		**6,461,761**	**6,349,097**	**23,212**	**2,431,252**	**46,595**	**149,991,650**	**2.4495**	**83,318,628**	**23,659**	**7,440,687**	**14,798**	**6,051,241**	**31,850**	**13,661,875**	**6,542,819**	**4,257,803**	**Massachusetts**
Michigan (MI; Code 26; 83 Counties)																		
Alcona	.001	11,604	11,719	17,054	5,387	30,059	197,890	.0031	64,730	18	2,182	4	1,830	10	7,372	1,319	10,026	Alcona
Alger	.003	9,742	9,862	17,180	3,968	34,045	167,370	.0026	51,946	15	1,848	4	...	...	16,871	1,116	7,174	Alger
Allegan**	.005	113,751	105,665	19,208	41,694	42,208	2,184,890	.0356	1,046,144	297	93,684	186	13,807	73	182,805	68,800	84,345	Allegan
Alpena**	.007	30,453	31,314	17,393	13,083	32,860	529,670	.0102	416,716	118	101,964	203	18,159	96	30,944	26,418	23,654	Alpena
Antrim	.009	24,925	23,110	18,196	10,138	36,079	453,530	.0073	191,989	55	4,437	9	3,060	16	52,609	13,215	19,389	Antrim
Arenac	.011	17,344	17,269	15,533	7,012	31,205	269,400	.0048	145,691	41	10,662	21	1,842	10	19,682	12,008	13,196	Arenac
Baraga	.013	8,726	8,746	15,776	3,468	32,232	137,660	.0025	78,923	22	2,995	6	1,470	8	14,106	5,297	6,077	Baraga
Barry*	.015	60,188	56,755	19,907	22,537	42,916	1,198,160	.0181	428,765	122	43,598	87	4,996	26	67,630	29,424	47,972	Barry
Bay*	.017	109,101	110,157	18,772	45,419	36,538	2,048,080	.0391	1,641,352	466	360,529	717	52,994	279	163,796	79,616	83,466	Bay
Benzie**	.019	17,877	15,998	17,676	7,198	35,664	315,990	.0053	153,781	44	4,327	9	2,237	12	32,264	9,322	13,836	Benzie
Berrien*	.021	162,940	162,453	18,150	65,840	36,310	2,957,340	.0504	1,604,788	456	295,720	588	32,671	172	224,588	119,269	117,237	Berrien
Branch**	.023	46,683	45,787	16,572	17,090	36,540	773,610	.0150	598,513	170	110,115	219	14,850	78	91,822	22,197	32,384	Branch
Calhoun*	.025	139,305	137,985	18,350	56,104	36,856	2,556,210	.0448	1,546,564	439	425,650	846	40,673	214	155,361	106,743	98,834	Calhoun
Cass*	.027	51,672	51,104	19,254	20,869	38,668	994,910	.0141	236,281	67	8,492	17	2,862	15	43,499	16,066	41,313	Cass
Charlevoix	.029	27,067	26,090	19,785	11,520	37,602	535,530	.0090	298,064	85	26,021	52	9,353	49	70,823	21,360	21,870	Charlevoix
Cheboygan	.031	27,893	26,448	16,136	11,500	31,773	450,090	.0090	379,042	108	69,444	138	9,039	48	57,671	15,054	20,962	Cheboygan
Chippewa**	.033	38,909	38,543	14,657	14,104	32,807	570,280	.0105	342,564	97	70,969	141	15,402	81	48,391	14,897	24,156	Chippewa
Clare	.035	31,896	31,252	14,116	13,122	27,898	450,230	.0087	304,451	86	3,063	6	4,407	23	45,672	24,107	22,941	Clare
Clinton*	.037	69,693	64,753	24,253	28,213	48,652	1,690,240	.0247	617,577	175	70,799	141	18,697	98	80,644	39,479	59,725	Clinton
Crawford	.039	15,145	14,273	15,218	5,888	31,633	230,470	.0045	171,233	49	15,010	30	1,641	9	21,852	4,367	10,856	Crawford
Delta**	.041	38,252	38,520	17,903	16,466	33,859	684,840	.0116	361,182	103	55,041	109	14,328	75	55,073	19,578	30,039	Delta
Dickinson**	.043	27,189	27,472	17,451	11,607	33,127	474,480	.0094	399,102	113	79,948	159	13,082	69	51,438	19,909	20,702	Dickinson
Eaton*	.045	108,140	103,655	22,312	43,225	45,085	2,412,820	.0418	1,584,315	450	484,341	963	37,699	198	216,189	62,113	84,696	Eaton
Emmet	.047	33,636	31,437	19,213	13,866	37,800	646,250	.0135	656,136	186	98,883	197	38,903	205	69,420	33,357	25,166	Emmet
Genesee*	.049	445,626	436,141	18,240	166,917	39,688	8,128,190	.1460	5,313,381	1,509	1,042,068	2,072	191,549	1,008	611,856	393,603	314,173	Genesee
Gladwin	.051	27,546	26,023	15,623	11,431	30,783	430,350	.0074	212,446	60	18,577	37	2,136	11	19,893	12,174	20,892	Gladwin
Gogebic	.053	17,030	17,370	14,262	7,464	26,509	242,890	.0049	190,583	54	29,109	58	8,886	47	28,004	10,510	12,028	Gogebic
Grand Traverse**	.055	84,359	77,654	20,072	33,939	40,393	1,693,280	.0357	1,796,292	510	477,495	950	102,316	539	148,283	72,896	64,816	Grand Traverse
Gratiot**	.057	42,572	42,285	15,430	14,954	35,488	656,870	.0119	384,427	109	81,089	161	4,248	22	59,758	19,240	28,334	Gratiot
Hillsdale	.059	47,810	46,527	18,143	18,578	37,783	867,440	.0140	377,213	107	66,972	133	7,227	38	45,096	20,481	36,198	Hillsdale
Houghton**	.061	35,363	36,016	13,598	14,035	28,680	480,870	.0097	370,620	105	75,688	151	15,894	84	65,965	12,584	24,928	Houghton
Huron	.063	34,686	36,079	18,081	15,117	33,601	627,170	.0106	323,823	92	65,384	130	7,548	40	54,520	17,134	27,984	Huron
Ingham*	.065	283,613	279,320	19,755	118,545	38,359	5,602,790	.0992	3,683,780	1,046	789,072	1,569	173,675	914	374,268	230,599	206,651	Ingham
Ionia*	.067	64,985	61,518	17,130	22,308	40,397	1,113,210	.0184	511,290	145	110,374	219	2,331	12	82,579	28,066	45,702	Ionia
Iosco	.069	26,526	27,339	16,823	12,090	30,206	446,240	.0079	263,235	75	25,440	51	5,745	30	51,529	23,467	20,902	Iosco
Iron	.071	12,490	13,138	15,786	5,822	27,530	197,170	.0035	112,324	32	8,056	16	1,141	6	22,779	11,172	9,893	Iron
Isabella**	.073	64,951	63,351	16,333	26,151	32,588	1,060,870	.0192	661,655	188	250,622	498	25,797	136	49,937	21,803	52,014	Isabella
Jackson*	.075	164,674	158,422	18,936	62,458	40,597	3,118,220	.0547	1,930,675	548	510,788	1,016	53,668	282	204,847	103,303	115,792	Jackson
Kalamazoo*	.077	243,549	238,603	20,016	99,959	39,676	4,874,900	.0882	3,444,834	978	1,145,106	2,277	132,877	699	237,113	169,222	185,127	Kalamazoo
Kalkaska**	.079	17,500	16,571	16,587	6,862	34,248	290,280	.0053	191,192	54	2,041	4	...	...	28,014	9,036	13,255	Kalkaska
Kent*	.081	599,621	574,335	19,937	227,397	42,574	11,954,940	.2179	8,625,979	2,449	1,727,533	3,436	349,036	1,837	652,528	408,445	451,431	Kent
Keweenaw**	.083	2,184	2,301	15,879	1,010	27,767	34,680	.0005	5,017	1	...	...	...	...	...	...	1,804	Keweenaw
Lake	.085	12,027	11,333	13,031	4,928	25,949	156,720	.0027	60,497	17	2,423	5	...	...	11,636	2,127	8,405	Lake
Lapeer*	.087	93,745	87,904	20,831	33,286	47,487	1,952,820	.0318	1,000,034	284	223,306	444	17,103	90	109,282	60,379	71,570	Lapeer
Leelanau**	.089	22,397	21,119	21,909	9,164	43,277	490,700	.0071	159,202	45	1,093	2	12,641	67	51,570	13,436	18,228	Leelanau
Lenawee**	.091	102,302	98,890	19,568	38,178	42,470	2,001,830	.0349	1,245,869	354	245,964	489	16,924	89	129,296	80,319	75,249	Lenawee
Livingston*	.093	182,797	156,951	27,815	67,271	60,888	5,084,410	.0761	2,294,954	652	408,714	813	60,358	318	225,030	96,500	147,454	Livingston
Luce	.095	6,814	7,024	14,285	2,593	30,559	97,340	.0021	92,033	26	2,281	5	1,110	6	17,093	6,056	4,517	Luce
Mackinac	.097	11,210	11,943	18,541	5,296	31,654	207,850	.0037	128,527	36	3,370	7	7,697	41	26,272	2,821	8,968	Mackinac
Macomb*	.099	829,028	788,149	23,354	327,622	48,147	19,361,480	.3280	12,178,708	3,458	2,153,508	4,283	389,754	2,051	1,370,284	953,554	625,033	Macomb
Manistee	.101	25,439	24,527	16,470	10,387	32,648	418,990	.0081	322,471	92	65,260	130	8,149	43	41,717	15,675	18,987	Manistee
Marquette**	.103	64,463	64,634	17,151	26,450	33,883	1,105,580	.0207	790,361	224	177,899	354	26,144	138	89,360	43,137	48,674	Marquette
Mason	.105	29,164	28,274	16,554	11,912	32,937	482,780	.0095	387,208	110	88,179	175	8,467	45	53,106	31,147	21,899	Mason
Mecosta**	.107	42,462	40,553	14,991	16,033	32,293	636,540	.0125	480,330	136	120,824	240	13,840	73	74,586	28,318	29,854	Mecosta
Menominee**	.109	25,014	25,326	17,085	10,999	31,561	427,360	.0073	219,968	62	44,405	88	2,078	11	40,151	6,120	19,861	Menominee
Midland**	.111	85,259	82,874	20,556	33,541	41,842	1,752,580	.0309	1,164,005	331	267,047	531	47,752	251	97,804	89,900	65,166	Midland
Missaukee**	.113	15,576	14,478	15,216	5,770	33,274	237,000	.0044	148,820	42	7,100	14	...	...	17,416	1,765	11,127	Missaukee
Monroe*	.115	153,774	145,945	22,697	59,699	47,228	3,490,180	.0557	1,755,648	499	342,638	681	65,382	344	187,187	109,909	120,720	Monroe
Montcalm	.117	64,025	61,266	15,833	23,289	35,380	1,013,700	.0180	576,810	164	138,677	276	12,433	65	76,856	23,594	44,971	Montcalm
Montmorency	.119	10,565	10,315	15,448	4,641	28,536	163,210	.0030	99,435	28	5,288	11	...	...	24,678	8,113	8,600	Montmorency
Muskegon*	.121	175,106	170,200	17,302	67,837	36,318	3,029,740	.0553	2,018,064	573	535,830	1,066	55,245	291	188,469	141,432	125,580	Muskegon
Newaygo*	.123	50,404	47,874	16,247	18,760	35,382	818,890	.0137	368,354	105	46,751	93	5,034	26	41,031	24,123	36,960	Newaygo
Oakland*	.125	1,214,978	1,194,156	27,460	479,227	56,419	33,363,780	.5710	23,357,225	6,632	3,487,459	6,935	1,522,696	8,014	2,287,508	1,628,633	927,628	Oakland
Oceana	.127	28,778	26,873	14,603	10,142	33,661	420,250	.0073	195,019	55	7,022	14	1,775	9	46,033	8,209	20,230	Oceana
Ogemaw	.129	21,932	21,645	14,902	9,163	29,140	326,820	.0075	377,841	107	48,757	97	31,937	168	52,149	28,014	16,861	Ogemaw
Ontonagon	.131	7,461	7,818	16,463	3,525	28,334	122,830	.0022	72,759	21	7,953	16	1,074	6	9,470	1,257	6,254	Ontonagon
Osceola	.133	23,952	23,197	15,597	9,318	32,462	373,570	.0066	200,088	57	2,459	5	1,103	6	36,484	22,840	17,273	Osceola
Oscoda	.135	9,510	9,418	15,048	4,229	27,359	143,110	.0025	77,124	22	2,758	5	1,386	7	19,912	5,394	7,597	Oscoda
Otsego	.137	24,968	23,301	18,888	9,966	38,339	471,590	.0101	510,778	145	105,255	209	12,892	68	48,400	12,057	18,654	Otsego
Ottawa*	.139	255,839	238,314	21,326	91,969	48,074	5,455,970	.0912	3,108,964	883	819,109	1,629	101,983	537	267,200	119,978	187,532	Ottawa
Presque Isle	.141	14,269	14,411	16,996	6,488	30,549	242,520	.0044	158,725	45	5,135	10	1,320	7	40,614	10,887	12,078	Presque Isle
Roscommon	.143	26,602	25,469	16,038	12,025	28,938	426,630	.0089	397,678	113	74,425	148	3,033	16	62,685	8,645	20,022	Roscommon
Saginaw*	.145	208,826	210,039	18,088	83,826	36,564	3,777,280	.0745	3,243,013	921	628,319	1,250	299,025	1,574	277,335	166,225	150,478	Saginaw
St. Clair*	.147	172,724	164,235	21,056	68,553	42,889	3,636,870	.0598	1,945,190	552	405,654	807	84,113	443	236,014	99,806	132,299	St. Clair
St. Joseph**	.149	62,938	62,422	18,064	24,279	37,921	1,136,940	.0195	632,185	180	118,389	235	13,998	74	132,003	30,936	45,669	St. Joseph
Sanilac	.151	44,747	44,547	16,826	17,516	34,892	752,910	.0130	407,500	116	25,202	50	3,625	19	57,461	37,535	33,791	Sanilac
Schoolcraft	.153	8,712	8,903	15,573	3,745	29,637	135,670	.0026	101,516	29	3,709	7	2,352	12	12,772	7,472	6,522	Schoolcraft
Shiawassee**	.155	73,340	71,687	18,914	28,204	39,876	1,387,130	.0246	895,879	254	185,422	369	8,828	46	86,113	57,896	57,100	Shiawassee
Tuscola	.157	58,649	58,266	17,901	22,380	37,816	1,049,890	.0183	616,222	175	53,974	107	6,952	37	83,227	27,311	44,809	Tuscola
Van Buren*	.159	79,273	76,263	17,315	29,852	37,170	1,372,620	.0229	662,473	188	60,280	120	3,047	16	105,202	42,694	59,186	Van Buren
Washtenaw*	.161	347,941	322,895	23,471	138,498	48,125	8,166,530	.1404	5,391,343	1,531	894,465	1,779	250,305	1,317	593,151	281,683	265,897	Washtenaw
Wayne*	.163	2,008,158	2,061,162	17,599	746,956	38,349	35,340,730	.6260	21,515,241	6,109	3,238,824	6,441	950,938	5,005	3,072,231	1,890,405	1,252,417	Wayne
Wexford**	.165	31,804	30,484	16,583	12,775	33,411	527,420	.0117	578,450	164	117,001	233	14,084	74	72,734	32,513	23,468	Wexford
Michigan Total		**10,164,188**	**9,938,444**	**20,298**	**3,944,647**	**41,869**	**206,311,060**	**3.6011**	**131,655,124**	**37,381**	**24,038,233**	**47,805**	**5,507,978**	**28,989**	**15,029,183**	**8,587,582**	**7,369,528**	**Michigan**

Source: Devonshire Associates Ltd. and Scan/US, Inc. 2005. ...Data less than 1,000. (d) Data not available.
* Component of a Metropolitan Core Based Statistical Area.
** Component of a Micropolitan Core Based Statistical Area.

Counties: Population/Income/Sales, *Continued*

County or County Equivalent	FIPS County Code	Population: Estimate 7/1/05	Population: Census 4/1/00	Per Capita Income 2004	Households Estimate 7/1/05	Median Household Income 2004	Disposable Income 2004 ($1,000)	Market Ability Index 2004	Total Retail Sales: 2004 Sales ($1,000)	Total Retail Sales: Ranally Sales Units	General Merchandise: 2004 Sales ($1,000)	General Merchandise: Ranally Sales Units	Apparel Store: 2004 Sales ($1,000)	Apparel Store: Ranally Sales Units	Food Store Sales 2004 ($1,000)	Health & Drug Store 2004 ($1,000)	Passenger Car Registrations 2004	County or County Equivalent
Minnesota (MN; Code 27; 87 Counties)																		
Aitkin	.001	16,081	15,301	16,663	7,423	29,979	267,960	.0044	114,087	32	10,142	20	...	...	22,380	5,065	14,472	Aitkin
Anoka*	.003	323,274	298,084	23,978	120,322	53,013	7,751,620	.1195	3,563,696	1,012	659,896	1,312	71,903	378	562,009	179,786	264,469	Anoka
Becker	.005	32,093	30,000	16,263	12,978	33,083	521,940	.0101	398,749	113	59,161	118	10,738	57	53,272	9,838	26,422	Becker
Beltrami**	.007	43,008	39,650	14,136	15,729	31,775	607,970	.0141	695,224	197	132,436	263	40,961	216	99,899	21,363	30,310	Beltrami
Benton*	.009	39,583	34,226	19,139	15,790	39,405	757,560	.0112	224,630	64	30,810	61	...	...	32,116	12,364	31,563	Benton
Big Stone	.011	5,604	5,820	15,751	2,470	29,607	88,270	.0014	28,744	8	1,502	3	...	...	6,797	4,995	4,742	Big Stone
Blue Earth**	.013	57,980	55,941	18,502	23,959	36,658	1,072,720	.0216	980,390	278	250,057	497	54,938	289	142,454	49,122	48,860	Blue Earth
Brown**	.015	26,594	26,911	19,134	11,147	37,357	508,840	.0089	309,563	88	33,336	66	4,510	24	70,728	9,909	21,481	Brown
Carlton*	.017	34,001	31,671	18,347	13,607	37,381	623,830	.0101	282,492	80	39,923	79	...	...	42,696	15,125	27,643	Carlton
Carver*	.019	84,468	70,205	27,045	32,020	59,052	2,284,400	.0316	704,597	200	101,548	202	1,013	5	131,199	26,697	67,793	Carver
Cass**	.021	28,798	27,150	17,240	12,461	32,749	496,480	.0080	208,001	59	2,718	5	2,163	11	29,579	6,896	24,835	Cass
Chippewa	.023	12,551	13,088	18,527	5,628	34,048	232,530	.0039	118,829	34	13,355	27	1,193	6	13,307	5,706	11,073	Chippewa
Chisago*	.025	49,980	41,101	20,910	18,054	47,903	1,045,060	.0154	342,009	97	3,504	7	21,840	115	39,177	9,064	41,237	Chisago
Clay*	.027	52,627	51,229	17,306	20,836	35,802	910,760	.0163	573,031	163	116,453	232	6,650	35	72,019	22,144	41,177	Clay
Clearwater	.029	8,402	8,423	14,957	3,571	27,954	125,670	.0020	45,336	13	3,519	7	...	...	6,661	2,463	7,359	Clearwater
Cook	.031	5,320	5,168	21,380	2,676	35,104	113,740	.0019	61,437	17	8,009	16	1,424	7	10,834	1,535	4,761	Cook
Cottonwood	.033	11,811	12,167	16,168	5,102	30,903	190,960	.0037	144,044	41	8,790	17	...	...	18,954	7,810	9,793	Cottonwood
Crow Wing**	.035	60,383	55,099	18,465	25,676	35,985	1,114,950	.0222	995,180	283	239,300	476	8,660	46	115,095	25,928	49,517	Crow Wing
Dakota*	.037	383,221	355,904	27,144	151,566	56,468	10,401,970	.1729	6,651,969	1,889	1,051,790	2,092	163,516	861	873,323	238,128	332,254	Dakota
Dodge*	.039	19,687	17,731	20,555	7,588	43,868	404,670	.0058	106,175	30	3,796	8	1,044	5	23,598	4,027	16,719	Dodge
Douglas**	.041	34,954	32,821	19,254	15,544	35,638	673,020	.0126	510,801	145	150,815	300	14,365	76	71,813	18,683	31,009	Douglas
Faribault	.043	15,461	16,181	17,679	6,840	32,712	273,330	.0042	89,375	25	12,675	25	...	...	15,836	5,733	13,594	Faribault
Fillmore	.045	21,436	21,122	17,864	9,047	34,699	382,930	.0064	191,988	55	5,692	11	...	...	24,421	12,859	18,457	Fillmore
Freeborn**	.047	31,729	32,584	18,809	13,968	35,279	596,800	.0108	408,161	116	72,587	144	4,062	21	45,346	10,955	27,234	Freeborn
Goodhue**	.049	45,895	44,127	21,856	19,021	43,369	1,003,090	.0155	429,450	122	26,664	53	14,794	78	85,902	26,553	39,902	Goodhue
Grant	.051	6,187	6,289	16,845	2,656	32,251	104,220	.0018	55,331	16	...	...	...	...	4,168	2,387	5,457	Grant
Hennepin*	.053	1,123,455	1,116,200	24,488	476,779	47,667	27,511,100	.5292	25,156,032	7,143	3,489,342	6,939	1,225,659	6,451	2,481,545	1,181,332	878,753	Hennepin
Houston*	.055	19,996	19,718	18,965	8,172	37,920	379,220	.0057	119,451	34	5,318	11	...	...	19,453	2,437	16,300	Houston
Hubbard	.057	18,717	18,376	17,551	8,042	33,777	328,510	.0057	184,299	52	13,841	28	2,136	11	56,697	9,587	16,390	Hubbard
Isanti*	.059	38,010	31,287	20,782	14,217	45,724	789,910	.0120	303,121	86	59,908	119	3,040	16	43,010	9,346	32,501	Isanti
Itasca	.061	44,576	43,992	18,316	19,571	34,484	816,460	.0140	454,779	129	69,247	138	8,435	44	79,982	20,711	38,286	Itasca
Jackson	.063	11,160	11,268	17,909	4,737	34,672	199,860	.0030	59,211	17	1,262	3	...	...	8,821	1,673	9,875	Jackson
Kanabec	.065	16,486	14,996	17,333	6,485	36,186	285,750	.0049	150,936	43	14,736	29	...	...	28,515	3,129	14,064	Kanabec
Kandiyohi**	.067	41,091	41,203	19,113	17,325	37,143	785,360	.0142	536,205	152	112,429	224	14,632	77	64,270	21,136	34,004	Kandiyohi
Kittson	.069	4,718	5,285	18,304	2,256	31,548	86,360	.0014	34,949	10	...	...	...	...	5,302	1,601	4,354	Kittson
Koochiching	.071	13,743	14,355	19,404	6,452	34,180	266,670	.0044	134,044	38	14,650	29	3,242	17	26,266	7,592	11,852	Koochiching
Lac qui Parle	.073	7,732	8,067	16,762	3,406	30,968	129,600	.0022	60,504	17	2,836	6	...	...	9,387	3,247	7,180	Lac qui Parle
Lake	.075	11,310	11,058	20,696	5,101	37,644	234,070	.0040	139,537	40	7,107	14	...	...	15,393	2,452	9,955	Lake
Lake of the Woods	.077	4,256	4,522	18,952	2,080	31,857	80,660	.0013	32,090	9	1,053	2	...	...	8,955	1,550	4,169	Lake of the Woods
Le Sueur	.079	27,527	25,426	20,432	10,891	42,255	562,420	.0086	219,028	62	3,484	7	1,695	9	34,931	18,754	23,286	Le Sueur
Lincoln	.081	6,092	6,429	16,638	2,770	30,277	101,360	.0017	45,600	13	...	...	...	...	6,442	2,148	5,673	Lincoln
Lyon**	.083	24,418	25,425	19,466	10,564	36,872	475,330	.0086	327,147	93	51,006	101	6,376	34	49,103	11,071	20,740	Lyon
McLeod**	.085	36,399	34,898	21,202	14,954	42,268	771,720	.0122	352,887	100	88,888	177	15,539	82	60,246	14,190	30,537	McLeod
Mahnomen	.087	5,081	5,190	14,373	2,108	28,444	73,030	.0013	36,712	10	...	...	...	...	4,632	1,182	4,155	Mahnomen
Marshall	.089	9,940	10,155	17,672	4,370	32,921	175,660	.0030	94,870	27	...	...	...	...	8,641	4,765	9,127	Marshall
Martin**	.091	20,808	21,802	18,636	9,529	33,459	387,780	.0072	280,211	80	33,318	66	4,084	21	38,114	9,267	18,135	Martin
Meeker	.093	23,493	22,644	18,904	9,466	38,405	444,100	.0068	162,014	46	10,531	21	...	...	21,064	4,725	19,500	Meeker
Mille Lacs	.095	25,759	22,330	16,416	9,889	35,122	422,870	.0068	166,760	47	11,255	22	...	...	43,266	7,047	20,239	Mille Lacs
Morrison	.097	33,023	31,712	17,452	13,552	34,793	576,330	.0108	418,026	119	43,055	86	3,186	17	92,299	7,585	27,891	Morrison
Mower**	.099	38,928	38,603	18,247	16,735	35,278	710,320	.0117	338,304	96	58,920	117	12,324	65	69,814	15,723	31,869	Mower
Murray	.101	8,900	9,165	18,062	3,946	33,383	160,750	.0025	59,559	17	1,025	2	...	...	17,118	2,545	8,180	Murray
Nicollet**	.103	31,136	29,771	20,144	12,064	42,646	627,200	.0090	164,350	47	4,244	8	...	...	26,312	3,603	24,434	Nicollet
Nobles**	.105	20,362	20,832	16,721	8,229	33,945	340,470	.0065	255,265	72	26,634	53	11,862	62	44,355	10,518	16,188	Nobles
Norman	.107	6,986	7,442	16,869	3,106	31,262	117,850	.0023	100,148	28	1,072	2	...	...	8,119	2,642	6,255	Norman
Olmsted*	.109	135,319	124,277	24,235	57,362	47,221	3,279,440	.0552	2,060,541	585	513,789	1,022	68,601	361	189,607	77,452	110,488	Olmsted
Otter Tail**	.111	58,074	57,159	16,919	24,107	33,509	982,530	.0175	596,373	169	91,196	181	8,041	42	75,613	19,227	49,084	Otter Tail
Pennington	.113	13,587	13,584	17,373	5,954	32,511	236,050	.0044	163,068	46	21,135	42	5,418	29	32,999	6,920	11,349	Pennington
Pine	.115	28,442	26,530	16,427	10,805	35,741	467,210	.0078	208,473	59	21,517	43	...	...	30,065	3,633	22,453	Pine
Pipestone	.117	9,530	9,895	16,524	4,243	30,739	157,470	.0029	108,774	31	6,502	13	...	...	13,408	5,571	8,046	Pipestone
Polk*	.119	30,767	31,369	16,811	12,790	33,480	517,230	.0087	246,354	70	17,944	36	1,754	9	48,196	11,192	24,476	Polk
Pope	.121	11,182	11,236	20,131	5,489	33,698	225,100	.0033	72,208	21	6,899	14	1,102	6	10,020	5,037	11,175	Pope
Ramsey*	.123	502,508	511,035	20,542	199,968	42,303	10,322,350	.1863	7,360,441	2,090	1,095,851	2,179	300,991	1,584	1,096,491	432,245	386,496	Ramsey
Red Lake	.125	4,293	4,299	15,961	1,837	30,047	68,520	.0012	42,139	12	2,200	4	...	...	4,635	1,279	3,761	Red Lake
Redwood	.127	15,972	16,815	18,986	6,977	35,685	303,250	.0053	187,221	53	24,562	49	1,047	6	27,267	7,635	13,719	Redwood
Renville	.129	16,652	17,154	18,479	7,024	35,875	307,710	.0051	147,348	42	4,076	8	...	...	19,123	5,849	14,147	Renville
Rice**	.131	61,423	56,665	19,279	21,864	44,570	1,184,200	.0194	581,887	165	76,527	152	14,288	75	105,214	18,047	44,520	Rice
Rock	.133	9,612	9,721	18,270	4,029	35,856	175,610	.0030	93,101	26	7,023	14	...	...	12,179	3,091	8,087	Rock
Roseau	.135	16,302	16,338	18,824	6,746	37,168	306,870	.0049	132,932	38	12,016	24	3,063	16	21,486	6,976	14,082	Roseau
St. Louis*	.137	197,532	200,528	18,408	86,474	34,734	3,636,230	.0659	2,457,585	698	486,555	968	73,624	388	310,373	144,469	160,350	St. Louis
Scott*	.139	120,628	89,498	25,417	42,234	60,267	3,065,980	.0410	727,333	207	53,457	106	6,093	32	100,854	25,769	93,268	Scott
Sherburne*	.141	82,041	64,417	21,911	28,278	52,272	1,797,600	.0290	918,235	261	64,046	127	3,864	20	124,421	21,443	65,374	Sherburne
Sibley	.143	15,188	15,356	19,271	6,221	38,939	292,690	.0043	82,572	23	3,997	8	...	...	12,295	5,401	13,390	Sibley
Stearns*	.145	144,296	133,166	18,342	54,426	40,160	2,646,740	.0551	2,620,760	744	536,744	1,067	69,121	364	308,096	77,026	112,989	Stearns
Steele**	.147	35,425	33,680	20,805	14,259	42,274	737,000	.0130	495,899	141	71,682	143	38,268	201	77,471	18,527	28,690	Steele
Stevens	.149	9,827	10,053	17,280	3,946	35,404	169,810	.0034	146,623	42	6,519	13	2,825	15	18,609	7,965	7,762	Stevens
Swift	.151	11,423	11,956	16,143	4,557	33,705	184,400	.0030	76,462	22	3,794	8	...	...	14,218	3,929	8,938	Swift
Todd	.153	24,400	24,426	15,622	10,069	31,421	381,180	.0059	109,914	31	5,748	11	...	...	19,587	7,304	20,197	Todd
Traverse	.155	3,740	4,134	17,174	1,794	29,812	64,230	.0011	29,373	8	...	...	...	...	4,847	1,041	3,469	Traverse
Wabasha*	.157	22,485	21,610	19,911	9,250	39,667	447,710	.0068	158,791	45	4,322	9	...	...	30,178	9,351	19,805	Wabasha
Wadena	.159	13,528	13,713	15,387	5,881	29,347	208,150	.0039	132,731	38	9,140	18	1,344	7	23,044	8,951	11,143	Wadena
Waseca	.161	19,353	19,526	18,961	7,591	39,751	366,950	.0057	135,930	39	22,353	44	...	...	22,708	3,672	16,000	Waseca
Washington*	.163	221,394	201,130	27,303	83,930	59,649	6,044,810	.0927	2,963,651	842	545,711	1,085	70,434	371	440,239	124,645	178,954	Washington
Watonwan	.165	11,367	11,876	17,329	4,798	33,662	196,980	.0031	70,983	20	5,248	10	...	...	14,115	4,646	9,284	Watonwan
Wilkin**	.167	6,827	7,138	18,629	2,903	35,780	127,180	.0018	31,139	9	...	...	...	...	2,510	2,004	5,880	Wilkin
Winona**	.169	48,918	49,985	18,440	20,299	36,672	902,030	.0156	521,084	148	90,146	179	14,604	77	71,377	10,020	39,417	Winona
Wright*	.171	110,736	89,986	22,020	40,698	49,504	2,438,460	.0384	1,139,027	323	124,478	248	2,771	15	151,736	32,168	90,395	Wright
Yellow Medicine	.173	10,486	11,080	17,565	4,618	32,643	184,190	.0033	110,688	31	2,037	4	...	...	23,362	4,676	9,610	Yellow Medicine
Minnesota Total		**5,148,487**	**4,919,479**	**21,914**	**2,083,896**	**44,100**	**112,821,870**	**1.9553**	**73,548,970**	**20,883**	**11,103,652**	**22,080**	**2,444,651**	**12,869**	**9,441,980**	**3,233,862**	**4,172,823**	**Minnesota**
Mississippi (MS; Code 28; 82 Counties)																		
Adams**	.001	32,569	34,340	12,964	13,177	24,567	422,240	.0094	420,176	119	164,017	326	19,555	103	32,226	19,058	22,908	Adams
Alcorn**	.003	35,170	34,558	14,527	13,993	28,175	510,900	.0109	475,955	135	149,113	297	22,928	121	30,235	21,201	27,545	Alcorn
Amite**	.005	13,498	13,599	12,490	5,195	25,039	168,590	.0029	56,996	16	1,927	4	...	...	6,490	2,724	9,790	Amite
Attala	.007	19,686	19,661	12,045	7,505	23,989	237,110	.0053	226,735	64	45,568	91	9,391	49	31,648	25,793	12,980	Attala
Benton	.009	7,697	8,026	11,883	2,949	23,791	91,460	.0015	24,468	7	1,870	4	...	...	5,152	1,553	5,822	Benton
Bolivar**	.011	38,629	40,633	10,562	13,494	23,005	407,990	.0096	403,654	115	59,066	117	11,638	61	50,037	16,427	21,563	Bolivar
Calhoun	.013	14,786	15,069	13,536	5,910	26,028	200,150	.0035	92,982	26	8,008	16	3,725	20	24,172	7,936	11,037	Calhoun
Carroll**	.015	10,406	10,769	14,016	4,035	27,797	145,850	.0022	23,229	7	1,379	3	...	...	...	1,194	7,880	Carroll
Chickasaw	.017	19,175	19,440	12,579	7,157	26,060	241,210	.0046	137,396	39	33,822	67	2,452	13	21,844	7,982	13,812	Chickasaw
Choctaw	.019	9,663	9,758	12,692	3,614	25,569	122,640	.0022	59,510	17	5,494	11	...	...	10,456	5,719	6,951	Choctaw
Claiborne	.021	11,298	11,831	9,381	3,643	22,004	105,990	.0022	60,938	17	4,416	9	...	...	10,246	2,496	6,004	Claiborne
Clarke**	.023	17,453	17,955	13,459	6,915	26,050	234,900	.0036	43,638	12	6,420	13	...	...	10,822	4,946	13,347	Clarke
Clay**	.025	21,277	21,979	13,252	8,009	27,014	281,960	.0051	139,150	40	24,261	48	2,734	14	20,812	10,106	14,606	Clay
Coahoma**	.027	28,776	30,622	10,294	10,187	21,720	296,210	.0069	281,645	80	43,446	86	12,521	66	37,090	18,164	15,378	Coahoma
Copiah*	.029	29,216	28,757	11,411	9,913	25,871	333,380	.0062	152,724	43	35,577	71	2,104	11	28,485	14,887	18,114	Copiah
Covington	.031	20,605	19,407	11,583	7,097	25,656	238,660	.0047	149,054	42	9,103	18	...	...	21,434	10,232	13,733	Covington
DeSoto*	.033	135,003	107,199	20,535	47,647	44,971	2,772,250	.0456	1,457,962	414	303,713	604	16,206	85	152,386	101,291	99,245	DeSoto
Forrest*	.035	75,059	72,604	12,816	27,415	26,779	961,960	.0242	1,261,704	358	418,169	832	16,387	86	74,026	89,889	49,176	Forrest
Franklin	.037	8,259	8,448	12,072	3,187	23,994	99,700	.0017	32,744	9	1,570	3	...	...	4,780	1,872	6,140	Franklin
George*	.039	21,369	19,144	13,491	6,658	33,136	288,290	.0051	132,055	38	43,222	86	...	...	18,484	10,017	13,869	George
Greene	.041	13,282	13,299	11,065	4,140	26,984	146,970	.0025	41,657	12	5,093	10	...	...	6,496	4,079	8,293	Greene
Grenada**	.043	22,531	23,263	13,714	8,717	27,197	309,000	.0072	356,666	101	101,247	201	6,929	36	35,179	11,668	15,322	Grenada
Hancock*	.045	46,503	42,967	17,028	18,134	33,540	791,860	.0127	315,763	90	68,019	135	2,956	16	56,251	8,412	34,863	Hancock
Harrison*	.047	190,466	189,601	17,587	75,484	34,084	3,349,750	.0638	2,567,514	729	678,743	1,350	119,510	629	208,251	124,548	142,088	Harrison
Hinds*	.049	248,051	250,800	15,450	90,327	32,396	3,832,300	.0815	3,689,606	1,048	779,230	1,550	179,821	946	327,621	240,366	162,383	Hinds
Holmes	.051	20,923	21,609	8,013	7,264	17,301	167,650	.0039	120,169	34	9,367	19	1,515	8	19,305	11,200	11,265	Holmes
Humphreys	.053	10,379	11,206	9,237	3,594	20,374	95,870	.0022	75,041	21	4,621	9	1,242	7	10,853	3,683	5,439	Humphreys
Issaquena	.055	1,948	2,274	9,379	699	20,261	18,270	.0003	2,861	1	...	...	...	...	2,827	...	1,165	Issaquena
Itawamba**	.057	23,385	22,770	14,480	8,738	29,850	338,620	.0057	136,153	39	31,590	63	1,638	9	16,462	11,736	17,930	Itawamba
Jackson*	.059	134,789	131,420	17,907	49,941	37,004	2,413,600	.0413	1,314,283	373	324,507	645	29,560	156	158,772	52,809	99,624	Jackson
Jasper**	.061	18,161	18,149	11,583	6,729	24,682	210,350	.0039	100,045	28	4,761	9	...	...	7,965	7,319	12,846	Jasper
Jefferson	.063	9,393	9,740	8,470	3,303	18,739	79,560	.0015	19,704	6	1,529	3	...	...	3,571	1,334	5,542	Jefferson
Jefferson Davis	.065	13,084	13,962	11,095	5,117	21,446	145,170	.0027	60,313	17	8,761	17	...	...	13,038	7,353	9,458	Jefferson Davis
Jones**	.067	65,261	64,958	13,356	23,822	28,107	871,620	.0172	610,713	173	155,679	310	23,477	124	65,469	40,569	45,665	Jones
Kemper**	.069	10,434	10,453	11,473	3,865	22,473	119,710	.0021	45,508	13	4,430	9	...	...	8,710	2,997	7,251	Kemper
Lafayette**	.071	40,791	38,744	13,110	14,876	27,540	534,790	.0108	396,160	112	86,992	173	29,713	156	53,924	33,287	28,655	Lafayette
Lamar*	.073	43,669	39,070	15,299	14,237	35,571	668,100	.0120	376,217	107	81,430	162	52,148	274	29,680	30,455	29,360	Lamar
Lauderdale**	.075	77,477	78,161	14,483	29,239	29,712	1,122,110	.0242	1,076,983	306	277,176	551	36,939	194	117,622	58,352	52,735	Lauderdale
Lawrence	.077	13,590	13,258	13,347	5,003	27,593	181,390	.0029	49,930	14	3,590	7	...	...	5,766	6,621	10,184	Lawrence
Leake	.079	22,451	20,940	11,471	7,536	26,362	257,540	.0052	172,437	49	42,310	84	7,414	39	21,341	8,155	14,087	Leake
Lee**	.081	78,812	75,755	16,233	28,467	34,366	1,279,340	.0286	1,426,957	405	444,364	884	101,978	537	81,659	57,384	54,339	Lee
Leflore**	.083	35,483	37,947	10,006	12,633	21,272	355,030	.0083	336,633	96	56,868	113	23,765	125	44,974	20,532	18,714	Leflore
Lincoln**	.085	33,858	33,166	12,733	12,344	26,876	431,130	.0101	478,162	136	156,219	311	19,413	102	32,549	18,847	23,668	Lincoln
Lowndes**	.087	60,078	61,586	15,138	22,559	30,916	909,490	.0196	894,880	254	213,242	424	43,659	230	99,694	45,896	42,014	Lowndes
Madison*	.089	82,974	74,674	20,072	29,273	43,674	1,665,460	.0299	1,154,099	328	352,806	702	91,195	480	97,145	61,693	64,516	Madison
Marion	.091	25,073	25,595	11,370	9,135	23,871	285,090	.0063	254,394	72	60,248	120	6,820	36	33,663	13,613	17,093	Marion
Marshall*	.093	35,935	34,993	12,358	12,173	28,085	444,070	.0075	137,778	39	29,979	60	2,066	11	19,363	14,597	23,434	Marshall
Monroe	.095	37,866	38,014	14,370	14,335	29,178	544,140	.0097	287,578	82	83,174	165	5,201	27	25,867	23,375	27,662	Monroe
Montgomery	.097	11,743	12,189	13,355	4,877	24,488	156,830	.0030	93,334	27	26,121	52	2,218	12	10,939	6,213	8,762	Montgomery
Neshoba	.099	29,435	28,684	12,739	10,522	27,495	374,960	.0075	262,089	74	71,876	143	8,506	45	32,206	12,111	20,257	Neshoba
Newton	.101	22,259	21,838	13,267	8,109	28,051	295,310	.0054	151,694	43	21,844	43	1,355	7	17,991	16,447	15,646	Newton
Noxubee	.103	12,138	12,548	10,564	4,407	22,044	128,220	.0025	60,658	17	3,860	8	...	...	10,080	7,739	7,388	Noxubee
Oktibbeha**	.105	40,856	42,902	13,109	16,974	24,461	535,580	.0106	369,168	105	98,244	195	22,125	116	40,146	7,981	33,141	Oktibbeha
Panola	.107	35,664	34,274	11,549	12,183	26,136	411,870	.0093	384,634	109	58,390	116	22,131	116	37,253	16,414	22,021	Panola
Pearl River**	.109	52,398	48,621	13,936	18,853	29,902	730,230	.0145	545,236	155	157,760	314	18,907	100	44,686	28,744	37,011	Pearl River
Perry*	.111	12,247	12,138	12,435	4,381	26,600	152,290	.0025	41,729	12	5,925	12	...	...	8,187	4,396	8,713	Perry
Pike**	.113	39,137	38,940	11,491	14,393	23,932	449,710	.0109	512,610	146	94,898	189	28,001	147	52,749	35,817	26,011	Pike
Pontotoc**	.115	28,310	26,726	14,667	10,170	31,233	415,220	.0072	202,857	58	44,762	89	5,549	29	29,532	12,898	20,278	Pontotoc
Prentiss	.117	25,682	25,556	13,662	9,740	27,440	350,880	.0062	172,178	49	31,505	63	2,328	12	23,007	10,001	19,644	Prentiss
Quitman	.119	9,474	10,117	9,594	3,427	20,104	90,890	.0019	61,120	17	15,269	30	...	...	6,969	2,931	5,344	Quitman
Rankin*	.121	130,428	115,327	18,995	45,358	41,763	2,477,540	.0429	1,475,189	419	230,825	459	13,785	73	142,089	66,817	92,870	Rankin
Scott	.123	28,594	28,423	12,078	10,121	26,386	345,360	.0067	201,868	57	32,557	65	4,002	21	41,045	20,658	18,520	Scott
Sharkey	.125	6,037	6,580	10,146	2,121	21,749	61,250	.0012	32,005	9	4,420	9	...	...	8,878	4,265	3,267	Sharkey
Simpson*	.127	27,657	27,639	12,663	9,832	27,078	350,230	.0069	232,784	66	53,182	106	3,386	18	26,354	24,468	18,902	Simpson
Smith	.129	15,641	16,182	14,761	5,997	29,530	230,880	.0036	59,911	17	4,914	10	...	...	12,991	4,836	12,155	Smith

Source: Devonshire Associates Ltd. and Scan/US, Inc. 2005. …Data less than 1,000. (d) Data not available.
* Component of a Metropolitan Core Based Statistical Area.
** Component of a Micropolitan Core Based Statistical Area.

Continued on next page

Counties: Population/Income/Sales, *Continued*

County or County Equivalent	FIPS County Code	Population Estimate 7/1/05	Population Census 4/1/00	Per Capita Income 2004	House-holds Estimate 7/1/05	Median Household Income 2004	Disposable Income 2004 ($1,000)	Market Ability Index 2004	Total Retail Sales 2004 Sales ($1,000)	Total Retail Sales Ranally Sales Units	General Merchandise 2004 Sales ($1,000)	General Merchandise Ranally Sales Units	Apparel Store 2004 Sales ($1,000)	Apparel Store Ranally Sales Units	Food Store Sales 2004 ($1,000)	Health & Drug Store 2004 ($1,000)	Passenger Car Regis-trations 2004	County or County Equivalent
Stone*	131	14,616	13,622	12,499	4,765	29,875	182,680	.0034	94,391	27	6,811	14	...	...	16,756	9,543	9,674	Stone
Sunflower**	133	32,962	34,369	9,119	9,423	24,764	300,570	.0078	345,273	98	29,253	58	6,110	32	52,785	22,487	15,659	Sunflower
Tallahatchie	135	14,071	14,903	10,725	5,184	21,970	150,910	.0028	66,386	19	8,319	17	...	...	4,492	8,089	8,674	Tallahatchie
Tate*	137	26,167	25,370	15,863	9,315	34,368	415,080	.0078	280,316	80	68,996	137	3,462	18	13,273	11,117	18,418	Tate
Tippah	139	21,049	20,826	13,907	8,015	27,970	292,730	.0051	129,648	37	31,510	63	...	...	16,255	11,373	15,931	Tippah
Tishomingo	141	18,922	19,163	14,576	7,734	27,238	275,800	.0048	137,907	39	27,930	56	...	...	17,583	11,643	16,137	Tishomingo
Tunica*	143	10,455	9,227	10,744	3,791	23,592	112,330	.0024	86,972	25	9,038	18	...	...	6,975	1,564	5,721	Tunica
Union	145	26,510	25,362	14,770	9,646	31,131	391,560	.0071	226,254	64	66,844	133	8,265	44	32,654	12,878	19,726	Union
Walthall	147	15,261	15,156	10,864	5,492	23,027	165,800	.0031	76,435	22	8,605	17	2,655	14	12,354	2,425	10,582	Walthall
Warren**	149	48,605	49,644	16,362	18,220	33,821	795,280	.0154	608,263	173	128,959	256	31,903	168	72,086	26,423	33,315	Warren
Washington**	151	58,568	62,977	12,236	21,983	25,109	716,650	.0160	677,659	192	185,861	370	38,008	200	55,209	28,610	35,013	Washington
Wayne	153	21,225	21,216	12,042	7,829	25,008	255,600	.0051	166,479	47	51,070	102	2,934	15	15,703	11,782	14,579	Wayne
Webster	155	10,044	10,294	13,710	3,831	27,548	137,700	.0024	57,688	16	5,724	11	...	...	10,890	2,078	7,531	Webster
Wilkinson	157	10,299	10,312	8,548	3,541	19,118	88,040	.0018	34,669	10	4,200	8	...	...	9,585	5,334	6,016	Wilkinson
Winston	159	19,693	20,160	13,337	7,451	26,940	262,640	.0049	146,455	42	39,869	79	4,479	24	20,082	7,730	14,158	Winston
Yalobusha	161	13,484	13,051	12,814	5,234	25,388	172,790	.0030	73,952	21	8,167	16	...	...	19,513	7,114	9,478	Yalobusha
Yazoo**	163	28,221	28,149	9,914	8,923	24,220	279,790	.0065	250,910	71	30,773	61	4,621	24	28,153	11,194	15,329	Yazoo
Mississippi Total		**2,904,093**	**2,844,658**	**14,560**	**1,061,226**	**30,550**	**42,282,620**	**.8232**	**30,449,639**	**8,646**	**7,094,418**	**14,111**	**1,152,431**	**6,062**	**3,145,066**	**1,768,487**	**2,001,366**	**Mississippi**

Missouri (MO; Code 29; 114 Counties, 1 Independent City)

County or County Equivalent	FIPS County Code	Population Estimate 7/1/05	Population Census 4/1/00	Per Capita Income 2004	House-holds Estimate 7/1/05	Median Household Income 2004	Disposable Income 2004 ($1,000)	Market Ability Index 2004	Total Retail Sales 2004 Sales ($1,000)	Total Retail Sales Ranally Sales Units	General Merchandise 2004 Sales ($1,000)	General Merchandise Ranally Sales Units	Apparel Store 2004 Sales ($1,000)	Apparel Store Ranally Sales Units	Food Store Sales 2004 ($1,000)	Health & Drug Store 2004 ($1,000)	Passenger Car Regis-trations 2004	County or County Equivalent
Adair**	001	24,596	24,977	13,597	10,272	26,102	334,440	.0069	272,931	78	52,259	104	10,892	57	35,960	18,796	19,914	Adair
Andrew*	003	17,141	16,492	18,958	6,736	38,234	324,960	.0049	103,843	29	24,749	49	...	...	7,359	5,278	14,693	Andrew
Atchison	005	6,230	6,430	16,772	2,796	29,932	104,490	.0019	68,614	19	1,891	4	1,135	6	6,363	3,032	5,567	Atchison
Audrain**	007	25,776	25,853	15,774	10,267	31,737	406,580	.0072	220,499	63	29,408	58	5,234	28	31,501	18,098	19,273	Audrain
Barry	009	35,483	34,010	14,426	14,559	27,819	511,890	.0099	355,185	101	47,836	95	5,222	27	56,221	11,420	28,783	Barry
Barton	011	13,431	12,541	13,691	5,168	28,344	183,890	.0035	113,947	32	14,912	30	...	...	13,892	3,654	10,799	Barton
Bates*	013	17,254	16,653	14,817	6,901	29,477	255,650	.0042	92,128	26	10,863	22	...	...	16,983	3,358	14,448	Bates
Benton	015	18,758	17,180	13,724	7,890	26,202	257,440	.0048	148,216	42	24,278	48	...	...	12,665	10,932	15,643	Benton
Bollinger**	017	12,532	12,029	14,327	4,912	28,528	179,540	.0029	59,531	17	2,713	5	...	...	8,837	1,739	10,332	Bollinger
Boone*	019	143,667	135,454	19,229	61,157	35,733	2,762,520	.0501	1,920,330	545	319,106	635	60,113	316	197,448	85,118	116,809	Boone
Buchanan*	021	84,810	85,998	17,049	34,760	33,261	1,445,950	.0279	1,130,955	321	284,811	566	22,370	118	139,637	45,469	63,310	Buchanan
Butler**	023	41,022	40,867	14,375	17,763	26,742	589,680	.0124	524,376	149	121,848	242	17,267	91	39,525	36,175	31,433	Butler
Caldwell*	025	9,345	8,969	14,684	3,667	30,035	137,220	.0021	29,931	9	...	...	...	...	6,134	1,597	7,631	Caldwell
Callaway*	027	42,867	40,766	16,962	15,756	36,488	727,110	.0115	264,544	75	32,363	64	1,494	8	24,272	7,062	32,757	Callaway
Camden	029	39,133	37,051	18,438	16,795	33,933	721,530	.0142	618,229	176	131,995	262	79,087	416	53,325	12,836	33,508	Camden
Cape Girardeau**	031	70,762	68,693	17,947	29,060	34,980	1,269,980	.0268	1,290,011	366	324,903	646	34,152	180	102,966	60,497	55,332	Cape Girardeau
Carroll	033	10,137	10,285	15,726	4,317	29,644	159,410	.0025	46,596	13	6,792	14	1,239	7	8,075	3,426	8,770	Carroll
Carter	035	6,012	5,941	12,275	2,564	22,657	73,800	.0012	23,311	7	...	...	...	...	7,152	...	4,980	Carter
Cass*	037	93,436	82,092	21,914	35,805	45,399	2,047,510	.0302	713,177	203	162,950	324	1,426	8	90,776	29,874	76,523	Cass
Cedar	039	14,032	13,733	14,190	6,038	26,592	199,120	.0035	94,380	27	5,404	11	...	...	20,979	4,166	11,609	Cedar
Chariton	041	8,140	8,438	17,220	3,642	30,876	140,170	.0024	79,357	23	1,381	3	...	...	8,515	6,972	7,780	Chariton
Christian*	043	66,271	54,285	17,166	24,720	36,334	1,137,640	.0180	429,382	122	32,974	66	1,891	10	43,043	24,988	51,685	Christian
Clark**	045	7,438	7,416	15,173	3,125	28,590	112,860	.0019	52,571	15	2,655	5	...	...	5,255	4,049	6,672	Clark
Clay*	047	201,582	184,006	22,310	80,163	45,028	4,497,380	.0820	3,437,845	976	630,421	1,254	71,468	376	316,802	172,876	158,218	Clay
Clinton*	049	20,940	18,979	18,797	7,988	39,367	393,610	.0068	226,802	64	49,856	99	...	...	11,165	8,452	17,243	Clinton
Cole*	051	72,592	71,397	21,311	30,347	40,464	1,547,000	.0295	1,310,475	372	282,097	561	24,587	129	158,790	60,921	59,672	Cole
Cooper	053	17,339	16,670	15,579	6,379	33,572	270,120	.0045	119,117	34	16,201	32	...	...	21,548	1,521	13,403	Cooper
Crawford	055	24,032	22,804	14,683	9,501	29,753	352,850	.0075	332,221	94	16,069	32	...	...	25,076	8,082	19,068	Crawford
Dade	057	7,872	7,923	15,067	3,364	27,272	118,610	.0018	28,731	8	...	...	...	...	4,742	...	7,237	Dade
Dallas*	059	16,430	15,661	13,492	6,537	26,719	221,670	.0038	84,853	24	9,597	19	...	...	17,723	2,404	13,298	Dallas
Daviess	061	8,111	8,016	15,229	3,348	29,519	123,520	.0019	36,573	10	1,118	2	...	...	7,902	3,265	6,807	Daviess
DeKalb*	063	12,234	11,597	11,864	3,802	30,390	145,150	.0027	71,786	20	1,561	3	...	...	11,777	2,775	7,677	DeKalb
Dent	065	15,088	14,927	14,120	6,377	26,535	213,050	.0041	140,040	40	25,380	50	...	...	31,223	6,265	12,286	Dent
Douglas	067	13,548	13,084	12,943	5,581	24,855	175,350	.0029	53,663	15	11,924	24	...	...	14,963	2,712	11,401	Douglas
Dunklin**	069	32,637	33,155	13,257	14,269	24,046	432,680	.0086	313,110	89	67,221	134	5,380	28	55,808	22,312	24,139	Dunklin
Franklin*	071	99,506	93,807	19,928	38,626	40,781	1,982,980	.0329	1,047,389	297	228,480	454	17,638	93	76,833	50,874	81,045	Franklin
Gasconade	073	15,689	15,342	17,573	6,555	33,298	275,700	.0046	133,264	38	21,863	43	...	...	17,210	4,540	13,460	Gasconade
Gentry	075	6,399	6,861	15,373	2,846	27,435	98,370	.0018	54,739	16	...	...	...	...	9,271	5,771	5,567	Gentry
Greene*	077	249,887	240,391	18,048	109,627	32,971	4,509,950	.0927	4,306,088	1,223	698,711	1,390	108,033	569	342,687	187,637	205,250	Greene
Grundy	079	10,252	10,432	14,904	4,571	26,492	152,800	.0028	91,015	26	15,571	31	2,294	12	22,181	5,268	8,460	Grundy
Harrison	081	8,820	8,850	15,063	3,825	27,575	132,860	.0029	134,353	38	22,884	46	...	...	16,130	1,300	7,888	Harrison
Henry	083	22,889	21,997	15,782	9,698	29,865	361,240	.0068	250,522	71	26,289	52	6,161	32	36,441	18,381	18,848	Henry
Hickory	085	9,199	8,940	14,212	4,264	24,269	130,740	.0020	25,230	7	...	...	...	...	4,643	1,803	8,686	Hickory
Holt	087	5,025	5,351	16,446	2,321	28,372	82,640	.0015	47,572	14	...	...	...	...	3,866	1,373	4,631	Holt
Howard*	089	9,909	10,212	15,603	4,048	30,657	154,610	.0023	33,357	9	1,055	2	...	...	9,412	2,064	8,181	Howard
Howell**	091	37,961	37,238	13,108	15,956	25,045	497,590	.0109	474,815	135	144,427	287	16,096	85	36,691	26,606	31,031	Howell
Iron	093	10,158	10,697	13,990	4,476	25,394	142,110	.0024	59,587	17	2,619	5	...	...	16,007	4,482	8,467	Iron
Jackson*	095	665,173	654,880	19,289	273,954	37,299	12,830,360	.2330	8,997,248	2,555	1,327,520	2,640	302,007	1,590	955,431	528,017	505,505	Jackson
Jasper*	097	110,824	104,686	15,133	44,544	30,292	1,677,080	.0346	1,473,014	418	332,736	662	47,922	252	102,050	63,113	84,548	Jasper
Jefferson*	099	213,724	198,099	20,496	80,687	42,959	4,380,500	.0657	1,551,121	440	304,616	606	13,829	73	284,430	61,994	171,803	Jefferson
Johnson**	101	51,438	48,258	15,559	18,893	33,852	800,330	.0133	333,501	95	100,107	199	5,107	27	29,073	8,787	38,976	Johnson
Knox	103	4,232	4,361	14,421	1,870	25,746	61,030	.0011	33,878	10	1,874	4	...	...	9,637	2,265	3,922	Knox
Laclede**	105	33,928	32,513	14,864	14,049	28,618	504,320	.0103	426,690	121	76,261	152	16,759	88	47,581	9,089	27,198	Laclede
Lafayette*	107	33,226	32,960	18,369	13,266	36,573	610,340	.0100	286,303	81	20,018	40	22,232	117	38,251	19,179	27,782	Lafayette
Lawrence	109	37,328	35,204	14,571	14,497	30,246	543,890	.0088	399,382	113	25,888	51	1,444	8	45,060	12,685	28,811	Lawrence
Lewis**	111	10,183	10,494	15,106	4,199	29,387	153,820	.0025	59,656	17	5,202	10	...	...	6,535	2,435	8,618	Lewis
Lincoln*	113	47,892	38,944	16,346	15,507	39,873	782,860	.0132	376,309	107	76,088	151	1,215	6	36,729	20,132	34,121	Lincoln
Linn	115	13,261	13,754	15,306	5,884	27,406	202,970	.0035	98,144	28	19,067	38	1,345	7	12,774	4,404	11,645	Linn
Livingston	117	14,322	14,558	16,450	6,071	30,855	235,600	.0043	172,849	49	30,672	61	7,343	39	32,110	3,451	11,630	Livingston
McDonald*	119	22,320	21,681	12,935	8,759	26,069	288,710	.0051	127,583	36	2,751	5	...	...	50,413	4,611	16,976	McDonald
Macon	121	15,620	15,762	15,791	6,802	28,827	246,650	.0041	101,055	29	19,102	38	1,041	5	13,957	7,473	13,560	Macon
Madison	123	11,830	11,800	13,149	4,991	25,555	155,550	.0029	85,475	24	7,467	15	...	...	18,116	2,413	9,706	Madison
Maries	125	8,678	8,903	16,647	3,782	31,012	144,460	.0022	37,201	11	2,267	5	...	...	5,737	1,351	8,261	Maries
Marion**	127	28,484	28,289	15,610	11,496	31,072	444,630	.0091	384,663	109	75,923	151	3,864	20	61,128	24,828	21,397	Marion
Mercer	129	3,575	3,757	16,862	1,690	28,268	60,280	.0009	17,313	5	...	...	...	...	...	1,062	3,502	Mercer
Miller	131	24,740	23,564	15,269	10,143	29,643	377,750	.0072	266,230	76	14,375	29	2,608	14	44,211	8,825	20,603	Miller
Mississippi	133	13,745	13,427	11,816	5,654	22,598	162,410	.0033	115,904	33	7,825	16	...	...	15,070	6,145	9,231	Mississippi
Moniteau*	135	15,162	14,827	16,311	5,582	35,534	247,300	.0044	141,417	40	5,188	10	...	...	15,807	2,547	11,538	Moniteau
Monroe	137	9,509	9,311	15,257	3,913	29,641	145,080	.0024	52,543	15	3,732	7	...	...	1,840	2,866	8,278	Monroe
Montgomery	139	12,025	12,136	16,971	5,164	31,389	204,080	.0035	108,114	31	4,556	9	...	...	22,979	3,225	11,060	Montgomery
Morgan	141	20,477	19,309	14,954	8,353	29,192	306,220	.0056	187,518	53	12,327	25	1,630	9	42,358	7,424	16,521	Morgan
New Madrid	143	18,921	19,760	14,497	8,357	26,163	274,290	.0056	226,356	64	7,840	16	1,839	10	17,194	9,521	14,153	New Madrid
Newton*	145	55,238	52,636	16,545	21,793	32,977	913,930	.0149	384,770	109	111,103	221	3,304	17	45,091	21,146	44,493	Newton
Nodaway**	147	21,740	21,912	15,390	8,695	30,446	334,570	.0060	190,447	54	23,670	47	5,719	30	52,631	1,852	17,441	Nodaway
Oregon	149	10,407	10,344	12,159	4,545	21,822	126,540	.0024	72,360	21	14,788	29	...	...	17,978	2,422	8,593	Oregon
Osage*	151	13,470	13,062	18,076	5,201	37,028	243,480	.0041	126,213	36	1,025	2	1,326	7	10,720	2,976	12,080	Osage
Ozark	153	9,542	9,542	14,048	4,262	25,044	134,050	.0023	54,875	16	...	...	...	...	13,159	1,022	9,018	Ozark
Pemiscot	155	19,582	20,047	11,533	8,267	21,662	225,840	.0047	164,244	47	16,745	33	...	...	31,958	16,139	13,239	Pemiscot
Perry	157	18,346	18,132	17,439	7,350	34,420	319,930	.0061	239,118	68	42,786	85	...	...	9,002	...	15,336	Perry
Pettis**	159	39,656	39,403	15,796	16,186	30,918	626,400	.0122	480,645	136	114,392	227	16,413	86	46,068	25,221	30,774	Pettis
Phelps**	161	42,060	39,825	14,763	17,347	28,317	620,950	.0121	453,050	129	91,512	182	12,382	65	49,824	13,846	32,431	Phelps
Pike	163	18,517	18,351	14,309	6,771	31,058	264,960	.0046	124,715	35	15,304	30	...	...	19,415	14,425	13,636	Pike
Platte*	165	83,253	73,781	26,358	33,998	51,278	2,194,370	.0335	1,034,822	294	46,296	92	6,121	32	115,458	41,238	69,786	Platte
Polk*	167	28,841	26,992	13,413	10,849	28,837	386,850	.0076	266,803	76	55,152	110	2,622	14	52,591	15,457	22,268	Polk
Pulaski**	169	46,136	41,165	12,885	14,497	33,001	594,450	.0105	263,461	75	39,123	78	2,125	11	15,989	7,874	28,886	Pulaski
Putnam	171	5,112	5,223	14,722	2,344	25,543	75,260	.0012	23,200	7	...	...	...	...	9,575	1,582	4,739	Putnam
Ralls**	173	9,687	9,626	18,298	3,981	35,420	177,250	.0025	36,432	10	...	...	...	...	8,232	...	8,794	Ralls
Randolph**	175	25,228	24,663	14,535	9,645	30,583	366,690	.0067	321,223	91	78,498	156	6,530	34	33,888	17,440	18,235	Randolph
Ray*	177	24,400	23,354	19,192	9,434	39,478	468,280	.0070	145,489	41	12,542	25	...	...	22,185	7,755	20,652	Ray
Reynolds	179	6,518	6,689	14,118	2,919	25,205	92,020	.0015	26,255	7	1,563	3	...	...	9,247	2,727	5,807	Reynolds
Ripley	181	13,999	13,509	11,866	5,835	22,488	166,110	.0032	93,161	26	7,228	14	...	...	22,309	1,672	11,001	Ripley
St. Charles*	183	329,900	283,883	24,863	123,928	52,326	8,202,170	.1192	3,010,569	855	474,871	944	115,107	606	391,344	175,903	278,709	St. Charles
St. Clair	185	9,573	9,652	14,024	4,340	24,737	134,250	.0023	54,728	16	1,866	4	...	...	12,756	1,187	8,734	St. Clair
Ste. Genevieve	186	18,451	17,842	17,656	6,988	36,772	325,780	.0050	110,230	31	9,620	19	...	...	13,509	6,357	14,954	Ste. Genevieve
St. Francois**	187	61,536	55,641	13,656	22,279	30,237	840,360	.0166	598,069	170	168,802	336	18,760	99	70,841	55,007	42,230	St. Francois
St. Louis*	189	1,015,417	1,016,315	23,155	402,919	46,326	23,511,940	.4117	16,296,065	4,627	2,295,446	4,565	727,471	3,829	2,128,216	1,178,575	787,231	St. Louis
Saline**	195	22,334	23,756	16,938	9,483	31,557	378,290	.0062	162,564	46	23,778	47	2,975	16	33,253	15,398	17,782	Saline
Schuyler**	197	4,300	4,170	14,730	1,861	27,008	63,340	.0011	27,680	8	...	...	...	...	3,669	...	3,850	Schuyler
Scotland	199	4,886	4,983	13,629	1,975	26,617	66,590	.0011	25,418	7	...	...	...	...	4,372	1,318	4,210	Scotland
Scott**	201	41,150	40,422	15,273	16,700	30,254	628,500	.0118	412,610	117	60,352	120	17,018	90	53,213	31,326	30,467	Scott
Shannon	203	8,354	8,324	11,096	3,570	20,502	92,700	.0016	30,120	9	5,925	12	...	...	6,867	2,728	7,085	Shannon
Shelby	205	6,702	6,799	15,079	2,858	28,079	101,060	.0016	36,895	10	...	...	...	...	4,060	1,871	5,883	Shelby
Stoddard	207	29,869	29,705	14,209	12,864	26,182	424,420	.0085	330,687	94	29,627	59	1,986	10	41,907	26,972	24,345	Stoddard
Stone**	209	31,189	28,658	16,095	12,726	31,125	501,990	.0080	180,048	51	53,183	106	...	...	32,965	7,378	25,764	Stone
Sullivan	211	6,976	7,219	14,048	3,087	25,499	98,000	.0018	56,947	16	1,229	2	...	...	6,537	4,675	6,208	Sullivan
Taney**	213	42,474	39,703	16,292	18,574	29,819	691,970	.0138	583,339	166	87,742	174	84,017	442	64,978	27,821	35,256	Taney
Texas	215	24,551	23,003	12,333	10,086	23,826	302,790	.0057	162,806	46	15,814	31	3,390	18	23,271	9,212	20,095	Texas
Vernon	217	20,324	20,454	14,924	8,383	28,829	303,310	.0055	172,966	49	31,249	62	2,444	13	20,394	31,236	16,982	Vernon
Warren*	219	28,605	24,525	18,535	10,909	39,095	530,200	.0089	280,234	80	37,407	74	23,410	123	25,832	15,863	23,816	Warren
Washington*	221	24,204	23,344	12,404	9,148	26,106	300,230	.0054	139,719	40	21,608	43	...	...	27,036	1,370	18,060	Washington
Wayne	223	13,122	13,259	13,550	6,029	22,737	177,800	.0031	80,116	23	8,876	18	...	...	16,629	5,942	11,415	Wayne
Webster*	225	34,597	31,045	13,586	12,186	30,787	470,040	.0060	210,355	60	21,165	42	...	...	30,564	6,091	25,414	Webster
Worth	227	2,262	2,382	15,287	1,038	26,441	34,580	.0005	7,190	2	...	...	...	...	...	...	2,274	Worth
Wright	229	18,424	17,955	12,255	7,458	24,174	225,790	.0046	166,945	47	43,837	87	...	...	17,749	8,713	14,716	Wright
INDEPENDENT CITY																		
St. Louis*	510	324,238	348,189	14,896	145,556	26,297	4,829,690	.0861	2,615,125	743	252,331	502	84,483	445	382,754	292,732	215,741	St. Louis
Missouri Total		**5,792,159**	**5,595,211**	**18,733**	**2,340,090**	**36,310**	**108,504,190**	**1.9115**	**67,777,368**	**19,246**	**10,713,022**	**21,302**	**2,080,546**	**10,947**	**8,113,431**	**3,921,735**	**4,547,989**	**Missouri**

Montana (MT; Code 30; 56 Counties)

County or County Equivalent	FIPS County Code	Population Estimate 7/1/05	Population Census 4/1/00	Per Capita Income 2004	House-holds Estimate 7/1/05	Median Household Income 2004	Disposable Income 2004 ($1,000)	Market Ability Index 2004	Total Retail Sales 2004 Sales ($1,000)	Total Retail Sales Ranally Sales Units	General Merchandise 2004 Sales ($1,000)	General Merchandise Ranally Sales Units	Apparel Store 2004 Sales ($1,000)	Apparel Store Ranally Sales Units	Food Store Sales 2004 ($1,000)	Health & Drug Store 2004 ($1,000)	Passenger Car Regis-trations 2004	County or County Equivalent
Beaverhead	001	8,780	9,202	14,856	3,665	28,216	130,440	.0025	95,951	27	...	...	3,217	17	20,098	2,947	7,886	Beaverhead
Big Horn	003	13,029	12,671	10,064	3,937	26,518	131,130	.0026	71,411	20	...	...	...	...	17,760	...	7,626	Big Horn
Blaine	005	6,601	7,009	11,727	2,489	24,965	77,410	.0014	37,018	11	...	...	...	...	8,069	1,983	5,208	Blaine
Broadwater	007	4,469	4,385	15,608	1,771	32,125	69,750	.0010	15,108	4	...	...	...	...	4,577	...	4,166	Broadwater
Carbon*	009	9,919	9,552	16,092	4,049	31,250	159,620	.0024	46,138	13	...	...	1,039	5	7,405	1,956	8,938	Carbon
Carter	011	1,319	1,360	13,328	537	25,937	17,580	.0003	2,545	1	...	...	...	...	...	...	1,441	Carter
Cascade*	013	79,409	80,357	16,614	32,956	31,584	1,319,290	.0256	1,027,263	292	244,590	486	25,008	132	107,838	48,119	66,005	Cascade
Chouteau	015	5,349	5,970	14,754	2,198	28,872	78,920	.0013	35,327	10	...	...	...	...	4,330	1,575	5,198	Chouteau
Custer	017	11,163	11,696	15,507	4,749	28,974	173,110	.0036	158,550	45	28,915	57	6,363	33	30,290	4,096	10,002	Custer
Daniels	019	1,856	2,017	15,857	875	26,624	29,430	.0006	27,639	8	...	...	...	...	7,441	2,539	1,980	Daniels
Dawson	021	8,549	9,059	15,950	3,595	30,034	136,360	.0026	92,865	26	7,784	15	1,406	7	7,094	10,279	7,792	Dawson
Deer Lodge	023	8,755	9,417	14,771	3,957	26,312	129,320	.0023	64,945	18	...	...	...	...	18,048	7,638	7,739	Deer Lodge
Fallon	025	2,738	2,837	14,996	1,132	28,807	41,060	.0008	34,295	10	1,192	2	...	...	9,155	4,262	2,640	Fallon
Fergus	027	11,478	11,893	15,396	4,824	29,017	176,720	.0033	114,934	33	7,130	14	3,805	20	21,727	3,920	10,700	Fergus
Flathead**	029	82,627	74,471	15,631	31,183	32,727	1,291,570	.0256	1,031,483	293	243,893	485	21,762	115	138,613	27,548	70,547	Flathead
Gallatin**	031	76,679	67,831	17,493	29,261	36,154	1,341,380	.0265	1,134,821	322	116,089	231	34,225	180	167,743	26,467	64,335	Gallatin

Source: Devonshire Associates Ltd. and Scan/US, Inc. 2005. ...Data less than 1,000. (d) Data not available.
* Component of a Metropolitan Core Based Statistical Area.
** Component of a Micropolitan Core Based Statistical Area.

Counties: Population/Income/Sales, *Continued*

County or County Equivalent	FIPS County Code	Population Estimate 7/1/05	Population Census 4/1/00	Per Capita Income 2004	House-holds Estimate 7/1/05	Median Household Income 2004	Disposable Income 2004 ($1,000)	Market Ability Index 2004	Total Retail Sales 2004 Sales ($1,000)	Total Retail Sales Ranally Sales Units	General Merchandise 2004 Sales ($1,000)	General Merchandise Ranally Sales Units	Apparel Store 2004 Sales ($1,000)	Apparel Store Ranally Sales Units	Food Store Sales 2004 ($1,000)	Health & Drug Store 2004 ($1,000)	Passenger Car Regis-trations 2004	County or County Equivalent
Garfield	.033	1,223	1,279	13,475	523	25,207	16,480	.0003	6,117	2	...	...	...	...	3,347	1,259	1,347	Garfield
Glacier	.035	13,321	13,247	10,818	4,277	26,647	144,110	.0029	87,963	25	2,005	4	4,673	25	24,577	1,140	8,055	Glacier
Golden Valley	.037	1,080	1,042	11,019	356	26,241	11,900	.0002	1,569	0	...	...	...	...	1,113	...	816	Golden Valley
Granite	.039	2,905	2,830	14,182	1,179	27,378	41,200	.0007	17,079	5	...	...	...	...	4,794	...	2,606	Granite
Hill**	.041	16,117	16,673	14,908	6,444	29,858	240,280	.0046	170,017	48	26,616	53	7,152	38	32,547	3,322	13,454	Hill
Jefferson**	.043	10,875	10,049	16,972	3,717	39,629	184,570	.0026	26,855	8	...	...	...	...	9,666	1,445	9,086	Jefferson
Judith Basin	.045	2,111	2,329	15,343	929	27,639	32,390	.0005	5,242	1	...	...	...	...	2,148	...	2,402	Judith Basin
Lake	.047	27,862	26,507	13,111	10,386	28,008	365,290	.0071	242,612	69	29,269	58	1,338	7	52,517	7,625	22,743	Lake
Lewis and Clark**	.049	58,051	55,716	17,913	23,120	35,557	1,039,890	.0196	776,207	220	139,665	278	12,068	64	122,176	23,048	48,239	Lewis and Clark
Liberty	.051	1,962	2,158	15,520	819	29,193	30,450	.0005	11,951	3	...	...	...	...	5,951	1,258	1,883	Liberty
Lincoln	.053	18,921	18,837	13,592	7,813	25,983	257,180	.0045	117,287	33	8,501	17	1,475	8	28,148	5,474	15,925	Lincoln
McCone	.055	1,719	1,977	16,905	800	28,925	29,060	.0004	8,851	3	...	...	...	...	1,987	...	2,057	McCone
Madison	.057	6,980	6,851	15,342	2,921	29,367	107,090	.0017	36,144	10	...	...	...	...	10,910	3,503	6,492	Madison
Meagher	.059	1,994	1,932	13,591	784	27,168	27,100	.0004	8,950	3	...	...	...	...	1,076	1,310	1,629	Meagher
Mineral	.061	3,869	3,884	14,017	1,601	26,650	54,230	.0010	29,624	8	...	...	...	...	8,214	...	3,366	Mineral
Missoula*	.063	100,118	95,802	17,414	41,813	33,144	1,743,480	.0355	1,600,814	455	351,579	699	41,311	217	176,081	45,603	86,431	Missoula
Musselshell	.065	4,474	4,497	13,020	1,857	25,363	58,250	.0009	16,376	5	...	...	...	...	6,995	1,121	4,260	Musselshell
Park	.067	15,825	15,694	16,682	6,880	30,770	264,000	.0046	148,304	42	6,301	13	3,227	17	17,599	6,450	14,042	Park
Petroleum	.069	487	493	12,608	207	22,965	6,140	.0001	...	...	...	...	...	...	...	...	490	Petroleum
Phillips	.071	4,070	4,601	15,671	1,815	27,770	63,780	.0012	37,949	11	...	...	...	...	7,044	1,108	4,093	Phillips
Pondera	.073	6,077	6,424	14,288	2,385	28,737	86,830	.0017	61,838	18	1,083	2	...	...	9,124	3,850	5,370	Pondera
Powder River	.075	1,815	1,858	14,171	733	27,783	25,720	.0004	12,057	3	...	...	...	...	6,155	...	1,988	Powder River
Powell	.077	6,784	7,180	13,101	2,395	29,647	88,880	.0014	21,859	6	...	...	...	...	9,927	...	5,212	Powell
Prairie	.079	1,152	1,199	14,384	528	25,074	16,570	.0003	6,017	2	...	...	...	...	1,120	...	1,298	Prairie
Ravalli	.081	40,335	36,070	14,175	14,565	31,200	571,750	.0102	296,127	84	34,094	68	5,416	29	83,047	11,338	32,203	Ravalli
Richland	.083	8,887	9,667	16,850	3,874	30,610	149,750	.0027	96,495	27	4,998	10	4,632	24	18,266	5,946	8,295	Richland
Roosevelt	.085	10,328	10,620	10,519	3,555	24,116	108,640	.0023	71,803	20	...	...	1,931	10	14,015	2,255	7,016	Roosevelt
Rosebud	.087	9,257	9,383	15,534	3,343	34,073	143,800	.0024	57,830	16	...	...	...	...	10,669	...	7,416	Rosebud
Sanders	.089	10,697	10,227	13,079	4,291	25,957	139,910	.0024	50,365	14	...	...	...	...	17,186	1,836	9,386	Sanders
Sheridan	.091	3,397	4,105	18,075	1,714	28,388	61,400	.0010	32,330	9	...	...	...	...	7,610	2,007	3,855	Sheridan
Silver Bow**	.093	32,391	34,606	16,278	14,352	29,522	527,260	.0110	492,355	140	82,505	164	30,620	161	70,561	21,072	28,569	Silver Bow
Stillwater	.095	8,584	8,195	17,732	3,288	36,421	152,210	.0024	56,389	16	...	...	...	...	6,647	1,500	7,842	Stillwater
Sweet Grass	.097	3,602	3,609	16,882	1,515	31,672	60,810	.0012	45,755	13	...	...	...	...	5,525	1,426	3,306	Sweet Grass
Teton	.099	6,349	6,445	14,541	2,518	29,094	92,320	.0018	61,573	17	...	...	...	...	5,023	2,366	5,899	Teton
Toole	.101	5,038	5,267	14,206	1,947	29,177	71,570	.0013	34,070	10	7,967	16	...	...	7,809	1,416	4,171	Toole
Treasure	.103	681	861	18,253	352	27,651	12,430	.0002	2,739	1	...	...	...	...	...	...	802	Treasure
Valley	.105	7,069	7,675	16,582	3,108	30,000	117,220	.0021	67,962	19	2,699	5	2,119	11	14,992	3,963	7,002	Valley
Wheatland	.107	2,009	2,259	12,658	831	24,302	25,430	.0005	13,755	4	...	...	...	...	3,996	...	1,844	Wheatland
Wibaux	.109	932	1,068	15,311	415	27,311	14,270	.0002	1,029	0	...	...	...	...	...	...	983	Wibaux
Yellowstone*	.111	135,784	129,352	17,833	54,868	35,052	2,421,380	.0489	2,199,002	624	431,695	858	77,026	405	224,767	63,476	110,168	Yellowstone
Montana Total		**927,852**	**902,195**	**16,067**	**369,996**	**32,014**	**14,908,110**	**.2861**	**11,022,426**	**3,127**	**1,781,479**	**3,540**	**300,276**	**1,579**	**1,606,684**	**373,333**	**784,244**	**Montana**

Nebraska (NE; Code 31; 93 Counties)

County or County Equivalent	FIPS County Code	Population Estimate 7/1/05	Population Census 4/1/00	Per Capita Income 2004	House-holds Estimate 7/1/05	Median Household Income 2004	Disposable Income 2004 ($1,000)	Market Ability Index 2004	Total Retail Sales 2004 Sales ($1,000)	Total Retail Sales Ranally Sales Units	General Merchandise 2004 Sales ($1,000)	General Merchandise Ranally Sales Units	Apparel Store 2004 Sales ($1,000)	Apparel Store Ranally Sales Units	Food Store Sales 2004 ($1,000)	Health & Drug Store 2004 ($1,000)	Passenger Car Regis-trations 2004	County or County Equivalent
Adams**	.001	30,836	31,151	16,928	12,182	34,955	521,990	.0098	373,570	106	62,448	124	8,176	43	72,155	23,376	23,715	Adams
Antelope	.003	7,038	7,452	14,420	2,890	29,002	101,490	.0018	57,590	16	...	...	...	...	7,107	...	6,207	Antelope
Arthur	.005	387	444	15,866	188	27,021	6,140	.0001	...	...	...	...	...	...	...	...	445	Arthur
Banner**	.007	730	819	16,315	312	31,061	11,910	.0002	...	...	...	...	...	...	...	...	803	Banner
Blaine	.009	508	583	14,390	240	24,836	7,310	.0001	...	...	...	...	...	...	...	...	574	Blaine
Boone	.011	5,694	6,259	15,741	2,445	30,251	89,630	.0018	74,627	21	1,495	3	...	...	3,242	2,140	5,353	Boone
Box Butte	.013	11,270	12,158	19,106	4,726	37,026	215,330	.0036	111,662	32	12,654	25	2,086	11	20,402	4,712	9,832	Box Butte
Boyd	.015	2,240	2,438	14,107	1,015	25,292	31,600	.0005	11,158	3	...	...	...	...	2,093	...	2,248	Boyd
Brown	.017	3,436	3,525	14,703	1,515	27,243	50,520	.0010	33,157	9	...	...	...	...	2,599	1,097	3,042	Brown
Buffalo**	.019	43,441	42,259	16,405	16,605	35,244	712,650	.0147	651,955	185	151,819	302	25,606	135	57,215	27,873	35,426	Buffalo
Burt	.021	7,286	7,791	16,941	3,111	32,240	123,430	.0021	60,295	17	...	...	...	...	3,517	4,424	6,420	Burt
Butler	.023	8,834	8,767	17,019	3,542	34,724	150,350	.0023	43,632	12	...	...	...	...	9,837	1,863	8,164	Butler
Cass*	.025	25,823	24,334	19,665	9,626	42,967	507,810	.0077	181,103	51	10,341	21	...	...	16,540	5,920	21,572	Cass
Cedar	.027	8,954	9,615	15,795	3,640	31,780	141,430	.0026	88,983	25	...	...	...	...	6,104	2,540	7,739	Cedar
Chase	.029	4,013	4,068	15,776	1,653	31,275	63,310	.0013	57,901	16	...	...	...	...	6,872	...	3,466	Chase
Cherry	.031	5,976	6,148	14,655	2,509	28,643	87,580	.0019	82,577	23	7,530	15	2,598	14	14,938	1,198	5,479	Cherry
Cheyenne	.033	9,968	9,830	16,127	4,133	31,862	160,750	.0108	1,024,444	291	28,684	57	3,441	18	24,956	20,556	8,009	Cheyenne
Clay**	.035	6,765	7,039	16,034	2,706	32,744	108,470	.0019	60,391	17	...	...	...	...	12,392	...	5,920	Clay
Colfax	.037	10,512	10,441	14,395	3,634	33,917	151,320	.0029	102,263	29	...	...	...	...	15,395	3,237	7,604	Colfax
Cuming	.039	9,635	10,203	15,942	3,922	31,910	153,600	.0030	117,560	33	4,140	8	1,246	7	17,538	6,353	8,212	Cuming
Custer	.041	11,302	11,793	15,186	4,771	29,585	171,630	.0032	114,434	32	6,078	12	...	...	19,737	12,010	10,390	Custer
Dakota*	.043	20,799	20,253	15,454	7,196	36,002	321,420	.0052	120,434	34	18,037	36	...	...	32,577	7,665	13,902	Dakota
Dawes	.045	8,815	9,060	13,698	3,470	28,033	120,750	.0028	137,513	39	27,381	54	1,902	10	21,673	7,574	7,385	Dawes
Dawson**	.047	24,642	24,365	14,842	8,715	34,180	365,730	.0070	254,821	72	34,954	70	3,690	19	37,735	15,211	17,910	Dawson
Deuel	.049	2,013	2,098	16,940	876	31,769	34,100	.0006	21,259	6	...	...	...	...	3,396	1,139	1,929	Deuel
Dixon*	.051	6,020	6,339	16,028	2,398	32,882	96,490	.0015	24,388	7	...	...	...	...	3,580	1,385	5,281	Dixon
Dodge**	.053	35,807	36,160	17,514	14,619	35,030	627,110	.0141	735,318	209	120,916	240	15,655	82	64,993	50,469	27,946	Dodge
Douglas*	.055	483,981	463,585	18,981	185,006	41,092	9,186,290	.1794	7,852,521	2,230	901,902	1,794	329,346	1,733	954,433	462,063	349,593	Douglas
Dundy	.057	2,158	2,292	14,319	947	26,838	30,900	.0005	15,893	5	...	...	...	...	2,257	...	2,045	Dundy
Fillmore	.059	6,363	6,634	16,841	2,642	33,504	107,160	.0018	52,169	15	...	...	...	...	4,309	3,029	5,584	Fillmore
Franklin	.061	3,402	3,574	14,471	1,429	28,297	49,230	.0008	15,864	5	...	...	...	...	5,240	...	3,309	Franklin
Frontier	.063	2,790	3,099	16,161	1,183	31,108	45,090	.0007	8,374	2	...	...	...	...	1,285	...	2,814	Frontier
Furnas	.065	5,130	5,324	15,388	2,225	29,162	78,940	.0015	53,190	15	...	...	...	...	5,185	...	4,594	Furnas
Gage**	.067	23,611	22,993	16,593	9,633	33,312	391,770	.0069	228,316	65	28,139	56	7,093	37	34,137	14,118	19,722	Gage
Garden	.069	2,177	2,292	14,410	1,000	25,964	31,370	.0005	11,610	3	...	...	...	...	3,193	...	2,247	Garden
Garfield	.071	1,811	1,902	14,130	803	25,973	25,590	.0007	37,378	11	...	...	...	...	...	...	1,744	Garfield
Gosper**	.073	2,030	2,143	17,916	851	34,904	36,370	.0005	3,105	1	...	...	...	...	...	...	1,998	Gosper
Grant	.075	661	747	17,776	293	32,518	11,750	.0002	3,633	1	...	...	...	...	...	...	696	Grant
Greeley	.077	2,550	2,714	14,102	1,066	27,389	35,960	.0008	42,702	12	...	...	...	...	2,483	...	2,398	Greeley
Hall**	.079	54,771	53,534	16,254	20,694	35,279	890,240	.0193	924,084	262	259,065	515	37,718	199	54,224	28,627	40,210	Hall
Hamilton	.081	9,513	9,403	17,024	3,513	37,857	161,950	.0024	45,779	13	...	...	...	...	3,015	3,638	7,920	Hamilton
Harlan	.083	3,608	3,786	15,870	1,609	29,160	57,260	.0009	23,939	7	...	...	...	...	3,249	...	3,541	Harlan
Hayes	.085	1,118	1,068	12,021	427	25,661	13,440	.0002	1,253	0	...	...	...	...	1,087	...	1,071	Hayes
Hitchcock	.087	2,992	3,111	14,248	1,273	26,575	42,630	.0007	18,633	5	...	...	...	...	2,179	...	2,949	Hitchcock
Holt	.089	10,821	11,551	15,467	4,649	29,621	167,370	.0033	131,409	37	12,970	26	2,056	11	12,399	17,472	9,924	Holt
Hooker	.091	720	783	15,083	326	26,936	10,860	.0002	3,619	1	...	...	...	...	...	...	766	Hooker
Howard**	.093	6,688	6,567	15,474	2,631	32,041	103,490	.0017	36,335	10	...	...	...	...	2,428	...	5,992	Howard
Jefferson	.095	7,950	8,333	16,375	3,470	30,909	130,180	.0024	81,135	23	13,729	27	...	...	12,111	...	7,282	Jefferson
Johnson	.097	4,505	4,488	16,107	1,890	31,327	72,560	.0013	39,542	11	...	...	...	...	5,425	...	4,071	Johnson
Kearney**	.099	6,816	6,882	17,218	2,588	36,810	117,360	.0018	32,713	9	...	...	...	...	6,048	1,009	5,965	Kearney
Keith	.101	8,230	8,875	18,424	3,952	31,387	151,630	.0030	134,674	38	13,012	26	1,651	9	13,746	6,735	8,361	Keith
Keya Paha	.103	928	983	13,082	410	24,020	12,140	.0002	2,691	1	...	...	...	...	...	...	1,025	Keya Paha
Kimball	.105	3,700	4,089	16,508	1,706	29,457	61,080	.0010	30,337	9	...	...	...	...	3,742	1,023	3,667	Kimball
Knox	.107	8,860	9,374	13,743	3,761	26,438	121,760	.0025	94,580	27	...	...	...	...	15,065	2,992	7,591	Knox
Lancaster*	.109	266,575	250,291	18,286	101,357	39,774	4,874,460	.0883	3,277,448	931	625,758	1,244	120,834	636	456,411	225,440	212,087	Lancaster
Lincoln**	.111	34,717	34,632	17,655	14,378	34,610	612,930	.0111	402,899	114	99,033	197	9,485	50	45,920	21,293	29,899	Lincoln
Logan**	.113	676	774	17,899	316	31,126	12,100	.0002	1,402	0	...	...	...	...	...	...	837	Logan
Loup	.115	760	712	11,579	286	25,122	8,800	.0001	2,397	1	...	...	...	...	...	...	695	Loup
McPherson**	.117	533	533	11,839	205	25,123	6,310	.0001	1,416	0	...	...	...	...	...	...	526	McPherson
Madison**	.119	36,184	35,226	15,563	13,538	33,991	563,130	.0129	655,868	186	151,340	301	26,631	140	80,767	26,463	25,882	Madison
Merrick**	.121	8,057	8,204	15,992	3,194	32,916	128,850	.0020	42,142	12	...	...	...	...	3,652	...	6,957	Merrick
Morrill	.123	5,188	5,440	14,410	2,114	28,920	74,760	.0013	32,326	9	2,390	5	...	...	7,613	...	4,706	Morrill
Nance	.125	3,585	4,038	15,604	1,514	30,405	55,940	.0009	17,451	5	...	...	...	...	4,039	...	3,378	Nance
Nemaha	.127	6,883	7,576	16,783	3,027	31,376	115,520	.0021	75,594	21	5,370	11	...	...	15,818	9,542	6,223	Nemaha
Nuckolls	.129	4,743	5,057	15,440	2,169	27,512	73,230	.0014	52,828	15	5,012	10	...	...	9,219	1,238	4,552	Nuckolls
Otoe	.131	15,427	15,396	17,629	6,218	35,767	271,970	.0045	125,847	36	1,298	3	11,781	62	17,090	10,575	12,861	Otoe
Pawnee	.133	2,762	3,087	16,434	1,328	28,012	45,390	.0007	13,193	4	...	...	...	...	...	2,185	2,844	Pawnee
Perkins	.135	2,955	3,200	17,036	1,258	32,640	50,340	.0008	15,178	4	...	...	...	...	...	...	2,865	Perkins
Phelps	.137	9,526	9,747	17,463	3,820	35,424	166,350	.0030	111,198	32	2,793	6	...	...	17,298	10,948	8,458	Phelps
Pierce**	.139	7,616	7,857	14,684	2,960	31,076	111,830	.0021	70,682	20	...	...	...	...	8,087	...	6,596	Pierce
Platte**	.141	30,978	31,662	17,819	12,218	36,772	552,000	.0100	365,807	104	58,414	116	11,139	59	58,563	23,667	24,826	Platte
Polk	.143	5,385	5,639	18,260	2,248	35,528	98,330	.0015	32,072	9	...	...	...	...	6,224	2,065	4,958	Polk
Red Willow	.145	11,063	11,448	16,275	4,710	31,311	180,050	.0044	240,970	68	61,153	122	6,213	33	25,761	14,118	9,777	Red Willow
Richardson	.147	8,592	9,531	15,713	3,892	28,472	135,010	.0024	78,591	22	4,256	8	1,077	6	12,540	6,590	7,853	Richardson
Rock	.149	1,511	1,756	15,354	768	24,735	23,200	.0004	7,273	2	...	...	...	...	...	...	1,661	Rock
Saline	.151	14,444	13,843	14,954	5,175	34,069	216,000	.0038	114,209	32	4,145	8	...	...	17,322	7,463	11,618	Saline
Sarpy*	.153	137,701	122,595	22,194	50,911	50,002	3,056,190	.0457	1,151,923	327	331,403	659	23,341	123	130,544	45,819	106,140	Sarpy
Saunders*	.155	20,179	19,830	18,660	7,794	39,444	376,550	.0058	131,661	37	4,183	8	1,303	7	26,893	4,128	17,455	Saunders
Scotts Bluff**	.157	36,634	36,951	15,286	14,939	30,781	559,990	.0114	477,941	136	117,010	233	13,788	73	61,678	13,914	28,656	Scotts Bluff
Seward*	.159	16,447	16,496	18,388	6,160	40,118	302,430	.0047	115,164	33	18,773	37	...	...	4,998	6,386	13,668	Seward
Sheridan	.161	5,617	6,198	15,409	2,513	28,261	86,550	.0017	68,101	19	5,049	10	...	...	14,975	1,095	5,306	Sheridan
Sherman	.163	3,050	3,318	14,757	1,346	27,457	45,010	.0008	24,799	7	...	...	...	...	6,401	1,455	2,815	Sherman
Sioux	.165	1,492	1,475	14,229	607	28,712	21,230	.0003	3,000	1	...	...	...	...	...	...	1,439	Sioux
Stanton**	.167	6,664	6,455	14,775	2,291	35,231	98,460	.0014	12,805	4	...	...	...	...	1,369	...	5,270	Stanton
Thayer	.169	5,357	6,055	16,903	2,515	29,704	90,550	.0017	63,550	18	...	...	...	...	8,749	...	5,261	Thayer
Thomas	.171	629	729	17,361	329	26,941	10,920	.0002	6,026	2	...	...	...	...	...	...	769	Thomas
Thurston	.173	7,097	7,171	10,397	2,222	27,049	73,790	.0016	58,237	17	...	...	...	...	7,608	2,000	4,303	Thurston
Valley	.175	4,582	4,647	13,780	1,919	27,055	63,140	.0011	31,005	9	2,838	6	...	...	3,880	...	3,924	Valley
Washington*	.177	20,017	18,780	19,769	7,250	44,750	395,710	.0086	451,610	128	22,010	44	11,644	61	47,462	30,662	16,114	Washington
Wayne	.179	9,086	9,851	14,171	3,413	30,996	128,760	.0023	69,759	20	4,111	8	1,319	7	12,560	6,557	7,587	Wayne
Webster	.181	3,774	4,061	15,464	1,667	28,791	58,360	.0010	28,669	8	...	...	...	...	4,426	...	3,629	Webster
Wheeler	.183	790	886	14,696	353	26,651	11,610	.0002	2,337	1	...	...	...	...	...	...	803	Wheeler
York	.185	14,071	14,598	17,338	5,650	35,274	243,960	.0052	246,132	70	35,754	71	4,411	23	31,777	11,098	11,448	York
Nebraska Total		**1,751,975**	**1,711,263**	**17,853**	**681,188**	**37,483**	**31,277,930**	**.5874**	**23,147,225**	**6,567**	**3,290,557**	**6,545**	**703,014**	**3,700**	**2,777,602**	**1,239,022**	**1,386,698**	**Nebraska**

Nevada (NV; Code 32; 16 Counties, 1 Independent City)

County or County Equivalent	FIPS County Code	Population Estimate 7/1/05	Population Census 4/1/00	Per Capita Income 2004	House-holds Estimate 7/1/05	Median Household Income 2004	Disposable Income 2004 ($1,000)	Market Ability Index 2004	Total Retail Sales 2004 Sales ($1,000)	Total Retail Sales Ranally Sales Units	General Merchandise 2004 Sales ($1,000)	General Merchandise Ranally Sales Units	Apparel Store 2004 Sales ($1,000)	Apparel Store Ranally Sales Units	Food Store Sales 2004 ($1,000)	Health & Drug Store 2004 ($1,000)	Passenger Car Regis-trations 2004	County or County Equivalent
Churchill**	.001	24,399	23,982	18,380	9,182	38,770	448,450	.0075	225,689	64	20,168	40	...	...	41,947	8,344	18,520	Churchill
Clark*	.003	1,697,755	1,375,765	19,197	620,452	43,184	32,591,720	.5707	20,294,277	5,763	2,891,887	5,751	1,375,438	7,239	3,018,726	841,646	1,074,001	Clark
Douglas**	.005	45,940	41,259	24,635	18,845	47,850	1,131,720	.0155	300,566	85	...	...	1,600	8	88,857	21,131	39,484	Douglas
Elko**	.007	43,415	45,291	20,497	15,859	44,946	889,860	.0144	444,093	126	49,011	97	11,210	59	90,799	25,959	30,872	Elko
Esmeralda	.009	781	971	23,611	460	31,896	18,440	.0002	1,006	0	...	...	...	...	...	...	845	Esmeralda
Eureka**	.011	1,395	1,651	23,462	679	38,251	32,730	.0004	3,180	1	...	...	...	...	...	...	1,352	Eureka
Humboldt	.013	16,980	16,106	18,713	5,755	43,798	317,740	.0056	198,125	56	4,327	9	...	...	14,494	8,354	11,632	Humboldt
Lander	.015	4,682	5,794	23,648	2,078	42,181	110,720	.0015	29,130	8	...	...	...	...	6,497	4,335	4,156	Lander
Lincoln	.017	4,343	4,165	13,977	1,541	31,319	60,700	.0010	17,244	5	...	...	...	...	1,956	4,591	2,718	Lincoln
Lyon	.019	43,895	34,501	15,671	14,344	38,095	687,900	.0112	264,466	75	1,774	4	...	...	62,869	12,472	29,727	Lyon
Mineral	.021	4,638	5,071	18,370	2,181	31,053	85,200	.0013	26,304	7	...	...	...	...	3,497	...	4,039	Mineral
Nye**	.023	37,749	32,485	15,460	13,509	34,208	583,600	.0096	235,500	67	1,288	3	...	...	42,533	49,871	26,166	Nye
Pershing	.027	6,305	6,693	14,744	1,944	37,592	92,960	.0015	32,957	9	...	...	...	...	1,734	...	3,743	Pershing
Storey*	.029	3,623	3,399	23,574	1,556	43,296	85,410	.0011	9,841	3	...	...	...	...	...	...	3,121	Storey
Washoe*	.031	390,302	339,486	20,811	151,394	42,847	8,122,740	.1409	5,166,455	1,467	834,750	1,660	170,959	900	705,819	218,418	296,523	Washoe
White Pine	.033	8,240	9,181	17,522	3,207	35,771	144,380	.0022	43,388	12	...	...	1,584	8	9,622	6,643	6,129	White Pine

Source: Devonshire Associates Ltd. and Scan/US, Inc. 2005. ...Data less than 1,000. (d) Data not available.
* Component of a Metropolitan Core Based Statistical Area.
** Component of a Micropolitan Core Based Statistical Area.

Continued on next page

Counties: Population/Income/Sales, *Continued*

County or County Equivalent	FIPS County Code	Population Estimate 7/1/05	Population Census 4/1/00	Per Capita Income 2004	House-holds Estimate 7/1/05	Median Household Income 2004	Disposable Income 2004 ($1,000)	Market Ability Index 2004	Total Retail Sales 2004 Sales ($1,000)	Total Retail Sales Ranally Sales Units	General Merchandise 2004 Sales ($1,000)	General Merchandise Ranally Sales Units	Apparel Store 2004 Sales ($1,000)	Apparel Store Ranally Sales Units	Food Store Sales 2004 ($1,000)	Health & Drug Store 2004 ($1,000)	Passenger Car Regis-trations 2004	County or County Equivalent
INDEPENDENT CITY																		
Carson City*	.510	57,139	52,457	18,725	21,471	39,258	1,069,920	.0212	948,543	269	50,822	101	1,398	7	156,413	109,780	38,608	Carson City
Nevada Total		**2,391,581**	**1,998,257**	**19,432**	**884,457**	**43,134**	**46,474,190**	**.8058**	**28,240,763**	**8,017**	**3,855,163**	**7,667**	**1,565,859**	**8,241**	**4,246,589**	**1,312,355**	**1,591,636**	**Nevada**
New Hampshire (NH; Code 33; 10 Counties)																		
Belknap**	.001	62,646	56,325	19,396	24,180	40,711	1,215,070	.0242	1,104,531	314	154,583	307	69,796	367	181,841	33,910	46,869	Belknap
Carroll	.003	47,487	43,666	19,180	19,603	37,498	910,810	.0172	709,101	201	28,412	56	76,729	404	146,146	23,815	38,785	Carroll
Cheshire**	.005	77,820	73,825	18,732	29,567	39,931	1,457,710	.0311	1,544,554	439	168,588	335	29,373	155	211,183	47,862	58,865	Cheshire
Coos**	.007	33,515	33,111	16,767	14,222	32,129	561,940	.0120	566,616	161	12,923	26	5,836	31	82,958	32,432	25,485	Coos
Grafton**	.009	84,673	81,743	19,072	33,232	39,308	1,614,880	.0334	1,600,896	455	170,697	339	46,588	245	345,344	64,471	62,497	Grafton
Hillsborough*	.011	403,350	380,841	22,648	151,152	49,235	9,135,020	.1760	8,150,622	2,314	1,197,089	2,381	345,041	1,816	1,015,559	278,338	332,832	Hillsborough
Merrimack**	.013	148,696	136,225	20,716	55,922	44,768	3,080,410	.0576	2,435,732	692	275,660	548	56,924	300	386,125	113,023	110,808	Merrimack
Rockingham*	.015	298,070	277,359	24,957	112,962	53,396	7,438,890	.1430	6,837,798	1,942	1,369,355	2,723	315,870	1,663	1,120,791	216,562	265,151	Rockingham
Strafford*	.017	120,636	112,233	19,646	46,025	41,625	2,370,060	.0426	1,629,887	463	146,439	291	33,405	176	336,659	83,783	90,014	Strafford
Sullivan**	.019	43,085	40,458	19,189	17,370	38,548	826,760	.0146	532,226	151	77,105	153	8,364	44	113,062	26,358	33,791	Sullivan
New Hampshire Total		**1,319,978**	**1,235,786**	**21,676**	**504,235**	**45,699**	**28,611,550**	**.5517**	**25,111,964**	**7,132**	**3,600,853**	**7,159**	**987,927**	**5,201**	**3,939,668**	**920,553**	**1,065,097**	**New Hampshire**
New Jersey (NJ; Code 34; 21 Counties)																		
Atlantic*	.001	261,127	252,552	23,217	106,895	41,073	6,062,550	.0989	3,352,942	952	390,047	776	238,389	1,255	677,404	206,415	174,273	Atlantic
Bergen*	.003	906,873	884,118	29,952	334,596	58,828	27,162,500	.4224	14,689,636	4,171	1,122,047	2,231	1,120,494	5,897	2,609,949	1,027,825	613,623	Bergen
Burlington*	.005	458,701	423,394	27,501	170,181	53,526	12,614,840	.1970	6,626,422	1,882	671,042	1,334	236,039	1,242	1,073,853	398,827	327,639	Burlington
Camden*	.007	518,146	508,932	21,721	184,104	44,199	11,254,830	.1868	6,338,456	1,800	467,956	931	387,219	2,038	1,099,932	454,604	327,805	Camden
Cape May*	.009	101,669	102,326	23,772	44,851	39,101	2,416,840	.0394	1,357,446	385	56,349	112	104,810	552	368,926	106,599	69,983	Cape May
Cumberland*	.011	151,331	146,438	17,001	50,414	37,029	2,572,830	.0457	1,545,886	439	141,137	281	57,136	301	329,106	128,153	79,636	Cumberland
Essex*	.013	800,056	793,633	20,002	276,836	41,584	16,002,500	.2461	6,228,174	1,769	427,748	851	678,474	3,571	1,452,794	617,675	398,283	Essex
Gloucester*	.015	275,154	254,673	25,140	101,309	49,838	6,917,480	.1070	3,325,785	944	527,958	1,050	206,642	1,088	466,625	181,016	216,158	Gloucester
Hudson*	.017	607,051	608,975	19,048	220,754	38,221	11,563,320	.1812	4,658,618	1,323	361,795	719	554,459	2,918	870,328	384,860	269,178	Hudson
Hunterdon*	.019	132,353	121,989	34,058	46,575	70,392	4,507,620	.0692	2,478,422	704	75,218	150	110,288	580	511,235	105,319	97,720	Hunterdon
Mercer*	.021	369,496	350,761	24,296	124,536	52,210	8,977,430	.1416	4,534,000	1,287	431,841	859	361,412	1,902	714,006	472,475	231,930	Mercer
Middlesex*	.023	800,915	750,162	26,500	274,736	56,224	21,224,180	.3235	9,983,512	2,835	972,789	1,935	677,432	3,565	1,540,211	591,887	537,098	Middlesex
Monmouth*	.025	644,487	615,301	29,638	238,052	58,476	19,101,530	.2872	9,123,567	2,591	864,002	1,718	697,011	3,669	1,716,845	583,879	472,932	Monmouth
Morris*	.027	492,011	470,212	33,152	173,146	68,182	16,311,390	.2625	10,268,969	2,916	699,821	1,392	744,571	3,919	1,554,501	572,965	343,694	Morris
Ocean*	.029	568,520	510,916	22,488	215,572	42,885	12,784,930	.2051	6,532,589	1,855	542,894	1,080	286,099	1,506	1,325,531	413,887	396,538	Ocean
Passaic*	.031	504,035	489,049	20,162	163,392	45,024	10,162,330	.1732	5,972,666	1,696	679,201	1,351	560,664	2,951	982,004	375,269	263,915	Passaic
Salem*	.033	65,361	64,285	22,435	25,034	42,364	1,466,390	.0215	515,299	146	41,111	82	19,272	101	104,938	39,065	43,428	Salem
Somerset*	.035	321,061	297,490	34,405	117,880	68,345	11,045,950	.1663	5,713,295	1,622	457,036	909	333,523	1,755	901,973	278,164	248,774	Somerset
Sussex*	.037	155,440	144,166	28,121	53,979	58,971	4,371,060	.0607	1,430,438	406	48,589	97	27,609	145	344,215	75,296	109,430	Sussex
Union*	.039	534,259	522,541	25,356	192,874	50,679	13,546,510	.2137	7,027,513	1,995	323,058	642	358,739	1,888	1,285,743	507,211	352,870	Union
Warren*	.041	113,479	102,437	26,679	42,471	52,020	3,027,550	.0459	1,395,229	396	124,115	247	47,020	247	272,967	77,574	77,652	Warren
New Jersey Total		**8,781,525**	**8,414,350**	**25,405**	**3,158,187**	**50,687**	**223,094,560**	**3.4949**	**113,098,864**	**32,114**	**9,425,753**	**18,747**	**7,807,303**	**41,090**	**20,203,086**	**7,598,965**	**5,652,559**	**New Jersey**
New Mexico (NM; Code 35; 33 Counties)																		
Bernalillo*	.001	598,254	556,678	19,004	239,638	36,968	11,369,390	.2126	8,620,223	2,448	1,740,137	3,461	317,923	1,673	638,809	468,309	481,415	Bernalillo
Catron	.003	3,383	3,543	15,658	1,737	23,443	52,970	.0007	3,812	1	1,058	2	...	...	...	...	3,424	Catron
Chaves**	.005	61,197	61,382	13,025	22,410	27,630	797,120	.0155	517,472	147	126,804	252	20,603	108	64,639	37,188	39,488	Chaves
Cibola**	.006	27,991	25,595	10,560	8,468	26,832	295,580	.0064	226,036	64	11,933	24	2,722	14	35,612	2,643	15,752	Cibola
Colfax	.007	13,790	14,189	15,933	5,761	29,923	219,720	.0041	142,338	40	12,876	26	3,518	19	16,345	6,373	10,955	Colfax
Curry**	.009	45,360	45,044	13,379	16,791	28,006	606,890	.0122	455,899	129	121,330	241	24,644	130	50,517	24,124	30,154	Curry
De Baca	.011	2,009	2,240	15,271	969	25,074	30,680	.0005	12,467	4	...	...	...	...	2,995	...	1,794	De Baca
Dona Ana*	.013	187,285	174,682	12,484	63,506	28,841	2,338,100	.0450	1,409,430	400	290,364	577	45,270	238	147,833	81,908	119,072	Dona Ana
Eddy**	.015	51,414	51,658	14,760	19,363	30,665	758,860	.0137	428,156	122	75,227	150	14,770	78	75,411	26,416	35,068	Eddy
Grant**	.017	29,153	31,002	15,180	12,264	28,163	442,550	.0079	249,095	71	58,293	116	6,950	37	49,472	7,407	22,745	Grant
Guadalupe	.019	4,598	4,680	11,427	1,714	23,288	52,540	.0011	35,079	10	...	...	...	...	2,115	...	3,033	Guadalupe
Harding	.021	730	810	18,233	412	25,000	13,310	.0002	8,001	2	2,970	6	...	...	...	...	849	Harding
Hidalgo	.023	4,943	5,932	14,153	2,258	23,936	69,960	.0016	72,014	20	...	...	...	...	7,966	1,549	4,034	Hidalgo
Lea**	.025	56,128	55,511	12,940	19,605	28,880	726,310	.0144	504,459	143	93,373	186	17,430	92	62,107	25,056	35,313	Lea
Lincoln	.027	20,841	19,411	17,059	8,516	32,527	355,530	.0065	235,671	67	54,318	108	9,675	51	37,605	9,794	16,153	Lincoln
Los Alamos**	.028	19,001	18,343	37,666	8,065	68,446	715,700	.0083	91,036	26	2,269	5	2,933	15	43,594	2,743	17,214	Los Alamos
Luna**	.029	26,168	25,016	9,741	9,600	20,622	254,890	.0061	249,364	71	33,636	67	2,795	15	37,956	2,453	16,404	Luna
McKinley**	.031	71,137	74,798	9,589	21,759	24,148	682,140	.0171	742,366	211	148,031	294	51,690	272	97,964	18,854	35,295	McKinley
Mora	.033	5,295	5,180	11,715	2,038	23,226	62,030	.0010	10,913	3	...	...	...	...	2,190	...	3,990	Mora
Otero**	.035	61,969	62,298	14,452	23,448	29,835	895,600	.0153	393,021	112	74,162	147	17,636	93	51,611	16,174	43,295	Otero
Quay	.037	9,355	10,155	14,111	4,254	24,186	132,010	.0028	124,876	35	11,931	24	1,270	7	13,639	8,560	7,651	Quay
Rio Arriba**	.039	40,597	41,190	13,781	15,277	28,452	559,460	.0103	322,577	92	11,435	23	2,678	14	60,641	39,436	30,747	Rio Arriba
Roosevelt**	.041	18,342	18,018	12,214	6,706	25,917	224,030	.0043	126,289	36	10,537	21	2,309	12	18,134	4,221	12,256	Roosevelt
Sandoval*	.043	104,283	89,908	17,713	34,335	41,562	1,847,150	.0264	389,733	111	12,783	25	14,290	75	73,522	15,005	67,261	Sandoval
San Juan*	.045	127,992	113,801	12,484	38,249	32,186	1,597,810	.0348	1,437,477	408	384,722	765	44,763	236	142,782	43,540	73,505	San Juan
San Miguel**	.047	29,205	30,126	12,717	11,227	25,795	371,390	.0070	209,875	60	36,484	73	3,920	21	39,989	15,173	20,079	San Miguel
Santa Fe*	.049	141,278	129,292	19,564	53,845	39,553	2,763,920	.0503	1,960,868	557	417,468	830	156,790	825	196,529	123,851	101,716	Santa Fe
Sierra	.051	13,029	13,270	14,571	6,275	23,429	189,840	.0033	85,108	24	6,718	13	1,491	8	23,450	2,416	10,776	Sierra
Socorro	.053	18,193	18,078	11,515	6,920	23,295	209,490	.0037	75,567	21	2,504	5	1,458	8	17,802	2,088	12,114	Socorro
Taos**	.055	31,943	29,979	13,670	12,965	26,237	436,670	.0083	272,340	77	39,220	78	18,155	96	56,219	11,880	23,926	Taos
Torrance*	.057	16,716	16,911	14,052	6,238	29,788	234,900	.0041	108,351	31	...	...	...	...	13,466	3,954	12,153	Torrance
Union	.059	3,657	4,174	17,427	1,804	27,364	63,730	.0010	18,891	5	...	...	...	...	4,363	...	3,471	Union
Valencia*	.061	69,672	66,152	14,480	24,051	32,317	1,008,840	.0185	587,973	167	153,191	305	8,232	43	90,082	27,992	49,846	Valencia
New Mexico Total		**1,914,908**	**1,819,046**	**15,865**	**710,468**	**33,027**	**30,379,110**	**.5650**	**20,126,775**	**5,715**	**3,935,122**	**7,827**	**796,560**	**4,194**	**2,175,450**	**1,031,154**	**1,360,948**	**New Mexico**
New York (NY; Code 36; 62 Counties)																		
Albany*	.001	300,976	294,565	21,389	119,170	40,516	6,437,440	.1147	4,514,798	1,282	553,638	1,101	364,216	1,917	463,271	266,287	207,387	Albany
Allegany	.003	50,878	49,927	14,927	18,541	30,727	759,460	.0121	238,672	68	16,800	33	5,402	28	52,691	28,116	31,444	Allegany
Bronx*	.005	1,385,071	1,332,650	12,499	480,811	26,842	17,312,080	.2806	4,302,652	1,222	316,644	630	493,247	2,596	1,052,902	712,213	265,303	Bronx
Broome*	.007	197,991	200,536	18,584	81,699	33,795	3,679,400	.0648	2,289,715	650	360,040	716	99,962	526	412,314	181,389	129,680	Broome
Cattaraugus**	.009	83,138	83,955	16,759	32,752	31,902	1,393,300	.0248	832,880	237	125,308	249	30,089	158	138,620	63,036	54,530	Cattaraugus
Cayuga**	.011	82,152	81,963	18,201	31,225	35,822	1,495,270	.0242	659,356	187	93,033	185	21,039	111	111,499	67,622	52,870	Cayuga
Chautauqua**	.013	136,986	139,750	17,230	55,411	31,978	2,360,230	.0399	1,194,716	339	183,712	365	31,959	168	221,135	87,985	89,027	Chautauqua
Chemung*	.015	90,031	91,070	18,393	35,794	34,866	1,655,900	.0303	1,148,737	326	193,665	385	58,842	310	156,337	77,465	57,688	Chemung
Chenango	.017	52,058	51,401	16,836	20,443	32,248	876,450	.0142	360,297	102	40,683	81	1,787	9	40,643	35,926	35,877	Chenango
Clinton**	.019	82,512	79,894	17,509	30,826	35,146	1,444,720	.0258	899,746	255	130,388	259	52,672	277	136,739	55,316	53,552	Clinton
Columbia**	.021	63,685	63,094	21,308	25,860	39,592	1,357,030	.0211	591,829	168	64,359	128	2,441	13	126,578	27,083	45,527	Columbia
Cortland**	.023	49,245	48,599	16,456	18,471	32,881	810,380	.0153	577,388	164	57,362	114	9,809	52	129,772	32,181	31,284	Cortland
Delaware	.025	46,922	48,055	17,626	19,744	31,369	827,060	.0136	384,861	109	23,764	47	4,887	26	56,368	24,523	33,586	Delaware
Dutchess*	.027	297,806	280,150	22,445	102,228	49,154	6,684,180	.1041	3,035,458	862	364,401	725	207,370	1,091	575,075	167,837	192,255	Dutchess
Erie*	.029	936,770	950,265	20,218	387,148	36,596	18,940,050	.3141	10,128,257	2,876	1,001,036	1,991	563,691	2,967	1,816,172	800,999	638,494	Erie
Essex	.031	39,212	38,851	17,709	15,669	33,088	694,390	.0125	452,403	128	24,899	50	13,633	72	94,776	23,655	26,670	Essex
Franklin**	.033	51,230	51,134	14,299	18,291	30,347	732,550	.0130	369,021	105	22,754	45	...	...	63,837	35,504	29,990	Franklin
Fulton**	.035	55,594	55,073	17,116	22,238	32,089	951,520	.0159	458,443	130	48,496	96	...	...	100,105	39,810	36,888	Fulton
Genesee**	.037	59,736	60,370	19,801	23,203	38,088	1,182,840	.0184	474,440	135	62,639	125	18,892	99	71,456	22,249	41,972	Genesee
Greene	.039	49,325	48,195	17,798	18,877	34,894	877,870	.0143	391,131	111	25,264	50	5,145	27	84,467	29,801	32,788	Greene
Hamilton	.041	5,189	5,379	19,146	2,422	30,739	99,350	.0015	30,590	9	4,103	8	4,741	25	4,953	...	4,382	Hamilton
Herkimer*	.043	63,402	64,427	17,426	26,193	31,779	1,104,820	.0173	403,282	115	32,477	65	9,315	49	70,347	48,949	42,738	Herkimer
Jefferson**	.045	114,448	111,738	15,461	40,813	32,571	1,769,530	.0347	1,360,604	386	149,294	297	67,911	357	173,006	94,890	66,214	Jefferson
Kings*	.047	2,480,420	2,465,326	14,611	872,191	31,137	36,242,150	.5758	10,970,708	3,115	847,248	1,685	1,264,957	6,658	2,092,774	1,620,360	559,335	Kings
Lewis	.049	26,386	26,944	17,606	10,645	32,740	464,540	.0074	184,884	53	6,069	12	3,454	18	28,982	18,514	19,937	Lewis
Livingston*	.051	64,792	64,328	18,854	23,160	39,450	1,221,600	.0197	558,417	159	42,609	85	5,264	28	115,194	37,894	44,108	Livingston
Madison*	.053	70,875	69,441	18,732	26,136	37,725	1,327,660	.0219	648,959	184	55,213	110	6,802	36	125,877	59,420	46,582	Madison
Monroe*	.055	738,925	735,343	21,936	290,346	41,738	16,209,150	.2640	8,593,168	2,440	939,333	1,868	423,910	2,231	1,726,847	409,234	552,051	Monroe
Montgomery**	.057	49,061	49,708	17,073	20,222	31,191	837,620	.0146	468,428	133	46,496	92	17,305	91	79,064	35,253	31,991	Montgomery
Nassau*	.059	1,343,675	1,334,544	27,741	432,740	64,264	37,274,930	.6060	22,464,430	6,379	2,092,700	4,162	2,219,797	11,683	2,950,865	1,618,495	892,018	Nassau
New York*	.061	1,588,044	1,537,195	26,832	730,318	43,660	42,609,670	.7445	31,346,074	8,901	3,426,024	6,813	8,658,940	45,574	3,042,648	3,214,471	216,437	New York
Niagara*	.063	217,756	219,846	20,085	90,214	36,316	4,373,660	.0691	1,920,658	545	229,222	456	160,821	846	339,519	177,262	147,865	Niagara
Oneida*	.065	234,252	235,469	17,880	91,660	34,370	4,188,500	.0729	2,427,049	689	399,195	794	97,786	515	353,373	226,771	145,700	Oneida
Onondaga*	.067	462,726	458,336	20,646	185,938	38,491	9,553,310	.1615	5,544,935	1,575	585,852	1,165	368,834	1,941	1,003,122	379,355	341,702	Onondaga
Ontario*	.069	104,413	100,224	21,587	40,515	41,560	2,253,930	.0405	1,622,363	461	283,735	564	122,376	644	237,641	91,965	73,980	Ontario
Orange*	.071	377,527	341,367	21,229	125,035	48,210	8,014,490	.1301	4,108,957	1,167	650,185	1,293	426,239	2,243	540,066	245,035	259,345	Orange
Orleans*	.073	43,876	44,171	17,172	15,632	35,963	753,420	.0117	254,760	72	22,034	44	2,965	16	66,350	18,539	28,358	Orleans
Oswego*	.075	124,250	122,377	17,614	47,022	34,940	2,188,500	.0353	927,547	263	86,207	171	15,508	82	190,428	67,493	81,197	Oswego
Otsego**	.077	62,947	61,676	17,663	25,936	32,155	1,111,820	.0197	680,122	193	82,889	165	16,230	85	91,384	30,625	44,898	Otsego
Putnam*	.079	102,260	95,745	29,059	34,303	64,905	2,971,600	.0382	647,969	184	28,894	57	4,603	24	169,153	63,625	72,778	Putnam
Queens*	.081	2,225,143	2,229,379	18,665	773,138	40,171	41,531,430	.6132	11,981,875	3,402	898,792	1,787	1,043,787	5,494	2,418,562	1,713,694	829,192	Queens
Rensselaer*	.083	153,917	152,538	21,594	61,650	40,413	3,323,610	.0500	1,261,200	358	132,107	263	12,731	67	265,926	118,481	102,046	Rensselaer
Richmond*	.085	470,056	443,728	24,609	170,972	50,531	11,567,790	.1582	3,040,329	863	268,197	533	320,240	1,686	724,948	313,667	258,235	Richmond
Rockland*	.087	297,018	286,753	26,159	94,119	61,332	7,769,710	.1153	3,255,514	924	349,907	696	251,969	1,326	533,042	273,440	189,093	Rockland
St. Lawrence**	.089	110,838	111,931	15,516	41,553	31,029	1,719,710	.0306	964,644	274	125,351	249	31,062	163	177,627	97,491	67,980	St. Lawrence
Saratoga*	.091	216,567	200,635	23,552	84,300	45,310	5,100,660	.0775	2,180,435	619	245,312	488	121,206	638	265,750	120,924	153,680	Saratoga
Schenectady*	.093	148,278	146,555	21,418	60,774	39,133	3,175,870	.0510	1,575,601	447	191,257	380	59,105	311	246,310	109,095	96,036	Schenectady
Schoharie*	.095	31,992	31,582	17,947	12,339	35,141	574,170	.0098	308,450	88	36,047	72	17,939	94	44,507	13,456	22,634	Schoharie
Schuyler	.097	19,648	19,224	17,595	7,602	34,034	345,710	.0056	153,878	44	2,255	4	11,227	59	55,963	...	14,064	Schuyler
Seneca**	.099	35,799	33,342	16,899	12,842	35,212	604,970	.0110	394,280	112	30,414	60	89,406	471	42,220	20,139	22,579	Seneca
Steuben**	.101	99,314	98,726	18,266	40,281	33,734	1,814,050	.0299	875,908	249	93,430	186	17,283	91	179,152	54,426	68,159	Steuben
Suffolk*	.103	1,498,863	1,419,369	26,283	501,523	58,944	39,394,130	.6151	20,136,013	5,718	2,044,905	4,067	1,428,479	7,518	3,233,887	1,319,179	1,106,624	Suffolk
Sullivan	.105	76,088	73,966	17,820	28,912	35,176	1,355,860	.0222	624,487	177	32,718	65	8,609	45	124,507	50,065	47,948	Sullivan
Tioga*	.107	51,865	51,784	19,873	20,336	37,665	1,030,730	.0150	303,636	86	6,466	13	3,422	18	42,674	25,326	37,760	Tioga
Tompkins*	.109	100,996	96,501	18,164	38,542	35,482	1,834,480	.0295	790,679	225	80,341	160	35,530	187	182,026	55,756	62,907	Tompkins
Ulster*	.111	183,995	177,749	20,416	70,360	39,892	3,756,450	.0597	1,713,351	487	147,662	294	68,026	358	318,658	119,290	124,781	Ulster
Warren*	.113	65,852	63,303	20,290	27,038	36,897	1,336,110	.0251	1,063,260	302	108,815	216	103,497	545	158,772	43,465	45,578	Warren
Washington*	.115	62,872	61,042	17,801	23,257	35,970	1,119,170	.0169	339,064	96	17,986	36	3,263	17	48,273	38,108	41,156	Washington
Wayne*	.117	94,278	93,765	21,175	36,255	40,965	1,996,310	.0302	761,222	216	51,019	101	2,562	13	129,936	46,139	67,991	Wayne
Westchester*	.119	951,137	923,459	27,386	336,611	58,055	26,047,630	.4013	12,998,481	3,691	1,345,677	2,676	1,180,669	6,214	2,165,138	960,620	600,726	Westchester
Wyoming	.121	42,979	43,424	17,777	15,252	37,227	764,030	.0121	304,357	86	25,939	52	2,583	14	66,398	17,512	28,157	Wyoming
Yates	.123	24,809	24,621	16,566	9,267	33,167	410,980	.0067	164,831	47	9,662	19	2,523	13	41,063	13,270	16,143	Yates
New York Total		**19,348,846**	**18,976,457**	**20,757**	**7,156,765**	**40,835**	**401,615,930**	**6.4460**	**193,660,204**	**54,990**	**19,962,926**	**39,698**	**20,699,290**	**108,942**	**30,771,689**	**16,761,435**	**9,761,897**	**New York**
North Carolina (NC; Code 37; 100 Counties)																		
Alamance*	.001	140,105	130,800	18,162	54,708	36,808	2,544,520	.0467	1,771,538	503	233,033	463	113,462	597	219,919	99,591	106,644	Alamance
Alexander*	.003	35,588	33,603	17,737	13,653	36,019	631,210	.0098	223,340	63	30,144	60	1,990	10	42,164	6,936	29,473	Alexander
Alleghany	.005	10,966	10,677	15,490	4,777	28,221	169,860	.0030	97,111	28	3,870	8	...	...	21,817	7,891	9,506	Alleghany
Anson*	.007	25,186	25,275	13,140	9,150	28,751	330,940	.0059	151,826	43	22,252	44	4,649	24	35,401	17,931	16,825	Anson
Ashe	.009	25,406	24,384	15,145	11,025	27,895	384,780	.0071	237,894	68	36,084	72	3,329	18	37,827	15,487	21,807	Ashe

Source: Devonshire Associates Ltd. and Scan/US, Inc. 2005. ...Data less than 1,000. (d) Data not available.
* Component of a Metropolitan Core Based Statistical Area.
** Component of a Micropolitan Core Based Statistical Area.

Counties: Population/Income/Sales, *Continued*

County or County Equivalent	FIPS County Code	Population Estimate 7/1/05	Population Census 4/1/00	Per Capita Income 2004	House-holds Estimate 7/1/05	Median Household Income 2004	Disposable Income 2004 ($1,000)	Market Ability Index 2004	Total Retail Sales 2004 Sales ($1,000)	Total Retail Sales Ranally Sales Units	General Merchandise 2004 Sales ($1,000)	General Merchandise Ranally Sales Units	Apparel Store 2004 Sales ($1,000)	Apparel Store Ranally Sales Units	Food Store Sales 2004 ($1,000)	Health & Drug Store 2004 ($1,000)	Passenger Car Regis-trations 2004	County or County Equivalent
Avery	.011	17,957	17,167	13,601	6,639	29,328	244,240	.0050	198,806	56	38,695	77	6,352	33	45,730	13,020	13,402	Avery
Beaufort**	.013	45,889	44,958	15,051	18,550	29,941	690,670	.0142	601,430	171	80,292	160	17,212	91	103,906	44,021	34,235	Beaufort
Bertie	.015	19,376	19,773	12,229	7,744	24,162	236,940	.0043	104,945	30	3,478	7	...	...	17,894	9,703	13,689	Bertie
Bladen	.017	32,934	32,278	13,018	12,964	26,419	428,720	.0078	213,842	61	29,091	58	8,406	44	41,700	22,561	23,944	Bladen
Brunswick*	.019	86,905	73,143	17,548	35,455	34,105	1,524,990	.0258	788,049	224	108,460	216	17,660	93	165,635	67,032	66,286	Brunswick
Buncombe*	.021	217,531	206,330	18,402	91,046	35,131	4,003,020	.0769	3,224,184	916	538,059	1,070	178,449	939	355,022	192,281	167,709	Buncombe
Burke*	.023	89,829	89,148	16,690	35,089	33,915	1,499,280	.0256	765,791	217	80,278	160	22,763	120	113,647	60,551	69,094	Burke
Cabarrus*	.025	150,533	131,063	20,217	56,447	43,440	3,043,400	.0560	2,275,592	646	394,680	785	94,239	496	269,669	134,227	113,124	Cabarrus
Caldwell*	.027	79,837	77,415	17,044	31,802	33,940	1,360,740	.0232	696,788	198	88,183	175	11,777	62	104,041	45,057	66,074	Caldwell
Camden**	.029	8,501	6,885	16,662	2,990	37,471	141,640	.0020	25,322	7	2,228	4	...	...	4,260	...	6,669	Camden
Carteret**	.031	62,124	59,383	19,152	25,900	36,311	1,189,770	.0220	877,612	249	191,194	380	27,059	142	126,297	41,209	47,867	Carteret
Caswell	.033	23,819	23,501	15,846	8,912	33,658	377,430	.0054	65,809	19	3,804	8	...	...	18,325	3,620	18,813	Caswell
Catawba*	.035	150,785	141,685	19,008	59,599	38,069	2,866,120	.0570	2,573,243	731	397,658	791	123,224	649	240,821	164,647	119,536	Catawba
Chatham*	.037	59,157	49,329	18,364	21,338	41,189	1,086,360	.0164	352,830	100	46,211	92	10,403	55	68,466	10,943	43,306	Chatham
Cherokee	.039	25,461	24,298	14,787	11,055	26,935	376,500	.0079	337,965	96	90,512	180	10,910	57	53,648	12,459	21,243	Cherokee
Chowan	.041	14,562	14,526	14,235	5,569	30,092	207,290	.0042	160,394	46	8,331	17	4,841	25	32,555	9,702	9,467	Chowan
Clay	.043	9,666	8,775	16,443	4,212	30,107	158,940	.0032	138,467	39	4,505	9	2,479	13	23,446	7,005	8,254	Clay
Cleveland**	.045	99,439	96,287	16,216	37,963	33,659	1,612,550	.0281	870,703	247	135,175	269	30,607	161	133,721	63,624	73,469	Cleveland
Columbus	.047	54,523	54,749	12,799	21,339	26,078	697,830	.0146	570,968	162	78,617	156	17,211	91	89,268	46,103	38,454	Columbus
Craven**	.049	91,416	91,436	17,051	36,161	34,222	1,558,760	.0291	1,098,768	312	143,458	285	42,898	226	144,866	46,324	64,521	Craven
Cumberland*	.051	306,556	302,963	16,580	112,683	35,624	5,082,570	.0957	3,616,858	1,027	706,497	1,405	191,060	1,006	419,738	163,935	216,141	Cumberland
Currituck*	.053	22,484	18,190	17,020	7,928	38,191	382,680	.0064	185,622	53	7,123	14	4,234	22	42,553	1,645	16,144	Currituck
Dare**	.055	34,986	29,967	20,837	14,343	40,346	729,000	.0153	772,156	219	121,374	241	65,582	345	170,374	36,264	26,793	Dare
Davidson**	.057	155,335	147,246	18,078	60,668	36,538	2,808,080	.0452	1,209,095	343	147,396	293	35,828	189	197,473	97,758	123,216	Davidson
Davie*	.059	38,755	34,835	18,495	14,814	38,182	716,790	.0113	288,494	82	41,172	82	3,007	16	38,619	17,253	31,373	Davie
Duplin	.061	52,526	49,063	12,668	18,535	28,580	665,390	.0125	375,443	107	50,662	101	7,599	40	69,443	26,950	35,573	Duplin
Durham*	.063	243,802	223,314	21,100	100,170	41,305	5,144,330	.0876	3,105,698	882	354,647	705	237,908	1,252	451,825	209,248	172,324	Durham
Edgecombe*	.065	54,620	55,606	14,250	20,852	29,804	778,360	.0130	294,908	84	25,068	50	13,308	70	51,140	38,979	35,003	Edgecombe
Forsyth*	.067	325,303	306,067	19,331	125,965	39,653	6,288,550	.1208	5,183,134	1,472	748,200	1,488	283,587	1,493	549,490	275,430	237,675	Forsyth
Franklin*	.069	55,425	47,260	16,191	19,341	36,886	897,360	.0141	299,005	85	39,465	78	6,894	36	61,256	19,310	38,916	Franklin
Gaston*	.071	195,391	190,365	18,409	76,615	37,180	3,596,920	.0626	2,125,297	603	322,736	642	95,076	500	286,961	163,132	144,258	Gaston
Gates	.073	10,936	10,516	15,008	3,872	33,574	164,130	.0025	44,601	13	1,347	3	...	...	7,910	...	7,930	Gates
Graham	.075	8,046	7,993	13,765	3,439	25,693	110,750	.0021	65,697	19	2,897	6	...	...	10,154	6,195	6,398	Graham
Granville	.077	54,864	48,498	15,640	18,253	37,298	858,070	.0139	326,538	93	35,083	70	6,963	37	62,872	30,238	36,922	Granville
Greene*	.079	20,517	18,974	12,593	6,762	30,330	258,370	.0042	63,863	18	2,524	5	...	...	16,267	2,497	12,943	Greene
Guilford*	.081	442,093	421,048	20,198	176,286	40,413	8,929,590	.1676	7,062,888	2,006	831,891	1,654	366,030	1,927	737,610	382,138	350,559	Guilford
Halifax**	.083	55,838	57,370	12,678	21,942	25,700	707,910	.0150	602,020	171	97,779	194	29,776	157	93,660	43,862	37,120	Halifax
Harnett**	.085	104,103	91,025	14,550	36,119	33,516	1,514,720	.0263	714,028	203	121,207	241	11,294	59	114,501	50,140	69,250	Harnett
Haywood*	.087	56,679	54,033	17,290	23,944	32,551	980,000	.0193	817,761	232	116,084	231	21,749	114	92,048	41,379	46,421	Haywood
Henderson*	.089	96,658	89,173	18,908	40,011	36,076	1,827,620	.0348	1,458,504	414	149,112	297	56,990	300	180,171	74,002	76,158	Henderson
Hertford	.091	23,602	22,601	12,169	8,898	25,803	287,210	.0066	298,614	85	38,821	77	12,990	68	63,696	29,048	15,748	Hertford
Hoke*	.093	39,794	33,646	12,683	12,657	32,203	504,690	.0079	97,882	28	7,254	14	...	...	32,568	7,418	24,058	Hoke
Hyde	.095	5,391	5,826	13,825	2,137	27,757	74,530	.0013	39,620	11	10,172	20	...	...	5,686	...	3,690	Hyde
Iredell**	.097	140,000	122,660	19,191	54,116	39,864	2,686,700	.0474	1,715,762	487	259,854	517	76,025	400	204,058	109,592	109,926	Iredell
Jackson	.099	35,487	33,121	16,164	14,540	31,278	573,600	.0106	383,178	109	112,604	224	6,127	32	57,841	17,617	27,674	Jackson
Johnston*	.101	146,138	121,965	17,506	52,937	38,913	2,558,340	.0438	1,379,463	392	152,332	303	93,553	492	188,882	54,092	103,226	Johnston
Jones**	.103	10,062	10,381	14,721	4,027	29,977	148,120	.0025	59,024	17	1,325	3	...	...	6,645	...	7,619	Jones
Lee**	.105	49,188	49,040	18,263	19,307	36,823	898,300	.0186	879,978	250	98,276	195	27,704	146	137,024	42,311	37,354	Lee
Lenoir**	.107	58,000	59,648	15,702	24,048	30,385	910,720	.0183	757,690	215	107,204	213	35,243	185	108,175	45,513	41,779	Lenoir
Lincoln**	.109	69,482	63,780	19,101	26,968	39,228	1,327,200	.0220	683,406	194	102,933	205	8,402	44	115,247	73,560	58,217	Lincoln
McDowell	.111	43,478	42,151	15,191	16,879	31,179	660,460	.0122	415,015	118	58,107	116	7,926	42	75,549	17,083	32,691	McDowell
Macon	.113	31,979	29,811	15,953	13,195	30,770	510,150	.0111	529,495	150	90,059	179	28,454	150	70,638	13,508	24,672	Macon
Madison*	.115	20,139	19,635	15,261	8,265	29,605	307,340	.0047	72,896	21	3,808	8	1,415	7	21,077	11,610	16,182	Madison
Martin	.117	24,783	25,593	13,983	9,923	27,888	346,530	.0068	243,340	69	37,234	74	8,590	45	37,579	13,845	17,150	Martin
Mecklenburg*	.119	787,867	695,454	23,125	311,927	47,386	18,219,660	.3172	12,410,603	3,524	1,733,721	3,448	688,385	3,623	1,397,245	621,767	612,023	Mecklenburg
Mitchell	.121	15,868	15,687	15,190	6,566	28,710	241,030	.0047	180,264	51	5,309	11	4,599	24	31,051	20,916	12,680	Mitchell
Montgomery	.123	27,614	26,822	14,222	9,890	31,704	392,740	.0073	239,724	68	7,999	16	8,087	43	42,587	20,205	19,091	Montgomery
Moore**	.125	81,519	74,769	19,491	32,473	38,746	1,588,870	.0274	953,265	271	140,641	280	55,010	290	116,223	100,372	62,483	Moore
Nash*	.127	91,159	87,420	17,273	35,288	35,587	1,574,620	.0297	1,159,162	329	160,436	319	71,295	375	113,181	58,915	66,959	Nash
New Hanover*	.129	173,836	160,307	20,505	74,665	37,924	3,564,580	.0746	3,744,350	1,063	521,632	1,037	172,997	911	379,059	173,172	130,508	New Hanover
Northampton**	.131	21,514	22,086	13,122	8,696	25,800	282,310	.0049	111,539	32	15,721	31	...	...	11,524	3,126	15,566	Northampton
Onslow*	.133	149,754	150,355	14,047	51,435	32,283	2,103,590	.0423	1,637,736	465	298,217	593	55,104	290	193,779	64,913	95,703	Onslow
Orange*	.135	118,085	118,227	20,689	48,280	40,544	2,443,020	.0409	1,369,033	389	71,752	143	33,271	175	273,364	65,950	92,297	Orange
Pamlico**	.137	12,746	12,934	16,999	5,218	32,888	216,670	.0033	67,330	19	3,287	7	...	...	20,721	7,570	9,481	Pamlico
Pasquotank**	.139	36,831	34,897	13,154	13,155	29,465	484,460	.0120	625,608	178	95,393	190	22,660	119	71,045	32,544	22,740	Pasquotank
Pender*	.141	45,203	41,082	16,191	17,017	33,744	731,870	.0116	253,490	72	8,206	16	7,684	40	68,396	14,399	33,064	Pender
Perquimans**	.143	11,824	11,368	14,343	4,749	28,513	169,590	.0026	43,039	12	3,060	6	...	...	15,935	4,603	8,599	Perquimans
Person*	.145	37,629	35,623	17,243	14,549	35,587	648,830	.0113	365,234	104	51,402	102	11,329	60	72,047	20,467	31,024	Person
Pitt*	.147	141,666	133,798	16,773	59,080	32,196	2,376,140	.0479	2,073,721	589	230,337	458	132,141	695	247,586	103,215	103,300	Pitt
Polk	.149	19,102	18,324	18,971	8,288	34,619	362,380	.0053	96,240	27	1,735	3	...	...	29,279	10,687	16,172	Polk
Randolph*	.151	137,787	130,454	17,642	53,133	36,203	2,430,830	.0411	1,254,564	356	198,058	394	48,921	257	188,485	113,695	108,805	Randolph
Richmond**	.153	46,738	46,564	13,865	18,577	27,777	648,020	.0128	472,278	134	53,682	107	18,614	98	69,167	28,198	32,713	Richmond
Robeson**	.155	127,419	123,339	11,988	44,631	27,283	1,527,540	.0326	1,261,165	358	154,962	308	53,976	284	157,332	63,363	81,191	Robeson
Rockingham*	.157	93,254	91,928	16,486	37,350	32,810	1,537,400	.0264	795,696	226	108,730	216	22,939	121	141,374	64,312	74,433	Rockingham
Rowan**	.159	136,277	130,340	17,188	51,994	35,793	2,342,380	.0402	1,247,881	354	143,440	285	52,129	274	204,021	83,451	101,982	Rowan
Rutherford**	.161	64,035	62,899	15,058	25,682	30,203	964,210	.0180	617,574	175	100,796	200	18,020	95	96,606	43,132	48,871	Rutherford
Sampson	.163	63,147	60,161	13,743	22,463	30,850	867,810	.0165	549,676	156	53,718	107	7,385	39	89,121	39,164	43,519	Sampson
Scotland**	.165	36,031	35,998	14,092	13,604	30,309	507,760	.0096	319,912	91	74,103	147	16,690	88	55,851	18,884	24,057	Scotland
Stanly**	.167	59,255	58,100	17,100	22,896	35,252	1,013,290	.0189	710,630	202	76,577	152	18,380	97	112,277	44,598	48,126	Stanly
Stokes*	.169	45,460	44,711	18,132	17,899	36,175	824,270	.0122	230,875	66	13,655	27	2,389	13	39,896	30,166	39,775	Stokes
Surry**	.171	73,080	71,219	15,714	28,687	31,745	1,148,370	.0240	1,064,749	302	197,293	392	41,543	219	133,041	72,164	58,407	Surry
Swain	.173	13,158	12,968	14,369	5,426	27,794	189,070	.0035	115,129	33	4,738	9	2,599	14	26,696	11,821	10,010	Swain
Transylvania**	.175	29,531	29,334	19,935	12,792	36,427	588,710	.0092	242,966	69	60,342	120	9,253	49	48,401	10,391	24,532	Transylvania
Tyrrell	.177	4,228	4,149	11,459	1,548	25,163	48,450	.0009	23,086	7	2,449	5	...	...	4,736	...	2,602	Tyrrell
Union*	.179	159,636	123,677	19,691	53,939	46,752	3,143,350	.0483	1,203,030	342	147,777	294	36,873	194	141,478	53,501	114,348	Union
Vance**	.181	44,153	42,954	13,849	16,365	30,179	611,490	.0136	618,425	176	90,177	179	24,439	129	80,789	32,081	29,097	Vance
Wake*	.183	737,573	627,846	24,201	279,880	50,939	17,849,910	.3106	12,410,844	3,524	1,838,820	3,657	624,028	3,284	1,461,740	489,136	573,971	Wake
Warren	.185	19,765	19,972	13,688	7,826	28,292	270,540	.0043	70,731	20	5,350	11	...	...	24,103	3,873	15,099	Warren
Washington	.187	13,278	13,723	13,841	5,260	28,078	183,780	.0034	102,489	29	6,397	13	4,189	22	23,577	4,059	8,854	Washington
Watauga**	.189	42,666	42,695	16,192	17,467	31,594	690,840	.0156	787,972	224	104,961	209	62,217	327	79,518	39,220	34,780	Watauga
Wayne*	.191	113,461	113,329	15,801	43,498	32,698	1,792,770	.0345	1,320,622	375	253,513	504	59,248	312	168,453	67,902	80,217	Wayne
Wilkes**	.193	67,997	65,632	16,288	26,943	32,520	1,107,550	.0219	898,777	255	128,604	256	34,485	182	85,940	56,114	56,091	Wilkes
Wilson**	.195	76,408	73,814	15,855	30,032	32,298	1,211,430	.0246	1,049,296	298	127,383	253	47,768	251	126,972	62,754	53,833	Wilson
Yadkin*	.197	37,851	36,348	17,168	14,828	34,814	649,820	.0103	240,560	68	7,254	14	4,143	22	41,750	18,070	32,220	Yadkin
Yancey	.199	18,184	17,774	14,838	7,532	28,442	269,810	.0050	163,618	46	19,469	39	1,695	9	27,925	10,635	14,732	Yancey
North Carolina Total		**8,642,524**	**8,049,313**	**18,446**	**3,356,054**	**37,498**	**159,421,340**	**2.8862**	**107,693,075**	**30,583**	**15,111,629**	**30,052**	**4,973,209**	**26,175**	**14,001,045**	**6,043,252**	**6,488,469**	**North Carolina**

North Dakota (ND; Code 38; 53 Counties)

County or County Equivalent	FIPS County Code	Population Estimate 7/1/05	Population Census 4/1/00	Per Capita Income 2004	House-holds Estimate 7/1/05	Median Household Income 2004	Disposable Income 2004 ($1,000)	Market Ability Index 2004	Total Retail Sales 2004 Sales ($1,000)	Total Retail Sales Ranally Sales Units	General Merchandise 2004 Sales ($1,000)	General Merchandise Ranally Sales Units	Apparel Store 2004 Sales ($1,000)	Apparel Store Ranally Sales Units	Food Store Sales 2004 ($1,000)	Health & Drug Store 2004 ($1,000)	Passenger Car Regis-trations 2004	County or County Equivalent
Adams	.001	2,392	2,593	14,929	1,053	27,527	35,710	.0009	45,840	13	...	...	...	...	7,364	3,479	2,439	Adams
Barnes	.003	10,814	11,775	15,673	4,580	30,261	169,490	.0031	100,736	29	3,548	7	...	...	14,242	7,761	10,141	Barnes
Benson	.005	6,819	6,964	10,529	2,225	26,128	71,800	.0012	18,506	5	...	...	...	...	1,193	1,235	4,719	Benson
Billings**	.007	833	888	15,618	343	30,640	13,010	.0002	2,385	1	...	...	...	...	...	...	1,012	Billings
Bottineau	.009	6,682	7,149	14,939	2,828	28,851	99,820	.0019	64,893	18	4,274	8	...	...	7,699	2,562	6,453	Bottineau
Bowman	.011	2,978	3,242	16,273	1,275	30,919	48,460	.0011	61,125	17	...	...	...	...	6,962	1,384	3,034	Bowman
Burke	.013	2,012	2,242	14,299	948	24,806	28,770	.0005	13,466	4	...	...	...	...	5,861	...	2,462	Burke
Burleigh*	.015	73,166	69,416	18,735	28,627	38,815	1,370,800	.0274	1,233,523	350	257,311	512	35,237	185	137,747	85,234	60,582	Burleigh
Cass*	.017	128,908	123,138	18,841	54,138	36,451	2,428,790	.0525	2,661,292	756	349,333	695	93,538	492	208,819	127,818	110,383	Cass
Cavalier	.019	4,319	4,831	16,455	1,908	30,577	71,070	.0013	49,252	14	2,600	5	...	...	5,463	2,038	4,414	Cavalier
Dickey	.021	5,302	5,757	13,961	2,154	28,038	74,020	.0016	65,160	19	...	...	...	...	5,631	1,594	4,764	Dickey
Divide	.023	2,165	2,283	15,182	938	28,473	32,870	.0005	11,342	3	...	...	...	...	1,044	1,071	2,455	Divide
Dunn	.025	3,491	3,600	12,959	1,294	28,396	45,240	.0010	41,947	12	...	...	...	...	8,854	1,411	3,112	Dunn
Eddy	.027	2,539	2,757	14,537	1,101	27,218	36,910	.0006	14,813	4	...	...	...	...	5,718	...	2,457	Eddy
Emmons	.029	3,828	4,331	13,621	1,690	25,279	52,140	.0012	54,856	16	...	...	...	...	5,338	1,127	3,805	Emmons
Foster	.031	3,369	3,759	16,483	1,440	31,143	55,530	.0012	54,231	15	5,029	10	...	...	6,848	4,615	3,097	Foster
Golden Valley	.033	1,758	1,924	14,164	708	28,469	24,900	.0005	22,162	6	...	...	...	...	2,199	...	1,684	Golden Valley
Grand Forks*	.035	63,757	66,109	16,076	24,409	34,315	1,024,980	.0249	1,371,355	389	297,566	592	45,473	239	100,901	50,034	48,565	Grand Forks
Grant	.037	2,562	2,841	12,592	1,137	22,855	32,260	.0006	14,731	4	...	...	...	...	2,008	...	2,786	Grant
Griggs	.039	2,467	2,754	15,780	1,105	28,523	38,930	.0007	28,441	8	...	...	...	...	5,338	2,262	2,697	Griggs
Hettinger	.041	2,510	2,715	14,721	1,084	27,541	36,950	.0007	20,735	6	...	...	...	...	3,533	3,340	2,545	Hettinger
Kidder	.043	2,499	2,753	13,573	1,123	24,404	33,920	.0006	19,472	6	...	...	...	...	1,594	1,391	2,815	Kidder
LaMoure	.045	4,421	4,701	14,743	1,859	28,576	65,180	.0011	24,676	7	...	...	...	...	3,183	1,081	4,510	LaMoure
Logan	.047	2,015	2,308	14,903	910	26,616	30,030	.0005	16,419	5	...	...	...	...	1,022	1,139	2,143	Logan
McHenry**	.049	5,555	5,987	14,347	2,407	26,747	79,700	.0012	12,635	4	...	...	...	...	2,332	...	5,748	McHenry
McIntosh	.051	3,092	3,390	13,972	1,386	25,250	43,200	.0009	35,750	10	...	...	...	...	5,713	2,027	3,081	McIntosh
McKenzie	.053	5,503	5,737	12,977	2,068	28,082	71,410	.0013	30,909	9	...	...	...	...	4,217	2,441	4,834	McKenzie
McLean	.055	8,705	9,311	16,008	3,610	31,084	139,350	.0023	56,579	16	...	...	...	...	8,698	3,650	8,942	McLean
Mercer	.057	8,403	8,644	18,798	3,198	40,063	157,960	.0025	68,358	19	2,641	5	...	...	12,515	7,354	8,267	Mercer
Morton*	.059	25,137	25,303	17,019	9,857	35,320	427,800	.0076	256,234	73	1,542	3	...	...	15,083	7,898	22,625	Morton
Mountrail	.061	6,402	6,631	11,956	2,406	25,903	76,540	.0016	61,195	17	...	...	...	...	12,518	3,750	5,434	Mountrail
Nelson	.063	3,260	3,715	16,169	1,530	27,947	52,710	.0008	14,853	4	...	...	...	...	2,315	1,074	3,230	Nelson
Oliver	.065	1,808	2,065	17,583	736	37,369	31,790	.0004	4,371	1	...	...	...	...	1,306	...	2,091	Oliver
Pembina	.067	7,995	8,585	17,730	3,293	34,949	141,750	.0028	125,866	36	2,123	4	2,133	11	16,820	4,307	7,192	Pembina
Pierce	.069	4,333	4,675	13,732	1,866	25,945	59,500	.0013	56,372	16	4,781	10	1,255	7	6,545	3,381	4,030	Pierce
Ramsey	.071	11,321	12,066	17,177	4,699	33,873	194,460	.0039	166,910	47	32,216	64	3,402	18	19,055	7,424	9,489	Ramsey
Ransom	.073	5,808	5,890	17,744	2,345	35,453	103,060	.0017	50,202	14	2,676	5	...	...	7,440	2,900	5,400	Ransom
Renville**	.075	2,433	2,610	15,368	1,033	29,432	37,390	.0007	28,389	8	...	...	...	...	...	...	2,538	Renville
Richland**	.077	17,458	17,998	15,896	6,517	34,559	277,520	.0050	170,324	48	4,927	10	3,296	17	30,543	8,942	14,221	Richland
Rolette	.079	13,754	13,674	9,646	4,299	25,319	132,670	.0029	96,129	27	3,562	7	...	...	19,463	1,906	8,646	Rolette
Sargent	.081	4,125	4,366	17,918	1,695	35,015	73,910	.0012	33,587	10	...	...	...	...	3,415	...	4,088	Sargent
Sheridan	.083	1,430	1,710	14,196	685	24,708	20,300	.0003	6,729	2	...	...	...	...	1,482	...	1,705	Sheridan
Sioux	.085	4,172	4,044	7,100	1,072	22,038	29,620	.0007	16,639	5	...	...	...	...	1,613	...	2,095	Sioux
Slope	.087	740	767	11,973	296	24,106	8,860	.0001	...	...	...	...	...	...	...	...	900	Slope
Stark**	.089	21,753	22,636	15,270	8,638	31,005	332,170	.0073	349,550	99	53,585	107	9,988	53	32,665	19,920	18,235	Stark
Steele	.091	1,978	2,258	18,418	868	34,069	36,430	.0006	19,515	6	...	...	...	...	1,630	...	2,077	Steele
Stutsman**	.093	20,655	21,908	16,238	8,483	32,147	335,390	.0068	286,940	81	44,516	89	13,708	72	32,592	21,349	17,998	Stutsman
Towner	.095	2,525	2,876	17,402	1,144	31,008	43,940	.0006	9,768	3	...	...	...	...	1,048	...	2,553	Towner
Traill	.097	8,176	8,477	16,947	3,141	35,623	138,560	.0023	58,980	17	2,559	5	...	...	4,271	6,030	6,974	Traill
Walsh	.099	11,353	12,389	16,530	4,699	32,279	187,660	.0035	133,582	38	7,257	14	...	...	23,365	7,624	10,047	Walsh
Ward**	.101	54,872	58,795	16,166	22,233	32,300	887,070	.0200	1,004,533	285	152,340	303	26,588	140	94,593	43,289	48,473	Ward
Wells	.103	4,493	5,102	17,476	2,088	30,510	78,520	.0014	53,967	15	...	...	...	...	6,493	4,161	4,679	Wells
Williams**	.105	19,144	19,761	14,706	7,655	30,099	281,540	.0062	292,506	83	51,200	102	8,046	42	38,625	14,678	16,064	Williams
North Dakota Total		**627,989**	**642,200**	**16,565**	**252,824**	**33,330**	**10,402,360**	**.2137**	**9,512,875**	**2,700**	**1,290,581**	**2,567**	**250,028**	**1,313**	**956,600**	**477,987**	**544,730**	**North Dakota**

Source: Devonshire Associates Ltd. and Scan/US, Inc. 2005. ...Data less than 1,000. (d) Data not available.
* Component of a Metropolitan Core Based Statistical Area.
** Component of a Micropolitan Core Based Statistical Area.

Continued on next page

Counties: Population/Income/Sales, *Continued*

County or County Equivalent	FIPS County Code	Population Estimate 7/1/05	Population Census 4/1/00	Per Capita Income 2004	Households Estimate 7/1/05	Median Household Income 2004	Disposable Income 2004 ($1,000)	Market Ability Index 2004	Total Retail Sales 2004 Sales ($1,000)	Total Retail Sales Ranally Sales Units	General Merchandise 2004 Sales ($1,000)	General Merchandise Ranally Sales Units	Apparel Store 2004 Sales ($1,000)	Apparel Store Ranally Sales Units	Food Store Sales 2004 ($1,000)	Health & Drug Store 2004 ($1,000)	Passenger Car Registrations 2004	County or County Equivalent
Ohio (OH; Code 39; 88 Counties)																		
Adams	.001	28,624	27,330	13,297	10,844	28,054	380,610	.0069	192,769	55	31,392	62	1,506	8	24,959	17,192	21,729	Adams
Allen*	.003	106,543	108,473	16,950	40,979	35,403	1,805,860	.0372	1,684,654	478	408,689	813	47,477	250	125,580	104,889	77,132	Allen
Ashland**	.005	54,594	52,523	17,021	20,133	36,816	929,220	.0156	445,580	127	53,232	106	10,455	55	70,817	31,589	40,999	Ashland
Ashtabula**	.007	103,185	102,728	16,748	40,666	34,272	1,728,100	.0294	873,011	248	125,687	250	26,267	138	150,692	75,500	77,941	Ashtabula
Athens**	.009	63,652	62,223	11,797	22,730	23,776	750,930	.0147	457,922	130	51,314	102	21,902	115	113,734	33,820	44,858	Athens
Auglaize**	.011	46,791	46,611	19,306	17,843	40,546	903,340	.0148	440,314	125	44,672	89	19,450	102	55,039	25,390	36,828	Auglaize
Belmont*	.013	69,040	70,226	14,443	28,120	28,586	997,160	.0223	1,056,978	300	226,091	450	62,799	331	169,448	79,654	51,460	Belmont
Brown*	.015	44,709	42,285	16,443	16,281	36,146	735,140	.0112	209,128	59	16,340	32	2,962	16	49,229	20,319	36,036	Brown
Butler*	.017	349,225	332,807	20,901	132,118	44,295	7,298,990	.1152	3,315,271	941	441,690	878	68,628	361	546,611	174,591	258,968	Butler
Carroll*	.019	29,941	28,836	15,712	11,145	34,019	470,440	.0078	203,585	58	3,790	8	2,311	12	45,525	26,928	23,634	Carroll
Champaign**	.021	39,898	38,890	19,642	15,494	40,658	783,690	.0121	309,928	88	31,820	63	3,014	16	64,605	16,904	30,904	Champaign
Clark*	.023	141,771	144,742	19,206	57,550	38,083	2,722,860	.0463	1,530,971	435	237,291	472	35,580	187	246,663	151,117	108,627	Clark
Clermont*	.025	190,233	177,977	21,548	72,719	45,270	4,099,100	.0676	2,247,176	638	474,648	944	55,753	293	210,504	70,991	151,848	Clermont
Clinton**	.027	42,495	40,543	18,223	16,259	38,070	774,380	.0150	638,116	181	66,141	132	7,090	37	94,749	19,700	32,295	Clinton
Columbiana**	.029	111,181	112,075	16,097	43,951	32,672	1,789,730	.0318	1,025,022	291	106,839	212	21,773	115	166,091	77,945	85,435	Columbiana
Coshocton**	.031	37,286	36,655	16,073	14,497	33,146	599,290	.0099	259,532	74	37,564	75	9,325	49	55,351	14,781	29,005	Coshocton
Crawford**	.033	45,458	46,966	18,139	19,153	34,703	824,540	.0131	332,711	94	18,466	37	5,909	31	55,436	46,158	37,017	Crawford
Cuyahoga*	.035	1,344,252	1,393,978	19,182	557,717	36,978	25,785,490	.4635	17,454,772	4,956	1,677,803	3,337	1,093,042	5,753	2,709,994	2,056,841	905,392	Cuyahoga
Darke**	.037	52,876	53,309	18,312	20,850	37,144	968,270	.0166	544,103	155	82,809	165	16,543	87	81,293	18,501	43,079	Darke
Defiance**	.039	38,831	39,500	20,933	15,591	41,635	812,850	.0146	576,022	164	83,031	165	12,100	64	82,072	22,248	31,860	Defiance
Delaware*	.041	151,233	109,989	27,406	54,583	60,904	4,144,650	.0604	1,660,053	471	129,819	258	20,091	106	291,637	42,528	116,996	Delaware
Erie*	.043	78,323	79,551	20,617	32,271	40,251	1,614,780	.0275	965,059	274	200,248	398	52,598	277	121,844	78,924	61,068	Erie
Fairfield*	.045	139,046	122,759	20,266	51,061	44,379	2,817,900	.0442	1,212,251	344	157,672	314	67,951	358	213,637	63,369	107,915	Fairfield
Fayette**	.047	28,010	28,433	17,752	11,388	35,009	497,220	.0107	529,336	150	39,442	78	145,216	764	71,583	19,857	21,882	Fayette
Franklin*	.049	1,100,544	1,068,978	19,441	425,624	40,555	21,395,270	.4219	18,973,154	5,387	2,325,256	4,624	971,342	5,112	1,977,266	772,272	816,702	Franklin
Fulton*	.051	42,582	42,084	19,541	16,153	41,078	832,090	.0134	384,087	109	38,538	77	3,258	17	62,794	25,235	34,580	Fulton
Gallia**	.053	31,347	31,069	13,840	12,079	28,979	433,840	.0093	396,852	113	47,585	95	8,252	43	59,604	20,671	23,958	Gallia
Geauga*	.055	95,917	90,895	24,004	33,562	54,642	2,302,350	.0337	852,850	242	27,926	56	14,136	74	205,145	82,616	72,313	Geauga
Greene*	.057	152,045	147,886	22,108	60,239	45,071	3,361,400	.0557	1,909,483	542	344,914	686	146,383	770	217,643	65,301	123,039	Greene
Guernsey**	.059	41,593	40,792	14,370	16,623	28,961	597,680	.0117	438,468	125	59,717	119	7,611	40	76,349	19,369	32,267	Guernsey
Hamilton*	.061	809,794	845,303	19,942	335,551	38,570	16,149,060	.2995	12,266,060	3,483	1,547,940	3,078	874,702	4,604	1,737,505	790,611	623,286	Hamilton
Hancock**	.063	74,326	71,295	19,948	29,041	40,847	1,482,630	.0282	1,206,927	343	265,644	528	31,557	166	102,711	49,066	56,808	Hancock
Hardin	.065	31,758	31,945	15,625	12,060	32,794	496,210	.0084	224,914	64	26,108	52	3,846	20	47,467	13,685	23,607	Hardin
Harrison	.067	16,069	15,856	14,493	6,439	29,019	232,890	.0038	78,053	22	3,654	7	...	...	16,520	7,306	13,066	Harrison
Henry	.069	29,483	29,210	18,969	11,215	39,810	559,260	.0091	263,551	75	20,452	41	3,667	19	35,041	21,028	23,674	Henry
Highland	.071	42,760	40,875	15,488	15,843	33,443	662,270	.0115	338,207	96	63,748	127	4,825	25	48,353	25,027	32,194	Highland
Hocking	.073	29,005	28,241	15,275	10,827	32,938	443,060	.0076	211,275	60	18,328	36	2,915	15	45,287	16,076	21,846	Hocking
Holmes	.075	41,788	38,943	11,891	11,325	35,225	496,900	.0104	377,678	107	33,080	66	2,328	12	43,091	17,898	19,268	Holmes
Huron**	.077	60,500	59,487	18,063	22,929	37,998	1,092,820	.0185	574,811	163	54,240	108	9,092	48	95,576	41,739	45,014	Huron
Jackson	.079	33,408	32,641	14,435	13,233	29,358	482,240	.0092	325,335	92	56,622	113	2,843	15	58,275	24,480	25,720	Jackson
Jefferson*	.081	70,461	73,894	16,058	30,679	29,950	1,131,470	.0204	686,418	195	101,334	202	20,125	106	129,348	74,763	55,282	Jefferson
Knox**	.083	58,657	54,500	16,644	21,251	36,785	976,310	.0163	451,239	128	66,280	132	13,536	71	83,856	31,838	42,504	Knox
Lake*	.085	232,832	227,511	22,269	92,768	44,750	5,184,900	.0945	3,955,705	1,123	499,556	993	145,957	768	455,190	318,056	179,578	Lake
Lawrence*	.087	62,567	62,319	14,019	25,141	28,105	877,140	.0158	460,504	131	147,803	294	5,100	27	73,012	38,138	46,329	Lawrence
Licking*	.089	153,841	145,491	20,207	60,353	41,227	3,108,720	.0521	1,729,156	491	229,300	456	52,055	274	217,562	72,421	122,729	Licking
Logan**	.091	46,813	46,005	19,601	18,923	38,757	917,560	.0147	414,743	118	59,192	118	12,844	68	81,058	25,855	37,687	Logan
Lorain*	.093	295,342	284,664	18,988	107,046	42,040	5,607,930	.0965	3,266,939	928	432,268	860	99,800	525	447,072	328,226	216,414	Lorain
Lucas*	.095	452,909	455,054	17,874	179,516	36,154	8,095,090	.1564	6,508,999	1,848	1,048,213	2,085	297,542	1,566	837,264	399,591	327,278	Lucas
Madison*	.097	40,930	40,213	18,184	14,454	41,004	744,280	.0126	396,235	113	25,479	51	2,290	12	55,485	15,392	29,821	Madison
Mahoning*	.099	248,058	257,555	16,383	96,905	33,748	4,063,900	.0774	2,980,092	846	382,352	760	141,580	745	364,799	185,998	174,199	Mahoning
Marion**	.101	66,455	66,217	17,218	25,158	36,401	1,144,210	.0207	736,968	209	177,105	352	22,091	116	96,521	40,751	46,417	Marion
Medina*	.103	168,198	151,095	23,201	61,124	51,065	3,902,400	.0621	1,976,163	561	189,512	377	59,385	313	240,206	175,378	131,021	Medina
Meigs	.105	23,466	23,072	13,003	9,345	26,313	305,130	.0054	131,704	37	9,700	19	1,870	10	29,616	11,787	18,757	Meigs
Mercer**	.107	41,093	40,924	18,688	15,239	40,208	767,950	.0135	473,480	134	32,140	64	8,788	46	63,808	27,356	32,129	Mercer
Miami*	.109	100,836	98,868	19,945	39,147	40,984	2,011,140	.0334	1,069,903	304	163,151	324	43,784	230	136,545	63,767	79,290	Miami
Monroe	.111	14,858	15,180	14,707	5,997	29,416	218,510	.0034	60,241	17	1,148	2	1,476	8	16,419	6,234	12,419	Monroe
Montgomery*	.113	547,810	559,062	19,352	224,247	37,774	10,601,050	.1900	7,146,156	2,029	1,152,638	2,292	260,529	1,371	987,131	369,266	427,932	Montgomery
Morgan	.115	14,848	14,897	13,784	5,894	27,875	204,670	.0033	60,038	17	4,767	9	1,246	7	15,315	2,969	12,161	Morgan
Morrow*	.117	34,782	31,628	16,286	11,810	38,272	566,450	.0088	176,601	50	9,399	19	2,163	11	38,904	10,046	26,457	Morrow
Muskingum**	.119	85,731	84,585	16,060	32,886	33,714	1,376,870	.0277	1,169,837	332	163,216	325	80,846	426	157,669	82,761	64,086	Muskingum
Noble	.121	14,079	14,058	13,000	4,629	31,611	183,020	.0032	72,586	21	1,339	3	1,331	7	17,165	6,511	9,927	Noble
Ottawa*	.123	41,432	40,985	21,184	17,002	41,158	877,710	.0148	509,193	145	29,838	59	6,510	34	79,647	24,281	34,113	Ottawa
Paulding	.125	19,368	20,293	19,839	8,166	37,500	384,240	.0059	144,262	41	5,516	11	1,393	7	23,202	8,131	17,593	Paulding
Perry	.127	35,396	34,078	14,714	12,662	33,042	520,810	.0081	144,892	41	11,448	23	1,526	8	42,874	12,954	26,127	Perry
Pickaway*	.129	53,572	52,727	17,182	18,361	40,253	920,490	.0149	387,108	110	63,075	125	6,202	33	59,221	26,984	38,373	Pickaway
Pike	.131	28,517	27,695	14,262	10,807	30,275	406,710	.0074	229,038	65	44,709	89	3,412	18	47,266	20,830	21,482	Pike
Portage*	.133	155,370	152,061	19,948	60,110	41,277	3,099,270	.0499	1,464,259	416	96,055	191	83,246	438	216,094	95,850	123,653	Portage
Preble*	.135	42,629	42,337	19,216	16,591	39,470	819,150	.0127	312,133	89	16,719	33	4,369	23	45,925	19,938	35,993	Preble
Putnam	.137	34,791	34,726	19,553	12,711	42,639	680,280	.0103	243,676	69	22,774	45	5,462	29	35,859	38,011	27,900	Putnam
Richland*	.139	127,690	128,852	17,821	51,202	35,618	2,275,620	.0425	1,656,330	470	368,119	732	53,257	280	172,943	81,571	97,710	Richland
Ross**	.141	75,026	73,345	16,439	28,051	35,274	1,233,350	.0221	745,545	212	171,903	342	23,229	122	128,770	40,086	55,589	Ross
Sandusky**	.143	61,596	61,792	18,761	24,120	38,133	1,155,610	.0195	623,014	177	102,167	203	13,965	74	98,689	33,724	48,061	Sandusky
Scioto**	.145	76,419	79,195	14,096	31,867	27,171	1,077,230	.0202	667,085	189	106,080	211	25,281	133	114,583	51,735	59,039	Scioto
Seneca**	.147	57,462	58,683	17,826	22,825	35,845	1,024,290	.0174	545,091	155	43,489	86	18,482	97	85,219	33,767	45,068	Seneca
Shelby**	.149	48,854	47,910	19,495	18,357	41,505	952,430	.0156	468,965	133	48,182	96	10,684	56	77,440	28,705	36,960	Shelby
Stark*	.151	377,190	378,098	18,259	146,969	37,487	6,887,110	.1295	5,181,811	1,471	691,936	1,376	278,530	1,466	755,809	476,326	291,619	Stark
Summit*	.153	549,026	542,899	19,289	212,381	40,137	10,590,380	.1979	8,074,226	2,293	824,382	1,639	318,103	1,674	1,104,975	747,813	396,561	Summit
Trumbull*	.155	219,265	225,116	18,710	90,119	36,441	4,102,490	.0706	2,360,583	670	315,828	628	88,072	464	339,684	165,241	168,683	Trumbull
Tuscarawas**	.157	92,174	90,914	16,496	36,067	33,803	1,520,510	.0277	970,512	276	139,211	277	42,474	224	174,290	78,315	69,933	Tuscarawas
Union*	.159	45,412	40,909	21,736	16,672	47,836	987,070	.0152	417,644	119	49,933	99	5,283	28	67,396	20,285	36,220	Union
Van Wert**	.161	29,040	29,659	18,782	11,762	36,987	545,440	.0091	281,684	80	41,429	82	6,014	32	43,954	15,177	23,729	Van Wert
Vinton	.163	13,511	12,806	12,900	5,002	27,908	174,290	.0027	37,286	11	1,915	4	...	...	13,160	2,683	10,061	Vinton
Warren*	.165	196,541	158,383	23,142	68,640	53,284	4,548,430	.0691	1,911,891	543	242,059	481	24,655	130	332,056	68,807	145,568	Warren
Washington*	.167	62,162	63,251	16,813	25,469	33,070	1,045,120	.0192	698,181	198	85,886	171	10,833	57	123,124	34,981	49,870	Washington
Wayne**	.169	114,151	111,564	18,320	43,062	38,804	2,091,220	.0352	1,097,041	312	107,505	214	32,286	170	193,656	58,586	85,560	Wayne
Williams	.171	38,609	39,188	19,366	15,650	38,199	747,710	.0119	322,539	92	53,131	106	7,401	39	52,793	23,300	31,036	Williams
Wood*	.173	123,284	121,065	20,534	48,903	41,402	2,531,460	.0415	1,313,308	373	162,987	324	31,852	168	225,687	59,594	98,588	Wood
Wyandot	.175	22,712	22,908	18,268	9,081	36,401	414,900	.0064	152,321	43	7,004	14	1,704	9	23,888	17,406	19,039	Wyandot
Ohio Total		**11,485,881**	**11,353,140**	**19,054**	**4,501,807**	**38,837**	**218,856,530**	**3.8858**	**141,869,295**	**40,284**	**18,429,412**	**36,651**	**6,276,437**	**33,033**	**19,867,867**	**9,854,297**	**8,606,795**	**Ohio**
Oklahoma (OK; Code 40; 77 Counties)																		
Adair	.001	21,905	21,038	10,835	7,596	24,213	237,350	.0043	87,880	25	18,289	36	...	...	12,236	3,278	13,691	Adair
Alfalfa	.003	5,749	6,105	13,561	2,092	28,836	77,960	.0013	23,223	7	2,995	6	...	...	3,594	2,022	4,331	Alfalfa
Atoka	.005	14,370	13,879	10,674	4,967	23,789	153,380	.0031	99,142	28	28,829	57	1,198	6	11,935	4,546	8,982	Atoka
Beaver	.007	5,366	5,857	18,423	2,194	34,937	98,860	.0014	17,791	5	1,986	4	...	...	2,425	...	4,894	Beaver
Beckham**	.009	19,255	19,799	13,166	7,332	26,850	253,510	.0061	302,008	86	64,218	128	7,263	38	30,719	10,931	13,503	Beckham
Blaine	.011	11,058	11,976	13,036	4,037	27,517	144,150	.0024	50,478	14	6,615	13	...	...	10,511	2,679	8,156	Blaine
Bryan**	.013	37,565	36,534	13,664	14,672	27,159	513,290	.0093	267,810	76	50,210	100	4,094	22	36,479	11,802	26,502	Bryan
Caddo	.015	29,994	30,150	12,353	10,753	26,591	370,520	.0069	191,045	54	40,434	80	3,026	16	30,459	15,150	19,783	Caddo
Canadian*	.017	96,179	87,697	19,368	34,116	42,233	1,862,800	.0295	804,119	228	221,762	441	6,309	33	44,235	36,963	68,025	Canadian
Carter**	.019	47,108	45,621	13,970	18,027	28,330	658,080	.0140	598,297	170	145,400	289	25,640	135	48,873	37,747	32,116	Carter
Cherokee**	.021	44,488	42,521	12,484	16,674	26,031	555,390	.0107	336,470	96	76,098	151	9,705	51	67,008	12,605	30,035	Cherokee
Choctaw	.023	15,333	15,342	11,655	6,201	22,170	178,710	.0033	89,146	25	23,303	46	2,074	11	13,934	5,336	10,671	Choctaw
Cimarron	.025	2,858	3,148	15,966	1,215	29,140	45,630	.0009	35,145	10	...	...	...	...	5,147	1,767	2,414	Cimarron
Cleveland*	.027	225,695	208,016	19,067	84,366	39,710	4,303,430	.0691	1,937,693	550	480,144	955	69,434	365	233,684	131,103	162,545	Cleveland
Coal	.029	5,962	6,031	11,667	2,327	23,223	69,560	.0012	20,774	6	2,829	6	...	...	5,231	1,405	4,182	Coal
Comanche*	.031	109,018	114,996	15,172	39,373	32,739	1,654,020	.0287	814,320	231	282,458	562	24,492	129	71,642	32,806	70,251	Comanche
Cotton	.033	6,520	6,614	13,725	2,556	27,200	89,490	.0014	27,046	8	4,596	9	...	...	6,265	3,024	4,983	Cotton
Craig	.035	14,793	14,950	14,268	5,537	30,230	211,070	.0039	128,007	36	23,916	48	1,031	5	16,411	6,756	10,643	Craig
Creek*	.037	69,584	67,367	15,196	25,557	31,751	1,057,420	.0174	416,198	118	92,569	184	5,200	27	64,212	34,070	49,355	Creek
Custer	.039	24,574	26,142	14,659	10,008	27,933	360,220	.0075	315,989	90	66,394	132	10,903	57	40,194	17,694	18,382	Custer
Delaware	.041	39,577	37,077	13,575	15,178	27,479	537,240	.0090	190,460	54	70,818	141	1,897	10	13,899	7,443	28,497	Delaware
Dewey	.043	4,494	4,743	14,915	1,915	26,987	67,030	.0011	20,108	6	1,475	3	...	...	1,572	1,187	4,171	Dewey
Ellis	.045	3,904	4,075	15,348	1,698	27,291	59,920	.0010	22,252	6	1,890	4	...	...	4,869	1,639	3,508	Ellis
Garfield**	.047	56,753	57,813	16,418	22,797	31,679	931,760	.0174	639,603	182	159,589	317	17,110	90	89,321	29,742	41,570	Garfield
Garvin	.049	27,208	27,210	13,930	10,723	27,363	379,020	.0073	254,843	72	38,917	77	4,528	24	38,761	12,004	19,660	Garvin
Grady*	.051	48,624	45,516	14,713	17,555	31,754	715,400	.0125	349,360	99	42,971	85	9,843	52	51,890	17,469	34,358	Grady
Grant	.053	4,882	5,144	14,877	2,004	28,109	72,630	.0011	12,986	4	2,010	4	...	...	2,616	1,033	4,259	Grant
Greer	.055	5,719	6,061	12,070	2,160	24,541	69,030	.0011	17,800	5	1,650	3	...	...	5,816	1,604	4,049	Greer
Harmon	.057	2,930	3,283	12,150	1,236	22,013	35,600	.0007	17,823	5	2,275	5	...	...	3,533	1,183	2,192	Harmon
Harper	.059	3,283	3,562	18,657	1,459	32,310	61,250	.0009	14,800	4	1,533	3	...	...	3,712	1,653	3,221	Harper
Haskell	.061	12,217	11,792	11,780	4,647	22,963	143,920	.0027	73,207	21	19,737	39	1,141	6	12,104	1,998	8,494	Haskell
Hughes	.063	13,826	14,154	11,081	5,207	22,563	153,210	.0028	68,550	19	16,107	32	...	...	9,610	2,876	9,275	Hughes
Jackson**	.065	26,651	28,439	14,841	10,341	30,182	395,540	.0078	300,008	85	93,249	185	11,234	59	34,949	10,768	17,976	Jackson
Jefferson	.067	6,372	6,818	12,522	2,657	23,198	79,790	.0014	37,443	11	5,897	12	...	...	5,635	4,481	4,923	Jefferson
Johnston	.069	10,513	10,513	11,951	4,071	23,793	125,640	.0021	36,653	10	2,199	4	...	...	9,001	4,981	7,440	Johnston
Kay**	.071	46,817	48,080	15,098	18,589	29,677	706,850	.0137	517,974	147	146,203	291	12,736	67	49,501	34,730	33,170	Kay
Kingfisher	.073	14,199	13,926	16,827	5,233	35,387	238,930	.0041	127,015	36	17,898	36	...	...	12,127	9,313	10,732	Kingfisher
Kiowa	.075	9,841	10,227	13,424	4,053	25,320	132,110	.0023	53,439	15	11,520	23	...	...	11,352	7,598	7,231	Kiowa
Latimer	.077	10,448	10,692	11,477	3,944	23,527	119,910	.0020	30,479	9	9,706	19	...	...	6,136	2,577	7,158	Latimer
Le Flore*	.079	49,394	48,109	12,509	17,999	26,572	617,870	.0119	374,940	106	118,636	236	3,461	18	57,659	11,259	33,780	Le Flore
Lincoln*	.081	32,331	32,080	14,530	12,194	30,108	469,760	.0075	142,208	40	17,285	34	14,985	79	16,548	5,074	24,233	Lincoln
Logan*	.083	36,508	33,924	15,290	12,303	35,457	558,210	.0090	200,034	57	30,979	62	...	...	22,265	6,179	25,189	Logan
Love**	.085	9,059	8,831	15,367	3,446	30,908	139,210	.0025	74,142	21	5,338	11	...	...	20,166	3,470	6,915	Love
McClain*	.087	29,188	27,740	17,159	10,862	35,564	500,840	.0085	249,880	71	40,618	81	1,091	6	24,561	11,212	22,751	McClain
McCurtain	.089	33,866	34,402	11,990	13,258	23,615	406,050	.0078	228,801	65	57,830	115	6,619	35	36,684	11,136	22,990	McCurtain
McIntosh	.091	20,057	19,456	13,232	8,176	25,325	265,390	.0055	215,989	61	69,323	138	3,138	17	38,018	7,322	15,015	McIntosh
Major	.093	7,340	7,545	15,614	2,977	30,102	114,610	.0022	78,281	22	6,030	12	...	...	7,683	4,770	6,215	Major
Marshall	.095	13,994	13,184	12,772	5,398	25,677	178,730	.0032	84,659	24	20,340	40	...	...	21,103	7,933	9,852	Marshall
Mayes	.097	39,343	38,369	14,719	15,089	29,310	579,070	.0099	258,119	73	47,787	95	3,082	16	51,468	15,744	29,649	Mayes
Murray	.099	12,753	12,623	14,524	4,961	29,135	185,230	.0036	135,529	38	24,775	49	...	...	14,975	5,264	9,263	Murray
Muskogee**	.101	70,975	69,451	13,218	26,491	27,498	938,150	.0189	695,489	197	160,505	319	17,203	91	81,722	48,482	45,706	Muskogee
Noble	.103	11,182	11,411	16,588	4,431	32,513	185,490	.0032	95,898	27	9,440	19	...	...	7,284	4,749	9,118	Noble
Nowata	.105	11,060	10,569	13,626	4,110	28,192	150,700	.0023	25,603	7	3,845	8	...	...	4,416	2,226	7,872	Nowata
Okfuskee	.107	11,617	11,814	11,178	4,245	23,307	129,860	.0023	46,436	13	5,453	11	...	...	5,390	6,290	7,781	Okfuskee
Oklahoma*	.109	687,070	660,448	17,050	271,354	33,692	11,714,620	.2318	9,815,970	2,787	1,539,214	3,061	345,467	1,818	1,031,109	537,882	491,025	Oklahoma
Okmulgee*	.111	40,003	39,685	13,072	15,053	27,385	522,910	.0096	281,315	80	86,679	172	4,857	26	35,145	8,209	26,631	Okmulgee
Osage*	.113	45,632	44,437	15,619	16,758	32,963	712,730	.0103	122,483	35	11,930	24	...	...	33,432	10,102	32,632	Osage
Ottawa**	.115	32,406	33,194	13,607	12,850	26,682	440,960	.0081	242,305	69	41,863	83	3,379	18	32,853	14,072	23,580	Ottawa
Pawnee*	.117	17,006	16,612	14,556	6,306	30,528	247,540	.0042	101,681	29	24,675	49	1,528	8	23,071	8,444	12,644	Pawnee
Payne**	.119	70,126	68,190	13,841	26,959	28,292	970,630	.0190	684,911	194	204,937	408	26,603	140	64,075	37,353	49,843	Payne
Pittsburg**	.121	44,083	43,953	13,792	17,186	27,464	607,990	.0123	468,830	133	137,603	274	13,668	72	28,264	17,944	30,212	Pittsburg
Pontotoc**	.123	34,877	35,143	13,645	13,854	27,192	475,900	.0096	359,834	102	109,559	218	13,487	71	35,615	21,242	25,201	Pontotoc
Pottawatomie**	.125	67,866	65,521	14,150	24,516	30,469	960,320	.0175	534,896	152	141,264	281	25,517	134	60,179	48,651	45,681	Pottawatomie
Pushmataha	.127	11,739	11,667	11,497	4,721	21,846	134,960	.0025	57,802	16	4,791	10	...	...	10,467	6,418	8,424	Pushmataha

Source: Devonshire Associates Ltd. and Scan/US, Inc. 2005. ...Data less than 1,000. (d) Data not available.
* Component of a Metropolitan Core Based Statistical Area.
** Component of a Micropolitan Core Based Statistical Area.

Counties: Population/Income/Sales, *Continued*

County or County Equivalent	FIPS County Code	Population Estimate 7/1/05	Population Census 4/1/00	Per Capita Income 2004	House-holds Estimate 7/1/05	Median Household Income 2004	Disposable Income 2004 ($1,000)	Market Ability Index 2004	Total Retail Sales 2004 Sales ($1,000)	Total Retail Sales Ranally Sales Units	General Merchandise 2004 Sales ($1,000)	General Merchandise Ranally Sales Units	Apparel Store 2004 Sales ($1,000)	Apparel Store Ranally Sales Units	Food Store Sales 2004 ($1,000)	Health & Drug Store 2004 ($1,000)	Passenger Car Regis-trations 2004	County or County Equivalent
Roger Mills	.129	3,069	3,436	16,865	1,391	28,681	51,760	.0009	26,429	8	3,917	8	...	...	1,117	2,452	3,175	Roger Mills
Rogers*	.131	81,199	70,641	18,006	27,301	41,261	1,462,050	.0224	494,375	140	126,693	252	8,299	44	46,622	23,439	56,623	Rogers
Seminole	.133	24,269	24,894	12,452	9,463	24,693	302,190	.0056	157,491	45	32,494	65	3,440	18	26,008	11,864	16,938	Seminole
Sequoyah*	.135	40,620	38,972	12,893	15,218	26,578	523,710	.0098	291,953	83	38,484	77	1,781	9	58,534	14,572	27,593	Sequoyah
Stephens**	.137	42,200	43,182	15,460	17,219	29,534	652,410	.0129	519,068	147	111,336	221	13,261	70	52,541	34,344	32,171	Stephens
Texas**	.139	19,768	20,107	16,201	7,308	33,823	320,270	.0054	155,245	44	36,413	72	2,849	15	20,571	7,659	14,163	Texas
Tillman	.141	8,665	9,287	12,545	3,446	24,391	108,700	.0019	38,294	11	4,653	9	2,929	15	9,907	3,325	6,240	Tillman
Tulsa*	.143	574,848	563,299	17,228	210,356	36,646	9,903,560	.2024	9,098,051	2,583	1,842,757	3,665	330,944	1,742	841,269	553,409	409,916	Tulsa
Wagoner*	.145	64,436	57,491	18,610	23,724	39,105	1,199,150	.0167	226,279	64	65,784	131	1,673	9	34,858	12,091	48,375	Wagoner
Washington**	.147	49,163	48,996	17,800	19,855	34,685	875,090	.0145	417,857	119	150,301	299	15,166	80	31,628	23,568	36,538	Washington
Washita	.149	11,230	11,508	14,500	4,426	28,571	162,830	.0027	61,036	17	3,281	7	...	...	9,389	3,808	8,642	Washita
Woods	.151	8,442	9,089	14,921	3,534	27,764	125,960	.0025	93,717	27	31,066	62	1,312	7	11,715	4,367	6,624	Woods
Woodward**	.153	18,697	18,486	15,624	7,007	32,218	292,130	.0062	276,656	79	85,767	171	7,515	40	27,150	13,349	13,654	Woodward
Oklahoma Total		**3,541,713**	**3,450,654**	**15,842**	**1,340,812**	**32,476**	**56,107,160**	**1.0405**	**36,779,875**	**10,439**	**7,733,198**	**15,381**	**1,114,063**	**5,863**	**4,057,057**	**2,095,771**	**2,518,182**	**Oklahoma**

Oregon (OR; Code 41; 36 Counties)

County or County Equivalent	FIPS County Code	Population Estimate 7/1/05	Population Census 4/1/00	Per Capita Income 2004	House-holds Estimate 7/1/05	Median Household Income 2004	Disposable Income 2004 ($1,000)	Market Ability Index 2004	Total Retail Sales 2004 Sales ($1,000)	Total Retail Sales Ranally Sales Units	General Merchandise 2004 Sales ($1,000)	General Merchandise Ranally Sales Units	Apparel Store 2004 Sales ($1,000)	Apparel Store Ranally Sales Units	Food Store Sales 2004 ($1,000)	Health & Drug Store 2004 ($1,000)	Passenger Car Regis-trations 2004	County or County Equivalent
Baker	.001	16,341	16,741	16,137	7,300	29,072	263,700	.0048	170,164	48	3,683	7	1,416	7	38,429	12,778	14,485	Baker
Benton*	.003	79,778	78,153	20,737	33,621	39,321	1,654,350	.0250	619,285	176	82,101	163	24,988	132	143,655	30,072	65,820	Benton
Clackamas*	.005	369,163	338,391	22,779	140,180	47,656	8,408,980	.1353	4,391,350	1,247	796,615	1,584	178,915	942	604,593	124,490	293,645	Clackamas
Clatsop**	.007	36,264	35,630	18,477	15,467	34,715	670,050	.0121	453,282	129	115,410	230	26,665	140	72,232	21,688	27,660	Clatsop
Columbia*	.009	48,039	43,560	20,356	18,435	42,303	977,900	.0143	298,325	85	25,185	50	3,588	19	73,103	30,634	40,292	Columbia
Coos**	.011	63,447	62,779	16,346	27,391	30,442	1,037,130	.0187	635,885	181	138,845	276	13,127	69	112,584	25,949	51,366	Coos
Crook**	.013	21,549	19,182	16,966	8,596	34,117	365,600	.0058	140,988	40	...	...	1,952	10	37,972	6,738	18,345	Crook
Curry**	.015	22,083	21,137	17,024	10,418	29,029	375,940	.0065	204,461	58	53,211	106	2,973	16	32,637	17,674	19,145	Curry
Deschutes*	.017	138,176	115,367	20,225	56,974	39,129	2,794,630	.0517	2,124,592	603	522,176	1,038	63,805	336	282,969	50,914	121,379	Deschutes
Douglas**	.019	103,471	100,399	16,693	43,031	31,954	1,727,220	.0299	926,696	263	187,051	372	23,687	125	170,593	49,089	87,114	Douglas
Gilliam	.021	1,715	1,915	19,644	834	32,268	33,690	.0005	12,573	4	...	...	...	...	2,472	1,390	1,726	Gilliam
Grant	.023	7,180	7,935	19,192	3,529	31,176	137,800	.0023	66,741	19	1,240	2	...	...	24,304	7,623	7,247	Grant
Harney	.025	6,968	7,609	16,906	3,165	29,857	117,800	.0022	81,038	23	...	...	1,134	6	23,905	3,565	6,550	Harney
Hood River**	.027	21,109	20,411	17,356	8,012	36,157	366,360	.0069	269,146	76	46,145	92	7,680	40	73,661	13,741	16,520	Hood River
Jackson*	.029	196,043	181,269	18,053	81,232	34,871	3,539,120	.0732	3,428,121	973	602,138	1,197	88,759	467	352,409	91,518	160,782	Jackson
Jefferson	.031	20,186	19,009	16,142	7,658	34,041	325,840	.0055	156,601	44	2,130	4	3,297	17	41,623	4,130	16,356	Jefferson
Josephine**	.033	80,986	75,726	15,787	34,298	30,001	1,278,490	.0234	800,316	227	186,784	371	16,337	86	123,035	34,787	68,466	Josephine
Klamath**	.035	65,599	63,775	15,374	26,815	30,344	1,008,510	.0193	718,536	204	157,255	313	12,785	67	124,159	24,379	52,781	Klamath
Lake	.037	7,459	7,422	15,477	3,261	28,283	115,440	.0020	61,168	17	...	...	...	...	21,168	5,055	6,521	Lake
Lane*	.039	335,284	322,959	18,570	141,340	35,235	6,226,310	.1146	4,441,395	1,261	819,155	1,629	129,203	680	689,971	164,173	285,037	Lane
Lincoln	.041	45,186	44,479	18,025	20,643	31,422	814,490	.0147	542,285	154	102,256	203	58,251	307	118,105	29,347	35,726	Lincoln
Linn**	.043	108,650	103,069	17,895	43,171	35,863	1,944,340	.0338	1,119,783	318	308,440	613	32,018	169	164,919	42,140	87,818	Linn
Malheur**	.045	31,247	31,615	12,490	10,766	28,905	390,290	.0089	404,013	115	113,018	225	13,314	70	65,511	14,734	21,567	Malheur
Marion*	.047	306,501	284,834	16,417	105,803	37,785	5,031,780	.0959	3,699,429	1,050	815,557	1,622	143,367	755	490,160	119,269	206,376	Marion
Morrow**	.049	12,009	10,995	14,987	4,047	35,431	179,980	.0029	64,646	18	...	...	...	...	7,578	4,713	8,986	Morrow
Multnomah*	.051	688,787	660,486	20,245	286,135	38,576	13,944,220	.2615	11,016,058	3,128	1,750,833	3,482	731,462	3,850	1,432,122	356,373	460,028	Multnomah
Polk*	.053	68,485	62,380	18,584	25,455	39,770	1,272,700	.0182	298,514	85	34,724	69	1,799	9	87,259	16,241	51,969	Polk
Sherman	.055	1,693	1,934	20,343	829	33,209	34,440	.0006	20,051	6	1,608	3	...	...	8,568	...	1,762	Sherman
Tillamook	.057	24,989	24,262	18,141	11,034	32,801	453,330	.0073	199,072	57	32,043	64	3,395	18	45,611	10,563	20,272	Tillamook
Umatilla**	.059	74,284	70,548	15,905	27,311	34,540	1,181,500	.0244	1,065,935	303	159,395	317	30,908	163	193,362	36,756	56,871	Umatilla
Union**	.061	24,483	24,530	16,761	10,121	32,177	410,350	.0081	338,026	96	56,301	112	12,168	64	64,938	13,357	20,696	Union
Wallowa	.063	7,006	7,226	17,612	3,207	30,649	123,390	.0022	81,182	23	1,138	2	...	...	19,270	3,169	6,669	Wallowa
Wasco**	.065	23,581	23,791	17,821	9,780	34,344	420,240	.0079	312,445	89	67,398	134	9,213	48	36,928	14,936	19,786	Wasco
Washington*	.067	500,313	445,342	23,091	192,236	47,739	11,552,810	.2039	8,188,900	2,325	1,697,503	3,376	468,873	2,468	930,500	181,498	378,697	Washington
Wheeler	.069	1,504	1,547	15,838	672	28,270	23,820	.0004	11,997	3	...	...	...	...	3,022	...	1,470	Wheeler
Yamhill*	.071	92,229	84,992	18,563	33,205	40,996	1,712,020	.0280	807,766	229	160,933	320	19,918	105	93,450	33,221	70,101	Yamhill
Oregon Total		**3,651,787**	**3,421,399**	**19,419**	**1,455,972**	**38,529**	**70,914,560**	**1.2727**	**48,170,766**	**13,677**	**9,043,205**	**17,982**	**2,126,499**	**11,193**	**6,806,775**	**1,597,000**	**2,810,031**	**Oregon**

Pennsylvania (PA; Code 42; 67 Counties)

County or County Equivalent	FIPS County Code	Population Estimate 7/1/05	Population Census 4/1/00	Per Capita Income 2004	House-holds Estimate 7/1/05	Median Household Income 2004	Disposable Income 2004 ($1,000)	Market Ability Index 2004	Total Retail Sales 2004 Sales ($1,000)	Total Retail Sales Ranally Sales Units	General Merchandise 2004 Sales ($1,000)	General Merchandise Ranally Sales Units	Apparel Store 2004 Sales ($1,000)	Apparel Store Ranally Sales Units	Food Store Sales 2004 ($1,000)	Health & Drug Store 2004 ($1,000)	Passenger Car Regis-trations 2004	County or County Equivalent
Adams**	.001	99,533	91,292	18,367	36,146	40,145	1,828,120	.0277	593,215	168	61,243	122	12,637	67	126,110	25,354	70,459	Adams
Allegheny*	.003	1,249,911	1,281,666	19,001	518,543	36,324	23,749,790	.4335	16,756,392	4,758	1,758,024	3,496	932,020	4,905	2,767,469	1,152,625	811,277	Allegheny
Armstrong*	.005	71,316	72,392	15,595	29,348	30,565	1,112,170	.0197	609,338	173	63,857	127	9,122	48	106,426	84,607	51,114	Armstrong
Beaver*	.007	177,681	181,412	18,305	73,460	35,385	3,252,440	.0524	1,428,397	406	259,767	517	59,363	312	285,712	132,313	123,762	Beaver
Bedford	.009	50,045	49,984	15,897	20,257	31,279	795,550	.0167	756,527	215	56,786	113	4,221	22	77,887	30,071	39,325	Bedford
Berks*	.011	393,253	373,638	19,745	147,995	41,706	7,764,710	.1320	4,459,882	1,266	520,167	1,034	360,634	1,898	665,140	278,677	275,607	Berks
Blair*	.013	126,465	129,144	16,251	51,843	31,712	2,055,160	.0421	1,839,118	522	340,485	677	66,222	349	262,688	130,976	86,596	Blair
Bradford**	.015	62,544	62,761	16,614	24,861	33,103	1,039,120	.0188	649,910	185	74,937	149	14,325	75	81,387	37,516	44,109	Bradford
Bucks*	.017	622,393	597,635	24,908	226,010	54,755	15,502,700	.2671	10,608,647	3,012	906,388	1,803	427,256	2,249	1,629,157	600,178	452,286	Bucks
Butler*	.019	183,231	174,083	19,252	70,408	40,041	3,527,510	.0609	2,102,186	597	300,893	598	53,921	284	322,101	130,404	130,787	Butler
Cambria*	.021	147,675	152,598	14,830	60,359	28,910	2,190,070	.0418	1,496,756	425	197,260	392	36,268	191	280,379	106,411	97,764	Cambria
Cameron	.023	5,664	5,974	16,969	2,459	31,047	96,110	.0015	36,166	10	1,082	2	1,184	6	7,969	3,012	3,897	Cameron
Carbon*	.025	61,398	58,802	16,611	24,234	33,403	1,019,910	.0174	510,645	145	49,251	98	1,167	6	137,431	43,607	43,406	Carbon
Centre*	.027	141,710	135,758	16,078	52,454	34,755	2,278,390	.0430	1,600,239	454	218,370	434	91,218	480	222,490	77,825	92,574	Centre
Chester*	.029	471,979	433,501	26,126	166,783	58,937	12,331,100	.2238	9,955,995	2,827	297,766	592	204,567	1,077	806,704	334,670	336,851	Chester
Clarion	.031	41,049	41,765	14,704	16,353	29,641	603,570	.0119	457,168	130	44,515	89	15,456	81	89,626	27,648	28,606	Clarion
Clearfield**	.033	82,756	83,382	15,115	33,199	30,341	1,250,840	.0250	999,608	284	163,065	324	38,856	205	137,401	48,654	58,147	Clearfield
Clinton**	.035	37,145	37,914	15,181	15,163	30,047	563,900	.0109	408,903	116	36,186	72	17,614	93	63,774	20,082	25,673	Clinton
Columbia**	.037	65,170	64,151	16,081	25,579	32,621	1,047,970	.0191	655,500	186	74,614	148	21,521	113	103,612	42,328	46,481	Columbia
Crawford**	.039	89,827	90,366	15,924	35,359	32,191	1,430,410	.0255	822,751	234	91,572	182	23,839	125	128,960	55,416	59,651	Crawford
Cumberland*	.041	223,224	213,674	21,296	87,343	43,124	4,753,730	.0917	4,148,191	1,178	400,741	797	123,260	649	485,034	177,038	158,272	Cumberland
Dauphin*	.043	251,422	251,798	20,901	106,799	39,074	5,254,940	.0908	3,306,386	939	344,474	685	188,453	992	503,157	230,020	197,796	Dauphin
Delaware*	.045	556,280	550,864	20,552	198,206	45,910	11,432,720	.1901	6,249,010	1,774	564,538	1,123	356,062	1,874	1,351,257	580,140	345,349	Delaware
Elk**	.047	33,752	35,112	19,035	14,200	35,935	642,480	.0101	264,689	75	33,904	67	4,440	23	56,674	28,363	24,216	Elk
Erie*	.049	279,281	280,843	17,187	109,682	34,993	4,799,900	.0894	3,381,763	960	451,424	898	142,791	752	538,747	194,570	194,833	Erie
Fayette*	.051	144,770	148,644	14,061	60,538	26,825	2,035,650	.0389	1,346,280	382	249,110	495	48,540	255	225,132	106,925	100,995	Fayette
Forest	.053	4,912	4,946	13,774	2,043	26,429	67,660	.0013	44,017	13	...	...	...	...	5,347	...	3,503	Forest
Franklin**	.055	135,052	129,313	19,117	53,769	38,061	2,581,770	.0451	1,589,982	451	178,405	355	37,191	196	263,811	90,426	102,493	Franklin
Fulton	.057	14,764	14,261	16,914	5,951	33,155	249,720	.0040	100,579	29	3,524	7	...	...	13,654	1,371	12,155	Fulton
Greene	.059	39,988	40,672	14,081	15,371	29,261	563,060	.0104	332,869	95	9,591	19	...	...	48,993	34,669	26,500	Greene
Huntingdon**	.061	46,112	45,586	15,061	17,269	32,583	694,510	.0122	361,275	103	16,741	33	4,881	26	69,738	27,101	32,115	Huntingdon
Indiana**	.063	89,103	89,605	14,272	34,918	29,095	1,271,710	.0253	971,024	276	165,326	329	26,432	139	139,506	52,438	61,421	Indiana
Jefferson	.065	46,018	45,932	15,503	18,678	30,644	713,410	.0121	325,911	93	8,687	17	3,068	16	63,237	29,722	32,120	Jefferson
Juniata	.067	23,358	22,821	15,686	8,781	32,904	366,400	.0063	175,253	50	3,647	7	1,306	7	21,999	5,900	17,178	Juniata
Lackawanna*	.069	208,594	213,295	17,113	86,402	33,139	3,569,700	.0679	2,676,456	760	347,635	691	163,621	861	522,145	187,078	135,462	Lackawanna
Lancaster*	.071	490,254	470,658	19,871	183,207	42,188	9,741,670	.1767	6,915,084	1,964	618,456	1,230	403,743	2,125	1,058,381	357,146	343,004	Lancaster
Lawrence**	.073	92,801	94,643	16,282	37,654	32,155	1,510,980	.0272	913,512	259	109,326	217	14,722	77	148,663	61,782	64,483	Lawrence
Lebanon*	.075	124,776	120,327	18,857	48,779	38,264	2,352,950	.0432	1,679,715	477	197,472	393	29,535	155	218,373	74,543	87,079	Lebanon
Lehigh*	.077	325,977	312,090	18,917	119,965	40,954	6,166,560	.1185	5,038,571	1,431	587,507	1,168	281,287	1,480	747,767	349,055	226,538	Lehigh
Luzerne*	.079	310,470	319,250	16,348	124,905	32,479	5,075,640	.0977	3,826,022	1,086	516,120	1,026	181,698	956	613,615	277,040	217,402	Luzerne
Lycoming*	.081	117,787	120,044	16,584	47,746	32,660	1,953,340	.0380	1,538,724	437	234,178	466	69,595	366	245,666	120,115	79,638	Lycoming
McKean**	.083	44,562	45,936	16,176	18,020	31,714	720,840	.0127	408,069	116	20,587	41	5,236	28	86,851	42,878	28,733	McKean
Mercer*	.085	119,699	120,293	16,717	47,949	33,218	2,001,010	.0409	1,811,143	514	258,804	515	176,771	930	225,340	118,242	80,797	Mercer
Mifflin**	.087	46,250	46,486	15,806	18,682	31,305	731,050	.0133	444,636	126	67,569	134	19,886	105	73,994	23,747	32,004	Mifflin
Monroe**	.089	164,314	138,687	17,826	54,370	42,803	2,929,020	.0519	1,798,093	511	250,720	499	181,531	955	350,567	123,096	105,625	Monroe
Montgomery*	.091	785,423	750,097	25,705	288,624	55,699	20,189,250	.3371	12,752,083	3,621	1,386,418	2,757	1,131,124	5,953	1,961,407	903,981	518,141	Montgomery
Montour**	.093	18,104	18,236	18,352	7,263	36,349	332,240	.0057	182,334	52	4,299	9	2,670	14	40,801	3,606	12,488	Montour
Northampton*	.095	284,960	267,066	20,332	109,627	42,142	5,793,790	.0911	2,523,459	717	189,646	377	62,392	328	495,270	189,518	223,039	Northampton
Northumberland**	.097	92,367	94,556	15,819	38,821	30,527	1,461,180	.0259	815,460	232	39,125	78	8,020	42	111,949	72,754	63,191	Northumberland
Perry*	.099	44,778	43,602	19,094	17,297	39,345	854,970	.0132	318,435	90	2,766	5	...	...	67,622	16,842	33,736	Perry
Philadelphia*	.101	1,456,998	1,517,550	14,450	567,762	29,655	21,053,750	.3663	9,981,344	2,834	794,491	1,580	1,203,647	6,335	2,107,907	1,457,217	612,457	Philadelphia
Pike*	.103	55,957	46,302	17,411	18,605	41,618	974,270	.0144	253,972	72	66,711	133	5,836	31	39,219	9,179	35,272	Pike
Potter	.105	18,093	18,080	15,629	7,184	31,150	282,770	.0048	129,642	37	5,125	10	...	...	31,310	11,119	12,403	Potter
Schuylkill**	.107	146,247	150,336	15,643	57,934	31,516	2,287,810	.0429	1,543,237	438	139,705	278	32,868	173	283,819	206,102	107,089	Schuylkill
Snyder**	.109	38,279	37,546	15,790	14,040	34,320	604,420	.0131	613,689	174	154,712	308	26,368	139	91,193	22,187	26,227	Snyder
Somerset**	.111	79,207	80,023	14,900	31,802	29,761	1,180,200	.0214	685,749	195	46,194	92	24,309	128	71,131	53,129	56,061	Somerset
Sullivan	.113	6,369	6,556	15,309	2,664	29,296	97,500	.0015	30,690	9	1,936	4	...	...	6,196	2,800	4,834	Sullivan
Susquehanna	.115	41,700	42,238	16,373	16,830	32,193	682,740	.0114	306,642	87	6,426	13	...	...	55,521	19,510	30,764	Susquehanna
Tioga	.117	41,888	41,373	15,129	16,482	30,725	633,730	.0112	340,831	97	44,735	89	6,129	32	55,350	17,574	29,643	Tioga
Union**	.119	42,775	41,624	15,149	13,630	38,336	647,980	.0111	307,871	87	30,293	60	3,667	19	62,260	10,713	24,736	Union
Venango**	.121	56,115	57,565	16,084	22,932	31,353	902,530	.0169	617,678	175	81,803	163	18,054	95	109,794	42,210	38,377	Venango
Warren**	.123	42,271	43,863	18,124	17,796	34,257	766,100	.0169	872,189	248	64,551	128	20,899	110	59,481	20,691	30,139	Warren
Washington*	.125	206,014	202,897	18,394	83,889	35,920	3,789,350	.0635	1,954,746	555	176,229	350	63,300	333	345,763	143,035	144,059	Washington
Wayne	.127	49,976	47,722	15,452	18,842	32,554	772,220	.0152	600,163	170	52,585	105	9,427	50	119,493	43,996	34,046	Wayne
Westmoreland*	.129	367,421	369,993	17,678	146,379	35,452	6,495,420	.1193	4,467,532	1,269	508,415	1,011	166,658	877	563,105	338,268	270,979	Westmoreland
Wyoming*	.131	28,230	28,080	17,124	11,101	34,677	483,420	.0087	301,621	86	43,043	86	3,262	17	57,183	14,844	21,012	Wyoming
York*	.133	403,361	381,751	20,209	154,303	41,939	8,151,520	.1339	4,206,302	1,194	585,240	1,164	159,393	839	714,134	198,492	285,327	York
Pennsylvania Total		**12,420,798**	**12,281,054**	**18,844**	**4,815,847**	**38,021**	**234,057,120**	**4.1520**	**150,200,264**	**42,651**	**15,579,866**	**30,982**	**7,805,821**	**41,081**	**23,829,978**	**10,453,945**	**8,202,103**	**Pennsylvania**

Rhode Island (RI; Code 44; 5 Counties)

County or County Equivalent	FIPS County Code	Population Estimate 7/1/05	Population Census 4/1/00	Per Capita Income 2004	House-holds Estimate 7/1/05	Median Household Income 2004	Disposable Income 2004 ($1,000)	Market Ability Index 2004	Total Retail Sales 2004 Sales ($1,000)	Total Retail Sales Ranally Sales Units	General Merchandise 2004 Sales ($1,000)	General Merchandise Ranally Sales Units	Apparel Store 2004 Sales ($1,000)	Apparel Store Ranally Sales Units	Food Store Sales 2004 ($1,000)	Health & Drug Store 2004 ($1,000)	Passenger Car Regis-trations 2004	County or County Equivalent
Bristol*	.001	53,538	50,648	21,281	19,476	46,271	1,139,350	.0160	293,454	83	15,600	31	19,097	101	67,997	39,679	36,932	Bristol
Kent*	.003	174,124	167,090	22,197	69,663	43,794	3,864,970	.0674	2,588,307	735	422,174	840	143,410	755	269,388	269,758	130,724	Kent
Newport*	.005	85,506	85,433	24,837	36,479	46,095	2,123,730	.0325	965,165	274	26,927	54	69,527	366	159,623	101,602	65,948	Newport
Providence*	.007	653,201	621,602	16,192	237,843	35,316	10,576,640	.1849	5,740,257	1,630	350,084	696	422,619	2,224	1,150,284	659,724	443,235	Providence
Washington*	.009	130,736	123,546	23,601	50,060	49,107	3,085,450	.0494	1,616,144	459	132,229	263	69,023	363	374,540	141,543	101,346	Washington
Rhode Island Total		**1,097,105**	**1,048,319**	**18,950**	**413,521**	**39,859**	**20,790,140**	**.3502**	**11,203,327**	**3,181**	**947,014**	**1,884**	**723,676**	**3,809**	**2,021,832**	**1,212,306**	**778,185**	**Rhode Island**

South Carolina (SC; Code 45; 46 Counties)

County or County Equivalent	FIPS County Code	Population Estimate 7/1/05	Population Census 4/1/00	Per Capita Income 2004	House-holds Estimate 7/1/05	Median Household Income 2004	Disposable Income 2004 ($1,000)	Market Ability Index 2004	Total Retail Sales 2004 Sales ($1,000)	Total Retail Sales Ranally Sales Units	General Merchandise 2004 Sales ($1,000)	General Merchandise Ranally Sales Units	Apparel Store 2004 Sales ($1,000)	Apparel Store Ranally Sales Units	Food Store Sales 2004 ($1,000)	Health & Drug Store 2004 ($1,000)	Passenger Car Regis-trations 2004	County or County Equivalent
Abbeville	.001	26,448	26,167	14,911	9,903	31,393	394,370	.0061	105,335	30	4,778	9	...	...	33,915	10,920	19,359	Abbeville
Aiken*	.003	149,719	142,552	17,455	56,936	35,920	2,613,360	.0431	1,209,775	344	239,642	477	55,010	290	208,831	66,424	106,548	Aiken
Allendale	.005	10,876	11,211	9,217	3,844	20,578	100,240	.0022	75,165	21	1,634	3	...	...	13,077	4,649	5,633	Allendale
Anderson*	.007	175,558	165,740	17,283	68,265	35,050	3,034,240	.0560	2,090,904	594	326,516	649	101,958	537	310,355	140,498	130,149	Anderson
Bamberg	.009	15,631	16,658	11,511	5,991	23,560	179,930	.0037	130,926	37	8,985	18	3,070	16	30,773	19,285	9,426	Bamberg
Barnwell	.011	23,437	23,478	13,237	8,803	27,745	310,240	.0055	144,919	41	37,737	75	4,882	26	31,246	14,456	15,314	Barnwell
Beaufort**	.013	138,811	120,937	20,991	52,292	44,381	2,913,760	.0526	2,103,582	597	319,978	636	208,128	1,095	300,692	78,254	93,017	Beaufort
Berkeley*	.015	150,053	142,651	16,780	52,569	37,823	2,517,950	.0405	993,797	282	95,642	190	21,042	111	230,206	45,478	98,994	Berkeley
Calhoun*	.017	15,398	15,185	15,798	6,056	31,453	243,250	.0035	46,115	13	1,392	3	1,107	6	9,599	7,456	11,698	Calhoun
Charleston*	.019	327,786	309,969	16,915	120,761	36,101	5,544,500	.1118	4,876,398	1,385	932,007	1,853	389,073	2,048	625,410	202,109	209,915	Charleston
Cherokee**	.021	54,193	52,537	15,568	20,445	32,414	843,680	.0159	579,066	164	75,109	149	83,192	438	77,718	30,648	36,904	Cherokee
Chester**	.023	33,738	34,068	15,062	12,768	31,459	508,150	.0088	246,544	70	27,229	54	5,902	31	48,275	16,654	23,151	Chester
Chesterfield	.025	43,493	42,768	13,794	16,676	28,479	599,950	.0119	436,844	124	50,081	100	12,682	67	88,311	36,116	29,477	Chesterfield
Clarendon	.027	33,132	32,502	12,151	11,805	27,086	402,600	.0078	245,611	70	32,584	65	7,440	39	57,936	15,306	19,535	Clarendon
Colleton**	.029	39,740	38,264	13,279	14,476	28,632	527,720	.0102	339,345	96	52,614	105	11,007	58	66,025	18,499	24,597	Colleton
Darlington*	.031	68,159	67,394	14,326	25,673	30,100	976,420	.0177	543,492	154	62,226	124	23,721	125	107,565	40,358	43,986	Darlington
Dillon**	.033	31,472	30,722	11,556	11,012	26,053	363,680	.0077	278,926	79	43,318	86	8,824	46	46,594	21,660	17,881	Dillon
Dorchester*	.035	109,033	96,413	17,795	37,416	40,724	1,940,280	.0305	738,076	210	171,728	342	8,280	44	137,647	49,870	69,908	Dorchester
Edgefield*	.037	24,910	24,595	14,191	8,304	33,625	353,510	.0058	120,558	34	1,808	4	1,161	6	18,665	8,808	16,252	Edgefield
Fairfield*	.039	24,030	23,454	13,399	8,693	29,682	321,970	.0052	92,841	26	14,434	29	...	...	22,302	12,654	15,958	Fairfield

Source: Devonshire Associates Ltd. and Scan/US, Inc. 2005. ...Data less than 1,000. (d) Data not available.
* Component of a Metropolitan Core Based Statistical Area.
** Component of a Micropolitan Core Based Statistical Area.

Continued on next page

Counties: Population/Income/Sales, *Continued*

County or County Equivalent	FIPS County Code	Population Estimate 7/1/05	Population Census 4/1/00	Per Capita Income 2004	Households Estimate 7/1/05	Median Household Income 2004	Disposable Income 2004 ($1,000)	Market Ability Index 2004	Total Retail Sales 2004 Sales ($1,000)	Total Retail Sales Ranally Sales Units	General Merchandise 2004 Sales ($1,000)	General Merchandise Ranally Sales Units	Apparel Store 2004 Sales ($1,000)	Apparel Store Ranally Sales Units	Food Store Sales 2004 ($1,000)	Health & Drug Store 2004 ($1,000)	Passenger Car Registrations 2004	County or County Equivalent
Florence*	.041	130,435	125,761	15,344	47,128	33,172	2,001,340	.0424	1,899,095	539	331,941	660	101,088	532	222,876	102,627	82,577	Florence
Georgetown**	.043	60,729	55,797	16,302	22,990	34,475	990,000	.0186	691,651	196	153,616	305	62,466	329	108,029	50,153	40,303	Georgetown
Greenville*	.045	405,039	379,616	18,551	152,278	38,987	7,513,850	.1435	5,971,576	1,696	790,767	1,573	347,199	1,827	627,421	314,950	301,138	Greenville
Greenwood**	.047	68,219	66,271	15,901	25,853	32,911	1,084,740	.0206	776,900	221	156,638	311	44,852	236	108,764	43,753	45,429	Greenwood
Hampton	.049	21,500	21,386	11,911	7,301	27,532	256,080	.0050	151,365	43	8,701	17	4,841	25	34,948	9,394	12,050	Hampton
Horry*	.051	219,791	196,629	18,431	91,467	34,935	4,050,980	.0826	3,819,977	1,085	609,030	1,211	439,072	2,311	501,810	168,795	159,066	Horry
Jasper**	.053	21,135	20,678	12,759	7,145	30,166	269,670	.0049	129,583	37	2,848	6	...	...	22,062	6,267	12,268	Jasper
Kershaw*	.055	55,859	52,647	17,429	20,902	36,323	973,550	.0161	459,047	130	86,796	173	12,168	64	79,234	24,757	39,959	Kershaw
Lancaster**	.057	63,554	61,351	15,884	23,843	33,281	1,009,490	.0172	486,426	138	86,552	172	13,212	70	90,019	31,843	45,296	Lancaster
Laurens*	.059	70,753	69,567	15,300	26,332	32,477	1,082,530	.0180	442,495	126	70,542	140	9,008	47	80,596	30,757	49,099	Laurens
Lee	.061	20,528	20,119	11,019	6,796	27,176	226,190	.0042	97,985	28	3,637	7	2,602	14	18,923	6,563	11,134	Lee
Lexington*	.063	233,853	216,014	19,715	87,030	41,176	4,610,410	.0798	2,814,613	799	373,784	743	84,123	443	437,861	153,804	169,398	Lexington
McCormick	.065	10,462	9,958	13,412	3,676	30,850	140,320	.0022	28,178	8	1,203	2	...	...	10,394	4,401	6,650	McCormick
Marion	.067	34,821	35,466	12,299	13,110	25,941	428,250	.0083	266,012	76	34,375	68	11,274	59	49,472	23,388	20,827	Marion
Marlboro**	.069	28,041	28,818	11,890	10,181	25,801	333,410	.0062	165,706	47	9,139	18	3,851	20	40,604	14,822	15,705	Marlboro
Newberry**	.071	37,538	36,108	14,853	13,867	31,954	557,550	.0098	283,373	80	54,873	109	9,145	48	45,930	16,075	25,697	Newberry
Oconee**	.073	69,933	66,215	17,855	28,237	34,780	1,248,670	.0208	613,337	174	124,138	247	17,087	90	95,174	44,915	54,724	Oconee
Orangeburg**	.075	90,679	91,582	13,687	34,396	28,252	1,241,080	.0250	946,702	269	133,307	265	42,639	224	146,671	59,531	59,438	Orangeburg
Pickens*	.077	112,937	110,757	16,733	42,845	34,826	1,889,760	.0328	1,025,562	291	136,504	271	23,997	126	200,794	82,582	85,390	Pickens
Richland*	.079	339,314	320,677	18,581	131,397	37,506	6,304,950	.1201	4,980,042	1,414	1,220,096	2,426	346,416	1,823	504,896	248,227	258,588	Richland
Saluda*	.081	18,966	19,181	16,034	7,024	34,600	304,100	.0048	107,544	31	5,515	11	1,744	9	21,227	10,054	13,768	Saluda
Spartanburg*	.083	264,032	253,791	17,007	98,341	35,881	4,490,450	.0847	3,268,756	928	533,561	1,061	138,696	730	398,905	232,753	191,126	Spartanburg
Sumter*	.085	106,517	104,646	14,511	37,845	31,896	1,545,670	.0291	1,000,202	284	156,992	312	57,119	301	121,933	48,459	67,662	Sumter
Union**	.087	28,761	29,881	15,660	11,695	30,524	450,390	.0078	224,886	64	41,506	83	10,147	53	41,410	17,432	20,668	Union
Williamsburg	.089	35,050	37,217	11,593	13,527	23,338	406,350	.0075	190,686	54	14,044	28	5,622	30	35,884	17,590	22,624	Williamsburg
York*	.091	186,816	164,614	20,027	70,793	41,347	3,741,340	.0618	1,961,913	557	272,071	541	70,887	373	310,687	109,098	137,754	York
South Carolina Total		**4,230,879**	**4,012,012**	**16,980**	**1,588,687**	**35,611**	**71,840,920**	**1.3203**	**48,201,831**	**13,686**	**7,911,617**	**15,731**	**2,807,751**	**14,777**	**6,821,670**	**2,713,093**	**2,946,040**	**South Carolina**

South Dakota (SD; Code 46; 66 Counties)

County or County Equivalent	FIPS County Code	Population Estimate 7/1/05	Population Census 4/1/00	Per Capita Income 2004	Households Estimate 7/1/05	Median Household Income 2004	Disposable Income 2004 ($1,000)	Market Ability Index 2004	Total Retail Sales 2004 Sales ($1,000)	Total Retail Sales Ranally Sales Units	General Merchandise 2004 Sales ($1,000)	General Merchandise Ranally Sales Units	Apparel Store 2004 Sales ($1,000)	Apparel Store Ranally Sales Units	Food Store Sales 2004 ($1,000)	Health & Drug Store 2004 ($1,000)	Passenger Car Registrations 2004	County or County Equivalent
Aurora	.003	2,828	3,058	14,455	1,145	29,064	40,880	.0009	37,130	11	...	...	...	...	...	...	2,834	Aurora
Beadle**	.005	15,775	17,023	16,241	7,088	29,425	256,200	.0055	263,540	75	9,419	19	7,555	40	8,976	11,720	14,407	Beadle
Bennett	.007	3,455	3,574	9,841	1,130	23,959	34,000	.0008	31,411	9	...	...	...	...	...	...	2,167	Bennett
Bon Homme	.009	7,022	7,260	13,389	2,599	29,316	94,020	.0018	64,100	18	1,166	2	...	...	1,217	2,274	5,865	Bon Homme
Brookings**	.011	27,984	28,220	16,936	11,259	33,963	473,930	.0088	330,039	94	42,368	84	13,004	68	13,059	4,147	25,237	Brookings
Brown**	.013	34,450	35,460	17,701	14,716	33,410	609,790	.0164	1,026,807	292	57,686	115	8,457	45	48,950	3,939	29,417	Brown
Brule	.015	5,100	5,364	15,202	2,000	31,202	77,530	.0018	89,933	26	3,437	7	...	...	8,361	...	4,490	Brule
Buffalo	.017	2,070	2,032	3,889	547	11,342	8,050	.0002	3,334	1	...	...	...	...	1,110	...	955	Buffalo
Butte	.019	9,232	9,094	13,449	3,577	28,064	124,160	.0028	125,882	36	2,430	5	...	...	11,570	1,347	8,520	Butte
Campbell	.021	1,589	1,782	15,500	718	27,365	24,630	.0004	11,609	3	...	...	...	...	...	...	1,821	Campbell
Charles Mix	.023	9,054	9,350	11,394	3,320	25,377	103,160	.0024	106,306	30	3,661	7	...	...	15,207	...	6,999	Charles Mix
Clark	.025	3,842	4,143	14,344	1,547	28,780	55,110	.0010	33,948	10	...	...	...	...	...	...	3,618	Clark
Clay**	.027	13,025	13,537	12,495	4,979	26,744	162,750	.0034	134,285	38	5,080	10	...	...	14,845	2,336	10,677	Clay
Codington**	.029	25,915	25,897	17,520	10,650	34,756	454,020	.0112	640,873	182	43,533	87	23,268	122	59,509	6,375	22,446	Codington
Corson	.031	4,361	4,181	7,374	1,282	20,196	32,160	.0007	13,302	4	...	...	...	...	...	...	2,770	Corson
Custer	.033	7,598	7,275	18,242	3,230	34,536	138,600	.0023	65,892	19	...	...	...	...	2,275	2,997	7,359	Custer
Davison**	.035	18,848	18,741	16,358	7,826	31,774	308,310	.0084	517,848	147	74,344	148	9,849	52	27,142	9,720	16,191	Davison
Day	.037	5,678	6,267	16,078	2,548	29,171	91,290	.0018	75,606	21	1,435	3	...	...	3,759	...	5,615	Day
Deuel	.039	4,244	4,498	16,461	1,866	30,283	69,860	.0012	37,393	11	1,775	4	...	...	...	...	4,279	Deuel
Dewey	.041	6,253	5,972	8,887	1,914	23,554	55,570	.0012	32,875	9	1,244	2	...	...	...	...	3,834	Dewey
Douglas	.043	3,227	3,458	13,855	1,301	27,629	44,710	.0010	47,708	14	...	...	...	...	1,073	2,700	3,044	Douglas
Edmunds**	.045	4,107	4,367	15,459	1,675	30,735	63,490	.0013	54,357	15	...	...	...	...	1,662	...	3,934	Edmunds
Fall River	.047	7,265	7,453	15,398	3,182	28,526	111,870	.0021	76,917	22	2,956	6	...	...	5,166	...	6,657	Fall River
Faulk	.049	2,391	2,640	15,069	1,018	28,635	36,030	.0007	26,757	8	...	...	...	...	...	...	2,257	Faulk
Grant	.051	7,546	7,847	16,020	3,126	31,706	120,890	.0027	129,506	37	3,832	8	...	...	12,233	2,504	6,778	Grant
Gregory	.053	4,257	4,792	13,347	2,014	22,484	56,820	.0011	40,364	11	1,522	3	...	...	4,523	...	4,642	Gregory
Haakon	.055	1,949	2,196	16,254	878	29,298	31,680	.0007	29,073	8	1,306	3	...	...	...	...	2,120	Haakon
Hamlin**	.057	5,600	5,540	14,775	2,048	32,559	82,740	.0015	44,972	13	...	...	...	...	...	...	4,846	Hamlin
Hand	.059	3,399	3,741	17,223	1,521	30,871	58,540	.0011	39,633	11	...	...	...	...	...	...	3,431	Hand
Hanson**	.061	3,742	3,139	11,817	1,116	31,960	44,220	.0007	9,197	3	...	...	...	...	...	...	2,751	Hanson
Harding	.063	1,264	1,353	11,978	506	24,121	15,140	.0003	7,705	2	...	...	...	...	...	...	1,416	Harding
Hughes**	.065	16,860	16,481	19,355	6,681	39,572	326,320	.0070	360,270	102	49,032	98	12,476	66	6,777	2,258	13,703	Hughes
Hutchinson	.067	7,594	8,075	14,804	3,149	28,928	112,420	.0025	118,659	34	2,986	6	...	...	3,413	2,985	7,005	Hutchinson
Hyde	.069	1,561	1,671	15,708	665	30,272	24,520	.0004	14,682	4	...	...	...	...	...	...	1,595	Hyde
Jackson	.071	2,820	2,930	9,794	962	22,676	27,620	.0007	27,724	8	1,033	2	...	...	...	...	2,146	Jackson
Jerauld	.073	2,095	2,295	16,563	973	28,920	34,700	.0010	66,246	19	1,986	4	...	...	1,858	...	2,159	Jerauld
Jones	.075	1,017	1,193	17,788	505	28,719	18,090	.0004	20,524	6	...	...	...	...	...	...	1,277	Jones
Kingsbury	.077	5,407	5,815	16,582	2,409	30,302	89,660	.0015	45,049	13	...	...	...	...	7,228	...	5,650	Kingsbury
Lake	.079	10,858	11,276	16,771	4,507	32,906	182,100	.0043	228,328	65	8,689	17	1,402	7	13,520	6,867	10,291	Lake
Lawrence**	.081	22,208	21,802	15,854	9,342	30,703	352,080	.0083	437,431	124	56,020	111	3,978	21	12,812	5,226	20,565	Lawrence
Lincoln*	.083	32,370	24,131	22,086	12,980	46,437	714,910	.0120	426,915	121	1,489	3	...	...	15,919	2,848	31,021	Lincoln
Lyman	.085	4,004	3,895	11,976	1,407	27,444	47,950	.0012	64,087	18	1,316	3	...	...	3,253	...	3,150	Lyman
McCook*	.087	5,854	5,832	16,324	2,274	33,794	95,560	.0019	79,014	22	...	...	...	...	...	1,781	5,372	McCook
McPherson	.089	2,678	2,904	12,465	1,190	22,268	33,380	.0007	22,284	6	...	...	...	...	4,607	...	2,572	McPherson
Marshall	.091	4,087	4,576	16,291	1,842	29,302	66,580	.0012	45,812	13	...	...	...	...	2,817	...	4,129	Marshall
Meade*	.093	24,726	24,253	16,295	9,332	35,094	402,910	.0070	218,709	62	5,115	10	1,522	8	10,224	2,216	22,126	Meade
Mellette	.095	2,147	2,083	9,115	708	22,241	19,570	.0004	10,605	3	...	...	...	...	4,750	...	1,583	Mellette
Miner	.097	2,570	2,884	16,019	1,175	28,696	41,170	.0007	24,299	7	...	...	...	...	2,210	...	2,823	Miner
Minnehaha*	.099	158,995	148,281	19,625	62,877	40,150	3,120,270	.0743	4,274,959	1,214	692,683	1,378	67,861	357	301,523	188,182	131,527	Minnehaha
Moody	.101	6,474	6,595	16,112	2,486	33,822	104,310	.0017	41,619	12	1,515	3	...	...	...	...	5,813	Moody
Pennington*	.103	93,346	88,565	17,313	36,862	35,378	1,616,070	.0387	2,156,687	612	458,899	913	84,210	443	161,146	78,277	79,183	Pennington
Perkins	.105	3,127	3,363	15,098	1,425	26,629	47,210	.0009	26,918	8	1,881	4	...	...	...	...	3,498	Perkins
Potter	.107	2,383	2,693	17,583	1,170	28,949	41,900	.0010	52,907	15	1,584	3	...	...	...	1,638	2,524	Potter
Roberts	.109	10,068	10,016	12,368	3,674	27,388	124,520	.0024	78,648	22	3,965	8	...	...	...	1,693	8,275	Roberts
Sanborn	.111	2,584	2,675	15,364	1,013	31,601	39,700	.0007	17,269	5	...	...	...	...	...	...	2,620	Sanborn
Shannon	.113	13,740	12,466	5,590	2,912	20,877	76,800	.0020	45,440	13	1,294	3	...	...	7,600	3,098	5,251	Shannon
Spink	.115	6,723	7,454	15,398	2,760	30,519	103,520	.0021	85,040	24	5,480	11	...	...	1,267	...	6,068	Spink
Stanley**	.117	2,744	2,772	20,740	1,178	38,800	56,910	.0010	37,317	11	1,344	3	...	...	4,414	...	2,814	Stanley
Sully	.119	1,397	1,556	17,981	643	31,524	25,120	.0006	33,942	10	...	...	...	...	...	...	1,524	Sully
Todd	.121	9,791	9,050	6,283	2,524	19,564	61,520	.0015	31,087	9	...	...	...	...	8,022	...	4,656	Todd
Tripp	.123	6,108	6,430	14,108	2,559	27,131	86,170	.0019	92,255	26	5,508	11	...	...	7,881	1,324	5,879	Tripp
Turner*	.125	8,495	8,849	17,404	3,489	34,167	147,850	.0024	57,750	16	...	...	...	...	1,332	1,878	8,508	Turner
Union*	.127	13,465	12,584	20,010	5,234	40,901	269,440	.0523	5,761,053	1,636	...	...	...	...	17,689	1,810	11,835	Union
Walworth	.129	5,302	5,974	15,651	2,485	26,911	82,980	.0019	95,815	27	8,328	17	...	...	...	1,873	4,876	Walworth
Yankton**	.135	21,471	21,652	16,163	8,349	34,215	347,040	.0081	429,096	122	63,340	126	19,708	104	9,737	8,419	17,283	Yankton
Ziebach	.137	2,616	2,519	6,831	773	17,753	17,870	.0004	8,289	2	...	...	...	...	1,738	...	1,523	Ziebach
South Dakota Total		**770,755**	**754,844**	**16,658**	**304,840**	**34,111**	**12,838,890**	**.3313**	**19,685,031**	**5,591**	**1,631,533**	**3,249**	**261,080**	**1,374**	**862,978**	**371,687**	**662,201**	**South Dakota**

Tennessee (TN; Code 47; 95 Counties)

County or County Equivalent	FIPS County Code	Population Estimate 7/1/05	Population Census 4/1/00	Per Capita Income 2004	Households Estimate 7/1/05	Median Household Income 2004	Disposable Income 2004 ($1,000)	Market Ability Index 2004	Total Retail Sales 2004 Sales ($1,000)	Total Retail Sales Ranally Sales Units	General Merchandise 2004 Sales ($1,000)	General Merchandise Ranally Sales Units	Apparel Store 2004 Sales ($1,000)	Apparel Store Ranally Sales Units	Food Store Sales 2004 ($1,000)	Health & Drug Store 2004 ($1,000)	Passenger Car Registrations 2004	County or County Equivalent
Anderson*	.001	72,469	71,330	18,297	30,630	33,706	1,325,940	.0243	920,343	261	177,812	354	28,792	152	128,579	61,356	59,696	Anderson
Bedford**	.003	41,827	37,586	15,784	14,658	35,092	660,200	.0117	363,439	103	77,012	153	6,156	32	61,682	12,515	30,157	Bedford
Benton	.005	16,603	16,537	15,132	7,085	27,481	251,230	.0043	117,585	33	23,894	48	1,811	10	20,039	5,796	13,496	Benton
Bledsoe	.007	12,801	12,367	12,847	4,578	27,937	164,460	.0026	36,723	10	6,133	12	...	...	7,001	3,727	9,520	Bledsoe
Blount*	.009	115,094	105,823	17,853	44,481	35,784	2,054,760	.0391	1,587,317	451	248,574	494	26,007	137	159,597	81,970	90,561	Blount
Bradley*	.011	91,502	87,965	17,123	36,430	33,325	1,566,750	.0284	1,009,211	287	202,468	403	35,106	185	111,908	66,518	73,532	Bradley
Campbell**	.013	40,199	39,854	12,744	16,318	24,481	512,290	.0096	290,109	82	50,294	100	5,457	29	62,779	26,569	29,442	Campbell
Cannon*	.015	13,427	12,826	15,633	5,155	31,496	209,900	.0032	57,817	16	4,557	9	1,063	6	10,834	4,199	10,998	Cannon
Carroll	.017	29,355	29,475	15,354	12,049	29,136	450,720	.0072	151,773	43	26,604	53	3,005	16	29,037	12,108	23,763	Carroll
Carter*	.019	58,964	56,742	13,975	24,039	26,581	824,010	.0141	346,772	98	72,045	143	2,545	13	67,795	17,661	48,686	Carter
Cheatham*	.021	38,152	35,912	20,214	14,141	42,352	771,210	.0110	206,244	59	25,281	50	1,577	8	40,380	12,314	31,127	Cheatham
Chester*	.023	15,642	15,540	16,272	5,998	32,866	254,530	.0045	143,465	41	8,181	16	2,546	13	13,382	9,813	11,957	Chester
Claiborne	.025	30,854	29,862	13,609	13,064	24,985	419,880	.0072	173,896	49	56,312	112	2,210	12	39,580	15,295	26,025	Claiborne
Clay	.027	7,940	7,976	13,356	3,509	23,214	106,050	.0017	31,182	9	1,144	2	...	...	11,543	4,848	7,170	Clay
Cocke**	.029	34,965	33,565	12,853	14,166	24,712	449,400	.0083	233,636	66	72,616	144	7,904	42	42,600	14,879	28,033	Cocke
Coffee**	.031	50,789	48,014	16,651	19,762	33,048	845,700	.0171	738,169	210	161,552	321	27,542	145	95,402	36,566	39,692	Coffee
Crockett	.033	14,486	14,532	14,572	5,723	28,764	211,090	.0036	87,481	25	9,896	20	...	...	12,555	12,835	10,419	Crockett
Cumberland**	.035	50,826	46,802	15,138	20,332	29,556	769,380	.0152	594,644	169	154,627	307	46,548	245	71,476	21,262	39,460	Cumberland
Davidson*	.037	570,911	569,891	19,575	231,320	37,471	11,175,760	.2364	11,824,729	3,358	1,697,954	3,377	706,536	3,719	1,165,989	802,806	412,285	Davidson
Decatur	.039	11,598	11,731	15,395	5,046	26,931	178,550	.0029	67,462	19	9,358	19	1,057	6	8,232	4,995	9,783	Decatur
DeKalb	.041	18,375	17,423	14,449	7,098	29,327	265,500	.0044	103,591	29	6,739	13	1,972	10	19,660	14,163	13,973	DeKalb
Dickson*	.043	46,096	43,156	18,748	18,086	37,043	864,190	.0152	539,325	153	141,030	280	16,587	87	53,645	17,531	36,647	Dickson
Dyer**	.045	37,453	37,279	16,625	15,389	31,573	622,640	.0123	513,468	146	122,941	244	31,737	167	59,767	25,938	27,642	Dyer
Fayette*	.047	34,492	28,806	15,638	11,151	38,005	539,370	.0082	138,158	39	23,593	47	...	...	13,499	12,156	22,608	Fayette
Fentress	.049	17,289	16,625	11,685	6,903	22,745	202,030	.0038	104,611	30	22,852	45	1,456	8	29,676	6,349	13,060	Fentress
Franklin**	.051	41,102	39,270	17,337	16,183	34,313	712,600	.0115	301,760	86	71,348	142	5,020	26	48,060	17,511	33,199	Franklin
Gibson**	.053	47,853	48,152	15,994	20,042	30,126	765,380	.0128	338,749	96	63,027	125	5,821	31	42,814	17,782	36,584	Gibson
Giles	.055	29,274	29,447	17,492	12,008	33,139	512,070	.0090	297,084	84	43,304	86	6,693	35	45,054	10,673	24,663	Giles
Grainger*	.057	22,098	20,659	13,498	8,603	26,842	298,280	.0047	72,741	21	1,752	3	...	...	18,192	6,768	18,305	Grainger
Greene**	.059	64,950	62,909	15,605	27,009	29,374	1,013,540	.0200	799,855	227	134,187	267	25,058	132	146,565	66,284	55,093	Greene
Grundy	.061	14,427	14,332	11,495	5,717	22,291	165,840	.0029	55,510	16	4,723	9	...	...	8,968	6,827	11,348	Grundy
Hamblen*	.063	59,329	58,128	16,404	24,246	31,177	973,230	.0214	1,052,543	299	175,730	349	44,724	235	106,393	64,580	47,750	Hamblen
Hamilton*	.065	310,232	307,896	18,346	119,980	36,886	5,691,610	.1078	4,390,151	1,247	716,331	1,425	305,682	1,609	546,552	293,956	247,586	Hamilton
Hancock	.067	6,566	6,786	10,602	2,801	19,237	69,610	.0012	18,593	5	1,452	3	...	...	5,274	1,870	5,177	Hancock
Hardeman	.069	28,266	28,105	12,390	9,793	27,811	350,210	.0061	136,103	39	30,165	60	1,305	7	15,716	12,614	17,913	Hardeman
Hardin	.071	26,174	25,578	14,284	10,801	26,801	373,880	.0071	246,935	70	52,812	105	2,739	14	31,917	12,597	20,820	Hardin
Hawkins*	.073	56,299	53,563	15,656	22,866	30,044	881,420	.0141	306,858	87	36,262	72	6,597	35	66,140	27,452	46,648	Hawkins
Haywood**	.075	19,464	19,797	13,807	7,841	26,626	268,740	.0054	201,959	57	23,004	46	2,316	12	25,339	6,987	13,255	Haywood
Henderson	.077	26,319	25,522	16,156	10,721	30,934	425,220	.0074	231,338	66	37,096	74	4,683	25	30,338	17,520	21,272	Henderson
Henry**	.079	31,445	31,115	15,870	13,379	29,033	499,020	.0096	371,909	106	105,435	210	9,555	50	52,606	14,544	25,269	Henry
Hickman*	.081	23,877	22,295	13,280	8,334	29,890	317,080	.0050	73,808	21	2,893	6	...	...	23,047	4,625	16,630	Hickman
Houston	.083	8,096	8,088	15,053	3,322	28,490	121,870	.0019	35,868	10	1,914	4	...	...	13,866	2,235	6,724	Houston
Humphreys	.085	18,272	17,929	18,042	7,524	34,039	329,670	.0052	129,855	37	20,675	41	...	...	17,702	12,983	15,156	Humphreys
Jackson**	.087	11,294	10,984	13,373	4,584	25,670	151,040	.0024	34,362	10	6,524	13	...	...	13,005	1,152	9,562	Jackson
Jefferson*	.089	48,669	44,294	15,621	18,668	31,750	760,270	.0127	329,109	93	95,772	190	1,287	7	41,716	17,470	38,763	Jefferson
Johnson	.091	18,226	17,499	11,649	7,224	22,668	212,310	.0041	115,898	33	8,387	17	1,428	8	25,102	11,018	14,038	Johnson
Knox*	.093	400,313	382,032	18,989	165,094	35,881	7,601,590	.1610	7,978,192	2,265	1,330,630	2,646	402,501	2,118	765,561	422,959	327,040	Knox
Lake	.095	7,749	7,954	8,690	2,388	21,807	67,340	.0014	33,011	9	5,777	11	...	...	8,760	3,965	3,809	Lake
Lauderdale	.097	27,008	27,101	13,562	10,040	28,639	366,270	.0065	175,902	50	40,039	80	6,435	34	27,998	15,722	17,405	Lauderdale
Lawrence**	.099	41,266	39,926	14,325	15,761	29,509	591,120	.0116	429,288	122	102,801	204	8,068	42	58,839	26,368	31,301	Lawrence
Lewis	.101	11,563	11,367	14,648	4,526	29,344	169,370	.0030	89,791	26	15,363	31	1,113	6	13,576	4,356	9,143	Lewis
Lincoln	.103	32,273	31,340	16,224	12,688	32,203	523,600	.0093	297,221	84	72,999	145	8,812	46	40,136	13,985	26,245	Lincoln
Loudon*	.105	43,287	39,086	18,887	16,825	37,727	817,560	.0133	387,690	110	38,184	76	...	...	51,039	27,786	34,770	Loudon
McMinn**	.107	51,547	49,015	15,327	20,185	30,723	790,040	.0144	481,007	137	88,725	176	11,206	59	72,668	29,840	40,483	McMinn
McNairy	.109	25,085	24,653	15,055	10,256	28,448	377,650	.0066	190,681	54	25,911	52	1,565	8	22,169	13,422	20,588	McNairy
Macon*	.111	21,439	20,386	14,241	8,229	29,024	305,310	.0053	142,427	40	38,318	76	2,460	13	24,972	10,286	16,946	Macon
Madison*	.113	95,082	91,837	18,227	38,165	35,328	1,733,070	.0355	1,642,562	466	369,190	734	111,444	587	146,968	88,794	70,606	Madison
Marion*	.115	27,902	27,776	16,613	11,994	30,240	463,540	.0086	317,062	90	71,431	142	6,711	35	54,643	19,250	24,476	Marion

Source: Devonshire Associates Ltd. and Scan/US, Inc. 2005. ...Data less than 1,000. (d) Data not available.
* Component of a Metropolitan Core Based Statistical Area.
** Component of a Micropolitan Core Based Statistical Area.

Counties: Population/Income/Sales, *Continued*

County or County Equivalent	FIPS County Code	Population Estimate 7/1/05	Population Census 4/1/00	Per Capita Income 2004	House-holds Estimate 7/1/05	Median Household Income 2004	Disposable Income 2004 ($1,000)	Market Ability Index 2004	Total Retail Sales 2004 Sales ($1,000)	Total Retail Sales Ranally Sales Units	General Merchandise 2004 Sales ($1,000)	General Merchandise Ranally Sales Units	Apparel Store 2004 Sales ($1,000)	Apparel Store Ranally Sales Units	Food Store Sales 2004 ($1,000)	Health & Drug Store 2004 ($1,000)	Passenger Car Regis-trations 2004	County or County Equivalent
Marshall**	117	28,119	26,767	18,670	11,197	36,637	524,980	.0085	236,004	67	28,486	57	7,556	40	44,337	14,533	22,925	Marshall
Maury**	119	75,379	69,498	19,517	29,258	39,232	1,471,150	.0240	718,466	204	134,621	268	33,667	177	109,193	36,369	59,009	Maury
Meigs	121	11,583	11,086	14,009	4,482	28,160	162,270	.0025	34,605	10	1,688	3	...	...	11,379	1,306	9,231	Meigs
Monroe	123	42,438	38,961	14,021	16,028	29,006	595,040	.0111	364,280	103	65,274	130	5,764	30	75,458	27,011	33,007	Monroe
Montgomery*	125	142,262	134,768	18,135	54,559	36,866	2,579,930	.0459	1,631,217	463	468,790	932	77,691	409	112,942	42,667	106,765	Montgomery
Moore**	127	6,039	5,740	17,875	2,425	34,631	107,950	.0014	10,268	3	1,282	3	...	...	3,949	1,216	5,337	Moore
Morgan	129	20,337	19,757	12,412	7,251	26,867	252,430	.0039	37,963	11	7,058	14	...	...	9,228	2,714	15,324	Morgan
Obion**	131	32,244	32,450	16,820	13,386	31,610	542,350	.0102	390,063	111	112,524	224	28,130	148	19,499	11,570	25,324	Obion
Overton**	133	20,231	20,118	13,963	8,352	26,663	282,480	.0046	90,833	26	7,676	15	1,647	9	21,811	8,268	16,664	Overton
Perry	135	7,646	7,631	14,346	3,112	27,565	109,690	.0017	30,524	9	10,930	22	...	...	7,780	...	6,388	Perry
Pickett	137	4,963	4,945	13,490	2,141	24,862	66,950	.0012	34,722	10	5,848	12	...	...	1,244	3,229	4,317	Pickett
Polk*	139	16,204	16,050	15,143	6,640	28,939	245,370	.0039	75,090	21	2,779	6	...	...	13,077	7,322	13,811	Polk
Putnam**	141	66,540	62,315	14,977	26,151	29,928	996,540	.0207	882,655	251	189,139	376	49,168	259	100,994	37,538	52,666	Putnam
Rhea	143	30,009	28,400	14,644	11,818	29,038	439,440	.0074	178,026	51	38,448	76	4,011	21	36,746	13,036	23,910	Rhea
Roane**	145	52,994	51,910	16,974	21,781	32,068	899,530	.0149	415,761	118	73,601	146	3,160	17	75,940	31,056	44,775	Roane
Robertson*	147	60,561	54,433	19,281	22,518	40,257	1,167,690	.0187	529,315	150	84,992	169	6,600	35	106,498	32,881	47,130	Robertson
Rutherford*	149	214,830	182,023	20,889	81,467	42,497	4,487,530	.0736	2,354,677	669	577,247	1,148	68,622	361	263,011	88,905	170,275	Rutherford
Scott	151	22,108	21,127	11,532	8,457	23,134	254,940	.0049	144,523	41	35,336	70	...	...	32,172	19,161	16,727	Scott
Sequatchie*	153	12,475	11,370	14,224	4,656	29,970	177,440	.0031	82,221	23	9,854	20	...	...	7,705	4,644	10,050	Sequatchie
Sevier**	155	78,085	71,170	17,924	32,863	33,052	1,399,600	.0287	1,319,387	375	147,328	293	260,968	1,374	157,459	39,760	72,386	Sevier
Shelby*	157	912,260	897,472	18,368	348,231	37,820	16,756,180	.3085	11,890,926	3,376	2,029,744	4,037	833,803	4,389	1,136,381	872,261	613,625	Shelby
Smith*	159	18,675	17,712	16,538	7,101	34,094	308,840	.0052	144,859	41	31,143	62	5,229	28	20,883	9,652	14,859	Smith
Stewart*	161	13,128	12,370	15,849	5,075	31,748	208,070	.0032	61,220	17	8,504	17	...	...	10,059	2,327	10,695	Stewart
Sullivan*	163	153,049	153,048	17,759	65,722	32,159	2,717,930	.0509	1,988,588	565	453,786	902	66,156	348	214,080	115,079	130,307	Sullivan
Sumner*	165	143,900	130,449	20,623	54,252	42,243	2,967,690	.0450	1,119,031	318	231,962	461	22,121	116	200,873	78,569	110,503	Sumner
Tipton*	167	55,893	51,271	18,715	20,581	39,956	1,046,050	.0160	362,591	103	48,141	96	4,434	23	60,603	15,770	40,814	Tipton
Trousdale*	169	7,565	7,259	15,446	2,903	31,471	116,850	.0019	41,020	12	1,872	4	...	...	10,059	6,110	5,863	Trousdale
Unicoi*	171	17,796	17,667	15,752	7,631	28,560	280,320	.0042	65,177	19	4,060	8	...	...	14,451	9,750	15,786	Unicoi
Union*	173	19,486	17,808	12,896	7,366	26,564	251,290	.0039	48,669	14	6,209	12	...	...	7,839	5,413	15,173	Union
Van Buren	175	5,480	5,508	14,569	2,263	27,339	79,840	.0012	13,538	4	...	...	...	...	2,362	...	4,577	Van Buren
Warren**	177	39,934	38,276	14,839	15,548	30,127	592,580	.0111	377,908	107	140,550	280	16,292	86	59,578	25,810	30,465	Warren
Washington*	179	111,810	107,198	16,749	45,954	31,571	1,872,720	.0384	1,712,431	486	330,282	657	136,881	720	151,048	108,343	88,744	Washington
Wayne	181	16,865	16,842	12,062	6,164	25,670	203,420	.0035	65,387	19	7,783	15	...	...	16,204	13,154	12,447	Wayne
Weakley**	183	33,864	34,895	15,531	14,075	29,395	525,950	.0088	222,798	63	40,674	81	5,881	31	31,489	12,995	26,693	Weakley
White	185	23,872	23,102	14,466	9,523	28,130	345,340	.0069	270,212	77	29,039	58	2,061	11	33,525	15,704	19,057	White
Williamson*	187	150,607	126,638	27,506	51,852	61,641	4,142,610	.0692	2,707,926	769	435,015	865	192,885	1,015	348,866	111,989	113,706	Williamson
Wilson*	189	99,771	88,809	21,692	36,555	45,616	2,164,200	.0328	846,124	240	159,862	318	29,899	157	147,338	35,604	78,414	Wilson
Tennessee Total		**5,937,857**	**5,689,283**	**17,807**	**2,334,246**	**34,908**	**105,738,070**	**1.9467**	**73,585,974**	**20,895**	**13,197,164**	**26,243**	**3,815,354**	**20,082**	**8,624,391**	**4,471,274**	**4,556,048**	**Tennessee**

Texas (TX; Code 48; 254 Counties)

County or County Equivalent	FIPS County Code	Population Estimate 7/1/05	Population Census 4/1/00	Per Capita Income 2004	House-holds Estimate 7/1/05	Median Household Income 2004	Disposable Income 2004 ($1,000)	Market Ability Index 2004	Total Retail Sales 2004 Sales ($1,000)	Total Retail Sales Ranally Sales Units	General Merchandise 2004 Sales ($1,000)	General Merchandise Ranally Sales Units	Apparel Store 2004 Sales ($1,000)	Apparel Store Ranally Sales Units	Food Store Sales 2004 ($1,000)	Health & Drug Store 2004 ($1,000)	Passenger Car Regis-trations 2004	County or County Equivalent
Anderson**	001	56,568	55,109	11,144	16,074	30,331	630,410	.0126	390,317	111	92,004	183	16,626	88	52,419	18,113	28,064	Anderson
Andrews**	003	12,721	13,004	15,608	4,686	32,473	198,550	.0033	81,715	23	2,819	6	...	...	4,528	5,140	8,377	Andrews
Angelina**	005	81,450	80,130	15,268	29,634	32,435	1,243,560	.0243	933,356	265	206,929	412	31,071	164	147,034	32,412	51,880	Angelina
Aransas*	007	24,347	22,497	15,069	9,589	29,354	366,880	.0062	156,457	44	31,315	62	5,756	30	45,732	1,770	16,167	Aransas
Archer*	009	9,260	8,854	17,082	3,344	36,287	158,180	.0023	38,084	11	...	...	...	...	2,217	1,203	6,873	Archer
Armstrong*	011	2,041	2,148	18,290	790	36,452	37,330	.0005	3,250	1	...	...	...	...	...	...	1,760	Armstrong
Atascosa*	013	43,553	38,628	12,530	13,308	31,636	545,720	.0103	306,528	87	37,838	75	3,468	18	82,809	8,280	24,302	Atascosa
Austin*	015	26,140	23,590	16,606	9,080	36,877	434,070	.0080	291,595	83	26,122	52	18,468	97	33,476	12,178	17,448	Austin
Bailey	017	6,623	6,594	12,238	2,313	26,847	81,050	.0015	41,889	12	2,285	5	...	...	6,231	...	4,202	Bailey
Bandera*	019	20,429	17,645	16,862	7,156	37,082	344,470	.0052	91,892	26	...	...	1,354	7	21,177	9,107	13,764	Bandera
Bastrop*	021	72,404	57,733	15,801	21,436	41,074	1,144,040	.0202	632,324	180	86,712	172	4,121	22	96,554	7,860	41,393	Bastrop
Baylor	023	3,830	4,093	14,078	1,729	24,191	53,920	.0009	21,212	6	3,740	7	...	...	2,682	...	2,985	Baylor
Bee**	025	33,460	32,359	9,796	9,100	27,541	327,760	.0067	186,162	53	21,351	42	7,368	39	36,232	9,708	15,069	Bee
Bell*	027	255,627	237,974	17,090	95,731	35,611	4,368,780	.0762	2,467,412	701	337,643	671	86,719	456	336,720	45,060	169,389	Bell
Bexar*	029	1,512,995	1,392,931	16,421	525,519	36,844	24,844,960	.4782	18,807,064	5,340	2,686,228	5,342	1,143,594	6,019	2,849,856	754,871	895,728	Bexar
Blanco	031	9,114	8,418	17,665	3,365	37,215	161,000	.0025	52,006	15	...	...	...	...	2,486	...	6,508	Blanco
Borden	033	654	729	16,468	292	28,205	10,770	.0002	4,244	1	...	...	...	...	4,244	...	609	Borden
Bosque	035	18,153	17,204	15,629	6,736	33,119	283,710	.0046	104,007	30	1,821	4	...	...	23,578	6,351	12,797	Bosque
Bowie*	037	89,875	89,306	15,542	33,979	32,008	1,396,810	.0294	1,309,256	372	257,635	512	74,808	394	98,501	36,016	58,783	Bowie
Brazoria*	039	276,715	241,767	19,374	92,366	45,490	5,361,020	.0852	2,345,214	666	569,951	1,133	62,344	328	318,997	90,787	175,565	Brazoria
Brazos*	041	156,700	152,415	14,404	62,130	28,774	2,257,060	.0460	1,859,016	528	361,493	719	99,437	523	226,349	46,272	111,164	Brazos
Brewster	043	9,481	8,866	13,448	3,750	26,570	127,500	.0025	84,578	24	6,600	13	...	...	22,855	7,039	6,195	Brewster
Briscoe	045	1,621	1,790	16,360	721	28,184	26,520	.0004	7,238	2	...	...	...	...	1,566	...	1,375	Briscoe
Brooks	047	7,604	7,976	8,624	2,714	18,729	65,580	.0015	51,832	15	5,729	11	...	...	6,744	1,388	3,931	Brooks
Brown**	049	38,227	37,674	14,412	14,365	29,888	550,930	.0110	429,878	122	96,920	193	19,007	100	38,951	27,607	25,626	Brown
Burleson*	051	17,184	16,470	15,539	6,546	31,501	267,020	.0046	126,928	36	16,062	32	...	...	28,095	...	12,047	Burleson
Burnet	053	41,569	34,147	16,519	14,837	36,121	686,660	.0128	478,474	136	111,111	221	9,355	49	76,435	16,953	27,622	Burnet
Caldwell*	055	37,547	32,194	14,160	11,715	35,750	531,650	.0089	200,999	57	13,042	26	...	...	44,985	8,199	21,448	Caldwell
Calhoun*	057	20,251	20,647	16,375	7,617	33,302	331,600	.0056	162,786	46	19,598	39	5,131	27	45,151	1,477	13,306	Calhoun
Callahan*	059	13,188	12,905	15,640	5,120	31,036	206,260	.0034	79,854	23	...	...	...	...	6,375	1,469	9,637	Callahan
Cameron*	061	379,998	335,227	8,453	97,445	25,552	3,212,080	.0778	2,844,598	808	682,514	1,357	195,900	1,031	495,642	117,593	159,954	Cameron
Camp	063	11,873	11,549	14,112	4,389	29,560	167,550	.0037	171,589	49	2,290	5	5,320	28	29,673	15,382	7,774	Camp
Carson*	065	6,540	6,516	18,670	2,488	37,535	122,100	.0018	32,201	9	...	...	...	...	...	...	5,238	Carson
Cass	067	29,757	30,438	14,934	12,450	27,629	444,400	.0075	189,936	54	34,031	68	3,686	19	25,110	14,793	22,011	Cass
Castro	069	7,645	8,285	13,529	2,730	29,348	103,430	.0020	66,185	19	7,775	15	...	...	14,131	3,079	5,134	Castro
Chambers*	071	28,434	26,031	21,189	10,550	43,885	602,500	.0083	132,191	38	3,573	7	1,037	5	14,792	5,153	20,300	Chambers
Cherokee**	073	48,315	46,659	12,938	17,040	28,998	625,110	.0120	390,599	111	81,250	162	7,834	41	64,037	14,646	29,960	Cherokee
Childress	075	7,530	7,688	11,404	2,393	27,602	85,870	.0017	57,075	16	17,013	34	...	...	5,097	1,812	4,014	Childress
Clay*	077	11,441	11,006	16,831	4,365	34,186	192,560	.0031	82,144	23	...	...	...	...	6,474	1,215	8,933	Clay
Cochran	079	3,327	3,730	13,709	1,300	27,003	45,610	.0008	16,534	5	...	...	...	...	1,329	...	2,387	Cochran
Coke	081	3,695	3,864	15,085	1,553	27,712	55,740	.0010	30,743	9	...	...	...	...	3,144	1,034	2,886	Coke
Coleman	083	8,504	9,235	14,434	3,825	25,065	122,750	.0022	61,305	17	1,455	3	...	...	8,728	4,276	6,777	Coleman
Collin*	085	660,783	491,675	29,477	236,366	64,239	19,477,740	.2816	7,954,314	2,259	1,215,534	2,417	493,002	2,595	1,122,993	303,737	479,877	Collin
Collingsworth	087	2,976	3,206	13,317	1,238	25,000	39,630	.0007	22,025	6	...	...	...	...	5,311	...	2,396	Collingsworth
Colorado	089	20,877	20,390	14,820	7,665	31,398	309,400	.0061	237,830	68	21,157	42	1,693	9	38,417	10,882	13,659	Colorado
Comal*	091	93,631	78,021	20,385	34,407	42,845	1,908,690	.0301	848,117	241	133,602	266	24,349	128	93,054	33,799	67,063	Comal
Comanche	093	13,249	14,026	14,690	5,531	27,363	194,630	.0034	96,635	27	1,689	3	...	...	17,141	3,918	10,211	Comanche
Concho	095	3,701	3,966	11,040	1,051	30,113	40,860	.0007	14,702	4	...	...	...	...	4,011	...	2,040	Concho
Cooke**	097	39,041	36,363	16,560	13,887	36,207	646,500	.0129	544,515	155	61,572	122	46,378	244	62,927	20,208	26,289	Cooke
Coryell*	099	75,531	74,978	12,060	20,340	35,200	910,870	.0164	401,975	114	98,736	196	5,363	28	72,934	8,671	39,217	Coryell
Cottle	101	1,673	1,904	15,003	785	24,880	25,100	.0005	14,132	4	...	...	1,691	9	1,419	...	1,335	Cottle
Crane	103	3,787	3,996	14,465	1,339	31,398	54,780	.0009	21,067	6	...	...	...	...	4,141	...	2,377	Crane
Crockett	105	3,845	4,099	14,783	1,537	28,331	56,840	.0010	32,057	9	...	...	...	...	5,951	...	2,585	Crockett
Crosby*	107	6,558	7,072	12,063	2,460	24,974	79,110	.0017	64,048	18	...	...	...	...	20,158	2,549	4,339	Crosby
Culberson	109	2,667	2,975	12,801	1,067	24,554	34,140	.0010	58,735	17	...	...	...	...	1,807	...	1,863	Culberson
Dallam	111	6,047	6,222	13,708	2,328	27,360	82,890	.0019	88,970	25	7,067	14	...	...	5,449	...	4,113	Dallam
Dallas*	113	2,319,427	2,218,899	17,628	772,468	40,691	40,885,960	.8073	34,683,969	9,849	5,131,277	10,204	2,013,339	10,597	3,983,118	1,304,871	1,433,930	Dallas
Dawson**	115	14,211	14,985	11,554	4,665	26,967	164,190	.0033	111,713	32	10,436	21	2,606	14	19,590	6,465	7,737	Dawson
Deaf Smith**	117	18,298	18,561	12,338	6,110	28,508	225,760	.0044	138,665	39	4,596	9	2,820	15	22,604	2,819	10,755	Deaf Smith
Delta*	119	5,417	5,327	14,504	2,105	29,072	78,570	.0012	16,770	5	...	...	...	...	2,632	...	3,596	Delta
Denton*	121	558,392	432,976	23,061	185,789	53,874	12,876,850	.1968	5,542,632	1,574	1,160,247	2,307	279,879	1,473	907,692	355,892	372,045	Denton
DeWitt	123	20,263	20,013	12,810	7,212	27,655	259,570	.0046	119,222	34	10,875	22	2,340	12	24,773	11,276	12,294	DeWitt
Dickens	125	2,671	2,762	11,606	966	24,794	31,000	.0005	9,167	3	...	...	...	...	1,537	...	1,803	Dickens
Dimmit	127	10,361	10,248	8,929	3,318	21,284	92,510	.0021	75,352	21	17,796	35	...	...	5,479	1,035	5,322	Dimmit
Donley	129	3,969	3,828	14,351	1,573	27,947	56,960	.0010	31,089	9	1,122	2	...	...	5,847	1,192	2,976	Donley
Duval	131	12,397	13,120	10,307	4,426	22,019	127,770	.0023	43,242	12	1,048	2	...	...	6,861	1,161	7,020	Duval
Eastland	133	18,292	18,297	13,371	7,207	26,148	244,580	.0048	172,836	49	22,199	44	...	...	24,071	9,227	12,972	Eastland
Ector*	135	124,311	121,123	14,158	45,309	29,963	1,760,030	.0368	1,535,143	436	363,065	722	49,705	262	203,323	70,887	76,897	Ector
Edwards	137	1,962	2,162	12,722	792	24,496	24,960	.0004	6,911	2	...	...	...	...	1,464	...	1,516	Edwards
Ellis*	139	132,726	111,360	19,114	42,413	46,205	2,536,980	.0394	986,222	280	161,258	321	17,992	95	191,017	56,159	85,534	Ellis
El Paso*	141	720,147	679,622	11,701	218,789	30,082	8,426,220	.1787	6,673,517	1,895	1,498,168	2,979	459,278	2,417	781,502	305,744	391,428	El Paso
Erath**	143	33,521	33,001	14,581	12,789	30,093	488,780	.0097	379,166	108	81,264	162	17,631	93	42,275	19,512	23,163	Erath
Falls	145	17,547	18,576	12,345	6,477	27,225	216,620	.0039	95,919	27	17,489	35	...	...	29,580	3,499	10,949	Falls
Fannin**	147	32,906	31,242	14,702	11,338	33,622	483,780	.0090	303,454	86	49,026	97	1,651	9	27,426	13,520	21,284	Fannin
Fayette	149	22,745	21,804	16,203	8,639	32,684	368,540	.0070	265,945	76	25,231	50	6,198	33	38,324	6,439	16,187	Fayette
Fisher	151	4,090	4,344	15,279	1,763	27,266	62,490	.0009	12,931	4	...	...	...	...	4,016	...	3,263	Fisher
Floyd	153	7,313	7,771	12,631	2,670	26,513	92,370	.0017	49,038	14	...	...	...	...	4,753	1,492	4,896	Floyd
Foard	155	1,513	1,622	13,952	652	25,149	21,110	.0003	5,629	2	...	...	...	...	...	...	1,224	Foard
Fort Bend*	157	459,581	354,452	20,499	125,540	58,325	9,421,150	.1504	4,403,988	1,251	908,063	1,806	193,800	1,020	501,094	171,263	264,251	Fort Bend
Franklin	159	10,140	9,458	14,738	3,773	30,910	149,440	.0025	60,554	17	2,041	4	...	...	3,448	2,480	7,046	Franklin
Freestone	161	18,928	17,867	14,113	6,804	30,730	267,130	.0052	188,297	53	7,905	16	2,354	12	32,137	11,158	12,721	Freestone
Frio	163	16,418	16,252	9,014	4,805	24,225	148,000	.0035	128,816	37	17,125	34	1,613	8	22,455	2,369	7,644	Frio
Gaines	165	14,394	14,467	12,379	4,748	28,961	178,190	.0036	130,923	37	19,928	40	1,456	8	34,742	4,847	8,545	Gaines
Galveston*	167	277,119	250,158	20,343	108,269	40,256	5,637,460	.0889	2,484,736	706	458,480	912	150,792	794	482,952	159,029	183,474	Galveston
Garza	169	5,129	4,872	11,018	1,644	26,213	56,510	.0010	20,884	6	...	...	...	...	3,603	1,292	2,781	Garza
Gillespie	171	23,046	20,814	18,037	8,847	36,020	415,690	.0073	255,361	73	25,530	51	9,921	52	65,049	4,811	16,862	Gillespie
Glasscock	173	1,317	1,406	16,606	484	35,428	21,870	.0003	6,163	2	...	...	...	...	...	...	1,038	Glasscock
Goliad*	175	7,260	6,928	15,534	2,684	32,569	112,780	.0017	28,671	8	1,318	3	...	...	8,079	1,364	5,031	Goliad
Gonzales	177	19,254	18,628	12,633	6,820	27,518	243,240	.0046	141,846	40	24,245	48	2,046	11	30,963	5,173	11,550	Gonzales
Gray**	179	21,030	22,744	16,150	8,622	30,464	339,640	.0063	227,174	65	32,414	64	7,431	39	35,205	9,663	15,803	Gray
Grayson*	181	117,502	110,595	17,315	43,814	36,026	2,034,550	.0385	1,514,081	430	384,275	764	35,926	189	174,651	59,560	80,686	Grayson
Gregg*	183	115,857	111,379	16,267	43,356	33,431	1,884,600	.0420	2,085,909	592	424,354	844	77,896	410	245,870	87,146	74,751	Gregg
Grimes	185	25,947	23,552	12,408	7,903	31,210	321,960	.0059	163,466	46	11,666	23	...	...	40,764	...	14,025	Grimes
Guadalupe*	187	101,471	89,023	17,778	33,817	41,432	1,804,000	.0297	843,488	240	113,731	226	23,469	124	88,843	30,792	65,330	Guadalupe
Hale**	189	35,016	36,602	13,408	12,082	30,143	469,490	.0092	320,218	91	64,491	128	16,662	88	44,113	11,547	21,129	Hale
Hall	191	3,755	3,782	11,148	1,493	21,501	41,860	.0010	46,357	13	1,648	3	...	...	1,885	1,863	2,381	Hall
Hamilton	193	8,070	8,229	16,015	3,337	30,142	129,240	.0022	66,077	19	...	...	...	...	14,463	5,889	6,284	Hamilton
Hansford	195	5,131	5,369	16,714	1,972	33,416	85,760	.0015	53,216	15	...	...	4,140	22	5,780	...	3,920	Hansford
Hardeman	197	4,303	4,724	15,480	1,884	27,209	66,610	.0010	18,424	5	1,174	2	...	...	5,123	1,205	3,477	Hardeman
Hardin*	199	50,484	48,073	16,770	18,473	35,398	846,620	.0152	515,454	146	77,989	155	3,254	17	75,494	12,318	33,881	Hardin
Harris*	201	3,713,507	3,400,578	17,676	1,258,645	40,526	65,639,600	1.2294	47,930,192	13,610	7,461,373	14,838	2,977,973	15,674	7,117,190	2,349,763	2,297,170	Harris
Harrison**	203	62,247	62,110	15,769	23,459	32,307	981,570	.0176	572,291	163	86,822	173	21,489	113	69,377	26,090	42,967	Harrison
Hartley	205	5,487	5,537	16,441	1,616	43,271	90,210	.0013	16,066	5	...	...	1,406	7	9,317	...	3,137	Hartley
Haskell	207	5,490	6,093	13,987	2,517	23,281	76,790	.0016	63,089	18	...	...	...	...	6,892	1,042	4,422	Haskell
Hays*	209	126,250	97,589	17,421	40,584	40,662	2,199,370	.0380	1,212,621	344	100,442	200	266,573	1,403	154,573	49,901	79,535	Hays
Hemphill	211	3,323	3,351	16,196	1,246	33,163	53,820	.0009	24,509	7	4,843	10	...	...	1,645	1,562	2,495	Hemphill
Henderson**	213	79,774	73,277	15,287	29,819	31,489	1,219,480	.0209	571,521	162	129,846	258	14,302	75	115,467	36,870	53,957	Henderson
Hidalgo*	215	675,597	569,463	8,316	179,247	24,020	5,618,500	.1432	5,723,037	1,625	1,172,978	2,333	428,765	2,257	870,770	248,513	322,531	Hidalgo
Hill	217	35,663	32,321	13,501	12,275	30,708	481,490	.0109	508,216	144	31,654	63	89,747	472	76,677	14,621	22,235	Hill
Hockley**	219	22,926	22,716	13,599	8,074	30,108	311,760	.0062	223,177	63	29,400	58	4,848	26	31,662	8,032	14,469	Hockley
Hood**	221	47,627	41,100	18,672	16,786	40,723	889,290	.0157	562,980	160	88,093	175	7,377	39	73,530	18,064	32,200	Hood
Hopkins**	223	33,033	31,960	15,369	12,539	31,230	507,690	.0106	463,489	132	42,477	84	30,400	160	33,108	25,616	22,722	Hopkins
Houston	225	23,137	23,185	12,580	8,301	26,945	291,060	.0057	186,292	53	19,053	38	2,916	15	37,197	14,977	13,917	Houston
Howard**	227	32,531	33,627	13,267	11,405	29,416	431,600	.0088	329,673	94	56,768	113	9,442	50	38,570	14,924	18,780	Howard
Hudspeth	229	3,196	3,344	9,484	1,125	20,634	30,310	.0006	8,417	2	...	...	...	...	2,021	...	2,027	Hudspeth
Hunt*	231	82,483	76,596	16,129	29,259	35,918	1,330,350	.0237	768,237	218	158,612	315	27,363	144	129,967	41,383	54,438	Hunt
Hutchinson**	233	22,266	23,857	18,640	9,237	34,732	415,040	.0067	184,357	52	25,359	50	8,338	44	36,927	8,704	17,760	Hutchinson
Irion*	235	1,750	1,771	17,874	688	35,000	31,280	.0004	1,510	0	...	...	...	...	...	...	1,335	Irion

Source: Devonshire Associates Ltd. and Scan/US, Inc. 2005. ...Data less than 1,000. (d) Data not available.
* Component of a Metropolitan Core Based Statistical Area.
** Component of a Micropolitan Core Based Statistical Area.

Continued on next page

Counties: Population/Income/Sales, *Continued*

County or County Equivalent	FIPS County Code	Population Estimate 7/1/05	Population Census 4/1/00	Per Capita Income 2004	Households Estimate 7/1/05	Median Household Income 2004	Disposable Income 2004 ($1,000)	Market Ability Index 2004	Total Retail Sales 2004 Sales ($1,000)	Total Retail Sales Ranally Sales Units	General Merchandise 2004 Sales ($1,000)	General Merchandise Ranally Sales Units	Apparel Store 2004 Sales ($1,000)	Apparel Store Ranally Sales Units	Food Store Sales 2004 ($1,000)	Health & Drug Store 2004 ($1,000)	Passenger Car Registrations 2004	County or County Equivalent
Jack	237	9,060	8,763	13,477	3,034	30,791	122,100	.0019	27,866	8	...	...	...	...	6,445	3,651	5,539	Jack
Jackson	239	14,222	14,391	16,425	5,341	33,740	233,590	.0038	93,360	27	5,955	12	...	...	17,321	...	9,563	Jackson
Jasper	241	35,540	35,604	14,728	13,740	29,499	523,450	.0100	362,643	103	79,738	159	7,843	41	54,888	21,318	23,865	Jasper
Jeff Davis	243	2,253	2,207	15,890	884	31,406	35,800	.0005	4,706	1	...	...	...	...	3,656	...	1,648	Jeff Davis
Jefferson*	245	246,195	252,051	16,425	94,064	33,193	4,043,810	.0815	3,490,149	991	596,856	1,187	186,618	982	417,661	218,638	151,758	Jefferson
Jim Hogg	247	4,873	5,281	12,114	1,837	24,866	59,030	.0012	39,122	11	1,119	2	...	...	6,091	...	2,794	Jim Hogg
Jim Wells**	249	41,141	39,326	11,371	13,093	27,382	467,810	.0098	350,099	99	51,719	103	14,689	77	62,126	19,000	21,880	Jim Wells
Johnson*	251	147,080	126,811	17,235	47,005	41,345	2,534,890	.0412	1,090,262	310	212,709	423	33,621	177	145,171	40,172	93,399	Johnson
Jones*	253	19,799	20,785	11,501	6,188	28,587	227,700	.0051	211,580	60	16,403	33	...	...	9,683	3,739	11,253	Jones
Karnes	255	15,291	15,446	9,716	4,451	25,660	148,560	.0031	91,899	26	11,835	24	...	...	18,019	1,395	7,540	Karnes
Kaufman*	257	88,739	71,313	16,357	26,808	41,397	1,451,470	.0272	1,003,480	285	77,160	153	49,582	261	151,021	32,931	53,145	Kaufman
Kendall*	259	27,913	23,743	21,012	10,000	45,144	586,520	.0116	537,404	153	40,083	80	2,728	14	93,660	1,374	20,577	Kendall
Kenedy**	261	396	414	10,960	136	24,238	4,340	.0001	...	...	...	...	...	...	...	...	212	Kenedy
Kent	263	738	859	18,401	355	29,284	13,580	.0002	5,678	2	...	...	...	...	...	...	699	Kent
Kerr**	265	45,977	43,653	17,014	18,467	32,591	782,240	.0160	712,280	202	113,739	226	42,047	221	217,166	43,498	31,601	Kerr
Kimble	267	4,539	4,468	14,904	1,833	28,408	67,650	.0013	45,194	13	...	...	...	...	11,906	...	3,357	Kimble
King	269	302	356	15,331	108	32,795	4,630	.0001	...	...	...	...	...	...	...	...	211	King
Kinney	271	3,300	3,379	14,027	1,309	27,403	46,290	.0007	6,124	2	...	...	...	...	3,717	...	2,119	Kinney
Kleberg**	273	30,799	31,549	12,691	10,791	27,864	390,870	.0082	319,599	91	76,201	152	14,771	78	44,536	13,160	16,979	Kleberg
Knox	275	3,774	4,253	14,126	1,677	24,916	53,310	.0009	27,224	8	...	...	...	...	5,734	...	2,821	Knox
Lamar**	277	50,016	48,499	15,271	19,498	31,025	763,780	.0159	687,370	195	137,580	274	32,578	171	68,717	37,578	33,763	Lamar
Lamb	279	14,650	14,709	12,704	5,294	27,098	186,110	.0034	94,173	27	5,525	11	1,620	9	23,627	2,279	9,587	Lamb
Lampasas*	281	20,209	17,762	14,683	6,684	34,869	296,720	.0052	150,022	43	8,329	17	1,327	7	16,767	8,048	12,650	Lampasas
La Salle	283	5,878	5,866	8,505	1,803	21,134	49,990	.0011	32,320	9	1,869	4	...	...	3,439	1,497	2,651	La Salle
Lavaca	285	18,859	19,210	14,825	7,628	28,663	279,580	.0052	170,397	48	17,404	35	1,993	10	36,601	7,320	13,853	Lavaca
Lee	287	16,933	15,657	15,277	5,835	34,255	258,690	.0044	122,468	35	19,667	39	2,014	11	15,599	2,448	10,957	Lee
Leon	289	16,397	15,335	14,769	6,336	29,464	242,170	.0043	122,546	35	...	...	...	...	35,552	3,470	11,314	Leon
Liberty*	291	76,373	70,154	15,082	24,383	36,651	1,151,850	.0203	603,523	171	130,040	259	19,438	102	105,180	30,647	42,862	Liberty
Limestone	293	22,867	22,051	12,733	7,926	28,528	291,170	.0057	196,305	56	21,636	43	2,539	13	45,096	9,549	14,208	Limestone
Lipscomb	295	3,128	3,057	14,946	1,174	30,605	46,750	.0007	13,745	4	...	...	...	...	1,896	...	2,323	Lipscomb
Live Oak	297	11,530	12,309	14,725	4,254	30,971	169,780	.0031	99,741	28	1,287	3	...	...	10,980	2,596	7,490	Live Oak
Llano	299	18,715	17,044	19,596	8,425	33,512	366,730	.0053	104,470	30	...	...	1,227	6	27,689	6,951	15,140	Llano
Loving	301	62	67	27,581	31	42,386	1,710	...	...	...	...	...	...	...	...	...	71	Loving
Lubbock*	303	255,027	242,628	16,025	101,319	31,092	4,086,700	.0845	3,724,640	1,058	576,586	1,147	183,780	967	535,172	115,234	188,346	Lubbock
Lynn	305	6,036	6,550	13,024	2,331	26,223	78,610	.0013	28,178	8	...	...	...	...	...	1,123	4,297	Lynn
McCulloch	307	7,784	8,205	13,722	3,301	25,307	106,810	.0024	112,241	32	30,004	60	1,898	10	7,238	1,929	5,490	McCulloch
McLennan*	309	222,879	213,517	15,287	81,749	32,361	3,407,130	.0644	2,317,504	658	441,422	878	85,844	452	368,221	97,552	142,946	McLennan
McMullen	311	900	851	16,411	361	31,553	14,770	.0002	2,399	1	...	...	...	...	...	...	676	McMullen
Madison	313	13,032	12,940	11,333	4,011	28,534	147,690	.0043	254,447	72	41,105	82	...	...	31,907	11,441	6,965	Madison
Marion	315	11,193	10,941	13,481	4,706	24,897	150,890	.0026	67,880	19	...	...	...	...	9,104	...	7,907	Marion
Martin	317	4,422	4,746	15,045	1,696	30,680	66,530	.0013	47,719	14	...	...	...	...	4,018	2,255	3,081	Martin
Mason	319	3,785	3,738	15,768	1,562	29,670	59,680	.0009	16,675	5	...	...	...	...	4,532	1,127	3,000	Mason
Matagorda**	321	38,394	37,957	14,728	13,985	31,549	565,480	.0102	311,702	89	36,975	74	12,481	66	81,855	13,134	23,706	Matagorda
Maverick**	323	51,449	47,297	7,453	14,027	21,016	383,460	.0101	381,100	108	83,153	165	56,609	298	106,462	11,488	21,868	Maverick
Medina*	325	42,885	39,304	13,692	13,231	34,273	587,190	.0109	344,521	98	22,615	45	1,745	9	56,805	5,960	25,482	Medina
Menard	327	2,310	2,360	13,307	977	24,469	30,740	.0006	16,071	5	...	...	...	...	...	...	1,707	Menard
Midland*	329	120,852	116,009	17,296	43,353	37,295	2,090,260	.0408	1,702,551	483	319,844	636	87,217	459	191,235	56,316	76,630	Midland
Milam	331	25,480	24,238	15,073	9,322	31,723	384,050	.0063	148,537	42	25,055	50	1,565	8	32,849	9,116	16,858	Milam
Mills	333	4,998	5,151	15,008	1,995	29,101	75,010	.0015	61,929	18	...	...	1,124	6	4,809	...	3,770	Mills
Mitchell	335	9,254	9,698	9,776	2,805	24,826	90,470	.0018	43,727	12	...	...	1,677	9	9,936	3,313	4,820	Mitchell
Montague	337	19,639	19,117	15,427	7,847	30,109	302,970	.0050	125,134	36	15,514	31	1,757	9	24,219	9,130	14,866	Montague
Montgomery*	339	375,519	293,768	16,341	101,158	47,202	6,136,350	.1129	4,023,010	1,142	908,203	1,806	222,964	1,174	606,624	134,824	216,646	Montgomery
Moore**	341	20,232	20,121	14,695	6,883	33,129	297,300	.0053	163,238	46	28,654	57	6,183	33	29,519	6,482	13,401	Moore
Morris	343	13,298	13,048	14,500	5,282	28,193	192,820	.0031	60,821	17	1,742	3	...	...	14,398	4,984	9,336	Morris
Motley	345	1,242	1,426	16,602	592	27,222	20,620	.0003	7,580	2	...	...	...	...	...	...	1,146	Motley
Nacogdoches**	347	59,701	59,203	13,679	23,087	27,470	816,660	.0176	765,321	217	131,566	262	46,309	244	107,888	28,551	40,389	Nacogdoches
Navarro**	349	48,525	45,124	13,314	16,589	30,654	646,080	.0129	473,807	135	68,775	137	24,534	129	70,372	17,255	28,748	Navarro
Newton	351	14,689	15,072	13,845	5,731	27,214	203,370	.0030	29,075	8	...	...	...	...	14,150	...	9,861	Newton
Nolan**	353	14,739	15,802	13,612	6,028	25,827	200,630	.0040	149,850	43	17,030	34	5,492	29	18,164	8,241	10,033	Nolan
Nueces*	355	316,026	313,645	15,439	109,778	34,684	4,879,190	.0962	3,806,144	1,081	684,567	1,361	197,335	1,039	567,342	155,543	206,391	Nueces
Ochiltree	357	8,929	9,006	17,237	3,274	36,068	153,910	.0026	82,840	24	5,616	11	3,062	16	8,965	5,560	6,088	Ochiltree
Oldham	359	2,148	2,185	14,441	733	32,627	31,020	.0005	12,195	3	...	...	...	...	...	...	1,368	Oldham
Orange*	361	84,104	84,966	17,889	32,445	35,843	1,504,510	.0246	691,793	196	122,822	244	20,616	109	112,052	45,328	58,328	Orange
Palo Pinto**	363	27,466	27,026	14,850	10,563	30,233	407,880	.0073	220,242	63	30,974	62	17,396	92	38,395	11,244	18,661	Palo Pinto
Panola	365	22,816	22,756	15,650	9,034	30,489	357,070	.0061	170,829	49	18,708	37	4,780	25	38,941	17,651	15,860	Panola
Parker*	367	103,201	88,495	17,695	33,227	42,001	1,826,160	.0319	1,066,328	303	135,908	270	25,891	136	174,528	40,974	67,154	Parker
Parmer	369	9,815	10,016	12,863	3,322	29,422	126,250	.0022	57,223	16	...	...	...	...	5,555	1,504	6,349	Parmer
Pecos	371	15,522	16,809	11,999	5,161	27,803	186,250	.0035	100,485	29	17,042	34	1,751	9	14,077	1,561	9,443	Pecos
Polk	373	48,082	41,133	12,104	15,378	29,499	582,000	.0119	417,998	119	108,584	216	12,286	65	63,470	13,324	26,116	Polk
Potter*	375	119,630	113,546	13,022	42,381	28,484	1,557,880	.0386	1,994,542	566	263,550	524	105,189	554	148,314	96,571	70,258	Potter
Presidio	377	7,768	7,304	8,977	2,752	19,254	69,730	.0014	32,547	9	12,027	24	...	...	5,925	...	4,374	Presidio
Rains	379	11,915	9,139	13,012	3,712	31,528	155,040	.0025	42,321	12	...	...	...	...	19,042	1,292	7,042	Rains
Randall*	381	108,926	104,312	20,469	42,619	40,379	2,229,610	.0360	1,082,809	307	190,429	379	24,459	129	102,982	29,019	80,374	Randall
Reagan	383	2,928	3,326	15,652	1,121	31,639	45,830	.0008	19,094	5	...	...	...	...	3,427	...	2,087	Reagan
Real	385	3,036	3,047	13,333	1,279	24,843	40,480	.0006	8,467	2	...	...	...	...	2,075	...	2,323	Real
Red River	387	13,363	14,314	15,160	5,878	26,763	202,580	.0032	66,957	19	10,499	21	...	...	8,703	5,807	10,694	Red River
Reeves**	389	11,644	13,137	10,189	4,026	22,443	118,640	.0025	84,873	24	18,574	37	2,696	14	2,505	9,672	6,421	Reeves
Refugio	391	7,402	7,828	14,828	2,960	28,803	109,760	.0021	73,658	21	...	...	...	...	12,015	2,268	4,879	Refugio
Roberts**	393	784	887	23,839	353	41,085	18,690	.0002	2,161	1	...	...	...	...	...	...	738	Roberts
Robertson*	395	15,890	16,000	14,341	6,266	27,848	227,880	.0038	82,880	24	3,528	7	...	...	20,651	5,974	10,652	Robertson
Rockwall*	397	61,874	43,080	25,037	20,274	58,496	1,549,160	.0231	644,685	183	114,593	228	17,650	93	167,967	37,010	42,582	Rockwall
Runnels	399	10,572	11,495	14,283	4,320	26,770	151,000	.0027	80,611	23	3,064	6	...	...	9,473	1,610	8,024	Runnels
Rusk*	401	47,694	47,372	15,010	17,573	31,283	715,870	.0120	294,650	84	56,959	113	7,329	39	54,126	16,581	32,044	Rusk
Sabine	403	10,400	10,469	14,875	4,592	25,977	154,700	.0025	52,621	15	1,124	2	...	...	12,815	4,743	7,868	Sabine
San Augustine	405	8,806	8,946	14,044	3,643	26,798	123,670	.0022	58,849	17	1,116	2	...	...	13,644	3,907	6,268	San Augustine
San Jacinto*	407	24,863	22,246	14,283	8,866	30,739	355,110	.0052	48,435	14	...	...	...	...	20,471	1,269	15,647	San Jacinto
San Patricio*	409	67,922	67,138	14,994	23,548	33,356	1,018,450	.0181	546,514	155	57,756	115	9,457	50	140,924	28,379	40,613	San Patricio
San Saba	411	5,947	6,186	14,347	2,292	28,477	85,320	.0018	76,295	22	6,220	12	...	...	7,768	4,220	4,184	San Saba
Schleicher	413	2,701	2,935	15,498	1,113	28,998	41,860	.0006	8,177	2	...	...	...	...	...	...	2,061	Schleicher
Scurry**	415	15,814	16,361	14,261	5,716	30,601	225,520	.0046	186,688	53	25,127	50	2,966	16	18,516	9,467	9,907	Scurry
Shackelford	417	3,278	3,302	14,878	1,286	29,801	48,770	.0008	19,213	5	...	...	...	...	1,612	...	2,395	Shackelford
Shelby	419	26,305	25,224	13,470	9,818	27,793	354,330	.0068	229,533	65	21,875	43	4,010	21	58,438	18,680	16,751	Shelby
Sherman	421	3,123	3,186	16,045	1,194	32,342	50,110	.0007	9,562	3	1,525	3	...	...	...	...	2,269	Sherman
Smith*	423	189,133	174,706	16,668	68,560	35,523	3,152,460	.0649	2,900,030	823	492,616	980	195,885	1,031	351,168	135,119	122,512	Smith
Somervell**	425	7,614	6,809	16,466	2,589	37,423	125,370	.0020	47,045	13	11,800	23	...	...	4,325	7,808	5,034	Somervell
Starr**	427	60,785	53,597	5,155	14,585	16,208	313,340	.0095	316,856	90	57,220	114	14,363	76	83,674	8,153	22,739	Starr
Stephens	429	9,377	9,674	14,350	3,614	28,847	134,560	.0024	67,812	19	8,855	18	1,554	8	11,326	4,364	6,246	Stephens
Sterling	431	1,292	1,393	17,229	514	33,184	22,260	.0003	6,917	2	...	...	...	...	...	...	973	Sterling
Stonewall	433	1,326	1,693	18,808	710	26,785	24,940	.0004	7,811	2	...	...	...	...	...	...	1,250	Stonewall
Sutton	435	4,065	4,077	15,798	1,499	32,546	64,220	.0014	67,439	19	...	...	...	...	6,100	...	2,648	Sutton
Swisher	437	7,706	8,378	14,120	2,896	29,153	108,810	.0018	39,169	11	2,771	6	...	...	3,870	...	5,184	Swisher
Tarrant*	439	1,626,962	1,446,219	19,074	558,390	43,459	31,032,520	.5681	22,136,303	6,286	2,479,052	4,930	1,063,464	5,597	2,745,265	937,248	1,077,111	Tarrant
Taylor*	441	123,775	126,555	16,487	48,220	32,527	2,040,720	.0405	1,697,028	482	377,627	751	62,994	332	188,548	70,018	85,264	Taylor
Terrell	443	981	1,081	13,833	446	23,346	13,570	.0002	2,114	1	...	...	...	...	...	...	809	Terrell
Terry	445	12,398	12,761	12,175	4,236	27,287	150,940	.0029	87,709	25	11,133	22	1,879	10	13,971	4,153	7,610	Terry
Throckmorton	447	1,581	1,850	17,084	757	27,218	27,010	.0004	5,565	2	...	...	...	...	...	...	1,446	Throckmorton
Titus**	449	29,131	28,118	13,642	9,765	31,582	397,410	.0087	384,249	109	85,137	169	16,357	86	37,009	21,606	17,358	Titus
Tom Green*	451	103,625	104,010	15,895	40,080	31,763	1,647,170	.0317	1,216,496	345	260,149	517	51,673	272	166,583	40,858	68,491	Tom Green
Travis*	453	882,137	812,280	21,969	344,485	44,208	19,380,040	.4426	25,198,059	7,155	1,838,931	3,657	740,524	3,898	2,214,813	1,244,357	652,744	Travis
Trinity	455	14,414	13,779	13,696	5,845	26,116	197,410	.0032	59,744	17	...	...	...	...	24,292	...	9,704	Trinity
Tyler	457	20,450	20,871	14,314	7,906	28,716	292,730	.0047	89,999	26	13,035	26	...	...	18,500	3,449	13,697	Tyler
Upshur*	459	38,037	35,291	14,907	13,634	31,988	567,000	.0092	203,217	58	42,520	85	1,887	10	36,475	9,320	25,759	Upshur
Upton	461	3,057	3,404	14,985	1,243	28,587	45,810	.0007	14,058	4	...	...	...	...	2,354	...	2,305	Upton
Uvalde**	463	26,870	25,926	11,115	8,668	26,379	298,660	.0065	250,967	71	33,837	67	7,180	38	60,196	6,833	14,397	Uvalde
Val Verde**	465	47,764	44,856	10,893	14,699	27,527	520,290	.0115	437,238	124	91,484	182	25,432	134	84,060	6,683	25,651	Val Verde
Van Zandt	467	52,458	48,140	15,404	18,714	33,142	808,050	.0136	360,714	102	78,328	156	3,635	19	39,062	25,247	35,802	Van Zandt
Victoria*	469	86,168	84,088	17,025	30,781	36,791	1,467,050	.0289	1,213,957	345	245,245	488	55,150	290	155,184	57,549	54,241	Victoria
Walker**	471	62,539	61,758	12,027	19,080	30,805	752,170	.0156	573,591	163	118,028	235	25,865	136	56,646	27,254	32,448	Walker
Waller*	473	35,721	32,663	15,758	11,878	36,219	562,890	.0131	683,185	194	65,642	131	5,483	29	48,436	10,642	21,337	Waller
Ward	475	9,974	10,909	14,530	3,955	28,116	144,920	.0025	67,828	19	7,766	15	1,452	8	11,971	1,283	6,717	Ward
Washington**	477	31,249	30,373	16,736	11,612	34,898	522,990	.0100	395,739	112	69,201	138	18,054	95	59,077	15,933	20,760	Washington
Webb*	479	224,381	193,117	9,241	58,794	27,107	2,073,610	.0538	2,426,335	689	508,362	1,011	297,333	1,565	374,549	102,163	97,606	Webb
Wharton**	481	41,343	41,188	14,407	15,030	30,682	595,620	.0117	433,525	123	37,487	75	9,561	50	96,376	14,944	25,571	Wharton
Wheeler	483	4,569	5,284	17,457	2,094	29,585	79,760	.0013	37,565	11	...	...	...	...	6,562	2,573	3,947	Wheeler
Wichita*	485	125,947	131,664	16,433	49,046	32,514	2,069,690	.0398	1,559,140	443	323,578	643	48,523	255	226,701	77,594	85,482	Wichita
Wilbarger**	487	13,882	14,676	14,391	5,409	28,570	199,770	.0039	149,469	42	10,121	20	3,492	18	25,980	13,709	9,482	Wilbarger
Willacy**	489	20,054	20,082	8,270	5,828	21,665	165,840	.0035	81,942	23	7,197	14	...	...	8,551	9,363	9,205	Willacy
Williamson*	491	335,518	249,967	22,961	107,222	55,982	7,703,790	.1144	2,915,306	828	402,242	800	89,653	472	527,955	183,402	195,867	Williamson
Wilson*	493	37,038	32,408	15,256	11,547	37,627	565,060	.0089	177,774	50	17,644	35	...	...	28,051	10,611	23,600	Wilson
Winkler	495	6,570	7,173	14,624	2,537	29,243	96,080	.0017	51,601	15	2,332	5	...	...	4,587	...	4,446	Winkler
Wise*	497	57,616	48,793	16,020	17,999	40,162	923,020	.0218	1,158,706	329	300,668	598	13,196	69	44,035	10,435	36,496	Wise
Wood	499	40,942	36,752	14,733	14,787	31,601	603,190	.0106	304,781	87	80,063	159	3,103	16	37,770	12,689	27,024	Wood
Yoakum	501	7,254	7,322	13,601	2,494	30,720	98,660	.0017	40,655	12	...	...	1,205	6	8,312	1,693	4,665	Yoakum
Young	503	17,950	17,943	15,143	7,121	29,802	271,820	.0048	141,972	40	27,207	54	2,317	12	29,753	8,701	12,793	Young
Zapata	505	13,368	12,182	9,381	4,054	23,814	125,410	.0023	39,136	11	...	...	...	...	13,846	...	6,510	Zapata
Zavala	507	11,654	11,600	6,611	3,455	16,959	77,040	.0017	30,501	9	1,281	3	...	...	13,047	...	5,085	Zavala
Texas Total		**22,865,855**	**20,851,820**	**16,999**	**7,783,329**	**38,155**	**388,698,090**	**7.2816**	**277,178,962**	**78,714**	**42,317,101**	**84,157**	**14,059,461**	**73,993**	**37,556,608**	**12,056,216**	**14,286,277**	**Texas**

Utah (UT; Code 49; 29 Counties)

County or County Equivalent	FIPS County Code	Population Estimate 7/1/05	Population Census 4/1/00	Per Capita Income 2004	Households Estimate 7/1/05	Median Household Income 2004	Disposable Income 2004 ($1,000)	Market Ability Index 2004	Total Retail Sales 2004 Sales ($1,000)	Total Retail Sales Ranally Sales Units	General Merchandise 2004 Sales ($1,000)	General Merchandise Ranally Sales Units	Apparel Store 2004 Sales ($1,000)	Apparel Store Ranally Sales Units	Food Store Sales 2004 ($1,000)	Health & Drug Store 2004 ($1,000)	Passenger Car Registrations 2004	County or County Equivalent
Beaver	001	6,051	6,005	13,844	2,087	32,926	83,770	.0015	46,322	13	...	...	...	...	8,533	4,183	4,560	Beaver
Box Elder**	003	45,266	42,745	16,485	14,622	41,759	746,230	.0130	411,961	117	44,269	88	9,872	52	69,947	6,505	33,332	Box Elder
Cache*	005	98,441	91,391	14,422	31,258	37,274	1,419,740	.0278	1,032,725	293	218,575	435	32,483	171	147,131	26,099	70,971	Cache
Carbon**	007	19,333	20,422	15,949	7,785	32,632	308,350	.0062	258,331	73	79,641	158	9,029	48	31,754	3,128	17,245	Carbon
Daggett	009	875	921	15,611	369	30,285	13,660	.0002	2,478	1	...	...	...	...	...	...	745	Daggett
Davis*	011	287,557	238,994	17,981	86,418	48,877	5,170,480	.0884	2,840,684	807	443,893	883	79,695	419	420,836	67,441	218,769	Davis
Duchesne	013	15,108	14,371	12,209	5,036	30,301	184,460	.0039	147,724	42	4,368	9	...	...	27,369	2,764	10,782	Duchesne
Emery	015	10,515	10,860	15,762	3,666	36,913	165,740	.0027	69,418	20	...	...	...	...	4,870	4,763	8,890	Emery
Garfield	017	4,370	4,735	16,446	1,769	33,156	71,870	.0011	23,691	7	...	...	...	...	2,640	1,366	4,008	Garfield
Grand	019	8,773	8,485	17,006	3,923	31,212	149,190	.0028	102,433	29	2,598	5	1,814	10	27,853	5,581	7,334	Grand
Iron**	021	36,286	33,779	13,422	12,379	32,427	487,030	.0104	441,947	125	86,941	173	8,077	43	68,296	5,836	26,845	Iron
Juab*	023	9,022	8,238	13,711	2,824	35,756	123,700	.0022	63,617	18	3,711	7	...	...	4,769	1,217	6,668	Juab
Kane	025	6,029	6,046	16,868	2,564	32,663	101,700	.0016	34,916	10	...	...	...	...	11,443	1,777	5,128	Kane
Millard	027	12,268	12,405	13,933	4,080	34,514	170,930	.0033	115,773	33	...	...	1,369	7	25,424	4,753	9,027	Millard
Morgan*	029	7,623	7,129	17,319	2,333	46,522	132,020	.0020	42,743	12	...	...	...	...	6,733	1,909	6,139	Morgan
Piute	031	1,329	1,435	13,634	524	28,153	18,120	.0003	4,188	1	...	...	...	...	1,220	...	1,209	Piute
Rich	033	2,048	1,961	17,358	775	37,828	35,550	.0005	7,393	2	...	...	...	...	...	...	1,817	Rich
Salt Lake*	035	930,006	898,387	17,953	307,564	44,586	16,696,420	.3331	14,700,927	4,174	2,318,808	4,611	680,631	3,582	1,899,566	323,003	643,149	Salt Lake
San Juan	037	13,346	14,413	10,668	4,281	27,010	142,370	.0026	48,609	14	...	...	...	...	12,275	2,127	7,810	San Juan

Source: Devonshire Associates Ltd. and Scan/US, Inc. 2005. ...Data less than 1,000. (d) Data not available.
* Component of a Metropolitan Core Based Statistical Area.
** Component of a Micropolitan Core Based Statistical Area.

Counties: Population/Income/Sales, *Continued*

County or County Equivalent	FIPS County Code	Population Estimate 7/1/05	Population Census 4/1/00	Per Capita Income 2004	Households Estimate 7/1/05	Median Household Income 2004	Disposable Income 2004 ($1,000)	Market Ability Index 2004	Total Retail Sales 2004 Sales ($1,000)	Total Retail Sales Ranally Sales Units	General Merchandise 2004 Sales ($1,000)	General Merchandise Ranally Sales Units	Apparel Store 2004 Sales ($1,000)	Apparel Store Ranally Sales Units	Food Store Sales 2004 ($1,000)	Health & Drug Store 2004 ($1,000)	Passenger Car Registrations 2004	County or County Equivalent
Sanpete	.039	24,063	22,763	11,364	7,089	31,571	273,440	.0053	156,837	45	...	...	...	...	48,537	5,855	15,987	Sanpete
Sevier	.041	19,166	18,842	14,331	6,578	34,283	274,660	.0059	265,467	75	32,789	65	8,546	45	42,975	6,356	14,515	Sevier
Summit*	.043	34,273	29,736	25,057	11,937	59,187	858,770	.0136	451,107	128	33,979	68	77,304	407	112,106	11,299	26,276	Summit
Tooele*	.045	51,817	40,735	16,209	16,145	42,913	839,880	.0135	315,317	90	23,129	46	1,541	8	92,245	6,645	35,391	Tooele
Uintah**	.047	26,736	25,224	13,467	8,885	33,353	360,060	.0074	294,633	84	65,683	131	6,386	34	52,694	...	18,907	Uintah
Utah*	.049	409,622	368,536	15,081	119,096	42,310	6,177,510	.1186	4,378,818	1,243	892,140	1,774	147,868	778	679,220	84,277	277,886	Utah
Wasatch**	.051	18,878	15,215	17,464	5,939	45,734	329,680	.0052	127,974	36	9,013	18	1,098	6	25,591	2,082	13,070	Wasatch
Washington*	.053	112,063	90,354	14,745	38,015	35,593	1,652,320	.0358	1,634,619	464	208,871	415	56,203	296	210,035	29,423	75,206	Washington
Wayne	.055	2,431	2,509	14,875	952	31,258	36,160	.0007	20,191	6	1,068	2	...	...	5,967	...	2,128	Wayne
Weber*	.057	209,328	196,533	17,847	74,367	41,209	3,735,900	.0693	2,668,508	758	641,547	1,276	85,622	451	399,161	57,477	150,313	Weber
Utah Total		**2,422,623**	**2,233,169**	**16,825**	**783,260**	**42,735**	**40,759,710**	**.7789**	**30,709,350**	**8,720**	**5,112,456**	**10,166**	**1,209,753**	**6,369**	**4,439,600**	**666,059**	**1,714,107**	**Utah**

Vermont (VT; Code 50; 14 Counties)

County or County Equivalent	FIPS County Code	Population Estimate 7/1/05	Population Census 4/1/00	Per Capita Income 2004	Households Estimate 7/1/05	Median Household Income 2004	Disposable Income 2004 ($1,000)	Market Ability Index 2004	Total Retail Sales 2004 Sales ($1,000)	Total Retail Sales Ranally Sales Units	General Merchandise 2004 Sales ($1,000)	General Merchandise Ranally Sales Units	Apparel Store 2004 Sales ($1,000)	Apparel Store Ranally Sales Units	Food Store Sales 2004 ($1,000)	Health & Drug Store 2004 ($1,000)	Passenger Car Registrations 2004	County or County Equivalent
Addison	.001	37,083	35,974	17,993	13,353	40,335	667,220	.0126	498,732	142	14,813	29	7,359	39	69,921	23,045	27,391	Addison
Bennington**	.003	37,189	36,994	18,637	14,991	37,273	693,080	.0151	772,366	219	46,266	92	88,457	466	105,687	38,270	28,493	Bennington
Caledonia	.005	30,350	29,702	15,772	11,722	33,125	478,680	.0087	291,883	83	18,844	37	13,555	71	48,088	23,527	22,404	Caledonia
Chittenden*	.007	150,099	146,571	21,076	57,876	44,395	3,163,560	.0621	2,868,775	815	282,526	562	153,094	806	456,485	139,448	112,415	Chittenden
Essex**	.009	6,643	6,459	13,739	2,543	29,077	91,270	.0013	9,655	3	...	...	...	...	5,122	...	4,848	Essex
Franklin*	.011	48,164	45,417	17,296	17,259	39,075	833,040	.0149	516,699	147	19,815	39	15,114	80	85,694	44,776	34,663	Franklin
Grand Isle*	.013	7,858	6,901	17,764	2,778	40,587	139,590	.0019	22,476	6	...	...	...	...	6,029	...	5,839	Grand Isle
Lamoille	.015	24,840	23,233	17,738	9,545	37,184	440,600	.0074	221,972	63	11,339	23	8,127	43	59,381	17,989	18,755	Lamoille
Orange**	.017	29,610	28,226	16,977	10,802	37,424	502,680	.0081	208,415	59	5,558	11	...	...	35,231	11,623	22,143	Orange
Orleans	.019	27,635	26,277	13,828	10,406	30,098	382,140	.0079	317,765	90	24,493	49	3,441	18	50,773	24,651	19,502	Orleans
Rutland**	.021	63,632	63,400	17,125	25,181	35,141	1,089,680	.0215	910,422	259	71,392	142	42,833	225	145,714	63,633	46,546	Rutland
Washington**	.023	59,549	58,039	19,041	23,794	38,469	1,133,900	.0205	782,474	222	31,024	62	27,634	145	155,920	56,791	43,995	Washington
Windham	.025	44,579	44,216	18,602	18,416	36,262	829,240	.0150	563,247	160	11,791	23	16,116	85	91,596	35,405	35,072	Windham
Windsor**	.027	58,380	57,418	19,628	24,251	38,151	1,145,860	.0184	530,158	151	17,409	35	13,269	70	77,190	18,172	47,094	Windsor
Vermont Total		**625,611**	**608,827**	**18,527**	**242,917**	**38,559**	**11,590,540**	**.2154**	**8,515,041**	**2,419**	**555,792**	**1,105**	**389,736**	**2,051**	**1,392,833**	**497,331**	**469,160**	**Vermont**

Virginia (VA; Code 51; 95 Counties, 39 Independent Cities)

County or County Equivalent	FIPS County Code	Population Estimate 7/1/05	Population Census 4/1/00	Per Capita Income 2004	Households Estimate 7/1/05	Median Household Income 2004	Disposable Income 2004 ($1,000)	Market Ability Index 2004	Total Retail Sales 2004 Sales ($1,000)	Total Retail Sales Ranally Sales Units	General Merchandise 2004 Sales ($1,000)	General Merchandise Ranally Sales Units	Apparel Store 2004 Sales ($1,000)	Apparel Store Ranally Sales Units	Food Store Sales 2004 ($1,000)	Health & Drug Store 2004 ($1,000)	Passenger Car Registrations 2004	County or County Equivalent
Accomack	.001	39,480	38,305	13,594	15,336	28,734	536,710	.0092	215,789	61	16,953	34	8,833	46	42,096	12,328	26,941	Accomack
Albemarle*	.003	89,294	79,236	22,763	35,752	46,246	2,032,640	.0332	1,112,752	316	240,412	478	53,144	280	140,197	62,036	70,885	Albemarle
Alleghany[3]	.005	16,506	12,926	17,161	6,935	33,821	283,260	.0046	119,790	34	11,999	24	1,385	7	18,546	12,721	13,957	Alleghany
Amelia*	.007	11,902	11,400	17,237	4,457	37,120	205,150	.0029	38,268	11	...	...	...	...	8,221	1,512	10,041	Amelia
Amherst*	.009	31,991	31,894	16,406	12,120	35,599	524,830	.0089	255,020	72	53,310	106	2,234	12	52,700	18,719	25,519	Amherst
Appomattox*	.011	13,764	13,705	16,789	5,487	34,280	231,090	.0038	104,576	30	3,228	6	1,524	8	27,764	9,514	11,681	Appomattox
Arlington*	.013	185,858	189,453	32,500	86,155	57,737	6,040,410	.0857	2,428,168	689	378,511	753	332,014	1,747	314,640	149,013	132,071	Arlington
Augusta**	.015	68,777	65,615	18,778	26,235	40,427	1,291,470	.0205	549,786	156	20,540	41	18,706	98	82,648	41,112	59,980	Augusta
Bath	.017	5,004	5,048	17,118	2,074	33,796	85,660	.0012	12,633	4	...	...	...	...	2,221	...	4,810	Bath
Bedford*	.019	64,051	60,371	19,615	25,309	40,525	1,256,390	.0162	112,967	32	...	...	...	...	8,303	7,554	57,615	Bedford
Bland	.021	7,021	6,871	13,632	2,686	29,452	95,710	.0015	18,228	5	...	...	...	...	...	...	5,866	Bland
Botetourt*	.023	31,989	30,496	20,567	12,173	44,301	657,910	.0096	202,734	58	...	...	1,326	7	33,027	12,183	28,539	Botetourt
Brunswick	.025	17,961	18,419	12,793	6,304	29,818	229,780	.0038	73,552	21	1,172	2	3,284	17	15,893	6,364	12,063	Brunswick
Buchanan	.027	24,693	26,978	11,449	10,413	22,089	282,700	.0051	117,068	33	...	...	1,645	9	31,047	26,579	19,915	Buchanan
Buckingham	.029	15,981	15,623	11,896	5,431	28,812	190,110	.0032	53,841	15	4,512	9	...	...	5,884	1,225	10,974	Buckingham
Campbell*	.031	51,615	51,078	18,130	21,585	35,561	935,800	.0150	401,277	114	23,030	46	13,686	72	72,228	11,833	44,822	Campbell
Caroline*	.033	23,809	22,121	16,577	8,578	37,682	394,670	.0064	156,440	44	1,834	4	1,431	8	15,411	5,864	18,569	Caroline
Carroll	.035	29,271	29,245	15,194	12,579	29,171	444,740	.0078	225,823	64	7,336	15	10,657	56	32,792	13,974	25,211	Carroll
Charles City*	.036	7,266	6,926	18,362	2,786	39,559	133,420	.0017	6,014	2	...	...	...	...	3,404	...	6,421	Charles City
Charlotte	.037	12,323	12,472	14,249	5,192	28,308	175,590	.0029	61,821	18	...	...	...	...	14,226	3,818	9,983	Charlotte
Chesterfield*	.041	286,764	259,903	21,996	96,724	53,374	6,307,570	.1037	3,470,025	985	732,014	1,456	162,406	855	457,684	168,556	221,920	Chesterfield
Clarke*	.043	13,896	12,652	21,755	5,244	47,486	302,310	.0042	69,202	20	...	...	...	...	11,197	1,170	11,654	Clarke
Craig*	.045	5,124	5,091	17,611	2,138	34,548	90,240	.0012	7,630	2	...	...	...	...	3,575	...	4,804	Craig
Culpeper**	.047	41,320	34,262	16,811	13,527	42,096	694,640	.0127	458,128	130	61,209	122	8,879	47	47,180	22,837	28,510	Culpeper
Cumberland*	.049	9,230	9,017	14,658	3,641	30,605	135,290	.0022	49,146	14	...	...	...	...	8,184	2,308	7,568	Cumberland
Dickenson	.051	16,070	16,395	11,567	6,706	22,620	185,880	.0034	82,275	23	1,761	3	...	...	18,507	6,193	12,102	Dickenson
Dinwiddie*	.053	25,886	24,533	18,481	9,662	39,353	463,620	.0064	77,293	22	2,275	5	...	...	25,030	8,510	20,770	Dinwiddie
Essex	.057	10,491	9,989	17,118	4,132	35,540	179,580	.0038	175,000	50	60,350	120	4,563	24	14,869	7,656	8,526	Essex
Fairfax*	.059	1,016,742	969,749	31,192	367,922	70,784	31,713,770	.4513	12,565,689	3,568	1,817,553	3,615	1,007,026	5,300	1,974,501	569,883	769,581	Fairfax
Fauquier*	.061	64,828	55,139	23,738	22,305	56,221	1,538,870	.0226	566,800	161	42,870	85	14,922	79	111,734	34,359	52,331	Fauquier
Floyd	.063	14,630	13,874	15,157	6,008	30,561	221,740	.0035	69,464	20	1,367	3	1,158	6	7,051	4,594	13,211	Floyd
Fluvanna*	.065	24,716	20,047	18,785	8,901	42,978	464,290	.0061	41,163	12	...	...	...	...	11,820	1,779	19,334	Fluvanna
Franklin*	.067	50,120	47,286	17,839	20,322	36,175	894,070	.0148	427,731	121	54,512	108	8,402	44	53,182	11,212	44,523	Franklin
Frederick*	.069	68,153	59,209	19,025	24,525	43,190	1,296,590	.0211	617,549	175	94,067	187	20,652	109	44,513	46,543	54,154	Frederick
Giles*	.071	17,084	16,657	16,699	7,104	32,955	285,290	.0049	144,274	41	8,935	18	...	...	33,636	8,372	13,963	Giles
Gloucester*	.073	37,812	34,780	18,538	13,670	41,926	700,940	.0115	337,823	96	60,610	121	9,064	48	60,351	31,159	29,165	Gloucester
Goochland*	.075	18,934	16,863	23,401	7,064	50,753	443,080	.0060	105,361	30	...	...	...	...	11,881	1,109	15,981	Goochland
Grayson	.077	16,331	17,917	15,565	7,544	27,586	254,200	.0037	45,271	13	...	...	...	...	11,656	1,146	15,040	Grayson
Greene*	.079	17,587	15,244	18,580	6,354	41,794	326,770	.0045	55,505	16	...	...	...	...	8,407	2,382	14,272	Greene
Greensville	.081	11,518	11,560	11,354	3,500	30,907	130,770	.0022	33,535	10	...	...	...	...	...	...	7,163	Greensville
Halifax	.083	36,141	37,355	14,489	14,941	29,048	523,650	.0100	357,858	102	67,382	134	8,294	44	68,885	26,839	29,805	Halifax
Hanover*	.085	98,498	86,320	23,207	34,716	54,099	2,285,810	.0361	1,127,353	320	123,803	246	12,677	67	213,374	58,778	78,651	Hanover
Henrico*	.087	275,628	262,300	20,328	102,206	45,255	5,603,040	.1059	4,529,717	1,286	944,138	1,878	295,946	1,558	508,706	321,421	207,842	Henrico
Henry**	.089	56,419	57,930	15,740	23,916	30,726	888,050	.0151	418,245	119	49,267	98	12,752	67	70,189	34,422	47,704	Henry
Highland	.091	2,497	2,536	15,635	1,115	28,778	39,040	.0006	5,557	2	...	...	...	...	...	...	2,407	Highland
Isle of Wight*	.093	33,202	29,728	19,242	12,374	42,486	638,870	.0096	210,506	60	3,776	8	3,947	21	52,309	11,386	26,975	Isle of Wight
James City*	.095	56,330	48,102	25,433	22,844	51,469	1,432,660	.0196	398,505	113	28,803	57	84,522	445	78,193	16,155	45,316	James City
King and Queen*	.097	6,541	6,630	17,201	2,727	33,910	112,510	.0015	7,922	2	...	...	...	...	...	...	6,077	King and Queen
King George	.099	19,561	16,803	19,182	6,774	44,673	375,220	.0053	83,040	24	...	...	1,118	6	19,028	2,748	15,558	King George
King William*	.101	14,688	13,146	19,431	5,167	45,360	285,400	.0046	133,161	38	...	...	...	...	19,122	8,307	11,511	King William
Lancaster	.103	12,120	11,567	16,279	5,070	31,840	197,300	.0037	139,028	39	3,364	7	4,023	21	33,505	8,116	9,385	Lancaster
Lee	.105	23,816	23,589	11,297	9,776	22,347	269,050	.0049	117,652	33	2,169	4	...	...	32,144	18,523	17,575	Lee
Loudoun*	.107	252,089	169,599	29,191	85,646	71,514	7,358,620	.1027	2,551,093	724	580,622	1,155	86,604	456	399,522	110,156	180,794	Loudoun
Louisa*	.109	29,516	25,627	16,808	10,948	36,985	496,110	.0072	110,397	31	3,328	7	...	...	26,630	4,083	23,921	Louisa
Lunenburg	.111	13,101	13,146	12,217	4,946	26,406	160,060	.0028	59,012	17	1,737	3	...	...	9,058	5,987	9,254	Lunenburg
Madison	.113	13,415	12,520	17,018	5,013	37,234	228,300	.0041	144,893	41	...	...	...	...	14,384	2,231	11,135	Madison
Mathews*	.115	9,283	9,207	20,716	3,922	40,196	192,310	.0026	40,940	12	...	...	...	...	9,690	1,227	8,063	Mathews
Mecklenburg	.117	32,515	32,380	14,848	13,163	30,298	482,780	.0094	358,895	102	48,341	96	11,432	60	55,878	21,618	25,134	Mecklenburg
Middlesex	.119	10,491	9,932	17,872	4,335	35,459	187,490	.0030	73,319	21	...	...	...	...	9,146	2,987	8,531	Middlesex
Montgomery*	.121	83,778	83,629	14,756	32,455	31,045	1,236,240	.0256	1,084,898	308	259,010	515	37,330	196	81,031	45,121	67,783	Montgomery
Nelson*	.125	15,141	14,445	16,837	5,956	34,862	254,930	.0037	52,980	15	...	...	...	...	16,961	2,621	12,836	Nelson
New Kent*	.127	15,806	13,462	21,570	5,656	49,888	340,940	.0047	78,881	22	...	...	1,710	9	23,302	6,329	13,335	New Kent
Northampton	.131	13,218	13,093	13,669	5,458	27,140	180,680	.0033	99,698	28	18,517	37	1,347	7	31,157	6,933	9,121	Northampton
Northumberland	.133	12,986	12,259	19,253	5,653	36,261	250,020	.0035	58,611	17	...	...	...	...	14,969	5,155	11,144	Northumberland
Nottoway	.135	15,629	15,725	13,025	5,723	29,692	203,570	.0040	133,951	38	3,668	7	4,052	21	26,102	13,257	10,594	Nottoway
Orange	.137	29,303	25,881	18,593	11,185	39,887	544,830	.0085	206,916	59	5,141	10	...	...	46,730	31,570	22,955	Orange
Page	.139	23,888	23,177	15,206	9,310	31,865	363,240	.0060	147,060	42	9,434	19	7,667	40	28,965	16,430	19,265	Page
Patrick	.141	19,063	19,407	14,785	8,287	27,891	281,850	.0044	81,219	23	1,970	4	...	...	18,711	9,771	17,926	Patrick
Pittsylvania*	.143	61,661	61,745	16,567	25,209	33,281	1,021,540	.0167	428,242	122	63,961	127	13,118	69	101,518	14,478	53,804	Pittsylvania
Powhatan*	.145	26,540	22,377	19,039	8,406	49,320	505,290	.0074	140,862	40	...	...	...	...	15,897	2,443	20,236	Powhatan
Prince Edward	.147	20,310	19,720	12,722	7,044	30,252	258,380	.0063	311,089	88	90,406	180	7,208	38	27,666	8,006	12,787	Prince Edward
Prince George*	.149	34,896	33,047	17,258	10,878	45,281	602,240	.0086	116,666	33	...	...	1,926	10	17,031	13,575	23,775	Prince George
Prince William*	.153	352,321	280,813	24,362	119,044	60,702	8,583,190	.1292	3,615,105	1,027	522,800	1,040	339,578	1,787	381,768	101,710	305,570	Prince William
Pulaski*	.155	34,887	35,127	16,718	14,701	32,761	583,230	.0103	332,431	94	46,664	93	4,069	21	70,264	28,425	28,166	Pulaski
Rappahannock	.157	7,202	6,983	20,710	2,859	42,658	149,150	.0024	71,948	20	...	...	...	...	1,155	1,571	6,680	Rappahannock
Richmond	.159	9,076	8,809	12,664	2,957	32,039	114,940	.0024	91,381	26	10,717	21	...	...	21,230	8,368	5,951	Richmond
Roanoke*	.161	88,219	85,778	22,034	36,308	43,814	1,943,820	.0274	536,183	152	27,475	55	19,606	103	108,716	18,507	75,869	Roanoke
Rockbridge	.163	21,000	20,808	18,282	9,146	34,558	383,930	.0068	241,271	69	23,312	46	...	...	34,426	1,286	20,069	Rockbridge
Rockingham*	.165	70,537	67,725	17,478	26,471	38,111	1,232,860	.0208	622,581	177	3,179	6	...	...	93,518	39,753	57,775	Rockingham
Russell	.167	28,667	30,308	13,124	11,828	26,279	376,230	.0070	205,983	58	7,758	15	...	...	29,932	14,494	22,974	Russell
Scott*	.169	22,744	23,403	13,781	9,842	26,284	313,430	.0059	187,942	53	5,099	10	1,143	6	47,950	12,145	18,400	Scott
Shenandoah	.171	38,397	35,075	17,710	15,058	36,924	680,000	.0122	428,350	122	8,270	16	2,623	14	59,651	22,194	31,835	Shenandoah
Smyth	.173	32,402	33,081	14,435	13,438	28,675	467,720	.0088	301,811	86	45,934	91	4,609	24	62,734	26,026	25,366	Smyth
Southampton	.175	17,248	17,482	14,777	6,392	32,722	254,870	.0038	52,538	15	2,248	4	...	...	8,264	11,424	12,430	Southampton
Spotsylvania*	.177	118,182	90,395	20,874	38,603	52,259	2,466,890	.0410	1,357,978	386	428,658	852	26,006	137	153,991	49,969	87,213	Spotsylvania
Stafford*	.179	121,019	92,446	22,695	37,855	60,056	2,746,570	.0372	611,614	174	84,702	168	7,147	38	95,097	35,720	87,033	Stafford
Surry*	.181	7,064	6,829	16,281	2,708	34,850	115,010	.0016	12,686	4	...	...	...	...	1,098	...	5,663	Surry
Sussex*	.183	11,648	12,504	12,682	4,071	30,095	147,720	.0029	99,901	28	1,416	3	1,446	8	8,338	7,458	7,533	Sussex
Tazewell**	.185	44,463	44,598	13,306	18,192	26,761	591,620	.0138	669,167	190	175,041	348	11,007	58	100,800	46,591	33,727	Tazewell
Warren*	.187	35,096	31,584	17,743	12,806	40,133	622,700	.0112	397,441	113	37,145	74	12,463	66	81,340	16,293	26,703	Warren
Washington*	.191	51,736	51,103	16,241	21,793	31,674	840,270	.0170	731,595	208	79,474	158	24,956	131	89,922	31,648	43,018	Washington
Westmoreland	.193	17,150	16,718	16,742	6,959	33,992	287,120	.0046	117,028	33	...	...	2,300	12	31,818	6,555	13,452	Westmoreland
Wise	.195	41,379	40,123	11,907	15,968	25,504	492,720	.0102	372,219	106	48,695	97	10,391	55	64,123	35,841	29,246	Wise
Wythe	.197	28,133	27,599	15,437	11,587	30,987	434,300	.0100	503,230	143	31,883	63	28,122	148	38,453	20,955	22,662	Wythe
York*	.199	62,330	56,297	23,650	22,865	52,786	1,474,110	.0208	444,061	126	109,950	219	44,986	237	58,973	38,347	49,675	York
INDEPENDENT CITIES																		
Alexandria*	.510	128,132	128,283	32,416	65,709	52,722	4,153,470	.0643	2,290,886	651	311,114	619	106,628	561	256,217	138,112	97,730	Alexandria
Bedford*	.515	6,206	6,299	13,302	2,497	27,233	82,550	.0026	176,576	50	27,180	54	3,580	19	33,134	17,692	4,185	Bedford
Bristol*	.520	17,230	17,367	14,352	7,646	26,704	247,290	.0066	390,106	111	134,453	267	10,710	56	40,302	28,585	12,249	Bristol
Buena Vista	.530	6,258	6,349	15,713	2,579	31,594	98,330	.0016	43,345	12	...	...	...	...	13,265	1,423	4,488	Buena Vista
Charlottesville*	.540	36,403	45,049	16,410	16,513	29,818	597,360	.0171	1,112,758	316	84,794	169	81,811	431	217,859	56,252	28,918	Charlottesville
Chesapeake*	.550	215,873	199,184	19,324	73,909	46,396	4,171,500	.0787	3,276,187	930	846,522	1,683	172,362	907	315,585	124,193	146,016	Chesapeake
Clifton Forge[3]	.560	(d)	4,289	(d)	(d)	(d)	(d)	(d)	(d)	(d)	(d)	(d)	(d)	(d)	(d)	(d)	(d)	Clifton Forge
Colonial Heights*	.570	17,418	16,897	20,330	7,186	40,291	354,110	.0108	770,869	219	351,838	700	60,217	317	40,515	26,955	13,652	Colonial Heights
Covington	.580	6,254	6,303	15,453	2,739	29,052	96,640	.0025	148,393	42	5,868	12	7,382	39	37,306	5,987	4,516	Covington
Danville*	.590	46,092	48,411	13,830	20,021	26,278	637,430	.0147	707,238	201	147,506	293	21,857	115	87,811	49,827	31,718	Danville
Emporia	.595	5,681	5,665	15,272	2,457	29,032	86,760	.0023	132,282	38	...	...	5,812	31	28,549	12,920	3,681	Emporia
Fairfax*	.600	22,200	21,498	28,664	8,468	61,840	636,330	.0234	1,927,229	547	128,819	256	91,348	481	186,146	61,419	16,830	Fairfax
Falls Church*	.610	10,716	10,377	32,569	4,324	66,604	349,010	.0081	510,751	145	11,591	23	11,038	58	53,856	31,489	7,034	Falls Church
Franklin	.620	8,347	8,346	14,802	3,376	30,565	123,550	.0029	144,018	41	3,805	8	6,160	32	26,539	8,339	5,648	Franklin
Fredericksburg*	.630	20,769	19,279	15,743	8,069	32,814	326,970	.0116	865,934	246	108,676	216	48,935	258	61,450	45,844	13,220	Fredericksburg
Galax	.640	6,551	6,837	14,743	2,899	27,132	96,580	.0031	217,986	62	60,600	121	5,046	27	30,380	15,174	4,642	Galax
Hampton*	.650	144,708	146,437	16,802	53,698	37,020	2,431,340	.0490	2,127,173	604	420,800	837	97,218	512	172,091	85,145	96,816	Hampton
Harrisonburg*	.660	41,264	40,468	11,720	13,780	28,766	483,600	.0151	956,977	272	235,070	467	38,810	204	107,221	25,286	28,665	Harrisonburg
Hopewell*	.670	22,404	22,354	15,501	9,019	31,681	347,280	.0055	115,787	33	2,714	5	4,953	26	24,955	9,884	15,317	Hopewell
Lexington	.678	6,909	6,867	10,494	2,163	27,620	72,500	.0025	163,045	46	17,580	35	5,468	29	22,374	20,339	3,376	Lexington
Lynchburg*	.680	64,615	65,269	15,188	25,910	31,385	981,370	.0264	1,586,593	451	272,942	543	57,803	304	137,909	133,853	42,569	Lynchburg
Manassas*	.683	38,088	35,135	21,209	12,001	55,394	807,790	.0185	1,049,143	298	194,037	386	25,144	132	154,411	32,309	23,872	Manassas
Manassas Park*	.685	11,429	10,290	23,175	3,914	56,265	264,870	.0036	59,571	17	...	...	...	...	13,893	2,182	8,318	Manassas Park
Martinsville**	.690	14,971	15,416	13,860	6,389	26,513	207,500	.0058	348,066	99	119,065	237	22,912	121	35,056	15,987	10,085	Martinsville
Newport News*	.700	182,551	180,150	16,595	71,189	34,888	3,029,380	.0568	2,128,411	604	277,991	553	100,964	531	239,986	69,935	120,794	Newport News
Norfolk*	.710	238,106	234,403	13,459	86,008	30,737	3,204,570	.0633	2,280,371	648	361,702	719	130,039	684	264,008	85,054	128,884	Norfolk
Norton	.720	3,886	3,904	11,963	1,696	22,226	46,490	.0021	173,449	49	68,801	137	12,683	67	18,752	6,387	2,612	Norton
Petersburg*	.730	32,717	33,740	13,883	13,295	28,131	454,200	.0093	374,084	106	2,500	5	5,711	30	45,825	23,610	19,674	Petersburg
Poquoson*	.735	11,837	11,566	24,260	4,229	55,605	287,160	.0038	54,561	15	...	...	...	...	19,197	3,578	9,796	Poquoson
Portsmouth*	.740	98,061	100,565	15,144	37,291	32,573	1,485,070	.0243	559,132	159	19,630	39	11,724	62	141,144	96,294	60,571	Portsmouth

Source: Devonshire Associates Ltd. and Scan/US, Inc. 2005.
* Component of a Metropolitan Core Based Statistical Area.
** Component of a Micropolitan Core Based Statistical Area.

...Data less than 1,000. (d) Data not available.
[3] Clifton Forge independent city merged with Alleghany county on July 1, 2001.

Continued on next page

Counties: Population/Income/Sales, *Continued*

County or County Equivalent	FIPS County Code	Population Estimate 7/1/05	Population Census 4/1/00	Per Capita Income 2004	Households Estimate 7/1/05	Median Household Income 2004	Disposable Income 2004 ($1,000)	Market Ability Index 2004	Total Retail Sales 2004 Sales ($1,000)	Total Retail Sales Ranally Sales Units	General Merchandise 2004 Sales ($1,000)	General Merchandise Ranally Sales Units	Apparel Store 2004 Sales ($1,000)	Apparel Store Ranally Sales Units	Food Store Sales 2004 ($1,000)	Health & Drug Store 2004 ($1,000)	Passenger Car Registrations 2004	County or County Equivalent
Radford*	.750	14,413	15,859	11,817	5,792	24,414	170,320	.0032	88,992	25	...	...	1,767	9	14,926	7,720	11,142	Radford
Richmond*	.760	191,700	197,790	15,549	81,933	30,215	2,980,720	.0582	2,273,802	646	157,737	314	159,049	837	381,907	185,742	114,269	Richmond
Roanoke*	.770	91,029	94,911	16,372	41,716	29,563	1,490,350	.0405	2,518,073	715	506,736	1,008	144,120	759	212,407	129,276	67,700	Roanoke
Salem*	.775	24,289	24,747	18,210	9,937	36,316	442,310	.0104	582,392	165	50,454	100	8,422	44	88,008	21,055	18,794	Salem
Staunton**	.790	23,887	23,853	15,353	9,516	31,754	366,740	.0091	503,561	143	154,204	307	13,219	70	66,080	27,679	16,860	Staunton
Suffolk*	.800	79,362	63,677	16,410	27,724	38,686	1,302,310	.0217	595,794	169	102,476	204	4,758	25	87,531	22,240	52,159	Suffolk
Virginia Beach*	.810	447,757	425,257	19,490	160,377	44,630	8,726,910	.1461	4,702,261	1,335	626,959	1,247	309,382	1,628	678,813	207,923	365,791	Virginia Beach
Waynesboro**	.820	20,940	19,520	15,575	8,463	31,209	326,150	.0066	270,731	77	33,805	67	10,692	56	61,297	18,255	14,949	Waynesboro
Williamsburg*	.830	11,046	11,998	16,707	4,197	36,615	184,540	.0068	523,921	149	5,676	11	78,957	416	75,931	23,110	6,818	Williamsburg
Winchester*	.840	24,730	23,585	16,908	10,413	33,158	418,130	.0135	966,374	274	296,218	589	42,132	222	110,724	52,134	17,712	Winchester
Virginia Total		**7,538,791**	**7,078,515**	**21,002**	**2,846,317**	**44,120**	**158,329,450**	**2.6441**	**89,195,181**	**25,329**	**13,870,118**	**27,583**	**4,762,573**	**25,068**	**12,155,350**	**4,663,419**	**5,690,714**	**Virginia**

Washington (WA; Code 53; 39 Counties)

County or County Equivalent	FIPS County Code	Population Estimate 7/1/05	Population Census 4/1/00	Per Capita Income 2004	Households Estimate 7/1/05	Median Household Income 2004	Disposable Income 2004 ($1,000)	Market Ability Index 2004	Total Retail Sales 2004 Sales ($1,000)	Total Retail Sales Ranally Sales Units	General Merchandise 2004 Sales ($1,000)	General Merchandise Ranally Sales Units	Apparel Store 2004 Sales ($1,000)	Apparel Store Ranally Sales Units	Food Store Sales 2004 ($1,000)	Health & Drug Store 2004 ($1,000)	Passenger Car Registrations 2004	County or County Equivalent
Adams	.001	16,743	16,428	13,219	5,465	32,927	221,330	.0042	136,463	39	19,880	40	2,257	12	12,277	8,121	11,073	Adams
Asotin*	.003	20,584	20,551	16,888	8,687	32,114	347,630	.0062	208,351	59	87,948	175	2,042	11	36,156	13,965	17,092	Asotin
Benton*	.005	161,100	142,475	19,866	59,142	43,399	3,200,350	.0544	1,848,040	525	481,142	957	64,535	340	363,801	80,875	121,522	Benton
Chelan*	.007	68,844	66,616	16,899	26,298	35,425	1,163,400	.0234	1,016,516	289	174,577	347	19,976	105	149,012	39,268	50,806	Chelan
Clallam**	.009	68,528	64,525	18,414	29,213	34,762	1,261,880	.0212	653,227	185	140,515	279	19,624	103	156,332	34,902	53,778	Clallam
Clark*	.011	401,099	345,238	19,696	142,782	44,582	7,899,990	.1258	3,525,551	1,001	722,397	1,437	109,090	574	564,363	200,372	305,086	Clark
Columbia	.013	4,190	4,064	16,826	1,757	32,235	70,500	.0012	30,303	9	9,821	20	...	...	2,674	...	3,609	Columbia
Cowlitz*	.015	96,590	92,948	18,627	38,508	37,449	1,799,210	.0308	1,018,200	289	228,810	455	18,571	98	178,499	42,485	76,338	Cowlitz
Douglas*	.017	34,494	32,603	16,919	12,774	36,332	583,620	.0100	305,078	87	85,292	170	11,336	60	90,506	8,881	26,183	Douglas
Ferry	.019	7,518	7,260	14,159	2,973	28,881	106,450	.0018	45,601	13	...	...	1,173	6	9,768	...	6,155	Ferry
Franklin*	.021	60,835	49,347	13,161	17,526	36,658	800,620	.0170	696,854	198	59,305	118	4,522	24	39,807	25,464	35,853	Franklin
Garfield	.023	2,357	2,397	16,309	982	32,080	38,440	.0006	13,001	4	...	...	...	...	4,141	...	1,939	Garfield
Grant**	.025	81,412	74,698	13,765	27,001	33,226	1,120,600	.0217	755,475	215	99,885	199	14,144	74	128,324	29,193	53,991	Grant
Grays Harbor**	.027	70,148	67,194	15,996	27,800	32,440	1,122,090	.0195	587,646	167	100,097	199	8,968	47	149,230	46,775	51,185	Grays Harbor
Island**	.029	81,610	71,558	19,687	30,606	42,017	1,606,630	.0234	459,975	131	41,637	83	7,139	38	102,588	27,578	62,185	Island
Jefferson	.031	28,498	25,953	20,097	12,791	35,975	572,720	.0087	210,864	60	25,311	50	5,042	27	62,831	5,764	24,564	Jefferson
King*	.033	1,776,888	1,737,034	25,356	740,874	49,031	45,055,510	.7566	28,773,498	8,170	4,043,337	8,041	1,871,552	9,850	3,667,624	1,227,647	1,373,484	King
Kitsap*	.035	241,196	231,969	20,793	92,982	43,330	5,015,170	.0800	2,360,051	670	567,682	1,129	73,505	387	316,380	119,693	184,355	Kitsap
Kittitas**	.037	36,010	33,362	16,082	14,841	30,928	579,130	.0103	332,098	94	28,287	56	4,059	21	68,094	7,038	29,736	Kittitas
Klickitat	.039	19,961	19,161	16,190	7,947	32,664	323,170	.0048	75,654	21	5,490	11	...	...	20,637	3,445	16,443	Klickitat
Lewis**	.041	72,039	68,600	16,017	27,409	33,876	1,153,860	.0222	861,472	245	175,188	348	35,148	185	158,325	41,544	57,132	Lewis
Lincoln	.043	10,268	10,184	17,350	4,268	33,432	178,150	.0028	68,572	19	...	...	1,418	7	7,006	4,041	9,237	Lincoln
Mason**	.045	54,163	49,405	17,609	20,603	36,990	953,750	.0149	343,830	98	60,371	120	4,781	25	79,701	14,220	42,668	Mason
Okanogan	.047	38,804	39,564	14,472	15,909	28,640	561,590	.0096	242,328	69	40,294	80	...	...	60,482	12,549	31,525	Okanogan
Pacific	.049	21,260	20,984	16,303	9,354	29,928	346,600	.0054	115,523	33	11,946	24	2,396	13	27,479	13,959	16,880	Pacific
Pend Oreille	.051	12,561	11,732	14,727	4,900	30,604	184,990	.0028	43,398	12	1,675	3	...	...	23,154	...	10,093	Pend Oreille
Pierce*	.053	765,698	700,820	19,356	283,473	42,060	14,820,820	.2482	7,947,017	2,257	1,476,200	2,936	288,392	1,518	1,044,483	335,167	586,648	Pierce
San Juan	.055	15,292	14,077	24,167	7,337	40,195	369,560	.0053	127,270	36	3,067	6	1,447	8	56,361	9,805	14,175	San Juan
Skagit*	.057	113,129	102,979	18,878	42,775	40,059	2,135,630	.0395	1,562,875	444	309,228	615	69,381	365	201,334	68,712	87,761	Skagit
Skamania*	.059	10,526	9,872	17,495	3,953	37,316	184,150	.0025	20,562	6	...	...	...	...	7,133	...	8,815	Skamania
Snohomish*	.061	659,426	606,024	23,485	255,643	48,830	15,486,600	.2411	7,278,603	2,067	1,241,281	2,469	356,259	1,875	1,036,480	254,645	553,617	Snohomish
Spokane*	.063	439,273	417,939	18,223	180,505	35,565	8,004,860	.1437	5,223,271	1,483	985,255	1,959	248,626	1,309	753,870	200,787	357,490	Spokane
Stevens	.065	41,414	40,066	15,683	15,778	33,021	649,490	.0106	255,115	72	52,334	104	6,787	36	72,335	8,703	33,444	Stevens
Thurston*	.067	229,500	207,355	21,189	90,231	43,121	4,862,910	.0830	2,958,276	840	761,569	1,515	83,210	438	469,563	106,737	176,941	Thurston
Wahkiakum	.069	3,639	3,824	20,632	1,625	36,850	75,080	.0010	9,195	3	1,718	3	...	...	...	...	3,476	Wahkiakum
Walla Walla**	.071	57,748	55,180	15,167	20,655	34,127	875,850	.0155	462,889	131	76,510	152	16,841	89	100,251	19,940	38,749	Walla Walla
Whatcom*	.073	182,534	166,814	18,455	71,812	37,510	3,368,700	.0612	2,303,589	654	435,895	867	99,789	525	459,114	114,322	139,293	Whatcom
Whitman**	.075	39,812	40,740	14,027	16,288	27,361	558,450	.0100	293,515	83	61,342	122	4,183	22	21,506	10,623	30,545	Whitman
Yakima*	.077	229,468	222,581	13,955	77,113	33,372	3,202,190	.0607	2,041,424	580	479,903	954	65,560	345	329,172	58,849	167,079	Yakima
Washington Total		**6,275,159**	**5,894,121**	**20,854**	**2,450,580**	**42,730**	**130,861,670**	**2.2016**	**75,211,170**	**21,358**	**13,095,191**	**26,043**	**3,524,707**	**18,553**	**11,031,248**	**3,198,774**	**4,870,945**	**Washington**

West Virginia (WV; Code 54; 55 Counties)

County or County Equivalent	FIPS County Code	Population Estimate 7/1/05	Population Census 4/1/00	Per Capita Income 2004	Households Estimate 7/1/05	Median Household Income 2004	Disposable Income 2004 ($1,000)	Market Ability Index 2004	Total Retail Sales 2004 Sales ($1,000)	Total Retail Sales Ranally Sales Units	General Merchandise 2004 Sales ($1,000)	General Merchandise Ranally Sales Units	Apparel Store 2004 Sales ($1,000)	Apparel Store Ranally Sales Units	Food Store Sales 2004 ($1,000)	Health & Drug Store 2004 ($1,000)	Passenger Car Registrations 2004	County or County Equivalent
Barbour	.001	15,652	15,557	12,076	6,009	23,871	189,010	.0033	73,481	21	5,708	11	...	...	12,777	7,839	11,283	Barbour
Berkeley*	.003	91,401	75,905	17,576	33,175	36,903	1,606,430	.0263	722,840	205	122,684	244	58,730	309	91,626	49,106	65,438	Berkeley
Boone*	.005	25,896	25,535	12,723	10,090	25,000	329,480	.0060	166,016	47	8,151	16	...	...	33,804	24,818	17,180	Boone
Braxton	.007	14,918	14,702	11,900	5,681	23,584	177,520	.0038	144,557	41	4,131	8	5,587	29	23,057	8,801	10,309	Braxton
Brooke*	.009	24,717	25,447	16,842	9,971	31,608	416,290	.0062	111,841	32	8,487	17	1,445	8	24,096	17,044	18,368	Brooke
Cabell*	.011	93,961	96,784	15,407	39,898	27,801	1,447,660	.0304	1,347,087	383	242,420	482	84,013	442	121,728	204,652	65,870	Cabell
Calhoun	.013	7,207	7,582	11,687	3,028	20,860	84,230	.0014	26,441	8	3,319	7	...	...	7,357	4,235	5,392	Calhoun
Clay*	.015	10,320	10,330	11,138	3,951	21,773	114,940	.0022	53,986	15	3,338	7	...	...	14,673	1,538	7,038	Clay
Doddridge**	.017	7,502	7,403	12,565	2,760	25,810	94,260	.0014	13,428	4	3,278	7	...	...	...	...	5,310	Doddridge
Fayette**	.019	47,157	47,579	12,563	18,684	24,068	592,410	.0117	397,402	113	86,024	171	10,381	55	54,226	28,193	31,869	Fayette
Gilmer	.021	6,947	7,160	11,471	2,714	22,091	79,690	.0014	24,647	7	2,211	4	...	...	7,767	1,812	5,018	Gilmer
Grant	.023	11,543	11,299	14,515	4,646	27,416	167,550	.0028	60,861	17	1,819	4	...	...	8,198	7,252	9,065	Grant
Greenbrier	.025	34,969	34,453	14,078	14,438	26,054	492,280	.0100	398,013	113	94,446	188	9,891	52	35,504	17,947	27,186	Greenbrier
Hampshire*	.027	21,905	20,203	14,706	8,028	30,520	322,140	.0050	84,504	24	2,867	6	...	...	13,372	9,914	17,083	Hampshire
Hancock*	.029	31,270	32,667	18,087	13,234	32,446	565,580	.0092	250,361	71	65,860	131	12,418	65	54,340	18,873	24,515	Hancock
Hardy	.031	13,308	12,669	16,068	5,321	31,153	213,830	.0035	91,299	26	14,868	30	1,395	7	23,490	...	10,983	Hardy
Harrison**	.033	67,829	68,652	15,320	27,065	29,288	1,039,160	.0225	1,044,191	297	219,072	436	50,513	266	104,319	66,857	48,047	Harrison
Jackson	.035	28,355	28,000	15,866	10,982	31,691	449,890	.0093	405,522	115	75,321	150	2,500	13	39,764	19,380	21,256	Jackson
Jefferson*	.037	49,069	42,190	19,945	17,962	41,607	978,660	.0148	345,418	98	21,568	43	3,999	21	59,862	42,797	38,998	Jefferson
Kanawha*	.039	193,206	200,073	18,539	84,325	32,253	3,581,870	.0700	3,027,557	860	535,250	1,064	139,779	736	303,260	256,471	140,208	Kanawha
Lewis	.041	17,217	16,919	13,489	6,744	26,282	232,240	.0046	169,851	48	50,943	101	2,492	13	14,240	7,997	12,374	Lewis
Lincoln*	.043	22,614	22,108	11,284	8,654	22,157	255,170	.0043	69,518	20	7,930	16	...	...	28,774	2,265	14,560	Lincoln
Logan	.045	36,230	37,710	12,845	14,772	23,927	465,380	.0105	476,546	135	73,984	147	13,947	73	68,700	53,166	24,434	Logan
McDowell	.047	24,188	27,329	9,850	10,691	16,585	238,260	.0046	110,564	31	31,637	63	...	...	18,854	17,862	16,190	McDowell
Marion**	.049	56,491	56,598	14,717	22,825	27,826	831,350	.0155	522,818	148	120,843	240	8,107	43	78,585	38,941	41,144	Marion
Marshall*	.051	34,564	35,519	15,453	13,637	30,193	534,120	.0090	234,577	67	52,411	104	4,688	25	43,104	10,488	25,542	Marshall
Mason**	.053	26,170	25,957	13,936	10,509	26,568	364,700	.0059	115,143	33	4,248	8	...	...	20,359	20,647	19,610	Mason
Mercer**	.055	61,684	62,980	14,085	25,631	25,812	868,840	.0187	817,321	232	163,775	326	28,251	149	81,466	72,584	44,629	Mercer
Mineral*	.057	27,200	27,078	15,830	11,058	29,891	430,580	.0076	242,736	69	85,450	170	2,706	14	33,530	19,621	22,126	Mineral
Mingo	.059	27,327	28,253	11,487	11,328	20,924	313,910	.0061	179,744	51	8,662	17	1,693	9	33,089	16,337	18,039	Mingo
Monongalia*	.061	84,446	81,866	14,264	32,976	28,026	1,204,510	.0241	929,642	264	188,870	376	68,319	360	99,454	64,972	59,517	Monongalia
Monroe	.063	13,636	14,583	14,077	5,371	27,182	191,960	.0029	37,644	11	3,664	7	...	...	7,670	1,970	11,124	Monroe
Morgan*	.065	15,940	14,943	17,763	6,481	33,099	283,150	.0043	85,207	24	4,317	9	...	...	12,774	9,534	13,469	Morgan
Nicholas	.067	26,107	26,562	14,049	10,735	26,081	366,770	.0074	288,740	82	56,776	113	7,892	42	25,649	22,130	19,864	Nicholas
Ohio*	.069	44,633	47,427	16,162	18,612	29,924	721,360	.0131	448,707	127	21,558	43	7,107	37	58,508	30,628	29,720	Ohio
Pendleton	.071	7,742	8,196	16,166	3,302	28,905	125,160	.0019	38,848	11	2,019	4	...	...	5,405	6,610	7,135	Pendleton
Pleasants*	.073	7,347	7,514	15,600	2,795	31,247	114,610	.0020	58,761	17	7,305	15	...	...	6,958	1,661	5,172	Pleasants
Pocahontas	.075	8,908	9,131	13,852	3,694	25,493	123,390	.0022	61,567	17	1,044	2	2,242	12	6,133	6,327	7,117	Pocahontas
Preston*	.077	30,071	29,334	13,341	11,328	26,967	401,180	.0072	199,545	57	21,325	42	...	...	18,685	14,397	22,510	Preston
Putnam*	.079	53,879	51,589	19,799	20,566	39,330	1,066,760	.0175	540,817	154	52,442	104	3,754	20	67,857	29,053	41,207	Putnam
Raleigh**	.081	79,333	79,220	14,064	31,178	27,201	1,115,770	.0238	1,031,087	293	229,306	456	20,084	106	88,109	75,911	54,273	Raleigh
Randolph	.083	28,261	28,262	13,469	10,865	26,597	380,660	.0076	280,447	80	74,896	149	6,541	34	35,149	18,109	19,197	Randolph
Ritchie	.085	10,628	10,343	13,514	4,038	26,879	143,630	.0024	47,385	13	3,282	7	...	...	9,579	5,784	7,856	Ritchie
Roane	.087	15,339	15,446	12,361	6,048	23,876	189,600	.0036	105,965	30	3,241	6	...	...	25,201	12,188	10,886	Roane
Summers	.089	13,710	12,999	10,643	5,319	20,795	145,920	.0026	49,609	14	7,320	15	...	...	13,291	7,008	9,652	Summers
Taylor**	.091	16,183	16,089	13,088	6,123	26,160	211,800	.0035	69,979	20	6,198	12	...	...	10,916	2,312	11,156	Taylor
Tucker	.093	7,068	7,321	13,981	2,950	25,496	98,820	.0018	56,421	16	...	...	...	...	12,105	5,483	5,413	Tucker
Tyler	.095	9,336	9,592	14,734	3,704	28,329	137,560	.0021	30,632	9	4,590	9	...	...	9,459	3,486	6,967	Tyler
Upshur	.097	23,976	23,404	12,898	8,946	26,590	309,240	.0063	236,531	67	22,201	44	2,574	14	39,867	11,798	17,027	Upshur
Wayne*	.099	42,169	42,903	14,011	16,939	26,447	590,820	.0100	239,759	68	52,697	105	2,590	14	25,858	15,352	29,664	Wayne
Webster	.101	9,827	9,719	10,867	3,942	20,406	106,790	.0019	41,455	12	7,038	14	...	...	12,820	1,716	7,052	Webster
Wetzel	.103	16,750	17,693	16,016	6,938	29,245	268,260	.0051	195,487	56	33,819	67	2,941	15	33,434	20,075	12,582	Wetzel
Wirt*	.105	5,752	5,873	14,976	2,239	29,379	86,140	.0013	14,091	4	1,926	4	...	...	4,642	...	4,496	Wirt
Wood*	.107	87,089	87,986	17,177	35,693	31,882	1,495,930	.0307	1,384,558	393	359,685	715	54,147	285	97,914	88,717	64,629	Wood
Wyoming	.109	24,416	25,708	12,761	10,164	23,151	311,580	.0055	134,936	38	18,236	36	...	...	26,965	27,653	17,213	Wyoming
West Virginia Total		**1,813,363**	**1,808,344**	**15,258**	**728,757**	**28,840**	**27,668,800**	**.5188**	**18,336,092**	**5,208**	**3,305,329**	**6,574**	**628,422**	**3,309**	**2,208,983**	**1,532,224**	**1,313,962**	**West Virginia**

Wisconsin (WI; Code 55; 72 Counties)

County or County Equivalent	FIPS County Code	Population Estimate 7/1/05	Population Census 4/1/00	Per Capita Income 2004	Households Estimate 7/1/05	Median Household Income 2004	Disposable Income 2004 ($1,000)	Market Ability Index 2004	Total Retail Sales 2004 Sales ($1,000)	Total Retail Sales Ranally Sales Units	General Merchandise 2004 Sales ($1,000)	General Merchandise Ranally Sales Units	Apparel Store 2004 Sales ($1,000)	Apparel Store Ranally Sales Units	Food Store Sales 2004 ($1,000)	Health & Drug Store 2004 ($1,000)	Passenger Car Registrations 2004	County or County Equivalent
Adams	.001	20,816	18,643	15,791	8,569	32,125	328,710	.0051	97,223	28	15,007	30	1,173	6	16,791	...	17,033	Adams
Ashland	.003	16,683	16,866	14,694	6,782	30,563	245,140	.0052	223,432	63	46,578	93	5,079	27	23,100	8,544	11,688	Ashland
Barron	.005	45,819	44,963	17,471	19,008	35,338	800,520	.0155	639,793	182	163,277	325	14,199	75	82,512	15,637	37,106	Barron
Bayfield	.007	15,215	15,013	15,897	6,368	31,760	241,870	.0037	65,441	19	4,870	10	...	...	14,075	2,125	12,778	Bayfield
Brown*	.009	238,847	226,778	20,437	95,295	43,168	4,881,200	.0880	3,453,490	981	921,590	1,833	93,558	492	323,144	107,664	175,861	Brown
Buffalo	.011	13,896	13,804	17,512	5,776	35,325	243,340	.0037	73,754	21	11,016	22	...	...	12,097	...	12,046	Buffalo
Burnett	.013	16,745	15,674	16,364	6,997	32,630	274,020	.0044	99,631	28	5,950	12	1,034	5	17,618	3,526	14,033	Burnett
Calumet*	.015	45,019	40,631	21,876	17,222	48,158	984,840	.0145	343,304	97	33,645	67	4,592	24	90,621	...	35,239	Calumet
Chippewa*	.017	59,690	55,195	17,496	23,499	37,124	1,044,340	.0196	757,829	215	113,447	226	5,573	29	68,156	20,588	47,474	Chippewa
Clark	.019	34,159	33,557	14,067	12,238	32,898	480,530	.0088	268,710	76	22,650	45	...	...	37,179	7,217	24,669	Clark
Columbia*	.021	55,054	52,468	19,676	21,669	41,815	1,083,230	.0180	569,976	162	71,460	142	8,379	44	71,548	22,669	43,477	Columbia
Crawford	.023	16,875	17,243	15,890	6,883	32,500	268,150	.0056	250,633	71	71,113	141	7,596	40	31,910	6,051	13,076	Crawford
Dane*	.025	463,177	426,526	22,795	196,124	45,190	10,558,140	.1825	6,977,606	1,981	914,396	1,818	244,878	1,289	756,141	323,059	360,324	Dane
Dodge**	.027	88,215	85,897	18,638	32,806	41,855	1,644,110	.0269	780,863	222	163,556	325	15,089	79	77,920	14,294	64,519	Dodge
Door	.029	28,616	27,961	19,711	12,780	36,904	564,060	.0101	384,993	109	54,190	108	18,145	96	63,739	12,974	25,343	Door
Douglas*	.031	44,257	43,287	16,552	18,288	33,707	732,530	.0132	449,971	128	77,784	155	5,755	30	70,047	14,707	34,226	Douglas
Dunn**	.033	41,813	39,858	16,384	15,674	36,517	685,080	.0129	487,724	138	90,814	181	4,456	23	49,757	55,101	33,839	Dunn
Eau Claire*	.035	94,647	93,142	18,232	38,825	37,181	1,725,580	.0377	1,914,448	544	456,448	908	99,885	526	202,419	78,512	75,962	Eau Claire
Florence**	.037	5,005	5,088	16,943	2,154	32,899	84,800	.0012	18,161	5	...	...	...	...	5,734	...	4,172	Florence
Fond du Lac*	.039	98,664	97,296	19,585	38,452	41,781	1,932,370	.0330	1,116,093	317	218,023	434	23,248	122	144,958	55,570	73,815	Fond du Lac
Forest	.041	9,871	10,024	15,486	4,168	30,949	152,860	.0025	64,275	18	6,745	13	...	...	8,535	...	7,615	Forest
Grant**	.043	49,417	49,597	15,522	18,693	34,348	767,070	.0140	473,549	134	74,787	149	8,356	44	64,121	12,903	37,068	Grant
Green**	.045	34,678	33,647	19,445	13,998	40,320	674,310	.0145	735,651	209	65,089	129	5,930	31	43,972	11,884	27,615	Green
Green Lake	.047	19,181	19,105	18,127	7,813	37,108	347,690	.0064	238,917	68	23,530	47	3,627	19	59,747	6,133	15,255	Green Lake
Iowa*	.049	23,578	22,780	19,379	9,545	39,640	456,910	.0177	1,419,938	403	62,825	125	2,183	11	20,429	4,339	19,892	Iowa
Iron	.051	6,680	6,861	15,937	3,134	28,488	106,460	.0019	56,461	16	1,872	4	...	...	16,059	...	5,522	Iron
Jackson	.053	19,785	19,100	15,669	7,389	35,226	310,010	.0054	164,752	47	30,694	61	...	...	20,383	4,957	14,673	Jackson
Jefferson**	.055	78,765	74,021	19,692	30,006	43,187	1,551,070	.0253	759,282	216	122,446	243	10,206	54	111,528	20,178	59,278	Jefferson
Juneau	.057	25,808	24,316	16,124	10,414	33,557	416,130	.0073	232,305	66	17,344	34	1,616	9	29,903	16,764	20,411	Juneau
Kenosha*	.059	160,165	149,577	19,412	59,894	43,522	3,109,160	.0487	1,281,385	364	195,888	390	91,653	482	198,533	80,426	109,770	Kenosha
Kewaunee*	.061	20,693	20,187	19,059	8,097	40,740	394,390	.0061	145,604	41	6,531	13	...	...	24,342	2,177	17,026	Kewaunee
La Crosse*	.063	109,413	107,120	17,696	43,638	37,140	1,936,220	.0382	1,645,896	467	343,934	684	37,325	196	187,544	47,093	81,311	La Crosse
Lafayette	.065	16,437	16,137	16,212	6,312	35,398	266,470	.0043	105,616	30	...	...	...	...	10,268	4,147	13,027	Lafayette
Langlade	.067	20,949	20,740	16,008	8,782	31,965	335,350	.0071	328,689	93	59,802	119	3,915	21	52,994	1,291	16,496	Langlade
Lincoln**	.069	30,417	29,641	17,744	12,311	36,652	539,710	.0093	300,186	85	43,908	87	4,485	24	35,920	12,675	23,921	Lincoln
Manitowoc**	.071	81,467	82,887	20,138	34,006	40,367	1,640,590	.0259	725,976	206	159,448	317	10,470	55	114,801	16,936	64,155	Manitowoc
Marathon*	.073	128,048	125,834	19,994	51,263	41,676	2,560,230	.0472	1,913,179	543	394,943	785	40,798	215	199,109	39,650	101,039	Marathon
Marinette**	.075	43,337	43,384	16,725	18,179	33,358	724,830	.0126	391,762	111	93,048	185	12,271	65	52,332	24,215	34,609	Marinette
Marquette	.077	14,963	15,832	16,872	6,259	33,845	252,450	.0039	81,864	23	...	...	...	...	12,111	...	12,603	Marquette
Menominee	.078	4,636	4,562	10,550	1,431	29,088	48,910	.0009	24,132	7	...	...	...	...	5,134	...	2,452	Menominee
Milwaukee*	.079	927,823	940,164	17,202	369,437	36,173	15,960,420	.2778	8,974,974	2,548	1,369,742	2,724	368,054	1,937	1,235,264	828,625	620,735	Milwaukee

Source: Devonshire Associates Ltd. and Scan/US, Inc. 2005. ...Data less than 1,000. (d) Data not available.
* Component of a Metropolitan Core Based Statistical Area.
** Component of a Micropolitan Core Based Statistical Area.

Counties: Population/Income/Sales, *Continued*

County or County Equivalent	FIPS County Code	Population Estimate 7/1/05	Population Census 4/1/00	Per Capita Income 2004	Households Estimate 7/1/05	Median Household Income 2004	Disposable Income 2004 ($1,000)	Market Ability Index 2004	Total Retail Sales 2004 Sales ($1,000)	Total Retail Ranally Sales Units	General Merchandise 2004 Sales ($1,000)	General Merchandise Ranally Sales Units	Apparel Store 2004 Sales ($1,000)	Apparel Store Ranally Sales Units	Food Store Sales 2004 ($1,000)	Health & Drug Store 2004 ($1,000)	Passenger Car Registrations 2004	County or County Equivalent
Monroe	.081	42,227	40,899	16,112	16,176	35,343	680,360	.0124	431,576	123	68,545	136	3,628	19	51,477	13,471	31,269	Monroe
Oconto*	.083	37,980	35,634	18,480	15,274	38,607	701,860	.0108	245,415	70	8,079	16	...	...	44,219	8,368	31,626	Oconto
Oneida	.085	37,592	36,776	18,175	16,124	35,498	683,220	.0147	725,885	206	144,857	288	22,055	116	66,859	10,843	30,344	Oneida
Outagamie*	.087	171,486	160,971	21,109	66,869	45,705	3,619,950	.0662	2,722,045	773	441,832	879	116,620	614	278,010	90,879	129,050	Outagamie
Ozaukee*	.089	86,503	82,317	26,089	33,111	56,967	2,256,810	.0363	1,268,092	360	109,246	217	26,263	138	151,177	50,094	67,159	Ozaukee
Pepin	.091	7,443	7,213	16,645	2,920	35,348	123,890	.0026	118,561	34	10,523	21	1,278	7	5,210	1,973	6,028	Pepin
Pierce*	.093	38,572	36,804	20,163	14,383	45,384	777,730	.0109	175,855	50	3,129	6	...	...	38,402	7,955	32,255	Pierce
Polk	.095	44,455	41,319	18,182	17,525	38,351	808,270	.0129	335,837	95	53,414	106	1,231	6	44,037	13,645	36,299	Polk
Portage**	.097	67,357	67,182	19,429	26,944	40,793	1,308,670	.0222	734,357	209	170,669	339	20,832	110	83,416	5,646	53,330	Portage
Price	.099	15,253	15,822	18,191	6,974	33,376	277,460	.0047	152,432	43	13,379	27	1,511	8	31,854	5,073	13,287	Price
Racine*	.101	194,975	188,831	19,876	73,303	44,385	3,875,310	.0640	2,014,987	572	340,901	678	46,824	246	298,620	135,936	134,043	Racine
Richland	.103	18,375	17,924	15,485	7,334	32,624	284,530	.0055	207,455	59	43,739	87	6,853	36	18,149	11,182	14,294	Richland
Rock*	.105	156,477	152,307	19,832	61,510	42,232	3,103,240	.0553	2,090,244	594	382,774	761	34,271	180	272,604	109,715	116,116	Rock
Rusk	.107	15,167	15,347	15,320	6,501	30,301	232,360	.0039	101,510	29	12,311	24	...	...	17,317	4,529	12,561	Rusk
St. Croix*	.109	76,388	63,155	23,216	29,378	50,259	1,773,400	.0281	887,081	252	232,132	462	4,716	25	80,198	13,603	63,751	St. Croix
Sauk**	.111	57,305	55,225	19,836	24,156	39,340	1,136,710	.0215	905,166	257	148,643	296	18,332	96	109,269	34,082	46,347	Sauk
Sawyer	.113	17,102	16,196	15,226	7,082	31,002	260,400	.0051	193,759	55	19,047	38	4,657	25	32,548	3,538	13,444	Sawyer
Shawano	.115	41,250	40,664	17,221	16,547	35,858	710,380	.0118	332,485	94	69,762	139	7,814	41	42,947	10,292	32,855	Shawano
Sheboygan*	.117	114,016	112,646	20,368	45,505	42,758	2,322,260	.0378	1,160,993	330	251,599	500	16,223	85	172,267	56,215	83,247	Sheboygan
Taylor	.119	19,466	19,680	17,431	7,780	36,489	339,320	.0061	219,647	62	39,866	79	1,650	9	21,584	1,049	15,887	Taylor
Trempealeau	.121	27,431	27,010	17,501	11,199	35,848	480,060	.0079	224,085	64	5,265	10	2,025	11	23,694	6,224	22,682	Trempealeau
Vernon	.123	28,805	28,056	14,828	11,227	31,792	427,120	.0076	231,154	66	22,702	45	3,392	18	27,963	14,553	21,642	Vernon
Vilas	.125	22,705	21,033	15,877	9,360	32,328	360,480	.0062	183,367	52	13,050	26	...	...	26,914	9,406	17,766	Vilas
Walworth**	.127	99,826	93,759	18,995	37,087	42,765	1,896,150	.0308	886,238	252	159,285	317	16,158	85	131,383	44,985	74,018	Walworth
Washburn	.129	16,746	16,036	16,450	7,145	32,337	275,470	.0053	213,168	61	24,674	49	2,022	11	31,441	3,381	13,827	Washburn
Washington*	.131	125,320	117,493	23,551	47,535	51,723	2,951,350	.0484	1,673,482	475	163,804	326	18,387	97	185,301	58,399	97,002	Washington
Waukesha*	.133	381,827	360,767	26,377	147,756	57,186	10,071,340	.1637	5,917,022	1,680	976,173	1,941	193,250	1,017	887,937	294,711	324,286	Waukesha
Waupaca*	.135	52,974	51,731	18,292	21,118	38,223	968,980	.0169	575,452	163	92,784	185	4,913	26	86,213	24,747	41,832	Waupaca
Waushara	.137	23,988	23,154	17,402	9,986	35,023	417,450	.0069	199,341	57	11,546	23	...	...	27,795	...	20,344	Waushara
Winnebago*	.139	159,732	156,763	20,158	65,214	41,332	3,219,810	.0561	2,030,094	576	271,497	540	72,095	379	199,281	121,453	121,977	Winnebago
Wood*	.141	75,060	75,555	19,773	31,752	39,521	1,484,150	.0284	1,228,624	349	262,537	522	16,027	84	113,346	16,564	60,313	Wood
Wisconsin Total		**5,543,126**	**5,363,675**	**19,697**	**2,204,953**	**41,215**	**109,182,290**	**1.8976**	**67,422,874**	**19,144**	**11,096,962**	**22,069**	**1,823,731**	**9,595**	**8,263,929**	**3,068,802**	**4,200,034**	**Wisconsin**

Wyoming (WY; Code 56; 23 Counties)

County or County Equivalent	FIPS County Code	Population Estimate 7/1/05	Population Census 4/1/00	Per Capita Income 2004	Households Estimate 7/1/05	Median Household Income 2004	Disposable Income 2004 ($1,000)	Market Ability Index 2004	Total Retail Sales 2004 Sales ($1,000)	Total Retail Ranally Sales Units	General Merchandise 2004 Sales ($1,000)	General Merchandise Ranally Sales Units	Apparel Store 2004 Sales ($1,000)	Apparel Store Ranally Sales Units	Food Store Sales 2004 ($1,000)	Health & Drug Store 2004 ($1,000)	Passenger Car Registrations 2004	County or County Equivalent
Albany**	.001	31,324	32,014	15,236	13,989	27,577	477,250	.0103	473,284	134	123,039	245	6,800	36	46,843	5,588	30,204	Albany
Big Horn	.003	11,058	11,461	15,265	4,374	30,871	168,800	.0028	63,238	18	2,610	5	...	...	11,838	2,173	10,045	Big Horn
Campbell**	.005	38,069	33,698	19,128	12,989	45,187	728,200	.0123	397,319	113	90,833	181	7,730	41	52,620	4,801	32,048	Campbell
Carbon	.007	15,270	15,639	17,226	6,232	34,192	263,040	.0050	196,971	56	12,975	26	1,257	7	28,137	4,748	13,963	Carbon
Converse	.009	12,451	12,052	17,987	4,803	37,870	223,950	.0036	95,666	27	8,608	17	...	...	18,737	5,311	11,129	Converse
Crook	.011	6,046	5,887	17,147	2,450	34,124	103,670	.0016	36,033	10	...	...	...	...	5,269	...	6,279	Crook
Fremont**	.013	36,221	35,804	14,987	14,092	31,253	542,850	.0109	443,569	126	81,415	162	5,870	31	53,388	7,229	30,590	Fremont
Goshen	.015	12,005	12,538	16,199	5,130	30,691	194,470	.0032	83,496	24	8,818	18	...	...	17,191	8,789	11,268	Goshen
Hot Springs	.017	4,459	4,882	17,141	2,134	29,250	76,430	.0012	29,861	8	3,391	7	...	...	9,660	1,254	4,521	Hot Springs
Johnson	.019	7,850	7,075	16,042	3,116	32,686	125,930	.0021	58,478	17	...	...	...	...	6,988	3,804	6,773	Johnson
Laramie*	.021	86,122	81,607	17,927	33,481	37,087	1,543,880	.0305	1,326,732	377	210,135	418	24,046	127	135,941	26,824	71,287	Laramie
Lincoln	.023	15,651	14,573	18,099	5,957	38,292	283,260	.0047	137,996	39	4,729	9	1,170	6	27,398	5,198	13,570	Lincoln
Natrona*	.025	69,348	66,533	17,101	27,462	35,148	1,185,920	.0231	956,827	272	208,531	415	22,617	119	100,078	22,464	58,140	Natrona
Niobrara	.027	2,170	2,407	15,917	1,003	27,712	34,540	.0006	17,115	5	...	...	...	...	4,197	...	2,491	Niobrara
Park	.029	26,709	25,786	17,131	10,902	34,192	457,540	.0088	350,342	99	69,091	137	7,586	40	47,279	7,617	24,108	Park
Platte	.031	8,590	8,807	17,515	3,707	32,659	150,450	.0028	108,659	31	9,556	19	...	...	15,067	1,404	8,679	Platte
Sheridan*	.033	27,462	26,560	17,094	11,541	32,916	469,440	.0090	358,932	102	68,126	135	7,342	39	37,249	4,865	24,162	Sheridan
Sublette**	.035	6,629	5,920	17,669	2,586	38,481	117,130	.0019	46,213	13	5,313	11	...	...	8,958	1,855	5,915	Sublette
Sweetwater**	.037	36,923	37,613	20,667	14,332	43,023	763,080	.0139	564,572	160	95,934	191	14,333	75	72,737	8,285	33,204	Sweetwater
Teton**	.039	18,930	18,251	27,578	8,526	49,862	522,060	.0096	448,453	127	55,108	110	38,506	203	74,010	7,133	18,974	Teton
Uinta**	.041	19,787	19,742	18,471	7,132	41,216	365,490	.0067	258,257	73	36,354	72	1,795	9	38,557	3,558	16,365	Uinta
Washakie	.043	7,703	8,289	17,805	3,331	33,263	137,150	.0025	91,854	26	15,508	31	1,225	6	9,985	2,898	7,082	Washakie
Weston	.045	6,690	6,644	15,419	2,691	31,171	103,150	.0017	41,272	12	6,280	12	...	...	9,429	1,777	6,780	Weston
Wyoming Total		**507,467**	**493,782**	**17,809**	**201,960**	**36,174**	**9,037,680**	**.1688**	**6,585,140**	**1,869**	**1,118,329**	**2,225**	**144,598**	**762**	**831,556**	**138,844**	**447,577**	**Wyoming**
United States Total		**296,460,358**	**281,421,906**	**19,402**	**110,228,421**	**39,828**	**5,752,025,490**	**100.0000**	**3,521,709,000**	**1,000,000**	**502,845,000**	**1,000,000**	**189,997,000**	**1,000,000**	**498,151,000**	**205,404,000**	**203,446,969**	**United States**

Source: Devonshire Associates Ltd. and Scan/US, Inc. 2005.   ...Data less than 1,000.   (d) Data not available.
* Component of a Metropolitan Core Based Statistical Area.
** Component of a Micropolitan Core Based Statistical Area.

Principal Business Centers and Other Places with 30,000 or More: Population/Income/Sales

This table presents, for Principal Business Centers and other selected places over 30,000 in population, July 1, 2005 estimates of population and households; and 2004 estimates of per capita income; median household income; disposable income and market ability index; total retail sales; and general merchandise, apparel, food, and health and drug store sales. Ranally Sales Units are shown for total retail sales, general merchandise store sales and apparel store sales. Also shown are 1997 manufacturers value added and Ranally Manufacturing Units. Source for population, income, and sales estimates: Devonshire Associates Ltd. and Scan/US, Inc. 2005. Place Codes are from the Federal Information Processing Standards (FIPS) of the National Bureau of Standards. Each place carries a number unique in its relationship to the state in which it is located. Central cities of Ranally Metro Areas (RMAs) and suburbs located within them are identified by the abbreviation of the Metro Area name. An alphabetical list of RMAs appears on pages 126-127. The Ranally City Rating classifies Principal Business Centers according to their relative business and economic importance; for a complete explanation, see the Introduction on pages 5-9. A list of cities and other places of 35,000 or more, ranked according to 2000 Census population, appears on pages 129-131. Statistics for Total Retail Sales, General Merchandise Sales, Apparel Store Sales, Food Store Sales, and Health and Drug Store Sales in this edition are estimates based on data from the U.S. Census Bureau, and utilize the 1997 North American Industry Classification System (NAICS).

Place Name	Ranally Metro Area	FIPS Place Code	Ranally City Rating	Population Estimate 7/1/05	Population Census 4/1/00	Per Capita Income 2004	Households Estimate 7/1/05	Median Household Income 2004	Disposable Income 2004 ($1,000)	Market Ability Index 2004	Total Retail Sales 2004 Sales ($1,000)	Total Retail Sales Ranally Sales Units	General Merchandise 2004 Sales ($1,000)	General Merchandise Ranally Sales Units	Apparel Store 2004 Sales ($1,000)	Apparel Store Ranally Sales Units	Food Store Sales 2004 ($1,000)	Health & Drug Store 2004 ($1,000)	Manufacturers Value Added 1997* ($1,000)	Manufacturers Ranally Mfg. Units	Place Type
Alabama																					
Anniston	ANNI	01852	3-A	23,842	24,276	17,724	10,233	29,094	422,580	.0090	441,236	125	62,269	124	15,386	81	67,803	25,077	355,623	195	Inc. Place
Auburn	AU-OP	03076	3-B	44,194	42,987	14,395	19,416	20,725	636,178	.0127	493,548	140	130,138	259	35,714	188	85,747	18,310	149,929	82	Inc. Place
Bessemer	BIR	05980	4-S	28,367	29,672	12,208	11,041	25,308	346,296	.0087	442,701	126	135,454	269	12,684	67	52,806	17,108	162,160	89	Inc. Place
Birmingham	BIR	07000	2-AA	231,588	242,820	14,636	94,182	27,479	3,389,472	.0777	3,832,095	1,088	339,574	675	225,923	1,189	352,494	175,308	1,239,064	678	Inc. Place
Cullman		18976	4-C	13,731	13,995	17,544	5,819	29,912	240,894	.0066	417,152	118	91,897	183	13,130	69	57,787	24,938	281,334	154	Inc. Place
Decatur	DEC	20104	3-A	53,051	53,929	19,002	21,146	35,280	1,008,082	.0212	1,036,872	294	147,219	293	47,248	249	80,906	58,622	1,218,480	667	Inc. Place
Dothan	DOTH	21184	3-A	60,222	57,737	17,982	24,223	33,369	1,082,903	.0246	1,310,356	372	303,254	603	63,789	336	83,677	52,427	622,171	341	Inc. Place
Enterprise		24184	4-B	21,267	21,178	16,838	8,339	35,115	358,102	.0076	358,299	102	91,152	181	11,794	62	26,742	12,615	102,743	56	Inc. Place
Florence	FLO	26896	3-AA	32,128	36,264	16,957	14,162	26,099	544,809	.0137	803,569	228	269,772	536	68,554	361	65,286	35,574	345,750	189	Inc. Place
Gadsden	GAD	28696	3-A	37,087	38,978	15,904	15,704	27,508	589,847	.0120	508,501	144	115,463	230	33,436	176	88,661	28,127	568,276	311	Inc. Place
Homewood	BIR	35800	4-Sm	25,160	25,043	20,931	10,759	38,011	526,623	.0137	869,963	247	244,125	485	69,759	367	64,110	34,662	103,797	57	Inc. Place
Hoover	BIR	35896		64,171	62,742	27,595	25,781	55,788	1,770,773	.0273	888,527	252	150,183	299	31,334	165	90,059	56,572	(d)	...	Inc. Place
Huntsville	HNTS	37000	3-AA	164,021	158,216	22,646	68,841	40,728	3,714,409	.0683	2,928,555	832	655,320	1,303	171,096	901	299,689	112,146	2,668,556	1,461	Inc. Place
Jasper		38416	4-C	13,611	14,052	16,566	5,586	29,628	225,473	.0067	447,868	127	120,632	240	24,505	129	39,627	17,884	57,480	31	Inc. Place
Madison	HNTS	45784		35,125	29,329	24,241	13,279	55,714	851,459	.0128	355,666	101	101,442	202	2,217	12	80,260	21,214	...	...	Inc. Place
Mobile	MOB	50000	2-A	195,666	198,915	14,334	67,034	30,695	2,804,716	.0588	2,492,806	708	434,099	863	129,936	684	271,507	158,574	968,844	530	Inc. Place
Montgomery	MTGY	51000	2-A	202,006	201,568	17,322	79,434	35,565	3,499,065	.0698	3,026,652	859	611,833	1,217	173,811	915	327,188	160,588	901,160	493	Inc. Place
Opelika	AU-OP	57048	3-A	22,979	23,498	16,508	9,221	31,411	379,334	.0086	445,857	127	76,466	152	17,717	93	90,767	12,940	502,652	275	Inc. Place
Selma		69120	4-A	18,934	20,512	12,191	7,785	23,971	230,827	.0050	197,496	56	46,892	93	12,176	64	27,236	13,945	405,078	222	Inc. Place
Talladega		74592	4-C	14,528	15,143	15,192	5,643	29,051	220,703	.0040	125,427	36	29,149	58	5,684	30	27,171	9,283	91,562	50	Inc. Place
Tuscaloosa	TUSC	77256	3-AA	75,894	77,906	17,199	31,568	29,663	1,305,288	.0265	1,180,151	335	210,875	419	60,306	317	90,433	76,788	415,687	228	Inc. Place
Alaska																					
Anchorage	ANCH	03000	2-A	278,263	260,283	23,461	103,824	50,900	6,528,250	.1139	4,510,522	1,281	1,086,418	2,161	230,765	1,215	522,594	52,268	157,819	86	Inc. Place
Fairbanks	FRBK	24230	3-A	30,903	30,224	18,093	11,055	38,762	559,136	.0141	843,316	239	167,085	332	34,133	180	69,555	8,234	(d)	...	Inc. Place
Juneau		36400	4-A	31,260	30,711	26,710	11,972	56,604	834,950	.0123	342,867	97	116,565	232	21,689	114	39,607	9,140	(d)	...	Inc. Place
Ketchikan		38970	4-B	7,585	7,922	26,496	3,520	47,240	200,971	.0041	219,245	62	9,221	18	22,140	117	70,278	6,084	...	...	Inc. Place
Arizona																					
Apache Junction	PHOE	02830		42,941	31,814	17,816	18,658	34,467	765,048	.0109	158,476	45	35,929	71	2,289	12	48,553	10,701	(d)	...	Inc. Place
Avondale	PHOE	04720		51,405	35,883	14,000	14,896	45,369	719,654	.0122	293,427	83	94,914	189	1,135	6	60,228	14,346	(d)	...	Inc. Place
Bullhead City		08220		39,967	33,769	15,467	16,092	28,737	618,181	.0109	326,549	93	84,097	167	12,802	67	41,419	27,676	(d)	...	Inc. Place
Casas Adobes	TUC	10670		58,997	54,011	20,330	23,811	44,269	1,199,391	.0198	634,991	180	136,688	272	39,550	208	145,251	48,296	(d)	...	CDP
Catalina Foothills	TUC	11230		58,762	53,794	38,161	25,938	57,597	2,242,426	.0251	192,121	55	12,483	25	14,274	75	63,175	18,459	(d)	...	CDP
Chandler	PHOE	12000		222,237	176,581	19,711	76,649	52,413	4,380,514	.0681	1,761,811	500	318,790	634	22,237	117	253,805	103,946	3,984,780	2,182	Inc. Place
Douglas		20050	4-B	14,644	14,312	9,821	4,716	20,526	143,812	.0033	120,959	34	29,375	58	7,084	37	42,697	3,745	(d)	...	Inc. Place
Flagstaff		23620	3-A	55,772	52,894	18,337	20,513	38,281	1,022,676	.0183	663,937	189	185,518	369	14,395	76	78,346	15,360	307,423	168	Inc. Place
Gilbert	PHOE	27400		151,950	109,697	19,940	47,858	60,861	3,029,811	.0440	871,599	247	65,101	129	11,385	60	167,241	54,960	150,797	83	Inc. Place
Glendale	PHOE	27820	3-S	254,336	218,812	16,440	85,906	43,284	4,181,298	.0746	2,471,413	702	370,746	737	65,954	347	360,643	111,552	649,555	356	Inc. Place
Lake Havasu City		39370		51,293	41,938	17,349	21,446	33,746	889,898	.0166	630,481	179	91,298	182	11,582	61	129,634	20,784	139,072	76	Inc. Place
Mesa	PHOE	46000	2-S	456,830	396,375	16,845	165,121	40,231	7,695,184	.1538	6,585,896	1,870	1,211,370	2,409	244,222	1,285	807,605	323,928	2,404,733	1,317	Inc. Place
Nogales	NOGLS	49640	4-A	20,329	20,878	10,623	6,302	23,412	215,957	.0061	339,243	96	105,696	210	42,730	225	60,014	11,732	25,820	14	Inc. Place
Oro Valley	TUC	51600		36,123	29,700	24,521	14,759	54,650	885,756	.0111	118,590	34	33,605	67	1,284	7	45,654	1,363	(d)	...	Inc. Place
Peoria	PHOE	54050		151,162	108,364	19,183	53,453	48,390	2,899,694	.0445	1,070,363	304	123,114	245	20,930	110	153,184	44,930	30,265	17	Inc. Place
Phoenix	PHOE	55000	1-A	1,510,889	1,321,045	17,866	521,109	40,564	26,993,077	.4882	17,794,945	5,053	2,464,183	4,900	702,515	3,698	2,164,522	944,603	10,283,805	5,630	Inc. Place
Prescott		57380	4-A	36,460	33,938	21,812	16,382	34,929	795,257	.0151	668,870	190	171,713	341	22,674	119	107,485	31,041	106,421	58	Inc. Place
Prescott Valley		57450		32,047	23,535	14,031	12,311	32,386	449,665	.0073	143,704	41	37,744	75	1,398	7	24,460	3,711	(d)	...	Inc. Place
Scottsdale	PHOE	65000	3-SS	225,617	202,705	33,970	98,660	57,675	7,664,116	.1224	4,766,837	1,354	656,856	1,306	346,335	1,823	493,584	244,844	756,260	414	Inc. Place
Sierra Vista		66820	4-A	40,149	37,775	16,941	15,320	35,869	680,163	.0120	394,164	112	113,090	225	13,730	72	70,444	11,106	(d)	...	Inc. Place
Sun City	PHOE	70320		44,667	38,309	24,492	26,843	32,231	1,093,984	.0148	271,468	77	...	...	12,606	66	92,543	48,642	(d)	...	CDP
Sun City West	PHOE	70355		30,719	26,344	28,124	17,096	40,285	863,951	.0104	92,954	26	7,661	15	4,671	25	31,789	20,371	(d)	...	CDP
Surprise	PHOE	71510		44,192	30,848	18,430	17,454	42,209	814,454	.0110	110,354	31	22,267	44	2,196	12	9,072	4,625	(d)	...	Inc. Place
Tempe	PHOE	73000	3-S	163,483	158,625	19,471	64,054	41,589	3,183,205	.0731	4,043,261	1,148	351,427	699	152,686	804	322,516	183,558	3,345,256	1,831	Inc. Place
Tucson	TUC	77000	2-AA	524,996	486,699	14,941	205,995	31,062	7,844,028	.1560	6,152,409	1,747	904,739	1,799	244,678	1,288	856,739	388,571	1,767,480	968	Inc. Place
Yuma	YUMA	85540	3-A	84,868	77,515	14,452	29,347	31,695	1,226,519	.0244	946,502	269	237,871	473	21,899	115	95,272	60,252	136,486	75	Inc. Place
Arkansas																					
Batesville		04030	4-C	9,320	9,445	16,546	3,793	30,614	154,210	.0033	152,810	43	59,831	119	8,045	42	8,686	6,937	454,299	249	Inc. Place
Benton	L.R.	05290	4-S	23,090	21,906	21,981	9,642	39,082	507,543	.0109	579,671	165	93,543	186	8,168	43	14,728	15,845	54,892	30	Inc. Place
Blytheville		07330	4-A	15,749	18,272	15,462	6,701	28,089	243,518	.0049	204,134	58	51,439	102	6,980	37	22,639	7,339	503,204	275	Inc. Place
Camden		10720	4-B	11,697	13,154	15,816	5,161	28,286	184,997	.0037	150,965	43	37,374	74	7,452	39	20,071	6,927	159,485	87	Inc. Place
Conway		15190	4-C	49,847	43,167	17,586	18,438	36,066	876,605	.0145	418,565	119	136,932	272	18,637	98	20,797	16,646	570,840	313	Inc. Place
El Dorado		21070	4-A	20,846	21,530	15,838	8,693	29,519	330,165	.0067	284,978	81	85,102	169	13,283	70	25,171	20,057	739,456	405	Inc. Place
Fayetteville	FAY-	23290	3-A	65,643	58,047	17,749	27,025	31,459	1,165,102	.0252	1,253,000	356	550,873	1,096	60,529	319	99,348	32,682	449,049	246	Inc. Place
Fort Smith	FTSM	24550	3-AA	81,788	80,268	17,263	33,318	31,628	1,411,924	.0330	1,787,152	507	604,076	1,201	64,745	341	121,327	75,762	1,786,206	978	Inc. Place
Harrison		30460	4-A	12,696	12,152	15,996	5,420	28,985	203,080	.0049	265,813	75	83,038	165	7,465	39	14,488	7,887	210,623	115	Inc. Place
Hot Springs	HTSPR	33400	3-A	37,180	35,750	16,729	16,117	28,005	621,967	.0136	669,022	190	161,042	320	24,238	128	66,936	32,888	180,271	99	Inc. Place
Jacksonville	L.R.	34750	4-S	30,311	29,916	13,986	11,429	33,432	423,918	.0081	277,003	79	68,609	136	4,109	22	28,488	3,396	127,726	70	Inc. Place
Jonesboro	JONES	35710	3-A	59,648	55,515	16,385	24,019	31,659	977,340	.0209	978,202	278	317,528	631	69,348	365	68,328	42,019	469,336	257	Inc. Place
Little Rock	L.R.	41000	2-AA	187,938	183,133	21,622	81,971	38,039	4,063,664	.0792	3,660,338	1,039	757,735	1,507	196,945	1,037	342,629	132,359	977,106	535	Inc. Place
Magnolia		43460	4-B	10,483	10,858	14,517	4,317	27,210	152,179	.0030	118,097	34	37,590	75	8,632	45	15,218	3,432	248,206	136	Inc. Place
North Little Rock	L.R.	50450	3-S	59,512	60,433	18,147	26,068	34,126	1,079,946	.0271	1,610,912	457	367,856	732	71,127	374	119,934	55,420	582,299	319	Inc. Place
Paragould		53390	4-B	23,517	22,017	15,762	9,670	30,564	370,671	.0070	257,422	73	87,860	175	6,260	33	26,055	10,891	390,803	214	Inc. Place
Pine Bluff	PNBLF	55310	3-A	54,348	55,085	13,993	19,688	29,887	760,485	.0164	719,277	204	178,204	354	52,429	276	82,230	77,570	...	...	Inc. Place
Rogers		60410	4-B	45,808	38,829	17,649	15,840	38,059	808,458	.0147	532,805	151	151,317	301	12,891	68	25,336	22,466	533,180	292	Inc. Place
Russellville		61670	4-A	22,843	23,682	16,018	9,185	30,159	365,905	.0093	541,644	154	159,753	318	18,368	97	54,388	20,880	457,849	251	Inc. Place
Searcy		63020	4-C	20,365	18,928	15,306	7,273	31,890	311,715	.0074	393,236	112	147,416	293	20,736	109	20,730	18,336	260,338	143	Inc. Place
Springdale	FAY-	66080	4-B	54,143	45,798	15,573	19,219	35,696	843,175	.0165	642,891	183	182,208	362	12,701	67	65,444	15,477	...	...	Inc. Place
Texarkana	TEXR-	68810	4-B	28,484	26,448	15,269	11,088	29,486	434,920	.0079	258,799	73	59,130	118	8,182	43	51,299	7,621	261,331	143	Inc. Place
West Memphis	MEM	74540	4-S	27,956	27,666	14,078	10,692	26,822	393,572	.0092	460,004	131	119,252	237	10,914	57	36,342	33,259	...	...	Inc. Place
California																					
Alameda	SF-O-	00562	3-S	71,020	72,259	27,854	28,791	52,459	1,978,171	.0272	607,018	172	70,955	141	26,287	138	134,735	59,108	578,741	317	Inc. Place
Alhambra	L.A.	00884	3-S	89,730	85,804	14,054	29,261	37,232	1,261,023	.0268	1,151,551	327	135,780	270	35,080	185	140,117	46,596	175,929	96	Inc. Place
Aliso Viejo	L.A.	00947		43,019	40,166	30,080	17,213	64,203	1,293,993	.0187	539,066	153	96,029	191	32,185	169	89,930	28,081	(d)	...	CDP
Altadena	L.A.	01290		45,104	42,610	21,510	15,064	54,659	970,196	.0124	103,416	29	5,131	10	1,463	8	33,638	26,351	(d)	...	CDP
Anaheim	L.A.	02000	2-S	351,174	328,014	16,520	103,319	46,052	5,801,537	.1077	3,944,186	1,120	363,171	722	115,454	608	652,142	204,089	3,402,548	1,863	Inc. Place
Antioch	SF-O-	02252	3-S	107,455	90,532	18,404	32,580	53,156	1,977,558	.0324	932,473	265	213,203	424	41,609	219	196,839	35,852	61,317	34	Inc. Place
Apple Valley	HESP-	02364		59,511	54,239	16,403	19,414	37,590	976,141	.0149	276,655	79	59,601	119	1,916	10	85,358	24,136	(d)	...	Inc. Place
Arcadia	L.A.	02462	3-Sm	58,581	53,054	22,651	20,340	49,744	1,326,903	.0215	705,349	200	142,280	283	190,576	1,003	110,570	60,065	151,017	83	Inc. Place
Auburn	SAC	03204	4-C	12,632	12,462	27,370	5,576	43,963	345,738	.0073	399,279	113	36,469	73	12,037	63	62,948	29,147	70,443	39	Inc. Place
Azusa	L.A.	03386		49,250	44,712	11,702	13,316	40,108	576,313	.0111	325,421	92	71,582	142	4,262	22	27,232	10,486	488,689	268	Inc. Place
Bakersfield	BAK	03526	2-A	309,140	247,057	15,652	104,326	36,838	4,838,600	.0898	3,160,888	898	500,370	995	162,167	854	388,584	236,186	217,840	119	Inc. Place
Baldwin Park	L.A.	03666		82,385	75,837	9,113	17,750	39,193	750,789	.0155	397,142	113	41,584	83	6,647	35	48,773	23,159	146,985	80	Inc. Place
Barstow		04030	4-C	22,092	21,119	15,479	7,623	35,343	341,966	.0075	350,788	100	29,909	59	79,537	419	33,635	8,208	(d)	...	Inc. Place
Bell	L.A.	04870		39,225	36,664	7,750	9,190	28,756	303,978	.0067	170,176	48	16,924	34	10,604	56	35,850	12,585	68,969	38	Inc. Place
Bellflower	L.A.	04982	4-S	80,301	72,878	12,571	24,763	36,947	1,009,497	.0190	569,391	162	38,318	76	14,390	76	79,850	37,558	(d)	...	Inc. Place
Bell Gardens	L.A.	04996		45,384	44,054	6,830	9,380	28,714	309,982	.0075	199,139	57	18,203	36	14,852	78	38,866	13,792	81,355	45	Inc. Place
Berkeley	SF-O-	06000	3-S	101,172	102,743	28,947	42,798	44,217	2,928,667	.0444	1,425,337	405	6,600	13	84,402	444	336,278	67,122	656,470	359	Inc. Place
Beverly Hills	L.A.	06308	3-SS	36,214	33,784	54,570	15,535	69,475	1,976,180	.0293	1,140,449	324	102,464	204	318,379	1,676	249,247	65,370	21,698	12	Inc. Place
Brea	L.A.	08100	3-Sm	37,733	35,410	23,264	13,876	52,433	877,814	.0198	1,128,657	320	276,072	549	203,418	1,071	100,414	49,562	603,175	330	Inc. Place
Buena Park	L.A.	08786	3-S	84,050	78,282	15,854	24,949	45,244	1,332,493	.0282	1,286,731	365	194,300	386	72,804	383	191,267	61,946	675,959	370	Inc. Place
Burbank	L.A.	08954	3-S	105,804	100,316	20,825	42,200	43,892	2,203,391	.0478	2,524,766	717	345,133	686	211,865	1,115	436,925	308,728	725,796	397	Inc. Place
Burlingame	SF-O-	09066	4-Sr	27,584	28,158	57,399	12,242	71,496	1,583,299	.0227	835,589	237	...	...	51,585	272	107,317	65,113	237,210	130	Inc. Place
Calexico	CLEX	09710	4-B	30,726	27,109	9,353	7,933	27,986	287,388	.0084	447,875	127	72,429	144	73,539	387	117,044	18,467	(d)	...	Inc. Place
Camarillo	OXN-	10046	4-Sr	58,697	57,077	29,581	22,068	59,241	1,736,299	.0257	777,730	221	35,530	71	98,670	519	106,717	47,498	875,556	479	Inc. Place
Campbell	SF-O-	10345	4-S	36,567	38,138	31,448	15,127	61,716	1,149,976	.0191	777,692	221	54,618	109	44,259	233	135,205	36,467	351,993	193	Inc. Place
Carlsbad	SDGO	11194	4-S	88,195	78,247	29,304	34,473	59,854	2,584,432	.0422	1,615,478	459	233,024	463	149,562	787	184,114	75,179	1,482,216	811	Inc. Place
Carmichael	SAC	11390		56,746	49,742	24,230	22,434	43,270	1,374,969	.0192	399,948	114	13,935	28	12,388	65	113,217	31,636	(d)	...	CDP
Carson	L.A.	11530	3-S	94,591	89,730	13,148	25,014	46,974	1,243,685	.0252	937,492	266	204,482	407	30,690	162	111,876	31,612	2,235,168	1,224	Inc. Place
Castro Valley	SF-O-	11964		58,191	57,292	24,956	21,285	56,784	1,452,194	.0199	398,803	113	12,296	24	21,679	114	157,070	39,089	(d)	...	CDP
Cathedral City	PSPR-	12048		55,965	42,647	16,306	18,527	37,318	912,540	.0184	788,380	224	110,336	219	10,186	54	95,974	18,783	(d)	...	Inc. Place
Ceres	MOD	12524		40,078	34,609	12,223	11,543	34,094	489,892	.0095	298,233	85	66,888	133	2,804	15	54,974	29,266	67,702	37	Inc. Place
Cerritos	L.A.	12552	3-Sm	52,832	51,488	19,457	15,178	63,791	1,027,961	.0262	1,608,933	457	259,578	516	121,114	637	5,228	32,621	347,984	191	Inc. Place
Chico	CHICO	13014	3-A	68,339	59,954	16,259	26,892	30,851	1,111,140	.0232	1,052,842	299	209,648	417	44,575	235	141,823	56,951	195,298	107	Inc. Place
Chino	L.A.	13210	4-Sr	74,453	67,168	14,813	18,311	49,757	1,102,844	.0207	714,380	203	99,835	199	54,011	284	131,556	27,664	621,175	340	Inc. Place
Chino Hills	L.A.	13214		88,424	66,787	23,117	25,317	68,934	2,044,062	.0269	374,167	106	53,320	106	9,252	49	121,382	21,583	(d)	...	Inc. Place
Chula Vista	SDGO	13392	3-S	200,903	173,556	16,430	64,961	43,549	3,300,789	.0589	1,960,427	557	516,642	1,027	142,652	751	266,890	134,060	390,041	214	Inc. Place
Citrus Heights	SAC	13588		92,677	85,071	19,413	34,772	40,928	1,799,112	.0319	1,172,104	333	363,465	723	117,655	619	158,690	46,619	(d)	...	Inc. Place
Claremont	L.A.	13756		35,118	33,998	22,343	11,225	58,192	784,637	.0117	291,500	83	1,670	3	7,040	37	52,697	19,232	100,936	55	Inc. Place
Clovis	FRES	14218	4-Sr	79,242	68,468	16,694	27,405	42,149	1,322,896	.0257	1,041,332	296	217,234	432	55,870	294	146,904	50,635	117,467	64	Inc. Place
Colton	RIV-	14890		56,354	47,662	13,635	16,379	34,852	768,387	.0138	388,245	110	52,710	105	5,189	27	67,352	24,994	139,694	76	Inc. Place
Commerce	L.A.	14974	4-S	13,352	12,568	9,080	3,356	31,900	121,242	.0050	357,487	102	4,066	8	74,340	391	9,200	6,596	1,853,748	1,015	Inc. Place
Compton	L.A.	15044	4-Sr	97,467	93,493	8,686	22,399	31,061	846,585	.0167	328,463	93	45,592	91	12,269	65	82,905	14,407	562,951	308	Inc. Place
Concord	SF-O-	16000	3-SS	129,829	121,780	21,379	43,894	52,203	2,775,565	.0530	2,361,279	670	349,918	696	168,712	888	253,977	76,753	167,754	92	Inc. Place
Corona	RIV-	16350	4-S	163,735	124,966	19,471	49,796	54,457	3,188,131	.0497	1,282,003	364	161,694	322	36,088	190	211,978	42,649	859,544	471	Inc. Place
Costa Mesa	L.A.	16532	2-S	115,406	108,724	21,180	41,377	47,066	2,444,277	.0583	3,430,940	974	509,604	1,013	702,912	3,700	263,107	106,058	985,993	540	Inc. Place
Covina	L.A.	16742	3-S	50,522	46,837	16,177	16,588	44,664	817,294	.0156	599,945	170	95,044	189	14,319	75	91,256	31,836	236,567	130	Inc. Place
Culver City	L.A.	17568	3-S	39,821	38,816	22,441	16,425	44,472	893,609	.0179	878,878	250	134,972	268	81,706	430	79,521	32,182	160,294	88	Inc. Place
Cupertino	SF-O-	17610	3-Sm	55,098	50,546	41,661	19,688	82,751	2,295,447	.0326	1,043,661	296	267,766	533	121,250	638	181,140	41,654	188,380	103	Inc. Place
Cypress	L.A.	17750		48,381	46,229	23,739	16,295	56,427	1,148,498	.0163	357,959	102	79,558	158	21,002	111	36,490	28,736	132,698	73	Inc. Place
Daly City	SF-O-	17918	3-Sm	105,630	103,621	17,783	31,346	56,238	1,878,444	.0398	1,923,400	546	446,833	889	161,063	848	237,965	82,974	(d)	...	Inc. Place
Dana Point	L.A.	17946		36,731	35,110	36,444	15,059	58,000	1,338,641	.0166	289,504	82	...	...	18,854	99	85,768	16,943	(d)	...	Inc. Place
Danville	SF-O-	17988		44,392	41,715	47,354	14,796	99,848	2,102,136	.0250	440,920	125	84,855	169	20,858	110	68,906	25,224	(d)	...	Inc. Place
Davis	DAV	18100		67,477	60,308	21,043	25,257	39,515	1,419,890	.0209	469,139	133	3,174	6	6,846	36	105,630	31,585	(d)	...	Inc. Place
Delano		18394		47,283	38,824	7,986	10,236	26,438	377,601	.0087	258,369	73	32,995	66	17,058	90	65,117	17,497	(d)	...	Inc. Place
Diamond Bar	L.A.	19192		60,198	56,287	20,282	18,158	62,261	1,220,955	.0170	272,962	78	27,260	54	7,387	39	62,289	20,670	(d)	...	Inc. Place
Downey	L.A.	19766	3-S	118,310	107,323	15,018	36,025	42,702	1,776,760	.0351	1,369,014	389	277,091	551	84,437	444	133,662	86,167	841,582	461	Inc. Place
Dublin	SF-O-	20018		32,016	29,973	23,942	9,643	67,783	766,538	.0190	1,198,367	340	106,122	211	61,224	322	61,580	20,944	50,125	27	Inc. Place
East Los Angeles	L.A.	20802		131,563	124,283	7,879	30,380	27,219	1,036,587	.0230	601,030	171	127,366	253	49,365	260	109,176	36,012	(d)	...	CDP

Source: Devonshire Associates Ltd. and Scan/US, Inc. 2005.
* Source: 1997 Census of Manufactures.
Not classified as a Principal Business Center.

...Data less than 1,000.
(d) Data not available.

Principal Business Centers and Other Places with 30,000 or More: Population/Income/Sales, *Continued*

Place Name	Ranally Metro Area	FIPS Place Code	Ranally City Rating	Population: Estimate 7/1/05	Population: Census 4/1/00	Per Capita Income 2004	House-holds Estimate 7/1/05	Median Household Income 2004	Disposable Income 2004 ($1,000)	Market Ability Index 2004	Total Retail Sales: 2004 Sales ($1,000)	Total Retail Sales: Ranally Sales Units	General Merchandise: 2004 Sales ($1,000)	General Merchandise: Ranally Sales Units	Apparel Store: 2004 Sales ($1,000)	Apparel Store: Ranally Sales Units	Food Store Sales 2004 ($1,000)	Health & Drug Store 2004 ($1,000)	Manufacturers: Value Added 1997* ($1,000)	Manufacturers: Ranally Mfg. Units	Place Type
East Palo Alto	SF-O-	20956		31,380	29,506	21,111	7,406	59,461	662,465	.0084	61,678	18	...	...	...	...	9,396	...	117,577	64	Inc. Place
El Cajon	SDGO	21712	3-SS	97,440	94,869	17,200	34,113	38,313	1,675,922	.0352	1,648,758	468	276,838	551	107,678	567	167,400	73,583	390,270	214	Inc. Place
El Centro		21782	3-A	38,817	37,835	13,507	12,049	33,062	524,286	.0113	483,256	137	145,154	289	12,590	66	50,592	23,081	(d)	...	Inc. Place
Elk Grove	SAC	22020		68,552	59,984	18,161	20,244	53,930	1,244,947	.0198	516,488	147	47,311	94	16,105	85	157,809	14,245	(d)	...	CDP
El Monte	L.A.	22230	4-S	125,088	115,965	8,430	28,078	31,721	1,054,437	.0304	1,497,038	425	105,832	210	28,302	149	172,414	31,499	484,262	265	Inc. Place
El Segundo	L.A.	22412	4-Sr	16,505	16,033	25,948	6,988	55,920	428,270	.0067	214,076	61	...	...	12,109	64	22,797	16,943	5,336,252	2,921	Inc. Place
El Toro	L.A.	39496		60,888	58,707	24,341	20,646	59,745	1,482,053	.0224	634,437	180	4,201	8	37,841	199	123,946	57,225	161,562	88	Inc. Place
Encinitas	SDGO	22678		60,092	58,014	31,049	23,026	58,830	1,865,814	.0273	822,578	234	34,666	69	46,634	245	152,289	48,231	(d)	...	Inc. Place
Escondido	SDGO	22804	3-S	147,309	133,559	17,553	47,007	42,528	2,585,700	.0515	2,243,013	637	328,867	654	182,568	961	320,382	96,836	296,410	162	Inc. Place
Eureka	EUR-	23042	3-A	26,208	26,128	16,205	11,258	27,743	424,708	.0099	520,798	148	86,071	171	35,709	188	67,644	57,056	61,779	34	Inc. Place
Fairfield	FRFL-	23182	3-C	106,069	96,178	20,568	34,211	48,358	2,181,599	.0369	1,261,234	358	359,819	716	74,721	393	209,525	32,364	561,814	308	Inc. Place
Fair Oaks	SAC	23294		31,953	28,008	27,466	12,180	54,013	877,608	.0115	197,379	56	2,388	5	11,597	61	85,513	5,331	(d)	...	CDP
Fallbrook	SDGO	23462		30,927	29,100	18,132	9,679	44,610	560,781	.0084	168,713	48	...	...	2,994	16	63,090	18,445	(d)	...	CDP
Florin	SAC	24498		31,546	27,653	15,464	9,994	40,394	487,833	.0082	217,369	62	30,509	61	6,657	35	54,629	14,421	(d)	...	CDP
Folsom	SAC	24638		65,265	51,884	25,074	20,677	65,335	1,636,467	.0285	1,157,630	329	176,204	350	89,453	471	138,155	47,699	44,599	24	Inc. Place
Fontana	RIV-	24680	4-Sr	174,749	128,929	13,224	43,992	43,174	2,310,845	.0386	791,090	225	99,300	197	25,615	135	157,302	44,532	460,803	252	Inc. Place
Fountain Valley	L.A.	25380	3-S	57,386	54,978	23,165	18,883	61,733	1,329,337	.0244	1,055,684	300	186,545	371	31,576	166	141,844	61,183	737,093	404	Inc. Place
Fremont	SF-O-	26000	3-SS	208,143	203,413	28,667	67,503	69,075	5,966,779	.0845	2,179,330	619	85,770	171	42,299	223	414,582	135,218	4,280,594	2,343	Inc. Place
Fresno	FRES	27000	2-A	479,143	427,652	13,940	152,211	34,407	6,679,242	.1283	4,449,443	1,263	638,906	1,271	229,253	1,207	709,354	311,113	1,298,165	711	Inc. Place
Fullerton	L.A.	28000	3-SS	132,685	126,003	21,928	45,768	46,500	2,909,552	.0476	1,564,440	444	234,278	466	78,085	411	269,580	81,287	1,202,024	658	Inc. Place
Gardena	L.A.	28168	3-S	62,463	57,746	13,801	21,155	36,463	862,038	.0173	661,992	188	66,050	131	8,449	44	96,094	27,352	469,309	257	Inc. Place
Garden Grove	L.A.	29000	3-S	175,563	165,196	14,215	48,513	43,912	2,495,644	.0460	1,459,663	414	175,293	349	39,482	208	243,479	83,136	1,158,058	634	Inc. Place
Gilroy	SF-O-	29504		45,370	41,464	19,739	12,885	57,679	895,539	.0188	936,452	266	87,678	174	163,149	859	115,576	34,855	145,886	80	Inc. Place
Glendale	L.A.	30000	3-SS	210,003	194,973	17,998	74,523	40,618	3,779,682	.0651	2,123,650	603	247,971	493	75,739	399	290,607	145,883	511,036	280	Inc. Place
Glendora	L.A.	30014	4-S	50,770	49,415	19,868	16,612	54,127	1,008,705	.0163	486,983	138	77,838	155	4,734	25	80,251	26,538	131,403	72	Inc. Place
Goleta	S.BAR	30378		55,972	55,204	21,917	20,479	47,447	1,226,734	.0178	398,414	113	32,384	64	7,225	38	101,890	27,761	(d)	...	CDP
Hacienda Heights	L.A.	31596		56,233	53,122	17,705	16,300	53,203	995,606	.0154	346,484	98	37,691	75	9,578	50	102,381	48,678	(d)	...	CDP
Hanford		31960	4-B	47,941	41,686	15,333	15,415	35,287	735,089	.0134	447,846	127	68,379	136	26,389	139	114,851	26,374	113,947	62	Inc. Place
Hawthorne	L.A.	32548	3-S	92,552	84,112	12,805	30,180	32,105	1,185,143	.0218	611,033	174	78,197	156	39,549	208	97,642	33,107	793,906	435	Inc. Place
Hayward	SF-O-	33000	3-SS	142,700	140,030	17,846	44,217	47,932	2,546,627	.0482	1,925,783	547	183,328	365	78,161	411	270,124	98,537	1,036,271	567	Inc. Place
Hemet	HEM	33182	3-C	69,382	58,812	16,711	29,938	27,524	1,159,440	.0229	961,019	273	204,752	407	14,497	76	131,399	78,181	69,079	38	Inc. Place
Hesperia	HESP-	33434		71,480	62,582	15,120	21,765	38,972	1,080,811	.0173	364,910	104	13,282	26	7,078	37	97,694	22,280	68,444	37	Inc. Place
Highland	RIV-	33588		53,616	44,605	14,457	15,442	38,888	775,100	.0124	234,239	67	68,203	136	8,408	44	57,735	10,604	(d)	...	Inc. Place
Hollister		34120		40,158	34,413	20,257	11,499	53,124	813,482	.0124	308,014	87	45,460	90	...	...	60,998	19,268	105,640	58	Inc. Place
Huntington Beach	L.A.	36000	3-SS	200,325	189,594	28,456	77,371	58,404	5,700,517	.0873	2,840,022	806	200,496	399	193,496	1,018	333,798	195,826	906,253	496	Inc. Place
Huntington Park	L.A.	36056	4-S	66,103	61,348	7,943	15,412	28,962	525,038	.0119	339,237	96	23,410	47	64,166	338	81,084	30,709	301,720	165	Inc. Place
Indio	IND-	36448	3-C	65,001	49,116	12,973	18,488	35,365	843,243	.0162	523,803	149	89,249	177	12,647	67	61,702	26,192	(d)	...	Inc. Place
Industry	L.A.	36490	3-Sm	801	777	7,693	121	45,980	6,162	.0119	1,378,857	392	179,876	358	36,847	194	248,581	95,252	2,335,206	1,278	Inc. Place
Inglewood	L.A.	36546	3-S	115,454	112,580	12,035	36,299	32,888	1,389,454	.0248	574,709	163	92,511	184	20,262	107	132,776	47,331	204,869	112	Inc. Place
Irvine	L.A.	36770	4-Sr	158,626	143,072	29,357	56,468	64,602	4,656,719	.0756	2,866,430	814	236,246	470	108,832	573	235,424	140,454	4,143,406	2,268	Inc. Place
Laguna	SAC	39173		39,140	34,309	22,343	12,318	60,898	874,523	.0124	248,616	71	81,457	162	4,183	22	54,017	1,734	(d)	...	CDP
Laguna Hills	L.A.	39220		32,428	31,178	24,685	11,303	44,599	800,470	.0143	601,852	171	138,181	275	67,797	357	70,262	43,825	59,032	32	Inc. Place
Laguna Niguel	L.A.	39248		67,137	61,891	35,558	25,060	69,049	2,387,234	.0311	686,864	195	120,218	239	32,389	170	97,718	33,225	(d)	...	Inc. Place
La Habra	L.A.	39290	4-S	62,624	58,974	19,474	20,014	46,857	1,219,514	.0221	852,728	242	132,911	264	20,889	110	350,072	32,423	95,388	52	Inc. Place
Lake Elsinore		39486		36,820	28,928	14,779	11,299	38,592	544,151	.0105	389,369	111	59,123	118	49,079	258	94,605	21,368	36,935	20	Inc. Place
Lakewood	L.A.	39892	3-S	84,510	79,345	17,353	27,558	51,619	1,466,478	.0258	867,099	246	204,744	407	111,018	584	194,590	43,867	(d)	...	Inc. Place
La Mesa	SDGO	40004	3-S	54,396	54,749	22,171	23,322	40,933	1,206,031	.0229	1,028,225	292	163,464	325	65,146	343	165,126	45,856	(d)	...	Inc. Place
La Mirada	L.A.	40032	4-S	51,190	46,783	16,662	15,345	54,903	852,944	.0157	563,807	160	17,630	35	12,778	67	74,819	24,173	360,387	197	Inc. Place
Lancaster	L.A.	40130	3-C	125,514	118,718	13,015	38,829	38,263	1,633,509	.0345	1,392,104	395	175,693	349	51,520	271	165,436	112,552	56,845	31	Inc. Place
La Presa	SDGO	40326		34,777	32,721	14,832	10,350	42,901	515,822	.0079	121,589	35	17,308	34	1,510	8	17,349	9,510	(d)	...	CDP
La Puente	L.A.	40340		44,613	41,063	10,198	9,899	42,558	454,972	.0092	264,216	75	41,251	82	5,480	29	38,733	11,689	(d)	...	Inc. Place
La Quinta	PSPR-	40354		35,740	23,694	26,817	12,798	49,401	958,446	.0137	350,520	100	94,728	188	4,620	24	57,539	2,096	(d)	...	Inc. Place
La Verne	L.A.	40830		33,022	31,638	20,044	11,106	55,907	661,891	.0106	309,080	88	56,861	113	14,039	74	48,499	8,563	105,763	58	Inc. Place
Lawndale	L.A.	40886		35,161	31,711	11,689	10,192	38,055	411,000	.0081	257,769	73	47,113	94	5,289	28	32,267	5,819	(d)	...	Inc. Place
Livermore	SF-O-	41992	4-S	76,642	73,345	28,198	26,443	65,600	2,161,167	.0309	815,770	232	146,089	291	13,163	69	156,047	36,295	210,999	116	Inc. Place
Lodi	STOC	42202	4-C	64,381	56,999	17,877	21,687	37,715	1,150,920	.0205	718,732	204	85,336	170	17,141	90	97,690	71,081	220,170	121	Inc. Place
Lompoc	LOMP	42524	4-C	40,222	41,103	14,670	12,900	39,375	590,068	.0106	318,005	90	80,264	160	8,551	45	74,428	22,603	(d)	...	Inc. Place
Long Beach	L.A.	43000	2-S	506,236	461,522	15,747	172,054	37,406	7,971,540	.1350	3,699,729	1,051	454,285	903	153,931	810	634,061	218,546	2,238,957	1,226	Inc. Place
Los Angeles	L.A.	44000	1-AAA	3,909,172	3,694,820	16,805	1,296,650	37,592	65,694,610	1.1132	32,687,410	9,282	3,435,537	6,832	3,118,718	16,415	5,629,688	2,129,160	14,314,915	7,837	Inc. Place
Los Banos		44028		36,108	25,869	13,883	10,262	40,582	501,289	.0087	223,337	63	48,912	97	11,159	59	45,078	7,471	...	...	Inc. Place
Los Gatos	SF-O-	44112	4-Sr	27,211	28,592	56,540	11,303	86,506	1,538,517	.0206	631,574	179	2,440	5	19,008	100	148,950	48,944	80,486	44	Inc. Place
Lynwood	L.A.	44574	4-S	76,973	69,845	7,212	15,256	33,775	555,108	.0117	193,384	55	4,704	9	7,624	40	80,356	14,875	119,863	66	Inc. Place
Madera	FRES	45022		53,993	43,207	11,887	14,240	34,471	641,810	.0118	302,087	86	42,239	84	6,122	32	91,902	21,597	90,532	50	Inc. Place
Manhattan Beach	L.A.	45400	4-S	35,946	33,852	52,051	14,764	86,024	1,871,037	.0238	598,604	170	77,508	154	56,439	297	99,692	35,956	(d)	...	Inc. Place
Manteca		45484		58,389	49,258	16,303	18,036	43,107	951,888	.0164	488,020	139	78,224	156	7,304	38	112,344	26,261	92,914	51	Inc. Place
Martinez	SF-O-	46114		36,334	35,866	24,447	13,551	54,744	888,240	.0131	347,572	99	35,699	71	2,497	13	73,296	20,791	...	...	Inc. Place
Marysville	YUCY	46170	3-B	13,441	12,268	14,615	4,939	28,078	196,445	.0036	119,802	34	10,118	20	...	...	23,724	18,770	41,157	23	Inc. Place
Menlo Park	SF-O-	46870	4-Sr	30,445	30,785	46,833	12,215	75,219	1,425,821	.0207	737,982	210	...	...	23,057	121	172,872	41,363	950,119	520	Inc. Place
Merced	MRCD	46898	3-A	74,941	63,893	13,416	22,791	31,605	1,005,398	.0200	729,766	207	164,638	327	20,632	109	117,894	41,172	208,550	114	Inc. Place
Milpitas	SF-O-	47766		63,514	62,698	24,699	17,253	72,707	1,568,742	.0317	1,622,094	461	188,637	375	310,754	1,636	233,065	64,727	4,486,657	2,456	Inc. Place
Mission Viejo	L.A.	48256		97,578	93,102	28,563	33,893	68,458	2,787,086	.0413	1,232,502	350	206,909	411	72,017	379	193,725	69,033	151,272	83	Inc. Place
Modesto	MOD	48354	2-A	208,952	188,856	16,631	68,637	37,738	3,475,048	.0662	2,568,317	729	459,031	913	131,234	691	316,019	170,690	946,491	518	Inc. Place
Monrovia	L.A.	48648	4-S	38,195	36,929	16,851	13,455	42,539	643,614	.0135	624,281	177	34,164	68	15,663	82	78,713	8,971	395,645	217	Inc. Place
Montclair	L.A.	48788	3-Sm	38,496	33,049	12,136	9,768	36,991	467,193	.0158	1,071,020	304	252,581	502	181,287	954	64,309	31,963	40,858	22	Inc. Place
Montebello	L.A.	48816	4-S	65,468	62,150	12,902	19,091	36,268	844,672	.0192	870,903	247	235,885	469	111,768	588	115,500	46,685	367,836	201	Inc. Place
Monterey	MTRY-	48872	3-BB	29,425	29,674	26,712	12,863	45,693	785,995	.0132	512,630	146	69,686	139	39,871	210	135,325	47,013	80,163	44	Inc. Place
Monterey Park	L.A.	48914	4-S	62,518	60,051	13,918	19,592	38,298	870,137	.0158	468,020	133	1,077	2	33,387	176	149,718	71,070	106,065	58	Inc. Place
Moorpark	L.A.	49138		34,869	31,415	22,811	9,963	67,247	795,385	.0108	174,859	50	24,537	49	1,686	9	55,232	17,457	221,189	121	Inc. Place
Moreno Valley	RIV-	49270		161,665	142,381	14,514	44,844	44,362	2,346,330	.0408	1,109,899	315	225,045	448	57,211	301	206,641	73,501	58,033	32	Inc. Place
Morgan Hill	SF-O-	49278		35,830	33,556	29,333	11,485	71,548	1,051,007	.0149	391,080	111	101,155	201	11,731	62	58,821	16,686	220,090	120	Inc. Place
Mountain View	SF-O-	49670	3-SS	68,284	70,708	35,869	29,989	62,242	2,449,268	.0375	1,364,926	388	273,759	544	40,802	215	253,764	118,985	6,251,610	3,423	Inc. Place
Murrieta		50076		81,049	44,282	20,837	26,399	53,830	1,688,830	.0249	557,232	158	8,992	18	9,837	52	176,940	15,091	71,974	39	Inc. Place
Napa	NAPA	50258	3-S	80,790	72,585	22,757	29,491	47,451	1,838,565	.0290	888,644	252	77,600	154	63,437	334	175,789	48,407	400,475	219	Inc. Place
National City	SDGO	50398	3-S	54,034	54,260	9,897	14,527	29,211	534,767	.0217	1,579,281	448	187,878	374	119,069	627	125,544	48,475	133,607	73	Inc. Place
Newark	SF-O-	50916		43,023	42,471	20,795	12,762	61,210	894,663	.0184	908,437	258	259,765	517	93,807	494	137,359	27,215	337,105	185	Inc. Place
Newport Beach	L.A.	51182	3-SS	74,623	70,032	56,865	35,045	73,454	4,243,420	.0556	1,603,296	455	240,449	478	172,470	908	259,757	89,552	1,295,162	709	Inc. Place
North Highlands	SAC	51924		50,405	44,187	13,884	16,745	32,186	699,830	.0156	719,933	204	57,632	115	4,576	24	92,878	11,820	(d)	...	CDP
Norwalk	L.A.	52526	4-S	111,927	103,298	11,186	28,061	41,834	1,251,964	.0252	791,715	225	134,711	268	15,866	84	158,916	27,283	73,073	40	Inc. Place
Novato	SF-O-	52582		46,515	47,630	25,698	18,595	59,921	1,195,327	.0184	572,832	163	101,984	203	33,094	174	98,864	21,961	122,525	67	Inc. Place
Oakland	SF-O-	53000	2-BB	394,830	399,484	20,901	144,415	40,109	8,252,269	.1270	3,364,473	955	167,794	334	92,103	485	765,992	254,466	1,196,774	655	Inc. Place
Oceanside	SDGO	53322	3-C	176,878	161,029	17,364	60,403	42,582	3,071,242	.0485	1,161,977	330	227,676	453	31,258	165	213,359	68,182	256,252	140	Inc. Place
Oildale	BAK	53448		31,346	27,885	17,169	12,321	31,894	538,188	.0099	360,270	102	24,015	48	1,498	8	48,889	15,088	(d)	...	CDP
Ontario	L.A.	53896	3-S	183,556	158,007	13,445	48,235	40,346	2,467,916	.0524	2,184,261	620	216,236	430	217,532	1,145	261,107	60,642	1,692,554	927	Inc. Place
Orange	L.A.	53980	3-SS	135,977	128,821	21,397	43,044	53,865	2,909,470	.0500	1,823,303	518	206,604	411	185,714	977	129,703	113,025	767,521	420	Inc. Place
Orangevale	SAC	54092		30,467	26,705	22,149	10,716	50,684	674,815	.0089	118,014	34	1,169	2	10,076	53	23,265	1,865	(d)	...	CDP
Oroville		54386	4-B	13,543	13,004	13,048	5,110	27,040	176,716	.0040	182,932	52	27,568	55	2,890	15	37,768	19,695	79,370	43	Inc. Place
Oxnard	OXN-	54652	3-CC	198,439	170,358	14,544	50,757	44,307	2,886,034	.0539	1,806,542	513	211,321	420	98,098	516	216,492	64,915	749,006	410	Inc. Place
Pacifica	SF-O-	54806		35,551	38,390	24,062	12,920	63,116	855,432	.0117	215,702	61	5,183	10	6,227	33	114,241	16,573	(d)	...	Inc. Place
Palmdale	L.A.	55156		130,724	116,670	13,042	37,002	44,503	1,704,907	.0327	1,068,318	303	232,136	462	68,646	361	200,570	38,633	...	...	Inc. Place
Palm Desert	PSPR-	55184		53,835	41,155	31,297	25,283	43,192	1,684,847	.0267	993,113	282	197,913	394	175,439	923	196,196	53,337	40,973	22	Inc. Place
Palm Springs	PSPR-	55254	3-C	46,389	42,807	25,909	22,411	33,927	1,201,889	.0185	579,208	164	19,751	39	70,452	371	148,663	41,412	73,771	40	Inc. Place
Palo Alto	SF-O-	55282	3-SS	56,451	58,598	47,645	24,155	72,129	2,689,602	.0434	1,898,115	539	392,307	780	379,558	1,998	201,512	73,586	1,825,277	999	Inc. Place
Paramount	L.A.	55618		60,926	55,266	9,483	14,812	34,743	577,749	.0118	316,908	90	92,850	185	8,203	43	72,742	13,597	450,626	247	Inc. Place
Pasadena	L.A.	56000	2-S	139,277	133,936	22,596	51,906	43,626	3,147,118	.0536	1,975,003	561	212,507	423	158,841	836	317,258	92,612	207,570	114	Inc. Place
Perris	RIV-	56700		47,519	36,189	11,458	12,760	35,630	544,453	.0144	754,801	214	82,222	164	2,866	15	37,272	8,222	170,290	93	Inc. Place
Petaluma	SF-O-	56784	4-S	56,946	54,548	25,964	20,601	57,113	1,478,527	.0233	771,281	219	77,191	154	52,266	275	106,174	70,111	665,302	364	Inc. Place
Pico Rivera	L.A.	56924	4-S	68,539	63,428	10,828	17,140	39,096	742,174	.0140	339,182	96	85,335	170	9,176	48	60,109	23,845	259,350	142	Inc. Place
Pittsburg	SF-O-	57456	4-S	65,268	56,769	15,308	19,111	44,789	999,114	.0166	411,504	117	95,478	190	27,587	145	98,201	12,410	616,901	338	Inc. Place
Placentia	L.A.	57526		50,755	46,488	20,935	16,326	55,578	1,062,572	.0166	459,494	130	7,626	15	10,003	53	67,233	43,236	288,940	158	Inc. Place
Pleasant Hill	SF-O-	57764	4-Sm	32,902	32,837	28,937	12,885	61,181	952,093	.0157	613,597	174	172,417	343	26,686	140	93,099	29,050	(d)	...	Inc. Place
Pleasanton	SF-O-	57792	4-S	66,329	63,654	36,712	23,553	77,462	2,435,086	.0373	1,371,877	390	272,429	542	158,486	834	218,738	77,317	188,177	103	Inc. Place
Pomona	L.A.	58072	3-SS	166,429	149,473	10,696	40,566	38,065	1,780,097	.0363	1,128,648	320	87,985	175	11,059	58	200,733	60,954	742,598	407	Inc. Place
Porterville	PORT	58240	4-B	46,135	39,615	11,317	13,783	29,892	522,112	.0105	339,281	96	62,850	125	12,321	65	62,017	26,970	96,988	53	Inc. Place
Poway	SDGO	58520		49,020	48,044	25,159	15,341	63,029	1,233,312	.0207	780,216	222	137,272	273	9,892	52	91,987	20,193	104,298	57	Inc. Place
Rancho Cordova	SAC	59444		62,489	55,060	19,458	22,143	41,028	1,215,933	.0213	767,206	218	138,513	275	29,006	153	118,526	22,272	(d)	...	CDP
Rancho Cucamonga	L.A.	59451		156,372	127,743	19,925	47,766	55,765	3,115,723	.0457	944,126	268	190,003	378	28,613	151	221,956	52,098	977,336	535	Inc. Place
Rancho Palos Verdes	L.A.	59514		42,559	41,145	40,634	15,159	81,094	1,729,357	.0187	91,493	26	...	...	5,355	28	8,357	9,321	(d)	...	Inc. Place
Rancho Santa Margarita	L.A.	59587		50,799	47,214	30,844	17,403	72,247	1,566,824	.0195	293,744	83	34,724	69	17,299	91	56,878	13,244	(d)	...	Inc. Place
Redding	REDD	59920	3-A	91,286	80,865	17,356	34,887	33,690	1,584,350	.0288	1,042,406	296	222,710	443	23,053	121	167,814	60,957	77,257	42	Inc. Place
Redlands	RIV-	59962	3-S	66,518	63,591	22,271	23,543	43,714	1,481,422	.0243	815,071	231	139,856	278	22,354	118	139,966	53,517	99,920	55	Inc. Place
Redondo Beach	L.A.	60018	3-S	66,319	63,261	29,841	28,835	61,386	1,979,050	.0305	1,034,643	294	173,196	344	257,448	1,355	149,011	70,102	...	...	Inc. Place
Redwood City	SF-O-	60102	3-S	75,996	75,402	30,069	28,232	65,142	2,285,086	.0358	1,265,958	359	198,484	395	41,208	217	240,981	43,674	632,348	346	Inc. Place
Rialto	RIV-	60466		107,770	91,873	12,791	27,564	38,240	1,378,480	.0225	377,678	107	58,260	116	9,521	50	128,141	27,673	140,246	77	Inc. Place
Richmond	SF-O-	60620	3-S	108,182	99,216	16,514	35,428	40,187	1,786,478	.0282	636,447	181	110,683	220	31,164	164	121,527	33,402	985,497	540	Inc. Place
Riverside	RIV-	62000	2-C	283,180	255,166	18,039	91,644	41,221	5,108,254	.0905	3,170,912	900	559,099	1,112	187,184	985	374,674	189,494	789,082	432	Inc. Place
Rocklin	SAC	62364		50,732	36,330	26,292	19,206	58,528	1,333,849	.0192	487,858	139	127,505	254	1,575	8	107,270	17,406	85,041	47	Inc. Place
Rohnert Park	S.ROS	62546		42,831	42,236	21,224	15,552	47,953	909,050	.0159	604,364	172	118,256	235	17,661	93	136,583	24,165	80,853	44	Inc. Place
Rosemead	L.A.	62896	4-S	55,405	53,505	10,139	13,855	36,229	561,759	.0111	292,363	83	40,120	80	18,272	96	65,615	19,447	86,277	47	Inc. Place
Roseville	SAC	62938	4-Sr	107,649	79,921	25,882	43,113	51,591	2,786,170	.0512	2,318,695	658	200,917	400	77,000	405	234,461	99,272	...	...	Inc. Place
Rowland Heights	L.A.	63218		51,396	48,553	16,213	14,422	49,306	833,273	.0229	1,433,763	407	233,433	464	90,454	476	117,871	29,934	(d)	...	CDP
Rubidoux	RIV-	63260		36,438	29,180	14,302	10,025	42,019	521,134	.0085	172,439	49	9,698	19	2,740	14	42,670	3,790	(d)	...	CDP
Sacramento	SAC	64000	2-AA	441,061	407,018	17,315	159,845	36,327	7,636,857	.1370	4,794,318	1,361	734,619	1,461	471,784	2,483	771,968	212,507	1,965,437	1,076	Inc. Place
Salinas	SLNS	64224	3-AA	164,953	151,060	12,949	43,046	41,555	2,136,049	.0447	1,755,586	499	228,712	455	109,264	575	243,539	117,190	345,127	189	Inc. Place
San Bernardino	RIV-	65000	2-C	197,088	185,401	12,225	57,111	30,227	2,409,396	.0527	2,170,521	616	381,116	758	88,482	466	226,952	69,461	269,114	147	Inc. Place
San Bruno	SF-O-	65028	4-Sm	38,923	40,165	21,385	14,197	55,992	832,381	.0188	1,049,954	298	394,321	784	39,890	210	143,384	38,421	(d)	...	Inc. Place
San Clemente	L.A.	65084		54,388	49,936	31,612	21,006	59,222	1,719,312	.0214	323,682	92	28,921	58	11,713	62	91,620	32,176	100,164	55	Inc. Place
San Diego	SDGO	66000	1-A	1,286,347	1,223,400	20,706	460,279	44,645	26,635,297	.4458	14,969,315	4,251	1,477,564	2,938	1,371,184	7,217	2,427,103	804,593	6,680,426	3,657	Inc. Place
San Dimas	L.A.	66070		36,094	34,980	21,721	12,097	57,113	783,981	.0119	305,659	87	41,583	83	24,429	129	79,592	24,017	183,111	100	Inc. Place
San Francisco	SF-O-	67000	1-AA	734,587	776,733	29,289	317,359	50,717	21,515,350	.3346	11,511,398	3,269	1,090,215	2,168	2,270,361	11,949	1,932,648	783,829	1,998,438	1,094	Inc. Place
San Gabriel	L.A.	67042	4-S	43,691	39,804	12,815	13,304	39,029	559,917	.0112	391,830	111	39,946	79	16,084	85	88,475	13,411	22,580	12	Inc. Place
San Jose	SF-O-	68000	2-BB	916,491	894,943	23,541	281,135	62,589	21,575,265	.3497	11,775,651	3,344	1,412,778	2,810	606,683	3,193	1,998,802	664,724	14,933,197	8,175	Inc. Place
San Juan Capistrano	L.A.	68028		37,139	33,826	26,772	11,946	57,053	994,286	.0175	747,079	212	91,666	182	26,356	139	81,578	35,659	125,726	69	Inc. Place
San Leandro	SF-O-	68084	3-SS	80,665	79,452	21,913	30,070	46,888	1,767,613	.0338	1,527,156	434	307,577	612	134,712	709	190,198	53,005	1,027,711	563	Inc. Place
San Luis Obispo	S.LUIS	68154	3-A	44,733	44,174	22,904	20,121	33,469	1,024,554	.0191	847,869	241	60,847	121	52,734	278	125,458	61,368	124,966	68	Inc. Place
San Marcos	SDGO	68196		63,295	54,977	17,117	20,265	44,129	1,083,418	.0187	589,419	167	36,403	72	16,476	87	88,151	22,707	500,039	274	Inc. Place
San Mateo	SF-O-	68252	3-SS	91,909	92,482	30,296	37,024	59,659	2,784,444	.0537	2,729,904	775	595,156	1,184	388,663	2,046	338,865	174,961	39,341	22	Inc. Place
San Pablo	SF-O-	68294	4-S	35,203	30,215	13,913	9,876	40,921	489,795	.0100	397,180	113	79,645	158	33,862	178	63,022	12,534	(d)	...	Inc. Place
San Rafael	SF-O-	68364	3-S	56,569	56,063	28,096	23,156	56,509	1,589,370	.0275	1,154,710	328	124,616	248	38,837	204	133,029	35,220	129,558	71	Inc. Place
San Ramon	SF-O-	68378		46,337	44,722	36,414	16,435	82,649	1,687,298	.0228	590,333	168	44,327	88	14,855	78	179,481	38,673	(d)	...	Inc. Place
Santa Ana	L.A.	69000	2-S	358,533	337,977	11,252	77,128	42,327	4,034,151	.0852	3,042,348	864	343,619	683	289,840	1,525	507,057	128,847	2,343,812	1,283	Inc. Place
Santa Barbara	S.BAR	69070	3-AA	95,136	92,325	24,330	37,083	46,000	2,314,630	.0409	1,682,032	478	70,979	141	198,688	1,046	251,094	108,215	146,777	80	Inc. Place
Santa Clara	SF-O-	69084	3-S	103,078	102,361	26,957	38,488	61,826	2,778,651	.0594	3,321,693	943	411,077	818	455,008	2,395	305,498	168,948	7,469,243	4,089	Inc. Place
Santa Clarita	L.A.	69088		172,048	151,088	21,736	55,727	59,862	3,739,601	.0564	1,442,135	409	246,870	491	81,013	426	195,153	78,173	101,915	56	Inc. Place
Santa Cruz	S.CRZ	69112	3-C	53,121	54,593	23,690	19,651	47,875	1,258,458	.0195	580,150	165	42,226	84	34,877	184	93,453	75,322	498,363	273	Inc. Place
Santa Fe Springs	L.A.	69154	4-S	19,518	17,438	11,542	5,204	42,248	225,276	.0090	666,495	189	40,941	81	8,430	44	24,305	15,494	1,504,180	823	Inc. Place
Santa Maria	S.MAR	69196	3-B	81,179	77,423	12,524	23,438	35,405	1,016,645	.0233	1,050,840	298	183,932	366	53,963	284	134,035	63,181	283,543	155	Inc. Place
Santa Monica	L.A.	70000	3-SS	88,492	84,084	36,628	44,955	49,594	3,241,266	.0553	2,487,664	706	169,174	336	328,498	1,729	241,767	151,761	330,028	181	Inc. Place
Santa Paula	OXN-	70042		31,207	28,598	16,197	8,867	39,898	505,462	.0080	179,461	51	17,186	34	2,840	15	50,225	13,121	(d)	...	Inc. Place

Source: Devonshire Associates Ltd. and Scan/US, Inc. 2005.
* Source: 1997 Census of Manufactures.
Not classified as a Principal Business Center.

...Data less than 1,000.
(d) Data not available.

Continued on next page

Principal Business Centers and Other Places with 30,000 or More: Population/Income/Sales, *Continued*

Place Name	Ranally Metro Area	FIPS Place Code	Ranally City Rating	Population: Estimate 7/1/05	Population: Census 4/1/00	Per Capita Income 2004	House-holds Estimate 7/1/05	Median Household Income 2004	Disposable Income 2004 ($1,000)	Market Ability Index 2004	Total Retail Sales: 2004 Sales ($1,000)	Total Retail Sales: Ranally Sales Units	General Merchandise: 2004 Sales ($1,000)	General Merchandise: Ranally Sales Units	Apparel Store: 2004 Sales ($1,000)	Apparel Store: Ranally Sales Units	Food Store Sales 2004 ($1,000)	Health & Drug Store 2004 ($1,000)	Manufacturers: Value Added 1997* ($1,000)	Manufacturers: Ranally Mfg. Units	Place Type
Santa Rosa	S.ROS	70098	3-CC	157,459	147,595	23,708	59,121	47,742	3,733,027	.0646	2,524,896	717	316,954	630	181,187	954	404,840	177,817	1,199,566	657	Inc. Place
Santee	SDGO	70224		53,186	52,975	17,946	18,036	49,219	954,500	.0163	520,062	148	130,462	259	9,997	53	41,496	26,353	132,407	72	Inc. Place
Seaside	MTRY-	70742		33,842	31,696	14,364	10,821	38,591	486,119	.0114	572,061	162	75,462	150	13,830	73	27,098	17,657	(d)	...	Inc. Place
Simi Valley	L.A.	72016	3-S	119,795	111,351	25,190	39,152	62,773	3,017,599	.0459	1,355,320	385	134,929	268	55,570	292	232,144	72,209	646,633	354	Inc. Place
South Gate	L.A.	73080	4-Sr	106,454	96,375	8,632	24,700	33,901	918,924	.0197	537,160	153	86,391	172	12,467	66	108,312	28,406	591,688	324	Inc. Place
South Lake Tahoe		73108	4-C	25,925	23,609	20,877	10,178	37,543	541,233	.0082	205,691	58	15,917	32	33,382	176	48,119	10,706	(d)	...	Inc. Place
South San Francisco	SF-O-	73262	4-S	61,754	60,552	19,033	20,046	55,492	1,175,393	.0234	1,062,036	302	109,811	218	8,070	42	208,423	61,278	1,477,988	809	Inc. Place
South Whittier	L.A.	73430		58,426	55,193	13,100	14,958	45,349	765,409	.0131	297,492	84	1,147	2	8,678	46	57,176	6,736	(d)	...	CDP
Stanton	L.A.	73962		39,807	37,403	13,280	11,409	39,063	528,634	.0100	324,381	92	49,410	98	11,154	59	80,792	12,007	66,689	37	Inc. Place
Stockton	STOC	75000	2-A	281,628	243,771	14,223	84,193	35,760	4,005,633	.0706	1,972,525	560	270,225	537	131,060	690	388,474	138,423	774,595	424	Inc. Place
Sunnyvale	SF-O-	77000	3-S	132,339	131,760	32,188	52,355	66,361	4,259,720	.0667	2,432,162	691	258,129	513	112,882	594	335,778	108,862	7,469,489	4,089	Inc. Place
Temecula		78120		94,672	57,716	19,922	30,154	55,434	1,886,093	.0313	996,133	283	149,946	298	31,318	165	129,779	29,873	843,028	462	Inc. Place
Temple City	L.A.	78148		36,263	33,377	16,377	11,866	44,333	593,884	.0095	224,034	64	41,613	83	22,071	116	54,413	18,672	(d)	...	Inc. Place
Thousand Oaks	OXN-	78582	3-S	125,350	117,005	33,355	44,772	68,104	4,181,037	.0635	2,190,413	622	238,526	474	148,878	784	366,173	136,340	342,749	188	Inc. Place
Torrance	L.A.	80000	2-S	142,372	137,946	21,726	54,102	50,545	3,093,146	.0655	3,405,448	967	431,706	859	328,399	1,728	259,207	160,114	1,849,269	1,012	Inc. Place
Tracy		80238		80,177	56,929	17,593	23,007	57,190	1,410,558	.0247	822,868	234	148,414	295	70,766	372	118,739	44,256	264,366	145	Inc. Place
Tulare	VISL	80644		50,806	43,994	12,629	15,598	32,186	641,613	.0117	318,427	90	64,441	128	23,923	126	43,216	13,445	206,316	113	Inc. Place
Turlock	MOD	80812	4-C	68,654	55,810	15,151	21,662	36,607	1,040,193	.0193	663,449	188	100,234	199	26,158	138	158,858	34,623	409,913	224	Inc. Place
Tustin	L.A.	80854	4-S	73,152	67,504	23,541	25,676	53,746	1,722,080	.0331	1,554,563	441	126,920	252	110,066	579	177,853	71,469	833,818	456	Inc. Place
Ukiah		81134	4-C	15,855	15,497	18,251	6,113	34,530	289,366	.0060	279,194	79	40,885	81	2,536	13	60,896	14,192	39,321	22	Inc. Place
Union City	SF-O-	81204		69,333	66,869	19,823	18,738	63,688	1,374,398	.0213	548,503	156	81,029	161	8,068	42	168,302	29,978	360,615	197	Inc. Place
Upland	L.A.	81344	3-S	74,823	68,393	21,209	25,630	45,458	1,586,916	.0250	717,472	204	86,694	172	16,304	86	144,019	49,333	99,138	54	Inc. Place
Vacaville	FRFL-	81554		96,835	88,625	21,578	30,935	52,692	2,089,486	.0338	1,064,357	302	178,541	355	85,045	448	216,534	41,215	217,827	119	Inc. Place
Vallejo	SF-O-	81666	3-S	121,895	116,760	20,703	41,580	46,245	2,523,611	.0392	1,067,060	303	216,581	431	25,390	134	145,024	56,056	84,067	46	Inc. Place
Ventura	OXN-	65042	3-CC	106,061	100,916	23,647	40,486	48,020	2,508,070	.0445	1,829,133	519	135,707	270	59,860	315	244,664	107,620	225,031	123	Inc. Place
Victorville	HESP-	82590	4-C	70,621	64,029	14,534	21,991	36,194	1,026,437	.0221	986,843	280	193,944	386	54,345	286	129,276	45,173	128,099	70	Inc. Place
Visalia	VISL	82954	3-AA	104,116	91,565	16,811	34,968	38,738	1,750,341	.0312	1,054,926	300	181,754	361	53,749	283	202,332	55,885	373,411	204	Inc. Place
Vista	SDGO	82996		98,831	89,857	16,294	30,829	42,326	1,610,385	.0274	792,213	225	112,957	225	25,432	134	139,886	43,737	390,261	214	Inc. Place
Walnut	L.A.	83332		31,234	30,004	18,176	8,282	64,352	567,717	.0085	170,999	49	...	...	4,927	26	32,136	5,715	77,308	42	Inc. Place
Walnut Creek	SF-O-	83346	3-SS	65,452	64,296	36,455	28,882	60,367	2,386,075	.0370	1,384,877	393	132,553	264	189,525	998	185,013	87,522	239,193	131	Inc. Place
Watsonville	WATS	83668	4-C	47,163	44,265	13,728	11,990	41,801	647,451	.0116	326,099	93	41,169	82	10,178	54	71,919	11,510	268,444	147	Inc. Place
West Covina	L.A.	84200	3-S	114,953	105,080	15,397	33,023	48,709	1,769,933	.0347	1,352,065	384	311,797	620	168,378	886	143,902	53,112	(d)	...	Inc. Place
West Hollywood	L.A.	84410		35,955	35,716	41,282	22,391	41,574	1,484,311	.0201	555,341	158	22,887	46	90,656	477	110,980	51,611	(d)	...	Inc. Place
Westminster	L.A.	84550	3-S	93,208	88,207	15,749	27,749	44,782	1,467,905	.0347	1,835,577	521	353,934	704	145,265	765	275,129	73,682	96,068	53	Inc. Place
Westmont	L.A.	84592		33,474	31,623	8,905	9,420	25,990	298,074	.0055	71,927	20	16,337	32	3,197	17	25,108	4,523	(d)	...	CDP
West Sacramento	SAC	84816		34,307	31,615	14,625	12,149	31,672	501,735	.0097	352,459	100	5,520	11	9,173	48	93,295	8,343	342,378	187	Inc. Place
Whittier	L.A.	85292	3-S	89,752	83,680	17,555	29,169	45,433	1,575,616	.0257	694,484	197	112,223	223	44,451	234	119,392	46,723	158,062	87	Inc. Place
Willowbrook	L.A.	85614		36,137	34,138	8,049	8,634	25,722	290,878	.0057	83,796	24	3,569	7	1,518	8	24,238	5,547	(d)	...	CDP
Woodland		86328	4-C	55,759	49,151	16,256	18,671	41,128	906,417	.0165	569,961	162	92,933	185	10,885	57	120,750	38,151	205,393	112	Inc. Place
Yorba Linda	L.A.	86832		63,551	58,918	31,653	20,707	76,204	2,011,589	.0268	594,520	169	97,061	193	12,294	65	135,324	30,749	116,866	64	Inc. Place
Yuba City	YUCY	86972	3-A	44,111	36,758	15,291	15,336	34,134	674,520	.0132	507,063	144	127,041	253	22,526	119	85,259	26,873	116,044	64	Inc. Place
Yucaipa	RIV-	87042		52,154	41,207	19,271	18,323	37,130	1,005,071	.0138	176,046	50	6,132	12	2,362	12	64,025	17,853	(d)	...	Inc. Place
Colorado																					
Arvada	DEN	03455	4-S	102,459	102,153	23,758	41,541	51,111	2,434,264	.0345	752,048	214	111,464	222	18,795	99	199,385	42,460	251,554	138	Inc. Place
Aurora	DEN	04000	3-SS	312,274	276,393	19,326	127,498	44,877	6,034,980	.1099	4,273,955	1,214	812,498	1,616	175,878	926	597,550	176,126	172,675	95	Inc. Place
Boulder	BOUL-	07850	3-CC	94,846	94,673	25,487	39,867	46,159	2,417,329	.0402	1,502,318	427	100,459	200	86,442	455	327,041	50,950	1,002,806	549	Inc. Place
Broomfield	DEN	09280		44,052	38,272	31,400	18,953	59,463	1,383,230	.0174	283,136	80	45,927	91	...	...	56,649	10,761	919,582	503	Inc. Place
Castle Rock	DEN	12415		33,043	20,224	29,898	12,540	65,145	987,912	.0135	310,495	88	22,339	44	66,891	352	41,453	9,074	(d)	...	Inc. Place
Colorado Springs	CSPG	16000	2-A	386,372	360,890	21,324	155,608	42,966	8,239,095	.1508	6,235,192	1,771	1,127,794	2,243	186,673	983	606,349	241,873	2,600,880	1,424	Inc. Place
Denver	DEN	20000	1-A	558,088	554,636	21,096	252,189	37,304	11,773,190	.2076	7,942,001	2,255	917,312	1,824	422,490	2,224	952,255	320,196	2,525,048	1,382	Inc. Place
Durango		22035	4-B	15,026	13,922	20,497	6,500	36,049	307,982	.0064	320,643	91	27,642	55	13,442	71	49,196	9,986	(d)	...	Inc. Place
Englewood	DEN	24785	3-S	32,330	31,727	30,098	15,648	39,217	973,084	.0192	1,006,726	286	56,901	113	22,483	118	121,176	41,504	351,086	192	Inc. Place
Fort Collins	FTCL-	27425	3-A	129,345	118,652	23,790	56,026	43,756	3,077,096	.0517	1,906,977	541	400,004	795	70,785	373	244,360	63,210	1,099,468	602	Inc. Place
Grand Junction	GDJC	31660	3-A	43,112	41,986	20,527	19,898	33,133	884,967	.0195	1,038,789	295	280,392	558	25,362	133	82,696	28,762	241,154	132	Inc. Place
Greeley	GRLY	32155	3-A	86,804	76,930	18,602	34,066	36,729	1,614,706	.0300	1,190,603	338	254,091	505	21,618	114	118,742	39,108	376,315	206	Inc. Place
Highlands Ranch	DEN	36410		102,257	70,931	31,291	37,600	74,826	3,199,747	.0394	545,060	155	164,294	327	51,423	271	96,057	24,997	(d)	...	CDP
Ken Caryl	DEN	40377		31,626	30,887	28,184	11,868	63,429	891,353	.0123	282,354	80	67,577	134	13,108	69	50,474	21,491	(d)	...	CDP
Lakewood	DEN	43000	3-SS	146,362	144,126	24,939	65,350	45,048	3,650,096	.0595	2,096,608	595	481,908	958	105,950	558	306,494	87,367	278,422	152	Inc. Place
Littleton	DEN	45255	4-S	41,368	40,340	26,171	18,992	48,310	1,082,650	.0215	1,091,545	310	196,572	391	50,820	267	139,543	73,001	165,055	90	Inc. Place
Longmont	BOUL-	45970	4-C	82,830	71,093	20,162	31,165	49,201	1,670,005	.0315	1,336,328	379	254,185	505	24,422	129	210,080	61,353	305,367	167	Inc. Place
Loveland	FTCL-	46465	4-B	55,915	50,608	23,560	24,410	46,349	1,317,365	.0216	747,554	212	150,203	299	39,794	209	103,689	17,286	734,884	402	Inc. Place
Northglenn	DEN	54330	4-Sm	38,024	31,575	21,645	15,053	47,764	823,019	.0124	310,410	88	29,907	59	1,310	7	39,444	12,276	47,252	26	Inc. Place
Parker	DEN	57630		44,563	23,558	29,081	15,945	70,695	1,295,919	.0156	160,530	46	28,097	56	2,163	11	61,509	3,390	(d)	...	Inc. Place
Pueblo	PUEB	62000	3-AA	99,671	102,121	15,774	42,012	29,053	1,572,252	.0327	1,447,070	411	411,500	818	26,489	139	173,914	53,243	264,716	145	Inc. Place
Southglenn	DEN	72505		47,415	43,520	32,856	19,139	63,963	1,557,855	.0306	1,632,400	464	284,134	565	104,718	551	242,916	37,597	(d)	...	CDP
Sterling		73935	4-C	11,069	11,360	16,946	4,753	31,236	187,572	.0037	157,712	45	39,390	78	4,023	21	13,200	7,061	(d)	...	Inc. Place
Thornton	DEN	77290	4-S	102,959	82,384	20,575	38,904	47,870	2,118,409	.0309	650,368	185	89,141	177	1,975	10	116,870	14,286	122,070	67	Inc. Place
Westminster	DEN	83835	4-S	114,512	100,940	25,234	46,876	51,498	2,889,588	.0439	1,293,051	367	208,718	415	63,332	333	206,737	45,936	203,426	111	Inc. Place
Wheat Ridge	DEN	84440	4-Sr	33,993	32,913	21,322	15,987	36,961	724,787	.0158	851,123	242	115,776	230	13,497	71	145,076	20,527	145,842	80	Inc. Place
Connecticut																					
Ansonia	N.Y.	01150	4-S	19,171	18,554	19,161	7,521	40,280	367,336	.0066	244,860	70	...	...	3,153	17	79,309	18,678	74,334	41	Inc. Place
Branford	N.HAV	07310		30,042	28,683	31,232	12,717	51,742	938,283	.0148	544,275	155	37,642	75	18,521	97	77,360	34,836	269,377	147	MCD-Town
Bridgeport	N.Y.	08000	2-C	139,666	139,529	12,890	49,752	33,054	1,800,339	.0358	1,263,909	359	21,174	42	38,852	204	152,684	97,859	757,957	415	Inc. Place
Bristol	H-NB	08420	3-S	60,307	60,062	23,102	25,148	43,458	1,393,203	.0222	704,957	200	36,351	72	32,063	169	175,926	55,712	361,069	198	Inc. Place
Cheshire	N.HAV	14160		30,597	28,543	31,338	9,714	67,969	958,863	.0160	660,606	188	...	...	10,991	58	49,119	29,738	187,434	103	MCD-Town
Danbury	N.Y.	18430	3-SS	79,449	74,848	18,971	28,507	50,028	1,507,213	.0389	2,402,542	682	290,937	579	248,905	1,310	292,606	114,247	731,675	401	Inc. Place
Derby	N.Y.	19480	4-S	12,738	12,391	22,185	5,232	42,444	282,591	.0053	237,076	67	39,364	78	15,497	82	3,705	27,943	(d)	...	Inc. Place
East Hartford	H-NB	22630	4-S	51,182	49,575	21,392	20,994	39,073	1,094,877	.0199	808,223	229	30,538	61	33,426	176	118,014	68,029	867,842	475	MCD-Town
Enfield	H-NB	25990	4-S	46,680	45,212	22,076	17,049	48,153	1,030,498	.0181	700,256	199	121,696	242	56,063	295	131,548	49,960	269,800	148	MCD-Town
Fairfield	N.Y.	26620	4-S	59,608	57,340	33,821	20,932	73,881	2,016,027	.0338	1,437,306	408	73,514	146	88,452	466	160,483	67,151	103,514	57	MCD-Town
Glastonbury	H-NB	31240		33,841	31,876	36,959	13,077	69,734	1,250,733	.0164	382,509	109	...	...	28,879	152	87,251	26,187	93,391	51	MCD-Town
Greenwich	N.Y.	33620	3-S	63,082	61,101	55,153	23,668	86,223	3,479,187	.0472	1,485,927	422	13,974	28	128,988	679	141,890	61,380	169,150	93	MCD-Town
Groton	N.LON-	34250		40,496	39,907	24,531	16,084	43,619	993,423	.0188	877,779	249	117,139	233	39,154	206	122,960	48,017	59,542	33	MCD-Town
Hamden	N.HAV	35650	4-S	60,392	56,913	26,085	23,039	48,094	1,575,332	.0234	664,624	189	38,048	76	86,355	455	132,913	51,033	114,958	63	MCD-Town
Hartford	H-NB	37000	2-AA	121,656	121,578	14,404	45,262	24,298	1,752,333	.0324	1,055,985	300	19,026	38	58,431	308	119,187	108,629	130,684	72	Inc. Place
Manchester	H-NB	44700	3-S	56,492	54,740	25,972	24,058	45,125	1,467,194	.0314	1,737,408	493	362,890	722	143,089	753	176,344	67,502	456,245	250	MCD-Town
Meriden	N.HAV	46450	3-B	59,125	58,244	19,931	22,555	40,738	1,178,395	.0207	757,494	215	118,361	235	104,589	550	99,674	54,751	378,759	207	Inc. Place
Middletown	H-NB	47290	3-S	43,758	43,167	27,420	18,592	44,250	1,199,848	.0181	553,783	157	29,106	58	22,879	120	66,630	69,193	705,669	386	Inc. Place
Milford	N.Y.	47515	3-S	53,781	50,594	26,946	20,680	55,030	1,449,202	.0271	1,276,364	362	159,844	318	111,677	588	88,511	61,599	720,445	394	Inc. Place
Naugatuck	WATB	49880		31,597	30,989	22,122	11,685	46,450	698,992	.0107	295,033	84	39,293	78	3,932	21	109,576	16,535	378,644	207	Inc. Place
New Britain	H-NB	50370	3-C	71,663	71,538	18,672	28,689	32,982	1,338,071	.0209	524,021	149	41,414	82	11,238	59	63,564	46,589	497,710	272	Inc. Place
New Haven	N.HAV	52000	2-AA	123,849	123,626	17,509	45,625	29,913	2,168,414	.0363	1,064,711	302	58,388	116	79,158	417	156,719	126,503	413,807	227	Inc. Place
New London	N.LON-	52280	3-AA	25,722	25,671	19,946	10,460	32,932	513,049	.0101	458,662	130	...	...	21,046	111	20,770	27,250	(d)	...	Inc. Place
New Milford	N.Y.	52630		30,499	27,121	29,222	11,151	60,240	891,237	.0136	441,565	125	45,367	90	6,128	32	86,185	18,821	612,707	335	MCD-Town
Norwalk	N.Y.	55990	3-SS	85,736	82,951	26,324	33,307	55,456	2,256,884	.0472	2,555,229	726	84,684	168	91,403	481	261,499	61,677	889,946	487	Inc. Place
Norwich	N.LON-	56200	4-B	36,626	36,117	22,521	15,709	36,932	824,849	.0143	551,982	157	98,860	197	18,748	99	100,847	42,548	138,999	76	Inc. Place
Orange	N.HAV	57600	4-Sm	13,888	13,233	34,571	4,822	68,116	480,120	.0115	747,141	212	125,458	249	23,129	122	114,213	33,381	60,288	33	MCD-Town
Shelton	N.Y.	68100		39,349	38,101	22,562	14,434	60,217	887,808	.0149	536,428	152	43,835	87	12,443	65	122,008	4,656	441,241	242	Inc. Place
Southington	H-NB	70550	4-S	40,724	39,728	25,136	15,556	54,336	1,023,640	.0168	607,323	172	45,725	91	20,238	107	115,050	59,863	181,417	99	MCD-Town
Stamford	N.Y.	73000	2-S	120,873	117,083	26,720	46,229	56,073	3,229,724	.0552	2,227,322	632	177,043	352	175,142	922	211,606	84,077	1,644,778	900	Inc. Place
Stratford	N.Y.	74190	4-S	50,232	49,976	20,344	19,747	48,913	1,021,939	.0254	1,546,371	439	24,350	48	46,077	243	150,334	51,273	1,119,345	613	MCD-Town
Torrington	TORR	76500	4-C	37,137	35,202	22,464	15,402	39,481	834,242	.0160	735,887	209	75,831	151	28,729	151	126,652	43,563	240,502	132	Inc. Place
Trumbull	N.Y.	77200	4-Sm	35,144	34,243	25,614	12,040	68,269	900,195	.0191	1,042,797	296	209,750	417	137,893	726	85,553	27,644	41,104	23	MCD-Town
Vernon	H-NB	78250	4-S	27,717	28,063	27,597	11,787	43,568	764,905	.0123	441,183	125	25,105	50	27,079	143	87,594	55,195	44,272	24	MCD-Town
Wallingford	N.HAV	78740	4-S	45,327	43,026	25,567	17,022	52,358	1,158,878	.0196	754,608	214	100,156	199	12,568	66	103,727	28,467	596,755	327	MCD-Town
Waterbury	WATB	80000	3-BB	108,093	107,271	17,403	41,564	33,223	1,881,142	.0351	1,344,688	382	243,535	484	88,102	464	204,662	100,789	531,402	291	Inc. Place
West Hartford	H-NB	82590	3-S	66,565	63,589	33,684	25,821	55,784	2,242,180	.0303	745,350	212	93,003	185	101,360	533	89,174	83,607	319,242	175	MCD-Town
West Haven	N.HAV	82800	4-S	52,594	52,360	20,560	20,468	39,813	1,081,306	.0161	365,260	104	15,260	30	9,266	49	53,178	46,191	1,116,307	611	Inc. Place
Westport	N.Y.	83500	4-S	26,866	25,749	65,855	9,855	104,873	1,769,251	.0244	843,298	239	2,969	6	124,434	655	93,737	43,926	(d)	...	MCD-Town
Wethersfield	H-NB	84900	4-S	26,958	26,271	28,090	11,579	49,372	757,238	.0106	254,317	72	5,714	11	25,581	135	65,644	40,922	(d)	...	MCD-Town
Delaware																					
Dover	DOVR	21200	3-A	34,548	32,135	18,835	13,253	38,453	650,720	.0130	583,050	166	164,334	327	20,827	110	66,901	26,725	845,914	463	Inc. Place
Newark	PHIL-	50670	4-S	29,271	28,547	19,109	8,715	54,232	559,354	.0113	525,725	149	27,510	55	14,727	78	92,654	31,436	...	...	Inc. Place
Wilmington	PHIL-	77580	2-BB	73,279	72,664	17,665	27,337	34,364	1,294,490	.0241	926,338	263	54,130	108	35,114	185	141,391	64,764	...	...	Inc. Place
District of Columbia																					
Washington	WASH	50000	1-AA	548,902	572,059	26,120	245,648	37,484	14,337,490	.1918	3,540,123	1,005	143,774	286	501,970	2,642	938,614	520,795	170,849	94	Inc. Place
Florida																					
Altamonte Springs	ORL	00950	3-Sm	43,311	41,200	22,395	18,822	39,762	969,971	.0192	926,460	263	249,980	497	123,802	652	83,638	55,486	(d)	...	Inc. Place
Apopka	ORL	01700		34,306	26,642	17,714	12,074	41,025	607,683	.0094	217,048	62	28,287	56	4,148	22	53,645	12,083	72,884	40	Inc. Place
Bal Harbour	MIA-	03275	4-Sm	3,413	3,305	36,083	1,869	41,721	123,153	.0023	115,569	33	24,362	48	65,224	343	4,006	8,151	(d)	...	Inc. Place
Boca Raton	MIA-	07300	3-B	77,736	74,764	33,180	30,611	52,459	2,579,303	.0424	1,728,041	491	276,779	550	395,393	2,081	251,718	151,236	300,389	164	Inc. Place
Bonita Springs	NAP	07525		36,136	32,797	30,833	15,991	45,608	1,114,174	.0160	454,977	129	34,555	69	9,350	49	60,156	36,264	(d)	...	Inc. Place
Boynton Beach	MIA-	07875		69,912	60,389	18,536	28,006	37,833	1,295,900	.0257	1,136,912	323	272,947	543	138,362	728	168,151	97,857	...	...	Inc. Place
Bradenton	SAR-B	07950	3-B	51,873	49,504	20,799	23,559	34,060	1,078,886	.0202	861,378	245	148,604	296	83,839	441	110,925	69,197	...	...	Inc. Place
Brandon	TAM	08150		87,256	77,895	19,974	31,252	47,404	1,742,882	.0317	1,250,127	355	335,270	667	108,970	574	144,520	101,106	(d)	...	CDP
Cape Coral	FTMY-	10275		125,952	102,286	18,651	49,271	40,903	2,349,082	.0383	1,099,040	312	235,231	468	44,772	236	188,861	88,668	24,819	14	Inc. Place
Carol City	MIA-	10650		63,081	59,443	10,261	16,509	36,589	647,255	.0114	173,942	49	2,442	5	3,334	18	29,518	14,904	(d)	...	CDP
Clearwater	ST.PET	12875	2-B	111,078	108,787	21,645	48,714	35,576	2,404,242	.0535	2,941,852	835	437,139	869	168,004	884	296,779	137,979	198,000	108	Inc. Place
Cocoa	MELB-	13150	3-S	16,128	16,412	16,574	6,756	26,554	267,310	.0058	277,395	79	5,508	11	2,840	15	35,921	9,682	(d)	...	Inc. Place
Coconut Creek	MIA-	13275		54,310	43,566	22,230	24,076	42,261	1,207,330	.0213	835,263	237	9,018	18	22,483	118	55,197	30,086	(d)	...	Inc. Place
Coral Gables	MIA-	14250	3-S	42,494	42,249	31,674	16,064	53,604	1,345,959	.0229	972,997	276	79,781	159	91,064	479	113,044	53,406	(d)	...	Inc. Place
Coral Springs	MIA-	14400		130,366	117,549	22,574	42,136	56,412	2,942,859	.0464	1,416,538	402	283,895	565	126,622	666	269,992	112,740	70,588	39	Inc. Place
Country Club	MIA-	14895		38,529	36,310	15,307	13,015	40,383	589,748	.0109	377,674	107	65,357	130	7,404	39	72,418	48,207	(d)	...	CDP
Davie	MIA-	16475		90,853	75,720	20,778	33,133	47,186	1,887,737	.0312	1,015,803	288	100,475	200	53,074	279	185,258	72,110	85,217	47	Inc. Place
Daytona Beach	D.BCH	16525	2-A	62,175	64,112	16,290	26,457	25,896	1,012,843	.0301	2,009,619	571	318,511	633	143,300	754	125,453	111,774	102,946	56	Inc. Place
Deerfield Beach	MIA-	16725		73,178	64,583	21,614	34,165	33,247	1,581,691	.0302	1,351,553	384	117,543	234	45,078	237	186,836	107,037	174,195	95	Inc. Place
De Land	DL	16875	4-C	24,470	20,904	16,925	9,367	32,325	414,162	.0083	360,033	102	40,673	81	15,020	79	73,647	32,794	92,053	50	Inc. Place
Delray Beach	MIA-	17100	4-S	68,711	60,020	22,208	28,386	40,863	1,525,944	.0332	1,792,992	509	95,539	190	85,594	450	108,849	49,671	44,625	24	Inc. Place
Deltona	ORL	17200		86,892	69,543	15,095	29,686	37,710	1,311,606	.0190	203,484	58	2,009	4	1,212	6	125,154	21,264	(d)	...	Inc. Place
Dunedin	ST.PET	18575		35,159	35,691	21,600	16,685	33,843	759,447	.0119	346,316	98	5,473	11	7,600	40	139,016	34,593	(d)	...	Inc. Place
Egypt Lake-Leto	TAM	20108		36,723	32,782	15,693	14,614	31,858	576,288	.0137	732,473	208	4,530	9	16,687	88	30,989	26,996	(d)	...	CDP
Fort Lauderdale	MIA-	24000	2-BB	158,667	152,397	24,979	68,762	37,001	3,963,289	.0767	3,702,995	1,051	219,508	437	239,300	1,259	409,331	242,194	543,417	298	Inc. Place
Fort Myers	FTMY-	24125	2-A	53,143	48,208	15,426	20,623	28,930	819,764	.0253	1,706,933	485	317,487	631	115,891	610	72,606	82,178	179,260	98	Inc. Place
Fort Pierce	FTPI	24300	3-A	38,461	37,516	15,581	14,402	26,645	599,272	.0128	590,809	168	85,523	170	13,871	73	59,070	43,082	(d)	...	Inc. Place
Fort Walton Beach	FTWL	24475	3-A	19,972	19,973	20,692	8,593	36,197	413,266	.0110	707,658	201	34,042	68	13,805	73	55,314	21,871	113,486	62	Inc. Place
Fountainbleau	MIA-	24562		63,193	59,549	11,847	21,049	31,773	748,643	.0182	870,562	247	226,814	451	86,696	456	46,290	48,123	(d)	...	CDP
Gainesville	GAIN	25175	3-AA	89,956	95,447	16,228	37,460	30,090	1,459,778	.0313	1,473,371	418	234,460	466	106,872	562	207,789	65,811	162,917	89	Inc. Place
Golden Glades	MIA-	26375		34,619	32,623	10,639	9,904	30,503	368,308	.0088	380,490	108	26,556	53	19,142	101	42,737	23,985	(d)	...	CDP
Greenacres City	MIA-	27322		32,808	27,569	17,277	13,258	38,341	566,831	.0100	333,343	95	82,450	164	16,948	89	41,678	30,867	(d)	...	Inc. Place
Hallandale Beach	MIA-	28450	4-S	39,223	34,282	19,318	19,846	26,590	757,693	.0136	518,444	147	38,038	76	21,705	114	110,523	37,644	43,814	24	Inc. Place
Hialeah	MIA-	30000	2-S	239,534	226,419	10,993	71,085	30,008	2,633,188	.0590	2,337,043	664	262,162	521	203,054	1,069	419,206	227,391	939,116	514	Inc. Place

Source: Devonshire Associates Ltd. and Scan/US, Inc. 2005.
* Source: 1997 Census of Manufactures.
Not classified as a Principal Business Center.

...Data less than 1,000.
(d) Data not available.

Principal Business Centers and Other Places with 30,000 or More: Population/Income/Sales, *Continued*

Place Name	Ranally Metro Area	FIPS Place Code	Ranally City Rating	Population: Estimate 7/1/05	Population: Census 4/1/00	Per Capita Income 2004	Households Estimate 7/1/05	Median Household Income 2004	Disposable Income 2004 ($1,000)	Market Ability Index 2004	Total Retail Sales: 2004 Sales ($1,000)	Total Retail Sales: Ranally Sales Units	General Merchandise: 2004 Sales ($1,000)	General Merchandise: Ranally Sales Units	Apparel Store: 2004 Sales ($1,000)	Apparel Store: Ranally Sales Units	Food Store Sales 2004 ($1,000)	Health & Drug Store 2004 ($1,000)	Manufacturers: Value Added 1997* ($1,000)	Manufacturers: Ranally Mfg. Units	Place Type
Hollywood	MIA-	32000	2-S	150,163	139,357	20,077	62,018	36,134	3,014,830	.0561	2,317,474	658	108,570	216	109,289	575	275,198	136,846	461,892	253	Inc. Place
Homestead	MIA-	32275	4-S	32,990	31,909	10,198	9,915	28,438	336,448	.0078	313,177	89	15,817	31	6,891	36	85,814	20,700	(d)	...	Inc. Place
Jacksonville	JAX	35000	2-AA	798,525	735,617	19,623	308,062	38,462	15,669,193	.2880	11,494,549	3,264	1,611,285	3,204	522,574	2,750	1,472,795	551,619	3,878,378	2,123	Inc. Place
Jupiter	MIA-	35875		49,085	39,328	28,106	19,579	52,262	1,379,600	.0202	570,507	162	70,925	141	25,937	137	148,183	45,022	(d)	...	Inc. Place
Kendale Lakes	MIA-	36062		60,381	56,901	14,308	18,202	42,233	863,956	.0146	353,571	100	56,508	112	66,206	348	62,167	31,502	(d)	...	CDP
Kendall	MIA-	36100		79,830	75,226	25,883	28,697	51,238	2,066,215	.0362	1,503,854	427	264,555	526	264,118	1,390	152,534	110,831	(d)	...	CDP
Key West		36550	4-C	25,759	25,478	22,520	11,190	40,234	580,088	.0105	431,683	123	42,211	84	66,748	351	94,963	34,875	(d)	...	Inc. Place
Kissimmee	KISS	36950	4-C	59,892	47,814	16,579	21,679	33,114	992,969	.0182	651,723	185	90,978	181	34,232	180	87,532	39,251	37,813	21	Inc. Place
Lake City		37775	4-C	10,320	9,980	15,376	3,929	28,557	158,681	.0042	253,511	72	59,728	119	7,919	42	25,917	12,049	41,231	23	Inc. Place
Lakeland	LKLD	38250	3-AA	82,329	78,452	19,578	35,403	33,491	1,611,798	.0317	1,430,170	406	223,342	444	58,804	310	237,110	76,908	349,513	191	Inc. Place
Lake Magdalene	TAM	38350		32,211	28,755	21,048	13,087	36,159	677,970	.0146	763,020	217	159,040	316	43,183	227	78,147	50,732	(d)	...	CDP
Lake Park	MIA-	38600	4-S	9,787	8,721	13,400	3,470	32,462	131,149	.0070	615,531	175	59,601	119	12,071	64	12,627	5,753	(d)	...	Inc. Place
Lakeside	JAX	38813		36,659	30,927	20,167	12,673	44,525	739,295	.0128	462,302	131	73,501	146	23,492	124	57,389	27,425	(d)	...	CDP
Lake Worth	MIA-	39075	4-S	39,326	35,133	12,196	14,327	29,482	479,633	.0086	207,681	59	2,707	5	11,041	58	34,267	35,295	22,295	12	Inc. Place
Largo	ST.PET	39425	4-S	68,892	69,371	20,523	33,175	32,600	1,413,848	.0261	1,070,517	304	94,120	187	34,978	184	198,002	86,039	135,963	74	Inc. Place
Lauderdale Lakes	MIA-	39525	4-S	34,680	31,705	14,367	12,743	31,114	498,258	.0091	288,231	82	7,256	14	15,506	82	31,005	30,705	(d)	...	Inc. Place
Lauderhill	MIA-	39550	4-S	64,571	57,585	15,034	24,664	31,056	970,733	.0169	478,094	136	54,668	109	27,906	147	63,295	52,912	(d)	...	Inc. Place
Leesburg		39875	4-C	16,150	15,956	17,181	6,429	31,532	277,481	.0065	349,062	99	66,712	133	11,213	59	35,601	31,278	39,462	22	Inc. Place
Lehigh Acres	FTMY-	39925		39,697	33,430	15,409	14,761	36,942	611,695	.0101	247,158	70	107,701	214	8,249	43	60,687	12,210	(d)	...	CDP
Margate	MIA-	43125		56,621	53,909	17,532	22,991	36,869	992,679	.0190	773,427	220	56,549	112	13,335	70	149,490	71,455	(d)	...	Inc. Place
Melbourne	MELB-	43975	2-A	77,012	71,382	19,500	32,960	33,654	1,501,733	.0318	1,589,161	451	180,373	359	67,927	358	152,612	100,984	737,586	404	Inc. Place
Merritt Island	MELB-	44275		39,677	36,090	23,714	16,344	43,550	940,920	.0173	751,641	213	200,157	398	32,268	170	64,845	39,748	(d)	...	CDP
Miami	MIA-	45000	1-AA	371,978	362,470	13,099	130,757	26,446	4,872,398	.1003	3,861,375	1,096	264,375	526	488,934	2,573	449,488	386,086	546,582	299	Inc. Place
Miami Beach	MIA-	45025	3-S	90,783	87,933	23,965	45,277	29,152	2,175,610	.0307	664,798	189	20,165	40	116,000	611	177,750	123,312	(d)	...	Inc. Place
Miramar	MIA-	45975		92,007	72,739	14,495	28,050	41,351	1,333,610	.0242	756,424	215	101,481	202	9,095	48	94,089	32,028	73,431	40	Inc. Place
Naples	NAP	47625	3-A	20,517	20,976	45,631	10,743	54,314	936,209	.0194	1,163,927	331	154,542	307	190,038	1,000	127,449	81,248	48,299	26	Inc. Place
New Port Richey	ST.PET	48500	4-S	17,532	16,117	17,249	7,498	28,337	302,416	.0052	165,005	47	36,199	72	4,660	25	26,445	18,144	(d)	...	Inc. Place
North Fort Myers	FTMY-	49350		47,752	40,214	19,334	22,892	32,294	923,244	.0144	371,102	105	102,825	204	8,661	46	76,610	23,407	(d)	...	CDP
North Lauderdale	MIA-	49425		36,487	32,264	13,378	11,755	37,201	488,123	.0083	188,830	54	49,569	99	3,916	21	34,343	4,754	(d)	...	Inc. Place
North Miami	MIA-	49450	4-Sr	62,665	59,880	12,550	20,443	29,355	786,461	.0174	739,739	210	61,854	123	7,663	40	72,874	37,762	24,279	13	Inc. Place
North Miami Beach	MIA-	49475	3-S	42,661	40,786	13,052	13,870	31,378	556,832	.0118	482,506	137	48,770	97	50,330	265	55,409	34,972	42,539	23	Inc. Place
North Port	PUN-	49675		30,097	22,797	13,691	11,307	35,168	412,068	.0062	67,695	19	3,350	7	1,382	7	27,356	5,779	(d)	...	Inc. Place
Oakland Park	MIA-	50575	4-S	34,430	30,966	18,061	14,467	35,265	621,825	.0118	481,883	137	37,927	75	24,966	131	57,521	41,267	99,232	54	Inc. Place
Ocala	OCA	50750	3-AA	47,889	45,943	17,756	19,469	31,227	850,308	.0232	1,474,526	419	309,967	616	50,487	266	109,553	85,269	510,922	280	Inc. Place
Orlando	ORL	53000	2-AA	201,139	185,951	20,448	85,875	35,335	4,112,932	.0813	3,755,756	1,066	378,185	752	213,923	1,126	452,900	171,854	1,553,663	851	Inc. Place
Ormond Beach	D.BCH	53150		38,332	36,301	22,002	15,748	38,177	843,392	.0127	326,722	93	71,882	143	9,105	48	70,743	27,857	56,129	31	Inc. Place
Oviedo	ORL	53575		32,369	26,316	20,327	9,989	56,149	657,952	.0102	269,857	77	57,830	115	32,695	172	72,208	20,999	(d)	...	Inc. Place
Palatka		53875	4-C	10,383	10,033	14,111	3,944	27,820	146,518	.0032	138,265	39	32,107	64	6,491	34	14,410	10,194	277,085	152	Inc. Place
Palm Bay	MELB-	54000		89,432	79,413	16,377	33,876	35,055	1,464,602	.0228	473,202	134	58,374	116	11,707	62	106,408	42,947	544,829	298	Inc. Place
Palm Beach	MIA-	54025	4-S	11,058	10,468	73,066	5,654	75,512	807,968	.0098	234,347	67	3,430	7	134,205	706	27,414	9,601	(d)	...	Inc. Place
Palm Beach Gardens	MIA-	54075		39,614	35,058	29,369	16,292	54,797	1,163,424	.0200	842,821	239	181,344	361	197,053	1,037	126,263	48,349	(d)	...	Inc. Place
Palm Coast		54200		47,876	32,732	19,893	18,967	38,801	952,412	.0130	179,498	51	50,255	100	6,588	35	39,628	22,031	(d)	...	Inc. Place
Palm Harbor	ST.PET	54350		59,617	59,248	22,398	25,243	41,943	1,335,317	.0208	604,666	172	60,033	119	17,699	93	169,101	49,291	(d)	...	CDP
Panama City	PNCY	54700	3-A	38,060	36,417	17,063	15,402	30,353	649,425	.0155	859,246	244	173,205	344	35,581	187	82,324	44,719	247,806	136	Inc. Place
Pembroke Pines	MIA-	55775		170,837	137,427	20,709	62,302	50,147	3,537,778	.0555	1,553,790	441	392,694	781	128,669	677	213,689	103,432	54,183	30	Inc. Place
Pensacola	PENS	55925	2-A	51,998	56,255	22,000	24,703	31,842	1,143,958	.0235	1,175,452	334	285,116	567	112,764	594	132,200	92,796	226,643	124	Inc. Place
Pine Hills	ORL	56825		46,879	41,764	12,877	14,707	32,598	603,657	.0159	883,588	251	90,652	180	20,480	108	64,777	29,130	(d)	...	CDP
Pinellas Park	ST.PET	56975	4-S	44,729	45,658	16,957	18,698	33,932	758,450	.0181	1,001,262	284	242,717	483	26,009	137	80,220	142,184	630,218	345	Inc. Place
Plantation	MIA-	57425	3-Sm	86,418	82,934	21,272	33,406	41,955	1,838,305	.0365	1,729,072	491	185,708	369	153,856	810	207,990	80,806	...	...	Inc. Place
Plant City	TAM	57550		32,993	29,915	15,697	11,560	34,766	517,892	.0105	437,039	124	82,739	165	10,437	55	71,551	20,213	461,663	253	Inc. Place
Pompano Beach	MIA-	58050	3-S	80,914	78,191	21,410	35,066	35,192	1,732,404	.0353	1,740,590	494	83,187	165	41,733	220	151,595	68,278	436,553	239	Inc. Place
Port Charlotte	PUN-	58350		52,467	46,451	17,708	22,515	32,028	929,074	.0187	828,126	235	290,258	577	54,391	286	85,091	58,060	(d)	...	CDP
Port Orange	D.BCH	58575		50,068	45,823	19,223	20,395	37,385	962,471	.0139	254,419	72	79,688	158	2,874	15	39,463	30,322	(d)	...	Inc. Place
Port Saint Lucie	FTPI	58715		116,407	88,769	17,613	43,420	37,899	2,050,321	.0306	581,176	165	112,133	223	16,099	85	149,258	78,991	(d)	...	Inc. Place
Riviera Beach	MIA-	60975		31,934	29,884	15,084	11,237	31,976	481,704	.0100	434,662	123	26,935	54	22,547	119	27,890	34,474	127,279	70	Inc. Place
Saint Augustine		62500	4-C	11,243	11,592	20,100	4,623	34,197	225,979	.0043	180,781	51	6,330	13	17,052	90	28,350	9,863	38,415	21	Inc. Place
Saint Petersburg	ST.PET	63000	2-BB	250,426	248,232	19,093	108,853	33,076	4,781,348	.0899	3,696,424	1,050	349,764	696	148,707	783	505,680	233,181	650,404	356	Inc. Place
Sanford	ORL	63650	4-S	42,218	38,291	16,458	14,924	34,506	694,806	.0150	721,088	205	143,827	286	68,945	363	71,694	46,464	124,812	68	Inc. Place
Sarasota	SAR-B	64175	2-A	53,082	52,715	19,019	22,257	33,629	1,009,582	.0225	1,196,314	340	40,833	81	138,345	728	94,114	79,713	85,588	47	Inc. Place
South Miami Heights	MIA-	67575		35,572	33,522	13,450	9,996	42,676	478,443	.0089	278,269	79	37,163	74	6,181	33	44,753	15,128	(d)	...	CDP
Spring Hill	SPR.H	68350		79,904	69,078	16,337	31,298	32,727	1,305,354	.0217	579,944	165	75,484	150	16,339	86	176,495	52,055	(d)	...	CDP
Stuart	STU	68875	3-B	16,501	14,633	23,082	7,980	34,114	380,873	.0082	439,408	125	28,125	56	19,825	104	59,167	31,971	194,673	107	Inc. Place
Sunrise	MIA-	69700		92,607	85,779	18,400	34,555	40,569	1,703,969	.0351	1,642,908	467	262,716	522	301,016	1,584	147,711	127,056	104,360	57	Inc. Place
Tallahassee	TALL	70600	3-AA	156,589	150,624	19,426	70,870	33,396	3,041,916	.0607	2,776,290	788	482,395	959	152,698	804	401,543	186,438	...	...	Inc. Place
Tamarac	MIA-	70675		60,883	55,588	19,455	28,984	32,878	1,184,493	.0189	527,160	150	43,862	87	24,710	130	199,728	65,068	(d)	...	Inc. Place
Tamiami	MIA-	70700		58,139	54,788	14,048	16,385	45,436	816,717	.0128	207,245	59	23,548	47	9,708	51	68,327	31,951	(d)	...	CDP
Tampa	TAM	71000	2-AA	324,897	303,447	20,418	129,296	35,745	6,633,846	.1274	5,614,605	1,594	605,033	1,203	358,016	1,884	616,846	384,085	1,125,623	616	Inc. Place
The Hammocks	MIA-	71569		50,277	47,379	15,496	15,302	48,963	779,098	.0126	289,635	82	68,785	137	13,238	70	58,464	27,991	(d)	...	CDP
Titusville	TITUS	71900	4-B	41,172	40,670	20,402	17,249	36,333	839,990	.0142	484,010	137	147,958	294	11,089	58	80,177	38,580	29,319	16	Inc. Place
Town 'n' Country	TAM	72145		81,239	72,523	19,109	31,300	39,985	1,552,426	.0285	1,118,587	318	117,835	234	16,300	86	88,624	66,778	(d)	...	CDP
Venice	VEN	73900	4-C	17,921	17,764	23,156	9,198	36,073	414,983	.0067	216,842	62	5,314	11	12,821	67	37,724	11,279	(d)	...	Inc. Place
Vero Beach	VERO	74150	3-B	17,193	17,705	31,353	8,607	45,512	539,058	.0093	403,449	115	16,503	33	23,368	123	73,845	41,636	39,036	21	Inc. Place
Wellington	MIA-	75812		47,575	38,216	20,735	14,872	62,368	986,446	.0139	242,651	69	79,650	158	4,548	24	47,427	27,293	(d)	...	Inc. Place
Westchester	MIA-	76075		32,123	30,271	13,372	9,839	38,472	429,542	.0091	378,820	108	22,930	46	26,281	138	76,408	42,405	(d)	...	CDP
West Little River	MIA-	76487		34,484	32,498	8,203	9,577	21,631	282,884	.0062	165,892	47	2,744	5	6,675	35	22,992	16,621	(d)	...	CDP
Weston	MIA-	76582		58,794	49,286	30,421	19,067	71,817	1,788,601	.0212	193,526	55	...	...	10,921	57	77,860	30,948	(d)	...	Inc. Place
West Palm Beach	MIA-	76600	2-AA	92,336	82,103	17,066	36,207	34,118	1,575,803	.0403	2,397,340	681	294,119	585	156,507	824	267,559	120,915	1,886,388	1,033	Inc. Place
Winter Haven	WNHV	78275	3-B	27,440	26,487	19,832	12,327	31,360	544,179	.0102	420,574	119	60,439	120	17,277	91	67,693	27,717	74,698	41	Inc. Place
Winter Park	ORL	78300	3-S	24,193	24,090	34,221	10,558	42,127	827,905	.0149	713,411	203	61,168	122	38,156	201	62,572	46,495	(d)	...	Inc. Place
Winter Springs	ORL	78325		36,180	31,666	22,987	12,789	48,734	831,663	.0105	94,946	27	15,717	31	1,178	6	23,495	21,197	(d)	...	Inc. Place
Georgia																					
Albany	ALB	01052	3-AA	76,098	76,939	14,229	28,572	30,884	1,082,801	.0246	1,181,152	335	277,967	553	60,379	318	161,455	53,489	...	...	Inc. Place
Alpharetta	ATL	01696		40,050	34,854	29,198	15,944	70,075	1,169,364	.0187	679,707	193	93,627	186	35,446	187	110,052	22,125	330,203	181	Inc. Place
Athens	ATH	03440	3-A	105,535	100,266	14,754	43,875	27,966	1,557,083	.0331	1,466,169	416	307,832	612	78,063	411	215,259	65,112	577,408	316	Inc. Place
Atlanta	ATL	04000	1-AA	399,217	416,474	18,753	160,865	37,396	7,486,364	.1360	5,167,026	1,467	663,666	1,320	680,327	3,581	639,579	261,165	3,093,862	1,694	Inc. Place
Augusta	AUG	04204	2-A	190,195	195,182	15,474	72,062	31,902	2,942,988	.0602	2,561,078	727	495,999	986	172,972	910	268,785	127,419	...	...	Inc. Place
Brunswick	BRUNS	11560	3-A	15,982	15,600	13,208	6,228	24,318	211,089	.0064	409,418	116	13,171	26	8,461	45	71,948	22,772	370,515	203	Inc. Place
Carrollton		13492	4-C	23,976	19,843	16,869	8,701	33,189	404,460	.0077	304,845	87	74,998	149	16,618	87	45,723	17,383	462,998	253	Inc. Place
Cartersville		13688	4-C	18,954	15,925	19,116	6,945	40,999	362,324	.0072	330,869	94	70,200	140	5,316	28	41,968	15,651	1,157,973	634	Inc. Place
Chamblee	ATL	15172	4-Sr	10,227	9,552	16,326	2,844	46,397	166,963	.0044	269,433	77	...	...	2,506	13	21,208	5,295	190,956	105	Inc. Place
Columbus	COL	19007	3-AA	182,354	185,781	16,496	71,716	33,741	3,008,082	.0596	2,481,631	705	441,082	877	169,101	890	303,883	169,549	...	...	Inc. Place
Dalton		21380	3-A	32,872	27,912	17,664	11,328	37,137	580,643	.0136	743,919	211	137,269	273	35,068	185	81,762	25,548	1,986,334	1,087	Inc. Place
Decatur	ATL	22052	4-Sr	17,354	18,147	22,881	7,647	42,697	397,069	.0055	100,598	29	...	...	4,769	25	6,905	6,876	(d)	...	Inc. Place
Doraville	ATL	23536	4-S	10,796	9,862	15,480	3,268	40,017	167,126	.0037	176,154	50	11,679	23	3,466	18	11,120	5,991	...	...	Inc. Place
Dublin		24376	4-C	16,730	15,857	14,505	6,113	31,072	242,672	.0061	331,153	94	65,773	131	14,359	76	54,303	15,364	367,801	201	Inc. Place
Dunwoody	ATL	24768		33,494	32,808	37,244	13,955	66,062	1,247,453	.0212	947,341	269	185,999	370	164,493	866	79,007	44,427	(d)	...	CDP
East Point	ATL	25720	4-Sr	40,437	39,595	12,022	14,796	30,954	486,127	.0107	436,747	124	36,126	72	10,005	53	133,224	38,836	122,681	67	Inc. Place
Gainesville		31908	3-A	33,675	25,578	15,865	10,774	35,452	534,244	.0129	708,290	201	172,355	343	28,409	150	68,105	42,039	598,564	328	Inc. Place
Griffin		35324	4-C	25,050	23,451	17,281	9,532	35,967	432,884	.0078	280,931	80	43,987	87	12,986	68	52,745	14,533	381,753	209	Inc. Place
Hinesville		38964		34,471	30,392	15,127	13,043	33,011	521,439	.0096	321,347	91	85,161	169	16,701	88	48,214	8,903	(d)	...	Inc. Place
Lagrange		44340	4-A	27,514	25,998	16,614	10,708	34,748	457,113	.0093	410,305	117	67,104	133	21,387	113	63,151	14,464	651,225	357	Inc. Place
Lawrenceville	ATL	45488	4-Sr	26,509	22,397	19,471	8,381	50,128	516,146	.0124	719,683	204	68,676	137	7,941	42	68,865	18,733	305,851	167	Inc. Place
Mableton	ATL	48288		33,155	29,733	17,925	11,195	44,013	594,306	.0106	379,546	108	65,547	130	6,487	34	96,269	24,435	(d)	...	CDP
Macon	MAC	49000	3-AA	96,074	97,255	14,349	37,779	28,823	1,378,530	.0345	1,876,864	533	407,015	809	87,946	463	232,268	110,162	3,709,119	2,031	Inc. Place
Marietta	ATL	49756	3-S	68,491	58,748	24,598	25,664	50,081	1,684,757	.0285	1,085,550	308	97,724	194	25,743	135	160,101	37,939	462,440	253	Inc. Place
Martinez	AUG	50036		31,786	27,749	22,764	11,250	50,805	723,586	.0127	501,521	142	95,684	190	7,968	42	79,911	15,769	(d)	...	CDP
Milledgeville		51492	4-C	18,521	18,757	10,974	4,778	34,142	203,252	.0053	263,851	75	71,746	143	11,194	59	42,339	12,493	...	...	Inc. Place
Morrow	ATL	53004	4-Sm	4,648	4,882	17,010	1,623	38,065	79,062	.0034	279,589	79	88,679	176	19,847	104	12,414	8,172	(d)	...	Inc. Place
Moultrie		53060	4-C	14,079	14,387	12,975	5,263	26,800	182,669	.0045	235,400	67	38,597	77	9,714	51	40,902	8,075	99,754	55	Inc. Place
North Atlanta	ATL	56000		39,386	38,579	28,466	16,140	50,770	1,121,173	.0151	317,762	90	16,859	34	13,700	72	89,749	28,688	(d)	...	CDP
Peachtree City	ATL	59724		34,389	31,580	28,564	11,560	66,136	982,284	.0136	325,944	93	30,753	61	20,098	106	82,116	12,384	597,925	327	Inc. Place
Redan	ATL	63952		34,549	33,841	18,036	11,946	46,631	623,128	.0087	115,467	33	2,477	5	1,609	8	47,699	6,135	(d)	...	CDP
Rome	ROME	66668	3-A	36,825	34,980	15,728	13,733	32,843	579,167	.0121	535,556	152	139,359	277	26,989	142	43,599	39,800	425,547	233	Inc. Place
Roswell	ATL	67284	4-S	86,891	79,334	26,968	33,009	67,962	2,343,305	.0416	1,799,806	511	123,467	246	88,419	465	254,615	42,875	85,639	47	Inc. Place
Sandy Springs	ATL	68516		86,511	85,781	34,377	39,497	57,345	2,974,018	.0437	1,413,667	401	137,691	274	78,422	413	167,975	43,980	(d)	...	CDP
Savannah	SAV	69000	2-A	127,884	131,510	15,804	50,773	30,475	2,021,049	.0411	1,745,215	496	343,856	684	117,108	616	234,587	69,057	450,528	247	Inc. Place
Smyrna	ATL	71492	3-S	48,106	40,999	23,052	19,885	43,745	1,108,950	.0214	1,004,300	285	122,068	243	26,311	138	103,301	50,959	75,948	42	Inc. Place
Statesboro		73256	4-C	23,508	22,698	12,579	8,976	24,059	295,705	.0074	382,393	109	117,600	234	23,543	124	53,568	23,933	169,079	93	Inc. Place
Thomasville		76224	4-C	18,357	18,162	14,773	6,922	30,568	271,184	.0071	411,550	117	90,350	180	16,438	87	48,793	28,521	374,101	205	Inc. Place
Tifton		76476	4-B	15,940	15,060	14,042	5,649	30,397	223,827	.0056	298,055	85	59,966	119	11,856	62	39,027	14,678	162,820	89	Inc. Place
Union City	ATL	78324	4-Sm	12,212	11,621	14,408	5,216	35,880	175,945	.0093	816,915	232	137,614	274	42,879	226	33,660	22,876	(d)	...	Inc. Place
Valdosta	VALD	78800	3-A	43,557	43,724	15,429	16,948	31,005	672,040	.0159	833,304	237	128,736	256	51,688	272	88,167	22,253	366,069	200	Inc. Place
Warner Robins	MAC	80508	4-B	55,477	48,804	19,828	22,428	40,020	1,099,986	.0187	628,975	179	102,451	204	8,951	47	82,534	20,277	...	...	Inc. Place
Waycross		80956	3-A	15,168	15,333	13,915	5,967	27,069	211,057	.0051	267,345	76	90,282	180	7,324	39	36,946	17,884	89,718	49	Inc. Place
Hawaii																					
'Aiea	HON	00550	4-Sm	9,371	9,019	20,318	2,909	54,078	190,405	.0047	284,129	81	62,236	124	35,073	185	16,826	21,149	105,365	58	CDP
Hilo	HILO	14650	3-A	44,700	40,759	17,037	16,088	36,664	761,541	.0163	777,522	221	131,194	261	38,536	203	175,712	57,200	34,467	19	CDP
Honolulu	HON	17000	2-AA	390,815	371,657	23,237	149,838	43,412	9,081,341	.1580	6,184,298	1,756	1,185,913	2,358	1,012,104	5,327	773,253	542,311	446,893	245	CDP
Kahului		22700	4-A	21,831	20,146	17,181	6,368	43,827	375,080	.0133	1,002,093	285	278,159	553	64,566	340	95,795	65,179	41,776	23	CDP
Kailua	HON	23150	4-S	37,945	36,513	25,118	12,888	59,590	953,084	.0131	264,096	75	39,167	78	5,139	27	57,308	16,793	(d)	...	CDP
Kāne'ohe	HON	28250	4-S	36,342	34,970	22,148	11,567	61,068	804,904	.0123	338,566	96	39,698	79	37,157	196	61,338	36,336	(d)	...	CDP
Lahaina		42950	4-B	9,881	9,118	17,896	2,818	49,234	176,830	.0042	232,288	66	9,895	20	69,920	368	58,341	16,493	(d)	...	CDP
Lihue		45200	4-A	5,963	5,674	21,146	2,333	44,521	126,093	.0032	200,749	57	58,653	117	4,476	24	25,549	12,856	(d)	...	CDP
Pearl City	HON	62600		32,188	30,976	19,157	9,416	55,722	616,617	.0095	229,230	65	103,193	205	24,953	131	18,642	20,090	(d)	...	CDP
Wailuku		77450	4-B	13,322	12,296	20,315	4,922	46,072	270,636	.0041	103,955	30	7,263	14	2,877	15	34,262	5,491	(d)	...	CDP
Waimalu	HON	77750		30,521	29,371	23,839	11,113	54,471	727,597	.0117	387,505	110	93,343	186	47,300	249	23,757	29,327	(d)	...	CDP
Waipahu	HON	79700		34,402	33,108	14,534	7,987	54,322	499,989	.0104	436,639	124	105,455	210	39,906	210	63,811	28,890	(d)	...	CDP
Idaho																					
Boise	BOIS	08830	3-AA	202,968	185,787	21,869	84,380	40,654	4,438,729	.0830	3,605,400	1,024	658,740	1,310	180,318	949	509,862	132,979	1,990,826	1,090	Inc. Place
Caldwell		12250		33,300	25,967	14,120	11,474	30,308	470,206	.0105	484,659	138	19,718	39	1,088	6	79,570	22,576	75,740	41	Inc. Place
Coeur d'Alene		16750	4-C	38,565	34,514	18,125	15,769	33,870	698,973	.0153	778,346	221	168,681	335	23,183	122	94,021	27,711	81,665	45	Inc. Place
Idaho Falls	IDFL	39700	3-A	55,034	50,730	19,082	20,719	40,366	1,050,136	.0187	688,103	195	203,457	405	22,770	120	74,049	37,937	110,555	61	Inc. Place
Lewiston	LEW	46540	3-A	31,683	30,904	18,306	13,344	34,869	579,974	.0116	513,552	146	107,195	213	9,912	52	78,581	16,282	...	...	Inc. Place
Meridian	BOIS	52120		46,902	34,919	19,247	16,458	49,485	902,739	.0147	429,607	122	98,216	195	1,973	10	55,361	7,363	56,374	31	Inc. Place
Moscow		54550	4-B	21,599	21,291	13,867	8,284	27,519	299,515	.0063	262,981	75	57,292	114	10,359	55	62,319	13,968	(d)	...	Inc. Place
Nampa	BOIS	56260	3-B	74,247	51,867	14,597	25,852	35,161	1,083,797	.0211	780,915	222	161,769	322	21,025	111	96,952	29,754	936,799	513	Inc. Place
Pocatello	POC	64090	3-A	49,963	51,466	17,040	19,674	33,937	851,368	.0168	702,094	199	78,600	156	11,924	63	131,617	42,716	208,058	114	Inc. Place
Twin Falls		82810	3-A	37,475	34,469	16,225	14,450	32,793	608,036	.0145	786,473	223	214,161	426	32,903	173	70,435	29,368	177,258	97	Inc. Place
Illinois																					
Addison	CHI	00243	4-S	37,465	35,914	19,033	12,070	48,962	713,078	.0144	666,430	189	60,227	120	11,741	62	76,140	17,755	820,700	449	Inc. Place
Alton	ST.L	01114	3-S	30,058	30,496	18,285	12,985	33,433	549,613	.0113	530,249	151	115,713	230	12,267	65	70,130	37,771	76,615	42	Inc. Place
Arlington Heights	CHI	02154	3-S	73,459	76,031	25,265	28,655	57,603	1,855,955	.0311	1,172,989	333	100,287	199	63,480	334	233,348	115,896	902,885	494	Inc. Place

Source: Devonshire Associates Ltd. and Scan/US, Inc. 2005.
* Source: 1997 Census of Manufactures.
Not classified as a Principal Business Center.

...Data less than 1,000.
(d) Data not available.

Continued on next page

Principal Business Centers and Other Places with 30,000 or More: Population/Income/Sales, *Continued*

Place Name	Ranally Metro Area	FIPS Place Code	Ranally City Rating	Population Estimate 7/1/05	Population Census 4/1/00	Per Capita Income 2004	Households Estimate 7/1/05	Median Household Income 2004	Disposable Income 2004 ($1,000)	Market Ability Index 2004	Total Retail Sales 2004 Sales ($1,000)	Total Retail Ranally Sales Units	General Merchandise 2004 Sales ($1,000)	General Merchandise Ranally Sales Units	Apparel Store 2004 Sales ($1,000)	Apparel Store Ranally Sales Units	Food Store Sales 2004 ($1,000)	Health & Drug Store 2004 ($1,000)	Manufacturers Value Added 1997* ($1,000)	Manufacturers Ranally Mfg. Units	Place Type
Aurora	CHI	03012	3-SS	188,282	142,990	20,056	58,546	52,545	3,776,247	.0579	1,452,098	412	318,750	634	124,182	654	195,361	141,355	1,415,118	775	Inc. Place
Bartlett	CHI	04013		39,220	36,706	24,334	12,930	68,784	954,365	.0122	153,043	43	...	...	2,685	14	32,442	24,965	147,760	81	Inc. Place
Belleville	ST.L	04845	3-S	42,617	41,410	20,372	18,104	38,136	868,213	.0144	466,434	132	48,432	96	8,133	43	60,445	54,316	159,016	87	Inc. Place
Berwyn	CHI	05573	4-S	54,996	54,016	16,155	19,339	40,620	888,449	.0155	475,850	135	13,372	27	21,978	116	89,718	66,584	47,120	26	Inc. Place
Bloomingdale	CHI	06587	4-Sm	22,685	21,675	28,559	8,558	61,212	647,858	.0145	857,514	243	284,852	566	105,485	555	28,421	60,809	37,434	20	Inc. Place
Bloomington	BLOOM-	06613	3-AA	71,392	64,808	24,045	30,083	45,738	1,716,591	.0302	1,227,611	349	156,666	312	85,874	452	126,538	95,127	...	...	Inc. Place
Bolingbrook	CHI	07133		64,879	56,321	21,388	18,697	62,004	1,387,622	.0226	724,237	206	158,322	315	10,122	53	83,640	60,718	530,148	290	Inc. Place
Buffalo Grove	CHI	09447		43,380	42,909	28,664	15,403	70,717	1,243,445	.0199	721,361	205	1,919	4	6,527	34	53,384	77,016	337,885	185	Inc. Place
Calumet City	CHI	10487	3-Sm	40,107	39,071	14,904	14,978	36,729	597,770	.0160	946,646	269	283,078	563	114,553	603	50,530	63,987	77,996	43	Inc. Place
Canton		11007	4-C	15,465	15,288	15,456	5,811	31,446	239,023	.0046	170,622	48	35,628	71	5,068	27	25,178	18,165	(d)	...	Inc. Place
Carbondale	CARB-	11163	3-A	19,222	20,681	12,770	9,877	15,785	245,472	.0070	421,532	120	125,791	250	23,061	121	39,217	24,126	(d)	...	Inc. Place
Carol Stream	CHI	11332		41,852	40,438	22,579	14,271	59,762	944,981	.0149	457,066	130	14,334	29	1,943	10	37,052	17,345	503,514	276	Inc. Place
Carpentersville	CHI	11358		41,858	30,586	15,923	11,620	50,958	666,513	.0092	72,821	21	7,796	16	2,883	15	19,102	7,006	137,041	75	Inc. Place
Centralia		12164	4-B	13,769	14,136	19,365	5,896	32,387	266,642	.0049	194,585	55	46,078	92	7,906	42	29,425	10,411	103,956	57	Inc. Place
Champaign	CH-U	12385	3-AA	68,053	67,518	17,673	27,894	32,485	1,202,676	.0255	1,223,801	348	406,412	808	76,032	400	107,909	88,915	219,205	120	Inc. Place
Chicago	CHI	14000	1-AAA	2,896,965	2,896,016	16,607	1,022,399	37,697	48,110,282	.7868	20,332,249	5,773	1,979,030	3,936	1,821,890	9,589	3,836,315	2,959,137	13,497,813	7,390	Inc. Place
Chicago Heights	CHI	14026	4-S	32,461	32,776	13,163	10,220	38,869	427,295	.0087	332,378	94	3,031	6	1,186	6	65,511	30,902	419,292	230	Inc. Place
Cicero	CHI	14351	4-Sr	90,190	85,616	10,030	23,485	35,893	904,606	.0174	410,186	116	83,164	165	17,409	92	64,638	37,780	499,866	274	Inc. Place
Crystal Lake	CHI	17887	4-S	45,028	38,000	26,807	15,461	62,446	1,207,080	.0212	900,155	256	187,037	372	22,842	120	80,707	49,581	449,038	246	Inc. Place
Danville	DANV	18563	3-A	33,617	33,904	15,967	13,441	30,429	536,775	.0113	514,036	146	134,310	267	17,717	93	70,238	39,669	507,484	278	Inc. Place
Decatur	DEC	18823	3-AA	78,430	81,860	18,953	34,645	33,543	1,486,484	.0283	1,181,629	336	223,906	445	39,096	206	153,205	90,193	...	...	Inc. Place
DeKalb	DKLB	19161	4-C	40,994	39,018	15,305	13,619	32,455	627,431	.0121	460,961	131	84,107	167	15,259	80	57,765	31,195	271,271	149	Inc. Place
Des Plaines	CHI	19642	3-S	58,857	58,720	18,261	21,561	45,644	1,074,797	.0188	643,718	183	52,538	104	9,289	49	114,033	72,735	988,977	541	Inc. Place
Downers Grove	CHI	20591	4-S	49,739	48,724	28,056	19,279	58,647	1,395,481	.0302	1,724,455	490	53,957	107	34,009	179	122,968	69,831	426,765	234	Inc. Place
East St. Louis	ST.L	22255	4-S	30,888	31,542	11,028	10,927	21,270	340,643	.0061	122,100	35	3,017	6	...	...	43,450	13,109	63,825	35	Inc. Place
Effingham		22736	4-B	12,278	12,384	20,748	5,341	36,628	254,743	.0068	442,487	126	58,214	116	17,595	93	33,579	14,670	288,900	158	Inc. Place
Elgin	CHI	23074	3-S	109,858	94,487	19,152	35,071	50,476	2,103,983	.0341	987,788	280	84,155	167	5,511	29	157,636	59,443	909,017	498	Inc. Place
Elk Grove Village	CHI	23256	4-Sr	33,377	34,727	21,674	12,275	55,324	723,414	.0152	784,870	223	114,261	227	2,415	13	93,050	21,046	2,109,266	1,155	Inc. Place
Elmhurst	CHI	23620	4-Sr	44,011	42,762	28,381	15,997	62,310	1,249,073	.0237	1,162,074	330	...	...	14,980	79	129,065	99,815	226,566	124	Inc. Place
Evanston	CHI	24582	3-S	74,008	74,239	26,695	28,522	51,327	1,975,654	.0310	1,040,795	296	89,507	178	43,431	229	202,202	160,738	167,457	92	Inc. Place
Evergreen Park	CHI	24634	3-Sm	20,361	20,821	18,568	7,031	49,525	378,073	.0072	300,075	85	96,850	193	61,017	321	19,369	10,737	(d)	...	Inc. Place
Fairview Heights	ST.L	25141	3-Sm	15,901	15,034	21,296	6,373	42,183	338,632	.0113	858,185	244	306,608	610	116,061	611	50,239	52,674	(d)	...	Inc. Place
Franklin Park	CHI	27702	4-S	19,997	19,434	13,812	6,422	42,588	276,201	.0060	267,472	76	30,715	61	2,915	15	39,218	11,675	1,963,752	1,075	Inc. Place
Freeport		27884	4-C	25,951	26,443	20,332	11,276	36,194	527,628	.0094	358,644	102	76,626	152	12,116	64	62,696	30,445	595,642	326	Inc. Place
Galesburg	GLSB	28326	3-A	33,001	33,706	16,913	13,463	31,579	558,144	.0115	517,736	147	118,717	236	11,700	62	72,649	34,056	...	...	Inc. Place
Glendale Heights	CHI	29730		32,738	31,765	19,364	11,049	52,123	633,942	.0101	284,248	81	36,093	72	...	...	41,095	21,953	190,122	104	Inc. Place
Glenview	CHI	29938	4-Sr	41,916	41,847	34,490	14,902	65,261	1,445,664	.0211	675,466	192	49,105	98	25,313	133	79,037	60,342	102,240	56	Inc. Place
Granite City	ST.L	30926	4-S	31,515	31,301	19,129	13,503	35,596	602,843	.0100	305,632	87	48,478	96	5,661	30	75,754	24,417	813,853	446	Inc. Place
Gurnee	CHI	32018		34,847	28,834	22,785	12,464	65,187	794,003	.0160	790,173	224	187,135	372	156,614	824	69,344	51,613	278,780	153	Inc. Place
Hanover Park	CHI	32746		39,396	38,278	16,897	11,002	56,436	665,694	.0096	138,250	39	8,967	18	2,279	12	22,372	14,771	(d)	...	Inc. Place
Harvey	CHI	33383	4-Sr	29,380	30,000	10,582	8,474	32,834	310,885	.0067	236,604	67	2,984	6	7,177	38	33,535	23,573	315,510	173	Inc. Place
Highland Park	CHI	34722	4-S	31,942	31,365	44,732	11,383	85,468	1,428,824	.0223	901,468	256	38,134	76	68,504	361	137,133	59,446	...	...	Inc. Place
Hinsdale	CHI	35307	4-S	18,407	17,349	55,744	6,299	89,743	1,026,073	.0128	314,193	89	57,443	114	65,731	346	9,022	16,913	(d)	...	Inc. Place
Hoffman Estates	CHI	35411		48,948	49,495	21,588	16,207	59,792	1,056,690	.0175	589,110	167	24,259	48	30,549	161	72,714	33,306	104,649	57	Inc. Place
Homewood	CHI	35879	4-S	19,269	19,543	21,371	7,169	51,915	411,798	.0092	501,711	142	65,761	131	14,401	76	78,874	37,866	(d)	...	Inc. Place
Jacksonville		38115	3-A	18,836	18,940	17,943	7,598	34,463	337,966	.0065	272,802	77	56,552	112	11,305	60	34,600	20,759	...	...	Inc. Place
Joliet	CHI	38570	3-SS	139,724	106,221	18,328	44,390	45,849	2,560,842	.0455	1,616,020	459	266,795	531	60,666	319	172,922	179,600	1,304,353	714	Inc. Place
Kankakee	KANK	38934	3-A	27,624	27,491	16,829	10,047	34,367	464,878	.0087	331,166	94	11,454	23	1,679	9	56,802	46,429	288,232	158	Inc. Place
Lake in the Hills	CHI	41183		30,142	23,152	25,897	9,940	64,992	780,589	.0091	32,936	9	1,021	2	3,802	20	7,141	4,056	(d)	...	Inc. Place
La Salle		42184	3-A	9,789	9,796	19,951	4,215	32,883	195,302	.0036	150,395	43	3,860	8	2,322	12	14,273	5,545	77,519	42	Inc. Place
Libertyville	CHI	43250	4-Sr	21,592	20,742	34,633	7,369	78,781	747,800	.0166	1,017,841	289	...	...	8,024	42	76,585	14,237	1,937,093	1,060	Inc. Place
Lombard	CHI	44407	3-Sm	42,512	42,322	24,531	16,477	54,628	1,042,880	.0199	940,307	267	170,944	340	111,991	589	52,652	33,093	146,397	80	Inc. Place
Macomb		45889	4-C	18,829	18,558	13,799	7,062	28,101	259,817	.0056	245,384	70	72,992	145	9,158	48	41,505	24,037	59,507	33	Inc. Place
Marion	CARB-	46916	4-B	16,277	16,035	19,183	6,999	31,848	312,249	.0076	441,415	125	144,544	287	13,318	70	34,881	11,180	...	...	Inc. Place
Matteson	CHI	47540	4-Sm	12,656	12,928	19,191	4,308	50,693	242,885	.0083	620,964	176	214,477	427	83,915	442	32,030	15,291	(d)	...	Inc. Place
Mattoon		47553	4-A	17,608	18,291	18,392	8,166	32,955	323,844	.0075	405,972	115	137,346	273	4,522	24	16,532	20,601	497,769	273	Inc. Place
Melrose Park	CHI	48242	3-S	23,839	23,171	13,940	7,556	38,226	332,315	.0094	571,216	162	74,510	148	24,816	131	68,484	29,351	1,093,761	599	Inc. Place
Moline	D-RI-M	49867	3-B	43,548	43,768	20,376	18,568	36,675	887,317	.0194	1,026,933	292	208,515	415	72,119	380	89,915	109,700	237,831	130	Inc. Place
Morton Grove	CHI	50647	4-S	22,067	22,451	21,585	7,759	57,630	476,317	.0098	484,218	137	4,112	8	30,136	159	34,375	42,549	717,167	393	Inc. Place
Mount Prospect	CHI	51089	3-S	56,928	56,265	21,526	21,016	52,054	1,225,408	.0217	844,925	240	217,334	432	55,199	291	112,145	80,503	270,726	148	Inc. Place
Mount Vernon		51180	3-A	16,339	16,269	17,650	7,128	30,447	288,378	.0076	466,742	133	83,073	165	14,512	76	33,218	28,093	368,582	202	Inc. Place
Mundelein	CHI	51349		34,287	30,935	20,811	10,585	62,499	713,546	.0111	307,977	87	25,755	51	9,865	52	49,041	36,545	305,034	167	Inc. Place
Naperville	CHI	51622	4-S	140,522	128,358	31,242	47,589	75,769	4,390,159	.0645	1,978,092	562	198,174	394	72,024	379	193,875	128,556	193,251	106	Inc. Place
Niles	CHI	53000	3-S	29,671	30,068	18,869	11,389	45,056	559,862	.0188	1,400,022	398	235,643	469	49,608	261	222,969	86,131	588,352	322	Inc. Place
Normal	BLOOM-	53234	4-S	48,193	45,386	16,653	16,491	37,845	802,578	.0156	635,574	180	173,867	346	48,967	258	65,850	40,240	...	...	Inc. Place
Norridge	CHI	53377	4-Sm	14,373	14,582	19,233	5,430	42,802	276,431	.0059	298,155	85	...	...	36,936	194	93,177	27,328	48,441	27	Inc. Place
Northbrook	CHI	53481	3-Sm	32,773	33,435	40,119	11,525	75,416	1,314,828	.0202	772,714	219	121,871	242	115,244	607	60,431	40,313	474,909	260	Inc. Place
North Chicago	CHI	53559		36,390	35,918	8,580	7,521	36,745	312,213	.0068	190,127	54	...	...	...	...	28,064	3,930	130,015	71	Inc. Place
North Riverside	CHI	54144	4-Sm	6,875	6,688	25,258	2,905	50,298	173,651	.0049	345,423	98	90,692	180	75,081	395	38,023	16,234	(d)	...	Inc. Place
Oak Brook	CHI	54534	3-S	8,834	8,702	53,490	3,154	84,501	472,532	.0096	578,885	164	236,221	470	82,603	435	2,649	8,129	220,093	120	Inc. Place
Oak Lawn	CHI	54820	3-S	51,900	55,245	20,145	20,083	43,742	1,045,528	.0254	1,509,392	429	121,361	241	46,485	245	217,649	109,462	30,654	17	Inc. Place
Oak Park	CHI	54885	4-S	48,993	52,524	29,964	20,704	53,458	1,468,035	.0195	405,609	115	...	...	29,205	154	107,682	61,174	49,041	27	Inc. Place
Olney		55912	4-C	8,049	8,631	17,824	3,692	30,108	143,464	.0033	177,223	50	25,201	50	2,941	15	28,154	8,318	(d)	...	Inc. Place
Orland Park	CHI	56640	3-Sm	49,921	51,077	23,944	17,554	62,225	1,195,309	.0265	1,499,212	426	319,123	635	163,309	860	105,202	125,306	359,992	197	Inc. Place
Ottawa		56926	4-B	18,309	18,307	20,228	7,623	36,659	370,351	.0077	379,370	108	88,379	176	7,597	40	54,029	22,915	54,605	30	Inc. Place
Palatine	CHI	57225		69,393	65,479	26,288	26,015	58,880	1,824,193	.0260	636,069	181	41,327	82	15,335	81	111,396	49,489	258,005	141	Inc. Place
Park Ridge	CHI	57875	4-S	37,087	37,775	29,235	13,433	64,211	1,084,225	.0151	373,228	106	...	...	16,109	85	67,360	43,025	(d)	...	Inc. Place
Pekin	PEOR	58447	3-S	33,996	33,857	19,142	13,756	37,413	650,757	.0128	568,630	161	60,328	120	17,310	91	68,465	28,069	...	...	Inc. Place
Peoria	PEOR	59000	2-AA	112,199	112,936	19,049	46,445	35,991	2,137,328	.0416	1,816,151	516	319,190	635	35,375	186	260,651	157,115	541,527	296	Inc. Place
Peru		59234	3-B	9,743	9,835	20,686	4,159	36,291	201,540	.0070	539,702	153	164,116	326	24,973	131	58,367	27,095	133,136	73	Inc. Place
Quincy	QUIN	62367	3-A	38,548	40,366	16,964	16,289	30,503	653,940	.0152	812,962	231	167,160	332	24,576	129	123,969	49,354	405,817	222	Inc. Place
Rockford	RKFD	65000	2-A	153,501	150,115	19,669	59,596	39,131	3,019,231	.0535	1,987,747	564	296,690	590	49,430	260	380,282	141,367	2,524,850	1,382	Inc. Place
Rock Island	D-RI-M	65078	3-C	39,812	39,684	17,914	16,352	33,284	713,192	.0112	275,719	78	18,273	36	4,530	24	44,407	25,846	137,352	75	Inc. Place
Round Lake Beach	CHI	66040		30,046	25,859	13,521	8,273	51,949	406,243	.0082	307,091	87	76,538	152	10,046	53	48,711	13,991	(d)	...	Inc. Place
St. Charles	CHI	66703	4-S	33,777	27,896	31,696	11,981	62,891	1,070,604	.0177	721,502	205	124,212	247	32,839	173	156,266	51,455	764,899	419	Inc. Place
Schaumburg	CHI	68003	3-SSm	72,765	75,386	24,683	29,581	55,709	1,796,055	.0411	2,416,365	686	347,440	691	304,739	1,604	94,992	111,769	920,387	504	Inc. Place
Skokie	CHI	70122	3-SSm	66,139	63,348	22,197	23,342	53,081	1,468,081	.0293	1,420,838	403	217,790	433	262,340	1,381	107,168	130,731	1,176,843	644	Inc. Place
Springfield	SPRG	72000	2-A	114,607	111,454	21,113	50,265	37,931	2,419,645	.0451	1,923,234	546	418,396	832	71,548	377	237,344	137,045	211,854	116	Inc. Place
Sterling		72546	3-B	15,350	15,451	20,988	6,315	38,125	322,163	.0060	254,387	72	82,388	164	5,110	27	20,792	14,383	226,595	124	Inc. Place
Streamwood	CHI	73157		36,398	36,407	19,039	11,650	58,643	692,965	.0100	177,712	50	59,147	118	9,518	50	35,380	...	84,209	46	Inc. Place
Streator		73170	4-B	13,805	14,190	17,234	5,677	33,819	237,910	.0043	152,783	43	13,774	27	5,920	31	24,403	15,174	101,438	56	Inc. Place
Tinley Park	CHI	75484		48,211	48,401	19,326	16,769	56,010	931,704	.0177	744,790	211	126,949	252	25,651	135	74,939	49,062	104,667	57	Inc. Place
Urbana	CH-U	77005	4-B	36,818	36,395	15,075	14,794	26,991	555,038	.0106	389,025	110	43,925	87	6,176	33	101,832	54,576	...	...	Inc. Place
Vernon Hills	CHI	77694	4-Sm	23,405	20,120	24,079	8,528	63,420	563,580	.0235	1,999,316	568	238,851	475	118,946	626	23,325	42,690	179,070	98	Inc. Place
Villa Park	CHI	77993	4-S	22,281	22,075	21,475	7,840	50,267	478,482	.0104	550,588	156	141,854	282	16,073	85	39,229	43,182	79,212	43	Inc. Place
Waukegan	CHI	79293	3-SS	99,347	87,901	13,272	30,474	41,187	1,318,489	.0299	1,377,795	391	150,209	299	31,698	167	189,979	162,042	453,546	248	Inc. Place
Wheaton	CHI	81048		55,555	55,416	31,923	19,275	66,731	1,773,475	.0246	640,955	182	70,101	139	58,803	309	133,432	60,972	37,664	21	Inc. Place
Wheeling	CHI	81087		36,460	34,496	20,887	13,511	50,732	761,543	.0129	443,528	126	70,120	139	5,734	30	82,346	44,123	1,234,260	676	Inc. Place
Woodridge	CHI	83245		32,458	30,934	23,712	11,884	56,924	769,658	.0111	264,296	75	110,696	220	16,070	85	26,759	10,674	92,332	51	Inc. Place
Indiana																					
Anderson	AND	01468	3-A	58,561	59,734	18,094	25,062	34,281	1,059,620	.0198	778,815	221	187,700	373	24,352	128	72,198	59,851	717,721	393	Inc. Place
Bedford		04114	4-B	13,450	13,768	18,364	5,783	35,316	246,999	.0047	196,849	56	49,041	98	10,576	56	20,194	12,860	311,883	171	Inc. Place
Bloomington	BLMNG	05860	3-A	67,861	69,291	15,542	26,871	31,609	1,054,662	.0209	837,078	238	176,921	352	38,457	202	128,105	37,856	641,806	351	Inc. Place
Carmel	IND	10342		40,018	37,733	34,669	13,579	80,827	1,387,402	.0189	489,563	139	155,239	309	18,606	98	45,251	26,933	77,728	43	Inc. Place
Clarksville	LOU	12934	4-Sm	21,633	21,400	19,881	9,306	32,798	430,090	.0106	637,701	181	87,038	173	24,936	131	37,698	33,854	149,981	82	Inc. Place
Columbus	COL	14734	3-A	40,526	39,059	20,305	16,128	41,100	822,861	.0138	464,772	132	92,648	184	30,671	161	57,399	35,255	1,055,077	578	Inc. Place
Crawfordsville		15742	4-C	15,300	15,243	18,976	6,088	38,152	290,334	.0052	189,793	54	37,911	75	2,689	14	27,459	13,104	...	...	Inc. Place
East Chicago	CHI	19486	4-S	32,403	32,414	12,874	11,136	25,768	417,157	.0071	156,162	44	...	...	6,453	34	44,637	22,233	2,405,111	1,317	Inc. Place
Elkhart	ELK	20728	3-A	53,488	51,874	18,971	20,598	38,862	1,014,733	.0187	741,312	210	85,847	171	13,142	69	93,254	42,565	1,481,111	811	Inc. Place
Evansville	EV	22000	2-A	117,092	121,582	17,117	50,139	33,053	2,004,239	.0471	2,553,716	725	518,971	1,032	155,321	817	232,915	128,738	2,148,005	1,176	Inc. Place
Fishers	IND	23278		66,374	37,835	24,513	23,192	65,450	1,627,032	.0258	847,143	241	132,750	264	6,914	36	85,257	27,848	50,937	28	Inc. Place
Fort Wayne	FTWA	25000	2-A	210,534	205,727	16,130	78,829	36,679	3,395,960	.0697	3,049,195	866	643,018	1,279	173,347	912	260,367	203,336	2,043,352	1,119	Inc. Place
Gary	CHI	27000	3-S	102,928	102,746	12,940	36,433	27,315	1,331,852	.0233	566,350	161	26,679	53	18,081	95	91,529	69,974	1,802,488	987	Inc. Place
Goshen	ELK	28386	4-S	32,233	29,383	17,665	11,691	41,550	569,386	.0122	598,066	170	192,292	382	7,113	37	34,877	19,479	449,604	246	Inc. Place
Greenwood	IND	29898	4-Sm	41,418	36,037	25,261	17,083	50,553	1,046,275	.0184	765,507	217	296,985	591	51,297	270	38,176	32,854	78,753	43	Inc. Place
Hammond	CHI	31000	3-S	83,018	83,048	14,538	30,411	33,558	1,206,902	.0231	826,191	235	50,310	100	21,267	112	121,155	71,062	556,299	305	Inc. Place
Highland	CHI	33466	4-Sr	23,737	23,546	20,935	9,232	46,793	496,944	.0115	649,064	184	106,213	211	16,747	88	83,562	36,682	(d)	...	Inc. Place
Indianapolis	IND	36003	1-A	784,519	781,870	17,744	303,743	38,910	13,920,500	.2923	13,889,919	3,944	2,235,730	4,446	687,021	3,616	1,090,211	1,078,663	11,048,165	6,049	Inc. Place
Jasper		37782	4-C	12,838	12,100	22,154	5,127	42,660	284,414	.0067	397,448	113	64,861	129	15,230	80	24,530	6,742	474,014	260	Inc. Place
Jeffersonville	LOU	38358	4-S	28,460	27,362	19,418	12,455	38,280	552,624	.0105	444,862	126	122,170	243	11,299	59	37,395	18,251	252,575	138	Inc. Place
Kokomo	KOK	40392	3-A	45,835	46,113	21,500	20,278	39,235	985,448	.0179	733,914	208	217,496	433	22,544	119	68,653	60,049	...	...	Inc. Place
Lafayette	LAF-	40788	3-AA	60,240	56,397	19,356	27,104	37,007	1,165,995	.0230	1,037,041	294	263,805	525	47,589	250	59,400	56,226	...	...	Inc. Place
La Porte	MICH	42246	4-B	21,556	21,621	19,889	8,888	40,741	428,726	.0071	221,728	63	30,085	60	5,634	30	32,398	13,797	308,059	169	Inc. Place
Lawrence	IND	42426		41,659	38,915	20,837	15,078	49,041	868,042	.0127	271,649	77	17,640	35	3,744	20	33,236	38,559	30,313	17	Inc. Place
Logansport		44658	4-B	19,447	19,684	16,886	7,567	35,219	328,381	.0063	255,418	73	40,875	81	11,936	63	28,713	16,901	202,466	111	Inc. Place
Madison		45990	4-C	11,859	12,004	18,669	5,010	35,922	221,392	.0044	194,957	55	52,382	104	7,773	41	19,070	6,964	230,263	126	Inc. Place
Marion	MRN	46908	3-A	30,890	31,320	16,922	12,620	33,250	522,715	.0105	448,972	127	62,886	125	11,062	58	38,578	29,172	642,317	352	Inc. Place
Merrillville	CHI	48528	3-S	30,856	30,560	18,880	11,217	44,445	582,566	.0199	1,500,693	426	443,587	882	127,213	670	88,135	61,653	44,774	25	Inc. Place
Michigan City	MICH	48798	3-A	32,433	32,900	17,793	12,349	36,553	577,085	.0116	514,050	146	124,137	247	77,179	406	37,449	36,737	516,876	283	Inc. Place
Mishawaka	S.B.	49932	3-B	46,864	46,557	16,258	18,680	35,109	761,907	.0218	1,416,224	402	369,644	735	86,463	455	83,046	66,492	360,347	197	Inc. Place
Muncie	MUN	51876	3-AA	65,540	67,430	15,081	26,326	30,962	988,421	.0204	868,890	247	223,341	444	30,784	162	83,670	47,129	614,293	336	Inc. Place
New Albany	LOU	52326	4-S	37,232	37,603	18,526	15,831	36,804	689,769	.0111	304,245	86	64,694	129	4,219	22	38,705	36,619	634,275	347	Inc. Place
New Castle		52740	4-C	17,542	17,780	18,500	7,565	35,094	324,529	.0060	234,703	67	35,550	71	4,032	21	22,990	16,995	212,960	117	Inc. Place
Noblesville	IND	54180		36,150	28,590	22,817	12,583	56,596	824,820	.0140	517,448	147	88,883	177	4,526	24	39,273	9,558	201,491	110	Inc. Place
Portage	CHI	61092		36,206	33,496	19,278	13,644	43,772	697,982	.0106	250,895	71	126,442	251	1,172	6	28,512	29,797	359,426	197	Inc. Place
Richmond	RICH	64260	3-A	39,345	39,124	16,428	16,195	31,956	646,373	.0139	654,931	186	154,002	306	16,010	84	83,131	30,034	660,737	362	Inc. Place
Shelbyville		69318	4-S	18,449	17,951	18,809	7,441	38,599	347,005	.0060	207,069	59	30,405	60	...	...	26,441	8,267	383,386	210	Inc. Place
South Bend	S.B.	71000	2-A	110,443	107,789	14,945	40,163	33,731	1,650,623	.0309	1,073,333	305	183,995	366	22,520	119	127,993	82,068	956,514	524	Inc. Place
Terre Haute	T.H.	75428	3-AA	60,280	59,614	14,409	23,381	29,905	868,553	.0301	2,174,489	617	243,230	484	50,817	267	107,397	48,464	788,416	432	Inc. Place
Valparaiso	CHI	78326	4-S	29,589	27,428	23,339	11,595	48,014	690,592	.0118	441,084	125	88,851	177	9,987	53	57,205	41,950	276,909	152	Inc. Place
Vincennes		79208	3-A	18,334	18,701	14,529	7,418	30,147	266,379	.0061	296,117	84	72,906	145	18,350	97	25,986	18,335	92,644	51	Inc. Place
Warsaw		80306	4-C	12,757	12,415	19,060	4,980	39,433	243,146	.0050	242,761	69	53,758	107	9,124	48	30,044	14,024	966,257	529	Inc. Place
Washington		80504	4-B	11,060	11,380	15,178	4,422	30,844	167,864	.0036	163,134	46	12,643	25	3,268	17	18,357	12,475	95,059	52	Inc. Place
Iowa																					
Ames	AMES	01855	3-C	50,915	50,731	17,483	18,955	36,577	890,137	.0171	701,642	199	162,391	323	29,169	154	113,645	30,450	568,081	311	Inc. Place
Ankeny	DES	02305		30,293	27,117	21,665	11,325	53,193	656,308	.0110	378,909	108	33,045	66	4,022	21	55,782	13,701	487,377	267	Inc. Place
Bettendorf	D-RI-M	06355	4-S	31,155	31,275	24,953	12,516	49,787	777,404	.0120	365,355	104	39,946	79	15,851	83	59,476	20,515	72,831	40	Inc. Place
Burlington	BUR	09550	3-A	25,728	26,839	17,858	10,856	33,398	459,460	.0085	327,210	93	55,134	110	5,067	27	89,558	22,274	295,043	162	Inc. Place
Cedar Falls	WATL	11755	4-B	35,983	36,145	16,568	12,944	38,538	596,154	.0117	474,530	135	45,025	90	25,420	134	60,844	18,675	162,403	89	Inc. Place
Cedar Rapids	CEDR	12000	3-AA	123,877	120,758	21,563	52,691	41,254	2,671,128	.0508	2,260,449	642	466,110	927	112,225	591	247,921	131,921	3,517,315	1,926	Inc. Place
Clinton	CLNT	14430	3-A	26,916	27,772	17,018	11,038	32,859	458,046	.0090	374,826	106	59,778	119	7,277	38	47,447	25,827	909,683	498	Inc. Place
Council Bluffs	OMA	16860	3-S	59,630	58,268	17,703	23,805	36,607	1,055,610	.0229	1,137,123	323	123,977	247	36,653	193	117,840	64,647	...	...	Inc. Place
Davenport	D-RI-M	19000	2-A	99,998	98,359	17,435	40,174	36,200	1,743,499	.0381	1,896,517	539	372,748	741	95,481	503	180,148	111,468	1,363,190	746	Inc. Place
Des Moines	DES	21000	2-AA	200,756	198,682	17,386	79,605	37,034	3,490,270	.0677	2,798,082	795	533,207	1,060	130,230	685	391,905	157,439	1,027,848	563	Inc. Place
Dubuque	DUB	22395	3-A	58,271	57,686	17,440	22,921	35,971	1,016,222	.0202	867,720	246	158,808	316	26,420	139	115,184	60,717	...	...	Inc. Place

Source: Devonshire Associates Ltd. and Scan/US, Inc. 2005.
* Source: 1997 Census of Manufactures.
Not classified as a Principal Business Center.

...Data less than 1,000.
(d) Data not available.

Principal Business Centers and Other Places with 30,000 or More: Population/Income/Sales, *Continued*

Place Name	Ranally Metro Area	FIPS Place Code	Ranally City Rating	Population Estimate 7/1/05	Population Census 4/1/00	Per Capita Income 2004	Households Estimate 7/1/05	Median Household Income 2004	Disposable Income 2004 ($1,000)	Market Ability Index 2004	Total Retail Sales 2004 Sales ($1,000)	Total Retail Sales Ranally Sales Units	General Merchandise 2004 Sales ($1,000)	General Merchandise Ranally Sales Units	Apparel Store 2004 Sales ($1,000)	Apparel Store Ranally Sales Units	Food Store Sales 2004 ($1,000)	Health & Drug Store 2004 ($1,000)	Manufacturers Value Added 1997* ($1,000)	Manufacturers Ranally Mfg. Units	Place Type
Fort Dodge		28515	3-A	23,321	25,136	16,767	9,838	32,753	391,021	.0086	424,847	121	105,526	210	10,184	54	55,687	23,966	634,072	347	Inc. Place
Iowa City	IACY	38595	3-A	61,916	62,220	19,144	26,073	35,678	1,185,330	.0213	802,151	228	81,304	162	19,826	104	170,204	47,031	1,769,541	969	Inc. Place
Marshalltown		49755	4-A	26,083	26,009	17,186	10,150	35,443	448,273	.0082	300,478	85	60,877	121	18,061	95	48,252	19,664	...	...	Inc. Place
Mason City		50160	3-A	28,211	29,172	18,106	12,128	33,566	510,797	.0113	581,459	165	184,418	367	15,024	79	65,287	11,570	252,177	138	Inc. Place
Muscatine		55110	4-C	22,792	22,697	19,039	8,851	38,775	433,937	.0080	314,226	89	62,346	124	7,740	41	48,223	18,227	564,392	309	Inc. Place
Ottumwa		60465	4-A	25,213	24,998	15,187	10,300	30,627	382,905	.0077	308,309	88	75,750	151	11,719	62	46,237	16,686	...	...	Inc. Place
Sioux City	SXCY	73335	3-AA	83,976	85,013	16,833	31,344	36,538	1,413,559	.0284	1,223,832	348	231,169	460	55,215	291	166,931	48,617	476,963	261	Inc. Place
Urbandale	DES	79950		31,585	29,072	24,213	12,227	55,484	764,754	.0132	521,428	148	35,919	71	6,013	32	74,286	28,927	126,660	69	Inc. Place
Waterloo	WATL	82425	3-AA	69,817	68,747	16,984	29,041	33,724	1,185,779	.0243	1,089,742	309	260,675	518	30,019	158	128,219	79,532	2,082,662	1,140	Inc. Place
West Des Moines	DES	83910	4-Sm	50,242	46,403	27,210	21,029	50,130	1,367,073	.0202	577,433	164	79,890	159	68,057	358	81,800	36,193	113,983	62	Inc. Place
Kansas																					
Coffeyville		14600	4-A	9,815	11,021	15,117	4,362	28,275	148,371	.0028	104,977	30	26,549	53	4,502	24	17,890	8,124	53,112	29	Inc. Place
Dodge City		18250	4-A	25,928	25,176	14,610	8,634	35,766	378,820	.0082	368,552	105	76,980	153	11,158	59	34,082	9,476	...	...	Inc. Place
Emporia		21275	4-A	27,054	26,760	14,732	10,412	30,795	398,558	.0081	331,145	94	67,531	134	17,302	91	49,259	14,807	...	...	Inc. Place
Garden City		25325	4-A	29,096	28,451	15,519	10,332	35,983	451,535	.0091	379,340	108	80,535	160	23,622	124	49,973	7,555	(d)	...	Inc. Place
Great Bend		28300	3-A	14,876	15,345	16,092	6,371	31,076	239,378	.0052	249,916	71	45,114	90	5,182	27	34,147	13,081	44,919	25	Inc. Place
Hays		31100	4-A	19,796	20,013	16,891	8,333	32,301	334,382	.0076	396,754	113	72,090	143	24,169	127	48,220	13,042	43,301	24	Inc. Place
Hutchinson	HUCH	33625	3-A	40,172	40,787	17,005	16,454	33,960	683,124	.0131	517,636	147	102,041	203	16,536	87	60,191	21,140	232,041	127	Inc. Place
Junction City		35750	4-B	16,423	18,886	16,772	7,308	30,042	275,446	.0053	210,812	60	48,011	95	1,614	8	36,201	2,558	(d)	...	Inc. Place
Kansas City	K.C.	36000	3-SS	145,825	146,866	14,837	55,350	32,425	2,163,563	.0386	1,167,136	331	143,532	285	19,122	101	190,187	78,829	2,826,709	1,548	Inc. Place
Lawrence	LAWR	38900	3-A	83,085	80,098	17,822	34,579	35,637	1,480,782	.0270	1,003,452	285	153,499	305	58,890	310	175,953	47,009	325,174	178	Inc. Place
Leavenworth	LEAV	39000	4-C	34,091	35,420	17,537	11,625	40,182	597,865	.0096	249,955	71	55,076	110	5,392	28	33,292	17,823	(d)	...	Inc. Place
Leawood	K.C.	39075		31,074	27,656	37,826	10,936	81,475	1,175,404	.0152	342,054	97	...	...	69,304	365	58,306	31,327	(d)	...	Inc. Place
Lenexa	K.C.	39350	4-Sr	44,921	40,238	25,858	17,220	61,324	1,161,587	.0200	809,655	230	123,357	245	21,306	112	79,777	48,659	658,743	361	Inc. Place
Liberal		39825	4-A	20,849	19,666	13,386	6,614	34,961	279,080	.0065	310,961	88	66,024	131	23,977	126	46,938	7,545	...	...	Inc. Place
Manhattan	MANH	44250	3-A	50,396	44,831	14,453	19,450	30,977	728,353	.0145	559,431	159	131,108	261	31,812	167	46,717	16,614	(d)	...	Inc. Place
Olathe	K.C.	52575	4-S	113,035	92,962	20,735	38,951	55,829	2,343,773	.0431	1,768,653	502	223,579	445	58,187	306	166,438	54,555	523,679	287	Inc. Place
Overland Park	K.C.	53775	3-SSm	171,864	149,080	27,330	68,261	60,927	4,696,981	.0808	3,330,876	946	758,636	1,509	284,255	1,496	257,953	160,962	115,593	63	Inc. Place
Parsons		54675	4-B	11,230	11,514	16,199	4,758	29,570	181,918	.0035	132,686	38	22,871	45	3,321	17	22,604	8,621	101,120	55	Inc. Place
Pittsburg		56025	4-A	19,177	19,243	14,584	8,142	26,904	279,678	.0060	264,386	75	109,044	217	6,681	35	35,528	7,948	187,244	103	Inc. Place
Salina	SLN	62700	3-A	46,054	45,679	17,556	18,953	35,203	808,546	.0173	845,596	240	221,854	441	45,041	237	92,159	32,084	329,695	180	Inc. Place
Shawnee	K.C.	64500		56,781	47,996	24,000	21,682	56,276	1,362,755	.0227	819,613	233	111,911	223	72,452	381	131,901	40,171	...	...	Inc. Place
Topeka	TOP	71000	3-AA	122,260	122,377	19,158	53,118	36,010	2,342,313	.0462	2,060,564	585	504,036	1,002	70,910	373	236,089	144,483	...	...	Inc. Place
Wichita	WICH	79000	2-AA	359,396	344,284	18,390	140,228	39,215	6,609,148	.1208	4,594,886	1,305	977,336	1,944	228,277	1,201	589,755	258,208	4,011,147	2,196	Inc. Place
Kentucky																					
Ashland	HNTG	02368	3-B	21,498	21,981	17,448	9,191	30,323	375,102	.0093	543,100	154	101,639	202	35,726	188	60,938	44,327	...	...	Inc. Place
Bowling Green	BOWLG	08902	3-A	53,680	49,296	17,405	21,039	33,814	934,286	.0191	860,344	244	176,277	351	51,719	272	77,552	37,492	...	...	Inc. Place
Corbin		17362	4-A	7,535	7,742	12,953	3,050	24,186	97,604	.0033	224,016	64	52,669	105	4,699	25	12,894	14,836	51,297	28	Inc. Place
Covington	CIN	17848	4-S	43,955	43,370	19,024	18,560	34,341	836,179	.0131	334,943	95	23,804	47	8,443	44	75,314	39,331	148,337	81	Inc. Place
Danville		19882	4-C	15,084	15,477	17,667	6,107	33,272	266,483	.0057	273,155	78	77,401	154	14,710	77	23,921	13,387	313,948	172	Inc. Place
Elizabethtown		24274	4-C	23,909	22,542	21,386	10,119	36,994	511,311	.0105	520,437	148	156,998	312	38,116	201	28,862	33,168	693,186	379	Inc. Place
Florence	CIN	27982	3-S	28,038	23,551	22,461	11,507	44,472	629,767	.0166	1,082,244	307	266,361	530	52,741	278	41,543	28,384	476,098	261	Inc. Place
Frankfort		28900	4-C	27,972	27,741	21,794	12,468	37,788	609,632	.0101	336,798	96	72,279	144	11,609	61	33,389	19,849	266,113	146	Inc. Place
Glasgow		31114	4-B	13,499	13,019	15,685	5,494	30,776	211,728	.0048	246,225	70	66,004	131	6,194	33	25,499	13,536	298,275	163	Inc. Place
Harlan		34732	4-B	1,866	2,081	11,972	864	20,386	22,340	.0011	95,526	27	31,519	63	3,779	20	15,924	7,607	(d)	...	Inc. Place
Henderson	EV	35866	4-S	28,085	27,373	18,306	11,795	33,144	514,121	.0098	403,517	115	63,889	127	12,481	66	44,280	38,240	784,611	430	Inc. Place
Hopkinsville	HPKNV	37918	4-B	28,430	30,089	16,484	12,018	30,847	468,636	.0092	382,011	108	91,935	183	17,301	91	35,053	26,265	329,419	180	Inc. Place
Lexington	LEX	46027	2-AA	271,787	260,512	20,800	116,259	38,503	5,653,273	.1044	4,338,325	1,232	637,967	1,269	295,918	1,557	406,099	292,471	2,147,695	1,176	Inc. Place
Louisville	LOU	48000	2-AA	249,089	256,231	16,096	103,413	28,743	4,009,413	.0732	2,528,862	718	206,833	411	97,241	512	345,007	205,768	9,819,972	5,376	Inc. Place
Madisonville		49368	4-A	19,053	19,307	16,625	7,835	30,873	316,753	.0066	300,895	85	73,341	146	16,846	89	31,482	26,205	...	...	Inc. Place
Mayfield		50898	4-B	9,759	10,349	15,120	4,007	27,745	147,559	.0032	142,509	40	31,793	63	2,539	13	10,574	8,915	105,930	58	Inc. Place
Maysville		51024	4-C	8,896	8,993	15,174	3,693	28,685	134,992	.0035	204,381	58	50,945	101	12,743	67	34,861	6,607	...	...	Inc. Place
Middlesboro		51924	4-A	10,205	10,384	11,135	4,405	19,655	113,630	.0035	212,972	60	84,231	168	11,063	58	45,000	7,829	...	...	Inc. Place
Murray		54642	4-B	14,579	14,950	14,712	5,785	28,560	214,491	.0051	266,748	76	54,050	107	10,898	57	17,138	13,155	...	...	Inc. Place
Newport	CIN	55884	4-S	16,721	17,048	17,003	6,831	31,041	284,310	.0058	252,561	72	23,625	47	7,978	42	49,962	19,724	187,672	103	Inc. Place
Owensboro	OWNS	58620	3-A	54,311	54,067	19,477	24,110	33,781	1,057,833	.0193	751,257	213	181,004	360	27,230	143	82,983	55,534	...	...	Inc. Place
Paducah	PAD	58836	3-A	25,541	26,307	19,954	11,636	33,310	509,636	.0125	744,212	211	240,290	478	46,138	243	50,907	36,577	152,607	84	Inc. Place
Pikeville		60852	4-B	6,396	6,295	15,022	2,874	24,402	96,081	.0031	213,919	61	48,211	96	13,030	69	19,615	12,422	(d)	...	Inc. Place
Richmond		65226	4-C	29,847	27,152	15,780	11,371	31,462	470,981	.0094	380,875	108	73,367	146	24,072	127	50,640	21,019	314,947	172	Inc. Place
Saint Matthews	LOU	67944	4-Sm	15,668	15,852	33,642	7,524	49,106	527,101	.0108	602,321	171	111,200	221	66,232	349	36,935	40,614	(d)	...	Inc. Place
Somerset		71688	4-A	12,032	11,352	13,153	4,767	26,003	158,258	.0045	276,377	78	50,125	100	14,988	79	33,034	19,503	138,120	76	Inc. Place
Louisiana																					
Alexandria	ALEX	00975	3-AA	46,250	46,342	14,497	18,183	25,637	670,479	.0179	1,047,862	298	296,675	590	61,721	325	82,015	60,068	...	...	Inc. Place
Baton Rouge	B.R.	05000	2-AA	228,423	227,818	16,000	84,407	31,112	3,654,788	.0814	4,021,107	1,142	750,185	1,492	188,945	994	410,011	185,690	547,351	300	Inc. Place
Bossier City	SHRE	08920	3-S	59,392	56,461	18,032	22,764	35,972	1,070,958	.0222	1,041,958	296	256,571	510	42,632	224	88,467	27,504	87,128	48	Inc. Place
Chalmette	N.O.	14135		30,826	32,069	18,123	12,436	34,983	558,669	.0090	241,155	68	80,792	161	12,304	65	42,789	31,541	(d)	...	CDP
Gretna	N.O.	31915	4-S	17,736	17,423	14,341	6,850	26,644	254,358	.0085	602,603	171	187,812	373	69,132	364	34,845	21,415	45,832	25	Inc. Place
Hammond		32755	3-A	18,136	17,639	13,305	6,569	27,424	241,304	.0076	505,727	144	146,398	291	20,103	106	40,399	32,542	63,528	35	Inc. Place
Houma	HOMA-	36255	3-A	32,484	32,393	17,855	12,047	35,501	580,015	.0144	839,298	238	219,239	436	29,251	154	84,918	37,689	157,888	86	Inc. Place
Kenner	N.O.	39475	4-S	67,402	70,517	17,714	23,746	38,199	1,193,949	.0239	1,059,186	301	280,939	559	114,589	603	101,909	69,823	88,945	49	Inc. Place
Lafayette	LAF	40735	2-A	105,390	110,257	19,371	43,367	35,039	2,041,523	.0474	2,651,705	753	601,422	1,196	165,519	871	207,658	211,532	258,729	142	Inc. Place
Lake Charles	LKCH	41155	3-AA	69,412	71,757	17,913	28,670	30,726	1,243,370	.0262	1,253,563	356	343,175	682	73,217	385	145,362	92,032	...	...	Inc. Place
Marrero	N.O.	48785		35,535	36,165	14,391	11,826	35,795	511,382	.0088	229,406	65	25,584	51	13,016	69	58,041	30,224	(d)	...	CDP
Metairie	N.O.	50115		143,582	146,136	22,389	60,565	38,510	3,214,707	.0655	3,274,420	930	711,474	1,415	222,817	1,173	336,164	255,892	(d)	...	CDP
Monroe	MONR	51410	3-AA	53,098	53,107	16,079	19,870	29,392	853,737	.0197	1,026,485	291	270,756	538	51,617	272	105,566	39,860	182,363	100	Inc. Place
Morgan City		52040	4-C	11,616	12,703	16,179	4,855	28,927	187,940	.0033	102,328	29	18,520	37	...	...	16,683	8,893	102,469	56	Inc. Place
New Iberia	LAF	54035	3-B	32,229	32,623	14,118	11,698	30,063	455,021	.0096	411,525	117	53,047	105	25,281	133	50,596	26,127	100,458	55	Inc. Place
New Orleans	N.O.	55000	1-A	456,285	484,674	13,448	174,662	26,719	6,136,230	.1143	3,541,633	1,006	389,671	775	339,037	1,784	628,347	314,738	1,064,555	583	Inc. Place
Opelousas		58045	4-C	23,249	22,860	11,023	8,875	20,950	256,275	.0060	256,482	73	83,487	166	13,559	71	37,329	22,380	38,738	21	Inc. Place
Ruston		66655	4-C	20,124	20,546	13,778	7,799	25,060	277,271	.0061	278,921	79	74,799	149	11,245	59	31,543	8,315	103,768	57	Inc. Place
Shreveport	SHRE	70000	2-AA	226,284	200,145	15,881	89,829	30,853	3,593,528	.0694	2,683,840	762	497,489	989	141,272	744	315,190	139,946	...	...	Inc. Place
Slidell	N.O.	70805	3-S	26,116	25,695	20,163	9,603	41,833	526,566	.0107	514,611	146	85,649	170	18,177	96	47,383	36,099	27,179	15	Inc. Place
Thibodaux	HOMA-	75425	4-B	14,624	14,431	17,018	5,641	32,557	248,878	.0043	139,592	40	22,893	46	3,519	19	32,684	9,715	38,585	21	Inc. Place
West Monroe	MONR	80955	4-S	12,640	13,250	18,944	5,594	35,880	239,457	.0047	205,156	58	68,057	135	5,964	31	30,341	13,684	61,912	34	Inc. Place
Maine																					
Auburn	LEW-	02060	4-B	23,733	23,203	19,041	10,086	33,839	451,903	.0114	686,999	195	134,379	267	17,147	90	83,683	25,864	441,155	242	Inc. Place
Augusta	AUG	02100	3-B	18,367	18,560	19,033	8,650	31,447	349,581	.0094	597,692	170	109,276	217	8,293	44	81,227	16,066	76,394	42	Inc. Place
Bangor	BANG	02795	3-AA	31,246	31,473	19,419	13,919	31,175	606,765	.0157	976,106	277	176,454	351	34,433	181	144,864	45,547	...	...	Inc. Place
Biddeford		04860	4-S	20,570	20,942	17,156	8,396	34,098	352,907	.0066	250,547	71	32,578	65	5,560	29	74,053	6,100	153,791	84	Inc. Place
Brunswick	BR-BA	08430	4-B	21,723	21,172	17,255	8,331	38,036	374,836	.0094	549,930	156	114,091	227	20,387	107	86,706	13,842	72,496	40	MCD-Town
Lewiston	LEW-	38740	3-A	35,524	35,690	16,347	15,358	28,331	580,712	.0144	816,651	232	62,608	125	4,216	22	97,402	31,769	...	...	Inc. Place
Portland	POR	60545	2-A	65,563	64,249	19,495	30,175	34,268	1,278,129	.0305	1,757,296	499	47,047	94	31,728	167	273,383	73,223	319,168	175	Inc. Place
Presque Isle		60825	4-A	9,318	9,511	16,456	4,053	28,278	153,341	.0038	214,348	61	55,427	110	9,964	52	43,280	11,144	(d)	...	Inc. Place
South Portland	POR	71990	4-Sm	23,468	23,324	19,235	10,053	40,103	451,406	.0147	1,075,440	305	183,290	365	123,532	650	126,260	45,658	...	...	Inc. Place
Waterville	WATRVL	80740	3-A	15,541	15,605	16,536	6,320	30,870	256,979	.0058	299,891	85	36,254	72	14,270	75	84,081	11,084	103,350	57	Inc. Place
Maryland																					
Annapolis	ANPLS	01600	3-C	38,325	35,838	33,140	16,396	56,601	1,270,107	.0194	683,283	194	77,772	155	77,415	407	82,879	23,266	(d)	...	Inc. Place
Aspen Hill	WASH	02825		54,498	50,228	24,093	19,380	58,664	1,313,011	.0166	182,565	52	19,144	38	3,362	18	60,132	15,970	(d)	...	CDP
Baltimore	BAL	04000	1-A	617,204	651,154	14,301	240,250	28,904	8,826,780	.1515	3,887,601	1,104	195,612	389	271,094	1,427	766,785	536,954	4,452,897	2,438	Independent City
Bel Air	BAL	05550	4-Sm	10,892	10,080	30,553	4,602	56,453	332,782	.0063	313,263	89	46,299	92	14,846	78	34,442	11,834	(d)	...	Inc. Place
Bethesda	WASH	07125		59,975	55,277	51,583	25,154	85,842	3,093,698	.0427	1,385,118	393	106,940	213	231,686	1,219	131,169	55,432	(d)	...	CDP
Bowie	WASH	08775		58,311	50,269	30,192	21,305	66,830	1,760,517	.0235	497,512	141	107,676	214	10,371	55	105,651	15,098	(d)	...	Inc. Place
Catonsville	BAL	14125		41,776	39,820	21,498	15,842	49,399	898,111	.0166	696,197	198	74,042	147	26,918	142	77,235	32,216	(d)	...	CDP
Chillum	WASH	16875		36,900	34,252	19,641	13,149	40,882	724,760	.0110	260,830	74	38,875	77	39,264	207	102,803	24,257	(d)	...	CDP
Columbia	BAL	19125		95,378	88,254	31,114	35,920	63,369	2,967,555	.0429	1,252,470	356	249,165	496	129,670	682	210,151	51,889	(d)	...	CDP
Cumberland	CUMB	21325	3-A	19,864	21,518	17,189	8,839	29,963	341,450	.0069	299,669	85	66,617	132	17,663	93	36,527	28,388	35,080	19	Inc. Place
Dundalk	BAL	23975		65,370	62,306	15,886	25,282	36,111	1,038,464	.0189	636,616	181	34,439	68	12,419	65	132,796	75,256	(d)	...	CDP
Easton		24475	4-C	12,710	11,708	22,595	5,744	38,807	287,182	.0064	355,783	101	38,188	76	15,751	83	43,351	18,605	368,001	201	Inc. Place
Eldersburg	BAL	25575		30,724	27,741	25,945	10,031	63,099	797,137	.0108	216,231	61	29,726	59	5,152	27	91,859	10,353	(d)	...	CDP
Ellicott City	BAL	26000		62,436	56,397	31,269	21,822	70,216	1,952,313	.0275	747,217	212	121,304	241	15,611	82	171,675	25,604	(d)	...	CDP
Essex	BAL	26600		40,998	39,078	15,821	16,311	34,339	648,622	.0106	255,577	73	22,344	44	6,136	32	66,211	11,492	(d)	...	CDP
Frederick	WASH	30325	3-C	63,712	52,767	25,899	24,942	49,716	1,650,069	.0294	1,262,997	359	264,904	527	64,884	341	194,332	49,199	221,392	121	Inc. Place
Gaithersburg	WASH	31175	3-S	63,475	52,613	25,476	23,247	62,136	1,617,100	.0273	1,051,017	298	194,303	386	74,203	391	117,993	24,135	205,980	113	Inc. Place
Germantown	WASH	32025		60,129	55,419	23,504	22,270	59,342	1,413,245	.0196	383,814	109	69,771	139	8,019	42	135,817	15,672	(d)	...	CDP
Glen Burnie	BAL	32650		41,118	38,922	20,344	16,073	42,778	836,503	.0169	801,909	228	190,325	378	32,483	171	98,053	20,130	(d)	...	CDP
Hagerstown	HAG	36075	3-A	38,790	36,687	19,730	16,894	35,074	765,308	.0142	584,674	166	146,389	291	21,923	115	72,401	32,394	347,549	190	Inc. Place
Laurel	WASH	45900	3-Sm	22,145	19,960	29,372	10,014	49,440	650,450	.0126	645,600	183	88,304	176	47,466	250	63,497	26,086	(d)	...	Inc. Place
Montgomery Village	WASH	53325		41,284	38,051	23,631	15,063	58,741	975,568	.0134	249,110	71	21,799	43	2,502	13	36,042	9,839	(d)	...	CDP
North Bethesda	WASH	56337		41,894	38,610	37,580	18,438	62,824	1,574,363	.0284	1,394,961	396	28,879	57	126,269	665	180,471	68,538	(d)	...	CDP
Olney	WASH	58900		34,110	31,438	27,921	10,940	77,818	952,394	.0119	149,299	42	...	...	2,861	15	79,348	10,586	(d)	...	CDP
Oxon Hill-Glassmanor	WASH	59505		38,086	35,355	24,828	14,887	48,833	945,607	.0130	260,663	74	24,793	49	20,125	106	76,800	13,400	(d)	...	CDP
Parkville	BAL	60275		32,649	31,118	19,554	13,317	41,782	638,434	.0116	447,283	127	23,600	47	11,517	61	83,159	25,042	(d)	...	CDP
Perry Hall	BAL	60975		30,118	28,705	20,614	11,602	46,908	620,864	.0129	647,019	184	200,801	399	51,357	270	98,118	27,662	(d)	...	CDP
Pikesville	BAL	61400		30,554	29,123	29,858	13,009	48,424	912,275	.0118	215,610	61	1,091	2	16,317	86	73,750	18,645	(d)	...	CDP
Potomac	WASH	63300		48,631	44,822	54,461	16,688	114,068	2,648,505	.0296	386,575	110	38,730	77	86,320	454	73,553	18,110	(d)	...	CDP
Randallstown	BAL	64950		32,391	30,870	21,214	11,645	51,464	687,127	.0109	316,680	90	21,218	42	7,261	38	69,944	15,535	(d)	...	CDP
Rockville	WASH	67675	3-SS	51,809	47,388	29,824	18,491	67,098	1,545,170	.0230	711,404	202	...	...	37,092	195	156,183	34,857	102,631	56	Inc. Place
St. Charles	WASH	69350		38,693	33,379	23,244	13,364	53,517	899,371	.0140	421,257	120	142,672	284	45,550	240	47,868	15,063	(d)	...	CDP
Salisbury	SLSB	69925	3-A	26,307	23,743	18,367	10,436	36,427	483,187	.0113	622,030	177	159,555	317	28,067	148	73,070	35,924	419,783	230	Inc. Place
Severn	BAL	71150		37,058	35,076	22,539	12,694	57,931	835,250	.0108	125,469	36	2,593	5	3,764	20	30,927	16,020	(d)	...	CDP
Severna Park	BAL	71200		30,118	28,507	32,446	10,281	70,882	977,203	.0127	255,405	73	25,666	51	6,951	37	70,908	12,061	(d)	...	CDP
Silver Spring	WASH	72450		83,049	76,540	22,923	32,345	49,212	1,903,697	.0273	602,684	171	40,716	81	52,929	279	181,516	42,771	(d)	...	CDP
South Gate	BAL	73550		30,290	28,672	22,832	11,934	46,753	691,591	.0149	807,113	229	172,648	343	49,636	261	90,924	24,063	(d)	...	CDP
Towson	BAL	78425		54,342	51,793	28,264	21,532	47,140	1,535,913	.0266	1,128,793	321	143,950	286	214,154	1,127	150,473	79,896	(d)	...	CDP
Woodlawn	BAL	86475		37,853	36,079	18,466	14,243	43,238	698,991	.0126	461,420	131	76,217	152	23,701	125	63,058	25,334	(d)	...	CDP
Massachusetts																					
Amherst	SPRG	01325		35,099	34,874	16,234	9,373	39,498	569,782	.0087	157,077	45	...	...	3,629	19	58,991	12,331	(d)	...	MCD-Town
Andover	BOS	01465		31,763	31,247	36,758	11,209	75,107	1,167,550	.0140	196,095	56	...	...	25,341	133	55,923	23,977	1,585,271	868	MCD-Town
Arlington	BOS	01605		40,424	42,389	29,582	17,593	57,427	1,195,839	.0164	389,371	111	...	...	4,111	22	64,293	69,881	(d)	...	MCD-Town
Attleboro	PROV-	02690	3-S	44,845	42,068	21,080	16,794	46,221	945,313	.0187	880,279	250	88,236	175	26,591	140	104,498	49,732	704,774	386	Inc. Place
Barnstable	BARN	03600		48,874	47,821	23,510	20,039	43,370	1,149,036	.0240	1,254,485	356	141,254	281	90,103	474	153,658	85,395	...	...	Inc. Place
Beverly	BOS	05595	4-S	40,104	39,862	24,230	15,499	49,566	971,705	.0161	580,035	165	13,023	26	12,440	65	107,772	62,841	469,110	257	Inc. Place
Billerica	BOS	05805		38,347	38,981	21,045	12,309	60,477	807,003	.0134	444,809	126	17,844	35	33,555	177	91,412	39,586	1,045,186	572	MCD-Town
Boston	BOS	07000	1-AA	581,578	589,141	18,643	220,121	38,185	10,842,276	.1881	6,406,993	1,819	338,279	673	1,160,426	6,108	1,343,944	762,962	2,424,545	1,327	Inc. Place
Braintree	BOS	07665	3-Sm	33,810	33,828	24,070	12,499	56,293	813,791	.0190	1,129,845	321	300,752	598	156,692	825	66,871	70,666	333,808	183	MCD-Town
Brockton	BOS	09000	3-SS	97,470	94,304	16,994	34,345	37,231	1,656,406	.0337	1,495,941	425	129,001	257	48,455	255	186,727	105,335	217,622	119	Inc. Place
Brookline	BOS	09175	4-Sr	56,639	57,107	39,692	25,090	59,432	2,248,135	.0275	485,904	138	50,716	101	70,342	370	106,042	82,937	(d)	...	MCD-Town
Burlington	BOS	09840	3-SSm	22,362	22,876	26,500	7,856	64,870	592,589	.0159	1,084,179	308	304,533	606	186,451	981	42,552	44,883	219,369	120	MCD-Town
Cambridge	BOS	11000	3-SS	102,925	101,355	26,270	41,960	45,265	2,703,875	.0497	2,254,404	640	141,250	281	375,010	1,974	392,147	162,689	356,954	195	Inc. Place
Chelmsford	BOS	13135	4-S	33,537	33,858	25,196	12,321	61,631	845,012	.0141	524,586	149	52,005	103	24,210	127	82,260	25,725	483,546	265	MCD-Town

Source: Devonshire Associates Ltd. and Scan/US, Inc. 2005.
* Source: 1997 Census of Manufactures.
Not classified as a Principal Business Center.

...Data less than 1,000.
(d) Data not available.

Continued on next page

Principal Business Centers and Other Places with 30,000 or More: Population/Income/Sales, *Continued*

Place Name	Ranally Metro Area	FIPS Place Code	Ranally City Rating	Population Estimate 7/1/05	Population Census 4/1/00	Per Capita Income 2004	Households Estimate 7/1/05	Median Household Income 2004	Disposable Income 2004 ($1,000)	Market Ability Index 2004	Total Retail Sales 2004 Sales ($1,000)	Total Retail Sales Ranally Sales Units	General Merchandise 2004 Sales ($1,000)	General Merchandise Ranally Sales Units	Apparel Store 2004 Sales ($1,000)	Apparel Store Ranally Sales Units	Food Store Sales 2004 ($1,000)	Health & Drug Store 2004 ($1,000)	Manufacturers Value Added 1997* ($1,000)	Manufacturers Ranally Mfg. Units	Place Type
Chelsea	BOS	13205	4-S	36,760	35,080	11,591	11,595	29,320	426,102	.0083	242,849	69	13,304	26	9,102	48	97,566	26,043	163,069	89	Inc. Place
Chicopee	SPRG	13660	4-S	55,285	54,653	18,609	23,426	34,059	1,028,784	.0161	408,053	116	67,570	134	13,703	72	69,844	52,203	560,843	307	Inc. Place
Danvers	BOS	16250	3-S	25,785	25,212	22,772	9,549	52,432	587,187	.0155	1,018,522	289	150,186	299	76,434	402	87,915	38,406	364,443	200	MCD-Town
Dartmouth	N.BED	16425		32,055	30,666	21,118	10,842	45,831	676,950	.0129	570,051	162	163,291	325	53,721	283	38,133	34,710	17,896	10	MCD-Town
Dedham	BOS	16495	3-Sm	23,317	23,464	24,337	8,493	55,655	567,469	.0103	442,908	126	80,257	160	38,423	202	26,360	31,304	(d)	...	MCD-Town
Everett	BOS	21990		38,559	38,037	17,056	15,145	37,731	657,663	.0105	254,371	72	3,484	7	4,315	23	18,558	41,443	172,010	94	Inc. Place
Fall River	F.R.	23000	3-BB	91,764	91,938	16,246	38,006	28,183	1,490,796	.0252	710,832	202	58,732	117	57,786	304	148,511	55,773	720,215	394	Inc. Place
Falmouth		23105		33,391	32,660	25,218	14,156	44,140	842,050	.0137	486,461	138	15,801	31	32,274	170	98,654	51,244	(d)	...	MCD-Town
Fitchburg	BOS	23875	3-B	38,376	39,102	16,560	14,317	35,229	635,502	.0124	506,340	144	35,502	71	18,758	99	90,986	34,340	349,671	191	Inc. Place
Framingham	BOS	24925	3-SS	67,188	66,910	23,796	25,456	50,188	1,598,796	.0321	1,600,771	455	113,718	226	109,628	577	146,176	89,521	348,488	191	MCD-Town
Franklin	BOS	25100		30,267	29,560	24,597	10,263	62,678	744,469	.0124	458,462	130	17,373	35	20,394	107	71,622	20,082	333,457	183	Inc. Place
Gloucester	BOS	26150	4-Sr	30,597	30,273	21,637	12,416	43,528	662,035	.0101	268,274	76	13,193	26	7,479	39	53,748	42,002	419,058	229	Inc. Place
Greenfield		27025	4-C	18,030	18,168	19,663	7,987	32,221	354,530	.0072	334,832	95	26,347	52	9,315	49	63,690	20,601	52,231	29	MCD-Town
Haverhill	BOS	29405	4-S	62,209	58,969	19,958	23,667	45,269	1,241,539	.0194	523,219	149	17,845	35	17,286	91	97,355	69,044	260,228	142	Inc. Place
Holyoke	SPRG	30840	3-B	40,207	39,838	14,762	15,172	29,418	593,537	.0135	664,853	189	89,187	177	120,831	636	60,985	58,197	410,882	225	Inc. Place
Lawrence	BOS	34550	3-SS	74,271	72,043	12,453	24,605	27,943	924,903	.0172	484,485	138	2,301	5	11,344	60	43,752	47,483	607,999	333	Inc. Place
Leominster	BOS	35075	3-B	42,811	41,303	20,118	16,674	41,837	861,253	.0173	816,670	232	73,802	147	73,879	389	112,805	49,886	547,996	300	Inc. Place
Lexington	BOS	35215		30,540	30,355	42,434	10,848	82,150	1,295,922	.0154	244,303	69	...	...	14,752	78	28,034	32,479	180,585	99	MCD-Town
Lowell	BOS	37000	3-SS	106,431	105,167	15,328	37,124	36,706	1,631,423	.0286	852,020	242	28,420	57	9,261	49	136,347	78,863	454,856	249	Inc. Place
Lynn	BOS	37490	3-S	91,717	89,050	15,855	33,708	36,065	1,454,161	.0260	836,813	238	53,864	107	15,314	81	106,303	70,756	788,084	431	Inc. Place
Malden	BOS	37875	4-S	57,362	56,340	19,538	22,713	42,135	1,120,758	.0180	511,807	145	36,690	73	15,937	84	129,966	35,809	162,999	89	Inc. Place
Marlborough	BOS	38715	4-S	37,546	36,255	23,702	14,569	51,867	889,911	.0171	796,575	226	139,860	278	129,537	682	82,569	86,260	1,102,649	604	Inc. Place
Medford	BOS	39835	3-S	53,715	55,765	21,618	20,594	47,626	1,161,224	.0214	896,718	255	74,221	148	58,171	306	178,080	63,296	66,273	36	Inc. Place
Methuen	BOS	40710	3-Sm	45,506	43,789	19,549	16,787	45,208	889,607	.0134	303,265	86	14,698	29	5,512	29	57,120	42,852	88,104	48	Inc. Place
Milford	BOS	41165	4-S	28,544	26,799	21,714	10,857	46,722	619,791	.0106	385,849	110	29,766	59	20,730	109	77,733	51,706	467,394	256	MCD-Town
Natick	BOS	43895	3-S	32,227	32,170	31,441	12,709	61,730	1,013,233	.0263	1,796,750	510	371,827	739	195,393	1,028	80,673	66,987	387,534	212	MCD-Town
Needham	BOS	44105	4-S	29,078	28,911	39,720	10,551	76,597	1,154,968	.0151	359,826	102	...	...	6,760	36	59,925	42,032	618,775	339	MCD-Town
New Bedford	N.BED	45000	3-BB	91,785	93,768	15,825	36,769	27,631	1,452,474	.0246	680,014	193	49,459	98	16,693	88	188,032	81,132	650,558	356	Inc. Place
Newton	BOS	45560	3-SS	85,656	83,829	40,801	30,880	75,845	3,494,859	.0463	1,195,829	340	81,679	162	128,053	674	200,824	84,252	282,327	155	Inc. Place
North Adams		46225	4-C	13,750	14,681	16,060	6,155	28,043	220,819	.0043	174,958	50	29,101	58	3,454	18	42,839	14,256	45,824	25	Inc. Place
Northampton	SPRG	46330	4-C	28,972	28,978	22,044	12,053	39,576	638,652	.0112	434,462	123	20,248	40	25,490	134	89,160	30,724	133,498	73	Inc. Place
Norwood	BOS	50250	4-S	28,696	28,587	24,754	11,519	52,639	710,327	.0193	1,309,096	372	14,136	28	29,384	155	92,194	38,830	300,302	164	MCD-Town
Peabody	BOS	52490	3-Sm	48,823	48,129	21,272	18,431	49,744	1,038,563	.0215	1,079,830	307	192,856	384	146,123	769	68,387	94,264	370,468	203	Inc. Place
Pittsfield	PTSF	53960	3-A	43,780	45,793	20,099	19,601	34,785	879,916	.0150	519,691	148	33,502	67	13,939	73	146,905	29,369	...	...	Inc. Place
Plymouth	BOS	54310		56,353	51,701	21,955	19,858	50,440	1,237,244	.0178	382,476	109	41,167	82	9,750	51	120,008	19,769	133,330	73	MCD-Town
Quincy	BOS	55745	3-S	88,764	88,025	23,016	38,795	43,623	2,042,960	.0322	993,792	282	46,274	92	23,313	123	253,176	104,366	54,217	30	Inc. Place
Randolph	BOS	55955		31,003	30,963	19,844	11,167	50,949	615,222	.0093	213,888	61	1,155	2	18,817	99	44,210	33,242	134,611	74	MCD-Town
Revere	BOS	56585		50,064	47,283	16,385	19,184	35,371	820,283	.0134	335,576	95	14,976	30	38,944	205	63,956	68,003	(d)	...	Inc. Place
Salem	BOS	59105	3-S	41,844	40,407	21,230	17,719	40,958	888,359	.0147	489,798	139	50,946	101	10,059	53	66,565	65,715	120,791	66	Inc. Place
Saugus	BOS	60015	4-Sm	26,442	26,078	22,239	9,867	51,171	588,043	.0136	791,307	225	184,363	367	127,948	673	96,971	37,980	51,042	28	MCD-Town
Shrewsbury	WORC	61800	4-S	35,864	31,640	27,970	13,694	57,191	1,003,129	.0167	656,810	187	62,108	124	19,836	104	95,122	32,819	110,480	60	MCD-Town
Somerville	BOS	62535	4-S	78,295	77,478	19,903	30,877	43,239	1,558,267	.0252	747,845	212	56,870	113	14,254	75	193,451	71,916	244,804	134	Inc. Place
Springfield	SPRG	67000	2-AA	153,765	152,082	15,295	58,022	29,686	2,351,869	.0441	1,564,942	444	169,263	337	59,802	315	248,772	172,509	665,713	364	Inc. Place
Swansea	F.R.	68750	4-Sm	16,075	15,901	21,206	5,841	48,160	340,887	.0068	321,746	91	92,929	185	53,208	280	22,153	19,742	(d)	...	MCD-Town
Taunton	BOS	69170	4-C	58,882	55,976	19,194	22,748	40,294	1,130,160	.0197	688,087	195	111,702	222	87,297	459	98,437	54,243	396,091	217	Inc. Place
Waltham	BOS	72600	3-S	59,162	59,226	22,049	22,504	49,022	1,304,469	.0234	943,478	268	59,770	119	42,391	223	101,684	69,981	622,299	341	Inc. Place
Watertown	BOS	73440		32,560	32,986	29,998	13,982	53,685	976,748	.0169	729,019	207	47,250	94	76,201	401	97,385	31,828	436,208	239	Inc. Place
Wellesley	BOS	74175	4-S	26,534	26,613	46,904	8,473	96,218	1,244,554	.0163	433,924	123	...	...	44,689	235	70,954	30,254	(d)	...	MCD-Town
Westfield	SPRG	76030	4-S	40,996	40,072	19,396	15,182	42,150	795,143	.0135	445,681	127	47,510	94	13,293	70	82,479	36,510	321,101	176	Inc. Place
West Springfield	SPRG	77885	4-S	28,316	27,899	20,379	12,048	37,589	577,057	.0137	793,538	225	43,123	86	34,487	182	106,705	34,266	(d)	...	CDP
Weymouth	BOS	78865	4-S	54,454	53,988	22,053	21,946	47,438	1,200,867	.0196	645,211	183	80,333	160	10,427	55	105,866	73,666	106,560	58	MCD-Town
Woburn	BOS	81035	3-S	36,591	37,258	22,354	14,256	50,750	817,964	.0193	1,146,780	326	73,926	147	28,110	148	93,441	60,410	526,184	288	Inc. Place
Worcester	WORC	82000	2-A	179,225	172,648	17,755	67,902	34,072	3,182,205	.0595	2,320,703	659	133,779	266	176,784	930	362,012	274,511	1,210,485	663	Inc. Place

Michigan

Place Name	Ranally Metro Area	FIPS Place Code	Ranally City Rating	Population Estimate 7/1/05	Population Census 4/1/00	Per Capita Income 2004	Households Estimate 7/1/05	Median Household Income 2004	Disposable Income 2004 ($1,000)	Market Ability Index 2004	Total Retail Sales 2004 Sales ($1,000)	Total Retail Sales Ranally Sales Units	General Merchandise 2004 Sales ($1,000)	General Merchandise Ranally Sales Units	Apparel Store 2004 Sales ($1,000)	Apparel Store Ranally Sales Units	Food Store Sales 2004 ($1,000)	Health & Drug Store 2004 ($1,000)	Manufacturers Value Added 1997* ($1,000)	Manufacturers Ranally Mfg. Units	Place Type
Adrian		00440	3-A	21,131	21,574	18,969	7,953	39,335	400,832	.0084	413,396	117	123,717	246	7,788	41	24,949	23,144	353,205	193	Inc. Place
Alpena		01740	4-A	10,795	11,304	18,433	4,888	32,969	198,980	.0040	179,825	51	47,075	94	8,401	44	14,020	12,221	234,813	129	Inc. Place
Ann Arbor	DET	03000	2-C	117,933	114,024	26,235	48,530	47,141	3,094,021	.0530	2,135,596	606	303,024	603	153,270	807	256,670	114,629	347,274	190	Inc. Place
Battle Creek	BTLCK	05920	3-A	54,163	53,364	18,862	22,271	36,304	1,021,633	.0188	735,972	209	241,309	480	24,936	131	64,085	51,534	1,726,943	945	Inc. Place
Bay City	SAG-	06020	3-B	36,645	36,817	18,334	15,823	33,430	671,853	.0130	552,944	157	104,069	207	21,619	114	43,494	27,673	317,934	174	Inc. Place
Bedford	TOL	06740		31,464	28,606	24,227	11,981	52,822	762,281	.0111	279,456	79	...	...	2,627	14	51,905	16,958	79,050	43	MCD-Township
Benton Harbor	BNTH-	07520	3-A	10,972	11,182	11,749	3,820	25,504	128,914	.0036	202,996	58	72,661	144	6,736	35	9,911	6,396	159,131	87	Inc. Place
Birmingham	DET	08640	4-S	18,615	19,291	52,326	8,821	70,068	974,046	.0133	422,700	120	1,196	2	92,284	486	41,602	30,639	34,681	19	Inc. Place
Bloomfield	DET	09110		42,603	43,023	58,562	16,628	90,433	2,494,915	.0316	831,399	236	36,915	73	27,442	144	82,097	41,293	(d)	...	MCD-Township
Burton	FLN	12060	4-Sm	32,301	30,308	17,827	11,986	40,903	575,828	.0134	731,297	208	234,242	466	52,578	277	60,743	63,708	...	...	Inc. Place
Cadillac		12320	4-C	9,959	10,000	18,888	4,246	34,522	188,108	.0045	261,240	74	57,080	114	6,871	36	29,979	12,564	336,875	184	Inc. Place
Canton	DET	13120		77,350	76,366	23,747	27,824	64,024	1,836,803	.0281	813,339	231	252,019	501	12,112	64	82,266	54,227	201,543	110	MCD-Charter Township
Chesterfield	DET	15340		42,819	37,405	22,701	15,408	55,468	972,018	.0140	315,661	90	43,032	86	1,542	8	40,777	36,081	629,160	344	MCD-Charter Township
Clinton	DET	16520		96,236	95,648	24,859	40,795	45,535	2,392,349	.0380	1,253,034	356	80,782	161	10,239	54	107,158	61,186	489,177	268	MCD-Charter Township
Commerce	DET	17640		36,722	34,764	24,199	13,052	59,456	888,639	.0159	663,746	188	229,093	456	4,071	21	92,393	35,644	139,482	76	MCD-Charter Township
Dearborn	DET	21000	2-S	97,508	97,775	19,023	36,525	41,557	1,854,920	.0516	3,392,027	963	563,665	1,121	199,331	1,049	329,622	222,538	2,440,365	1,336	Inc. Place
Dearborn Heights	DET	21020	4-Sr	58,035	58,264	19,704	23,130	43,545	1,143,508	.0180	488,293	139	26,949	54	6,861	36	108,229	89,338	(d)	...	Inc. Place
Delta	LANS	21520		31,275	29,682	24,908	13,641	44,535	778,997	.0157	798,839	227	344,397	685	28,530	150	84,115	29,001	(d)	...	MCD-Charter Township
Detroit	DET	22000	1-AA	928,992	951,270	13,207	328,246	28,864	12,268,844	.2052	4,217,129	1,197	289,540	576	156,578	824	1,022,847	455,984	6,445,938	3,529	Inc. Place
East Lansing	LANS	24120	4-S	47,732	46,525	16,499	15,887	32,278	787,513	.0128	325,711	92	102,240	203	8,194	43	52,097	9,235	(d)	...	Inc. Place
Eastpointe	DET	24290	4-Sr	34,367	34,077	20,979	13,808	42,834	720,969	.0135	571,375	162	32,919	65	8,835	46	54,891	96,630	(d)	...	Inc. Place
Escanaba		26360	4-A	13,023	13,140	18,573	6,011	31,054	241,873	.0057	313,664	89	55,084	110	14,325	75	44,626	16,228	331,046	181	Inc. Place
Farmington Hills	DET	27440	4-S	83,799	82,111	30,996	34,181	60,878	2,597,474	.0407	1,458,722	414	136,888	272	95,305	502	152,762	144,566	476,776	261	Inc. Place
Flint	FLN	29000	2-A	122,883	124,943	14,995	46,135	29,113	1,842,614	.0395	1,788,335	508	396,302	788	70,088	369	167,135	129,781	...	...	Inc. Place
Georgetown	GDR	31880		44,308	41,658	21,424	15,749	51,642	949,263	.0174	726,949	206	296,794	590	6,629	35	72,690	12,900	38,852	21	MCD-Charter Township
Grand Blanc	FLN	33300		31,961	29,827	23,437	12,142	52,443	749,055	.0126	457,224	130	73,089	145	16,548	87	42,759	32,882	138,255	76	MCD-Charter Township
Grand Haven		33340	4-C	10,751	11,168	27,122	5,038	46,364	291,588	.0054	253,041	72	92,421	184	5,754	30	13,992	12,606	518,674	284	Inc. Place
Grand Rapids	GDR	34000	2-AA	198,345	197,800	18,174	74,990	37,726	3,604,736	.0665	2,552,540	725	500,071	994	90,601	477	292,604	158,126	3,123,985	1,710	Inc. Place
Greenville	GDR	35100	4-C	8,206	7,935	19,839	3,452	35,751	162,799	.0032	143,369	41	63,682	127	5,779	30	9,121	2,995	383,569	210	Inc. Place
Grosse Pointe	DET	35480	4-S	5,599	5,670	44,209	2,354	70,215	247,527	.0032	74,113	21	...	...	17,820	94	17,135	12,367	(d)	...	Inc. Place
Harper Woods	DET	36700	4-Sm	13,516	14,254	21,216	5,960	43,271	286,755	.0067	383,249	109	152,732	304	55,960	295	50,502	39,605	(d)	...	Inc. Place
Highland Park	DET	38180	4-S	15,426	16,746	11,553	5,692	21,325	178,216	.0034	95,409	27	...	...	4,375	23	19,284	6,198	(d)	...	Inc. Place
Holland	HLND	38640	3-C	35,160	35,048	20,558	12,584	42,184	722,810	.0117	357,322	101	47,175	94	5,483	29	47,540	32,504	1,757,132	962	Inc. Place
Houghton		39360	4-A	6,548	7,010	10,861	2,044	29,105	71,120	.0017	69,459	20	18,441	37	9,058	48	1,956	...	(d)	...	Inc. Place
Independence	DET	40400		34,166	32,581	25,841	12,319	64,302	882,898	.0127	323,552	92	...	...	4,939	26	43,715	33,279	(d)	...	MCD-Charter Township
Iron Mountain		40960	4-A	7,705	8,154	18,463	3,372	33,776	142,261	.0034	192,531	55	55,158	110	5,664	30	25,585	11,612	(d)	...	Inc. Place
Ironwood		41060	4-A	5,968	6,293	14,601	2,764	25,260	87,138	.0019	91,277	26	20,754	41	4,917	26	15,056	5,308	(d)	...	Inc. Place
Jackson	JAC	41420	3-AA	36,575	36,316	18,671	14,766	36,467	682,891	.0146	726,145	206	237,074	471	24,922	131	63,542	34,747	425,876	233	Inc. Place
Kalamazoo	KZOO	42160	2-A	75,698	77,145	16,680	30,226	32,644	1,262,612	.0273	1,319,424	375	467,015	929	40,614	214	107,422	61,350	699,046	383	Inc. Place
Kentwood	GDR	42820	4-Sm	48,123	45,255	20,869	20,133	42,085	1,004,270	.0304	2,164,589	615	517,822	1,030	130,111	685	48,285	77,637	859,766	471	Inc. Place
Lansing	LANS	46000	2-A	117,694	119,128	17,952	52,615	34,440	2,112,886	.0429	1,953,691	555	338,658	673	37,509	197	181,091	151,691	...	...	Inc. Place
Lincoln Park	DET	47800	4-S	37,915	40,008	17,748	15,295	40,126	672,923	.0123	456,055	129	111,807	222	19,376	102	89,044	52,408	(d)	...	Inc. Place
Livonia	DET	49000	3-SS	100,717	100,545	23,316	38,014	57,094	2,348,300	.0454	2,139,740	608	371,665	739	189,430	997	266,050	163,737	1,810,408	991	Inc. Place
Macomb	DET	50480		57,783	50,478	24,478	19,530	64,466	1,414,410	.0186	284,153	81	...	...	7,815	41	78,841	27,370	68,537	38	MCD-Township
Madison Heights	DET	50560	4-S	29,928	31,101	19,993	12,784	40,247	598,363	.0149	897,635	255	169,653	337	27,969	147	83,488	47,410	586,821	321	Inc. Place
Marquette		51900	4-A	18,997	19,661	18,775	8,016	33,876	356,667	.0073	344,347	98	99,527	198	14,282	75	25,259	14,800	(d)	...	Inc. Place
Menominee		53020	4-B	9,121	9,131	18,643	4,295	31,842	170,044	.0030	111,496	32	20,386	41	1,498	8	22,006	4,219	196,657	108	Inc. Place
Meridian	LANS	53140		40,134	39,116	28,405	18,094	48,000	1,139,994	.0203	898,508	255	305,495	608	107,774	567	55,142	30,888	(d)	...	MCD-Charter Township
Midland	SAG-	53780	3-C	42,553	41,685	23,066	17,527	44,055	981,531	.0172	678,972	193	169,598	337	30,579	161	52,951	51,400	760,472	416	Inc. Place
Monroe	MONR	55020	3-C	22,585	22,076	22,897	9,276	42,403	517,124	.0097	433,941	123	131,247	261	23,459	123	30,289	29,964	756,010	414	Inc. Place
Mount Clemens	DET	55820	3-S	17,103	17,312	20,891	7,041	35,692	357,304	.0082	462,907	131	36,969	74	13,439	71	69,592	49,915	531,194	291	Inc. Place
Mount Pleasant		56020	4-A	26,857	25,946	14,683	9,960	29,973	394,341	.0083	358,519	102	146,366	291	15,033	79	20,897	10,878	...	...	Inc. Place
Muskegon	MUS	56320	3-AA	39,661	40,105	15,702	15,021	32,440	622,740	.0126	524,300	149	113,299	225	23,514	124	41,207	51,058	630,574	345	Inc. Place
Muskegon Heights	MUS	56360	4-Sm	11,870	12,049	16,286	4,631	31,733	193,319	.0042	199,874	57	54,852	109	7,426	39	16,150	3,635	130,874	72	Inc. Place
Novi	DET	59440	3-Sm	50,252	47,386	28,872	19,847	64,582	1,450,891	.0285	1,470,690	418	387,482	771	107,829	568	75,956	77,112	204,136	112	Inc. Place
Orion	DET	61100		35,373	33,463	24,384	12,943	62,126	862,545	.0123	279,686	79	40,884	81	3,507	18	39,331	14,773	...	...	MCD-Charter Township
Owosso		61940	4-C	16,040	15,713	18,911	6,643	35,973	303,339	.0060	272,467	77	41,868	83	3,913	21	25,136	21,598	135,157	74	Inc. Place
Petoskey		63820	4-A	6,351	6,080	22,447	2,904	38,380	142,559	.0035	213,746	61	36,752	73	11,187	59	23,946	12,272	30,212	17	Inc. Place
Pittsfield	DET	64560		34,215	30,167	21,857	13,747	46,422	747,848	.0151	734,174	208	213,759	425	57,234	301	46,423	30,596	96,264	53	MCD-Charter Township
Plainfield	GDR	64660		31,689	30,195	22,633	11,849	49,065	717,219	.0119	416,214	118	127,036	253	2,339	12	10,165	3,624	145,495	80	MCD-Charter Township
Pontiac	DET	65440	3-SS	64,121	66,337	13,974	23,461	30,415	896,041	.0199	911,640	259	39,875	79	21,241	112	102,366	69,590	1,526,591	836	Inc. Place
Portage	KZOO	65560	3-Sm	45,536	44,897	22,586	19,292	45,617	1,028,492	.0208	1,031,298	293	383,809	763	59,099	311	29,452	44,864	400,741	219	Inc. Place
Port Huron	PTHU	65820	3-C	32,228	32,338	18,043	13,586	32,244	581,475	.0112	462,291	131	74,590	148	14,861	78	53,934	24,591	519,145	284	Inc. Place
Redford	DET	67625		48,375	51,622	19,358	18,903	44,575	936,428	.0166	615,210	175	27,801	55	22,122	116	55,345	37,081	222,469	122	MCD-Charter Township
Rochester Hills	DET	69035		70,646	68,825	31,616	27,043	66,985	2,233,541	.0319	903,195	256	64,837	129	47,021	247	77,653	120,506	638,058	349	Inc. Place
Roseville	DET	69800	3-S	46,750	48,129	19,690	19,569	38,687	920,487	.0221	1,285,523	365	349,971	696	57,000	300	84,621	41,789	551,795	302	Inc. Place
Royal Oak	DET	70040	3-S	57,449	60,062	26,788	27,622	48,394	1,538,920	.0306	1,563,316	444	261,608	520	28,380	149	138,355	157,379	274,330	150	Inc. Place
Saginaw	SAG-	70520	2-A	60,406	61,799	14,365	23,755	28,310	867,732	.0160	511,406	145	33,665	67	31,640	167	66,182	70,782	738,336	404	Inc. Place
St. Clair Shores	DET	70760	4-S	60,990	63,096	24,732	26,760	44,774	1,508,407	.0234	725,847	206	26,958	54	31,362	165	147,226	79,662	158,426	87	Inc. Place
St. Joseph	BNTH-	70960	4-C	8,591	8,789	27,824	4,163	45,430	239,035	.0032	59,315	17	...	...	1,578	8	18,488	12,237	172,813	95	Inc. Place
Sault Ste. Marie	SOO	71740	4-A	17,343	16,542	14,615	6,238	31,794	253,468	.0052	211,710	60	53,842	107	10,684	56	25,969	10,909	17,447	10	Inc. Place
Shelby	DET	72820		70,729	65,159	26,969	26,802	58,517	1,907,468	.0278	756,980	215	190,467	379	16,147	85	52,481	56,983	517,779	283	MCD-Charter Township
Southfield	DET	74900	2-S	79,622	78,296	24,759	34,604	48,411	1,971,378	.0448	2,617,384	743	392,833	781	209,830	1,104	155,059	151,580	326,834	179	Inc. Place
Southgate	DET	74960	4-S	28,822	30,136	19,890	12,273	43,132	573,274	.0157	1,035,374	294	240,093	477	21,945	116	59,206	45,793	(d)	...	Inc. Place
Sterling Heights	DET	76460	3-SSm	130,930	124,471	23,443	49,059	54,355	3,069,401	.0542	2,196,012	624	740,654	1,473	134,760	709	165,747	125,897	2,423,167	1,327	Inc. Place
Taylor	DET	79000	3-Sm	62,459	65,868	16,689	23,397	40,136	1,042,400	.0247	1,346,926	382	319,963	636	74,847	394	108,083	97,734	225,464	123	Inc. Place
Traverse City		80340	3-A	13,855	14,532	24,072	6,325	40,693	333,520	.0069	359,886	102	96,870	193	20,907	110	28,070	14,016	254,006	139	Inc. Place
Troy	DET	80700	2-Sm	82,569	80,959	28,874	30,663	71,104	2,384,107	.0528	3,110,872	883	657,814	1,308	502,221	2,643	192,072	157,519	898,252	492	Inc. Place
Walker	GDR	82960	4-Sm	23,755	21,842	21,051	9,778	44,204	500,059	.0094	400,810	114	79,112	157	5,595	29	8,130	7,909	574,342	314	Inc. Place
Warren	DET	84000	3-SS	136,376	138,247	21,028	55,236	41,691	2,867,725	.0520	2,103,016	597	208,811	415	40,804	215	303,582	179,274	2,210,392	1,210	Inc. Place
Waterford	DET	84240		73,281	73,150	21,929	29,408	49,460	1,606,986	.0336	1,722,600	489	482,451	959	71,747	378	121,399	99,407	77,419	42	MCD-Charter Township
West Bloomfield	DET	85480		67,589	64,860	37,554	24,372	79,039	2,538,242	.0310	511,600	145	4,080	8	39,404	207	116,838	53,777	(d)	...	MCD-Charter Township
West Bloomfield Township	DET	85510		65,994	64,862	37,636	23,797	79,168	2,483,754	.0304	510,285	145	4,070	8	39,302	207	116,542	53,639	(d)	...	CDP
Westland	DET	86000	3-S	87,414	86,602	19,668	36,750	42,579	1,719,294	.0323	1,340,504	381	392,980	782	60,545	319	169,028	119,427	199,408	109	Inc. Place
Wyandotte	DET	88900	4-Sr	26,405	28,006	20,426	11,101	41,631	539,341	.0082	207,078	59	...	...	5,199	27	35,254	47,080	175,763	96	Inc. Place
Wyoming	GDR	88940	3-S	72,132	69,368	17,562	28,212	39,959	1,266,764	.0256	1,137,556	323	283,732	564	59,777	315	83,129	53,903	965,374	529	Inc. Place
Ypsilanti	DET	89140	4-S	22,792	22,362	18,985	8,947	40,430	432,708	.0088	411,778	117	116,933	233	4,407	23	45,156	20,926	...	...	Inc. Place

Minnesota

Place Name	Ranally Metro Area	FIPS Place Code	Ranally City Rating	Population Estimate 7/1/05	Population Census 4/1/00	Per Capita Income 2004	Households Estimate 7/1/05	Median Household Income 2004	Disposable Income 2004 ($1,000)	Market Ability Index 2004	Total Retail Sales 2004 Sales ($1,000)	Total Retail Sales Ranally Sales Units	General Merchandise 2004 Sales ($1,000)	General Merchandise Ranally Sales Units	Apparel Store 2004 Sales ($1,000)	Apparel Store Ranally Sales Units	Food Store Sales 2004 ($1,000)	Health & Drug Store 2004 ($1,000)	Manufacturers Value Added 1997* ($1,000)	Manufacturers Ranally Mfg. Units	Place Type
Albert Lea		00694	4-B	17,926	18,356	19,105	8,154	33,448	342,471	.0067	294,760	84	59,765	119	3,451	18	33,201	9,307	186,785	102	Inc. Place
Andover	MPLS-	01486		32,119	26,588	26,112	10,215	64,189	838,703	.0103	103,049	29	...	...	2,618	14	16,999	5,680	(d)	...	Inc. Place
Apple Valley	MPLS-	01900		50,039	45,527	29,369	19,260	60,650	1,469,606	.0234	851,989	242	195,492	389	9,130	48	138,634	28,437	(d)	...	Inc. Place
Austin		02908	4-B	23,715	23,314	19,099	10,739	33,211	452,930	.0076	247,923	70	51,313	102	10,564	56	51,663	13,333	...	...	Inc. Place
Bemidji		05068	4-A	12,459	11,917	16,080	4,938	33,625	200,345	.0047	252,738	72	52,935	105	16,353	86	36,822	8,610	34,085	19	Inc. Place
Blaine	MPLS-	06382	4-Sm	49,600	44,942	23,226	18,300	54,048	1,151,988	.0190	659,286	187	134,997	268	32,863	173	141,357	40,682	240,778	132	Inc. Place
Bloomington	MPLS-	06616	3-SS	80,881	85,172	25,643	35,853	50,753	2,073,996	.0510	3,233,354	918	524,958	1,044	411,626	2,166	211,306	129,610	783,566	429	Inc. Place
Brainerd		07300	4-A	13,344	13,178	19,424	6,007	34,540	259,192	.0056	287,154	82	59,913	119	3,166	17	23,499	8,646	158,562	87	Inc. Place
Brooklyn Center	MPLS-	07948	3-S	28,962	29,172	16,728	11,781	39,332	484,487	.0130	802,608	228	219,429	436	19,010	100	20,337	13,816	147,969	81	Inc. Place
Brooklyn Park	MPLS-	07966		70,025	67,388	20,332	26,414	52,722	1,423,771	.0280	1,277,684	363	148,815	296	22,579	119	114,375	45,518	416,075	228	Inc. Place
Burnsville	MPLS-	08794	3-Sm	61,674	60,220	27,846	26,085	52,148	1,717,377	.0352	1,887,960	536	427,674	851	104,804	552	195,180	67,138	384,578	211	Inc. Place
Coon Rapids	MPLS-	13114	4-S	62,183	61,607	23,677	23,788	50,687	1,472,308	.0233	737,585	209	207,036	412	7,669	40	70,756	26,684	220,496	121	Inc. Place
Cottage Grove	MPLS-	13456		31,413	30,582	22,562	10,868	58,985	708,754	.0111	333,809	95	68,273	136	1,465	8	71,347	26,847	...	...	Inc. Place

Source: Devonshire Associates Ltd. and Scan/US, Inc. 2005.
* Source: 1997 Census of Manufactures.
Not classified as a Principal Business Center.

...Data less than 1,000.
(d) Data not available.

Principal Business Centers and Other Places with 30,000 or More: Population/Income/Sales, *Continued*

Place Name	Ranally Metro Area	FIPS Place Code	Ranally City Rating	Population: Estimate 7/1/05	Population: Census 4/1/00	Per Capita Income 2004	Households Estimate 7/1/05	Median Household Income 2004	Disposable Income 2004 ($1,000)	Market Ability Index 2004	Total Retail Sales: 2004 Sales ($1,000)	Total Retail Sales: Ranally Sales Units	General Merchandise: 2004 Sales ($1,000)	General Merchandise: Ranally Sales Units	Apparel Store: 2004 Sales ($1,000)	Apparel Store: Ranally Sales Units	Food Store Sales 2004 ($1,000)	Health & Drug Store 2004 ($1,000)	Manufacturers: Value Added 1997* ($1,000)	Manufacturers: Ranally Mfg. Units	Place Type
Duluth	DUL	17000	3-AA	87,481	86,918	18,401	38,038	33,618	1,609,774	.0304	1,233,145	350	242,018	481	40,985	216	134,926	89,235	286,310	157	Inc. Place
Eagan	MPLS-	17288		67,250	63,557	29,780	26,952	60,120	2,002,678	.0325	1,243,909	353	237,582	472	19,670	104	186,061	57,916	1,114,607	610	Inc. Place
Eden Prairie	MPLS-	18116		58,399	54,901	31,788	22,603	69,855	1,856,366	.0296	1,112,618	316	289,749	576	10,107	53	163,211	29,574	917,355	502	Inc. Place
Edina	MPLS-	18188	3-SSm	46,762	47,425	38,231	21,462	59,296	1,787,745	.0401	2,515,114	714	627,544	1,248	168,170	885	157,398	104,221	289,215	158	Inc. Place
Fairmont		20330	4-B	10,390	10,889	20,583	4,947	33,661	213,854	.0040	174,458	50	27,044	54	3,315	17	26,657	7,284	151,114	83	Inc. Place
Fergus Falls		20906	4-A	13,514	13,471	19,522	5,923	33,675	263,819	.0051	226,562	64	56,649	113	3,465	18	20,794	3,973	101,735	56	Inc. Place
Fridley	MPLS-	22814	3-Sm	27,125	27,449	23,852	11,669	43,623	646,973	.0115	469,141	133	97,750	194	6,637	35	50,924	21,811	866,141	474	Inc. Place
Golden Valley	MPLS-	24308	4-Sr	19,241	20,281	23,506	8,317	48,286	452,272	.0122	822,263	233	56,458	112	11,764	62	171,830	87,111	734,806	402	Inc. Place
Hibbing		28790	4-C	16,283	17,071	19,471	7,546	33,000	317,054	.0054	182,636	52	38,669	77	4,985	26	27,643	11,500	93,067	51	Inc. Place
Inver Grove Heights	MPLS-	31076		33,395	29,751	25,726	13,588	53,928	859,115	.0148	595,037	169	43,244	86	1,045	6	58,684	1,934	(d)	...	Inc. Place
Lakeville	MPLS-	35180		50,461	43,128	25,692	17,087	64,494	1,296,454	.0190	504,172	143	15,366	31	3,249	17	56,311	14,088	285,133	156	Inc. Place
Mankato	MNKT	39878	3-A	33,995	32,427	18,653	14,206	35,108	634,107	.0141	734,183	208	214,012	426	46,209	243	102,567	37,108	340,281	186	Inc. Place
Maple Grove	MPLS-	40166		51,026	50,365	24,891	18,441	67,813	1,270,063	.0195	589,908	168	146,613	292	25,238	133	77,641	33,300	616,158	337	Inc. Place
Maplewood	MPLS-	40382	4-S	34,021	34,947	19,432	13,522	43,742	661,102	.0150	817,021	232	164,803	328	41,360	218	95,170	29,341	46,245	25	Inc. Place
Marshall		40688	4-B	12,500	12,735	20,465	5,465	37,565	255,816	.0052	244,964	70	45,402	90	5,155	27	33,276	8,811	100,289	55	Inc. Place
Minneapolis	MPLS-	43000	1-AA	390,008	382,618	19,471	172,150	36,800	7,593,762	.1315	4,600,789	1,306	581,495	1,156	231,261	1,217	606,643	354,983	2,106,593	1,153	Inc. Place
Minnetonka	MPLS-	43252	3-Sm	49,066	51,301	33,497	21,206	59,257	1,643,573	.0347	2,003,844	569	440,733	876	103,355	544	148,938	89,656	971,589	532	Inc. Place
Moorhead	FAR-	43864		32,401	32,177	17,448	12,777	34,498	565,342	.0106	409,804	116	74,430	148	6,150	32	58,533	17,844	44,584	24	Inc. Place
New Ulm		46042	4-C	13,360	13,594	19,613	5,750	38,688	262,033	.0049	203,114	58	27,923	56	2,690	14	46,896	5,738	734,237	402	Inc. Place
Owatonna		49300	4-C	23,839	22,434	21,339	9,756	42,359	508,709	.0090	351,775	100	59,114	118	4,883	26	57,169	13,446	505,543	277	Inc. Place
Plymouth	MPLS-	51730		68,602	65,894	29,597	26,853	66,790	2,030,421	.0407	2,162,546	614	88,003	175	13,807	73	160,671	27,124	1,138,178	623	Inc. Place
Richfield	MPLS-	54214	4-S	33,358	34,439	20,521	15,177	41,795	684,531	.0164	958,019	272	26,032	52	25,800	136	94,586	42,925	(d)	...	Inc. Place
Rochester	ROCH	54880	3-AA	96,182	85,806	25,707	42,106	47,683	2,472,535	.0426	1,711,159	486	455,419	906	57,508	303	161,675	67,128	...	...	Inc. Place
Roseville	MPLS-	55852	3-Sm	31,560	33,690	23,900	13,791	47,355	754,276	.0222	1,586,975	451	335,316	667	118,451	623	163,968	99,141	248,830	136	Inc. Place
St. Cloud	ST.CLD	56896	3-A	62,922	59,107	20,040	25,448	37,555	1,260,955	.0264	1,318,640	374	362,165	720	47,678	251	109,680	39,493	499,285	273	Inc. Place
St. Louis Park	MPLS-	57220	4-S	43,478	44,126	27,371	21,273	46,870	1,190,046	.0256	1,443,521	410	199,219	396	33,366	176	101,271	64,262	388,369	213	Inc. Place
St. Paul	MPLS-	58000	2-BB	290,701	287,151	18,246	114,631	37,759	5,304,232	.0878	2,587,172	735	248,116	493	93,234	491	528,378	190,889	2,873,925	1,573	Inc. Place
Shakopee	MPLS-	59350		33,851	20,568	23,731	12,680	54,342	803,319	.0119	303,713	86	48,432	96	3,639	19	18,315	11,415	(d)	...	Inc. Place
Virginia		67288	4-C	9,025	9,157	18,061	4,540	29,928	162,997	.0040	237,042	67	66,389	132	8,845	47	22,440	10,120	(d)	...	Inc. Place
West St. Paul	MPLS-	69700	4-Sm	19,166	19,405	31,859	9,156	45,231	610,616	.0093	320,392	91	58,449	116	10,078	53	85,486	20,298	67,097	37	Inc. Place
Willmar		70420	3-A	17,615	18,351	19,140	7,645	34,983	337,160	.0074	381,851	108	91,198	181	11,759	62	45,884	14,871	142,260	78	Inc. Place
Winona		71032	4-B	26,947	27,069	18,354	11,347	34,793	494,589	.0087	308,153	88	68,304	136	10,969	58	41,672	5,520	425,999	233	Inc. Place
Woodbury	MPLS-	71428		56,562	46,463	31,015	21,688	66,359	1,754,244	.0262	837,264	238	204,507	407	60,187	317	121,526	43,074	96,502	53	Inc. Place
Worthington		71734	4-A	11,517	11,283	17,595	4,666	34,610	202,646	.0042	200,434	57	23,914	48	10,650	56	26,996	8,562	233,396	128	Inc. Place
Mississippi																					
Biloxi	BIL-	06220	3-AA	51,853	50,644	16,980	21,090	32,480	880,478	.0180	804,479	228	312,542	622	58,012	305	43,699	37,391	...	...	Inc. Place
Brookhaven		08820	4-B	9,688	9,861	12,992	3,606	26,091	125,870	.0033	182,240	52	64,170	128	8,135	43	13,639	7,897	119,874	66	Inc. Place
Clarksdale		13820	4-C	20,033	20,645	10,575	7,213	22,042	211,850	.0051	218,120	62	34,308	68	9,979	53	28,460	14,476	60,412	33	Inc. Place
Columbus	COL	15380	3-A	25,025	25,944	15,271	9,812	27,849	382,151	.0096	543,803	154	153,338	305	30,833	162	65,185	27,651	...	...	Inc. Place
Corinth		15700	4-B	13,902	14,054	15,702	5,937	28,029	218,283	.0049	241,068	68	79,331	158	11,871	62	15,607	11,318	...	...	Inc. Place
Greenville	GRNV	29180	3-A	39,712	41,633	12,543	15,017	25,446	498,119	.0112	496,238	141	158,305	315	32,623	172	41,612	17,875	416,767	228	Inc. Place
Greenwood		29340	4-B	16,649	18,425	11,235	6,518	21,449	187,055	.0047	229,239	65	42,994	86	17,790	94	29,088	15,158	...	...	Inc. Place
Gulfport	BIL-	29700	3-B	73,890	71,127	16,614	29,368	32,535	1,227,626	.0260	1,211,953	344	234,455	466	47,730	251	94,867	59,432	115,299	63	Inc. Place
Hattiesburg	HATT	31020	3-A	46,507	44,779	13,336	17,519	26,338	620,228	.0161	884,561	251	303,114	603	25,798	136	55,447	71,155	387,501	212	Inc. Place
Jackson	JAC	36000	2-AA	181,458	184,256	15,396	67,000	30,699	2,793,745	.0646	3,298,446	937	699,904	1,392	172,436	908	264,413	211,469	828,738	454	Inc. Place
Laurel	LAUR	39640	3-A	17,337	18,393	14,278	6,366	25,606	247,531	.0069	416,129	118	127,765	254	18,653	98	47,465	29,806	412,886	226	Inc. Place
McComb		43280	4-A	13,152	13,337	11,882	5,025	23,017	156,269	.0043	244,639	69	58,141	116	16,182	85	26,096	20,202	19,427	11	Inc. Place
Meridian	MRID	46640	3-A	37,372	39,968	14,642	14,692	28,290	547,210	.0133	711,233	202	200,599	399	23,297	123	77,533	39,494	...	...	Inc. Place
Natchez	NCHZ	50440	3-A	17,226	18,464	13,317	7,203	24,465	229,398	.0054	265,845	75	116,725	232	13,905	73	22,723	13,685	89,625	49	Inc. Place
Olive Branch	MEM	54040		33,950	21,054	22,324	11,858	51,829	757,899	.0110	250,327	71	8,493	17	...	...	28,525	3,181	(d)	...	Inc. Place
Pascagoula	PSCG	55360	3-B	25,860	26,200	17,510	9,960	30,913	452,807	.0121	757,299	215	161,541	321	14,290	75	98,567	22,430	...	...	Inc. Place
Southaven	MEM	69280		37,350	28,977	20,817	13,842	43,926	777,514	.0160	789,638	224	293,728	584	11,707	62	61,298	56,672	(d)	...	Inc. Place
Starkville		70240	4-B	20,996	21,869	15,233	10,161	24,393	319,823	.0059	198,166	56	57,486	114	12,059	63	22,179	4,225	...	...	Inc. Place
Tupelo		74840	3-A	35,693	34,211	17,129	13,111	35,055	611,392	.0153	893,223	254	306,014	609	69,235	364	47,525	37,532	664,511	364	Inc. Place
Vicksburg	VICK	76720	3-A	25,599	26,407	16,847	9,952	34,068	431,278	.0081	312,829	89	21,115	42	19,923	105	44,602	16,011	236,691	130	Inc. Place
Missouri																					
Ballwin	ST.L	03160		31,495	31,283	26,345	11,842	62,750	829,736	.0150	664,072	189	59,048	117	13,809	73	77,417	37,003	(d)	...	Inc. Place
Blue Springs	K.C.	06652	4-S	48,966	48,080	20,935	17,862	50,500	1,025,098	.0176	629,329	179	77,417	154	2,417	13	113,634	23,318	74,315	41	Inc. Place
Bridgeton	ST.L	08398	3-S	15,260	15,550	19,004	6,108	44,463	289,993	.0094	681,936	194	101,326	202	14,831	78	35,975	43,058	481,935	264	Inc. Place
Cape Girardeau	CPGIR	11242	3-A	35,568	35,349	18,470	15,123	32,688	656,947	.0156	874,568	248	222,275	442	24,542	129	42,659	52,601	721,404	395	Inc. Place
Chesterfield	ST.L	13600		47,983	46,802	39,606	18,460	77,080	1,900,419	.0248	593,104	168	160,025	318	70,061	369	89,301	56,652	108,081	59	Inc. Place
Clayton	ST.L	14572	3-S	12,708	12,825	42,968	5,299	57,961	546,033	.0095	452,961	129	...	...	9,214	48	12,225	8,063	(d)	...	Inc. Place
Columbia	COL	15670	3-A	91,697	84,531	19,681	39,703	34,962	1,804,722	.0336	1,376,856	391	259,439	516	48,583	256	122,861	64,553	739,533	405	Inc. Place
Crestwood	ST.L	17218	4-Sm	11,770	11,863	21,923	5,057	48,281	258,030	.0064	391,793	111	122,838	244	35,787	188	28,265	33,625	81,873	45	Inc. Place
Creve Coeur	ST.L	17272	4-S	16,556	16,500	47,921	6,993	68,956	793,380	.0123	501,726	142	...	...	17,651	93	132,923	43,921	305,915	167	Inc. Place
Des Peres	ST.L	19270	4-Sm	8,811	8,592	43,532	3,069	86,533	383,558	.0059	232,312	66	84,561	168	40,080	211	15,955	10,696	(d)	...	Inc. Place
Florissant	ST.L	24778	4-S	49,238	50,497	18,734	19,867	44,243	922,449	.0160	548,112	156	61,996	123	11,214	59	111,414	68,951	(d)	...	Inc. Place
Frontenac	ST.L	26110	4-Sm	3,561	3,483	50,134	1,323	92,213	178,528	.0027	102,364	29	39,178	78	18,739	99	6,549	4,496	(d)	...	Inc. Place
Hannibal		30214	4-B	17,368	17,757	16,390	7,091	30,434	284,663	.0058	253,837	72	58,428	116	2,802	15	43,865	17,769	...	...	Inc. Place
Independence	K.C.	35000	3-S	114,540	113,288	18,137	48,628	36,904	2,077,365	.0398	1,647,861	468	372,097	740	70,129	369	139,219	123,697	521,830	286	Inc. Place
Jefferson City	JFCY	37000	3-A	40,564	39,636	22,290	17,814	39,911	904,176	.0172	774,964	220	166,857	332	15,000	79	101,160	40,135	610,123	334	Inc. Place
Jennings	ST.L	37178	4-Sm	15,473	15,469	14,345	6,168	30,213	221,960	.0045	182,787	52	42,033	84	4,946	26	36,413	12,105	(d)	...	Inc. Place
Joplin	JOP	37592	3-A	47,216	45,504	17,365	20,167	31,071	819,903	.0174	827,016	235	193,117	384	29,504	155	52,022	43,456	390,960	214	Inc. Place
Kansas City	K.C.	38000	1-A	457,970	441,545	19,799	193,617	36,463	9,067,328	.1668	6,700,431	1,903	1,099,910	2,187	249,877	1,315	621,139	439,419	4,235,403	2,319	Inc. Place
Kirksville		39026	4-A	16,429	16,988	13,612	6,872	25,283	223,629	.0049	221,280	63	43,507	87	9,068	48	28,996	15,648	221,671	121	Inc. Place
Kirkwood	ST.L	39044	4-S	27,008	27,324	30,694	11,605	53,973	828,987	.0127	430,827	122	44,101	88	10,066	53	53,906	30,303	74,903	41	Inc. Place
Lees Summit	K.C.	41348		73,797	70,700	24,291	27,927	56,667	1,792,596	.0258	618,886	176	80,431	160	11,496	61	142,990	32,343	296,146	162	Inc. Place
Mexico		47648	4-C	10,138	11,320	18,123	4,496	31,823	183,734	.0034	128,827	37	17,457	35	3,783	20	21,005	11,612	150,391	82	Inc. Place
Moberly		49034	4-C	12,011	11,945	16,153	5,155	29,306	194,008	.0047	262,119	74	65,336	130	5,435	29	28,206	14,516	78,951	43	Inc. Place
North Kansas City	K.C.	53102	4-S	5,290	4,714	28,019	2,877	34,749	148,220	.0028	137,079	39	...	...	...	...	2,191	5,475	441,655	242	Inc. Place
Oakville	ST.L	53876		35,279	35,309	19,541	12,506	54,932	689,396	.0114	356,095	101	134,369	267	33,546	177	45,455	36,319	(d)	...	CDP
O'Fallon	ST.L	54074		69,237	46,169	22,390	24,218	52,793	1,550,183	.0219	444,919	126	88,651	176	9,940	52	54,391	28,702	...	...	Inc. Place
Poplar Bluff		59096	3-A	15,603	16,651	15,205	7,027	26,904	237,240	.0062	358,609	102	90,793	181	12,142	64	25,057	26,517	249,438	137	Inc. Place
Raytown	K.C.	60788		30,309	30,388	19,839	12,976	39,972	601,306	.0118	536,663	152	166,782	332	15,629	82	44,852	29,195	32,176	18	Inc. Place
Rolla		62912	4-A	17,631	16,367	15,135	7,354	29,427	266,850	.0056	250,253	71	61,662	123	7,720	41	25,175	8,095	83,013	45	Inc. Place
Saint Ann	ST.L	63956	4-Sm	13,299	13,607	16,312	6,027	32,377	216,929	.0075	550,874	156	211,087	420	53,707	283	36,806	33,609	(d)	...	Inc. Place
Saint Charles	ST.L	64082	3-S	63,789	60,321	25,689	26,901	44,367	1,638,679	.0241	655,342	186	78,392	156	16,542	87	86,600	47,824	187,380	103	Inc. Place
Saint Joseph	ST.JO	64550	3-AA	74,379	73,990	17,104	30,667	33,278	1,272,189	.0249	1,037,062	294	276,628	550	21,549	113	124,813	43,572	...	...	Inc. Place
St. Louis	ST.L	65000	1-AA	324,238	348,189	14,896	145,556	26,297	4,829,690	.0861	2,615,125	743	252,331	502	84,483	445	382,754	292,732	5,088,636	2,786	Independent City
Saint Peters	ST.L	65126		54,787	51,381	25,840	20,611	54,545	1,415,701	.0233	860,313	244	118,759	236	57,906	305	87,034	42,864	1,227,392	672	Inc. Place
Sedalia		66440	4-A	19,471	20,339	16,892	8,518	30,706	328,909	.0067	292,877	83	73,320	146	10,203	54	29,318	16,165	269,557	148	Inc. Place
Sikeston		67790	4-B	16,915	16,992	15,529	7,076	28,933	262,680	.0056	252,398	72	41,175	82	12,303	65	29,733	22,126	145,424	80	Inc. Place
Springfield	SPRG	70000	2-A	153,675	151,580	17,734	70,735	30,849	2,725,217	.0601	3,052,351	867	572,446	1,138	101,162	532	244,270	150,563	1,670,752	915	Inc. Place
University City	ST.L	75220		36,969	37,428	26,038	16,237	41,678	962,589	.0149	470,153	134	23,547	47	11,159	59	134,871	38,391	(d)	...	Inc. Place
West Plains		78928	4-A	10,241	10,866	14,031	4,514	25,978	143,690	.0037	211,104	60	65,740	131	7,843	41	10,837	11,771	168,465	92	Inc. Place
Wildwood	ST.L	79820		33,966	32,884	28,217	11,163	74,355	958,406	.0108	18,786	5	1,474	3	...	...	2,872	1,161	(d)	...	Inc. Place
Montana																					
Billings	BIL	06550	3-AA	94,441	89,847	18,090	39,536	34,980	1,708,408	.0361	1,751,167	497	428,626	852	71,103	374	179,279	53,764	...	...	Inc. Place
Bozeman		08950	3-A	32,783	27,509	17,740	12,756	34,816	581,566	.0118	537,349	153	45,517	91	20,337	107	58,633	14,888	41,788	23	Inc. Place
Butte	BUT	11397	3-A	31,829	33,892	16,229	14,100	29,445	516,569	.0103	431,035	122	79,895	159	29,290	154	68,107	20,473	(d)	...	Inc. Place
Great Falls	GTFA	32800	3-A	55,249	56,690	16,898	23,776	31,345	933,609	.0183	761,000	216	184,899	368	18,585	98	82,441	38,713	54,936	30	Inc. Place
Havre		35050	4-C	8,799	9,621	16,259	3,798	29,682	143,060	.0029	119,781	34	19,816	39	5,325	28	24,024	2,473	(d)	...	Inc. Place
Helena		35600	3-A	26,009	25,780	19,533	11,333	34,002	508,032	.0111	580,587	165	128,883	256	10,640	56	99,977	21,249	(d)	...	Inc. Place
Kalispell		40075	4-A	15,980	14,223	16,791	6,551	31,891	268,314	.0057	266,145	76	83,641	166	4,964	26	31,497	7,030	(d)	...	Inc. Place
Missoula	MSLA	50200	3-A	56,672	57,053	17,061	24,910	30,435	966,878	.0221	1,156,995	329	325,088	646	38,922	205	147,911	37,717	65,422	36	Inc. Place
Nebraska																					
Beatrice		03390	4-C	12,845	12,496	17,679	5,587	33,049	227,088	.0043	170,385	48	23,603	47	6,001	32	25,608	11,618	42,581	23	Inc. Place
Bellevue	OMA	03950	4-Sm	47,773	44,382	21,697	19,057	43,570	1,036,526	.0167	524,360	149	151,266	301	5,674	30	70,145	24,114	86,962	48	Inc. Place
Columbus		10110	4-C	20,007	20,971	18,641	8,175	37,279	372,957	.0068	259,509	74	46,485	92	6,554	34	44,375	18,932	197,603	108	Inc. Place
Fremont		17670	4-C	25,038	25,174	18,255	10,340	35,715	457,065	.0101	515,713	146	103,037	205	13,262	70	51,155	40,554	107,041	59	Inc. Place
Grand Island	GDIS	19595	3-A	44,007	42,940	16,336	16,760	34,999	718,899	.0154	728,499	207	235,200	468	32,455	171	44,871	23,976	414,467	227	Inc. Place
Hastings		21415	3-A	25,184	24,064	17,231	10,176	34,433	433,937	.0081	311,941	89	57,456	114	7,379	39	65,054	21,508	196,653	108	Inc. Place
Kearney		25055	4-B	27,512	27,431	16,895	10,738	35,083	464,802	.0101	492,603	140	138,604	276	15,974	84	46,147	24,747	129,585	71	Inc. Place
Lincoln	LINC	28000	3-AA	240,192	225,581	18,175	92,308	39,580	4,365,498	.0808	3,132,141	889	589,217	1,172	119,764	630	445,566	224,579	...	...	Inc. Place
McCook		29925	4-A	7,729	7,994	17,041	3,378	31,433	131,708	.0033	192,683	55	52,204	104	5,304	28	21,991	12,052	(d)	...	Inc. Place
Norfolk		34615	3-A	24,242	23,516	16,327	9,450	34,505	395,791	.0091	477,483	136	120,190	239	20,996	111	52,882	20,252	56,492	31	Inc. Place
North Platte		35000	3-A	23,693	23,878	18,192	10,049	34,154	431,013	.0080	306,625	87	84,132	167	7,772	41	36,488	18,089	(d)	...	Inc. Place
Omaha	OMA	37000	2-AA	401,817	390,007	18,140	157,230	39,868	7,289,021	.1503	7,018,683	1,993	838,601	1,668	325,366	1,712	855,774	436,739	2,939,121	1,609	Inc. Place
Scottsbluff		44245	3-A	14,355	14,732	15,802	6,006	29,934	226,840	.0058	335,545	95	93,278	185	11,084	58	47,450	9,803	45,664	25	Inc. Place
Nevada																					
Carson City		09700	4-C	57,139	52,457	18,725	21,471	39,258	1,069,920	.0212	948,543	269	50,822	101	1,398	7	156,413	109,780	297,324	163	Independent City
Henderson	LASV	31900		226,988	175,381	22,618	84,245	52,836	5,134,057	.0816	2,548,288	724	409,369	814	96,916	510	341,290	81,511	544,072	298	Inc. Place
Las Vegas	LASV	40000	2-AA	574,733	478,434	20,094	208,586	44,178	11,548,611	.1967	6,759,971	1,920	943,006	1,875	217,070	1,142	1,054,266	321,478	272,972	149	Inc. Place
North Las Vegas	LASV	51800		161,757	115,488	13,517	46,792	44,177	2,186,437	.0382	967,430	275	154,210	307	10,897	57	210,542	56,994	195,723	107	Inc. Place
Paradise	LASV	54600		229,619	186,070	18,711	93,709	38,774	4,296,445	.0885	4,186,539	1,189	801,625	1,594	599,009	3,153	626,864	177,044	(d)	...	CDP
Reno	RENO	60600	2-A	209,477	180,480	21,133	85,514	40,987	4,426,810	.0813	3,366,049	956	652,546	1,298	142,298	749	432,378	133,759	446,658	245	Inc. Place
Sparks	RENO	68400	4-S	78,062	66,346	17,464	28,810	43,681	1,363,282	.0261	1,056,056	300	148,179	295	9,149	48	157,138	58,476	390,132	214	Inc. Place
Spring Valley	LASV	68585		144,864	117,390	22,987	58,155	46,230	3,330,044	.0567	2,105,871	598	134,663	268	38,788	204	164,684	56,460	(d)	...	CDP
Sunrise Manor	LASV	71400		192,656	156,120	14,347	65,114	37,914	2,763,996	.0496	1,476,149	419	160,512	319	29,988	158	222,294	65,087	(d)	...	CDP
Winchester	LASV	84600		33,268	26,958	17,773	14,542	31,593	591,270	.0181	1,253,615	356	315,238	627	273,270	1,438	190,068	58,992	(d)	...	CDP
New Hampshire																					
Claremont		12900	4-B	12,790	13,151	18,438	5,450	33,502	235,820	.0054	291,277	83	60,659	121	4,684	25	64,650	18,614	223,256	122	Inc. Place
Concord	CONC	14200	3-B	42,465	40,687	20,801	16,781	39,542	883,313	.0212	1,245,724	354	185,149	368	36,490	192	206,203	55,545	216,070	118	Inc. Place
Derry	BOS	17940		36,958	34,021	21,051	13,463	50,584	778,017	.0124	364,770	104	60,915	121	3,558	19	54,872	14,260	163,961	90	MCD-Town
Dover	PTSM-	18820	4-C	28,329	26,884	21,819	12,277	41,801	618,120	.0112	459,007	130	33,989	68	12,531	66	111,790	26,918	291,829	160	Inc. Place
Keene		39300	4-A	23,295	22,563	19,052	9,153	36,368	443,826	.0118	752,885	214	74,760	149	21,947	116	71,019	34,581	257,672	141	Inc. Place
Laconia		40180	4-C	15,728	16,411	16,330	6,232	35,864	256,835	.0080	555,815	158	91,005	181	45,424	239	81,721	14,619	191,406	105	Inc. Place
Lebanon		41300	3-A	12,906	12,568	22,290	5,736	39,693	287,669	.0078	515,201	146	111,420	222	17,860	94	84,646	23,399	172,031	94	Inc. Place
Manchester	MNCH	45140	3-AA	111,484	107,006	19,846	45,578	38,809	2,212,523	.0466	2,325,358	660	375,054	746	119,979	631	232,610	101,880	705,764	386	Inc. Place
Nashua	BOS	50260	3-B	90,383	86,605	22,636	35,621	48,036	2,045,884	.0494	2,999,471	852	506,752	1,008	189,047	995	310,850	100,873	1,255,871	688	Inc. Place
Portsmouth	PTSM-	62900	3-C	20,139	20,784	26,650	9,607	42,611	536,698	.0195	1,579,363	448	314,398	625	79,692	419	216,575	42,889	159,643	87	Inc. Place
Rochester	PTSM-	65140	4-C	29,894	28,461	19,020	12,067	38,157	568,597	.0110	471,448	134	42,727	85	10,932	58	83,398	26,336	808,492	443	Inc. Place
Salem	BOS	66660	4-S	29,661	28,112	25,539	11,045	52,958	757,517	.0233	1,722,191	489	610,814	1,215	142,888	752	186,932	50,791	...	...	MCD-Town
New Jersey																					
Asbury Park	N.Y.	01960	4-S	17,104	16,930	23,814	6,920	37,728	407,319	.0064	201,780	57	41,598	83	5,540	29	24,243	26,113	(d)	...	Inc. Place
Atlantic City	ATCY	02080	3-AA	40,750	40,517	18,751	17,331	26,193	764,109	.0145	601,844	171	58,825	117	86,980	458	134,813	56,304	(d)	...	Inc. Place
Bayonne	N.Y.	03580	4-S	57,535	61,842	19,649	22,818	39,093	1,130,486	.0169	371,513	105	5,743	11	23,413	123	98,732	40,325	243,949	134	Inc. Place
Belleville	N.Y.	04695	4-Sr	36,292	35,928	17,488	13,400	43,971	634,666	.0106	312,246	89	23,176	46	11,532	61	105,449	12,324	219,662	120	MCD-Township
Berkeley	N.Y.	05305		39,599	39,991	23,382	19,017	35,290	925,902	.0116	105,571	30	1,328	3	1,360	7	42,048	9,910	(d)	...	MCD-Township
Bloomfield	N.Y.	06260	4-S	48,089	47,683	20,307	18,535	49,410	976,546	.0156	457,829	130	1,452	3	26,811	141	148,362	46,490	163,327	89	MCD-Township

Source: Devonshire Associates Ltd. and Scan/US, Inc. 2005.
* Source: 1997 Census of Manufactures.
Not classified as a Principal Business Center.

...Data less than 1,000.
(d) Data not available.

Continued on next page

Principal Business Centers and Other Places with 30,000 or More: Population/Income/Sales, *Continued*

Place Name	Ranally Metro Area	FIPS Place Code	Ranally City Rating	Population: Estimate 7/1/05	Population: Census 4/1/00	Per Capita Income 2004	Households Estimate 7/1/05	Median Household Income 2004	Disposable Income 2004 ($1,000)	Market Ability Index 2004	Total Retail Sales: 2004 Sales ($1,000)	Total Retail Sales: Ranally Sales Units	General Merchandise: 2004 Sales ($1,000)	General Merchandise: Ranally Sales Units	Apparel Store: 2004 Sales ($1,000)	Apparel Store: Ranally Sales Units	Food Store Sales 2004 ($1,000)	Health & Drug Store 2004 ($1,000)	Manufacturers: Value Added 1997* ($1,000)	Manufacturers: Ranally Mfg. Units	Place Type
Brick	N.Y.	07420	4-S	79,322	76,119	24,050	29,678	48,020	1,907,713	.0296	904,713	257	145,476	289	58,596	308	225,899	45,741	(d)	...	MCD-Township
Bridgewater	N.Y.	07720	4-S	47,529	42,940	36,698	17,265	74,976	1,744,232	.0308	1,462,947	415	383,316	762	234,861	1,236	70,197	47,005	609,867	334	MCD-Township
Burlington	PHIL-	08920	4-S	10,263	9,736	25,955	4,186	50,126	266,379	.0053	274,710	78	61,908	123	15,603	82	29,690	14,573	181,828	100	Inc. Place
Camden	PHIL-	10000	3-S	80,611	79,904	9,837	23,768	23,412	793,002	.0146	264,640	75	4,999	10	9,490	50	69,765	36,006	340,536	186	Inc. Place
Cherry Hill	PHIL-	12280	3-SS	71,980	69,965	30,567	26,251	61,638	2,200,237	.0380	1,640,668	466	134,040	267	222,762	1,172	215,805	91,972	468,629	257	MCD-Township
City of Orange	N.Y.	13045	4-S	33,444	32,868	13,440	11,723	35,339	449,504	.0081	228,487	65	6,669	13	18,946	100	28,905	28,128	35,818	20	MCD-Township
Clifton	N.Y.	13690	4-S	81,294	78,672	22,876	30,216	46,810	1,859,681	.0299	973,526	276	96,898	193	57,025	300	166,542	64,036	932,625	511	Inc. Place
Deptford	PHIL-	17710		30,855	26,763	24,609	11,933	46,357	759,317	.0154	793,967	225	176,074	350	83,451	439	49,723	30,650	43,727	24	MCD-Township
Dover	N.Y.	18070	4-S	19,071	18,188	17,063	5,551	52,681	325,403	.0072	366,009	104	35,922	71	10,225	54	98,577	4,422	61,647	34	Inc. Place
Dover	N.Y.	18130	3-S	96,908	89,706	23,994	35,036	49,465	2,325,179	.0415	1,728,372	491	282,186	561	109,810	578	293,629	123,754	53,097	29	MCD-Township
East Brunswick	N.Y.	19000	3-S	50,845	46,756	31,885	17,224	66,106	1,621,173	.0265	1,055,130	300	180,656	359	109,662	577	131,728	61,116	70,733	39	MCD-Township
East Orange	N.Y.	19390	4-Sr	68,982	69,824	13,273	24,901	31,324	915,612	.0142	187,444	53	3,736	7	21,751	114	59,270	24,187	(d)	...	Inc. Place
Eatontown	N.Y.	19840	4-Sm	14,429	14,008	27,326	6,031	52,835	394,288	.0090	534,638	152	92,881	185	98,807	520	46,335	17,748	154,367	85	Inc. Place
Edison	N.Y.	20230	3-S	103,611	97,687	29,664	36,110	61,716	3,073,486	.0509	2,014,060	572	184,482	367	220,614	1,161	211,250	130,686	1,317,847	721	MCD-Township
Egg Harbor	ATCY	20290		34,865	30,726	23,883	13,804	48,289	832,683	.0132	428,476	122	27,894	55	26,242	138	18,493	23,274	(d)	...	MCD-Township
Elizabeth	N.Y.	21000	3-S	126,938	120,568	14,483	43,136	33,504	1,838,472	.0319	864,468	245	27,312	54	64,651	340	211,658	70,848	544,705	298	Inc. Place
Englewood	N.Y.	21480	4-S	27,068	26,203	30,280	9,462	53,701	819,629	.0142	611,444	174	...	...	27,859	147	88,834	16,294	181,081	99	Inc. Place
Evesham	PHIL-	22110		49,152	42,275	28,530	18,619	59,868	1,402,311	.0230	881,708	250	112,093	223	50,983	268	182,789	51,282	(d)	...	MCD-Township
Ewing	PHIL-	22185		37,535	35,707	18,358	12,398	43,958	689,059	.0112	312,055	89	3,626	7	24,644	130	72,448	33,665	161,663	89	MCD-Township
Fair Lawn	N.Y.	22470		32,225	31,637	28,716	11,853	63,171	925,384	.0130	331,960	94	...	...	4,981	26	55,319	34,000	346,422	190	Inc. Place
Flemington	N.Y.	23700	4-S	4,369	4,200	42,422	1,845	69,945	185,342	.0034	176,747	50	4,686	9	14,863	78	30,194	6,105	297,403	163	Inc. Place
Fort Lee	N.Y.	24420		37,439	35,461	35,055	17,246	52,262	1,312,424	.0167	327,897	93	1,221	2	19,329	102	132,431	57,324	(d)	...	Inc. Place
Franklin	N.Y.	24900		54,595	50,903	27,065	20,813	61,123	1,477,630	.0228	732,471	208	41,820	83	24,457	129	167,470	59,227	368,354	202	MCD-Township
Freehold	N.Y.	25230		33,155	31,537	26,427	11,525	59,632	876,185	.0188	1,050,092	298	106,325	211	152,091	800	105,109	43,690	143,750	79	MCD-Township
Galloway	ATCY	25560		34,029	31,209	22,873	12,776	46,447	778,358	.0096	63,333	18	1,578	3	...	...	13,210	2,484	...	...	MCD-Township
Garfield	N.Y.	25770		30,759	29,786	17,078	11,442	40,577	525,316	.0085	219,396	62	1,337	3	...	...	46,411	18,846	293,514	161	Inc. Place
Gloucester	PHIL-	26760		65,958	64,350	20,899	23,098	47,585	1,378,469	.0205	473,239	134	55,554	110	12,286	65	99,879	27,978	95,649	52	MCD-Township
Hackensack	N.Y.	28680	3-SS	44,075	42,677	23,498	18,410	45,193	1,035,674	.0225	1,240,091	352	230,183	458	98,276	517	172,150	145,390	191,180	105	Inc. Place
Hamilton	PHIL-	29310		90,639	87,109	21,641	32,829	51,037	1,961,529	.0308	900,454	256	50,491	100	31,247	164	194,243	126,316	338,838	186	MCD-Township
Hillsborough	N.Y.	31890		39,371	36,634	29,021	13,611	73,128	1,142,586	.0138	147,840	42	1,112	2	1,839	10	96,148	...	363,691	199	MCD-Township
Hoboken	N.Y.	32250	4-S	41,321	38,577	36,940	20,028	58,031	1,526,404	.0175	170,507	48	2,078	4	8,976	47	66,576	33,776	120,572	66	Inc. Place
Howell	N.Y.	33300		53,360	48,903	23,854	17,755	61,463	1,272,853	.0181	402,989	114	64,956	129	28,252	149	80,910	16,546	73,223	40	MCD-Township
Irvington	N.Y.	34450	4-S	61,055	60,695	13,192	21,478	35,123	805,408	.0130	224,031	64	24,611	49	21,189	112	47,541	27,463	94,478	52	MCD-Township
Jackson	N.Y.	34680		50,477	42,816	22,377	16,134	58,611	1,129,531	.0154	259,563	74	1,018	2	50,841	268	65,574	20,061	(d)	...	MCD-Township
Jersey City	N.Y.	36000	3-SS	228,275	240,055	17,679	80,840	36,852	4,035,658	.0650	1,705,229	484	251,675	501	196,046	1,032	250,696	138,866	534,551	293	Inc. Place
Kearny	N.Y.	36510	4-S	42,062	40,513	18,089	13,502	44,039	760,877	.0128	388,632	110	37,069	74	25,128	132	147,980	28,908	180,388	99	Inc. Place
Lakewood	N.Y.	38550	4-Sr	78,556	60,352	16,589	25,026	33,905	1,303,171	.0308	1,659,211	471	9,894	20	5,688	30	110,181	56,984	364,429	200	MCD-Township
Lawrence	PHIL-	39510		31,154	29,159	26,844	10,824	60,674	836,302	.0197	1,214,763	345	233,652	465	137,426	723	83,361	80,354	37,003	20	MCD-Township
Linden	N.Y.	40350	4-S	41,546	39,394	19,340	16,112	42,553	803,516	.0156	681,313	193	76,278	152	41,339	218	99,262	41,039	1,951,317	1,068	Inc. Place
Livingston	N.Y.	40890	3-Sm	27,357	27,391	36,704	9,001	83,893	1,004,099	.0165	698,557	198	150,725	300	112,248	591	100,416	75,395	43,463	24	MCD-Township
Long Branch	N.Y.	41310	4-Sr	32,808	31,340	21,080	13,382	37,335	691,598	.0099	196,396	56	2,039	4	1,593	8	104,313	19,746	31,106	17	Inc. Place
Manalapan	N.Y.	42990		35,450	33,423	30,080	11,604	73,623	1,066,331	.0145	329,428	94	37,109	74	19,864	105	94,486	18,789	(d)	...	MCD-Township
Manchester	N.Y.	43140		41,512	38,928	22,557	21,314	27,244	936,381	.0117	94,098	27	...	...	...	...	45,406	25,517	(d)	...	MCD-Township
Marlboro	N.Y.	44070		39,111	36,398	36,135	12,521	85,099	1,413,294	.0161	135,237	38	11,887	24	3,387	18	44,686	14,937	76,189	42	MCD-Township
Middletown	N.Y.	45990		67,428	66,327	30,830	23,931	63,200	2,078,781	.0302	884,999	251	104,432	208	42,278	223	235,294	75,921	(d)	...	MCD-Township
Millburn	N.Y.	46380	4-Sm	20,038	19,765	63,754	6,874	122,711	1,277,510	.0178	628,172	178	110,755	220	239,845	1,262	85,006	44,808	(d)	...	MCD-Township
Millville	VINL	46680	4-S	27,588	26,847	19,257	10,228	37,964	531,272	.0083	217,662	62	27,307	54	4,446	23	71,585	16,900	344,652	189	Inc. Place
Monroe	PHIL-	47250		30,511	28,967	22,547	11,455	45,389	687,930	.0101	243,730	69	...	...	6,074	32	73,526	12,991	54,788	30	MCD-Township
Monroe	N.Y.	47280		31,311	27,999	33,295	13,542	51,739	1,042,493	.0118	70,560	20	...	...	...	...	19,334	7,106	80,316	44	MCD-Township
Montclair	N.Y.	47500	4-S	39,585	38,977	37,175	14,786	66,966	1,471,561	.0182	322,853	92	...	...	19,848	104	115,047	33,712	(d)	...	MCD-Township
Moorestown	PHIL-	47880	3-Sm	22,525	19,017	47,489	8,407	69,723	1,069,683	.0161	614,573	175	108,223	215	80,563	424	18,494	55,477	742,519	407	MCD-Township
Morristown	N.Y.	48300	3-S	19,642	18,544	42,690	7,490	70,572	838,520	.0124	439,610	125	14,964	30	29,139	153	37,134	17,670	182,698	100	Inc. Place
Mount Laurel	PHIL-	49020		45,508	40,221	34,545	19,100	58,002	1,572,070	.0226	683,624	194	...	...	9,643	51	109,503	29,407	162,553	89	MCD-Township
Newark	N.Y.	51000	2-CC	275,652	273,546	10,693	89,188	26,296	2,947,420	.0566	1,449,454	412	50,811	101	119,640	630	345,996	159,683	1,817,277	995	Inc. Place
New Brunswick	N.Y.	51210	3-S	51,222	48,573	14,293	13,340	34,979	732,141	.0121	262,045	74	60,603	121	19,085	100	35,529	25,130	497,120	272	Inc. Place
Newton	N.Y.	51930	4-S	8,830	8,244	28,523	3,437	53,795	251,854	.0043	180,045	51	5,902	12	2,114	11	35,065	8,062	(d)	...	Inc. Place
North Bergen	N.Y.	52470	4-Sr	60,721	58,092	17,407	21,347	38,307	1,056,993	.0165	376,569	107	35,288	70	10,266	54	149,177	23,922	358,769	196	MCD-Township
North Brunswick	N.Y.	52560		39,072	36,287	28,970	14,232	55,727	1,131,933	.0182	671,186	191	81,872	163	27,363	144	78,444	23,340	256,716	141	MCD-Township
Ocean Township	N.Y.	54270	4-Sm	27,809	26,959	24,572	10,736	44,385	683,312	.0112	397,423	113	45,186	90	9,437	50	54,289	45,893	(d)	...	MCD-Township
Old Bridge	N.Y.	54705		65,007	60,456	25,718	22,334	58,242	1,671,826	.0242	614,667	175	24,542	49	13,237	70	149,677	33,425	159,870	88	MCD-Township
Orange	N.Y.	55020		33,133	32,868	13,417	11,613	35,324	444,559	.0080	228,569	65	6,672	13	18,952	100	28,916	28,138	(d)	...	CDP
Paramus	N.Y.	55950	2-Sm	26,001	25,737	24,515	8,060	66,353	637,408	.0341	3,149,138	894	635,038	1,263	627,605	3,303	128,624	105,767	124,562	68	Inc. Place
Parsippany-Troy Hills	N.Y.	56460	4-S	53,082	50,649	27,627	20,082	61,387	1,466,482	.0291	1,502,127	427	72,195	144	54,189	285	196,540	64,757	693,569	380	MCD-Township
Passaic	N.Y.	56550	4-S	70,103	67,861	12,669	19,431	32,266	888,146	.0159	408,254	116	13,294	26	40,415	213	139,181	34,135	237,872	130	Inc. Place
Paterson	N.Y.	57000	3-S	151,585	149,222	13,052	43,897	32,098	1,978,541	.0325	593,371	168	20,408	41	36,211	191	164,035	56,481	929,443	509	Inc. Place
Pennsauken	PHIL-	57660	4-S	36,078	35,737	18,972	12,195	43,051	684,460	.0121	433,102	123	6,494	13	14,116	74	45,992	26,848	601,437	329	MCD-Township
Perth Amboy	N.Y.	58200	4-S	50,990	47,303	15,475	15,202	36,396	789,072	.0129	308,509	88	2,423	5	16,408	86	78,382	26,398	220,395	121	Inc. Place
Piscataway	N.Y.	59010		54,338	50,482	25,289	17,204	60,849	1,374,143	.0174	213,246	61	31,937	64	1,323	7	53,619	10,134	879,274	481	MCD-Township
Plainfield	N.Y.	59190	4-S	48,731	47,829	18,381	15,620	45,971	895,716	.0166	647,260	184	69,388	138	28,190	148	111,308	48,620	64,566	35	Inc. Place
Pleasantville	ATCY	59640	4-S	19,439	19,012	17,577	7,126	36,624	341,677	.0092	575,739	163	54,002	107	23,276	123	92,792	30,966	(d)	...	Inc. Place
Princeton		60900	4-C	14,935	14,203	25,005	3,289	73,351	373,449	.0072	341,380	97	21,921	44	51,249	270	37,863	25,697	(d)	...	Inc. Place
Red Bank	N.Y.	62430	4-S	12,433	11,844	32,240	5,541	53,995	400,840	.0071	325,686	92	2,985	6	40,369	212	45,869	19,890	(d)	...	Inc. Place
Ridgewood	N.Y.	63000	4-S	25,118	24,936	49,048	8,538	88,563	1,231,999	.0161	429,326	122	...	...	42,843	225	66,735	25,856	(d)	...	Inc. Place
Sayreville	N.Y.	65790		43,862	40,377	25,059	15,739	52,953	1,099,150	.0144	224,538	64	1,392	3	13,044	69	69,614	11,733	540,416	296	Inc. Place
Secaucus	N.Y.	66570	4-S	16,592	15,931	26,403	6,220	54,722	438,072	.0128	918,313	261	29,134	58	191,031	1,005	42,109	17,790	280,395	154	Inc. Place
Somerville	N.Y.	68460	4-S	13,084	12,423	29,032	5,007	60,356	379,861	.0086	517,732	147	9,889	20	9,185	48	43,727	19,915	400,495	219	Inc. Place
South Brunswick	N.Y.	68790		41,757	37,734	31,742	14,398	69,036	1,325,450	.0186	498,566	142	8,798	17	9,181	48	55,684	19,175	435,944	239	MCD-Township
South Plainfield	N.Y.	69390	4-S	23,720	21,810	24,310	7,534	60,292	576,643	.0116	586,370	167	86,281	172	19,426	102	92,475	28,010	391,340	214	Inc. Place
Summit	N.Y.	71430	4-S	22,134	21,131	59,491	8,392	81,445	1,316,780	.0162	377,972	107	...	...	17,711	93	20,023	18,571	244,006	134	Inc. Place
Teaneck	N.Y.	72360	4-Sr	39,453	39,260	28,686	13,273	64,552	1,131,756	.0147	255,679	73	...	...	3,691	19	74,029	49,005	(d)	...	MCD-Township
Toms River	N.Y.	73110		96,061	86,327	23,748	34,091	50,525	2,281,258	.0412	1,742,381	495	287,782	572	110,906	584	291,403	124,516	(d)	...	CDP
Trenton	PHIL-	74000	2-B	86,529	85,403	14,439	27,989	34,543	1,249,366	.0206	456,393	130	7,615	15	32,870	173	91,319	86,387	185,692	102	Inc. Place
Union	N.Y.	74480	4-S	57,436	54,405	22,749	20,917	53,021	1,306,604	.0257	1,232,666	350	44,233	88	70,545	371	195,274	93,548	433,782	237	MCD-Township
Union City	N.Y.	74630	3-S	69,907	67,088	12,870	22,898	29,493	899,707	.0161	415,140	118	5,411	11	47,102	248	76,524	66,666	61,780	34	Inc. Place
Vineland	VINL	76070	3-C	57,614	56,271	18,558	20,224	38,610	1,069,207	.0197	762,929	217	88,555	176	45,679	240	93,029	62,387	494,402	271	Inc. Place
Washington	PHIL-	77180		51,374	47,114	26,588	17,616	56,705	1,365,958	.0199	529,776	150	67,267	134	15,272	80	123,248	35,616	(d)	...	MCD-Township
Watchung	N.Y.	77600	4-Sm	5,856	5,613	59,292	2,191	86,394	347,215	.0043	108,475	31	...	...	5,039	27	3,462	40,295	(d)	...	Inc. Place
Wayne	N.Y.	77840	3-SSm	56,158	54,069	32,993	18,852	71,891	1,852,845	.0367	1,967,484	559	502,325	999	336,862	1,773	164,658	105,297	419,140	229	MCD-Township
Westfield	N.Y.	79040		30,073	29,644	43,480	10,913	82,786	1,307,578	.0157	270,980	77	35,984	72	30,636	161	51,242	31,392	(d)	...	Inc. Place
West New York	N.Y.	79610	4-S	49,125	45,768	17,190	17,208	34,066	844,437	.0122	187,198	53	5,255	10	30,042	158	38,059	27,972	73,110	40	Inc. Place
West Orange	N.Y.	79800	4-S	45,871	44,943	26,888	16,255	62,113	1,233,400	.0160	260,345	74	51,259	102	16,808	88	71,803	30,330	302,909	166	MCD-Township
Willingboro	PHIL-	81440	4-S	32,352	33,008	24,330	10,694	54,556	787,116	.0105	176,097	50	13,283	26	2,235	12	86,722	18,487	(d)	...	MCD-Township
Winslow	PHIL-	81740		35,630	34,611	20,438	11,677	51,397	728,192	.0108	240,454	68	9,391	19	3,358	18	66,409	13,639	(d)	...	MCD-Township
Woodbridge Township	N.Y.	82000	3-SSm	102,534	97,203	25,134	35,353	54,994	2,577,041	.0471	2,082,314	591	265,829	529	216,748	1,141	182,324	87,645	753,472	413	MCD-Township
Woodbury	PHIL-	82120	4-S	10,268	10,307	25,771	4,174	45,266	264,614	.0070	471,247	134	116,573	232	56,229	296	21,067	19,756	(d)	...	Inc. Place
New Mexico																					
Alamogordo		01780	4-C	39,405	35,582	15,369	15,535	30,555	605,608	.0106	316,574	90	63,737	127	14,573	77	40,691	13,899	45,990	25	Inc. Place
Albuquerque	ALBU	02000	2-AA	495,118	448,607	19,082	204,106	37,191	9,447,740	.1803	7,607,001	2,160	1,515,991	3,015	287,712	1,514	591,314	438,902	...	...	Inc. Place
Carlsbad		12150	4-A	25,652	25,625	15,937	10,010	31,375	408,816	.0071	217,278	62	43,808	87	9,931	52	33,111	16,042	(d)	...	Inc. Place
Clovis	CLOV	16420	4-A	32,931	32,667	13,853	12,490	28,203	456,201	.0091	336,976	96	94,010	187	18,675	98	38,479	17,962	(d)	...	Inc. Place
Farmington	FARM	25800	3-A	42,422	37,844	15,036	14,144	33,993	637,871	.0163	926,574	263	325,435	647	33,957	179	57,268	25,262	46,426	25	Inc. Place
Gallup		28460	3-A	17,432	20,209	12,745	6,266	27,653	222,178	.0063	376,501	107	83,591	166	35,537	187	27,882	11,031	(d)	...	Inc. Place
Hobbs		32520	4-A	29,711	28,657	12,875	10,239	27,980	382,541	.0085	371,604	106	73,091	145	13,097	69	39,867	20,194	(d)	...	Inc. Place
Las Cruces	LSCR	39380	3-A	77,806	74,267	14,632	30,379	30,398	1,138,482	.0230	922,259	262	246,050	489	33,247	175	93,702	63,797	106,241	58	Inc. Place
Rio Rancho	ALBU	63460		64,262	51,765	17,863	22,232	43,522	1,147,886	.0173	351,340	100	15,337	31	6,408	34	76,138	15,679	...	...	Inc. Place
Roswell	RSWL	64930	3-A	43,708	45,293	13,410	16,383	27,963	586,109	.0111	358,241	102	101,558	202	16,501	87	39,155	21,202	...	...	Inc. Place
Santa Fe	S.FE	70500	3-A	64,470	62,203	21,787	26,772	38,829	1,404,611	.0315	1,753,886	498	397,987	791	151,774	799	179,910	119,204	55,489	30	Inc. Place
South Valley	ALBU	74520		41,978	39,060	12,262	13,890	30,375	514,723	.0095	256,264	73	44,568	89	3,829	20	33,181	14,078	(d)	...	CDP
New York																					
Albany	A-S-T	01000	2-AA	97,769	95,658	18,153	40,247	31,695	1,774,768	.0315	1,115,625	317	100,395	200	132,329	696	109,522	105,132	157,323	86	Inc. Place
Amherst	BUF	02000		118,412	116,510	27,201	47,292	50,202	3,220,871	.0567	2,428,032	689	250,976	499	191,988	1,010	425,720	129,422	247,985	136	MCD-Town
Amsterdam	A-S-T	02066	4-S	17,489	18,355	18,747	7,769	30,910	327,864	.0058	204,563	58	24,595	49	10,173	54	36,092	16,860	128,831	71	Inc. Place
Auburn	SYR	03078	3-C	27,847	28,574	19,401	11,317	34,082	540,264	.0096	360,777	102	63,168	126	5,554	29	55,495	41,273	275,943	151	Inc. Place
Babylon	N.Y.	04000		218,314	211,792	22,509	71,963	54,051	4,913,931	.0770	2,298,238	653	180,740	359	113,764	599	425,229	177,742	1,166,916	639	MCD-Town
Batavia		04715	4-C	16,493	16,256	19,587	6,752	33,142	323,048	.0059	231,370	66	43,203	86	12,585	66	25,805	10,962	155,700	85	Inc. Place
Bethlehem	A-S-T	06354		32,681	31,304	28,390	12,249	55,666	927,827	.0120	207,269	59	24,984	50	15,214	80	54,128	18,675	377,096	206	MCD-Town
Binghamton	BING	06607	3-AA	46,069	47,380	18,596	21,040	30,495	856,684	.0140	401,453	114	22,357	44	7,101	37	96,134	45,372	718,099	393	Inc. Place
Brentwood	N.Y.	08026		56,937	53,917	15,294	13,450	52,931	870,808	.0139	297,892	85	15,265	30	14,321	75	80,012	23,510	(d)	...	CDP
Brighton	ROCH	08246		36,029	35,588	32,670	16,165	47,301	1,177,064	.0184	677,816	192	67,377	134	77,101	406	77,025	46,545	64,018	35	MCD-Town
Brookhaven	N.Y.	10000		484,643	448,248	23,468	160,803	57,089	11,373,417	.1794	5,611,318	1,593	834,269	1,659	469,059	2,469	986,365	343,698	279,526	153	MCD-Town
Buffalo	BUF	11000	2-AA	278,583	292,648	15,801	120,650	25,053	4,401,991	.0717	1,720,198	488	88,819	177	75,569	398	408,630	224,963	2,491,343	1,364	Inc. Place
Carmel	N.Y.	12529		35,678	33,006	28,080	11,522	66,594	1,001,840	.0132	242,124	69	20,879	42	...	...	59,242	29,201	67,685	37	MCD-Town
Central Islip	N.Y.	13552		33,738	31,950	17,888	9,400	52,069	603,503	.0096	247,057	70	1,907	4	22,185	117	70,820	18,659	(d)	...	CDP
Cheektowaga	BUF	15011		90,709	94,019	19,157	39,789	34,729	1,737,682	.0345	1,555,349	442	239,072	475	174,578	919	288,344	105,728	433,728	237	MCD-Town
Clarkstown	N.Y.	15968		84,750	82,082	29,774	28,042	70,108	2,523,373	.0418	1,663,691	472	302,047	601	186,505	982	172,952	142,082	377,465	207	MCD-Town
Clay	SYR	16067		59,681	58,805	20,960	22,965	45,274	1,250,891	.0225	893,847	254	143,000	284	61,638	324	177,050	65,525	113,254	62	MCD-Town
Clifton Park	A-S-T	16353		35,129	32,995	27,453	13,408	53,900	964,393	.0143	417,220	118	60,581	120	33,051	174	61,261	21,733	40,758	22	MCD-Town
Colonie	A-S-T	17343		80,128	79,258	21,613	30,269	45,254	1,731,808	.0421	2,535,155	720	376,812	749	156,698	825	162,503	88,188	198,300	109	MCD-Town
Commack	N.Y.	17530		38,403	36,367	28,103	12,495	70,887	1,079,239	.0198	917,763	261	151,705	302	68,402	360	145,281	51,419	(d)	...	CDP
Coram	N.Y.	18157		36,880	34,923	24,069	13,381	55,552	887,680	.0124	254,593	72	4,352	9	9,033	48	91,445	12,844	(d)	...	CDP
Corning		18256	4-B	10,627	10,842	24,119	5,014	35,577	256,317	.0038	104,883	30	...	...	2,092	11	41,022	11,640	131,021	72	Inc. Place
Cortland		18388	4-C	19,150	18,740	15,162	7,075	29,852	290,348	.0067	341,864	97	37,611	75	5,799	31	73,133	20,897	287,213	157	Inc. Place
Cortlandt	N.Y.	18410		39,722	38,467	23,867	13,522	66,343	948,063	.0125	182,124	52	3,655	7	1,067	6	53,971	13,524	(d)	...	MCD-Town
Dunkirk		21105	4-B	12,909	13,131	18,436	5,574	28,203	237,992	.0041	133,370	38	23,240	46	7,225	38	42,962	14,807	138,438	76	Inc. Place
Eastchester	N.Y.	21820		32,314	31,318	39,017	12,641	70,339	1,260,793	.0161	347,867	99	27,555	55	30,818	162	107,984	29,265	(d)	...	MCD-Town
East Meadow	N.Y.	22502		37,718	37,461	22,304	11,801	59,758	841,262	.0145	539,811	153	9,367	19	32,023	169	125,257	61,012	(d)	...	CDP
Elmira	ELM	24229	3-AA	30,246	30,940	15,414	11,591	29,526	466,204	.0084	272,060	77	2,903	6	9,631	51	60,281	20,292	221,899	121	Inc. Place
Elmont	N.Y.	24273		32,880	32,657	17,777	9,570	57,152	584,516	.0100	312,278	89	3,317	7	9,430	50	76,367	26,590	(d)	...	CDP
Endicott	BING	24515	4-S	12,774	13,038	22,033	6,023	36,327	281,456	.0042	106,847	30	11,791	23	2,515	13	28,267	10,351	...	...	Inc. Place
Freeport	N.Y.	27485	4-Sr	44,999	43,783	17,409	13,339	51,271	783,370	.0155	664,034	189	34,701	69	16,654	88	60,481	39,303	175,742	96	Inc. Place
Garden City	N.Y.	28178	3-Sm	21,423	21,672	42,116	7,022	82,415	902,244	.0213	1,409,454	400	380,697	757	313,763	1,651	41,666	105,620	76,856	42	Inc. Place
Geneva		28640	3-C	13,628	13,617	17,069	5,090	34,216	232,618	.0049	225,738	64	35,411	70	5,505	29	55,305	11,863	76,547	42	Inc. Place
Glen Cove	N.Y.	29113	4-Sr	27,716	26,622	23,342	9,473	51,738	646,937	.0110	415,458	118	...	...	9,071	48	99,617	48,563	245,265	134	Inc. Place
Glens Falls	GLFLS	29333	3-A	14,064	14,354	19,156	6,212	29,463	269,407	.0061	335,315	95	15,658	31	27,684	146	109,312	10,160	350,068	192	Inc. Place
Gloversville		29443	4-C	15,350	15,413	18,292	6,511	29,964	280,788	.0046	136,593	39	29,026	58	...	...	36,448	11,430	121,622	67	Inc. Place
Greece	ROCH	30290		94,850	94,141	21,347	37,528	43,013	2,024,770	.0365	1,468,807	417	257,587	512	94,752	499	241,634	65,751	65,108	36	MCD-Town
Greenburgh	N.Y.	30367		89,538	86,764	31,825	33,031	70,774	2,849,529	.0426	1,380,154	392	137,461	273	122,383	644	234,992	103,876	124,255	68	MCD-Town
Guilderland	A-S-T	31104		33,721	32,688	23,335	13,422	45,159	786,863	.0117	302,191	86	37,147	74	44,980	237	74,100	25,440	(d)	...	MCD-Town
Hamburg	BUF	31654		57,303	56,259	21,353	23,065	43,556	1,223,565	.0229	983,551	279	169,865	338	55,833	294	107,049	47,352	415,458	227	MCD-Town
Haverstraw	N.Y.	32765		34,628	33,811	21,853	11,305	51,039	756,740	.0094	61,498	17	...	...	...	...	17,018	2,536	(d)	...	MCD-Town
Hempstead	N.Y.	33139	3-S	58,656	56,554	14,356	15,145	42,396	842,062	.0173	702,678	200	5,347	11	13,142	69	43,809	47,125	44,926	25	Inc. Place
Henrietta	ROCH	34099		40,287	39,028	18,750	13,363	47,289	755,394	.0214	1,426,367	405	242,579	482	106,790	562	123,053	45,692	361,255	198	MCD-Town
Hicksville	N.Y.	34374		41,541	41,260	23,193	13,256	61,812	963,475	.0245	1,566,019	445	152,874	304	126,837	668	86,381	98,789	(d)	...	CDP
Hornell		35672	4-B	8,833	9,019	15,575	3,615	29,682	137,572	.0029	128,263	36	22,239	44	3,019	16	27,476	7,040	...	...	Inc. Place
Huntington	N.Y.	37000		198,533	195,289	38,784	67,883	72,468	7,699,820	.1041	2,788,146	792	285,165	567	273,527	1,440	403,226	187,712	1,680,966	920	MCD-Town

Source: Devonshire Associates Ltd. and Scan/US, Inc. 2005.
* Source: 1997 Census of Manufactures.
Not classified as a Principal Business Center.

...Data less than 1,000.
(d) Data not available.

Principal Business Centers and Other Places with 30,000 or More: Population/Income/Sales, *Continued*

Place Name	Ranally Metro Area	FIPS Place Code	Ranally City Rating	Population: Estimate 7/1/05	Population: Census 4/1/00	Per Capita Income 2004	Households Estimate 7/1/05	Median Household Income 2004	Disposable Income 2004 ($1,000)	Market Ability Index 2004	Total Retail Sales: 2004 Sales ($1,000)	Total Retail Sales: Ranally Sales Units	General Merchandise: 2004 Sales ($1,000)	General Merchandise: Ranally Sales Units	Apparel Store: 2004 Sales ($1,000)	Apparel Store: Ranally Sales Units	Food Store Sales 2004 ($1,000)	Health & Drug Store 2004 ($1,000)	Manufacturers: Value Added 1997* ($1,000)	Manufacturers: Ranally Mfg. Units	Place Type
Huntington Station	N.Y.	37044		31,585	29,910	33,337	10,411	67,943	1,052,953	.0154	482,900	137	50,688	101	66,891	352	48,224	28,703	(d)	...	CDP
Irondequoit	ROCH	37726		52,385	52,354	22,314	22,402	40,644	1,168,944	.0178	485,393	138	104,313	207	50,503	266	104,476	38,628	(d)	...	MCD-Town
Islip	N.Y.	38000		339,846	322,612	23,122	105,474	58,641	7,857,972	.1262	4,106,014	1,166	375,207	746	192,014	1,011	733,851	292,414	2,893,322	1,584	MCD-Town
Ithaca	ITH	38077	3-A	30,368	29,287	17,373	10,771	32,292	527,590	.0096	348,192	99	40,824	81	17,880	94	77,763	26,396	246,969	135	Inc. Place
Jamestown	JMST	38264	3-A	29,933	31,730	17,761	13,257	28,197	531,633	.0099	381,718	108	48,361	96	3,269	17	65,944	25,974	405,316	222	Inc. Place
Johnson City	BING	38748	3-Sm	15,204	15,535	17,728	7,007	28,939	269,543	.0064	354,642	101	81,107	161	45,873	241	87,530	28,937	22,369	12	Inc. Place
Kingston	KNGST	39727	3-B	23,364	23,456	21,181	9,913	33,876	494,867	.0104	530,062	151	88,771	177	34,191	180	92,005	32,567	60,921	33	Inc. Place
Lancaster	BUF	41146		39,466	39,019	20,786	15,701	45,262	820,353	.0116	208,291	59	11,603	23	4,602	24	46,327	14,190	61,943	34	MCD-Town
Levittown	N.Y.	42081		53,430	53,067	21,770	16,661	61,938	1,163,149	.0194	671,699	191	119,175	237	47,996	253	100,319	57,970	(d)	...	CDP
Lockport	LOCK	43082	3-C	21,608	22,279	22,735	9,525	38,442	491,254	.0084	308,019	87	39,828	79	7,823	41	47,130	26,454	1,104,815	605	Inc. Place
Long Beach	N.Y.	43335		36,334	35,462	27,619	14,664	53,448	1,003,517	.0122	120,885	34	...	...	4,938	26	42,065	21,223	(d)	...	Inc. Place
Manlius	SYR	45029		32,557	31,872	30,415	13,024	52,567	990,221	.0129	246,140	70	20,090	40	6,673	35	73,794	12,330	(d)	...	MCD-Town
Middletown	MIDD	47042	3-C	27,507	25,388	21,759	10,089	41,147	598,533	.0126	647,278	184	197,461	393	51,678	272	59,845	31,813	110,409	60	Inc. Place
Mineola	N.Y.	47636	4-Sr	19,322	19,234	24,439	7,221	55,678	472,216	.0092	445,031	126	...	...	18,406	97	54,092	59,313	85,962	47	Inc. Place
Monroe	N.Y.	47999		40,157	31,407	16,347	10,359	50,959	656,428	.0106	250,784	71	15,384	31	10,493	55	57,160	21,266	(d)	...	MCD-Town
Mount Kisco	N.Y.	48890	4-S	10,422	9,983	44,065	4,045	65,212	459,243	.0078	362,986	103	...	...	40,654	214	21,525	20,441	49,380	27	Inc. Place
Mount Pleasant	N.Y.	49011		44,857	43,221	27,272	13,816	73,352	1,223,321	.0197	708,951	201	3,860	8	9,721	51	106,748	36,539	(d)	...	MCD-Town
Mount Vernon	N.Y.	49121	4-Sr	69,499	68,381	15,416	25,349	39,412	1,071,424	.0179	457,468	130	4,814	10	27,369	144	137,590	51,174	287,052	157	Inc. Place
Newburgh	NWBG	50034	3-C	31,219	28,259	18,445	9,964	40,157	575,836	.0108	429,555	122	83,414	166	20,589	108	55,461	26,759	59,176	32	Inc. Place
New City	N.Y.	50100		35,258	34,038	32,221	11,212	77,396	1,136,061	.0151	329,257	93	40,609	81	31,296	165	87,552	48,435	(d)	...	CDP
New Rochelle	N.Y.	50617	3-S	73,824	72,182	25,197	25,951	56,779	1,860,178	.0275	739,845	210	94,370	188	31,794	167	97,945	49,313	84,171	46	Inc. Place
New York	N.Y.	51000	1-AAAA	8,148,734	8,008,278	18,317	3,027,430	36,878	149,263,120	2.3723	61,641,638	17,503	5,756,905	11,449	11,781,171	62,007	9,331,833	7,574,405	13,875,950	7,597	Inc. Place
Niagara Falls	BUF	51055	3-BB	53,593	55,593	17,467	24,035	27,330	936,110	.0165	556,114	158	73,864	147	87,354	460	106,770	54,093	683,992	374	Inc. Place
North Hempstead	N.Y.	53000		229,177	222,611	36,981	75,903	74,147	8,475,243	.1374	5,665,248	1,609	340,272	677	683,446	3,597	596,189	304,608	539,300	295	MCD-Town
North Tonawanda	BUF	53682	4-S	33,109	33,262	21,297	14,113	39,906	705,126	.0097	151,134	43	12,759	25	3,092	16	28,584	17,616	300,857	165	Inc. Place
Oceanside	N.Y.	54441		32,957	32,733	24,378	10,841	65,578	803,429	.0151	697,147	198	64,276	128	63,400	334	97,951	89,067	(d)	...	CDP
Olean		54716	3-A	14,720	15,347	18,985	6,374	30,694	279,457	.0061	316,556	90	51,055	102	19,119	101	46,776	19,781	394,390	216	Inc. Place
Oneonta		54881	4-A	13,611	13,292	14,091	4,746	28,444	191,798	.0048	259,767	74	47,648	95	7,917	42	34,095	9,263	86,341	47	Inc. Place
Orangetown	N.Y.	55211		49,077	47,711	32,301	17,479	62,777	1,585,221	.0206	410,848	117	11,959	24	19,055	100	101,824	46,586	711,652	390	MCD-Town
Ossining	N.Y.	55541		37,925	36,534	27,030	12,431	66,271	1,025,102	.0135	237,813	68	...	...	3,082	16	61,206	26,591	(d)	...	MCD-Town
Oswego		55574	4-C	18,080	17,954	19,251	7,517	32,929	348,057	.0053	124,211	35	18,047	36	5,388	28	28,349	12,212	...	...	Inc. Place
Oyster Bay	N.Y.	56000		293,385	293,925	30,873	95,200	70,656	9,057,529	.1474	5,737,038	1,629	515,033	1,024	455,190	2,396	793,998	393,754	2,026,739	1,110	MCD-Town
Patchogue	N.Y.	56660	4-S	12,654	11,919	24,289	4,985	50,530	307,357	.0058	271,371	77	25,191	50	19,420	102	38,012	12,195	(d)	...	Inc. Place
Peekskill	N.Y.	56979	3-S	23,652	22,441	16,836	8,894	43,026	398,216	.0084	394,054	112	42,498	85	2,625	14	92,293	27,217	(d)	...	Inc. Place
Penfield	ROCH	57144		36,006	34,645	27,003	13,758	55,965	972,255	.0141	373,804	106	18,854	37	5,391	28	98,476	12,090	99,688	55	MCD-Town
Perinton	ROCH	57221		45,587	46,090	29,744	17,554	62,392	1,355,941	.0171	266,889	76	12,787	25	3,831	20	134,159	7,020	121,601	67	MCD-Town
Plattsburgh	PLATT	58574	3-A	19,267	18,816	18,927	7,905	31,931	364,673	.0081	423,670	120	73,636	146	29,823	157	63,497	25,675	220,743	121	Inc. Place
Port Chester	N.Y.	59223	4-S	28,365	27,867	20,190	9,393	49,533	572,699	.0098	336,096	95	30,672	61	17,764	93	107,627	30,553	70,946	39	Inc. Place
Port Washington North	N.Y.	59531	4-Sm	2,671	2,700	45,094	1,009	75,103	120,445	.0019	80,086	23	...	...	...	...	3,795	1,723	(d)	...	Inc. Place
Poughkeepsie	POK	59641	3-AA	31,661	29,871	20,153	12,295	37,130	638,076	.0126	575,959	164	112,246	223	93,963	495	75,514	28,668	...	...	Inc. Place
Ramapo	N.Y.	60510		113,591	108,905	21,965	32,246	54,584	2,495,013	.0362	806,292	229	33,450	67	46,417	244	151,267	56,102	(d)	...	MCD-Town
Riverhead		61984		31,610	27,680	24,128	12,406	42,886	762,685	.0143	646,272	184	73,812	147	128,593	677	61,195	18,716	57,507	31	MCD-Town
Rochester	ROCH	63000	2-AA	216,407	219,773	16,669	88,408	28,621	3,607,389	.0586	1,480,520	420	42,515	85	47,741	251	260,849	113,448	7,098,433	3,886	Inc. Place
Rockville Centre	N.Y.	63264	4-S	24,248	24,568	36,200	8,722	69,050	877,768	.0128	418,682	119	...	...	13,712	72	68,030	37,099	(d)	...	Inc. Place
Rome	UT-R	63418	3-B	34,318	34,950	17,771	13,625	34,859	609,868	.0103	312,644	89	75,098	149	9,887	52	39,698	26,652	148,075	81	Inc. Place
Rye	N.Y.	64320		45,100	43,880	22,188	15,354	51,238	1,000,663	.0165	556,179	158	40,287	80	25,728	135	170,187	47,868	(d)	...	MCD-Town
Salina	SYR	64815		33,725	33,290	21,264	14,840	38,283	717,117	.0123	440,227	125	39,012	78	5,168	27	58,527	62,407	112,281	61	MCD-Town
Saratoga Springs	A-S-T	65255	4-S	28,267	26,186	26,188	11,639	43,624	740,261	.0136	622,111	177	105,105	209	47,108	248	69,181	31,430	174,855	96	Inc. Place
Schenectady	A-S-T	65508	3-BB	62,065	61,821	19,550	26,594	33,253	1,213,353	.0205	677,238	192	67,748	135	20,699	109	71,523	55,231	568,643	311	Inc. Place
Smithtown	N.Y.	68000		118,318	115,715	30,408	39,781	69,264	3,597,816	.0570	2,077,204	590	175,919	350	87,617	461	305,715	128,183	701,960	384	MCD-Town
Southampton		68473		61,460	54,712	29,667	24,407	50,094	1,823,330	.0293	1,086,440	308	62,041	123	84,013	442	128,352	58,627	(d)	...	MCD-Town
Syracuse	SYR	73000	2-AA	146,651	147,306	15,360	60,089	25,835	2,252,490	.0418	1,452,198	412	106,255	211	80,263	422	182,360	96,921	1,111,876	609	Inc. Place
Tonawanda	BUF	75000		74,925	78,155	20,507	32,866	38,189	1,536,493	.0243	693,610	197	44,712	89	11,437	60	104,322	101,077	907,013	497	MCD-Town
Troy	A-S-T	75484	3-C	48,811	49,170	19,864	20,288	33,835	969,560	.0154	427,752	121	46,189	92	4,329	23	83,901	45,577	77,144	42	Inc. Place
Union	BING	76056		55,409	56,298	19,629	24,749	33,847	1,087,624	.0178	545,587	155	95,408	190	44,453	234	139,128	48,244	171,412	94	MCD-Town
Utica	UT-R	76540	3-AA	60,264	60,651	16,095	25,422	25,688	969,928	.0161	418,477	119	82,611	164	3,464	18	84,924	46,205	251,483	138	Inc. Place
Valley Stream	N.Y.	76705	4-S	37,234	36,368	22,965	12,290	59,316	855,064	.0165	771,325	219	171,904	342	91,684	483	67,385	51,053	(d)	...	Inc. Place
Warwick	N.Y.	78366		34,340	30,764	25,171	11,927	56,082	864,356	.0115	198,944	56	...	...	2,584	14	60,312	15,358	(d)	...	MCD-Town
Watertown	WATN	78608	3-A	25,961	26,705	17,982	10,682	30,595	466,834	.0115	666,436	189	103,276	205	45,751	241	71,206	57,739	138,761	76	Inc. Place
Webster	ROCH	78971		39,417	37,926	24,874	15,473	52,805	980,455	.0146	401,144	114	73,141	145	4,322	23	137,631	13,593	76,243	42	MCD-Town
West Babylon	N.Y.	79246		45,884	43,452	21,625	15,224	54,353	992,262	.0163	533,093	151	73,622	146	34,963	184	111,482	25,083	(d)	...	CDP
West Islip	N.Y.	80302		30,524	28,907	28,824	9,502	65,785	879,835	.0146	570,111	162	12,874	26	3,982	21	87,132	52,504	(d)	...	CDP
West Seneca	BUF	80918		44,468	45,920	20,099	18,330	41,375	893,774	.0156	568,802	162	25,807	51	15,665	82	134,965	44,192	222,121	122	MCD-Town
White Plains	N.Y.	81677	2-S	55,123	53,077	23,638	21,055	55,545	1,302,985	.0290	1,634,988	464	276,178	549	410,272	2,159	79,637	97,827	(d)	...	Inc. Place
Yonkers	N.Y.	84000	3-SS	201,122	196,086	17,542	73,913	42,904	3,528,034	.0620	2,079,598	591	236,145	470	186,418	981	394,020	214,274	274,591	150	Inc. Place
Yorktown	N.Y.	84077		37,551	36,318	23,331	12,606	70,315	876,121	.0198	1,132,245	322	275,058	547	123,717	651	132,934	62,142	(d)	...	MCD-Town
North Carolina																					
Asheboro		02080	3-C	23,654	21,672	16,411	9,501	31,490	388,192	.0106	660,688	188	103,512	206	31,778	167	76,400	56,137	978,623	536	Inc. Place
Asheville	ASHE	02140	3-AA	70,396	68,889	19,443	31,525	33,008	1,368,744	.0309	1,669,175	474	332,951	662	104,456	550	149,936	93,572	628,646	344	Inc. Place
Burlington	BUR	09060	3-A	46,902	44,917	18,456	18,938	36,301	865,629	.0181	875,073	248	173,588	345	81,490	429	89,162	47,706	600,468	329	Inc. Place
Cary	RAL	10740		109,847	94,536	27,991	39,917	63,307	3,074,686	.0518	2,076,526	590	495,197	985	152,664	804	277,974	113,655	217,430	119	Inc. Place
Chapel Hill	DUR	11800	3-C	50,516	48,715	22,390	19,473	41,849	1,131,072	.0185	611,831	174	47,483	94	27,369	144	184,706	45,040	(d)	...	Inc. Place
Charlotte	CHRLT	12000	2-AA	588,566	540,828	23,187	235,890	47,284	13,646,996	.2370	9,235,045	2,622	1,185,752	2,358	515,400	2,713	1,073,897	473,328	3,235,192	1,771	Inc. Place
Clinton		13240	4-C	8,316	8,600	15,096	3,104	30,568	125,541	.0027	123,036	35	15,495	31	2,007	11	17,606	6,920	63,816	35	Inc. Place
Concord	CHRLT	14100	4-C	67,394	55,977	20,836	25,048	44,242	1,404,201	.0243	882,205	251	186,489	371	45,082	237	93,154	53,604	5,678,518	3,109	Inc. Place
Dunn		18320	4-C	9,958	9,196	16,275	3,842	30,615	162,071	.0034	149,790	43	21,404	43	2,835	15	22,043	13,982	84,152	46	Inc. Place
Durham	DUR	19000	3-BB	212,990	187,035	20,718	88,085	40,440	4,412,710	.0762	2,751,551	781	340,284	677	237,618	1,251	396,312	192,750	...	...	Inc. Place
Eden	MRTNV	20080	4-C	16,225	15,908	14,904	6,755	28,864	241,812	.0047	178,112	51	30,084	60	5,854	31	35,585	16,269	501,895	275	Inc. Place
Elizabeth City		20580	4-C	18,527	17,188	13,613	6,844	29,465	252,215	.0060	301,754	86	47,169	94	10,522	55	35,256	16,150	...	...	Inc. Place
Fayetteville	FAY	22920	2-A	128,929	121,015	19,274	53,413	34,892	2,484,983	.0480	2,075,359	589	505,761	1,006	134,247	707	187,958	81,409	1,107,190	606	Inc. Place
Forest City		24080	4-C	7,434	7,549	16,312	3,194	28,290	121,265	.0031	175,669	50	35,025	70	5,119	27	14,381	9,787	167,023	91	Inc. Place
Gastonia	CHRLT	25580	3-BB	69,232	66,277	18,205	27,382	35,464	1,260,394	.0248	1,079,394	306	256,767	511	65,516	345	88,477	74,760	1,193,568	653	Inc. Place
Goldsboro	GLDS	26880	3-A	34,875	39,043	16,019	13,309	33,062	558,658	.0126	630,096	179	128,712	256	34,005	179	86,309	37,184	305,196	167	Inc. Place
Greensboro	GRNS-	28000	2-A	238,862	223,891	21,059	98,093	40,280	5,030,143	.0937	3,969,136	1,127	567,051	1,128	239,539	1,261	386,995	255,641	3,497,301	1,915	Inc. Place
Greenville	GRNV	28080	3-A	66,126	60,476	17,890	29,234	32,320	1,182,968	.0239	1,069,697	304	134,876	268	88,535	466	106,141	47,086	1,330,242	728	Inc. Place
Henderson		30660	4-C	15,776	16,095	13,614	6,104	24,033	214,773	.0072	499,460	142	75,631	150	20,497	108	67,758	26,907	...	...	Inc. Place
Hendersonville		30720	3-B	11,106	10,420	19,706	4,815	35,284	218,855	.0063	433,383	123	58,490	116	16,525	87	55,772	24,778	146,708	80	Inc. Place
Hickory	HICK	31060	3-A	43,522	37,222	21,147	18,106	38,238	920,341	.0199	1,053,686	299	155,088	308	59,470	313	121,240	69,631	965,332	528	Inc. Place
High Point	GRNS-	31400	3-B	93,102	85,839	18,379	36,143	39,053	1,711,146	.0339	1,496,492	425	162,211	323	75,536	398	176,717	70,624	972,213	532	Inc. Place
Huntersville	CHRLT	33120		31,783	24,960	22,575	11,755	62,146	717,504	.0109	291,763	83	67,620	134	9,563	50	34,090	12,958	(d)	...	Inc. Place
Jacksonville	JAX	34200	3-A	63,742	66,715	10,988	17,611	32,600	700,427	.0164	702,547	199	151,744	302	22,693	119	59,752	25,197	(d)	...	Inc. Place
Kannapolis	CHRLT	35200	3-C	39,450	36,910	17,550	15,723	35,294	692,342	.0136	581,964	165	127,445	253	16,280	86	66,554	30,477	...	...	Inc. Place
Kinston		35920	3-B	21,679	23,688	15,391	9,312	27,637	333,657	.0078	398,686	113	76,291	152	19,314	102	63,104	32,199	345,211	189	Inc. Place
Lenoir		37760	4-B	16,755	16,793	17,046	6,910	31,812	285,600	.0057	246,704	70	43,473	86	4,264	22	34,581	14,432	528,077	289	Inc. Place
Lexington		38060	4-C	20,556	19,953	17,486	8,076	34,325	359,435	.0077	369,607	105	65,155	130	11,149	59	47,247	23,512	446,189	244	Inc. Place
Lumberton		39700	4-B	20,638	20,795	12,721	7,670	28,443	262,535	.0077	468,963	133	65,431	130	25,634	135	43,995	17,637	344,256	188	Inc. Place
Monroe		43920	3-S	33,914	26,228	18,522	11,255	42,512	628,154	.0109	368,548	105	58,722	117	14,668	77	44,499	11,820	964,429	528	Inc. Place
Morganton		44400	4-B	17,665	17,310	17,427	7,027	33,955	307,854	.0058	232,218	66	29,764	59	8,616	45	37,020	14,089	496,535	272	Inc. Place
Mount Airy		44800	4-C	8,679	8,484	16,951	3,689	30,525	147,115	.0042	277,743	79	49,712	99	11,542	61	27,799	18,385	442,323	242	Inc. Place
New Bern		46340	3-A	23,957	23,128	20,798	10,821	36,233	498,249	.0099	461,525	131	88,525	176	20,600	108	54,429	17,833	144,518	79	Inc. Place
Raleigh	RAL	55000	2-AA	312,857	276,093	24,555	125,753	47,304	7,682,244	.1440	6,583,148	1,869	908,069	1,806	376,718	1,983	702,171	256,691	1,057,542	579	Inc. Place
Roanoke Rapids		56900	4-A	16,875	16,957	14,197	7,000	27,632	239,579	.0056	280,742	80	54,303	108	16,626	88	39,171	17,485	95,705	52	Inc. Place
Rockingham		57260	4-C	9,530	9,672	15,392	4,046	27,666	146,683	.0039	227,596	65	35,409	70	11,881	63	33,671	11,308	253,762	139	Inc. Place
Rocky Mount	RKYMT	57500	3-A	57,607	55,893	16,718	22,219	33,471	963,089	.0195	849,107	241	142,473	283	63,910	336	80,952	50,425	767,332	420	Inc. Place
Salisbury	SLSB	58860	3-C	27,322	26,462	17,698	10,579	32,653	483,534	.0100	459,261	130	100,272	199	28,690	151	59,265	36,563	456,869	250	Inc. Place
Sanford		59280	4-C	24,244	23,220	17,508	9,293	36,553	424,471	.0097	508,108	144	59,080	117	16,516	87	78,470	25,436	1,091,937	598	Inc. Place
Shelby		61200	4-C	19,820	19,477	17,508	8,004	32,913	347,016	.0066	262,285	74	58,357	116	12,560	66	44,195	19,056	605,864	332	Inc. Place
Statesville		64740	4-C	25,926	23,320	17,908	10,408	34,184	464,275	.0095	434,675	123	73,537	146	27,562	145	48,361	32,769	878,716	481	Inc. Place
Thomasville	GRNS-	67420	4-S	21,289	19,788	17,500	8,499	34,061	372,568	.0061	163,902	47	19,165	38	3,027	16	33,212	15,365	352,217	193	Inc. Place
Washington		71220	4-B	9,798	9,583	14,789	4,021	29,899	144,902	.0034	168,385	48	28,265	56	6,345	33	21,729	13,290	119,903	66	Inc. Place
Wilmington	WILM	74440	3-AA	87,653	75,838	19,203	40,173	31,880	1,683,204	.0441	2,764,447	785	468,426	932	147,535	777	298,469	133,218	700,865	384	Inc. Place
Wilson		74540	3-B	46,986	44,405	16,215	18,562	32,283	761,879	.0158	710,154	202	102,354	204	37,423	197	82,228	45,682	833,769	456	Inc. Place
Winston Salem	WNS	75000	2-B	197,537	185,776	19,533	77,727	37,628	3,858,539	.0770	3,540,183	1,005	608,435	1,210	236,820	1,246	326,725	193,802	2,444,535	1,338	Inc. Place
North Dakota																					
Bismarck	BIS	07200	3-A	57,609	55,532	19,536	23,602	38,630	1,125,432	.0225	1,037,674	295	224,314	446	30,260	159	119,272	70,454	...	...	Inc. Place
Dickinson		19620	4-A	15,122	16,010	15,972	6,182	31,283	241,522	.0054	263,002	75	45,379	90	7,979	42	26,540	15,600	(d)	...	Inc. Place
Fargo	FAR-	25700	3-AA	93,589	90,599	19,330	40,946	35,374	1,809,044	.0414	2,270,927	645	353,001	702	83,204	438	137,284	112,488	493,433	270	Inc. Place
Grand Forks	GDFK	32060	3-A	50,680	49,321	16,643	20,125	33,445	843,447	.0209	1,188,736	338	293,662	584	44,881	236	94,122	45,613	131,601	72	Inc. Place
Jamestown		40580	4-C	14,493	15,527	16,363	6,096	31,690	237,156	.0047	199,577	57	38,035	76	10,129	53	27,151	18,241	...	...	Inc. Place
Minot		53380	3-A	35,404	36,567	17,895	15,549	32,458	633,542	.0138	695,007	197	127,235	253	22,101	116	74,176	34,047	...	...	Inc. Place
Williston		86220	4-A	12,353	12,512	15,076	5,061	30,257	186,236	.0042	203,596	58	40,585	81	6,271	33	28,468	10,742	(d)	...	Inc. Place
Ohio																					
Akron	AKR	01000	2-BB	216,322	217,074	15,442	86,568	31,453	3,340,408	.0672	2,764,254	785	340,330	677	131,413	692	261,490	279,567	1,129,973	619	Inc. Place
Alliance	ALLI	01420	4-C	23,405	23,253	15,772	8,904	32,582	369,153	.0082	396,201	113	65,893	131	15,902	84	50,830	31,379	208,454	114	Inc. Place
Ashland		02568	4-C	21,383	21,249	17,881	8,317	36,115	382,360	.0067	232,230	66	32,977	66	5,545	29	36,439	18,947	378,066	207	Inc. Place
Ashtabula	ASHT	02638	3-A	20,838	20,962	16,395	8,630	31,059	341,634	.0066	255,973	73	65,227	130	13,690	72	37,311	21,931	166,562	91	Inc. Place
Athens		02736	4-A	20,774	21,342	9,477	6,029	20,087	196,873	.0052	245,249	70	31,136	62	15,380	81	53,247	17,961	59,591	33	Inc. Place
Barberton	AKR	03828	4-S	28,275	27,899	16,537	11,268	35,113	467,588	.0085	296,256	84	20,476	41	5,801	31	64,181	26,363	233,165	128	Inc. Place
Beachwood	CLEV	04500	4-Sm	12,257	12,186	36,466	5,169	53,833	446,962	.0081	400,966	114	31,470	63	120,340	633	30,954	42,453	(d)	...	Inc. Place
Beavercreek	DAY	04720		39,295	37,984	24,447	15,417	52,800	960,657	.0157	555,935	158	85,626	170	65,572	345	76,823	22,321	76,333	42	Inc. Place
Bedford	CLEV	04878	4-Sr	14,207	14,214	18,768	6,725	36,461	266,638	.0082	574,495	163	46,407	92	5,408	28	36,738	11,225	122,475	67	Inc. Place
Bellefontaine		05130	4-C	13,451	13,069	20,852	5,664	37,962	280,479	.0051	207,845	59	38,038	76	8,201	43	38,556	13,905	...	...	Inc. Place
Bowling Green		07972	4-C	30,151	29,636	15,761	11,097	33,242	475,197	.0093	368,614	105	51,749	103	11,854	62	67,174	11,253	255,711	140	Inc. Place
Brooklyn	CLEV	09246	4-Sm	11,553	11,586	18,096	5,392	35,023	209,058	.0054	326,404	93	50,482	100	18,440	97	79,961	79,649	220,033	120	Inc. Place
Brunswick	CLEV	09680		35,590	33,388	22,076	12,772	51,249	785,682	.0126	401,280	114	18,330	36	19,000	100	35,187	26,696	48,428	27	Inc. Place
Cambridge		10996	4-B	11,633	11,520	15,970	5,043	28,170	185,785	.0039	174,589	50	31,275	62	3,480	18	29,625	8,438	125,188	69	Inc. Place
Canton	CAN	12000	2-A	80,935	80,806	15,961	32,281	31,304	1,291,767	.0251	984,549	280	104,216	207	40,657	214	176,677	117,881	1,745,086	955	Inc. Place
Celina		12868	4-C	10,150	10,303	20,592	4,249	37,520	209,013	.0037	145,012	41	16,444	33	4,211	22	16,914	6,339	255,222	140	Inc. Place
Chillicothe		14184	3-A	22,254	21,796	19,458	9,766	35,147	433,007	.0078	297,801	85	74,075	147	10,010	53	48,699	17,066	...	...	Inc. Place
Cincinnati	CIN	15000	1-A	315,137	331,285	17,727	142,565	30,570	5,586,428	.0996	3,501,499	994	269,010	535	247,300	1,302	617,321	296,374	3,778,697	2,069	Inc. Place
Cleveland	CLEV	16000	1-AA	440,844	478,403	13,395	177,765	26,359	5,905,006	.1154	4,028,078	1,144	199,322	396	220,230	1,159	822,399	494,799	4,128,581	2,260	Inc. Place
Cleveland Heights	CLEV	16014	4-S	45,905	49,958	21,059	19,444	40,401	966,700	.0155	468,066	133	41,559	83	11,912	63	123,250	108,752	(d)	...	Inc. Place
Columbus	COL	18000	1-A	741,747	711,470	18,787	296,187	38,632	13,935,326	.2835	13,182,911	3,743	1,477,357	2,938	704,685	3,709	1,375,200	553,405	4,498,713	2,463	Inc. Place
Coshocton		18868	4-C	11,744	11,682	18,006	5,029	31,466	211,459	.0038	134,154	38	20,994	42	4,311	23	29,319	8,335	407,354	223	Inc. Place
Cuyahoga Falls	AKR	19778	4-S	49,501	49,374	19,692	20,943	40,744	974,766	.0200	962,876	273	60,454	120	24,445	129	118,408	104,325	315,078	172	Inc. Place
Dayton	DAY	21000	2-AA	161,888	166,179	15,013	65,583	28,308	2,430,352	.0449	1,513,480	430	134,395	267	38,497	203	273,200	115,330	1,599,319	876	Inc. Place
Defiance		21308	4-C	16,507	16,465	21,918	6,890	42,028	361,808	.0067	285,877	81	46,370	92	6,720	35	42,871	12,061	493,455	270	Inc. Place
Delaware		21434	4-C	28,177	25,243	22,184	10,647	46,557	625,069	.0119	532,700	151	13,806	27	6,742	35	65,452	15,142	497,673	272	Inc. Place
Dover		22456	3-C	12,016	12,210	18,647	4,896	37,077	224,063	.0041	158,349	45	5,447	11	1,901	10	37,484	11,773	256,287	140	Inc. Place
Dublin	COL	22694		34,302	31,392	28,673	11,538	66,090	983,533	.0192	974,955	277	188,993	376	92,793	488	71,732	38,525	100,764	55	Inc. Place
East Liverpool	E.LIV	23730	4-A	13,074	13,089	14,750	5,407	26,930	192,836	.0040	171,242	49	41,821	83	6,507	34	26,037	11,647	46,553	25	Inc. Place
Elyria	CLEV	25256	3-S	55,970	55,953	18,256	21,856	37,176	1,021,805	.0217	1,064,009	302	232,874	463	58,004	305	86,203	69,303	858,688	470	Inc. Place
Euclid	CLEV	25704	3-S	52,731	52,717	18,008	24,611	33,455	949,585	.0163	526,258	149	112,076	223	26,230	138	51,697	73,209	725,724	397	Inc. Place
Fairborn	DAY	25914		33,114	32,052	19,690	14,880	35,229	652,021	.0116	431,588	123	85,259	170	8,388	44	36,694	10,955	83,286	46	Inc. Place

Source: Devonshire Associates Ltd. and Scan/US, Inc. 2005.
* Source: 1997 Census of Manufactures.
Not classified as a Principal Business Center.

...Data less than 1,000.
(d) Data not available.

Continued on next page

Principal Business Centers and Other Places with 30,000 or More: Population/Income/Sales, *Continued*

Place Name	Ranally Metro Area	FIPS Place Code	Ranally City Rating	Population Estimate 7/1/05	Population Census 4/1/00	Per Capita Income 2004	Households Estimate 7/1/05	Median Household Income 2004	Disposable Income 2004 ($1,000)	Market Ability Index 2004	Total Retail Sales 2004 Sales ($1,000)	Total Retail Sales Ranally Sales Units	General Merchandise 2004 Sales ($1,000)	General Merchandise Ranally Sales Units	Apparel Store 2004 Sales ($1,000)	Apparel Store Ranally Sales Units	Food Store Sales 2004 ($1,000)	Health & Drug Store 2004 ($1,000)	Manufacturers Value Added 1997* ($1,000)	Manufacturers Ranally Mfg. Units	Place Type
Fairfield	CIN	25970	4-S	42,975	42,097	23,177	17,740	45,789	996,043	.0198	961,822	273	46,294	92	32,504	171	129,096	30,079	245,037	134	Inc. Place
Fairlawn	AKR	26166	4-Sm	7,457	7,307	36,416	2,935	65,983	271,551	.0054	301,699	86	35,863	71	40,705	214	43,312	29,795	(d)	...	Inc. Place
Findlay	FIND	27048	3-A	38,590	38,967	21,149	15,709	40,590	816,129	.0165	799,997	227	191,726	381	22,776	120	63,632	32,990	696,898	382	Inc. Place
Fremont		28826	4-C	17,347	17,375	19,282	6,975	36,066	334,483	.0062	245,796	70	53,552	106	7,161	38	35,681	8,816	573,001	314	Inc. Place
Gahanna	COL	29106		34,075	32,636	21,888	11,799	55,627	745,825	.0121	390,965	111	93,469	186	8,137	43	68,410	13,378	36,513	20	Inc. Place
Garfield Heights	CLEV	29428		30,776	30,734	16,367	12,611	36,738	503,716	.0094	340,163	97	17,060	34	3,997	21	39,992	53,756	102,517	56	Inc. Place
Greenville		32340	4-C	13,386	13,294	20,009	5,851	35,138	267,842	.0049	190,965	54	32,113	64	9,120	48	24,971	8,438	398,008	218	Inc. Place
Hamilton	CIN	33012	3-C	61,120	60,690	21,016	24,928	41,122	1,284,504	.0192	454,548	129	93,782	187	5,778	30	90,091	31,683	363,002	199	Inc. Place
Huber Heights	DAY	36610		36,719	38,212	19,169	13,804	45,513	703,854	.0123	439,208	125	185,983	370	10,986	58	61,910	26,288	...	...	Inc. Place
Kent	AKR	39872	4-S	27,752	27,906	16,254	10,113	32,828	451,077	.0087	336,529	96	18,632	37	7,951	42	34,658	14,007	155,054	85	Inc. Place
Kettering	DAY	40040	3-S	56,932	57,502	24,411	25,339	43,172	1,389,791	.0213	634,155	180	89,840	179	30,335	160	82,266	47,795	457,138	250	Inc. Place
Lakewood	CLEV	41664	4-Sr	56,174	56,646	20,753	26,838	37,780	1,165,754	.0177	443,130	126	...	...	20,736	109	87,431	89,753	103,812	57	Inc. Place
Lancaster	LANC	41720	3-C	37,145	35,335	19,399	15,492	36,187	720,564	.0131	506,225	144	98,180	195	40,105	211	64,025	29,382	366,487	201	Inc. Place
Lima	LIMA	43554	3-AA	38,642	40,081	15,859	15,274	31,367	612,817	.0139	701,165	199	215,458	428	23,312	123	50,241	44,642	623,253	341	Inc. Place
Lorain	CLEV	44856	3-S	69,031	68,652	15,810	25,912	32,770	1,091,414	.0189	555,820	158	76,902	153	17,188	90	81,395	83,687	3,215,673	1,760	Inc. Place
Mansfield	MANS	47138	3-AA	47,231	49,346	18,287	20,173	33,244	863,716	.0168	711,177	202	188,228	374	31,371	165	89,712	40,945	643,978	353	Inc. Place
Marietta	PRKB	47628	4-B	13,699	14,515	17,528	5,754	32,292	240,121	.0055	291,970	83	46,430	92	5,824	31	41,652	9,754	151,178	83	Inc. Place
Marion	MRN	47754	3-A	34,800	35,318	17,333	13,627	35,084	603,176	.0114	449,974	128	115,157	229	14,364	76	57,872	25,220	300,441	164	Inc. Place
Massillon	CAN	48244	4-C	31,432	31,325	18,077	12,639	37,625	568,206	.0096	297,203	84	31,417	62	5,711	30	52,195	33,887	273,150	150	Inc. Place
Maumee	TOL	48342	4-S	14,800	15,237	24,750	6,072	47,041	366,294	.0078	430,155	122	97,669	194	2,854	15	11,725	17,439	283,703	155	Inc. Place
Mayfield Heights	CLEV	48482	4-S	19,471	19,386	29,802	10,015	42,911	580,272	.0096	376,363	107	1,180	2	30,467	160	45,754	43,734	...	...	Inc. Place
Medina	CLEV	48790	4-S	29,455	25,139	25,597	11,171	53,069	753,970	.0119	393,414	112	68,239	136	12,389	65	44,416	25,824	348,114	191	Inc. Place
Mentor	CLEV	49056	3-Sm	51,783	50,278	23,119	19,543	50,860	1,197,166	.0264	1,473,260	418	278,996	555	93,167	490	122,625	112,728	870,739	477	Inc. Place
Middleburg Heights	CLEV	49644	3-S	16,124	15,542	18,396	7,037	39,895	296,623	.0079	495,953	141	88,830	177	14,742	78	25,749	43,004	39,752	22	Inc. Place
Middletown	MIDD	49840	3-C	51,813	51,605	21,170	22,013	38,886	1,096,883	.0162	375,021	106	55,101	110	5,503	29	61,969	26,395	2,807,989	1,537	Inc. Place
Mount Vernon		53102	4-C	14,608	14,375	19,104	6,213	33,500	279,065	.0050	188,873	54	34,807	69	6,926	36	29,849	14,194	285,930	157	Inc. Place
Newark	NWRK	54040	3-C	48,382	46,279	18,387	20,698	34,753	889,624	.0143	392,092	111	54,810	109	1,784	9	69,275	22,334	441,871	242	Inc. Place
New Philadelphia		55216	3-B	16,841	17,056	18,380	7,216	32,986	309,531	.0063	290,467	82	85,044	169	26,225	138	22,767	27,849	239,302	131	Inc. Place
Niles	YNGS-	55916	3-Sm	20,514	20,932	18,810	9,014	33,286	385,864	.0085	443,250	126	86,070	171	54,326	286	55,502	36,949	294,789	161	Inc. Place
North Olmsted	CLEV	56882	4-Sm	34,145	34,113	21,157	13,714	48,300	722,419	.0185	1,161,511	330	208,791	415	95,381	502	111,479	94,147	(d)	...	Inc. Place
Ontario	MANS	58520	4-Sm	5,397	5,303	18,899	2,324	34,447	102,000	.0044	373,698	106	156,996	312	17,459	92	12,644	13,631	222,232	122	Inc. Place
Painesville	CLEV	59416	4-S	17,744	17,503	20,960	6,697	43,239	371,917	.0057	153,596	44	...	...	...	...	29,567	18,104	431,320	236	Inc. Place
Parma	CLEV	61000	3-S	85,873	85,655	17,776	35,624	40,390	1,526,441	.0319	1,502,554	427	257,863	513	92,670	488	197,474	189,963	388,141	212	Inc. Place
Piqua		62848	4-C	20,914	20,738	18,497	8,336	35,855	386,848	.0074	313,147	89	22,285	44	27,449	144	46,273	16,478	313,018	171	Inc. Place
Portsmouth	PTSM	64304	3-A	19,217	20,909	15,026	8,962	24,037	288,758	.0067	340,822	97	67,165	134	16,997	89	59,871	25,535	46,428	25	Inc. Place
Ravenna	AKR	65592	4-Sr	11,636	11,771	20,002	5,124	38,683	232,749	.0037	108,757	31	13,603	27	...	...	15,677	6,832	213,918	117	Inc. Place
Reynoldsburg	COL	66390		34,347	32,069	18,948	12,944	46,538	650,798	.0103	278,470	79	39,095	78	14,482	76	33,838	9,533	95,827	52	Inc. Place
Richmond Heights	CLEV	66894	4-Sm	11,034	10,944	26,745	4,966	49,531	295,108	.0051	207,461	59	33,586	67	10,013	53	43,013	12,822	(d)	...	Inc. Place
St. Clairsville	WHL	69526	4-Sm	5,101	5,057	19,029	2,309	34,815	97,067	.0028	188,669	54	65,818	131	19,697	104	19,143	14,469	(d)	...	Inc. Place
Salem		69834	4-B	12,371	12,197	19,597	5,377	34,485	242,438	.0040	119,590	34	6,270	12	3,005	16	21,340	14,663	297,446	163	Inc. Place
Sandusky	SNDSK	70380	3-A	26,547	27,844	19,791	11,682	34,728	525,390	.0103	464,424	132	122,790	244	30,342	160	44,212	36,105	303,519	166	Inc. Place
Springdale	CIN	74104	3-Sm	10,517	10,563	19,974	4,438	42,337	210,071	.0099	868,873	247	188,437	375	118,030	621	17,136	52,682	823,722	451	Inc. Place
Springfield	SPR	74118	3-BB	63,432	65,358	18,297	26,382	34,328	1,160,631	.0203	701,958	199	67,926	135	19,860	105	128,805	73,475	...	...	Inc. Place
Steubenville	STU-	74608	3-A	17,901	19,015	17,200	8,316	26,916	307,900	.0075	428,335	122	83,065	165	15,898	84	71,818	46,761	...	...	Inc. Place
Stow	AKR	74944		32,644	32,139	21,888	12,058	51,755	714,523	.0122	447,142	127	77,139	153	9,700	51	105,742	61,726	179,497	98	Inc. Place
Strongsville	CLEV	75098		45,577	43,858	23,429	17,017	61,048	1,067,821	.0190	784,233	223	167,234	333	97,362	512	103,474	65,018	340,221	186	Inc. Place
Tiffin		76778	4-B	17,985	18,135	19,515	7,591	36,012	350,981	.0057	173,030	49	19,628	39	8,666	46	22,651	10,653	271,920	149	Inc. Place
Toledo	TOL	77000	2-AA	308,876	313,619	16,047	125,166	32,148	4,956,443	.0964	3,815,882	1,084	541,086	1,076	228,477	1,203	560,986	262,846	2,764,850	1,514	Inc. Place
Trotwood	DAY	77504	4-Sm	26,485	27,420	16,102	10,729	33,236	426,462	.0102	551,409	157	111,823	222	30,044	158	62,005	16,957	43,093	24	Inc. Place
Troy		77588	4-C	22,278	21,999	20,793	9,026	41,144	463,219	.0085	343,902	98	95,119	189	5,994	32	28,803	10,599	718,818	394	Inc. Place
Upper Arlington	COL	79002	4-S	34,592	33,686	27,837	13,526	52,396	962,935	.0140	385,081	109	38,731	77	37,187	196	58,213	33,402	(d)	...	Inc. Place
Warren	YNGS-	80892	3-B	44,275	46,832	18,090	18,968	32,614	800,933	.0149	586,275	166	98,182	195	5,845	31	91,347	39,931	1,097,861	601	Inc. Place
Westerville	COL	83342		35,606	35,318	22,945	12,019	58,766	816,991	.0125	349,684	99	37,227	74	3,221	17	71,676	12,121	99,567	55	Inc. Place
Westlake	CLEV	83622		32,515	31,719	30,884	13,325	57,822	1,004,191	.0165	649,840	185	24,078	48	12,170	64	51,739	74,078	145,672	80	Inc. Place
Whitehall	COL	84742	4-S	18,300	19,201	17,660	7,499	33,482	323,184	.0089	573,069	163	53,516	106	19,366	102	105,554	20,069	...	...	Inc. Place
Willoughby	CLEV	85484	4-Sr	22,881	22,621	26,670	10,488	43,306	610,247	.0110	482,110	137	27,900	55	7,010	37	65,650	46,260	583,386	319	Inc. Place
Wooster		86548	3-C	25,694	24,811	21,367	10,828	38,473	548,994	.0098	384,711	109	60,870	121	7,301	38	62,185	20,660	856,510	469	Inc. Place
Xenia	DAY	86772	4-S	24,433	24,164	19,433	10,037	39,264	474,804	.0077	228,407	65	21,461	43	6,857	36	33,683	7,720	45,847	25	Inc. Place
Youngstown	YNGS-	88000	2-AA	75,560	82,026	13,247	29,103	25,842	1,000,976	.0191	617,275	175	55,021	109	20,141	106	100,429	61,843	413,577	226	Inc. Place
Zanesville	ZAN	88084	3-A	25,548	25,586	17,191	10,536	31,805	439,185	.0095	459,563	130	74,374	148	35,861	189	61,938	32,157	356,455	195	Inc. Place

Oklahoma

Place Name	Ranally Metro Area	FIPS Place Code	Ranally City Rating	Population Estimate 7/1/05	Population Census 4/1/00	Per Capita Income 2004	Households Estimate 7/1/05	Median Household Income 2004	Disposable Income 2004 ($1,000)	Market Ability Index 2004	Total Retail Sales 2004 Sales ($1,000)	Total Retail Sales Ranally Sales Units	General Merchandise 2004 Sales ($1,000)	General Merchandise Ranally Sales Units	Apparel Store 2004 Sales ($1,000)	Apparel Store Ranally Sales Units	Food Store Sales 2004 ($1,000)	Health & Drug Store 2004 ($1,000)	Manufacturers Value Added 1997* ($1,000)	Manufacturers Ranally Mfg. Units	Place Type
Ada		00200	4-A	15,606	15,691	14,777	6,651	27,145	230,614	.0048	209,786	60	67,908	135	8,291	44	20,262	11,675	44,306	24	Inc. Place
Altus		01700	4-C	20,422	21,447	14,950	7,839	29,995	305,309	.0061	246,807	70	87,176	173	10,502	55	32,277	9,728	...	...	Inc. Place
Ardmore		02600	3-A	24,711	23,711	15,033	9,764	29,209	371,491	.0082	387,872	110	105,010	209	17,643	93	30,022	23,004	...	...	Inc. Place
Bartlesville	BART	04450	3-A	34,901	34,748	19,015	14,332	35,565	663,657	.0115	399,403	113	146,025	290	14,831	78	32,811	25,459	86,510	47	Inc. Place
Broken Arrow	TUL	09050	4-S	76,774	74,859	16,737	24,380	49,113	1,284,935	.0241	906,807	257	181,940	362	11,828	62	112,259	45,001	340,699	187	Inc. Place
Chickasha		13950	4-C	16,143	15,850	15,820	6,200	27,721	255,381	.0050	202,912	58	34,748	69	7,960	42	35,614	11,138	347,937	190	Inc. Place
Duncan		21900	4-B	22,609	22,505	16,931	9,521	30,606	382,792	.0076	316,897	90	61,997	123	8,778	46	28,246	22,265	279,551	153	Inc. Place
Edmond	O.C.	23200	4-S	72,631	68,315	22,377	26,228	49,930	1,625,257	.0234	510,766	145	73,895	147	16,352	86	95,747	39,355	56,473	31	Inc. Place
Elk City		23500	4-C	10,040	10,510	14,842	4,070	28,682	149,014	.0037	202,123	57	52,417	104	6,110	32	21,104	8,467	(d)	...	Inc. Place
Enid	ENID	23950	3-A	47,555	47,045	16,643	19,186	31,872	791,456	.0145	522,198	148	151,039	300	10,540	55	59,592	27,007	...	...	Inc. Place
Lawton	LAWT	41850	3-AA	94,389	92,757	14,962	33,693	32,102	1,412,271	.0250	741,247	210	270,040	537	22,101	116	62,535	29,295	...	...	Inc. Place
McAlester		44800	4-A	17,688	17,783	13,798	6,552	28,680	244,058	.0053	236,064	67	85,772	171	8,647	46	12,491	9,267	79,959	44	Inc. Place
Miami		48000	4-B	12,986	13,704	14,788	5,366	26,654	192,034	.0037	134,750	38	32,974	66	2,482	13	19,632	11,152	76,290	42	Inc. Place
Midwest City	O.C.	48350	3-S	54,029	54,088	15,050	21,678	33,372	813,146	.0182	880,264	250	284,890	567	20,360	107	56,534	39,892	...	...	Inc. Place
Moore	O.C.	49200		44,425	41,138	17,324	15,738	41,370	769,598	.0129	374,584	106	184,692	367	6,691	35	43,580	25,766	(d)	...	Inc. Place
Muskogee	MSKOG	50050	3-A	39,255	38,310	14,727	15,570	27,685	578,104	.0115	444,673	126	120,533	240	11,859	62	26,148	36,481	475,830	261	Inc. Place
Norman	O.C.	52500	3-S	101,820	95,694	19,920	40,635	36,104	2,028,247	.0360	1,352,929	384	266,285	530	61,704	325	149,488	77,683	331,946	182	Inc. Place
Oklahoma City	O.C.	55000	1-A	544,097	506,132	16,854	214,773	34,577	9,170,296	.1815	7,639,440	2,169	1,182,395	2,351	283,573	1,493	700,065	397,133	4,451,920	2,437	Inc. Place
Ponca City		59850	4-A	24,724	25,919	16,078	10,091	31,202	397,502	.0081	351,790	100	116,510	232	8,958	47	27,797	24,970	...	...	Inc. Place
Shawnee		66800	3-C	29,259	28,692	15,260	11,124	30,149	446,487	.0088	351,268	100	99,591	198	18,374	97	35,766	33,806	272,407	149	Inc. Place
Stillwater		70300	4-A	39,318	39,065	14,293	15,403	28,254	561,976	.0111	420,152	119	145,829	290	19,398	102	37,014	16,922	438,949	240	Inc. Place
Tulsa	TUL	75000	2-AA	396,188	393,049	17,962	151,826	35,417	7,116,142	.1493	7,130,693	2,025	1,518,763	3,020	300,927	1,584	602,616	461,804	2,656,935	1,455	Inc. Place
Woodward		82150	4-C	11,779	11,853	16,122	4,607	31,711	189,901	.0043	214,249	61	73,706	147	6,354	33	19,759	11,472	(d)	...	Inc. Place

Oregon

Place Name	Ranally Metro Area	FIPS Place Code	Ranally City Rating	Population Estimate 7/1/05	Population Census 4/1/00	Per Capita Income 2004	Households Estimate 7/1/05	Median Household Income 2004	Disposable Income 2004 ($1,000)	Market Ability Index 2004	Total Retail Sales 2004 Sales ($1,000)	Total Retail Sales Ranally Sales Units	General Merchandise 2004 Sales ($1,000)	General Merchandise Ranally Sales Units	Apparel Store 2004 Sales ($1,000)	Apparel Store Ranally Sales Units	Food Store Sales 2004 ($1,000)	Health & Drug Store 2004 ($1,000)	Manufacturers Value Added 1997* ($1,000)	Manufacturers Ranally Mfg. Units	Place Type
Albany	CORV-	01000	3-B	44,289	40,852	19,104	18,115	38,541	846,097	.0159	656,473	186	221,393	440	22,759	120	61,559	17,919	345,138	189	Inc. Place
Aloha	POR	01650		45,654	41,741	20,832	15,716	48,323	951,082	.0137	281,265	80	76,960	153	18,218	96	53,051	9,074	(d)	...	CDP
Beaverton	POR	05350	3-S	87,474	76,129	22,696	35,841	44,323	1,985,304	.0412	2,112,790	600	294,536	586	148,612	782	181,545	30,067	1,336,393	732	Inc. Place
Bend		05800	3-A	75,817	52,029	20,618	31,982	40,631	1,563,192	.0283	1,125,891	320	324,506	645	42,047	221	96,703	24,091	225,835	124	Inc. Place
Coos Bay		15250	4-A	15,490	15,374	15,873	6,779	30,244	245,877	.0052	239,698	68	68,252	136	...	...	23,691	4,936	16,077	9	Inc. Place
Corvallis	CORV-	15800	3-B	50,080	49,322	20,313	21,743	36,454	1,017,294	.0164	485,145	138	68,110	135	20,930	110	112,985	23,555	553,900	303	Inc. Place
Eugene	EUG	23850	2-A	149,779	137,893	20,086	65,754	34,270	3,008,516	.0593	2,709,468	769	459,032	913	93,482	492	381,010	119,179	614,945	337	Inc. Place
Grants Pass		30550	3-B	24,932	23,003	16,285	10,505	30,846	406,008	.0086	403,315	115	108,440	216	10,085	53	53,355	17,015	125,680	69	Inc. Place
Gresham	POR	31250	4-S	96,478	90,205	17,749	35,911	41,451	1,712,410	.0325	1,303,736	370	207,942	414	26,451	139	213,946	49,183	476,797	261	Inc. Place
Hillsboro	POR	34100	4-S	85,646	70,186	20,661	30,955	48,361	1,769,513	.0313	1,188,124	337	179,934	358	17,514	92	151,056	34,853	788,238	432	Inc. Place
Keizer	SAL	38500		36,962	32,203	15,361	13,431	36,449	567,771	.0095	237,927	68	27,542	55	1,178	6	40,872	10,553	(d)	...	Inc. Place
Klamath Falls		39700	3-A	19,683	19,462	15,794	8,292	28,804	310,877	.0064	275,116	78	18,311	36	6,553	34	63,369	6,266	123,925	68	Inc. Place
Lake Oswego	POR	40550		37,535	35,278	36,758	15,778	62,635	1,379,727	.0174	332,902	95	...	...	13,797	73	113,422	27,048	70,004	38	Inc. Place
Medford	MEDF	47000	3-AA	70,365	63,154	19,276	29,412	36,568	1,356,381	.0347	2,128,851	604	412,276	820	53,556	282	151,451	38,998	132,508	73	Inc. Place
Milwaukie	POR	48650	4-S	22,014	20,490	19,058	9,215	38,414	419,534	.0072	243,346	69	88,068	175	5,273	28	18,144	9,996	365,995	200	Inc. Place
North Bend		53000	4-B	9,421	9,544	17,768	4,054	33,279	167,395	.0030	105,639	30	24,917	50	7,039	37	26,379	6,620	(d)	...	Inc. Place
Ontario		54900	4-C	10,032	10,985	15,546	3,979	29,169	155,953	.0038	206,659	59	65,358	130	7,699	41	28,089	6,120	...	...	Inc. Place
Oregon City	POR	55200	4-S	31,153	25,754	19,819	11,500	46,418	617,423	.0101	310,350	88	99,917	199	14,377	76	42,566	8,869	90,863	50	Inc. Place
Pendleton		57150	4-B	16,283	16,354	16,093	6,109	36,000	262,049	.0052	211,441	60	22,762	45	12,189	64	51,524	4,000	69,300	38	Inc. Place
Portland	POR	59000	1-A	551,781	529,121	20,484	234,846	38,323	11,302,849	.2115	8,929,909	2,536	1,448,302	2,880	630,018	3,316	1,120,506	291,841	3,465,307	1,897	Inc. Place
Roseburg		63650	3-A	20,547	20,017	18,829	8,857	34,082	386,877	.0080	385,786	110	103,282	205	10,380	55	52,288	19,913	54,371	30	Inc. Place
Salem	SAL	64900	2-A	150,116	136,924	18,482	53,742	39,879	2,774,424	.0499	1,840,674	523	470,599	936	73,982	389	246,782	67,733	644,920	353	Inc. Place
Springfield	EUG	69600	3-B	56,018	52,864	16,350	22,679	34,265	915,882	.0166	575,566	163	165,071	328	20,870	110	106,172	12,888	373,038	204	Inc. Place
The Dalles		13425	4-C	12,056	12,156	18,145	5,100	34,624	218,761	.0047	236,576	67	51,663	103	7,085	37	26,228	11,486	(d)	...	Inc. Place
Tigard	POR	73650		45,697	41,223	23,592	18,499	46,236	1,078,088	.0236	1,306,557	371	425,089	845	123,600	651	103,652	32,573	290,001	159	Inc. Place
Tualatin	POR	74950	4-Sm	25,449	22,791	26,041	9,756	51,305	662,715	.0100	298,916	85	126,866	252	5,309	28	37,091	2,640	364,262	199	Inc. Place

Pennsylvania

Place Name	Ranally Metro Area	FIPS Place Code	Ranally City Rating	Population Estimate 7/1/05	Population Census 4/1/00	Per Capita Income 2004	Households Estimate 7/1/05	Median Household Income 2004	Disposable Income 2004 ($1,000)	Market Ability Index 2004	Total Retail Sales 2004 Sales ($1,000)	Total Retail Sales Ranally Sales Units	General Merchandise 2004 Sales ($1,000)	General Merchandise Ranally Sales Units	Apparel Store 2004 Sales ($1,000)	Apparel Store Ranally Sales Units	Food Store Sales 2004 ($1,000)	Health & Drug Store 2004 ($1,000)	Manufacturers Value Added 1997* ($1,000)	Manufacturers Ranally Mfg. Units	Place Type
Abington Township	PHIL-	00156	3-S	55,631	56,103	26,454	20,727	54,426	1,471,657	.0261	1,118,928	318	43,896	87	78,436	413	134,742	112,381	(d)	...	MCD-Township
Allentown	ALL-	02000	2-AA	108,777	106,632	15,963	40,426	33,359	1,736,376	.0342	1,378,234	391	102,516	204	44,766	236	261,280	105,643	3,362,309	1,841	Inc. Place
Altoona	ALT	02184	3-AA	48,534	49,523	15,236	20,163	29,258	739,472	.0176	932,327	265	242,566	482	45,896	242	124,214	66,909	253,069	139	Inc. Place
Beaver	PGH	04688	4-S	4,673	4,775	24,761	2,134	40,897	115,707	.0018	59,739	17	...	...	...	...	7,729	7,605	...	...	Inc. Place
Bensalem Township	PHIL-	05616	3-Sm	59,340	58,434	20,330	22,805	45,530	1,206,387	.0269	1,462,145	415	189,175	376	53,589	282	182,596	84,081	292,518	160	MCD-Township
Bethel Park	PGH	06064		33,031	33,556	22,255	13,013	49,351	735,109	.0123	429,792	122	41,832	83	18,819	99	149,657	30,002	28,725	16	Inc. Place
Bethlehem	ALL-	06088	3-B	73,153	71,329	20,296	29,124	38,069	1,484,690	.0248	816,586	232	52,644	105	18,399	97	152,831	64,125	527,214	289	Inc. Place
Bloomsburg		07128	4-C	12,295	12,375	14,299	4,091	33,747	175,805	.0041	206,174	59	30,652	61	8,330	44	22,692	11,002	128,049	70	Inc. Place
Bradford		08040	4-B	8,645	9,175	18,008	3,803	30,873	155,681	.0030	119,639	34	9,208	18	2,311	12	19,760	8,714	240,008	131	Inc. Place
Bristol	PHIL-	08768		54,738	55,521	17,906	19,308	43,188	980,121	.0180	677,417	192	40,562	81	18,323	96	125,718	45,099	478,417	262	MCD-Township
Butler	BUTL	10464	3-C	15,070	15,121	19,382	6,830	33,755	292,094	.0062	312,102	89	68,830	137	11,918	63	38,828	24,227	76,227	42	Inc. Place
Camp Hill	HRBG	11000	3-Sm	7,745	7,636	25,884	3,463	45,403	200,472	.0040	203,998	58	51,444	102	18,291	96	17,488	18,540	...	...	Inc. Place
Carlisle	CARL	11272	3-C	18,272	17,970	21,313	7,595	40,792	389,434	.0065	224,423	64	23,863	47	5,580	29	29,687	6,198	569,478	312	Inc. Place
Chambersburg		12536	3-B	18,359	17,862	21,462	8,078	37,290	394,013	.0078	365,493	104	58,244	116	11,997	63	56,804	19,839	196,945	108	Inc. Place
Charleroi	PGH	12704	4-S	5,066	4,871	16,745	2,387	29,605	84,831	.0014	42,288	12	7,712	15	2,061	11	7,660	4,219	84,346	46	Inc. Place
Cheltenham Township	PHIL-	12968	4-S	38,307	36,875	27,084	14,384	54,600	1,037,495	.0135	227,811	65	34,210	68	9,029	48	50,472	30,943	136,174	75	MCD-Township
Chester	PHIL-	13208	4-Sr	36,914	36,854	10,377	12,197	25,062	383,059	.0072	166,845	47	6,522	13	4,112	22	27,518	17,835	534,383	293	Inc. Place
Clearfield		14064	4-B	6,488	6,631	17,163	3,058	27,876	111,354	.0026	141,880	40	30,937	62	5,458	29	15,321	6,986	92,597	51	Inc. Place
Connellsville		15776	4-C	9,164	9,146	16,053	4,121	26,733	147,107	.0027	89,191	25	6,088	12	...	...	5,443	7,772	(d)	...	Inc. Place
Doylestown	PHIL-	19784	4-S	8,172	8,227	41,410	3,900	65,966	338,403	.0053	208,195	59	9,009	18	6,338	33	25,475	12,393	(d)	...	Inc. Place
Du Bois		20136	4-A	7,865	8,123	20,114	3,574	34,091	158,194	.0037	206,739	59	39,689	79	11,380	60	32,281	11,349	92,425	51	Inc. Place
Easton	ALL-	21648	3-B	26,971	26,263	15,916	9,915	34,762	429,278	.0076	235,236	67	11,738	23	9,860	52	42,100	29,844	430,301	236	Inc. Place
Erie	ERIE	24000	2-A	103,797	103,717	14,962	42,430	29,385	1,552,960	.0286	954,668	271	100,289	199	25,367	134	181,832	87,486	937,786	513	Inc. Place
Falls	PHIL-	25112	4-S	35,665	34,865	24,537	13,344	52,576	875,099	.0155	641,343	182	60,484	120	28,108	148	111,694	45,121	187,571	103	MCD-Township
Franklin	OILC-F	27456	4-B	7,106	7,212	18,531	3,081	31,668	131,681	.0025	102,611	29	10,893	22	1,004	5	20,294	7,936	195,969	107	Inc. Place
Greensburg	PGH	31200	3-SS	15,885	15,889	21,240	7,032	36,694	337,394	.0091	592,978	168	100,450	200	49,431	260	54,439	39,554	73,940	40	Inc. Place
Hanover	HANV	32448	3-B	14,614	14,535	23,025	6,550	40,793	336,490	.0065	309,467	88	50,686	101	10,034	53	42,685	9,068	588,939	322	Inc. Place
Harrisburg	HRBG	32800	2-AA	46,556	48,950	17,832	20,396	28,895	830,188	.0141	441,035	125	7,020	14	13,714	72	63,242	36,663	223,366	122	Inc. Place
Hatboro	PHIL-	33088	4-S	7,276	7,393	20,574	2,878	47,012	149,695	.0023	57,572	16	8,712	17	4,025	21	4,475	3,743	36,287	20	Inc. Place
Haverford Township	PHIL-	33144		48,531	48,498	26,032	17,172	58,030	1,263,373	.0176	387,123	110	31,300	62	31,990	168	72,988	49,230	(d)	...	MCD-Township
Hazleton	HAZ	33408	3-B	22,221	23,329	17,366	9,643	27,498	385,887	.0099	587,865	167	118,787	236	31,562	166	92,745	37,650	625,358	342	Inc. Place
Hempfield	PGH	33792		40,016	40,721	18,052	15,473	36,546	722,366	.0099	106,069	30	15,148	30	7,517	40	10,586	7,234	45,275	25	MCD-Township
Hermitage	SHAR	34064	4-Sm	16,182	16,157	22,095	7,039	36,721	357,542	.0085	499,729	142	162,143	322	11,403	60	72,334	23,569	67,573	37	Inc. Place
Indiana		36816	3-A	14,666	14,895	13,364	4,875	28,083	195,993	.0050	272,582	77	62,148	124	9,929	52	33,149	14,401	34,285	19	Inc. Place
Jenkintown	PHIL-	38000	4-S	4,542	4,478	39,641	1,984	55,812	180,050	.0031	143,603	41	...	...	7,767	41	9,779	10,977	(d)	...	Inc. Place
Johnstown	JNST	38288	3-AA	21,928	23,906	14,287	10,533	22,897	313,293	.0057	171,006	49	6,110	12	2,055	11	21,390	18,779	348,876	191	Inc. Place
Lancaster	LANC	41216	2-A	56,093	56,348	18,026	21,262	35,391	1,011,129	.0189	742,124	211	69,432	138	111,940	589	96,184	55,236	1,148,243	629	Inc. Place
Lansdale	PHIL-	41432	4-S	15,986	16,071	25,740	6,349	56,698	411,473	.0064	209,674	60	12,152	24	13,678	72	40,143	20,893	305,402	167	Inc. Place
Latrobe	LTROB	41680	4-C	8,776	8,994	18,103	3,816	33,866	158,868	.0029	104,235	30	8,864	18	1,829	10	9,707	8,941	272,124	149	Inc. Place
Lebanon	LEB	42168	3-C	24,433	24,461	19,493	10,369	35,285	476,270	.0088	350,344	99	52,415	104	6,691	35	37,728	14,869	307,861	169	Inc. Place
Levittown	PHIL-	42928	4-Sr	56,202	53,966	18,347	19,207	46,331	1,031,122	.0149	247,832	70	4,096	8	8,305	44	80,611	38,201	(d)	...	CDP
Lewistown		43000	4-C	8,865	8,998	16,809	4,035	28,825	149,015	.0027	99,183	28	19,661	39	4,250	22	7,435	4,156	165,264	90	Inc. Place

Source: Devonshire Associates Ltd. and Scan/US, Inc. 2005.
* Source: 1997 Census of Manufactures.
Not classified as a Principal Business Center.

...Data less than 1,000.
(d) Data not available.

Principal Business Centers and Other Places with 30,000 or More: Population/Income/Sales, *Continued*

Place Name	Ranally Metro Area	FIPS Place Code	Ranally City Rating	Population: Estimate 7/1/05	Population: Census 4/1/00	Per Capita Income 2004	Households Estimate 7/1/05	Median Household Income 2004	Disposable Income 2004 ($1,000)	Market Ability Index 2004	Total Retail Sales: 2004 Sales ($1,000)	Total Retail Sales: Ranally Sales Units	General Merchandise: 2004 Sales ($1,000)	General Merchandise: Ranally Sales Units	Apparel Store: 2004 Sales ($1,000)	Apparel Store: Ranally Sales Units	Food Store Sales 2004 ($1,000)	Health & Drug Store 2004 ($1,000)	Manufacturers: Value Added 1997* ($1,000)	Manufacturers: Ranally Mfg. Units	Place Type
Lock Haven	WMSPT	44128	4-C	8,894	9,149	13,718	3,369	27,951	122,008	.0024	84,901	24	1,136	2	1,821	10	16,835	4,494	(d)	...	Inc. Place
Lower Makefield	PHIL-	44968		33,490	32,681	31,905	11,899	62,905	1,068,493	.0126	122,121	35	7,645	15	2,359	12	41,373	21,110	(d)	...	MCD-Township
Lower Merion Township	PHIL-	44976	3-S	62,041	59,850	44,302	22,850	74,661	2,748,511	.0358	904,242	257	42,545	85	113,873	599	200,186	73,082	48,584	27	MCD-Township
Lower Paxton	HRBG	45056		45,119	44,424	23,430	19,684	44,529	1,057,117	.0196	866,304	246	137,091	273	54,172	285	123,804	32,020	(d)	...	MCD-Township
Manheim	LANC	46896		35,320	33,697	25,283	13,853	48,804	893,003	.0192	1,062,178	302	174,023	346	72,932	384	73,756	55,471	265,430	145	MCD-Township
Marple Township	PHIL-	47616	4-Sm	23,965	23,737	22,635	8,294	53,848	542,447	.0102	455,527	129	50,205	100	22,567	119	99,674	30,045	(d)	...	MCD-Township
McKeesport	PGH	46256	4-S	23,572	24,040	11,075	9,361	23,889	261,049	.0054	182,607	52	12,416	25	3,856	20	40,584	7,077	67,127	37	Inc. Place
Meadville		48360	3-A	13,042	13,685	17,533	5,304	31,734	228,662	.0051	257,759	73	40,561	81	10,241	54	34,254	22,973	345,762	189	Inc. Place
Mechanicsburg	HRBG	48376	4-Sr	8,959	9,042	26,298	4,007	46,320	235,605	.0066	465,626	132	18,966	38	5,124	27	36,771	10,187	116,324	64	Inc. Place
Middletown	PHIL-	49120		44,733	44,141	21,325	15,393	54,713	953,943	.0248	1,581,135	449	178,212	354	131,878	694	90,525	84,698	119,874	66	MCD-Township
Middletown	PHIL-	49136	4-Sm	16,253	16,064	24,653	5,315	55,951	400,688	.0080	405,119	115	50,757	101	29,893	157	36,031	19,876	82,097	45	MCD-Township
Millcreek	ERIE	49548	4-Sm	51,609	52,129	23,442	21,789	40,824	1,209,794	.0243	1,210,713	344	260,292	518	101,407	534	148,638	60,959	413,260	226	MCD-Township
Monessen	PGH	50344	4-S	8,457	8,669	14,459	3,761	26,170	122,284	.0021	51,711	15	...	...	...	...	3,155	7,363	(d)	...	Inc. Place
Monroeville	PGH	52330	3-Sm	29,190	29,349	19,646	12,182	41,148	573,476	.0189	1,407,805	400	238,329	474	130,734	688	94,339	53,823	42,987	24	Inc. Place
Mount Lebanon	PGH	51696		32,466	33,017	25,461	13,267	49,091	826,610	.0115	246,218	70	...	...	28,550	150	55,645	18,227	(d)	...	MCD-Township
Natrona Heights	PGH	32868	4-S	10,663	10,934	15,171	4,626	32,544	161,767	.0036	174,582	50	27,762	55	2,712	14	40,941	10,752	(d)	...	CDP
New Castle	NWCS	53368	3-A	26,060	26,309	16,887	11,003	31,231	440,067	.0081	291,643	83	48,849	97	5,102	27	48,906	20,151	201,272	110	Inc. Place
New Kensington	PGH	53736	4-S	14,589	14,701	17,865	6,372	33,483	260,633	.0045	151,962	43	24,017	48	3,851	20	21,385	17,259	41,339	23	Inc. Place
Norristown	PHIL-	54656	3-S	32,320	31,282	16,705	11,995	37,048	539,919	.0094	292,466	83	25,613	51	17,813	94	78,189	35,357	113,434	62	Inc. Place
Northampton	PHIL-	54688		40,792	39,384	26,105	13,385	63,673	1,064,864	.0154	398,326	113	14,785	29	9,094	48	102,252	29,762	133,943	73	MCD-Township
North Wales	PHIL-	55512	4-Sm	3,313	3,342	28,344	1,239	62,132	93,903	.0017	77,607	22	20,959	42	14,306	75	7,201	7,303	(d)	...	Inc. Place
Oil City	OILC-F	56456	4-A	11,283	11,504	15,735	4,831	29,213	177,540	.0028	63,808	18	1,862	4	...	...	21,859	7,610	(d)	...	Inc. Place
Penn Hills	PGH	59032		44,656	46,809	17,718	18,402	38,034	791,235	.0142	506,325	144	22,989	46	2,559	13	44,573	12,051	40,186	22	MCD-Township
Philadelphia	PHIL-	60000	1-AA	1,456,998	1,517,550	14,450	567,762	29,655	21,053,750	.3663	9,981,344	2,834	794,491	1,580	1,203,647	6,335	2,107,907	1,457,217	3,997,488	2,188	Inc. Place
Pittsburgh	PGH	61000	1-AA	314,857	334,563	16,530	133,660	28,726	5,204,710	.0952	3,365,785	956	193,388	385	256,368	1,349	627,832	343,102	1,183,746	648	Inc. Place
Plymouth Township	PHIL-	61664	4-Sm	15,966	16,045	24,127	6,238	51,300	385,210	.0086	494,238	140	47,613	95	48,509	255	37,236	38,876	41,577	23	MCD-Township
Pottstown	PTSTN	62416	3-C	21,958	21,859	18,277	8,868	40,801	401,325	.0080	361,478	103	84,184	167	20,709	109	49,523	28,956	476,162	261	Inc. Place
Pottsville	PTSVL	62432	3-A	14,791	15,549	17,050	5,981	32,205	252,182	.0056	281,704	80	26,261	52	5,014	26	35,081	79,722	123,763	68	Inc. Place
Radnor	PHIL-	63264	4-Sm	31,148	30,878	37,429	9,944	73,897	1,165,831	.0153	358,933	102	13,270	26	26,724	141	103,170	30,516	144,564	79	MCD-Township
Radnor Township	PHIL-	63268		31,185	30,878	37,808	9,957	74,783	1,179,034	.0154	360,922	102	13,343	27	26,872	141	103,741	30,685	(d)	...	CDP
Reading	READ	63624	2-A	83,596	81,207	13,879	30,840	27,602	1,160,255	.0205	557,781	158	24,247	48	110,891	584	81,258	61,663	1,893,280	1,037	Inc. Place
Ridley Township	PHIL-	64800		31,032	30,791	18,682	11,630	44,188	579,749	.0111	461,206	131	37,302	74	11,656	61	178,900	44,354	(d)	...	MCD-Township
Ross	PGH	66264	4-S	31,729	32,551	21,680	13,412	44,240	687,887	.0137	652,136	185	143,761	286	66,805	352	111,330	34,544	(d)	...	MCD-Township
Scranton	SCR-	69000	2-A	73,981	76,415	15,170	31,005	28,188	1,122,284	.0244	1,128,531	320	197,239	392	117,732	620	191,403	85,202	340,419	186	Inc. Place
Shamokin		69600	4-B	7,448	8,009	12,639	3,556	20,989	94,137	.0022	107,581	31	3,402	7	2,088	11	16,908	18,395	(d)	...	Inc. Place
Sharon	SHAR	69720	3-A	16,335	16,328	15,813	7,015	26,424	258,300	.0057	272,780	77	40,475	80	40,388	213	27,599	33,380	132,316	72	Inc. Place
Springfield	PHIL-	73032	3-Sm	23,862	23,677	23,370	8,258	57,813	557,645	.0139	874,860	248	148,260	295	102,329	539	90,001	42,599	(d)	...	MCD-Township
State College	STCOL	73808	3-A	37,681	38,420	12,995	12,005	28,541	489,672	.0119	603,554	171	114,012	227	58,209	306	71,134	33,140	172,952	95	Inc. Place
Stroudsburg		74888	3-A	6,092	5,756	21,783	2,375	41,919	132,703	.0029	160,847	46	31,564	63	9,404	49	21,173	8,838	(d)	...	Inc. Place
Sunbury		75304	4-A	10,293	10,610	15,696	4,513	30,668	161,557	.0037	184,947	53	6,516	13	1,915	10	28,103	13,486	125,470	69	Inc. Place
Swatara Township	HRBG	75672	4-S	23,362	22,611	19,312	9,367	41,266	451,169	.0096	476,292	135	97,875	195	36,705	193	18,924	21,681	84,204	46	MCD-Township
Uniontown	UNTN	78528	3-C	12,530	12,422	15,405	5,659	25,501	193,020	.0050	285,703	81	90,032	179	15,947	84	27,900	20,595	125,513	69	Inc. Place
Upper Darby	PHIL-	79000	3-S	82,461	81,821	17,425	31,153	39,799	1,436,850	.0249	801,925	228	69,484	138	37,543	198	186,256	81,647	(d)	...	MCD-Township
Upper Merion Township	PHIL-	79136	3-Sm	27,151	26,863	26,563	11,249	56,478	721,202	.0231	1,765,553	501	471,546	938	416,910	2,194	101,908	79,616	743,921	407	MCD-Township
Upper St. Clair	PGH	79274	4-Sm	19,941	20,053	32,638	6,867	71,230	650,842	.0106	421,165	120	106,774	212	72,967	384	24,005	20,181	(d)	...	MCD-Township
Warminster	PHIL-	80952	4-Sr	31,738	31,383	21,847	11,399	52,264	693,391	.0139	669,530	190	70,532	140	24,816	131	100,067	23,068	281,222	154	MCD-Township
Warren		81000	4-B	9,788	10,259	20,615	4,552	33,979	201,779	.0075	593,849	169	50,624	101	15,764	83	27,185	9,116	267,826	147	Inc. Place
Washington	WASH	81328	3-C	15,896	15,268	17,685	6,627	33,452	281,120	.0053	203,763	58	27,817	55	13,634	72	33,783	10,655	384,068	210	Inc. Place
Waynesboro	HAG	81824	4-C	9,726	9,614	21,315	4,356	36,716	207,314	.0031	80,748	23	7,109	14	...	...	15,253	8,096	130,961	72	Inc. Place
West Chester	PHIL-	82704	4-S	17,874	17,861	27,000	6,083	62,438	482,601	.0150	1,123,665	319	7,393	15	3,127	16	41,889	16,206	221,308	121	Inc. Place
West Mifflin	PGH	83512	3-Sm	21,765	22,464	15,763	9,122	35,083	343,084	.0109	755,773	215	251,644	500	36,688	193	147,503	21,526	327,381	179	Inc. Place
Wilkes Barre	SCR-	85152	3-BB	41,202	43,123	14,735	16,833	28,261	607,106	.0170	1,044,928	297	225,041	448	77,541	408	143,203	60,009	241,438	132	Inc. Place
Williamsport	WMSPT	85312	3-A	30,147	30,706	16,629	12,408	28,903	501,311	.0108	511,748	145	35,838	71	16,201	85	102,941	46,332	587,735	322	Inc. Place
Wyomissing	READ	86880	4-Sm	8,910	8,587	35,954	3,468	55,518	320,353	.0065	368,983	105	73,748	147	104,640	551	31,960	21,291	206,410	113	Inc. Place
York	YORK	87048	3-AA	41,172	40,862	19,265	16,037	35,043	793,172	.0135	449,608	128	47,106	94	17,662	93	64,156	30,518	1,257,244	688	Inc. Place
Rhode Island																					
Coventry	PROV-	18640		35,069	33,668	20,330	13,020	47,163	712,968	.0103	209,573	60	28,892	57	...	...	45,703	24,839	...	...	MCD-Town
Cranston	PROV-	19180	4-S	81,669	79,269	17,735	30,127	40,335	1,448,377	.0257	888,473	252	29,038	58	124,251	654	92,424	79,204	523,274	286	Inc. Place
Cumberland	PROV-	20080		33,209	31,840	20,020	12,015	49,450	664,829	.0107	315,246	90	87,718	174	20,469	108	93,107	20,234	92,384	51	MCD-Town
East Providence	PROV-	22960	4-S	49,475	48,688	16,977	19,721	36,678	839,939	.0162	657,242	187	21,336	42	51,017	269	101,352	41,807	328,540	180	Inc. Place
Newport	NWPT	49960	3-C	26,693	26,475	23,805	12,057	38,855	635,423	.0115	486,087	138	17,887	36	69,510	366	114,286	76,979	(d)	...	Inc. Place
North Providence	PROV-	51760		33,104	32,411	17,795	13,840	34,064	589,075	.0107	392,226	111	14,768	29	13,299	70	75,907	38,583	62,544	34	MCD-Town
Pawtucket	PROV-	54640	3-BB	75,407	72,958	15,096	29,310	30,552	1,138,372	.0199	575,623	163	51,366	102	15,077	79	126,117	69,802	682,512	374	Inc. Place
Providence	PROV-	59000	2-AA	188,570	173,618	14,381	64,037	28,485	2,711,758	.0466	1,204,794	342	26,080	52	96,481	508	280,280	145,687	739,896	405	Inc. Place
South Kingstown	PROV-	67460		30,153	27,921	21,334	10,079	51,711	643,286	.0106	346,272	98	5,620	11	10,649	56	63,895	50,777	224,186	123	MCD-Town
Warwick	PROV-	74300	3-CC	87,724	85,808	22,153	36,097	43,192	1,943,390	.0371	1,672,541	475	318,979	634	131,573	692	171,634	159,631	611,016	335	Inc. Place
Westerly	N.LON-	77000	4-S	23,329	22,966	23,566	9,627	41,261	549,761	.0105	484,544	138	58,629	117	12,247	64	109,909	32,469	71,213	39	MCD-Town
West Warwick	PROV-	78440		30,077	29,581	19,390	12,640	37,303	583,198	.0106	416,788	118	1,317	3	8,255	43	23,990	50,177	95,186	52	MCD-Town
Woonsocket	PROV-	80780	3-S	43,654	43,224	13,745	16,898	29,671	600,011	.0126	518,237	147	44,944	89	26,222	138	134,871	115,016	169,199	93	Inc. Place
South Carolina																					
Aiken	AUG	00550	4-C	27,604	25,337	19,772	10,931	39,359	545,795	.0095	338,190	96	75,842	151	15,524	82	52,055	25,000	652,632	357	Inc. Place
Anderson	AND	01360	3-A	24,820	25,514	18,988	10,149	35,229	471,285	.0105	549,291	156	111,201	221	38,406	202	62,049	32,330	962,649	527	Inc. Place
Charleston	CHAS	13330	2-A	106,231	96,650	17,700	41,509	34,216	1,880,331	.0379	1,686,142	479	283,115	563	218,944	1,152	254,727	93,142	362,268	198	Inc. Place
Columbia	COL	16000	2-AA	118,299	116,278	17,152	44,363	32,856	2,029,122	.0424	1,967,768	559	420,995	837	159,738	841	205,340	110,101	763,766	418	Inc. Place
Florence	FLO	25810	3-A	30,506	30,248	17,850	11,574	35,981	544,540	.0118	587,678	167	121,170	241	33,673	177	64,059	33,381	343,276	188	Inc. Place
Goose Creek	CHAS	29815		31,911	29,208	15,208	9,788	40,949	485,302	.0072	98,792	28	1,855	4	1,499	8	39,508	8,829	388,649	213	Inc. Place
Greenville	GRNV	30850	2-A	54,857	56,002	20,000	22,782	33,908	1,097,137	.0302	1,992,232	566	312,023	621	176,014	926	120,574	94,524	1,955,952	1,071	Inc. Place
Greenwood	GREEN	30895	3-A	22,083	22,071	15,592	8,297	32,210	344,326	.0076	362,166	103	80,646	160	20,624	109	66,533	23,450	581,116	318	Inc. Place
Hilton Head Island		34045		38,072	33,862	31,923	16,206	55,500	1,215,358	.0194	733,289	208	136,442	271	108,153	569	134,187	35,795	(d)	...	Inc. Place
Mount Pleasant	CHAS	48535		52,845	47,609	22,764	19,566	53,661	1,202,977	.0183	498,149	141	98,446	196	35,609	187	110,514	30,696	(d)	...	Inc. Place
Myrtle Beach	MYR.B	49075	3-A	23,504	22,759	22,950	10,777	34,843	539,409	.0168	1,237,040	351	267,190	531	201,420	1,060	105,223	52,348	...	...	Inc. Place
North Charleston	CHAS	50875	3-S	82,553	79,641	12,157	28,605	29,854	1,003,556	.0258	1,353,686	384	281,787	560	73,536	387	94,252	39,338	573,669	314	Inc. Place
Orangeburg		53080	3-A	11,827	12,765	13,064	4,260	28,345	154,511	.0041	231,963	66	45,063	90	12,214	64	33,454	15,901	293,434	161	Inc. Place
Rock Hill	CHRLT	61405	3-C	56,260	49,765	19,529	21,690	39,268	1,098,698	.0197	742,555	211	112,406	224	32,574	171	114,503	37,567	420,258	230	Inc. Place
Spartanburg	SPRT	68290	3-BB	38,163	39,673	18,082	14,881	32,493	690,072	.0145	697,141	198	154,665	308	33,748	178	66,374	54,808	754,617	413	Inc. Place
Summerville	CHAS	70270		33,949	27,752	18,789	12,095	42,335	637,864	.0109	356,522	101	95,029	189	3,838	20	69,652	21,227	114,427	63	Inc. Place
Sumter	SUMT	70405	3-A	38,359	39,643	14,815	13,874	30,645	568,288	.0132	661,072	188	118,389	235	41,465	218	79,168	35,560	810,636	444	Inc. Place
South Dakota																					
Aberdeen		00100	3-A	23,864	24,658	18,378	10,577	33,136	438,584	.0122	799,416	227	49,485	98	6,743	35	39,615	3,329	...	...	Inc. Place
Huron		31060	4-A	11,002	11,893	16,903	5,156	28,645	185,969	.0043	223,541	63	8,060	16	6,465	34	7,622	10,029	...	...	Inc. Place
Mitchell		43100	4-A	14,387	14,558	17,064	6,211	31,418	245,498	.0064	390,996	111	68,101	135	9,022	47	24,661	8,904	192,540	105	Inc. Place
Rapid City	RAP	52980	3-A	63,322	59,607	17,866	25,746	34,435	1,131,297	.0287	1,712,434	486	435,857	867	75,071	395	143,414	55,966	268,013	147	Inc. Place
Sioux Falls	SXFL	59020	3-AA	135,425	123,975	20,287	54,884	40,490	2,747,401	.0667	3,959,122	1,124	652,984	1,299	67,755	357	265,622	180,844	579,979	318	Inc. Place
Watertown		69300	4-A	20,019	20,237	17,966	8,506	34,328	359,651	.0091	548,320	156	37,649	75	20,123	106	51,465	5,514	...	...	Inc. Place
Yankton		73060	4-C	12,675	13,528	17,123	5,174	34,290	217,032	.0054	317,413	90	47,395	94	14,747	78	6,642	6,300	116,134	64	Inc. Place
Tennessee																					
Alcoa	KNOX	00540	4-S	8,137	7,734	18,691	3,516	30,992	152,090	.0099	946,000	269	132,095	263	5,337	28	59,481	37,230	...	...	Inc. Place
Athens		02320	4-C	13,723	13,220	15,768	5,610	30,847	216,378	.0052	275,265	78	62,893	125	7,547	40	41,853	13,495	303,516	166	Inc. Place
Bartlett	MEM	03440		43,732	40,543	18,004	15,026	50,868	787,332	.0135	438,578	125	107,518	214	39,322	207	34,827	29,463	59,149	32	Inc. Place
Bristol	JNSC-	08540	3-B	24,494	24,821	17,521	10,851	30,022	429,152	.0082	333,282	95	54,514	108	2,582	14	36,597	16,678	89,082	49	Inc. Place
Chattanooga	CHTN	14000	2-A	156,076	155,554	17,282	62,755	32,321	2,697,292	.0577	2,783,247	790	409,023	813	216,226	1,138	293,615	190,085	1,844,947	1,010	Inc. Place
Clarksville	CLRKV	15160	3-A	111,150	103,455	17,610	42,525	36,218	1,957,388	.0356	1,304,376	370	393,426	782	61,842	325	74,291	34,357	688,667	377	Inc. Place
Cleveland	CLEV	15400	3-A	38,471	37,192	17,240	15,901	31,722	663,251	.0137	621,396	176	122,403	243	20,605	108	66,914	45,776	1,440,780	789	Inc. Place
Collierville	MEM	16420		34,537	31,872	25,056	11,364	69,394	865,362	.0127	334,905	95	72,751	145	5,663	30	30,396	15,571	188,553	103	Inc. Place
Columbia		16540	4-C	35,333	33,055	20,489	14,217	38,791	723,926	.0128	479,233	136	102,197	203	25,897	136	56,791	24,873	...	...	Inc. Place
Cookeville		16920	3-A	25,634	23,923	14,990	10,489	28,400	384,244	.0096	526,010	149	129,105	257	28,602	151	61,279	21,951	605,190	331	Inc. Place
Dyersburg		22200	4-A	17,615	17,452	17,137	7,363	30,987	301,862	.0062	276,500	79	72,186	144	18,908	100	31,492	13,290	338,169	185	Inc. Place
Elizabethton	JNSC-	23500	4-S	13,395	13,372	13,700	5,374	26,645	183,514	.0041	191,979	55	45,166	90	4,366	23	32,724	10,120	118,140	65	Inc. Place
Franklin	NASH	27740		62,018	41,842	27,199	23,294	60,628	1,686,814	.0306	1,383,907	393	286,740	570	104,844	552	130,594	54,878	299,224	164	Inc. Place
Germantown	MEM	28960		37,345	37,348	35,627	13,377	80,746	1,330,498	.0181	468,657	133	96,485	192	68,850	362	73,280	46,501	(d)	...	Inc. Place
Goodlettsville	NASH	29920	4-Sm	13,711	13,780	19,004	5,425	42,618	260,557	.0059	315,494	90	100,381	200	43,246	228	26,738	13,338	(d)	...	Inc. Place
Greeneville		30980	4-C	15,113	15,198	17,116	6,718	28,452	258,671	.0057	291,020	83	58,347	116	9,947	52	55,088	26,125	343,548	188	Inc. Place
Hendersonville	NASH	33280		44,453	40,620	24,315	17,432	47,118	1,080,890	.0152	325,466	92	26,326	52	8,343	44	78,525	39,835	78,734	43	Inc. Place
Jackson	JAC	37640	3-A	64,212	59,643	18,023	26,234	34,227	1,157,285	.0243	1,167,972	332	269,031	535	79,273	417	111,290	68,095	...	...	Inc. Place
Johnson City	JNSC-	38320	3-B	58,172	55,469	16,575	24,748	29,335	964,174	.0216	1,085,650	308	239,995	477	99,905	526	81,683	70,768	444,653	243	Inc. Place
Kingsport	JNSC-	39560	3-AA	46,066	44,905	18,035	20,855	31,074	830,778	.0177	869,266	247	250,923	499	35,597	187	83,971	54,500	...	...	Inc. Place
Knoxville	KNOX	40000	2-AA	181,674	173,890	16,817	79,893	29,478	3,055,211	.0734	4,055,548	1,152	586,051	1,165	212,105	1,116	412,287	226,119	1,060,551	581	Inc. Place
Lebanon		41520	4-C	22,722	20,235	19,984	8,907	38,102	454,065	.0088	389,268	111	99,594	198	9,514	50	58,424	10,845	318,155	174	Inc. Place
Maryville	KNOX	46380	4-C	24,987	23,120	17,643	9,359	37,013	440,836	.0079	274,537	78	43,128	86	7,037	37	46,111	23,341	523,202	286	Inc. Place
Memphis	MEM	48000	2-AA	669,066	650,100	16,316	260,938	32,627	10,916,753	.2161	8,930,602	2,536	1,239,754	2,465	580,141	3,053	866,680	700,295	3,593,510	1,967	Inc. Place
Morristown	MORR	50280	3-C	25,484	24,965	16,734	10,734	30,273	426,445	.0100	542,453	154	84,096	167	23,820	125	57,124	35,134	896,655	491	Inc. Place
Murfreesboro	MUR	51560	3-C	88,210	68,816	20,976	35,295	37,740	1,850,291	.0310	1,053,937	299	235,111	468	35,966	189	138,850	41,651	661,302	362	Inc. Place
Nashville	NASH	52006	2-AA	551,402	545,524	19,467	223,636	38,382	10,733,948	.2243	11,008,212	3,126	1,515,290	3,013	589,626	3,103	1,100,310	763,341	...	...	Inc. Place
Oak Ridge	KNOX	55120	3-C	27,503	27,387	23,529	12,259	39,389	647,127	.0126	605,593	172	88,449	176	26,901	142	76,310	47,321	774,483	424	Inc. Place
Paris		56720	4-C	9,279	9,763	17,452	4,255	28,594	161,934	.0036	187,335	53	54,864	109	4,934	26	26,351	7,651	142,382	78	Inc. Place
Union City		75940	4-B	11,040	10,876	18,536	4,736	32,843	204,633	.0044	218,430	62	76,139	151	18,418	97	9,276	6,230	595,958	326	Inc. Place
Texas																					
Abilene	ABIL	01000	3-AA	117,535	115,930	15,745	43,955	32,284	1,850,580	.0381	1,651,025	469	373,165	742	60,624	319	180,871	70,214	519,341	284	Inc. Place
Addison	D-FW	01240	4-Sr	14,756	14,166	30,111	7,248	46,022	444,322	.0076	326,747	93	49,145	98	9,104	48	47,077	9,135	48,687	27	Inc. Place
Allen	D-FW	01924		59,143	43,554	25,731	18,654	72,915	1,521,813	.0205	388,599	110	53,078	106	9,675	51	116,941	6,052	57,494	31	Inc. Place
Amarillo	AMA	03000	2-A	179,315	173,627	16,594	68,945	34,177	2,975,483	.0593	2,504,465	711	374,653	745	128,940	679	244,600	124,211	...	...	Inc. Place
Arlington	D-FW	04000	2-S	377,827	332,969	18,916	131,743	45,607	7,147,156	.1357	5,647,919	1,604	676,859	1,346	323,786	1,704	663,882	231,584	1,374,814	753	Inc. Place
Atascocita	HOU	04462		39,046	35,757	18,749	11,479	61,030	732,092	.0107	201,443	57	44,148	88	6,666	35	64,762	6,614	(d)	...	CDP
Austin	AUS	05000	2-AA	709,517	656,562	20,857	283,457	43,672	14,798,442	.3643	22,044,179	6,260	1,609,364	3,201	648,958	3,416	1,886,787	1,095,864	10,541,882	5,771	Inc. Place
Bay City		05984	4-C	18,197	18,667	14,625	6,703	31,103	266,139	.0052	198,334	56	26,903	54	10,178	54	48,924	9,212	(d)	...	Inc. Place
Baytown	HOU	06128	3-S	69,956	66,430	15,820	23,608	40,190	1,106,727	.0191	555,489	158	127,073	253	38,441	202	76,149	25,735	...	...	Inc. Place
Beaumont	B-PA	07000	2-A	110,037	113,866	18,004	44,476	34,003	1,981,150	.0410	1,919,632	545	355,125	706	125,825	662	199,470	135,721	1,210,461	663	Inc. Place
Bedford	D-FW	07132		48,351	47,152	24,463	19,320	50,113	1,182,829	.0183	556,571	158	71,580	142	8,590	45	92,833	34,520	...	...	Inc. Place
Big Spring		08236	3-A	25,965	25,233	12,583	8,695	29,097	326,706	.0068	259,231	74	47,293	94	7,757	41	30,933	12,433	...	...	Inc. Place
Borger		09556	4-C	13,124	14,302	19,315	5,463	34,207	253,490	.0042	135,498	38	24,222	48	7,783	41	27,381	7,241	(d)	...	Inc. Place
Brownsville	BRNS	10768	3-AA	155,791	139,722	7,353	37,638	23,518	1,145,498	.0305	1,178,218	335	318,271	633	97,931	515	231,063	42,434	443,267	243	Inc. Place
Brownwood		10780	4-A	18,461	18,813	13,905	6,907	28,281	256,705	.0058	277,993	79	71,312	142	7,526	40	23,490	16,753	476,667	261	Inc. Place
Bryan	BRY-	10912	3-A	65,889	65,660	13,647	26,089	31,799	899,164	.0200	912,928	259	129,993	259	15,013	79	106,025	17,622	134,588	74	Inc. Place
Carrollton	D-FW	13024	4-S	119,002	109,576	23,757	38,567	56,567	2,827,089	.0447	1,421,079	404	186,894	372	43,227	228	225,039	103,665	1,362,395	746	Inc. Place
Cedar Hill	D-FW	13492		35,781	32,093	16,977	10,955	53,344	607,448	.0093	190,723	54	33,158	66	1,822	10	48,837	6,009	(d)	...	Inc. Place
Cedar Park	AUS	13552		39,272	26,049	22,849	11,966	61,090	897,344	.0143	456,670	130	152,439	303	51,216	270	30,578	58,278	...	...	Inc. Place
Channelview	HOU	14236		32,419	29,685	13,078	9,590	39,704	423,963	.0072	152,989	43	10,773	21	4,175	22	26,650	17,709	(d)	...	CDP
Cleburne	D-FW	15364	4-S	28,365	26,005	17,139	9,472	36,907	486,141	.0095	389,813	111	78,780	157	11,896	63	36,005	14,494	288,797	158	Inc. Place
College Station	BRY-	15976	3-B	70,334	67,890	13,697	28,054	26,565	963,335	.0202	831,835	236	233,585	465	82,848	436	106,015	26,948	(d)	...	Inc. Place
Conroe		16432	3-S	39,648	36,811	11,862	10,843	34,120	470,310	.0189	1,422,159	404	295,774	588	45,091	237	141,074	31,652	321,502	176	Inc. Place
Coppell	D-FW	16612		39,815	35,958	28,155	12,355	80,889	1,120,987	.0149	289,807	82	...	...	3,402	18	91,933	17,657	(d)	...	Inc. Place
Corpus Christi	CRPX	17000	2-A	278,068	277,454	15,812	97,704	35,609	4,396,811	.0877	3,602,354	1,023	686,210	1,365	189,224	996	522,557	153,346	...	...	Inc. Place

Source: Devonshire Associates Ltd. and Scan/US, Inc. 2005.
* Source: 1997 Census of Manufactures.
Not classified as a Principal Business Center.

...Data less than 1,000.
(d) Data not available.

Continued on next page

Principal Business Centers and Other Places with 30,000 or More: Population/Income/Sales, *Continued*

Place Name	Ranally Metro Area	FIPS Place Code	Ranally City Rating	Population Estimate 7/1/05	Population Census 4/1/00	Per Capita Income 2004	Households Estimate 7/1/05	Median Household Income 2004	Disposable Income 2004 ($1,000)	Market Ability Index 2004	Total Retail Sales 2004 Sales ($1,000)	Total Retail Sales Ranally Sales Units	General Merchandise 2004 Sales ($1,000)	General Merchandise Ranally Sales Units	Apparel Store 2004 Sales ($1,000)	Apparel Store Ranally Sales Units	Food Store Sales 2004 ($1,000)	Health & Drug Store 2004 ($1,000)	Manufacturers Value Added 1997* ($1,000)	Manufacturers Ranally Mfg. Units	Place Type
Corsicana		17060	4-C	25,448	24,485	13,049	8,516	28,583	332,072	.0077	364,050	103	57,497	114	20,788	109	52,303	13,445	...	...	Inc. Place
Dallas	D-FW	19000	1-AA	1,264,288	1,188,580	17,954	439,885	37,629	22,698,485	.4283	17,108,998	4,858	2,233,769	4,442	1,224,928	6,447	1,974,764	564,763	9,756,190	5,341	Inc. Place
Del Rio		19792	4-B	34,977	33,867	11,004	10,863	27,615	384,904	.0085	333,258	95	72,812	145	20,052	106	66,205	5,319	(d)	...	Inc. Place
Denison	SHRM-	19900	4-B	21,973	22,773	18,048	8,524	33,540	396,578	.0078	341,384	97	74,473	148	6,008	32	35,991	11,951	463,961	254	Inc. Place
Denton	DENT	19972	3-S	93,660	80,537	17,094	32,564	35,866	1,600,982	.0317	1,346,912	382	329,806	656	47,894	252	232,836	85,942	519,941	285	Inc. Place
Desoto	D-FW	20092		39,142	37,646	18,650	13,026	52,078	729,980	.0123	394,443	112	24,841	49	29,116	153	156,035	22,500	(d)	...	Inc. Place
Duncanville	D-FW	21628	4-Sr	35,891	36,081	17,863	11,733	47,757	641,107	.0123	500,583	142	122,731	244	10,623	56	67,418	17,401	146,646	80	Inc. Place
Eagle Pass		21892	4-A	24,631	22,413	8,376	7,495	21,126	206,308	.0050	181,564	52	42,412	84	27,242	143	52,476	5,859	...	...	Inc. Place
Edinburg	MCAL	22660	4-C	60,235	48,465	8,752	16,985	25,534	527,204	.0112	297,665	85	55,416	110	11,287	59	63,103	10,212	236,144	129	Inc. Place
El Paso	ELP	24000	2-AA	602,267	563,662	12,642	191,117	32,127	7,614,112	.1613	6,393,016	1,815	1,520,108	3,023	464,781	2,446	679,253	304,151	3,115,892	1,706	Inc. Place
Euless	D-FW	24768		49,693	46,005	20,129	19,276	44,683	1,000,249	.0161	480,785	137	2,465	5	22,771	120	116,481	19,695	68,365	37	Inc. Place
Flower Mound	D-FW	26232		67,419	50,702	27,292	19,484	80,990	1,839,986	.0226	241,848	69	...	...	3,736	20	148,286	34,812	(d)	...	Inc. Place
Fort Hood	KILL-	26736		36,213	33,711	6,426	6,518	31,411	232,714	.0045	2,959	1	...	...	...	...	...	...	(d)	...	CDP
Fort Worth	D-FW	27000	2-BB	623,477	534,694	16,148	211,843	36,324	10,067,756	.2012	8,402,967	2,386	855,131	1,701	375,551	1,977	954,407	369,404	5,885,255	3,222	Inc. Place
Friendswood	HOU	27648	4-Sm	32,216	29,037	25,440	11,554	62,187	819,564	.0124	360,561	102	108,645	216	48,052	253	67,537	36,684	(d)	...	Inc. Place
Frisco	D-FW	27684		54,501	33,714	28,228	18,853	69,275	1,538,457	.0195	287,860	82	3,548	7	3,694	19	73,892	24,193	84,976	47	Inc. Place
Galveston	GLV-	28068	3-C	56,763	57,247	18,818	24,344	29,607	1,068,165	.0172	476,667	135	70,083	139	35,050	184	112,633	35,645	24,149	13	Inc. Place
Garland	D-FW	29000	3-S	226,153	215,768	15,254	70,178	45,267	3,449,640	.0632	2,110,730	599	439,602	874	51,255	270	301,908	98,943	1,467,003	803	Inc. Place
Georgetown	AUS	29336		31,496	28,339	24,007	10,654	54,072	756,114	.0120	392,509	111	19,688	39	3,426	18	109,392	16,096	...	...	Inc. Place
Grand Prairie	D-FW	30464	4-S	139,132	127,427	15,126	43,767	44,121	2,104,551	.0419	1,672,589	475	189,995	378	13,820	73	176,968	73,960	1,121,505	614	Inc. Place
Grapevine	D-FW	30644		45,765	42,059	25,836	15,897	62,250	1,182,379	.0239	1,236,617	351	85,449	170	164,827	868	155,438	24,684	139,495	76	Inc. Place
Greenville		30920	4-C	25,184	23,960	17,042	9,081	36,003	429,176	.0085	365,066	104	92,523	184	19,820	104	46,323	21,074	146,685	80	Inc. Place
Haltom City	D-FW	31928		42,083	39,018	16,513	14,953	40,104	694,904	.0135	538,777	153	33,079	66	3,844	20	75,406	20,796	183,132	100	Inc. Place
Harlingen	BRNS	32372	3-B	62,809	57,564	10,804	18,339	28,620	678,566	.0168	776,450	220	137,971	274	46,105	243	121,699	32,327	229,228	125	Inc. Place
Houston	HOU	35000	1-AA	2,136,305	1,953,631	17,263	749,999	37,569	36,879,617	.7013	27,773,194	7,886	3,768,904	7,495	1,981,043	10,427	4,114,442	1,455,408	13,318,807	7,292	Inc. Place
Humble	HOU	35348	4-S	15,757	14,579	15,568	5,636	40,797	245,307	.0093	717,355	204	248,067	493	54,656	288	29,163	15,407	57,767	32	Inc. Place
Huntsville		35528	4-C	35,000	35,078	11,826	10,546	30,490	413,913	.0095	416,525	118	93,505	186	20,290	107	38,179	21,072	(d)	...	Inc. Place
Hurst	D-FW	35576	3-Sm	37,646	36,273	20,747	13,585	49,544	781,035	.0187	1,101,953	313	242,115	481	81,405	428	136,457	42,529	48,617	27	Inc. Place
Irving	D-FW	37000	3-S	200,225	191,615	18,724	72,982	42,898	3,749,025	.0805	4,042,015	1,148	439,633	874	153,050	806	288,261	144,623	1,256,787	688	Inc. Place
Jacksonville		37216	4-C	14,175	13,868	12,736	4,935	27,648	180,538	.0038	154,980	44	51,465	102	4,785	25	14,383	5,208	141,924	78	Inc. Place
Keller	D-FW	38632		34,556	27,345	23,439	10,377	65,981	809,968	.0105	128,279	36	2,110	4	...	...	54,667	5,478	(d)	...	Inc. Place
Kerrville		39040	4-C	20,974	20,425	17,937	8,656	32,275	376,212	.0081	401,559	114	65,504	130	24,808	131	127,549	26,600	33,970	19	Inc. Place
Killeen	KILL-	39148	3-B	96,187	86,911	15,663	37,478	34,579	1,506,559	.0279	972,753	276	142,198	283	40,849	215	119,718	13,909	(d)	...	Inc. Place
Lake Jackson	L.JAC-	40588	3-C	27,697	26,386	25,207	9,894	54,885	698,164	.0120	476,512	135	228,130	454	23,238	122	17,308	25,188	(d)	...	Inc. Place
La Porte	HOU	41440		34,307	31,880	17,269	11,261	51,940	592,440	.0101	305,076	87	5,443	11	5,580	29	66,840	21,227	785,420	430	Inc. Place
Laredo	LAR	41464	3-AA	201,702	176,576	9,400	53,394	28,580	1,896,026	.0498	2,311,202	656	516,539	1,027	253,224	1,333	354,245	103,374	...	...	Inc. Place
League City	HOU	41980		54,268	45,444	23,507	19,950	57,989	1,275,669	.0181	388,928	110	4,177	8	3,815	20	110,014	20,500	(d)	...	Inc. Place
Lewisville	D-FW	42508		94,217	77,737	22,972	33,010	51,925	2,164,391	.0446	2,283,149	648	533,595	1,061	189,933	1,000	136,391	136,184	617,939	338	Inc. Place
Longview	LNGV	43888	3-AA	75,614	73,344	16,920	28,579	34,052	1,279,359	.0294	1,548,714	440	316,640	630	68,522	361	179,074	55,304	1,249,706	684	Inc. Place
Lubbock	LUB	45000	2-A	207,716	199,564	16,254	84,177	31,777	3,376,230	.0702	3,152,093	895	536,024	1,066	176,790	930	425,800	104,309	828,864	454	Inc. Place
Lufkin	LUFK	45072	3-A	32,042	32,709	16,146	12,176	32,818	517,335	.0114	553,029	157	140,487	279	20,892	110	79,280	18,618	283,175	155	Inc. Place
Mansfield	D-FW	46452		36,975	28,031	19,807	10,893	60,097	732,358	.0106	208,643	59	57,826	115	1,616	9	56,436	8,055	180,286	99	Inc. Place
Marshall	MAR	46776	4-B	22,663	23,935	14,346	8,384	29,089	325,125	.0068	286,542	81	65,104	129	15,885	84	37,821	12,119	105,716	58	Inc. Place
McAllen	MCAL	45384	2-A	121,404	106,414	12,320	36,482	32,551	1,495,739	.0440	2,679,506	761	739,318	1,470	317,827	1,673	274,205	139,303	260,836	143	Inc. Place
McKinney	D-FW	45744		101,539	54,369	23,818	32,775	62,570	2,418,478	.0379	1,178,005	334	152,475	303	24,259	128	168,963	40,979	720,084	394	Inc. Place
Mesquite	D-FW	47892	3-Sm	132,562	124,523	15,333	42,724	45,671	2,032,527	.0512	2,885,259	819	804,294	1,599	239,800	1,262	217,175	147,951	739,695	405	Inc. Place
Midland	MIDL-	48072	3-AA	98,355	94,996	17,427	35,935	38,283	1,714,017	.0345	1,526,954	434	269,454	536	77,354	407	185,104	54,775	77,473	42	Inc. Place
Mission	MCAL	48768		54,662	45,408	8,646	15,977	23,714	472,615	.0101	264,744	75	55,234	110	6,817	36	51,217	8,579	88,371	48	Inc. Place
Mission Bend	HOU	48772		39,975	30,831	14,830	10,167	50,285	592,844	.0107	338,855	96	84,501	168	4,615	24	63,655	15,633	(d)	...	CDP
Missouri City	HOU	48804		60,188	52,913	20,777	16,937	62,196	1,250,521	.0182	380,863	108	106,998	213	6,250	33	102,504	31,766	75,115	41	Inc. Place
Mount Pleasant		49800	4-C	13,979	13,935	13,372	4,513	30,782	186,930	.0048	259,382	74	64,898	129	11,321	60	23,822	16,509	178,062	97	Inc. Place
Nacogdoches		50256	4-B	27,576	29,914	14,044	10,774	27,705	387,270	.0083	366,599	104	70,696	141	24,767	130	55,330	14,855	232,756	127	Inc. Place
New Braunfels		50820		41,311	36,494	17,625	15,143	38,996	728,111	.0130	452,107	128	64,362	128	10,938	58	41,225	12,564	274,768	150	Inc. Place
North Richland Hills	D-FW	52356	4-S	60,541	55,635	20,608	21,031	51,121	1,247,606	.0250	1,185,275	337	117,138	233	33,436	176	84,825	56,671	233,129	128	Inc. Place
Odessa	MIDL-	53388	3-AA	93,895	90,943	14,883	35,047	30,375	1,397,395	.0290	1,231,162	350	341,368	679	41,955	221	163,126	38,419	201,812	110	Inc. Place
Orange	B-PA	54132	3-C	17,314	18,643	18,431	7,031	34,674	319,113	.0055	182,206	52	32,327	64	7,098	37	23,352	13,845	377,681	207	Inc. Place
Palestine		54708	4-C	17,847	17,598	15,099	6,740	29,851	269,468	.0053	206,442	59	60,547	120	10,623	56	13,433	10,654	48,160	26	Inc. Place
Pampa		54912	4-C	17,119	17,887	17,186	7,507	30,633	294,212	.0053	182,653	52	29,159	58	6,746	36	30,568	8,399	(d)	...	Inc. Place
Paris		55080	3-A	25,953	25,898	15,789	10,505	28,543	409,765	.0100	550,156	156	127,867	254	25,956	137	53,118	33,692	1,329,043	728	Inc. Place
Pasadena	HOU	56000	3-S	152,410	141,674	13,700	48,368	38,427	2,087,957	.0419	1,579,469	448	380,723	757	70,641	372	215,163	79,999	1,434,970	786	Inc. Place
Pearland	HOU	56348		48,135	37,640	23,500	16,592	56,893	1,131,193	.0168	441,464	125	121,866	242	18,804	99	79,268	23,724	39,435	22	Inc. Place
Pharr	MCAL	57200	4-S	54,540	46,660	8,128	14,408	23,987	443,280	.0119	510,662	145	48,896	97	18,078	95	83,403	10,640	(d)	...	Inc. Place
Plainview		57980	4-C	20,844	22,336	13,774	7,515	30,270	287,110	.0056	204,566	58	40,035	80	13,122	69	30,134	8,420	...	...	Inc. Place
Plano	D-FW	58016	3-S	236,270	222,030	34,038	83,223	70,559	8,042,087	.1309	5,290,824	1,502	921,806	1,833	403,199	2,122	670,948	212,411	1,478,608	809	Inc. Place
Port Arthur	B-PA	58820	3-B	54,950	57,755	13,920	21,537	25,783	764,887	.0154	588,387	167	81,994	163	52,412	276	100,530	39,554	1,454,445	796	Inc. Place
Richardson	D-FW	61796	3-S	97,955	91,802	23,067	34,343	57,705	2,259,511	.0435	2,022,061	574	239,193	476	98,723	520	253,294	77,534	1,883,412	1,031	Inc. Place
Rosenberg	HOU	63284	4-S	27,260	24,043	13,317	7,848	35,437	363,027	.0110	708,013	201	111,396	222	15,875	84	51,072	26,355	154,345	84	Inc. Place
Round Rock	AUS	63500		72,731	61,136	23,255	23,076	57,371	1,691,372	.0274	916,802	260	90,756	180	16,199	85	212,639	44,465	...	...	Inc. Place
Rowlett	D-FW	63572		49,665	44,503	18,725	14,575	62,183	929,962	.0133	215,894	61	9,914	20	2,362	12	78,041	12,642	33,283	18	Inc. Place
San Angelo	SANG	64472	3-AA	87,129	88,439	16,012	34,101	31,681	1,395,074	.0271	1,065,161	302	231,086	460	43,600	229	147,841	37,088	353,578	194	Inc. Place
San Antonio	SANT	65000	1-A	1,237,338	1,144,646	16,054	433,239	37,173	19,863,847	.3998	16,860,069	4,787	2,526,052	5,024	1,082,496	5,697	2,564,780	707,518	2,552,048	1,397	Inc. Place
San Juan	MCAL	65516		32,548	26,229	6,769	7,904	21,794	220,316	.0048	82,669	23	1,679	3	1,988	10	27,350	3,250	(d)	...	Inc. Place
San Marcos		65600		35,759	34,733	14,831	12,222	30,000	530,328	.0125	640,696	182	63,246	126	174,979	921	82,379	29,153	122,874	67	Inc. Place
Sherman	SHRM-	67496	3-A	35,939	35,082	17,592	13,559	34,834	632,222	.0141	722,582	205	235,874	469	21,753	114	66,114	33,912	1,681,085	920	Inc. Place
Spring	HOU	69596		39,732	36,385	16,744	12,866	51,448	665,256	.0115	362,112	103	48,446	96	9,897	52	144,994	34,333	(d)	...	CDP
Sugar Land	HOU	70808		72,884	63,328	26,391	20,644	70,552	1,923,518	.0295	922,886	262	207,713	413	65,957	347	115,870	54,464	414,019	227	Inc. Place
Temple	KILL-	72176	3-A	55,307	54,514	20,091	22,742	34,669	1,111,178	.0206	843,716	240	133,249	265	28,522	150	90,725	17,105	596,066	326	Inc. Place
Texarkana	TEXR-	72368	3-AA	35,024	34,782	18,523	13,964	35,385	648,733	.0140	702,823	200	135,947	270	55,798	294	50,980	18,631	289,887	159	Inc. Place
Texas City	GLV-	72392	3-C	42,915	41,521	16,309	16,481	34,335	699,908	.0138	563,120	160	213,411	424	27,981	147	56,801	30,922	1,632,210	894	Inc. Place
The Colony	D-FW	72530		31,295	26,531	19,193	9,044	57,225	600,638	.0087	164,978	47	66,852	133	5,655	30	46,196	9,062	(d)	...	Inc. Place
The Woodlands	HOU	72656		71,133	55,649	25,047	19,453	72,644	1,781,702	.0274	834,080	237	278,137	553	81,570	429	177,638	54,424	(d)	...	CDP
Tyler	TYL	74144	3-AA	87,433	83,650	17,856	32,757	33,984	1,561,209	.0368	2,030,996	577	342,734	682	146,171	769	215,487	107,202	996,129	545	Inc. Place
Victoria	VICT	75428	3-A	61,620	60,603	17,408	22,491	37,031	1,072,676	.0225	1,052,963	299	216,793	431	48,626	256	150,794	55,261	569,184	312	Inc. Place
Waco	WACO	76000	3-AA	119,965	113,726	13,928	44,280	28,054	1,670,821	.0371	1,702,349	483	353,717	703	80,112	422	244,188	72,997	1,987,836	1,088	Inc. Place
Weslaco	MCAL	77272		30,246	26,935	8,928	8,976	23,867	270,028	.0071	315,729	90	76,382	152	23,896	126	49,471	11,716	12,374	7	Inc. Place
Wichita Falls	WIFL	79000	3-AA	102,794	104,197	16,347	39,721	32,008	1,680,387	.0330	1,350,039	383	281,084	559	44,891	236	175,122	67,492	570,299	312	Inc. Place

Utah

Place Name	Ranally Metro Area	FIPS Place Code	Ranally City Rating	Population Estimate 7/1/05	Population Census 4/1/00	Per Capita Income 2004	Households Estimate 7/1/05	Median Household Income 2004	Disposable Income 2004 ($1,000)	Market Ability Index 2004	Total Retail Sales 2004 Sales ($1,000)	Total Retail Sales Ranally Sales Units	General Merchandise 2004 Sales ($1,000)	General Merchandise Ranally Sales Units	Apparel Store 2004 Sales ($1,000)	Apparel Store Ranally Sales Units	Food Store Sales 2004 ($1,000)	Health & Drug Store 2004 ($1,000)	Manufacturers Value Added 1997* ($1,000)	Manufacturers Ranally Mfg. Units	Place Type
Bountiful	S.L.C.	07690	4-S	44,668	41,301	23,122	14,567	49,598	1,032,796	.0174	636,015	181	60,443	120	6,672	35	92,830	29,651	26,982	15	Inc. Place
Clearfield	OGD	13850		31,863	25,974	14,815	9,788	42,206	472,048	.0074	133,425	38	3,051	6	1,085	6	40,484	2,780	297,448	163	Inc. Place
Kearns	S.L.C.	40470		34,844	33,659	14,030	9,587	45,150	488,875	.0084	213,529	61	26,375	52	1,472	8	85,549	4,539	(d)	...	CDP
Layton	OGD	43660	4-S	71,596	58,474	17,633	22,545	48,428	1,262,446	.0251	1,092,012	310	270,686	538	57,658	303	119,582	24,008	(d)	...	Inc. Place
Logan	LOGN	45860	4-A	45,734	42,670	14,376	15,714	32,243	657,478	.0146	679,147	193	184,084	366	24,860	131	86,581	15,082	283,940	155	Inc. Place
Millcreek	S.L.C.	50150		31,446	30,377	22,062	13,084	41,463	693,756	.0150	799,136	227	129,275	257	59,447	313	76,495	20,155	(d)	...	CDP
Murray	S.L.C.	53230	3-S	34,494	34,024	17,243	12,912	38,277	594,790	.0193	1,381,346	392	225,497	448	87,523	461	78,412	21,611	136,911	75	Inc. Place
Ogden	OGD	55980	3-BB	81,032	77,226	17,517	30,542	36,264	1,419,414	.0281	1,208,971	343	275,022	547	29,504	155	178,590	32,477	1,546,457	847	Inc. Place
Orem	PRVO-	57300	3-B	91,794	84,324	16,006	27,292	44,003	1,469,299	.0346	1,835,205	521	391,832	779	75,335	397	205,748	22,906	142,014	78	Inc. Place
Provo	PRVO-	62470	3-AA	113,165	105,166	13,118	33,645	32,895	1,484,508	.0295	1,050,996	298	254,728	507	57,452	302	179,310	33,735	191,371	105	Inc. Place
Roy	OGD	65110		36,076	32,885	17,688	12,450	45,501	638,102	.0098	214,000	61	...	...	4,564	24	72,568	4,549	...	...	Inc. Place
St. George		65330	4-A	61,449	49,663	15,923	21,982	35,097	978,451	.0246	1,399,679	397	196,457	391	56,222	296	135,719	27,972	107,637	59	Inc. Place
Salt Lake City	S.L.C.	67000	2-AA	180,579	181,743	19,364	71,586	36,193	3,496,687	.0712	3,359,068	954	302,320	601	163,029	858	466,055	61,064	2,306,155	1,263	Inc. Place
Sandy	S.L.C.	67440		88,548	88,418	20,441	25,918	58,543	1,809,969	.0362	1,701,507	483	431,002	857	80,815	425	168,594	28,472	187,820	103	Inc. Place
South Jordan	S.L.C.	70850		32,015	29,437	16,965	8,224	62,782	543,119	.0075	77,244	22	2,313	5	...	...	3,622	...	...	...	Inc. Place
Taylorsville	S.L.C.	75360		55,894	57,439	15,681	18,156	42,754	876,463	.0162	569,800	162	124,551	248	8,567	45	103,161	8,842	...	...	Inc. Place
Tooele		76680		31,404	22,502	17,747	10,410	43,419	557,331	.0087	208,937	59	18,664	37	1,105	6	61,731	3,900	...	...	Inc. Place
West Jordan	S.L.C.	82950		74,187	68,336	14,917	20,635	50,523	1,106,682	.0188	493,551	140	141,299	281	5,433	29	110,675	5,442	155,966	85	Inc. Place
West Valley	S.L.C.	83470	3-S	117,966	108,896	13,542	35,143	41,620	1,597,455	.0387	1,981,934	563	342,767	682	42,814	225	177,415	30,090	637,803	349	Inc. Place

Vermont

Place Name	Ranally Metro Area	FIPS Place Code	Ranally City Rating	Population Estimate 7/1/05	Population Census 4/1/00	Per Capita Income 2004	Households Estimate 7/1/05	Median Household Income 2004	Disposable Income 2004 ($1,000)	Market Ability Index 2004	Total Retail Sales 2004 Sales ($1,000)	Total Retail Sales Ranally Sales Units	General Merchandise 2004 Sales ($1,000)	General Merchandise Ranally Sales Units	Apparel Store 2004 Sales ($1,000)	Apparel Store Ranally Sales Units	Food Store Sales 2004 ($1,000)	Health & Drug Store 2004 ($1,000)	Manufacturers Value Added 1997* ($1,000)	Manufacturers Ranally Mfg. Units	Place Type
Barre		03175	4-C	9,238	9,291	19,092	4,108	34,000	176,372	.0034	148,480	42	4,614	9	5,493	29	28,007	14,945	63,395	35	Inc. Place
Bennington		04825	4-B	15,666	15,737	15,395	6,155	32,733	241,173	.0063	368,555	105	41,912	83	16,135	85	63,079	18,798	156,465	86	MCD-Town
Burlington	BUR	10675	3-AA	38,653	38,889	17,260	15,781	31,910	667,164	.0144	702,104	199	59,098	118	55,068	290	119,965	35,762	...	...	Inc. Place
Rutland		61225	3-A	17,616	17,292	18,026	7,403	32,053	317,541	.0080	472,787	134	52,479	104	31,683	167	61,786	36,781	189,099	104	Inc. Place
South Burlington	BUR	66175	4-S	16,558	15,814	23,170	6,625	48,211	383,643	.0103	690,758	196	103,860	207	23,940	126	28,695	35,580	(d)	...	Inc. Place

Virginia

Place Name	Ranally Metro Area	FIPS Place Code	Ranally City Rating	Population Estimate 7/1/05	Population Census 4/1/00	Per Capita Income 2004	Households Estimate 7/1/05	Median Household Income 2004	Disposable Income 2004 ($1,000)	Market Ability Index 2004	Total Retail Sales 2004 Sales ($1,000)	Total Retail Sales Ranally Sales Units	General Merchandise 2004 Sales ($1,000)	General Merchandise Ranally Sales Units	Apparel Store 2004 Sales ($1,000)	Apparel Store Ranally Sales Units	Food Store Sales 2004 ($1,000)	Health & Drug Store 2004 ($1,000)	Manufacturers Value Added 1997* ($1,000)	Manufacturers Ranally Mfg. Units	Place Type
Alexandria	WASH	01000	3-SS	128,132	128,283	32,416	65,709	52,722	4,153,470	.0643	2,290,886	651	311,114	619	106,628	561	256,217	138,112	194,752	107	Independent City
Annandale	WASH	01912		57,526	54,994	27,444	20,839	64,491	1,578,762	.0217	480,055	136	42,148	84	6,919	36	133,118	39,867	(d)	...	CDP
Arlington	WASH	03000	3-SS	185,858	189,453	32,500	86,155	57,737	6,040,410	.0857	2,428,168	689	378,511	753	332,014	1,747	314,640	149,013	(d)	...	CDP
Blacksburg		07784		41,698	39,573	12,695	14,502	25,077	529,339	.0094	230,838	66	...	...	6,581	35	40,860	16,539	149,272	82	Inc. Place
Bristol	JNSC-	09816	3-B	17,230	17,367	14,352	7,646	26,704	247,290	.0066	390,106	111	134,453	267	10,710	56	40,302	28,585	474,903	260	Independent City
Burke	WASH	11464		60,533	57,737	28,470	20,174	77,165	1,723,399	.0218	323,348	92	29,518	59	8,785	46	123,255	17,978	(d)	...	CDP
Centreville	WASH	14440		51,020	48,661	27,232	18,686	69,056	1,389,370	.0173	212,172	60	...	...	1,352	7	118,862	8,614	(d)	...	CDP
Chantilly	WASH	14744		43,030	41,041	29,382	15,589	71,931	1,264,310	.0250	1,309,380	372	416,010	827	139,674	735	110,167	28,832	(d)	...	CDP
Charlottesville	CHRLTV	14968	3-AA	36,403	45,049	16,410	16,513	29,818	597,360	.0171	1,112,758	316	84,794	169	81,811	431	217,859	56,252	...	...	Independent City
Chesapeake	NORF-	16000	3-S	215,873	199,184	19,324	73,909	46,396	4,171,500	.0787	3,276,187	930	846,522	1,683	172,362	907	315,585	124,193	336,679	184	Independent City
Dale City	WASH	21088		70,223	55,971	21,615	22,159	60,606	1,517,869	.0198	215,620	61	38,484	77	6,055	32	49,659	5,805	(d)	...	CDP
Danville	DANV	21344	3-A	46,092	48,411	13,830	20,021	26,278	637,430	.0147	707,238	201	147,506	293	21,857	115	87,811	49,827	...	...	Independent City
Fairfax	WASH	26496	3-SS	22,200	21,498	28,664	8,468	61,840	636,330	.0234	1,927,229	547	128,819	256	91,348	481	186,146	61,419	(d)	...	Independent City
Falls Church	WASH	27200	3-S	10,716	10,377	32,569	4,324	66,604	349,010	.0081	510,751	145	11,591	23	11,038	58	53,856	31,489	(d)	...	Independent City
Franconia	WASH	29552		33,452	31,907	31,461	13,936	69,484	1,052,420	.0130	188,478	54	96,940	193	4,827	25	41,696	5,379	(d)	...	CDP
Fredericksburg	FRED	29744	3-A	20,769	19,279	15,743	8,069	32,814	326,970	.0116	865,934	246	108,676	216	48,935	258	61,450	45,844	88,499	48	Independent City
Hampton	NN-H	35000	3-BB	144,708	146,437	16,802	53,698	37,020	2,431,340	.0490	2,127,173	604	420,800	837	97,218	512	172,091	85,145	422,730	231	Independent City
Harrisonburg		35624	3-A	41,264	40,468	11,720	13,780	28,766	483,600	.0151	956,977	272	235,070	467	38,810	204	107,221	25,286	254,261	139	Independent City
Hopewell	RICH	38424	4-S	22,404	22,354	15,501	9,019	31,681	347,280	.0055	115,787	33	2,714	5	4,953	26	24,955	9,884	743,916	407	Independent City
Lake Ridge	WASH	43432		38,145	30,404	28,018	13,824	63,395	1,068,739	.0174	652,575	185	107,972	215	145,858	768	56,582	29,778	(d)	...	CDP
Leesburg	WASH	44984		34,507	28,311	30,444	12,115	66,342	1,050,518	.0164	575,555	163	96,336	192	26,710	141	101,254	32,498	(d)	...	Inc. Place
Lynchburg	LYNCH	47672	3-AA	64,615	65,269	15,188	25,910	31,385	981,370	.0264	1,586,593	451	272,942	543	57,803	304	137,909	133,853	1,602,612	877	Independent City
Manassas	WASH	48952	4-S	38,088	35,135	21,209	12,001	55,394	807,790	.0185	1,049,143	298	194,037	386	25,144	132	154,411	32,309	594,660	326	Independent City
Martinsville	MRTNV	49784	3-A	14,971	15,416	13,860	6,389	26,513	207,500	.0058	348,066	99	119,065	237	22,912	121	35,056	15,987	345,425	189	Independent City
McLean	WASH	48376		40,818	38,929	49,259	15,059	94,231	2,010,642	.0263	714,177	203	194,840	387	119,517	629	155,765	36,007	(d)	...	CDP
Mechanicsville	RICH	50856		34,762	30,464	23,926	12,952	53,379	831,726	.0129	393,318	112	79,011	157	3,155	17	93,999	29,070	(d)	...	CDP
Newport News	NN-H	56000	2-B	182,551	180,150	16,595	71,189	34,888	3,029,380	.0568	2,128,411	604	277,991	553	100,964	531	239,986	69,935	1,653,589	905	Independent City
Norfolk	NORF-	57000	2-AA	238,106	234,403	13,459	86,008	30,737	3,204,570	.0633	2,280,701	648	361,702	719	130,039	684	264,608	85,054	2,789,712	1,527	Independent City
Oakton	WASH	58472		30,771	29,348	42,289	11,654	88,180	1,301,262	.0159	300,161	85	8,863	18	17,830	94	27,899	15,229	(d)	...	CDP
Petersburg	RICH	61832	3-B	32,717	33,740	13,883	13,295	28,131	454,200	.0093	374,084	106	2,500	5	5,711	30	45,825	23,610	145,376	80	Independent City
Portsmouth	NORF-	64000	3-C	98,061	100,565	15,144	37,716	32,573	1,485,070	.0243	559,132	159	19,630	39	11,724	62	141,144	96,294	143,648	79	Independent City
Reston	WASH	66672		59,140	56,407	35,337	24,434	70,235	2,089,825	.0275	626,163	178	37,897	75	50,697	267	155,094	38,462	(d)	...	CDP
Richmond	RICH	67000	2-AA	191,700	197,790	15,549	81,933	30,215	2,980,720	.0582	2,273,802	646	157,737	314	159,049	837	381,907	185,742	8,229,631	4,505	Independent City
Roanoke	ROAN	68000	2-A	91,029	94,911	16,372	41,716	29,563	1,490,350	.0405	2,518,073	715	506,736	1,008	144,120	759	212,407	129,276	1,213,436	664	Independent City
Salem	ROAN	70000	4-S	24,289	24,747	18,210	9,937	36,316	442,310	.0104	582,392	165	50,454	100	8,422	44	88,008	21,055	555,145	304	Independent City
Springfield	WASH	74592		31,891	30,417	23,251	10,995	61,389	741,509	.0182	1,128,185	320	142,621	284	142,593	751	61,578	68,433	(d)	...	CDP
Staunton		75216	3-A	23,887	23,853	15,353	9,516	31,754	366,740	.0091	503,561	143	154,204	307	13,219	70	66,080	27,679	(d)	...	Independent City
Suffolk	NORF-	76432	4-S	79,362	63,677	16,410	27,724	38,686	1,302,310	.0217	595,794	169	102,476	204	4,758	25	87,531	22,240	539,571	295	Independent City
Tuckahoe	RICH	79560		45,439	43,242	28,762	17,155	53,789	1,306,904	.0205	710,606	202	227,846	453	132,840	699	99,301	62,175	(d)	...	CDP
Virginia Beach	NORF-	82000	2-B	447,757	425,257	19,490	160,377	44,630	8,726,910	.1461	4,702,261	1,335	626,959	1,247	309,382	1,628	678,813	207,923	380,394	208	Independent City
Waynesboro		83680	4-B	20,940	19,520	15,575	8,463	31,209	326,150	.0066	270,731	77	33,805	67	10,692	56	61,297	18,255	452,490	248	Independent City

Source: Devonshire Associates Ltd. and Scan/US, Inc. 2005.
* Source: 1997 Census of Manufactures.
Not classified as a Principal Business Center.

...Data less than 1,000.
(d) Data not available.

Principal Business Centers and Other Places with 30,000 or More: Population/Income/Sales, *Continued*

Place Name	Ranally Metro Area	FIPS Place Code	Ranally City Rating	Population: Estimate 7/1/05	Population: Census 4/1/00	Per Capita Income 2004	Households Estimate 7/1/05	Median Household Income 2004	Disposable Income 2004 ($1,000)	Market Ability Index 2004	Total Retail Sales: 2004 Sales ($1,000)	Total Retail Sales: Ranally Sales Units	General Merchandise: 2004 Sales ($1,000)	General Merchandise: Ranally Sales Units	Apparel Store: 2004 Sales ($1,000)	Apparel Store: Ranally Sales Units	Food Store Sales 2004 ($1,000)	Health & Drug Store 2004 ($1,000)	Manufacturers: Value Added 1997* ($1,000)	Manufacturers: Ranally Mfg. Units	Place Type
Williamsburg	NN-H	86160	4-S	11,046	11,998	16,707	4,197	36,615	184,540	.0068	523,921	149	5,676	11	78,957	416	75,931	23,110	...	...	Independent City
Winchester		86720	3-A	24,730	23,585	16,908	10,413	33,158	418,130	.0135	966,374	274	296,218	589	42,132	222	110,724	52,134	791,080	433	Independent City
Woodbridge	WASH	87312		40,072	31,941	18,962	13,450	46,974	759,839	.0157	747,328	212	23,613	47	12,990	68	63,459	6,661	(d)	...	CDP
Washington																					
Aberdeen		00100	4-A	16,937	16,461	16,338	6,651	31,671	276,719	.0061	296,531	84	74,488	148	5,609	30	74,698	20,155	(d)	...	Inc. Place
Auburn	SEAT	03180	4-S	42,869	40,314	17,652	17,460	39,117	756,708	.0182	1,030,390	293	143,327	285	29,142	153	186,138	18,055	1,205,661	660	Inc. Place
Bellevue	SEAT	05210	3-SS	112,592	109,569	32,538	47,968	58,014	3,663,496	.0623	2,683,550	762	383,911	763	319,697	1,683	223,384	115,215	281,164	154	Inc. Place
Bellingham	BELNG	05280	3-A	76,238	67,171	18,320	32,299	33,748	1,396,677	.0275	1,202,693	342	267,605	532	48,969	258	211,014	59,576	235,158	129	Inc. Place
Bothell	SEAT	07380		30,405	30,150	24,321	12,237	56,236	739,475	.0127	490,248	139	...	...	18,594	98	145,743	34,898	383,068	210	Inc. Place
Bremerton	BREM	07695	3-A	35,703	37,259	17,989	14,984	34,171	642,250	.0115	408,661	116	79,755	159	2,718	14	33,701	26,210	(d)	...	Inc. Place
Burien	SEAT	08850		33,819	31,881	22,061	14,468	41,646	746,073	.0118	352,540	100	25,804	51	8,669	46	71,948	27,071	(d)	...	Inc. Place
Centralia		11160	3-B	15,652	14,742	17,613	6,254	31,508	275,682	.0050	178,701	51	...	...	17,131	90	34,134	18,836	(d)	...	Inc. Place
Edmonds	SEAT	20750		39,167	39,515	32,004	17,469	51,874	1,253,497	.0158	269,999	77	12,924	26	16,428	86	73,533	11,604	(d)	...	Inc. Place
Everett	SEAT	22640	3-CC	99,688	91,488	22,151	41,287	41,174	2,208,236	.0419	1,870,376	531	247,616	492	32,977	174	197,843	41,901	...	...	Inc. Place
Federal Way	SEAT	23515		87,058	83,259	20,233	33,451	46,517	1,761,437	.0304	1,082,435	307	351,861	700	55,526	292	155,401	28,934	46,205	25	Inc. Place
Kennewick	RICH-	35275	3-A	64,342	54,693	18,638	24,230	38,547	1,199,231	.0246	1,152,755	327	356,469	709	54,081	285	190,509	45,044	...	...	Inc. Place
Kent	SEAT	35415	4-S	83,699	79,524	19,387	33,421	43,902	1,622,712	.0308	1,297,745	368	308,352	613	21,104	111	145,533	69,684	2,503,653	1,371	Inc. Place
Kirkland	SEAT	35940	4-S	43,896	45,054	34,393	20,597	59,400	1,509,708	.0242	953,174	271	142,223	283	24,311	128	167,831	35,991	194,142	106	Inc. Place
Lacey	OLYM	36745		34,451	31,226	20,661	13,731	43,131	711,788	.0125	471,935	134	196,516	391	4,922	26	76,156	17,290	(d)	...	Inc. Place
Lakewood	SEAT	38038		60,396	58,211	19,681	24,596	35,283	1,188,630	.0211	787,998	224	186,886	372	34,339	181	131,147	45,902	33,679	18	Inc. Place
Longview	LNGV	40245	3-A	35,658	34,660	19,822	14,979	36,004	706,805	.0129	515,871	146	120,041	239	2,871	15	87,173	16,986	336,920	184	Inc. Place
Lynnwood	SEAT	40840	3-Sm	34,396	33,847	22,209	14,134	45,186	763,907	.0167	905,051	257	247,270	492	117,892	620	76,831	29,688	75,004	41	Inc. Place
Marysville	SEAT	43955		30,327	25,315	21,290	11,767	47,174	645,652	.0096	226,170	64	84,608	168	11,562	61	31,257	9,554	91,262	50	Inc. Place
Mount Vernon		47560	4-C	29,890	26,232	17,992	10,602	39,790	537,782	.0101	399,015	113	59,047	117	4,163	22	63,912	19,863	32,585	18	Inc. Place
Olympia	OLYM	51300	3-A	47,525	42,514	24,284	20,863	42,212	1,154,092	.0209	896,448	255	196,831	391	38,447	202	119,676	26,182	155,664	85	Inc. Place
Pasco	RICH-	53545	3-B	44,582	32,066	13,331	12,796	37,612	594,302	.0122	468,686	133	45,256	90	3,451	18	28,717	17,218	...	...	Inc. Place
Port Angeles		55365	4-A	18,371	18,397	19,098	8,158	34,593	350,855	.0062	228,871	65	61,565	122	6,398	34	37,848	9,904	108,889	60	Inc. Place
Puyallup	SEAT	56695	4-S	37,513	33,011	21,323	14,560	45,017	799,881	.0159	748,449	213	146,944	292	13,284	70	57,846	10,240	223,122	122	Inc. Place
Redmond	SEAT	57535	4-S	45,240	45,256	30,346	19,436	62,021	1,372,834	.0231	954,522	271	156,841	312	79,546	419	126,545	70,641	1,297,879	711	Inc. Place
Renton	SEAT	57745	3-S	53,549	50,052	24,315	23,706	47,086	1,302,045	.0289	1,634,249	464	313,913	624	15,028	79	144,218	41,201	...	...	Inc. Place
Richland	RICH-	58235	3-B	44,029	38,708	24,074	17,513	49,288	1,059,954	.0161	461,049	131	96,843	193	5,486	29	120,392	31,021	138,617	76	Inc. Place
Sammamish	SEAT	61115		35,073	34,104	37,826	11,671	86,011	1,326,683	.0139	2,311	1	...	...	...	...	1,054	...	(d)	...	Inc. Place
Seattle	SEAT	63000	1-A	574,178	563,374	25,595	268,184	42,504	14,695,840	.2498	9,786,383	2,779	618,138	1,229	708,103	3,727	1,278,568	466,574	2,722,952	1,491	Inc. Place
Shoreline	SEAT	63960		53,823	53,025	21,636	21,408	46,672	1,164,489	.0193	649,883	185	161,440	321	12,481	66	116,473	29,305	(d)	...	Inc. Place
South Hill	SEAT	65922		34,549	31,623	19,803	11,879	51,125	684,186	.0111	331,495	94	115,495	230	18,310	96	42,982	12,165	(d)	...	CDP
Spokane	SPOK	67000	2-AA	204,483	195,629	18,152	89,358	32,864	3,711,819	.0687	2,655,483	754	536,039	1,066	175,408	923	380,100	124,313	447,426	245	Inc. Place
Tacoma	SEAT	70000	2-B	215,273	193,556	18,253	84,217	36,453	3,929,278	.0741	2,983,966	847	635,797	1,264	155,038	816	339,844	118,120	1,037,083	568	Inc. Place
Tukwila	SEAT	72625	4-Sm	17,591	17,181	18,754	7,494	38,769	329,897	.0112	836,689	238	236,247	470	99,176	522	59,042	18,289	200,283	110	Inc. Place
University Place	SEAT	73465		34,329	29,933	23,671	13,867	44,837	812,619	.0107	151,803	43	19,320	38	3,143	17	22,118	22,832	(d)	...	Inc. Place
Vancouver	POR	74060	3-SS	184,786	143,560	19,444	70,333	40,605	3,592,887	.0565	1,498,589	426	378,674	753	38,886	205	264,435	113,637	1,316,796	721	Inc. Place
Walla Walla	WALL	75775	3-A	31,182	29,686	15,572	11,194	33,869	485,567	.0092	334,394	95	60,381	120	13,196	69	67,150	15,768	95,598	52	Inc. Place
Wenatchee		77105	3-A	29,849	27,856	17,973	11,688	35,095	536,461	.0119	615,751	175	132,680	264	10,896	57	78,173	23,312	42,191	23	Inc. Place
Yakima	YAK	80010	3-AA	72,971	71,845	15,141	27,170	31,299	1,104,829	.0230	998,045	283	252,666	502	33,969	179	121,207	33,447	320,084	175	Inc. Place
West Virginia																					
Barboursville	HNTG	04276	4-Sm	2,859	3,183	18,343	1,222	34,900	52,443	.0030	270,703	77	65,625	131	32,868	173	15,314	56,544	(d)	...	Inc. Place
Beckley	BECK	05332	3-A	16,381	17,254	15,882	7,125	27,701	260,171	.0065	362,264	103	107,954	215	9,358	49	21,624	24,536	(d)	...	Inc. Place
Bluefield		08524	3-A	10,555	11,451	14,585	4,589	25,584	153,942	.0039	222,028	63	71,421	142	13,646	72	19,175	20,608	(d)	...	Inc. Place
Charleston	CHAS	14600	2-A	49,941	53,421	23,304	23,246	34,627	1,163,821	.0205	828,067	235	167,958	334	26,968	142	85,268	89,702	113,803	62	Inc. Place
Clarksburg	CLRKB	15628	3-A	16,440	16,743	15,663	7,175	26,007	257,507	.0061	319,374	91	82,935	165	3,990	21	49,165	21,030	(d)	...	Inc. Place
Elkins		24580	4-B	6,904	7,032	15,817	2,876	27,501	109,198	.0025	131,580	37	38,115	76	3,347	18	16,128	8,928	(d)	...	Inc. Place
Fairmont	FAIRM	26452	3-A	18,634	19,097	16,055	7,953	28,650	299,178	.0056	210,291	60	54,243	108	3,445	18	28,412	12,788	129,865	71	Inc. Place
Huntington	HNTG	39460	2-A	47,494	51,475	15,620	21,124	25,202	741,880	.0150	628,140	178	93,880	187	17,947	94	66,360	67,218	569,709	312	Inc. Place
Logan		48148	4-A	1,454	1,630	15,551	693	23,712	22,611	.0006	32,760	9	9,292	18	1,076	6	1,425	1,787	(d)	...	Inc. Place
Martinsburg		52060	4-B	14,647	14,972	20,384	6,099	35,343	298,558	.0054	218,003	62	43,188	86	20,874	110	27,982	16,959	212,791	116	Inc. Place
Morgantown	MORG	55756	3-A	26,278	26,809	12,830	10,101	22,453	337,140	.0085	447,918	127	102,477	204	36,285	191	51,450	37,192	...	...	Inc. Place
Parkersburg	PRKB	62140	3-AA	32,774	33,099	16,152	14,261	27,915	529,352	.0123	648,908	184	112,166	223	27,178	143	61,019	45,890	67,949	37	Inc. Place
Vienna	PRKB	83500	4-Sm	10,350	10,861	21,237	4,483	36,491	219,803	.0056	354,058	101	203,484	405	17,465	92	11,109	14,909	(d)	...	Inc. Place
Weirton	STU-	85156	4-B	19,642	20,411	19,270	8,706	33,664	378,501	.0064	209,468	59	62,923	125	11,864	62	41,378	14,265	760,589	416	Inc. Place
Wheeling	WHL	86452	3-AA	28,403	31,419	17,224	12,432	29,982	489,217	.0089	324,031	92	17,047	34	5,535	29	45,044	24,220	...	...	Inc. Place
Williamson		87508	4-A	3,177	3,414	14,420	1,512	21,918	45,812	.0012	72,180	20	1,225	2	1,469	8	16,734	7,159	(d)	...	Inc. Place
Wisconsin																					
Antigo		02250	4-C	8,331	8,560	17,242	3,642	32,214	143,642	.0034	183,933	52	34,872	69	2,371	12	30,592	...	73,861	40	Inc. Place
Appleton	APP	02375	3-AA	73,932	70,087	21,830	29,340	44,670	1,613,943	.0308	1,378,404	391	225,075	448	68,508	361	134,403	56,303	949,942	520	Inc. Place
Beaver Dam		05900	4-C	15,470	15,169	20,906	6,592	39,026	323,416	.0066	325,596	92	108,902	217	9,178	48	21,368	5,539	108,005	59	Inc. Place
Beloit	RKFD	06500	3-B	35,906	35,775	17,586	13,689	37,263	631,442	.0111	375,106	107	83,552	166	2,563	13	41,575	21,343	666,913	365	Inc. Place
Brookfield	MILW	10025	3-Sm	40,191	38,649	33,906	14,918	65,941	1,362,709	.0261	1,359,823	386	245,287	488	133,650	703	208,882	54,013	244,100	134	Inc. Place
Eau Claire	EAUC	22300	3-AA	62,148	61,704	18,398	25,848	37,128	1,143,416	.0261	1,408,526	400	351,753	700	77,208	406	121,686	61,739	369,935	203	Inc. Place
Fond du Lac	FDLC	26275	3-A	42,791	42,203	20,003	17,316	40,368	855,946	.0145	486,701	138	149,983	298	16,983	89	81,308	23,822	888,756	487	Inc. Place
Franklin	MILW	27300		30,239	29,494	21,037	10,779	58,502	636,131	.0099	278,359	79	83,806	167	...	...	47,994	5,842	179,206	98	Inc. Place
Glendale	MILW	29400	4-S	12,723	13,367	25,364	5,438	43,103	322,708	.0067	352,091	100	52,922	105	17,162	90	60,273	44,956	302,716	166	Inc. Place
Green Bay	GRBY	31000	2-A	102,844	102,313	19,154	43,292	38,709	1,969,898	.0417	2,071,056	588	551,644	1,097	54,565	287	206,154	67,037	1,768,420	968	Inc. Place
Greendale	MILW	31125	4-Sm	13,683	14,405	23,402	5,653	50,019	320,209	.0066	337,050	96	187,573	373	47,228	249	13,306	25,158	40,895	22	Inc. Place
Greenfield	MILW	31175	4-S	34,800	35,476	19,410	15,272	41,520	675,483	.0137	647,125	184	85,150	169	11,974	63	63,092	48,599	(d)	...	Inc. Place
Janesville	JNSV	37825	3-A	61,458	59,498	21,585	25,225	43,538	1,326,559	.0248	1,074,753	305	209,989	418	25,209	133	126,347	60,965	3,016,117	1,651	Inc. Place
Kenosha	KEN	39225	3-S	93,826	90,352	18,731	35,617	40,240	1,757,413	.0296	934,818	265	147,681	294	68,475	360	132,020	65,061	533,449	292	Inc. Place
La Crosse	LACRO	40775	3-AA	51,379	51,818	18,188	21,527	32,624	934,502	.0189	858,903	244	148,034	294	26,330	139	73,131	27,240	367,439	201	Inc. Place
Madison	MAD	48000	2-AA	223,674	208,054	22,032	99,477	39,767	4,927,899	.0914	3,934,145	1,117	733,833	1,459	213,755	1,125	483,901	211,710	1,344,489	736	Inc. Place
Manitowoc	MNTW	48500	3-A	34,167	34,053	20,880	15,088	37,780	713,419	.0119	398,195	113	123,779	246	6,331	33	50,418	12,973	819,379	449	Inc. Place
Marinette		49300	3-A	11,296	11,749	19,116	5,066	33,980	215,929	.0042	185,325	53	67,944	135	8,863	47	21,330	8,131	332,748	182	Inc. Place
Marshfield		49675	3-B	17,831	18,800	23,973	8,298	38,495	427,462	.0094	524,526	149	112,880	224	3,815	20	28,045	6,381	199,746	109	Inc. Place
Menomonee Falls	MILW	51000	4-S	34,920	32,647	24,302	14,197	51,907	848,637	.0162	762,129	216	180,734	359	12,000	63	74,879	57,761	745,816	408	Inc. Place
Milwaukee	MILW	53000	1-A	592,470	596,974	14,653	228,512	31,870	8,681,248	.1512	4,196,177	1,192	442,975	881	152,381	802	644,602	455,672	4,168,514	2,282	Inc. Place
Neenah	APP	55750	4-S	23,858	24,507	24,542	10,022	46,210	585,526	.0094	313,444	89	41,814	83	4,347	23	36,731	25,341	966,968	529	Inc. Place
New Berlin	MILW	56375		40,678	38,220	27,385	15,906	60,462	1,113,977	.0154	352,691	100	33,972	68	3,832	20	59,103	8,141	732,623	401	Inc. Place
Oshkosh	OSH	60500	3-B	64,849	62,916	17,720	25,985	37,518	1,149,135	.0249	1,238,664	352	178,724	355	49,310	260	118,196	68,527	718,814	394	Inc. Place
Racine	MILW	66000	3-CC	80,827	81,855	19,374	31,129	39,905	1,565,947	.0242	605,039	172	101,051	201	17,796	94	98,274	52,257	1,118,610	612	Inc. Place
Rhinelander		67200	4-B	7,377	7,735	17,211	3,160	34,555	126,968	.0031	180,747	51	32,270	64	6,292	33	14,251	2,383	151,695	83	Inc. Place
Sheboygan	SHEB	72975	3-A	49,965	50,792	19,911	21,112	39,233	994,841	.0178	672,886	191	191,913	382	11,421	60	87,696	41,579	664,045	364	Inc. Place
Stevens Point		77200	3-A	24,742	24,551	18,816	10,059	37,890	465,558	.0087	355,780	101	99,150	197	12,690	67	38,757	3,437	192,516	105	Inc. Place
Superior	DUL	78650	4-C	27,561	27,368	16,667	11,718	31,798	459,372	.0090	365,165	104	67,706	135	5,158	27	58,164	13,182	...	...	Inc. Place
Watertown		83975	4-C	22,969	21,598	18,253	8,527	41,172	419,264	.0072	231,409	66	69,117	137	3,315	17	37,509	7,293	240,119	131	Inc. Place
Waukesha	MILW	84250	3-S	68,491	64,825	23,139	27,954	49,151	1,584,825	.0284	1,172,929	333	237,766	473	18,558	98	121,763	47,671	1,361,225	745	Inc. Place
Wausau	WAUS	84475	3-A	38,366	38,426	21,827	16,505	39,441	837,411	.0165	781,312	222	202,238	402	21,211	112	56,184	21,711	564,657	309	Inc. Place
Wauwatosa	MILW	84675	3-S	46,661	47,271	22,510	19,945	46,736	1,050,319	.0196	857,140	243	168,314	335	64,744	341	59,209	77,103	877,711	481	Inc. Place
West Allis	MILW	85300	3-S	60,032	61,254	17,830	26,821	37,002	1,070,381	.0211	908,284	258	102,556	204	12,293	65	75,053	53,230	422,228	231	Inc. Place
West Bend		85350	4-C	29,249	28,152	24,945	11,998	48,344	729,602	.0130	544,788	155	83,288	166	6,438	34	53,172	19,533	327,249	179	Inc. Place
Wisconsin Rapids		88200	3-B	17,949	18,435	20,836	8,245	39,158	373,978	.0063	221,264	63	50,054	100	5,610	30	35,798	3,585	395,393	216	Inc. Place
Wyoming																					
Casper	CASP	13150	3-A	50,742	49,644	17,544	20,409	35,371	890,204	.0175	742,821	211	204,581	407	20,967	110	78,229	17,769	(d)	...	Inc. Place
Cheyenne	CHEY	13900	3-A	55,016	53,011	19,220	23,060	37,893	1,057,401	.0196	790,416	224	148,649	296	17,572	92	101,876	21,541	...	...	Inc. Place
Gillette		31855	4-B	21,565	19,646	19,391	7,645	44,097	418,158	.0072	249,185	71	55,543	110	5,333	28	32,477	2,614	(d)	...	Inc. Place
Laramie		45050	4-C	26,205	27,204	15,128	11,789	27,638	396,432	.0084	378,163	107	96,900	193	5,441	29	37,077	4,497	(d)	...	Inc. Place
Riverton		66220	4-A	9,633	9,310	15,590	4,066	30,717	150,182	.0032	147,069	42	35,282	70	2,038	11	17,727	2,706	(d)	...	Inc. Place
Rock Springs		67235	4-A	18,801	18,708	20,378	7,653	41,071	383,136	.0075	336,135	95	68,506	136	10,741	57	39,002	4,117	(d)	...	Inc. Place
Sheridan		69845	4-C	16,294	15,804	18,232	7,232	32,790	297,078	.0058	243,187	69	48,598	97	5,141	27	25,399	3,470	(d)	...	Inc. Place

Source: Devonshire Associates Ltd. and Scan/US, Inc. 2005.
* Source: 1997 Census of Manufactures.
Not classified as a Principal Business Center.

...Data less than 1,000.
(d) Data not available.

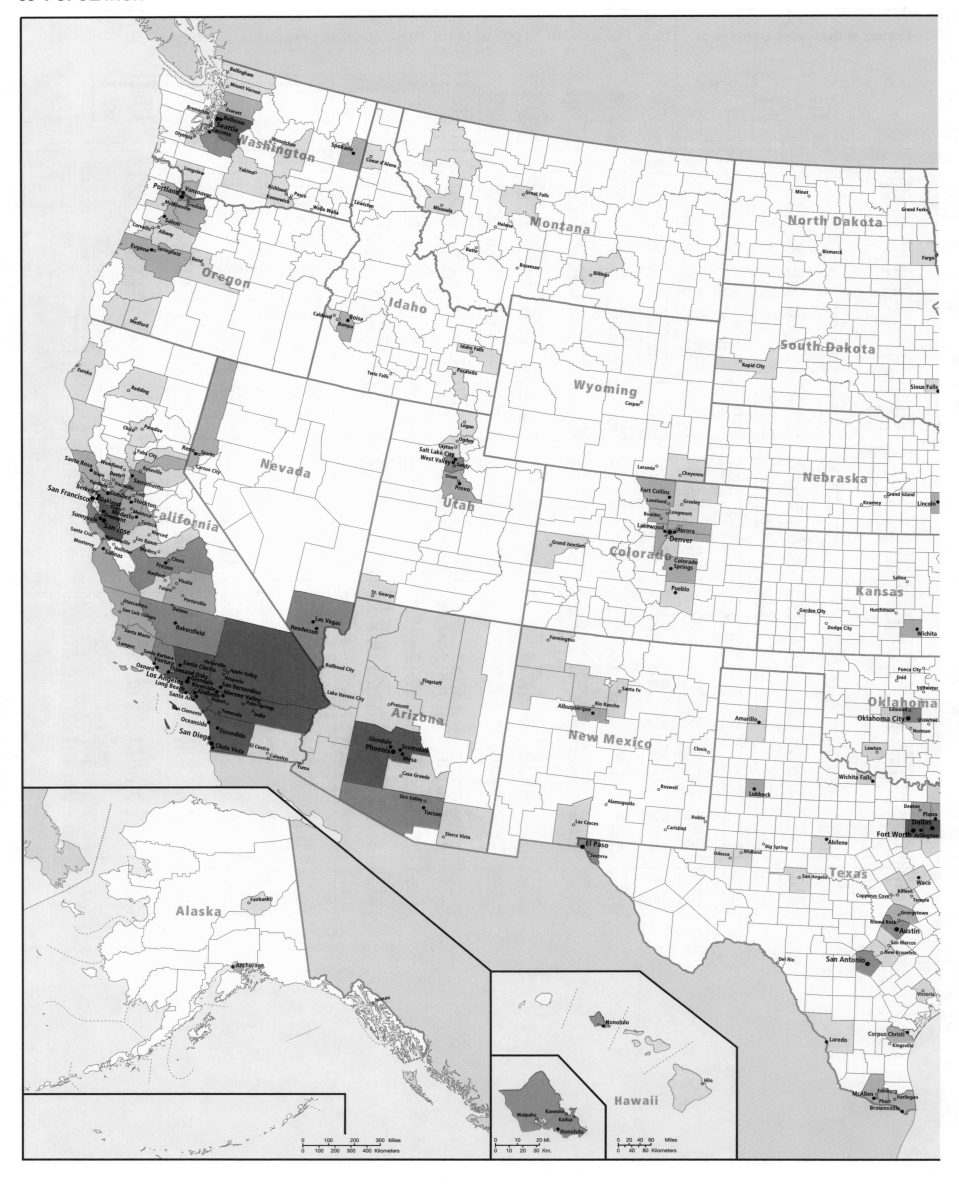

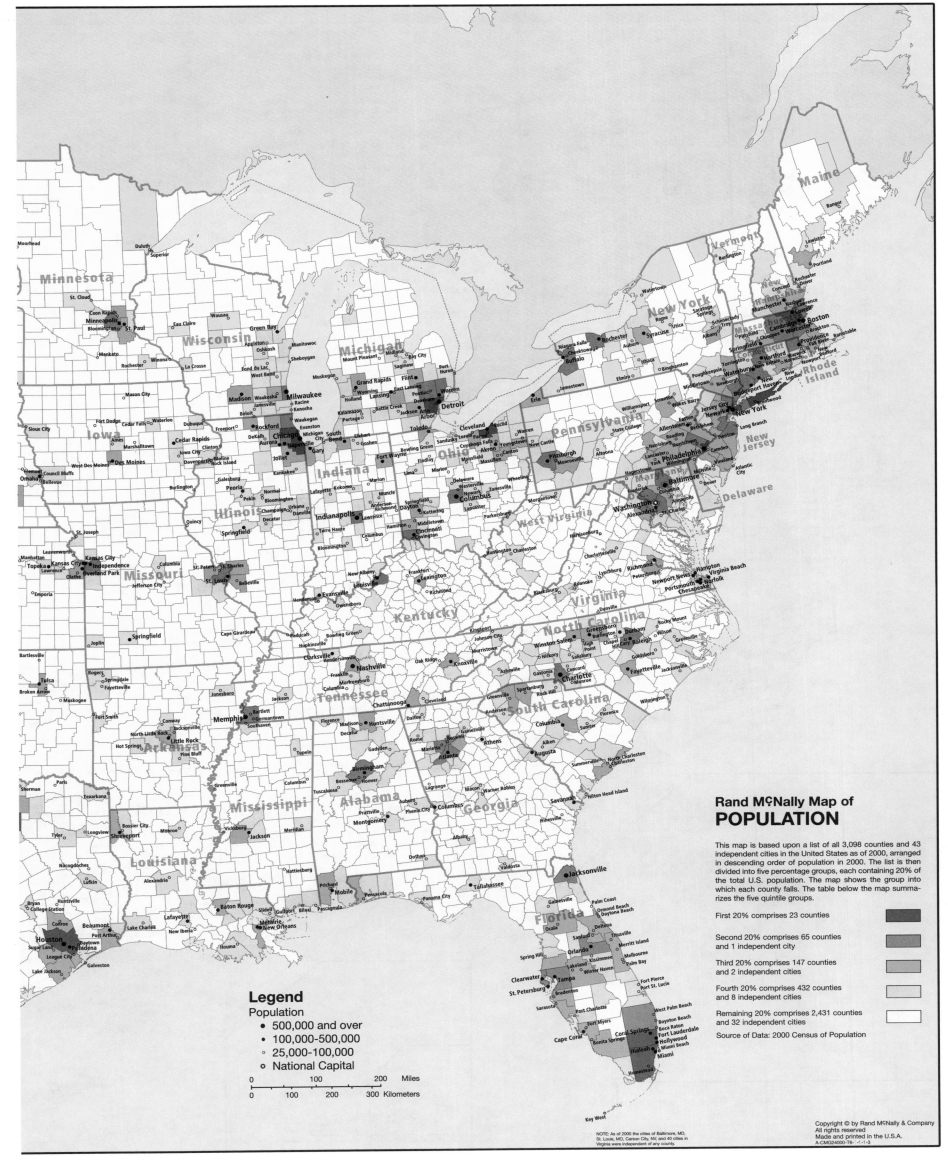

Rand McNally Map of
POPULATION

This map is based upon a list of all 3,098 counties and 43 independent cities in the United States as of 2000, arranged in descending order of population in 2000. The list is then divided into five percentage groups, each containing 20% of the total U.S. population. The map shows the group into which each county falls. The table below the map summarizes the five quintile groups.

First 20% comprises 23 counties

Second 20% comprises 65 counties and 1 independent city

Third 20% comprises 147 counties and 2 independent cities

Fourth 20% comprises 432 counties and 8 independent cities

Remaining 20% comprises 2,431 counties and 32 independent cities

Source of Data: 2000 Census of Population

Legend
Population
- ● 500,000 and over
- ● 100,000-500,000
- ○ 25,000-100,000
- ○ National Capital

0   100   200   Miles
0   100   200   300 Kilometers

NOTE: As of 2000 the cities of Baltimore, MD, St. Louis, MO, Carson City, NV, and 40 cities in Virginia were independent of any county.

QUINTILE GROUPING OF COUNTIES AND INDEPENDENT CITIES ACCORDING TO TOTAL POPULATION, 2000

Group	Range in population of counties and independent cities in each group — Largest	Smallest	Total population of each group	Population of each group plus all preceding groups	% of total U.S. population contained in each group	% of total U.S. population contained in each group plus all preceding groups	Number of counties & indep. cities in each group	% of the total number of counties & indep. cities in each group	Numbers of counties & indep. cities in each group plus all preceding groups	% of the total number of counties & indep. cities in each group plus all preceding groups
1	9,519,338 to	1,393,978	56,777,962	56,777,962	20.1	20.1	23	0.7	23	0.7
2	1,392,931 to	607,751	56,207,218	112,985,180	20.0	40.1	66	2.1	89	2.8
3	606,024 to	241,767	55,968,411	168,953,591	19.9	60.0	149	4.8	238	7.6
4	240,391 to	73,825	56,234,029	225,187,620	20.0	80.0	440	14.0	678	21.6
5	73,814 to	67	56,234,286	281,421,906	20.0	100.0	2,463	78.4	3,141	100.0

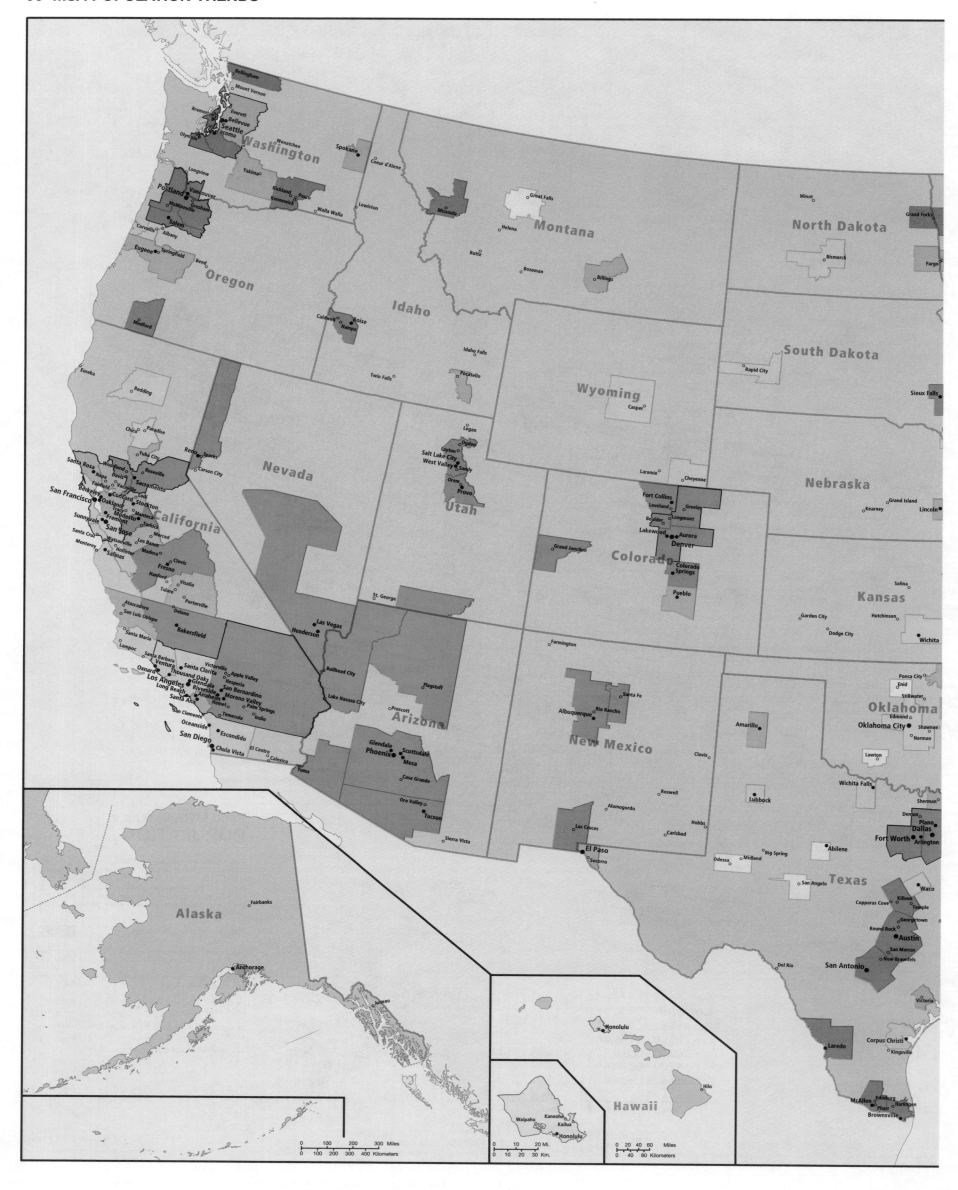

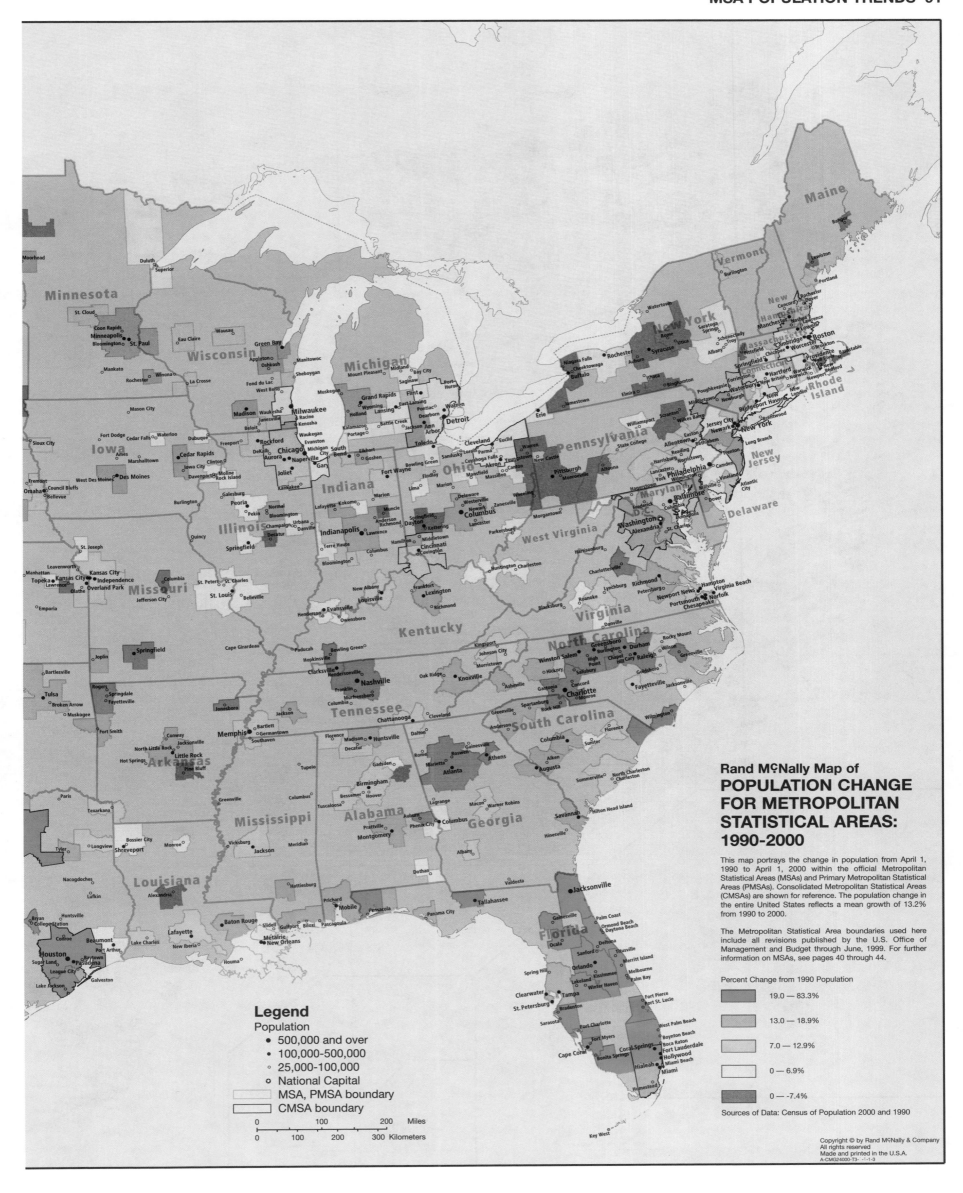

Rand McNally Map of

POPULATION CHANGE FOR METROPOLITAN STATISTICAL AREAS: 1990-2000

This map portrays the change in population from April 1, 1990 to April 1, 2000 within the official Metropolitan Statistical Areas (MSAs) and Primary Metropolitan Statistical Areas (PMSAs). Consolidated Metropolitan Statistical Areas (CMSAs) are shown for reference. The population change in the entire United States reflects a mean growth of 13.2% from 1990 to 2000.

The Metropolitan Statistical Area boundaries used here include all revisions published by the U.S. Office of Management and Budget through June, 1999. For further information on MSAs, see pages 40 through 44.

Percent Change from 1990 Population

19.0 — 83.3%

13.0 — 18.9%

7.0 — 12.9%

0 — 6.9%

0 — -7.4%

Sources of Data: Census of Population 2000 and 1990

Legend

Population

● 500,000 and over

● 100,000-500,000

○ 25,000-100,000

⊙ National Capital

▭ MSA, PMSA boundary

▭ CMSA boundary

| 0 | 100 | 200 | Miles |

| 0 | 100 | 200 | 300 | Kilometers |

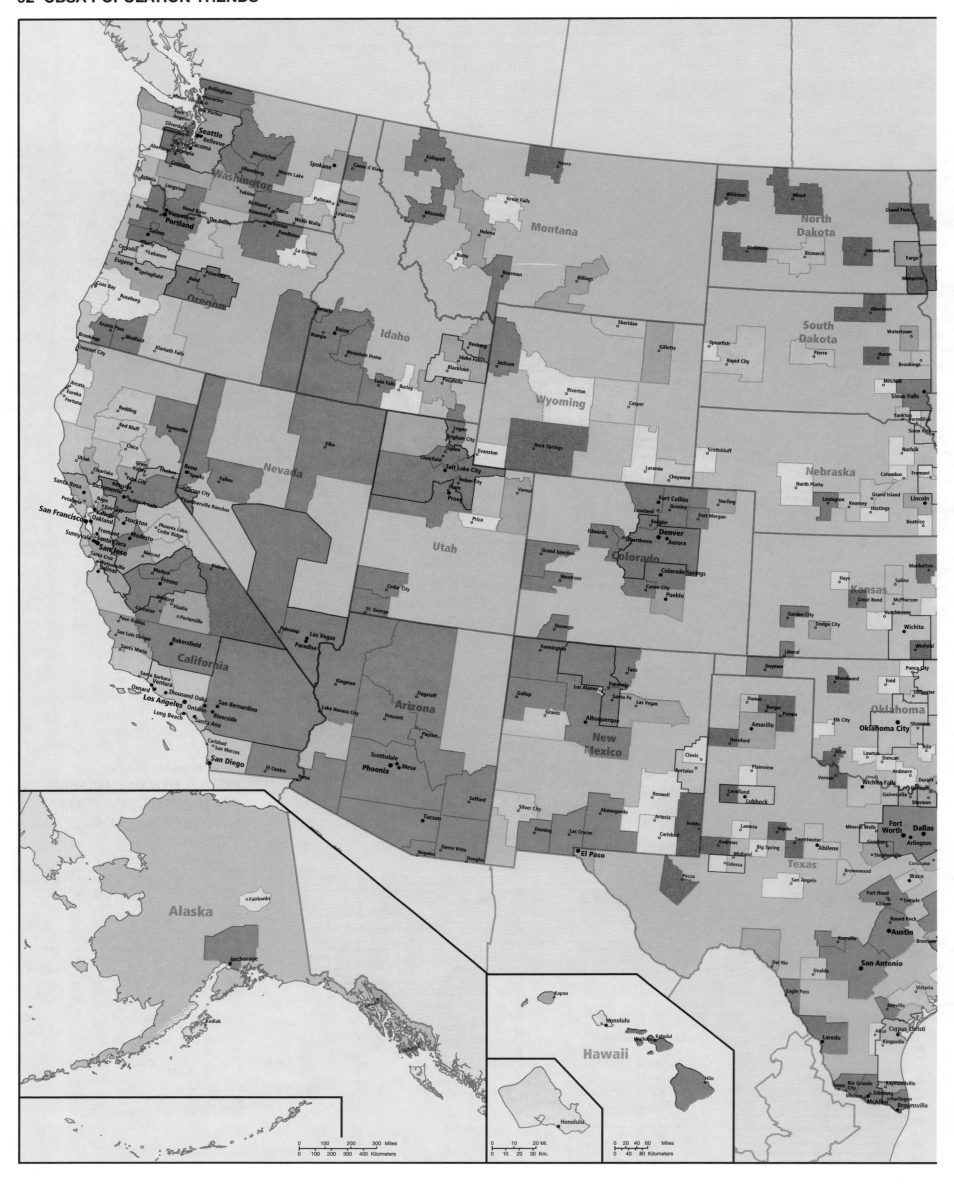

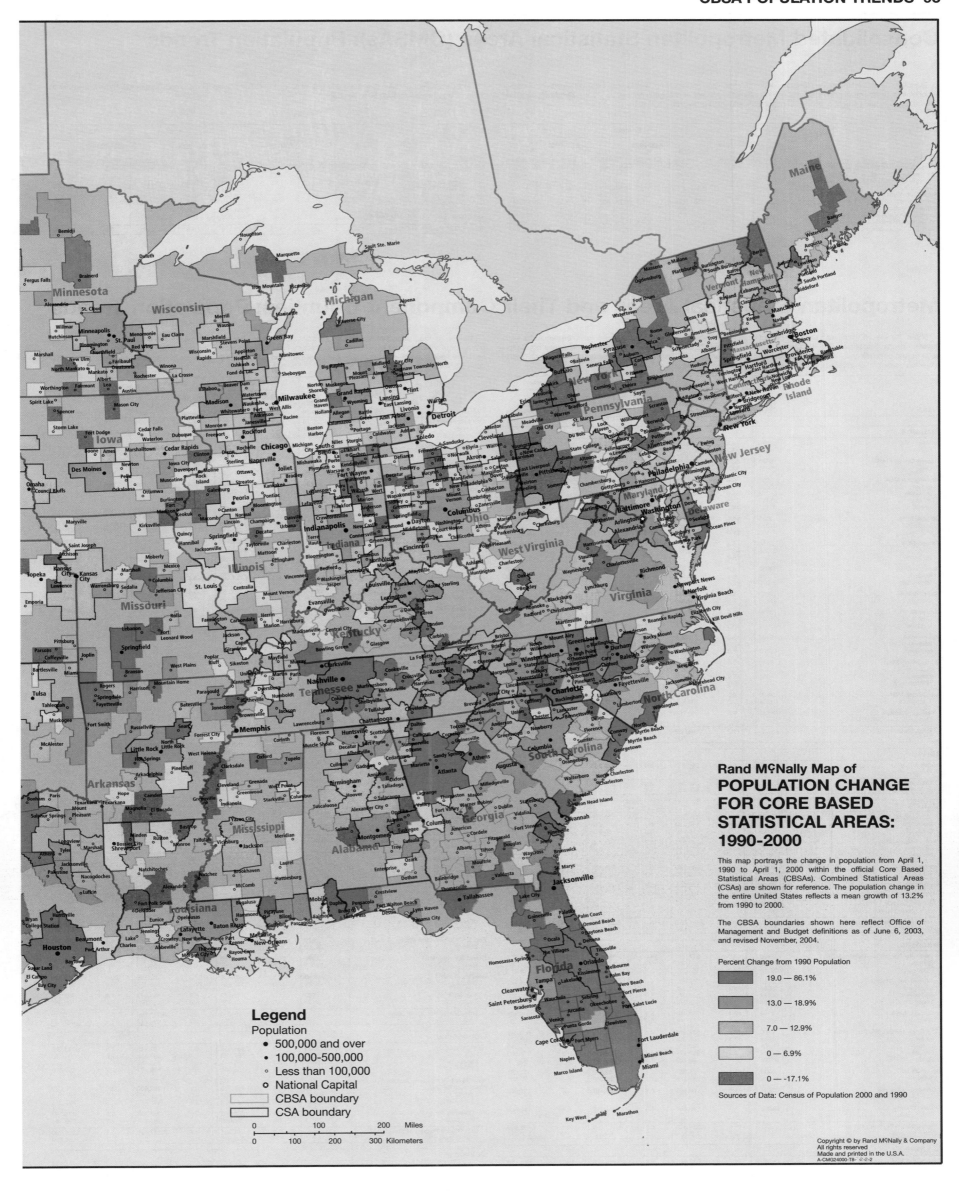

Rand McNally Map of
POPULATION CHANGE FOR CORE BASED STATISTICAL AREAS: 1990-2000

This map portrays the change in population from April 1, 1990 to April 1, 2000 within the official Core Based Statistical Areas (CBSAs). Combined Statistical Areas (CSAs) are shown for reference. The population change in the entire United States reflects a mean growth of 13.2% from 1990 to 2000.

The CBSA boundaries shown here reflect Office of Management and Budget definitions as of June 6, 2003, and revised November, 2004.

Percent Change from 1990 Population

	19.0 — 86.1%
	13.0 — 18.9%
	7.0 — 12.9%
	0 — 6.9%
	0 — -17.1%

Sources of Data: Census of Population 2000 and 1990

Legend
Population
- ● 500,000 and over
- • 100,000-500,000
- ○ Less than 100,000
- ◉ National Capital
- ▭ CBSA boundary
- ▭ CSA boundary

0   100   200   Miles
0   100   200   300 Kilometers

Consolidated Metropolitan Statistical Areas (CMSAs): Population Trends

The following data are presented for Consolidated Metropolitan Statistical Areas (CMSAs): 1990-2000 percent of change in population; 2000 **actual** population; 2000-2005 estimated percent of change in population; 2005 **estimated** population; 2005-2010 projected percent of change in population; and 2010 **projected** population.

The data reflect CMSAs as defined and published by the Office of Management and Budget (OMB) on December 31, 1992, and as revised through June 30, 1999.

CMSA	Past: 1990-2000 % Change	Past: 2000 Census	Present: 2000-2005 % Change	Present: 7/1/05 Estimate	Future: 2005-2010 % Change	Future: 2010 Projection
Boston-Worcester-Lawrence, MA-NH-ME-CT	6.7	5,819,100	2.7	5,974,626	1.8	6,084,353
Chicago-Gary-Kenosha, IL-IN-WI	11.1	9,157,540	4.1	9,532,924	3.7	9,886,288
Cincinnati-Hamilton, OH-KY-IN	8.9	1,979,202	3.0	2,037,766	2.7	2,092,279
Cleveland-Akron, OH	3.0	2,945,831	-0.1	2,944,122	-0.1	2,941,865
Dallas-Fort Worth, TX	29.3	5,221,801	13.2	5,909,068	11.0	6,560,123
Denver-Boulder-Greeley, CO	30.4	2,581,506	7.9	2,784,667	8.1	3,009,541
Detroit-Ann Arbor-Flint, MI	5.2	5,456,428	1.7	5,551,073	1.6	5,637,222
Houston-Galveston-Brazoria, TX	25.2	4,669,571	12.3	5,242,969	10.4	5,789,739
Los Angeles-Riverside-Orange County, CA	12.7	16,373,645	8.7	17,797,954	7.6	19,155,356
Miami-Fort Lauderdale, FL	21.4	3,876,380	8.0	4,185,259	7.0	4,477,647
Milwaukee-Racine, WI	5.1	1,689,572	1.6	1,716,448	1.5	1,741,701
New York-Northern NJ-Long Island, NY-NJ-CT-PA	8.4	21,199,865	3.2	21,887,706	2.9	22,522,136
Philadelphia-Wilmington-Atlantic City, PA-NJ-DE-MD	5.0	6,188,463	2.5	6,345,752	2.4	6,496,961
Portland-Salem, OR-WA	26.3	2,265,223	9.2	2,474,616	8.1	2,674,742
Sacramento-Yolo, CA	21.3	1,796,857	15.8	2,081,634	13.1	2,354,217
San Francisco-Oakland-San Jose, CA	12.6	7,039,362	1.1	7,114,596	0.8	7,171,589
Seattle-Tacoma-Bremerton, WA	19.7	3,554,760	5.6	3,754,318	5.1	3,943,943
Washington-Baltimore, DC-MD-VA-WV	13.1	7,608,070	7.9	8,207,016	6.9	8,776,496
Total: CMSA Portion of Country	**12.5**	**109,423,176**	**5.6**	**115,542,514**	**5.0**	**121,316,198**

Metropolitan Statistical Areas and Their Component Counties: Population Trends

MSAs, PMSAs, NECMAs, and their component counties are listed by state. The following data are presented for each: the Metropolitan Statistical Area FIPS Code and State-County FIPS Code(s); 1990-2000 percent of change in population; 2000 **actual** population; 2000-2005 estimated percent of change in population; 2005 **estimated** population; 2005-2010 projected percent of change in population; and 2010 **projected** population.

The total metropolitan population within the state (**Total: Metro Portion of State**) and the total state population are also given. Data shown in **bold face** represent in-state metropolitan area totals. The data reflect MSAs, PMSAs, and NECMAs as defined and published by the Office of Management and Budget (OMB) on December 31, 1992, and as revised through June 30, 1999.

MSA	FIPS Code	Past: 1990-2000 % Change	Past: 2000 Census	Present: 2000-2005 % Change	Present: 7/1/05 Estimate	Future: 2005-2010 % Change	Future: 2010 Projection
Alabama							
Anniston MSA	**.0450**	**-3.3**	**112,249**	**0.3**	**112,624**	**1.1**	**113,834**
Calhoun	01015	-3.3	112,249	0.3	112,624	1.1	113,834
Auburn-Opelika MSA	**.0580**	**32.1**	**115,092**	**5.7**	**121,616**	**5.1**	**127,779**
Lee	01081	32.1	115,092	5.7	121,616	5.1	127,779
Birmingham MSA	**.1000**	**9.6**	**921,106**	**3.4**	**952,851**	**3.1**	**982,594**
Blount	01009	30.0	51,024	10.1	56,200	8.9	61,174
Jefferson	01073	1.6	662,047	-0.9	655,970	-0.9	649,779
St. Clair	01115	29.5	64,742	9.5	70,917	8.2	76,697
Shelby	01117	44.2	143,293	18.5	169,764	14.8	194,944
Decatur MSA	**.2030**	**10.9**	**145,867**	**1.7**	**148,289**	**1.5**	**150,474**
Lawrence	01079	10.4	34,803	-1.4	34,317	-1.6	33,772
Morgan	01103	11.0	111,064	2.6	113,972	2.4	116,702
Dothan MSA	**.2180**	**5.3**	**137,916**	**3.6**	**142,862**	**3.4**	**147,650**
Dale	01045	-1.0	49,129	0.8	49,503	0.8	49,897
Houston	01069	9.2	88,787	5.1	93,359	4.7	97,753
Florence MSA	**.2650**	**8.9**	**142,950**	**-1.4**	**140,981**	**-1.4**	**138,945**
Colbert	01033	6.4	54,984	-1.0	54,455	-1.1	53,872
Lauderdale	01077	10.4	87,966	-1.6	86,526	-1.7	85,073
Gadsden MSA	**.2880**	**3.6**	**103,459**	**-0.4**	**103,021**	**-0.3**	**102,701**
Etowah	01055	3.6	103,459	-0.4	103,021	-0.3	102,701
Huntsville MSA	**.3440**	**16.8**	**342,376**	**7.3**	**367,395**	**6.4**	**390,910**
Limestone	01083	21.3	65,676	6.3	69,788	5.5	73,608
Madison	01089	15.8	276,700	7.6	297,607	6.6	317,302
Mobile MSA	**.5160**	**13.3**	**540,258**	**3.3**	**558,139**	**3.0**	**574,645**
Baldwin	01003	42.9	140,415	12.8	158,412	10.7	175,379
Mobile	01097	5.6	399,843	-0.0	399,727	-0.1	399,266
Montgomery MSA	**.5240**	**13.9**	**333,055**	**3.0**	**343,079**	**2.8**	**352,515**
Autauga	01001	27.6	43,671	9.9	47,987	8.5	52,052
Elmore	01051	33.9	65,874	11.3	73,325	9.6	80,363
Montgomery	01101	6.9	223,510	-0.8	221,767	-0.8	220,100
Tuscaloosa MSA	**.8600**	**9.5**	**164,875**	**1.5**	**167,273**	**1.3**	**169,516**
Tuscaloosa	01125	9.5	164,875	1.5	167,273	1.3	169,516
* **Russell County** (See Columbus, GA-AL MSA.)	**.01113**	**6.2**	**49,756**	**-2.4**	**48,555**	**-2.3**	**47,428**
Total: Metro Portion of State		**11.2**	**3,108,959**	**3.1**	**3,206,685**	**2.9**	**3,298,991**
Total: Alabama		10.1	4,447,100	2.0	4,537,634	1.9	4,622,960
Alaska							
Anchorage MSA	**.0380**	**15.0**	**260,283**	**6.9**	**278,263**	**6.3**	**295,713**
Anchorage	02020	15.0	260,283	6.9	278,263	6.3	295,713
Total: Metro Portion of State		**15.0**	**260,283**	**6.9**	**278,263**	**6.3**	**295,713**
Total: Alaska		14.0	626,932	5.6	662,020	5.2	696,537
Arizona							
Flagstaff, AZ-UT MSA	.2620	20.2	122,366	6.3	130,122	5.7	137,503
Coconino	**04005**	**20.4**	**116,320**	**6.7**	**124,093**	**6.0**	**131,518**
Kane, UT	49025	17.0	6,046	-0.3	6,029	-0.7	5,985
Phoenix-Mesa MSA	**.6200**	**45.3**	**3,251,876**	**16.9**	**3,801,803**	**13.8**	**4,325,342**
Maricopa	04013	44.8	3,072,149	16.6	3,582,040	13.5	4,067,317
Pinal	04021	54.4	179,727	22.3	219,763	17.4	258,025
Tucson MSA	**.8520**	**26.5**	**843,746**	**9.2**	**921,681**	**7.9**	**994,799**
Pima	04019	26.5	843,746	9.2	921,681	7.9	994,799
Yuma MSA	**.9360**	**49.7**	**160,026**	**10.6**	**177,064**	**9.2**	**193,373**
Yuma	04027	49.7	160,026	10.6	177,064	9.2	193,373
* **Mohave County** (See Las Vegas, NV-AZ MSA.)	**.04015**	**65.8**	**155,032**	**17.9**	**182,775**	**14.5**	**209,264**
Total: Metro Portion of State		**41.4**	**4,527,000**	**15.0**	**5,207,416**	**12.4**	**5,854,296**
Total: Arizona		40.0	5,130,632	14.1	5,854,746	11.8	6,543,549
Arkansas							
Fayetteville-Springdale-Rogers MSA	**.2580**	**47.5**	**311,121**	**16.0**	**360,974**	**13.1**	**408,202**
Benton	05007	57.3	153,406	19.9	183,859	15.7	212,752
Washington	05143	39.1	157,715	12.3	177,115	10.4	195,450
Fort Smith, AR-OK MSA	.2720	17.8	207,290	4.4	216,321	3.8	224,493
Crawford	**05033**	**25.3**	**53,247**	**7.4**	**57,169**	**6.5**	**60,900**
Sebastian	**05131**	**15.5**	**115,071**	**3.0**	**118,532**	**2.5**	**121,438**
Sequoyah, OK	40135	15.2	38,972	4.2	40,620	3.8	42,155
Jonesboro MSA	**.3700**	**19.1**	**82,148**	**5.1**	**86,335**	**4.4**	**90,134**
Craighead	05031	19.1	82,148	5.1	86,335	4.4	90,134
Little Rock-North Little Rock MSA	**.4400**	**13.8**	**583,845**	**4.8**	**612,049**	**4.3**	**638,447**
Faulkner	05045	43.3	86,014	12.5	96,723	10.6	106,971
Lonoke	05085	34.5	52,828	11.9	59,112	10.0	65,019
Pulaski	05119	3.4	361,474	1.4	366,433	1.2	370,906
Saline	05125	30.1	83,529	7.5	89,781	6.4	95,551
Pine Bluff MSA	**.6240**	**-1.4**	**84,278**	**-2.7**	**82,043**	**-2.6**	**79,881**
Jefferson	05069	-1.4	84,278	-2.7	82,043	-2.6	79,881
* **Crittenden County** (See Memphis, TN-AR-MS MSA.)	**.05035**	**1.9**	**50,866**	**0.8**	**51,287**	**0.5**	**51,532**
* **Miller County** (See Texarkana, TX-AR MSA.)	**.05091**	**5.1**	**40,443**	**6.3**	**42,971**	**5.8**	**45,456**
Total: Metro Portion of State		**19.1**	**1,321,019**	**6.8**	**1,411,360**	**6.0**	**1,495,990**
Total: Arkansas		13.7	2,673,400	3.2	2,759,439	2.9	2,840,378
California							
Bakersfield MSA	**.0680**	**21.7**	**661,645**	**12.4**	**743,729**	**10.7**	**823,538**
Kern	06029	21.7	661,645	12.4	743,729	10.7	823,538
Chico-Paradise MSA	**.1620**	**11.6**	**203,171**	**6.1**	**215,649**	**5.5**	**227,494**
Butte	06007	11.6	203,171	6.1	215,649	5.5	227,494
Fresno MSA	**.2840**	**22.1**	**922,516**	**11.0**	**1,023,612**	**9.5**	**1,121,239**
Fresno	06019	19.8	799,407	10.3	881,918	9.0	961,546
Madera	06039	39.8	123,109	15.1	141,694	12.7	159,693
Los Angeles-Long Beach PMSA	**.4480**	**7.4**	**9,519,338**	**5.9**	**10,076,928**	**5.3**	**10,607,471**
Los Angeles	06037	7.4	9,519,338	5.9	10,076,928	5.3	10,607,471
Merced MSA	**.4940**	**18.0**	**210,554**	**15.7**	**243,619**	**13.1**	**275,515**
Merced	06047	18.0	210,554	15.7	243,619	13.1	275,515
Modesto MSA	**.5170**	**20.6**	**446,997**	**16.3**	**519,823**	**13.4**	**589,650**
Stanislaus	06099	20.6	446,997	16.3	519,823	13.4	589,650
Oakland PMSA	**.5775**	**14.9**	**2,392,557**	**4.4**	**2,497,921**	**3.8**	**2,591,744**
Alameda	06001	12.9	1,443,741	1.6	1,466,375	1.1	1,482,425
Contra Costa	06013	18.1	948,816	8.7	1,031,546	7.5	1,109,319
Orange County PMSA	**.5945**	**18.1**	**2,846,289**	**6.1**	**3,020,648**	**5.4**	**3,184,136**
Orange	06059	18.1	2,846,289	6.1	3,020,648	5.4	3,184,136
Redding MSA	**.6690**	**11.0**	**163,256**	**12.3**	**183,315**	**10.6**	**202,753**
Shasta	06089	11.0	163,256	12.3	183,315	10.6	202,753
Riverside-San Bernardino PMSA	**.6780**	**25.7**	**3,254,821**	**19.4**	**3,886,808**	**15.6**	**4,493,354**
Riverside	06065	32.0	1,545,387	24.9	1,929,673	19.1	2,298,625
San Bernardino	06071	20.5	1,709,434	14.5	1,957,135	12.1	2,194,729
Sacramento PMSA	**.6920**	**21.5**	**1,628,197**	**16.2**	**1,891,938**	**13.4**	**2,144,620**
El Dorado	06017	24.1	156,299	13.2	176,979	11.2	196,724
Placer	06061	43.8	248,399	28.5	319,191	21.2	386,916
Sacramento	06067	17.5	1,223,499	14.1	1,395,768	11.8	1,560,980
Salinas MSA	**.7120**	**13.0**	**401,762**	**4.9**	**421,269**	**4.3**	**439,362**
Monterey	06053	13.0	401,762	4.9	421,269	4.3	439,362
San Diego MSA	**.7320**	**12.6**	**2,813,833**	**6.3**	**2,990,693**	**5.5**	**3,156,599**
San Diego	06073	12.6	2,813,833	6.3	2,990,693	5.5	3,156,599
San Francisco PMSA	**.7360**	**8.0**	**1,731,183**	**-3.6**	**1,669,327**	**-3.6**	**1,608,889**
Marin	06041	7.5	247,289	-0.8	245,317	-0.9	243,027
San Francisco	06075	7.3	776,733	-5.4	734,587	-5.4	694,890
San Mateo	06081	8.9	707,161	-2.5	689,423	-2.7	670,972
San Jose PMSA	**.7400**	**12.4**	**1,682,585**	**-0.7**	**1,669,973**	**-1.0**	**1,653,999**
Santa Clara	06085	12.4	1,682,585	-0.7	1,669,973	-1.0	1,653,999
San Luis Obispo-Atascadero-Paso Robles MSA	**.7460**	**13.6**	**246,681**	**4.3**	**257,381**	**3.8**	**267,045**
San Luis Obispo	06079	13.6	246,681	4.3	257,381	3.8	267,045
Santa Barbara-Santa Maria-Lompoc MSA	**.7480**	**8.0**	**399,347**	**1.3**	**404,582**	**1.2**	**409,485**
Santa Barbara	06083	8.0	399,347	1.3	404,582	1.2	409,485
Santa Cruz-Watsonville PMSA	**.7485**	**11.3**	**255,602**	**-2.8**	**248,347**	**-2.9**	**241,190**
Santa Cruz	06087	11.3	255,602	-2.8	248,347	-2.9	241,190
Santa Rosa PMSA	**.7500**	**18.1**	**458,614**	**2.7**	**470,813**	**2.2**	**481,193**
Sonoma	06097	18.1	458,614	2.7	470,813	2.2	481,193
Stockton-Lodi MSA	**.8120**	**17.3**	**563,598**	**19.6**	**674,080**	**15.7**	**779,783**
San Joaquin	06077	17.3	563,598	19.6	674,080	15.7	779,783
Vallejo-Fairfield-Napa PMSA	**.8720**	**15.0**	**518,821**	**7.6**	**558,215**	**6.5**	**594,574**
Napa	06055	12.2	124,279	9.8	136,414	8.6	148,203
Solano	06095	15.9	394,542	6.9	421,801	5.8	446,371
Ventura PMSA	**.8735**	**12.6**	**753,197**	**8.0**	**813,570**	**7.0**	**870,395**
Ventura	06111	12.6	753,197	8.0	813,570	7.0	870,395
Visalia-Tulare-Porterville MSA	**.8780**	**18.0**	**368,021**	**10.0**	**404,818**	**8.9**	**440,650**
Tulare	06107	18.0	368,021	10.0	404,818	8.9	440,650
Yolo PMSA	**.9270**	**19.5**	**168,660**	**12.5**	**189,696**	**10.5**	**209,597**
Yolo	06113	19.5	168,660	12.5	189,696	10.5	209,597
Yuba City MSA	**.9340**	**13.5**	**139,149**	**10.6**	**153,877**	**9.3**	**168,208**
Sutter	06101	22.5	78,930	11.8	88,233	10.2	97,260
Yuba	06115	3.4	60,219	9.0	65,644	8.1	70,948
Total: Metro Portion of State		**13.7**	**32,750,394**	**7.6**	**35,230,631**	**6.7**	**37,582,483**
Total: California		13.8	33,871,648	7.6	36,430,227	6.7	38,857,985
Colorado							
Boulder-Longmont PMSA[1]	**.1125**	**29.3**	**291,288**	**-3.0**	**282,452**	**3.9**	**293,577**
Boulder[1]	08013	29.3	291,288	-3.0	282,452	3.9	293,577
Colorado Springs MSA	**.1720**	**30.2**	**516,929**	**10.4**	**570,479**	**9.0**	**621,578**
El Paso	08041	30.2	516,929	10.4	570,479	9.0	621,578
Denver PMSA[1]	**.2080**	**30.0**	**2,109,282**	**7.7**	**2,271,459**	**7.3**	**2,437,644**
Adams[1]	08001	37.3	363,857	9.7	399,121	12.0	446,996
Arapahoe	08005	24.6	487,967	9.0	531,667	7.5	571,739
Denver	08031	18.6	554,636	0.6	558,088	0.5	560,809
Douglas	08035	191.0	175,766	44.2	253,393	28.7	326,199
Jefferson[1]	08059	20.2	527,056	0.4	529,190	0.5	531,901
Fort Collins-Loveland MSA	**.2670**	**35.1**	**251,494**	**9.5**	**275,364**	**8.1**	**297,783**
Larimer	08069	35.1	251,494	9.5	275,364	8.1	297,783
Grand Junction MSA	**.2995**	**24.8**	**116,255**	**11.3**	**129,419**	**9.2**	**141,326**
Mesa	08077	24.8	116,255	11.3	129,419	9.2	141,326
Greeley PMSA[1]	**.3060**	**37.3**	**180,936**	**27.5**	**230,756**	**20.6**	**278,320**
Weld[1]	08123	37.3	180,936	27.5	230,756	20.6	278,320
Pueblo MSA	**.6560**	**15.0**	**141,472**	**8.6**	**153,579**	**7.6**	**165,291**
Pueblo	08101	15.0	141,472	8.6	153,579	7.6	165,291
Total: Metro Portion of State		**29.8**	**3,607,656**	**8.5**	**3,913,508**	**8.2**	**4,235,519**
Total: Colorado		30.6	4,301,261	9.1	4,694,778	7.8	5,062,536
Connecticut							
Hartford NECMA	**.3283**	**2.2**	**1,148,618**	**4.2**	**1,197,175**	**3.9**	**1,243,285**
Hartford	09003	0.6	857,183	2.8	881,552	2.6	904,560
Middlesex	09007	8.3	155,071	6.9	165,752	6.1	175,863
Tolland	09013	6.0	136,364	9.9	149,871	8.7	162,862
New Haven-Bridgeport-Stamford-Danbury-Waterbury NECMA	**.5483**	**4.6**	**1,706,575**	**3.3**	**1,762,900**	**3.0**	**1,815,942**
Fairfield	09001	6.6	882,567	3.0	909,263	2.7	933,729
New Haven	09009	2.5	824,008	3.6	853,637	3.3	882,213
New London-Norwich NECMA	**.5523**	**1.6**	**259,088**	**3.2**	**267,325**	**2.9**	**275,163**
New London	09011	1.6	259,088	3.2	267,325	2.9	275,163
Total: Metro Portion of State		**3.4**	**3,114,281**	**3.6**	**3,227,400**	**3.3**	**3,334,390**
Total: Connecticut		3.6	3,405,565	3.8	3,534,280	3.5	3,656,299
Delaware							
Dover MSA	**.2190**	**14.1**	**126,697**	**10.2**	**139,558**	**8.9**	**152,015**
Kent	10001	14.1	126,697	10.2	139,558	8.9	152,015
Wilmington-Newark, DE-MD PMSA	.9160	14.2	586,216	6.0	621,190	5.3	654,010
New Castle	**10003**	**13.2**	**500,265**	**4.7**	**523,864**	**4.2**	**545,859**
Cecil, MD	24015	20.5	85,951	13.2	97,326	11.1	108,151
Total: Metro Portion of State		**13.4**	**626,962**	**5.8**	**663,422**	**5.2**	**697,874**
Total: Delaware		17.6	783,600	7.1	839,169	6.3	891,897
District of Columbia							
Washington, DC-MD-VA-WV PMSA	.8840	16.6	4,923,153	9.8	5,407,889	8.5	5,867,015
District of Columbia	**11001**	**-5.7**	**572,059**	**-4.0**	**548,902**	**-3.9**	**527,662**
Calvert, MD	24009	45.1	74,563	21.0	90,186	16.6	105,178
Charles, MD	24017	19.2	120,546	15.9	139,740	13.2	158,178
Frederick, MD	24021	30.0	195,277	15.4	225,299	12.7	253,983

* Indicates county is included from metro in different state.
Source: Devonshire Associates Ltd. and Scan/US, Inc. 2005.

[1] Census population includes a portion of Broomfield county.

Metropolitan Statistical Areas and Their Component Counties: Population Trends, *Continued*

MSA	FIPS Code	Past: 1990-2000 % Change	Past: 2000 Census	Present: 2000-2005 % Change	Present: 7/1/05 Estimate	Future: 2005-2010 % Change	Future: 2010 Projection
Montgomery, MD	24031	15.4	873,341	8.5	947,578	7.3	1,017,181
Prince George's, MD	24033	9.9	801,515	7.7	863,468	6.9	923,099
Alexandria, VA (Ind. City)	51510	15.4	128,283	-0.1	128,132	-0.8	127,123
Arlington, VA	51013	10.8	189,453	-1.9	185,858	-1.8	182,475
Clarke, VA	51043	4.6	12,652	9.8	13,896	8.5	15,075
Culpeper, VA	51047	23.3	34,262	20.6	41,320	16.4	48,099
Fairfax, VA	51059	18.5	969,749	4.8	1,016,742	4.2	1,059,612
Fairfax, VA (Ind. City)	51600	9.6	21,498	3.3	22,200	2.8	22,824
Falls Church, VA (Ind. City)	51610	8.3	10,377	3.3	10,716	2.9	11,022
Fauquier, VA	51061	13.1	55,139	17.6	64,828	14.2	74,034
Fredericksburg, VA (Ind. City)	51630	1.3	19,279	7.7	20,769	6.8	22,189
King George, VA	51099	24.2	16,803	16.4	19,561	13.5	22,193
Loudoun, VA	51107	96.9	169,599	48.6	252,089	30.9	329,892
Manassas, VA (Ind. City)	51683	25.7	35,135	8.4	38,088	7.0	40,756
Manassas Park, VA (Ind. City)	51685	52.8	10,290	11.1	11,429	9.5	12,518
Prince William, VA	51153	30.2	280,813	25.5	352,321	19.4	420,534
Spotsylvania, VA	51177	57.5	90,395	30.7	118,182	22.4	144,675
Stafford, VA	51179	51.0	92,446	30.9	121,019	22.6	148,329
Warren, VA	51187	20.8	31,584	11.1	35,096	9.6	38,451
Berkeley, WV	54003	28.1	75,905	20.4	91,401	16.3	106,284
Jefferson, WV	54037	17.4	42,190	16.3	49,069	13.4	55,649
Total: Metro Portion of District		-5.7	572,059	-4.0	548,902	-3.9	527,662
Total: District of Columbia		-5.7	572,059	-4.0	548,902	-3.9	527,662
Florida							
Daytona Beach MSA	2020	23.5	493,175	12.3	554,014	10.5	612,372
Flagler	12035	73.6	49,832	41.6	70,570	28.3	90,512
Volusia	12127	19.6	443,343	9.0	483,444	7.9	521,860
Fort Lauderdale PMSA	2680	29.3	1,623,018	10.5	1,794,053	9.0	1,955,383
Broward	12011	29.3	1,623,018	10.5	1,794,053	9.0	1,955,383
Fort Myers-Cape Coral MSA	2700	31.6	440,888	18.7	523,512	15.2	603,036
Lee	12071	31.6	440,888	18.7	523,512	15.2	603,036
Fort Pierce-Port St. Lucie MSA	2710	27.2	319,426	15.1	367,537	12.8	414,409
Martin	12085	25.6	126,731	10.6	140,204	9.3	153,278
St. Lucie	12111	28.3	192,695	18.0	227,333	14.9	261,131
Fort Walton Beach MSA	2750	18.6	170,498	6.9	182,186	6.2	193,464
Okaloosa	12091	18.6	170,498	6.9	182,186	6.2	193,464
Gainesville MSA	2900	20.0	217,955	2.5	223,316	2.3	228,469
Alachua	12001	20.0	217,955	2.5	223,316	2.3	228,469
Jacksonville MSA	3600	21.4	1,100,491	11.3	1,224,737	9.9	1,345,578
Clay	12019	32.9	140,814	18.5	166,915	15.1	192,116
Duval	12031	15.7	778,879	7.7	838,841	7.1	897,985
Nassau	12089	31.2	57,663	10.9	63,967	9.4	69,968
St. Johns	12109	46.9	123,135	25.9	155,014	19.7	185,509
Lakeland-Winter Haven MSA	3980	19.4	483,924	8.7	526,208	7.7	566,911
Polk	12105	19.4	483,924	8.7	526,208	7.7	566,911
Melbourne-Titusville-Palm Bay MSA	4900	19.4	476,230	9.9	523,567	8.7	569,284
Brevard	12009	19.4	476,230	9.9	523,567	8.7	569,284
Miami PMSA	5000	16.3	2,253,362	6.1	2,391,206	5.5	2,522,264
Miami-Dade	12086	16.3	2,253,362	6.1	2,391,206	5.5	2,522,264
Naples MSA	5345	65.3	251,377	22.1	306,973	17.2	359,758
Collier	12021	65.3	251,377	22.1	306,973	17.2	359,758
Ocala MSA	5790	32.9	258,916	13.8	294,555	11.6	328,736
Marion	12083	32.9	258,916	13.8	294,555	11.6	328,736
Orlando MSA	5960	34.3	1,644,561	15.6	1,900,560	12.8	2,144,445
Lake	12069	38.4	210,528	27.8	269,070	20.9	325,184
Orange	12095	32.3	896,344	12.2	1,006,134	10.3	1,109,877
Osceola	12097	60.1	172,493	31.5	226,787	23.1	279,286
Seminole	12117	27.0	365,196	9.1	398,569	7.9	430,098
Panama City MSA	6015	16.7	148,217	7.3	159,012	6.8	169,776
Bay	12005	16.7	148,217	7.3	159,012	6.8	169,776
Pensacola MSA	6080	19.7	412,153	6.1	437,128	5.6	461,430
Escambia	12033	12.0	294,410	0.4	295,558	0.4	296,781
Santa Rosa	12113	44.3	117,743	20.2	141,570	16.3	164,649
Punta Gorda MSA	6580	27.6	141,627	12.9	159,967	11.0	177,627
Charlotte	12015	27.6	141,627	12.9	159,967	11.0	177,627
Sarasota-Bradenton MSA	7510	20.5	589,959	11.8	659,642	10.1	726,472
Manatee	12081	24.7	264,002	13.7	300,298	11.5	334,840
Sarasota	12115	17.3	325,957	10.2	359,344	9.0	391,632
Tallahassee MSA	8240	21.8	284,539	1.8	289,597	1.7	294,535
Gadsden	12039	9.7	45,087	1.7	45,844	1.7	46,633
Leon	12073	24.4	239,452	1.8	243,753	1.7	247,902
Tampa-St. Petersburg-Clearwater MSA	8280	15.9	2,395,997	9.1	2,613,412	8.0	2,822,434
Hernando	12053	29.4	130,802	15.7	151,302	13.1	171,067
Hillsborough	12057	19.8	998,948	12.0	1,118,988	10.3	1,234,723
Pasco	12101	22.6	344,765	20.6	415,912	16.4	484,329
Pinellas	12103	8.2	921,482	0.6	927,210	0.6	932,315
West Palm Beach-Boca Raton MSA	8960	31.0	1,131,184	12.0	1,267,148	10.4	1,398,390
Palm Beach	12099	31.0	1,131,184	12.0	1,267,148	10.4	1,398,390
Total: Metro Portion of State		23.4	14,837,497	10.5	16,398,330	9.1	17,894,773
Total: Florida		23.5	15,982,378	10.3	17,633,938	9.0	19,219,041
Georgia							
Albany MSA	0120	7.3	120,822	5.1	126,968	4.8	133,030
Dougherty	13095	-0.3	96,065	-0.6	95,460	-0.6	94,904
Lee	13177	52.4	24,757	27.3	31,508	21.0	38,126
Athens MSA	0500	21.5	153,444	5.8	162,302	5.0	170,474
Clarke	13059	15.9	101,489	3.3	104,888	2.9	107,919
Madison	13195	22.2	25,730	9.1	28,081	7.9	30,297
Oconee	13219	48.9	26,225	11.9	29,333	10.0	32,258
Atlanta MSA	0520	38.9	4,112,198	13.3	4,657,401	11.0	5,168,849
Barrow	13013	55.3	46,144	25.9	58,111	19.9	69,674
Bartow	13015	36.0	76,019	19.4	90,793	15.5	104,872
Carroll	13045	22.2	87,268	21.6	106,138	17.0	124,223
Cherokee	13057	57.3	141,903	28.6	182,558	21.3	221,356
Clayton	13063	29.9	236,517	1.9	241,082	1.0	243,517
Cobb	13067	35.7	607,751	11.5	677,675	9.6	742,723
Coweta	13077	65.7	89,215	22.7	109,445	17.6	128,756
DeKalb	13089	22.0	665,865	2.1	679,804	1.6	690,779
Douglas	13097	29.6	92,174	17.5	108,297	14.4	123,916
Fayette	13113	46.2	91,263	13.5	103,541	11.0	114,966
Forsyth	13117	123.2	98,407	42.5	140,241	28.4	180,032
Fulton	13121	25.7	816,006	0.9	822,956	0.7	828,558
Gwinnett	13135	66.7	588,448	23.4	725,943	17.8	855,451
Henry	13151	103.2	119,341	42.0	169,496	28.3	217,404
Newton	13217	48.3	62,001	38.2	85,695	26.6	108,499
Paulding	13223	96.3	81,678	36.6	111,558	25.6	140,064
Pickens	13227	59.3	22,983	27.9	29,406	20.6	35,452
Rockdale	13247	29.6	70,111	11.3	78,002	9.5	85,415
Spalding	13255	7.3	58,417	5.9	61,851	5.4	65,194
Walton	13297	57.3	60,687	23.3	74,809	17.6	87,998
Augusta-Aiken, GA-SC MSA	0600	15.0	477,441	3.6	494,516	3.3	510,890
Columbia	13073	35.2	89,288	14.5	102,278	12.2	114,723
McDuffie	13189	5.5	21,231	1.7	21,591	1.4	21,894
Richmond	13245	5.3	199,775	-1.9	196,018	-1.8	192,421
Aiken, SC	45003	17.9	142,552	5.0	149,719	4.6	156,610
Edgefield, SC	45037	33.9	24,595	1.3	24,910	1.3	25,242
Columbus, GA-AL MSA	1800	5.3	274,624	-1.6	270,357	-0.8	268,314
Russell, AL	01113	6.2	49,756	-2.4	48,555	-2.3	47,428
Chattahoochee	13053	-12.1	14,882	-11.2	13,213	-3.0	12,813
Harris	13145	33.2	23,695	15.7	27,412	13.1	31,009
Muscogee	13215	3.9	186,291	-2.7	181,177	-2.3	177,064
Macon MSA	4680	10.9	322,549	6.6	343,865	5.9	364,318
Bibb	13021	2.6	153,887	0.9	155,253	0.8	156,539
Houston	13153	24.2	110,765	14.1	126,391	11.9	141,461
Jones	13169	14.0	23,639	13.4	26,799	11.6	29,899
Peach	13225	11.7	23,668	5.2	24,889	4.2	25,943
Twiggs	13289	8.0	10,590	-0.5	10,533	-0.5	10,476
Savannah MSA	7520	13.5	293,000	6.6	312,351	5.9	330,822
Bryan	13029	51.7	23,417	19.4	27,955	15.9	32,387
Chatham	13051	7.0	232,048	2.6	238,192	2.4	243,819
Effingham	13103	46.1	37,535	23.1	46,204	18.2	54,616
* **Catoosa County**	13047	25.5	53,282	15.1	61,327	12.5	68,977
* **Dade County**	13083	15.3	15,154	8.0	16,361	7.0	17,514
* **Walker County** (See Chattanooga, TN-GA MSA.)	13295	4.7	61,053	4.4	63,750	4.1	66,335
Total: Metro Portion of State		30.2	5,666,664	10.9	6,286,014	9.3	6,870,243
Total: Georgia		26.4	8,186,453	9.6	8,969,042	8.2	9,707,997
Hawaii							
Honolulu MSA	3320	4.8	876,156	3.9	910,475	3.9	945,789
Honolulu	15003	4.8	876,156	3.9	910,475	3.9	945,789
Total: Metro Portion of State		4.8	876,156	3.9	910,475	3.9	945,789
Total: Hawaii		9.3	1,211,537	5.1	1,273,900	4.9	1,335,692
Idaho							
Boise City MSA	1080	46.1	432,345	16.6	504,057	13.4	571,805
Ada	16001	46.2	300,904	12.8	339,342	10.7	375,504
Canyon	16027	45.9	131,441	25.3	164,715	19.2	196,301
Pocatello MSA	6340	14.4	75,565	-0.1	75,502	-0.1	75,389
Bannock	16005	14.4	75,565	-0.1	75,502	-0.1	75,389
Total: Metro Portion of State		40.4	507,910	14.1	579,559	11.7	647,194
Total: Idaho		28.5	1,293,953	9.1	1,411,270	7.9	1,522,862
Illinois							
Bloomington-Normal MSA	1040	16.5	150,433	6.7	160,498	6.0	170,048
McLean	17113	16.5	150,433	6.7	160,498	6.0	170,048
Champaign-Urbana MSA	1400	3.8	179,669	3.6	186,135	3.3	192,360
Champaign	17019	3.8	179,669	3.6	186,135	3.3	192,360
Chicago PMSA	1600	11.6	8,272,768	4.2	8,619,113	3.8	8,944,692
Cook	17031	5.3	5,376,741	-0.8	5,332,321	-0.9	5,286,501
DeKalb	17037	14.2	88,969	8.2	96,267	7.2	103,181
DuPage	17043	15.7	904,161	3.7	937,264	3.2	967,550
Grundy	17063	16.1	37,535	8.8	40,846	7.7	43,999
Kane	17089	27.3	404,119	21.3	490,051	16.8	572,298
Kendall	17093	38.4	54,544	37.3	74,879	26.2	94,525
Lake	17097	24.8	644,356	9.4	704,726	8.0	761,208
McHenry	17111	41.9	260,077	16.2	302,316	13.4	342,870
Will	17197	40.6	502,266	27.5	640,443	20.6	772,560
Decatur MSA	2040	-2.1	114,706	-4.9	109,127	-4.7	104,032
Macon	17115	-2.1	114,706	-4.9	109,127	-4.7	104,032
Kankakee PMSA	3740	7.9	103,833	3.7	107,719	3.5	111,511
Kankakee	17091	7.9	103,833	3.7	107,719	3.5	111,511
Peoria-Pekin MSA	6120	2.4	347,387	-0.2	346,545	-0.2	345,823
Peoria	17143	0.3	183,433	-1.2	181,293	-1.1	179,349
Tazewell	17179	3.9	128,485	-0.1	128,302	-0.2	128,094
Woodford	17203	8.6	35,469	4.2	36,950	3.9	38,380
Rockford MSA	6880	12.6	371,236	5.5	391,588	4.9	410,833
Boone	17007	35.6	41,786	18.7	49,590	15.1	57,085
Ogle	17141	11.0	51,032	6.2	54,203	5.6	57,225
Winnebago	17201	10.1	278,418	3.4	287,795	3.0	296,523
Springfield MSA	7880	6.3	201,437	2.5	206,549	2.4	211,478
Menard	17129	11.8	12,486	2.0	12,738	1.7	12,958
Sangamon	17167	5.9	188,951	2.6	193,811	2.4	198,520
* **Henry County**	17073	-0.3	51,020	-0.9	50,536	-1.0	50,012
* **Rock Island County** (See Davenport-Moline-Rock Island, IA-IL MSA.)	17161	0.4	149,374	-1.6	146,919	-1.5	144,712
* **Clinton County**	17027	4.7	35,535	2.1	36,286	2.0	36,996
* **Jersey County**	17083	5.5	21,668	3.4	22,415	3.3	23,156
* **Madison County**	17119	3.9	258,941	1.7	263,396	1.6	267,624
* **Monroe County**	17133	23.2	27,619	12.4	31,030	10.5	34,284
* **St. Clair County** (See St. Louis, MO-IL MSA.)	17163	-2.6	256,082	1.6	260,165	1.5	264,081
Total: Metro Portion of State		10.1	10,541,708	3.8	10,938,021	3.4	11,311,642
Total: Illinois		8.6	12,419,293	3.0	12,788,145	2.7	13,136,615
Indiana							
Bloomington MSA	1020	10.6	120,563	0.2	120,813	0.2	121,016
Monroe	18105	10.6	120,563	0.2	120,813	0.2	121,016
Elkhart-Goshen MSA	2330	17.0	182,791	5.4	192,614	4.7	201,665
Elkhart	18039	17.0	182,791	5.4	192,614	4.7	201,665
Evansville-Henderson, IN-KY MSA	2440	6.2	296,195	1.8	301,479	1.7	306,597
Posey	18129	4.2	27,061	-0.8	26,837	-0.9	26,598
Vanderburgh	18163	4.2	171,922	0.6	173,036	0.7	174,191
Warrick	18173	16.6	52,383	7.2	56,136	6.3	59,690
Henderson, KY	21101	4.1	44,829	1.4	45,470	1.4	46,118
Fort Wayne MSA	2760	10.1	502,141	3.5	519,862	3.2	536,419
Adams	18001	8.1	33,625	0.6	33,818	0.6	34,010
Allen	18003	10.3	331,849	4.1	345,326	3.6	357,869
De Kalb	18033	14.0	40,285	3.4	41,636	2.9	42,862
Huntington	18069	7.5	38,075	0.8	38,393	0.8	38,682
Wells	18179	6.4	27,600	2.1	28,181	2.0	28,737
Whitley	18183	11.1	30,707	5.9	32,508	5.4	34,259
Gary PMSA	2960	4.4	631,362	2.3	645,927	2.2	659,848
Lake	18089	1.9	484,564	1.0	489,391	1.0	494,044
Porter	18127	13.9	146,798	6.6	156,536	5.9	165,804
Indianapolis MSA	3480	16.4	1,607,486	7.3	1,724,043	6.4	1,834,827
Boone	18011	20.9	46,107	12.0	51,660	10.2	56,921
Hamilton	18057	67.7	182,740	33.8	244,530	24.2	303,639
Hancock	18059	21.7	55,391	12.4	62,264	10.6	68,861
Hendricks	18063	37.5	104,093	22.9	127,940	17.6	150,445
Johnson	18081	30.8	115,209	11.7	128,689	9.9	141,367
Madison	18095	2.1	133,358	-2.7	129,750	-2.7	126,277
Marion	18097	7.9	860,454	0.6	865,538	0.6	870,495
Morgan	18109	19.3	66,689	5.1	70,108	4.6	73,307
Shelby	18145	7.8	43,445	0.3	43,564	-0.1	43,515
Kokomo MSA	3850	4.7	101,541	-0.3	101,209	-0.3	100,883
Howard	18067	5.1	84,964	-0.3	84,735	-0.3	84,494
Tipton	18159	2.8	16,577	-0.6	16,474	-0.5	16,389
Lafayette MSA	3920	13.2	182,821	2.1	186,643	1.9	190,161
Clinton	18023	9.3	33,866	0.6	34,053	0.2	34,122
Tippecanoe	18157	14.1	148,955	2.4	152,590	2.3	156,039
Muncie MSA	5280	-0.7	118,769	-0.8	117,847	-0.7	117,042
Delaware	18035	-0.7	118,769	-0.8	117,847	-0.7	117,042
South Bend MSA	7800	7.5	265,559	0.5	266,795	0.3	267,686
St. Joseph	18141	7.5	265,559	0.5	266,795	0.3	267,686
Terre Haute MSA	8320	1.1	149,192	-2.1	146,116	-1.9	143,291
Clay	18021	7.5	26,556	1.8	27,038	1.7	27,500
Vermillion	18165	0.1	16,788	-2.7	16,339	-2.6	15,909
Vigo	18167	-0.2	105,848	-2.9	102,739	-2.8	99,882
* **Clark County**	18019	9.9	96,472	5.0	101,296	4.4	105,779
* **Floyd County**	18043	10.0	70,823	1.2	71,650	1.0	72,393
* **Harrison County**	18061	14.8	34,325	6.5	36,550	5.6	38,587
* **Scott County** (See Louisville, KY-IN MSA.)	18143	9.4	22,960	4.2	23,934	3.7	24,816
* **Dearborn County**	18029	18.7	46,109	6.6	49,138	5.7	51,918
* **Ohio County** (See Cincinnati, OH-KY-IN PMSA.)	18115	5.8	5,623	3.3	5,809	2.8	5,974
Total: Metro Portion of State		10.8	4,389,903	4.0	4,566,255	3.6	4,732,784
Total: Indiana		9.7	6,080,485	3.1	6,270,352	2.8	6,448,758
Iowa							
Cedar Rapids MSA	1360	13.6	191,701	3.5	198,432	3.1	204,502
Linn	19113	13.6	191,701	3.5	198,432	3.1	204,502
Davenport-Moline-Rock Island, IA-IL MSA	1960	2.3	359,062	-0.5	357,408	-0.4	355,816
Henry, IL	17073	-0.3	51,020	-0.9	50,536	-1.0	50,012
Rock Island, IL	17161	0.4	149,374	-1.6	146,919	-1.5	144,712
Scott	19163	5.1	158,668	0.8	159,953	0.7	161,092
Des Moines MSA	2120	16.1	456,022	7.5	490,399	6.6	522,858
Dallas	19049	37.0	40,750	23.1	50,179	18.1	59,282
Polk	19153	14.5	374,601	6.0	397,152	5.3	418,267
Warren	19181	12.9	40,671	5.9	43,068	5.2	45,309
Dubuque MSA	2200	3.2	89,143	2.3	91,167	2.0	93,009
Dubuque	19061	3.2	89,143	2.3	91,167	2.0	93,009
Iowa City MSA	3500	15.5	111,006	5.6	117,205	5.0	123,052
Johnson	19103	15.5	111,006	5.6	117,205	5.0	123,052
Sioux City, IA-NE MSA	7720	7.9	124,130	-0.4	123,592	-0.5	122,975
Woodbury	19193	5.7	103,877	-1.0	102,793	-1.1	101,679
Dakota, NE	31043	21.0	20,253	2.7	20,799	2.4	21,296
Waterloo-Cedar Falls MSA	8920	3.4	128,012	-2.1	125,273	-2.0	122,736
Black Hawk	19013	3.4	128,012	-2.1	125,273	-2.0	122,736
* **Pottawattamie County** (See Omaha, NE-IA MSA.)	19155	6.1	87,704	1.3	88,801	0.9	89,567
Total: Metro Portion of State		10.5	1,326,133	3.6	1,374,023	3.2	1,418,495
Total: Iowa		5.4	2,926,324	0.9	2,951,374	0.8	2,974,324
Kansas							
Lawrence MSA	4150	22.2	99,962	3.3	103,269	3.0	106,337
Douglas	20045	22.2	99,962	3.3	103,269	3.0	106,337

* Indicates county is included from metro in different state.
Source: Devonshire Associates Ltd. and Scan/US, Inc. 2005.

Continued on next page

Metropolitan Statistical Areas and Their Component Counties: Population Trends, *Continued*

MSA	FIPS Code	Past: 1990-2000 % Change	Past: 2000 Census	Present: 2000-2005 % Change	Present: 7/1/05 Estimate	Future: 2005-2010 % Change	Future: 2010 Projection
Topeka MSA	.8440	5.5	169,871	1.3	172,022	1.1	173,843
Shawnee	20177	5.5	169,871	1.3	172,022	1.1	173,843
Wichita MSA[2]	.9040	12.8	512,351	3.6	530,928	3.3	548,235
Butler	20015	17.6	59,482	4.3	62,010	3.7	64,277
Sedgwick	20173	12.2	452,869	3.5	468,918	3.2	483,958
* Johnson County	20091	27.0	451,086	12.5	507,661	10.4	560,260
* Leavenworth County	20103	6.7	68,691	8.0	74,179	6.9	79,330
* Miami County	20121	20.8	28,351	4.6	29,658	3.8	30,790
* Wyandotte County (See Kansas City, MO-KS MSA.)	20209	-2.5	157,882	-0.9	156,403	-1.0	154,859
Total: Metro Portion of State		14.3	1,488,194	5.8	1,574,120	5.1	1,653,654
Total: Kansas		8.5	2,688,418	2.1	2,746,171	1.9	2,799,691

Kentucky

MSA	FIPS Code	Past: 1990-2000 % Change	Past: 2000 Census	Present: 2000-2005 % Change	Present: 7/1/05 Estimate	Future: 2005-2010 % Change	Future: 2010 Projection
Lexington MSA	.4280	18.0	479,198	5.9	507,373	5.2	533,961
Bourbon	21017	0.6	19,360	1.4	19,637	1.3	19,898
Clark	21049	12.4	33,144	3.6	34,351	3.2	35,453
Fayette	21067	15.6	260,512	4.0	270,888	3.7	280,831
Jessamine	21113	28.0	39,041	10.1	42,965	8.7	46,710
Madison	21151	23.2	70,872	8.2	76,677	7.0	82,079
Scott	21209	38.5	33,061	17.9	38,974	14.2	44,504
Woodford	21239	16.3	23,208	2.9	23,881	2.5	24,486
Louisville, KY-IN MSA	.4520	8.1	1,025,598	2.9	1,055,433	2.6	1,082,969
Clark, IN	18019	9.9	96,472	5.0	101,296	4.4	105,779
Floyd, IN	18043	10.0	70,823	1.2	71,650	1.0	72,393
Harrison, IN	18061	14.8	34,325	6.5	36,550	5.6	38,587
Scott, IN	18143	9.4	22,960	4.2	23,934	3.7	24,816
Bullitt	21029	28.7	61,236	9.8	67,211	8.3	72,761
Jefferson	21111	4.3	693,604	1.2	701,817	1.1	709,724
Oldham	21185	38.8	46,178	14.7	52,975	11.2	58,909
Owensboro MSA	.5990	5.0	91,545	1.5	92,957	1.4	94,290
Daviess	21059	5.0	91,545	1.5	92,957	1.4	94,290
* Henderson County (See Evansville-Henderson, IN-KY MSA.)	21101	4.1	44,829	1.4	45,470	1.4	46,118
* Boone County	21015	49.3	85,991	20.8	103,836	16.2	120,627
* Campbell County	21037	5.7	88,616	-1.7	87,132	-1.7	85,641
* Gallatin County	21077	45.9	7,870	3.2	8,122	3.2	8,384
* Grant County	21081	42.2	22,384	11.8	25,032	9.9	27,503
* Kenton County	21117	6.6	151,464	0.9	152,794	0.7	153,919
* Pendleton County (See Cincinnati, OH-KY-IN PMSA.)	21191	19.6	14,390	7.0	15,401	5.8	16,296
* Christian County (See Clarksville-Hopkinsville, TN-KY MSA.)	21047	4.8	72,265	-2.8	70,255	-2.8	68,296
* Boyd County	21019	-2.7	49,752	0.3	49,908	0.5	50,148
* Carter County	21043	10.5	26,889	2.6	27,587	2.6	28,295
* Greenup County (See Huntington-Ashland, WV-KY-OH MSA.)	21089	0.4	36,891	0.8	37,186	0.9	37,530
Total: Metro Portion of State		10.9	1,973,102	3.6	2,045,056	3.3	2,112,402
Total: Kentucky		9.7	4,041,769	3.0	4,164,333	2.8	4,279,671

Louisiana (Parishes)

MSA	FIPS Code	Past: 1990-2000 % Change	Past: 2000 Census	Present: 2000-2005 % Change	Present: 7/1/05 Estimate	Future: 2005-2010 % Change	Future: 2010 Projection
Alexandria MSA	.0220	-4.0	126,337	0.6	127,099	0.5	127,698
Rapides	22079	-4.0	126,337	0.6	127,099	0.5	127,698
Baton Rouge MSA	.0760	14.1	602,894	4.0	627,014	3.5	649,179
Ascension	22005	31.6	76,627	15.5	88,503	12.4	99,442
East Baton Rouge	22033	8.6	412,852	-0.9	409,249	-0.9	405,635
Livingston	22063	30.2	91,814	17.2	107,626	13.7	122,405
West Baton Rouge	22121	11.2	21,601	0.2	21,636	0.3	21,667
Houma MSA	.3350	6.4	194,477	1.9	198,122	1.8	201,610
Lafourche	22057	4.8	89,974	2.0	91,749	1.9	93,469
Terrebonne	22109	7.8	104,503	1.8	106,373	1.7	108,141
Lafayette MSA	.3880	11.8	385,647	2.1	393,730	1.9	401,337
Acadia	22001	5.3	58,861	0.3	59,013	0.3	59,164
Lafayette	22055	15.6	190,503	2.3	194,974	2.2	199,223
St. Landry	22097	9.2	87,700	1.8	89,252	1.6	90,680
St. Martin	22099	10.5	48,583	3.9	50,491	3.5	52,270
Lake Charles MSA	.3960	9.2	183,577	-0.2	183,193	-0.2	182,785
Calcasieu	22019	9.2	183,577	-0.2	183,193	-0.2	182,785
Monroe MSA	.5200	3.6	147,250	0.1	147,371	0.1	147,574
Ouachita	22073	3.6	147,250	0.1	147,371	0.1	147,574
New Orleans MSA	.5560	4.1	1,337,726	-0.6	1,329,657	-0.5	1,323,366
Jefferson	22051	1.6	455,466	-1.7	447,509	-1.6	440,244
Orleans	22071	-2.5	484,674	-5.9	456,285	-5.7	430,487
Plaquemines	22075	4.6	26,757	6.8	28,584	6.3	30,379
St. Bernard	22087	0.9	67,229	-3.9	64,622	-3.6	62,286
St. Charles	22089	13.3	48,072	3.6	49,807	3.1	51,375
St. James	22093	1.6	21,216	-0.9	21,026	-0.8	20,854
St. John The Baptist	22095	7.6	43,044	6.3	45,754	5.6	48,304
St. Tammany	22103	32.4	191,268	13.0	216,070	10.8	239,437
Shreveport-Bossier City MSA	.7680	4.2	392,302	7.2	420,461	6.6	448,010
Bossier	22015	14.2	98,310	5.6	103,854	4.9	108,957
Caddo	22017	1.6	252,161	9.4	275,910	8.5	299,381
Webster	22119	-0.4	41,831	-2.7	40,697	-2.5	39,672
Total: Metro Portion of State		6.7	3,370,210	1.7	3,426,647	1.6	3,481,559
Total: Louisiana		5.9	4,468,976	0.9	4,510,134	0.9	4,550,648

Maine

MSA	FIPS Code	Past: 1990-2000 % Change	Past: 2000 Census	Present: 2000-2005 % Change	Present: 7/1/05 Estimate	Future: 2005-2010 % Change	Future: 2010 Projection
Bangor NECMA	.0733	-1.1	144,919	3.2	149,585	3.1	154,285
Penobscot	23019	-1.1	144,919	3.2	149,585	3.1	154,285
Lewiston-Auburn NECMA	.4243	-1.4	103,793	3.7	107,666	3.5	111,467
Androscoggin	23001	-1.4	103,793	3.7	107,666	3.5	111,467
Portland NECMA	.6403	9.2	265,612	3.9	275,908	3.6	285,820
Cumberland	23005	9.2	265,612	3.9	275,908	3.6	285,820
Total: Metro Portion of State		3.9	514,324	3.7	533,159	3.5	551,572
Total: Maine		3.8	1,274,923	4.2	1,328,582	3.9	1,379,771

Maryland

MSA	FIPS Code	Past: 1990-2000 % Change	Past: 2000 Census	Present: 2000-2005 % Change	Present: 7/1/05 Estimate	Future: 2005-2010 % Change	Future: 2010 Projection
Baltimore PMSA	.0720	7.2	2,552,994	4.1	2,658,807	3.8	2,761,004
Anne Arundel	24003	14.6	489,656	5.6	517,299	5.0	543,077
Baltimore	24005	9.0	754,292	4.9	791,384	4.4	826,495
Baltimore (Ind. City)	24510	-11.5	651,154	-5.2	617,204	-4.9	587,263
Carroll	24013	22.3	150,897	13.4	171,167	11.4	190,663
Harford	24025	20.0	218,590	10.1	240,719	8.8	261,870
Howard	24027	32.3	247,842	10.7	274,373	9.0	299,101
Queen Anne's	24035	19.5	40,563	15.0	46,661	12.6	52,535
Cumberland, MD-WV MSA	.1900	0.4	102,008	-1.5	100,474	-1.4	99,073
Allegany	24001	-0.0	74,930	-2.2	73,274	-2.1	71,735
Mineral, WV	54057	1.4	27,078	0.5	27,200	0.5	27,338
Hagerstown PMSA	.3180	8.7	131,923	6.4	140,320	5.8	148,477
Washington	24043	8.7	131,923	6.4	140,320	5.8	148,477
* Cecil County (See Wilmington-Newark, DE-MD PMSA.)	24015	20.5	85,951	13.2	97,326	11.1	108,151
* Calvert County	24009	45.1	74,563	21.0	90,186	16.6	105,178
* Charles County	24017	19.2	120,546	15.9	139,740	13.2	158,178
* Frederick County	24021	30.0	195,277	15.4	225,299	12.7	253,983
* Montgomery County	24031	15.4	873,341	8.5	947,578	7.3	1,017,181
* Prince George's County (See Washington, DC-MD-VA-WV PMSA.)	24033	9.9	801,515	7.7	863,468	6.9	923,099
Total: Metro Portion of State		10.6	4,911,040	6.6	5,235,998	5.9	5,546,986
Total: Maryland		10.8	5,296,486	6.6	5,645,286	5.9	5,979,065

Massachusetts

MSA	FIPS Code	Past: 1990-2000 % Change	Past: 2000 Census	Present: 2000-2005 % Change	Present: 7/1/05 Estimate	Future: 2005-2010 % Change	Future: 2010 Projection
Barnstable-Yarmouth NECMA	.0743	19.1	222,230	4.5	232,312	3.9	241,347
Barnstable	25001	19.1	222,230	4.5	232,312	3.9	241,347
Boston-Worcester-Lawrence-Lowell-Brockton, MA-NH NECMA	.1123	6.5	6,057,826	2.4	6,204,190	2.1	6,335,887
Bristol	25005	5.6	534,678	3.4	553,046	3.1	569,949
Essex	25009	8.0	723,419	2.9	744,047	2.5	762,420
Middlesex	25017	4.8	1,465,396	0.3	1,469,958	0.1	1,471,162
Norfolk	25021	5.6	650,308	0.7	655,077	0.6	659,014
Plymouth	25023	8.6	472,822	4.9	495,811	4.3	517,008
Suffolk	25025	3.9	689,807	-2.3	673,720	-2.3	657,995
Worcester	25027	5.8	750,963	5.3	790,475	4.8	828,032
Hillsborough, NH	33011	13.3	380,841	5.9	403,350	5.2	424,307
Rockingham, NH	33015	12.8	277,359	7.5	298,070	6.5	317,391
Strafford, NH	33017	7.7	112,233	7.5	120,636	6.6	128,609
Pittsfield NECMA	.6323	-3.2	134,953	-2.5	131,527	-2.4	128,335
Berkshire	25003	-3.2	134,953	-2.5	131,527	-2.4	128,335
Springfield NECMA	.8003	0.9	608,479	1.5	617,467	1.4	625,916
Hampden	25013	-0.0	456,228	1.5	463,031	1.4	469,420
Hampshire	25015	3.9	152,251	1.4	154,436	1.3	156,496
Total: Metro Portion of State		5.5	6,253,055	1.8	6,363,440	1.5	6,461,178
Total: Massachusetts		5.5	6,349,097	1.8	6,461,761	1.5	6,561,659

Michigan

MSA	FIPS Code	Past: 1990-2000 % Change	Past: 2000 Census	Present: 2000-2005 % Change	Present: 7/1/05 Estimate	Future: 2005-2010 % Change	Future: 2010 Projection
Ann Arbor PMSA	.0440	18.1	578,736	9.4	633,040	8.1	684,095
Lenawee	26091	8.1	98,890	3.5	102,302	3.1	105,474
Livingston	26093	35.7	156,951	16.5	182,797	13.3	207,062
Washtenaw	26161	14.1	322,895	7.8	347,941	6.8	371,559
Benton Harbor MSA	.0870	0.7	162,453	0.3	162,940	0.2	163,248
Berrien	26021	0.7	162,453	0.3	162,940	0.2	163,248
Detroit PMSA	.2160	4.1	4,441,551	0.7	4,472,407	0.6	4,498,955
Lapeer	26087	17.6	87,904	6.6	93,745	5.8	99,150
Macomb	26099	9.9	788,149	5.2	829,028	4.6	866,942
Monroe	26115	9.2	145,945	5.4	153,774	4.7	161,017
Oakland	26125	10.2	1,194,156	1.7	1,214,978	1.5	1,233,145
St. Clair	26147	12.8	164,235	5.2	172,724	4.6	180,692
Wayne	26163	-2.4	2,061,162	-2.6	2,008,158	-2.5	1,958,009
Flint PMSA	.2640	1.3	436,141	2.2	445,626	1.9	454,172
Genesee	26049	1.3	436,141	2.2	445,626	1.9	454,172
Grand Rapids-Muskegon-Holland MSA	.3000	16.1	1,088,514	5.1	1,144,317	4.5	1,195,956
Allegan	26005	16.7	105,665	7.7	113,751	6.7	121,352
Kent	26081	14.7	574,335	4.4	599,621	3.9	622,847
Muskegon	26121	7.1	170,200	2.9	175,106	2.6	179,638
Ottawa	26139	26.9	238,314	7.4	255,839	6.4	272,119
Jackson MSA	.3520	5.8	158,422	3.9	164,674	3.6	170,566
Jackson	26075	5.8	158,422	3.9	164,674	3.6	170,566
Kalamazoo-Battle Creek MSA	.3720	5.4	452,851	2.0	462,127	1.9	470,878
Calhoun	26025	1.5	137,985	1.0	139,305	0.9	140,493
Kalamazoo	26077	6.8	238,603	2.1	243,549	1.9	248,213
Van Buren	26159	8.9	76,263	3.9	79,273	3.7	82,172
Lansing-East Lansing MSA	.4040	3.5	447,728	3.1	461,446	2.8	474,468
Clinton	26037	11.9	64,753	7.6	69,693	6.8	74,398
Eaton	26045	11.6	103,655	4.3	108,140	3.9	112,348
Ingham	26065	-0.9	279,320	1.5	283,613	1.4	287,722
Saginaw-Bay City-Midland MSA	.6960	0.9	403,070	0.0	403,186	0.0	403,247
Bay	26017	-1.4	110,157	-1.0	109,101	-1.0	108,063
Midland	26111	9.5	82,874	2.9	85,259	2.6	87,498
Saginaw	26145	-0.9	210,039	-0.6	208,826	-0.5	207,686
Total: Metro Portion of State		6.1	8,169,466	2.2	8,349,763	2.0	8,515,585
Total: Michigan		6.9	9,938,444	2.3	10,164,188	2.0	10,372,286

Minnesota

MSA	FIPS Code	Past: 1990-2000 % Change	Past: 2000 Census	Present: 2000-2005 % Change	Present: 7/1/05 Estimate	Future: 2005-2010 % Change	Future: 2010 Projection
Duluth-Superior, MN-WI MSA	.2240	1.6	243,815	-0.8	241,789	-0.8	239,875
St. Louis	27137	1.2	200,528	-1.5	197,532	-1.4	194,767
Douglas, WI	55031	3.7	43,287	2.2	44,257	1.9	45,108
Minneapolis-St. Paul, MN-WI MSA	.5120	16.9	2,968,806	6.3	3,154,675	5.5	3,327,749
Anoka	27003	22.3	298,084	8.5	323,274	7.2	346,641
Carver	27019	46.5	70,205	20.3	84,468	16.0	98,024
Chisago	27025	34.7	41,101	21.6	49,980	16.8	58,375
Dakota	27037	29.3	355,904	7.7	383,221	6.6	408,473
Hennepin	27053	8.1	1,116,200	0.6	1,123,455	0.5	1,129,139
Isanti	27059	20.7	31,287	21.5	38,010	17.0	44,466
Ramsey	27123	5.2	511,035	-1.7	502,508	-1.7	493,791
Scott	27139	54.7	89,498	34.8	120,628	24.4	150,073
Sherburne	27141	53.6	64,417	27.4	82,041	20.3	98,726
Washington	27163	37.9	201,130	10.1	221,394	8.4	240,076
Wright	27171	31.0	89,986	23.1	110,736	18.0	130,635
Pierce, WI	55093	12.3	36,804	4.8	38,572	4.3	40,236
St. Croix, WI	55109	25.7	63,155	21.0	76,388	16.6	89,094
Rochester MSA	.6820	16.7	124,277	8.9	135,319	7.7	145,757
Olmsted	27109	16.7	124,277	8.9	135,319	7.7	145,757
St. Cloud MSA	.6980	12.4	167,392	9.8	183,879	8.6	199,661
Benton	27009	13.4	34,226	15.7	39,583	12.8	44,666
Stearns	27145	12.1	133,166	8.4	144,296	7.4	154,995
* Clay County (See Fargo-Moorhead, ND-MN MSA.)	27027	1.6	51,229	2.7	52,627	2.5	53,940
* Polk County (See Grand Forks, ND-MN MSA.)	27119	-3.5	31,369	-1.9	30,767	-2.0	30,162
* Houston County (See La Crosse, WI-MN MSA.)	27055	6.6	19,718	1.4	19,996	1.2	20,236
Total: Metro Portion of State		15.0	3,463,360	5.7	3,659,835	5.0	3,842,942
Total: Minnesota		12.4	4,919,479	4.7	5,148,487	4.2	5,363,223

Mississippi

MSA	FIPS Code	Past: 1990-2000 % Change	Past: 2000 Census	Present: 2000-2005 % Change	Present: 7/1/05 Estimate	Future: 2005-2010 % Change	Future: 2010 Projection
Biloxi-Gulfport-Pascagoula MSA	.0920	16.5	363,988	2.1	371,758	1.8	378,455
Hancock	28045	35.3	42,967	8.2	46,503	6.9	49,696
Harrison	28047	14.7	189,601	0.5	190,466	0.3	191,127
Jackson	28059	14.0	131,420	2.6	134,789	2.1	137,632
Hattiesburg MSA	.3285	13.1	111,674	6.3	118,728	5.5	125,259
Forrest	28035	6.3	72,604	3.4	75,059	3.0	77,299
Lamar	28073	28.4	39,070	11.8	43,669	9.8	47,960
Jackson MSA	.3560	11.5	440,801	4.7	461,453	4.2	480,793
Hinds	28049	-1.4	250,800	-1.1	248,051	-1.1	245,399
Madison	28089	38.8	74,674	11.1	82,974	9.5	90,825
Rankin	28121	32.3	115,327	13.1	130,428	10.8	144,569
* DeSoto County (See Memphis, TN-AR-MS MSA.)	28033	57.9	107,199	25.9	135,003	19.5	161,295
Total: Metro Portion of State		17.1	1,023,662	6.2	1,086,942	5.4	1,145,802
Total: Mississippi		10.5	2,844,658	2.1	2,904,093	1.9	2,959,451

Missouri

MSA	FIPS Code	Past: 1990-2000 % Change	Past: 2000 Census	Present: 2000-2005 % Change	Present: 7/1/05 Estimate	Future: 2005-2010 % Change	Future: 2010 Projection
Columbia MSA	.1740	20.5	135,454	6.1	143,667	5.5	151,543
Boone	29019	20.5	135,454	6.1	143,667	5.5	151,543
Joplin MSA	.3710	16.6	157,322	5.6	166,062	5.0	174,350
Jasper	29097	15.7	104,686	5.9	110,824	5.2	116,636
Newton	29145	18.4	52,636	4.9	55,238	4.5	57,714
Kansas City, MO-KS MSA	.3760	12.2	1,776,062	6.4	1,889,911	5.6	1,996,129
Johnson, KS	20091	27.0	451,086	12.5	507,661	10.4	560,260
Leavenworth, KS	20103	6.7	68,691	8.0	74,179	6.9	79,330
Miami, KS	20121	20.8	28,351	4.6	29,658	3.8	30,790
Wyandotte, KS	20209	-2.5	157,882	-0.9	156,403	-1.0	154,859
Cass	29037	28.7	82,092	13.8	93,436	11.6	104,263
Clay	29047	19.9	184,006	9.6	201,582	8.3	218,355
Clinton	29049	14.4	18,979	10.3	20,940	9.0	22,831
Jackson	29095	3.4	654,880	1.6	665,173	1.4	674,318
Lafayette	29107	6.0	32,960	0.8	33,226	0.5	33,399
Platte	29165	27.5	73,781	12.8	83,253	10.9	92,321
Ray	29177	6.3	23,354	4.5	24,400	4.1	25,403
St. Joseph MSA	.7000	4.9	102,490	-0.5	101,951	-0.7	101,261
Andrew	29003	12.7	16,492	3.9	17,141	3.5	17,741
Buchanan	29021	3.5	85,998	-1.4	84,810	-1.5	83,520
St. Louis, MO-IL MSA	.7040	4.5	2,603,607	2.6	2,672,574	2.5	2,739,104
Clinton, IL	17027	4.7	35,535	2.1	36,286	2.0	36,996
Jersey, IL	17083	5.5	21,668	3.4	22,415	3.3	23,156
Madison, IL	17119	3.9	258,941	1.7	263,396	1.6	267,624
Monroe, IL	17133	23.2	27,619	12.4	31,030	10.5	34,284
St. Clair, IL	17163	-2.6	256,082	1.6	260,165	1.5	264,081
Franklin	29071	16.4	93,807	6.1	99,506	5.4	104,904
Jefferson	29099	15.6	198,099	7.9	213,724	7.0	228,606
Lincoln	29113	34.8	38,944	23.0	47,892	18.1	56,559
St. Charles	29183	33.3	283,883	16.2	329,900	13.3	373,721
St. Louis	29189	2.3	1,016,315	-0.1	1,015,417	-0.2	1,013,712
St. Louis (Ind. City)	29510	-12.2	348,189	-6.9	324,238	-6.6	302,974
Warren	29219	25.6	24,525	16.6	28,605	13.6	32,487
Springfield MSA	.7920	23.2	325,721	7.7	350,755	6.8	374,623
Christian	29043	66.3	54,285	22.1	66,271	17.2	77,639
Greene	29077	15.6	240,391	4.0	249,887	3.7	259,037
Webster	29225	30.7	31,045	11.4	34,597	9.7	37,947
Total: Metro Portion of State		8.7	3,794,801	3.9	3,943,727	3.6	4,085,630
Total: Missouri		9.3	5,595,211	3.5	5,792,159	3.2	5,978,071

Montana

MSA	FIPS Code	Past: 1990-2000 % Change	Past: 2000 Census	Present: 2000-2005 % Change	Present: 7/1/05 Estimate	Future: 2005-2010 % Change	Future: 2010 Projection
Billings MSA	.0880	14.0	129,352	5.0	135,784	4.5	141,861
Yellowstone	30111	14.0	129,352	5.0	135,784	4.5	141,861
Great Falls MSA	.3040	3.4	80,357	-1.2	79,409	-1.1	78,518
Cascade	30013	3.4	80,357	-1.2	79,409	-1.1	78,518
Missoula MSA	.5140	21.8	95,802	4.5	100,118	3.9	104,056
Missoula	30063	21.8	95,802	4.5	100,118	3.9	104,056
Total: Metro Portion of State		13.2	305,511	3.2	315,311	2.9	324,435
Total: Montana		12.9	902,195	2.8	927,852	2.6	952,203

* Indicates county is included from metro in different state.
Source: Devonshire Associates Ltd. and Scan/US, Inc. 2005.

[2] Data excludes Harvey county, Kansas (2000 Census population 32,869; 2005 estimated population 34,021; and 2010 projected population 35,130) which fails to meet published standards for MSA inclusion, but has been included with the Wichita MSA as the result of Congressional action.

Metropolitan Statistical Areas and Their Component Counties: Population Trends, *Continued*

MSA	FIPS Code	Past: 1990-2000 % Change	Past: 2000 Census	Present: 2000-2005 % Change	Present: 7/1/05 Estimate	Future: 2005-2010 % Change	Future: 2010 Projection
Nebraska							
Lincoln MSA	.4360	17.2	250,291	6.5	266,575	5.7	281,788
Lancaster	31109	17.2	250,291	6.5	266,575	5.7	281,788
Omaha, NE-IA MSA	.5920	12.1	716,998	5.5	756,323	4.9	793,109
Pottawattamie, IA	19155	6.1	87,704	1.3	88,801	0.9	89,567
Cass	31025	14.1	24,334	6.1	25,823	5.4	27,226
Douglas	31055	11.3	463,585	4.4	483,981	3.9	503,039
Sarpy	31153	19.5	122,595	12.3	137,701	10.4	152,053
Washington	31177	13.1	18,780	6.6	20,017	6.0	21,224
* **Dakota County** (See Sioux City, IA-NE MSA.)	.31043	21.0	20,253	2.7	20,799	2.4	21,296
Total: Metro Portion of State		14.3	899,838	6.1	954,896	5.4	1,006,626
Total: Nebraska		8.4	1,711,263	2.4	1,751,975	2.2	1,790,712
Nevada							
Las Vegas, NV-AZ MSA	.4120	83.3	1,563,282	22.7	1,918,279	17.5	2,253,767
Mohave, AZ	04015	65.8	155,032	17.9	182,775	14.5	209,264
Clark	32003	85.5	1,375,765	23.4	1,697,755	17.9	2,001,933
Nye	32023	82.7	32,485	16.2	37,749	12.8	42,570
Reno MSA	.6720	33.3	339,486	15.0	390,302	12.5	439,196
Washoe	32031	33.3	339,486	15.0	390,302	12.5	439,196
Total: Metro Portion of State		72.4	1,747,736	21.6	2,125,806	16.8	2,483,699
Total: Nevada		66.3	1,998,257	19.7	2,391,581	15.6	2,764,949
New Hampshire							
* **Hillsborough County**	.33011	13.3	380,841	5.9	403,350	5.2	424,307
* **Rockingham County**	.33015	12.8	277,359	7.5	298,070	6.5	317,391
* **Strafford County** (See Boston-Worcester-Lawrence-Lowell-Brockton, MA-NH NECMA.)	.33017	7.7	112,233	7.5	120,636	6.6	128,609
Total: Metro Portion of State		12.3	770,433	6.7	822,056	5.9	870,307
Total: New Hampshire		11.4	1,235,786	6.8	1,319,978	6.0	1,399,401
New Jersey							
Atlantic-Cape May PMSA	.0560	11.1	354,878	2.2	362,796	2.0	370,154
Atlantic	34001	12.6	252,552	3.4	261,127	3.1	269,137
Cape May	34009	7.6	102,326	-0.6	101,669	-0.6	101,017
Bergen-Passaic PMSA	.0875	7.4	1,373,167	2.7	1,410,908	2.4	1,444,821
Bergen	34003	7.1	884,118	2.6	906,873	2.3	927,845
Passaic	34031	7.9	489,049	3.1	504,035	2.6	516,976
Jersey City PMSA	.3640	10.1	608,975	-0.3	607,051	-0.4	604,565
Hudson	34017	10.1	608,975	-0.3	607,051	-0.4	604,565
Middlesex-Somerset-Hunterdon PMSA	.5015	14.7	1,169,641	7.2	1,254,329	6.4	1,334,138
Hunterdon	34019	13.2	121,989	8.5	132,353	7.4	142,102
Middlesex	34023	11.7	750,162	6.8	800,915	6.0	848,816
Somerset	34035	23.8	297,490	7.9	321,061	6.9	343,220
Monmouth-Ocean PMSA	.5190	14.2	1,126,217	7.7	1,213,007	6.8	1,295,131
Monmouth	34025	11.2	615,301	4.7	644,487	4.2	671,700
Ocean	34029	17.9	510,916	11.3	568,520	9.7	623,431
Newark PMSA	.5640	6.1	2,032,989	3.1	2,095,245	2.9	2,155,281
Essex	34013	2.0	793,633	0.8	800,056	0.9	807,383
Morris	34027	11.6	470,212	4.6	492,011	4.2	512,552
Sussex	34037	10.1	144,166	7.8	155,440	6.9	166,205
Union	34039	5.8	522,541	2.2	534,259	2.0	545,156
Warren	34041	11.8	102,437	10.8	113,479	9.3	123,985
Trenton PMSA	.8480	7.7	350,761	5.3	369,496	4.9	387,426
Mercer	34021	7.7	350,761	5.3	369,496	4.9	387,426
Vineland-Millville-Bridgeton PMSA	.8760	6.1	146,438	3.3	151,331	3.2	156,244
Cumberland	34011	6.1	146,438	3.3	151,331	3.2	156,244
* **Burlington County**	.34005	7.2	423,394	8.3	458,701	7.4	492,773
* **Camden County**	.34007	1.2	508,932	1.8	518,146	1.8	527,433
* **Gloucester County**	.34015	10.7	254,673	8.0	275,154	7.2	294,986
* **Salem County** (See Philadelphia, PA-NJ PMSA.)	.34033	-1.5	64,285	1.7	65,361	1.7	66,484
Total: Metro Portion of State		8.9	8,414,350	4.4	8,781,525	4.0	9,129,436
Total: New Jersey		8.9	8,414,350	4.4	8,781,525	4.0	9,129,436
New Mexico							
Albuquerque MSA	.0200	21.0	712,738	8.3	772,209	7.4	829,520
Bernalillo	35001	15.8	556,678	7.5	598,254	6.8	638,753
Sandoval	35043	42.0	89,908	16.0	104,283	13.1	117,912
Valencia	35061	46.2	66,152	5.3	69,672	4.6	72,855
Las Cruces MSA	.4100	28.9	174,682	7.2	187,285	6.5	199,509
Dona Ana	35013	28.9	174,682	7.2	187,285	6.5	199,509
Santa Fe MSA	.7490	26.1	147,635	8.6	160,279	7.6	172,399
Los Alamos	35028	1.3	18,343	3.6	19,001	3.7	19,707
Santa Fe	35049	30.7	129,292	9.3	141,278	8.1	152,692
Total: Metro Portion of State		23.0	1,035,055	8.2	1,119,773	7.3	1,201,428
Total: New Mexico		20.1	1,819,046	5.3	1,914,908	4.9	2,008,321
New York							
Albany-Schenectady-Troy MSA	.0160	1.6	875,583	2.9	900,791	2.7	925,250
Albany	36001	0.7	294,565	2.2	300,976	2.1	307,368
Montgomery	36057	-4.4	49,708	-1.3	49,061	-1.3	48,445
Rensselaer	36083	-1.2	152,538	0.9	153,917	0.9	155,278
Saratoga	36091	10.7	200,635	7.9	216,567	7.0	231,679
Schenectady	36093	-1.8	146,555	1.2	148,278	1.2	150,092
Schoharie	36095	-0.9	31,582	1.3	31,992	1.2	32,388
Binghamton MSA	.0960	-4.6	252,320	-1.0	249,856	-0.9	247,721
Broome	36007	-5.5	200,536	-1.3	197,991	-1.1	195,750
Tioga	36107	-1.1	51,784	0.2	51,865	0.2	51,971
Buffalo-Niagara Falls MSA	.1280	-1.6	1,170,111	-1.3	1,154,526	-1.2	1,140,186
Erie	36029	-1.9	950,265	-1.4	936,770	-1.3	924,278
Niagara	36063	-0.4	219,846	-1.0	217,756	-0.8	215,908
Dutchess County PMSA	.2281	8.0	280,150	6.3	297,806	5.7	314,780
Dutchess	36027	8.0	280,150	6.3	297,806	5.7	314,780
Elmira MSA	.2335	-4.3	91,070	-1.1	90,031	-1.1	89,021
Chemung	36015	-4.3	91,070	-1.1	90,031	-1.1	89,021
Glens Falls MSA	.2975	4.9	124,345	3.5	128,724	3.4	133,094
Warren	36113	6.9	63,303	4.0	65,852	3.8	68,356
Washington	36115	2.9	61,042	3.0	62,872	3.0	64,738
Jamestown MSA	.3610	-1.5	139,750	-2.0	136,986	-1.9	134,415
Chautauqua	36013	-1.5	139,750	-2.0	136,986	-1.9	134,415
Nassau-Suffolk PMSA	.5380	5.5	2,753,913	3.2	2,842,538	2.9	2,924,418
Nassau	36059	3.7	1,334,544	0.7	1,343,675	0.5	1,350,776
Suffolk	36103	7.4	1,419,369	5.6	1,498,863	5.0	1,573,642
Newburgh, NY-PA PMSA	.5660	15.5	387,669	11.8	433,484	10.1	477,278
Orange	36071	11.0	341,367	10.6	377,527	9.1	412,040
Pike, PA	42103	65.6	46,302	20.9	55,957	16.6	65,238
New York PMSA	.5600	9.0	9,314,235	2.0	9,499,149	1.8	9,670,524
Bronx	36005	10.7	1,332,650	3.9	1,385,071	3.6	1,435,428
Kings	36047	7.2	2,465,326	0.6	2,480,420	0.5	2,493,914
New York	36061	3.3	1,537,195	3.3	1,588,044	3.1	1,636,531
Putnam	36079	14.1	95,745	6.8	102,260	6.0	108,401
Queens	36081	14.2	2,229,379	-0.2	2,225,143	-0.3	2,218,858
Richmond	36085	17.1	443,728	5.9	470,056	5.2	494,633
Rockland	36087	8.0	286,753	3.6	297,018	3.2	306,523
Westchester	36119	5.6	923,459	3.0	951,137	2.6	976,236
Rochester MSA	.6840	3.4	1,098,201	0.7	1,106,020	0.6	1,113,174
Genesee	36037	0.5	60,370	-1.1	59,736	-1.0	59,138
Livingston	36051	3.1	64,328	0.7	64,792	0.6	65,187
Monroe	36055	3.0	735,343	0.5	738,925	0.4	742,088
Ontario	36069	5.4	100,224	4.2	104,413	3.8	108,420
Orleans	36073	5.6	44,171	-0.7	43,876	-0.7	43,571
Wayne	36117	5.2	93,765	0.5	94,278	0.5	94,770
Syracuse MSA	.8160	-1.4	732,117	1.1	740,003	1.0	747,586
Cayuga	36011	-0.4	81,963	0.2	82,152	0.2	82,352
Madison	36053	0.5	69,441	2.1	70,875	2.0	72,294
Onondaga	36067	-2.3	458,336	1.0	462,726	0.9	466,993
Oswego	36075	0.5	122,377	1.5	124,250	1.4	125,947
Utica-Rome MSA	.8680	-5.3	299,896	-0.7	297,654	-0.7	295,683
Herkimer	36043	-2.1	64,427	-1.6	63,402	-1.6	62,418
Oneida	36065	-6.1	235,469	-0.5	234,252	-0.4	233,265
Total: Metro Portion of State		5.8	17,473,058	2.0	17,821,611	1.8	18,147,892
Total: New York		5.5	18,976,457	2.0	19,348,846	1.8	19,698,950
North Carolina							
Asheville MSA	.0480	17.8	225,965	5.2	237,670	4.6	248,633
Buncombe	37021	18.0	206,330	5.4	217,531	4.8	228,057
Madison	37115	15.8	19,635	2.6	20,139	2.2	20,576
Charlotte-Gastonia-Rock Hill, NC-SC MSA	.1520	29.0	1,499,293	12.5	1,686,002	10.5	1,862,599
Cabarrus	37025	32.5	131,063	14.9	150,533	12.1	168,822
Gaston	37071	8.7	190,365	2.6	195,391	2.4	200,065
Lincoln	37109	26.8	63,780	8.9	69,482	7.8	74,908
Mecklenburg	37119	36.0	695,454	13.3	787,867	11.1	875,406
Rowan	37159	17.8	130,340	4.6	136,277	4.1	141,864
Union	37179	46.9	123,677	29.1	159,636	21.3	193,627
York, SC	45091	25.2	164,614	13.5	186,816	11.3	207,907
Fayetteville MSA	.2560	10.3	302,963	1.2	306,556	1.2	310,229
Cumberland	37051	10.3	302,963	1.2	306,556	1.2	310,229
Goldsboro MSA	.2980	8.3	113,329	0.1	113,461	0.1	113,549
Wayne	37191	8.3	113,329	0.1	113,461	0.1	113,549
Greensboro—Winston-Salem—High Point MSA	.3120	19.2	1,251,509	5.7	1,322,689	5.0	1,389,241
Alamance	37001	20.9	130,800	7.1	140,105	6.2	148,722
Davidson	37057	16.2	147,246	5.5	155,335	4.9	162,985
Davie	37059	25.0	34,835	11.3	38,755	9.5	42,443
Forsyth	37067	15.1	306,067	6.3	325,303	5.6	343,635
Guilford	37081	21.2	421,048	5.0	442,093	4.4	461,760
Randolph	37151	22.4	130,454	5.6	137,787	4.8	144,465
Stokes	37169	20.1	44,711	1.7	45,460	1.3	46,050
Yadkin	37197	19.2	36,348	4.1	37,851	3.5	39,181
Greenville MSA	.3150	24.0	133,798	5.9	141,666	5.3	149,202
Pitt	37147	24.0	133,798	5.9	141,666	5.3	149,202
Hickory-Morganton-Lenoir MSA	.3290	16.9	341,851	4.2	356,039	3.6	368,980
Alexander	37003	22.0	33,603	5.9	35,588	5.4	37,498
Burke	37023	17.7	89,148	0.8	89,829	0.6	90,378
Caldwell	37027	9.5	77,415	3.1	79,837	2.8	82,046
Catawba	37035	19.7	141,685	6.4	150,785	5.5	159,058
Jacksonville MSA	.3605	0.3	150,355	-0.4	149,754	0.2	150,057
Onslow	37133	0.3	150,355	-0.4	149,754	0.2	150,057
Raleigh-Durham-Chapel Hill MSA	.6640	38.9	1,187,941	14.5	1,360,180	12.2	1,526,072
Chatham	37037	27.3	49,329	19.9	59,157	16.0	68,596
Durham	37063	22.8	223,314	9.2	243,802	7.9	263,055
Franklin	37069	29.8	47,260	17.3	55,425	14.1	63,240
Johnston	37101	50.0	121,965	19.8	146,138	15.6	168,989
Orange	37135	26.0	118,227	-0.1	118,085	1.8	120,243
Wake	37183	48.3	627,846	17.5	737,573	14.2	841,949
Rocky Mount MSA	.6895	7.3	143,026	1.9	145,779	1.9	148,498
Edgecombe	37065	-1.7	55,606	-1.8	54,620	-1.3	53,931
Nash	37127	14.0	87,420	4.3	91,159	3.7	94,567
Wilmington MSA	.9200	36.3	233,450	11.7	260,741	10.1	287,032
Brunswick	37019	43.5	73,143	18.8	86,905	15.1	100,046
New Hanover	37129	33.3	160,307	8.4	173,836	7.6	186,986
* **Currituck County** (See Norfolk-Virginia Beach-Newport News, VA-NC MSA.)	.37053	32.4	18,190	23.6	22,484	18.4	26,629
Total: Metro Portion of State		24.3	5,437,056	8.8	5,916,205	7.7	6,372,814
Total: North Carolina		21.4	8,049,313	7.4	8,642,524	6.5	9,206,675
North Dakota							
Bismarck MSA	.1010	13.0	94,719	3.8	98,303	3.3	101,535
Burleigh	38015	15.4	69,416	5.4	73,166	4.8	76,649
Morton	38059	6.8	25,303	-0.7	25,137	-1.0	24,886
Fargo-Moorhead, ND-MN MSA	.2520	13.7	174,367	4.1	181,535	3.6	188,090
Clay, MN	27027	1.6	51,229	2.7	52,627	2.5	53,940
Cass	38017	19.7	123,138	4.7	128,908	4.1	134,150
Grand Forks, ND-MN MSA	.2985	-5.5	97,478	-3.0	94,524	-2.9	91,810
Polk, MN	27119	-3.5	31,369	-1.9	30,767	-2.0	30,162
Grand Forks	38035	-6.5	66,109	-3.6	63,757	-3.3	61,648
Total: Metro Portion of State		10.3	283,966	2.5	290,968	2.2	297,333
Total: North Dakota		0.5	642,200	-2.2	627,989	-2.0	615,176
Ohio							
Akron PMSA	.0080	5.7	694,960	1.4	704,396	1.2	712,569
Portage	39133	6.6	152,061	2.2	155,370	1.9	158,307
Summit	39153	5.4	542,899	1.1	549,026	1.0	554,262
Canton-Massillon MSA	.1320	3.3	406,934	0.0	407,131	-0.0	407,088
Carroll	39019	8.7	28,836	3.8	29,941	3.5	30,982
Stark	39151	2.9	378,098	-0.2	377,190	-0.3	376,106
Cincinnati, OH-KY-IN PMSA	.1640	7.9	1,646,395	2.6	1,688,541	2.3	1,727,719
Dearborn, IN	18029	18.7	46,109	6.6	49,138	5.7	51,918
Ohio, IN	18115	5.8	5,623	3.3	5,809	2.8	5,974
Boone, KY	21015	49.3	85,991	20.8	103,836	16.2	120,627
Campbell, KY	21037	5.7	88,616	-1.7	87,132	-1.7	85,641
Gallatin, KY	21077	45.9	7,870	3.2	8,122	3.2	8,384
Grant, KY	21081	42.2	22,384	11.8	25,032	9.9	27,503
Kenton, KY	21117	6.6	151,464	0.9	152,794	0.7	153,919
Pendleton, KY	21191	19.6	14,390	7.0	15,401	5.8	16,296
Brown	39015	20.9	42,285	5.7	44,709	4.7	46,813
Clermont	39025	18.5	177,977	6.9	190,233	6.0	201,712
Hamilton	39061	-2.4	845,303	-4.2	809,794	-4.1	776,764
Warren	39165	39.0	158,383	24.1	196,541	18.1	232,168
Cleveland-Lorain-Elyria PMSA	.1680	2.2	2,250,871	-0.5	2,239,726	-0.5	2,229,296
Ashtabula	39007	2.9	102,728	0.4	103,185	0.3	103,544
Cuyahoga	39035	-1.3	1,393,978	-3.6	1,344,252	-3.5	1,297,572
Geauga	39055	12.0	90,895	5.5	95,917	4.8	100,533
Lake	39085	5.6	227,511	2.3	232,832	2.2	237,905
Lorain	39093	5.0	284,664	3.8	295,342	3.4	305,320
Medina	39103	23.5	151,095	11.3	168,198	9.6	184,422
Columbus MSA	.1840	14.5	1,540,157	6.4	1,639,166	5.6	1,731,644
Delaware	39041	64.3	109,989	37.5	151,233	26.0	190,621
Fairfield	39045	18.7	122,759	13.3	139,046	11.2	154,580
Franklin	39049	11.2	1,068,978	3.0	1,100,544	2.6	1,129,032
Licking	39089	13.4	145,491	5.7	153,841	5.0	161,531
Madison	39097	8.5	40,213	1.8	40,930	1.7	41,613
Pickaway	39129	9.3	52,727	1.6	53,572	1.3	54,267
Dayton-Springfield MSA	.2000	-0.1	950,558	-0.9	942,462	-0.8	934,629
Clark	39023	-1.9	144,742	-2.1	141,771	-1.9	139,024
Greene	39057	8.2	147,886	2.8	152,045	2.5	155,847
Miami	39109	6.1	98,868	2.0	100,836	1.8	102,636
Montgomery	39113	-2.6	559,062	-2.0	547,810	-2.0	537,122
Hamilton-Middletown PMSA	.3200	14.2	332,807	4.9	349,225	4.4	364,560
Butler	39017	14.2	332,807	4.9	349,225	4.4	364,560
Lima MSA	.4320	0.5	155,084	-1.1	153,334	-1.1	151,722
Allen	39003	-1.2	108,473	-1.8	106,543	-1.7	104,784
Auglaize	39011	4.5	46,611	0.4	46,791	0.3	46,938
Mansfield MSA	.4800	1.0	175,818	-1.5	173,148	-1.5	170,578
Crawford	39033	-1.9	46,966	-3.2	45,458	-3.1	44,043
Richland	39139	2.2	128,852	-0.9	127,690	-0.9	126,535
Steubenville-Weirton, OH-WV MSA	.8080	-7.4	132,008	-4.2	126,448	-4.0	121,361
Jefferson	39081	-8.0	73,894	-4.6	70,461	-4.4	67,356
Brooke, WV	54009	-5.7	25,447	-2.9	24,717	-2.7	24,058
Hancock, WV	54029	-7.3	32,667	-4.3	31,270	-4.2	29,947
Toledo MSA	.8400	0.7	618,203	0.1	618,775	0.1	619,136
Fulton	39051	9.3	42,084	1.2	42,582	1.0	43,007
Lucas	39095	-1.6	455,054	-0.5	452,909	-0.5	450,819
Wood	39173	6.9	121,065	1.8	123,284	1.6	125,310
Youngstown-Warren MSA	.9320	-1.0	594,746	-2.7	578,504	-2.7	563,099
Columbiana	39029	3.5	112,075	-0.8	111,181	-0.9	110,205
Mahoning	39099	-2.7	257,555	-3.7	248,058	-3.5	239,280
Trumbull	39155	-1.2	225,116	-2.6	219,265	-2.6	213,614
* **Lawrence County** (See Huntington-Ashland, WV-KY-OH MSA.)	.39087	0.8	62,319	0.4	62,567	0.4	62,824
* **Washington County** (See Parkersburg-Marietta, WV-OH MSA.)	.39167	1.6	63,251	-1.7	62,162	-1.7	61,134
* **Belmont County** (See Wheeling, WV-OH MSA.)	.39013	-1.2	70,226	-1.7	69,040	-1.6	67,943
Total: Metro Portion of State		4.4	9,213,776	1.1	9,311,374	1.0	9,401,035
Total: Ohio		4.7	11,353,140	1.2	11,485,881	1.1	11,607,960
Oklahoma							
Enid MSA	.2340	1.9	57,813	-1.8	56,753	-1.7	55,789
Garfield	40047	1.9	57,813	-1.8	56,753	-1.7	55,789
Lawton MSA	.4200	3.1	114,996	-5.2	109,018	-3.7	104,954
Comanche	40031	3.1	114,996	-5.2	109,018	-3.7	104,954

* Indicates county is included from metro in different state.
Source: Devonshire Associates Ltd. and Scan/US, Inc. 2005.

Continued on next page

Metropolitan Statistical Areas and Their Component Counties: Population Trends, *Continued*

MSA	FIPS Code	Past: 1990-2000 % Change	Past: 2000 Census	Present: 2000-2005 % Change	Present: 7/1/05 Estimate	Future: 2005-2010 % Change	Future: 2010 Projection
Oklahoma City MSA	**.5880**	**13.0**	**1,083,346**	**5.5**	**1,142,506**	**4.9**	**1,198,501**
Canadian	40017	17.9	87,697	9.7	96,179	8.3	104,171
Cleveland	40027	19.4	208,016	8.5	225,695	7.6	242,817
Logan	40083	16.9	33,924	7.6	36,508	6.8	38,983
McClain	40087	21.7	27,740	5.2	29,188	4.5	30,516
Oklahoma	40109	10.1	660,448	4.0	687,070	3.6	711,865
Pottawatomie	40125	11.5	65,521	3.6	67,866	3.4	70,149
Tulsa MSA	**.8560**	**13.3**	**803,235**	**4.0**	**835,699**	**3.6**	**865,868**
Creek	40037	10.6	67,367	3.3	69,584	2.9	71,575
Osage	40113	6.7	44,437	2.7	45,632	2.3	46,662
Rogers	40131	28.0	70,641	14.9	81,199	12.1	90,987
Tulsa	40143	11.9	563,299	2.1	574,848	1.9	585,531
Wagoner	40145	20.1	57,491	12.1	64,436	10.4	71,113
* **Sequoyah County** (See Fort Smith, AR-OK MSA.)	**.40135**	**15.2**	**38,972**	**4.2**	**40,620**	**3.8**	**42,155**
Total: Metro Portion of State		**12.2**	**2,098,362**	**4.1**	**2,184,596**	**3.8**	**2,267,267**
Total: Oklahoma		9.7	3,450,654	2.6	3,541,713	2.5	3,629,142

Oregon

MSA	FIPS Code	Past: 1990-2000 % Change	Past: 2000 Census	Present: 2000-2005 % Change	Present: 7/1/05 Estimate	Future: 2005-2010 % Change	Future: 2010 Projection
Corvallis MSA	**.1890**	**10.4**	**78,153**	**2.1**	**79,778**	**2.1**	**81,434**
Benton	41003	10.4	78,153	2.1	79,778	2.1	81,434
Eugene-Springfield MSA	**.2400**	**14.2**	**322,959**	**3.8**	**335,284**	**3.5**	**347,119**
Lane	41039	14.2	322,959	3.8	335,284	3.5	347,119
Medford-Ashland MSA	**.4890**	**23.8**	**181,269**	**8.2**	**196,043**	**7.2**	**210,212**
Jackson	41029	23.8	181,269	8.2	196,043	7.2	210,212
Portland-Vancouver, OR-WA PMSA	.6440	26.6	1,918,009	9.5	2,099,630	8.3	2,273,070
Clackamas	**41005**	**21.4**	**338,391**	**9.1**	**369,163**	**8.0**	**398,673**
Columbia	**41009**	**16.0**	**43,560**	**10.3**	**48,039**	**9.1**	**52,406**
Multnomah	**41051**	**13.1**	**660,486**	**4.3**	**688,787**	**4.0**	**716,054**
Washington	**41067**	**42.9**	**445,342**	**12.3**	**500,313**	**10.3**	**552,092**
Yamhill	**41071**	**29.7**	**84,992**	**8.5**	**92,229**	**7.5**	**99,169**
Clark, WA	53011	45.0	345,238	16.2	401,099	13.4	454,676
Salem PMSA	**.7080**	**24.9**	**347,214**	**8.0**	**374,986**	**7.1**	**401,672**
Marion	41047	24.7	284,834	7.6	306,501	6.8	327,358
Polk	41053	25.9	62,380	9.8	68,485	8.5	74,314
Total: Metro Portion of State		**21.7**	**2,502,366**	**7.3**	**2,684,622**	**6.5**	**2,858,831**
Total: Oregon		20.4	3,421,399	6.7	3,651,787	6.0	3,872,508

Pennsylvania

MSA	FIPS Code	Past: 1990-2000 % Change	Past: 2000 Census	Present: 2000-2005 % Change	Present: 7/1/05 Estimate	Future: 2005-2010 % Change	Future: 2010 Projection
Allentown-Bethlehem-Easton MSA	**.0240**	**7.2**	**637,958**	**5.4**	**672,335**	**4.9**	**705,413**
Carbon	42025	3.4	58,802	4.4	61,398	4.1	63,927
Lehigh	42077	7.2	312,090	4.4	325,977	4.0	339,160
Northampton	42095	8.1	267,066	6.7	284,960	6.1	302,326
Altoona MSA	**.0280**	**-1.1**	**129,144**	**-2.1**	**126,465**	**-2.0**	**123,875**
Blair	42013	-1.1	129,144	-2.1	126,465	-2.0	123,875
Erie MSA	**.2360**	**1.9**	**280,843**	**-0.6**	**279,281**	**-0.5**	**277,775**
Erie	42049	1.9	280,843	-0.6	279,281	-0.5	277,775
Harrisburg-Lebanon-Carlisle MSA	**.3240**	**7.0**	**629,401**	**2.4**	**644,200**	**2.2**	**658,322**
Cumberland	42041	9.4	213,674	4.5	223,224	4.1	232,401
Dauphin	42043	5.9	251,798	-0.1	251,422	-0.2	250,927
Lebanon	42075	5.8	120,327	3.7	124,776	3.4	129,072
Perry	42099	5.9	43,602	2.7	44,778	2.6	45,922
Johnstown MSA	**.3680**	**-3.6**	**232,621**	**-2.5**	**226,882**	**-2.3**	**221,631**
Cambria	42021	-6.4	152,598	-3.2	147,675	-3.0	143,243
Somerset	42111	2.3	80,023	-1.0	79,207	-1.0	78,388
Lancaster MSA	**.4000**	**11.3**	**470,658**	**4.2**	**490,254**	**3.7**	**508,588**
Lancaster	42071	11.3	470,658	4.2	490,254	3.7	508,588
Philadelphia, PA-NJ PMSA	.6160	3.6	5,100,931	2.1	5,210,435	2.0	5,316,553
Burlington, NJ	34005	7.2	423,394	8.3	458,701	7.4	492,773
Camden, NJ	34007	1.2	508,932	1.8	518,146	1.8	527,433
Gloucester, NJ	34015	10.7	254,673	8.0	275,154	7.2	294,986
Salem, NJ	34033	-1.5	64,285	1.7	65,361	1.7	66,484
Bucks	**42017**	**10.4**	**597,635**	**4.1**	**622,393**	**3.6**	**645,062**
Chester	**42029**	**15.2**	**433,501**	**8.9**	**471,979**	**7.6**	**507,963**
Delaware	**42045**	**0.6**	**550,864**	**1.0**	**556,280**	**0.7**	**560,150**
Montgomery	**42091**	**10.6**	**750,097**	**4.7**	**785,423**	**4.3**	**819,588**
Philadelphia	**42101**	**-4.3**	**1,517,550**	**-4.0**	**1,456,998**	**-3.8**	**1,402,114**
Pittsburgh MSA	**.6280**	**-1.5**	**2,358,695**	**-1.3**	**2,329,028**	**-1.2**	**2,301,195**
Allegheny	42003	-4.1	1,281,666	-2.5	1,249,911	-2.4	1,220,311
Beaver	42007	-2.5	181,412	-2.1	177,681	-2.0	174,204
Butler	42019	14.5	174,083	5.3	183,231	4.7	191,805
Fayette	42051	2.3	148,644	-2.6	144,770	-2.6	141,062
Washington	42125	-0.8	202,897	1.5	206,014	1.4	208,908
Westmoreland	42129	-0.1	369,993	-0.7	367,421	-0.7	364,905
Reading MSA	**.6680**	**11.0**	**373,638**	**5.2**	**393,253**	**4.7**	**411,802**
Berks	42011	11.0	373,638	5.2	393,253	4.7	411,802
Scranton—Wilkes-Barre—Hazleton MSA	**.7560**	**-2.1**	**624,776**	**-2.0**	**612,464**	**-1.8**	**601,397**
Columbia	42037	1.5	64,151	1.6	65,170	1.6	66,204
Lackawanna	42069	-2.6	213,295	-2.2	208,594	-2.1	204,297
Luzerne	42079	-2.7	319,250	-2.8	310,470	-2.6	302,479
Wyoming	42131	0.0	28,080	0.5	28,230	0.7	28,417
Sharon MSA	**.7610**	**-0.6**	**120,293**	**-0.5**	**119,699**	**-0.4**	**119,167**
Mercer	42085	-0.6	120,293	-0.5	119,699	-0.4	119,167
State College MSA	**.8050**	**9.7**	**135,758**	**4.4**	**141,710**	**4.1**	**147,551**
Centre	42027	9.7	135,758	4.4	141,710	4.1	147,551
Williamsport MSA	**.9140**	**1.1**	**120,044**	**-1.9**	**117,787**	**-1.8**	**115,625**
Lycoming	42081	1.1	120,044	-1.9	117,787	-1.8	115,625
York MSA	**.9280**	**12.4**	**381,751**	**5.7**	**403,361**	**5.1**	**423,825**
York	42133	12.4	381,751	5.7	403,361	5.1	423,825
* **Pike County** (See Newburgh, NY-PA PMSA.)	**.42103**	**65.6**	**46,302**	**20.9**	**55,957**	**16.6**	**65,238**
Total: Metro Portion of State		**3.1**	**10,391,529**	**1.1**	**10,505,749**	**1.1**	**10,616,281**
Total: Pennsylvania		3.4	12,281,054	1.1	12,420,798	1.1	12,555,326

Rhode Island

MSA	FIPS Code	Past: 1990-2000 % Change	Past: 2000 Census	Present: 2000-2005 % Change	Present: 7/1/05 Estimate	Future: 2005-2010 % Change	Future: 2010 Projection
Providence-Warwick-Pawtucket NECMA	**.6483**	**5.1**	**962,886**	**5.1**	**1,011,599**	**4.6**	**1,058,106**
Bristol	44001	3.7	50,648	5.7	53,538	5.2	56,344
Kent	44003	3.7	167,090	4.2	174,124	3.8	180,732
Providence	44007	4.2	621,602	5.1	653,201	4.7	683,578
Washington	44009	12.3	123,546	5.8	130,736	5.1	137,452
Total: Metro Portion of State		**5.1**	**962,886**	**5.1**	**1,011,599**	**4.6**	**1,058,106**
Total: Rhode Island		4.5	1,048,319	4.7	1,097,105	4.2	1,143,471

South Carolina

MSA	FIPS Code	Past: 1990-2000 % Change	Past: 2000 Census	Present: 2000-2005 % Change	Present: 7/1/05 Estimate	Future: 2005-2010 % Change	Future: 2010 Projection
Charleston-North Charleston MSA	**.1440**	**8.3**	**549,033**	**6.9**	**586,872**	**6.2**	**623,170**
Berkeley	45015	10.8	142,651	5.2	150,053	4.6	157,004
Charleston	45019	5.1	309,969	5.7	327,786	5.2	344,833
Dorchester	45035	16.1	96,413	13.1	109,033	11.3	121,333
Columbia MSA	**.1760**	**18.4**	**536,691**	**6.8**	**573,167**	**6.1**	**608,077**
Lexington	45063	28.9	216,014	8.3	233,853	7.2	250,806
Richland	45079	12.2	320,677	5.8	339,314	5.3	357,271
Florence MSA	**.2655**	**10.0**	**125,761**	**3.7**	**130,435**	**3.5**	**135,045**
Florence	45041	10.0	125,761	3.7	130,435	3.5	135,045
Greenville-Spartanburg-Anderson MSA	**.3160**	**15.9**	**962,441**	**5.1**	**1,011,759**	**4.6**	**1,058,021**
Anderson	45007	14.1	165,740	5.9	175,558	5.2	184,764
Cherokee	45021	18.0	52,537	3.2	54,193	2.8	55,701
Greenville	45045	18.6	379,616	6.7	405,039	5.9	428,939
Pickens	45077	18.0	110,757	2.0	112,937	1.8	115,019
Spartanburg	45083	11.9	253,791	4.0	264,032	3.6	273,598
Myrtle Beach MSA	**.5330**	**36.5**	**196,629**	**11.8**	**219,791**	**9.9**	**241,524**
Horry	45051	36.5	196,629	11.8	219,791	9.9	241,524
Sumter MSA	**.8140**	**2.0**	**104,646**	**1.8**	**106,517**	**1.7**	**108,314**
Sumter	45085	2.0	104,646	1.8	106,517	1.7	108,314
* **Aiken County**	**.45003**	**17.9**	**142,552**	**5.0**	**149,719**	**4.6**	**156,610**
* **Edgefield County** (See Augusta-Aiken, GA-SC MSA.)	**.45037**	**33.9**	**24,595**	**1.3**	**24,910**	**1.3**	**25,242**
* **York County** (See Charlotte-Gastonia-Rock Hill, NC-SC MSA.)	**.45091**	**25.2**	**164,614**	**13.5**	**186,816**	**11.3**	**207,907**
Total: Metro Portion of State		**15.9**	**2,806,962**	**6.5**	**2,989,986**	**5.8**	**3,163,910**
Total: South Carolina		15.1	4,012,012	5.5	4,230,879	4.9	4,438,211

South Dakota

MSA	FIPS Code	Past: 1990-2000 % Change	Past: 2000 Census	Present: 2000-2005 % Change	Present: 7/1/05 Estimate	Future: 2005-2010 % Change	Future: 2010 Projection
Rapid City MSA	**.6660**	**8.9**	**88,565**	**5.4**	**93,346**	**4.8**	**97,800**
Pennington	46103	8.9	88,565	5.4	93,346	4.8	97,800
Sioux Falls MSA	**.7760**	**23.8**	**172,412**	**11.0**	**191,365**	**9.2**	**208,880**
Lincoln	46083	56.4	24,131	34.1	32,370	24.0	40,135
Minnehaha	46099	19.8	148,281	7.2	158,995	6.1	168,745
Total: Metro Portion of State		**18.3**	**260,977**	**9.1**	**284,711**	**7.7**	**306,680**
Total: South Dakota		8.5	754,844	2.1	770,755	1.9	785,776

Tennessee

MSA	FIPS Code	Past: 1990-2000 % Change	Past: 2000 Census	Present: 2000-2005 % Change	Present: 7/1/05 Estimate	Future: 2005-2010 % Change	Future: 2010 Projection
Chattanooga, TN-GA MSA	.1560	9.6	465,161	3.1	479,572	2.9	493,272
Catoosa, GA	13047	25.5	53,282	15.1	61,327	12.5	68,977
Dade, GA	13083	15.3	15,154	8.0	16,361	7.0	17,514
Walker, GA	13295	4.7	61,053	4.4	63,750	4.1	66,335
Hamilton	**47065**	**7.8**	**307,896**	**0.8**	**310,232**	**0.7**	**312,422**
Marion	**47115**	**11.7**	**27,776**	**0.5**	**27,902**	**0.4**	**28,024**
Clarksville-Hopkinsville, TN-KY MSA	.1660	22.2	207,033	2.6	212,517	2.4	217,575
Christian, KY	21047	4.8	72,265	-2.8	70,255	-2.8	68,296
Montgomery	**47125**	**34.1**	**134,768**	**5.6**	**142,262**	**4.9**	**149,279**
Jackson MSA	**.3580**	**18.3**	**107,377**	**3.1**	**110,724**	**2.9**	**113,912**
Chester	47023	21.2	15,540	0.7	15,642	0.8	15,774
Madison	47113	17.8	91,837	3.5	95,082	3.2	98,138
Johnson City-Kingsport-Bristol, TN-VA MSA	.3660	10.1	480,091	2.0	489,628	1.9	498,754
Carter	**47019**	**10.2**	**56,742**	**3.9**	**58,964**	**3.6**	**61,077**
Hawkins	**47073**	**20.2**	**53,563**	**5.1**	**56,299**	**4.6**	**58,887**
Sullivan	**47163**	**6.6**	**153,048**	**0.0**	**153,049**	**0.1**	**153,145**
Unicoi	**47171**	**6.8**	**17,667**	**0.7**	**17,796**	**0.8**	**17,936**
Washington	**47179**	**16.1**	**107,198**	**4.3**	**111,810**	**3.9**	**116,145**
Bristol, VA (Ind. City)	51520	-5.7	17,367	-0.8	17,230	-0.5	17,149
Scott, VA	51169	0.9	23,403	-2.8	22,744	-2.7	22,125
Washington, VA	51191	11.4	51,103	1.2	51,736	1.1	52,290
Knoxville MSA	**.3840**	**17.3**	**687,249**	**6.0**	**728,734**	**5.4**	**768,308**
Anderson	47001	4.5	71,330	1.6	72,469	1.6	73,642
Blount	47009	23.1	105,823	8.8	115,094	7.7	123,944
Knox	47093	13.8	382,032	4.8	400,313	4.4	417,807
Loudon	47105	25.1	39,086	10.7	43,287	9.4	47,348
Sevier	47155	39.4	71,170	9.7	78,085	8.2	84,466
Union	47173	30.0	17,808	9.4	19,486	8.3	21,101
Memphis, TN-AR-MS MSA	.4920	12.7	1,135,614	4.7	1,188,935	4.2	1,239,110
Crittenden, AR	05035	1.9	50,866	0.8	51,287	0.5	51,532
DeSoto, MS	28033	57.9	107,199	25.9	135,003	19.5	161,295
Fayette	**47047**	**12.7**	**28,806**	**19.7**	**34,492**	**15.6**	**39,865**
Shelby	**47157**	**8.6**	**897,472**	**1.6**	**912,260**	**1.5**	**926,191**
Tipton	**47167**	**36.5**	**51,271**	**9.0**	**55,893**	**7.8**	**60,227**
Nashville MSA	**.5360**	**25.0**	**1,231,311**	**7.6**	**1,324,828**	**6.7**	**1,413,321**
Cheatham	47021	32.3	35,912	6.2	38,152	5.3	40,188
Davidson	47037	11.6	569,891	0.2	570,911	0.2	571,793
Dickson	47043	23.1	43,156	6.8	46,096	6.0	48,853
Robertson	47147	31.2	54,433	11.3	60,561	9.4	66,265
Rutherford	47149	53.5	182,023	18.0	214,830	14.6	246,213
Sumner	47165	26.3	130,449	10.3	143,900	8.9	156,643
Williamson	47187	56.3	126,638	18.9	150,607	14.9	173,113
Wilson	47189	31.2	88,809	12.3	99,771	10.5	110,253
Total: Metro Portion of State		**16.7**	**3,862,144**	**4.7**	**4,045,245**	**4.3**	**4,218,739**
Total: Tennessee		16.7	5,689,283	4.4	5,937,857	4.0	6,172,676

Texas

MSA	FIPS Code	Past: 1990-2000 % Change	Past: 2000 Census	Present: 2000-2005 % Change	Present: 7/1/05 Estimate	Future: 2005-2010 % Change	Future: 2010 Projection
Abilene MSA	**.0040**	**5.8**	**126,555**	**-2.2**	**123,775**	**-2.1**	**121,186**
Taylor	48441	5.8	126,555	-2.2	123,775	-2.1	121,186
Amarillo MSA	**.0320**	**16.2**	**217,858**	**4.9**	**228,556**	**4.4**	**238,712**
Potter	48375	16.0	113,546	5.4	119,630	4.9	125,515
Randall	48381	16.3	104,312	4.4	108,926	3.9	113,197
Austin-San Marcos MSA	**.0640**	**47.7**	**1,249,763**	**16.3**	**1,453,856**	**13.0**	**1,642,751**
Bastrop	48021	50.9	57,733	25.4	72,404	19.4	86,450
Caldwell	48055	22.0	32,194	16.6	37,547	13.5	42,608
Hays	48209	48.7	97,589	29.4	126,250	21.5	153,406
Travis	48453	40.9	812,280	8.6	882,137	7.1	944,453
Williamson	48491	79.1	249,967	34.2	335,518	23.9	415,834
Beaumont-Port Arthur MSA	**.0840**	**6.6**	**385,090**	**-1.1**	**380,783**	**-1.0**	**376,981**
Hardin	48199	16.3	48,073	5.0	50,484	4.6	52,821
Jefferson	48245	5.3	252,051	-2.3	246,195	-2.1	240,914
Orange	48361	5.5	84,966	-1.0	84,104	-1.0	83,246
Brazoria PMSA	**.1145**	**26.1**	**241,767**	**14.5**	**276,715**	**12.1**	**310,079**
Brazoria	48039	26.1	241,767	14.5	276,715	12.1	310,079
Brownsville-Harlingen-San Benito MSA	**.1240**	**28.9**	**335,227**	**13.4**	**379,998**	**11.3**	**423,084**
Cameron	48061	28.9	335,227	13.4	379,998	11.3	423,084
Bryan-College Station MSA	**.1260**	**25.1**	**152,415**	**2.8**	**156,700**	**2.7**	**160,854**
Brazos	48041	25.1	152,415	2.8	156,700	2.7	160,854
Corpus Christi MSA	**.1880**	**8.8**	**380,783**	**0.8**	**383,948**	**1.0**	**387,760**
Nueces	48355	7.7	313,645	0.8	316,026	0.8	318,647
San Patricio	48409	14.3	67,138	1.2	67,922	1.8	69,113
Dallas PMSA	**.1920**	**31.5**	**3,519,176**	**13.2**	**3,984,198**	**11.0**	**4,424,108**
Collin	48085	86.2	491,675	34.4	660,783	24.3	821,038
Dallas	48113	19.8	2,218,899	4.5	2,319,427	4.1	2,413,468
Denton	48121	58.3	432,976	29.0	558,392	21.4	677,656
Ellis	48139	30.8	111,360	19.2	132,726	15.2	152,908
Henderson	48213	25.2	73,277	8.9	79,774	7.7	85,944
Hunt	48231	19.0	76,596	7.7	82,483	6.7	87,979
Kaufman	48257	36.6	71,313	24.4	88,739	18.6	105,279
Rockwall	48397	68.3	43,080	43.6	61,874	29.0	79,836
El Paso MSA	**.2320**	**14.9**	**679,622**	**6.0**	**720,147**	**5.4**	**758,748**
El Paso	48141	14.9	679,622	6.0	720,147	5.4	758,748
Fort Worth-Arlington PMSA	**.2800**	**25.1**	**1,702,625**	**13.1**	**1,924,870**	**11.0**	**2,136,015**
Hood	48221	41.8	41,100	15.9	47,627	12.8	53,725
Johnson	48251	30.5	126,811	16.0	147,080	12.9	166,061
Parker	48367	36.6	88,495	16.6	103,201	13.5	117,084
Tarrant	48439	23.6	1,446,219	12.5	1,626,962	10.6	1,799,145
Galveston-Texas City PMSA	**.2920**	**15.1**	**250,158**	**10.8**	**277,119**	**9.5**	**303,434**
Galveston	48167	15.1	250,158	10.8	277,119	9.5	303,434
Houston PMSA	**.3360**	**25.8**	**4,177,646**	**12.2**	**4,689,135**	**10.4**	**5,176,226**
Chambers	48071	29.6	26,031	9.2	28,434	7.9	30,689
Fort Bend	48157	57.2	354,452	29.7	459,581	21.8	559,909
Harris	48201	20.7	3,400,578	9.2	3,713,507	8.0	4,011,640
Liberty	48291	33.1	70,154	8.9	76,373	7.5	82,084
Montgomery	48339	61.2	293,768	27.8	375,519	20.7	453,313
Waller	48473	39.6	32,663	9.4	35,721	8.0	38,591
Killeen-Temple MSA	**.3810**	**22.6**	**312,952**	**5.8**	**331,158**	**5.2**	**348,347**
Bell	48027	24.5	237,974	7.4	255,627	6.6	272,474
Coryell	48099	16.8	74,978	0.7	75,531	0.5	75,873
Laredo MSA	**.4080**	**44.9**	**193,117**	**16.2**	**224,381**	**13.2**	**254,024**
Webb	48479	44.9	193,117	16.2	224,381	13.2	254,024
Longview-Marshall MSA	**.4420**	**7.7**	**208,780**	**3.5**	**216,141**	**3.4**	**223,500**
Gregg	48183	6.1	111,379	4.0	115,857	3.9	120,411
Harrison	48203	8.0	62,110	0.2	62,247	0.3	62,404
Upshur	48459	12.5	35,291	7.8	38,037	7.0	40,685
Lubbock MSA	**.4600**	**9.0**	**242,628**	**5.1**	**255,027**	**4.8**	**267,172**
Lubbock	48303	9.0	242,628	5.1	255,027	4.8	267,172
McAllen-Edinburg-Mission MSA	**.4880**	**48.5**	**569,463**	**18.6**	**675,597**	**15.0**	**776,946**
Hidalgo	48215	48.5	569,463	18.6	675,597	15.0	776,946
Odessa-Midland MSA	**.5800**	**5.1**	**237,132**	**3.4**	**245,163**	**3.6**	**254,060**
Ector	48135	1.8	121,123	2.6	124,311	2.9	127,900
Midland	48329	8.8	116,009	4.2	120,852	4.4	126,160
San Angelo MSA	**.7200**	**5.6**	**104,010**	**-0.4**	**103,625**	**-0.3**	**103,277**
Tom Green	48451	5.6	104,010	-0.4	103,625	-0.3	103,277
San Antonio MSA	**.7240**	**20.2**	**1,592,383**	**9.6**	**1,745,135**	**8.3**	**1,890,824**
Bexar	48029	17.5	1,392,931	8.6	1,512,995	7.6	1,628,001
Comal	48091	50.5	78,021	20.0	93,631	15.8	108,430
Guadalupe	48187	37.2	89,023	14.0	101,471	11.4	113,047
Wilson	48493	43.1	32,408	14.3	37,038	11.6	41,346
Sherman-Denison MSA	**.7640**	**16.4**	**110,595**	**6.2**	**117,502**	**5.5**	**123,951**
Grayson	48181	16.4	110,595	6.2	117,502	5.5	123,951
Texarkana, TX-AR MSA	.8360	8.0	129,749	2.4	132,846	2.3	135,906
Miller, AR	05091	5.1	40,443	6.3	42,971	5.8	45,456
Bowie	**48037**	**9.4**	**89,306**	**0.6**	**89,875**	**0.6**	**90,450**
Tyler MSA	**.8640**	**15.5**	**174,706**	**8.3**	**189,133**	**7.2**	**202,798**
Smith	48423	15.5	174,706	8.3	189,133	7.2	202,798
Victoria MSA	**.8750**	**13.1**	**84,088**	**2.5**	**86,168**	**2.5**	**88,308**
Victoria	48469	13.1	84,088	2.5	86,168	2.5	88,308
Waco MSA	**.8800**	**12.9**	**213,517**	**4.4**	**222,879**	**4.0**	**231,707**
McLennan	48309	12.9	213,517	4.4	222,879	4.0	231,707
Wichita Falls MSA	**.9080**	**7.8**	**140,518**	**-3.8**	**135,207**	**-3.6**	**130,347**
Archer	48009	11.0	8,854	4.6	9,260	3.2	9,553
Wichita	48485	7.6	131,664	-4.3	125,947	-4.1	120,794
Total: Metro Portion of State		**24.9**	**17,691,880**	**10.9**	**19,616,791**	**9.3**	**21,445,649**
Total: Texas		22.8	20,851,820	9.7	22,865,855	8.4	24,782,576

Utah

MSA	FIPS Code	Past: 1990-2000 % Change	Past: 2000 Census	Present: 2000-2005 % Change	Present: 7/1/05 Estimate	Future: 2005-2010 % Change	Future: 2010 Projection
Provo-Orem MSA	**.6520**	**39.8**	**368,536**	**11.1**	**409,622**	**9.5**	**448,415**
Utah	49049	39.8	368,536	11.1	409,622	9.5	448,415

* Indicates county is included from metro in different state.
Source: Devonshire Associates Ltd. and Scan/US, Inc. 2005.

Metropolitan Statistical Areas and Their Component Counties: Population Trends, *Continued*

MSA	FIPS Code	Past: 1990-2000 % Change	Past: 2000 Census	Present: 2000-2005 % Change	Present: 7/1/05 Estimate	Future: 2005-2010 % Change	Future: 2010 Projection
Salt Lake City-Ogden MSA	.7160	**24.4**	**1,333,914**	**7.0**	**1,426,891**	**6.2**	**1,515,491**
Davis	49011	27.2	238,994	20.3	287,557	16.2	334,268
Salt Lake	49035	23.8	898,387	3.5	930,006	3.2	959,978
Weber	49057	24.1	196,533	6.5	209,328	5.7	221,245
* **Kane County**	.49025	**17.0**	**6,046**	**-0.3**	**6,029**	**-0.7**	**5,985**
(See Flagstaff, AZ-UT MSA.)							
Total: Metro Portion of State		**27.4**	**1,708,496**	**7.8**	**1,842,542**	**6.9**	**1,969,891**
Total: Utah		29.6	2,233,169	8.5	2,422,623	7.4	2,602,113

Vermont

MSA	FIPS Code	Past: 1990-2000 % Change	Past: 2000 Census	Present: 2000-2005 % Change	Present: 7/1/05 Estimate	Future: 2005-2010 % Change	Future: 2010 Projection
Burlington NECMA	.1303	**12.3**	**198,889**	**3.6**	**206,121**	**3.2**	**212,728**
Chittenden	50007	11.2	146,571	2.4	150,099	2.1	153,222
Franklin	50011	13.6	45,417	6.0	48,164	5.3	50,729
Grand Isle	50013	29.8	6,901	13.9	7,858	11.7	8,777
Total: Metro Portion of State		**12.3**	**198,889**	**3.6**	**206,121**	**3.2**	**212,728**
Total: Vermont		8.2	608,827	2.8	625,611	2.5	641,281

Virginia

MSA	FIPS Code	Past: 1990-2000 % Change	Past: 2000 Census	Present: 2000-2005 % Change	Present: 7/1/05 Estimate	Future: 2005-2010 % Change	Future: 2010 Projection
Charlottesville MSA	.1540	**21.7**	**159,576**	**5.3**	**168,000**	**4.7**	**175,962**
Albemarle	51003	16.5	79,236	12.7	89,294	5.2	93,894
Charlottesville (Ind. City)	51540	11.7	45,049	-19.2	36,403	-9.1	33,104
Fluvanna	51065	61.3	20,047	23.3	24,716	18.0	29,167
Greene	51079	48.0	15,244	15.4	17,587	12.6	19,797
Danville MSA	.1950	**1.3**	**110,156**	**-2.2**	**107,753**	**-2.0**	**105,549**
Danville (Ind. City)	51590	-8.8	48,411	-4.8	46,092	-4.5	44,017
Pittsylvania	51143	10.9	61,745	-0.1	61,661	-0.2	61,532
Lynchburg MSA	.4640	**10.8**	**214,911**	**1.7**	**218,478**	**1.4**	**221,618**
Amherst	51009	11.6	31,894	0.3	31,991	0.2	32,065
Bedford	51019	32.2	60,371	6.1	64,051	5.3	67,444
Bedford (Ind. City)	51515	3.7	6,299	-1.5	6,206	-1.7	6,103
Campbell	51031	7.4	51,078	1.1	51,615	0.9	52,085
Lynchburg (Ind. City)	51680	-1.2	65,269	-1.0	64,615	-1.1	63,921
Norfolk-Virginia Beach-Newport News, VA-NC MSA	.5720	8.8	1,569,541	5.2	1,650,742	4.7	1,728,713
Currituck, NC	37053	32.4	18,190	23.6	22,484	18.4	26,629
Chesapeake (Ind. City)	**51550**	**31.1**	**199,184**	**8.4**	**215,873**	**7.1**	**231,265**
Gloucester	**51073**	**15.4**	**34,780**	**8.7**	**37,812**	**7.7**	**40,725**
Hampton (Ind. City)	**51650**	**9.5**	**146,437**	**-1.2**	**144,708**	**-1.2**	**142,906**
Isle of Wight	**51093**	**18.7**	**29,728**	**11.7**	**33,202**	**9.9**	**36,500**
James City	**51095**	**38.0**	**48,102**	**17.1**	**56,330**	**13.9**	**64,132**
Mathews	**51115**	**10.3**	**9,207**	**0.8**	**9,283**	**0.9**	**9,363**
Newport News (Ind. City)	**51700**	**5.9**	**180,150**	**1.3**	**182,551**	**1.9**	**186,096**
Norfolk (Ind. City)	**51710**	**-10.3**	**234,403**	**1.6**	**238,106**	**1.5**	**241,716**
Poquoson (Ind. City)	**51735**	**5.1**	**11,566**	**2.3**	**11,837**	**2.1**	**12,087**
Portsmouth (Ind. City)	**51740**	**-3.2**	**100,565**	**-2.5**	**98,061**	**-2.4**	**95,703**
Suffolk (Ind. City)	**51800**	**22.1**	**63,677**	**24.6**	**79,362**	**19.0**	**94,429**
Virginia Beach (Ind. City)	**51810**	**8.2**	**425,257**	**5.3**	**447,757**	**4.7**	**468,941**
Williamsburg (Ind. City)	**51830**	**4.1**	**11,998**	**-7.9**	**11,046**	**-7.9**	**10,177**
York	**51199**	**32.7**	**56,297**	**10.7**	**62,330**	**9.2**	**68,044**
Richmond-Petersburg MSA	.6760	**15.1**	**996,512**	**5.7**	**1,053,657**	**5.1**	**1,107,479**
Charles City	51036	10.3	6,926	4.9	7,266	4.6	7,600
Chesterfield	51041	24.2	259,903	10.3	286,764	8.9	312,369
Colonial Heights (Ind. City)	51570	5.2	16,897	3.1	17,418	2.9	17,922
Dinwiddie	51053	17.0	24,533	2.3	25,086	2.0	25,576
Goochland	51075	19.1	16,863	12.3	18,934	10.4	20,902
Hanover	51085	36.4	86,320	14.1	98,498	11.6	109,899
Henrico	51087	20.4	262,300	5.1	275,628	4.4	287,842
Hopewell (Ind. City)	51670	-3.2	22,354	0.2	22,404	0.5	22,509
New Kent	51127	28.9	13,462	17.4	15,806	14.3	18,065
Petersburg (Ind. City)	51730	-12.1	33,740	-3.0	32,717	-2.6	31,864
Powhatan	51145	46.0	22,377	18.6	26,540	14.6	30,413
Prince George	51149	20.6	33,047	5.6	34,896	4.6	36,515
Richmond (Ind. City)	51760	-2.6	197,790	-3.1	191,700	-3.0	186,003
Roanoke MSA	.6800	**5.1**	**235,932**	**-0.2**	**235,526**	**-0.1**	**235,254**
Botetourt	51023	22.0	30,496	4.9	31,989	4.4	33,392
Roanoke	51161	8.1	85,778	2.8	88,219	2.7	90,636
Roanoke (Ind. City)	51770	-1.5	94,911	-4.1	91,029	-3.9	87,440
Salem (Ind. City)	51775	4.2	24,747	-1.9	24,289	-2.1	23,786
* **Alexandria City**	.51510	**15.4**	**128,283**	**-0.1**	**128,132**	**-0.8**	**127,123**
* **Arlington County**	.51013	**10.8**	**189,453**	**-1.9**	**185,858**	**-1.8**	**182,475**
* **Clarke County**	.51043	**4.6**	**12,652**	**9.8**	**13,896**	**8.5**	**15,075**
* **Culpeper County**	.51047	**23.3**	**34,262**	**20.6**	**41,320**	**16.4**	**48,099**
* **Fairfax County**	.51059	**18.5**	**969,749**	**4.8**	**1,016,742**	**4.2**	**1,059,612**
* **Fairfax City**	.51600	**9.6**	**21,498**	**3.3**	**22,200**	**2.8**	**22,824**
* **Falls Church City**	.51610	**8.3**	**10,377**	**3.3**	**10,716**	**2.9**	**11,022**
* **Fauquier County**	.51061	**13.1**	**55,139**	**17.6**	**64,828**	**14.2**	**74,034**
* **Fredericksburg City**	.51630	**1.3**	**19,279**	**7.7**	**20,769**	**6.8**	**22,189**
* **King George County**	.51099	**24.2**	**16,803**	**16.4**	**19,561**	**13.5**	**22,193**
* **Loudoun County**	.51107	**96.9**	**169,599**	**48.6**	**252,089**	**30.9**	**329,892**
* **Manassas City**	.51683	**25.7**	**35,135**	**8.4**	**38,088**	**7.0**	**40,756**
* **Manassas Park City**	.51685	**52.8**	**10,290**	**11.1**	**11,429**	**9.5**	**12,518**
* **Prince William County**	.51153	**30.2**	**280,813**	**25.5**	**352,321**	**19.4**	**420,534**
* **Spotsylvania County**	.51177	**57.5**	**90,395**	**30.7**	**118,182**	**22.4**	**144,675**
* **Stafford County**	.51179	**51.0**	**92,446**	**30.9**	**121,019**	**22.6**	**148,329**
* **Warren County**	.51187	**20.8**	**31,584**	**11.1**	**35,096**	**9.6**	**38,451**
(See Washington, DC-MD-VA-WV PMSA.)							
* **Bristol City**	.51520	**-5.7**	**17,367**	**-0.8**	**17,230**	**-0.5**	**17,149**
* **Scott County**	.51169	**0.9**	**23,403**	**-2.8**	**22,744**	**-2.7**	**22,125**
* **Washington County**	.51191	**11.4**	**51,103**	**1.2**	**51,736**	**1.1**	**52,290**
(See Johnson City-Kingsport-Bristol, TN-VA MSA.)							
Total: Metro Portion of State		**15.8**	**5,528,068**	**7.7**	**5,955,628**	**6.8**	**6,359,311**
Total: Virginia		14.4	7,078,515	6.5	7,538,791	5.8	7,973,549

Washington

MSA	FIPS Code	Past: 1990-2000 % Change	Past: 2000 Census	Present: 2000-2005 % Change	Present: 7/1/05 Estimate	Future: 2005-2010 % Change	Future: 2010 Projection
Bellingham MSA	.0860	**30.5**	**166,814**	**9.4**	**182,534**	**8.2**	**197,436**
Whatcom	53073	30.5	166,814	9.4	182,534	8.2	197,436
Bremerton PMSA	.1150	**22.3**	**231,969**	**4.0**	**241,196**	**3.7**	**250,057**
Kitsap	53035	22.3	231,969	4.0	241,196	3.7	250,057
Olympia PMSA	.5910	**28.6**	**207,355**	**10.7**	**229,500**	**9.2**	**250,695**
Thurston	53067	28.6	207,355	10.7	229,500	9.2	250,695
Richland-Kennewick-Pasco MSA	.6740	**27.9**	**191,822**	**15.7**	**221,935**	**13.2**	**251,185**
Benton	53005	26.6	142,475	13.1	161,100	11.2	179,077
Franklin	53021	31.7	49,347	23.3	60,835	18.5	72,108
Seattle-Bellevue-Everett PMSA	.7600	**18.8**	**2,414,616**	**4.3**	**2,517,924**	**3.9**	**2,615,828**
Island	53029	18.9	71,558	14.0	81,610	11.9	91,341
King	53033	15.2	1,737,034	2.3	1,776,888	2.1	1,814,815
Snohomish	53061	30.1	606,024	8.8	659,426	7.6	709,672
Spokane MSA	.7840	**15.7**	**417,939**	**5.1**	**439,273**	**4.7**	**459,829**
Spokane	53063	15.7	417,939	5.1	439,273	4.7	459,829
Tacoma PMSA	.8200	**19.6**	**700,820**	**9.3**	**765,698**	**8.1**	**827,363**
Pierce	53053	19.6	700,820	9.3	765,698	8.1	827,363
Yakima MSA	.9260	**17.9**	**222,581**	**3.1**	**229,468**	**2.9**	**236,174**
Yakima	53077	17.9	222,581	3.1	229,468	2.9	236,174
* **Clark County**	.53011	**45.0**	**345,238**	**16.2**	**401,099**	**13.4**	**454,676**
(See Portland-Vancouver, OR-WA PMSA.)							
Total: Metro Portion of State		**21.4**	**4,899,154**	**6.7**	**5,228,627**	**6.0**	**5,543,243**
Total: Washington		21.1	5,894,121	6.5	6,275,159	5.8	6,639,135

West Virginia

MSA	FIPS Code	Past: 1990-2000 % Change	Past: 2000 Census	Present: 2000-2005 % Change	Present: 7/1/05 Estimate	Future: 2005-2010 % Change	Future: 2010 Projection
Charleston MSA	.1480	**0.5**	**251,662**	**-1.8**	**247,085**	**-1.7**	**242,780**
Kanawha	54039	-3.6	200,073	-3.4	193,206	-3.3	186,813
Putnam	54079	20.4	51,589	4.4	53,879	3.9	55,967
Huntington-Ashland, WV-KY-OH MSA	.3400	1.0	315,538	-0.7	313,378	-0.6	311,495
Boyd, KY	21019	-2.7	49,752	0.3	49,908	0.5	50,148
Carter, KY	21043	10.5	26,889	2.6	27,587	2.6	28,295
Greenup, KY	21089	0.4	36,891	0.8	37,186	0.9	37,530
Lawrence, OH	39087	0.8	62,319	0.4	62,567	0.4	62,824
Cabell	**54011**	**-0.0**	**96,784**	**-2.9**	**93,961**	**-2.8**	**91,287**
Wayne	**54099**	**3.0**	**42,903**	**-1.7**	**42,169**	**-1.8**	**41,411**
Parkersburg-Marietta, WV-OH MSA	.6020	1.4	151,237	-1.3	149,251	-1.3	147,362
Washington, OH	39167	1.6	63,251	-1.7	62,162	-1.7	61,134
Wood	**54107**	**1.2**	**87,986**	**-1.0**	**87,089**	**-1.0**	**86,228**
Wheeling, WV-OH MSA	.9000	-3.8	153,172	-3.2	148,237	-3.0	143,718
Belmont, OH	39013	-1.2	70,226	-1.7	69,040	-1.6	67,943
Marshall	**54051**	**-4.9**	**35,519**	**-2.7**	**34,564**	**-2.4**	**33,723**
Ohio	**54069**	**-6.8**	**47,427**	**-5.9**	**44,633**	**-5.8**	**42,052**
* **Berkeley County**	.54003	**28.1**	**75,905**	**20.4**	**91,401**	**16.3**	**106,284**
* **Jefferson County**	.54037	**17.4**	**42,190**	**16.3**	**49,069**	**13.4**	**55,649**
(See Washington, DC-MD-VA-WV PMSA.)							
* **Mineral County**	.54057	**1.4**	**27,078**	**0.5**	**27,200**	**0.5**	**27,338**
(See Cumberland, MD-WV MSA.)							
* **Brooke County**	.54009	**-5.7**	**25,447**	**-2.9**	**24,717**	**-2.7**	**24,058**
* **Hancock County**	.54029	**-7.3**	**32,667**	**-4.3**	**31,270**	**-4.2**	**29,947**
(See Steubenville-Weirton, OH-WV MSA.)							
Total: Metro Portion of State		**2.3**	**765,568**	**1.0**	**773,158**	**1.0**	**780,757**
Total: West Virginia		0.8	1,808,344	0.3	1,813,363	0.3	1,819,289

Wisconsin

MSA	FIPS Code	Past: 1990-2000 % Change	Past: 2000 Census	Present: 2000-2005 % Change	Present: 7/1/05 Estimate	Future: 2005-2010 % Change	Future: 2010 Projection
Appleton-Oshkosh-Neenah MSA	.0460	**13.7**	**358,365**	**5.0**	**376,237**	**4.4**	**392,863**
Calumet	55015	18.5	40,631	10.8	45,019	9.5	49,298
Outagamie	55087	14.6	160,971	6.5	171,486	5.6	181,135
Winnebago	55139	11.7	156,763	1.9	159,732	1.7	162,430
Eau Claire MSA	.2290	**7.8**	**148,337**	**4.0**	**154,337**	**3.7**	**160,041**
Chippewa	55017	5.4	55,195	8.1	59,690	7.3	64,022
Eau Claire	55035	9.3	93,142	1.6	94,647	1.4	96,019
Green Bay MSA	.3080	**16.5**	**226,778**	**5.3**	**238,847**	**4.8**	**250,395**
Brown	55009	16.5	226,778	5.3	238,847	4.8	250,395
Janesville-Beloit MSA	.3620	**9.2**	**152,307**	**2.7**	**156,477**	**2.5**	**160,406**
Rock	55105	9.2	152,307	2.7	156,477	2.5	160,406
Kenosha PMSA	.3800	**16.7**	**149,577**	**7.1**	**160,165**	**6.3**	**170,237**
Kenosha	55059	16.7	149,577	7.1	160,165	6.3	170,237
La Crosse, WI-MN MSA	.3870	9.0	126,838	2.0	129,409	1.8	131,800
Houston, MN	27055	6.6	19,718	1.4	19,996	1.2	20,236
La Crosse	**55063**	**9.4**	**107,120**	**2.1**	**109,413**	**2.0**	**111,564**
Madison MSA	.4720	**16.2**	**426,526**	**8.6**	**463,177**	**7.5**	**497,973**
Dane	55025	16.2	426,526	8.6	463,177	7.5	497,973
Milwaukee-Waukesha PMSA	.5080	**4.8**	**1,500,741**	**1.4**	**1,521,473**	**1.3**	**1,540,762**
Milwaukee	55079	-2.0	940,164	-1.3	927,823	-1.3	916,196
Ozaukee	55089	13.0	82,317	5.1	86,503	4.5	90,435
Washington	55131	23.3	117,493	6.7	125,320	5.8	132,639
Waukesha	55133	18.4	360,767	5.8	381,827	5.2	401,492
Racine PMSA	.6600	**7.9**	**188,831**	**3.3**	**194,975**	**3.1**	**200,939**
Racine	55101	7.9	188,831	3.3	194,975	3.1	200,939
Sheboygan MSA	.7620	**8.4**	**112,646**	**1.2**	**114,016**	**1.1**	**115,256**
Sheboygan	55117	8.4	112,646	1.2	114,016	1.1	115,256
Wausau MSA	.8940	**9.0**	**125,834**	**1.8**	**128,048**	**1.7**	**130,168**
Marathon	55073	9.0	125,834	1.8	128,048	1.7	130,168
* **Douglas County**	.55031	**3.7**	**43,287**	**2.2**	**44,257**	**1.9**	**45,108**
(See Duluth-Superior, MN-WI MSA.)							
* **Pierce County**	.55093	**12.3**	**36,804**	**4.8**	**38,572**	**4.3**	**40,236**
* **St. Croix County**	.55109	**25.7**	**63,155**	**21.0**	**76,388**	**16.6**	**89,094**
(See Minneapolis-St. Paul, MN-WI MSA.)							
Total: Metro Portion of State		**9.3**	**3,640,308**	**3.7**	**3,776,382**	**3.4**	**3,905,042**
Total: Wisconsin		9.6	5,363,675	3.3	5,543,126	3.0	5,711,860

Wyoming

MSA	FIPS Code	Past: 1990-2000 % Change	Past: 2000 Census	Present: 2000-2005 % Change	Present: 7/1/05 Estimate	Future: 2005-2010 % Change	Future: 2010 Projection
Casper MSA	.1350	**8.7**	**66,533**	**4.2**	**69,348**	**4.0**	**72,107**
Natrona	56025	8.7	66,533	4.2	69,348	4.0	72,107
Cheyenne MSA	.1580	**11.6**	**81,607**	**5.5**	**86,122**	**5.1**	**90,483**
Laramie	56021	11.6	81,607	5.5	86,122	5.1	90,483
Total: Metro Portion of State		**10.2**	**148,140**	**4.9**	**155,470**	**4.6**	**162,590**
Total: Wyoming		8.9	493,782	2.8	507,467	2.6	520,799
Total: Metro Portion of United States		**13.9**	**226,042,306**	**6.0**	**239,679,703**	**5.4**	**252,645,178**
Total: United States		13.2	281,421,906	5.3	296,460,358	4.8	310,730,123

* Indicates county is included from metro in different state.
Source: Devonshire Associates Ltd. and Scan/US, Inc. 2005.

150 Largest Metropolitan Statistical Areas: Population Trends

The following data are presented for the 150 largest MSAs, PMSAs, and NECMAs (based on 2010 population projections): the Metropolitan Statistical Area FIPS Code, 1990-2000 percent of change in population; 2000 actual population; 2000-2005 estimated percent of change in population; 2005 estimated population; 2005-2010 projected percent of change in population; and 2010 projected population. MSAs, PMSAs, and NECMAs are ranked and listed in descending order according to their 2010 projected population figures. (A ranking of MSAs and PMSAs according to their 2005 estimated population figures can be found on page 44).

The data reflect MSAs, PMSAs, and NECMAs as defined and published by the Office of Management and Budget (OMB) on December 31, 1992, and as revised through June 30, 1999.

		Past		Present		Future		
MSA	FIPS Code	1990-2000 % Change	2000 Census	2000-2005 % Change	7/1/05 Estimate	2005-2010 % Change	2010 Projection	2010 Rank
Los Angeles-Long Beach, CA PMSA	.4480	7.4	9,519,338	5.9	10,076,928	5.3	10,607,471	1
New York, NY PMSA	.5600	9.0	9,314,235	2.0	9,499,149	1.8	9,670,524	2
Chicago, IL PMSA	.1600	11.6	8,272,768	4.2	8,619,113	3.8	8,944,692	3
Boston-Worcester-Lawrence-Lowell-Brockton, MA-NH NECMA	.1123	6.5	6,057,826	2.4	6,204,190	2.1	6,335,887	4
Washington, DC-MD-VA-WV PMSA	.8840	16.6	4,923,153	9.8	5,407,889	8.5	5,867,015	5
Philadelphia, PA-NJ PMSA	.6160	3.6	5,100,931	2.1	5,210,435	2.0	5,316,553	6
Houston, TX PMSA	.3360	25.8	4,177,646	12.2	4,689,135	10.4	5,176,226	7
Atlanta, GA MSA	.0520	38.9	4,112,198	13.3	4,657,401	11.0	5,168,849	8
Detroit, MI PMSA	.2160	4.1	4,441,551	0.7	4,472,407	0.6	4,498,955	9
Riverside-San Bernardino, CA PMSA	.6780	25.7	3,254,821	19.4	3,886,808	15.6	4,493,354	10
Dallas, TX PMSA	.1920	31.5	3,519,176	13.2	3,984,198	11.0	4,424,108	11
Phoenix-Mesa, AZ MSA	.6200	45.3	3,251,876	16.9	3,801,803	13.8	4,325,342	12
Minneapolis-St. Paul, MN-WI MSA	.5120	16.9	2,968,806	6.3	3,154,675	5.5	3,327,749	13
Orange County, CA PMSA	.5945	18.1	2,846,289	6.1	3,020,648	5.4	3,184,136	14
San Diego, CA MSA	.7320	12.6	2,813,833	6.3	2,990,693	5.5	3,156,599	15
Nassau-Suffolk, NY PMSA	.5380	5.5	2,753,913	3.2	2,842,538	2.9	2,924,418	16
Tampa-St. Petersburg-Clearwater, FL MSA	.8280	15.9	2,395,997	9.1	2,613,412	8.0	2,822,434	17
Baltimore, MD PMSA	.0720	7.2	2,552,994	4.1	2,658,807	3.8	2,761,004	18
St. Louis, MO-IL MSA	.7040	4.5	2,603,607	2.6	2,672,574	2.5	2,739,104	19
Seattle-Bellevue-Everett, WA PMSA	.7600	18.8	2,414,616	4.3	2,517,924	3.9	2,615,828	20
Oakland, CA PMSA	.5775	14.9	2,392,557	4.4	2,497,921	3.8	2,591,744	21
Miami, FL PMSA	.5000	16.3	2,253,362	6.1	2,391,206	5.5	2,522,264	22
Denver, CO PMSA[1]	.2080	30.0	2,109,282	7.7	2,271,459	7.3	2,437,644	23
Pittsburgh, PA MSA	.6280	-1.5	2,358,695	-1.3	2,329,028	-1.2	2,301,195	24
Portland-Vancouver, OR-WA PMSA	.6440	26.6	1,918,009	9.5	2,099,630	8.3	2,273,070	25
Las Vegas, NV-AZ MSA	.4120	83.3	1,563,282	22.7	1,918,279	17.5	2,253,767	26
Cleveland-Lorain-Elyria, OH PMSA	.1680	2.2	2,250,871	-0.5	2,239,726	-0.5	2,229,296	27
Newark, NJ PMSA	.5640	6.1	2,032,989	3.1	2,095,245	2.9	2,155,281	28
Sacramento, CA PMSA	.6920	21.5	1,628,197	16.2	1,891,938	13.4	2,144,620	29
Orlando, FL MSA	.5960	34.3	1,644,561	15.6	1,900,560	12.8	2,144,445	30
Fort Worth-Arlington, TX PMSA	.2800	25.1	1,702,625	13.1	1,924,870	11.0	2,136,015	31
Kansas City, MO-KS MSA	.3760	12.2	1,776,062	6.4	1,889,911	5.6	1,996,129	32
Fort Lauderdale, FL PMSA	.2680	29.3	1,623,018	10.5	1,794,053	9.0	1,955,383	33
San Antonio, TX MSA	.7240	20.2	1,592,383	9.6	1,745,135	8.3	1,890,824	34
Charlotte-Gastonia-Rock Hill, NC-SC MSA	.1520	29.0	1,499,293	12.5	1,686,002	10.5	1,862,599	35
Indianapolis, IN MSA	.3480	16.4	1,607,486	7.3	1,724,043	6.4	1,834,827	36
New Haven-Bridgeport-Stamford-Danbury-Waterbury, CT NECMA	.5483	4.6	1,706,575	3.3	1,762,900	3.0	1,815,942	37
Columbus, OH MSA	.1840	14.5	1,540,157	6.4	1,639,166	5.6	1,731,644	38
Norfolk-Virginia Beach-Newport News, VA-NC MSA	.5720	8.8	1,569,541	5.2	1,650,742	4.7	1,728,713	39
Cincinnati, OH-KY-IN PMSA	.1640	7.9	1,646,395	2.6	1,688,541	2.3	1,727,719	40
San Jose, CA PMSA	.7400	12.4	1,682,585	-0.7	1,669,973	-1.0	1,653,999	41
Austin-San Marcos, TX MSA	.0640	47.7	1,249,763	16.3	1,453,856	13.0	1,642,751	42
San Francisco, CA PMSA	.7360	8.0	1,731,183	-3.6	1,669,327	-3.6	1,608,889	43
Milwaukee-Waukesha, WI PMSA	.5080	4.8	1,500,741	1.4	1,521,473	1.3	1,540,762	44
Raleigh-Durham-Chapel Hill, NC MSA	.6640	38.9	1,187,941	14.5	1,360,180	12.2	1,526,072	45
Salt Lake City-Ogden, UT MSA	.7160	24.4	1,333,914	7.0	1,426,891	6.2	1,515,491	46
Bergen-Passaic, NJ PMSA	.0875	7.4	1,373,167	2.7	1,410,908	2.4	1,444,821	47
Nashville, TN MSA	.5360	25.0	1,231,311	7.6	1,324,828	6.7	1,413,321	48
West Palm Beach-Boca Raton, FL MSA	.8960	31.0	1,131,184	12.0	1,267,148	10.4	1,398,390	49
Greensboro—Winston-Salem—High Point, NC MSA	.3120	19.2	1,251,509	5.7	1,322,689	5.0	1,389,241	50
Jacksonville, FL MSA	.3600	21.4	1,100,491	11.3	1,224,737	9.9	1,345,578	51
Middlesex-Somerset-Hunterdon, NJ PMSA	.5015	14.7	1,169,641	7.2	1,254,329	6.4	1,334,138	52
New Orleans, LA MSA	.5560	4.1	1,337,726	-0.6	1,329,657	-0.5	1,323,366	53
Monmouth-Ocean, NJ PMSA	.5190	14.2	1,126,217	7.7	1,213,007	6.8	1,295,131	54
Hartford, CT NECMA	.3283	2.2	1,148,618	4.2	1,197,175	3.9	1,243,285	55
Memphis, TN-AR-MS MSA	.4920	12.7	1,135,614	4.7	1,188,935	4.2	1,239,110	56
Oklahoma City, OK MSA	.5880	13.0	1,083,346	5.5	1,142,506	4.9	1,198,501	57
Grand Rapids-Muskegon-Holland, MI MSA	.3000	16.1	1,088,514	5.1	1,144,317	4.5	1,195,956	58
Buffalo-Niagara Falls, NY MSA	.1280	-1.6	1,170,111	-1.3	1,154,526	-1.2	1,140,186	59
Fresno, CA MSA	.2840	22.1	922,516	11.0	1,023,612	9.5	1,121,239	60
Rochester, NY MSA	.6840	3.4	1,098,201	0.7	1,106,020	0.6	1,113,174	61
Richmond-Petersburg, VA MSA	.6760	15.1	996,512	5.7	1,053,657	5.1	1,107,479	62
Louisville, KY-IN MSA	.4520	8.1	1,025,598	2.9	1,055,433	2.6	1,082,969	63
Providence-Warwick-Pawtucket, RI NECMA	.6483	5.1	962,886	5.1	1,011,599	4.6	1,058,106	64
Greenville-Spartanburg-Anderson, SC MSA	.3160	15.9	962,441	5.1	1,011,759	4.6	1,058,021	65
Tucson, AZ MSA	.8520	26.5	843,746	9.2	921,681	7.9	994,799	66
Birmingham, AL MSA	.1000	9.6	921,106	3.4	952,851	3.1	982,594	67
Honolulu, HI MSA	.3320	4.8	876,156	3.9	910,475	3.9	945,789	68
Dayton-Springfield, OH MSA	.2000	-0.1	950,558	-0.9	942,462	-0.8	934,629	69
Albany-Schenectady-Troy, NY MSA	.0160	1.6	875,583	2.9	900,791	2.7	925,250	70
Ventura, CA PMSA	.8735	12.6	753,197	8.0	813,570	7.0	870,395	71
Tulsa, OK MSA	.8560	13.3	803,235	4.0	835,699	3.6	865,868	72
Albuquerque, NM MSA	.0200	21.0	712,738	8.3	772,209	7.4	829,520	73
Tacoma, WA PMSA	.8200	19.6	700,820	9.3	765,698	8.1	827,363	74
Bakersfield, CA MSA	.0680	21.7	661,645	12.4	743,729	10.7	823,538	75
Omaha, NE-IA MSA	.5920	12.1	716,998	5.5	756,323	4.9	793,109	76
Stockton-Lodi, CA MSA	.8120	17.3	563,598	19.6	674,080	15.7	779,783	77
McAllen-Edinburg-Mission, TX MSA	.4880	48.5	569,463	18.6	675,597	15.0	776,946	78
Knoxville, TN MSA	.3840	17.3	687,249	6.0	728,734	5.4	768,308	79
El Paso, TX MSA	.2320	14.9	679,622	6.0	720,147	5.4	758,748	80
Syracuse, NY MSA	.8160	-1.4	732,117	1.1	740,003	1.0	747,586	81
Sarasota-Bradenton, FL MSA	.7510	20.5	589,959	11.8	659,642	10.1	726,472	82
Akron, OH PMSA	.0080	5.7	694,960	1.4	704,396	1.2	712,569	83
Allentown-Bethlehem-Easton, PA MSA	.0240	7.2	637,958	5.4	672,335	4.9	705,413	84
Ann Arbor, MI PMSA	.0440	18.1	578,736	9.4	633,040	8.1	684,095	85
Gary, IN PMSA	.2960	4.4	631,362	2.3	645,927	2.2	659,848	86
Harrisburg-Lebanon-Carlisle, PA MSA	.3240	7.0	629,401	2.4	644,200	2.2	658,322	87
Wilmington-Newark, DE-MD PMSA	.9160	14.2	586,216	6.0	621,190	5.3	654,010	88
Baton Rouge, LA MSA	.0760	14.1	602,894	4.0	627,014	3.5	649,179	89
Little Rock-North Little Rock, AR MSA	.4400	13.8	583,845	4.8	612,049	4.3	638,447	90
Springfield, MA NECMA	.8003	0.9	608,479	1.5	617,467	1.4	625,916	91
Charleston-North Charleston, SC MSA	.1440	8.3	549,033	6.9	586,872	6.2	623,170	92
Colorado Springs, CO MSA	.1720	30.2	516,929	10.4	570,479	9.0	621,578	93
Toledo, OH MSA	.8400	0.7	618,203	0.1	618,775	0.1	619,136	94
Daytona Beach, FL MSA	.2020	23.5	493,175	12.3	554,014	10.5	612,372	95
Columbia, SC MSA	.1760	18.4	536,691	6.8	573,167	6.1	608,077	96
Jersey City, NJ PMSA	.3640	10.1	608,975	-0.3	607,051	-0.4	604,565	97
Fort Myers-Cape Coral, FL MSA	.2700	31.6	440,888	18.7	523,512	15.2	603,036	98
Scranton—Wilkes-Barre—Hazleton, PA MSA	.7560	-2.1	624,776	-2.0	612,464	-1.8	601,397	99
Vallejo-Fairfield-Napa, CA PMSA	.8720	15.0	518,821	7.6	558,215	6.5	594,574	100
Modesto, CA MSA	.5170	20.6	446,997	16.3	519,823	13.4	589,650	101
Mobile, AL MSA	.5160	13.3	540,258	3.3	558,139	3.0	574,645	102
Boise City, ID MSA	.1080	46.1	432,345	16.6	504,057	13.4	571,805	103
Melbourne-Titusville-Palm Bay, FL MSA	.4900	19.4	476,230	9.9	523,567	8.7	569,284	104
Lakeland-Winter Haven, FL MSA	.3980	19.4	483,924	8.7	526,208	7.7	566,911	105
Youngstown-Warren, OH MSA	.9320	-1.0	594,746	-2.7	578,504	-2.7	563,099	106
Wichita, KS MSA[2]	.9040	12.8	512,351	3.6	530,928	3.3	548,235	107
Fort Wayne, IN MSA	.2760	10.1	502,141	3.5	519,862	3.2	536,419	108
Lexington, KY MSA	.4280	18.0	479,198	5.9	507,373	5.2	533,961	109
Des Moines, IA MSA	.2120	16.1	456,022	7.5	490,399	6.6	522,858	110
Augusta-Aiken, GA-SC MSA	.0600	15.0	477,441	3.6	494,516	3.3	510,890	111
Lancaster, PA MSA	.4000	11.3	470,658	4.2	490,254	3.7	508,588	112
Johnson City-Kingsport-Bristol, TN-VA MSA	.3660	10.1	480,091	2.0	489,628	1.9	498,754	113
Madison, WI MSA	.4720	16.2	426,526	8.6	463,177	7.5	497,973	114
Chattanooga, TN-GA MSA	.1560	9.6	465,161	3.1	479,572	2.9	493,272	115
Santa Rosa, CA PMSA	.7500	18.1	458,614	2.7	470,813	2.2	481,193	116
Jackson, MS MSA	.3560	11.5	440,801	4.7	461,453	4.2	480,793	117
Newburgh, NY-PA PMSA	.5660	15.5	387,669	11.8	433,484	10.1	477,278	118
Lansing-East Lansing, MI MSA	.4040	3.5	447,728	3.1	461,446	2.8	474,468	119
Kalamazoo-Battle Creek, MI MSA	.3720	5.4	452,851	2.0	462,127	1.9	470,878	120
Pensacola, FL MSA	.6080	19.7	412,153	6.1	437,128	5.6	461,430	121
Spokane, WA MSA	.7840	15.7	417,939	5.1	439,273	4.7	459,829	122
Flint, MI PMSA	.2640	1.3	436,141	2.2	445,626	1.9	454,172	123
Provo-Orem, UT MSA	.6520	39.8	368,536	11.1	409,622	9.5	448,415	124
Shreveport-Bossier City, LA MSA	.7680	4.2	392,302	7.2	420,461	6.6	448,010	125
Visalia-Tulare-Porterville, CA MSA	.8780	18.0	368,021	10.0	404,818	8.9	440,650	126
Salinas, CA MSA	.7120	13.0	401,762	4.9	421,269	4.3	439,362	127
Reno, NV MSA	.6720	33.3	339,486	15.0	390,302	12.5	439,196	128
York, PA MSA	.9280	12.4	381,751	5.7	403,361	5.1	423,825	129
Brownsville-Harlingen-San Benito, TX MSA	.1240	28.9	335,227	13.4	379,998	11.3	423,084	130
Fort Pierce-Port St. Lucie, FL MSA	.2710	27.2	319,426	15.1	367,537	12.8	414,409	131
Reading, PA MSA	.6680	11.0	373,638	5.2	393,253	4.7	411,802	132
Rockford, IL MSA	.6880	12.6	371,236	5.5	391,588	4.9	410,833	133
Santa Barbara-Santa Maria-Lompoc, CA MSA	.7480	8.0	399,347	1.3	404,582	1.2	409,485	134
Fayetteville-Springdale-Rogers, AR MSA	.2580	47.5	311,121	16.0	360,974	13.1	408,202	135
Canton-Massillon, OH MSA	.1320	3.3	406,934	0.0	407,131	-0.0	407,088	136
Saginaw-Bay City-Midland, MI MSA	.6960	0.9	403,070	0.0	403,186	0.0	403,247	137
Salem, OR PMSA	.7080	24.9	347,214	8.0	374,986	7.1	401,672	138
Lafayette, LA MSA	.3880	11.8	385,647	2.1	393,730	1.9	401,337	139
Appleton-Oshkosh-Neenah, WI MSA	.0460	13.7	358,365	5.0	376,237	4.4	392,863	140
Huntsville, AL MSA	.3440	16.8	342,376	7.3	367,395	6.4	390,910	141
Corpus Christi, TX MSA	.1880	8.8	380,783	0.8	383,948	1.0	387,760	142
Trenton, NJ PMSA	.8480	7.7	350,761	5.3	369,496	4.9	387,426	143
Biloxi-Gulfport-Pascagoula, MS MSA	.0920	16.5	363,988	2.1	371,758	1.8	378,455	144
Beaumont-Port Arthur, TX MSA	.0840	6.6	385,090	-1.1	380,783	-1.0	376,981	145
Springfield, MO MSA	.7920	23.2	325,721	7.7	350,755	6.8	374,623	146
Atlantic-Cape May, NJ PMSA	.0560	11.1	354,878	2.2	362,796	2.0	370,154	147
Hickory-Morganton-Lenoir, NC MSA	.3290	16.9	341,851	4.2	356,039	3.6	368,980	148
Hamilton-Middletown, OH PMSA	.3200	14.2	332,807	4.9	349,225	4.4	364,560	149
Macon, GA MSA	.4680	10.9	322,549	6.6	343,865	5.9	364,318	150

Source: Devonshire Associates Ltd. and Scan/US, Inc. 2005.

[1] Census population includes a portion of Broomfield county.

[2] Data excludes Harvey county, Kansas (2000 Census population 32,869; 2005 estimated population 34,021; and 2010 projected population 35,130), which fails to meet published standards for MSA inclusion, but has been included with the Wichita MSA as the result of Congressional action.

Combined Statistical Areas (CSAs): Population Trends

The following data are presented for Combined Statistical Areas (CSAs): 1990-2000 percent of change in population; 2000 actual population; 2000-2005 estimated percent of change in population; 2005 estimated population; 2005-2010 projected percent of change in population; and 2010 projected population.

CSA	Past 1990-2000 % Change	Past 2000 Census	Present 2000-2005 % Change	Present 7/1/05 Estimate	Future 2005-2010 % Change	Future 2010 Projection
Albany-Corvallis-Lebanon, OR	11.8	181,222	4.0	188,428	3.8	195,675
Albany-Schenectady-Amsterdam, NY	1.9	1,118,095	2.7	1,148,794	2.6	1,178,825
Ames-Boone, IA	6.8	106,205	0.5	106,698	0.3	107,040
Appleton-Oshkosh-Neenah, WI	13.7	358,365	5.0	376,237	4.4	392,863
Asheville-Brevard, NC	19.5	398,505	5.5	420,538	4.9	441,225
Atlanta-Sandy Springs-Gainesville, GA-AL	37.1	4,548,344	13.1	5,142,784	10.8	5,700,560
Baton Rouge-Pierre Part, LA	12.8	729,361	2.9	750,528	2.6	769,752
Beckley-Oak Hill, WV	1.6	126,799	-0.2	126,490	-0.2	126,278
Bend-Prineville, OR	51.1	134,549	18.7	159,725	14.9	183,493
Birmingham-Hoover-Cullman, AL	10.3	1,129,721	3.1	1,165,267	2.9	1,199,356
Boston-Worcester-Manchester, MA-NH	6.9	5,715,698	2.6	5,862,486	2.3	5,995,339
Brownsville-Harlingen-Raymondville, TX	27.9	355,309	12.6	400,052	10.8	443,123
Buffalo-Niagara-Cattaraugus, NY	-1.5	1,254,066	-1.3	1,237,664	-1.2	1,222,546
Cape Girardeau-Sikeston-Jackson, MO-IL	6.9	130,734	2.1	133,531	2.0	136,213
Charlotte-Gastonia-Salisbury, NC-SC	26.3	1,897,034	11.1	2,107,174	9.4	2,305,727
Chattanooga-Cleveland-Athens, TN-GA	11.8	629,561	3.5	651,300	3.2	671,853
Chicago-Naperville-Michigan City, IL-IN-WI	11.1	9,312,255	4.0	9,688,795	3.7	10,043,074
Cincinnati-Middletown-Wilmington, OH-KY-IN	9.0	2,050,175	3.0	2,112,096	2.7	2,169,708
Claremont-Lebanon, NH-VT	7.3	207,845	3.8	215,748	3.5	223,295
Cleveland-Akron-Elyria, OH	3.0	2,945,831	-0.1	2,944,122	-0.1	2,941,865
Clovis-Portales, NM	7.0	63,062	1.0	63,702	1.2	64,498
Columbia-Newberry, SC	17.5	683,266	6.1	724,958	5.5	764,679
Columbus-Auburn-Opelika, GA-AL	11.2	420,965	0.3	422,147	0.7	425,226
Columbus-Marion-Chillicothe, OH	13.7	1,835,189	6.1	1,947,508	5.4	2,052,482
Columbus-West Point, MS	3.9	83,565	-2.6	81,355	-2.6	79,262
Corbin-London, KY	15.4	88,580	7.2	94,979	6.4	101,057
Corpus Christi-Kingsville, TX	9.2	435,243	1.0	439,490	1.1	444,409
Dallas-Fort Worth, TX	29.2	5,377,361	13.1	6,079,128	10.9	6,743,666
Dayton-Springfield-Greenville, OH	0.4	1,085,094	-0.7	1,077,865	-0.7	1,070,768
Deltona-Daytona Beach-Palm Coast, FL	23.5	493,175	12.3	554,014	10.5	612,372
Denver-Aurora-Boulder, CO	30.6	2,449,054	8.4	2,653,866	7.1	2,842,711
Des Moines-Newton-Pella, IA	14.4	550,659	6.7	587,776	6.0	622,798
Detroit-Warren-Flint, MI	5.1	5,357,538	1.7	5,448,771	1.5	5,531,748
Dothan-Enterprise-Ozark, AL	6.4	223,605	2.8	229,971	2.7	236,153
Eau Claire-Menomonie, WI	8.5	188,195	4.2	196,150	3.9	203,706
Fairmont-Clarksburg, WV	-0.0	148,742	-0.5	148,005	-0.5	147,322
Fargo-Wahpeton, ND-MN	11.5	199,503	3.2	205,820	2.8	211,570
Findlay-Tiffin, OH	3.8	129,978	1.4	131,788	1.4	133,600
Fond du Lac-Beaver Dam, WI	9.9	183,193	2.0	186,879	1.8	190,335
Fort Polk South-De Ridder, LA	-7.1	85,517	-3.5	82,559	-3.3	79,794
Fort Wayne-Huntington-Auburn, IN	11.0	548,416	3.4	567,257	3.1	584,765
Fresno-Madera, CA	22.1	922,516	11.0	1,023,612	9.5	1,121,239
Grand Rapids-Muskegon-Holland, MI	15.8	1,254,661	5.2	1,319,894	4.6	1,380,466
Greensboro—Winston-Salem—High Point, NC	18.1	1,414,656	5.3	1,489,023	4.7	1,558,676
Greenville-Spartanburg-Anderson, SC	15.5	1,128,104	4.7	1,181,206	4.2	1,230,965
Gulfport-Biloxi-Pascagoula, MS	16.8	396,754	2.8	407,743	2.4	417,527
Harrisburg-Carlisle-Lebanon, PA	7.0	629,401	2.4	644,200	2.2	658,322
Hartford-West Hartford-Willimantic, CT	2.6	1,257,709	4.3	1,312,381	4.0	1,364,506
Houston-Baytown-Huntsville, TX	24.9	4,815,122	12.0	5,394,905	10.2	5,947,711
Huntsville-Decatur, AL	15.0	488,243	5.6	515,684	5.0	541,384
Idaho Falls-Blackfoot, ID	13.5	143,412	7.9	154,711	6.9	165,437
Indianapolis-Anderson-Columbus, IN	15.6	1,843,588	6.5	1,963,161	5.8	2,076,447
Ithaca-Cortland, NY	1.4	145,100	3.5	150,241	3.4	155,349
Jackson-Humboldt, TN	13.4	155,529	2.0	158,577	1.8	161,442
Jackson-Yazoo City, MS	11.2	525,346	4.0	546,547	3.6	566,315
Johnson City-Kingsport-Bristol (Tri-Cities), TN-VA	10.1	480,091	2.0	489,628	1.9	498,754
Kansas City-Overland Park-Kansas City, MO-KS	12.1	1,901,070	6.3	2,021,011	5.5	2,132,864
Knoxville-Sevierville-La Follette, TN	16.6	779,013	5.5	821,927	5.0	862,794
Kokomo-Peru, IN	2.8	137,623	-0.2	137,399	-0.2	137,072
Lafayette-Acadiana, LA	10.7	512,720	1.8	521,932	1.7	530,607
Lafayette-Frankfort, IN	11.9	212,407	2.0	216,614	1.8	220,553
Lake Charles-Jennings, LA	8.1	225,003	-0.7	223,358	-0.7	221,780
Lansing-East Lansing-Owosso, MI	3.4	519,415	3.0	534,786	2.7	549,427
Las Vegas-Paradise-Pahrump, NV	85.5	1,408,250	23.2	1,735,504	17.8	2,044,503
Lexington-Fayette—Frankfort—Richmond, KY	17.4	602,773	5.3	634,845	4.7	664,830
Lima-Van Wert-Wapakoneta, OH	-0.0	184,743	-1.3	182,374	-1.2	180,163
Little Rock-North Little Rock-Pine Bluff, AR	12.7	785,024	3.9	815,978	3.5	844,883
Longview-Marshall, TX	7.8	256,152	3.0	263,835	2.9	271,529
Los Angeles-Long Beach-Riverside, CA	12.7	16,373,645	8.7	17,797,954	7.6	19,155,356
Louisville-Elizabethtown-Scottsburg, KY-IN	9.7	1,292,482	3.7	1,340,908	3.3	1,385,790
Lubbock-Levelland, TX	7.2	272,416	4.4	284,511	4.2	296,455
Lumberton-Laurinburg, NC	14.7	159,337	2.6	163,450	2.4	167,447
Macon-Warner Robins-Fort Valley, GA	12.6	356,801	6.8	381,000	6.1	404,256
Madison-Baraboo, WI	16.2	556,999	7.6	599,114	6.7	639,055
Mansfield-Bucyrus, OH	1.0	175,818	-1.5	173,148	-1.5	170,578
Midland-Odessa, TX	5.1	237,132	3.4	245,163	3.6	254,060
Milwaukee-Racine-Waukesha, WI	5.1	1,689,572	1.6	1,716,448	1.5	1,741,701
Minneapolis-St. Paul-St. Cloud, MN-WI	16.4	3,271,888	6.4	3,482,271	5.6	3,678,948
Mobile-Daphne-Fairhope, AL	13.3	540,258	3.3	558,139	3.0	574,645
Monroe-Bastrop, LA	3.2	201,074	-0.3	200,434	-0.2	199,939
Montgomery-Alexander City, AL	12.7	400,205	2.0	408,053	1.8	415,449
Morristown-Newport, TN	20.7	156,646	5.4	165,061	4.8	172,954
Myrtle Beach-Conway-Georgetown, SC	32.6	252,426	11.1	280,520	9.4	306,868
Nashville-Davidson—Murfreesboro—Columbia, TN	25.2	1,381,287	7.5	1,485,190	6.6	1,583,363
New Orleans-Metairie-Bogalusa, LA	4.0	1,360,436	-0.6	1,352,374	-0.5	1,346,083
New York-Newark-Bridgeport, NY-NJ-CT-PA	8.4	21,361,797	3.2	22,048,103	2.9	22,691,080
Oklahoma City-Shawnee, OK	12.7	1,160,942	5.4	1,223,461	4.8	1,282,631
Omaha-Council Bluffs-Fremont, NE-IA	11.5	803,201	5.0	843,112	4.4	880,281
Orlando-The Villages, FL	35.1	1,697,906	15.6	1,962,360	12.8	2,214,415
Paducah-Mayfield, KY-IL	6.0	135,793	-0.6	134,919	-0.6	134,095
Peoria-Canton, IL	2.1	405,149	-0.5	402,994	-0.5	401,025
Philadelphia-Camden-Vineland, PA-NJ-DE-MD	4.7	5,833,585	2.6	5,982,956	2.4	6,126,807
Pittsburgh-New Castle, PA	-1.5	2,525,730	-1.3	2,493,145	-1.2	2,462,488
Portland-Lewiston-South Portland, ME	8.2	591,361	5.9	626,031	5.2	658,838
Raleigh-Durham-Cary, NC	37.9	1,314,589	14.2	1,501,912	12.0	1,682,183
Rochester-Batavia-Seneca Falls, NY	3.2	1,131,543	0.9	1,141,819	0.8	1,151,392
Rockford-Freeport-Rochelle, IL	11.2	420,215	4.6	439,376	4.1	457,518
Sacramento—Arden-Arcade—Truckee, CA-NV	21.6	1,930,149	15.3	2,226,161	12.7	2,509,259
Saginaw-Bay City-Saginaw Township North, MI	-1.1	320,196	-0.7	317,927	-0.7	315,749
St. Louis-St. Charles-Farmington, MO-IL	4.7	2,754,328	2.8	2,830,590	2.6	2,904,114
Salisbury-Ocean Pines, MD	17.4	155,934	6.0	165,220	5.3	174,006
Salt Lake City-Ogden-Clearfield, UT	26.0	1,469,474	7.8	1,584,748	6.9	1,693,853
San Jose-San Francisco-Oakland, CA	12.8	7,092,596	1.1	7,172,262	0.8	7,233,057
Santa Fe-Espanola, NM	27.9	170,482	6.7	181,875	5.9	192,627
Savannah-Hinesville-Fort Stewart, GA	15.1	364,914	4.7	382,074	4.4	398,731
Seattle-Tacoma-Olympia, WA	19.8	3,604,165	5.7	3,808,481	5.1	4,002,690
Shreveport-Bossier City-Minden, LA	4.0	417,796	6.9	444,519	6.3	474,587
Sioux City-Vermillion, IA-NE-SD	8.3	156,590	-0.3	156,102	-0.3	155,603
Sunbury-Lewisburg-Selinsgrove, PA	2.4	173,726	-0.2	173,421	-0.1	173,163
Syracuse-Auburn, NY	-1.4	732,117	1.1	740,003	1.0	747,586
Toledo-Fremont, OH	0.7	720,980	0.1	721,803	0.1	722,330
Tulsa-Bartlesville, OK	12.3	908,528	3.7	941,871	3.3	972,818
Tyler-Jacksonville, TX	15.1	221,365	7.3	237,448	6.5	252,774
Union City-Martin, TN-KY	4.4	75,097	-2.2	73,415	-2.0	71,915
Washington-Baltimore-Northern Virginia, DC-MD-VA-WV	13.1	7,572,647	7.9	8,167,341	6.9	8,732,566
Wausau-Merrill, WI	9.2	155,475	1.9	158,465	1.8	161,286
Wichita-Winfield, KS	10.8	607,457	2.9	625,277	2.6	641,777
Williamsport-Lock Haven, PA	1.3	157,958	-1.9	154,932	-1.9	151,996
York-Hanover-Gettysburg, PA	13.2	473,043	6.3	502,894	5.6	531,245
Youngstown-Warren-East Liverpool, OH-PA	-1.0	715,039	-2.4	698,203	-2.3	682,266
Total: CSA Portion of Country	**12.7**	**174,094,288**	**5.5**	**183,624,479**	**4.9**	**192,627,974**

Core Based Statistical Areas and Their Component Counties: Population Trends

Metropolitan CBSAs and their component counties are listed by state. The following data are presented for each: the CBSA FIPS Code and State-County FIPS Code(s); 1990-2000 percent of change in population; 2000 **actual** population; 2000-2005 estimated percent of change in population; 2005 **estimated** population; 2005-2010 projected percent of change in population; and 2010 **projected** population.

The total metropolitan CBSA population within the state (**Total: Metro Portion of State**), the total Micropolitan CBSA population within the state (Total: Micro Portion of State), and the total state population are also given. Data shown in **bold face** represent the in-state metropolitan area totals. A U.S. total for Micropolitan CBSAs is also provided.

		Past		Present		Future	
CBSA	FIPS Code	1990-2000 % Change	2000 Census	2000-2005 % Change	7/1/05 Estimate	2005-2010 % Change	2010 Projection
Alabama							
Anniston-Oxford AL	**11500**	**-3.3**	**112,249**	**0.3**	**112,624**	**1.1**	**113,834**
Calhoun	01015	-3.3	112,249	0.3	112,624	1.1	113,834
Auburn-Opelika AL	**12220**	**32.1**	**115,092**	**5.7**	**121,616**	**5.1**	**127,779**
Lee	01081	32.1	115,092	5.7	121,616	5.1	127,779
Birmingham-Hoover AL	**13820**	**10.0**	**1,052,238**	**3.2**	**1,086,137**	**3.0**	**1,118,703**
Bibb	01007	25.6	20,826	4.2	21,699	8.1	23,449
Blount	01009	30.0	51,024	10.1	56,200	8.9	61,174
Chilton	01021	22.0	39,593	5.6	41,805	4.8	43,797
Jefferson	01073	1.6	662,047	-0.9	655,970	-0.9	649,779
Shelby	01117	44.2	143,293	18.5	169,764	14.8	194,944
St. Clair	01115	29.5	64,742	9.5	70,917	8.2	76,697
Walker	01127	4.5	70,713	-1.3	69,782	-1.3	68,863
Decatur AL	**19460**	**10.9**	**145,867**	**1.7**	**148,289**	**1.5**	**150,474**
Lawrence	01079	10.4	34,803	-1.4	34,317	-1.6	33,772
Morgan	01103	11.0	111,064	2.6	113,972	2.4	116,702
Dothan AL	**20020**	**8.7**	**130,861**	**3.4**	**135,324**	**3.1**	**139,534**
Geneva	01061	9.0	25,764	-1.4	25,405	-1.6	25,010
Henry	01067	6.1	16,310	1.5	16,560	1.3	16,771
Houston	01069	9.2	88,787	5.1	93,359	4.7	97,753
Florence-Muscle Shoals AL	**22520**	**8.9**	**142,950**	**-1.4**	**140,981**	**-1.4**	**138,945**
Colbert	01033	6.4	54,984	-1.0	54,455	-1.1	53,872
Lauderdale	01077	10.4	87,966	-1.6	86,526	-1.7	85,073
Gadsden AL	**23460**	**3.6**	**103,459**	**-0.4**	**103,021**	**-0.3**	**102,701**
Etowah	01055	3.6	103,459	-0.4	103,021	-0.3	102,701
Huntsville AL	**26620**	**16.8**	**342,376**	**7.3**	**367,395**	**6.4**	**390,910**
Limestone	01083	21.3	65,676	6.3	69,788	5.5	73,608
Madison	01089	15.8	276,700	7.6	297,607	6.6	317,302
Mobile AL	**33660**	**5.6**	**399,843**	**-0.0**	**399,727**	**-0.1**	**399,266**
Mobile	01097	5.6	399,843	-0.0	399,727	-0.1	399,266
Montgomery AL	**33860**	**13.6**	**346,528**	**2.9**	**356,454**	**2.6**	**365,780**
Autauga	01001	27.6	43,671	9.9	47,987	8.5	52,052
Elmore	01051	33.9	65,874	11.3	73,325	9.6	80,363
Lowndes	01085	6.4	13,473	-0.7	13,375	-0.8	13,265
Montgomery	01101	6.9	223,510	-0.8	221,767	-0.8	220,100
Tuscaloosa AL	**46220**	**9.0**	**192,034**	**1.8**	**195,477**	**1.1**	**197,641**
Greene	01063	-1.8	9,974	-1.1	9,862	-1.0	9,760
Hale	01065	10.9	17,185	6.7	18,342	0.1	18,365
Tuscaloosa	01125	9.5	164,875	1.5	167,273	1.3	169,516
*** Russell** (See Columbus, GA-AL.)	**01113**	**6.2**	**49,756**	**-2.4**	**48,555**	**-2.3**	**47,428**
Total: Metro Portion of State		**10.2**	**3,133,253**	**2.6**	**3,215,600**	**2.4**	**3,292,995**
Total: Micro Portion of State		13.3	810,945	2.4	830,752	2.2	849,397
Total: Alabama		10.1	4,447,100	2.0	4,537,634	1.9	4,622,960
Alaska							
Anchorage AK	**11260**	**20.1**	**319,605**	**10.2**	**352,186**	**8.9**	**383,536**
Anchorage	02020	15.0	260,283	6.9	278,263	6.3	295,713
Matanuska-Susitna	02170	49.5	59,322	24.6	73,923	18.8	87,823
Fairbanks AK	**21820**	**6.6**	**82,840**	**4.8**	**86,784**	**4.6**	**90,770**
Fairbanks North Star	02090	6.6	82,840	4.8	86,784	4.6	90,770
Total: Metro Portion of State		**17.1**	**402,445**	**9.1**	**438,970**	**8.0**	**474,306**
Total: Micro Portion of State		8.9	58,694	-2.7	57,093	-2.4	55,700
Total: Alaska		14.0	626,932	5.6	662,020	5.2	696,537
Arizona							
Flagstaff AZ	**22380**	**20.4**	**116,320**	**6.7**	**124,093**	**6.0**	**131,518**
Coconino	04005	20.4	116,320	6.7	124,093	6.0	131,518
Phoenix-Mesa-Scottsdale AZ	**38060**	**45.3**	**3,251,876**	**16.9**	**3,801,803**	**13.8**	**4,325,342**
Maricopa	04013	44.8	3,072,149	16.6	3,582,040	13.5	4,067,317
Pinal	04021	54.4	179,727	22.3	219,763	17.4	258,025
Prescott AZ	**39140**	**55.5**	**167,517**	**16.3**	**194,839**	**13.3**	**220,681**
Yavapai	04025	55.5	167,517	16.3	194,839	13.3	220,681
Tucson AZ	**46060**	**26.5**	**843,746**	**9.2**	**921,681**	**7.9**	**994,799**
Pima	04019	26.5	843,746	9.2	921,681	7.9	994,799
Yuma AZ	**49740**	**49.7**	**160,026**	**10.6**	**177,064**	**9.2**	**193,373**
Yuma	04027	49.7	160,026	10.6	177,064	9.2	193,373
Total: Metro Portion of State		**41.1**	**4,539,485**	**15.0**	**5,219,480**	**12.4**	**5,865,713**
Total: Micro Portion of State		36.9	404,539	8.5	439,121	7.5	472,268
Total: Arizona		40.0	5,130,632	14.1	5,854,746	11.8	6,543,549
Arkansas							
Fayetteville-Springdale-Rogers, AR-MO	22220	44.9	347,045	14.6	397,806	12.1	445,885
Benton	**05007**	**57.3**	**153,406**	**19.9**	**183,859**	**15.7**	**212,752**
Madison	**05087**	**22.6**	**14,243**	**1.9**	**14,512**	**1.5**	**14,723**
Washington	**05143**	**39.1**	**157,715**	**12.3**	**177,115**	**10.4**	**195,450**
McDonald, MO	29119	28.0	21,681	2.9	22,320	2.9	22,960
Fort Smith, AR-OK	22900	16.7	273,170	3.9	283,847	3.4	293,593
Crawford	**05033**	**25.3**	**53,247**	**7.4**	**57,169**	**6.5**	**60,900**
Franklin	**05047**	**19.3**	**17,771**	**2.0**	**18,132**	**2.1**	**18,517**
Sebastian	**05131**	**15.5**	**115,071**	**3.0**	**118,532**	**2.5**	**121,438**
Le Flore, OK	40079	11.2	48,109	2.7	49,394	2.4	50,583
Sequoyah, OK	40135	15.2	38,972	4.2	40,620	3.8	42,155
Hot Springs AR	**26300**	**20.0**	**88,068**	**5.7**	**93,078**	**5.0**	**97,702**
Garland	05051	20.0	88,068	5.7	93,078	5.0	97,702
Jonesboro AR	**27860**	**15.1**	**107,762**	**3.5**	**111,567**	**3.0**	**114,962**
Craighead	05031	19.1	82,148	5.1	86,335	4.4	90,134
Poinsett	05111	3.9	25,614	-1.5	25,232	-1.6	24,828
Little Rock-North Little Rock AR	**30780**	**14.1**	**610,518**	**4.8**	**639,802**	**4.3**	**667,180**
Faulkner	05045	43.3	86,014	12.5	96,723	10.6	106,971
Grant	05053	18.0	16,464	4.7	17,241	4.2	17,962
Lonoke	05085	34.5	52,828	11.9	59,112	10.0	65,019
Perry	05105	28.1	10,209	3.0	10,512	2.5	10,771
Pulaski	05119	3.4	361,474	1.4	366,433	1.2	370,906
Saline	05125	30.1	83,529	7.5	89,781	6.4	95,551
Pine Bluff AR	**38220**	**0.4**	**107,341**	**-2.0**	**105,209**	**-1.9**	**103,228**
Cleveland	05025	10.2	8,571	3.5	8,871	3.6	9,186
Jefferson	05069	-1.4	84,278	-2.7	82,043	-2.6	79,881
Lincoln	05079	5.9	14,492	-1.4	14,295	-0.9	14,161
*** Crittenden** (See Memphis, TN-MS-AR.)	**05035**	**1.9**	**50,866**	**0.8**	**51,287**	**0.5**	**51,532**
*** Miller** (See Texarkana, TX-Texarkana, AR.)	**05091**	**5.1**	**40,443**	**6.3**	**42,971**	**5.8**	**45,456**
Total: Metro Portion of State		**18.8**	**1,516,451**	**6.4**	**1,613,233**	**5.6**	**1,703,840**
Total: Micro Portion of State		7.7	565,886	-0.8	561,240	-0.7	557,047
Total: Arkansas		13.7	2,673,400	3.2	2,759,439	2.9	2,840,378
California							
Bakersfield CA	**12540**	**21.7**	**661,645**	**12.4**	**743,729**	**10.7**	**823,538**
Kern	06029	21.7	661,645	12.4	743,729	10.7	823,538
Chico CA	**17020**	**11.6**	**203,171**	**6.1**	**215,649**	**5.5**	**227,494**
Butte	06007	11.6	203,171	6.1	215,649	5.5	227,494
El Centro CA	**20940**	**30.2**	**142,361**	**7.8**	**153,484**	**7.1**	**164,418**
Imperial	06025	30.2	142,361	7.8	153,484	7.1	164,418
Fresno CA	**23420**	**19.8**	**799,407**	**10.3**	**881,918**	**9.0**	**961,546**
Fresno	06019	19.8	799,407	10.3	881,918	9.0	961,546
Hanford-Corcoran CA	**25260**	**27.6**	**129,461**	**12.3**	**145,336**	**10.7**	**160,827**
Kings	06031	27.6	129,461	12.3	145,336	10.7	160,827
Los Angeles-Long Beach-Santa Ana CA	**31100**	**9.7**	**12,365,627**	**5.9**	**13,097,576**	**5.3**	**13,791,607**
Los Angeles	06037	7.4	9,519,338	5.9	10,076,928	5.3	10,607,471
Orange	06059	18.1	2,846,289	6.1	3,020,648	5.4	3,184,136
Madera CA	**31460**	**39.8**	**123,109**	**15.1**	**141,694**	**12.7**	**159,693**
Madera	06039	39.8	123,109	15.1	141,694	12.7	159,693
Merced CA	**32900**	**18.0**	**210,554**	**15.7**	**243,619**	**13.1**	**275,515**
Merced	06047	18.0	210,554	15.7	243,619	13.1	275,515
Modesto CA	**33700**	**20.6**	**446,997**	**16.3**	**519,823**	**13.4**	**589,650**
Stanislaus	06099	20.6	446,997	16.3	519,823	13.4	589,650
Napa CA	**34900**	**12.2**	**124,279**	**9.8**	**136,414**	**8.6**	**148,203**
Napa	06055	12.2	124,279	9.8	136,414	8.6	148,203
Oxnard-Thousand Oaks-Ventura CA	**37100**	**12.6**	**753,197**	**8.0**	**813,570**	**7.0**	**870,395**
Ventura	06111	12.6	753,197	8.0	813,570	7.0	870,395
Redding CA	**39820**	**11.0**	**163,256**	**12.3**	**183,315**	**10.6**	**202,753**
Shasta	06089	11.0	163,256	12.3	183,315	10.6	202,753
Riverside-San Bernardino-Ontario CA	**40140**	**25.7**	**3,254,821**	**19.4**	**3,886,808**	**15.6**	**4,493,354**
Riverside	06065	32.0	1,545,387	24.9	1,929,673	19.1	2,298,625
San Bernardino	06071	20.5	1,709,434	14.5	1,957,135	12.1	2,194,729
Sacramento—Arden-Arcade—Roseville CA	**40900**	**21.3**	**1,796,857**	**15.8**	**2,081,634**	**13.1**	**2,354,217**
El Dorado	06017	24.1	156,299	13.2	176,979	11.2	196,724
Placer	06061	43.8	248,399	28.5	319,191	21.2	386,916
Sacramento	06067	17.5	1,223,499	14.1	1,395,768	11.8	1,560,980
Yolo	06113	19.5	168,660	12.5	189,696	10.5	209,597
Salinas CA	**41500**	**13.0**	**401,762**	**4.9**	**421,269**	**4.3**	**439,362**
Monterey	06053	13.0	401,762	4.9	421,269	4.3	439,362
San Diego-Carlsbad-San Marcos CA	**41740**	**12.6**	**2,813,833**	**6.3**	**2,990,693**	**5.5**	**3,156,599**
San Diego	06073	12.6	2,813,833	6.3	2,990,693	5.5	3,156,599
San Francisco-Oakland-Fremont CA	**41860**	**11.9**	**4,123,740**	**1.1**	**4,167,248**	**0.8**	**4,200,633**
Alameda	06001	12.9	1,443,741	1.6	1,466,375	1.1	1,482,425
Contra Costa	06013	18.1	948,816	8.7	1,031,546	7.5	1,109,319
Marin	06041	7.5	247,289	-0.8	245,317	-0.9	243,027
San Francisco	06075	7.3	776,733	-5.4	734,587	-5.4	694,890
San Mateo	06081	8.9	707,161	-2.5	689,423	-2.7	670,972
San Jose-Sunnyvale-Santa Clara CA	**41940**	**13.1**	**1,735,819**	**-0.5**	**1,727,639**	**-0.7**	**1,715,467**
San Benito	06069	45.1	53,234	8.3	57,666	6.6	61,468
Santa Clara	06085	12.4	1,682,585	-0.7	1,669,973	-1.0	1,653,999
San Luis Obispo-Paso Robles CA	**42020**	**13.6**	**246,681**	**4.3**	**257,381**	**3.8**	**267,045**
San Luis Obispo	06079	13.6	246,681	4.3	257,381	3.8	267,045
Santa Barbara-Santa Maria CA	**42060**	**8.0**	**399,347**	**1.3**	**404,582**	**1.2**	**409,485**
Santa Barbara	06083	8.0	399,347	1.3	404,582	1.2	409,485
Santa Cruz-Watsonville CA	**42100**	**11.3**	**255,602**	**-2.8**	**248,347**	**-2.9**	**241,190**
Santa Cruz	06087	11.3	255,602	-2.8	248,347	-2.9	241,190
Santa Rosa-Petaluma CA	**42220**	**18.1**	**458,614**	**2.7**	**470,813**	**2.2**	**481,193**
Sonoma	06097	18.1	458,614	2.7	470,813	2.2	481,193
Stockton CA	**44700**	**17.3**	**563,598**	**19.6**	**674,080**	**15.7**	**779,783**
San Joaquin	06077	17.3	563,598	19.6	674,080	15.7	779,783
Vallejo-Fairfield CA	**46700**	**15.9**	**394,542**	**6.9**	**421,801**	**5.8**	**446,371**
Solano	06095	15.9	394,542	6.9	421,801	5.8	446,371
Visalia-Porterville CA	**47300**	**18.0**	**368,021**	**10.0**	**404,818**	**8.9**	**440,650**
Tulare	06107	18.0	368,021	10.0	404,818	8.9	440,650
Yuba City CA	**49700**	**13.5**	**139,149**	**10.6**	**153,877**	**9.3**	**168,208**
Sutter	06101	22.5	78,930	11.8	88,233	10.2	97,260
Yuba	06115	3.4	60,219	9.0	65,644	8.1	70,948
Total: Metro Portion of State		**13.9**	**33,075,450**	**7.6**	**35,587,117**	**6.7**	**37,969,196**
Total: Micro Portion of State		11.5	552,945	5.6	583,701	5.1	613,466
Total: California		13.8	33,871,648	7.6	36,430,227	6.7	38,857,985
Colorado							
Boulder CO	**14500**	**29.1**	**269,814**	**4.7**	**282,452**	**3.9**	**293,577**
Boulder	08013	29.1	269,814	4.7	282,452	3.9	293,577
Colorado Springs CO	**17820**	**31.3**	**537,484**	**10.3**	**592,836**	**8.9**	**645,614**
El Paso	08041	30.2	516,929	10.4	570,479	9.0	621,578
Teller	08119	64.9	20,555	8.8	22,357	7.5	24,036
Denver-Aurora CO	**19740**	**30.7**	**2,179,240**	**8.8**	**2,371,414**	**7.5**	**2,549,134**
Adams	08001	35.0	348,618	14.5	399,121	12.0	446,996
Arapahoe	08005	24.6	487,967	9.0	531,667	7.5	571,739
Broomfield	08014	55.3	38.272	15.1	44,052	10.4	48,630
Clear Creek	08019	22.4	9,322	3.3	9,627	3.2	9,939
Denver	08031	18.6	554,636	0.6	558,088	0.5	560,809
Douglas	08035	191.0	175,766	44.2	253,393	28.7	326,199
Elbert	08039	106.0	19,872	18.9	23,618	14.8	27,106
Gilpin	08047	55.0	4,757	4.0	4,945	3.0	5,093
Jefferson	08059	20.3	525,507	0.7	529,190	0.5	531,901
Park	08093	102.4	14,523	22.0	17,713	17.0	20,722
Fort Collins-Loveland CO	**22660**	**35.1**	**251,494**	**9.5**	**275,364**	**8.1**	**297,783**
Larimer	08069	35.1	251,494	9.5	275,364	8.1	297,783
Grand Junction CO	**24300**	**24.8**	**116,255**	**11.3**	**129,419**	**9.2**	**141,326**
Mesa	08077	24.8	116,255	11.3	129,419	9.2	141,326
Greeley CO	**24540**	**37.3**	**180,926**	**27.5**	**230,756**	**20.6**	**278,320**
Weld	08123	37.3	180,926	27.5	230,756	20.6	278,320
Pueblo CO	**39380**	**15.0**	**141,472**	**8.6**	**153,579**	**7.6**	**165,291**
Pueblo	08101	15.0	141,472	8.6	153,579	7.6	165,291
Total: Metro Portion of State		**30.4**	**3,676,685**	**9.8**	**4,035,820**	**8.3**	**4,371,045**
Total: Micro Portion of State		44.2	244,212	7.9	263,590	6.9	281,732
Total: Colorado		30.6	4,301,261	9.1	4,694,778	7.8	5,062,536
Connecticut							
Bridgeport-Stamford-Norwalk CT	**14860**	**6.6**	**882,567**	**3.0**	**909,263**	**2.7**	**933,729**
Fairfield	09001	6.6	882,567	3.0	909,263	2.7	933,729
Hartford-West Hartford-East Hartford CT	**25540**	**2.2**	**1,148,618**	**4.2**	**1,197,175**	**3.9**	**1,243,285**
Hartford	09003	0.6	857,183	2.8	881,552	2.6	904,560
Middlesex	09007	8.3	155,071	6.9	165,752	6.1	175,863
Tolland	09013	6.0	136,364	9.9	149,871	8.7	162,862
New Haven-Milford CT	**35300**	**2.5**	**824,008**	**3.6**	**853,637**	**3.3**	**882,213**
New Haven	09009	2.5	824,008	3.6	853,637	3.3	882,213
Norwich-New London CT	**35980**	**1.6**	**259,088**	**3.2**	**267,325**	**2.9**	**275,163**
New London	09011	1.6	259,088	3.2	267,325	2.9	275,163
Total: Metro Portion of State		**3.4**	**3,114,281**	**3.6**	**3,227,400**	**3.3**	**3,334,390**
Total: Micro Portion of State		5.3	291,284	5.4	306,880	4.9	321,909
Total: Connecticut		3.6	3,405,565	3.8	3,534,280	3.5	3,656,299
Delaware							
Dover DE	**20100**	**14.1**	**126,697**	**10.2**	**139,558**	**8.9**	**152,015**
Kent	10001	14.1	126,697	10.2	139,558	8.9	152,015
*** New Castle** (See Philadelphia-Camden-Wilmington, PA-NJ-DE-MD.)	**10003**	**13.2**	**500,265**	**4.7**	**523,864**	**4.2**	**545,859**
Total: Metro Portion of State		**13.4**	**626,962**	**5.8**	**663,422**	**5.2**	**697,874**
Total: Micro Portion of State		38.3	156,638	12.2	175,747	10.4	194,023
Total: Delaware		17.6	783,600	7.1	839,169	6.3	891,897
District of Columbia							
Washington-Arlington-Alexandria, DC-VA-MD-WV	47900	16.3	4,796,183	9.6	5,255,607	8.3	5,690,439
District of Columbia	**11001**	**-5.7**	**572,059**	**-4.0**	**548,902**	**-3.9**	**527,662**
Calvert, MD	24009	45.1	74,563	21.0	90,186	16.6	105,178
Charles, MD	24017	19.2	120,546	15.9	139,740	13.2	158,178
Frederick, MD	24021	30.0	195,277	15.4	225,299	12.7	253,983
Montgomery, MD	24031	15.4	873,341	8.5	947,578	7.3	1,017,181
Prince George's, MD	24033	9.9	801,515	7.7	863,468	6.9	923,099
Alexandria, VA (Ind. City)	51510	15.4	128,283	-0.1	128,132	-0.8	127,123
Arlington, VA	51013	10.8	189,453	-1.9	185,858	-1.8	182,475
Clarke, VA	51043	4.6	12,652	9.8	13,896	8.5	15,075
Fairfax, VA	51059	18.5	969,749	4.8	1,016,742	4.2	1,059,612
Fairfax, VA (Ind. City)	51600	9.6	21,498	3.3	22,200	2.8	22,824
Falls Church, VA (Ind. City)	51610	8.3	10,377	3.3	10,716	2.9	11,022
Fauquier, VA	51061	13.1	55,139	17.6	64,828	14.2	74,034
Fredericksburg, VA (Ind. City)	51630	1.3	19,279	7.7	20,769	6.8	22,189
Loudoun, VA	51107	96.9	169,599	48.6	252,089	30.9	329,892
Manassas, VA (Ind. City)	51683	25.7	35,135	8.4	38,088	7.0	40,756
Manassas Park, VA (Ind. City)	51685	52.8	10,290	11.1	11,429	9.5	12,518
Prince William, VA	51153	30.2	280,813	25.5	352,321	19.4	420,534
Spotsylvania, VA	51177	57.5	90,395	30.7	118,182	22.4	144,675
Stafford, VA	51179	51.0	92,446	30.9	121,019	22.6	148,329
Warren, VA	51187	20.8	31,584	11.1	35,096	9.6	38,451
Jefferson, WV	54037	17.4	42,190	16.3	49,069	13.4	55,649
Total: Metro Portion of District		**-5.7**	**572,059**	**-4.0**	**548,902**	**-3.9**	**527,662**
Total: District of Columbia		-5.7	572,059	-4.0	548,902	-3.9	527,662
Florida							
Cape Coral-Fort Myers FL	**15980**	**31.6**	**440,888**	**18.7**	**523,512**	**15.2**	**603,036**
Lee	12071	31.6	440,888	18.7	523,512	15.2	603,036
Deltona-Daytona Beach-Ormond Beach FL	**19660**	**19.6**	**443,343**	**9.0**	**483,444**	**7.9**	**521,860**
Volusia	12127	19.6	443,343	9.0	483,444	7.9	521,860
Fort Walton Beach-Crestview-Destin FL	**23020**	**18.6**	**170,498**	**6.9**	**182,186**	**6.2**	**193,464**
Okaloosa	12091	18.6	170,498	6.9	182,186	6.2	193,464
Gainesville FL	**23540**	**21.5**	**232,392**	**3.1**	**239,650**	**2.9**	**246,588**
Alachua	12001	20.0	217,955	2.5	223,316	2.3	228,469
Gilchrist	12041	49.3	14,437	13.1	16,334	10.9	18,119

* Indicates county is included from metro in different state.
Source: Devonshire Associates Ltd. and Scan/US, Inc. 2005.

Core Based Statistical Areas and Their Component Counties: Population Trends, *Continued*

CBSA	FIPS Code	Past: 1990-2000 % Change	Past: 2000 Census	Present: 2000-2005 % Change	Present: 7/1/05 Estimate	Future: 2005-2010 % Change	Future: 2010 Projection
Jacksonville FL	27260	21.4	1,122,750	11.2	1,248,873	9.8	1,371,454
Baker	12003	20.4	22,259	8.4	24,136	7.2	25,876
Clay	12019	32.9	140,814	18.5	166,915	15.1	192,116
Duval	12031	15.7	778,879	7.7	838,841	7.1	897,985
Nassau	12089	31.2	57,663	10.9	63,967	9.4	69,968
St. Johns	12109	46.9	123,135	25.9	155,014	19.7	185,509
Lakeland FL	29460	19.4	483,924	8.7	526,208	7.7	566,911
Polk	12105	19.4	483,924	8.7	526,208	7.7	566,911
Miami-Fort Lauderdale-Miami Beach FL	33100	23.5	5,007,564	8.9	5,452,407	7.8	5,876,037
Broward	12011	29.3	1,623,018	10.5	1,794,053	9.0	1,955,383
Miami-Dade	12086	16.3	2,253,362	6.1	2,391,206	5.5	2,522,264
Palm Beach	12099	31.0	1,131,184	12.0	1,267,148	10.4	1,398,390
Naples-Marco Island FL	34940	65.3	251,377	22.1	306,973	17.2	359,758
Collier	12021	65.3	251,377	22.1	306,973	17.2	359,758
Ocala FL	36100	32.9	258,916	13.8	294,555	11.6	328,736
Marion	12083	32.9	258,916	13.8	294,555	11.6	328,736
Orlando-Kissimmee FL	36740	34.3	1,644,561	15.6	1,900,560	12.8	2,144,445
Lake	12069	38.4	210,528	27.8	269,070	20.9	325,184
Orange	12095	32.3	896,344	12.2	1,006,134	10.3	1,109,877
Osceola	12097	60.1	172,493	31.5	226,787	23.1	279,286
Seminole	12117	27.0	365,196	9.1	398,569	7.9	430,098
Palm Bay-Melbourne-Titusville FL	37340	19.4	476,230	9.9	523,567	8.7	569,284
Brevard	12009	19.4	476,230	9.9	523,567	8.7	569,284
Panama City-Lynn Haven FL	37460	16.7	148,217	7.3	159,012	6.8	169,776
Bay	12005	16.7	148,217	7.3	159,012	6.8	169,776
Pensacola-Ferry Pass-Brent FL	37860	19.7	412,153	6.1	437,128	5.6	461,430
Escambia	12033	12.0	294,410	0.4	295,558	0.4	296,781
Santa Rosa	12113	44.3	117,743	20.2	141,570	16.3	164,649
Port St. Lucie-Fort Pierce FL	38940	27.2	319,426	15.1	367,537	12.8	414,409
Martin	12085	25.6	126,731	10.6	140,204	9.3	153,278
St. Lucie	12111	28.3	192,695	18.0	227,333	14.9	261,131
Punta Gorda FL	39460	27.6	141,627	12.9	159,967	11.0	177,627
Charlotte	12015	27.6	141,627	12.9	159,967	11.0	177,627
Sarasota-Bradenton-Venice FL	42260	20.5	589,959	11.8	659,642	10.1	726,472
Manatee	12081	24.7	264,002	13.7	300,298	11.5	334,840
Sarasota	12115	17.3	325,957	10.2	359,344	9.0	391,632
Tallahassee FL	45220	23.6	320,304	3.8	332,381	3.5	344,169
Gadsden	12039	9.7	45,087	1.7	45,844	1.7	46,633
Jefferson	12065	14.2	12,902	15.6	14,917	13.3	16,904
Leon	12073	24.4	239,452	1.8	243,753	1.7	247,902
Wakulla	12129	61.0	22,863	21.9	27,867	17.5	32,730
Tampa-St. Petersburg-Clearwater FL	45300	15.9	2,395,997	9.1	2,613,412	8.0	2,822,434
Hernando	12053	29.4	130,802	15.7	151,302	13.1	171,067
Hillsborough	12057	19.8	998,948	12.0	1,118,988	10.3	1,234,723
Pasco	12101	22.6	344,765	20.6	415,912	16.4	484,329
Pinellas	12103	8.2	921,482	0.6	927,210	0.6	932,315
Vero Beach FL	46940	25.2	112,947	10.3	124,614	9.0	135,839
Indian River	12061	25.2	112,947	10.3	124,614	9.0	135,839
Total: Metro Portion of State		23.4	14,973,073	10.4	16,535,628	9.1	18,033,729
Total: Micro Portion of State		27.6	646,420	10.0	711,177	8.9	774,140
Total: Florida		23.5	15,982,378	10.3	17,633,938	9.0	19,219,041

Georgia

CBSA	FIPS Code	Past: 1990-2000 % Change	Past: 2000 Census	Present: 2000-2005 % Change	Present: 7/1/05 Estimate	Future: 2005-2010 % Change	Future: 2010 Projection
Albany GA	10500	7.7	157,833	4.1	164,365	3.9	170,843
Baker	13007	12.7	4,074	9.4	4,458	9.1	4,864
Dougherty	13095	-0.3	96,065	-0.6	95,460	-0.6	94,904
Lee	13177	52.4	24,757	27.3	31,508	21.0	38,126
Terrell	13273	3.0	10,970	-0.2	10,948	-0.3	10,913
Worth	13321	11.3	21,967	0.1	21,991	0.2	22,036
Athens-Clarke County GA	12020	22.1	166,079	6.0	176,112	5.3	185,370
Clarke	13059	15.9	101,489	3.3	104,888	2.9	107,919
Madison	13195	22.2	25,730	9.1	28,081	7.9	30,297
Oconee	13219	48.9	26,225	11.9	29,333	10.0	32,258
Oglethorpe	13221	29.4	12,635	9.3	13,810	7.9	14,896
Atlanta-Sandy Springs-Marietta GA	12060	38.4	4,247,981	13.2	4,809,992	11.0	5,337,353
Barrow	13013	55.3	46,144	25.9	58,111	19.9	69,674
Bartow	13015	36.0	76,019	19.4	90,793	15.5	104,872
Butts	13035	27.4	19,522	21.3	23,687	16.8	27,670
Carroll	13045	22.2	87,268	21.6	106,138	17.0	124,223
Cherokee	13057	57.3	141,903	28.6	182,558	21.3	221,356
Clayton	13063	29.9	236,517	1.9	241,082	1.0	243,517
Cobb	13067	35.7	607,751	11.5	677,675	9.6	742,723
Coweta	13077	65.7	89,215	22.7	109,445	17.6	128,756
Dawson	13085	69.7	15,999	25.4	20,058	18.9	23,841
DeKalb	13089	22.0	665,865	2.1	679,804	1.6	690,779
Douglas	13097	29.6	92,174	17.5	108,297	14.4	123,916
Fayette	13113	46.2	91,263	13.5	103,541	11.0	114,966
Forsyth	13117	123.2	98,407	42.5	140,241	28.4	180,032
Fulton	13121	25.7	816,006	0.9	822,956	0.7	828,558
Gwinnett	13135	66.7	588,448	23.4	725,943	17.8	855,451
Haralson	13143	17.0	25,690	11.3	28,594	9.7	31,359
Heard	13149	27.6	11,012	2.4	11,272	1.4	11,433
Henry	13151	103.2	119,341	42.0	169,496	28.3	217,404
Jasper	13159	35.2	11,426	17.4	13,413	14.3	15,328
Lamar	13171	22.0	15,912	4.8	16,682	4.6	17,456
Meriwether	13199	0.5	22,534	1.6	22,899	1.5	23,249
Newton	13217	48.3	62,001	38.2	85,695	26.6	108,499
Paulding	13223	96.3	81,678	36.6	111,558	25.6	140,064
Pickens	13227	59.3	22,983	27.9	29,406	20.6	35,452
Pike	13231	33.9	13,688	16.8	15,986	13.6	18,168
Rockdale	13247	29.6	70,111	11.3	78,002	9.5	85,415
Spalding	13255	7.3	58,417	5.9	61,851	5.4	65,194
Walton	13297	57.3	60,687	23.3	74,809	17.6	87,998
Augusta-Richmond County, GA-SC	12260	14.7	499,684	3.7	517,953	3.4	535,459
Burke	13033	8.1	22,243	5.4	23,437	4.8	24,569
Columbia	13073	35.2	89,288	14.5	102,278	12.2	114,723
McDuffie	13189	5.5	21,231	1.7	21,591	1.4	21,894
Richmond	13245	5.3	199,775	-1.9	196,018	-1.8	192,421
Aiken, SC	45003	17.9	142,552	5.0	149,719	4.6	156,610
Edgefield, SC	45037	33.9	24,595	1.3	24,910	1.3	25,242
Brunswick GA	15260	13.2	93,044	6.6	99,197	6.0	105,114
Brantley	13025	32.1	14,629	9.0	15,951	7.9	17,210
Glynn	13127	8.1	67,568	6.8	72,136	6.1	76,558
McIntosh	13191	25.6	10,847	2.4	11,110	2.1	11,346
Columbus, GA-AL	17980	5.7	281,768	-1.5	277,462	-0.8	275,338
Russell, AL	01113	6.2	49,756	-2.4	48,555	-2.3	47,428
Chattahoochee	13053	-12.1	14,882	-11.2	13,213	-3.0	12,813
Harris	13145	33.2	23,695	15.7	27,412	13.1	31,009
Marion	13197	27.8	7,144	-0.5	7,105	-1.1	7,024
Muscogee	13215	3.9	186,291	-2.7	181,177	-2.3	177,064
Dalton GA	19140	21.7	120,031	10.2	132,298	8.6	143,632
Murray	13213	39.6	36,506	13.7	41,502	11.3	46,196
Whitfield	13313	15.3	83,525	8.7	90,796	7.3	97,436
Gainesville GA	23580	45.9	139,277	19.9	166,966	15.6	193,008
Hall	13139	45.9	139,277	19.9	166,966	15.6	193,008
Hinesville-Fort Stewart GA	25980	22.0	71,914	-3.0	69,723	-2.6	67,909
Liberty	13179	16.8	61,610	-4.8	58,683	-4.3	56,159
Long	13183	66.1	10,304	7.1	11,040	6.4	11,750
Macon GA	31420	7.6	222,368	3.3	229,720	3.1	236,852
Bibb	13021	2.6	153,887	0.9	155,253	0.8	156,539
Crawford	13079	39.0	12,495	2.5	12,802	2.7	13,143
Jones	13169	14.0	23,639	13.4	26,799	11.6	29,899
Monroe	13207	27.1	21,757	11.8	24,333	10.1	26,795
Twiggs	13289	8.0	10,590	-0.5	10,533	-0.5	10,476
Rome GA	40660	11.5	90,565	5.0	95,112	4.4	99,319
Floyd	13115	11.5	90,565	5.0	95,112	4.4	99,319
Savannah GA	42340	13.5	293,000	6.6	312,351	5.9	330,822
Bryan	13029	51.7	23,417	19.4	27,955	15.9	32,387
Chatham	13051	7.0	232,048	2.6	238,192	2.4	243,819
Effingham	13103	46.1	37,535	23.1	46,204	18.2	54,616
Valdosta GA	46660	20.5	119,560	3.8	124,076	3.5	128,379
Brooks	13027	6.8	16,450	-1.7	16,171	-1.9	15,858
Echols	13101	60.8	3,754	10.0	4,131	8.2	4,470
Lanier	13173	30.9	7,241	4.1	7,538	3.6	7,806
Lowndes	13185	21.2	92,115	4.5	96,236	4.2	100,245
Warner Robins GA	47580	24.2	110,765	14.1	126,391	11.9	141,461
Houston	13153	24.2	110,765	14.1	126,391	11.9	141,461
*** Catoosa**	13047	25.5	53,282	15.1	61,327	12.5	68,977
*** Dade**	13083	15.3	15,154	8.0	16,361	7.0	17,514
*** Walker**	13295	4.7	61,053	4.4	63,750	4.1	66,335
(See Chattanooga, TN-GA.)							
Total: Metro Portion of State		29.2	6,526,455	10.6	7,219,972	9.1	7,874,405
Total: Micro Portion of State		14.8	884,394	4.8	927,113	4.4	967,621
Total: Georgia		26.4	8,186,453	9.6	8,969,042	8.2	9,707,997

Hawaii

CBSA	FIPS Code	Past: 1990-2000 % Change	Past: 2000 Census	Present: 2000-2005 % Change	Present: 7/1/05 Estimate	Future: 2005-2010 % Change	Future: 2010 Projection
Honolulu HI	26180	4.8	876,156	3.9	910,475	3.9	945,789
Honolulu	15003	4.8	876,156	3.9	910,475	3.9	945,789
Total: Metro Portion of State		4.8	876,156	3.9	910,475	3.9	945,789
Total: Micro Portion of State		23.3	335,234	8.4	363,307	7.3	389,806
Total: Hawaii		9.3	1,211,537	5.1	1,273,900	4.9	1,335,69

* Indicates county is included from metro in different state.
Source: Devonshire Associates Ltd. and Scan/US, Inc. 2005.

Idaho

CBSA	FIPS Code	Past: 1990-2000 % Change	Past: 2000 Census	Present: 2000-2005 % Change	Present: 7/1/05 Estimate	Future: 2005-2010 % Change	Future: 2010 Projection
Boise City-Nampa ID	14260	45.4	464,840	16.0	539,170	13.0	609,364
Ada	16001	46.2	300,904	12.8	339,342	10.7	375,504
Boise	16015	90.1	6,670	13.4	7,566	10.8	8,384
Canyon	16027	45.9	131,441	25.3	164,715	19.2	196,301
Gem	16045	28.2	15,181	6.5	16,167	5.8	17,109
Owyhee	16073	26.8	10,644	6.9	11,380	6.0	12,066
Coeur d'Alene ID	17660	55.7	108,685	13.1	122,971	10.9	136,366
Kootenai	16055	55.7	108,685	13.1	122,971	10.9	136,366
Idaho Falls ID	26820	14.6	101,677	9.2	111,058	8.0	119,959
Bonneville	16019	14.3	82,522	9.3	90,159	8.0	97,393
Jefferson	16051	15.8	19,155	9.1	20,899	8.0	22,566
Lewiston, ID-WA	30300	12.9	57,961	0.9	58,492	0.9	59,015
Nez Perce	16069	10.8	37,410	1.3	37,908	1.3	38,413
Asotin, WA	53003	16.7	20,551	0.2	20,584	0.1	20,602
Pocatello ID	38540	13.7	83,103	-0.4	82,761	-0.4	82,400
Bannock	16005	14.4	75,565	-0.1	75,502	-0.1	75,389
Power	16077	6.4	7,538	-3.7	7,259	-3.4	7,011
*** Franklin**	16041	22.7	11,329	8.2	12,259	7.3	13,151
(See Logan, UT-ID.)							
Total: Metro Portion of State		35.8	807,044	12.3	906,127	10.3	999,653
Total: Micro Portion of State		17.6	295,879	4.5	309,285	4.3	322,620
Total: Idaho		28.5	1,293,953	9.1	1,411,270	7.9	1,522,862

Illinois

CBSA	FIPS Code	Past: 1990-2000 % Change	Past: 2000 Census	Present: 2000-2005 % Change	Present: 7/1/05 Estimate	Future: 2005-2010 % Change	Future: 2010 Projection
Bloomington-Normal IL	14060	16.5	150,433	6.7	160,498	6.0	170,048
McLean	17113	16.5	150,433	6.7	160,498	6.0	170,048
Champaign-Urbana IL	16580	3.7	210,275	3.0	216,661	2.8	222,813
Champaign	17019	3.8	179,669	3.6	186,135	3.3	192,360
Ford	17053	-0.2	14,241	-1.0	14,102	-0.9	13,979
Piatt	17147	5.3	16,365	0.4	16,424	0.3	16,474
Chicago-Naperville-Joliet, IL-IN-WI	16980	11.2	9,098,316	4.1	9,471,425	3.7	9,822,462
Cook	17031	5.3	5,376,741	-0.8	5,332,321	-0.9	5,286,501
DeKalb	17037	14.2	88,969	8.2	96,267	7.2	103,181
DuPage	17043	15.7	904,161	3.7	937,264	3.2	967,550
Grundy	17063	16.1	37,535	8.8	40,846	7.7	43,999
Kane	17089	27.3	404,119	21.3	490,051	16.8	572,298
Kendall	17093	38.4	54,544	37.3	74,879	26.2	94,525
Lake	17097	24.8	644,356	9.4	704,726	8.0	761,208
McHenry	17111	41.9	260,077	16.2	302,316	13.4	342,870
Will	17197	40.6	502,266	27.5	640,443	20.6	772,560
Jasper, IN	18073	20.4	30,043	6.0	31,839	5.1	33,475
Lake, IN	18089	1.9	484,564	1.0	489,391	1.0	494,044
Newton, IN	18111	7.5	14,566	-1.3	14,381	-1.2	14,210
Porter, IN	18127	13.9	146,798	6.6	156,536	5.9	165,804
Kenosha, WI	55059	16.7	149,577	7.1	160,165	6.3	170,237
Danville IL	19180	-4.9	83,919	-2.0	82,252	-1.9	80,685
Vermilion	17183	-4.9	83,919	-2.0	82,252	-1.9	80,685
Decatur IL	19500	-2.1	114,706	-4.9	109,127	-4.7	104,032
Macon	17115	-2.1	114,706	-4.9	109,127	-4.7	104,032
Kankakee-Bradley IL	28100	7.9	103,833	3.7	107,719	3.5	111,511
Kankakee	17091	7.9	103,833	3.7	107,719	3.5	111,511
Peoria IL	37900	2.3	366,899	-0.3	365,630	-0.3	364,530
Marshall	17123	2.6	13,180	-1.6	12,965	-1.4	12,780
Peoria	17143	0.3	183,433	-1.2	181,293	-1.1	179,349
Stark	17175	-3.1	6,332	-3.3	6,120	-3.2	5,927
Tazewell	17179	3.9	128,485	-0.1	128,302	-0.2	128,094
Woodford	17203	8.6	35,469	4.2	36,950	3.9	38,380
Rockford IL	40420	12.9	320,204	5.4	337,385	4.8	353,608
Boone	17007	35.6	41,786	18.7	49,590	15.1	57,085
Winnebago	17201	10.1	278,418	3.4	287,795	3.0	296,523
Springfield IL	44100	6.3	201,437	2.5	206,549	2.4	211,478
Menard	17129	11.8	12,486	2.0	12,738	1.7	12,958
Sangamon	17167	5.9	188,951	2.6	193,811	2.4	198,520
*** Henry**	17073	-0.3	51,020	-0.9	50,536	-1.0	50,012
*** Mercer**	17131	-1.9	16,957	-0.3	16,906	-0.4	16,846
*** Rock Island**	17161	0.4	149,374	-1.6	146,919	-1.5	144,712
(See Davenport-Moline-Rock Island, IA-IL.)							
*** Bond**	17005	17.6	17,633	2.4	18,049	2.2	18,440
*** Calhoun**	17013	-4.5	5,084	1.1	5,139	0.9	5,187
*** Clinton**	17027	4.7	35,535	2.1	36,286	2.0	36,996
*** Jersey**	17083	5.5	21,668	3.4	22,415	3.3	23,156
*** Macoupin**	17117	2.8	49,019	0.1	49,088	0.1	49,152
*** Madison**	17119	3.9	258,941	1.7	263,396	1.6	267,624
*** Monroe**	17133	23.2	27,619	12.4	31,030	10.5	34,284
*** St. Clair**	17163	-2.6	256,082	1.6	260,165	1.5	264,081
(See St. Louis, MO-IL.)							
Total: Metro Portion of State		9.9	10,713,406	3.7	11,104,863	3.3	11,473,887
Total: Micro Portion of State		2.2	1,081,896	-1.2	1,068,885	-1.1	1,057,178
Total: Illinois		8.6	12,419,293	3.0	12,788,145	2.7	13,136,615

Indiana

CBSA	FIPS Code	Past: 1990-2000 % Change	Past: 2000 Census	Present: 2000-2005 % Change	Present: 7/1/05 Estimate	Future: 2005-2010 % Change	Future: 2010 Projection
Anderson IN	11300	2.1	133,358	-2.7	129,750	-2.7	126,277
Madison	18095	2.1	133,358	-2.7	129,750	-2.7	126,277
Bloomington IN	14020	12.0	175,506	1.3	177,866	1.2	179,994
Greene	18055	9.0	33,157	0.9	33,439	0.6	33,653
Monroe	18105	10.6	120,563	0.2	120,813	0.2	121,016
Owen	18119	26.1	21,786	8.4	23,614	7.2	25,325
Columbus IN	18020	12.2	71,435	1.9	72,772	1.4	73,827
Bartholomew	18005	12.2	71,435	1.9	72,772	1.4	73,827
Elkhart-Goshen IN	21140	17.0	182,791	5.4	192,614	4.7	201,665
Elkhart	18039	17.0	182,791	5.4	192,614	4.7	201,665
Evansville, IN-KY	21780	5.5	342,815	1.8	348,860	1.7	354,678
Gibson	18051	1.8	32,500	2.6	33,333	2.3	34,109
Posey	18129	4.2	27,061	-0.8	26,837	-0.9	26,598
Vanderburgh	18163	4.2	171,922	0.6	173,036	0.7	174,191
Warrick	18173	16.6	52,383	7.2	56,136	6.3	59,690
Henderson, KY	21101	4.1	44,829	1.4	45,470	1.4	46,118
Webster, KY	21233	1.2	14,120	-0.5	14,048	-0.5	13,972
Fort Wayne IN	23060	10.1	390,156	4.1	406,015	3.7	420,865
Allen	18003	10.3	331,849	4.1	345,326	3.6	357,869
Wells	18179	6.4	27,600	2.1	28,181	2.0	28,737
Whitley	18183	11.1	30,707	5.9	32,508	5.4	34,259
Indianapolis IN	26900	17.8	1,525,104	8.0	1,646,860	7.0	1,762,556
Boone	18011	20.9	46,107	12.0	51,660	10.2	56,921
Brown	18013	6.2	14,957	3.7	15,508	3.3	16,013
Hamilton	18057	67.7	182,740	33.8	244,530	24.2	303,639
Hancock	18059	21.7	55,391	12.4	62,264	10.6	68,861
Hendricks	18063	37.5	104,093	22.9	127,940	17.6	150,445
Johnson	18081	30.8	115,209	11.7	128,689	9.9	141,367
Marion	18097	7.9	860,454	0.6	865,538	0.6	870,495
Morgan	18109	19.3	66,689	5.1	70,108	4.6	73,307
Putnam	18133	18.8	36,019	2.9	37,059	2.5	37,993
Shelby	18145	7.8	43,445	0.3	43,564	-0.1	43,515
Kokomo IN	29020	4.7	101,541	-0.3	101,209	-0.3	100,883
Howard	18067	5.1	84,964	-0.3	84,735	-0.3	84,494
Tipton	18159	2.8	16,577	-0.6	16,474	-0.5	16,389
Lafayette IN	29140	12.4	178,541	2.3	182,561	2.1	186,431
Benton	18007	-0.2	9,421	-3.0	9,138	-2.6	8,897
Carroll	18015	7.2	20,165	3.3	20,833	3.2	21,495
Tippecanoe	18157	14.1	148,955	2.4	152,590	2.3	156,039
Michigan City-La Porte IN	33140	2.8	110,106	-0.4	109,651	-0.5	109,101
LaPorte	18091	2.8	110,106	-0.4	109,651	-0.5	109,101
Muncie IN	34620	-0.7	118,769	-0.8	117,847	-0.7	117,042
Delaware	18035	-0.7	118,769	-0.8	117,847	-0.7	117,042
South Bend-Mishawaka, IN-MI	43780	6.8	316,663	0.6	318,467	0.4	319,857
St. Joseph	18141	7.5	265,559	0.5	266,795	0.3	267,686
Cass, MI	26027	3.3	51,104	1.1	51,672	1.0	52,171
Terre Haute IN	45460	2.6	170,943	-1.7	168,071	-1.6	165,449
Clay	18021	7.5	26,556	1.8	27,038	1.7	27,500
Sullivan	18153	14.5	21,751	0.9	21,955	0.9	22,158
Vermillion	18165	0.1	16,788	-2.7	16,339	-2.6	15,909
Vigo	18167	-0.2	105,848	-2.9	102,739	-2.8	99,882
*** Jasper**	18073	20.4	30,043	6.0	31,839	5.1	33,475
*** Lake**	18089	1.9	484,564	1.0	489,391	1.0	494,044
*** Newton**	18111	7.5	14,566	-1.3	14,381	-1.2	14,210
*** Porter**	18127	13.9	146,798	6.6	156,536	5.9	165,804
(See Chicago-Naperville-Joliet, IL-IN-WI.)							
*** Clark**	18019	9.9	96,472	5.0	101,296	4.4	105,779
*** Floyd**	18043	10.0	70,823	1.2	71,650	1.0	72,393
*** Harrison**	18061	14.8	34,325	6.5	36,550	5.6	38,587
*** Washington**	18175	14.8	27,223	2.7	27,951	2.4	28,626
(See Louisville, KY-IN.)							
*** Dearborn**	18029	18.7	46,109	6.6	49,138	5.7	51,918
*** Franklin**	18047	13.1	22,151	4.7	23,182	4.1	24,132
*** Ohio**	18115	5.8	5,623	3.3	5,809	2.8	5,974
(See Cincinnati-Middletown, OH-KY-IN.)							
Total: Metro Portion of State		10.7	4,686,372	3.9	4,869,076	3.5	5,041,306
Total: Micro Portion of State		6.5	1,028,340	0.5	1,033,732	0.4	1,038,229
Total: Indiana		9.7	6,080,485	3.1	6,270,352	2.8	6,448,758

Continued on next page

Core Based Statistical Areas and Their Component Counties: Population Trends, *Continued*

CBSA	FIPS Code	Past: 1990-2000 % Change	Past: 2000 Census	Present: 2000-2005 % Change	Present: 7/1/05 Estimate	Future: 2005-2010 % Change	Future: 2010 Projection
Iowa							
Ames IA	**11180**	**7.7**	**79,981**	**0.5**	**80,417**	**0.4**	**80,734**
Story	19169	7.7	79,981	0.5	80,417	0.4	80,734
Cedar Rapids IA	**16300**	**12.6**	**237,230**	**3.6**	**245,799**	**3.2**	**253,647**
Benton	19011	12.8	25,308	6.3	26,911	5.8	28,462
Jones	19105	4.0	20,221	1.2	20,456	1.1	20,683
Linn	19113	13.6	191,701	3.5	198,432	3.1	204,502
Davenport-Moline-Rock Island, IA-IL	19340	2.1	376,019	-0.5	374,314	-0.4	372,662
Henry, IL	17073	-0.3	51,020	-0.9	50,536	-1.0	50,012
Mercer, IL	17131	-1.9	16,957	-0.3	16,906	-0.4	16,846
Rock Island, IL	17161	0.4	149,374	-1.6	146,919	-1.5	144,712
Scott	**19163**	**5.1**	**158,668**	**0.8**	**159,953**	**0.7**	**161,092**
Des Moines IA	**19780**	**15.6**	**481,394**	**7.4**	**516,976**	**6.5**	**550,622**
Dallas	19049	37.0	40,750	23.1	50,179	18.1	59,282
Guthrie	19077	3.8	11,353	1.9	11,570	1.8	11,782
Madison	19121	12.3	14,019	7.0	15,007	6.5	15,982
Polk	19153	14.5	374,601	6.0	397,152	5.3	418,267
Warren	19181	12.9	40,671	5.9	43,068	5.2	45,309
Dubuque IA	**20220**	**3.2**	**89,143**	**2.3**	**91,167**	**2.0**	**93,009**
Dubuque	19061	3.2	89,143	2.3	91,167	2.0	93,009
Iowa City IA	**26980**	**13.8**	**131,676**	**5.4**	**138,810**	**4.8**	**145,535**
Johnson	19103	15.5	111,006	5.6	117,205	5.0	123,052
Washington	19183	5.4	20,670	4.5	21,605	4.1	22,483
Sioux City, IA-NE-SD	43580	8.9	143,053	0.0	143,077	-0.0	143,027
Woodbury	**19193**	**5.7**	**103,877**	**-1.0**	**102,793**	**-1.1**	**101,679**
Dakota, NE	31043	21.0	20,253	2.7	20,799	2.4	21,296
Dixon, NE	31051	3.2	6,339	-5.0	6,020	-4.7	5,735
Union, SD	46127	23.5	12,584	7.0	13,465	6.3	14,317
Waterloo-Cedar Falls IA	**47940**	**3.2**	**163,706**	**-1.6**	**161,128**	**-1.5**	**158,758**
Black Hawk	19013	3.4	128,012	-2.1	125,273	-2.0	122,736
Bremer	19017	2.2	23,325	0.8	23,518	0.9	23,723
Grundy	19075	2.8	12,369	-0.3	12,337	-0.3	12,299
*** Harrison**	**19085**	**6.4**	**15,666**	**0.3**	**15,710**	**-0.0**	**15,707**
*** Mills**	**19129**	**10.2**	**14,547**	**3.8**	**15,093**	**3.4**	**15,602**
*** Pottawattamie**	**19155**	**6.1**	**87,704**	**1.3**	**88,801**	**0.9**	**89,567**
(See Omaha-Council Bluffs, NE-IA.)							
Total: Metro Portion of State		**10.0**	**1,563,592**	**3.4**	**1,616,647**	**3.0**	**1,665,952**
Total: Micro Portion of State		1.9	526,441	-1.3	519,655	-1.2	513,220
Total: Iowa		5.4	2,926,324	0.9	2,951,374	0.8	2,974,324
Kansas							
Lawrence KS	**29940**	**22.2**	**99,962**	**3.3**	**103,269**	**3.0**	**106,337**
Douglas	20045	22.2	99,962	3.3	103,269	3.0	106,337
Topeka KS	**45820**	**6.8**	**224,551**	**1.6**	**228,099**	**1.3**	**231,160**
Jackson	20085	9.8	12,657	5.2	13,312	4.6	13,931
Jefferson	20087	15.9	18,426	3.2	19,009	2.8	19,534
Osage	20139	9.6	16,712	1.4	16,950	1.0	17,121
Shawnee	20177	5.5	169,871	1.3	172,022	1.1	173,843
Wabaunsee	20197	4.3	6,885	-1.1	6,806	-1.1	6,731
Wichita KS	**48620**	**11.7**	**571,166**	**3.3**	**589,782**	**2.9**	**607,077**
Butler	20015	17.6	59,482	4.3	62,010	3.7	64,277
Harvey	20079	5.9	32,869	3.5	34,021	3.3	35,130
Sedgwick	20173	12.2	452,869	3.5	468,918	3.2	483,958
Sumner	20191	0.4	25,946	-4.3	24,833	-4.5	23,712
*** Franklin**	**20059**	**12.7**	**24,784**	**6.5**	**26,406**	**5.7**	**27,916**
*** Johnson**	**20091**	**27.0**	**451,086**	**12.5**	**507,661**	**10.4**	**560,260**
*** Leavenworth**	**20103**	**6.7**	**68,691**	**8.0**	**74,179**	**6.9**	**79,330**
*** Linn**	**20107**	**15.9**	**9,570**	**2.9**	**9,844**	**2.4**	**10,077**
*** Miami**	**20121**	**20.8**	**28,351**	**4.6**	**29,658**	**3.8**	**30,790**
*** Wyandotte**	**20209**	**-2.5**	**157,882**	**-0.9**	**156,403**	**-1.0**	**154,859**
(See Kansas City, MO-KS.)							
*** Doniphan**	20043	1.4	8,249	-1.6	8,113	-1.7	7,974
(See St. Joseph, MO-KS.)							
Total: Metro Portion of State		**13.7**	**1,644,292**	**5.4**	**1,733,414**	**4.8**	**1,815,780**
Total: Micro Portion of State		3.6	603,665	-1.6	594,072	-1.5	584,959
Total: Kansas		8.5	2,688,418	2.1	2,746,171	1.9	2,799,691
Kentucky							
Bowling Green KY	**14540**	**19.7**	**104,166**	**5.0**	**109,420**	**4.5**	**114,363**
Edmonson	21061	12.4	11,644	3.5	12,050	3.1	12,428
Warren	21227	20.7	92,522	5.2	97,370	4.7	101,935
Elizabethtown KY	**21060**	**6.6**	**107,547**	**2.1**	**109,851**	**1.9**	**111,991**
Hardin	21093	5.5	94,174	2.4	96,438	2.2	98,566
Larue	21123	14.5	13,373	0.3	13,413	0.1	13,425
Lexington-Fayette KY	**30460**	**17.2**	**408,326**	**5.5**	**430,696**	**4.9**	**451,882**
Bourbon	21017	0.6	19,360	1.4	19,637	1.3	19,898
Clark	21049	12.4	33,144	3.6	34,351	3.2	35,453
Fayette	21067	15.6	260,512	4.0	270,888	3.6	280,831
Jessamine	21113	28.0	39,041	10.1	42,965	8.7	46,710
Scott	21209	38.5	33,061	17.9	38,974	14.2	44,504
Woodford	21239	16.3	23,208	2.9	23,881	2.5	24,486
Louisville, KY-IN	31140	10.0	1,161,975	3.9	1,207,123	3.5	1,248,983
Clark, IN	18019	9.9	96,472	5.0	101,296	4.4	105,779
Floyd, IN	18043	10.0	70,823	1.2	71,650	1.0	72,393
Harrison, IN	18061	14.8	34,325	6.5	36,550	5.6	38,587
Washington, IN	18175	14.8	27,223	2.7	27,951	2.4	28,626
Bullitt	**21029**	**28.7**	**61,236**	**9.8**	**67,211**	**8.3**	**72,761**
Henry	**21103**	**17.4**	**15,060**	**5.1**	**15,830**	**4.6**	**16,558**
Jefferson	**21111**	**4.3**	**693,604**	**1.2**	**701,817**	**1.1**	**709,724**
Meade	**21163**	**9.0**	**26,349**	**7.2**	**28,244**	**5.9**	**29,920**
Nelson	**21179**	**26.1**	**37,477**	**9.2**	**40,940**	**7.9**	**44,185**
Oldham	**21185**	**38.8**	**46,178**	**14.7**	**52,975**	**11.2**	**58,909**
Shelby	**21211**	**34.3**	**33,337**	**12.7**	**37,573**	**10.6**	**41,571**
Spencer	**21215**	**73.0**	**11,766**	**34.9**	**15,869**	**24.2**	**19,713**
Trimble	**21223**	**33.4**	**8,125**	**13.4**	**9,217**	**11.3**	**10,257**
Owensboro KY	**36980**	**5.0**	**109,875**	**1.3**	**111,282**	**1.1**	**112,535**
Daviess	21059	5.0	91,545	1.5	92,957	1.4	94,290
Hancock	21091	6.7	8,392	0.7	8,450	0.3	8,473
McLean	21149	3.2	9,938	-0.6	9,875	-1.0	9,772
*** Henderson**	**21101**	**4.1**	**44,829**	**1.4**	**45,470**	**1.4**	**46,118**
*** Webster**	**21233**	**1.2**	**14,120**	**-0.5**	**14,048**	**-0.5**	**13,972**
(See Evansville, IN-KY.)							
*** Boone**	**21015**	**49.3**	**85,991**	**20.8**	**103,836**	**16.2**	**120,627**
*** Bracken**	**21023**	**6.6**	**8,279**	**4.5**	**8,653**	**4.2**	**9,015**
*** Campbell**	**21037**	**5.7**	**88,616**	**-1.7**	**87,132**	**-1.7**	**85,641**
*** Gallatin**	**21077**	**45.9**	**7,870**	**3.2**	**8,122**	**3.2**	**8,384**
*** Grant**	**21081**	**42.2**	**22,384**	**11.8**	**25,032**	**9.9**	**27,503**
*** Kenton**	**21117**	**6.6**	**151,464**	**0.9**	**152,794**	**0.7**	**153,919**
*** Pendleton**	**21191**	**19.6**	**14,390**	**7.0**	**15,401**	**5.8**	**16,296**
(See Cincinnati-Middletown, OH-KY-IN.)							
*** Christian**	**21047**	**4.8**	**72,265**	**-2.8**	**70,255**	**-2.8**	**68,296**
*** Trigg**	**21221**	**21.6**	**12,597**	**3.4**	**13,027**	**2.9**	**13,410**
(See Clarksville, TN-KY.)							
*** Boyd**	**21019**	**-2.7**	**49,752**	**0.3**	**49,908**	**0.5**	**50,148**
*** Greenup**	**21089**	**0.4**	**36,891**	**0.8**	**37,186**	**0.9**	**37,530**
(See Huntington-Ashland, WV-KY-OH.)							
Total: Metro Portion of State		**11.4**	**2,272,494**	**3.9**	**2,361,789**	**3.5**	**2,445,228**
Total: Micro Portion of State		10.3	763,170	2.9	785,475	2.7	806,450
Total: Kentucky		9.7	4,041,769	3.0	4,164,333	2.8	4,279,671
Louisiana (Parishes)							
Alexandria LA	**10780**	**-2.7**	**145,035**	**0.6**	**145,923**	**0.5**	**146,627**
Grant	22043	6.7	18,698	0.7	18,824	0.6	18,929
Rapides	22079	-4.0	126,337	0.6	127,099	0.5	127,698
Baton Rouge LA	**12940**	**13.2**	**705,973**	**3.1**	**727,551**	**2.7**	**747,188**
Ascension	22005	31.6	76,627	15.5	88,503	12.4	99,442
East Baton Rouge	22033	8.6	412,852	-0.9	409,249	-0.9	405,635
East Feliciana	22037	11.2	21,360	-2.7	20,787	-2.8	20,210
Iberville	22047	7.3	33,320	-3.3	32,225	-3.3	31,161
Livingston	22063	30.2	91,814	17.2	107,626	13.7	122,405
Pointe Coupee	22077	1.0	22,763	-2.5	22,197	-2.5	21,634
St. Helena	22091	6.6	10,525	-3.8	10,124	-3.7	9,746
West Baton Rouge	22121	11.2	21,601	0.2	21,636	0.3	21,697
West Feliciana	22125	17.0	15,111	0.6	15,204	0.4	15,258
Houma-Bayou Cane-Thibodaux LA	**26380**	**6.4**	**194,477**	**1.9**	**198,122**	**1.8**	**201,610**
Lafourche	22057	4.8	89,974	2.0	91,749	1.9	93,469
Terrebonne	22109	7.8	104,503	1.8	106,373	1.7	108,141
Lafayette LA	**29180**	**14.5**	**239,086**	**2.7**	**245,465**	**2.5**	**251,493**
Lafayette	22055	15.6	190,503	2.3	194,974	2.2	199,223
St. Martin	22099	10.5	48,583	3.9	50,491	3.5	52,270
Lake Charles LA	**29340**	**9.1**	**193,568**	**-0.5**	**192,666**	**-0.5**	**191,797**
Calcasieu	22019	9.2	183,577	-0.2	183,193	-0.2	182,785
Cameron	22023	7.9	9,991	-5.2	9,473	-4.9	9,012
Monroe LA	**33740**	**4.4**	**170,053**	**0.1**	**170,239**	**0.2**	**170,521**
Ouachita	22073	3.6	147,250	0.1	147,371	0.1	147,574
Union	22111	10.2	22,803	0.3	22,868	0.3	22,947
New Orleans-Metairie-Kenner LA	**35380**	**4.1**	**1,316,510**	**-0.6**	**1,308,631**	**-0.5**	**1,302,512**
Jefferson	22051	1.6	455,466	-1.7	447,509	-1.6	440,244
Orleans	22071	-2.5	484,674	-5.9	456,285	-5.7	430,487
Plaquemines	22075	4.6	26,757	6.8	28,584	6.3	30,379
St. Bernard	22087	0.9	67,229	-3.9	64,622	-3.6	62,286
St. Charles	22089	13.3	48,072	3.6	49,807	3.1	51,375
St. John The Baptist	22095	7.6	43,044	6.3	45,754	5.6	48,304
St. Tammany	22103	32.4	191,268	13.0	216,070	10.8	239,437

CBSA	FIPS Code	Past: 1990-2000 % Change	Past: 2000 Census	Present: 2000-2005 % Change	Present: 7/1/05 Estimate	Future: 2005-2010 % Change	Future: 2010 Projection
Shreveport-Bossier City LA	**43340**	**4.5**	**375,965**	**7.9**	**405,822**	**7.2**	**434,915**
Bossier	22015	14.2	98,310	5.6	103,854	4.9	108,957
Caddo	22017	1.6	252,161	9.4	275,910	8.5	299,381
De Soto	22031	0.6	25,494	2.2	26,058	2.0	26,577
Total: Metro Portion of State		**6.8**	**3,340,667**	**1.6**	**3,394,419**	**1.5**	**3,446,663**
Total: Micro Portion of State		3.5	815,801	-0.7	810,236	-0.6	805,038
Total: Louisiana		5.9	4,468,976	0.9	4,510,134	0.9	4,550,648
Maine							
Bangor ME	**12620**	**-1.1**	**144,919**	**3.2**	**149,585**	**3.1**	**154,285**
Penobscot	23019	-1.1	144,919	3.2	149,585	3.1	154,285
Lewiston-Auburn ME	**30340**	**-1.4**	**103,793**	**3.7**	**107,666**	**3.5**	**111,467**
Androscoggin	23001	-1.4	103,793	3.7	107,666	3.5	111,467
Portland-South Portland-Biddeford ME	**38860**	**10.5**	**487,568**	**6.3**	**518,365**	**5.6**	**547,371**
Cumberland	23005	9.2	265,612	3.9	275,908	3.6	285,820
Sagadahoc	23023	5.0	35,214	6.9	37,650	6.4	40,063
York	23031	13.5	186,742	9.7	204,807	8.1	221,488
Total: Metro Portion of State		**6.2**	**736,280**	**5.3**	**775,616**	**4.8**	**813,123**
Total: Micro Portion of State		3.0	156,732	3.7	162,514	3.4	168,101
Total: Maine		3.8	1,274,923	4.2	1,328,582	3.9	1,379,771
Maryland							
Baltimore-Towson MD	**12580**	**7.2**	**2,552,994**	**4.1**	**2,658,807**	**3.8**	**2,761,004**
Anne Arundel	24003	14.6	489,656	5.6	517,299	5.0	543,077
Baltimore	24005	9.0	754,292	4.9	791,384	4.4	826,495
Baltimore (Ind. City)	24510	-11.5	651,154	-5.2	617,204	-4.9	587,263
Carroll	24013	22.3	150,897	13.4	171,167	11.4	190,663
Harford	24025	20.0	218,590	10.1	240,719	8.8	261,870
Howard	24027	32.3	247,842	10.7	274,373	9.0	299,101
Queen Anne's	24035	19.5	40,563	15.0	46,661	12.6	52,535
Cumberland, MD-WV	19060	0.4	102,008	-1.5	100,474	-1.4	99,073
Allegany	**24001**	**-0.0**	**74,930**	**-2.2**	**73,274**	**-2.1**	**71,735**
Mineral, WV	54057	1.4	27,078	0.5	27,200	0.5	27,338
Hagerstown-Martinsburg, MD-WV	25180	15.6	222,771	11.2	247,661	9.7	271,612
Washington	**24043**	**8.7**	**131,923**	**6.4**	**140,320**	**5.8**	**148,477**
Berkeley, WV	54003	28.1	75,905	20.4	91,401	16.3	106,284
Morgan, WV	54065	23.2	14,943	6.7	15,940	5.7	16,851
Salisbury MD	**41540**	**11.9**	**109,391**	**5.5**	**115,401**	**5.0**	**121,143**
Somerset	24039	5.6	24,747	4.9	25,960	4.7	27,181
Wicomico	24045	13.9	84,644	5.7	89,441	5.1	93,962
*** Calvert**	**24009**	**45.1**	**74,563**	**21.0**	**90,186**	**16.6**	**105,178**
*** Charles**	**24017**	**19.2**	**120,546**	**15.9**	**139,740**	**13.2**	**158,178**
*** Frederick**	**24021**	**30.0**	**195,277**	**15.4**	**225,299**	**12.7**	**253,983**
*** Montgomery**	**24031**	**15.4**	**873,341**	**8.5**	**947,578**	**7.3**	**1,017,181**
*** Prince George's**	**24033**	**9.9**	**801,515**	**7.7**	**863,468**	**6.9**	**923,099**
(See Washington-Arlington-Alexandria, DC-VA-MD-WV.)							
*** Cecil**	**24015**	**20.5**	**85,951**	**13.2**	**97,326**	**11.1**	**108,151**
(See Philadelphia-Camden-Wilmington, PA-NJ-DE-MD.)							
Total: Metro Portion of State		**10.7**	**5,020,431**	**6.6**	**5,351,399**	**5.9**	**5,668,129**
Total: Micro Portion of State		14.8	197,240	7.6	212,323	6.8	226,795
Total: Maryland		10.8	5,296,486	6.6	5,645,286	5.9	5,979,065
Massachusetts							
Barnstable Town MA	**12700**	**19.1**	**222,230**	**4.5**	**232,312**	**3.9**	**241,347**
Barnstable	25001	19.1	222,230	4.5	232,312	3.9	241,347
Boston-Cambridge-Quincy, MA-NH	14460	6.2	4,391,344	1.5	4,457,319	1.3	4,513,599
Essex	**25009**	**8.0**	**723,419**	**2.9**	**744,047**	**2.5**	**762,420**
Middlesex	**25017**	**4.8**	**1,465,396**	**0.3**	**1,469,958**	**0.1**	**1,471,162**
Norfolk	**25021**	**5.6**	**650,308**	**0.7**	**655,077**	**0.6**	**659,014**
Plymouth	**25023**	**8.6**	**472,822**	**4.9**	**495,811**	**4.3**	**517,008**
Suffolk	**25025**	**3.9**	**689,807**	**-2.3**	**673,720**	**-2.3**	**657,995**
Rockingham, NH	33015	12.8	277,359	7.5	298,070	6.5	317,391
Strafford, NH	33017	7.7	112,233	7.5	120,636	6.6	128,609
Pittsfield MA	**38340**	**-3.2**	**134,953**	**-2.5**	**131,527**	**-2.4**	**128,335**
Berkshire	25003	-3.2	134,953	-2.5	131,527	-2.4	128,335
Springfield MA	**44140**	**1.0**	**680,014**	**1.4**	**689,619**	**1.3**	**698,708**
Franklin	25011	2.1	71,535	0.9	72,152	0.9	72,792
Hampden	25013	-0.0	456,228	1.5	463,031	1.4	469,420
Hampshire	25015	3.9	152,251	1.4	154,436	1.3	156,496
Worcester MA	**49340**	**5.8**	**750,963**	**5.3**	**790,475**	**4.8**	**828,032**
Worcester	25027	5.8	750,963	5.3	790,475	4.8	828,032
*** Bristol**	**25005**	**5.6**	**534,678**	**3.4**	**553,046**	**3.1**	**569,949**
(See Providence-New Bedford-Fall River, RI-MA.)							
Total: Metro Portion of State		**5.4**	**6,324,590**	**1.8**	**6,435,592**	**1.5**	**6,533,970**
Total: Massachusetts		5.5	6,349,097	1.8	6,461,761	1.5	6,561,659
Michigan							
Ann Arbor MI	**11460**	**14.1**	**322,895**	**7.8**	**347,941**	**6.8**	**371,559**
Washtenaw	26161	14.1	322,895	7.8	347,941	6.8	371,559
Battle Creek MI	**12980**	**1.5**	**137,985**	**1.0**	**139,305**	**0.9**	**140,493**
Calhoun	26025	1.5	137,985	1.0	139,305	0.9	140,493
Bay City MI	**13020**	**-1.4**	**110,157**	**-1.0**	**109,101**	**-1.0**	**108,063**
Bay	26017	-1.4	110,157	-1.0	109,101	-1.0	108,063
Detroit-Warren-Livonia MI	**19820**	**4.8**	**4,452,557**	**1.1**	**4,501,430**	**1.0**	**4,545,000**
Lapeer	26087	17.6	87,904	6.6	93,745	5.8	99,150
Livingston	26093	35.7	156,951	16.5	182,797	13.3	207,062
Macomb	26099	9.9	788,149	5.2	829,028	4.6	866,942
Oakland	26125	10.2	1,194,156	1.7	1,214,978	1.5	1,233,145
St. Clair	26147	12.8	164,235	5.2	172,724	4.6	180,692
Wayne	26163	-2.4	2,061,162	-2.6	2,008,158	-2.5	1,958,009
Flint MI	**22420**	**1.3**	**436,141**	**2.2**	**445,626**	**1.9**	**454,172**
Genesee	26049	1.3	436,141	2.2	445,626	1.9	454,172
Grand Rapids-Wyoming MI	**24340**	**14.6**	**740,482**	**4.7**	**775,198**	**4.1**	**807,357**
Barry	26015	13.4	56,755	6.0	60,188	5.4	63,445
Ionia	26067	7.9	61,518	5.6	64,985	5.1	68,286
Kent	26081	14.7	574,335	4.4	599,621	3.9	622,847
Newaygo	26123	25.3	47,874	5.3	50,404	4.7	52,779
Holland-Grand Haven MI	**26100**	**26.9**	**238,314**	**7.4**	**255,839**	**6.4**	**272,119**
Ottawa	26139	26.9	238,314	7.4	255,839	6.4	272,119
Jackson MI	**27100**	**5.8**	**158,422**	**3.9**	**164,674**	**3.6**	**170,566**
Jackson	26075	5.8	158,422	3.9	164,674	3.6	170,566
Kalamazoo-Portage MI	**28020**	**7.3**	**314,866**	**2.5**	**322,822**	**2.3**	**330,385**
Kalamazoo	26077	6.8	238,603	2.1	243,549	1.9	248,213
Van Buren	26159	8.9	76,263	3.9	79,273	3.7	82,172
Lansing-East Lansing MI	**29620**	**3.5**	**447,728**	**3.1**	**461,446**	**2.8**	**474,468**
Clinton	26037	11.9	64,753	7.6	69,693	6.8	74,398
Eaton	26045	11.6	103,655	4.3	108,140	3.9	112,348
Ingham	26065	-0.9	279,320	1.5	283,613	1.4	287,722
Monroe MI	**33780**	**9.2**	**145,945**	**5.4**	**153,774**	**4.7**	**161,017**
Monroe	26115	9.2	145,945	5.4	153,774	4.7	161,017
Muskegon-Norton Shores MI	**34740**	**7.1**	**170,200**	**2.9**	**175,106**	**2.6**	**179,638**
Muskegon	26121	7.1	170,200	2.9	175,106	2.6	179,638
Niles-Benton Harbor MI	**35660**	**0.7**	**162,453**	**0.3**	**162,940**	**0.2**	**163,248**
Berrien	26021	0.7	162,453	0.3	162,940	0.2	163,248
Saginaw-Saginaw Township North MI	**40980**	**-0.9**	**210,039**	**-0.6**	**208,826**	**-0.5**	**207,686**
Saginaw	26145	-0.9	210,039	-0.6	208,826	-0.5	207,686
*** Cass**	**26027**	**3.3**	**51,104**	**1.1**	**51,672**	**1.0**	**52,171**
(See South Bend-Mishawaka, IN-MI.)							
Total: Metro Portion of State		**6.1**	**8,099,288**	**2.2**	**8,275,700**	**2.0**	**8,437,942**
Total: Micro Portion of State		9.0	1,053,944	3.0	1,085,598	2.7	1,115,242
Total: Michigan		6.9	9,938,444	2.3	10,164,188	2.0	10,372,286
Minnesota							
Duluth, MN-WI	20260	2.3	275,486	0.1	275,790	0.1	276,141
Carlton	**27017**	**8.2**	**31,671**	**7.4**	**34,001**	**6.7**	**36,266**
St. Louis	**27137**	**1.2**	**200,528**	**-1.5**	**197,532**	**-1.4**	**194,767**
Douglas, WI	55031	3.7	43,287	2.2	44,257	1.9	45,108
Minneapolis-St. Paul-Bloomington, MN-WI	33460	16.9	2,968,806	6.3	3,154,675	5.5	3,327,749
Anoka	**27003**	**22.3**	**298,084**	**8.5**	**323,274**	**7.2**	**346,641**
Carver	**27019**	**46.5**	**70,205**	**20.3**	**84,468**	**16.0**	**98,024**
Chisago	**27025**	**34.7**	**41,101**	**21.6**	**49,980**	**16.8**	**58,375**
Dakota	**27037**	**29.3**	**355,904**	**7.7**	**383,221**	**6.6**	**408,473**
Hennepin	**27053**	**8.1**	**1,116,200**	**0.6**	**1,123,455**	**0.5**	**1,129,139**
Isanti	**27059**	**20.7**	**31,287**	**21.5**	**38,010**	**17.0**	**44,466**
Ramsey	**27123**	**5.2**	**511,035**	**-1.7**	**502,508**	**-1.7**	**493,791**
Scott	**27139**	**54.7**	**89,498**	**34.8**	**120,628**	**24.4**	**150,073**
Sherburne	**27141**	**53.6**	**64,417**	**27.4**	**82,041**	**20.3**	**98,726**
Washington	**27163**	**37.9**	**201,130**	**10.1**	**221,394**	**8.4**	**240,076**
Wright	**27171**	**31.0**	**89,986**	**23.1**	**110,736**	**18.0**	**130,635**
Pierce, WI	55093	12.3	36,804	4.8	38,572	4.3	40,236
St. Croix, WI	55109	25.7	63,155	21.0	76,388	16.6	89,094

* Indicates county is included from metro in different state.
Source: Devonshire Associates Ltd. and Scan/US, Inc. 2005.

Core Based Statistical Areas and Their Component Counties: Population Trends, *Continued*

CBSA	FIPS Code	Past: 1990-2000 % Change	Past: 2000 Census	Present: 2000-2005 % Change	Present: 7/1/05 Estimate	Future: 2005-2010 % Change	Future: 2010 Projection
Rochester MN	40340	15.3	163,618	8.5	177,491	7.4	190,568
Dodge	27039	12.7	17,731	11.0	19,687	9.3	21,513
Olmsted	27109	16.7	124,277	8.9	135,319	7.7	145,757
Wabasha	27157	9.5	21,610	4.0	22,485	3.6	23,298
St. Cloud MN	41060	12.4	167,392	9.8	183,879	8.6	199,661
Benton	27009	13.4	34,226	15.7	39,583	12.8	44,666
Stearns	27145	12.1	133,166	8.4	144,296	7.4	154,995
* Clay	27027	1.6	51,229	2.7	52,627	2.5	53,940
(See Fargo, ND-MN.)							
* Polk	27119	-3.5	31,369	-1.9	30,767	-2.0	30,162
(See Grand Forks, ND-MN.)							
* Houston	27055	6.6	19,718	1.4	19,996	1.2	20,236
(See La Crosse, WI-MN.)							
Total: Metro Portion of State		14.9	3,534,372	5.7	3,736,008	5.0	3,924,019
Total: Micro Portion of State		8.5	731,444	3.0	753,150	2.8	773,956
Total: Minnesota		12.4	4,919,479	4.7	5,148,487	4.2	5,363,223
Mississippi							
Gulfport-Biloxi MS	25060	18.4	246,190	2.2	251,585	1.9	256,379
Hancock	28045	35.3	42,967	8.2	46,503	6.9	49,696
Harrison	28047	14.7	189,601	0.5	190,466	0.3	191,127
Stone	28131	26.7	13,622	7.3	14,616	6.4	15,556
Hattiesburg MS	25620	13.0	123,812	5.8	130,975	5.0	137,562
Forrest	28035	6.3	72,604	3.4	75,059	3.0	77,299
Lamar	28073	28.4	39,070	11.8	43,669	9.8	47,960
Perry	28111	11.7	12,138	0.9	12,247	0.5	12,303
Jackson MS	27140	11.2	497,197	4.2	518,326	3.8	538,054
Copiah	28029	4.2	28,757	1.6	29,216	1.5	29,642
Hinds	28049	-1.4	250,800	-1.1	248,051	-1.1	245,399
Madison	28089	38.8	74,674	11.1	82,974	9.5	90,825
Rankin	28121	32.3	115,327	13.1	130,428	10.8	144,569
Simpson	28127	15.4	27,639	0.1	27,657	-0.1	27,619
Pascagoula MS	37700	14.1	150,564	3.7	156,158	3.2	161,148
George	28039	14.8	19,144	11.6	21,369	10.0	23,516
Jackson	28059	14.0	131,420	2.6	134,789	2.1	137,632
* DeSoto	28033	57.9	107,199	25.9	135,003	19.5	161,295
* Marshall	28093	15.3	34,993	2.7	35,935	2.3	36,774
* Tate	28137	18.4	25,370	3.1	26,167	2.7	26,869
* Tunica	28143	13.0	9,227	13.3	10,455	11.6	11,672
(See Memphis, TN-MS-AR.)							
Total: Metro Portion of State		16.6	1,194,552	5.9	1,264,604	5.2	1,329,753
Total: Micro Portion of State		6.2	1,001,735	-0.9	993,106	-0.8	985,346
Total: Mississippi		10.5	2,844,658	2.1	2,904,093	1.9	2,959,451
Missouri							
Columbia MO	17860	19.4	145,666	5.4	153,576	4.9	161,175
Boone	29019	20.5	135,454	6.1	143,667	5.5	151,543
Howard	29089	6.0	10,212	-3.0	9,909	-2.8	9,632
Jefferson City MO	27620	16.0	140,052	2.9	144,091	2.8	148,117
Callaway	29027	24.3	40,766	5.2	42,867	4.9	44,966
Cole	29051	12.3	71,397	1.7	72,592	1.7	73,802
Moniteau	29135	20.6	14,827	2.3	15,162	2.2	15,496
Osage	29151	8.7	13,062	3.1	13,470	2.8	13,853
Joplin MO	27900	16.6	157,322	5.6	166,062	5.0	174,350
Jasper	29097	15.7	104,686	5.9	110,824	5.2	116,636
Newton	29145	18.4	52,636	4.9	55,238	4.5	57,714
Kansas City, MO-KS	28140	12.2	1,836,038	6.4	1,952,760	5.6	2,061,595
Franklin, KS	20059	12.7	24,784	6.5	26,406	5.7	27,916
Johnson, KS	20091	27.0	451,086	12.5	507,661	10.4	560,260
Leavenworth, KS	20103	6.7	68,691	8.0	74,179	6.9	79,330
Linn, KS	20107	15.9	9,570	2.9	9,844	2.4	10,077
Miami, KS	20121	20.8	28,351	4.6	29,658	3.8	30,790
Wyandotte, KS	20209	-2.5	157,882	-0.9	156,403	-1.0	154,859
Bates	29013	10.8	16,653	3.6	17,254	3.0	17,780
Caldwell	29025	7.0	8,969	4.2	9,345	3.7	9,693
Cass	29037	28.7	82,092	13.8	93,436	11.6	104,263
Clay	29047	19.9	184,006	9.6	201,582	8.3	218,355
Clinton	29049	14.4	18,979	10.3	20,940	9.0	22,831
Jackson	29095	3.4	654,880	1.6	665,173	1.4	674,318
Lafayette	29107	6.0	32,960	0.8	33,226	0.5	33,399
Platte	29165	27.5	73,781	12.8	83,253	10.9	92,321
Ray	29177	6.3	23,354	4.5	24,400	4.1	25,403
Springfield MO	44180	23.3	368,374	7.5	396,026	6.7	422,388
Christian	29043	66.3	54,285	22.1	66,271	17.2	77,639
Dallas	29059	23.8	15,661	4.9	16,430	4.5	17,165
Greene	29077	15.6	240,391	4.0	249,887	3.7	259,037
Polk	29167	23.7	26,992	6.9	28,841	6.1	30,600
Webster	29225	30.7	31,045	11.4	34,597	9.7	37,947
St. Joseph, MO-KS	41140	5.6	122,336	-0.0	122,298	-1.3	120,702
Doniphan, KS	20043	1.4	8,249	-1.6	8,113	-1.7	7,974
Andrew	29003	12.7	16,492	3.9	17,141	3.5	17,741
Buchanan	29021	3.5	85,998	-1.4	84,810	-1.5	83,520
DeKalb	29063	16.4	11,597	5.5	12,234	-6.3	11,467
St. Louis, MO-IL	41180	4.6	2,698,687	2.6	2,769,054	2.4	2,836,847
Bond, IL	17005	17.6	17,633	2.4	18,049	2.2	18,440
Calhoun, IL	17013	-4.5	5,084	1.1	5,139	0.9	5,187
Clinton, IL	17027	4.7	35,535	2.1	36,286	2.0	36,996
Jersey, IL	17083	5.5	21,668	3.4	22,415	3.3	23,156
Macoupin, IL	17117	2.8	49,019	0.1	49,088	0.1	49,152
Madison, IL	17119	3.9	258,941	1.7	263,396	1.6	267,624
Monroe, IL	17133	23.2	27,619	12.4	31,030	10.5	34,284
St. Clair, IL	17163	-2.6	256,082	1.6	260,165	1.5	264,081
Franklin	29071	16.4	93,807	6.1	99,506	5.4	104,904
Jefferson	29099	15.6	198,099	7.9	213,724	7.0	228,606
Lincoln	29113	34.8	38,944	23.0	47,892	18.1	56,559
St. Charles	29183	33.3	283,883	16.2	329,900	13.3	373,721
St. Louis	29189	2.3	1,016,315	-0.1	1,015,417	-0.2	1,013,712
St. Louis (Ind. City)	29510	-12.2	348,189	-6.9	324,238	-6.6	302,974
Warren	29219	25.6	24,525	16.6	28,605	13.6	32,487
Washington	29221	14.5	23,344	3.7	24,204	3.1	24,964
* McDonald	29119	28.0	21,681	2.9	22,320	2.9	22,960
(See Fayetteville-Springdale-Rogers, AR-MO.)							
Total: Metro Portion of State		9.2	4,069,962	3.9	4,228,355	3.5	4,378,008
Total: Micro Portion of State		10.9	738,726	3.5	764,247	3.1	788,230
Total: Missouri		9.3	5,595,211	3.5	5,792,159	3.2	5,978,071
Montana							
Billings MT	13740	14.3	138,904	4.9	145,703	4.4	152,133
Carbon	30009	18.2	9,552	3.8	9,919	3.6	10,272
Yellowstone	30111	14.0	129,352	5.0	135,784	4.5	141,861
Great Falls MT	24500	3.4	80,357	-1.2	79,409	-1.1	78,518
Cascade	30013	3.4	80,357	-1.2	79,409	-1.1	78,518
Missoula MT	33540	21.8	95,802	4.5	100,118	3.9	104,056
Missoula	30063	21.8	95,802	4.5	100,118	3.9	104,056
Total: Metro Portion of State		13.4	315,063	3.2	325,230	2.9	334,707
Total: Micro Portion of State		19.7	259,346	6.7	276,740	5.9	293,201
Total: Montana		12.9	902,195	2.8	927,852	2.6	952,203
Nebraska							
Lincoln NE	30700	16.5	266,787	6.1	283,022	5.3	298,141
Lancaster	31109	17.2	250,291	6.5	266,575	5.7	281,788
Seward	31159	6.8	16,496	-0.3	16,447	-0.6	16,353
Omaha-Council Bluffs, NE-IA	36540	11.8	767,041	5.2	807,305	4.7	844,907
Harrison, IA	19085	6.4	15,666	0.3	15,710	-0.0	15,707
Mills, IA	19129	10.2	14,547	3.8	15,093	3.4	15,602
Pottawattamie, IA	19155	6.1	87,704	1.3	88,801	0.9	89,567
Cass	31025	14.1	24,334	6.1	25,823	5.4	27,226
Douglas	31055	11.3	463,585	4.4	483,981	3.9	503,039
Sarpy	31153	19.5	122,595	12.3	137,701	10.4	152,053
Saunders	31155	8.4	19,830	1.8	20,179	1.5	20,489
Washington	31177	13.1	18,780	6.6	20,017	6.0	21,224
* Dakota	31043	21.0	20,253	2.7	20,799	2.4	21,296
* Dixon	31051	3.2	6,339	-5.0	6,020	-4.7	5,735
(See Sioux City, IA-NE-SD.)							
Total: Metro Portion of State		13.9	942,503	5.8	997,542	5.2	1,049,203
Total: Micro Portion of State		7.0	396,206	0.5	398,196	0.5	400,061
Total: Nebraska		8.4	1,711,263	2.4	1,751,975	2.2	1,790,712
Nevada							
Carson City NV	16180	29.7	52,457	8.9	57,139	8.0	61,722
Carson City (Ind. City)	32510	29.7	52,457	8.9	57,139	8.0	61,722
Las Vegas-Paradise NV	29820	85.5	1,375,765	23.4	1,697,755	17.9	2,001,933
Clark	32003	85.5	1,375,765	23.4	1,697,755	17.9	2,001,933
Reno-Sparks NV	39900	33.3	342,885	14.9	393,925	12.5	443,050
Storey	32029	34.6	3,399	6.6	3,623	6.4	3,854
Washoe	32031	33.3	339,486	15.0	390,302	12.5	439,196
Total: Metro Portion of State		70.4	1,771,107	21.3	2,148,819	16.7	2,506,705
Total: Micro Portion of State		47.0	144,668	5.7	152,898	5.0	160,561
Total: Nevada		66.3	1,998,257	19.7	2,391,581	15.6	2,764,949

CBSA	FIPS Code	Past: 1990-2000 % Change	Past: 2000 Census	Present: 2000-2005 % Change	Present: 7/1/05 Estimate	Future: 2005-2010 % Change	Future: 2010 Projection
New Hampshire							
Manchester-Nashua NH	31700	13.3	380,841	5.9	403,350	5.2	424,307
Hillsborough	33011	13.3	380,841	5.9	403,350	5.2	424,307
* Rockingham	33015	12.8	277,359	7.5	298,070	6.5	317,391
* Strafford	33017	7.7	112,233	7.5	120,636	6.6	128,609
(See Boston-Cambridge-Quincy, MA-NH.)							
Total: Metro Portion of State		12.3	770,433	6.7	822,056	5.9	870,307
Total: Micro Portion of State		8.8	421,687	6.8	450,435	6.1	478,037
Total: New Hampshire		11.4	1,235,786	6.8	1,319,978	6.0	1,399,401
New Jersey							
Atlantic City NJ	12100	12.6	252,552	3.4	261,127	3.1	269,137
Atlantic	34001	12.6	252,552	3.4	261,127	3.1	269,137
Ocean City NJ	36140	7.6	102,326	-0.6	101,669	-0.6	101,017
Cape May	34009	7.6	102,326	-0.6	101,669	-0.6	101,017
Trenton-Ewing NJ	45940	7.7	350,761	5.3	369,496	4.9	387,426
Mercer	34021	7.7	350,761	5.3	369,496	4.9	387,426
Vineland-Millville-Bridgeton NJ	47220	6.1	146,438	3.3	151,331	3.2	156,244
Cumberland	34011	6.1	146,438	3.3	151,331	3.2	156,244
* Bergen	34003	7.1	884,118	2.6	906,873	2.3	927,845
* Essex	34013	2.0	793,633	0.8	800,056	0.9	807,383
* Hudson	34017	10.1	608,975	-0.3	607,051	-0.4	604,565
* Hunterdon	34019	13.2	121,989	8.5	132,353	7.4	142,102
* Middlesex	34023	11.7	750,162	6.8	800,915	6.0	848,816
* Monmouth	34025	11.2	615,301	4.7	644,487	4.2	671,700
* Morris	34027	11.6	470,212	4.6	492,011	4.2	512,552
* Ocean	34029	17.9	510,916	11.3	568,520	9.7	623,431
* Passaic	34031	7.9	489,049	3.1	504,035	2.6	516,976
* Somerset	34035	23.8	297,490	7.9	321,061	6.9	343,220
* Sussex	34037	10.1	144,166	7.8	155,440	6.9	166,205
* Union	34039	5.8	522,541	2.2	534,259	2.0	545,156
(See New York-Northern New Jersey-Long Island, NY-NJ-PA.)							
* Warren	34041	11.8	102,437	10.8	113,479	9.3	123,985
(See Allentown-Bethlehem-Easton, PA-NJ.)							
* Burlington	34005	7.2	423,394	8.3	458,701	7.4	492,773
* Camden	34007	1.2	508,932	1.8	518,146	1.8	527,433
* Gloucester	34015	10.7	254,673	8.0	275,154	7.2	294,986
* Salem	34033	-1.5	64,285	1.7	65,361	1.7	66,484
(See Philadelphia-Camden-Wilmington, PA-NJ-DE-MD.)							
Total: Metro Portion of State		8.9	8,414,350	4.4	8,781,525	4.0	9,129,436
Total: New Jersey		8.9	8,414,350	4.4	8,781,525	4.0	9,129,436
New Mexico							
Albuquerque NM	10740	21.7	729,649	8.1	788,925	7.2	845,978
Bernalillo	35001	15.8	556,678	7.5	598,254	6.8	638,753
Sandoval	35043	42.0	89,908	16.0	104,283	13.1	117,912
Torrance	35057	64.4	16,911	-1.2	16,716	-1.5	16,458
Valencia	35061	46.2	66,152	5.3	69,672	4.6	72,855
Farmington NM	22140	24.2	113,801	12.5	127,992	10.7	141,716
San Juan	35045	24.2	113,801	12.5	127,992	10.7	141,716
Las Cruces NM	29740	28.9	174,682	7.2	187,285	6.5	199,509
Dona Ana	35013	28.9	174,682	7.2	187,285	6.5	199,509
Santa Fe NM	42140	30.7	129,292	9.3	141,278	8.1	152,692
Santa Fe	35049	30.7	129,292	9.3	141,278	8.1	152,692
Total: Metro Portion of State		24.0	1,147,424	8.5	1,245,480	7.6	1,339,895
Total: Micro Portion of State		12.9	569,960	-0.1	569,605	0.1	570,043
Total: New Mexico		20.1	1,819,046	5.3	1,914,908	4.9	2,008,321
New York							
Albany-Schenectady-Troy NY	10580	2.0	825,875	3.1	851,730	2.9	876,805
Albany	36001	0.7	294,565	2.2	300,976	2.1	307,368
Rensselaer	36083	-1.2	152,538	0.9	153,917	0.9	155,278
Saratoga	36091	10.7	200,635	7.9	216,567	7.0	231,679
Schenectady	36093	-1.8	146,555	1.2	148,278	1.2	150,092
Schoharie	36095	-0.9	31,582	1.3	31,992	1.2	32,388
Binghamton NY	13780	-4.6	252,320	-1.0	249,856	-0.9	247,721
Broome	36007	-5.5	200,536	-1.3	197,991	-1.1	195,750
Tioga	36107	-1.1	51,784	0.2	51,865	0.2	51,971
Buffalo-Niagara Falls NY	15380	-1.6	1,170,111	-1.3	1,154,526	-1.2	1,140,186
Erie	36029	-1.9	950,265	-1.4	936,770	-1.3	924,278
Niagara	36063	-0.4	219,846	-1.0	217,756	-0.8	215,908
Elmira NY	21300	-4.3	91,070	-1.1	90,031	-1.1	89,021
Chemung	36015	-4.3	91,070	-1.1	90,031	-1.1	89,021
Glens Falls NY	24020	4.9	124,345	3.5	128,724	3.4	133,094
Warren	36113	6.9	63,303	4.0	65,852	3.8	68,356
Washington	36115	2.9	61,042	3.0	62,872	3.0	64,738
Ithaca NY	27060	2.6	96,501	4.7	100,996	4.4	105,440
Tompkins	36109	2.6	96,501	4.7	100,996	4.4	105,440
Kingston NY	28740	7.5	177,749	3.5	183,995	3.3	190,073
Ulster	36111	7.5	177,749	3.5	183,995	3.3	190,073
New York-Northern New Jersey-Long Island, NY-NJ-PA	35620	8.8	18,323,002	3.0	18,864,705	2.7	19,370,131
Bergen, NJ	34003	7.1	884,118	2.6	906,873	2.3	927,845
Essex, NJ	34013	2.0	793,633	0.8	800,056	0.9	807,383
Hudson, NJ	34017	10.1	608,975	-0.3	607,051	-0.4	604,565
Hunterdon, NJ	34019	13.2	121,989	8.5	132,353	7.4	142,102
Middlesex, NJ	34023	11.7	750,162	6.8	800,915	6.0	848,816
Monmouth, NJ	34025	11.2	615,301	4.7	644,487	4.2	671,700
Morris, NJ	34027	11.6	470,212	4.6	492,011	4.2	512,552
Ocean, NJ	34029	17.9	510,916	11.3	568,520	9.7	623,431
Passaic, NJ	34031	7.9	489,049	3.1	504,035	2.6	516,976
Somerset, NJ	34035	23.8	297,490	7.9	321,061	6.9	343,220
Sussex, NJ	34037	10.1	144,166	7.8	155,440	6.9	166,205
Union, NJ	34039	5.8	522,541	2.2	534,259	2.0	545,156
Bronx	36005	10.7	1,332,650	3.9	1,385,071	3.6	1,435,428
Kings	36047	7.2	2,465,326	0.6	2,480,420	0.5	2,493,914
Nassau	36059	3.7	1,334,544	0.7	1,343,675	0.5	1,350,776
New York	36061	3.3	1,537,195	3.3	1,588,044	3.1	1,636,531
Putnam	36079	14.1	95,745	6.8	102,260	6.0	108,401
Queens	36081	14.2	2,229,379	-0.2	2,225,143	-0.3	2,218,858
Richmond	36085	17.1	443,728	5.9	470,056	5.2	494,633
Rockland	36087	8.0	286,753	3.6	297,018	3.2	306,523
Suffolk	36103	7.4	1,419,369	5.6	1,498,863	5.0	1,573,642
Westchester	36119	5.6	923,459	3.0	951,137	2.6	976,236
Pike, PA	42103	65.6	46,302	20.9	55,957	16.6	65,238
Poughkeepsie-Newburgh-Middletown NY	39100	9.6	621,517	8.7	675,333	7.6	726,820
Dutchess	36027	8.0	280,150	6.3	297,806	5.7	314,780
Orange	36071	11.0	341,367	10.6	377,527	9.1	412,040
Rochester NY	40380	3.5	1,037,831	0.8	1,046,284	0.7	1,054,036
Livingston	36051	3.1	64,328	0.7	64,792	0.6	65,187
Monroe	36055	3.0	735,343	0.5	738,925	0.4	742,088
Ontario	36069	5.4	100,224	4.2	104,413	3.8	108,420
Orleans	36073	5.6	44,171	-0.7	43,876	-0.7	43,571
Wayne	36117	5.2	93,765	0.5	94,278	0.5	94,770
Syracuse NY	45060	-1.5	650,154	1.2	657,851	1.1	665,234
Madison	36053	0.5	69,441	2.1	70,875	2.0	72,294
Onondaga	36067	-2.3	458,336	1.0	462,726	0.9	466,993
Oswego	36075	0.5	122,377	1.5	124,250	1.4	125,947
Utica-Rome NY	46540	-5.3	299,896	-0.7	297,654	-0.7	295,683
Herkimer	36043	-2.1	64,427	-1.6	63,402	-1.6	62,418
Oneida	36065	-6.1	235,469	-0.5	234,252	-0.4	233,265
Total: Metro Portion of State		5.9	17,415,517	2.1	17,778,667	1.9	18,119,055
Total: Micro Portion of State		-0.4	1,130,953	0.5	1,136,685	0.6	1,143,039
Total: New York		5.5	18,976,457	2.0	19,348,846	1.8	19,698,950
North Carolina							
Asheville NC	11700	19.9	369,171	5.9	391,007	5.3	411,544
Buncombe	37021	18.0	206,330	5.4	217,531	4.8	228,057
Haywood	37087	15.1	54,033	4.9	56,679	4.5	59,235
Henderson	37089	28.7	89,173	8.4	96,658	7.3	103,676
Madison	37115	15.8	19,635	2.6	20,139	2.2	20,576
Burlington NC	15500	20.9	130,800	7.1	140,105	6.2	148,722
Alamance	37001	20.9	130,800	7.1	140,105	6.2	148,722
Charlotte-Gastonia-Concord, NC-SC	16740	29.8	1,330,448	13.2	1,505,429	11.0	1,670,939
Anson	37007	7.7	25,275	-0.4	25,186	-0.3	25,112
Cabarrus	37025	32.5	131,063	14.9	150,533	12.1	168,822
Gaston	37071	8.7	190,365	2.6	195,391	2.4	200,065
Mecklenburg	37119	36.0	695,454	13.3	787,867	11.1	875,406
Union	37179	46.9	123,677	29.1	159,636	21.3	193,627
York, SC	45091	25.2	164,614	13.5	186,816	11.3	207,907
Durham NC	20500	23.8	426,493	7.5	458,673	7.1	491,391
Chatham	37037	27.3	49,329	19.9	59,157	16.0	68,596
Durham	37063	22.8	223,314	9.2	243,802	7.9	263,055
Orange	37135	26.0	118,227	-0.1	118,085	1.8	120,243
Person	37145	18.0	35,623	5.6	37,629	5.0	39,497

* Indicates county is included from metro in different state.
Source: Devonshire Associates Ltd. and Scan/US, Inc. 2005.

Continued on next page

Core Based Statistical Areas and Their Component Counties: Population Trends, *Continued*

CBSA	FIPS Code	Past: 1990-2000 % Change	Past: 2000 Census	Present: 2000-2005 % Change	Present: 7/1/05 Estimate	Future: 2005-2010 % Change	Future: 2010 Projection
Fayetteville NC	22180	13.2	336,609	2.9	346,350	2.8	355,917
Cumberland	37051	10.3	302,963	1.2	306,556	1.2	310,229
Hoke	37093	47.2	33,646	18.3	39,794	14.8	45,688
Goldsboro NC	24140	8.3	113,329	0.1	113,461	0.1	113,549
Wayne	37191	8.3	113,329	0.1	113,461	0.1	113,549
Greensboro-High Point NC	24660	19.1	643,430	4.6	673,134	4.1	700,749
Guilford	37081	21.2	421,048	5.0	442,093	4.4	461,760
Randolph	37151	22.4	130,454	5.6	137,787	4.8	144,465
Rockingham	37157	6.8	91,928	1.4	93,254	1.4	94,524
Greenville NC	24780	23.9	152,772	6.2	162,183	5.5	171,173
Greene	37079	23.3	18,974	8.1	20,517	7.1	21,971
Pitt	37147	24.0	133,798	5.9	141,666	5.3	149,202
Hickory-Lenoir-Morganton NC	25860	16.9	341,851	4.2	356,039	3.6	368,980
Alexander	37003	22.0	33,603	5.9	35,588	5.4	37,498
Burke	37023	17.7	89,148	0.8	89,829	0.6	90,378
Caldwell	37027	9.5	77,415	3.1	79,837	2.8	82,046
Catawba	37035	19.7	141,685	6.4	150,785	5.5	159,058
Jacksonville NC	27340	0.3	150,355	-0.4	149,754	0.2	150,057
Onslow	37133	0.3	150,355	-0.4	149,754	0.2	150,057
Raleigh-Cary NC	39580	47.3	797,071	17.8	939,136	14.4	1,074,178
Franklin	37069	29.8	47,260	17.3	55,425	14.1	63,240
Johnston	37101	50.0	121,965	19.8	146,138	15.6	168,989
Wake	37183	48.3	627,846	17.5	737,573	14.2	841,949
Rocky Mount NC	40580	7.3	143,026	1.9	145,779	1.9	148,498
Edgecombe	37065	-1.7	55,606	-1.8	54,620	-1.3	53,931
Nash	37127	14.0	87,420	4.3	91,159	3.7	94,567
Wilmington NC	48900	37.2	274,532	11.4	305,944	9.9	336,164
Brunswick	37019	43.5	73,143	18.8	86,905	15.1	100,046
New Hanover	37129	33.3	160,307	8.4	173,836	7.6	186,986
Pender	37141	42.4	41,082	10.0	45,203	8.7	49,132
Winston-Salem NC	49180	16.7	421,961	6.0	447,369	5.4	471,309
Davie	37059	25.0	34,835	11.3	38,755	9.5	42,443
Forsyth	37067	15.1	306,067	6.3	325,303	5.6	343,635
Stokes	37169	20.1	44,711	1.7	45,460	1.3	46,050
Yadkin	37197	19.2	36,348	4.1	37,851	3.5	39,181
* **Currituck**	37053	32.4	18,190	23.6	22,484	18.4	26,629
(See Virginia Beach-Norfolk-Newport News, VA-NC.)							
Total: Metro Portion of State		24.3	5,485,424	8.8	5,970,031	7.7	6,431,892
Total: Micro Portion of State		15.7	1,869,008	4.5	1,952,387	4.0	2,030,731
Total: North Carolina		21.4	8,049,313	7.4	8,642,524	6.5	9,206,675

North Dakota

CBSA	FIPS Code	Past: 1990-2000 % Change	Past: 2000 Census	Present: 2000-2005 % Change	Present: 7/1/05 Estimate	Future: 2005-2010 % Change	Future: 2010 Projection
Bismarck ND	13900	13.0	94,719	3.8	98,303	3.3	101,535
Burleigh	38015	15.4	69,416	5.4	73,166	4.8	76,649
Morton	38059	6.8	25,303	-0.7	25,137	-1.0	24,886
Fargo, ND-MN	22020	13.7	174,367	4.1	181,535	3.6	188,090
Clay, MN	27027	1.6	51,229	2.7	52,627	2.5	53,940
Cass	38017	19.7	123,138	4.7	128,908	4.1	134,150
Grand Forks, ND-MN	24220	-5.5	97,478	-3.0	94,524	-2.9	91,810
Polk, MN	27119	-3.5	31,369	-1.9	30,767	-2.0	30,162
Grand Forks	38035	-6.5	66,109	-3.6	63,757	-3.3	61,648
Total: Metro Portion of State		10.3	283,966	2.5	290,968	2.2	297,333
Total: Micro Portion of State		-1.6	150,583	-5.2	142,703	-5.1	135,465
Total: North Dakota		0.5	642,200	-2.2	627,989	-2.0	615,176

Ohio

CBSA	FIPS Code	Past: 1990-2000 % Change	Past: 2000 Census	Present: 2000-2005 % Change	Present: 7/1/05 Estimate	Future: 2005-2010 % Change	Future: 2010 Projection
Akron OH	10420	5.7	694,960	1.4	704,396	1.2	712,569
Portage	39133	6.6	152,061	2.2	155,370	1.9	158,307
Summit	39153	5.4	542,899	1.1	549,026	1.0	554,262
Canton-Massillon OH	15940	3.3	406,934	0.0	407,131	-0.0	407,088
Carroll	39019	8.7	28,836	3.8	29,941	3.5	30,982
Stark	39151	2.9	378,098	-0.2	377,190	-0.3	376,106
Cincinnati-Middletown, OH-KY-IN	17140	8.9	2,009,632	3.0	2,069,601	2.7	2,125,426
Dearborn, IN	18029	18.7	46,109	6.6	49,138	5.7	51,918
Franklin, IN	18047	13.1	22,151	4.7	23,182	4.1	24,132
Ohio, IN	18115	5.8	5,623	3.3	5,809	2.8	5,974
Boone, KY	21015	49.3	85,991	20.8	103,836	16.2	120,627
Bracken, KY	21023	6.6	8,279	4.5	8,653	4.2	9,015
Campbell, KY	21037	5.7	88,616	-1.7	87,132	-1.7	85,641
Gallatin, KY	21077	45.9	7,870	3.2	8,122	3.2	8,384
Grant, KY	21081	42.2	22,384	11.8	25,032	9.9	27,503
Kenton, KY	21117	6.6	151,464	0.9	152,794	0.7	153,919
Pendleton, KY	21191	19.6	14,390	7.0	15,401	5.8	16,296
Brown	39015	20.9	42,285	5.7	44,709	4.7	46,813
Butler	39017	14.2	332,807	4.9	349,225	4.4	364,560
Clermont	39025	18.5	177,977	6.9	190,233	6.0	201,712
Hamilton	39061	-2.4	845,303	-4.2	809,794	-4.1	776,764
Warren	39165	39.0	158,383	24.1	196,541	18.1	232,168
Cleveland-Elyria-Mentor OH	17460	2.2	2,148,143	-0.5	2,136,541	-0.5	2,125,752
Cuyahoga	39035	-1.3	1,393,978	-3.6	1,344,252	-3.5	1,297,572
Geauga	39055	12.0	90,895	5.5	95,917	4.8	100,533
Lake	39085	5.6	227,511	2.3	232,832	2.2	237,905
Lorain	39093	5.0	284,664	3.8	295,342	3.4	305,320
Medina	39103	23.5	151,095	11.3	168,198	9.6	184,422
Columbus OH	18140	14.8	1,612,694	6.6	1,719,360	5.8	1,818,975
Delaware	39041	64.3	109,989	37.5	151,233	26.0	190,621
Fairfield	39045	18.7	122,759	13.3	139,046	11.2	154,580
Franklin	39049	11.2	1,068,978	3.0	1,100,544	2.6	1,129,032
Licking	39089	13.4	145,491	5.7	153,841	5.0	161,531
Madison	39097	8.5	40,213	1.8	40,930	1.7	41,613
Morrow	39117	14.0	31,628	10.0	34,782	8.5	37,737
Pickaway	39129	9.3	52,727	1.6	53,572	1.3	54,267
Union	39159	28.0	40,909	11.0	45,412	9.2	49,594
Dayton OH	19380	0.5	848,153	-0.6	843,320	-0.6	838,487
Greene	39057	8.2	147,886	2.8	152,045	2.5	155,847
Miami	39109	6.1	98,868	2.0	100,836	1.8	102,636
Montgomery	39113	-2.6	559,062	-2.0	547,810	-2.0	537,122
Preble	39135	5.5	42,337	0.7	42,629	0.6	42,882
Lima OH	30620	-1.2	108,473	-1.8	106,543	-1.7	104,784
Allen	39003	-1.2	108,473	-1.8	106,543	-1.7	104,784
Mansfield OH	31900	2.2	128,852	-0.9	127,690	-0.9	126,535
Richland	39139	2.2	128,852	-0.9	127,690	-0.9	126,535
Sandusky OH	41780	3.6	79,551	-1.5	78,323	-1.6	77,033
Erie	39043	3.6	79,551	-1.5	78,323	-1.6	77,033
Springfield OH	44220	-1.9	144,742	-2.1	141,771	-1.9	139,024
Clark	39023	-1.9	144,742	-2.1	141,771	-1.9	139,024
Toledo OH	45780	0.8	659,188	0.2	660,207	0.1	660,975
Fulton	39051	9.3	42,084	1.2	42,582	1.0	43,007
Lucas	39095	-1.6	455,054	-0.5	452,909	-0.5	450,819
Ottawa	39123	2.4	40,985	1.1	41,432	1.0	41,839
Wood	39173	6.9	121,065	1.8	123,284	1.6	125,310
Youngstown-Warren-Boardman, OH-PA	49660	-1.7	602,964	-2.6	587,022	-2.5	572,061
Mahoning	39099	-2.7	257,555	-3.7	248,058	-3.5	239,280
Trumbull	39155	-1.2	225,116	-2.6	219,265	-2.6	213,614
Mercer, PA	42085	-0.6	120,293	-0.5	119,699	-0.4	119,167
* **Lawrence**	39087	0.8	62,319	0.4	62,567	0.4	62,824
(See Huntington-Ashland, WV-KY-OH.)							
* **Washington**	39167	1.6	63,251	-1.7	62,162	-1.7	61,134
(See Parkersburg-Marietta-Vienna, WV-OH.)							
* **Jefferson**	39081	-8.0	73,894	-4.6	70,461	-4.4	67,356
(See Weirton-Steubenville, WV-OH.)							
* **Belmont**	39013	-1.2	70,226	-1.7	69,040	-1.6	67,943
(See Wheeling, WV-OH.)							
Total: Metro Portion of State		4.6	9,140,806	1.2	9,247,337	1.1	9,345,390
Total: Micro Portion of State		4.5	1,708,392	1.0	1,725,494	0.9	1,740,978
Total: Ohio		4.7	11,353,140	1.2	11,485,881	1.1	11,607,960

Oklahoma

CBSA	FIPS Code	Past: 1990-2000 % Change	Past: 2000 Census	Present: 2000-2005 % Change	Present: 7/1/05 Estimate	Future: 2005-2010 % Change	Future: 2010 Projection
Lawton OK	30020	3.1	114,996	-5.2	109,018	-3.7	104,954
Comanche	40031	3.1	114,996	-5.2	109,018	-3.7	104,954
Oklahoma City OK	36420	12.8	1,095,421	5.5	1,155,595	4.9	1,212,482
Canadian	40017	17.9	87,697	9.7	96,179	8.3	104,171
Cleveland	40027	19.4	208,016	8.5	225,695	7.6	242,817
Grady	40051	9.0	45,516	6.8	48,624	6.2	51,631
Lincoln	40081	9.8	32,080	0.8	32,331	0.5	32,499
Logan	40083	16.9	33,924	7.6	36,508	6.8	38,983
McClain	40087	21.7	27,740	5.2	29,188	4.5	30,516
Oklahoma	40109	10.1	660,448	4.0	687,070	3.6	711,865
Tulsa OK	46140	12.9	859,532	3.9	892,708	3.5	923,510
Creek	40037	10.6	67,367	3.3	69,584	2.9	71,575
Okmulgee	40111	8.8	39,685	0.8	40,003	0.8	40,337
Osage	40113	6.7	44,437	2.7	45,632	2.3	46,662
Pawnee	40117	6.7	16,612	2.4	17,006	1.8	17,305
Rogers	40131	28.0	70,641	14.9	81,199	12.1	90,987
Tulsa	40143	11.9	563,299	2.1	574,848	1.9	585,531
Wagoner	40145	20.1	57,491	12.1	64,436	10.4	71,113
* **Le Flore**	40079	11.2	48,109	2.7	49,394	2.4	50,583
* **Sequoyah**	40135	15.2	38,972	4.2	40,620	3.8	42,155
(See Fort Smith, AR-OK.)							
Total: Metro Portion of State		12.3	2,157,030	4.2	2,247,335	3.8	2,333,684
Total: Micro Portion of State		6.5	733,861	0.5	737,857	0.5	741,653
Total: Oklahoma		9.7	3,450,654	2.6	3,541,713	2.5	3,629,142

Oregon

CBSA	FIPS Code	Past: 1990-2000 % Change	Past: 2000 Census	Present: 2000-2005 % Change	Present: 7/1/05 Estimate	Future: 2005-2010 % Change	Future: 2010 Projection
Bend OR	13460	53.9	115,367	19.8	138,176	15.6	159,740
Deschutes	41017	53.9	115,367	19.8	138,176	15.6	159,740
Corvallis OR	18700	10.4	78,153	2.1	79,778	2.1	81,434
Benton	41003	10.4	78,153	2.1	79,778	2.1	81,434
Eugene-Springfield OR	21660	14.2	322,959	3.8	335,284	3.5	347,119
Lane	41039	14.2	322,959	3.8	335,284	3.5	347,119
Medford OR	32780	23.8	181,269	8.2	196,043	7.2	210,212
Jackson	41029	23.8	181,269	8.2	196,043	7.2	210,212
Portland-Vancouver-Beaverton, OR-WA	38900	26.5	1,927,881	9.5	2,110,156	8.2	2,284,221
Clackamas	41005	21.4	338,391	9.1	369,163	8.0	398,673
Columbia	41009	16.0	43,560	10.3	48,039	9.1	52,406
Multnomah	41051	13.1	660,486	4.3	688,787	4.0	716,054
Washington	41067	42.9	445,342	12.3	500,313	10.3	552,092
Yamhill	41071	29.7	84,992	8.5	92,229	7.5	99,169
Clark, WA	53011	45.0	345,238	16.2	401,099	13.4	454,676
Skamania, WA	53059	19.1	9,872	6.6	10,526	5.9	11,151
Salem OR	41420	24.9	347,214	8.0	374,986	7.1	401,672
Marion	41047	24.7	284,834	7.6	306,501	6.8	327,358
Polk	41053	25.9	62,380	9.8	68,485	8.5	74,314
Total: Metro Portion of State		22.9	2,617,733	7.8	2,822,798	6.9	3,018,571
Total: Micro Portion of State		12.8	663,587	3.8	688,762	3.6	713,262
Total: Oregon		20.4	3,421,399	6.7	3,651,787	6.0	3,872,508

Pennsylvania

CBSA	FIPS Code	Past: 1990-2000 % Change	Past: 2000 Census	Present: 2000-2005 % Change	Present: 7/1/05 Estimate	Future: 2005-2010 % Change	Future: 2010 Projection
Allentown-Bethlehem-Easton, PA-NJ	10900	7.8	740,395	6.1	785,814	5.5	829,398
Warren, NJ	34041	11.8	102,437	10.8	113,479	9.3	123,985
Carbon	42025	3.4	58,802	4.4	61,398	4.1	63,927
Lehigh	42077	7.2	312,090	4.4	325,977	4.0	339,160
Northampton	42095	8.1	267,066	6.7	284,960	6.1	302,326
Altoona PA	11020	-1.1	129,144	-2.1	126,465	-2.0	123,875
Blair	42013	-1.1	129,144	-2.1	126,465	-2.0	123,875
Erie PA	21500	1.9	280,843	-0.6	279,281	-0.5	277,775
Erie	42049	1.9	280,843	-0.6	279,281	-0.5	277,775
Harrisburg-Carlisle PA	25420	7.3	509,074	2.0	519,424	1.9	529,250
Cumberland	42041	9.4	213,674	4.5	223,224	4.1	232,401
Dauphin	42043	5.9	251,798	-0.1	251,422	-0.2	250,927
Perry	42099	5.9	43,602	2.7	44,778	2.6	45,922
Johnstown PA	27780	-6.4	152,598	-3.2	147,675	-3.0	143,243
Cambria	42021	-6.4	152,598	-3.2	147,675	-3.0	143,243
Lancaster PA	29540	11.3	470,658	4.2	490,254	3.7	508,588
Lancaster	42071	11.3	470,658	4.2	490,254	3.7	508,588
Lebanon PA	30140	5.8	120,327	3.7	124,776	3.4	129,072
Lebanon	42075	5.8	120,327	3.7	124,776	3.4	129,072
Philadelphia-Camden-Wilmington, PA-NJ-DE-MD	37980	4.6	5,687,147	2.5	5,831,625	2.4	5,970,563
New Castle, DE	10003	13.2	500,265	4.7	523,864	4.2	545,859
Cecil, MD	24015	20.5	85,951	13.2	97,326	11.1	108,151
Burlington, NJ	34005	7.2	423,394	8.3	458,701	7.4	492,773
Camden, NJ	34007	1.2	508,932	1.8	518,146	1.8	527,433
Gloucester, NJ	34015	10.7	254,673	8.0	275,154	7.2	294,986
Salem, NJ	34033	-1.5	64,285	1.7	65,361	1.7	66,484
Bucks	42017	10.4	597,635	4.1	622,393	3.6	645,062
Chester	42029	15.2	433,501	8.9	471,979	7.6	507,963
Delaware	42045	0.6	550,864	1.0	556,280	0.7	560,150
Montgomery	42091	10.6	750,097	4.7	785,423	4.3	819,588
Philadelphia	42101	-4.3	1,517,550	-4.0	1,456,998	-3.8	1,402,114
Pittsburgh PA	38300	-1.5	2,431,087	-1.3	2,400,344	-1.2	2,371,504
Allegheny	42003	-4.1	1,281,666	-2.5	1,249,911	-2.4	1,220,311
Armstrong	42005	-1.5	72,392	-1.5	71,316	-1.4	70,309
Beaver	42007	-2.5	181,412	-2.1	177,681	-2.0	174,204
Butler	42019	14.5	174,083	5.3	183,231	4.7	191,805
Fayette	42051	2.3	148,644	-2.6	144,770	-2.6	141,062
Washington	42125	-0.8	202,897	1.5	206,014	1.4	208,908
Westmoreland	42129	-0.1	369,993	-0.7	367,421	-0.7	364,905
Reading PA	39740	11.0	373,638	5.2	393,253	4.7	411,802
Berks	42011	11.0	373,638	5.2	393,253	4.7	411,802
Scranton—Wilkes-Barre PA	42540	-2.5	560,625	-2.4	547,294	-2.2	535,193
Lackawanna	42069	-2.6	213,295	-2.2	208,594	-2.1	204,297
Luzerne	42079	-2.7	319,250	-2.8	310,470	-2.6	302,479
Wyoming	42131	0.0	28,080	0.5	28,230	0.7	28,417
State College PA	44300	9.7	135,758	4.4	141,710	4.1	147,551
Centre	42027	9.7	135,758	4.4	141,710	4.1	147,551
Williamsport PA	48700	1.1	120,044	-1.9	117,787	-1.8	115,625
Lycoming	42081	1.1	120,044	-1.9	117,787	-1.8	115,625
York-Hanover PA	49620	12.4	381,751	5.7	403,361	5.1	423,825
York	42133	12.4	381,751	5.7	403,361	5.1	423,825
* **Pike**	42103	65.6	46,302	20.9	55,957	16.6	65,238
(See New York-Northern New Jersey-Long Island, NY-NJ-PA.)							
* **Mercer**	42085	-0.6	120,293	-0.5	119,699	-0.4	119,167
(See Youngstown-Warren-Boardman, OH-PA.)							
Total: Metro Portion of State		3.0	10,319,747	1.1	10,432,688	1.0	10,541,998
Total: Micro Portion of State		5.1	1,578,983	1.6	1,604,286	1.5	1,628,421
Total: Pennsylvania		3.4	12,281,054	1.1	12,420,798	1.1	12,555,326

Rhode Island

CBSA	FIPS Code	Past: 1990-2000 % Change	Past: 2000 Census	Present: 2000-2005 % Change	Present: 7/1/05 Estimate	Future: 2005-2010 % Change	Future: 2010 Projection
Providence-New Bedford-Fall River, RI-MA	39300	4.8	1,582,997	4.2	1,650,151	3.8	1,713,420
Bristol, MA	25005	5.6	534,678	3.4	553,046	3.1	569,949
Bristol	44001	3.7	50,648	5.7	53,538	5.2	56,344
Kent	44003	3.7	167,090	4.2	174,124	3.8	180,732
Newport	44005	-2.0	85,433	0.1	85,506	-0.2	85,365
Providence	44007	4.2	621,602	5.1	653,201	4.7	683,578
Washington	44009	12.3	123,546	5.8	130,736	5.1	137,452
Total: Metro Portion of State		4.5	1,048,319	4.7	1,097,105	4.2	1,143,471
Total: Rhode Island		4.5	1,048,319	4.7	1,097,105	4.2	1,143,471

South Carolina

CBSA	FIPS Code	Past: 1990-2000 % Change	Past: 2000 Census	Present: 2000-2005 % Change	Present: 7/1/05 Estimate	Future: 2005-2010 % Change	Future: 2010 Projection
Anderson SC	11340	14.1	165,740	5.9	175,558	5.2	184,764
Anderson	45007	14.1	165,740	5.9	175,558	5.2	184,764
Charleston-North Charleston SC	16700	8.3	549,033	6.9	586,872	6.2	623,170
Berkeley	45015	10.8	142,651	5.2	150,053	4.6	157,004
Charleston	45019	5.1	309,969	5.7	327,786	5.2	344,833
Dorchester	45035	16.1	96,413	13.1	109,033	11.3	121,333
Columbia SC	17900	18.0	647,158	6.2	687,420	5.6	725,751
Calhoun	45017	19.1	15,185	1.4	15,398	1.0	15,555
Fairfield	45039	5.2	23,454	2.5	24,030	2.0	24,511
Kershaw	45055	20.8	52,647	6.1	55,859	5.4	58,861
Lexington	45063	28.9	216,014	8.3	233,853	7.2	250,806
Richland	45079	12.2	320,677	5.8	339,314	5.3	357,271
Saluda	45081	17.3	19,181	-1.1	18,966	-1.2	18,747
Florence SC	22500	9.6	193,155	2.8	198,594	2.7	203,862
Darlington	45031	9.0	67,394	1.1	68,159	1.0	68,817
Florence	45041	10.0	125,761	3.7	130,435	3.5	135,045
Greenville SC	24860	18.6	559,940	5.1	588,729	4.6	615,786
Greenville	45045	18.6	379,616	6.7	405,039	5.9	428,939
Laurens	45059	19.8	69,567	1.7	70,753	1.5	71,828
Pickens	45077	18.0	110,757	2.0	112,937	1.8	115,019
Myrtle Beach-Conway-North Myrtle Beach SC	34820	36.5	196,629	11.8	219,791	9.9	241,524
Horry	45051	36.5	196,629	11.8	219,791	9.9	241,524
Spartanburg SC	43900	11.9	253,791	4.0	264,032	3.6	273,598
Spartanburg	45083	11.9	253,791	4.0	264,032	3.6	273,598
Sumter SC	44940	2.0	104,646	1.8	106,517	1.7	108,314
Sumter	45085	2.0	104,646	1.8	106,517	1.7	108,314
* **Aiken**	45003	17.9	142,552	5.0	149,719	4.6	156,610
* **Edgefield**	45037	33.9	24,595	1.3	24,910	1.3	25,242
(See Augusta-Richmond County, GA-SC.)							
* **York**	45091	25.2	164,614	13.5	186,816	11.3	207,907
(See Charlotte-Gastonia-Concord, NC-SC.)							
Total: Metro Portion of State		15.8	3,001,853	6.2	3,188,958	5.6	3,366,528
Total: Micro Portion of State		15.0	733,229	4.5	766,543	4.1	797,850
Total: South Carolina		15.1	4,012,012	5.5	4,230,879	4.9	4,438,211

South Dakota

CBSA	FIPS Code	Past: 1990-2000 % Change	Past: 2000 Census	Present: 2000-2005 % Change	Present: 7/1/05 Estimate	Future: 2005-2010 % Change	Future: 2010 Projection
Rapid City SD	39660	9.3	112,818	4.7	118,072	4.2	122,982
Meade	46093	10.9	24,253	2.0	24,726	1.8	25,182
Pennington	46103	8.9	88,565	5.4	93,346	4.8	97,800
Sioux Falls SD	43620	21.9	187,093	10.0	205,714	8.3	222,865
Lincoln	46083	56.4	24,131	34.1	32,370	24.0	40,135
McCook	46087	2.5	5,832	0.4	5,854	-0.1	5,850
Minnehaha	46099	19.8	148,281	7.2	158,995	6.1	168,745
Turner	46125	3.2	8,849	-4.0	8,495	-4.2	8,135
* **Union**	46127	23.5	12,584	7.0	13,465	6.3	14,317
(See Sioux City, IA-NE-SD.)							
Total: Metro Portion of State		17.1	312,495	7.9	337,251	6.8	360,164
Total: Micro Portion of State		6.3	214,631	-0.9	212,729	-0.9	210,894
Total: South Dakota		8.5	754,844	2.1	770,755	1.9	785,776

* Indicates county is included from metro in different state.
Source: Devonshire Associates Ltd. and Scan/US, Inc. 2005.

Core Based Statistical Areas and Their Component Counties: Population Trends, *Continued*

CBSA	FIPS Code	Past 1990-2000 % Change	Past 2000 Census	Present 2000-2005 % Change	Present 7/1/05 Estimate	Future 2005-2010 % Change	Future 2010 Projection
Tennessee							
Chattanooga, TN-GA	16860	10.0	476,531	3.3	492,047	3.0	506,810
Catoosa, GA	13047	25.5	53,282	15.1	61,327	12.5	68,977
Dade, GA	13083	15.3	15,154	8.0	16,361	7.0	17,514
Walker, GA	13295	4.7	61,053	4.4	63,750	4.1	66,335
Hamilton	47065	7.8	307,896	0.8	310,232	0.7	312,422
Marion	47115	11.7	27,776	0.5	27,902	0.4	28,024
Sequatchie	47153	28.3	11,370	9.7	12,475	8.5	13,538
Clarksville, TN-KY	17300	22.6	232,000	2.9	238,672	2.6	244,792
Christian, KY	21047	4.8	72,265	-2.8	70,255	-2.8	68,296
Trigg, KY	21221	21.6	12,597	3.4	13,027	2.9	13,410
Montgomery	47125	34.1	134,768	5.6	142,262	4.9	149,279
Stewart	47161	30.5	12,370	6.1	13,128	5.2	13,807
Cleveland TN	17420	19.1	104,015	3.5	107,706	3.2	111,131
Bradley	47011	19.3	87,965	4.0	91,502	3.6	94,827
Polk	47139	17.6	16,050	1.0	16,204	0.6	16,304
Jackson TN	27180	18.3	107,377	3.1	110,724	2.9	113,912
Chester	47023	21.2	15,540	0.7	15,642	0.8	15,774
Madison	47113	17.8	91,837	3.5	95,082	3.2	98,138
Johnson City TN	27740	13.2	181,607	3.8	188,570	3.5	195,158
Carter	47019	10.2	56,742	3.9	58,964	3.6	61,077
Unicoi	47171	6.8	17,667	0.7	17,796	0.8	17,936
Washington	47179	16.1	107,198	4.3	111,810	3.9	116,145
Kingsport-Bristol-Bristol, TN-VA	28700	8.3	298,484	0.9	301,058	0.8	303,596
Hawkins	47073	20.2	53,563	5.1	56,299	4.6	58,887
Sullivan	47163	6.6	153,048	0.0	153,049	0.1	153,145
Bristol, VA (Ind. City)	51520	-5.7	17,367	-0.8	17,230	-0.5	17,149
Scott, VA	51169	0.9	23,403	-2.8	22,744	-2.7	22,125
Washington, VA	51191	11.4	51,103	1.2	51,736	1.1	52,290
Knoxville TN	28940	15.2	616,079	5.6	650,649	5.1	683,842
Anderson	47001	4.5	71,330	1.6	72,469	1.6	73,642
Blount	47009	23.1	105,823	8.8	115,094	7.7	123,944
Knox	47093	13.8	382,032	4.8	400,313	4.4	417,807
Loudon	47105	25.1	39,086	10.7	43,287	9.4	47,348
Union	47173	30.0	17,808	9.4	19,486	8.3	21,101
Memphis, TN-MS-AR	32820	12.9	1,205,204	4.7	1,261,492	4.2	1,314,425
Crittenden, AR	05035	1.9	50,866	0.8	51,287	0.5	51,532
DeSoto, MS	28033	57.9	107,199	25.9	135,003	19.5	161,295
Marshall, MS	28093	15.3	34,993	2.7	35,935	2.3	36,774
Tate, MS	28137	18.4	25,370	3.1	26,167	2.7	26,869
Tunica, MS	28143	13.0	9,227	13.3	10,455	11.6	11,672
Fayette	47047	12.7	28,806	19.7	34,492	15.6	39,865
Shelby	47157	8.6	897,472	1.6	912,260	1.5	926,191
Tipton	47167	36.5	51,271	9.0	55,893	7.8	60,227
Morristown TN	34100	22.4	123,081	5.7	130,096	5.0	136,646
Grainger	47057	20.8	20,659	7.0	22,098	6.2	23,477
Hamblen	47063	15.2	58,128	2.1	59,329	1.8	60,415
Jefferson	47089	34.2	44,294	9.9	48,669	8.4	52,754
Nashville-Davidson—Murfreesboro TN	34980	25.1	1,311,789	7.5	1,409,811	6.6	1,502,338
Cannon	47015	22.5	12,826	4.7	13,427	3.8	13,940
Cheatham	47021	32.3	35,912	6.2	38,152	5.3	40,188
Davidson	47037	11.6	569,891	0.2	570,911	0.2	571,793
Dickson	47043	23.1	43,156	6.8	46,096	6.0	48,853
Hickman	47081	33.1	22,295	7.1	23,877	6.0	25,313
Macon	47111	28.2	20,386	5.2	21,439	4.6	22,425
Robertson	47147	31.2	54,433	11.3	60,561	9.4	66,265
Rutherford	47149	53.5	182,023	18.0	214,830	14.6	246,213
Smith	47159	25.2	17,712	5.4	18,675	4.6	19,533
Sumner	47165	26.3	130,449	10.3	143,900	8.9	156,643
Trousdale	47169	22.6	7,259	4.2	7,565	3.2	7,806
Williamson	47187	56.3	126,638	18.9	150,607	14.9	173,113
Wilson	47189	31.2	88,809	12.3	99,771	10.5	110,253
Total: Metro Portion of State		16.8	4,122,288	4.7	4,315,548	4.2	4,498,412
Total: Micro Portion of State		16.6	957,407	4.3	998,409	3.8	1,036,823
Total: Tennessee		16.7	5,689,283	4.4	5,937,857	4.0	6,172,676
Texas							
Abilene TX	10180	8.3	160,245	-2.2	156,762	-2.0	153,556
Callahan	48059	8.8	12,905	2.2	13,188	2.0	13,454
Jones	48253	26.0	20,785	-4.7	19,799	-4.5	18,916
Taylor	48441	5.8	126,555	-2.2	123,775	-2.1	121,186
Amarillo TX	11100	15.5	226,522	4.7	237,137	4.2	247,208
Armstrong	48011	6.3	2,148	-5.0	2,041	-5.7	1,924
Carson	48065	-0.9	6,516	0.4	6,540	0.5	6,572
Potter	48375	16.0	113,546	5.4	119,630	4.9	125,515
Randall	48381	16.3	104,312	4.4	108,926	3.9	113,197
Austin-Round Rock TX	12420	47.7	1,249,763	16.3	1,453,856	13.0	1,642,751
Bastrop	48021	50.9	57,733	25.4	72,404	19.4	86,450
Caldwell	48055	22.0	32,194	16.6	37,547	13.5	42,608
Hays	48209	48.7	97,589	29.4	126,250	21.5	153,406
Travis	48453	40.9	812,280	8.6	882,137	7.1	944,453
Williamson	48491	79.1	249,967	34.2	335,518	23.9	415,834
Beaumont-Port Arthur TX	13140	6.6	385,090	-1.1	380,783	-1.0	376,981
Hardin	48199	16.3	48,073	5.0	50,484	4.6	52,821
Jefferson	48245	5.3	252,051	-2.3	246,195	-2.1	240,914
Orange	48361	5.5	84,966	-1.0	84,104	-1.0	83,246
Brownsville-Harlingen TX	15180	28.9	335,227	13.4	379,998	11.3	423,084
Cameron	48061	28.9	335,227	13.4	379,998	11.3	423,084
College Station-Bryan TX	17780	22.4	184,885	2.6	189,774	2.5	194,431
Brazos	48041	25.1	152,415	2.8	156,700	2.7	160,854
Burleson	48051	20.9	16,470	4.3	17,184	3.7	17,818
Robertson	48395	3.2	16,000	-0.7	15,890	-0.8	15,759
Corpus Christi TX	18580	9.7	403,280	1.2	408,295	1.4	413,914
Aransas	48007	25.7	22,497	8.2	24,347	7.4	26,154
Nueces	48355	7.7	313,645	0.8	316,026	0.8	318,647
San Patricio	48409	14.3	67,138	1.2	67,922	1.8	69,113
Dallas-Fort Worth-Arlington TX	19100	29.4	5,161,544	13.2	5,844,700	11.1	6,491,724
Collin	48085	86.2	491,675	34.4	660,783	24.3	821,038
Dallas	48113	19.8	2,218,899	4.5	2,319,427	4.1	2,413,468
Delta	48119	9.7	5,327	1.7	5,417	1.4	5,493
Denton	48121	58.3	432,976	29.0	558,392	21.4	677,656
Ellis	48139	30.8	111,360	19.2	132,726	15.2	152,908
Hunt	48231	19.0	76,596	7.7	82,483	6.7	87,979
Johnson	48251	30.5	126,811	16.0	147,080	12.9	166,061
Kaufman	48257	36.6	71,313	24.4	88,739	18.6	105,279
Parker	48367	36.6	88,495	16.6	103,201	13.5	117,084
Rockwall	48397	68.3	43,080	43.6	61,874	29.0	79,836
Tarrant	48439	23.6	1,446,219	12.5	1,626,962	10.6	1,799,145
Wise	48497	40.7	48,793	18.1	57,616	14.2	65,777
El Paso TX	21340	14.9	679,622	6.0	720,147	5.4	758,748
El Paso	48141	14.9	679,622	6.0	720,147	5.4	758,748
Houston-Sugar Land-Baytown TX	26420	25.2	4,715,407	12.3	5,293,972	10.4	5,845,518
Austin	48015	18.9	23,590	10.8	26,140	9.0	28,504
Brazoria	48039	26.1	241,767	14.5	276,715	12.1	310,079
Chambers	48071	29.6	26,031	9.2	28,434	7.9	30,689
Fort Bend	48157	57.2	354,452	29.7	459,581	21.8	559,909
Galveston	48167	15.1	250,158	10.8	277,119	9.5	303,434
Harris	48201	20.7	3,400,578	9.2	3,713,507	8.0	4,011,640
Liberty	48291	33.1	70,154	8.9	76,373	7.5	82,084
Montgomery	48339	61.2	293,768	27.8	375,519	20.7	453,313
San Jacinto	48407	35.9	22,246	11.8	24,863	9.7	27,275
Waller	48473	39.6	32,663	9.4	35,721	8.0	38,591
Killeen-Temple-Fort Hood TX	28660	23.0	330,714	6.2	351,367	5.5	370,854
Bell	48027	24.5	237,974	7.4	255,627	6.6	272,474
Coryell	48099	16.8	74,978	0.7	75,531	0.5	75,873
Lampasas	48281	31.4	17,762	13.8	20,209	11.4	22,507
Laredo TX	29700	44.9	193,117	16.2	224,381	13.2	254,024
Webb	48479	44.9	193,117	16.2	224,381	13.2	254,024
Longview TX	30980	7.8	194,042	3.9	201,588	3.7	209,125
Gregg	48183	6.1	111,379	4.0	115,857	3.9	120,411
Rusk	48401	8.3	47,372	0.7	47,694	0.7	48,029
Upshur	48459	12.5	35,291	7.8	38,037	7.0	40,685
Lubbock TX	31180	8.6	249,700	4.8	261,585	4.5	273,266
Crosby	48107	-3.2	7,072	-7.3	6,558	-7.1	6,094
Lubbock	48303	9.0	242,628	5.1	255,027	4.8	267,172
McAllen-Edinburg-Mission TX	32580	48.5	569,463	18.6	675,597	15.0	776,946
Hidalgo	48215	48.5	569,463	18.6	675,597	15.0	776,946
Midland TX	33260	8.8	116,009	4.2	120,852	4.4	126,160
Midland	48329	8.8	116,009	4.2	120,852	4.4	126,160
Odessa TX	36220	1.8	121,123	2.6	124,311	2.9	127,900
Ector	48135	1.8	121,123	2.6	124,311	2.9	127,900
San Angelo TX	41660	5.7	105,781	-0.4	105,375	-0.4	105,002
Irion	48235	8.7	1,771	-1.2	1,750	-1.4	1,725
Tom Green	48451	5.6	104,010	-0.4	103,625	-0.3	103,277
San Antonio TX	41700	21.6	1,711,703	9.8	1,879,915	8.5	2,040,162
Atascosa	48013	26.5	38,628	12.7	43,553	10.6	48,183
Bandera	48019	67.1	17,645	15.8	20,429	12.7	23,022
Bexar	48029	17.5	1,392,931	8.6	1,512,995	7.6	1,628,001
Comal	48091	50.5	78,021	20.0	93,631	15.8	108,430
Guadalupe	48187	37.2	89,023	14.0	101,471	11.4	113,047
Kendall	48259	62.7	23,743	17.6	27,913	14.1	31,848
Medina	48325	43.9	39,304	9.1	42,885	7.9	46,285
Wilson	48493	43.1	32,408	14.3	37,038	11.6	41,346

CBSA	FIPS Code	Past 1990-2000 % Change	Past 2000 Census	Present 2000-2005 % Change	Present 7/1/05 Estimate	Future 2005-2010 % Change	Future 2010 Projection
Sherman-Denison TX	43300	16.4	110,595	6.2	117,502	5.5	123,951
Grayson	48181	16.4	110,595	6.2	117,502	5.5	123,951
Texarkana, TX-Texarkana, AR	45500	8.0	129,749	2.4	132,846	2.3	135,906
Miller, AR	05091	5.1	40,443	6.3	42,971	5.8	45,456
Bowie	48037	9.4	89,306	0.6	89,875	0.6	90,450
Tyler TX	46340	15.5	174,706	8.3	189,133	7.2	202,798
Smith	48423	15.5	174,706	8.3	189,133	7.2	202,798
Victoria TX	47020	12.3	111,663	1.8	113,679	1.8	115,713
Calhoun	48057	8.4	20,647	-1.9	20,251	-1.9	19,857
Goliad	48175	15.9	6,928	4.8	7,260	4.0	7,548
Victoria	48469	13.1	84,088	2.5	86,168	2.5	88,308
Waco TX	47380	12.9	213,517	4.4	222,879	4.0	231,707
McLennan	48309	12.9	213,517	4.4	222,879	4.0	231,707
Wichita Falls TX	48660	7.9	151,524	-3.2	146,648	-3.1	142,117
Archer	48009	11.0	8,854	4.6	9,260	3.2	9,553
Clay	48077	9.8	11,006	4.0	11,441	2.9	11,770
Wichita	48485	7.6	131,664	-4.3	125,947	-4.1	120,794
Total: Metro Portion of State		24.9	17,944,548	10.8	19,890,111	9.3	21,738,090
Total: Micro Portion of State		12.0	1,520,819	2.8	1,563,476	2.7	1,605,358
Total: Texas		22.8	20,851,820	9.7	22,865,855	8.4	24,782,576
Utah							
Logan, UT-ID	30860	29.3	102,720	7.8	110,700	6.9	118,342
Franklin, ID	16041	22.7	11,329	8.2	12,259	7.3	13,151
Cache	49005	30.2	91,391	7.7	98,441	6.9	105,191
Ogden-Clearfield UT	36260	25.8	442,656	14.0	504,508	11.7	563,598
Davis	49011	27.2	238,994	20.3	287,557	16.2	334,268
Morgan	49029	29.0	7,129	6.9	7,623	6.1	8,085
Weber	49057	24.1	196,533	6.5	209,328	5.7	221,245
Provo-Orem UT	39340	39.9	376,774	11.1	418,644	9.4	458,173
Juab	49023	41.6	8,238	9.5	9,022	8.2	9,758
Utah	49049	39.8	368,536	11.1	409,622	9.5	448,415
Salt Lake City UT	41620	26.1	968,858	4.9	1,016,096	4.4	1,060,313
Salt Lake	49035	23.8	898,387	3.5	930,006	3.2	959,978
Summit	49043	91.6	29,736	15.3	34,273	12.4	38,516
Tooele	49045	53.1	40,735	27.2	51,817	19.3	61,819
St. George UT	41100	86.1	90,354	24.0	112,063	18.4	132,633
Washington	49053	86.1	90,354	24.0	112,063	18.4	132,633
Total: Metro Portion of State		30.6	1,970,033	9.1	2,149,752	7.9	2,319,908
Total: Micro Portion of State		25.1	137,385	6.6	146,499	5.9	155,159
Total: Utah		29.6	2,233,169	8.5	2,422,623	7.4	2,602,113
Vermont							
Burlington-South Burlington VT	15540	12.3	198,889	3.6	206,121	3.2	212,728
Chittenden	50007	11.2	146,571	2.4	150,099	2.1	153,222
Franklin	50011	13.6	45,417	6.0	48,164	5.3	50,729
Grand Isle	50013	29.8	6,901	13.9	7,858	11.7	8,777
Total: Metro Portion of State		12.3	198,889	3.6	206,121	3.2	212,728
Total: Micro Portion of State		4.6	250,536	1.8	255,003	1.7	259,248
Total: Vermont		8.2	608,827	2.8	625,611	2.5	641,281
Virginia							
Blacksburg-Christiansburg-Radford VA	13980	7.5	151,272	-0.7	150,162	-0.8	149,007
Giles	51071	1.8	16,657	2.6	17,084	2.2	17,460
Montgomery	51121	13.1	83,629	0.2	83,778	0.0	83,817
Pulaski	51155	1.8	35,127	-0.7	34,887	-0.8	34,619
Radford (Ind. City)	51750	-0.5	15,859	-9.1	14,413	-9.0	13,111
Charlottesville VA	16820	20.9	174,021	5.2	183,141	4.7	191,761
Albemarle	51003	16.5	79,236	12.7	89,294	5.2	93,894
Charlottesville (Ind. City)	51540	11.7	45,049	-19.2	36,403	-9.1	33,104
Fluvanna	51065	61.3	20,047	23.3	24,716	18.0	29,167
Greene	51079	48.0	15,244	15.4	17,587	12.6	19,797
Nelson	51125	13.0	14,445	4.8	15,141	4.3	15,799
Danville VA	19260	1.3	110,156	-2.2	107,753	-2.0	105,549
Danville (Ind. City)	51590	-8.8	48,411	-4.8	46,092	-4.5	44,017
Pittsylvania	51143	10.9	61,745	-0.1	61,661	-0.2	61,532
Harrisonburg VA	25500	22.7	108,193	3.3	111,801	3.1	115,317
Harrisonburg (Ind. City)	51660	31.8	40,468	2.0	41,264	2.0	42,095
Rockingham	51165	17.8	67,725	4.2	70,537	3.8	73,222
Lynchburg VA	31340	10.9	228,616	1.6	232,242	1.4	235,437
Amherst	51009	11.6	31,894	0.3	31,991	0.2	32,065
Appomattox	51011	11.4	13,705	0.4	13,764	0.4	13,819
Bedford	51019	32.2	60,371	6.1	64,051	5.3	67,444
Bedford (Ind. City)	51515	3.7	6,299	-1.5	6,206	-1.7	6,103
Campbell	51031	7.4	51,078	1.1	51,615	0.9	52,085
Lynchburg (Ind. City)	51680	-1.2	65,269	-1.0	64,615	-1.1	63,921
Richmond VA	40060	15.6	1,096,957	5.8	1,160,991	5.2	1,221,442
Amelia	51007	29.7	11,400	4.4	11,902	3.5	12,321
Caroline	51033	15.1	22,121	7.6	23,809	7.0	25,469
Charles City	51036	10.3	6,926	4.9	7,266	4.6	7,600
Chesterfield	51041	24.2	259,903	10.3	286,764	8.9	312,369
Colonial Heights (Ind. City)	51570	5.2	16,897	3.1	17,418	2.9	17,922
Cumberland	51049	15.2	9,017	2.4	9,230	2.4	9,454
Dinwiddie	51053	17.0	24,533	2.3	25,086	2.0	25,576
Goochland	51075	19.1	16,863	12.3	18,934	10.4	20,902
Hanover	51085	36.4	86,320	14.1	98,498	11.6	109,899
Henrico	51087	20.4	262,300	5.1	275,628	4.4	287,842
Hopewell (Ind. City)	51670	-3.2	22,354	0.2	22,404	0.5	22,509
King William	51101	20.5	13,146	11.7	14,688	10.0	16,160
King and Queen	51097	5.4	6,630	-1.3	6,541	-1.2	6,463
Louisa	51109	26.1	25,627	15.2	29,516	12.7	33,258
New Kent	51127	28.9	13,462	17.4	15,806	14.3	18,065
Petersburg (Ind. City)	51730	-12.1	33,740	-3.0	32,717	-2.6	31,864
Powhatan	51145	46.0	22,377	18.6	26,540	14.6	30,413
Prince George	51149	20.6	33,047	5.6	34,896	4.6	36,515
Richmond (Ind. City)	51760	-2.6	197,790	-3.1	191,700	-3.0	186,003
Sussex	51183	22.0	12,504	-6.8	11,648	-7.0	10,838
Roanoke VA	40220	7.4	288,309	0.9	290,770	0.8	293,152
Botetourt	51023	22.0	30,496	4.9	31,989	4.4	33,392
Craig	51045	16.4	5,091	0.6	5,124	0.4	5,147
Franklin	51067	19.6	47,286	6.0	50,120	5.2	52,751
Roanoke	51161	8.1	85,778	2.8	88,219	2.7	90,636
Roanoke (Ind. City)	51770	-1.5	94,911	-4.1	91,029	-3.9	87,440
Salem (Ind. City)	51775	4.2	24,747	-1.9	24,289	-2.1	23,786
Virginia Beach-Norfolk-Newport News, VA-NC	47260	8.8	1,576,370	5.2	1,657,806	4.7	1,735,996
Currituck, NC	37053	32.4	18,190	23.6	22,484	18.4	26,629
Chesapeake (Ind. City)	51550	31.1	199,184	8.4	215,873	7.1	231,265
Gloucester	51073	15.4	34,780	8.7	37,812	7.7	40,725
Hampton (Ind. City)	51650	9.5	146,437	-1.2	144,708	-1.2	142,906
Isle of Wight	51093	18.7	29,728	11.7	33,202	9.9	36,500
James City	51095	38.0	48,102	17.1	56,330	13.9	64,132
Mathews	51115	10.3	9,207	0.8	9,283	0.9	9,363
Newport News (Ind. City)	51700	5.9	180,150	1.3	182,551	1.9	186,096
Norfolk (Ind. City)	51710	-10.3	234,403	1.6	238,106	1.5	241,716
Poquoson (Ind. City)	51735	5.1	11,566	2.3	11,837	2.1	12,087
Portsmouth (Ind. City)	51740	-3.2	100,565	-2.5	98,061	-2.4	95,703
Suffolk (Ind. City)	51800	22.1	63,677	24.6	79,362	19.0	94,429
Surry	51181	11.1	6,829	3.4	7,064	3.1	7,283
Virginia Beach (Ind. City)	51810	8.2	425,257	5.3	447,757	4.7	468,941
Williamsburg (Ind. City)	51830	4.1	11,998	-7.9	11,046	-7.9	10,177
York	51199	32.7	56,297	10.7	62,330	9.2	68,044
Winchester, VA-WV	49020	22.4	102,997	11.4	114,788	9.7	125,934
Frederick	51069	29.5	59,209	15.1	68,153	12.5	76,670
Winchester (Ind. City)	51840	7.5	23,585	4.9	24,730	4.3	25,790
Hampshire, WV	54027	22.5	20,203	8.4	21,905	7.2	23,474
*** Alexandria City**	51510	15.4	128,283	-0.1	128,132	-0.8	127,123
*** Arlington County**	51013	10.8	189,453	-1.9	185,858	-1.8	182,475
*** Clarke County**	51043	4.6	12,652	9.8	13,896	8.5	15,075
*** Fairfax County**	51059	18.5	969,749	4.8	1,016,742	4.2	1,059,612
*** Fairfax City**	51600	9.6	21,498	3.3	22,200	2.8	22,824
*** Falls Church City**	51610	8.3	10,377	3.3	10,716	2.9	11,022
*** Fauquier County**	51061	13.1	55,139	17.6	64,828	14.2	74,034
*** Fredericksburg City**	51630	1.3	19,279	7.7	20,769	6.8	22,189
*** Loudoun County**	51107	96.9	169,599	48.6	252,089	30.9	329,892
*** Manassas City**	51683	25.7	35,135	8.4	38,088	7.0	40,756
*** Manassas Park City**	51685	52.8	10,290	11.1	11,429	9.5	12,518
*** Prince William County**	51153	30.2	280,813	25.5	352,321	19.4	420,534
*** Spotsylvania County**	51177	57.5	90,395	30.7	118,182	22.4	144,675
*** Stafford County**	51179	51.0	92,446	30.9	121,019	22.6	148,329
*** Warren County**	51187	20.8	31,584	11.1	35,096	9.6	38,451
(See Washington-Arlington-Alexandria, DC-VA-MD-WV.)							
*** Bristol City**	51520	-5.7	17,367	-0.8	17,230	-0.5	17,149
*** Scott County**	51169	0.9	23,403	-2.8	22,744	-2.7	22,125
*** Washington County**	51191	11.4	51,103	1.2	51,736	1.1	52,290
(See Kingsport-Bristol-Bristol, TN-VA.)							
Total: Metro Portion of State		15.8	6,007,063	7.3	6,448,140	6.5	6,864,565
Total: Micro Portion of State		6.8	261,194	3.7	270,777	3.4	279,987
Total: Virginia		14.4	7,078,515	6.5	7,538,791	5.8	7,973,549

* Indicates county is included from metro in different state.
Source: Devonshire Associates Ltd. and Scan/US, Inc. 2005.

Continued on next page

Core Based Statistical Areas and Their Component Counties: Population Trends, *Continued*

CBSA	FIPS Code	Past 1990-2000 % Change	Past 2000 Census	Present 2000-2005 % Change	Present 7/1/05 Estimate	Future 2005-2010 % Change	Future 2010 Projection
Washington							
Bellingham WA	13380	30.5	166,814	9.4	182,534	8.2	197,436
Whatcom	53073	30.5	166,814	9.4	182,534	8.2	197,436
Bremerton-Silverdale WA	14740	22.3	231,969	4.0	241,196	3.7	250,057
Kitsap	53035	22.3	231,969	4.0	241,196	3.7	250,057
Kennewick-Richland-Pasco WA	28420	27.9	191,822	15.7	221,935	13.2	251,185
Benton	53005	26.6	142,475	13.1	161,100	11.2	179,077
Franklin	53021	31.7	49,347	23.3	60,835	18.5	72,108
Longview WA	31020	13.2	92,948	3.9	96,590	3.7	100,131
Cowlitz	53015	13.2	92,948	3.9	96,590	3.7	100,131
Mount Vernon-Anacortes WA	34580	29.4	102,979	9.9	113,129	8.5	122,771
Skagit	53057	29.4	102,979	9.9	113,129	8.5	122,771
Olympia WA	36500	28.6	207,355	10.7	229,500	9.2	250,695
Thurston	53067	28.6	207,355	10.7	229,500	9.2	250,695
Seattle-Tacoma-Bellevue WA	42660	18.9	3,043,878	5.2	3,202,012	4.7	3,351,850
King	53033	15.2	1,737,034	2.3	1,776,888	2.1	1,814,815
Pierce	53053	19.6	700,820	9.3	765,698	8.1	827,363
Snohomish	53061	30.1	606,024	8.8	659,426	7.6	709,672
Spokane WA	44060	15.7	417,939	5.1	439,273	4.7	459,829
Spokane	53063	15.7	417,939	5.1	439,273	4.7	459,829
Wenatchee WA	48300	26.5	99,219	4.2	103,338	3.8	107,267
Chelan	53007	27.5	66,616	3.3	68,844	3.1	70,945
Douglas	53017	24.4	32,603	5.8	34,494	5.3	36,322
Yakima WA	49420	17.9	222,581	3.1	229,468	2.9	236,174
Yakima	53077	17.9	222,581	3.1	229,468	2.9	236,174
* Asotin	53003	16.7	20,551	0.2	20,584	0.1	20,602
(See Lewiston, ID-WA.)							
* Clark	53011	45.0	345,238	16.2	401,099	13.4	454,676
* Skamania	53059	19.1	9,872	6.6	10,526	5.9	11,151
(See Portland-Vancouver-Beaverton, OR-WA.)							
Total: Metro Portion of State		21.5	5,153,165	6.6	5,491,184	5.9	5,813,824
Total: Micro Portion of State		17.4	525,262	6.9	561,470	6.3	596,898
Total: Washington		21.1	5,894,121	6.5	6,275,159	5.8	6,639,135
West Virginia							
Charleston WV	16620	0.6	309,635	-1.2	305,915	-1.1	302,414
Boone	54005	-1.3	25,535	1.4	25,896	1.4	26,263
Clay	54015	3.5	10,330	-0.1	10,320	-0.3	10,291
Kanawha	54039	-3.6	200,073	-3.4	193,206	-3.3	186,813
Lincoln	54043	3.4	22,108	2.3	22,614	2.1	23,080
Putnam	54079	20.4	51,589	4.4	53,879	3.9	55,967
Huntington-Ashland, WV-KY-OH	26580	0.2	288,649	-1.0	285,791	-0.9	283,200
Boyd, KY	21019	-2.7	49,752	0.3	49,908	0.5	50,148
Greenup, KY	21089	0.4	36,891	0.8	37,186	0.9	37,530
Lawrence, OH	39087	0.8	62,319	0.4	62,567	0.4	62,824
Cabell	54011	-0.0	96,784	-2.9	93,961	-2.8	91,287
Wayne	54099	3.0	42,903	-1.7	42,169	-1.8	41,411
Morgantown WV	34060	6.4	111,200	3.0	114,517	2.8	117,764
Monongalia	54061	8.4	81,866	3.2	84,446	3.0	86,951
Preston	54077	1.0	29,334	2.5	30,071	2.5	30,813
Parkersburg-Marietta-Vienna, WV-OH	37620	1.7	164,624	-1.4	162,350	-1.3	160,169
Washington, OH	39167	1.6	63,251	-1.7	62,162	-1.7	61,134
Pleasants	54073	-0.4	7,514	-2.2	7,347	-2.2	7,184
Wirt	54105	13.1	5,873	-2.1	5,752	-2.2	5,623
Wood	54107	1.2	87,986	-1.0	87,089	-1.0	86,228
Weirton-Steubenville, WV-OH	48260	-7.4	132,008	-4.2	126,448	-4.0	121,361
Jefferson, OH	39081	-8.0	73,894	-4.6	70,461	-4.4	67,356
Brooke	54009	-5.7	25,447	-2.9	24,717	-2.7	24,058
Hancock	54029	-7.3	32,667	-4.3	31,270	-4.2	29,947
Wheeling, WV-OH	48540	-3.8	153,172	-3.2	148,237	-3.0	143,718
Belmont, OH	39013	-1.2	70,226	-1.7	69,040	-1.6	67,943
Marshall	54051	-4.9	35,519	-2.7	34,564	-2.4	33,723
Ohio	54069	-6.8	47,427	-5.9	44,633	-5.8	42,052
* Jefferson	54037	17.4	42,190	16.3	49,069	13.4	55,649
(See Washington-Arlington-Alexandria, DC-VA-MD-WV.)							
* Mineral	54057	1.4	27,078	0.5	27,200	0.5	27,338
(See Cumberland, MD-WV.)							

MSA	FIPS Code	Past 1990-2000 % Change	Past 2000 Census	Present 2000-2005 % Change	Present 7/1/05 Estimate	Future 2005-2010 % Change	Future 2010 Projection
* Berkeley	54003	28.1	75,905	20.4	91,401	16.3	106,284
* Morgan	54065	23.2	14,943	6.7	15,940	5.7	16,851
(See Hagerstown-Martinsburg, MD-WV.)							
* Hampshire	54027	22.5	20,203	8.4	21,905	7.2	23,474
(See Winchester, VA-WV.)							
Total: Metro Portion of State		3.4	983,274	1.4	997,449	1.4	1,011,287
Total: Micro Portion of State		0.2	364,478	-0.6	362,349	-0.5	360,407
Total: West Virginia		0.8	1,808,344	0.3	1,813,363	0.3	1,819,289
Wisconsin							
Appleton WI	11540	15.3	201,602	7.4	216,505	6.4	230,433
Calumet	55015	18.5	40,631	10.8	45,019	9.5	49,298
Outagamie	55087	14.6	160,971	6.5	171,486	5.6	181,135
Eau Claire WI	20740	7.8	148,337	4.0	154,337	3.7	160,041
Chippewa	55017	5.4	55,195	8.1	59,690	7.3	64,022
Eau Claire	55035	9.3	93,142	1.6	94,647	1.4	96,019
Fond du Lac WI	22540	8.0	97,296	1.4	98,664	1.3	99,927
Fond du Lac	55039	8.0	97,296	1.4	98,664	1.3	99,927
Green Bay WI	24580	16.0	282,599	5.3	297,520	4.8	311,749
Brown	55009	16.5	226,778	5.3	238,847	4.8	250,395
Kewaunee	55061	6.9	20,187	2.5	20,693	2.4	21,182
Oconto	55083	17.9	35,634	6.6	37,980	5.8	40,172
Janesville WI	27500	9.2	152,307	2.7	156,477	2.5	160,406
Rock	55105	9.2	152,307	2.7	156,477	2.5	160,406
La Crosse, WI-MN	29100	9.0	126,838	2.0	129,409	1.8	131,800
Houston, MN	27055	6.6	19,718	1.4	19,996	1.2	20,236
La Crosse	55063	9.4	107,120	2.1	109,413	2.0	111,564
Madison WI	31540	16.1	501,774	8.0	541,809	7.0	579,794
Columbia	55021	16.4	52,468	4.9	55,054	4.4	57,480
Dane	55025	16.2	426,526	8.6	463,177	7.5	497,973
Iowa	55049	13.1	22,780	3.5	23,578	3.2	24,341
Milwaukee-Waukesha-West Allis WI	33340	4.8	1,500,741	1.4	1,521,473	1.3	1,540,762
Milwaukee	55079	-2.0	940,164	-1.3	927,823	-1.3	916,196
Ozaukee	55089	13.0	82,317	5.1	86,503	4.5	90,435
Washington	55131	23.3	117,493	6.7	125,320	5.8	132,639
Waukesha	55133	18.4	360,767	5.8	381,827	5.2	401,492
Oshkosh-Neenah WI	36780	11.7	156,763	1.9	159,732	1.7	162,430
Winnebago	55139	11.7	156,763	1.9	159,732	1.7	162,430
Racine WI	39540	7.9	188,831	3.3	194,975	3.1	200,939
Racine	55101	7.9	188,831	3.3	194,975	3.1	200,939
Sheboygan WI	43100	8.4	112,646	1.2	114,016	1.1	115,256
Sheboygan	55117	8.4	112,646	1.2	114,016	1.1	115,256
Wausau WI	48140	9.0	125,834	1.8	128,048	1.7	130,168
Marathon	55073	9.0	125,834	1.8	128,048	1.7	130,168
* Kenosha	55059	16.7	149,577	7.1	160,165	6.3	170,237
(See Chicago-Naperville-Joliet, IL-IN-WI.)							
* Douglas	55031	3.7	43,287	2.2	44,257	1.9	45,108
(See Duluth, MN-WI.)							
* Pierce	55093	12.3	36,804	4.8	38,572	4.3	40,236
* St. Croix	55109	25.7	63,155	21.0	76,388	16.6	89,094
(See Minneapolis-St. Paul-Bloomington, MN-WI.)							
Total: Metro Portion of State		9.4	3,868,873	3.7	4,012,351	3.4	4,148,144
Total: Micro Portion of State		9.9	735,741	2.3	752,662	2.1	768,355
Total: Wisconsin		9.6	5,363,675	3.3	5,543,126	3.0	5,711,860
Wyoming							
Casper WY	16220	8.7	66,533	4.2	69,348	4.0	72,107
Natrona	56025	8.7	66,533	4.2	69,348	4.0	72,107
Cheyenne WY	16940	11.6	81,607	5.5	86,122	5.1	90,483
Laramie	56021	11.6	81,607	5.5	86,122	5.1	90,483
Total: Metro Portion of State		10.2	148,140	4.9	155,470	4.6	162,590
Total: Micro Portion of State		9.5	203,682	2.5	208,716	2.3	213,532
Total: Wyoming		8.9	493,782	2.8	507,467	2.6	520,799
Total: Metro Portion of United States		14.0	232,579,940	6.1	246,669,544	5.4	260,022,244
Total: Micro Portion of United States		10.0	29,477,802	2.6	30,246,680	2.4	30,982,436
Total: United States		13.2	281,421,906	5.3	296,460,358	4.8	310,730,123

* Indicates county is included from metro in different state.
Source: Devonshire Associates Ltd. and Scan/US, Inc. 2005.

Metropolitan Core Based Statistical Areas: Population Trends

The following data are presented for metropolitan CBSAs (based on 2010 population projections): the CBSA FIPS Code; 1990-2000 percent of change in population; 2000 actual population; 2000-2005 estimated percent of change in population; 2005 estimated population; 2005-2010 projected percent of change in population; and 2010 projected population. CBSAs are ranked and listed in descending order according to their 2010 projected population figures. (A ranking of CBSAs according to their 2005 estimated population figures can be found on page 50.)

		Past		Present		Future		
CBSA	FIPS Code	1990-2000 % Change	2000 Census	2000-2005 % Change	7/1/05 Estimate	2005-2010 % Change	2010 Projection	2010 Rank
New York-Northern New Jersey-Long Island, NY-NJ-PA	35620	8.8	18,323,002	3.0	18,864,705	2.7	19,370,131	1
Los Angeles-Long Beach-Santa Ana, CA	31100	9.7	12,365,627	5.9	13,097,576	5.3	13,791,607	2
Chicago-Naperville-Joliet, IL-IN-WI	16980	11.2	9,098,316	4.1	9,471,425	3.7	9,822,462	3
Dallas-Fort Worth-Arlington, TX	19100	29.4	5,161,544	13.2	5,844,700	11.1	6,491,724	4
Philadelphia-Camden-Wilmington, PA-NJ-DE-MD	37980	4.6	5,687,147	2.5	5,831,625	2.4	5,970,563	5
Miami-Fort Lauderdale-Miami Beach, FL	33100	23.5	5,007,564	8.9	5,452,407	7.8	5,876,037	6
Houston-Sugar Land-Baytown, TX	26420	25.2	4,715,407	12.3	5,293,972	10.4	5,845,518	7
Washington-Arlington-Alexandria, DC-VA-MD-WV	47900	16.3	4,796,183	9.6	5,255,607	8.3	5,690,439	8
Atlanta-Sandy Springs-Marietta, GA	12060	38.4	4,247,981	13.2	4,809,992	11.0	5,337,353	9
Detroit-Warren-Livonia, MI	19820	4.8	4,452,557	1.1	4,501,430	1.0	4,545,000	10
Boston-Cambridge-Quincy, MA-NH	14460	6.2	4,391,344	1.5	4,457,319	1.3	4,513,599	11
Riverside-San Bernardino-Ontario, CA	40140	25.7	3,254,821	19.4	3,886,808	15.6	4,493,354	12
Phoenix-Mesa-Scottsdale, AZ	38060	45.3	3,251,876	16.9	3,801,803	13.8	4,325,342	13
San Francisco-Oakland-Fremont, CA	41860	11.9	4,123,740	1.1	4,167,248	0.8	4,200,633	14
Seattle-Tacoma-Bellevue, WA	42660	18.9	3,043,878	5.2	3,202,012	4.7	3,351,850	15
Minneapolis-St. Paul-Bloomington, MN-WI	33460	16.9	2,968,806	6.3	3,154,675	5.5	3,327,749	16
San Diego-Carlsbad-San Marcos, CA	41740	12.6	2,813,833	6.3	2,990,693	5.5	3,156,599	17
St. Louis, MO-IL	41180	4.6	2,698,687	2.6	2,769,054	2.4	2,836,847	18
Tampa-St. Petersburg-Clearwater, FL	45300	15.9	2,395,997	9.1	2,613,412	8.0	2,822,434	19
Baltimore-Towson, MD	12580	7.2	2,552,994	4.1	2,658,807	3.8	2,761,004	20
Denver-Aurora, CO	19740	30.7	2,179,240	8.8	2,371,414	7.5	2,549,134	21
Pittsburgh, PA	38300	-1.5	2,431,087	-1.3	2,400,344	-1.2	2,371,504	22
Sacramento—Arden-Arcade—Roseville, CA	40900	21.3	1,796,857	15.8	2,081,634	13.1	2,354,217	23
Portland-Vancouver-Beaverton, OR-WA	38900	26.5	1,927,881	9.5	2,110,156	8.2	2,284,221	24
Orlando-Kissimmee, FL	36740	34.3	1,644,561	15.6	1,900,560	12.8	2,144,445	25
Cleveland-Elyria-Mentor, OH	17460	2.2	2,148,143	-0.5	2,136,541	-0.5	2,125,752	26
Cincinnati-Middletown, OH-KY-IN	17140	8.9	2,009,632	3.0	2,069,601	2.7	2,125,426	27
Kansas City, MO-KS	28140	12.2	1,836,038	6.4	1,952,760	5.6	2,061,595	28
San Antonio, TX	41700	21.6	1,711,703	9.8	1,879,915	8.5	2,040,162	29
Las Vegas-Paradise, NV	29820	85.5	1,375,765	23.4	1,697,755	17.9	2,001,933	30
Columbus, OH	18140	14.8	1,612,694	6.6	1,719,360	5.8	1,818,975	31
Indianapolis, IN	26900	17.8	1,525,104	8.0	1,646,860	7.0	1,762,556	32
Virginia Beach-Norfolk-Newport News, VA-NC	47260	8.8	1,576,370	5.2	1,657,806	4.7	1,735,996	33
San Jose-Sunnyvale-Santa Clara, CA	41940	13.1	1,735,819	-0.5	1,727,639	-0.7	1,715,467	34
Providence-New Bedford-Fall River, RI-MA	39300	4.8	1,582,997	4.2	1,650,151	3.8	1,713,420	35
Charlotte-Gastonia-Concord, NC-SC	16740	29.8	1,330,448	13.2	1,505,429	11.0	1,670,939	36
Austin-Round Rock, TX	12420	47.7	1,249,763	16.3	1,453,856	13.0	1,642,751	37
Milwaukee-Waukesha-West Allis, WI	33340	4.8	1,500,741	1.4	1,521,473	1.3	1,540,762	38
Nashville-Davidson—Murfreesboro, TN	34980	25.1	1,311,789	7.5	1,409,811	6.6	1,502,338	39
Jacksonville, FL	27260	21.4	1,122,750	11.2	1,248,873	9.8	1,371,454	40
Memphis, TN-MS-AR	32820	12.9	1,205,204	4.7	1,261,492	4.2	1,314,425	41
New Orleans-Metairie-Kenner, LA	35380	4.1	1,316,510	-0.6	1,308,631	-0.5	1,302,512	42
Louisville, KY-IN	31140	10.0	1,161,975	3.9	1,207,123	3.5	1,248,983	43
Hartford-West Hartford-East Hartford, CT	25540	2.2	1,148,618	4.2	1,197,175	3.9	1,243,285	44
Richmond, VA	40060	15.6	1,096,957	5.8	1,160,991	5.2	1,221,442	45
Oklahoma City, OK	36420	12.8	1,095,421	5.5	1,155,595	4.9	1,212,482	46
Buffalo-Niagara Falls, NY	15380	-1.6	1,170,111	-1.3	1,154,526	-1.2	1,140,186	47
Birmingham-Hoover, AL	13820	10.0	1,052,238	3.2	1,086,137	3.0	1,118,703	48
Raleigh-Cary, NC	39580	47.3	797,071	17.8	939,136	14.4	1,074,178	49
Salt Lake City, UT	41620	26.1	968,858	4.9	1,016,096	4.4	1,060,313	50
Rochester, NY	40380	3.5	1,037,831	0.8	1,046,284	0.7	1,054,036	51
Tucson, AZ	46060	26.5	843,746	9.2	921,681	7.9	994,799	52
Fresno, CA	23420	19.8	799,407	10.3	881,918	9.0	961,546	53
Honolulu, HI	26180	4.8	876,156	3.9	910,475	3.9	945,789	54
Bridgeport-Stamford-Norwalk, CT	14860	6.6	882,567	3.0	909,263	2.7	933,729	55
Tulsa, OK	46140	12.9	859,532	3.9	892,708	3.5	923,510	56
New Haven-Milford, CT	35300	2.5	824,008	3.6	853,637	3.3	882,213	57
Albany-Schenectady-Troy, NY	10580	2.0	825,875	3.1	851,730	2.9	876,805	58
Oxnard-Thousand Oaks-Ventura, CA	37100	12.6	753,197	8.0	813,570	7.0	870,395	59
Albuquerque, NM	10740	21.7	729,649	8.1	788,925	7.2	845,978	60
Omaha-Council Bluffs, NE-IA	36540	11.8	767,041	5.2	807,305	4.7	844,907	61
Dayton, OH	19380	0.5	848,153	-0.6	843,320	-0.6	838,487	62
Allentown-Bethlehem-Easton, PA-NJ	10900	7.8	740,395	6.1	785,814	5.5	829,398	63
Worcester, MA	49340	5.8	750,963	5.3	790,475	4.8	828,032	64
Bakersfield, CA	12540	21.7	661,645	12.4	743,729	10.7	823,538	65
Grand Rapids-Wyoming, MI	24340	14.6	740,482	4.7	775,198	4.1	807,357	66
Stockton, CA	44700	17.3	563,598	19.6	674,080	15.7	779,783	67
McAllen-Edinburg-Mission, TX	32580	48.5	569,463	18.6	675,597	15.0	776,946	68
El Paso, TX	21340	14.9	679,622	6.0	720,147	5.4	758,748	69
Baton Rouge, LA	12940	13.2	705,973	3.1	727,551	2.7	747,188	70
Poughkeepsie-Newburgh-Middletown, NY	39100	9.6	621,517	8.7	675,333	7.6	726,820	71
Sarasota-Bradenton-Venice, FL	42260	20.5	589,959	11.8	659,642	10.1	726,472	72
Columbia, SC	17900	18.0	647,158	6.2	687,420	5.6	725,751	73
Akron, OH	10420	5.7	694,960	1.4	704,396	1.2	712,569	74
Greensboro-High Point, NC	24660	19.1	643,430	4.6	673,134	4.1	700,749	75
Springfield, MA	44140	1.0	680,014	1.4	689,619	1.3	698,708	76
Knoxville, TN	28940	15.2	616,079	5.6	650,649	5.1	683,842	77
Little Rock-North Little Rock, AR	30780	14.1	610,518	4.8	639,802	4.3	667,180	78
Syracuse, NY	45060	-1.5	650,154	1.2	657,851	1.1	665,234	79
Toledo, OH	45780	0.8	659,188	0.2	660,207	0.1	660,975	80
Colorado Springs, CO	17820	31.3	537,484	10.3	592,836	8.9	645,614	81
Charleston-North Charleston, SC	16700	8.3	549,033	6.9	586,872	6.2	623,170	82
Greenville, SC	24860	18.6	559,940	5.1	588,729	4.6	615,786	83
Boise City-Nampa, ID	14260	45.4	464,840	16.0	539,170	13.0	609,364	84
Wichita, KS	48620	11.7	571,166	3.3	589,782	2.9	607,077	85
Cape Coral-Fort Myers, FL	15980	31.6	440,888	18.7	523,512	15.2	603,036	86
Modesto, CA	33700	20.6	446,997	16.3	519,823	13.4	589,650	87
Madison, WI	31540	16.1	501,774	8.0	541,809	7.0	579,794	88
Youngstown-Warren-Boardman, OH-PA	49660	-1.7	602,964	-2.6	587,022	-2.5	572,061	89
Palm Bay-Melbourne-Titusville, FL	37340	19.4	476,230	9.9	523,567	8.7	569,284	90
Lakeland, FL	29460	19.4	483,924	8.7	526,208	7.7	566,911	91
Ogden-Clearfield, UT	36260	25.8	442,656	14.0	504,508	11.7	563,598	92
Des Moines, IA	19780	15.6	481,394	7.4	516,976	6.5	550,622	93
Portland-South Portland-Biddeford, ME	38860	10.5	487,568	6.3	518,365	5.6	547,371	94
Jackson, MS	27140	11.2	497,197	4.2	518,326	3.8	538,054	95
Augusta-Richmond County, GA-SC	12260	14.7	499,684	3.7	517,953	3.4	535,459	96
Scranton—Wilkes-Barre, PA	42540	-2.5	560,625	-2.4	547,294	-2.2	535,193	97
Harrisburg-Carlisle, PA	25420	7.3	509,074	2.0	519,424	1.9	529,250	98
Deltona-Daytona Beach-Ormond Beach, FL	19660	19.6	443,343	9.0	483,444	7.9	521,860	99
Lancaster, PA	29540	11.3	470,658	4.2	490,254	3.7	508,588	100
Chattanooga, TN-GA	16860	10.0	476,531	3.3	492,047	3.0	506,810	101
Durham, NC	20500	23.8	426,493	7.5	458,673	7.1	491,391	102
Santa Rosa-Petaluma, CA	42220	18.1	458,614	2.7	470,813	2.2	481,193	103
Lansing-East Lansing, MI	29620	3.5	447,728	3.1	461,446	2.8	474,468	104
Winston-Salem, NC	49180	16.7	421,961	6.0	447,369	5.4	471,309	105
Pensacola-Ferry Pass-Brent, FL	37860	19.7	412,153	6.1	437,128	5.6	461,430	106
Spokane, WA	44060	15.7	417,939	5.1	439,273	4.7	459,829	107
Provo-Orem, UT	39340	39.9	376,774	11.1	418,644	9.4	458,173	108
Flint, MI	22420	1.3	436,141	2.2	445,626	1.9	454,172	109
Lexington-Fayette, KY	30460	17.2	408,326	5.5	430,696	4.9	451,882	110
Vallejo-Fairfield, CA	46700	15.9	394,542	6.9	421,801	5.8	446,371	111
Fayetteville-Springdale-Rogers, AR-MO	22220	44.9	347,045	14.6	397,806	12.1	445,885	112
Reno-Sparks, NV	39900	33.3	342,885	14.9	393,925	12.5	443,050	113
Visalia-Porterville, CA	47300	18.0	368,021	10.0	404,818	8.9	440,650	114
Salinas, CA	41500	13.0	401,762	4.9	421,269	4.3	439,362	115
Shreveport-Bossier City, LA	43340	4.5	375,965	7.9	405,822	7.2	434,915	116
Manchester-Nashua, NH	31700	13.3	380,841	5.9	403,350	5.2	424,307	117
York-Hanover, PA	49620	12.4	381,751	5.7	403,361	5.1	423,825	118
Brownsville-Harlingen, TX	15180	28.9	335,227	13.4	379,998	11.3	423,084	119
Springfield, MO	44180	23.3	368,374	7.5	396,026	6.7	422,388	120
Fort Wayne, IN	23060	10.1	390,156	4.1	406,015	3.7	420,865	121
Port St. Lucie-Fort Pierce, FL	38940	27.2	319,426	15.1	367,537	12.8	414,409	122
Corpus Christi, TX	18580	9.7	403,280	1.2	408,295	1.4	413,914	123
Reading, PA	39740	11.0	373,638	5.2	393,253	4.7	411,802	124
Asheville, NC	11700	19.9	369,171	5.9	391,007	5.3	411,544	125
Santa Barbara-Santa Maria, CA	42060	8.0	399,347	1.3	404,582	1.2	409,485	126
Canton-Massillon, OH	15940	3.3	406,934	0.0	407,131	-0.0	407,088	127
Salem, OR	41420	24.9	347,214	8.0	374,986	7.1	401,672	128
Mobile, AL	33660	5.6	399,843	-0.0	399,727	-0.1	399,266	129
Huntsville, AL	26620	16.8	342,376	7.3	367,395	6.4	390,910	130
Trenton-Ewing, NJ	45940	7.7	350,761	5.3	369,496	4.9	387,426	131
Anchorage, AK	11260	20.1	319,605	10.2	352,186	8.9	383,536	132
Beaumont-Port Arthur, TX	13140	6.6	385,090	-1.1	380,783	-1.0	376,981	133
Davenport-Moline-Rock Island, IA-IL	19340	2.1	376,019	-0.5	374,314	-0.4	372,662	134
Ann Arbor, MI	11460	14.1	322,895	7.8	347,941	6.8	371,559	135
Killeen-Temple-Fort Hood, TX	28660	23.0	330,714	6.2	351,367	5.5	370,854	136
Hickory-Lenoir-Morganton, NC	25860	16.9	341,851	4.2	356,039	3.6	368,980	137
Montgomery, AL	33860	13.6	346,528	2.9	356,454	2.6	365,780	138
Peoria, IL	37900	2.3	366,899	-0.3	365,630	-0.3	364,530	139
Naples-Marco Island, FL	34940	65.3	251,377	22.1	306,973	17.2	359,758	140
Fayetteville, NC	22180	13.2	336,609	2.9	346,350	2.8	355,917	141
Evansville, IN-KY	21780	5.5	342,815	1.8	348,860	1.7	354,678	142
Rockford, IL	40420	12.9	320,204	5.4	337,385	4.8	353,608	143
Eugene-Springfield, OR	21660	14.2	322,959	3.8	335,284	3.5	347,119	144
Tallahassee, FL	45220	23.6	320,304	3.8	332,381	3.5	344,169	145
Wilmington, NC	48900	37.2	274,532	11.4	305,944	9.9	336,164	146
Savannah, GA	42340	13.5	293,000	6.6	312,351	5.9	330,822	147
Kalamazoo-Portage, MI	28020	7.3	314,866	2.5	322,822	2.3	330,385	148
Ocala, FL	36100	32.9	258,916	13.8	294,555	11.6	328,736	149
South Bend-Mishawaka, IN-MI	43780	6.8	316,663	0.6	318,467	0.4	319,857	150
Green Bay, WI	24580	16.0	282,599	5.3	297,520	4.8	311,749	151
Kingsport-Bristol-Bristol, TN-VA	28700	8.3	298,484	0.9	301,058	0.8	303,596	152
Charleston, WV	16620	0.6	309,635	-1.2	305,915	-1.1	302,414	153
Lincoln, NE	30700	16.5	266,787	6.1	283,022	5.3	298,141	154
Fort Collins-Loveland, CO	22660	35.1	251,494	9.5	275,364	8.1	297,783	155
Utica-Rome, NY	46540	-5.3	299,896	-0.7	297,654	-0.7	295,683	156
Fort Smith, AR-OK	22900	16.7	273,170	3.9	283,847	3.4	293,593	157
Boulder, CO	14500	29.1	269,814	4.7	282,452	3.9	293,577	158
Roanoke, VA	40220	7.4	288,309	0.9	290,770	0.8	293,152	159
Huntington-Ashland, WV-KY-OH	26580	0.2	288,649	-1.0	285,791	-0.9	283,200	160
Greeley, CO	24540	37.3	180,926	27.5	230,756	20.6	278,320	161
Erie, PA	21500	1.9	280,843	-0.6	279,281	-0.5	277,775	162
Duluth, MN-WI	20260	2.3	275,486	0.1	275,790	0.1	276,141	163
Merced, CA	32900	18.0	210,554	15.7	243,619	13.1	275,515	164
Columbus, GA-AL	17980	5.7	281,768	-1.5	277,462	-0.8	275,338	165
Norwich-New London, CT	35980	1.6	259,088	3.2	267,325	2.9	275,163	166
Spartanburg, SC	43900	11.9	253,791	4.0	264,032	3.6	273,598	167
Lubbock, TX	31180	8.6	249,700	4.8	261,585	4.5	273,266	168
Holland-Grand Haven, MI	26100	26.9	238,314	7.4	255,839	6.4	272,119	169
Hagerstown-Martinsburg, MD-WV	25180	15.6	222,771	11.2	247,661	9.7	271,612	170
Atlantic City, NJ	12100	12.6	252,552	3.4	261,127	3.1	269,137	171
San Luis Obispo-Paso Robles, CA	42020	13.6	246,681	4.3	257,381	3.8	267,045	172
Gulfport-Biloxi, MS	25060	18.4	246,190	2.2	251,585	1.9	256,379	173
Laredo, TX	29700	44.9	193,117	16.2	224,381	13.2	254,024	174
Cedar Rapids, IA	16300	12.6	237,230	3.6	245,799	3.2	253,647	175
Lafayette, LA	29180	14.5	239,086	2.7	245,465	2.5	251,493	176
Kennewick-Richland-Pasco, WA	28420	27.9	191,822	15.7	221,935	13.2	251,185	177
Olympia, WA	36500	28.6	207,355	10.7	229,500	9.2	250,695	178
Bremerton-Silverdale, WA	14740	22.3	231,969	4.0	241,196	3.7	250,057	179
Binghamton, NY	13780	-4.6	252,320	-1.0	249,856	-0.9	247,721	180
Amarillo, TX	11100	15.5	226,522	4.7	237,137	4.2	247,208	181
Gainesville, FL	23540	21.5	232,392	3.1	239,650	2.9	246,588	182
Clarksville, TN-KY	17300	22.6	232,000	2.9	238,672	2.6	244,792	183
Myrtle Beach-Conway-North Myrtle Beach, SC	34820	36.5	196,629	11.8	219,791	9.9	241,524	184
Barnstable Town, MA	12700	19.1	222,230	4.5	232,312	3.9	241,347	185
Santa Cruz-Watsonville, CA	42100	11.3	255,602	-2.8	248,347	-2.9	241,190	186
Macon, GA	31420	7.6	222,368	3.3	229,720	3.1	236,852	187
Yakima, WA	49420	17.9	222,581	3.1	229,468	2.9	236,174	188
Lynchburg, VA	31340	10.9	228,616	1.6	232,242	1.4	235,437	189
Waco, TX	47380	12.9	213,517	4.4	222,879	4.0	231,707	190
Topeka, KS	45820	6.8	224,551	1.6	228,099	1.3	231,160	191
Appleton, WI	11540	15.3	201,602	7.4	216,505	6.4	230,433	192
Chico, CA	17020	11.6	203,171	6.1	215,649	5.5	227,494	193
Sioux Falls, SD	43620	21.9	187,093	10.0	205,714	8.3	222,865	194
Champaign-Urbana, IL	16580	3.7	210,275	3.0	216,661	2.8	222,813	195
Prescott, AZ	39140	55.5	167,517	16.3	194,839	13.3	220,681	196
Burlington-South Burlington, VT	15540	12.3	198,889	3.6	206,121	3.2	212,728	197
Springfield, IL	44100	6.3	201,437	2.5	206,549	2.4	211,478	198
Medford, OR	32780	23.8	181,269	8.2	196,043	7.2	210,212	199
Longview, TX	30980	7.8	194,042	3.9	201,588	3.7	209,125	200
Saginaw-Saginaw Township North, MI	40980	-0.9	210,039	-0.6	208,826	-0.5	207,686	201
Florence, SC	22500	9.6	193,155	2.8	198,594	2.7	203,862	202
Tyler, TX	46340	15.5	174,706	8.3	189,133	7.2	202,798	203
Redding, CA	39820	11.0	163,256	12.3	183,315	10.6	202,753	204
Elkhart-Goshen, IN	21140	17.0	182,791	5.4	192,614	4.7	201,665	205
Houma-Bayou Cane-Thibodaux, LA	26380	6.4	194,477	1.9	198,122	1.8	201,610	206
Racine, WI	39540	7.9	188,831	3.3	194,975	3.1	200,939	207
St. Cloud, MN	41060	12.4	167,392	9.8	183,879	8.6	199,661	208
Las Cruces, NM	29740	28.9	174,682	7.2	187,285	6.5	199,509	209
Tuscaloosa, AL	46220	9.0	192,034	1.8	195,477	1.1	197,641	210
Bellingham, WA	13380	30.5	166,814	9.4	182,534	8.2	197,436	211
Johnson City, TN	27740	13.2	181,607	3.8	188,570	3.5	195,158	212
College Station-Bryan, TX	17780	22.4	184,885	2.6	189,774	2.5	194,431	213
Fort Walton Beach-Crestview-Destin, FL	23020	18.6	170,498	6.9	182,186	6.2	193,464	214
Yuma, AZ	49740	49.7	160,026	10.6	177,064	9.2	193,373	215
Gainesville, GA	23580	45.9	139,277	19.9	166,966	15.6	193,008	216
Lake Charles, LA	29340	9.1	193,568	-0.5	192,666	-0.5	191,797	217
Charlottesville, VA	16820	20.9	174,021	5.2	183,141	4.7	191,761	218
Rochester, MN	40340	15.3	163,618	8.5	177,491	7.4	190,568	219
Kingston, NY	28740	7.5	177,749	3.5	183,995	3.3	190,073	220
Fargo, ND-MN	22020	13.7	174,367	4.1	181,535	3.6	188,090	221
Lafayette, IN	29140	12.4	178,541	2.3	182,561	2.1	186,431	222
Athens-Clarke County, GA	12020	22.1	166,079	6.0	176,112	5.3	185,370	223
Anderson, SC	11340	14.1	165,740	5.9	175,558	5.2	184,764	224
Bloomington, IN	14020	12.0	175,506	1.3	177,866	1.2	179,994	225
Muskegon-Norton Shores, MI	34740	7.1	170,200	2.9	175,106	2.6	179,638	226
Punta Gorda, FL	39460	27.6	141,627	12.9	159,967	11.0	177,627	227
Joplin, MO	27900	16.6	157,322	5.6	166,062	5.0	174,350	228
Greenville, NC	24780	23.9	152,772	6.2	162,183	5.5	171,173	229
Albany, GA	10500	7.7	157,833	4.1	164,365	3.9	170,843	230
Jackson, MI	27100	5.8	158,422	3.9	164,674	3.6	170,566	231
Monroe, LA	33740	4.4	170,053	0.1	170,239	0.2	170,521	232
Bloomington-Normal, IL	14060	16.5	150,433	6.7	160,498	6.0	170,048	233
Panama City-Lynn Haven, FL	37460	16.7	148,217	7.3	159,012	6.8	169,776	234
Yuba City, CA	49700	13.5	139,149	10.6	153,877	9.3	168,208	235
Terre Haute, IN	45460	2.6	170,943	-1.7	168,071	-1.6	165,449	236
Pueblo, CO	39380	15.0	141,472	8.6	153,579	7.6	165,291	237
El Centro, CA	20940	30.2	142,361	7.8	153,484	7.1	164,418	238
Niles-Benton Harbor, MI	35660	0.7	162,453	0.3	162,940	0.2	163,248	239
Oshkosh-Neenah, WI	36780	11.7	156,763	1.9	159,732	1.7	162,430	240
Columbia, MO	17860	19.4	145,666	5.4	153,576	4.9	161,175	241
Pascagoula, MS	37700	14.1	150,564	3.7	156,158	3.2	161,148	242
Monroe, MI	33780	9.2	145,945	5.4	153,774	4.7	161,017	243
Hanford-Corcoran, CA	25260	27.6	129,461	12.3	145,336	10.7	160,827	244
Janesville, WI	27500	9.2	152,307	2.7	156,477	2.5	160,406	245
Parkersburg-Marietta-Vienna, WV-OH	37620	1.7	164,624	-1.4	162,350	-1.3	160,169	246
Eau Claire, WI	20740	7.8	148,337	4.0	154,337	3.7	160,041	247
Bend, OR	13460	53.9	115,367	19.8	138,176	15.6	159,740	248
Madera, CA	31460	39.8	123,109	15.1	141,694	12.7	159,693	249
Waterloo-Cedar Falls, IA	47940	3.2	163,706	-1.6	161,128	-1.5	158,758	250
Vineland-Millville-Bridgeton, NJ	47220	6.1	146,438	3.3	151,331	3.2	156,244	251
Bangor, ME	12620	-1.1	144,919	3.2	149,585	3.1	154,285	252
Abilene, TX	10180	8.3	160,245	-2.2	156,762	-2.0	153,556	253
Santa Fe, NM	42140	30.7	129,292	9.3	141,278	8.1	152,692	254
Billings, MT	13740	14.3	138,904	4.9	145,703	4.4	152,133	255
Dover, DE	20100	14.1	126,697	10.2	139,558	8.9	152,015	256
Decatur, AL	19460	10.9	145,867	1.7	148,289	1.5	150,474	257
Jacksonville, NC	27340	0.3	150,355	-0.4	149,754	0.2	150,057	258
Blacksburg-Christiansburg-Radford, VA	13980	7.5	151,272	-0.7	150,162	-0.8	149,007	259
Burlington, NC	15500	20.9	130,800	7.1	140,105	6.2	148,722	260
Rocky Mount, NC	40580	7.3	143,026	1.9	145,779	1.9	148,498	261
Napa, CA	34900	12.2	124,279	9.8	136,414	8.6	148,203	262
Jefferson City, MO	27620	16.0	140,052	2.9	144,091	2.8	148,117	263
State College, PA	44300	9.7	135,758	4.4	141,710	4.1	147,551	264
Alexandria, LA	10780	-2.7	145,035	0.6	145,923	0.5	146,627	265
Iowa City, IA	26980	13.8	131,676	5.4	138,810	4.8	145,535	266
Wheeling, WV-OH	48540	-3.8	153,172	-3.2	148,237	-3.0	143,718	267
Dalton, GA	19140	21.7	120,031	10.2	132,298	8.6	143,632	268
Johnstown, PA	27780	-6.4	152,598	-3.2	147,675	-3.0	143,243	269
Sioux City, IA-NE-SD	43580	8.9	143,053	0.0	143,077	-0.0	143,027	270
Wichita Falls, TX	48660	7.9	151,524	-3.2	146,648	-3.1	142,117	271
Farmington, NM	22140	24.2	113,801	12.5	127,992	10.7	141,716	272
Warner Robins, GA	47580	24.2	110,765	14.1	126,391	11.9	141,461	273
Grand Junction, CO	24300	24.8	116,255	11.3	129,419	9.2	141,326	274
Battle Creek, MI	12980	1.5	137,985	1.0	139,305	0.9	140,493	275
Dothan, AL	20020	8.7	130,861	3.4	135,324	3.1	139,534	276
Springfield, OH	44220	-1.9	144,742	-2.1	141,771	-1.9	139,024	277
Florence-Muscle Shoals, AL	22520	8.9	142,950	-1.4	140,981	-1.4	138,945	278
Hattiesburg, MS	25620	13.0	123,812	5.8	130,975	5.0	137,562	279
Morristown, TN	34100	22.4	123,081	5.7	130,096	5.0	136,646	280
Coeur d'Alene, ID	17660	55.7	108,685	13.1	122,971	10.9	136,366	281
Texarkana, TX-Texarkana, AR	45500	8.0	129,749	2.4	132,846	2.3	135,906	282
Vero Beach, FL	46940	25.2	112,947	10.3	124,614	9.0	135,839	283
Glens Falls, NY	24020	4.9	124,345	3.5	128,724	3.4	133,094	284
St. George, UT	41100	86.1	90,354	24.0	112,063	18.4	132,633	285
La Crosse, WI-MN	29100	9.0	126,838	2.0	129,409	1.8	131,800	286
Flagstaff, AZ	22380	20.4	116,320	6.7	124,093	6.0	131,518	287
Wausau, WI	48140	9.0	125,834	1.8	128,048	1.7	130,168	288
Lebanon, PA	30140	5.8	120,327	3.7	124,776	3.4	129,072	289
Valdosta, GA	46660	20.5	119,560	3.8	124,076	3.5	128,379	290
Pittsfield, MA	38340	-3.2	134,953	-2.5	131,527	-2.4	128,335	291
Odessa, TX	36220	1.8	121,123	2.6	124,311	2.9	127,900	292

Source: Devonshire Associates Ltd. and Scan/US, Inc. 2005.

Continued on next page

Metropolitan Core Based Statistical Areas: Population Trends, *Continued*

CBSA	FIPS Code	Past		Present		Future		
		1990-2000 % Change	2000 Census	2000-2005 % Change	7/1/05 Estimate	2005-2010 % Change	2010 Projection	2010 Rank
Auburn-Opelika, AL	12220	32.1	115,092	5.7	121,616	5.1	127,779	293
Mansfield, OH	31900	2.2	128,852	-0.9	127,690	-0.9	126,535	294
Anderson, IN	11300	2.1	133,358	-2.7	129,750	-2.7	126,277	295
Midland, TX	33260	8.8	116,009	4.2	120,852	4.4	126,160	296
Winchester, VA-WV	49020	22.4	102,997	11.4	114,788	9.7	125,934	297
Sherman-Denison, TX	43300	16.4	110,595	6.2	117,502	5.5	123,951	298
Altoona, PA	11020	-1.1	129,144	-2.1	126,465	-2.0	123,875	299
Rapid City, SD	39660	9.3	112,818	4.7	118,072	4.2	122,982	300
Mount Vernon-Anacortes, WA	34580	29.4	102,979	9.9	113,129	8.5	122,771	301
Weirton-Steubenville, WV-OH	48260	-7.4	132,008	-4.2	126,448	-4.0	121,361	302
Salisbury, MD	41540	11.9	109,391	5.5	115,401	5.0	121,143	303
St. Joseph, MO-KS	41140	5.6	122,336	-0.0	122,298	-1.3	120,702	304
Idaho Falls, ID	26820	14.6	101,677	9.2	111,058	8.0	119,959	305
Logan, UT-ID	30860	29.3	102,720	7.8	110,700	6.9	118,342	306
Morgantown, WV	34060	6.4	111,200	3.0	114,517	2.8	117,764	307
Muncie, IN	34620	-0.7	118,769	-0.8	117,847	-0.7	117,042	308
Victoria, TX	47020	12.3	111,663	1.8	113,679	1.8	115,713	309
Williamsport, PA	48700	1.1	120,044	-1.9	117,787	-1.8	115,625	310
Harrisonburg, VA	25500	22.7	108,193	3.3	111,801	3.1	115,317	311
Sheboygan, WI	43100	8.4	112,646	1.2	114,016	1.1	115,256	312
Jonesboro, AR	27860	15.1	107,762	3.5	111,567	3.0	114,962	313
Bowling Green, KY	14540	19.7	104,166	5.0	109,420	4.5	114,363	314
Jackson, TN	27180	18.3	107,377	3.1	110,724	2.9	113,912	315
Anniston-Oxford, AL	11500	-3.3	112,249	0.3	112,624	1.1	113,834	316
Goldsboro, NC	24140	8.3	113,329	0.1	113,461	0.1	113,549	317
Owensboro, KY	36980	5.0	109,875	1.3	111,282	1.1	112,535	318
Elizabethtown, KY	21060	6.6	107,547	2.1	109,851	1.9	111,991	319
Kankakee-Bradley, IL	28100	7.9	103,833	3.7	107,719	3.5	111,511	320
Lewiston-Auburn, ME	30340	-1.4	103,793	3.7	107,666	3.5	111,467	321
Cleveland, TN	17420	19.1	104,015	3.5	107,706	3.2	111,131	322
Michigan City-La Porte, IN	33140	2.8	110,106	-0.4	109,651	-0.5	109,101	323
Sumter, SC	44940	2.0	104,646	1.8	106,517	1.7	108,314	324
Bay City, MI	13020	-1.4	110,157	-1.0	109,101	-1.0	108,063	325
Wenatchee, WA	48300	26.5	99,219	4.2	103,338	3.8	107,267	326
Lawrence, KS	29940	22.2	99,962	3.3	103,269	3.0	106,337	327
Danville, VA	19260	1.3	110,156	-2.2	107,753	-2.0	105,549	328
Ithaca, NY	27060	2.6	96,501	4.7	100,996	4.4	105,440	329
Brunswick, GA	15260	13.2	93,044	6.6	99,197	6.0	105,114	330
San Angelo, TX	41660	5.7	105,781	-0.4	105,375	-0.4	105,002	331
Lawton, OK	30020	3.1	114,996	-5.2	109,018	-3.7	104,954	332
Lima, OH	30620	-1.2	108,473	-1.8	106,543	-1.7	104,784	333
Missoula, MT	33540	21.8	95,802	4.5	100,118	3.9	104,056	334
Decatur, IL	19500	-2.1	114,706	-4.9	109,127	-4.7	104,032	335
Pine Bluff, AR	38220	0.4	107,341	-2.0	105,209	-1.9	103,228	336
Gadsden, AL	23460	3.6	103,459	-0.4	103,021	-0.3	102,701	337
Bismarck, ND	13900	13.0	94,719	3.8	98,303	3.3	101,535	338
Ocean City, NJ	36140	7.6	102,326	-0.6	101,669	-0.6	101,017	339
Kokomo, IN	29020	4.7	101,541	-0.3	101,209	-0.3	100,883	340
Longview, WA	31020	13.2	92,948	3.9	96,590	3.7	100,131	341
Fond du Lac, WI	22540	8.0	97,296	1.4	98,664	1.3	99,927	342
Rome, GA	40660	11.5	90,565	5.0	95,112	4.4	99,319	343
Cumberland, MD-WV	19060	0.4	102,008	-1.5	100,474	-1.4	99,073	344
Hot Springs, AR	26300	20.0	88,068	5.7	93,078	5.0	97,702	345
Dubuque, IA	20220	3.2	89,143	2.3	91,167	2.0	93,009	346
Grand Forks, ND-MN	24220	-5.5	97,478	-3.0	94,524	-2.9	91,810	347
Fairbanks, AK	21820	6.6	82,840	4.8	86,784	4.6	90,770	348
Cheyenne, WY	16940	11.6	81,607	5.5	86,122	5.1	90,483	349
Elmira, NY	21300	-4.3	91,070	-1.1	90,031	-1.1	89,021	350
Pocatello, ID	38540	13.7	83,103	-0.4	82,761	-0.4	82,400	351
Corvallis, OR	18700	10.4	78,153	2.1	79,778	2.1	81,434	352
Ames, IA	11180	7.7	79,981	0.5	80,417	0.4	80,734	353
Danville, IL	19180	-4.9	83,919	-2.0	82,252	-1.9	80,685	354
Great Falls, MT	24500	3.4	80,357	-1.2	79,409	-1.1	78,518	355
Sandusky, OH	41780	3.6	79,551	-1.5	78,323	-1.6	77,033	356
Columbus, IN	18020	12.2	71,435	1.9	72,772	1.4	73,827	357
Casper, WY	16220	8.7	66,533	4.2	69,348	4.0	72,107	358
Hinesville-Fort Stewart, GA	25980	22.0	71,914	-3.0	69,723	-2.6	67,909	359
Carson City, NV	16180	29.7	52,457	8.9	57,139	8.0	61,722	360
Lewiston, ID-WA	30300	12.9	57,961	0.9	58,492	0.9	59,015	361

Source: Devonshire Associates Ltd. and Scan/US, Inc. 2005.

Counties: Population Trends

Counties are arranged by state. The following data are provided for each county: the State-County FIPS Code, 2000-2005 estimated percent of change in population; 2005 estimated population; 2005-2010 projected percent of change in population; and 2010 projected population. Included are Ranally Population Units (RPUs) indicating how each county's population relates to the total population of the United States (due to the rounding of county RPUs, slight differences may occur between the state RPU totals shown and actual totals).

County	FIPS Code	Present: 2000-2005 % Change	Present: 7/1/05 Estimate	Present: 7/1/05 Ranally Population Units	Future: 2005-2010 % Change	Future: 2010 Projection	Future: 2010 Ranally Population Units
Alabama							
Autauga*	01001	9.9	47,987	162	8.5	52,052	168
Baldwin**	01003	12.8	158,412	534	10.7	175,379	564
Barbour**	01005	-1.6	28,584	96	-1.6	28,128	91
Bibb*	01007	4.2	21,699	73	8.1	23,449	75
Blount*	01009	10.1	56,200	190	8.9	61,174	197
Bullock	01011	-4.9	11,135	38	-4.1	10,675	34
Butler	01013	-4.7	20,400	69	-4.4	19,500	63
Calhoun*	01015	0.3	112,624	380	1.1	113,834	366
Chambers**	01017	-3.5	35,309	119	-3.5	34,076	110
Cherokee	01019	2.9	24,686	83	2.5	25,307	81
Chilton*	01021	5.6	41,805	141	4.8	43,797	141
Choctaw	01023	-5.7	15,018	51	-5.4	14,204	46
Clarke	01025	-2.4	27,198	92	-2.3	26,564	85
Clay	01027	-0.5	14,184	48	-0.6	14,101	45
Cleburne	01029	5.7	14,929	50	5.1	15,684	50
Coffee**	01031	3.5	45,144	152	3.5	46,722	150
Colbert*	01033	-1.0	54,455	184	-1.1	53,872	173
Conecuh	01035	-5.8	13,271	45	-5.6	12,527	40
Coosa**	01037	-6.8	11,373	38	-4.3	10,885	35
Covington	01039	-2.9	36,551	123	-2.6	35,598	115
Crenshaw	01041	-0.0	13,659	46	-0.3	13,617	44
Cullman**	01043	2.1	79,130	267	1.9	80,653	260
Dale**	01045	0.8	49,503	167	0.8	49,887	161
Dallas**	01047	-4.4	44,339	150	-4.1	42,520	137
DeKalb**	01049	4.8	67,523	228	4.2	70,363	226
Elmore*	01051	11.3	73,325	247	9.6	80,363	259
Escambia	01053	-0.6	38,227	129	-0.5	38,026	122
Etowah*	01055	-0.4	103,021	347	-0.3	102,701	331
Fayette	01057	-1.7	18,182	61	-1.6	17,890	58
Franklin	01059	-2.1	30,561	103	-2.1	29,909	96
Geneva*	01061	-1.4	25,405	86	-1.6	25,010	80
Greene*	01063	-1.1	9,862	33	-1.0	9,760	31
Hale*	01065	6.7	18,342	62	0.1	18,365	59
Henry*	01067	1.5	16,560	56	1.3	16,771	54
Houston*	01069	5.1	93,359	315	4.7	97,753	315
Jackson**	01071	-0.1	53,881	182	-0.3	53,725	173
Jefferson*	01073	-0.9	655,970	2,213	-0.9	649,779	2,091
Lamar	01075	-7.5	14,719	50	-7.5	13,612	44
Lauderdale*	01077	-1.6	86,526	292	-1.7	85,073	274
Lawrence*	01079	-1.4	34,317	116	-1.6	33,772	109
Lee*	01081	5.7	121,616	410	5.1	127,779	411
Limestone*	01083	6.3	69,788	235	5.5	73,608	237
Lowndes*	01085	-0.7	13,375	45	-0.8	13,265	43
Macon**	01087	-4.3	23,069	78	-4.2	22,109	71
Madison*	01089	7.6	297,607	1,004	6.6	317,302	1,021
Marengo	01091	-2.5	21,976	74	-2.6	21,399	69
Marion	01093	-5.0	29,666	100	-4.8	28,239	91
Marshall**	01095	3.8	85,329	288	3.5	88,318	284
Mobile*	01097	-0.0	399,727	1,348	-0.1	399,266	1,285
Monroe	01099	-3.2	23,551	79	-3.0	22,844	74
Montgomery*	01101	-0.8	221,767	748	-0.8	220,100	708
Morgan*	01103	2.6	113,972	384	2.4	116,702	376
Perry	01105	-2.6	11,552	39	-2.2	11,297	36
Pickens	01107	-3.1	20,303	68	-3.0	19,698	63
Pike**	01109	-2.4	28,893	97	-2.6	28,145	91
Randolph	01111	-0.1	22,368	75	-0.3	22,304	72
Russell*	01113	-2.4	48,555	164	-2.3	47,428	153
St. Clair*	01115	9.5	70,917	239	8.2	76,697	247
Shelby*	01117	18.5	169,764	573	14.8	194,944	627
Sumter	01119	-6.3	13,859	47	-6.1	13,019	42
Talladega**	01121	-0.4	80,037	270	-0.4	79,693	256
Tallapoosa**	01123	-3.0	40,226	136	-3.6	38,784	125
Tuscaloosa*	01125	1.5	167,273	564	1.3	169,516	546
Walker*	01127	-1.3	69,782	235	-1.3	68,863	222
Washington	01129	-1.5	17,817	60	-1.6	17,524	56
Wilcox	01131	-0.9	13,070	44	0.5	13,130	42
Winston	01133	-1.8	24,400	82	-2.0	23,900	77
Total: Alabama		**2.0**	**4,537,634**	**15,304**	**1.9**	**4,622,960**	**14,878**
Alaska (Boroughs and Census Areas)							
Aleutians East	02013	-0.3	2,690	9	0.1	2,694	9
Aleutians West	02016	-0.1	5,460	18	-0.0	5,458	18
Anchorage*	02020	6.9	278,263	939	6.3	295,713	952
Bethel	02050	7.8	17,248	58	6.6	18,389	59
Bristol Bay	02060	-17.0	1,044	4	-15.2	885	3
Denali	02068	-1.0	1,874	6	-0.9	1,858	6
Dillingham	02070	-0.8	4,882	16	-0.9	4,839	16
Fairbanks North Star*	02090	4.8	86,784	293	4.6	90,770	292
Haines	02100	-6.7	2,231	8	-7.0	2,075	7
Juneau**	02110	1.8	31,260	105	1.8	31,829	102
Kenai Peninsula	02122	5.1	52,237	176	4.8	54,747	176
Ketchikan Gateway**	02130	-8.5	12,871	43	-8.0	11,837	38
Kodiak Island**	02150	-6.8	12,962	44	-7.2	12,034	39
Lake and Peninsula	02164	-20.4	1,452	5	-19.8	1,165	4
Matanuska-Susitna*	02170	24.6	73,923	249	18.8	87,823	283
Nome	02180	-0.2	9,174	31	0.0	9,176	30
North Slope	02185	-4.1	7,080	24	-3.8	6,810	22
Northwest Arctic	02188	4.4	7,522	25	4.0	7,825	25
Prince of Wales-Outer Ketchikan	02201	-9.8	5,545	19	-9.8	5,002	16
Sitka	02220	0.5	8,879	30	0.5	8,924	29
Skagway-Hoonah-Angoon	02232	-13.5	2,973	10	-13.4	2,575	8
Southeast Fairbanks	02240	-11.1	5,487	19	-10.7	4,901	16
Valdez-Cordova	02261	-3.7	9,821	33	-4.1	9,416	30
Wade Hampton	02270	5.8	7,436	25	5.2	7,824	25
Wrangell-Petersburg	02280	-9.4	6,054	20	-9.4	5,484	18
Yakutat	02282	-17.6	666	2	-16.2	558	2
Yukon-Koyukuk	02290	-5.3	6,202	21	-4.5	5,926	19
Total: Alaska		**5.6**	**662,020**	**2,232**	**5.2**	**696,537**	**2,244**
Arizona							
Apache	04001	-2.3	67,835	229	-1.9	66,544	214
Cochise**	04003	5.4	124,122	419	4.9	130,214	419
Coconino*	04005	6.7	124,093	419	6.0	131,518	423
Gila**	04007	-0.1	51,287	173	-0.2	51,198	165
Graham**	04009	-2.2	32,757	110	-2.2	32,041	103
Greenlee**	04011	-18.8	6,942	23	-18.8	5,639	18
La Paz	04012	-0.0	19,709	66	0.3	19,762	64
Maricopa*	04013	16.6	3,582,040	12,083	13.5	4,067,317	13,090
Mohave**	04015	17.9	182,775	617	14.5	209,264	673
Navajo	04017	11.4	108,601	366	9.8	119,262	384
Pima*	04019	9.2	921,681	3,109	7.9	994,799	3,201
Pinal*	04021	22.3	219,763	741	17.4	258,025	830
Santa Cruz**	04023	7.4	41,238	139	6.5	43,912	141
Yavapai*	04025	16.3	194,839	657	13.3	220,681	710
Yuma*	04027	10.6	177,064	597	9.2	193,373	622
Total: Arizona		**14.1**	**5,854,746**	**19,748**	**11.8**	**6,543,549**	**21,057**
Arkansas							
Arkansas	05001	-4.5	19,811	67	-4.2	18,979	61
Ashley	05003	-3.2	23,444	79	-3.1	22,709	73
Baxter**	05005	3.1	39,577	133	2.7	40,660	131
Benton*	05007	19.9	183,859	620	15.7	212,752	685
Boone**	05009	3.9	35,283	119	3.4	36,477	117
Bradley	05011	-2.2	12,321	42	-2.3	12,036	39
Calhoun**	05013	-4.0	5,517	19	-3.8	5,307	17
Carroll	05015	7.0	27,143	92	6.3	28,847	93
Chicot	05017	-7.6	13,038	44	-7.5	12,066	39
Clark**	05019	-2.4	22,973	77	-2.3	22,455	72
Clay	05021	-6.2	16,521	56	-5.9	15,547	50
Cleburne	05023	4.8	25,192	85	4.2	26,258	85
Cleveland*	05025	3.5	8,871	30	3.6	9,186	30
Columbia**	05027	-4.7	24,407	82	-4.6	23,279	75
Conway	05029	1.6	20,660	70	1.5	20,973	67
Craighead*	05031	5.1	86,335	291	4.4	90,134	290
Crawford*	05033	7.4	57,169	193	6.5	60,900	196
Crittenden*	05035	0.8	51,287	173	0.5	51,532	166
Cross	05037	-2.9	18,969	64	-2.7	18,449	59
Dallas	05039	-8.3	8,445	28	-7.8	7,787	25
Desha	05041	-6.7	14,313	48	-6.7	13,361	43
Drew	05043	-1.2	18,493	62	-1.2	18,268	59
Faulkner*	05045	12.5	96,723	326	10.6	106,971	344
Franklin*	05047	2.0	18,132	61	2.1	18,517	60
Fulton	05049	0.2	11,665	39	-0.1	11,658	38
Garland*	05051	5.7	93,078	314	5.0	97,702	314
Grant*	05053	4.7	17,241	58	4.2	17,962	58
Greene**	05055	4.8	39,110	132	4.0	40,678	131
Hempstead**	05057	-1.3	23,287	79	-1.3	22,985	74
Hot Spring	05059	1.4	30,777	104	1.2	31,155	100
Howard	05061	2.1	14,604	49	2.2	14,931	48
Independence**	05063	1.1	34,597	117	0.8	34,874	112
Izard	05065	0.8	13,352	45	0.5	13,417	43
Jackson	05067	-8.3	16,885	57	-8.0	15,538	50
Jefferson*	05069	-2.7	82,043	277	-2.6	79,881	257
Johnson	05071	4.8	23,881	81	4.5	24,960	80
Lafayette	05073	-3.6	8,248	28	-3.5	7,959	26
Lawrence	05075	-2.2	17,378	59	-1.8	17,068	55
Lee	05077	-8.6	11,498	39	-8.2	10,555	34
Lincoln*	05079	-1.4	14,295	48	-0.9	14,161	46
Little River	05081	-2.7	13,264	45	-2.7	12,903	42
Logan	05083	2.4	23,032	78	2.2	23,535	76
Lonoke*	05085	11.9	59,112	199	10.0	65,019	209
Madison*	05087	1.9	14,512	49	1.5	14,723	47
Marion	05089	0.7	16,248	55	0.4	16,313	52
Miller*	05091	6.3	42,971	145	5.8	45,456	146
Mississippi**	05093	-9.2	47,179	159	-9.1	42,909	138
Monroe	05095	-8.9	9,342	32	-8.3	8,570	28
Montgomery	05097	-0.7	9,181	31	-1.2	9,073	29
Nevada**	05099	-4.5	9,503	32	-4.3	9,091	29
Newton**	05101	-0.5	8,568	29	-0.9	8,493	27
Ouachita**	05103	-6.1	27,020	91	-5.9	25,418	82
Perry*	05105	3.0	10,512	35	2.5	10,771	35
Phillips**	05107	-10.9	23,555	79	-10.4	21,101	68
Pike	05109	-3.5	10,907	37	-3.7	10,499	34
Poinsett*	05111	-1.5	25,232	85	-1.6	24,828	80
Polk	05113	-0.3	20,178	68	-0.5	20,070	65
Pope**	05115	2.0	55,567	187	1.9	56,604	182
Prairie	05117	-3.4	9,216	31	-3.2	8,924	29
Pulaski*	05119	1.4	366,433	1,236	1.2	370,906	1,194
Randolph	05121	0.2	18,232	61	0.2	18,273	59
St. Francis**	05123	-4.6	27,991	94	-4.5	26,738	86
Saline*	05125	7.5	89,781	303	6.4	95,551	308
Scott	05127	-0.1	10,981	37	-0.3	10,943	35
Searcy	05129	-5.7	7,786	26	-6.0	7,321	24
Sebastian*	05131	3.0	118,532	400	2.5	121,438	391
Sevier	05133	1.5	15,999	54	1.5	16,244	52
Sharp	05135	3.1	17,654	60	2.6	18,114	58
Stone	05137	1.3	11,647	39	0.9	11,750	38
Union**	05139	-2.5	44,474	150	-2.5	43,366	140
Van Buren	05141	2.5	16,590	56	2.2	16,950	55
Washington*	05143	12.3	177,115	597	10.4	195,450	629
White**	05145	5.7	70,967	239	4.9	74,475	240
Woodruff	05147	-7.7	8,071	27	-7.2	7,488	24
Yell**	05149	2.5	21,665	73	2.2	22,137	71
Total: Arkansas		**3.2**	**2,759,439**	**9,306**	**2.9**	**2,840,378**	**9,144**
California							
Alameda*	06001	1.6	1,466,375	4,946	1.1	1,482,425	4,771
Alpine	06003	-2.9	1,173	4	-2.6	1,142	4
Amador	06005	10.4	38,762	131	9.2	42,324	136
Butte*	06007	6.1	215,649	727	5.5	227,494	732
Calaveras	06009	16.7	47,324	160	13.9	53,904	173
Colusa	06011	8.2	20,353	69	7.4	21,868	70
Contra Costa*	06013	8.7	1,031,546	3,480	7.5	1,109,319	3,570
Del Norte**	06015	2.0	28,063	95	2.1	28,651	92
El Dorado*	06017	13.2	176,979	597	11.2	196,724	633
Fresno*	06019	10.3	881,918	2,975	9.0	961,546	3,094
Glenn	06021	4.8	27,715	93	4.5	28,975	93
Humboldt**	06023	1.7	128,714	434	1.8	131,095	422
Imperial*	06025	7.8	153,484	518	7.1	164,418	529
Inyo**	06027	3.8	18,631	63	3.8	19,337	62
Kern*	06029	12.4	743,729	2,509	10.7	823,538	2,650
Kings*	06031	12.3	145,336	490	10.7	160,827	518
Lake**	06033	14.0	66,477	224	11.8	74,339	239
Lassen**	06035	2.8	34,769	117	2.9	35,769	115
Los Angeles*	06037	5.9	10,076,928	33,991	5.3	10,607,471	34,137
Madera*	06039	15.1	141,694	478	12.7	159,693	514
Marin*	06041	-0.8	245,317	827	-0.9	243,027	782
Mariposa	06043	6.3	18,207	61	5.8	19,263	62
Mendocino**	06045	4.0	89,741	303	3.7	93,056	299
Merced*	06047	15.7	243,619	822	13.1	275,515	887
Modoc	06049	0.4	9,483	32	0.7	9,546	31
Mono	06051	-0.3	12,819	43	-0.3	12,786	41
Monterey*	06053	4.9	421,269	1,421	4.3	439,362	1,414
Napa*	06055	9.8	136,414	460	8.6	148,203	477
Nevada**	06057	7.1	98,587	333	6.1	104,633	337
Orange*	06059	6.1	3,020,648	10,189	5.4	3,184,136	10,247
Placer*	06061	28.5	319,191	1,077	21.2	386,916	1,245
Plumas	06063	3.0	21,450	72	3.1	22,122	71
Riverside*	06065	24.9	1,929,673	6,509	19.1	2,298,625	7,397
Sacramento*	06067	14.1	1,395,768	4,708	11.8	1,560,980	5,024
San Benito*	06069	8.3	57,666	195	6.6	61,468	198
San Bernardino*	06071	14.5	1,957,135	6,602	12.1	2,194,729	7,063
San Diego*	06073	6.3	2,990,693	10,088	5.5	3,156,599	10,159
San Francisco*	06075	-5.4	734,587	2,478	-5.4	694,890	2,236
San Joaquin*	06077	19.6	674,080	2,274	15.7	779,783	2,510
San Luis Obispo*	06079	4.3	257,381	868	3.8	267,045	859
San Mateo*	06081	-2.5	689,423	2,326	-2.7	670,972	2,159
Santa Barbara*	06083	1.3	404,582	1,365	1.2	409,485	1,318
Santa Clara*	06085	-0.7	1,669,973	5,633	-1.0	1,653,999	5,323
Santa Cruz*	06087	-2.8	248,347	838	-2.9	241,190	776
Shasta*	06089	12.3	183,315	618	10.6	202,753	653
Sierra	06091	-0.9	3,522	12	-1.5	3,469	11
Siskiyou	06093	1.1	44,782	151	1.2	45,302	146
Solano*	06095	6.9	421,801	1,423	5.8	446,371	1,437
Sonoma*	06097	2.7	470,813	1,588	2.2	481,193	1,549
Stanislaus*	06099	16.3	519,823	1,753	13.4	589,650	1,898
Sutter*	06101	11.8	88,233	298	10.2	97,260	313
Tehama**	06103	8.2	60,649	205	7.4	65,132	210
Trinity	06105	6.1	13,819	47	5.8	14,622	47
Tulare*	06107	10.0	404,818	1,366	8.9	440,650	1,418
Tuolumne**	06109	6.5	58,070	196	5.8	61,454	198
Ventura*	06111	8.0	813,570	2,744	7.0	870,395	2,801
Yolo*	06113	12.5	189,696	640	10.5	209,597	675
Yuba*	06115	9.0	65,644	221	8.1	70,948	228
Total: California		**7.6**	**36,430,227**	**122,887**	**6.7**	**38,857,985**	**125,053**
Colorado							
Adams*[1]	08001	9.7	399,121	1,346	12.0	446,996	1,439
Alamosa	08003	1.1	15,125	51	1.0	15,277	49
Arapahoe*	08005	9.0	531,667	1,793	7.5	571,739	1,840
Archuleta	08007	23.5	12,228	41	17.9	14,413	46
Baca	08009	-12.6	3,948	13	-12.3	3,464	11
Bent	08011	-8.7	5,474	18	-8.2	5,023	16
Boulder*[1]	08013	-3.0	282,452	953	3.9	293,577	945
Broomfield*[2]	08014	(d)	44,052	149	10.4	48,630	157
Chaffee	08015	6.1	17,225	58	5.3	18,146	58
Cheyenne	08017	-12.5	1,952	7	-12.1	1,716	6
Clear Creek*	08019	3.3	9,627	32	3.2	9,939	32
Conejos	08021	-0.4	8,365	28	-0.5	8,319	27
Costilla	08023	-4.3	3,504	12	-4.5	3,347	11
Crowley	08025	-1.6	5,427	18	-2.0	5,320	17
Custer	08027	13.8	3,988	13	11.8	4,460	14
Delta	08029	8.9	30,319	102	7.9	32,727	105
Denver*	08031	0.6	558,088	1,883	0.5	560,809	1,805
Dolores	08033	-3.1	1,787	6	-3.4	1,727	6
Douglas*	08035	44.2	253,393	855	28.7	326,199	1,050
Eagle**	08037	13.6	47,310	160	11.3	52,668	169
Elbert*	08039	18.9	23,618	80	14.8	27,106	87
El Paso*	08041	10.4	570,479	1,924	9.0	621,578	2,000
Fremont**	08043	5.0	48,435	163	4.4	50,545	163
Garfield	08045	14.4	50,094	169	11.7	55,958	180
Gilpin*	08047	4.0	4,945	17	3.0	5,093	16
Grand	08049	7.4	13,363	45	6.6	14,245	46
Gunnison	08051	-0.3	13,914	47	-0.5	13,840	45
Hinsdale	08053	-2.7	769	3	-2.2	752	2
Huerfano	08055	0.2	7,874	27	0.6	7,925	26

Source: Devonshire Associates Ltd. and Scan/US, Inc. 2005.
* Component of a Metropolitan Core Based Statistical Area.
** Component of a Micropolitan Core Based Statistical Area.

(d) Data not available.
[1] Census population includes a portion of Broomfield county.
[2] Created on November 15, 2001 from parts of Adams, Boulder, Jefferson and Weld counties.

Continued on next page

Counties: Population Trends, *Continued*

County	FIPS Code	Present			Future		
		2000-2005 % Change	7/1/05 Estimate	7/1/05 Ranally Population Units	2005-2010 % Change	2010 Projection	2010 Ranally Population Units
Jackson	08057	-9.4	1,429	5	-9.4	1,295	4
Jefferson*[1]	08059	0.4	529,190	1,785	0.5	531,901	1,712
Kiowa	08061	-15.5	1,370	5	-14.9	1,166	4
Kit Carson	08063	-3.3	7,743	26	-3.0	7,507	24
Lake**	08065	-2.7	7,603	26	-2.6	7,404	24
La Plata**	08067	7.9	47,411	160	6.8	50,641	163
Larimer*	08069	9.5	275,364	929	8.1	297,783	958
Las Animas	08071	3.1	15,674	53	2.5	16,060	52
Lincoln	08073	-5.5	5,750	19	-5.2	5,452	18
Logan**	08075	3.0	21,116	71	2.2	21,571	69
Mesa*	08077	11.3	129,419	437	9.2	141,326	455
Mineral	08079	10.7	920	3	8.9	1,002	3
Moffat	08081	2.9	13,569	46	2.9	13,960	45
Montezuma	08083	4.3	24,860	84	3.9	25,834	83
Montrose**	08085	12.0	37,456	126	10.3	41,310	133
Morgan**	08087	4.5	28,394	96	4.0	29,530	95
Otero	08089	-4.6	19,380	65	-4.3	18,542	60
Ouray	08091	10.9	4,150	14	8.9	4,520	15
Park*	08093	22.0	17,713	60	17.0	20,722	67
Phillips	08095	0.9	4,522	15	1.4	4,585	15
Pitkin	08097	0.3	14,924	50	1.0	15,080	49
Prowers	08099	-4.0	13,904	47	-3.8	13,369	43
Pueblo*	08101	8.6	153,579	518	7.6	165,291	532
Rio Blanco	08103	0.2	5,997	20	0.2	6,009	19
Rio Grande	08105	-1.6	12,217	41	-1.7	12,004	39
Routt	08107	8.4	21,335	72	7.0	22,839	73
Saguache	08109	20.2	7,113	24	15.9	8,241	27
San Juan	08111	3.0	575	2	3.3	594	2
San Miguel	08113	13.4	7,477	25	11.4	8,330	27
Sedgwick	08115	-5.8	2,588	9	-5.8	2,437	8
Summit**	08117	9.8	25,865	87	8.5	28,063	90
Teller*	08119	8.8	22,357	75	7.5	24,036	77
Washington	08121	-4.8	4,688	16	-5.3	4,440	14
Weld*[1]	08123	27.5	230,756	778	20.6	278,320	896
Yuma	08125	-0.1	9,827	33	0.1	9,834	32
Total: Colorado		**9.1**	**4,694,778**	**15,835**	**7.8**	**5,062,536**	**16,295**
Connecticut							
Fairfield*	09001	3.0	909,263	3,067	2.7	933,729	3,005
Hartford*	09003	2.8	881,552	2,974	2.6	904,560	2,911
Litchfield**	09005	5.2	191,674	647	4.7	200,688	646
Middlesex*	09007	6.9	165,752	559	6.1	175,863	566
New Haven*	09009	3.6	853,637	2,879	3.3	882,213	2,839
New London*	09011	3.2	267,325	902	2.9	275,163	886
Tolland*	09013	9.9	149,871	506	8.7	162,862	524
Windham**	09015	5.6	115,206	389	5.2	121,221	390
Total: Connecticut		**3.8**	**3,534,280**	**11,923**	**3.5**	**3,656,299**	**11,767**
Delaware							
Kent*	10001	10.2	139,558	471	8.9	152,015	489
New Castle*	10003	4.7	523,864	1,767	4.2	545,859	1,757
Sussex**	10005	12.2	175,747	593	10.4	194,023	624
Total: Delaware		**7.1**	**839,169**	**2,831**	**6.3**	**891,897**	**2,870**
District of Columbia (District)							
District of Columbia*	11001	-4.0	548,902	1,852	-3.9	527,662	1,698
Total: District of Columbia		**-4.0**	**548,902**	**1,852**	**-3.9**	**527,662**	**1,698**
Florida							
Alachua*	12001	2.5	223,316	753	2.3	228,469	735
Baker*	12003	8.4	24,136	81	7.2	25,876	83
Bay*	12005	7.3	159,012	536	6.8	169,776	546
Bradford	12007	7.1	27,952	94	6.6	29,804	96
Brevard*	12009	9.9	523,567	1,766	8.7	569,284	1,832
Broward*	12011	10.5	1,794,053	6,052	9.0	1,955,383	6,293
Calhoun	12013	0.3	13,051	44	0.1	13,059	42
Charlotte*	12015	12.9	159,967	540	11.0	177,627	572
Citrus**	12017	11.6	131,797	445	10.0	144,926	466
Clay*	12019	18.5	166,915	563	15.1	192,116	618
Collier*	12021	22.1	306,973	1,035	17.2	359,758	1,158
Columbia**	12023	10.6	62,510	211	9.2	68,247	220
DeSoto**	12027	9.0	35,115	118	8.0	37,936	122
Dixie	12029	4.5	14,447	49	4.3	15,062	48
Duval*	12031	7.7	838,841	2,830	7.1	897,985	2,890
Escambia*	12033	0.4	295,558	997	0.4	296,781	955
Flagler**	12035	41.6	70,570	238	28.3	90,512	291
Franklin	12037	-7.6	10,215	34	3.7	10,591	34
Gadsden*	12039	1.7	45,844	155	1.7	46,633	150
Gilchrist*	12041	13.1	16,334	55	10.9	18,119	58
Glades	12043	6.2	11,231	38	5.5	11,854	38
Gulf	12045	1.9	13,588	46	-3.1	13,163	42
Hamilton	12047	7.7	14,356	48	7.1	15,373	49
Hardee**	12049	3.8	27,971	94	3.8	29,023	93
Hendry**	12051	5.2	38,106	129	5.4	40,148	129
Hernando*	12053	15.7	151,302	510	13.1	171,067	551
Highlands**	12055	6.8	93,292	315	6.3	99,134	319
Hillsborough*	12057	12.0	1,118,988	3,774	10.3	1,234,723	3,974
Holmes	12059	3.6	19,226	65	3.6	19,913	64
Indian River*	12061	10.3	124,614	420	9.0	135,839	437
Jackson	12063	0.9	47,155	159	0.8	47,532	153
Jefferson*	12065	15.6	14,917	50	13.3	16,904	54
Lafayette	12067	9.4	7,682	26	8.1	8,305	27
Lake*	12069	27.8	269,070	908	20.9	325,184	1,047
Lee*	12071	18.7	523,512	1,766	15.2	603,036	1,941
Leon*	12073	1.8	243,753	822	1.7	247,902	798
Levy	12075	9.0	37,537	127	7.8	40,454	130
Liberty	12077	7.5	7,548	25	7.4	8,103	26
Madison	12079	0.7	18,873	64	0.7	19,000	61
Manatee*	12081	13.7	300,298	1,013	11.5	334,840	1,078
Marion*	12083	13.8	294,555	994	11.6	328,736	1,058
Martin*	12085	10.6	140,204	473	9.3	153,278	493
Miami-Dade*	12086	6.1	2,391,206	8,066	5.5	2,522,264	8,117
Monroe**	12087	-1.3	78,562	265	-1.1	77,671	250
Nassau*	12089	10.9	63,967	216	9.4	69,968	225
Okaloosa*	12091	6.9	182,186	615	6.2	193,464	623
Okeechobee**	12093	8.3	38,899	131	7.7	41,885	135
Orange*	12095	12.2	1,006,134	3,394	10.3	1,109,877	3,572
Osceola*	12097	31.5	226,787	765	23.1	279,286	899
Palm Beach*	12099	12.0	1,267,148	4,274	10.4	1,398,390	4,500
Pasco*	12101	20.6	415,912	1,403	16.4	484,329	1,559
Pinellas*	12103	0.6	927,210	3,128	0.6	932,315	3,000
Polk*	12105	8.7	526,208	1,775	7.7	566,911	1,824
Putnam**	12107	3.0	72,555	245	2.9	74,688	240
St. Johns*	12109	25.9	155,014	523	19.7	185,509	597
St. Lucie*	12111	18.0	227,333	767	14.9	261,131	840
Santa Rosa*	12113	20.2	141,570	478	16.3	164,649	530
Sarasota*	12115	10.2	359,344	1,212	9.0	391,632	1,260
Seminole*	12117	9.1	398,569	1,344	7.9	430,098	1,384
Sumter**	12119	15.8	61,800	208	13.2	69,970	225
Suwannee	12121	8.7	37,877	128	7.5	40,707	131
Taylor	12123	0.4	19,327	65	0.6	19,446	63
Union	12125	11.8	15,031	51	10.4	16,590	53
Volusia*	12127	9.0	483,444	1,631	7.9	521,860	1,679
Wakulla*	12129	21.9	27,867	94	17.5	32,730	105
Walton	12131	23.4	50,110	169	18.5	59,381	191
Washington	12133	4.5	21,927	74	4.1	22,835	73
Total: Florida		**10.3**	**17,633,938**	**59,483**	**9.0**	**19,219,041**	**61,846**
Georgia							
Appling	13001	4.4	18,178	61	4.1	18,924	61
Atkinson**	13003	8.1	8,225	28	7.5	8,843	28
Bacon	13005	2.4	10,350	35	2.0	10,562	34
Baker*	13007	9.4	4,458	15	9.1	4,864	16
Baldwin**	13009	1.0	45,160	152	0.6	45,436	146
Banks	13011	11.5	16,075	54	9.7	17,627	57
Barrow*	13013	25.9	58,111	196	19.9	69,674	224
Bartow*	13015	19.4	90,793	306	15.5	104,872	338
Ben Hill**	13017	-2.8	16,997	57	-2.9	16,504	53
Berrien	13019	3.0	16,729	56	2.7	17,174	55
Bibb*	13021	0.9	155,253	524	0.8	156,539	504
Bleckley	13023	3.5	12,076	41	3.0	12,444	40
Brantley*	13025	9.0	15,951	54	7.9	17,210	55

Source: Devonshire Associates Ltd. and Scan/US, Inc. 2005.
* Component of a Metropolitan Core Based Statistical Area.
** Component of a Micropolitan Core Based Statistical Area.

(d) Data not available.
[1] Census population includes a portion of Broomfield county.

County	FIPS Code	Present			Future		
		2000-2005 % Change	7/1/05 Estimate	7/1/05 Ranally Population Units	2005-2010 % Change	2010 Projection	2010 Ranally Population Units
Brooks*	13027	-1.7	16,171	55	-1.9	15,858	51
Bryan*	13029	19.4	27,955	94	15.9	32,387	104
Bulloch**	13031	8.4	60,709	205	7.4	65,176	210
Burke*	13033	5.4	23,437	79	4.8	24,569	79
Butts*	13035	21.3	23,687	80	16.8	27,670	89
Calhoun	13037	-4.5	6,034	20	-4.8	5,746	18
Camden**	13039	2.6	44,789	151	3.9	46,558	150
Candler	13043	8.3	10,374	35	7.5	11,156	36
Carroll*	13045	21.6	106,138	358	17.0	124,223	400
Catoosa*	13047	15.1	61,327	207	12.5	68,977	222
Charlton	13049	7.3	11,029	37	6.7	11,765	38
Chatham*	13051	2.6	238,192	803	2.4	243,819	785
Chattahoochee*	13053	-11.2	13,213	45	-3.0	12,813	41
Chattooga**	13055	6.5	27,124	91	5.9	28,724	92
Cherokee*	13057	28.6	182,558	616	21.3	221,356	712
Clarke*	13059	3.3	104,888	354	2.9	107,919	347
Clay	13061	0.6	3,378	11	0.5	3,396	11
Clayton*	13063	1.9	241,082	813	1.0	243,517	784
Clinch	13065	2.6	7,054	24	2.6	7,239	23
Cobb*	13067	11.5	677,675	2,286	9.6	742,723	2,390
Coffee**	13069	6.9	39,992	135	5.9	42,356	136
Colquitt**	13071	4.4	43,916	148	4.0	45,661	147
Columbia*	13073	14.5	102,278	345	12.2	114,723	369
Cook	13075	3.9	16,387	55	3.3	16,924	54
Coweta*	13077	22.7	109,445	369	17.6	128,756	414
Crawford*	13079	2.5	12,802	43	2.7	13,143	42
Crisp**	13081	0.4	22,085	74	0.4	22,166	71
Dade*	13083	8.0	16,361	55	7.0	17,514	56
Dawson*	13085	25.4	20,058	68	18.9	23,841	77
Decatur**	13087	0.9	28,502	96	0.8	28,738	92
DeKalb*	13089	2.1	679,804	2,293	1.6	690,779	2,223
Dodge	13091	2.3	19,612	66	2.2	20,042	64
Dooly	13093	1.6	11,706	39	1.5	11,887	38
Dougherty*	13095	-0.6	95,460	322	-0.6	94,904	305
Douglas*	13097	17.5	108,297	365	14.4	123,916	399
Early	13099	-1.7	12,148	41	-1.6	11,950	38
Echols*	13101	10.0	4,131	14	8.2	4,470	14
Effingham*	13103	23.1	46,204	156	18.2	54,616	176
Elbert	13105	1.7	20,869	70	1.7	21,223	68
Emanuel	13107	0.8	22,014	74	0.6	22,139	71
Evans	13109	11.9	11,740	40	9.8	12,896	42
Fannin	13111	11.7	22,120	75	9.8	24,295	78
Fayette*	13113	13.5	103,541	349	11.0	114,966	370
Floyd*	13115	5.0	95,112	321	4.4	99,319	320
Forsyth*	13117	42.5	140,241	473	28.4	180,032	579
Franklin	13119	7.6	21,827	74	6.8	23,308	75
Fulton*	13121	0.9	822,956	2,776	0.7	828,558	2,666
Gilmer	13123	17.3	27,505	93	13.6	31,235	101
Glascock	13125	2.3	2,616	9	2.2	2,673	9
Glynn*	13127	6.8	72,136	243	6.1	76,558	246
Gordon**	13129	14.0	50,284	170	11.8	56,195	181
Grady	13131	3.3	24,428	82	3.1	25,191	81
Greene	13133	10.9	15,970	54	9.4	17,477	56
Gwinnett*	13135	23.4	725,943	2,449	17.8	855,451	2,753
Habersham**	13137	11.9	40,178	136	10.0	44,186	142
Hall*	13139	19.9	166,966	563	15.6	193,008	621
Hancock**	13141	-1.4	9,935	34	-1.4	9,799	32
Haralson*	13143	11.3	28,594	96	9.7	31,359	101
Harris*	13145	15.7	27,412	92	13.1	31,009	100
Hart	13147	2.3	23,536	79	2.6	24,147	78
Heard*	13149	2.4	11,272	38	1.4	11,433	37
Henry*	13151	42.0	169,496	572	28.3	217,404	700
Houston*	13153	14.1	126,391	426	11.9	141,461	455
Irwin**	13155	2.6	10,193	34	2.1	10,403	33
Jackson	13157	22.5	50,957	172	17.7	59,992	193
Jasper*	13159	17.4	13,413	45	14.3	15,328	49
Jeff Davis	13161	1.8	12,914	44	1.5	13,104	42
Jefferson	13163	-2.7	16,800	57	-2.7	16,347	53
Jenkins	13165	2.7	8,803	30	2.2	9,000	29
Johnson**	13167	14.4	9,792	33	12.1	10,975	35
Jones*	13169	13.4	26,799	90	11.6	29,899	96
Lamar*	13171	4.8	16,682	56	4.6	17,456	56
Lanier*	13173	4.1	7,538	25	3.6	7,806	25
Laurens**	13175	5.8	47,465	160	5.2	49,925	161
Lee*	13177	27.3	31,508	106	21.0	38,126	123
Liberty*	13179	-4.8	58,683	198	-4.3	56,159	181
Lincoln	13181	2.9	8,590	29	2.7	8,822	28
Long*	13183	7.1	11,040	37	6.4	11,750	38
Lowndes*	13185	4.5	96,236	325	4.2	100,245	323
Lumpkin	13187	18.4	24,892	84	14.8	28,587	92
McDuffie*	13189	1.7	21,591	73	1.4	21,894	70
McIntosh*	13191	2.4	11,110	37	2.1	11,346	37
Macon	13193	-1.2	13,912	47	-1.2	13,748	44
Madison*	13195	9.1	28,081	95	7.9	30,297	98
Marion*	13197	-0.5	7,105	24	-1.1	7,024	23
Meriwether*	13199	1.6	22,899	77	1.5	23,249	75
Miller	13201	-2.8	6,207	21	-2.9	6,030	19
Mitchell	13205	-0.6	23,797	80	-0.9	23,589	76
Monroe*	13207	11.8	24,333	82	10.1	26,795	86
Montgomery**	13209	10.0	9,100	31	8.9	9,908	32
Morgan	13211	14.1	17,633	59	12.0	19,751	64
Murray*	13213	13.7	41,502	140	11.3	46,196	149
Muscogee*	13215	-2.7	181,177	611	-2.3	177,064	570
Newton*	13217	38.2	85,695	289	26.6	108,499	349
Oconee*	13219	11.9	29,333	99	10.0	32,258	104
Oglethorpe*	13221	9.3	13,810	47	7.9	14,896	48
Paulding*	13223	36.6	111,558	376	25.6	140,064	451
Peach**	13225	5.2	24,889	84	4.2	25,943	83
Pickens*	13227	27.9	29,406	99	20.6	35,452	114
Pierce**	13229	6.8	16,694	56	5.8	17,669	57
Pike*	13231	16.8	15,986	54	13.6	18,168	58
Polk**	13233	7.4	40,930	138	6.5	43,578	140
Pulaski	13235	2.8	9,861	33	2.5	10,109	33
Putnam	13237	6.4	20,017	68	6.1	21,236	68
Quitman**	13239	-7.2	2,412	8	-7.5	2,230	7
Rabun	13241	8.6	16,342	55	7.6	17,589	57
Randolph	13243	-8.5	7,128	24	-8.1	6,549	21
Richmond*	13245	-1.9	196,018	661	-1.8	192,421	619
Rockdale*	13247	11.3	78,002	263	9.5	85,415	275
Schley**	13249	8.1	4,070	14	7.0	4,356	14
Screven	13251	-0.6	15,277	52	-0.7	15,171	49
Seminole	13253	-2.5	9,135	31	-2.6	8,896	29
Spalding*	13255	5.9	61,851	209	5.4	65,194	210
Stephens**	13257	-1.4	25,083	85	-1.6	24,674	79
Stewart	13259	-6.4	4,915	17	-6.3	4,606	15
Sumter**	13261	-0.0	33,187	112	-0.3	33,090	106
Talbot	13263	1.3	6,583	22	0.8	6,635	21
Taliaferro	13265	-10.3	1,864	6	-10.3	1,672	5
Tattnall	13267	1.9	22,737	77	1.6	23,099	74
Taylor	13269	2.6	9,046	31	2.3	9,254	30
Telfair	13271	11.6	13,167	44	9.8	14,458	47
Terrell*	13273	-0.2	10,948	37	-0.3	10,913	35
Thomas**	13275	4.0	44,448	150	3.5	46,012	148
Tift**	13277	5.2	40,386	136	4.7	42,292	136
Toombs**	13279	2.7	26,767	90	2.4	27,409	88
Towns	13281	11.2	10,366	35	9.5	11,355	37
Treutlen	13283	2.1	6,997	24	1.5	7,099	23
Troup**	13285	4.5	61,418	207	4.0	63,860	206
Turner	13287	0.4	9,542	32	0.3	9,574	31
Twiggs*	13289	-0.5	10,533	36	-0.5	10,476	34
Union	13291	17.7	20,344	69	14.3	23,261	75
Upson**	13293	2.1	28,169	95	1.8	28,685	92
Walker*	13295	4.4	63,750	215	4.1	66,335	213
Walton*	13297	23.3	74,809	252	17.6	87,998	283
Ware**	13299	1.0	35,825	121	0.9	36,145	116
Warren	13301	-2.9	6,154	21	-2.4	6,006	19
Washington	13303	-1.4	20,879	70	-1.5	20,563	66
Wayne**	13305	6.9	28,389	96	6.1	30,125	97
Webster	13307	-5.5	2,258	8	-5.6	2,132	7
Wheeler	13309	9.0	6,736	23	7.8	7,263	23
White	13311	23.7	24,675	83	18.4	29,224	94
Whitfield*	13313	8.7	90,796	306	7.3	97,436	314
Wilcox	13315	2.1	8,759	30	1.9	8,923	29
Wilkes	13317	0.1	10,694	36	0.1	10,702	34
Wilkinson	13319	0.0	10,221	34	-0.2	10,205	33
Worth*	13321	0.1	21,991	74	0.2	22,036	71
Total: Georgia		**9.6**	**8,969,042**	**30,251**	**8.2**	**9,707,997**	**31,237**

Counties: Population Trends, *Continued*

County	FIPS Code	Present			Future		
		2000-2005 % Change	7/1/05 Estimate	7/1/05 Ranally Population Units	2005-2010 % Change	2010 Projection	2010 Ranally Population Units
Hawaii							
Hawaii**	15001	9.7	163,051	550	8.4	176,684	569
Honolulu*	15003	3.9	910,475	3,071	3.9	945,789	3,044
Kalawao	15005	-19.7	118	0	-17.8	97	0
Kauai**	15007	5.1	61,454	207	4.8	64,375	207
Maui**	15009	8.4	138,802	468	7.2	148,747	479
Total: Hawaii		**5.1**	**1,273,900**	**4,296**	**4.9**	**1,335,692**	**4,299**
Idaho							
Ada*	16001	12.8	339,342	1,145	10.7	375,504	1,208
Adams	16003	-0.1	3,472	12	0.1	3,476	11
Bannock*	16005	-0.1	75,502	255	-0.1	75,389	243
Bear Lake	16007	-2.2	6,270	21	-2.4	6,117	20
Benewah	16009	-2.6	8,929	30	-2.9	8,667	28
Bingham**	16011	4.6	43,653	147	4.2	45,478	146
Blaine	16013	14.8	21,809	74	12.3	24,486	79
Boise*	16015	13.4	7,566	26	10.8	8,384	27
Bonner	16017	10.4	40,662	137	8.9	44,286	143
Bonneville*	16019	9.3	90,159	304	8.0	97,393	313
Boundary	16021	4.8	10,340	35	4.0	10,749	35
Butte	16023	-2.3	2,832	10	-2.3	2,766	9
Camas	16025	8.2	1,072	4	8.4	1,162	4
Canyon*	16027	25.3	164,715	556	19.2	196,301	632
Caribou	16029	-2.5	7,121	24	-2.6	6,937	22
Cassia**	16031	1.0	21,629	73	1.0	21,840	70
Clark	16033	-18.0	838	3	-18.4	684	2
Clearwater	16035	-8.7	8,154	27	-8.2	7,483	24
Custer	16037	-8.4	3,978	13	-8.3	3,646	12
Elmore**	16039	-2.1	28,526	96	-2.0	27,956	90
Franklin*	16041	8.2	12,259	41	7.3	13,151	42
Fremont**	16043	4.9	12,398	42	4.9	13,000	42
Gem*	16045	6.5	16,167	55	5.8	17,109	55
Gooding	16047	1.9	14,420	49	1.5	14,635	47
Idaho	16049	-0.3	15,462	52	-0.1	15,444	50
Jefferson*	16051	9.1	20,899	70	8.0	22,566	73
Jerome**	16053	4.9	19,248	65	4.2	20,050	65
Kootenai*	16055	13.1	122,971	415	10.9	136,366	439
Latah**	16057	0.1	34,968	118	0.3	35,056	113
Lemhi	16059	-0.5	7,765	26	0.2	7,782	25
Lewis	16061	0.1	3,750	13	0.0	3,751	12
Lincoln	16063	10.5	4,467	15	9.2	4,877	16
Madison**	16065	14.3	31,407	106	13.0	35,477	114
Minidoka**	16067	-6.6	18,848	64	-6.2	17,671	57
Nez Perce*	16069	1.3	37,908	128	1.3	38,413	124
Oneida	16071	0.1	4,131	14	0.0	4,131	13
Owyhee*	16073	6.9	11,380	38	6.0	12,066	39
Payette**	16075	7.1	22,047	74	6.4	23,450	75
Power*	16077	-3.7	7,259	24	-3.4	7,011	23
Shoshone	16079	-9.2	12,506	42	-9.0	11,375	37
Teton**	16081	28.1	7,686	26	20.5	9,263	30
Twin Falls**	16083	7.1	68,875	232	6.5	73,379	236
Valley	16085	2.5	7,846	26	2.5	8,046	26
Washington	16087	0.6	10,034	34	0.5	10,089	32
Total: Idaho		**9.1**	**1,411,270**	**4,761**	**7.9**	**1,522,862**	**4,903**
Illinois							
Adams**	17001	-2.1	66,862	226	-2.0	65,532	211
Alexander**	17003	-5.2	9,087	31	-5.3	8,608	28
Bond*	17005	2.4	18,049	61	2.2	18,440	59
Boone*	17007	18.7	49,590	167	15.1	57,085	184
Brown	17009	-2.3	6,793	23	-2.5	6,625	21
Bureau**	17011	-0.9	35,168	119	-0.9	34,834	112
Calhoun*	17013	1.1	5,139	17	0.9	5,187	17
Carroll	17015	-2.7	16,220	55	-2.4	15,823	51
Cass	17017	1.5	13,901	47	1.5	14,116	45
Champaign*	17019	3.6	186,135	628	3.3	192,360	619
Christian**	17021	-1.0	35,006	118	-1.0	34,642	111
Clark	17023	-0.8	16,873	57	-0.8	16,746	54
Clay	17025	-3.2	14,093	48	-3.2	13,645	44
Clinton*	17027	2.1	36,286	122	2.0	36,996	119
Coles**	17029	-3.8	51,199	173	-3.2	49,566	160
Cook*	17031	-0.8	5,332,321	17,987	-0.9	5,286,501	17,013
Crawford	17033	-3.0	19,836	67	-2.8	19,276	62
Cumberland**	17035	-3.1	10,906	37	-3.2	10,557	34
DeKalb*	17037	8.2	96,267	325	7.2	103,181	332
De Witt	17039	-1.6	16,524	56	-1.6	16,258	52
Douglas	17041	-0.4	19,846	67	-0.4	19,768	64
DuPage*	17043	3.7	937,264	3,162	3.2	967,550	3,114
Edgar	17045	-2.8	19,157	65	-2.6	18,664	60
Edwards	17047	-3.2	6,747	23	-3.1	6,536	21
Effingham**	17049	1.1	34,652	117	1.1	35,030	113
Fayette	17051	-1.7	21,437	72	-1.7	21,069	68
Ford*	17053	-1.0	14,102	48	-0.9	13,979	45
Franklin	17055	0.9	39,352	133	0.8	39,660	128
Fulton**	17057	-2.3	37,364	126	-2.3	36,495	117
Gallatin	17059	-5.6	6,081	21	-5.5	5,747	18
Greene	17061	-1.0	14,612	49	-1.0	14,469	47
Grundy*	17063	8.8	40,846	138	7.7	43,999	142
Hamilton**	17065	-5.0	8,191	28	-4.8	7,801	25
Hancock	17067	-4.8	19,150	65	-4.7	18,246	59
Hardin	17069	-1.9	4,711	16	-1.6	4,637	15
Henderson**	17071	-3.4	7,935	27	-3.5	7,659	25
Henry*	17073	-0.9	50,536	170	-1.0	50,012	161
Iroquois	17075	-3.0	30,397	103	-3.0	29,489	95
Jackson**	17077	-3.3	57,629	194	-3.0	55,927	180
Jasper	17079	-1.5	9,969	34	-1.0	9,865	32
Jefferson**	17081	1.0	40,445	136	0.9	40,800	131
Jersey*	17083	3.4	22,415	76	3.3	23,156	75
Jo Daviess	17085	2.1	22,759	77	2.1	23,227	75
Johnson	17087	2.5	13,198	45	2.5	13,526	44
Kane*	17089	21.3	490,051	1,653	16.8	572,298	1,842
Kankakee*	17091	3.7	107,719	363	3.5	111,511	359
Kendall*	17093	37.3	74,879	253	26.2	94,525	304
Knox**	17095	-4.1	53,551	181	-4.0	51,408	165
Lake*	17097	9.4	704,726	2,377	8.0	761,208	2,450
La Salle**	17099	0.9	112,478	379	0.9	113,453	365
Lawrence	17101	4.5	16,147	54	4.5	16,877	54
Lee**	17103	-1.7	35,439	120	-1.6	34,855	112
Livingston**	17105	-1.8	38,958	131	-1.7	38,306	123
Logan**	17107	-2.3	30,451	103	-2.3	29,744	96
McDonough**	17109	-1.7	32,343	109	-1.6	31,829	102
McHenry*	17111	16.2	302,316	1,020	13.4	342,870	1,103
McLean*	17113	6.7	160,498	541	6.0	170,048	547
Macon*	17115	-4.9	109,127	368	-4.7	104,032	335
Macoupin*	17117	0.1	49,088	166	0.1	49,152	158
Madison*	17119	1.7	263,396	888	1.6	267,624	861
Marion**	17121	-3.3	40,297	136	-3.4	38,926	125
Marshall*	17123	-1.6	12,965	44	-1.4	12,780	41
Mason	17125	-1.3	15,822	53	-1.2	15,629	50
Massac**	17127	0.2	15,190	51	0.4	15,251	49
Menard*	17129	2.0	12,738	43	1.7	12,958	42
Mercer*	17131	-0.3	16,906	57	-0.4	16,846	54
Monroe*	17133	12.4	31,030	105	10.5	34,284	110
Montgomery	17135	-1.4	30,222	102	-1.5	29,781	96
Morgan**	17137	-2.5	35,707	120	-2.5	34,808	112
Moultrie	17139	1.2	14,456	49	0.8	14,565	47
Ogle**	17141	6.2	54,203	183	5.6	57,225	184
Peoria*	17143	-1.2	181,293	612	-1.1	179,349	577
Perry	17145	-2.5	22,506	76	-2.5	21,949	71
Piatt*	17147	0.4	16,424	55	0.3	16,474	53
Pike	17149	-3.5	16,771	57	-3.3	16,212	52
Pope	17151	-3.8	4,244	14	-4.0	4,075	13
Pulaski	17153	-6.4	6,877	23	-6.1	6,458	21
Putnam**	17155	1.0	6,149	21	1.0	6,208	20
Randolph	17157	-2.6	33,022	111	-2.6	32,165	104
Richland	17159	-2.3	15,777	53	-2.1	15,442	50
Rock Island*	17161	-1.6	146,919	496	-1.5	144,712	466
St. Clair*	17163	1.6	260,165	878	1.5	264,081	850
Saline**	17165	-3.5	25,795	87	-3.2	24,965	80
Sangamon*	17167	2.6	193,811	654	2.4	198,520	639
Schuyler	17169	-4.5	6,867	23	-4.5	6,561	21
Scott**	17171	-1.6	5,447	18	-1.9	5,346	17
Shelby	17173	-2.6	22,296	75	-2.4	21,769	70
Stark*	17175	-3.3	6,120	21	-3.2	5,927	19
Stephenson**	17177	-2.4	47,788	161	-2.3	46,685	150
Tazewell*	17179	-0.1	128,302	433	-0.2	128,094	412
Union	17181	-0.4	18,216	61	-0.2	18,172	58
Vermilion*	17183	-2.0	82,252	277	-1.9	80,685	260
Wabash	17185	-3.0	12,548	42	-2.8	12,202	39
Warren**	17187	-4.1	17,959	61	-3.9	17,253	56
Washington	17189	0.1	15,158	51	-0.1	15,142	49
Wayne	17191	-1.8	16,839	57	-1.7	16,551	53
White	17193	-2.6	14,973	51	-2.4	14,608	47
Whiteside**	17195	-1.9	59,513	201	-1.9	58,380	188
Will*	17197	27.5	640,443	2,160	20.6	772,560	2,486
Williamson**	17199	3.1	63,173	213	3.0	65,085	209
Winnebago*	17201	3.4	287,795	971	3.0	296,523	954
Woodford*	17203	4.2	36,950	125	3.9	38,380	124
Total: Illinois		**3.0**	**12,788,145**	**43,143**	**2.7**	**13,136,615**	**42,276**
Indiana							
Adams**	18001	0.6	33,818	114	0.6	34,010	109
Allen*	18003	4.1	345,326	1,165	3.6	357,869	1,152
Bartholomew*	18005	1.9	72,772	245	1.4	73,827	238
Benton*	18007	-3.0	9,138	31	-2.6	8,897	29
Blackford	18009	-1.7	13,816	47	-1.4	13,618	44
Boone*	18011	12.0	51,660	174	10.2	56,921	183
Brown*	18013	3.7	15,508	52	3.3	16,013	52
Carroll*	18015	3.3	20,833	70	3.2	21,495	69
Cass**	18017	-1.8	40,189	136	-1.9	39,413	127
Clark*	18019	5.0	101,296	342	4.4	105,779	340
Clay*	18021	1.8	27,038	91	1.7	27,500	88
Clinton**	18023	0.6	34,053	115	0.2	34,122	110
Crawford	18025	5.8	11,365	38	5.0	11,929	38
Daviess**	18027	1.4	30,227	102	1.3	30,625	99
Dearborn*	18029	6.6	49,138	166	5.7	51,918	167
Decatur**	18031	1.4	24,895	84	1.3	25,215	81
De Kalb**	18033	3.4	41,636	140	2.9	42,862	138
Delaware*	18035	-0.8	117,847	398	-0.7	117,042	377
Dubois**	18037	2.8	40,787	138	2.6	41,866	135
Elkhart*	18039	5.4	192,614	650	4.7	201,665	649
Fayette**	18041	-3.5	24,685	83	-3.4	23,847	77
Floyd*	18043	1.2	71,650	242	1.0	72,393	233
Fountain	18045	-1.9	17,607	59	-1.8	17,290	56
Franklin*	18047	4.7	23,182	78	4.1	24,132	78
Fulton	18049	0.0	20,511	69	-0.2	20,461	66
Gibson*	18051	2.6	33,333	112	2.3	34,109	110
Grant**	18053	-3.0	71,191	240	-2.8	69,190	223
Greene*	18055	0.9	33,439	113	0.6	33,653	108
Hamilton*	18057	33.8	244,530	825	24.2	303,639	977
Hancock*	18059	12.4	62,264	210	10.6	68,861	222
Harrison*	18061	6.5	36,550	123	5.6	38,587	124
Hendricks*	18063	22.9	127,940	432	17.6	150,445	484
Henry**	18065	-2.4	47,341	160	-2.3	46,232	149
Howard*	18067	-0.3	84,735	286	-0.3	84,494	272
Huntington**	18069	0.8	38,393	130	0.8	38,682	124
Jackson**	18071	1.4	41,918	141	1.2	42,419	137
Jasper*	18073	6.0	31,839	107	5.1	33,475	108
Jay	18075	-0.8	21,628	73	-0.8	21,448	69
Jefferson**	18077	2.0	32,343	109	1.9	32,969	106
Jennings**	18079	3.4	28,480	96	2.7	29,259	94
Johnson*	18081	11.7	128,689	434	9.9	141,367	455
Knox**	18083	-3.0	38,079	128	-2.8	37,012	119
Kosciusko**	18085	2.7	76,065	257	2.4	77,882	251
LaGrange	18087	5.5	36,821	124	5.1	38,689	125
Lake*	18089	1.0	489,391	1,651	1.0	494,044	1,590
LaPorte*	18091	-0.4	109,651	370	-0.5	109,101	351
Lawrence**	18093	1.6	46,645	157	1.5	47,334	152
Madison*	18095	-2.7	129,750	438	-2.7	126,277	406
Marion*	18097	0.6	865,538	2,920	0.6	870,495	2,801
Marshall**	18099	4.2	47,011	159	3.7	48,759	157
Martin	18101	0.4	10,412	35	0.5	10,468	34
Miami**	18103	0.3	36,190	122	-0.0	36,189	116
Monroe*	18105	0.2	120,813	408	0.2	121,016	389
Montgomery**	18107	0.9	37,958	128	0.9	38,296	123
Morgan*	18109	5.1	70,108	236	4.6	73,307	236
Newton*	18111	-1.3	14,381	49	-1.2	14,210	46
Noble**	18113	2.4	47,395	160	2.0	48,346	156
Ohio*	18115	3.3	5,809	20	2.8	5,974	19
Orange	18117	3.2	19,919	67	3.0	20,513	66
Owen*	18119	8.4	23,614	80	7.2	25,325	82
Parke	18121	1.2	17,452	59	1.2	17,661	57
Perry	18123	0.4	18,981	64	0.5	19,075	61
Pike**	18125	1.6	13,037	44	1.6	13,252	43
Porter*	18127	6.6	156,536	528	5.9	165,804	534
Posey*	18129	-0.8	26,837	91	-0.9	26,598	86
Pulaski	18131	1.0	13,893	47	1.0	14,032	45
Putnam*	18133	2.9	37,059	125	2.5	37,993	122
Randolph	18135	-3.1	26,547	90	-3.1	25,726	83
Ripley	18137	5.0	27,851	94	4.3	29,047	93
Rush	18139	-1.6	17,960	61	-1.4	17,701	57
St. Joseph*	18141	0.5	266,795	900	0.3	267,686	861
Scott**	18143	4.2	23,934	81	3.7	24,816	80
Shelby*	18145	0.3	43,564	147	-0.1	43,515	140
Spencer	18147	-0.9	20,210	68	-1.0	20,012	64
Starke	18149	-6.1	22,110	75	-6.1	20,758	67
Steuben**	18151	2.0	33,890	114	1.7	34,465	111
Sullivan*	18153	0.9	21,955	74	0.9	22,158	71
Switzerland	18155	6.6	9,665	33	5.9	10,234	33
Tippecanoe*	18157	2.4	152,590	515	2.3	156,039	502
Tipton*	18159	-0.6	16,474	56	-0.5	16,389	53
Union	18161	-2.0	7,200	24	-2.1	7,049	23
Vanderburgh*	18163	0.6	173,036	584	0.7	174,191	561
Vermillion*	18165	-2.7	16,339	55	-2.6	15,909	51
Vigo*	18167	-2.9	102,739	347	-2.8	99,882	321
Wabash**	18169	-3.1	33,885	114	-3.1	32,821	106
Warren	18171	5.6	8,891	30	5.0	9,336	30
Warrick*	18173	7.2	56,136	189	6.3	59,690	192
Washington*	18175	2.7	27,951	94	2.4	28,626	92
Wayne**	18177	-2.0	69,687	235	-1.9	68,346	220
Wells*	18179	2.1	28,181	95	2.0	28,737	92
White	18181	-2.2	24,705	83	-2.1	24,176	78
Whitley*	18183	5.9	32,508	110	5.4	34,259	110
Total: Indiana		**3.1**	**6,270,352**	**21,155**	**2.8**	**6,448,758**	**20,755**
Iowa							
Adair	19001	-5.1	7,823	26	-4.8	7,449	24
Adams	19003	-3.5	4,325	15	-3.4	4,176	13
Allamakee	19005	-0.7	14,567	49	-0.8	14,447	46
Appanoose	19007	-1.2	13,552	46	-1.2	13,395	43
Audubon	19009	-8.0	6,281	21	-7.8	5,792	19
Benton*	19011	6.3	26,911	91	5.8	28,462	92
Black Hawk*	19013	-2.1	125,273	423	-2.0	122,736	395
Boone**	19015	0.2	26,281	89	0.1	26,306	85
Bremer*	19017	0.8	23,518	79	0.9	23,723	76
Buchanan	19019	-1.5	20,777	70	-1.5	20,474	66
Buena Vista**	19021	-1.1	20,184	68	-0.9	19,995	64
Butler	19023	-2.8	14,884	50	-2.9	14,455	47
Calhoun	19025	-6.4	10,407	35	-6.1	9,774	31
Carroll	19027	-2.8	20,827	70	-2.6	20,291	65
Cass	19029	-3.6	14,155	48	-3.7	13,637	44
Cedar	19031	0.5	18,275	62	0.3	18,322	59
Cerro Gordo**	19033	-3.9	44,653	151	-3.7	43,018	138
Cherokee	19035	-6.0	12,250	41	-5.9	11,526	37
Chickasaw	19037	-4.8	12,463	42	-4.7	11,877	38
Clarke	19039	1.0	9,228	31	0.3	9,258	30
Clay**	19041	-3.7	16,737	56	-3.7	16,125	52
Clayton	19043	-2.8	18,164	61	-2.5	17,712	57
Clinton**	19045	-1.0	49,623	167	-0.9	49,155	158
Crawford	19047	-0.4	16,870	57	-0.4	16,797	54
Dallas*	19049	23.1	50,179	169	18.1	59,282	191
Davis	19051	0.6	8,594	29	0.5	8,633	28
Decatur	19053	-1.8	8,535	29	-1.7	8,392	27
Delaware	19055	-2.2	18,001	61	-2.2	17,604	57
Des Moines**	19057	-4.1	40,609	137	-4.0	38,993	125
Dickinson**	19059	0.1	16,443	55	-0.2	16,407	53
Dubuque*	19061	2.3	91,167	308	2.0	93,009	299
Emmet	19063	-4.0	10,581	36	-3.8	10,177	33
Fayette	19065	-4.2	21,084	71	-4.2	20,194	65
Floyd	19067	-2.9	16,410	55	-2.7	15,969	51
Franklin	19069	-0.0	10,700	36	0.1	10,709	34
Fremont	19071	-3.8	7,708	26	-3.7	7,421	24
Greene	19073	-5.0	9,847	33	-4.9	9,367	30
Grundy*	19075	-0.3	12,337	42	-0.3	12,299	40
Guthrie*	19077	1.9	11,570	39	1.8	11,782	38

Source: Devonshire Associates Ltd. and Scan/US, Inc. 2005.
* Component of a Metropolitan Core Based Statistical Area.
** Component of a Micropolitan Core Based Statistical Area.

(d) Data not available.

Continued on next page

Counties: Population Trends, *Continued*

County	FIPS Code	Present: 2000-2005 % Change	Present: 7/1/05 Estimate	Present: 7/1/05 Ranally Population Units	Future: 2005-2010 % Change	Future: 2010 Projection	Future: 2010 Ranally Population Units
Hamilton	19079	-1.1	16,250	55	-1.1	16,070	52
Hancock	19081	-3.0	11,732	40	-3.1	11,366	37
Hardin	19083	-4.8	17,900	60	-4.9	17,017	55
Harrison*	19085	0.3	15,710	53	-0.0	15,707	51
Henry	19087	-0.6	20,212	68	-0.5	20,106	65
Howard	19089	-1.8	9,754	33	-1.7	9,592	31
Humboldt	19091	-4.3	9,931	33	-4.3	9,504	31
Ida	19093	-6.3	7,345	25	-6.0	6,907	22
Iowa	19095	2.9	16,124	54	2.5	16,523	53
Jackson	19097	-0.5	20,203	68	-0.6	20,088	65
Jasper**	19099	2.2	38,018	128	1.9	38,759	125
Jefferson	19101	-1.8	15,888	54	-1.8	15,609	50
Johnson*	19103	5.6	117,205	395	5.0	123,052	396
Jones*	19105	1.2	20,456	69	1.1	20,683	67
Keokuk	19107	-0.7	11,318	38	-0.9	11,216	36
Kossuth	19109	-6.6	16,036	54	-6.4	15,009	48
Lee**	19111	-5.6	35,939	121	-5.3	34,028	110
Linn*	19113	3.5	198,432	669	3.1	204,502	658
Louisa**	19115	1.1	12,312	42	1.1	12,445	40
Lucas	19117	2.0	9,606	32	2.0	9,795	32
Lyon	19119	-0.4	11,711	39	-0.4	11,666	38
Madison*	19121	7.0	15,007	51	6.5	15,982	51
Mahaska**	19123	-1.8	21,924	74	-1.7	21,543	69
Marion**	19125	2.3	32,782	111	1.9	33,417	108
Marshall**	19127	-0.3	39,206	132	-0.4	39,066	126
Mills*	19129	3.8	15,093	51	3.4	15,602	50
Mitchell	19131	-0.2	10,855	37	-0.2	10,831	35
Monona	19133	-3.4	9,679	33	-3.3	9,357	30
Monroe	19135	-3.1	7,770	26	-2.9	7,547	24
Montgomery	19137	-6.1	11,050	37	-6.3	10,351	33
Muscatine**	19139	1.5	42,367	143	1.3	42,913	138
O'Brien	19141	-4.4	14,435	49	-4.2	13,823	44
Osceola	19143	-4.5	6,686	23	-4.3	6,399	21
Page	19145	-5.8	15,994	54	-5.6	15,103	49
Palo Alto	19147	-6.6	9,482	32	-6.6	8,860	29
Plymouth	19149	-0.6	24,707	83	-0.7	24,537	79
Pocahontas	19151	-7.2	8,037	27	-6.7	7,496	24
Polk*	19153	6.0	397,152	1,340	5.3	418,267	1,346
Pottawattamie*	19155	1.3	88,801	300	0.9	89,567	288
Poweshiek	19157	1.1	19,018	64	0.8	19,179	62
Ringgold	19159	-3.5	5,276	18	-3.5	5,092	16
Sac	19161	-8.7	10,523	35	-8.4	9,644	31
Scott*	19163	0.8	159,953	540	0.7	161,092	518
Shelby	19165	-4.0	12,642	43	-3.3	12,228	39
Sioux	19167	2.1	32,252	109	2.0	32,901	106
Story*	19169	0.5	80,417	271	0.4	80,734	260
Tama	19171	-1.9	17,756	60	-1.9	17,427	56
Taylor	19173	-4.8	6,624	22	-5.3	6,275	20
Union	19175	-4.7	11,732	40	-4.5	11,201	36
Van Buren	19177	-1.4	7,701	26	-1.6	7,578	24
Wapello**	19179	-0.7	35,794	121	-0.7	35,559	114
Warren*	19181	5.9	43,068	145	5.2	45,309	146
Washington*	19183	4.5	21,605	73	4.1	22,483	72
Wayne	19185	-1.8	6,607	22	-1.8	6,486	21
Webster**	19187	-2.6	39,183	132	-2.5	38,194	123
Winnebago	19189	-3.9	11,267	38	-4.1	10,802	35
Winneshiek	19191	-0.6	21,175	71	-0.7	21,027	68
Woodbury*	19193	-1.0	102,793	347	-1.1	101,679	327
Worth**	19195	-3.9	7,600	26	-4.0	7,297	23
Wright	19197	-5.9	13,486	45	-5.9	12,692	41
Total: Iowa		**0.9**	**2,951,374**	**9,955**	**0.8**	**2,974,324**	**9,572**
Kansas							
Allen	20001	-5.0	13,664	46	-5.0	12,979	42
Anderson	20003	2.3	8,295	28	2.3	8,485	27
Atchison**	20005	0.2	16,813	57	0.2	16,851	54
Barber	20007	-7.8	4,892	16	-7.6	4,519	15
Barton**	20009	-3.8	27,140	92	-3.6	26,169	84
Bourbon	20011	-2.4	15,011	51	-2.5	14,632	47
Brown	20013	-4.2	10,274	35	-4.1	9,849	32
Butler*	20015	4.3	62,010	209	3.7	64,277	207
Chase**	20017	-2.8	2,944	10	-3.0	2,856	9
Chautauqua	20019	-5.8	4,104	14	-5.7	3,869	12
Cherokee	20021	-5.0	21,484	72	-4.8	20,446	66
Cheyenne	20023	-8.9	2,884	10	-8.8	2,631	8
Clark	20025	-3.4	2,309	8	-3.2	2,235	7
Clay	20027	-4.8	8,399	28	-5.0	7,983	26
Cloud	20029	-5.9	9,665	33	-5.5	9,134	29
Coffey	20031	-0.6	8,814	30	-0.8	8,741	28
Comanche	20033	-4.1	1,887	6	-3.6	1,820	6
Cowley**	20035	-2.2	35,495	120	-2.2	34,700	112
Crawford**	20037	0.2	38,321	129	0.2	38,390	124
Decatur	20039	-7.4	3,215	11	-7.1	2,986	10
Dickinson	20041	-1.1	19,123	64	-1.4	18,864	61
Doniphan*	20043	-1.6	8,113	27	-1.7	7,974	26
Douglas*	20045	3.3	103,269	348	3.0	106,337	342
Edwards	20047	-7.8	3,181	11	-7.3	2,949	9
Elk	20049	-4.9	3,100	10	-4.0	2,977	10
Ellis**	20051	-1.5	27,084	91	-1.3	26,726	86
Ellsworth	20053	-3.5	6,295	21	-3.6	6,066	20
Finney**	20055	-6.0	38,083	128	-6.3	35,678	115
Ford**	20057	2.3	33,216	112	1.8	33,816	109
Franklin*	20059	6.5	26,406	89	5.7	27,916	90
Geary**	20061	-10.4	25,042	84	-9.8	22,600	73
Gove	20063	-9.7	2,769	9	-9.8	2,499	8
Graham	20065	-7.1	2,738	9	-6.3	2,566	8
Grant	20067	-3.0	7,668	26	-2.9	7,449	24
Gray	20069	2.7	6,062	20	2.4	6,207	20
Greeley	20071	-12.6	1,341	5	-13.1	1,165	4
Greenwood	20073	-2.6	7,475	25	-2.6	7,281	23
Hamilton	20075	1.5	2,709	9	1.7	2,756	9
Harper	20077	-5.8	6,157	21	-5.4	5,827	19
Harvey*	20079	3.5	34,021	115	3.3	35,130	113
Haskell	20081	-3.3	4,163	14	-3.4	4,020	13
Hodgeman	20083	4.2	2,172	7	4.0	2,259	7
Jackson*	20085	5.2	13,312	45	4.6	13,931	45
Jefferson*	20087	3.2	19,009	64	2.8	19,534	63
Jewell	20089	-14.2	3,251	11	-13.7	2,807	9
Johnson*	20091	12.5	507,661	1,712	10.4	560,260	1,803
Kearny	20093	-1.7	4,452	15	-1.3	4,393	14
Kingman	20095	-4.3	8,300	28	-4.5	7,929	26
Kiowa	20097	-7.1	3,044	10	-6.5	2,846	9
Labette**	20099	-3.4	22,059	74	-3.1	21,371	69
Lane	20101	-14.3	1,847	6	-14.0	1,589	5
Leavenworth*	20103	8.0	74,179	250	6.9	79,330	255
Lincoln	20105	-2.9	3,473	12	-2.9	3,371	11
Linn*	20107	2.9	9,844	33	2.4	10,077	32
Logan	20109	-9.3	2,764	9	-9.4	2,504	8
Lyon**	20111	-1.2	35,512	120	-1.3	35,043	113
McPherson**	20113	-1.1	29,232	99	-1.3	28,863	93
Marion	20115	-1.4	13,168	44	-1.6	12,951	42
Marshall	20117	-6.6	10,244	35	-6.4	9,588	31
Meade	20119	-0.2	4,620	16	-0.3	4,605	15
Miami*	20121	4.6	29,658	100	3.8	30,790	99
Mitchell	20123	-5.6	6,545	22	-5.4	6,192	20
Montgomery**	20125	-5.4	34,303	116	-5.3	32,485	105
Morris	20127	-3.5	5,892	20	-3.7	5,675	18
Morton	20129	-6.8	3,259	11	-6.4	3,051	10
Nemaha	20131	-3.2	10,377	35	-3.0	10,064	32
Neosho	20133	-3.7	16,372	55	-3.5	15,805	51
Ness	20135	-14.0	2,972	10	-13.7	2,565	8
Norton	20137	-3.3	5,759	19	-3.4	5,565	18
Osage*	20139	1.4	16,950	57	1.0	17,121	55
Osborne	20141	-10.6	3,982	13	-10.2	3,577	12
Ottawa**	20143	-0.0	6,160	21	-0.6	6,121	20
Pawnee	20145	-9.6	6,538	22	-9.4	5,925	19
Phillips	20147	-9.2	5,446	18	-9.3	4,938	16
Pottawatomie**	20149	4.2	18,976	64	3.5	19,649	63
Pratt	20151	-2.6	9,398	32	-2.5	9,166	29
Rawlins	20153	-7.3	2,750	9	-7.1	2,555	8
Reno**	20155	-2.3	63,269	213	-2.3	61,837	199
Republic	20157	-13.9	5,022	17	-13.6	4,341	14
Rice	20159	-4.7	10,259	35	-4.5	9,797	32
Riley**	20161	0.3	63,042	213	0.4	63,268	204
Rooks	20163	-7.5	5,259	18	-7.2	4,881	16
Rush	20165	-4.8	3,381	11	-4.6	3,225	10
Russell	20167	-9.3	6,688	23	-9.1	6,081	20
Saline**	20169	0.5	53,845	182	0.3	54,032	174
Scott	20171	-8.6	4,678	16	-8.4	4,287	14
Sedgwick*	20173	3.5	468,918	1,582	3.2	483,958	1,557
Seward**	20175	4.6	23,536	79	4.1	24,504	79
Shawnee*	20177	1.3	172,022	580	1.1	173,843	559
Sheridan	20179	-7.7	2,595	9	-7.4	2,402	8
Sherman	20181	-10.4	6,059	20	-10.1	5,445	18
Smith	20183	-10.3	4,069	14	-10.1	3,659	12
Stafford	20185	-7.2	4,442	15	-6.9	4,137	13
Stanton	20187	-1.2	2,377	8	-1.1	2,352	8
Stevens	20189	-3.8	5,258	18	-3.8	5,059	16
Sumner*	20191	-4.3	24,833	84	-4.5	23,712	76
Thomas	20193	-4.6	7,804	26	-4.6	7,442	24
Trego	20195	-9.9	2,989	10	-9.1	2,717	9
Wabaunsee*	20197	-1.1	6,806	23	-1.1	6,731	22
Wallace	20199	-11.9	1,541	5	-11.4	1,366	4
Washington	20201	-7.8	5,980	20	-7.6	5,525	18
Wichita	20203	-5.4	2,394	8	-5.1	2,271	7
Wilson	20205	-2.8	10,039	34	-2.7	9,770	31
Woodson	20207	-6.3	3,548	12	-5.9	3,340	11
Wyandotte*	20209	-0.9	156,403	528	-1.0	154,859	498
Total: Kansas		**2.1**	**2,746,171**	**9,260**	**1.9**	**2,799,691**	**9,013**
Kentucky							
Adair	21001	2.2	17,625	59	1.9	17,959	58
Allen	21003	4.4	18,589	63	4.1	19,355	62
Anderson**	21005	5.7	20,199	68	5.0	21,207	68
Ballard**	21007	-0.9	8,209	28	-1.2	8,112	26
Barren**	21009	4.5	39,743	134	4.1	41,353	133
Bath**	21011	5.1	11,651	39	4.4	12,169	39
Bell**	21013	-1.0	29,756	100	-1.0	29,470	95
Boone*	21015	20.8	103,836	350	16.2	120,627	388
Bourbon*	21017	1.4	19,637	66	1.3	19,898	64
Boyd*	21019	0.3	49,908	168	0.5	50,148	161
Boyle**	21021	1.1	27,990	94	1.0	28,280	91
Bracken*	21023	4.5	8,653	29	4.2	9,015	29
Breathitt	21025	-2.7	15,664	53	-2.5	15,273	49
Breckinridge	21027	3.5	19,300	65	3.2	19,909	64
Bullitt*	21029	9.8	67,211	227	8.3	72,761	234
Butler	21031	2.2	13,298	45	2.0	13,570	44
Caldwell	21033	-2.1	12,787	43	-1.9	12,540	40
Calloway**	21035	1.7	34,741	117	1.7	35,331	114
Campbell*	21037	-1.7	87,132	294	-1.7	85,641	276
Carlisle	21039	-0.4	5,332	18	-0.3	5,318	17
Carroll	21041	1.7	10,323	35	1.4	10,468	34
Carter	21043	2.6	27,587	93	2.6	28,295	91
Casey	21045	5.4	16,277	55	4.9	17,075	55
Christian*	21047	-2.8	70,255	237	-2.8	68,296	220
Clark*	21049	3.6	34,351	116	3.2	35,453	114
Clay	21051	-1.9	24,085	81	-1.7	23,683	76
Clinton	21053	-0.7	9,568	32	-0.7	9,503	31
Crittenden	21055	-5.0	8,916	30	-5.2	8,455	27
Cumberland	21057	0.8	7,206	24	0.5	7,244	23
Daviess*	21059	1.5	92,957	314	1.4	94,290	303
Edmonson*	21061	3.5	12,050	41	3.1	12,428	40
Elliott	21063	3.1	6,960	23	2.6	7,144	23
Estill	21065	-0.7	15,201	51	-0.7	15,093	49
Fayette*	21067	4.0	270,888	914	3.7	280,831	904
Fleming	21069	6.8	14,724	50	5.9	15,593	50
Floyd	21071	-0.7	42,157	142	-0.6	41,922	135
Franklin**	21073	0.7	48,023	162	0.4	48,200	155
Fulton**	21075	-5.7	7,307	25	-5.2	6,929	22
Gallatin*	21077	3.2	8,122	27	3.2	8,384	27
Garrard	21079	12.2	16,590	56	10.2	18,290	59
Grant*	21081	11.8	25,032	84	9.9	27,503	89
Graves**	21083	1.5	37,598	127	1.4	38,117	123
Grayson	21085	4.1	25,035	84	3.7	25,954	84
Green	21087	3.6	11,931	40	3.2	12,318	40
Greenup*	21089	0.8	37,186	125	0.9	37,530	121
Hancock*	21091	0.7	8,450	28	0.3	8,473	27
Hardin*	21093	2.4	96,438	325	2.2	98,566	317
Harlan	21095	-4.8	31,613	107	-4.3	30,256	97
Harrison	21097	2.3	18,398	62	2.0	18,766	60
Hart	21099	4.3	18,189	61	3.5	18,834	61
Henderson*	21101	1.4	45,470	153	1.4	46,118	148
Henry*	21103	5.1	15,830	53	4.6	16,558	53
Hickman	21105	-2.2	5,147	17	-1.9	5,048	16
Hopkins**	21107	1.0	46,972	158	1.0	47,462	153
Jackson	21109	1.3	13,664	46	1.1	13,812	44
Jefferson*	21111	1.2	701,817	2,367	1.1	709,724	2,284
Jessamine*	21113	10.1	42,965	145	8.7	46,710	150
Johnson	21115	1.1	23,704	80	1.5	24,057	77
Kenton*	21117	0.9	152,794	515	0.7	153,919	495
Knott	21119	0.4	17,716	60	0.5	17,796	57
Knox	21121	-0.4	31,664	107	-0.6	31,464	101
Larue*	21123	0.3	13,413	45	0.1	13,425	43
Laurel**	21125	8.1	57,008	192	7.1	61,079	197
Lawrence	21127	3.3	16,075	54	2.9	16,545	53
Lee	21129	-0.7	7,858	27	-0.9	7,789	25
Leslie	21131	-3.0	12,024	41	-2.9	11,674	38
Letcher	21133	-2.9	24,549	83	-2.7	23,878	77
Lewis**	21135	-4.1	13,510	46	-4.4	12,913	42
Lincoln**	21137	8.0	25,234	85	7.0	26,992	87
Livingston**	21139	-1.0	9,709	33	-1.1	9,603	31
Logan	21141	1.6	27,005	91	1.5	27,403	88
Lyon	21143	0.9	8,156	28	0.5	8,200	26
McCracken**	21145	-2.0	64,213	217	-1.9	63,012	203
McCreary	21147	0.4	17,152	58	0.5	17,241	55
McLean*	21149	-0.6	9,875	33	-1.0	9,772	31
Madison**	21151	8.2	76,677	259	7.0	82,079	264
Magoffin	21153	0.3	13,367	45	0.3	13,405	43
Marion	21155	3.0	18,754	63	2.8	19,285	62
Marshall	21157	2.6	30,902	104	2.5	31,662	102
Martin	21159	-1.0	12,456	42	-0.9	12,344	40
Mason**	21161	0.3	16,851	57	0.3	16,900	54
Meade*	21163	7.2	28,244	95	5.9	29,920	96
Menifee**	21165	2.7	6,736	23	2.0	6,869	22
Mercer	21167	3.7	21,579	73	3.4	22,317	72
Metcalfe**	21169	0.3	10,066	34	0.5	10,115	33
Monroe	21171	-0.3	11,716	40	-0.2	11,692	38
Montgomery**	21173	6.8	24,092	81	5.9	25,518	82
Morgan	21175	4.0	14,508	49	3.8	15,056	48
Muhlenberg**	21177	-0.5	31,670	107	-0.4	31,542	102
Nelson*	21179	9.2	40,940	138	7.9	44,185	142
Nicholas	21181	4.1	7,094	24	4.2	7,395	24
Ohio	21183	2.5	23,481	79	2.3	24,024	77
Oldham*	21185	14.7	52,975	179	11.2	58,909	190
Owen	21187	8.4	11,437	39	7.5	12,295	40
Owsley	21189	-4.5	4,637	16	-4.6	4,425	14
Pendleton*	21191	7.0	15,401	52	5.8	16,296	52
Perry	21193	1.8	29,906	101	2.0	30,497	98
Pike	21195	-2.8	66,804	225	-2.5	65,112	210
Powell	21197	1.7	13,460	45	1.3	13,637	44
Pulaski**	21199	5.0	59,052	199	4.6	61,776	199
Robertson	21201	4.0	2,356	8	3.9	2,448	8
Rockcastle**	21203	1.1	16,771	57	0.8	16,906	54
Rowan	21205	1.4	22,409	76	1.5	22,745	73
Russell	21207	3.0	16,798	57	2.8	17,260	56
Scott*	21209	17.9	38,974	131	14.2	44,504	143
Shelby*	21211	12.7	37,573	127	10.6	41,571	134
Simpson	21213	3.2	16,934	57	3.0	17,442	56
Spencer*	21215	34.9	15,869	54	24.2	19,713	63
Taylor**	21217	3.5	23,726	80	3.4	24,538	79
Todd	21219	-1.0	11,850	40	-0.9	11,744	38
Trigg*	21221	3.4	13,027	44	2.9	13,410	43
Trimble*	21223	13.4	9,217	31	11.3	10,257	33
Union	21225	0.6	15,724	53	0.7	15,841	51
Warren*	21227	5.2	97,370	328	4.7	101,935	328
Washington	21229	5.3	11,491	39	4.9	12,054	39
Wayne	21231	2.7	20,462	69	2.3	20,931	67
Webster*	21233	-0.5	14,048	47	-0.5	13,972	45
Whitley**	21235	5.9	37,971	128	5.3	39,978	129
Wolfe	21237	-2.7	6,875	23	-3.2	6,658	21
Woodford*	21239	2.9	23,881	81	2.5	24,486	79
Total: Kentucky		**3.0**	**4,164,333**	**14,044**	**2.8**	**4,279,671**	**13,770**
Louisiana (Parishes)							
Acadia**	22001	0.3	59,013	199	0.3	59,164	190
Allen	22003	-0.9	25,214	85	-0.8	25,005	80

Source: Devonshire Associates Ltd. and Scan/US, Inc. 2005.
* Component of a Metropolitan Core Based Statistical Area.
** Component of a Micropolitan Core Based Statistical Area.

(d) Data not available.

Counties: Population Trends, *Continued*

County	FIPS Code	Present: 2000-2005 % Change	Present: 7/1/05 Estimate	Present: 7/1/05 Ranally Population Units	Future: 2005-2010 % Change	Future: 2010 Projection	Future: 2010 Ranally Population Units
Ascension*	22005	15.5	88,503	299	12.4	99,442	320
Assumption**	22007	-1.8	22,977	77	-1.8	22,564	73
Avoyelles	22009	1.0	41,876	141	0.9	42,237	136
Beauregard**	22011	2.2	33,713	114	1.9	34,337	111
Bienville	22013	-5.0	14,968	50	-4.8	14,244	46
Bossier*	22015	5.6	103,854	350	4.9	108,957	351
Caddo*	22017	9.4	275,910	931	8.5	299,381	963
Calcasieu*	22019	-0.2	183,193	618	-0.2	182,785	588
Caldwell	22021	0.8	10,642	36	0.6	10,706	34
Cameron*	22023	-5.2	9,473	32	-4.9	9,012	29
Catahoula	22025	-4.5	10,428	35	-4.5	9,962	32
Claiborne	22027	-3.3	16,301	55	-2.8	15,845	51
Concordia**	22029	-4.3	19,369	65	-4.3	18,545	60
De Soto*	22031	2.2	26,058	88	2.0	26,577	86
East Baton Rouge*	22033	-0.9	409,249	1,380	-0.9	405,635	1,305
East Carroll	22035	-7.5	8,712	29	-7.3	8,077	26
East Feliciana*	22037	-2.7	20,787	70	-2.8	20,210	65
Evangeline	22039	-1.6	34,867	118	-1.6	34,326	110
Franklin	22041	-3.6	20,507	69	-3.6	19,766	64
Grant*	22043	0.7	18,824	63	0.6	18,929	61
Iberia**	22045	1.0	74,008	250	0.9	74,710	240
Iberville*	22047	-3.3	32,225	109	-3.3	31,161	100
Jackson**	22049	-1.9	15,103	51	-1.9	14,819	48
Jefferson*	22051	-1.7	447,509	1,510	-1.6	440,244	1,417
Jefferson Davis**	22053	-2.4	30,692	104	-2.3	29,983	96
Lafayette*	22055	2.3	194,974	658	2.2	199,223	641
Lafourche*	22057	2.0	91,749	309	1.9	93,469	301
La Salle	22059	-2.3	13,958	47	-2.3	13,635	44
Lincoln**	22061	-2.0	41,641	140	-2.0	40,799	131
Livingston*	22063	17.2	107,626	363	13.7	122,405	394
Madison**	22065	-9.1	12,480	42	-8.8	11,384	37
Morehouse**	22067	-2.7	30,195	102	-2.6	29,418	95
Natchitoches**	22069	-2.3	38,168	129	-2.4	37,264	120
Orleans*	22071	-5.9	456,285	1,539	-5.7	430,487	1,385
Ouachita*	22073	0.1	147,371	497	0.1	147,574	475
Plaquemines*	22075	6.8	28,584	96	6.3	30,379	98
Pointe Coupee*	22077	-2.5	22,197	75	-2.5	21,634	70
Rapides*	22079	0.6	127,099	429	0.5	127,698	411
Red River	22081	-0.8	9,543	32	-0.7	9,478	31
Richland	22083	-3.7	20,197	68	-3.6	19,466	63
Sabine	22085	-0.6	23,316	79	-0.8	23,127	74
St. Bernard*	22087	-3.9	64,622	218	-3.6	62,286	200
St. Charles*	22089	3.6	49,807	168	3.1	51,375	165
St. Helena*	22091	-3.8	10,124	34	-3.7	9,746	31
St. James	22093	-0.9	21,026	71	-0.8	20,854	67
St. John The Baptist*	22095	6.3	45,754	154	5.6	48,304	155
St. Landry**	22097	1.8	89,252	301	1.6	90,680	292
St. Martin*	22099	3.9	50,491	170	3.5	52,270	168
St. Mary**	22101	-3.9	51,413	173	-3.6	49,575	160
St. Tammany*	22103	13.0	216,070	729	10.8	239,437	771
Tangipahoa**	22105	4.1	104,732	353	3.6	108,536	349
Tensas	22107	-8.4	6,061	20	-7.9	5,580	18
Terrebonne*	22109	1.8	106,373	359	1.7	108,141	348
Union*	22111	0.3	22,868	77	0.3	22,947	74
Vermilion**	22113	0.7	54,194	183	0.7	54,560	176
Vernon**	22115	-7.0	48,846	165	-6.9	45,457	146
Washington**	22117	-0.4	43,743	148	-0.4	43,571	140
Webster**	22119	-2.7	40,697	137	-2.5	39,672	128
West Baton Rouge*	22121	0.2	21,636	73	0.3	21,697	70
West Carroll	22123	-2.6	11,994	40	-2.5	11,698	38
West Feliciana*	22125	0.6	15,204	51	0.4	15,258	49
Winn	22127	-6.1	15,869	54	-5.8	14,941	48
Total: Louisiana		**0.9**	**4,510,134**	**15,211**	**0.9**	**4,550,648**	**14,645**
Maine							
Androscoggin*	23001	3.7	107,666	363	3.5	111,467	359
Aroostook	23003	-1.5	72,859	246	-1.4	71,828	231
Cumberland*	23005	3.9	275,908	931	3.6	285,820	920
Franklin	23007	1.0	29,764	100	0.9	30,040	97
Hancock	23009	3.6	53,648	181	3.3	55,424	178
Kennebec**	23011	3.4	121,139	409	3.2	125,050	402
Knox**	23013	4.4	41,375	140	4.1	43,051	139
Lincoln	23015	5.7	35,525	120	5.1	37,341	120
Oxford	23017	3.9	56,888	192	3.6	58,951	190
Penobscot*	23019	3.2	149,585	505	3.1	154,285	497
Piscataquis	23021	1.9	17,564	59	1.7	17,861	57
Sagadahoc*	23023	6.9	37,650	127	6.4	40,063	129
Somerset	23025	1.5	51,674	174	1.4	52,423	169
Waldo	23027	8.3	39,306	133	7.2	42,120	136
Washington	23029	-2.1	33,224	112	-2.0	32,559	105
York*	23031	9.7	204,807	691	8.1	221,488	713
Total: Maine		**4.2**	**1,328,582**	**4,483**	**3.9**	**1,379,771**	**4,442**
Maryland							
Allegany*	24001	-2.2	73,274	247	-2.1	71,735	231
Anne Arundel*	24003	5.6	517,299	1,745	5.0	543,077	1,748
Baltimore*	24005	4.9	791,384	2,669	4.4	826,495	2,660
Calvert*	24009	21.0	90,186	304	16.6	105,178	338
Caroline	24011	6.2	31,608	107	5.5	33,357	107
Carroll*	24013	13.4	171,167	577	11.4	190,663	614
Cecil*	24015	13.2	97,326	328	11.1	108,151	348
Charles*	24017	15.9	139,740	471	13.2	158,178	509
Dorchester**	24019	-0.1	30,637	103	0.1	30,665	99
Frederick*	24021	15.4	225,299	760	12.7	253,983	817
Garrett	24023	1.6	30,309	102	1.5	30,774	99
Harford*	24025	10.1	240,719	812	8.8	261,870	843
Howard*	24027	10.7	274,373	925	9.0	299,101	963
Kent	24029	2.3	19,647	66	1.8	20,010	64
Montgomery*	24031	8.5	947,578	3,196	7.3	1,017,181	3,274
Prince George's*	24033	7.7	863,468	2,913	6.9	923,099	2,971
Queen Anne's*	24035	15.0	46,661	157	12.6	52,535	169
St. Mary's**	24037	12.3	96,819	327	10.6	107,090	345
Somerset*	24039	4.9	25,960	88	4.7	27,181	87
Talbot**	24041	3.7	35,048	118	3.2	36,177	116
Washington*	24043	6.4	140,320	473	5.8	148,477	478
Wicomico*	24045	5.7	89,441	302	5.1	93,962	302
Worcester**	24047	7.0	49,819	168	6.1	52,863	170
INDEPENDENT CITY							
Baltimore*	24510	-5.2	617,204	2,082	-4.9	587,263	1,890
Total: Maryland		**6.6**	**5,645,286**	**19,040**	**5.9**	**5,979,065**	**19,242**
Massachusetts							
Barnstable*	25001	4.5	232,312	784	3.9	241,347	777
Berkshire*	25003	-2.5	131,527	444	-2.4	128,335	413
Bristol*	25005	3.4	553,046	1,865	3.1	569,949	1,834
Dukes	25007	6.1	15,901	54	5.2	16,722	54
Essex*	25009	2.9	744,047	2,510	2.5	762,420	2,454
Franklin*	25011	0.9	72,152	243	0.9	72,792	234
Hampden*	25013	1.5	463,031	1,562	1.4	469,420	1,511
Hampshire*	25015	1.4	154,436	521	1.3	156,496	504
Middlesex*	25017	0.3	1,469,958	4,958	0.1	1,471,162	4,735
Nantucket	25019	7.9	10,268	35	6.8	10,967	35
Norfolk*	25021	0.7	655,077	2,210	0.6	659,014	2,121
Plymouth*	25023	4.9	495,811	1,672	4.3	517,008	1,664
Suffolk*	25025	-2.3	673,720	2,273	-2.3	657,995	2,118
Worcester*	25027	5.3	790,475	2,666	4.8	828,032	2,665
Total: Massachusetts		**1.8**	**6,461,761**	**21,797**	**1.5**	**6,561,659**	**21,119**
Michigan							
Alcona	26001	-1.0	11,604	39	-0.9	11,502	37
Alger	26003	-1.2	9,742	33	-1.1	9,639	31
Allegan**	26005	7.7	113,751	384	6.7	121,352	391
Alpena**	26007	-2.7	30,453	103	-2.7	29,631	95
Antrim	26009	7.9	24,925	84	6.6	26,578	86
Arenac	26011	0.4	17,344	58	0.2	17,384	56
Baraga	26013	-0.2	8,726	29	-0.2	8,710	28
Barry*	26015	6.0	60,188	203	5.4	63,445	204
Bay*	26017	-1.0	109,101	368	-1.0	108,063	348
Benzie**	26019	11.7	17,877	60	9.9	19,639	63
Berrien*	26021	0.3	162,940	550	0.2	163,248	525
Branch**	26023	2.0	46,683	157	1.7	47,487	153
Calhoun*	26025	1.0	139,305	470	0.9	140,493	452
Cass*	26027	1.1	51,672	174	1.0	52,171	168
Charlevoix	26029	3.7	27,067	91	3.3	27,970	90
Cheboygan	26031	5.5	27,893	94	4.7	29,214	94
Chippewa**	26033	0.9	38,909	131	0.9	39,244	126
Clare	26035	2.1	31,896	108	1.6	32,405	104
Clinton*	26037	7.6	69,693	235	6.8	74,398	239
Crawford	26039	6.1	15,145	51	5.3	15,941	51
Delta**	26041	-0.7	38,252	129	-0.8	37,932	122
Dickinson**	26043	-1.0	27,189	92	-1.1	26,894	87
Eaton*	26045	4.3	108,140	365	3.9	112,348	362
Emmet	26047	7.0	33,636	113	6.3	35,758	115
Genesee*	26049	2.2	445,626	1,503	1.9	454,172	1,462
Gladwin	26051	5.9	27,546	93	5.1	28,958	93
Gogebic	26053	-2.0	17,030	57	-1.3	16,803	54
Grand Traverse**	26055	8.6	84,359	285	7.5	90,710	292
Gratiot**	26057	0.7	42,572	144	0.6	42,821	138
Hillsdale	26059	2.8	47,810	161	2.3	48,927	157
Houghton**	26061	-1.8	35,363	119	-1.7	34,767	112
Huron	26063	-3.9	34,686	117	-3.8	33,364	107
Ingham*	26065	1.5	283,613	957	1.4	287,722	926
Ionia*	26067	5.6	64,985	219	5.1	68,286	220
Iosco	26069	-3.0	26,526	89	-3.0	25,732	83
Iron	26071	-4.9	12,490	42	-4.8	11,893	38
Isabella**	26073	2.5	64,951	219	2.5	66,549	214
Jackson*	26075	3.9	164,674	555	3.6	170,566	549
Kalamazoo*	26077	2.1	243,549	822	1.9	248,213	799
Kalkaska**	26079	5.6	17,500	59	5.0	18,370	59
Kent*	26081	4.4	599,621	2,023	3.9	622,847	2,004
Keweenaw**	26083	-5.1	2,184	7	-3.3	2,111	7
Lake	26085	6.1	12,027	41	5.3	12,659	41
Lapeer*	26087	6.6	93,745	316	5.8	99,150	319
Leelanau**	26089	6.1	22,397	76	5.0	23,527	76
Lenawee**	26091	3.5	102,302	345	3.1	105,474	339
Livingston*	26093	16.5	182,797	617	13.3	207,062	666
Luce	26095	-3.0	6,814	23	-2.8	6,620	21
Mackinac	26097	-6.1	11,210	38	-6.0	10,538	34
Macomb*	26099	5.2	829,028	2,796	4.6	866,942	2,790
Manistee	26101	3.7	25,439	86	3.2	26,264	85
Marquette**	26103	-0.3	64,463	217	-0.2	64,304	207
Mason	26105	3.1	29,164	98	2.8	29,978	96
Mecosta**	26107	4.7	42,462	143	4.2	44,262	142
Menominee**	26109	-1.2	25,014	84	-1.1	24,731	80
Midland**	26111	2.9	85,259	288	2.6	87,498	282
Missaukee**	26113	7.6	15,576	53	6.5	16,593	53
Monroe*	26115	5.4	153,774	519	4.7	161,017	518
Montcalm	26117	4.5	64,025	216	4.0	66,592	214
Montmorency	26119	2.4	10,565	36	1.8	10,754	35
Muskegon*	26121	2.9	175,106	591	2.6	179,638	578
Newaygo*	26123	5.3	50,404	170	4.7	52,779	170
Oakland*	26125	1.7	1,214,978	4,098	1.5	1,233,145	3,969
Oceana	26127	7.1	28,778	97	6.3	30,587	98
Ogemaw	26129	1.3	21,932	74	1.1	22,167	71
Ontonagon	26131	-4.6	7,461	25	-4.4	7,133	23
Osceola	26133	3.3	23,952	81	2.9	24,655	79
Oscoda	26135	1.0	9,510	32	0.9	9,596	31
Otsego	26137	7.2	24,968	84	6.1	26,502	85
Ottawa*	26139	7.4	255,839	863	6.4	272,119	876
Presque Isle	26141	-1.0	14,269	48	-0.8	14,159	46
Roscommon	26143	4.4	26,602	90	4.0	27,665	89
Saginaw*	26145	-0.6	208,826	704	-0.5	207,686	668
St. Clair*	26147	5.2	172,724	583	4.6	180,692	582
St. Joseph**	26149	0.8	62,938	212	0.6	63,329	204
Sanilac	26151	0.4	44,747	151	0.4	44,946	145
Schoolcraft	26153	-2.1	8,712	29	-2.3	8,512	27
Shiawassee**	26155	2.3	73,340	247	2.2	74,959	241
Tuscola	26157	0.7	58,649	198	0.6	58,997	190
Van Buren*	26159	3.9	79,273	267	3.7	82,172	264
Washtenaw*	26161	7.8	347,941	1,174	6.8	371,559	1,196
Wayne*	26163	-2.6	2,008,158	6,774	-2.5	1,958,009	6,301
Wexford**	26165	4.3	31,804	107	3.9	33,058	106
Total: Michigan		**2.3**	**10,164,188**	**34,283**	**2.0**	**10,372,286**	**33,378**
Minnesota							
Aitkin	27001	5.1	16,081	54	4.5	16,811	54
Anoka*	27003	8.5	323,274	1,090	7.2	346,641	1,116
Becker	27005	7.0	32,093	108	6.2	34,095	110
Beltrami**	27007	8.5	43,008	145	7.5	46,222	149
Benton*	27009	15.7	39,583	134	12.8	44,666	144
Big Stone	27011	-3.7	5,604	19	-3.3	5,420	17
Blue Earth**	27013	3.6	57,980	196	3.5	60,038	193
Brown**	27015	-1.2	26,594	90	-1.0	26,323	85
Carlton*	27017	7.4	34,001	115	6.7	36,266	117
Carver*	27019	20.3	84,468	285	16.0	98,024	315
Cass**	27021	6.1	28,798	97	5.2	30,293	97
Chippewa	27023	-4.1	12,551	42	-4.0	12,049	39
Chisago*	27025	21.6	49,980	169	16.8	58,375	188
Clay*	27027	2.7	52,627	178	2.5	53,940	174
Clearwater	27029	-0.2	8,402	28	0.2	8,419	27
Cook	27031	2.9	5,320	18	2.3	5,445	18
Cottonwood	27033	-2.9	11,811	40	-2.7	11,493	37
Crow Wing**	27035	9.6	60,383	204	8.3	65,416	211
Dakota*	27037	7.7	383,221	1,293	6.6	408,473	1,315
Dodge*	27039	11.0	19,687	66	9.3	21,513	69
Douglas**	27041	6.5	34,954	118	5.8	36,989	119
Faribault	27043	-4.4	15,461	52	-4.2	14,806	48
Fillmore	27045	1.5	21,436	72	1.3	21,707	70
Freeborn**	27047	-2.6	31,729	107	-2.5	30,921	100
Goodhue**	27049	4.0	45,895	155	3.8	47,619	153
Grant	27051	-1.6	6,187	21	-1.4	6,100	20
Hennepin*	27053	0.6	1,123,455	3,790	0.5	1,129,139	3,634
Houston*	27055	1.4	19,996	67	1.2	20,236	65
Hubbard	27057	1.9	18,717	63	1.5	18,998	61
Isanti*	27059	21.5	38,010	128	17.0	44,466	143
Itasca	27061	1.3	44,576	150	1.2	45,127	145
Jackson	27063	-1.0	11,160	38	-0.7	11,078	36
Kanabec	27065	9.9	16,486	56	8.6	17,897	58
Kandiyohi**	27067	-0.3	41,091	139	-0.2	41,018	132
Kittson	27069	-10.7	4,718	16	-10.4	4,226	14
Koochiching	27071	-4.3	13,743	46	-4.0	13,199	42
Lac qui Parle	27073	-4.2	7,732	26	-4.0	7,422	24
Lake	27075	2.3	11,310	38	2.1	11,552	37
Lake of the Woods	27077	-5.9	4,256	14	-5.6	4,017	13
Le Sueur	27079	8.3	27,527	93	7.4	29,552	95
Lincoln	27081	-5.2	6,092	21	-4.9	5,792	19
Lyon**	27083	-4.0	24,418	82	-4.0	23,453	75
McLeod**	27085	4.3	36,399	123	4.2	37,918	122
Mahnomen	27087	-2.1	5,081	17	-1.8	4,989	16
Marshall	27089	-2.1	9,940	34	-1.8	9,761	31
Martin**	27091	-4.6	20,808	70	-4.5	19,881	64
Meeker	27093	3.7	23,493	79	3.4	24,292	78
Mille Lacs	27095	15.4	25,759	87	12.8	29,050	93
Morrison	27097	4.1	33,023	111	3.7	34,245	110
Mower**	27099	0.8	38,928	131	0.6	39,152	126
Murray	27101	-2.9	8,900	30	-2.7	8,661	28
Nicollet**	27103	4.6	31,136	105	3.9	32,360	104
Nobles**	27105	-2.3	20,362	69	-2.1	19,925	64
Norman	27107	-6.1	6,986	24	-6.0	6,565	21
Olmsted*	27109	8.9	135,319	456	7.7	145,757	469
Otter Tail**	27111	1.6	58,074	196	1.6	58,984	190
Pennington	27113	0.0	13,587	46	0.3	13,623	44
Pine	27115	7.2	28,442	96	6.2	30,214	97
Pipestone	27117	-3.7	9,530	32	-3.3	9,219	30
Polk*	27119	-1.9	30,767	104	-2.0	30,162	97
Pope	27121	-0.5	11,182	38	-0.6	11,116	36
Ramsey*	27123	-1.7	502,508	1,695	-1.7	493,791	1,589
Red Lake	27125	-0.1	4,293	14	0.3	4,304	14
Redwood	27127	-5.0	15,972	54	-4.6	15,230	49
Renville	27129	-2.9	16,652	56	-2.8	16,179	52
Rice**	27131	8.4	61,423	207	7.5	66,001	212
Rock	27133	-1.1	9,612	32	-1.1	9,511	31
Roseau	27135	-0.2	16,302	55	-0.0	16,295	52
St. Louis*	27137	-1.5	197,532	666	-1.4	194,767	627
Scott*	27139	34.8	120,628	407	24.4	150,073	483
Sherburne*	27141	27.4	82,041	277	20.3	98,726	318
Sibley	27143	-1.1	15,188	51	-1.1	15,019	48
Stearns*	27145	8.4	144,296	487	7.4	154,995	499
Steele**	27147	5.2	35,425	119	4.6	37,046	119
Stevens	27149	-2.2	9,827	33	-1.9	9,644	31
Swift	27151	-4.5	11,423	39	-4.0	10,961	35
Todd	27153	-0.1	24,400	82	-0.1	24,373	78
Traverse	27155	-9.5	3,740	13	-9.3	3,393	11

Source: Devonshire Associates Ltd. and Scan/US, Inc. 2005.
* Component of a Metropolitan Core Based Statistical Area.
** Component of a Micropolitan Core Based Statistical Area.

(d) Data not available.

Continued on next page

Counties: Population Trends, *Continued*

County	FIPS Code	Present			Future		
		2000-2005 % Change	7/1/05 Estimate	7/1/05 Ranally Population Units	2005-2010 % Change	2010 Projection	2010 Ranally Population Units
Wabasha*	27157	4.0	22,485	76	3.6	23,298	75
Wadena	27159	-1.3	13,528	46	-1.4	13,340	43
Waseca	27161	-0.9	19,353	65	-0.9	19,176	62
Washington*	27163	10.1	221,394	747	8.4	240,076	773
Watonwan	27165	-4.3	11,367	38	-3.9	10,928	35
Wilkin**	27167	-4.4	6,827	23	-4.2	6,538	21
Winona**	27169	-2.1	48,918	165	-2.2	47,859	154
Wright*	27171	23.1	110,736	374	18.0	130,635	420
Yellow Medicine	27173	-5.4	10,486	35	-5.1	9,955	32
Total: Minnesota		**4.7**	**5,148,487**	**17,367**	**4.2**	**5,363,223**	**17,261**
Mississippi							
Adams**	28001	-5.2	32,569	110	-5.0	30,954	100
Alcorn**	28003	1.8	35,170	119	1.5	35,708	115
Amite**	28005	-0.7	13,498	46	-0.7	13,405	43
Attala	28007	0.1	19,686	66	0.1	19,706	63
Benton	28009	-4.1	7,697	26	-4.1	7,378	24
Bolivar**	28011	-4.9	38,629	130	-4.6	36,835	119
Calhoun	28013	-1.9	14,786	50	-1.8	14,521	47
Carroll**	28015	-3.4	10,406	35	-3.5	10,046	32
Chickasaw	28017	-1.4	19,175	65	-1.2	18,949	61
Choctaw	28019	-1.0	9,663	33	-1.0	9,565	31
Claiborne	28021	-4.5	11,298	38	-4.4	10,801	35
Clarke**	28023	-2.8	17,453	59	-2.9	16,941	55
Clay**	28025	-3.2	21,277	72	-3.1	20,623	66
Coahoma**	28027	-6.0	28,776	97	-5.9	27,078	87
Copiah*	28029	1.6	29,216	99	1.5	29,642	95
Covington	28031	6.2	20,605	69	5.5	21,743	70
DeSoto*	28033	25.9	135,003	455	19.5	161,295	519
Forrest*	28035	3.4	75,059	253	3.0	77,299	249
Franklin	28037	-2.2	8,259	28	-2.4	8,058	26
George*	28039	11.6	21,369	72	10.0	23,516	76
Greene	28041	-0.1	13,282	45	-0.3	13,245	43
Grenada**	28043	-3.1	22,531	76	-2.9	21,868	70
Hancock*	28045	8.2	46,503	157	6.9	49,696	160
Harrison*	28047	0.5	190,466	642	0.3	191,127	615
Hinds*	28049	-1.1	248,051	837	-1.1	245,399	790
Holmes	28051	-3.2	20,923	71	-3.1	20,273	65
Humphreys	28053	-7.4	10,379	35	-6.8	9,673	31
Issaquena	28055	-14.3	1,948	7	-13.8	1,680	5
Itawamba**	28057	2.7	23,385	79	2.2	23,899	77
Jackson*	28059	2.6	134,789	455	2.1	137,632	443
Jasper**	28061	0.1	18,161	61	0.1	18,185	59
Jefferson	28063	-3.6	9,393	32	-3.4	9,070	29
Jefferson Davis	28065	-6.3	13,084	44	-5.8	12,329	40
Jones**	28067	0.5	65,261	220	0.4	65,502	211
Kemper**	28069	-0.2	10,434	35	0.0	10,437	34
Lafayette**	28071	5.3	40,791	138	4.9	42,805	138
Lamar*	28073	11.8	43,669	147	9.8	47,960	154
Lauderdale**	28075	-0.9	77,477	261	-0.8	76,830	247
Lawrence	28077	2.5	13,590	46	2.1	13,873	45
Leake	28079	7.2	22,451	76	6.6	23,941	77
Lee**	28081	4.0	78,812	266	3.5	81,602	263
Leflore**	28083	-6.5	35,483	120	-6.3	33,236	107
Lincoln**	28085	2.1	33,858	114	2.0	34,520	111
Lowndes**	28087	-2.4	60,078	203	-2.4	58,639	189
Madison*	28089	11.1	82,974	280	9.5	90,825	292
Marion	28091	-2.0	25,073	85	-2.1	24,559	79
Marshall*	28093	2.7	35,935	121	2.3	36,774	118
Monroe	28095	-0.4	37,866	128	-0.4	37,701	121
Montgomery	28097	-3.7	11,743	40	-3.4	11,349	37
Neshoba	28099	2.6	29,435	99	2.4	30,141	97
Newton	28101	1.9	22,259	75	1.7	22,631	73
Noxubee	28103	-3.3	12,138	41	-3.3	11,740	38
Oktibbeha**	28105	-4.8	40,856	138	-4.8	38,878	125
Panola	28107	4.1	35,664	120	3.5	36,913	119
Pearl River**	28109	7.8	52,398	177	6.8	55,984	180
Perry*	28111	0.9	12,247	41	0.5	12,303	40
Pike**	28113	0.5	39,137	132	0.3	39,260	126
Pontotoc**	28115	5.9	28,310	95	5.4	29,835	96
Prentiss	28117	0.5	25,682	87	0.3	25,755	83
Quitman	28119	-6.4	9,474	32	-5.8	8,926	29
Rankin*	28121	13.1	130,428	440	10.8	144,569	465
Scott	28123	0.6	28,594	96	0.6	28,774	93
Sharkey	28125	-8.3	6,037	20	-7.8	5,566	18
Simpson*	28127	0.1	27,657	93	-0.1	27,619	89
Smith	28129	-3.3	15,641	53	-3.4	15,106	49
Stone*	28131	7.3	14,616	49	6.4	15,556	50
Sunflower**	28133	-4.1	32,962	111	-3.6	31,771	102
Tallahatchie	28135	-5.6	14,071	47	-5.5	13,299	43
Tate*	28137	3.1	26,167	88	2.7	26,869	86
Tippah	28139	1.1	21,049	71	0.8	21,219	68
Tishomingo	28141	-1.3	18,922	64	-1.3	18,678	60
Tunica*	28143	13.3	10,455	35	11.6	11,672	38
Union	28145	4.5	26,510	89	3.4	27,407	88
Walthall	28147	0.7	15,261	51	1.0	15,408	50
Warren**	28149	-2.1	48,605	164	-2.0	47,620	153
Washington**	28151	-7.0	58,568	198	-6.7	54,624	176
Wayne	28153	0.0	21,225	72	0.1	21,238	68
Webster	28155	-2.4	10,044	34	-2.5	9,792	32
Wilkinson	28157	-0.1	10,299	35	0.0	10,299	33
Winston	28159	-2.3	19,693	66	-2.4	19,224	62
Yalobusha	28161	3.3	13,484	45	2.5	13,822	44
Yazoo**	28163	0.3	28,221	95	0.1	28,261	91
Total: Mississippi		**2.1**	**2,904,093**	**9,796**	**1.9**	**2,959,451**	**9,527**
Missouri							
Adair**	29001	-1.5	24,596	83	-1.4	24,251	78
Andrew*	29003	3.9	17,141	58	3.5	17,741	57
Atchison	29005	-3.1	6,230	21	-2.9	6,051	19
Audrain**	29007	-0.3	25,776	87	-0.2	25,734	83
Barry	29009	4.3	35,483	120	4.0	36,897	119
Barton	29011	7.1	13,431	45	6.5	14,308	46
Bates*	29013	3.6	17,254	58	3.0	17,780	57
Benton	29015	9.2	18,758	63	8.0	20,261	65
Bollinger**	29017	4.2	12,532	42	3.7	12,993	42
Boone*	29019	6.1	143,667	485	5.5	151,543	488
Buchanan*	29021	-1.4	84,810	286	-1.5	83,520	269
Butler**	29023	0.4	41,022	138	0.4	41,192	133
Caldwell*	29025	4.2	9,345	32	3.7	9,693	31
Callaway*	29027	5.2	42,867	145	4.9	44,966	145
Camden	29029	5.6	39,133	132	4.8	41,027	132
Cape Girardeau**	29031	3.0	70,762	239	2.8	72,724	234
Carroll	29033	-1.4	10,137	34	-1.5	9,989	32
Carter	29035	1.2	6,012	20	1.0	6,075	20
Cass*	29037	13.8	93,436	315	11.6	104,263	336
Cedar	29039	2.2	14,032	47	2.1	14,326	46
Chariton	29041	-3.5	8,140	27	-3.4	7,863	25
Christian*	29043	22.1	66,271	224	17.2	77,639	250
Clark**	29045	0.3	7,438	25	0.5	7,478	24
Clay*	29047	9.6	201,582	680	8.3	218,355	703
Clinton*	29049	10.3	20,940	71	9.0	22,831	73
Cole*	29051	1.7	72,592	245	1.7	73,802	238
Cooper	29053	4.0	17,339	58	3.5	17,954	58
Crawford	29055	5.4	24,032	81	4.8	25,192	81
Dade	29057	-0.6	7,872	27	-0.6	7,823	25
Dallas*	29059	4.9	16,430	55	4.5	17,165	55
Daviess	29061	1.2	8,111	27	1.3	8,217	26
DeKalb*	29063	5.5	12,234	41	-6.3	11,467	37
Dent	29065	1.1	15,088	51	0.9	15,230	49
Douglas	29067	3.5	13,548	46	3.2	13,985	45
Dunklin**	29069	-1.6	32,637	110	-1.5	32,155	103
Franklin*	29071	6.1	99,506	336	5.4	104,904	338
Gasconade	29073	2.3	15,689	53	1.9	15,981	51
Gentry	29075	-6.7	6,399	22	-6.7	5,968	19
Greene*	29077	4.0	249,887	843	3.7	259,037	834
Grundy	29079	-1.7	10,252	35	-1.5	10,094	32
Harrison	29081	-0.3	8,820	30	-0.6	8,770	28
Henry	29083	4.1	22,889	77	3.4	23,669	76
Hickory	29085	2.9	9,199	31	2.7	9,446	30
Holt	29087	-6.1	5,025	17	-5.8	4,734	15
Howard*	29089	-3.0	9,909	33	-2.8	9,632	31
Howell**	29091	1.9	37,961	128	1.9	38,666	124
Iron	29093	-5.0	10,158	34	-4.5	9,696	31
Jackson*	29095	1.6	665,173	2,244	1.4	674,318	2,170
Jasper*	29097	5.9	110,824	374	5.2	116,636	375
Jefferson*	29099	7.9	213,724	721	7.0	228,606	736
Johnson**	29101	6.6	51,438	174	5.8	54,418	175
Knox	29103	-3.0	4,232	14	-3.0	4,103	13
Laclede**	29105	4.4	33,928	114	3.9	35,250	113
Lafayette*	29107	0.8	33,226	112	0.5	33,399	107
Lawrence	29109	6.0	37,328	126	5.3	39,318	127
Lewis**	29111	-3.0	10,183	34	-3.3	9,852	32
Lincoln*	29113	23.0	47,892	162	18.1	56,559	182
Linn	29115	-3.6	13,261	45	-3.5	12,803	41
Livingston	29117	-1.6	14,322	48	-1.3	14,131	45
McDonald*	29119	2.9	22,320	75	2.9	22,960	74
Macon	29121	-0.9	15,620	53	-0.9	15,479	50
Madison	29123	0.3	11,830	40	0.1	11,845	38
Maries	29125	-2.5	8,678	29	-2.7	8,448	27
Marion**	29127	0.7	28,484	96	0.6	28,665	92
Mercer	29129	-4.8	3,575	12	-5.1	3,391	11
Miller	29131	5.0	24,740	83	4.5	25,848	83
Mississippi	29133	2.4	13,745	46	2.8	14,129	45
Moniteau*	29135	2.3	15,162	51	2.2	15,496	50
Monroe	29137	2.1	9,509	32	1.8	9,680	31
Montgomery	29139	-0.9	12,025	41	-1.0	11,910	38
Morgan	29141	6.0	20,477	69	5.4	21,574	69
New Madrid	29143	-4.2	18,921	64	-3.9	18,187	59
Newton*	29145	4.9	55,238	186	4.5	57,714	186
Nodaway**	29147	-0.8	21,740	73	-0.6	21,600	70
Oregon	29149	0.6	10,407	35	0.8	10,487	34
Osage*	29151	3.1	13,470	45	2.8	13,853	45
Ozark	29153	0.0	9,542	32	0.0	9,542	31
Pemiscot	29155	-2.3	19,582	66	-2.3	19,133	62
Perry	29157	1.2	18,346	62	1.0	18,532	60
Pettis**	29159	0.6	39,656	134	0.5	39,838	128
Phelps**	29161	5.6	42,060	142	5.1	44,223	142
Pike	29163	0.9	18,517	62	1.0	18,706	60
Platte*	29165	12.8	83,253	281	10.9	92,321	297
Polk*	29167	6.9	28,841	97	6.1	30,600	98
Pulaski**	29169	12.1	46,136	156	9.4	50,463	162
Putnam	29171	-2.1	5,112	17	-2.6	4,981	16
Ralls**	29173	0.6	9,687	33	0.2	9,704	31
Randolph**	29175	2.3	25,228	85	2.2	25,778	83
Ray*	29177	4.5	24,400	82	4.1	25,403	82
Reynolds	29179	-2.6	6,518	22	-3.4	6,298	20
Ripley	29181	3.6	13,999	47	3.5	14,491	47
St. Charles*	29183	16.2	329,900	1,113	13.3	373,721	1,203
St. Clair	29185	-0.8	9,573	32	-1.3	9,453	30
Ste. Genevieve	29186	3.4	18,451	62	2.9	18,981	61
St. Francois**	29187	10.6	61,536	208	9.3	67,267	216
St. Louis*	29189	-0.1	1,015,417	3,425	-0.2	1,013,712	3,262
Saline**	29195	-6.0	22,334	75	-6.0	21,002	68
Schuyler**	29197	3.1	4,300	14	3.0	4,427	14
Scotland	29199	-1.9	4,886	16	-1.9	4,794	15
Scott**	29201	1.8	41,150	139	1.8	41,888	135
Shannon	29203	0.4	8,354	28	0.3	8,381	27
Shelby	29205	-1.4	6,702	23	-1.3	6,613	21
Stoddard	29207	0.6	29,869	101	0.5	30,013	97
Stone**	29209	8.8	31,189	105	7.9	33,639	108
Sullivan	29211	-3.4	6,976	24	-3.4	6,738	22
Taney**	29213	7.0	42,474	143	6.0	45,023	145
Texas	29215	6.7	24,551	83	6.2	26,071	84
Vernon	29217	-0.6	20,324	69	-0.5	20,216	65
Warren*	29219	16.6	28,605	96	13.6	32,487	105
Washington*	29221	3.7	24,204	82	3.1	24,964	80
Wayne	29223	-1.0	13,122	44	-1.1	12,977	42
Webster*	29225	11.4	34,597	117	9.7	37,947	122
Worth	29227	-5.0	2,262	8	-4.9	2,151	7
Wright	29229	2.6	18,424	62	2.4	18,873	61
INDEPENDENT CITY							
St. Louis*	29510	-6.9	324,238	1,094	-6.6	302,974	975
Total: Missouri		**3.5**	**5,792,159**	**19,536**	**3.2**	**5,978,071**	**19,235**
Montana							
Beaverhead	30001	-4.6	8,780	30	-4.6	8,375	27
Big Horn	30003	2.8	13,029	44	2.6	13,369	43
Blaine	30005	-5.8	6,601	22	-5.6	6,231	20
Broadwater	30007	1.9	4,469	15	2.1	4,563	15
Carbon*	30009	3.8	9,919	33	3.6	10,272	33
Carter	30011	-3.0	1,319	4	-2.4	1,288	4
Cascade*	30013	-1.2	79,409	268	-1.1	78,518	253
Chouteau	30015	-10.4	5,349	18	-10.6	4,781	15
Custer	30017	-4.6	11,163	38	-4.4	10,672	34
Daniels	30019	-8.0	1,856	6	-7.8	1,711	6
Dawson	30021	-5.6	8,549	29	-5.5	8,076	26
Deer Lodge	30023	-7.0	8,755	30	-6.8	8,157	26
Fallon	30025	-3.5	2,738	9	-2.7	2,664	9
Fergus	30027	-3.5	11,478	39	-3.6	11,064	36
Flathead**	30029	11.0	82,627	279	9.4	90,423	291
Gallatin**	30031	13.0	76,679	259	10.8	84,996	274
Garfield	30033	-4.4	1,223	4	-3.7	1,178	4
Glacier	30035	0.6	13,321	45	0.7	13,420	43
Golden Valley	30037	3.6	1,080	4	5.1	1,135	4
Granite	30039	2.7	2,905	10	2.1	2,966	10
Hill**	30041	-3.3	16,117	54	-3.2	15,600	50
Jefferson**	30043	8.2	10,875	37	7.1	11,652	37
Judith Basin	30045	-9.4	2,111	7	-9.7	1,907	6
Lake	30047	5.1	27,862	94	4.3	29,063	94
Lewis and Clark**	30049	4.2	58,051	196	3.6	60,165	194
Liberty	30051	-9.1	1,962	7	-8.8	1,789	6
Lincoln	30053	0.4	18,921	64	0.3	18,983	61
McCone	30055	-13.1	1,719	6	-12.7	1,501	5
Madison	30057	1.9	6,980	24	1.5	7,082	23
Meagher	30059	3.2	1,994	7	3.1	2,056	7
Mineral	30061	-0.4	3,869	13	-0.5	3,851	12
Missoula*	30063	4.5	100,118	338	3.9	104,056	335
Musselshell	30065	-0.5	4,474	15	-0.7	4,444	14
Park	30067	0.8	15,825	53	0.5	15,911	51
Petroleum	30069	-1.2	487	2	-1.2	481	2
Phillips	30071	-11.5	4,070	14	-10.7	3,634	12
Pondera	30073	-5.4	6,077	20	-4.8	5,787	19
Powder River	30075	-2.3	1,815	6	-2.4	1,771	6
Powell	30077	-5.5	6,784	23	-5.5	6,408	21
Prairie	30079	-3.9	1,152	4	-3.3	1,114	4
Ravalli	30081	11.8	40,335	136	9.8	44,286	143
Richland	30083	-8.1	8,887	30	-7.8	8,197	26
Roosevelt	30085	-2.7	10,328	35	-2.9	10,028	32
Rosebud	30087	-1.3	9,257	31	-1.5	9,121	29
Sanders	30089	4.6	10,697	36	4.1	11,133	36
Sheridan	30091	-17.2	3,397	11	-16.8	2,828	9
Silver Bow**	30093	-6.4	32,391	109	-6.3	30,365	98
Stillwater	30095	4.7	8,584	29	4.1	8,935	29
Sweet Grass	30097	-0.2	3,602	12	-1.0	3,567	11
Teton	30099	-1.5	6,349	21	-1.5	6,254	20
Toole	30101	-4.3	5,038	17	-4.1	4,831	16
Treasure	30103	-20.9	681	2	-20.4	542	2
Valley	30105	-7.9	7,069	24	-7.5	6,538	21
Wheatland	30107	-11.1	2,009	7	-10.7	1,794	6
Wibaux	30109	-12.7	932	3	-13.2	809	3
Yellowstone*	30111	5.0	135,784	458	4.5	141,861	457
Total: Montana		**2.8**	**927,852**	**3,131**	**2.6**	**952,203**	**3,070**
Nebraska							
Adams**	31001	-1.0	30,836	104	-1.1	30,486	98
Antelope	31003	-5.6	7,038	24	-5.5	6,648	21
Arthur	31005	-12.8	387	1	-12.9	337	1
Banner**	31007	-10.9	730	2	-11.4	647	2
Blaine	31009	-12.9	508	2	-12.6	444	1
Boone	31011	-9.0	5,694	19	-8.5	5,212	17
Box Butte	31013	-7.3	11,270	38	-7.0	10,478	34
Boyd	31015	-8.1	2,240	8	-7.7	2,067	7
Brown	31017	-2.5	3,436	12	-2.5	3,349	11
Buffalo**	31019	2.8	43,441	147	2.5	44,535	143
Burt	31021	-6.5	7,286	25	-6.6	6,807	22
Butler	31023	0.8	8,834	30	-0.4	8,801	28
Cass*	31025	6.1	25,823	87	5.4	27,226	88
Cedar	31027	-6.9	8,954	30	-6.6	8,360	27
Chase	31029	-1.4	4,013	14	-0.9	3,975	13
Cherry	31031	-2.8	5,976	20	-2.8	5,810	19
Cheyenne	31033	1.4	9,968	34	1.3	10,098	32
Clay**	31035	-3.9	6,765	23	-3.8	6,505	21
Colfax	31037	0.7	10,512	35	0.6	10,571	34
Cuming	31039	-5.6	9,635	32	-5.3	9,121	29

Source: Devonshire Associates Ltd. and Scan/US, Inc. 2005.
* Component of a Metropolitan Core Based Statistical Area.
** Component of a Micropolitan Core Based Statistical Area.

(d) Data not available.

Counties: Population Trends, *Continued*

County	FIPS Code	Present: 2000-2005 % Change	Present: 7/1/05 Estimate	Present: 7/1/05 Ranally Population Units	Future: 2005-2010 % Change	Future: 2010 Projection	Future: 2010 Ranally Population Units
Custer	31041	-4.2	11,302	38	-4.3	10,820	35
Dakota*	31043	2.7	20,799	70	2.4	21,296	69
Dawes	31045	-2.7	8,815	30	-2.4	8,600	28
Dawson**	31047	1.1	24,642	83	0.9	24,857	80
Deuel	31049	-4.1	2,013	7	-4.6	1,921	6
Dixon*	31051	-5.0	6,020	20	-4.7	5,735	18
Dodge**	31053	-1.0	35,807	121	-1.2	35,374	114
Douglas*	31055	4.4	483,981	1,633	3.9	503,039	1,619
Dundy	31057	-5.8	2,158	7	-5.9	2,031	7
Fillmore	31059	-4.1	6,363	21	-4.0	6,111	20
Franklin	31061	-4.8	3,402	11	-4.2	3,260	10
Frontier	31063	-10.0	2,790	9	-9.7	2,520	8
Furnas	31065	-3.6	5,130	17	-3.3	4,961	16
Gage**	31067	2.7	23,611	80	2.6	24,217	78
Garden	31069	-5.0	2,177	7	-4.5	2,078	7
Garfield	31071	-4.8	1,811	6	-4.5	1,729	6
Gosper**	31073	-5.3	2,030	7	-5.3	1,922	6
Grant	31075	-11.5	661	2	-11.5	585	2
Greeley	31077	-6.0	2,550	9	-5.8	2,403	8
Hall**	31079	2.3	54,771	185	2.2	56,002	180
Hamilton	31081	1.2	9,513	32	1.2	9,630	31
Harlan	31083	-4.7	3,608	12	-4.5	3,447	11
Hayes	31085	4.7	1,118	4	3.8	1,161	4
Hitchcock	31087	-3.8	2,992	10	-3.6	2,885	9
Holt	31089	-6.3	10,821	36	-5.9	10,182	33
Hooker	31091	-8.0	720	2	-7.6	665	2
Howard**	31093	1.8	6,688	23	1.9	6,816	22
Jefferson	31095	-4.6	7,950	27	-4.7	7,576	24
Johnson	31097	0.4	4,505	15	0.4	4,524	15
Kearney**	31099	-1.0	6,816	23	-1.1	6,744	22
Keith	31101	-7.3	8,230	28	-7.1	7,646	25
Keya Paha	31103	-5.6	928	3	-5.3	879	3
Kimball	31105	-9.5	3,700	12	-9.0	3,367	11
Knox	31107	-5.5	8,860	30	-5.2	8,397	27
Lancaster*	31109	6.5	266,575	899	5.7	281,788	907
Lincoln**	31111	0.2	34,717	117	0.1	34,754	112
Logan**	31113	-12.7	676	2	-12.4	592	2
Loup	31115	6.7	760	3	6.2	807	3
McPherson**	31117	0.0	533	2	0.6	536	2
Madison**	31119	2.7	36,184	122	2.7	37,178	120
Merrick**	31121	-1.8	8,057	27	-1.4	7,941	26
Morrill	31123	-4.6	5,188	17	-4.8	4,940	16
Nance	31125	-11.2	3,585	12	-11.3	3,179	10
Nemaha	31127	-9.1	6,883	23	-9.1	6,256	20
Nuckolls	31129	-6.2	4,743	16	-5.7	4,473	14
Otoe	31131	0.2	15,427	52	-0.1	15,417	50
Pawnee	31133	-10.5	2,762	9	-10.5	2,473	8
Perkins	31135	-7.7	2,955	10	-7.0	2,748	9
Phelps	31137	-2.3	9,526	32	-2.3	9,308	30
Pierce**	31139	-3.1	7,616	26	-3.1	7,383	24
Platte**	31141	-2.2	30,978	104	-1.8	30,413	98
Polk	31143	-4.5	5,385	18	-4.2	5,161	17
Red Willow	31145	-3.4	11,063	37	-3.4	10,686	34
Richardson	31147	-9.9	8,592	29	-9.7	7,758	25
Rock	31149	-14.0	1,511	5	-14.0	1,299	4
Saline	31151	4.3	14,444	49	4.0	15,017	48
Sarpy*	31153	12.3	137,701	464	10.4	152,053	489
Saunders*	31155	1.8	20,179	68	1.5	20,489	66
Scotts Bluff**	31157	-0.9	36,634	124	-1.0	36,259	117
Seward*	31159	-0.3	16,447	55	-0.6	16,353	53
Sheridan	31161	-9.4	5,617	19	-9.2	5,102	16
Sherman	31163	-8.1	3,050	10	-7.5	2,821	9
Sioux	31165	1.2	1,492	5	1.2	1,510	5
Stanton**	31167	3.2	6,664	22	3.5	6,900	22
Thayer	31169	-11.5	5,357	18	-11.4	4,747	15
Thomas	31171	-13.7	629	2	-14.1	540	2
Thurston	31173	-1.0	7,097	24	-1.2	7,009	23
Valley	31175	-1.4	4,582	15	-1.5	4,515	15
Washington*	31177	6.6	20,017	68	6.0	21,224	68
Wayne	31179	-7.8	9,086	31	-7.3	8,424	27
Webster	31181	-7.1	3,774	13	-6.9	3,512	11
Wheeler	31183	-10.8	790	3	-10.8	705	2
York	31185	-3.6	14,071	47	-3.5	13,585	44
Total: Nebraska		**2.4**	**1,751,975**	**5,906**	**2.2**	**1,790,712**	**5,767**
Nevada							
Churchill**	32001	1.7	24,399	82	1.5	24,773	80
Clark*	32003	23.4	1,697,755	5,727	17.9	2,001,933	6,443
Douglas**	32005	11.3	45,940	155	9.7	50,409	162
Elko**	32007	-4.1	43,415	146	-4.1	41,618	134
Esmeralda	32009	-19.6	781	3	-19.7	627	2
Eureka**	32011	-15.5	1,395	5	-14.6	1,191	4
Humboldt	32013	5.4	16,980	57	6.2	18,039	58
Lander	32015	-19.2	4,682	16	-18.0	3,841	12
Lincoln	32017	4.3	4,343	15	3.8	4,506	14
Lyon	32019	27.2	43,895	148	20.5	52,887	170
Mineral	32021	-8.5	4,638	16	-7.5	4,291	14
Nye**	32023	16.2	37,749	127	12.8	42,570	137
Pershing	32027	-5.8	6,305	21	-5.3	5,971	19
Storey*	32029	6.6	3,623	12	6.4	3,854	12
Washoe*	32031	15.0	390,302	1,317	12.5	439,196	1,413
White Pine	32033	-10.2	8,240	28	-8.7	7,521	24
INDEPENDENT CITY							
Carson City*	32510	8.9	57,139	193	8.0	61,722	199
Total: Nevada		**19.7**	**2,391,581**	**8,068**	**15.6**	**2,764,949**	**8,897**
New Hampshire							
Belknap**	33001	11.2	62,646	211	9.7	68,724	221
Carroll	33003	8.8	47,487	160	7.5	51,057	164
Cheshire**	33005	5.4	77,820	262	4.9	81,641	263
Coos**	33007	1.2	33,515	113	1.1	33,870	109
Grafton**	33009	3.6	84,673	286	3.4	87,515	282
Hillsborough*	33011	5.9	403,350	1,361	5.2	424,307	1,366
Merrimack**	33013	9.2	148,696	502	8.1	160,677	517
Rockingham*	33015	7.5	298,070	1,005	6.5	317,391	1,021
Strafford*	33017	7.5	120,636	407	6.6	128,609	414
Sullivan**	33019	6.5	43,085	145	5.9	45,610	147
Total: New Hampshire		**6.8**	**1,319,978**	**4,452**	**6.0**	**1,399,401**	**4,504**
New Jersey							
Atlantic*	34001	3.4	261,127	881	3.1	269,137	866
Bergen*	34003	2.6	906,873	3,059	2.3	927,845	2,986
Burlington*	34005	8.3	458,701	1,547	7.4	492,773	1,586
Camden*	34007	1.8	518,146	1,748	1.8	527,433	1,697
Cape May*	34009	-0.6	101,669	343	-0.6	101,017	325
Cumberland*	34011	3.3	151,331	510	3.2	156,244	503
Essex*	34013	0.8	800,056	2,699	0.9	807,383	2,598
Gloucester*	34015	8.0	275,154	928	7.2	294,986	949
Hudson*	34017	-0.3	607,051	2,048	-0.4	604,565	1,946
Hunterdon*	34019	8.5	132,353	446	7.4	142,102	457
Mercer*	34021	5.3	369,496	1,246	4.9	387,426	1,247
Middlesex*	34023	6.8	800,915	2,702	6.0	848,816	2,732
Monmouth*	34025	4.7	644,487	2,174	4.2	671,700	2,162
Morris*	34027	4.6	492,011	1,660	4.2	512,552	1,650
Ocean*	34029	11.3	568,520	1,918	9.7	623,431	2,006
Passaic*	34031	3.1	504,035	1,700	2.6	516,976	1,664
Salem*	34033	1.7	65,361	220	1.7	66,484	214
Somerset*	34035	7.9	321,061	1,083	6.9	343,220	1,105
Sussex*	34037	7.8	155,440	524	6.9	166,205	535
Union*	34039	2.2	534,259	1,802	2.0	545,156	1,754
Warren*	34041	10.8	113,479	383	9.3	123,985	399
Total: New Jersey		**4.4**	**8,781,525**	**29,621**	**4.0**	**9,129,436**	**29,381**
New Mexico							
Bernalillo*	35001	7.5	598,254	2,018	6.8	638,753	2,056
Catron	35003	-4.5	3,383	11	-5.1	3,210	10
Chaves**	35005	-0.3	61,197	206	-0.2	61,067	197
Cibola**	35006	9.4	27,991	94	8.2	30,298	98
Colfax	35007	-2.8	13,790	47	-2.9	13,384	43
Curry**	35009	0.7	45,360	153	1.0	45,804	147
De Baca	35011	-10.3	2,009	7	-9.4	1,820	6
Dona Ana*	35013	7.2	187,285	632	6.5	199,509	642
Eddy**	35015	-0.5	51,414	173	-0.1	51,357	165
Grant**	35017	-6.0	29,153	98	-5.7	27,479	88
Guadalupe	35019	-1.8	4,598	16	-1.7	4,522	15
Harding	35021	-9.9	730	2	-9.0	664	2
Hidalgo	35023	-16.7	4,943	17	-14.2	4,240	14
Lea**	35025	1.1	56,128	189	1.6	57,039	184
Lincoln	35027	7.4	20,841	70	6.2	22,135	71
Los Alamos**	35028	3.6	19,001	64	3.7	19,707	63
Luna**	35029	4.6	26,168	88	4.5	27,333	88
McKinley**	35031	-4.9	71,137	240	-5.1	67,514	217
Mora	35033	2.2	5,295	18	1.7	5,385	17
Otero**	35035	-0.5	61,969	209	-0.5	61,673	198
Quay	35037	-7.9	9,355	32	-7.2	8,680	28
Rio Arriba**	35039	-1.4	40,597	137	-1.6	39,935	129
Roosevelt**	35041	1.8	18,342	62	1.9	18,694	60
Sandoval*	35043	16.0	104,283	352	13.1	117,912	379
San Juan*	35045	12.5	127,992	432	10.7	141,716	456
San Miguel**	35047	-3.1	29,205	99	-2.9	28,345	91
Santa Fe*	35049	9.3	141,278	477	8.1	152,692	491
Sierra	35051	-1.8	13,029	44	-1.7	12,811	41
Socorro	35053	0.6	18,193	61	0.7	18,322	59
Taos**	35055	6.6	31,943	108	5.8	33,798	109
Torrance*	35057	-1.2	16,716	56	-1.5	16,458	53
Union	35059	-12.4	3,657	12	-12.2	3,210	10
Valencia*	35061	5.3	69,672	235	4.6	72,855	234
Total: New Mexico		**5.3**	**1,914,908**	**6,459**	**4.9**	**2,008,321**	**6,461**
New York							
Albany*	36001	2.2	300,976	1,015	2.1	307,368	989
Allegany	36003	1.9	50,878	172	1.9	51,844	167
Bronx*	36005	3.9	1,385,071	4,672	3.6	1,435,428	4,620
Broome*	36007	-1.3	197,991	668	-1.1	195,750	630
Cattaraugus**	36009	-1.0	83,138	280	-0.9	82,360	265
Cayuga**	36011	0.2	82,152	277	0.2	82,352	265
Chautauqua**	36013	-2.0	136,986	462	-1.9	134,415	433
Chemung*	36015	-1.1	90,031	304	-1.1	89,021	286
Chenango	36017	1.3	52,058	176	1.2	52,693	170
Clinton**	36019	3.3	82,512	278	3.1	85,084	274
Columbia**	36021	0.9	63,685	215	1.0	64,301	207
Cortland**	36023	1.3	49,245	166	1.3	49,909	161
Delaware	36025	-2.4	46,922	158	-2.2	45,893	148
Dutchess*	36027	6.3	297,806	1,005	5.7	314,780	1,013
Erie*	36029	-1.4	936,770	3,160	-1.3	924,278	2,975
Essex	36031	0.9	39,212	132	0.8	39,535	127
Franklin**	36033	0.2	51,230	173	0.2	51,339	165
Fulton**	36035	0.9	55,594	188	1.1	56,180	181
Genesee**	36037	-1.1	59,736	201	-1.0	59,138	190
Greene	36039	2.3	49,325	166	2.2	50,399	162
Hamilton	36041	-3.5	5,189	17	-3.7	4,999	16
Herkimer*	36043	-1.6	63,402	214	-1.6	62,418	201
Jefferson**	36045	2.4	114,448	386	2.6	117,428	378
Kings*	36047	0.6	2,480,420	8,367	0.5	2,493,914	8,026
Lewis	36049	-2.1	26,386	89	-2.3	25,792	83
Livingston*	36051	0.7	64,792	219	0.6	65,187	210
Madison*	36053	2.1	70,875	239	2.0	72,294	233
Monroe*	36055	0.5	738,925	2,492	0.4	742,088	2,388
Montgomery**	36057	-1.3	49,061	165	-1.3	48,445	156
Nassau*	36059	0.7	1,343,675	4,532	0.5	1,350,776	4,347
New York*	36061	3.3	1,588,044	5,357	3.1	1,636,531	5,267
Niagara*	36063	-1.0	217,756	735	-0.8	215,908	695
Oneida*	36065	-0.5	234,252	790	-0.4	233,265	751
Onondaga*	36067	1.0	462,726	1,561	0.9	466,993	1,503
Ontario*	36069	4.2	104,413	352	3.8	108,420	349
Orange*	36071	10.6	377,527	1,273	9.1	412,040	1,326
Orleans*	36073	-0.7	43,876	148	-0.7	43,571	140
Oswego*	36075	1.5	124,250	419	1.4	125,947	405
Otsego**	36077	2.1	62,947	212	2.0	64,231	207
Putnam*	36079	6.8	102,260	345	6.0	108,401	349
Queens*	36081	-0.2	2,225,143	7,506	-0.3	2,218,858	7,141
Rensselaer*	36083	0.9	153,917	519	0.9	155,278	500
Richmond*	36085	5.9	470,056	1,586	5.2	494,633	1,592
Rockland*	36087	3.6	297,018	1,002	3.2	306,523	986
St. Lawrence**	36089	-1.0	110,838	374	-0.9	109,831	353
Saratoga*	36091	7.9	216,567	731	7.0	231,679	746
Schenectady*	36093	1.2	148,278	500	1.2	150,092	483
Schoharie*	36095	1.3	31,992	108	1.2	32,388	104
Schuyler	36097	2.2	19,648	66	1.9	20,026	64
Seneca**	36099	7.4	35,799	121	6.8	38,218	123
Steuben**	36101	0.6	99,314	335	0.5	99,808	321
Suffolk*	36103	5.6	1,498,863	5,056	5.0	1,573,642	5,064
Sullivan	36105	2.9	76,088	257	2.6	78,104	251
Tioga*	36107	0.2	51,865	175	0.2	51,971	167
Tompkins*	36109	4.7	100,996	341	4.4	105,440	339
Ulster*	36111	3.5	183,995	621	3.3	190,073	612
Warren*	36113	4.0	65,852	222	3.8	68,356	220
Washington*	36115	3.0	62,872	212	3.0	64,738	208
Wayne*	36117	0.5	94,278	318	0.5	94,770	305
Westchester*	36119	3.0	951,137	3,208	2.6	976,236	3,142
Wyoming	36121	-1.0	42,979	145	-1.0	42,560	137
Yates	36123	0.8	24,809	84	0.8	25,011	80
Total: New York		**2.0**	**19,348,846**	**65,267**	**1.8**	**19,698,950**	**63,396**
North Carolina							
Alamance*	37001	7.1	140,105	473	6.2	148,722	479
Alexander*	37003	5.9	35,588	120	5.4	37,498	121
Alleghany	37005	2.7	10,966	37	2.4	11,229	36
Anson*	37007	-0.4	25,186	85	-0.3	25,112	81
Ashe	37009	4.2	25,406	86	3.7	26,351	85
Avery	37011	4.6	17,957	61	4.2	18,716	60
Beaufort**	37013	2.1	45,889	155	1.9	46,782	151
Bertie	37015	-2.0	19,376	65	-1.8	19,032	61
Bladen	37017	2.0	32,934	111	2.0	33,606	108
Brunswick*	37019	18.8	86,905	293	15.1	100,046	322
Buncombe*	37021	5.4	217,531	734	4.8	228,057	734
Burke*	37023	0.8	89,829	303	0.6	90,378	291
Cabarrus*	37025	14.9	150,533	508	12.1	168,822	543
Caldwell*	37027	3.1	79,837	269	2.8	82,046	264
Camden**	37029	23.5	8,501	29	18.5	10,074	32
Carteret**	37031	4.6	62,124	210	4.4	64,836	209
Caswell	37033	1.4	23,819	80	1.1	24,082	77
Catawba*	37035	6.4	150,785	509	5.5	159,058	512
Chatham*	37037	19.9	59,157	200	16.0	68,596	221
Cherokee	37039	4.8	25,461	86	4.2	26,529	85
Chowan	37041	0.2	14,562	49	3.0	15,001	48
Clay	37043	10.2	9,666	33	8.8	10,517	34
Cleveland**	37045	3.3	99,439	335	2.8	102,272	329
Columbus	37047	-0.4	54,523	184	-0.5	54,272	175
Craven**	37049	-0.0	91,416	308	-0.3	91,156	293
Cumberland*	37051	1.2	306,556	1,034	1.2	310,229	998
Currituck*	37053	23.6	22,484	76	18.4	26,629	86
Dare**	37055	16.7	34,986	118	13.7	39,777	128
Davidson**	37057	5.5	155,335	524	4.9	162,985	525
Davie*	37059	11.3	38,755	131	9.5	42,443	137
Duplin	37061	7.1	52,526	177	6.3	55,848	180
Durham*	37063	9.2	243,802	822	7.9	263,055	847
Edgecombe*	37065	-1.8	54,620	184	-1.3	53,931	174
Forsyth*	37067	6.3	325,303	1,097	5.6	343,635	1,106
Franklin*	37069	17.3	55,425	187	14.1	63,240	204
Gaston*	37071	2.6	195,391	659	2.4	200,065	644
Gates	37073	4.0	10,936	37	3.9	11,363	37
Graham	37075	0.7	8,046	27	0.6	8,095	26
Granville	37077	13.1	54,864	185	11.1	60,969	196
Greene*	37079	8.1	20,517	69	7.1	21,971	71
Guilford*	37081	5.0	442,093	1,491	4.4	461,760	1,486
Halifax**	37083	-2.7	55,838	188	-2.6	54,408	175
Harnett**	37085	14.4	104,103	351	12.0	116,614	375
Haywood*	37087	4.9	56,679	191	4.5	59,235	191
Henderson*	37089	8.4	96,658	326	7.3	103,676	334
Hertford	37091	4.4	23,602	80	2.9	24,290	78
Hoke*	37093	18.3	39,794	134	14.8	45,688	147
Hyde	37095	-7.5	5,391	18	-6.8	5,022	16
Iredell**	37097	14.1	140,000	472	11.7	156,391	503
Jackson	37099	7.1	35,487	120	6.2	37,697	121
Johnston*	37101	19.8	146,138	493	15.6	168,989	544
Jones**	37103	-3.1	10,062	34	-3.2	9,741	31
Lee**	37105	0.3	49,188	166	-0.5	48,942	158
Lenoir**	37107	-2.8	58,000	196	-2.5	56,528	182
Lincoln**	37109	8.9	69,482	234	7.8	74,908	241
McDowell	37111	3.1	43,478	147	2.9	44,723	144
Macon	37113	7.3	31,979	108	6.3	33,987	109

Source: Devonshire Associates Ltd. and Scan/US, Inc. 2005.
* Component of a Metropolitan Core Based Statistical Area.
** Component of a Micropolitan Core Based Statistical Area.
(d) Data not available.

Continued on next page

Counties: Population Trends, *Continued*

County	FIPS Code	Present: 2000-2005 % Change	Present: 7/1/05 Estimate	Present: 7/1/05 Ranally Population Units	Future: 2005-2010 % Change	Future: 2010 Projection	Future: 2010 Ranally Population Units
Madison*	37115	2.6	20,139	68	2.2	20,576	66
Martin	37117	-3.2	24,783	84	-2.9	24,065	77
Mecklenburg*	37119	13.3	787,867	2,658	11.1	875,406	2,817
Mitchell	37121	1.2	15,868	54	0.9	16,007	52
Montgomery	37123	3.0	27,614	93	2.4	28,284	91
Moore**	37125	9.0	81,519	275	7.8	87,878	283
Nash*	37127	4.3	91,159	307	3.7	94,567	304
New Hanover*	37129	8.4	173,836	586	7.6	186,986	602
Northampton**	37131	-2.6	21,514	73	-2.6	20,950	67
Onslow*	37133	-0.4	149,754	505	0.2	150,057	483
Orange*	37135	-0.1	118,085	398	1.8	120,243	387
Pamlico**	37137	-1.5	12,746	43	-1.5	12,550	40
Pasquotank**	37139	5.5	36,831	124	5.3	38,777	125
Pender*	37141	10.0	45,203	152	8.7	49,132	158
Perquimans**	37143	4.0	11,824	40	3.5	12,233	39
Person*	37145	5.6	37,629	127	5.0	39,497	127
Pitt*	37147	5.9	141,666	478	5.3	149,202	480
Polk	37149	4.2	19,102	64	3.6	19,791	64
Randolph*	37151	5.6	137,787	465	4.8	144,465	465
Richmond**	37153	0.4	46,738	158	0.3	46,883	151
Robeson**	37155	3.3	127,419	430	3.1	131,415	423
Rockingham*	37157	1.4	93,254	315	1.4	94,524	304
Rowan**	37159	4.6	136,277	460	4.1	141,864	457
Rutherford**	37161	1.8	64,035	216	1.6	65,064	209
Sampson	37163	5.0	63,147	213	4.5	65,970	212
Scotland**	37165	0.1	36,031	122	0.0	36,032	116
Stanly**	37167	2.0	59,255	200	1.8	60,312	194
Stokes*	37169	1.7	45,460	153	1.3	46,050	148
Surry**	37171	2.6	73,080	247	2.5	74,911	241
Swain	37173	1.5	13,158	44	1.0	13,293	43
Transylvania**	37175	0.7	29,531	100	0.5	29,681	96
Tyrrell	37177	1.9	4,228	14	2.0	4,311	14
Union*	37179	29.1	159,636	538	21.3	193,627	623
Vance**	37181	2.8	44,153	149	2.2	45,145	145
Wake*	37183	17.5	737,573	2,488	14.2	841,949	2,710
Warren	37185	-1.0	19,765	67	-0.9	19,592	63
Washington	37187	-3.2	13,278	45	-3.2	12,857	41
Watauga**	37189	-0.1	42,666	144	-0.2	42,578	137
Wayne*	37191	0.1	113,461	383	0.1	113,549	365
Wilkes**	37193	3.6	67,997	229	3.2	70,170	226
Wilson**	37195	3.5	76,408	258	3.2	78,874	254
Yadkin*	37197	4.1	37,851	128	3.5	39,181	126
Yancey	37199	2.3	18,184	61	2.0	18,553	60
Total: North Carolina		**7.4**	**8,642,524**	**29,155**	**6.5**	**9,206,675**	**29,630**
North Dakota							
Adams	38001	-7.8	2,392	8	-7.5	2,212	7
Barnes	38003	-8.2	10,814	36	-7.9	9,962	32
Benson	38005	-2.1	6,819	23	-2.2	6,667	21
Billings**	38007	-6.2	833	3	-5.0	791	3
Bottineau	38009	-6.5	6,682	23	-6.3	6,262	20
Bowman	38011	-8.1	2,978	10	-8.0	2,740	9
Burke	38013	-10.3	2,012	7	-10.0	1,810	6
Burleigh*	38015	5.4	73,166	247	4.8	76,649	247
Cass*	38017	4.7	128,908	435	4.1	134,150	432
Cavalier	38019	-10.6	4,319	15	-10.3	3,872	12
Dickey	38021	-7.9	5,302	18	-7.8	4,886	16
Divide	38023	-5.2	2,165	7	-4.6	2,065	7
Dunn	38025	-3.0	3,491	12	-3.2	3,379	11
Eddy	38027	-7.9	2,539	9	-7.5	2,348	8
Emmons	38029	-11.6	3,828	13	-11.2	3,398	11
Foster	38031	-10.4	3,369	11	-10.1	3,030	10
Golden Valley	38033	-8.6	1,758	6	-8.5	1,609	5
Grand Forks*	38035	-3.6	63,757	215	-3.3	61,648	198
Grant	38037	-9.8	2,562	9	-9.8	2,311	7
Griggs	38039	-10.4	2,467	8	-9.9	2,224	7
Hettinger	38041	-7.6	2,510	8	-6.5	2,347	8
Kidder	38043	-9.2	2,499	8	-8.8	2,278	7
LaMoure	38045	-6.0	4,421	15	-5.7	4,167	13
Logan	38047	-12.7	2,015	7	-12.3	1,767	6
McHenry**	38049	-7.2	5,555	19	-6.9	5,173	17
McIntosh	38051	-8.8	3,092	10	-8.6	2,826	9
McKenzie	38053	-4.1	5,503	19	-3.9	5,290	17
McLean	38055	-6.5	8,705	29	-6.2	8,161	26
Mercer	38057	-2.8	8,403	28	-2.6	8,188	26
Morton*	38059	-0.7	25,137	85	-1.0	24,886	80
Mountrail	38061	-3.5	6,402	22	-3.3	6,191	20
Nelson	38063	-12.2	3,260	11	-12.0	2,870	9
Oliver	38065	-12.4	1,808	6	-12.2	1,587	5
Pembina	38067	-6.9	7,995	27	-6.7	7,457	24
Pierce	38069	-7.3	4,333	15	-7.3	4,018	13
Ramsey	38071	-6.2	11,321	38	-6.0	10,639	34
Ransom	38073	-1.4	5,808	20	-1.7	5,710	18
Renville**	38075	-6.8	2,433	8	-6.4	2,278	7
Richland**	38077	-3.0	17,458	59	-3.0	16,942	55
Rolette	38079	0.6	13,754	46	0.3	13,793	44
Sargent	38081	-5.5	4,125	14	-5.5	3,897	13
Sheridan	38083	-16.4	1,430	5	-15.9	1,202	4
Sioux	38085	3.2	4,172	14	2.5	4,275	14
Slope	38087	-3.5	740	2	-2.7	720	2
Stark**	38089	-3.9	21,753	73	-3.7	20,952	67
Steele	38091	-12.4	1,978	7	-11.9	1,743	6
Stutsman**	38093	-5.7	20,655	70	-5.6	19,507	63
Towner	38095	-12.2	2,525	9	-11.8	2,228	7
Traill	38097	-3.6	8,176	28	-3.7	7,877	25
Walsh	38099	-8.4	11,353	38	-8.3	10,407	33
Ward**	38101	-6.7	54,872	185	-6.7	51,222	165
Wells	38103	-11.9	4,493	15	-11.8	3,965	13
Williams**	38105	-3.1	19,144	65	-2.8	18,600	60
Total: North Dakota		**-2.2**	**627,989**	**2,120**	**-2.0**	**615,176**	**1,979**
Ohio							
Adams	39001	4.7	28,624	97	4.4	29,895	96
Allen*	39003	-1.8	106,543	359	-1.7	104,784	337
Ashland**	39005	3.9	54,594	184	3.7	56,592	182
Ashtabula**	39007	0.4	103,185	348	0.3	103,544	333
Athens**	39009	2.3	63,652	215	2.1	64,962	209
Auglaize**	39011	0.4	46,791	158	0.3	46,938	151
Belmont*	39013	-1.7	69,040	233	-1.6	67,943	219
Brown*	39015	5.7	44,709	151	4.7	46,813	151
Butler*	39017	4.9	349,225	1,178	4.4	364,560	1,173
Carroll*	39019	3.8	29,941	101	3.5	30,982	100
Champaign**	39021	2.6	39,898	135	2.4	40,837	131
Clark*	39023	-2.1	141,771	478	-1.9	139,024	447
Clermont*	39025	6.9	190,233	642	6.0	201,712	649
Clinton**	39027	4.8	42,495	143	4.2	44,282	143
Columbiana**	39029	-0.8	111,181	375	-0.9	110,205	355
Coshocton**	39031	1.7	37,286	126	1.5	37,853	122
Crawford**	39033	-3.2	45,458	153	-3.1	44,043	142
Cuyahoga*	39035	-3.6	1,344,252	4,534	-3.5	1,297,572	4,176
Darke**	39037	-0.8	52,876	178	-0.9	52,420	169
Defiance**	39039	-1.7	38,831	131	-1.6	38,204	123
Delaware*	39041	37.5	151,233	510	26.0	190,621	613
Erie*	39043	-1.5	78,323	264	-1.6	77,033	248
Fairfield*	39045	13.3	139,046	469	11.2	154,580	497
Fayette**	39047	-1.5	28,010	94	-1.5	27,576	89
Franklin*	39049	3.0	1,100,544	3,712	2.6	1,129,032	3,633
Fulton*	39051	1.2	42,582	144	1.0	43,007	138
Gallia**	39053	0.9	31,347	106	0.8	31,596	102
Geauga*	39055	5.5	95,917	324	4.8	100,533	324
Greene*	39057	2.8	152,045	513	2.5	155,847	502
Guernsey**	39059	2.0	41,593	140	1.9	42,375	136
Hamilton*	39061	-4.2	809,794	2,732	-4.1	776,764	2,500
Hancock**	39063	4.3	74,326	251	4.0	77,299	249
Hardin	39065	-0.6	31,758	107	-0.6	31,570	102
Harrison	39067	1.3	16,069	54	1.2	16,268	52
Henry	39069	0.9	29,483	99	0.9	29,741	96
Highland	39071	4.6	42,760	144	4.0	44,472	143
Hocking	39073	2.7	29,005	98	2.6	29,748	96
Holmes	39075	7.3	41,788	141	6.5	44,494	143
Huron**	39077	1.7	60,500	204	1.4	61,366	197
Jackson	39079	2.3	33,408	113	2.2	34,159	110
Jefferson*	39081	-4.6	70,461	238	-4.4	67,356	217
Knox**	39083	7.6	58,657	198	6.8	62,627	202
Lake*	39085	2.3	232,832	785	2.2	237,905	766
Lawrence*	39087	0.4	62,567	211	0.4	62,824	202
Licking*	39089	5.7	153,841	519	5.0	161,531	520
Logan**	39091	1.8	46,813	158	1.7	47,589	153
Lorain*	39093	3.8	295,342	996	3.4	305,320	983
Lucas*	39095	-0.5	452,909	1,528	-0.5	450,819	1,451
Madison*	39097	1.8	40,930	138	1.7	41,613	134
Mahoning*	39099	-3.7	248,058	837	-3.5	239,280	770
Marion**	39101	0.4	66,455	224	0.4	66,733	215
Medina*	39103	11.3	168,198	567	9.6	184,422	594
Meigs	39105	1.7	23,466	79	1.8	23,883	77
Mercer**	39107	0.4	41,093	139	0.4	41,250	133
Miami*	39109	2.0	100,836	340	1.8	102,636	330
Monroe	39111	-2.1	14,858	50	-2.2	14,538	47
Montgomery*	39113	-2.0	547,810	1,848	-2.0	537,122	1,729
Morgan	39115	-0.3	14,848	50	-0.3	14,804	48
Morrow*	39117	10.0	34,782	117	8.5	37,737	121
Muskingum**	39119	1.4	85,731	289	1.1	86,692	279
Noble	39121	0.1	14,079	47	-0.2	14,053	45
Ottawa*	39123	1.1	41,432	140	1.0	41,839	135
Paulding	39125	-4.6	19,368	65	-4.3	18,532	60
Perry	39127	3.9	35,396	119	3.5	36,647	118
Pickaway*	39129	1.6	53,572	181	1.3	54,267	175
Pike	39131	3.0	28,517	96	2.6	29,266	94
Portage*	39133	2.2	155,370	524	1.9	158,307	509
Preble*	39135	0.7	42,629	144	0.6	42,882	138
Putnam	39137	0.2	34,791	117	0.0	34,807	112
Richland*	39139	-0.9	127,690	431	-0.9	126,535	407
Ross**	39141	2.3	75,026	253	2.1	76,571	246
Sandusky**	39143	-0.3	61,596	208	-0.4	61,355	197
Scioto**	39145	-3.5	76,419	258	-3.4	73,816	238
Seneca**	39147	-2.1	57,462	194	-2.0	56,301	181
Shelby**	39149	2.0	48,854	165	1.7	49,691	160
Stark*	39151	-0.2	377,190	1,272	-0.3	376,106	1,210
Summit*	39153	1.1	549,026	1,852	1.0	554,262	1,784
Trumbull*	39155	-2.6	219,265	740	-2.6	213,614	687
Tuscarawas**	39157	1.4	92,174	311	1.2	93,267	300
Union*	39159	11.0	45,412	153	9.2	49,594	160
Van Wert**	39161	-2.1	29,040	98	-2.1	28,441	92
Vinton	39163	5.5	13,511	46	5.1	14,203	46
Warren*	39165	24.1	196,541	663	18.1	232,168	747
Washington*	39167	-1.7	62,162	210	-1.7	61,134	197
Wayne**	39169	2.3	114,151	385	2.1	116,553	375
Williams	39171	-1.5	38,609	130	-1.6	38,006	122
Wood*	39173	1.8	123,284	416	1.6	125,310	403
Wyandot	39175	-0.9	22,712	77	-0.9	22,506	72
Total: Ohio		**1.2**	**11,485,881**	**38,744**	**1.1**	**11,607,960**	**37,359**
Oklahoma							
Adair	40001	4.1	21,905	74	3.7	22,717	73
Alfalfa	40003	-5.8	5,749	19	-5.9	5,409	17
Atoka	40005	3.5	14,370	48	3.4	14,855	48
Beaver	40007	-8.4	5,366	18	-7.3	4,972	16
Beckham**	40009	-2.7	19,255	65	-1.9	18,892	61
Blaine	40011	-7.7	11,058	37	-5.7	10,429	34
Bryan**	40013	2.8	37,565	127	2.4	38,479	124
Caddo	40015	-0.5	29,994	101	-0.5	29,833	96
Canadian*	40017	9.7	96,179	324	8.3	104,171	335
Carter**	40019	3.3	47,108	159	3.1	48,588	156
Cherokee**	40021	4.6	44,488	150	3.9	46,245	149
Choctaw	40023	-0.1	15,333	52	-0.2	15,310	49
Cimarron	40025	-9.2	2,858	10	-9.3	2,593	8
Cleveland*	40027	8.5	225,695	761	7.6	242,817	781
Coal	40029	-1.1	5,962	20	-0.8	5,913	19
Comanche*	40031	-5.2	109,018	368	-3.7	104,954	338
Cotton	40033	-1.4	6,520	22	-2.0	6,389	21
Craig	40035	-1.1	14,793	50	-1.2	14,610	47
Creek*	40037	3.3	69,584	235	2.9	71,575	230
Custer	40039	-6.0	24,574	83	-5.7	23,167	75
Delaware	40041	6.7	39,577	133	6.0	41,932	135
Dewey	40043	-5.2	4,494	15	-4.7	4,281	14
Ellis	40045	-4.2	3,904	13	-3.7	3,758	12
Garfield**	40047	-1.8	56,753	191	-1.7	55,789	180
Garvin	40049	-0.0	27,208	92	-0.3	27,119	87
Grady*	40051	6.8	48,624	164	6.2	51,631	166
Grant	40053	-5.1	4,882	16	-4.9	4,643	15
Greer	40055	-5.6	5,719	19	-5.3	5,418	17
Harmon	40057	-10.8	2,930	10	-10.8	2,614	8
Harper	40059	-7.8	3,283	11	-7.4	3,040	10
Haskell	40061	3.6	12,217	41	3.2	12,605	41
Hughes	40063	-2.3	13,826	47	-2.4	13,491	43
Jackson**	40065	-6.3	26,651	90	-5.7	25,125	81
Jefferson	40067	-6.5	6,372	21	-6.2	5,978	19
Johnston	40069	0.0	10,513	35	0.0	10,514	34
Kay**	40071	-2.6	46,817	158	-2.4	45,687	147
Kingfisher	40073	2.0	14,199	48	2.1	14,491	47
Kiowa	40075	-3.8	9,841	33	-3.7	9,481	31
Latimer	40077	-2.3	10,448	35	-2.3	10,207	33
Le Flore*	40079	2.7	49,394	167	2.4	50,583	163
Lincoln*	40081	0.8	32,331	109	0.5	32,499	105
Logan*	40083	7.6	36,508	123	6.8	38,983	125
Love**	40085	2.6	9,059	31	2.5	9,288	30
McClain*	40087	5.2	29,188	98	4.5	30,516	98
McCurtain	40089	-1.6	33,866	114	-1.6	33,314	107
McIntosh	40091	3.1	20,057	68	2.8	20,622	66
Major	40093	-2.7	7,340	25	-2.7	7,142	23
Marshall	40095	6.1	13,994	47	5.8	14,810	48
Mayes	40097	2.5	39,343	133	2.2	40,222	129
Murray	40099	1.0	12,753	43	1.0	12,882	41
Muskogee**	40101	2.2	70,975	239	2.0	72,396	233
Noble	40103	-2.0	11,182	38	-1.8	10,982	35
Nowata	40105	4.6	11,060	37	4.2	11,524	37
Okfuskee	40107	-1.7	11,617	39	-1.8	11,411	37
Oklahoma*	40109	4.0	687,070	2,318	3.6	711,865	2,291
Okmulgee*	40111	0.8	40,003	135	0.8	40,337	130
Osage*	40113	2.7	45,632	154	2.3	46,662	150
Ottawa**	40115	-2.4	32,406	109	-2.6	31,554	102
Pawnee*	40117	2.4	17,006	57	1.8	17,305	56
Payne**	40119	2.8	70,126	237	2.5	71,845	231
Pittsburg**	40121	0.3	44,083	149	0.1	44,127	142
Pontotoc**	40123	-0.8	34,877	118	-0.8	34,588	111
Pottawatomie**	40125	3.6	67,866	229	3.4	70,149	226
Pushmataha	40127	0.6	11,739	40	0.6	11,813	38
Roger Mills	40129	-10.7	3,069	10	-10.4	2,751	9
Rogers*	40131	14.9	81,199	274	12.1	90,987	293
Seminole	40133	-2.5	24,269	82	-2.6	23,645	76
Sequoyah*	40135	4.2	40,620	137	3.8	42,155	136
Stephens**	40137	-2.3	42,200	142	-2.1	41,318	133
Texas**	40139	-1.7	19,768	67	-2.1	19,352	62
Tillman	40141	-6.7	8,665	29	-6.5	8,106	26
Tulsa*	40143	2.1	574,848	1,939	1.9	585,531	1,884
Wagoner*	40145	12.1	64,436	217	10.4	71,113	229
Washington**	40147	0.3	49,163	166	0.3	49,308	159
Washita	40149	-2.4	11,230	38	-2.5	10,952	35
Woods	40151	-7.1	8,442	28	-6.9	7,860	25
Woodward**	40153	1.1	18,697	63	1.2	18,923	61
Total: Oklahoma		**2.6**	**3,541,713**	**11,944**	**2.5**	**3,629,142**	**11,679**
Oregon							
Baker	41001	-2.4	16,341	55	-2.3	15,960	51
Benton*	41003	2.1	79,778	269	2.1	81,434	262
Clackamas*	41005	9.1	369,163	1,245	8.0	398,673	1,283
Clatsop**	41007	1.8	36,264	122	1.8	36,934	119
Columbia*	41009	10.3	48,039	162	9.1	52,406	169
Coos**	41011	1.1	63,447	214	1.2	64,198	207
Crook**	41013	12.3	21,549	73	10.2	23,753	76
Curry**	41015	4.5	22,083	74	4.3	23,043	74
Deschutes*	41017	19.8	138,176	466	15.6	159,740	514
Douglas**	41019	3.1	103,471	349	2.9	106,452	343
Gilliam	41021	-10.4	1,715	6	-10.2	1,540	5
Grant	41023	-9.5	7,180	24	-9.1	6,527	21
Harney	41025	-8.4	6,968	23	-8.4	6,380	21
Hood River**	41027	3.4	21,109	71	3.0	21,734	70
Jackson*	41029	8.2	196,043	661	7.2	210,212	677
Jefferson	41031	6.2	20,186	68	5.3	21,261	68
Josephine**	41033	6.9	80,986	273	6.3	86,087	277
Klamath**	41035	2.9	65,599	221	2.5	67,262	216
Lake	41037	0.5	7,459	25	0.7	7,508	24
Lane*	41039	3.8	335,284	1,131	3.5	347,119	1,117
Lincoln	41041	1.6	45,186	152	1.9	46,031	148
Linn**	41043	5.4	108,650	366	5.1	114,241	368

Source: Devonshire Associates Ltd. and Scan/US, Inc. 2005.
* Component of a Metropolitan Core Based Statistical Area.
** Component of a Micropolitan Core Based Statistical Area.
(d) Data not available.

Counties: Population Trends, *Continued*

County	FIPS Code	Present: 2000-2005 % Change	Present: 7/1/05 Estimate	Present: 7/1/05 Ranally Population Units	Future: 2005-2010 % Change	Future: 2010 Projection	Future: 2010 Ranally Population Units
Malheur**	41045	-1.2	31,247	105	-0.9	30,957	100
Marion*	41047	7.6	306,501	1,034	6.8	327,358	1,054
Morrow**	41049	9.2	12,009	41	7.9	12,960	42
Multnomah*	41051	4.3	688,787	2,323	4.0	716,054	2,304
Polk*	41053	9.8	68,485	231	8.5	74,314	239
Sherman	41055	-12.5	1,693	6	-12.1	1,488	5
Tillamook	41057	3.0	24,989	84	2.9	25,715	83
Umatilla**	41059	5.3	74,284	251	4.8	77,879	251
Union**	41061	-0.2	24,483	83	-0.3	24,415	79
Wallowa	41063	-3.0	7,006	24	-2.9	6,800	22
Wasco**	41065	-0.9	23,581	80	-1.0	23,347	75
Washington*	41067	12.3	500,313	1,688	10.3	552,092	1,777
Wheeler	41069	-2.8	1,504	5	-2.6	1,465	5
Yamhill*	41071	8.5	92,229	311	7.5	99,169	319
Total: Oregon		**6.7**	**3,651,787**	**12,316**	**6.0**	**3,872,508**	**12,465**
Pennsylvania							
Adams**	42001	9.0	99,533	336	7.9	107,420	346
Allegheny*	42003	-2.5	1,249,911	4,216	-2.4	1,220,311	3,927
Armstrong*	42005	-1.5	71,316	241	-1.4	70,309	226
Beaver*	42007	-2.1	177,681	599	-2.0	174,204	561
Bedford	42009	0.1	50,045	169	-0.0	50,029	161
Berks*	42011	5.2	393,253	1,326	4.7	411,802	1,325
Blair*	42013	-2.1	126,465	427	-2.0	123,875	399
Bradford**	42015	-0.3	62,544	211	-0.4	62,271	200
Bucks*	42017	4.1	622,393	2,099	3.6	645,062	2,076
Butler*	42019	5.3	183,231	618	4.7	191,805	617
Cambria*	42021	-3.2	147,675	498	-3.0	143,243	461
Cameron	42023	-5.2	5,664	19	-4.7	5,396	17
Carbon*	42025	4.4	61,398	207	4.1	63,927	206
Centre*	42027	4.4	141,710	478	4.1	147,551	475
Chester*	42029	8.9	471,979	1,592	7.6	507,963	1,635
Clarion	42031	-1.7	41,049	138	-1.7	40,355	130
Clearfield**	42033	-0.8	82,756	279	-0.8	82,114	264
Clinton**	42035	-2.0	37,145	125	-2.1	36,371	117
Columbia**	42037	1.6	65,170	220	1.6	66,204	213
Crawford**	42039	-0.6	89,827	303	-0.7	89,236	287
Cumberland*	42041	4.5	223,224	753	4.1	232,401	748
Dauphin*	42043	-0.1	251,422	848	-0.2	250,927	808
Delaware*	42045	1.0	556,280	1,876	0.7	560,150	1,803
Elk**	42047	-3.9	33,752	114	-3.7	32,496	105
Erie*	42049	-0.6	279,281	942	-0.5	277,775	894
Fayette*	42051	-2.6	144,770	488	-2.6	141,062	454
Forest	42053	-0.7	4,912	17	-0.5	4,887	16
Franklin**	42055	4.4	135,052	456	4.0	140,509	452
Fulton	42057	3.5	14,764	50	3.3	15,257	49
Greene	42059	-1.7	39,988	135	-1.7	39,289	126
Huntingdon**	42061	1.2	46,112	156	1.1	46,610	150
Indiana**	42063	-0.6	89,103	301	-0.5	88,648	285
Jefferson	42065	0.2	46,018	155	0.1	46,071	148
Juniata	42067	2.4	23,358	79	2.1	23,851	77
Lackawanna*	42069	-2.2	208,594	704	-2.1	204,297	657
Lancaster*	42071	4.2	490,254	1,654	3.7	508,588	1,637
Lawrence**	42073	-1.9	92,801	313	-2.0	90,984	293
Lebanon*	42075	3.7	124,776	421	3.4	129,072	415
Lehigh*	42077	4.4	325,977	1,100	4.0	339,160	1,091
Luzerne*	42079	-2.8	310,470	1,047	-2.6	302,479	973
Lycoming*	42081	-1.9	117,787	397	-1.8	115,625	372
McKean**	42083	-3.0	44,562	150	-2.7	43,352	140
Mercer*	42085	-0.5	119,699	404	-0.4	119,167	384
Mifflin**	42087	-0.5	46,250	156	-0.6	45,984	148
Monroe**	42089	18.5	164,314	554	14.9	188,730	607
Montgomery*	42091	4.7	785,423	2,649	4.3	819,588	2,638
Montour**	42093	-0.7	18,104	61	-0.8	17,956	58
Northampton*	42095	6.7	284,960	961	6.1	302,326	973
Northumberland**	42097	-2.3	92,367	312	-2.3	90,286	291
Perry*	42099	2.7	44,778	151	2.6	45,922	148
Philadelphia*	42101	-4.0	1,456,998	4,915	-3.8	1,402,114	4,512
Pike*	42103	20.9	55,957	189	16.6	65,238	210
Potter	42105	0.1	18,093	61	-0.3	18,035	58
Schuylkill**	42107	-2.7	146,247	493	-2.6	142,436	458
Snyder**	42109	2.0	38,279	129	1.9	38,998	126
Somerset**	42111	-1.0	79,207	267	-1.0	78,388	252
Sullivan	42113	-2.9	6,369	21	-2.9	6,182	20
Susquehanna	42115	-1.3	41,700	141	-1.3	41,138	132
Tioga	42117	1.2	41,888	141	1.2	42,402	136
Union**	42119	2.8	42,775	144	2.6	43,879	141
Venango**	42121	-2.5	56,115	189	-2.4	54,766	176
Warren**	42123	-3.6	42,271	143	-3.5	40,783	131
Washington*	42125	1.5	206,014	695	1.4	208,908	672
Wayne	42127	4.7	49,976	169	4.1	52,015	167
Westmoreland*	42129	-0.7	367,421	1,239	-0.7	364,905	1,174
Wyoming*	42131	0.5	28,230	95	0.7	28,417	91
York*	42133	5.7	403,361	1,361	5.1	423,825	1,364
Total: Pennsylvania		**1.1**	**12,420,798**	**41,897**	**1.1**	**12,555,326**	**40,403**
Rhode Island							
Bristol*	44001	5.7	53,538	181	5.2	56,344	181
Kent*	44003	4.2	174,124	587	3.8	180,732	582
Newport*	44005	0.1	85,506	288	-0.2	85,365	275
Providence*	44007	5.1	653,201	2,203	4.7	683,578	2,200
Washington*	44009	5.8	130,736	441	5.1	137,452	442
Total: Rhode Island		**4.7**	**1,097,105**	**3,700**	**4.2**	**1,143,471**	**3,680**
South Carolina							
Abbeville	45001	1.1	26,448	89	0.8	26,671	86
Aiken*	45003	5.0	149,719	505	4.6	156,610	504
Allendale	45005	-3.0	10,876	37	-2.7	10,581	34
Anderson*	45007	5.9	175,558	592	5.2	184,764	595
Bamberg	45009	-6.2	15,631	53	-6.0	14,697	47
Barnwell	45011	-0.2	23,437	79	-0.2	23,400	75
Beaufort**	45013	14.8	138,811	468	12.1	155,602	501
Berkeley*	45015	5.2	150,053	506	4.6	157,004	505
Calhoun*	45017	1.4	15,398	52	1.0	15,555	50
Charleston*	45019	5.7	327,786	1,106	5.2	344,833	1,110
Cherokee**	45021	3.2	54,193	183	2.8	55,701	179
Chester**	45023	-1.0	33,738	114	-1.2	33,346	107
Chesterfield	45025	1.7	43,493	147	1.3	44,065	142
Clarendon	45027	1.9	33,132	112	1.7	33,708	108
Colleton**	45029	3.9	39,740	134	3.5	41,126	132
Darlington*	45031	1.1	68,159	230	1.0	68,817	221
Dillon**	45033	2.4	31,472	106	2.4	32,223	104
Dorchester*	45035	13.1	109,033	368	11.3	121,333	390
Edgefield*	45037	1.3	24,910	84	1.3	25,242	81
Fairfield*	45039	2.5	24,030	81	2.0	24,511	79
Florence*	45041	3.7	130,435	440	3.5	135,045	435
Georgetown**	45043	8.8	60,729	205	7.6	65,344	210
Greenville*	45045	6.7	405,039	1,366	5.9	428,939	1,380
Greenwood**	45047	2.9	68,219	230	2.8	70,099	226
Hampton	45049	0.5	21,500	73	0.6	21,629	70
Horry*	45051	11.8	219,791	741	9.9	241,524	777
Jasper**	45053	2.2	21,135	71	1.9	21,535	69
Kershaw*	45055	6.1	55,859	188	5.4	58,861	189
Lancaster**	45057	3.6	63,554	214	3.4	65,695	211
Laurens*	45059	1.7	70,753	239	1.5	71,828	231
Lee	45061	2.0	20,528	69	1.9	20,911	67
Lexington*	45063	8.3	233,853	789	7.2	250,806	807
McCormick	45065	5.1	10,462	35	4.5	10,928	35
Marion	45067	-1.8	34,821	117	-1.8	34,183	110
Marlboro**	45069	-2.7	28,041	95	-2.7	27,293	88
Newberry**	45071	4.0	37,538	127	3.7	38,928	125
Oconee**	45073	5.6	69,933	236	5.0	73,435	236
Orangeburg**	45075	-1.0	90,679	306	-0.9	89,842	289
Pickens*	45077	2.0	112,937	381	1.8	115,019	370
Richland*	45079	5.8	339,314	1,145	5.3	357,271	1,150
Saluda*	45081	-1.1	18,966	64	-1.2	18,747	60
Spartanburg*	45083	4.0	264,032	891	3.6	273,598	880
Sumter*	45085	1.8	106,517	359	1.7	108,314	349
Union**	45087	-3.7	28,761	97	-3.8	27,681	89
Williamsburg	45089	-5.8	35,050	118	-5.7	33,060	106
York*	45091	13.5	186,816	630	11.3	207,907	669
Total: South Carolina		**5.5**	**4,230,879**	**14,272**	**4.9**	**4,438,211**	**14,278**
South Dakota							
Aurora	46003	-7.5	2,828	10	-7.7	2,609	8
Beadle**	46005	-7.3	15,775	53	-7.2	14,639	47

Source: Devonshire Associates Ltd. and Scan/US, Inc. 2005.
* Component of a Metropolitan Core Based Statistical Area.
** Component of a Micropolitan Core Based Statistical Area.

(d) Data not available.

County	FIPS Code	Present: 2000-2005 % Change	Present: 7/1/05 Estimate	Present: 7/1/05 Ranally Population Units	Future: 2005-2010 % Change	Future: 2010 Projection	Future: 2010 Ranally Population Units
Bennett	46007	-3.3	3,455	12	-3.5	3,335	11
Bon Homme	46009	-3.3	7,022	24	-3.2	6,798	22
Brookings**	46011	-0.8	27,984	94	-1.1	27,685	89
Brown**	46013	-2.8	34,450	116	-2.7	33,511	108
Brule	46015	-4.9	5,100	17	-4.8	4,853	16
Buffalo	46017	1.9	2,070	7	3.0	2,133	7
Butte	46019	1.5	9,232	31	1.1	9,336	30
Campbell	46021	-10.8	1,589	5	-11.0	1,414	5
Charles Mix	46023	-3.2	9,054	31	-3.3	8,759	28
Clark	46025	-7.3	3,842	13	-7.0	3,572	11
Clay**	46027	-3.8	13,025	44	-3.4	12,576	40
Codington**	46029	0.1	25,915	87	-0.1	25,884	83
Corson	46031	4.3	4,361	15	3.3	4,503	14
Custer	46033	4.4	7,598	26	5.2	7,992	26
Davison**	46035	0.6	18,848	64	0.5	18,948	61
Day	46037	-9.4	5,678	19	-9.2	5,153	17
Deuel	46039	-5.6	4,244	14	-5.9	3,995	13
Dewey	46041	4.7	6,253	21	4.1	6,511	21
Douglas	46043	-6.7	3,227	11	-6.3	3,023	10
Edmunds**	46045	-6.0	4,107	14	-5.8	3,868	12
Fall River	46047	-2.5	7,265	25	-2.1	7,109	23
Faulk	46049	-9.4	2,391	8	-9.2	2,172	7
Grant	46051	-3.8	7,546	25	-3.8	7,262	23
Gregory	46053	-11.2	4,257	14	-10.8	3,799	12
Haakon	46055	-11.2	1,949	7	-10.5	1,745	6
Hamlin**	46057	1.1	5,600	19	0.7	5,640	18
Hand	46059	-9.1	3,399	11	-8.6	3,105	10
Hanson**	46061	19.2	3,742	13	15.6	4,324	14
Harding	46063	-6.6	1,264	4	-6.0	1,188	4
Hughes**	46065	2.3	16,860	57	2.0	17,195	55
Hutchinson	46067	-6.0	7,594	26	-6.1	7,132	23
Hyde	46069	-6.6	1,561	5	-6.6	1,458	5
Jackson	46071	-3.8	2,820	10	-4.1	2,703	9
Jerauld	46073	-8.7	2,095	7	-8.3	1,921	6
Jones	46075	-14.8	1,017	3	-14.2	873	3
Kingsbury	46077	-7.0	5,407	18	-7.1	5,023	16
Lake	46079	-3.7	10,858	37	-3.4	10,488	34
Lawrence**	46081	1.9	22,208	75	1.9	22,620	73
Lincoln*	46083	34.1	32,370	109	24.0	40,135	129
Lyman	46085	2.8	4,004	14	2.2	4,093	13
McCook*	46087	0.4	5,854	20	-0.1	5,850	19
McPherson	46089	-7.8	2,678	9	-7.5	2,476	8
Marshall	46091	-10.7	4,087	14	-10.8	3,646	12
Meade*	46093	2.0	24,726	83	1.8	25,182	81
Mellette	46095	3.1	2,147	7	2.7	2,204	7
Miner	46097	-10.9	2,570	9	-11.1	2,285	7
Minnehaha*	46099	7.2	158,995	536	6.1	168,745	543
Moody	46101	-1.8	6,474	22	-1.8	6,358	20
Pennington*	46103	5.4	93,346	315	4.8	97,800	315
Perkins	46105	-7.0	3,127	11	-6.3	2,929	9
Potter	46107	-11.5	2,383	8	-11.1	2,118	7
Roberts	46109	0.5	10,068	34	0.5	10,117	33
Sanborn	46111	-3.4	2,584	9	-3.4	2,496	8
Shannon	46113	10.2	13,740	46	8.6	14,917	48
Spink	46115	-9.8	6,723	23	-9.6	6,078	20
Stanley**	46117	-1.0	2,744	9	-1.5	2,704	9
Sully	46119	-10.2	1,397	5	-10.2	1,255	4
Todd	46121	8.2	9,791	33	7.0	10,475	34
Tripp	46123	-5.0	6,108	21	-4.5	5,834	19
Turner*	46125	-4.0	8,495	29	-4.2	8,135	26
Union*	46127	7.0	13,465	45	6.3	14,317	46
Walworth	46129	-11.2	5,302	18	-10.8	4,730	15
Yankton**	46135	-0.8	21,471	72	-0.8	21,300	69
Ziebach	46137	3.9	2,616	9	4.9	2,743	9
Total: South Dakota		**2.1**	**770,755**	**2,602**	**1.9**	**785,776**	**2,530**
Tennessee							
Anderson*	47001	1.6	72,469	244	1.6	73,642	237
Bedford**	47003	11.3	41,827	141	9.6	45,826	147
Benton	47005	0.4	16,603	56	0.4	16,673	54
Bledsoe	47007	3.5	12,801	43	3.0	13,184	42
Blount*	47009	8.8	115,094	388	7.7	123,944	399
Bradley*	47011	4.0	91,502	309	3.6	94,827	305
Campbell**	47013	0.9	40,199	136	0.6	40,454	130
Cannon*	47015	4.7	13,427	45	3.8	13,940	45
Carroll	47017	-0.4	29,355	99	-0.4	29,248	94
Carter*	47019	3.9	58,964	199	3.6	61,077	197
Cheatham*	47021	6.2	38,152	129	5.3	40,188	129
Chester*	47023	0.7	15,642	53	0.8	15,774	51
Claiborne	47025	3.3	30,854	104	3.0	31,788	102
Clay	47027	-0.5	7,940	27	-0.6	7,895	25
Cocke**	47029	4.2	34,965	118	3.8	36,308	117
Coffee**	47031	5.8	50,789	171	5.1	53,402	172
Crockett	47033	-0.3	14,486	49	-0.4	14,423	46
Cumberland**	47035	8.6	50,826	171	7.5	54,626	176
Davidson*	47037	0.2	570,911	1,926	0.2	571,793	1,840
Decatur	47039	-1.1	11,598	39	-0.9	11,488	37
DeKalb	47041	5.5	18,375	62	5.0	19,288	62
Dickson*	47043	6.8	46,096	155	6.0	48,853	157
Dyer**	47045	0.5	37,453	126	0.3	37,571	121
Fayette*	47047	19.7	34,492	116	15.6	39,865	128
Fentress	47049	4.0	17,289	58	3.7	17,934	58
Franklin**	47051	4.7	41,102	139	4.3	42,856	138
Gibson**	47053	-0.6	47,853	161	-0.7	47,530	153
Giles	47055	-0.6	29,274	99	-0.7	29,080	94
Grainger*	47057	7.0	22,098	75	6.2	23,477	76
Greene**	47059	3.2	64,950	219	2.9	66,843	215
Grundy	47061	0.7	14,427	49	0.7	14,522	47
Hamblen*	47063	2.1	59,329	200	1.8	60,415	194
Hamilton*	47065	0.8	310,232	1,046	0.7	312,422	1,005
Hancock	47067	-3.2	6,566	22	-3.1	6,364	20
Hardeman	47069	0.6	28,266	95	0.4	28,390	91
Hardin	47071	2.3	26,174	88	2.3	26,764	86
Hawkins*	47073	5.1	56,299	190	4.6	58,887	190
Haywood**	47075	-1.7	19,464	66	-1.8	19,108	61
Henderson	47077	3.1	26,319	89	2.7	27,026	87
Henry**	47079	1.1	31,445	106	0.9	31,738	102
Hickman*	47081	7.1	23,877	81	6.0	25,313	81
Houston	47083	0.1	8,096	27	0.9	8,170	26
Humphreys	47085	1.9	18,272	62	1.9	18,615	60
Jackson**	47087	2.8	11,294	38	2.4	11,560	37
Jefferson*	47089	9.9	48,669	164	8.4	52,754	170
Johnson	47091	4.2	18,226	61	3.9	18,936	61
Knox*	47093	4.8	400,313	1,350	4.4	417,807	1,345
Lake	47095	-2.6	7,749	26	-2.2	7,579	24
Lauderdale	47097	-0.3	27,008	91	-0.2	26,960	87
Lawrence**	47099	3.4	41,266	139	3.2	42,568	137
Lewis	47101	1.7	11,563	39	1.6	11,750	38
Lincoln	47103	3.0	32,273	109	2.7	33,129	107
Loudon*	47105	10.7	43,287	146	9.4	47,348	152
McMinn**	47107	5.2	51,547	174	4.6	53,912	173
McNairy	47109	1.8	25,085	85	1.4	25,445	82
Macon*	47111	5.2	21,439	72	4.6	22,425	72
Madison*	47113	3.5	95,082	321	3.2	98,138	316
Marion*	47115	0.5	27,902	94	0.4	28,024	90
Marshall**	47117	5.1	28,119	95	4.4	29,358	94
Maury**	47119	8.5	75,379	254	7.5	81,025	261
Meigs	47121	4.5	11,583	39	3.9	12,036	39
Monroe	47123	8.9	42,438	143	7.7	45,696	147
Montgomery*	47125	5.6	142,262	480	4.9	149,279	480
Moore**	47127	5.2	6,039	20	4.5	6,309	20
Morgan	47129	2.9	20,337	69	2.7	20,887	67
Obion**	47131	-0.6	32,244	109	-0.8	31,989	103
Overton**	47133	0.6	20,231	68	0.2	20,267	65
Perry	47135	0.2	7,646	26	0.0	7,647	25
Pickett	47137	0.4	4,963	17	0.6	4,991	16
Polk*	47139	1.0	16,204	55	0.6	16,304	52
Putnam**	47141	6.8	66,540	224	6.1	70,615	227
Rhea	47143	5.7	30,009	101	5.1	31,553	102
Roane**	47145	2.1	52,994	179	2.0	54,032	174
Robertson*	47147	11.3	60,561	204	9.4	66,265	213
Rutherford*	47149	18.0	214,830	725	14.6	246,213	792
Scott	47151	4.6	22,108	75	4.2	23,037	74
Sequatchie*	47153	9.7	12,475	42	8.5	13,538	44
Sevier**	47155	9.7	78,085	263	8.2	84,466	272
Shelby*	47157	1.6	912,260	3,077	1.5	926,191	2,981
Smith*	47159	5.4	18,675	63	4.6	19,533	63
Stewart*	47161	6.1	13,128	44	5.2	13,807	44
Sullivan*	47163	0.0	153,049	516	0.1	153,145	493

Continued on next page

Counties: Population Trends, *Continued*

County	FIPS Code	Present: 2000-2005 % Change	Present: 7/1/05 Estimate	Present: 7/1/05 Ranally Population Units	Future: 2005-2010 % Change	Future: 2010 Projection	Future: 2010 Ranally Population Units
Sumner*	47165	10.3	143,900	485	8.9	156,643	504
Tipton*	47167	9.0	55,893	189	7.8	60,227	194
Trousdale*	47169	4.2	7,565	26	3.2	7,806	25
Unicoi*	47171	0.7	17,796	60	0.8	17,936	58
Union*	47173	9.4	19,486	66	8.3	21,101	68
Van Buren	47175	-0.5	5,480	18	-0.7	5,442	18
Warren**	47177	4.3	39,934	135	3.8	41,463	133
Washington*	47179	4.3	111,810	377	3.9	116,145	374
Wayne	47181	0.1	16,865	57	0.2	16,894	54
Weakley**	47183	-3.0	33,864	114	-2.6	32,997	106
White	47185	3.3	23,872	81	3.1	24,607	79
Williamson*	47187	18.9	150,607	508	14.9	173,113	557
Wilson*	47189	12.3	99,771	337	10.5	110,253	355
Total: Tennessee		**4.4**	**5,937,857**	**20,028**	**4.0**	**6,172,676**	**19,861**
Texas							
Anderson**	48001	2.6	56,568	191	2.6	58,024	187
Andrews**	48003	-2.2	12,721	43	-1.6	12,512	40
Angelina**	48005	1.6	81,450	275	1.5	82,641	266
Aransas*	48007	8.2	24,347	82	7.4	26,154	84
Archer*	48009	4.6	9,260	31	3.2	9,553	31
Armstrong*	48011	-5.0	2,041	7	-5.7	1,924	6
Atascosa*	48013	12.7	43,553	147	10.6	48,183	155
Austin*	48015	10.8	26,140	88	9.0	28,504	92
Bailey	48017	0.4	6,623	22	0.5	6,656	21
Bandera*	48019	15.8	20,429	69	12.7	23,022	74
Bastrop*	48021	25.4	72,404	244	19.4	86,450	278
Baylor	48023	-6.4	3,830	13	-6.1	3,598	12
Bee**	48025	3.4	33,460	113	3.5	34,636	111
Bell*	48027	7.4	255,627	862	6.6	272,474	877
Bexar*	48029	8.6	1,512,995	5,104	7.6	1,628,001	5,239
Blanco	48031	8.3	9,114	31	7.1	9,762	31
Borden	48033	-10.3	654	2	-8.6	598	2
Bosque	48035	5.5	18,153	61	5.0	19,063	61
Bowie*	48037	0.6	89,875	303	0.6	90,450	291
Brazoria*	48039	14.5	276,715	933	12.1	310,079	998
Brazos*	48041	2.8	156,700	529	2.7	160,854	518
Brewster	48043	6.9	9,481	32	6.4	10,089	32
Briscoe	48045	-9.4	1,621	5	-8.8	1,478	5
Brooks	48047	-4.7	7,604	26	-4.4	7,269	23
Brown**	48049	1.5	38,227	129	1.4	38,772	125
Burleson*	48051	4.3	17,184	58	3.7	17,818	57
Burnet	48053	21.7	41,569	140	16.8	48,573	156
Caldwell*	48055	16.6	37,547	127	13.5	42,608	137
Calhoun*	48057	-1.9	20,251	68	-1.9	19,857	64
Callahan*	48059	2.2	13,188	44	2.0	13,454	43
Cameron*	48061	13.4	379,998	1,282	11.3	423,084	1,362
Camp	48063	2.8	11,873	40	2.3	12,151	39
Carson*	48065	0.4	6,540	22	0.5	6,572	21
Cass	48067	-2.2	29,757	100	-2.2	29,110	94
Castro	48069	-7.7	7,645	26	-7.0	7,110	23
Chambers*	48071	9.2	28,434	96	7.9	30,689	99
Cherokee**	48073	3.5	48,315	163	3.4	49,976	161
Childress	48075	-2.1	7,530	25	-1.9	7,389	24
Clay*	48077	4.0	11,441	39	2.9	11,770	38
Cochran	48079	-10.8	3,327	11	-10.3	2,985	10
Coke	48081	-4.4	3,695	12	-4.2	3,541	11
Coleman	48083	-7.9	8,504	29	-7.4	7,873	25
Collin*	48085	34.4	660,783	2,229	24.3	821,038	2,642
Collingsworth	48087	-7.2	2,976	10	-6.8	2,774	9
Colorado	48089	2.4	20,877	70	2.5	21,395	69
Comal*	48091	20.0	93,631	316	15.8	108,430	349
Comanche	48093	-5.5	13,249	45	-5.4	12,537	40
Concho	48095	-6.7	3,701	12	-6.3	3,466	11
Cooke**	48097	7.4	39,041	132	6.6	41,611	134
Coryell*	48099	0.7	75,531	255	0.5	75,873	244
Cottle	48101	-12.1	1,673	6	-11.1	1,487	5
Crane	48103	-5.2	3,787	13	-4.1	3,630	12
Crockett	48105	-6.2	3,845	13	-4.6	3,667	12
Crosby*	48107	-7.3	6,558	22	-7.1	6,094	20
Culberson	48109	-10.4	2,667	9	-9.4	2,416	8
Dallam	48111	-2.8	6,047	20	-2.9	5,873	19
Dallas*	48113	4.5	2,319,427	7,824	4.1	2,413,468	7,767
Dawson**	48115	-5.2	14,211	48	-4.9	13,517	43
Deaf Smith**	48117	-1.4	18,298	62	-1.2	18,081	58
Delta*	48119	1.7	5,417	18	1.4	5,493	18
Denton*	48121	29.0	558,392	1,884	21.4	677,656	2,181
DeWitt	48123	1.2	20,263	68	1.4	20,537	66
Dickens	48125	-3.3	2,671	9	-2.2	2,611	8
Dimmit	48127	1.1	10,361	35	1.4	10,504	34
Donley	48129	3.7	3,969	13	3.3	4,101	13
Duval	48131	-5.5	12,397	42	-4.9	11,789	38
Eastland	48133	-0.0	18,292	62	-0.1	18,280	59
Ector*	48135	2.6	124,311	419	2.9	127,900	412
Edwards	48137	-9.3	1,962	7	-8.9	1,788	6
Ellis*	48139	19.2	132,726	448	15.2	152,908	492
El Paso*	48141	6.0	720,147	2,429	5.4	758,748	2,442
Erath**	48143	1.6	33,521	113	1.4	34,006	109
Falls	48145	-5.5	17,547	59	-5.3	16,618	53
Fannin**	48147	5.3	32,906	111	4.6	34,428	111
Fayette	48149	4.3	22,745	77	4.1	23,675	76
Fisher	48151	-5.8	4,090	14	-5.6	3,859	12
Floyd	48153	-5.9	7,313	25	-5.6	6,907	22
Foard	48155	-6.7	1,513	5	-5.8	1,426	5
Fort Bend*	48157	29.7	459,581	1,550	21.8	559,909	1,802
Franklin	48159	7.2	10,140	34	6.6	10,807	35
Freestone	48161	5.9	18,928	64	5.3	19,937	64
Frio	48163	1.0	16,418	55	1.3	16,624	53
Gaines	48165	-0.5	14,394	49	-0.4	14,340	46
Galveston*	48167	10.8	277,119	935	9.5	303,434	977
Garza	48169	5.3	5,129	17	5.2	5,394	17
Gillespie	48171	10.7	23,046	78	9.2	25,163	81
Glasscock	48173	-6.3	1,317	4	-6.1	1,237	4
Goliad*	48175	4.8	7,260	24	4.0	7,548	24
Gonzales	48177	3.4	19,254	65	3.2	19,871	64
Gray**	48179	-7.5	21,030	71	-6.9	19,584	63
Grayson*	48181	6.2	117,502	396	5.5	123,951	399
Gregg*	48183	4.0	115,857	391	3.9	120,411	388
Grimes	48185	10.2	25,947	88	8.9	28,269	91
Guadalupe*	48187	14.0	101,471	342	11.4	113,047	364
Hale**	48189	-4.3	35,016	118	-4.2	33,552	108
Hall	48191	-0.7	3,755	13	-0.2	3,746	12
Hamilton	48193	-1.9	8,070	27	-1.9	7,916	25
Hansford	48195	-4.4	5,131	17	-4.1	4,919	16
Hardeman	48197	-8.9	4,303	15	-8.6	3,931	13
Hardin*	48199	5.0	50,484	170	4.6	52,821	170
Harris*	48201	9.2	3,713,507	12,526	8.0	4,011,640	12,910
Harrison**	48203	0.2	62,247	210	0.3	62,404	201
Hartley	48205	-0.9	5,487	19	-1.0	5,430	17
Haskell	48207	-9.9	5,490	19	-9.2	4,985	16
Hays*	48209	29.4	126,250	426	21.5	153,406	494
Hemphill	48211	-0.8	3,323	11	-0.0	3,322	11
Henderson**	48213	8.9	79,774	269	7.7	85,944	277
Hidalgo*	48215	18.6	675,597	2,279	15.0	776,946	2,500
Hill	48217	10.3	35,663	120	8.6	38,723	125
Hockley**	48219	0.9	22,926	77	1.1	23,189	75
Hood**	48221	15.9	47,627	161	12.8	53,725	173
Hopkins**	48223	3.4	33,033	111	3.1	34,046	110
Houston	48225	-0.2	23,137	78	-0.2	23,096	74
Howard**	48227	-3.3	32,531	110	-2.8	31,622	102
Hudspeth	48229	-4.4	3,196	11	-4.4	3,056	10
Hunt*	48231	7.7	82,483	278	6.7	87,979	283
Hutchinson**	48233	-6.7	22,266	75	-6.3	20,856	67
Irion*	48235	-1.2	1,750	6	-1.4	1,725	6
Jack	48237	3.4	9,060	31	3.2	9,352	30
Jackson	48239	-1.2	14,222	48	-1.5	14,008	45
Jasper	48241	-0.2	35,540	120	-0.2	35,464	114
Jeff Davis	48243	2.1	2,253	8	1.0	2,275	7
Jefferson*	48245	-2.3	246,195	830	-2.1	240,914	775
Jim Hogg	48247	-7.7	4,873	16	-7.5	4,507	15
Jim Wells**	48249	4.6	41,141	139	4.3	42,896	138
Johnson*	48251	16.0	147,080	496	12.9	166,061	534
Jones*	48253	-4.7	19,799	67	-4.5	18,916	61
Karnes	48255	-1.0	15,291	52	-1.0	15,133	49
Kaufman*	48257	24.4	88,739	299	18.6	105,279	339
Kendall*	48259	17.6	27,913	94	14.1	31,848	102
Kenedy**	48261	-4.3	396	1	-4.5	378	1
Kent	48263	-14.1	738	2	-12.9	643	2
Kerr**	48265	5.3	45,977	155	4.6	48,114	155
Kimble	48267	1.6	4,539	15	1.0	4,584	15
King	48269	-15.2	302	1	-15.6	255	1
Kinney	48271	-2.3	3,300	11	-2.4	3,220	10
Kleberg**	48273	-2.4	30,799	104	-2.2	30,117	97
Knox	48275	-11.3	3,774	13	-11.0	3,357	11
Lamar**	48277	3.1	50,016	169	2.8	51,398	165
Lamb	48279	-0.4	14,650	49	-0.1	14,631	47
Lampasas*	48281	13.8	20,209	68	11.4	22,507	72
La Salle	48283	0.2	5,878	20	-0.1	5,870	19
Lavaca	48285	-1.8	18,859	64	-1.7	18,532	60
Lee	48287	8.1	16,933	57	7.1	18,136	58
Leon	48289	6.9	16,397	55	5.8	17,351	56
Liberty*	48291	8.9	76,373	258	7.5	82,084	264
Limestone	48293	3.7	22,867	77	3.5	23,671	76
Lipscomb	48295	2.3	3,128	11	2.7	3,214	10
Live Oak	48297	-6.3	11,530	39	-6.1	10,823	35
Llano	48299	9.8	18,715	63	8.5	20,313	65
Loving	48301	-7.5	62	0	-4.8	59	0
Lubbock*	48303	5.1	255,027	860	4.8	267,172	860
Lynn	48305	-7.8	6,036	20	-7.2	5,601	18
McCulloch	48307	-5.1	7,784	26	-4.8	7,413	24
McLennan*	48309	4.4	222,879	752	4.0	231,707	746
McMullen	48311	5.8	900	3	4.9	944	3
Madison	48313	0.7	13,032	44	0.4	13,080	42
Marion	48315	2.3	11,193	38	2.2	11,438	37
Martin	48317	-6.8	4,422	15	-6.2	4,147	13
Mason	48319	1.3	3,785	13	1.1	3,825	12
Matagorda**	48321	1.2	38,394	130	1.1	38,834	125
Maverick**	48323	8.8	51,449	174	7.9	55,504	179
Medina*	48325	9.1	42,885	145	7.9	46,285	149
Menard	48327	-2.1	2,310	8	-1.9	2,266	7
Midland*	48329	4.2	120,852	408	4.4	126,160	406
Milam	48331	5.1	25,480	86	4.7	26,685	86
Mills	48333	-3.0	4,998	17	-2.8	4,860	16
Mitchell	48335	-4.6	9,254	31	-3.8	8,903	29
Montague	48337	2.7	19,639	66	2.6	20,157	65
Montgomery*	48339	27.8	375,519	1,267	20.7	453,313	1,459
Moore**	48341	0.6	20,232	68	0.6	20,354	66
Morris	48343	1.9	13,298	45	1.9	13,546	44
Motley	48345	-12.9	1,242	4	-13.6	1,073	3
Nacogdoches**	48347	0.8	59,701	201	0.8	60,175	194
Navarro**	48349	7.5	48,525	164	6.6	51,713	166
Newton	48351	-2.5	14,689	50	-2.4	14,336	46
Nolan**	48353	-6.7	14,739	50	-6.5	13,787	44
Nueces*	48355	0.8	316,026	1,066	0.8	318,647	1,025
Ochiltree	48357	-0.9	8,929	30	-0.7	8,870	29
Oldham	48359	-1.7	2,148	7	-2.1	2,103	7
Orange*	48361	-1.0	84,104	284	-1.0	83,246	268
Palo Pinto**	48363	1.6	27,466	93	1.4	27,847	90
Panola	48365	0.3	22,816	77	0.3	22,885	74
Parker*	48367	16.6	103,201	348	13.5	117,084	377
Parmer	48369	-2.0	9,815	33	-1.8	9,638	31
Pecos	48371	-7.7	15,522	52	-7.0	14,436	46
Polk	48373	16.9	48,082	162	13.5	54,566	176
Potter*	48375	5.4	119,630	404	4.9	125,515	404
Presidio	48377	6.4	7,768	26	5.5	8,192	26
Rains	48379	30.4	11,915	40	22.6	14,608	47
Randall*	48381	4.4	108,926	367	3.9	113,197	364
Reagan	48383	-12.0	2,928	10	-11.0	2,607	8
Real	48385	-0.4	3,036	10	1.0	3,067	10
Red River	48387	-6.6	13,363	45	-6.4	12,509	40
Reeves**	48389	-11.4	11,644	39	-10.7	10,395	33
Refugio	48391	-5.4	7,402	25	-5.4	7,000	23
Roberts**	48393	-11.6	784	3	-11.2	696	2
Robertson*	48395	-0.7	15,890	54	-0.8	15,759	51
Rockwall*	48397	43.6	61,874	209	29.0	79,836	257
Runnels	48399	-8.0	10,572	36	-7.9	9,732	31
Rusk*	48401	0.7	47,694	161	0.7	48,029	155
Sabine	48403	-0.7	10,400	35	-0.3	10,365	33
San Augustine	48405	-1.6	8,806	30	-1.5	8,673	28
San Jacinto*	48407	11.8	24,863	84	9.7	27,275	88
San Patricio*	48409	1.2	67,922	229	1.8	69,113	222
San Saba	48411	-3.9	5,947	20	-4.0	5,707	18
Schleicher	48413	-8.0	2,701	9	-7.6	2,497	8
Scurry**	48415	-3.3	15,814	53	-2.7	15,388	50
Shackelford	48417	-0.7	3,278	11	-0.4	3,265	11
Shelby	48419	4.3	26,305	89	3.9	27,337	88
Sherman	48421	-2.0	3,123	11	-2.0	3,060	10
Smith*	48423	8.3	189,133	638	7.2	202,798	653
Somervell**	48425	11.8	7,614	26	10.2	8,387	27
Starr**	48427	13.4	60,785	205	11.4	67,706	218
Stephens	48429	-3.1	9,377	32	-2.7	9,123	29
Sterling	48431	-7.3	1,292	4	-6.0	1,215	4
Stonewall	48433	-21.7	1,326	4	-20.8	1,050	3
Sutton	48435	-0.3	4,065	14	0.7	4,093	13
Swisher	48437	-8.0	7,706	26	-7.8	7,108	23
Tarrant*	48439	12.5	1,626,962	5,488	10.6	1,799,145	5,790
Taylor*	48441	-2.2	123,775	418	-2.1	121,186	390
Terrell	48443	-9.3	981	3	-7.4	908	3
Terry	48445	-2.8	12,398	42	-2.5	12,085	39
Throckmorton	48447	-14.5	1,581	5	-13.8	1,363	4
Titus**	48449	3.6	29,131	98	3.4	30,135	97
Tom Green*	48451	-0.4	103,625	350	-0.3	103,277	332
Travis*	48453	8.6	882,137	2,976	7.1	944,453	3,039
Trinity	48455	4.6	14,414	49	4.1	14,998	48
Tyler	48457	-2.0	20,450	69	-2.0	20,046	65
Upshur*	48459	7.8	38,037	128	7.0	40,685	131
Upton	48461	-10.2	3,057	10	-9.5	2,766	9
Uvalde**	48463	3.6	26,870	91	3.5	27,803	89
Val Verde**	48465	6.5	47,764	161	5.7	50,503	163
Van Zandt	48467	9.0	52,458	177	7.8	56,543	182
Victoria*	48469	2.5	86,168	291	2.5	88,308	284
Walker**	48471	1.3	62,539	211	1.3	63,359	204
Waller*	48473	9.4	35,721	120	8.0	38,591	124
Ward	48475	-8.6	9,974	34	-7.8	9,199	30
Washington**	48477	2.9	31,249	105	2.6	32,064	103
Webb*	48479	16.2	224,381	757	13.2	254,024	818
Wharton**	48481	0.4	41,343	139	0.3	41,467	133
Wheeler	48483	-13.5	4,569	15	-12.6	3,992	13
Wichita*	48485	-4.3	125,947	425	-4.1	120,794	389
Wilbarger**	48487	-5.4	13,882	47	-5.1	13,173	42
Willacy**	48489	-0.1	20,054	68	-0.1	20,039	64
Williamson*	48491	34.2	335,518	1,132	23.9	415,834	1,338
Wilson*	48493	14.3	37,038	125	11.6	41,346	133
Winkler	48495	-8.4	6,570	22	-7.3	6,091	20
Wise*	48497	18.1	57,616	194	14.2	65,777	212
Wood	48499	11.4	40,942	138	9.9	44,994	145
Yoakum	48501	-0.9	7,254	24	-0.4	7,228	23
Young	48503	0.0	17,950	61	0.1	17,972	58
Zapata	48505	9.7	13,368	45	8.6	14,511	47
Zavala	48507	0.5	11,654	39	0.4	11,703	38
Total: Texas		**9.7**	**22,865,855**	**77,132**	**8.4**	**24,782,576**	**79,755**
Utah							
Beaver	49001	0.8	6,051	20	0.6	6,090	20
Box Elder**	49003	5.9	45,266	153	5.3	47,663	153
Cache*	49005	7.7	98,441	332	6.9	105,191	339
Carbon**	49007	-5.3	19,333	65	-5.0	18,373	59
Daggett	49009	-5.0	875	3	-5.9	823	3
Davis*	49011	20.3	287,557	970	16.2	334,268	1,076
Duchesne	49013	5.1	15,108	51	4.9	15,841	51
Emery	49015	-3.2	10,515	35	-3.9	10,107	33
Garfield	49017	-7.7	4,370	15	-7.9	4,026	13
Grand	49019	3.4	8,773	30	4.2	9,145	29
Iron**	49021	7.4	36,286	122	6.5	38,636	124
Juab*	49023	9.5	9,022	30	8.2	9,758	31
Kane	49025	-0.3	6,029	20	-0.7	5,985	19
Millard	49027	-1.1	12,268	41	-1.0	12,144	39
Morgan*	49029	6.9	7,623	26	6.1	8,085	26
Piute	49031	-7.4	1,329	4	-7.4	1,230	4
Rich	49033	4.4	2,048	7	3.9	2,128	7
Salt Lake*	49035	3.5	930,006	3,137	3.2	959,978	3,089
San Juan	49037	-7.4	13,346	45	-7.0	12,413	40
Sanpete	49039	5.7	24,063	81	5.2	25,312	81
Sevier	49041	1.7	19,166	65	1.6	19,468	63
Summit*	49043	15.3	34,273	116	12.4	38,516	124
Tooele*	49045	27.2	51,817	175	19.3	61,819	199
Uintah**	49047	6.0	26,736	90	5.5	28,208	91
Utah*	49049	11.1	409,622	1,382	9.5	448,415	1,443

Source: Devonshire Associates Ltd. and Scan/US, Inc. 2005.
* Component of a Metropolitan Core Based Statistical Area.
** Component of a Micropolitan Core Based Statistical Area.

(d) Data not available.

Counties: Population Trends, *Continued*

County	FIPS Code	Present			Future		
		2000-2005 % Change	7/1/05 Estimate	7/1/05 Ranally Population Units	2005-2010 % Change	2010 Projection	2010 Ranally Population Units
Wasatch**	49051	24.1	18,878	64	18.0	22,279	72
Washington*	49053	24.0	112,063	378	18.4	132,633	427
Wayne	49055	-3.1	2,431	8	-4.0	2,334	8
Weber*	49057	6.5	209,328	706	5.7	221,245	712
Total: Utah		**8.5**	**2,422,623**	**8,171**	**7.4**	**2,602,113**	**8,375**
Vermont							
Addison	50001	3.1	37,083	125	2.8	38,128	123
Bennington**	50003	0.5	37,189	125	0.5	37,385	120
Caledonia	50005	2.2	30,350	102	1.9	30,939	100
Chittenden*	50007	2.4	150,099	506	2.1	153,222	493
Essex**	50009	2.8	6,643	22	2.7	6,823	22
Franklin*	50011	6.0	48,164	162	5.3	50,729	163
Grand Isle*	50013	13.9	7,858	27	11.7	8,777	28
Lamoille	50015	6.9	24,840	84	6.0	26,329	85
Orange**	50017	4.9	29,610	100	4.4	30,910	99
Orleans	50019	5.2	27,635	93	4.7	28,929	93
Rutland**	50021	0.4	63,632	215	0.3	63,846	205
Washington**	50023	2.6	59,549	201	2.5	61,024	196
Windham	50025	0.8	44,579	150	0.9	44,980	145
Windsor**	50027	1.7	58,380	197	1.5	59,260	191
Total: Vermont		**2.8**	**625,611**	**2,109**	**2.5**	**641,281**	**2,063**
Virginia							
Accomack	51001	3.1	39,480	133	2.7	40,555	131
Albemarle*	51003	12.7	89,294	301	5.2	93,894	302
Alleghany[3]	51005	27.7	16,506	56	-3.9	15,862	51
Amelia*	51007	4.4	11,902	40	3.5	12,321	40
Amherst*	51009	0.3	31,991	108	0.2	32,065	103
Appomattox*	51011	0.4	13,764	46	0.4	13,819	44
Arlington*	51013	-1.9	185,858	627	-1.8	182,475	587
Augusta**	51015	4.8	68,777	232	4.3	71,743	231
Bath	51017	-0.9	5,004	17	-0.8	4,964	16
Bedford*	51019	6.1	64,051	216	5.3	67,444	217
Bland	51021	2.2	7,021	24	2.2	7,172	23
Botetourt*	51023	4.9	31,989	108	4.4	33,392	107
Brunswick	51025	-2.5	17,961	61	-2.7	17,476	56
Buchanan	51027	-8.5	24,693	83	-7.9	22,742	73
Buckingham	51029	2.3	15,981	54	2.0	16,302	52
Campbell*	51031	1.1	51,615	174	0.9	52,085	168
Caroline*	51033	7.6	23,809	80	7.0	25,469	82
Carroll	51035	0.1	29,271	99	-0.1	29,242	94
Charles City*	51036	4.9	7,266	25	4.6	7,600	24
Charlotte	51037	-1.2	12,323	42	-1.1	12,187	39
Chesterfield*	51041	10.3	286,764	967	8.9	312,369	1,005
Clarke*	51043	9.8	13,896	47	8.5	15,075	49
Craig*	51045	0.6	5,124	17	0.4	5,147	17
Culpeper**	51047	20.6	41,320	139	16.4	48,099	155
Cumberland*	51049	2.4	9,230	31	2.4	9,454	30
Dickenson	51051	-2.0	16,070	54	-1.7	15,794	51
Dinwiddie*	51053	2.3	25,086	85	2.0	25,576	82
Essex	51057	5.0	10,491	35	4.7	10,984	35
Fairfax*	51059	4.8	1,016,742	3,430	4.2	1,059,612	3,410
Fauquier*	51061	17.6	64,828	219	14.2	74,034	238
Floyd	51063	5.4	14,630	49	4.6	15,306	49
Fluvanna*	51065	23.3	24,716	83	18.0	29,167	94
Franklin*	51067	6.0	50,120	169	5.2	52,751	170
Frederick*	51069	15.1	68,153	230	12.5	76,670	247
Giles*	51071	2.6	17,084	58	2.2	17,460	56
Gloucester*	51073	8.7	37,812	128	7.7	40,725	131
Goochland*	51075	12.3	18,934	64	10.4	20,902	67
Grayson	51077	-8.9	16,331	55	-3.3	15,792	51
Greene*	51079	15.4	17,587	59	12.6	19,797	64
Greensville	51081	-0.4	11,518	39	-0.7	11,436	37
Halifax	51083	-3.2	36,141	122	-3.2	34,983	113
Hanover*	51085	14.1	98,498	332	11.6	109,899	354
Henrico*	51087	5.1	275,628	930	4.4	287,842	926
Henry**	51089	-2.6	56,419	190	-2.6	54,955	177
Highland	51091	-1.5	2,497	8	-1.4	2,461	8
Isle of Wight*	51093	11.7	33,202	112	9.9	36,500	117
James City*	51095	17.1	56,330	190	13.9	64,132	206
King and Queen*	51097	-1.3	6,541	22	-1.2	6,463	21
King George	51099	16.4	19,561	66	13.5	22,193	71
King William*	51101	11.7	14,688	50	10.0	16,160	52
Lancaster	51103	4.8	12,120	41	4.2	12,626	41
Lee	51105	1.0	23,816	80	1.1	24,084	78
Loudoun*	51107	48.6	252,089	850	30.9	329,892	1,062
Louisa*	51109	15.2	29,516	100	12.7	33,258	107
Lunenburg	51111	-0.3	13,101	44	-0.1	13,092	42
Madison	51113	7.1	13,415	45	6.3	14,262	46
Mathews*	51115	0.8	9,283	31	0.9	9,363	30
Mecklenburg	51117	0.4	32,515	110	0.4	32,639	105
Middlesex	51119	5.6	10,491	35	4.9	11,009	35
Montgomery*	51121	0.2	83,778	283	0.0	83,817	270
Nelson*	51125	4.8	15,141	51	4.3	15,799	51
New Kent*	51127	17.4	15,806	53	14.3	18,065	58
Northampton	51131	1.0	13,218	45	1.1	13,368	43
Northumberland	51133	5.9	12,986	44	5.4	13,686	44
Nottoway	51135	-0.6	15,629	53	-0.8	15,500	50
Orange	51137	13.2	29,303	99	11.1	32,568	105
Page	51139	3.1	23,888	81	2.8	24,563	79
Patrick	51141	-1.8	19,063	64	-1.8	18,711	60
Pittsylvania*	51143	-0.1	61,661	208	-0.2	61,532	198
Powhatan*	51145	18.6	26,540	90	14.6	30,413	98
Prince Edward	51147	3.0	20,310	69	2.7	20,864	67
Prince George*	51149	5.6	34,896	118	4.6	36,515	118
Prince William*	51153	25.5	352,321	1,188	19.4	420,534	1,353
Pulaski*	51155	-0.7	34,887	118	-0.8	34,619	111
Rappahannock	51157	3.1	7,202	24	3.2	7,435	24
Richmond	51159	3.0	9,076	31	2.8	9,331	30
Roanoke*	51161	2.8	88,219	298	2.7	90,636	292
Rockbridge	51163	0.9	21,000	71	0.7	21,150	68
Rockingham*	51165	4.2	70,537	238	3.8	73,222	236
Russell	51167	-5.4	28,667	97	-2.1	28,056	90
Scott*	51169	-2.8	22,744	77	-2.7	22,125	71
Shenandoah	51171	9.5	38,397	130	8.2	41,538	134
Smyth	51173	-2.1	32,402	109	-2.1	31,720	102
Southampton	51175	-1.3	17,248	58	-1.5	16,995	55
Spotsylvania*	51177	30.7	118,182	399	22.4	144,675	466
Stafford*	51179	30.9	121,019	408	22.6	148,329	477
Surry*	51181	3.4	7,064	24	3.1	7,283	23
Sussex*	51183	-6.8	11,648	39	-7.0	10,838	35
Tazewell**	51185	-0.3	44,463	150	-0.0	44,461	143
Warren*	51187	11.1	35,096	118	9.6	38,451	124
Washington*	51191	1.2	51,736	175	1.1	52,290	168
Westmoreland	51193	2.6	17,150	58	2.7	17,610	57
Wise	51195	3.1	41,379	140	-2.0	40,548	130
Wythe	51197	1.9	28,133	95	1.7	28,625	92
York*	51199	10.7	62,330	210	9.2	68,044	219
INDEPENDENT CITIES							
Alexandria*	51510	-0.1	128,132	432	-0.8	127,123	409
Bedford*	51515	-1.5	6,206	21	-1.7	6,103	20
Bristol*	51520	-0.8	17,230	58	-0.5	17,149	55
Buena Vista	51530	-1.4	6,258	21	-1.6	6,157	20
Charlottesville*	51540	-19.2	36,403	123	-9.1	33,104	107
Chesapeake*	51550	8.4	215,873	728	7.1	231,265	744
Clifton Forge[3]	51560	(d)	(d)	(d)	(d)	(d)	(d)
Colonial Heights*	51570	3.1	17,418	59	2.9	17,922	58
Covington	51580	-0.8	6,254	21	-0.8	6,204	20
Danville*	51590	-4.8	46,092	155	-4.5	44,017	142
Emporia	51595	0.3	5,681	19	0.2	5,694	18
Fairfax*	51600	3.3	22,200	75	2.8	22,824	73
Falls Church*	51610	3.3	10,716	36	2.9	11,022	35
Franklin	51620	0.0	8,347	28	0.7	8,405	27
Fredericksburg*	51630	7.7	20,769	70	6.8	22,189	71
Galax	51640	-4.2	6,551	22	-4.4	6,260	20
Hampton*	51650	-1.2	144,708	488	-1.2	142,906	460
Harrisonburg*	51660	2.0	41,264	139	2.0	42,095	135
Hopewell*	51670	0.2	22,404	76	0.5	22,509	72
Lexington	51678	0.6	6,909	23	0.7	6,957	22
Lynchburg*	51680	-1.0	64,615	218	-1.1	63,921	206
Manassas*	51683	8.4	38,088	128	7.0	40,756	131
Manassas Park*	51685	11.1	11,429	39	9.5	12,518	40
Martinsville**	51690	-2.9	14,971	50	-2.7	14,563	47
Newport News*	51700	1.3	182,551	616	1.9	186,096	599
Norfolk*	51710	1.6	238,106	803	1.5	241,716	778
Norton	51720	-0.5	3,886	13	0.1	3,889	13
Petersburg*	51730	-3.0	32,717	110	-2.6	31,864	103

Source: Devonshire Associates Ltd. and Scan/US, Inc. 2005.
* Component of a Metropolitan Core Based Statistical Area.
** Component of a Micropolitan Core Based Statistical Area.

(d) Data not available.
[3] Clifton Forge independent city merged with Alleghany county on July 1, 2001.

County	FIPS Code	Present			Future		
		2000-2005 % Change	7/1/05 Estimate	7/1/05 Ranally Population Units	2005-2010 % Change	2010 Projection	2010 Ranally Population Units
Poquoson*	51735	2.3	11,837	40	2.1	12,087	39
Portsmouth*	51740	-2.5	98,061	331	-2.4	95,703	308
Radford*	51750	-9.1	14,413	49	-9.0	13,111	42
Richmond*	51760	-3.1	191,700	647	-3.0	186,003	599
Roanoke*	51770	-4.1	91,029	307	-3.9	87,440	281
Salem*	51775	-1.9	24,289	82	-2.1	23,786	77
Staunton**	51790	0.1	23,887	81	0.0	23,897	77
Suffolk*	51800	24.6	79,362	268	19.0	94,429	304
Virginia Beach*	51810	5.3	447,757	1,510	4.7	468,941	1,509
Waynesboro**	51820	7.3	20,940	71	6.3	22,269	72
Williamsburg*	51830	-7.9	11,046	37	-7.9	10,177	33
Winchester*	51840	4.9	24,730	83	4.3	25,790	83
Total: Virginia		**6.5**	**7,538,791**	**25,432**	**5.8**	**7,973,549**	**25,659**
Washington							
Adams	53001	1.9	16,743	56	1.7	17,020	55
Asotin*	53003	0.2	20,584	69	0.1	20,602	66
Benton*	53005	13.1	161,100	543	11.2	179,077	576
Chelan*	53007	3.3	68,844	232	3.1	70,945	228
Clallam**	53009	6.2	68,528	231	6.1	72,736	234
Clark*	53011	16.2	401,099	1,353	13.4	454,676	1,463
Columbia	53013	3.1	4,190	14	2.8	4,306	14
Cowlitz*	53015	3.9	96,590	326	3.7	100,131	322
Douglas*	53017	5.8	34,494	116	5.3	36,322	117
Ferry	53019	3.6	7,518	25	3.0	7,746	25
Franklin*	53021	23.3	60,835	205	18.5	72,108	232
Garfield	53023	-1.7	2,357	8	-1.5	2,322	7
Grant**	53025	9.0	81,412	275	7.8	87,794	283
Grays Harbor**	53027	4.4	70,148	237	4.2	73,085	235
Island**	53029	14.0	81,610	275	11.9	91,341	294
Jefferson	53031	9.8	28,498	96	7.2	30,548	98
King*	53033	2.3	1,776,888	5,994	2.1	1,814,815	5,840
Kitsap*	53035	4.0	241,196	814	3.7	250,057	805
Kittitas**	53037	7.9	36,010	121	7.0	38,526	124
Klickitat	53039	4.2	19,961	67	3.6	20,680	67
Lewis**	53041	5.0	72,039	243	4.7	75,418	243
Lincoln	53043	0.8	10,268	35	0.8	10,348	33
Mason**	53045	9.6	54,163	183	8.5	58,747	189
Okanogan	53047	-1.9	38,804	131	-2.0	38,042	122
Pacific	53049	1.3	21,260	72	1.5	21,576	69
Pend Oreille	53051	7.1	12,561	42	6.5	13,372	43
Pierce*	53053	9.3	765,698	2,583	8.1	827,363	2,663
San Juan	53055	8.6	15,292	52	7.4	16,425	53
Skagit*	53057	9.9	113,129	382	8.5	122,771	395
Skamania*	53059	6.6	10,526	36	5.9	11,151	36
Snohomish*	53061	8.8	659,426	2,224	7.6	709,672	2,284
Spokane*	53063	5.1	439,273	1,482	4.7	459,829	1,480
Stevens	53065	3.4	41,414	140	2.8	42,575	137
Thurston*	53067	10.7	229,500	774	9.2	250,695	807
Wahkiakum	53069	-4.8	3,639	12	-5.1	3,453	11
Walla Walla**	53071	4.7	57,748	195	4.2	60,198	194
Whatcom*	53073	9.4	182,534	616	8.2	197,436	635
Whitman**	53075	-2.3	39,812	134	-1.9	39,053	126
Yakima*	53077	3.1	229,468	774	2.9	236,174	760
Total: Washington		**6.5**	**6,275,159**	**21,167**	**5.8**	**6,639,135**	**21,365**
West Virginia							
Barbour	54001	0.6	15,652	53	0.6	15,750	51
Berkeley*	54003	20.4	91,401	308	16.3	106,284	342
Boone*	54005	1.4	25,896	87	1.4	26,263	85
Braxton	54007	1.5	14,918	50	1.3	15,110	49
Brooke*	54009	-2.9	24,717	83	-2.7	24,058	77
Cabell*	54011	-2.9	93,961	317	-2.8	91,287	294
Calhoun	54013	-4.9	7,207	24	-5.0	6,846	22
Clay*	54015	-0.1	10,320	35	-0.3	10,291	33
Doddridge**	54017	1.3	7,502	25	1.1	7,582	24
Fayette**	54019	-0.9	47,157	159	-0.8	46,767	151
Gilmer	54021	-3.0	6,947	23	-3.1	6,731	22
Grant	54023	2.2	11,543	39	2.2	11,793	38
Greenbrier	54025	1.5	34,969	118	1.5	35,490	114
Hampshire*	54027	8.4	21,905	74	7.2	23,474	76
Hancock*	54029	-4.3	31,270	105	-4.2	29,947	96
Hardy	54031	5.0	13,308	45	4.5	13,912	45
Harrison**	54033	-1.2	67,829	229	-1.1	67,058	216
Jackson	54035	1.3	28,355	96	1.0	28,634	92
Jefferson*	54037	16.3	49,069	166	13.4	55,649	179
Kanawha*	54039	-3.4	193,206	652	-3.3	186,813	601
Lewis	54041	1.8	17,217	58	1.9	17,542	56
Lincoln*	54043	2.3	22,614	76	2.1	23,080	74
Logan	54045	-3.9	36,230	122	-3.7	34,898	112
McDowell	54047	-11.5	24,188	82	-11.0	21,519	69
Marion**	54049	-0.2	56,491	191	-0.1	56,430	182
Marshall*	54051	-2.7	34,564	117	-2.4	33,723	109
Mason**	54053	0.8	26,170	88	0.7	26,354	85
Mercer**	54055	-2.1	61,684	208	-2.0	60,453	195
Mineral*	54057	0.5	27,200	92	0.5	27,338	88
Mingo	54059	-3.3	27,327	92	-2.6	26,620	86
Monongalia*	54061	3.2	84,446	285	3.0	86,951	280
Monroe	54063	-6.5	13,636	46	3.0	14,044	45
Morgan*	54065	6.7	15,940	54	5.7	16,851	54
Nicholas	54067	-1.7	26,107	88	-1.8	25,646	83
Ohio*	54069	-5.9	44,633	151	-5.8	42,052	135
Pendleton	54071	-5.5	7,742	26	-5.3	7,334	24
Pleasants*	54073	-2.2	7,347	25	-2.2	7,184	23
Pocahontas	54075	-2.4	8,908	30	-2.3	8,703	28
Preston*	54077	2.5	30,071	101	2.5	30,813	99
Putnam*	54079	4.4	53,879	182	3.9	55,967	180
Raleigh**	54081	0.1	79,333	268	0.2	79,511	256
Randolph	54083	-0.0	28,261	95	0.1	28,283	91
Ritchie	54085	2.8	10,628	36	2.7	10,913	35
Roane	54087	-0.7	15,339	52	-0.9	15,199	49
Summers	54089	5.5	13,710	46	-4.3	13,119	42
Taylor**	54091	0.6	16,183	55	0.4	16,252	52
Tucker	54093	-3.5	7,068	24	-3.2	6,841	22
Tyler	54095	-2.7	9,336	31	-2.8	9,079	29
Upshur	54097	2.4	23,976	81	2.3	24,520	79
Wayne*	54099	-1.7	42,169	142	-1.8	41,411	133
Webster	54101	1.1	9,827	33	1.2	9,947	32
Wetzel	54103	-5.3	16,750	56	-5.3	15,859	51
Wirt*	54105	-2.1	5,752	19	-2.2	5,623	18
Wood*	54107	-1.0	87,089	294	-1.0	86,228	277
Wyoming	54109	-5.0	24,416	82	-4.7	23,263	75
Total: West Virginia		**0.3**	**1,813,363**	**6,116**	**0.3**	**1,819,289**	**5,855**
Wisconsin							
Adams	55001	11.7	20,816	70	3.9	21,626	70
Ashland	55003	-1.1	16,683	56	-1.0	16,515	53
Barron	55005	1.9	45,819	155	1.7	46,590	150
Bayfield	55007	1.3	15,215	51	1.2	15,392	50
Brown*	55009	5.3	238,847	806	4.8	250,395	806
Buffalo	55011	0.7	13,896	47	0.5	13,970	45
Burnett	55013	6.8	16,745	56	6.1	17,766	57
Calumet*	55015	10.8	45,019	152	9.5	49,298	159
Chippewa*	55017	8.1	59,690	201	7.3	64,022	206
Clark	55019	1.8	34,159	115	1.5	34,679	112
Columbia*	55021	4.9	55,054	186	4.4	57,480	185
Crawford	55023	-2.1	16,875	57	-2.1	16,516	53
Dane*	55025	8.6	463,177	1,562	7.5	497,973	1,603
Dodge**	55027	2.7	88,215	298	2.5	90,408	291
Door	55029	2.3	28,616	97	2.0	29,202	94
Douglas*	55031	2.2	44,257	149	1.9	45,108	145
Dunn**	55033	4.9	41,813	141	4.4	43,665	141
Eau Claire*	55035	1.6	94,647	319	1.4	96,019	309
Florence**	55037	-1.6	5,005	17	-1.9	4,910	16
Fond du Lac*	55039	1.4	98,664	333	1.3	99,927	322
Forest	55041	-1.5	9,871	33	-1.7	9,701	31
Grant**	55043	-0.4	49,417	167	-0.2	49,303	159
Green**	55045	3.1	34,678	117	2.7	35,628	115
Green Lake	55047	0.4	19,181	65	0.4	19,264	62
Iowa*	55049	3.5	23,578	80	3.2	24,341	78
Iron	55051	-2.6	6,680	23	-2.6	6,506	21
Jackson	55053	3.6	19,785	67	3.3	20,435	66
Jefferson**	55055	6.4	78,765	266	3.6	81,583	263
Juneau	55057	6.1	25,808	87	5.6	27,248	88
Kenosha*	55059	7.1	160,165	540	6.3	170,237	548
Kewaunee*	55061	2.5	20,693	70	2.4	21,182	68

Continued on next page

Counties: Population Trends, *Continued*

County	FIPS Code	Present 2000-2005 % Change	7/1/05 Estimate	7/1/05 Ranally Population Units	Future 2005-2010 % Change	2010 Projection	2010 Ranally Population Units
La Crosse*	55063	2.1	109,413	369	2.0	111,564	359
Lafayette	55065	1.9	16,437	55	1.8	16,737	54
Langlade	55067	1.0	20,949	71	1.0	21,157	68
Lincoln**	55069	2.6	30,417	103	2.3	31,118	100
Manitowoc**	55071	-1.7	81,467	275	-1.8	80,025	258
Marathon*	55073	1.8	128,048	432	1.7	130,168	419
Marinette**	55075	-0.1	43,337	146	-0.3	43,216	139
Marquette	55077	-5.5	14,963	50	2.3	15,311	49
Menominee	55078	1.6	4,636	16	1.1	4,687	15
Milwaukee*	55079	-1.3	927,823	3,130	-1.3	916,196	2,949
Monroe	55081	3.2	42,227	142	2.9	43,436	140
Oconto*	55083	6.6	37,980	128	5.8	40,172	129
Oneida	55085	2.2	37,592	127	2.1	38,368	123
Outagamie*	55087	6.5	171,486	578	5.6	181,135	583
Ozaukee*	55089	5.1	86,503	292	4.5	90,435	291
Pepin	55091	3.2	7,443	25	3.3	7,690	25
Pierce*	55093	4.8	38,572	130	4.3	40,236	129
Polk	55095	7.6	44,455	150	6.7	47,437	153
Portage**	55097	0.3	67,357	227	0.2	67,470	217
Price	55099	-3.6	15,253	51	-3.6	14,704	47
Racine*	55101	3.3	194,975	658	3.1	200,939	647
Richland	55103	2.5	18,375	62	1.9	18,728	60
Rock*	55105	2.7	156,477	528	2.5	160,406	516
Rusk	55107	-1.2	15,167	51	-1.2	14,982	48
St. Croix*	55109	21.0	76,388	258	16.6	89,094	287
Sauk**	55111	3.8	57,305	193	3.4	59,261	191
Sawyer	55113	5.6	17,102	58	5.0	17,959	58
Shawano	55115	1.4	41,250	139	1.1	41,711	134
Sheboygan*	55117	1.2	114,016	385	1.1	115,256	371
Taylor	55119	-1.1	19,466	66	-1.3	19,212	62
Trempealeau	55121	1.6	27,431	93	1.3	27,785	89
Vernon	55123	2.7	28,805	97	2.5	29,538	95
Vilas	55125	7.9	22,705	77	6.9	24,278	78
Walworth**	55127	6.5	99,826	337	7.4	107,220	345
Washburn	55129	4.4	16,746	56	3.8	17,390	56
Washington*	55131	6.7	125,320	423	5.8	132,639	427
Waukesha*	55133	5.8	381,827	1,288	5.2	401,492	1,292
Waupaca	55135	2.4	52,974	179	1.9	53,976	174
Waushara	55137	3.6	23,988	81	3.7	24,865	80
Winnebago*	55139	1.9	159,732	539	1.7	162,430	523
Wood**	55141	-0.7	75,060	253	-0.7	74,548	240
Total: Wisconsin		3.3	5,543,126	18,701	3.0	5,711,860	18,386
Wyoming							
Albany**	56001	-2.2	31,324	106	-1.6	30,809	99
Big Horn	56003	-3.5	11,058	37	-3.2	10,701	34
Campbell**	56005	13.0	38,069	128	10.7	42,136	136
Carbon	56007	-2.4	15,270	52	-1.9	14,975	48
Converse	56009	3.3	12,451	42	2.7	12,792	41
Crook	56011	2.7	6,046	20	2.4	6,192	20
Fremont**	56013	1.2	36,221	122	1.0	36,586	118
Goshen	56015	-4.3	12,005	40	-4.4	11,473	37
Hot Springs	56017	-8.7	4,459	15	-8.4	4,085	13
Johnson	56019	11.0	7,850	26	9.4	8,591	28
Laramie*	56021	5.5	86,122	290	5.1	90,483	291
Lincoln	56023	7.4	15,651	53	6.4	16,659	54
Natrona*	56025	4.2	69,348	234	4.0	72,107	232
Niobrara	56027	-9.8	2,170	7	-9.3	1,969	6
Park	56029	3.6	26,709	90	3.4	27,604	89
Platte	56031	-2.5	8,590	29	-1.9	8,424	27
Sheridan*	56033	3.4	27,462	93	3.1	28,307	91
Sublette	56035	12.0	6,629	22	10.2	7,302	23
Sweetwater**	56037	-1.8	36,923	125	-1.6	36,341	117
Teton**	56039	3.7	18,930	64	3.0	19,496	63
Uinta**	56041	0.2	19,787	67	0.4	19,857	64
Washakie	56043	-7.1	7,703	26	-6.8	7,178	23
Weston	56045	0.7	6,690	23	0.6	6,732	22
Total: Wyoming		2.8	507,467	1,711	2.6	520,799	1,676
Total: United States		5.3	296,460,358	1,000,000	4.8	310,730,123	1,000,000

Source: Devonshire Associates Ltd. and Scan/US, Inc. 2005.　　(d) Data not available.
* Component of a Metropolitan Core Based Statistical Area.
** Component of a Micropolitan Core Based Statistical Area.

150 Largest Counties: Population Trends

The following data are provided for the 150 largest counties (or county equivalents): the State-County FIPS Code; 2000-2005 estimated percent of change in population; 2005 estimated population; 2005-2010 projected percent of change in population; and 2010 projected population. Counties are ranked by population according to their 2005 estimated and their 2010 projected figures. Counties are listed in descending order by their 2010 projected population figures.

County	FIPS Code	Present 2000-2005 % Change	Present 7/1/05 Estimate	Present 2005 Rank	Future 2005-2010 % Change	Future 2010 Projection	Future 2010 Rank
Los Angeles, CA	06037	5.9	10,076,928	1	5.3	10,607,471	1
Cook, IL	17031	-0.8	5,332,321	2	-0.9	5,286,501	2
Maricopa, AZ	04013	16.6	3,582,040	4	13.5	4,067,317	3
Harris, TX	48201	9.2	3,713,507	3	8.0	4,011,640	4
Orange, CA	06059	6.1	3,020,648	5	5.4	3,184,136	5
San Diego, CA	06073	6.3	2,990,693	6	5.5	3,156,599	6
Miami-Dade, FL	12086	6.1	2,391,206	8	5.5	2,522,264	7
Kings, NY	36047	0.6	2,480,420	7	0.5	2,493,914	8
Dallas, TX	48113	4.5	2,319,427	9	4.1	2,413,468	9
Riverside, CA	06065	24.9	1,929,673	13	19.1	2,298,625	10
Queens, NY	36081	-0.2	2,225,143	10	-0.3	2,218,858	11
San Bernardino, CA	06071	14.5	1,957,135	12	12.1	2,194,729	12
Clark, NV	32003	23.4	1,697,755	16	17.9	2,001,933	13
Wayne, MI	26163	-2.6	2,008,158	11	-2.5	1,958,009	14
Broward, FL	12011	10.5	1,794,053	14	9.0	1,955,383	15
King, WA	53033	2.3	1,776,888	15	2.1	1,814,815	16
Tarrant, TX	48439	12.5	1,626,962	18	10.6	1,799,145	17
Santa Clara, CA	06085	-0.7	1,669,973	17	-1.0	1,653,999	18
New York, NY	36061	3.3	1,588,044	19	3.1	1,636,531	19
Bexar, TX	48029	8.6	1,512,995	20	7.6	1,628,001	20
Suffolk, NY	36103	5.6	1,498,863	21	5.0	1,573,642	21
Sacramento, CA	06067	14.1	1,395,768	25	11.8	1,560,980	22
Alameda, CA	06001	1.6	1,466,375	23	1.1	1,482,425	23
Middlesex, MA	25017	0.3	1,469,958	22	0.1	1,471,162	24
Bronx, NY	36005	3.9	1,385,071	26	3.6	1,435,428	25
Philadelphia, PA	42101	-4.0	1,456,998	24	-3.8	1,402,114	26
Palm Beach, FL	12099	12.0	1,267,148	29	10.4	1,398,390	27
Nassau, NY	36059	0.7	1,343,675	28	0.5	1,350,776	28
Cuyahoga, OH	39035	-3.6	1,344,252	27	-3.5	1,297,572	29
Hillsborough, FL	12057	12.0	1,118,988	33	10.3	1,234,723	30
Oakland, MI	26125	1.7	1,214,978	31	1.5	1,233,145	31
Allegheny, PA	42003	-2.5	1,249,911	30	-2.4	1,220,311	32
Hennepin, MN	27053	0.6	1,123,455	32	0.5	1,129,139	33
Franklin, OH	39049	3.0	1,100,544	34	2.6	1,129,032	34
Orange, FL	12095	12.2	1,006,134	38	10.3	1,109,877	35
Contra Costa, CA	06013	8.7	1,031,546	35	7.5	1,109,319	36
Fairfax, VA (County)	51059	4.8	1,016,742	36	4.2	1,059,612	37
Montgomery, MD	24031	8.5	947,578	40	7.3	1,017,181	38
St. Louis, MO (County)	29189	-0.1	1,015,417	37	-0.2	1,013,712	39
Pima, AZ	04019	9.2	921,681	46	7.9	994,799	40
Westchester, NY	36119	3.0	951,137	39	2.6	976,236	41
DuPage, IL	17043	3.7	937,264	41	3.2	967,550	42
Fresno, CA	06019	10.3	881,918	52	9.0	961,546	43
Salt Lake, UT	49035	3.5	930,006	43	3.2	959,978	44
Honolulu, HI	15003	3.9	910,475	48	3.9	945,789	45
Travis, TX	48453	8.6	882,137	51	7.1	944,453	46
Fairfield, CT	09001	3.0	909,263	49	2.7	933,729	47
Pinellas, FL	12103	0.6	927,210	45	0.6	932,315	48
Bergen, NJ	34003	2.6	906,873	50	2.3	927,845	49
Shelby, TN	47157	1.6	912,260	47	1.5	926,191	50
Erie, NY	36029	-1.4	936,770	42	-1.3	924,278	51
Prince George's, MD	24033	7.7	863,468	55	6.9	923,099	52
Milwaukee, WI	55079	-1.3	927,823	44	-1.3	916,196	53
Hartford, CT	09003	2.8	881,552	53	2.6	904,560	54
Duval, FL	12031	7.7	838,841	57	7.1	897,985	55
New Haven, CT	09009	3.6	853,637	56	3.3	882,213	56
Mecklenburg, NC	37119	13.3	787,867	66	11.1	875,406	57
Marion, IN	18097	0.6	865,538	54	0.6	870,495	58
Ventura, CA	06111	8.0	813,570	60	7.0	870,395	59
Macomb, MI	26099	5.2	829,028	58	4.6	866,942	60
Gwinnett, GA	13135	23.4	725,943	74	17.8	855,451	61
Middlesex, NJ	34023	6.8	800,915	62	6.0	848,816	62
Wake, NC	37183	17.5	737,573	72	14.2	841,949	63
Fulton, GA	13121	0.9	822,956	59	0.7	828,558	64
Worcester, MA	25027	5.3	790,475	65	4.8	828,032	65
Pierce, WA	53053	9.3	765,698	68	8.1	827,363	66
Baltimore, MD (County)	24005	4.9	791,384	64	4.4	826,495	67
Kern, CA	06029	12.4	743,729	70	10.7	823,538	68
Collin, TX	48085	34.4	660,783	87	24.3	821,038	69
Montgomery, PA	42091	4.7	785,423	67	4.3	819,588	70
Essex, NJ	34013	0.8	800,056	63	0.9	807,383	71
San Joaquin, CA	06077	19.6	674,080	84	15.7	779,783	72
Hidalgo, TX	48215	18.6	675,597	83	15.0	776,946	73
Hamilton, OH	39061	-4.2	809,794	61	-4.1	776,764	74
Will, IL	17197	27.5	640,443	93	20.6	772,560	75
Essex, MA	25009	2.9	744,047	69	2.5	762,420	76
Lake, IL	17097	9.4	704,726	76	8.0	761,208	77
El Paso, TX	48141	6.0	720,147	75	5.4	758,748	78
Cobb, GA	13067	11.5	677,675	82	9.6	742,723	79
Monroe, NY	36055	0.5	738,925	71	0.4	742,088	80
Multnomah, OR	41051	4.3	688,787	79	4.0	716,054	81
Oklahoma, OK	40109	4.0	687,070	80	3.6	711,865	82
Jefferson, KY	21111	1.2	701,817	77	1.1	709,724	83
Snohomish, WA	53061	8.8	659,426	88	7.6	709,672	84
San Francisco, CA	06075	-5.4	734,587	73	-5.4	694,890	85
DeKalb, GA	13089	2.1	679,804	81	1.6	690,779	86
Providence, RI	44007	5.1	653,201	91	4.7	683,578	87
Denton, TX	48121	29.0	558,392	103	21.4	677,656	88
Jackson, MO	29095	1.6	665,173	86	1.4	674,318	89
Monmouth, NJ	34025	4.7	644,487	92	4.2	671,700	90
San Mateo, CA	06081	-2.5	689,423	78	-2.7	670,972	91
Norfolk, MA	25021	0.7	655,077	90	0.6	659,014	92
Suffolk, MA	25025	-2.3	673,720	85	-2.3	657,995	93
Jefferson, AL	01073	-0.9	655,970	89	-0.9	649,779	94
Bucks, PA	42017	4.1	622,393	94	3.6	645,062	95
Bernalillo, NM	35001	7.5	598,254	98	6.8	638,753	96
Ocean, NJ	34029	11.3	568,520	102	9.7	623,431	97
Kent, MI	26081	4.4	599,621	97	3.9	622,847	98
El Paso, CO	08041	10.4	570,479	101	9.0	621,578	99
Hudson, NJ	34017	-0.3	607,051	96	-0.4	604,565	100
Lee, FL	12071	18.7	523,512	116	15.2	603,036	101
Stanislaus, CA	06099	16.3	519,823	117	13.4	589,650	102
Baltimore, MD (Ind. City)	24510	-5.2	617,204	95	-4.9	587,263	103
Tulsa, OK	40143	2.1	574,848	99	1.9	585,531	104
Kane, IL	17089	21.3	490,051	127	16.8	572,298	105
Davidson, TN	47037	0.2	570,911	100	0.2	571,793	106
Arapahoe, CO	08005	9.0	531,667	111	7.5	571,739	107
Bristol, MA	25005	3.4	553,046	106	3.1	569,949	108
Brevard, FL	12009	9.9	523,567	115	8.7	569,284	109
Polk, FL	12105	8.7	526,208	113	7.7	566,911	110
Denver, CO	08031	0.6	558,088	104	0.5	560,809	111
Johnson, KS	20091	12.5	507,661	120	10.4	560,260	112
Delaware, PA	42045	1.0	556,280	105	0.7	560,150	113
Fort Bend, TX	48157	29.7	459,581	138	21.8	559,909	114
Summit, OH	39153	1.1	549,026	107	1.0	554,262	115
Washington, OR	41067	12.3	500,313	123	10.3	552,092	116
New Castle, DE	10003	4.7	523,864	114	4.2	545,859	117
Union, NJ	34039	2.2	534,259	110	2.0	545,156	118
Anne Arundel, MD	24003	5.6	517,299	119	5.0	543,077	119
Montgomery, OH	39113	-2.0	547,810	109	-2.0	537,122	120
Jefferson, CO[1]	08059	0.4	529,190	112	0.5	531,901	121
District of Columbia, DC	11001	-4.0	548,902	108	-3.9	527,662	122
Camden, NJ	34007	1.8	518,146	118	1.8	527,433	123
Volusia, FL	12127	9.0	483,444	130	7.9	521,860	124
Plymouth, MA	25023	4.9	495,811	124	4.3	517,008	125
Passaic, NJ	34031	3.1	504,035	121	2.6	516,976	126
Morris, NJ	34027	4.6	492,011	125	4.2	512,552	127
Lancaster, PA	42071	4.2	490,254	126	3.7	508,588	128
Chester, PA	42029	8.9	471,979	131	7.6	507,963	129
Douglas, NE	31055	4.4	483,981	129	3.9	503,039	130
Dane, WI	55025	8.6	463,177	135	7.5	497,973	131
Richmond, NY	36085	5.9	470,056	133	5.2	494,633	132
Lake, IN	18089	1.0	489,391	128	1.0	494,044	133
Ramsey, MN	27123	-1.7	502,508	122	-1.7	493,791	134
Burlington, NJ	34005	8.3	458,701	139	7.4	492,773	135
Pasco, FL	12101	20.6	415,912	149	16.4	484,329	136
Sedgwick, KS	20173	3.5	468,918	134	3.2	483,958	137
Sonoma, CA	06097	2.7	470,813	132	2.2	481,193	138
Hampden, MA	25013	1.5	463,031	136	1.4	469,420	139
Virginia Beach, VA (Ind. City)	51810	5.3	447,757	142	4.7	468,941	140
Onondaga, NY	36067	1.0	462,726	137	0.9	466,993	141
Guilford, NC	37081	5.0	442,093	145	4.4	461,760	142
Spokane, WA	53063	5.1	439,273	146	4.7	459,829	143
Clark, WA	53011	16.2	401,099	157	13.4	454,676	144
Genesee, MI	26049	2.2	445,626	144	1.9	454,172	145
Montgomery, TX	48339	27.8	375,519	170	20.7	453,313	146
Lucas, OH	39095	-0.5	452,909	141	-0.5	450,819	147
Utah, UT	49049	11.1	409,622	150	9.5	448,415	148
Adams, CO[1]	08001	9.7	399,121	160	12.0	446,996	149
Solano, CA	06095	6.9	421,801	147	5.8	446,371	150

Source: Devonshire Associates Ltd. and Scan/US, Inc. 2005.
[1] Census population includes a portion of Broomfield county.

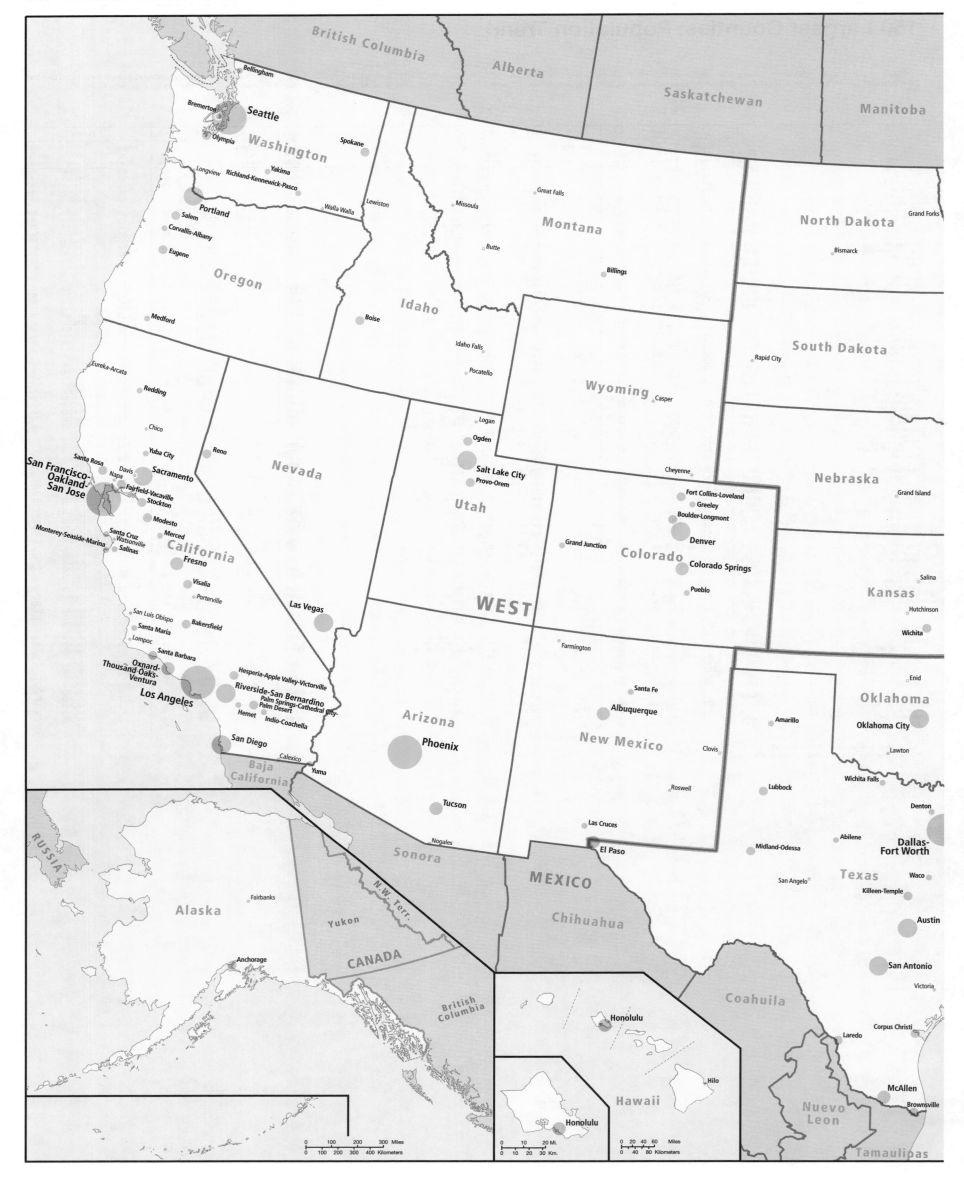

British Columbia
Alberta
Saskatchewan
Manitoba

Bellingham

Bremerton
Seattle
Olympia
Washington
Spokane

Longview
Richland-Kennewick-Pasco
Yakima

Walla Walla
Lewiston

Great Falls
Missoula
Montana
North Dakota
Grand Forks

Portland
Salem
Corvallis-Albany
Eugene
Oregon

Butte
Billings
Bismarck

Medford
Boise
Idaho

Idaho Falls
Pocatello

Wyoming
South Dakota
Rapid City

Eureka-Arcata
Redding

Chico
Yuba City
Reno
Nevada

Logan
Ogden
Salt Lake City
Provo-Orem
Cheyenne
Nebraska
Grand Island

Santa Rosa
San Francisco-Oakland-San Jose
Davis
Napa
Sacramento
Fairfield-Vacaville
Stockton
Modesto

Utah

Fort Collins-Loveland
Greeley
Boulder-Longmont
Denver

Salina

Monterey-Seaside-Marina
Santa Cruz
Watsonville
Salinas
Merced
California
Fresno
Visalia
Porterville

Grand Junction
Colorado
Colorado Springs
Pueblo

Kansas
Hutchinson
Wichita

San Luis Obispo
Santa Maria
Lompoc
Santa Barbara
Bakersfield
Las Vegas

WEST

Oxnard-Thousand Oaks-Ventura
Los Angeles
Hesperia-Apple Valley-Victorville
Riverside-San Bernardino
Palm Springs-Cathedral City-Palm Desert
Hemet
Indio-Coachella

Farmington

Santa Fe
Albuquerque
New Mexico

Enid
Oklahoma

Amarillo
Oklahoma City
Lawton

San Diego
Calexico
Yuma
Baja California

Arizona
Phoenix

Clovis

Wichita Falls
Denton

Tucson

Roswell
Lubbock
Dallas-Fort Worth

Russia

Nogales

Las Cruces
El Paso
Midland-Odessa
Abilene

Sonora

Fairbanks

N.W. Terr.

MEXICO
Chihuahua

San Angelo
Texas
Waco
Killeen-Temple

Alaska
Yukon

Austin

Anchorage
CANADA

San Antonio
Victoria

British Columbia

Coahuila

Honolulu

Corpus Christi
Laredo

Hilo
Hawaii

Nuevo Leon

McAllen
Brownsville

Honolulu

Tamaulipas

0   100   200   300 Miles
0   100   200   300   400 Kilometers

0   10   20 Mi.
0   10   20   30 Km.

0 20 40 60 Miles
0 40 80 Kilometers

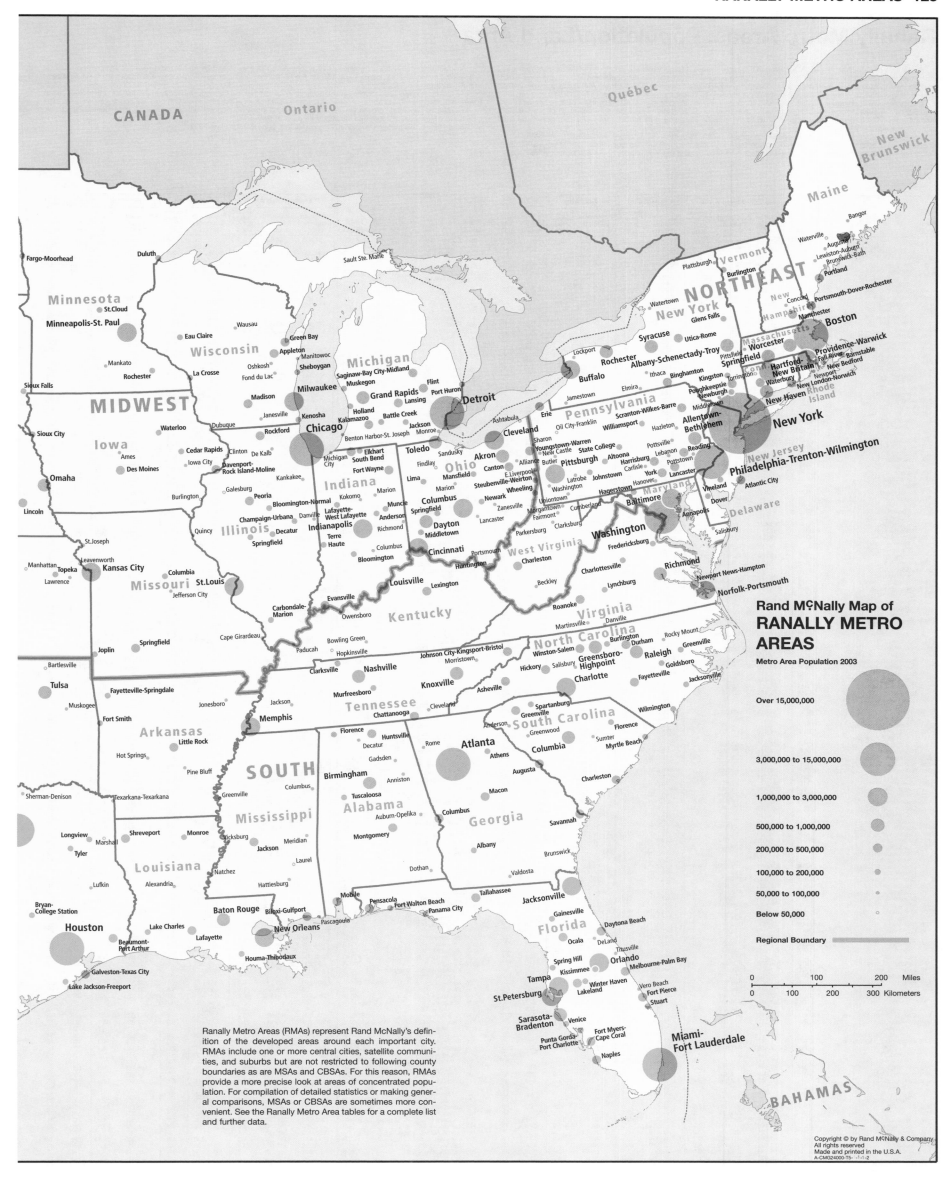

Rand McNally Map of
RANALLY METRO AREAS

Metro Area Population 2003

Over 15,000,000

3,000,000 to 15,000,000

1,000,000 to 3,000,000

500,000 to 1,000,000

200,000 to 500,000

100,000 to 200,000

50,000 to 100,000

Below 50,000

Regional Boundary

0   100   200 Miles
0 100 200 300 Kilometers

Ranally Metro Areas (RMAs) represent Rand McNally's definition of the developed areas around each important city.
RMAs include one or more central cities, satellite communities, and suburbs but are not restricted to following county
boundaries as are MSAs and CBSAs. For this reason, RMAs
provide a more precise look at areas of concentrated population. For compilation of detailed statistics or making general comparisons, MSAs or CBSAs are sometimes more convenient. See the Ranally Metro Area tables for a complete list
and further data.

Ranally Metro Areas: Population/Land Area

The Ranally Metropolitan Areas (RMAs) listed in this table represent Rand McNally's definitions of the metropolitan areas of the nation's major cities. They are designed to provide accurate information on the population change and areal extent of each metropolitan area. The RMAs are defined on a sub-county basis; this is in contrast with the U.S. government's Metropolitan Statistical Areas (MSAs), which are generally defined in terms of whole counties.

The RMAs have been defined for all areas with an estimated population of at least 50,000 and for selected areas of less than 50,000. A more detailed description of the criteria used for defining RMAs is in the Introduction on pages 5-9. The map on pages 124-125 shows the location of all RMAs and the individual state maps, pages 142-254, depict the areal extent of individual RMAs.

The table contains 2005 estimated populations for each RMA, its central city (or cities), and suburbs. All RMAs with a population over 50,000 are ranked, in addition the table presents the 2000 Census population for RMAs; a 2000-2005 percent of population change for RMAs, central cities, and suburbs; and the land area of RMAs and central cities.

Following this table are summaries of RMA population by region and by state, and a list of RMAs by population in descending order. Two tables on page 135 list the RMAs that are most rapidly growing, and most rapidly losing size in population.

The tables on page 128 indicate several population trends that are currently underway in the nation. Since 2000, most RMAs in the Northeast and Midwest have experienced lower rates of population growth than the country as a whole. The highest rates of population growth for RMAs have occurred in the South and West. In all regions, RMA Central Cities have grown more slowly since 2000 than the suburban parts of RMAs.

Source for city estimates: Devonshire Associates Ltd. and Scan/US, Inc. 2005.

Rank 2005	RMA	Abbrev.	Ranally Metro Area: Population Estimate 7/1/05	Ranally Metro Area: Population Census 4/1/00	Ranally Metro Area: Percent Change 2000-2005	Central City: Population Estimate 7/1/05	Central City: Percent Change 2000-2005	Suburbs: Population Estimate 7/1/05	Suburbs: Percent Change 2000-2005	Land Area (square miles): Metro Area	Land Area (square miles): City 2000
259	Abilene, TX	ABIL	117,735	117,689	.0	117,535	1.4	200	-88.6	211	103
62	Akron, OH	AKR	719,871	708,043	1.7	216,322	-.3	503,549	2.6	825	62
271	Albany, GA	ALB	109,970	107,244	2.5	76,098	-1.1	33,872	11.8	277	56
54	Albany-, NY	A-S-T	815,631	793,886	2.7	208,645	1.0	606,986	3.4	1,675	42
	Albany, NY					97,769	2.2				21
	Schenectady, NY					62,065	.4				11
	Troy, NY					48,811	-.7				10
59	Albuquerque, NM	ALBU	722,570	668,334	8.1	495,118	10.4	227,452	3.5	778	132
297	Alexandria, LA	ALEX	97,288	96,705	.6	46,250	-.2	51,038	1.3	394	25
65	Allentown-, PA-NJ	ALL-	646,337	608,943	6.1	181,930	2.2	464,407	7.8	790	37
	Allentown, PA					108,777	2.0				18
	Bethlehem, PA					73,153	2.6				19
414	Alliance, OH	ALLI	51,256	51,753	-1.0	23,405	.7	27,851	-2.3	167	8
244	Altoona, PA	ALT	122,908	125,517	-2.1	48,534	-2.0	74,374	-2.1	408	9
176	Amarillo, TX	AMA	197,504	188,149	5.0	179,315	3.3	18,189	25.3	153	88
388	Ames, IA	AMES	63,140	62,798	.5	50,915	.4	12,225	1.3	146	20
118	Anchorage, AK†	ANCH	319,384	293,276	8.9	278,263	6.9	41,121	24.6	1,754	1,698
232	Anderson, IN	AND	134,075	137,711	-2.6	58,561	-2.0	75,514	-3.2	440	38
288	Anderson, SC	AND	100,598	94,972	5.9	24,820	-2.7	75,778	9.1	294	12
204	Annapolis, MD	ANPLS	155,127	144,778	7.1	38,325	6.9	116,802	7.2	146	6
293	Anniston, AL	ANNI	98,851	98,571	.3	23,842	-1.8	75,009	1.0	382	20
161	Appleton, WI	APP	222,488	210,894	5.5	73,932	5.5	148,556	5.5	299	17
138	Asheville, NC	ASHE	265,012	251,012	5.6	70,396	2.2	194,616	6.9	727	35
	Ashtabula, OH	ASHT	42,278	42,091	.4	20,838	-.6	21,440	1.5	96	8
199	Athens, GA	ATH	163,451	151,357	8.0	105,535	5.3	57,916	13.4	452	17
12	Atlanta, GA	ATL	4,055,593	3,623,062	11.9	399,217	-4.1	3,656,376	14.0	3,132	132
128	Atlantic City, NJ	ATCY	291,892	281,933	3.5	40,750	.6	251,142	4.0	565	11
325	Auburn-, AL	AU-OP	85,407	80,826	5.7	67,173	1.0	18,234	27.1	137	78
	Auburn, AL					44,194	2.8				33
	Opelika, AL					22,979	-2.2				45
94	Augusta, GA-SC	AUG	417,212	402,891	3.6	190,195	-2.6	227,017	9.3	783	20
371	Augusta, ME	AUG	66,922	64,589	3.6	18,367	-1.0	48,555	5.5	365	55
37	Austin, TX	AUS	1,147,387	1,009,196	13.7	709,517	8.1	437,870	24.2	1,071	218
85	Bakersfield, CA	BAK	458,985	408,328	12.4	309,140	25.1	149,845	-7.1	492	92
18	Baltimore, MD-PA	BAL	2,319,491	2,241,860	3.5	617,204	-5.2	1,702,287	7.0	1,780	81
309	Bangor, ME	BANG	94,111	91,001	3.4	31,246	-.7	62,865	5.6	398	35
195	Barnstable, MA	BARN	168,066	160,772	4.5	48,874	2.2	119,192	5.5	260	60
	Bartlesville, OK	BART	40,913	40,774	.3	34,901	.4	6,012	-.2	40	21
72	Baton Rouge, LA	B.R.	557,929	542,403	2.9	228,423	.3	329,506	4.7	821	74
275	Battle Creek, MI	BTLCK	106,648	105,471	1.1	54,163	1.5	52,485	.7	251	43
108	Beaumont-, TX	B-PA	354,370	359,418	-1.4	164,987	-3.9	189,383	.8	722	157
	Beaumont, TX					110,037	-3.4				80
	Port Arthur, TX					54,950	-4.9				77
329	Beckley, WV	BECK	84,499	84,587	-.1	16,381	-5.1	68,118	1.2	441	9
209	Bellingham, WA	BELNG	152,279	139,165	9.4	76,238	13.5	76,041	5.6	338	22
292	Benton Harbor-, MI	BNTH-	99,038	98,418	.6	19,563	-2.0	79,475	1.3	278	7
	Benton Harbor, MI					10,972	-1.9				4
	St. Joseph, MI					8,591	-2.3				3
255	Billings, MT	BIL	119,066	113,426	5.0	94,441	5.1	24,625	4.4	107	33
143	Biloxi-, MS	BIL-	257,307	252,892	1.7	125,743	3.3	131,564	.3	309	43
	Biloxi, MS					51,853	2.4				20
	Gulfport, MS					73,890	3.9				23
164	Binghamton, NY-PA	BING	221,171	223,650	-1.1	46,069	-2.8	175,102	-.7	705	10
53	Birmingham, AL	BIR	815,670	800,495	1.9	231,588	-4.6	584,082	4.7	1,622	149
330	Bismarck, ND	BIS	84,042	80,754	4.1	57,609	3.7	26,433	4.8	159	24
253	Bloomington-, IL	BLOOM-	119,646	112,143	6.7	119,585	8.5	61	-96.9	76	29
	Bloomington, IL					71,392	10.2				17
	Normal, IL					48,193	6.2				12
262	Bloomington, IN	BLMNG	115,081	114,767	.3	67,861	-2.1	47,220	3.8	210	15
96	Boise, ID	BOIS	402,439	349,941	15.0	202,968	9.2	199,471	21.5	306	46
9	Boston, MA-NH	BOS	4,754,031	4,679,465	1.6	581,578	-1.3	4,172,453	2.0	3,609	48
147	Boulder-, CO	BOUL-	249,155	256,431	-2.8	177,676	7.2	71,479	-21.2	248	36
	Boulder, CO					94,846	.2				23
	Longmont, CO					82,830	16.5				13
405	Bowling Green, KY	BOWLG	53,880	48,992	10.0	53,680	8.9	200	.0	188	29
178	Bremerton, WA	BREM	192,778	185,060	4.2	35,703	-4.2	157,075	6.3	257	20
109	Brownsville, TX-MEX.	BRNS	348,413	307,363	13.4	155,791	11.5	192,622	14.9	393	28
	incl. Matamoros, MEX.		*798,413*	*587,363*	*35.9*					*418*	
370	Brunswick, GA	BRUNS	67,062	62,815	6.8	15,982	2.4	51,080	8.2	131	17
394	Brunswick-, ME††	BR-BA	60,423	57,361	5.3	24,340	1.1	36,083	8.4	211	22
	Brunswick, ME					15,325	3.4				13
	Bath, ME					9,015	-2.7				9
218	Bryan-, TX	BRY-	144,018	140,080	2.8	136,223	2.0	7,795	19.4	95	63
	Bryan, TX					65,889	.3				33
	College Station, TX					70,334	3.6				30
42	Buffalo, NY-CAN.	BUF	1,074,000	1,088,729	-1.4	278,583	-4.8	795,417	-.1	1,128	41
	incl. St. Catharines-Niagara Falls, CAN.		*1,465,900*	*1,451,929*	*1.0*					*1,668*	
	Burlington, IA	BUR	33,925	35,380	-4.1	25,728	-4.1	8,197	-4.0	83	13
225	Burlington, NC	BUR	137,092	128,179	7.0	46,902	4.4	90,190	8.3	317	20
189	Burlington, VT	BUR	175,046	169,535	3.3	38,653	-.6	136,393	4.4	562	11
367	Butler, PA	BUTL	68,464	65,046	5.3	15,070	-.3	53,394	6.9	170	3
	Butte, MT†	BUT	32,352	34,564	-6.4	31,829	-6.1	523	-22.2	718	716
	Calexico, CA-MEX.	CLEX	30,926	24,616	25.6	30,726	13.3	200	.0	8	4
	incl. Mexicali, MEX.		*650,926*	*474,616*	*37.1*					*48*	
111	Canton, OH	CAN	343,528	343,794	-.1	80,935	.2	262,593	-.2	585	20
372	Cape Girardeau, MO	CPGIR	66,854	65,017	2.8	35,568	.6	31,286	5.5	163	23
245	Carbondale-, IL	CARB-	122,593	122,444	.1	35,499	-3.3	87,094	1.6	504	21
	Carbondale, IL					19,222	-7.1				10
	Marion, IL					16,277	1.5				11
375	Carlisle, PA	CARL	66,306	63,470	4.5	18,272	1.7	48,034	5.6	197	5
380	Casper, WY	CASP	64,788	62,158	4.2	50,742	2.2	14,046	12.2	98	21
185	Cedar Rapids, IA	CEDR	178,126	172,024	3.5	123,877	2.6	54,249	5.8	259	54
231	Champaign-, IL	CH-U	134,149	129,489	3.6	104,871	.9	29,278	14.5	145	21
	Champaign, IL					68,053	.8				13
	Urbana, IL					36,818	1.2				8
77	Charleston, SC	CHAS	507,697	475,333	6.8	106,231	9.9	401,466	6.0	635	43
159	Charleston, WV	CHAS	230,125	234,573	-1.9	49,941	-6.5	180,184	-.5	826	30
32	Charlotte, NC-SC	CHRLT	1,458,942	1,301,901	12.1	588,566	8.8	870,376	14.4	2,106	174
256	Charlottesville, VA	CHRLTV	118,093	116,978	1.0	36,403	-19.2	81,690	13.6	373	10
91	Chattanooga, TN-GA	CHTN	425,810	412,643	3.2	156,076	.3	269,734	4.9	863	118
349	Cheyenne, WY	CHEY	76,888	72,857	5.5	55,016	3.8	21,872	10.2	56	19
3	Chicago, IL-IN-WI	CHI	9,086,842	8,748,587	3.9	2,896,965	.0	6,189,877	5.8	4,068	227
301	Chico, CA	CHICO	96,624	91,033	6.1	68,339	14.0	28,285	-9.0	135	22
25	Cincinnati, OH-KY-IN	CIN	1,717,698	1,691,894	1.5	315,137	-4.9	1,402,561	3.1	2,139	77
406	Clarksburg, WV	CLRKB	53,875	54,529	-1.2	16,440	-1.8	37,435	-.9	195	8
210	Clarksville, TN-KY	CLRKV	151,779	145,582	4.3	111,150	7.4	40,629	-3.6	299	73
20	Cleveland, OH	CLEV	2,165,087	2,182,254	-.8	440,844	-7.9	1,724,243	1.2	1,985	77
314	Cleveland, TN	CLEV	91,487	87,951	4.0	38,471	3.4	53,016	4.4	329	20
	Clinton, IA-IL	CLNT	37,213	37,644	-1.1	26,916	-3.1	10,297	4.3	73	36
	Clovis, NM	CLOV	39,334	39,060	.7	32,931	.8	6,403	.2	32	14
71	Colorado Springs, CO	CSPG	558,730	506,440	10.3	386,372	7.1	172,358	18.4	510	183
273	Columbia, MO	COL	107,770	101,609	6.1	91,697	8.5	16,073	-5.9	104	44
73	Columbia, SC	COL	546,557	512,179	6.7	118,299	1.7	428,258	8.2	1,070	117
152	Columbus, GA-AL	COL	241,854	248,565	-2.7	182,354	-1.8	59,500	-5.2	315	216
365	Columbus, IN	COL	68,749	66,969	2.7	40,526	3.8	28,223	1.1	262	20
409	Columbus, MS	COL	52,776	54,101	-2.4	25,025	-3.5	27,751	-1.4	150	12
33	Columbus, OH	COL	1,283,920	1,225,821	4.7	741,747	4.3	542,173	5.4	1,211	191
313	Concord, NH	CONC	92,312	84,570	9.2	42,465	4.4	49,847	13.6	329	64
117	Corpus Christi, TX	CRPX	320,199	317,717	.8	278,068	.2	42,131	4.6	334	135
264	Corvallis-, OR	CORV-	113,579	109,900	3.3	94,369	4.7	19,210	-2.6	194	25
	Corvallis, OR					50,080	1.5				13
	Albany, OR					44,289	8.4				12
345	Cumberland, MD-WV	CUMB	77,648	79,128	-1.9	19,864	-7.7	57,784	.3	289	8
7	Dallas-, TX	D-FW	5,259,868	4,681,646	12.4	1,887,765	9.5	3,372,103	14.0	3,360	623
	Dallas, TX					1,264,288	6.4				342
	Fort Worth, TX					623,477	16.6				281
383	Danville, IL	DANV	64,119	65,418	-2.0	33,617	-.8	30,502	-3.2	238	15
355	Danville, VA-NC	DANV	71,669	73,986	-3.1	46,092	-4.8	25,577	.0	265	43
122	Davenport-, IA-IL	D-RI-M	300,841	302,080	-.4	183,358	.9	117,483	-2.3	446	91
	Davenport, IA					99,998	1.7				61
	Moline, IL					43,548	-.5				15
	Rock Island, IL					39,812	.3				15
366	Davis, CA	DAV	68,569	60,966	12.5	67,477	11.9	1,092	66.0	38	8
56	Dayton, OH	DAY	784,334	785,027	-.1	161,888	-2.6	622,446	.6	1,100	55
119	Daytona Beach, FL	D.BCH	315,626	286,852	10.0	62,175	-3.0	253,451	13.8	281	32
299	Decatur, AL	DEC	97,190	95,099	2.2	53,051	-1.6	44,139	7.2	248	47
294	Decatur, IL	DEC	98,786	103,836	-4.9	78,430	-4.2	20,356	-7.4	238	37
363	De Kalb, IL	DKLB	69,669	64,388	8.2	40,994	5.1	28,675	13.0	141	8
396	DeLand, FL	DL	58,033	53,219	9.0	24,470	17.1	33,563	3.9	114	10
196	Denton, TX	DENT	165,156	128,061	29.0	93,660	16.3	71,496	50.4	145	53
19	Denver, CO	DEN	2,240,633	2,088,925	7.3	558,088	.6	1,682,545	9.7	1,267	153
95	Des Moines, IA	DES	412,318	388,217	6.2	200,756	1.0	211,562	11.6	475	75
10	Detroit, MI-CAN.	DET	4,705,677	4,641,127	1.4	928,992	-2.3	3,776,685	2.4	3,656	139
	incl. Windsor, CAN.		*5,010,177*	*4,899,827*	*2.3*					*3,989*	
315	Dothan, AL	DOTH	90,744	86,801	4.5	60,222	4.3	30,522	5.0	387	80
224	Dover, DE	DOVR	139,119	126,206	10.2	34,548	7.5	104,571	11.2	428	21
350	Dubuque, IA-WI-IL	DUB	75,175	73,570	2.2	58,271	1.0	16,904	6.4	117	23
211	Duluth, MN-WI	DUL	151,008	150,470	.4	87,481	.6	63,527	.0	292	68
104	Durham, NC	DUR	379,729	355,621	6.8	212,990	13.9	166,739	-1.1	680	69
	East Liverpool, OH	E.LIV	38,400	38,759	-.9	13,074	-.1	25,326	-1.3	156	4
274	Eau Claire, WI	EAUC	107,265	103,894	3.2	62,148	.7	45,117	6.9	197	28
177	Elkhart, IN-MI	ELK	196,791	187,083	5.2	53,488	3.1	143,303	6.0	519	17
342	Elmira, NY	ELM	81,051	81,987	-1.1	30,246	-2.2	50,805	-.5	209	7
57	El Paso, TX-NM-MEX.	ELP	737,098	695,311	6.0	602,267	6.8	134,831	2.4	469	245
	incl. Ciudad Juarez, MEX.		*2,012,098*	*1,490,311*	*35.0*					*529*	
	Enid, OK	ENID	49,015	49,931	-1.8	47,555	1.1	1,460	-49.4	168	72
141	Erie, PA	ERIE	257,921	259,365	-.6	103,797	.1	154,124	-1.0	537	22
129	Eugene, OR	EUG	287,049	276,455	3.8	149,779	8.6	137,270	-.9	505	38
291	Eureka-, CA	EUR-	99,303	97,609	1.7	42,531	-.6	56,772	3.5	211	18
	Eureka, CA					26,208	.3				10
	Arcata, CA					16,323	-2.0				8
149	Evansville, IN-KY	EV	245,571	241,874	1.5	117,092	-3.7	128,479	6.8	403	41
374	Fairbanks, AK	FRBK	66,439	63,420	4.8	30,903	2.2	35,536	7.0	95	31
155	Fairfield-, CA	FRFL-	239,882	224,380	6.9	202,904	9.8	36,978	-6.6	222	59
	Fairfield, CA					106,069	10.3				36
	Vacaville, CA					96,835	9.3				23
400	Fairmont, WV	FAIRM	56,596	56,699	-.2	18,634	-2.4	37,962	1.0	236	8
193	Fall River, MA-RI	F.R.	169,838	164,759	3.1	91,764	-.2	78,074	7.2	162	31
214	Fargo-, ND-MN	FAR-	149,745	143,735	4.2	125,990	2.6	23,755	13.3	129	40
	Fargo, ND					93,589	3.3				30
	Moorhead, MN					32,401	.7				10
354	Farmington, NM	FARM	72,236	64,227	12.5	42,422	12.1	29,814	13.0	134	24
213	Fayetteville-, AR	FAY-	149,773	132,499	13.0	119,786	15.4	29,987	4.7	340	70
	Fayetteville, AR					65,643	13.1				40
	Springdale, AR					54,143	18.2				30
110	Fayetteville, NC	FAY	345,816	336,917	2.6	128,929	6.5	216,887	.5	724	41
416	Findlay, OH	FIND	50,809	48,737	4.3	38,590	-1.0	12,219	25.1	95	14
79	Flint, MI	FLN	499,449	488,625	2.2	122,883	-1.6	376,566	3.5	1,032	34
269	Florence, AL	FLO	111,986	113,578	-1.4	32,128	-11.4	79,858	3.3	455	24
285	Florence, SC	FLO	103,848	100,577	3.3	30,506	.9	73,342	4.3	298	15
397	Fond du Lac, WI	FDLC	57,392	56,596	1.4	42,791	1.4	14,601	1.4	115	13
142	Fort Collins-, CO	FTCL-	257,559	235,232	9.5	185,260	9.5	72,299	9.6	356	62
	Fort Collins, CO					129,345	9.0				41
	Loveland, CO					55,915	10.5				21
83	Fort Myers-, FL	FTMY-	469,130	395,089	18.7	179,095	19.0	290,035	18.6	438	127
	Fort Myers, FL					53,143	10.2				22
	Cape Coral, FL					125,952	23.1				105
168	Fort Pierce, FL	FTPI	216,478	183,494	18.0	38,461	2.5	178,017	21.9	205	12
190	Fort Smith, AR-OK	FTSM	175,043	168,369	4.0	81,788	1.9	93,255	5.9	441	47
212	Fort Walton Beach, FL	FTWL	149,896	139,781	7.2	19,972	.0	129,924	8.4	98	7
116	Fort Wayne, IN	FTWA	329,330	316,478	4.1	210,534	2.3	118,796	7.3	424	63
	Frederick, MD, *now part of Washington, DC-MD-VA*										
205	Fredericksburg, VA	FRED	154,791	121,747	27.1	20,769	7.7	134,022	30.8	242	11
55	Fresno, CA	FRES	807,860	729,375	10.8	479,143	12.0	328,717	8.9	7,516	99
319	Gadsden, AL	GAD	89,500	89,619	-.1	37,087	-4.9	52,413	3.5	332	36
184	Gainesville, FL	GAIN	178,682	174,392	2.5	89,956	-5.8	88,726	12.4	166	35
	Galesburg, IL	GLSB	42,827	44,654	-4.1	33,001	-2.1	9,826	-10.2	126	17
170	Galveston-, TX	GLV-	210,198	189,747	10.8	99,678	.9	110,520	21.5	278	108
	Galveston, TX					56,763	-.8				46
	Texas City, TX					42,915	3.4				62
	Gastonia, NC, *now part of Charlotte, NC-SC*										
268	Glens Falls, NY	GLFLS	112,767	107,250	5.1	14,064	-2.0	98,703	6.3	384	4
280	Goldsboro, NC	GLDS	104,801	104,826	.0	34,875	-10.7	69,926	6.3	371	21
407	Grand Forks, ND-MN	GDFK	53,806	55,642	-3.3	50,680	2.8	3,126	-50.5	61	14
	Grand Island, NE	GDIS	47,242	46,175	2.3	44,007	2.5	3,235	.0	61	21
260	Grand Junction, CO	GDJC	116,434	104,591	11.3	43,112	2.7	73,322	17.1	124	15
61	Grand Rapids, MI	GDR	720,302	686,981	4.9	198,345	.3	521,957	6.7	1,357	44
362	Great Falls, MT	GTFA	70,321	71,161	-1.2	55,249	-2.5	15,072	4.2	101	15
237	Greeley, CO	GRLY	130,765	102,533	27.5	86,804	12.8	43,961	71.7	101	28
166	Green Bay, WI	GRBY	219,657	208,515	5.3	102,844	.5	116,813	10.0	267	44
69	Greensboro-, NC	GRNS-	573,163	546,450	4.9	331,964	7.2	241,199	1.9	1,132	123
	Greensboro, NC					238,862	6.7				80
	High Point, NC					93,102	8.5				43
	Greenville, MS	GRNV	41,813	44,961	-7.0	39,712	-4.6	2,101	-36.9	70	26
250	Greenville, NC	GRNV	120,633	113,933	5.9	66,126	9.3	54,507	2.0	357	18
80	Greenville, SC	GRNV	496,789	468,255	6.1	54,857	-2.0	441,932	7.2	914	25
379	Greenwood, SC	GREEN	64,869	63,176	2.7	22,083	.1	42,786	4.1	223	13
188	Hagerstown, MD-PA-WV	HAG	175,582	164,726	6.6	38,790	5.7	136,792	6.8	452	10
357	Hanover, PA	HANV	71,599	66,826	7.1	14,614	.5	56,985	9.0	151	4
	Harlingen, TX, *now part of Brownsville, TX-MEX.*										
93	Harrisburg, PA	HRBG	417,776	410,150	1.9	46,556	-4.9	371,220	2.8	700	8
34	Hartford-, CT	H-NB	1,231,740	1,182,480	4.2	193,319	.1	1,038,421	5.0	1,677	30
	Hartford, CT					121,656	.1				17
	New Britain, CT					71,663	.2				13
335	Hattiesburg, MS	HATT	82,743	78,776	5.0	46,507	3.9	36,236	6.6	171	25
369	Hazleton, PA	HAZ	67,286	68,670	-2.0	22,221	-4.7	45,065	-.6	267	6
202	Hemet, CA	HEM	157,288	125,964	24.9	69,382	18.0	87,906	30.9	135	18
162	Hesperia-, CA	HESP-	221,332	193,320	14.5	201,612	11.5	19,720	58.1	209	157
	Hesperia, CA					71,480	14.2				48
	Victorville, CA					70,621	10.3				42
	Apple Valley, CA					59,511	9.7				67
156	Hickory, NC	HICK	238,644	224,463	6.3	43,522	16.9	195,122	4.2	791	20
381	Hilo, HI††	HILO	64,506	58,820	9.7	44,700	9.7	19,806	9.7	68	54
247	Holland, MI	HLND	121,086	112,747	7.4	35,160	.3	85,926	10.6	246	14
49	Honolulu, HI††	HON	910,439	876,121	3.9	390,815	5.2	519,624	3.0	600	83
	Hopkinsville, KY	HPKNV	33,527	34,486	-2.8	28,430	-5.5	5,097	15.9	88	20
356	Hot Springs, AR	HTSPR	71,651	67,794	5.7	37,180	4.0	34,471	7.6	165	29
240	Houma-, LA	HOMA-	126,419	124,143	1.8	47,108	.6	79,311	2.6	457	18
	Houma, LA					32,484	.3				14
	Thibodaux, LA					14,624	1.3				4
11	Houston, TX	HOU	4,561,009	4,080,199	11.8	2,136,305	9.4	2,424,704	14.0	2,576	540
150	Huntington, WV-KY-OH	HNTG	245,262	247,651	-1.0	47,494	-7.7	197,768	.8	756	15
126	Huntsville, AL	HNTS	295,682	274,980	7.5	164,021	3.7	131,661	12.8	639	164
	Hutchinson, KS	HUCH	47,460	48,601	-2.3	40,172	-1.5	7,288	-6.7	90	21
305	Idaho Falls, ID	IDFL	95,765	87,666	9.2	55,034	8.5	40,731	10.3	205	15
31	Indianapolis, IN	IND	1,482,014	1,371,830	8.0	784,519	.3	697,495	18.2	1,737	362
265	Indio-, CA	IND-	113,272	90,714	24.9	94,680	31.8	18,592	-1.5	92	37
	Indio, CA					65,001	32.3				17
	Coachella, CA					29,679	30.6				20
295	Iowa City, IA	IACY	98,770	93,546	5.6	61,916	-.5	36,854	17.6	113	22
300	Ithaca, NY	ITH	97,005	92,631	4.7	30,368	3.7	66,637	5.2	399	6
201	Jackson, MI	JAC	158,046	152,085	3.9	36,575	.7	121,471	4.9	544	11
105	Jackson, MS	JAC	374,526	361,423	3.6	181,458	-1.5	193,068	9.0	590	109
339	Jackson, TN	JAC	81,204	78,432	3.5	64,212	7.7	16,992	-9.6	201	40
44	Jacksonville, FL	JAX	1,049,213	955,200	9.8	798,525	8.6	250,688	14.2	1,212	759
236	Jacksonville, NC	JAX	132,646	133,062	-.3	63,742	-4.5	68,904	3.9	273	13
390	Jamestown, NY	JMST	61,979	63,230	-2.0	29,933	-5.7	32,046	1.7	224	9
331	Janesville, WI	JNSV	83,897	81,661	2.7	61,458	3.3	22,439	1.2	182	24
360	Jefferson City, MO	JFCY	71,126	69,692	2.1	40,564	2.3	30,562	1.7	190	27
106	Johnson City-, TN-VA	JNSC-	365,207	358,147	2.0	128,732	2.8	236,475	1.5	992	84
	Johnson City, TN					58,172	4.9				31
	Kingsport, TN					46,066	2.6				32
	Bristol, TN					24,494	-1.3				21
252	Johnstown, PA	JNST	119,949	123,321	-2.7	21,928	-8.3	98,021	-1.4	403	6
391	Jonesboro, AR	JONES	61,725	58,732	5.1	59,648	7.4	2,077	-35.4	150	73
248	Joplin, MO-KS	JOP	120,892	114,889	5.2	47,216	3.8	73,676	6.2	371	30
123	Kalamazoo, MI	KZOO	298,084	290,529	2.6	75,698	-1.9	222,386	4.2	839	25
317	Kankakee, IL	KANK	90,205	87,116	3.5	27,624	.5	62,581	5.0	301	10
	Kannapolis, NC, *now part of Charlotte, NC-SC*										
26	Kansas City, MO-KS	K.C.	1,661,220	1,563,527	6.2	457,970	3.7	1,203,250	7.2	1,929	312
241	Kenosha, WI	KEN	125,203	116,926	7.1	93,826	3.8	31,377	18.1	86	22
130	Killeen-, TX	KILL-	286,749	270,163	6.1	151,494	7.1	135,255	5.1	361	71
	Killeen, TX					96,187	10.7				28
	Temple, TX					55,307	1.5				43
277	Kingston, NY	KNGST	106,394	102,928	3.4	23,364	-.4	83,030	4.5	314	8
174	Kissimmee, FL	KISS	203,901	155,541	31.1	59,892	25.3	144,009	33.7	300	12
58	Knoxville, TN	KNOX	730,852	693,948	5.3	181,674	4.5	549,178	5.6	1,802	77
323	Kokomo, IN	KOK	86,524	86,817	-.3	45,835	-.6	40,689	.0	267	14
279	La Crosse, WI-MN	LACRO	105,111	102,982	2.1	51,379	-.8	53,732	5.0	196	18
223	Lafayette-, IN	LAF-	140,207	136,867	2.4	87,067	2.2	53,140	2.8	223	18
	Lafayette, IN					60,240	6.8				13
	West Lafayette, IN					26,827	-6.8				5
134	Lafayette, LA	LAF	274,156	268,116	2.3	105,390	-4.4	168,766	6.9	882	41
207	Lake Charles, LA	LKCH	153,737	154,060	-.2	69,412	-3.3	84,325	2.5	287	32
215	Lake Jackson-, TX	L.JAC-	149,396	130,528	14.5	41,642	6.5	107,754	17.8	508	26
	Lake Jackson, TX					27,697	5.0				14
	Freeport, TX					13,945	9.7				12
146	Lakeland, FL	LKLD	250,785	230,633	8.7	82,329	4.9	168,456	10.7	324	38
353	Lancaster, OH	LANC	72,439	63,954	13.3	37,145	5.1	35,294	23.3	166	16
121	Lancaster, PA	LANC	304,943	292,754	4.2	56,093	-.5	248,850	5.3	503	7
101	Lansing, MI	LANS	386,220	376,205	2.7	117,694	-1.2	268,526	4.5	737	34
171	Laredo, TX-MEX.	LAR	210,000	180,740	16.2	201,702	14.2	8,298	99.3	59	33
	incl. Nuevo Laredo, MEX.		*660,000*	*399,740*	*65.1*					*79*	
254	Las Cruces, NM	LSCR	119,411	111,375	7.2	77,806	4.8	41,605	12.1	226	38
27	Las Vegas, NV	LASV	1,659,386	1,344,673	23.4	574,733	20.1	1,084,653	25.2	565	83
403	Latrobe, PA	LTROB	54,952	55,327	-.7	8,776	-2.4	46,176	-.3	190	2
	Laurel, MS	LAUR	49,763	49,532	.5	17,337	-5.7	32,426	4.1	231	15
324	Lawrence, KS	LAWR	86,102	83,344	3.3	83,085	3.7	3,017	-7.1	89	23
308	Lawton, OK	LAWT	94,589	96,238	-1.7	94,389	1.8	200	-94.3	101	51
	Leavenworth, KS	LEAV	45,633	42,257	8.0	34,091	-3.8	11,542	68.8	47	23
306	Lebanon, PA	LEB	95,109	91,718	3.7	24,433	-.1	70,676	5.1	216	5
413	Lewiston, ID-WA	LEW	51,847	51,385	.9	31,683	2.5	20,164	-1.5	36	16
303	Lewiston-, ME	LEW-	95,843	92,395	3.7	59,257	.6	36,586	9.2	305	94
	Lewiston, ME					35,524	-.5				34
	Auburn, ME					23,733	2.3				60
102	Lexington, KY	LEX	381,311	361,983	5.3	271,787	4.3	109,524	7.9	566	285
283	Lima, OH	LIMA	104,210	105,770	-1.5	38,642	-3.6	65,568	-.2	286	13
148	Lincoln, NE	LINC	246,683	231,614	6.5	240,192	6.5	6,491	7.6	158	63
88	Little Rock, AR	L.R.	443,345	431,800	2.7	187,938	2.6	255,407	2.7	605	103
401	Lockport, NY	LOCK	55,830	56,366	-1.0	21,608	-3.0	34,222	.4	195	9
326	Logan, UT	LOGN	85,280	79,173	7.7	45,734	7.2	39,546	8.3	120	14
382	Lompoc, CA	LOMP	64,146	63,316	1.3	40,222	-2.1	23,924	7.7	44	11
228	Longview, TX	LNGV	136,348	131,492	3.7	75,614	3.1	60,734	4.4	456	52
343	Longview, WA-OR	LNGV	79,366	76,068	4.3	35,658	2.9	43,708	5.6	120	12
2	Los Angeles, CA	L.A.	13,814,274	12,996,023	6.3	3,909,172	5.8	9,905,102	6.5	3,224	469

† To avoid dividing incorporated cities, the Anchorage and Butte RMAs each include some sparsely settled territory that would otherwise be omitted from the RMA.

†† Brunswick, Hilo, and Honolulu are not incorporated cities. Central city data refer to the census designated place.

Ranally Metro Areas: Population/Land Area, *Continued*

			Ranally Metro Area			Central City		Suburbs		Land Area (square miles)	
Rank 2005		RMA Abbrev.	Population Estimate 7/1/05	Population Census 4/1/00	Percent Change 2000-2005	Population Estimate 7/1/05	Percent Change 2000-2005	Population Estimate 7/1/05	Percent Change 2000-2005	Metro Area	City 2000
46	Louisville, KY-IN	LOU	997,083	970,458	2.7	249,089	-2.8	747,994	4.7	1,171	62
158	Lubbock, TX	LUB	231,159	219,920	5.1	207,716	4.1	23,443	15.2	245	104
385	Lufkin, TX	LUFK	63,403	62,376	1.6	32,042	-2.0	31,361	5.7	143	24
235	Lynchburg, VA	LYNCH	133,066	132,504	.4	64,615	-1.0	68,451	1.8	388	49
132	Macon, GA	MAC	281,436	265,193	6.1	96,074	-1.2	185,362	10.4	464	48
92	Madison, WI	MAD	423,575	390,058	8.6	223,674	7.5	199,901	9.8	584	58
172	Manchester, NH	MNCH	209,328	196,727	6.4	111,484	4.2	97,844	9.1	317	33
417	Manhattan, KS	MANH	50,596	44,482	13.7	50,396	12.4	200	.0	51	11
404	Manitowoc, WI	MNTW	54,601	55,553	-1.7	34,167	.3	20,434	-5.0	118	14
411	Mankato, MN	MNKT	52,294	50,357	3.8	33,995	4.8	18,299	2.1	81	12
251	Mansfield, OH	MANS	120,620	121,311	-.6	47,231	-4.3	73,389	2.0	420	28
377	Marion, IN	MRN	65,365	67,396	-3.0	30,890	-1.4	34,475	-4.4	250	13
402	Marion, OH	MRN	55,729	55,530	.4	34,800	-1.5	20,929	3.5	150	8
	Marshall, TX	MAR	30,321	30,254	.2	22,663	-5.3	7,658	21.2	80	24
338	Martinsville, VA-NC	MRTNV	81,737	83,170	-1.7	14,971	-2.9	66,766	-1.5	288	11
75	McAllen, TX-MEX.	MCAL	532,485	448,834	18.6	121,404	14.1	411,081	20.1	615	32
	incl. Reynosa, MEX.		*922,485*	*716,834*	*28.7*					*635*	
203	Medford, OR	MEDF	156,954	145,126	8.2	70,365	11.4	86,589	5.6	240	18
87	Melbourne-, FL	MELB-	446,008	405,677	9.9	166,444	10.4	279,564	9.7	339	93
	Melbourne, FL					77,012	7.9				29
	Palm Bay, FL					89,432	12.6				64
38	Memphis, TN-AR-MS	MEM	1,108,006	1,066,097	3.9	669,066	2.9	438,940	5.5	1,272	256
220	Merced, CA	MRCD	143,246	123,804	15.7	74,941	17.3	68,305	14.0	134	16
389	Meridian, MS	MRID	62,141	62,690	-.9	37,372	-6.5	24,769	9.0	195	36
6	Miami-, FL	MIA-	5,383,018	4,944,670	8.9	530,645	3.1	4,852,373	9.5	1,660	67
	Miami, FL					371,978	2.6				36
	Fort Lauderdale, FL					158,667	4.1				31
310	Michigan City, IN	MICH	93,402	93,789	-.4	32,433	-1.4	60,969	.1	242	20
322	Middletown, NY	MIDD	86,988	79,163	9.9	27,507	8.3	59,481	10.6	211	5
222	Middletown, OH	MIDD	142,328	128,847	10.5	51,813	.4	90,515	17.2	164	20
160	Midland-, TX	MIDL-	224,122	216,880	3.3	192,250	3.4	31,872	3.0	234	101
	Midland, TX					98,355	3.5				66
	Odessa, TX					93,895	3.2				35
28	Milwaukee, WI	MILW	1,632,845	1,610,669	1.4	592,470	-.8	1,040,375	2.6	1,494	96
16	Minneapolis-, MN-WI	MPLS-	2,809,891	2,682,362	4.8	680,709	1.6	2,129,182	5.8	2,425	108
	Minneapolis, MN					390,008	1.9				55
	St. Paul, MN					290,701	1.2				53
328	Missoula, MT	MSLA	84,612	80,964	4.5	56,672	-.7	27,940	16.8	122	17
90	Mobile, AL	MOB	431,599	425,684	1.4	195,666	-1.6	235,933	4.0	849	118
84	Modesto, CA	MOD	464,791	399,512	16.3	208,952	10.6	255,839	21.4	213	30
230	Monroe, LA	MONR	135,254	135,143	.1	53,098	.0	82,156	.1	357	26
387	Monroe, MI	MONR	63,190	59,973	5.4	22,585	2.3	40,605	7.1	116	9
186	Monterey-, CA	MTRY-	176,251	168,089	4.9	89,680	3.7	86,571	6.1	195	26
	Monterey, CA					29,425	-.8				8
	Seaside, CA					33,842	6.8				9
	Marina, CA					26,413	5.2				9
133	Montgomery, AL	MTGY	277,966	273,001	1.8	202,006	.2	75,960	6.3	453	135
318	Morgantown, WV-PA	MORG	89,854	87,377	2.8	26,278	-2.0	63,576	5.0	360	8
289	Morristown, TN	MORR	99,986	96,411	3.7	25,484	2.1	74,502	4.3	401	16
242	Muncie, IN	MUN	124,827	126,023	-.9	65,540	-2.8	59,287	1.2	375	23
263	Murfreesboro, TN	MUR	114,328	96,869	18.0	88,210	28.2	26,118	-6.9	126	30
194	Muskegon, MI	MUS	168,177	163,319	3.0	39,661	-1.1	128,516	4.3	367	14
412	Muskogee, OK	MSKOG	52,135	50,853	2.5	39,255	2.5	12,880	2.7	122	35
187	Myrtle Beach, SC-NC	MYR.B	175,664	156,337	12.4	23,504	3.3	152,160	13.9	423	16
321	Napa, CA	NAPA	87,072	79,326	9.8	80,790	11.3	6,282	-6.8	50	17
140	Naples, FL	NAP	263,636	216,383	21.8	20,517	-2.2	243,119	24.4	250	11
47	Nashville, TN	NASH	956,771	907,017	5.5	551,402	1.1	405,369	12.1	1,464	398
	Natchez, MS-LA	NCHZ	40,371	42,455	-4.9	17,226	-6.7	23,145	-3.5	333	13
284	Newark, OH	NWRK	104,200	98,544	5.7	48,382	4.5	55,818	6.8	250	18
179	New Bedford, MA	N.BED	192,581	185,971	3.6	91,785	-2.1	100,796	9.3	214	20
257	Newburgh, NY	NWBG	118,018	107,327	10.0	31,219	10.5	86,799	9.8	154	4
398	New Castle, PA	NWCS	56,984	58,116	-1.9	26,060	-.9	30,924	-2.8	102	9
70	New Haven, CT	N.HAV	564,473	544,274	3.7	123,849	.2	440,624	4.7	431	19
	New Iberia, LA, *now part of Lafayette, LA*										
120	New London-, CT-RI	N.LON-	311,355	300,098	3.8	62,348	.9	249,007	4.5	662	34
	New London, CT					25,722	.2				6
	Norwich, CT					36,626	1.4				28
35	New Orleans, LA	N.O.	1,227,714	1,242,139	-1.2	456,285	-5.9	771,429	1.8	1,039	181
386	Newport, RI	NWPT	63,251	63,197	.1	26,693	.8	36,558	-.4	44	8
78	Newport News-, VA	NN-H	505,949	487,244	3.8	327,259	.2	178,690	11.2	686	120
	Newport News, VA					182,551	1.3				68
	Hampton, VA					144,708	-1.2				52
1	New York, NY-NJ-CT	N.Y.	19,935,203	19,360,664	3.0	8,424,386	1.7	11,510,817	3.9	6,905	333
	New York, NY					8,148,734	1.8				309
	Newark, NJ					275,652	.8				24
	Nogales, AZ-MEX.	NOGLS	27,097	25,220	7.4	20,329	-2.6	6,768	55.9	22	21
	incl. Nogales, MEX.		*192,097*	*131,220*	*46.4*					*34*	
40	Norfolk-, VA‡	NORF-	1,079,063	1,023,003	5.5	901,736	5.0	177,327	8.0	1,076	643
	Norfolk, VA					238,106	1.6				54
	Virginia Beach, VA					447,757	5.3				248
	Chesapeake, VA					215,873	8.4				341
154	Ocala, FL	OCA	240,534	211,431	13.8	47,889	4.2	192,645	16.4	588	29
	Odessa, TX, *now part of Midland-, TX*										
114	Ogden, UT	OGD	336,227	300,985	11.7	81,032	4.9	255,195	14.0	220	26
	Oil City-, PA	OILC-F	37,422	38,389	-2.5	18,389	-1.7	19,033	-3.3	176	10
	Oil City, PA					11,283	-1.9				5
	Franklin, PA					7,106	-1.5				5
45	Oklahoma City, OK	O.C.	1,027,131	973,684	5.5	544,097	7.5	483,034	3.3	1,606	608
163	Olympia, WA	OLYM	221,327	200,141	10.6	47,525	11.8	173,802	10.3	340	16
63	Omaha, NE-IA	OMA	686,194	650,384	5.5	401,817	3.0	284,377	9.2	513	101
30	Orlando, FL	ORL	1,496,169	1,342,878	11.4	201,139	8.2	1,295,030	11.9	978	67
333	Oshkosh, WI	OSH	83,668	82,112	1.9	64,849	3.1	18,819	-2.0	117	18
352	Owensboro, KY	OWNS	72,605	71,502	1.5	54,311	.5	18,294	4.9	142	15
64	Oxnard-, CA	OXN-	667,617	618,831	7.9	429,850	10.7	237,767	3.1	529	95
	Oxnard, CA					198,439	16.5				24
	Thousand Oaks, CA					125,350	7.1				50
	Ventura, CA					106,061	5.1				21
364	Paducah, KY-IL	PAD	69,636	70,799	-1.6	25,541	-2.9	44,095	-.9	167	18
144	Palm Springs-, CA	PSPR-	254,061	203,466	24.9	156,189	23.4	97,872	27.3	312	115
	Palm Springs, CA					46,389	8.4				77
	Cathedral City, CA					55,965	31.2				19
	Palm Desert, CA					53,835	30.8				19
216	Panama City, FL	PNCY	146,875	136,904	7.3	38,060	4.5	108,815	8.3	161	16
290	Parkersburg, WV-OH	PRKB	99,845	100,987	-1.1	32,774	-1.0	67,071	-1.2	363	11
327	Pascagoula, MS	PSCG	84,680	82,563	2.6	25,860	-1.3	58,820	4.4	157	15
100	Pensacola, FL	PENS	390,496	371,095	5.2	51,998	-7.6	338,498	7.5	494	23
124	Peoria, IL	PEOR	297,302	298,602	-.4	112,199	-.7	185,103	-.3	587	41
5	Philadelphia-, PA-NJ-DE-MD	PHIL-	5,964,370	5,814,079	2.6	1,616,806	-3.5	4,347,564	5.1	3,912	154
	Philadelphia, PA					1,456,998	-4.0				135
	Trenton, NJ					86,529	1.3				8
	Wilmington, DE					73,279	.8				11
13	Phoenix, AZ	PHOE	3,591,520	3,078,489	16.7	1,510,889	14.4	2,080,631	18.4	2,071	420
378	Pine Bluff, AR	PNBLF	65,356	67,137	-2.7	54,348	-1.3	11,008	-8.7	125	42
21	Pittsburgh, PA	PGH	1,977,290	2,010,337	-1.6	314,857	-5.9	1,662,433	-.8	2,608	56
332	Pittsfield, MA	PTSF	83,720	85,900	-2.5	43,780	-4.4	39,940	-.4	252	41
410	Plattsburgh, NY	PLATT	52,404	50,741	3.3	19,267	2.4	33,137	3.8	228	5
376	Pocatello, ID	POC	65,638	65,692	-.1	49,963	-2.9	15,675	10.2	99	28
348	Porterville, CA	PORT	77,089	70,082	10.0	46,135	16.5	30,954	1.6	164	11
287	Port Huron, MI-CAN.	PTHU	102,643	97,755	5.0	32,228	-.3	70,415	7.6	185	8
	incl. Sarnia, CAN.		*188,043*	*185,855*	*1.2*					*378*	
145	Portland, ME	POR	253,171	242,412	4.4	65,563	2.0	187,608	5.3	626	23
22	Portland, OR-WA	POR	1,930,764	1,764,702	9.4	551,781	4.3	1,378,983	11.6	1,533	125
137	Portsmouth-, NH-ME	PTSM-	266,496	247,111	7.8	78,362	2.9	188,134	10.0	628	88
	Portsmouth, NH					20,139	-3.1				16
	Rochester, NH					29,894	5.0				45
	Dover, NH					28,329	5.4				27
393	Portsmouth, OH-KY	PTSM	61,041	63,075	-3.2	19,217	-8.1	41,824	-.8	210	11
361	Pottstown, PA	PTSTN	70,361	66,225	6.2	21,958	.5	48,403	9.1	66	5
344	Pottsville, PA	PTSVL	78,210	80,397	-2.7	14,791	-4.9	63,419	-2.2	257	4
153	Poughkeepsie, NY	POK	241,604	227,751	6.1	31,661	6.0	209,943	6.1	355	5
41	Providence-, RI-MA	PROV-	1,074,586	1,024,698	4.9	276,294	6.5	798,292	4.3	979	55
	Providence, RI					188,570	8.6				19
	Warwick, RI					87,724	2.2				36
97	Provo-, UT	PRVO-	400,934	360,719	11.1	204,959	8.2	195,975	14.5	286	57
	Provo, UT					113,165	7.6				39
	Orem, UT					91,794	8.9				18
219	Pueblo, CO	PUEB	143,406	132,101	8.6	99,671	-2.4	43,735	45.9	163	36
221	Punta Gorda-, FL	PUN-	142,632	126,731	12.5	69,993	15.1	72,639	10.2	227	36
	Punta Gorda, FL					17,526	22.2				14
	Port Charlotte, FL					52,467	13.0				22
415	Quincy, IL	QUIN	51,191	52,274	-2.1	38,548	-4.5	12,643	6.2	113	13
	Racine, WI, *now part of Milwaukee, WI*										
51	Raleigh, NC	RAL	863,306	733,981	17.6	312,857	13.3	550,449	20.2	1,330	88
316	Rapid City, SD	RAP	90,663	86,248	5.1	63,322	6.2	27,341	2.6	147	35
127	Reading, PA	READ	294,834	280,128	5.2	83,596	2.9	211,238	6.2	410	10
206	Redding, CA	REDD	154,221	137,346	12.3	91,286	12.9	62,935	11.4	322	51
103	Reno, NV	RENO	380,849	331,264	15.0	209,477	16.1	171,372	13.7	473	58
181	Richland-, WA	RICH-	187,252	162,425	15.3	152,953	21.9	34,299	-7.2	213	75
	Richland, WA					44,029	13.7				32
	Kennewick, WA					64,342	17.6				20
	Pasco, WA					44,582	39.0				23
395	Richmond, IN-OH	RICH	60,064	61,141	-1.8	39,345	.6	20,719	-5.9	203	18
48	Richmond, VA	RICH	943,498	897,287	5.2	191,700	-3.1	751,798	7.5	1,060	60
23	Riverside-, CA	RIV-	1,902,477	1,587,954	19.8	480,268	9.0	1,422,209	24.0	938	133
	Riverside, CA					283,180	11.0				78
	San Bernardino, CA					197,088	6.3				55
151	Roanoke, VA	ROAN	244,638	244,825	-.1	91,029	-4.1	153,609	2.5	555	43
238	Rochester, MN	ROCH	130,763	119,927	9.0	96,182	12.1	34,581	1.3	264	30
50	Rochester, NY	ROCH	878,380	873,504	.6	216,407	-1.5	661,973	1.3	1,585	36
115	Rockford, IL-WI	RKFD	332,828	318,096	4.6	153,501	2.3	179,327	6.8	424	45
	Rock Hill, SC, *now part of Charlotte, NC-SC*										
302	Rocky Mount, NC	RKYMT	96,287	93,768	2.7	57,607	3.1	38,680	2.1	351	25
320	Rome, GA	ROME	87,677	83,486	5.0	36,825	5.3	50,852	4.8	269	24
408	Roswell, NM	RSWL	53,528	53,690	-.3	43,708	-3.5	9,820	16.9	81	29
24	Sacramento, CA	SAC	1,761,696	1,518,806	16.0	441,061	8.4	1,320,635	18.8	1,035	96
107	Saginaw-, MI	SAG-	359,420	359,538	.0	139,604	-.5	219,816	.3	1,028	55
	Saginaw, MI					60,406	-2.3				17
	Midland, MI					42,553	2.1				28
	Bay City, MI					36,645	-.5				10
258	St. Cloud, MN	ST.CLD	117,880	105,361	11.9	62,922	6.5	54,958	18.8	203	15
312	St. Joseph, MO-KS	ST.JO	92,493	93,230	-.8	74,379	.5	18,114	-5.9	238	43
17	St. Louis, MO-IL	ST.L	2,379,333	2,337,245	1.8	324,238	-6.9	2,055,095	3.3	2,437	62
36	St. Petersburg, FL	ST.PET	1,206,229	1,152,771	4.6	250,426	.9	955,803	5.7	514	59
125	Salem, OR	SAL	296,530	274,523	8.0	150,116	9.6	146,414	6.4	439	42
	Salina, KS	SLN	47,291	47,073	.5	46,054	.8	1,237	-11.3	42	21
192	Salinas, CA	SLNS	171,157	163,232	4.9	164,953	9.2	6,204	-49.0	234	19
336	Salisbury, MD-DE	SLSB	82,604	77,891	6.1	26,307	10.8	56,297	4.0	210	10
296	Salisbury, NC	SLSB	98,314	93,662	5.0	27,322	3.2	70,992	5.6	333	16
43	Salt Lake City, UT	S.L.C.	1,050,244	994,767	5.6	180,579	-.6	869,665	7.0	461	109
307	San Angelo, TX	SANG	94,724	95,076	-.4	87,129	-1.5	7,595	14.4	103	48
29	San Antonio, TX	SANT	1,528,650	1,405,646	8.8	1,237,338	8.1	291,312	11.6	1,032	333
15	San Diego, CA-MEX.	SDGO	2,908,419	2,736,424	6.3	1,286,347	5.1	1,622,072	7.2	1,373	324
	incl. Tijuana, MEX.		*4,408,419*	*3,471,424*	*27.0*					*1,453*	
337	Sandusky, OH	SNDSK	82,546	83,125	-.7	26,547	-4.7	55,999	1.3	172	10
4	San Francisco-, CA	SF-O-	6,033,647	5,990,557	.7	2,045,908	-1.2	3,987,739	1.7	2,041	274
	San Francisco, CA					734,587	-5.4				47
	San Jose, CA					916,491	2.4				171
	Oakland, CA					394,830	-1.2				56
392	San Luis Obispo, CA	S.LUIS	61,275	58,727	4.3	44,733	1.3	16,542	13.7	33	9
173	Santa Barbara, CA	S.BAR	208,198	205,504	1.3	95,136	3.0	113,062	-.1	153	19
183	Santa Cruz, CA	S.CRZ	179,773	185,025	-2.8	53,121	-2.7	126,652	-2.9	223	13
282	Santa Fe, NM	S.FE	104,250	95,406	9.3	64,470	3.6	39,780	19.8	172	37
270	Santa Maria, CA	S.MAR	111,365	109,581	1.6	81,179	4.9	30,186	-6.1	57	17
113	Santa Rosa, CA	S.ROS	336,900	328,170	2.7	157,459	6.7	179,441	-.6	457	34
76	Sarasota-, FL	SAR-B	523,362	466,778	12.1	104,955	2.7	418,407	14.8	242	26
	Sarasota, FL					53,082	.7				15
	Bradenton, FL					51,873	4.8				11
	Sault Ste. Marie, MI-CAN.	SOO	18,777	18,601	.9	17,343	4.8	1,434	-30.4	40	15
	incl. Sault Ste. Marie, CAN.		*101,277*	*105,001*	*-3.5*					*315*	
136	Savannah, GA	SAV	269,916	257,930	4.6	127,884	-2.8	142,032	12.3	550	63
86	Scranton-, PA	SCR-	458,365	469,087	-2.3	115,183	-3.6	343,182	-1.8	925	32
	Scranton, PA					73,981	-3.2				25
	Wilkes Barre, PA					41,202	-4.5				7
14	Seattle, WA	SEAT	3,196,664	3,036,889	5.3	574,178	1.9	2,622,486	6.0	2,604	84
358	Sharon, PA-OH	SHAR	71,293	71,902	-.8	16,335	.0	54,958	-1.1	158	4
281	Sheboygan, WI	SHEB	104,492	103,237	1.2	49,965	-1.6	54,527	4.0	314	13
340	Sherman-, TX	SHRM-	81,120	76,351	6.2	57,912	.1	23,208	25.5	194	59
	Sherman, TX					35,939	2.4				37
	Denison, TX					21,973	-3.5				22
112	Shreveport, LA-TX	SHRE	340,464	314,390	8.3	226,284	13.1	114,180	-.1	599	99
276	Sioux City, IA-NE-SD	SXCY	106,568	106,902	-.3	83,976	-1.2	22,592	3.2	130	54
229	Sioux Falls, SD	SXFL	135,625	125,549	8.0	135,425	9.2	200	-87.3	60	45
131	South Bend, IN-MI	S.B.	282,307	280,926	.5	110,443	2.5	171,864	-.7	364	36
180	Spartanburg, SC	SPRT	189,525	182,174	4.0	38,163	-3.8	151,362	6.2	399	18
99	Spokane, WA-ID	SPOK	392,250	371,509	5.6	204,483	4.5	187,767	6.8	315	56
191	Springfield, IL	SPRG	171,337	167,040	2.6	114,607	2.8	56,730	2.1	330	43
66	Springfield, MA	SPRG	602,027	593,284	1.5	153,765	1.1	448,262	1.6	745	32
135	Springfield, MO	SPRG	270,383	254,590	6.2	153,675	1.4	116,708	13.3	437	68
249	Springfield, OH	SPR	120,779	123,310	-2.1	63,432	-2.9	57,347	-1.0	293	20
266	Spring Hill, FL	SPR.H	113,111	97,754	15.7	79,904	15.7	33,207	15.8	117	23
278	State College, PA	STCOL	105,665	101,227	4.4	37,681	-1.9	67,984	8.2	234	5
286	Steubenville-, OH-WV	STU-	102,980	107,478	-4.2	37,543	-4.8	65,437	-3.8	348	26
	Steubenville, OH					17,901	-5.9				8
	Weirton, WV					19,642	-3.8				18
82	Stockton, CA	STOC	474,047	396,350	19.6	281,628	15.5	192,419	26.1	252	53
243	Stuart, FL	STU	123,042	110,885	11.0	16,501	12.8	106,541	10.7	107	4
311	Sumter, SC	SUMT	93,091	91,455	1.8	38,359	-3.2	54,732	5.6	293	23
68	Syracuse, NY	SYR	577,349	571,783	1.0	146,651	-.4	430,698	1.5	1,303	25
167	Tallahassee, FL	TALL	217,550	213,711	1.8	156,589	4.0	60,961	-3.4	241	63
39	Tampa, FL	TAM	1,105,461	984,692	12.3	324,897	7.1	780,564	14.6	870	109
	Temple, TX, *now part of Killeen-, TX*										
272	Terre Haute, IN	T.H.	109,341	112,034	-2.4	60,280	1.1	49,061	-6.4	322	28
304	Texarkana-, TX-AR	TEXR-	95,768	93,525	2.4	63,508	3.7	32,260	-.1	175	38
	Texarkana, TX					35,024	.7				21
	Texarkana, AR					28,484	7.7				17
351	Titusville, FL	TITUS	74,142	67,439	9.9	41,172	1.2	32,970	23.2	73	20
67	Toledo, OH-MI	TOL	592,509	590,723	.3	308,876	-1.5	283,633	2.4	879	81
200	Topeka, KS	TOP	163,072	161,033	1.3	122,260	-.1	40,812	5.6	256	55
	Torrington, CT	TORR	48,553	46,151	5.2	37,137	5.5	11,416	4.3	113	40
52	Tucson, AZ	TUC	840,582	769,505	9.2	524,996	7.9	315,586	11.6	778	156
60	Tulsa, OK	TUL	722,314	698,105	3.5	396,188	.8	326,126	6.9	1,169	184
226	Tuscaloosa, AL	TUSC	137,022	135,057	1.5	75,894	-2.6	61,128	7.0	249	47
208	Tyler, TX	TYL	152,366	140,749	8.3	87,433	4.5	64,933	13.7	359	40
346	Uniontown, PA	UNTN	77,390	79,461	-2.6	12,530	.9	64,860	-3.3	248	2
165	Utica-, NY	UT-R	220,258	221,518	-.6	94,582	-1.1	125,676	-.2	717	91
	Utica, NY					60,264	-.6				16
	Rome, NY					34,318	-1.8				75
341	Valdosta, GA	VALD	81,062	77,590	4.5	43,557	-.4	37,505	10.7	150	27
239	Venice, FL	VEN	130,649	117,800	10.9	17,921	.9	112,728	12.7	144	7
298	Vero Beach, FL	VERO	97,251	88,146	10.3	17,193	-2.9	80,058	13.7	108	11
	Vicksburg, MS-LA	VICK	40,498	41,403	-2.2	25,599	-3.1	14,899	-.6	258	13
368	Victoria, TX	VICT	68,252	66,604	2.5	61,620	1.7	6,632	10.5	63	30
198	Vineland, NJ	VINL	163,562	158,101	3.5	57,614	2.4	105,948	4.0	356	69
169	Visalia, CA	VISL	211,028	191,846	10.0	104,116	13.7	106,912	6.6	3,371	24
182	Waco, TX	WACO	184,669	176,912	4.4	119,965	5.5	64,704	2.4	287	76
399	Walla Walla, WA-OR	WALL	56,922	54,342	4.7	31,182	5.0	25,740	4.4	95	10
8	Washington, DC-MD-VA	WASH	4,967,224	4,581,114	8.4	548,902	-4.0	4,418,322	10.2	3,479	61
384	Washington, PA	WASH	64,044	63,075	1.5	15,896	4.1	48,148	.7	217	3
157	Waterbury, CT	WATB	236,743	227,899	3.9	108,093	.8	128,650	6.7	234	29
261	Waterloo, IA	WATL	115,459	117,984	-2.1	69,817	1.6	45,642	-7.3	233	61
373	Watertown, NY	WATN	66,641	65,063	2.4	25,961	-2.8	40,680	6.1	226	9
418	Waterville, ME	WATRVL	50,585	49,192	2.8	15,541	-.4	35,044	4.3	218	14
347	Watsonville, CA	WATS	77,154	78,222	-1.4	47,163	6.5	29,991	-11.7	129	6
334	Wausau, WI	WAUS	83,110	81,673	1.8	38,366	-.2	44,744	3.5	244	14
	West Palm Beach, FL, *now part of Miami-, FL*										
234	Wheeling, WV-OH	WHL	133,617	138,490	-3.5	28,403	-9.6	105,214	-1.7	487	14
81	Wichita, KS	WICH	476,548	460,520	3.5	359,396	4.4	117,152	.8	615	115
246	Wichita Falls, TX	WIFL	122,478	127,789	-4.2	102,794	-1.3	19,684	-16.6	225	54
233	Williamsport, PA	WMSPT	133,664	136,302	-1.9	30,147	-1.8	103,517	-2.0	471	9
175	Wilmington, NC	WILM	198,552	181,109	9.6	87,653	15.6	110,899	5.3	377	30
98	Winston-Salem, NC	WNS	395,576	373,267	6.0	197,537	6.3	198,039	5.6	754	71
217	Winter Haven, FL	WNHV	145,123	133,461	8.7	27,440	3.6	117,683	10.0	173	12
74	Worcester, MA-CT	WORC	532,710	506,130	5.3	179,225	3.8	353,485	6.0	860	38
227	Yakima, WA	YAK	136,595	132,496	3.1	72,971	1.6	63,624	4.9	240	15
139	York, PA	YORK	264,770	250,585	5.7	41,172	.8	223,598	6.6	416	5
89	Youngstown-, OH-PA	YNGS-	434,446	448,405	-3.1	119,835	-7.0	314,611	-1.5	809	50
	Youngstown, OH					75,560	-7.9				34
	Warren, OH					44,275	-5.5				16
267	Yuba City, CA	YUCY	113,093	102,089	10.8	44,111	20.0	68,982	5.6	81	7
197	Yuma, AZ-CA	YUMA	164,364	148,651	10.6	84,868	9.5	79,496	11.8	239	22
359	Zanesville, OH	ZAN	71,227	70,135	1.6	25,548	-.1	45,679	2.5	257	10

‡ To avoid dividing the independent cities of Chesapeake, Suffolk, and Virginia Beach, the Norfolk-Virginia Beach-Chesapeake RMA includes some sparsely settled territory that would otherwise be omitted from the RMA.

Ranally Metro Areas: Summary Tables

Grouped within Regions/Size Classes

	Ranally Metro Area			Central City		Suburbs		Land Area	
	Population Estimate 7/1/05	Population Census 4/1/00	Percent Change 2000-2005	Population Estimate 7/1/05	Percent Change 2000-2005	Population Estimate 7/1/05	Percent Change 2000-2005	Metro Area (mi²)	City 2000 (mi²)
Northeast (incl. DE, MD, DC and WV)									
New York, NY-NJ-CT	19,935,203	19,360,664	3.0	8,424,386	1.7	11,510,817	3.9	6,905	333
Philadelphia-, PA-NJ-DE-MD	5,964,370	5,814,079	2.6	1,616,806	-3.5	4,347,564	5.1	3,912	154
Boston, MA-NH	4,754,031	4,679,465	1.6	581,578	-1.3	4,172,453	2.0	3,609	48
2,500,000 - 4,999,999	2,903,380	2,723,237	6.6	548,902	-4.0	2,354,478	9.5	2,392	61
1,000,000 - 2,499,999	7,677,107	7,548,104	1.7	1,680,257	-2.9	5,996,850	3.1	8,172	263
500,000 - 999,999	4,616,907	4,491,804	2.8	1,210,472	.9	3,406,435	3.5	7,389	229
300,000 - 499,999	1,492,439	1,472,089	1.4	280,180	-2.2	1,212,259	2.3	2,790	81
200,000 - 299,999	2,988,313	2,893,652	3.3	855,070	.9	2,133,243	4.2	6,336	357
100,000 - 199,999	2,267,473	2,190,890	3.5	694,784	.2	1,572,689	5.0	5,237	288
70,000 - 99,999	1,518,157	1,485,636	2.2	503,202	-.4	1,014,955	3.5	4,866	332
50,000 - 69,999	1,026,093	1,014,518	1.1	339,414	-1.2	686,679	2.3	3,413	179
Less Than 50,000	143,944	144,475	-.4	75,168	1.1	68,776	-2.0	515	68
Total in RMAs	**55,287,417**	**53,818,613**	**2.7**	**16,810,219**	**.1**	**38,477,198**	**3.9**	**55,536**	**2,393**
Not in RMAs	8,477,789	8,236,254	2.9					142,587	
Total, Northeast	63,765,206	62,054,867	2.8					198,123	
Midwest (North Central)									
Chicago, IL-IN-WI	9,086,842	8,748,587	3.9	2,896,965	.0	6,189,877	5.8	4,068	227
Detroit, MI-CAN.	4,705,677	4,641,127	1.4	928,992	-2.3	3,776,685	2.4	3,656	139
Minneapolis-, MN-WI	2,809,891	2,682,362	4.8	680,709	1.6	2,129,182	5.8	2,425	108
1,000,000 - 2,499,999	11,983,196	11,660,846	2.8	3,656,925	-.9	8,326,271	4.5	12,429	1,177
500,000 - 999,999	3,503,210	3,421,158	2.4	1,287,248	.2	2,215,962	3.7	4,674	343
300,000 - 499,999	4,286,740	4,180,019	2.6	1,912,170	1.6	2,374,570	3.4	7,058	640
200,000 - 299,999	2,051,946	1,987,445	3.2	986,075	1.8	1,065,871	4.7	3,309	335
100,000 - 199,999	4,714,183	4,573,472	3.1	2,518,807	2.2	2,195,376	4.1	9,663	1,019
70,000 - 99,999	1,543,213	1,513,020	2.0	896,944	1.2	646,269	3.2	3,517	377
50,000 - 69,999	1,228,576	1,219,738	.7	678,930	1.1	549,646	.2	3,348	252
Less Than 50,000	438,656	439,415	-.2	301,224	-.8	137,432	1.3	965	179
Total in RMAs	**46,352,130**	**45,067,189**	**2.9**	**16,744,989**	**.4**	**29,607,141**	**4.3**	**55,112**	**4,796**
Not in RMAs	19,688,472	19,325,587	1.9					696,328	
Total, Midwest	66,040,602	64,392,776	2.6					751,440	
South (excl. DE, MD, DC and WV)									
Miami-, FL	5,383,018	4,944,670	8.9	530,645	3.1	4,852,373	9.5	1,660	67
Dallas-, TX	5,259,868	4,681,646	12.4	1,887,765	9.5	3,372,103	14.0	3,360	623
Houston, TX	4,561,009	4,080,199	11.8	2,136,305	9.4	2,424,704	14.0	2,576	540
Atlanta, GA	4,055,593	3,623,062	11.9	399,217	-4.1	3,656,376	14.0	3,132	132
1,000,000 - 2,499,999	15,497,809	14,315,084	8.3	6,681,592	5.8	8,816,217	10.2	13,863	3,407
500,000 - 999,999	10,307,395	9,677,593	6.5	4,055,300	3.1	6,252,095	8.9	14,813	1,798
300,000 - 499,999	7,780,547	7,368,626	5.6	3,191,007	4.2	4,589,540	6.6	12,423	1,737
200,000 - 299,999	5,201,723	4,849,620	7.3	2,466,936	3.2	2,734,787	11.2	8,770	1,390
100,000 - 199,999	5,697,751	5,349,456	6.5	2,712,213	3.8	2,985,538	9.1	11,484	1,368
70,000 - 99,999	2,368,587	2,302,252	2.9	1,205,686	1.0	1,162,901	4.9	6,389	842
50,000 - 69,999	729,177	711,422	2.5	451,066	2.0	278,111	3.3	1,737	339
Less Than 50,000	360,900	368,012	-1.9	233,423	-3.0	127,477	.1	1,333	204
Total in RMAs	**67,203,377**	**62,271,642**	**7.9**	**25,951,155**	**4.6**	**41,252,222**	**10.1**	**81,540**	**12,447**
Not in RMAs	31,032,855	29,504,689	5.2					753,416	
Total, South	98,236,232	91,776,331	7.0					834,956	
West									
Los Angeles, CA	13,814,274	12,996,023	6.3	3,909,172	5.8	9,905,102	6.5	3,224	469
San Francisco-, CA	6,033,647	5,990,557	.7	2,045,908	-1.2	3,987,739	1.7	2,041	274
Phoenix, AZ	3,591,520	3,078,489	16.7	1,510,889	14.4	2,080,631	18.4	2,071	420
Seattle, WA	3,196,664	3,036,889	5.3	574,178	1.9	2,622,486	6.0	2,604	84
San Diego, CA-MEX.	2,908,419	2,736,424	6.3	1,286,347	5.1	1,622,072	7.2	1,373	324
1,000,000 - 2,499,999	10,545,200	9,299,827	13.4	2,786,510	7.5	7,758,690	15.7	5,799	699
500,000 - 999,999	4,507,798	4,168,606	8.1	2,706,294	9.0	1,801,504	6.9	10,711	748
300,000 - 499,999	3,966,806	3,540,054	12.1	2,138,361	11.6	1,828,445	12.6	4,768	2,150
200,000 - 299,999	2,446,121	2,261,298	8.2	1,470,313	10.7	975,808	4.6	6,155	568
100,000 - 199,999	3,156,799	2,888,099	9.3	1,817,104	9.4	1,339,695	9.2	4,087	588
70,000 - 99,999	1,001,710	948,388	5.6	630,743	6.6	370,967	4.0	1,547	190
50,000 - 69,999	617,658	592,516	4.2	435,313	2.8	182,345	7.9	687	217
Less Than 50,000	157,628	149,500	5.4	115,815	1.1	41,813	19.6	836	755
Total in RMAs	**55,944,244**	**51,686,670**	**8.2**	**21,426,947**	**7.2**	**34,517,297**	**8.9**	**45,903**	**7,486**
Not in RMAs	12,474,074	11,511,262	8.4					1,707,045	
Total, West	68,418,318	63,197,932	8.3					1,752,948	
United States									
10,000,000 AND OVER	33,749,477	32,356,687	4.3	12,333,558	3.0	21,415,919	5.1	10,129	802
5,000,000 - 9,999,999	31,727,745	30,179,539	5.1	8,978,089	1.1	22,749,656	6.8	15,041	1,345
2,500,000 - 4,999,999	33,486,184	31,281,254	7.0	8,647,117	4.7	24,839,067	7.9	23,838	1,856
1,000,000 - 2,499,999	45,703,312	42,823,861	6.7	14,805,284	3.3	30,898,028	8.4	40,263	5,546
500,000 - 999,999	22,935,310	21,759,161	5.4	9,259,314	4.0	13,675,996	6.4	37,587	3,118
300,000 - 499,999	17,526,532	16,560,788	5.8	7,521,718	5.2	10,004,814	6.3	27,039	4,608
200,000 - 299,999	12,688,103	11,992,015	5.8	5,778,394	4.4	6,909,709	7.0	24,570	2,650
100,000 - 199,999	15,836,206	15,001,917	5.6	7,742,908	4.2	8,093,298	6.9	30,471	3,263
70,000 - 99,999	6,431,667	6,249,296	2.9	3,236,575	1.9	3,195,092	4.0	16,319	1,741
50,000 - 69,999	3,601,504	3,538,194	1.8	1,904,723	1.3	1,696,781	2.4	9,185	987
Less Than 50,000	1,101,128	1,101,402	-.0	725,630	-1.0	375,498	2.0	3,649	1,206
Total in RMAs	**224,787,168**	**212,844,114**	**5.6**	**80,933,310**	**3.4**	**143,853,858**	**6.9**	**238,091**	**27,122**
Not in RMAs	71,673,190	68,577,792	4.5					3,299,376	
United States: Total	296,460,358	281,421,906	5.3					3,537,467	

Population By State

	Ranally Metro Area			Central City		Suburbs		Land Area	
	Population Estimate 7/1/05	Population Census 4/1/00	Percent Change 2000-2005	Population Estimate 7/1/05	Percent Change 2000-2005	Population Estimate 7/1/05	Percent Change 2000-2005	Metro Area (mi²)	City 2000 (mi²)
Alabama	2,580,902	2,523,154	2.3	1,142,678	-1.2	1,438,224	5.3	5,843	898
Alaska	385,823	356,696	8.2	309,166	6.4	76,657	15.8	1,849	1,729
Arizona	4,619,210	4,017,828	15.0	2,141,082	12.3	2,478,128	17.4	3,068	619
Arkansas	1,015,558	973,549	4.3	569,172	5.4	446,386	3.0	1,833	381
California	32,751,391	30,562,624	7.2	12,020,334	6.7	20,731,057	7.5	24,664	2,383
Colorado	3,696,682	3,426,253	7.9	1,536,983	4.4	2,159,699	10.5	2,769	513
Connecticut	3,421,118	3,298,426	3.7	524,746	.7	2,896,372	4.3	3,886	152
Delaware	652,996	616,607	5.9	107,827	2.9	545,169	6.5	769	32
District of Columbia	548,902	572,059	-4.0	548,902	-4.0	0		61	61
Florida	15,137,032	13,763,407	10.0	3,518,558	6.2	11,618,474	11.2	10,424	1,708
Georgia	5,716,700	5,216,665	9.6	1,273,721	-1.8	4,442,979	13.4	6,459	620
Hawaii	974,945	934,941	4.3	435,515	5.6	539,430	3.2	668	137
Idaho	621,766	557,885	11.5	339,648	6.5	282,118	18.0	694	105
Illinois	10,659,742	10,302,563	3.5	3,872,801	.3	6,786,941	5.4	7,792	557
Indiana	4,318,469	4,164,390	3.7	1,804,414	.3	2,514,055	6.3	7,299	726
Iowa	1,311,972	1,277,865	2.7	802,170	.7	509,802	6.0	1,830	419
Kansas	1,584,366	1,500,851	5.6	735,454	3.1	848,912	7.8	1,800	269
Kentucky	1,893,064	1,832,624	3.3	682,838	.9	1,210,226	4.7	2,690	429
Louisiana	2,916,586	2,881,643	1.2	1,232,250	-.7	1,684,336	2.7	4,897	496
Maine	666,350	638,250	4.4	214,314	.7	452,036	6.3	2,285	243
Maryland	5,146,739	4,837,731	6.4	740,490	-3.7	4,406,249	8.3	5,010	115
Massachusetts	6,209,536	6,102,337	1.8	1,190,771	-.2	5,018,765	2.2	5,499	270
Michigan	7,891,987	7,733,798	2.0	1,840,494	-1.4	6,051,493	3.1	11,033	452
Minnesota	3,257,429	3,108,729	4.8	993,690	2.8	2,263,739	5.7	3,212	243
Mississippi	1,199,040	1,158,765	3.5	541,839	-1.1	657,201	7.6	2,681	307
Missouri	3,577,386	3,470,723	3.1	1,225,307	.4	2,352,079	4.5	4,164	609
Montana	306,351	300,115	2.1	238,191	.3	68,160	8.8	1,048	781
Nebraska	924,741	873,272	5.9	686,016	4.2	238,725	11.2	656	185
Nevada	2,040,235	1,675,937	21.7	784,210	19.0	1,256,025	23.5	1,038	141
New Hampshire	882,094	824,315	7.0	232,311	3.8	649,783	8.2	1,729	185
New Jersey	8,574,478	8,214,209	4.4	460,545	1.1	8,113,933	4.6	6,062	112
New Mexico	1,139,248	1,058,132	7.7	756,455	7.9	382,793	7.1	1,479	274
New York	17,261,405	16,918,374	2.0	9,424,869	1.4	7,836,536	2.8	12,422	625
North Carolina	5,295,334	4,873,505	8.7	2,270,988	8.4	3,024,346	8.9	10,378	764
North Dakota	240,882	234,263	2.8	201,878	3.3	39,004	.5	291	68
Ohio	8,920,056	8,857,600	.7	2,892,149	-1.6	6,027,907	1.9	12,292	809
Oklahoma	2,005,879	1,928,674	4.0	1,156,385	4.0	849,494	4.0	3,333	971
Oregon	2,409,434	2,248,265	7.2	1,016,410	6.2	1,393,024	7.9	2,553	248
Pennsylvania	9,807,083	9,723,499	.9	2,767,817	-3.0	7,039,266	2.5	13,127	403
Rhode Island	1,096,116	1,047,383	4.7	302,987	6.0	793,129	4.2	1,035	63
South Carolina	2,540,891	2,385,797	6.5	456,822	1.8	2,084,069	7.6	5,216	282
South Dakota	229,460	214,761	6.8	198,747	8.3	30,713	-1.5	224	80
Tennessee	3,790,524	3,642,045	4.1	2,014,477	3.6	1,776,047	4.6	6,871	1,112
Texas	17,701,077	16,038,228	10.4	9,396,853	7.3	8,304,224	14.0	14,831	3,489
Utah	1,872,685	1,735,644	7.9	512,304	4.3	1,360,381	9.3	1,087	206
Vermont	175,046	169,535	3.3	38,653	-.6	136,393	4.4	562	11
Virginia	5,410,790	5,053,586	7.1	1,694,574	1.4	3,716,216	9.9	6,084	990
Washington	4,984,798	4,677,335	6.6	1,230,891	5.4	3,753,907	7.0	4,832	310
West Virginia	845,554	855,888	-1.2	255,987	-5.1	589,567	.6	3,089	121
Wisconsin	3,435,640	3,328,374	3.2	1,491,869	1.5	1,943,771	4.5	4,519	379
Wyoming	141,676	135,015	4.9	105,758	3.0	35,918	11.0	154	40

Ranked by Population

Rank 2000	RMA	Census 4/1/00
1	New York, NY-NJ-CT	19,360,664
2	Los Angeles, CA	12,996,023
3	Chicago, IL-IN-WI	8,748,587
4	San Francisco-, CA	5,990,557
5	Philadelphia-, PA-NJ-DE-MD	5,814,079
6	Miami-, FL	4,944,670
7	Dallas-, TX	4,681,646
8	Boston, MA-NH	4,679,465
9	Detroit, MI-CAN.	4,641,127
10	Washington, DC-MD-VA	4,581,114
11	Houston, TX	4,080,199
12	Atlanta, GA	3,623,062
13	Phoenix, AZ	3,078,489
14	Seattle, WA	3,036,889
15	San Diego, CA-MEX.	2,736,424
16	Minneapolis-, MN-WI	2,682,362
17	St. Louis, MO-IL	2,337,245
18	Baltimore, MD-PA	2,241,860
19	Cleveland, OH	2,182,254
20	Denver, CO	2,088,925
21	Pittsburgh, PA	2,010,337
22	Portland, OR-WA	1,764,702
23	Cincinnati, OH-KY-IN	1,691,894
24	Milwaukee, WI	1,610,669
25	Riverside-, CA	1,587,954
26	Kansas City, MO-KS	1,563,527
27	Sacramento, CA	1,518,806
28	San Antonio, TX	1,405,646
29	Indianapolis, IN	1,371,830
30	Las Vegas, NV	1,344,673
31	Orlando, FL	1,342,878
32	Charlotte, NC-SC	1,301,901
33	New Orleans, LA	1,242,139
34	Columbus, OH	1,225,821
35	Hartford-, CT	1,182,480
36	St. Petersburg, FL	1,152,771
37	Buffalo, NY-CAN.	1,088,729
38	Memphis, TN-AR-MS	1,066,097
39	Providence-, RI-MA	1,024,698
40	Norfolk-, VA	1,023,003
41	Austin, TX	1,009,196
42	Salt Lake City, UT	994,767
43	Tampa, FL	984,692
44	Oklahoma City, OK	973,684
45	Louisville, KY-IN	970,458
46	Jacksonville, FL	955,200
47	Nashville, TN	907,017
48	Richmond, VA	897,287
49	Honolulu, HI	876,121
50	Rochester, NY	873,504
51	Birmingham, AL	800,495
52	Albany-, NY	793,886
53	Dayton, OH	785,027
54	Tucson, AZ	769,505
55	Raleigh, NC	733,981
56	Fresno, CA	729,375
57	Akron, OH	708,043
58	Tulsa, OK	698,105
59	El Paso, TX-NM-MEX.	695,311
60	Knoxville, TN	693,948
61	Grand Rapids, MI	686,981
62	Albuquerque, NM	668,334
63	Omaha, NE-IA	650,384
64	Oxnard-, CA	618,831
65	Allentown-, PA-NJ	608,943
66	Springfield, MA	593,284
67	Toledo, OH-MI	590,723
68	Syracuse, NY	571,783
69	Greensboro-, NC	546,450
70	New Haven, CT	544,274
71	Baton Rouge, LA	542,403
72	Columbia, SC	512,179
73	Colorado Springs, CO	506,440
74	Worcester, MA-CT	506,130
75	Flint, MI	488,625
76	Newport News-, VA	487,244
77	Charleston, SC	475,333
78	Scranton-, PA	469,087
79	Greenville, SC	468,255
80	Sarasota-, FL	466,778
81	Wichita, KS	460,520
82	McAllen, TX-MEX.	448,834
83	Youngstown-, OH-PA	448,405
84	Little Rock, AR	431,800
85	Mobile, AL	425,684
86	Chattanooga, TN-GA	412,643
87	Harrisburg, PA	410,150
88	Bakersfield, CA	408,328
89	Melbourne-, FL	405,677
90	Augusta, GA-SC	402,891
91	Modesto, CA	399,512
92	Stockton, CA	396,350
93	Fort Myers-, FL	395,089
94	Madison, WI	390,058
95	Des Moines, IA	388,217
96	Lansing, MI	376,205
97	Winston-Salem, NC	373,267
98	Spokane, WA-ID	371,509
99	Pensacola, FL	371,095
100	Lexington, KY	361,983
101	Jackson, MS	361,423
102	Provo-, UT	360,719
103	Saginaw-, MI	359,538
104	Beaumont-, TX	359,418
105	Johnson City-, TN-VA	358,147
106	Durham, NC	355,621
107	Boise, ID	349,941
108	Canton, OH	343,794
109	Fayetteville, NC	336,917
110	Reno, NV	331,264
111	Santa Rosa, CA	328,170
112	Rockford, IL-WI	318,096
113	Corpus Christi, TX	317,717
114	Fort Wayne, IN	316,478
115	Shreveport, LA-TX	314,390
116	Brownsville, TX-MEX.	307,363
117	Davenport-, IA-IL	302,080
118	Ogden, UT	300,985
119	New London-, CT-RI	300,098
120	Peoria, IL	298,602
121	Anchorage, AK	293,276
122	Lancaster, PA	292,754
123	Kalamazoo, MI	290,529
124	Daytona Beach, FL	286,852
125	Atlantic City, NJ	281,933
126	South Bend, IN-MI	280,926
127	Reading, PA	280,128
128	Eugene, OR	276,455
129	Huntsville, AL	274,980
130	Salem, OR	274,523
131	Montgomery, AL	273,001
132	Killeen-, TX	270,163
133	Lafayette, LA	268,116
134	Macon, GA	265,193
135	Erie, PA	259,365
136	Savannah, GA	257,930
137	Boulder-, CO	256,431
138	Springfield, MO	254,590
139	Biloxi-, MS	252,892
140	Asheville, NC	251,012
141	York, PA	250,585
142	Columbus, GA-AL	248,565
143	Huntington, WV-KY-OH	247,651
144	Portsmouth-, NH-ME	247,111
145	Roanoke, VA	244,825
146	Portland, ME	242,412
147	Evansville, IN-KY	241,874
148	Fort Collins-, CO	235,232
149	Charleston, WV	234,573
150	Lincoln, NE	231,614
151	Lakeland, FL	230,633
152	Waterbury, CT	227,899
153	Poughkeepsie, NY	227,751
154	Hickory, NC	224,463
155	Fairfield-, CA	224,380
156	Binghamton, NY-PA	223,650
157	Utica-, NY	221,518
158	Lubbock, TX	219,920
159	Midland-, TX	216,880
160	Naples, FL	216,383
161	Tallahassee, FL	213,711
162	Ocala, FL	211,431
163	Appleton, WI	210,894
164	Green Bay, WI	208,515
165	Santa Barbara, CA	205,504
166	Palm Springs-, CA	203,466
167	Olympia, WA	200,141
168	Manchester, NH	196,727
169	Hesperia-, CA	193,320
170	Visalia, CA	191,846
171	Galveston-, TX	189,747
172	Amarillo, TX	188,149
173	Elkhart, IN-MI	187,083
174	New Bedford, MA	185,971
175	Bremerton, WA	185,060
176	Santa Cruz, CA	185,025
177	Fort Pierce, FL	183,494
178	Spartanburg, SC	182,174
179	Wilmington, NC	181,109
180	Laredo, TX-MEX.	180,740
181	Waco, TX	176,912
182	Gainesville, FL	174,392
183	Cedar Rapids, IA	172,024
184	Burlington, VT	169,535
185	Fort Smith, AR-OK	168,369
186	Monterey-, CA	168,089
187	Springfield, IL	167,040
188	Fall River, MA-RI	164,759
189	Hagerstown, MD-PA-WV	164,726
190	Muskegon, MI	163,319
191	Salinas, CA	163,232
192	Richland-, WA	162,425
193	Topeka, KS	161,033
194	Barnstable, MA	160,772
195	Vineland, NJ	158,101
196	Myrtle Beach, SC-NC	156,337
197	Kissimmee, FL	155,541
198	Lake Charles, LA	154,060
199	Jackson, MI	152,085
200	Athens, GA	151,357
201	Duluth, MN-WI	150,470
202	Yuma, AZ-CA	148,651
203	Clarksville, TN-KY	145,582
204	Medford, OR	145,126
205	Annapolis, MD	144,778
206	Fargo-, ND-MN	143,735
207	Tyler, TX	140,749
208	Bryan-, TX	140,080
209	Fort Walton Beach, FL	139,781
210	Bellingham, WA	139,165
211	Wheeling, WV-OH	138,490
212	Anderson, IN	137,711
213	Redding, CA	137,346
214	Panama City, FL	136,904
215	Lafayette-, IN	136,867
216	Williamsport, PA	136,302
217	Monroe, LA	135,143
218	Tuscaloosa, AL	135,057
219	Winter Haven, FL	133,461
220	Jacksonville, NC	133,062
221	Lynchburg, VA	132,504
222	Fayetteville-, AR	132,499
223	Yakima, WA	132,496
224	Pueblo, CO	132,101
225	Longview, TX	131,492
226	Lake Jackson-, TX	130,528
227	Champaign-, IL	129,489
228	Middletown, OH	128,847
229	Burlington, NC	128,179
230	Denton, TX	128,061
231	Wichita Falls, TX	127,789
232	Punta Gorda-, FL	126,731
233	Dover, DE	126,206
234	Muncie, IN	126,023
235	Hemet, CA	125,964
236	Sioux Falls, SD	125,549
237	Altoona, PA	125,517
238	Houma-, LA	124,143
239	Merced, CA	123,804
240	Johnstown, PA	123,321
241	Springfield, OH	123,310
242	Carbondale-, IL	122,444
243	Fredericksburg, VA	121,747
244	Mansfield, OH	121,311
245	Rochester, MN	119,927
246	Waterloo, IA	117,984
247	Venice, FL	117,800
248	Abilene, TX	117,689
249	Charlottesville, VA	116,978
250	Kenosha, WI	116,926
251	Joplin, MO-KS	114,889
252	Bloomington, IN	114,767
253	Greenville, NC	113,933
254	Florence, AL	113,578
255	Billings, MT	113,426
256	Holland, MI	112,747
257	Bloomington-, IL	112,143
258	Terre Haute, IN	112,034
259	Las Cruces, NM	111,375
260	Stuart, FL	110,885
261	Corvallis-, OR	109,900
262	Santa Maria, CA	109,581
263	Steubenville-, OH-WV	107,478
264	Newburgh, NY	107,327
265	Glens Falls, NY	107,250
266	Albany, GA	107,244
267	Sioux City, IA-NE-SD	106,902
268	Lima, OH	105,770
269	Battle Creek, MI	105,471
270	St. Cloud, MN	105,361
271	Goldsboro, NC	104,826
272	Grand Junction, CO	104,591
273	Eau Claire, WI	103,894
274	Decatur, IL	103,836
275	Sheboygan, WI	103,237
276	La Crosse, WI-MN	102,982
277	Kingston, NY	102,928
278	Greeley, CO	102,533
279	Yuba City, CA	102,089
280	Columbia, MO	101,609
281	State College, PA	101,227
282	Parkersburg, WV-OH	100,987
283	Florence, SC	100,577
284	Anniston, AL	98,571
285	Newark, OH	98,544
286	Benton Harbor-, MI	98,418
287	Port Huron, MI-CAN.	97,755
288	Spring Hill, FL	97,754
289	Eureka-, CA	97,609
290	Murfreesboro, TN	96,869
291	Alexandria, LA	96,705
292	Morristown, TN	96,411
293	Lawton, OK	96,238
294	Santa Fe, NM	95,406
295	Decatur, AL	95,099
296	San Angelo, TX	95,076
297	Anderson, SC	94,972
298	Michigan City, IN	93,789
299	Rocky Mount, NC	93,768
300	Salisbury, NC	93,662
301	Iowa City, IA	93,546
302	Texarkana-, TX-AR	93,525
303	St. Joseph, MO-KS	93,230
304	Ithaca, NY	92,631
305	Lewiston-, ME	92,395
306	Lebanon, PA	91,718
307	Sumter, SC	91,455
308	Chico, CA	91,033
309	Bangor, ME	91,001
310	Indio-, CA	90,714
311	Gadsden, AL	89,619
312	Vero Beach, FL	88,146
313	Cleveland, TN	87,951
314	Idaho Falls, ID	87,666
315	Morgantown, WV-PA	87,377
316	Kankakee, IL	87,116
317	Kokomo, IN	86,817
318	Dothan, AL	86,801
319	Rapid City, SD	86,248
320	Pittsfield, MA	85,900
321	Beckley, WV	84,587
322	Concord, NH	84,570
323	Rome, GA	83,486
324	Lawrence, KS	83,344
325	Martinsville, VA-NC	83,170
326	Sandusky, OH	83,125
327	Pascagoula, MS	82,563
328	Oshkosh, WI	82,112
329	Elmira, NY	81,987
330	Wausau, WI	81,673
331	Janesville, WI	81,661
332	Missoula, MT	80,964
333	Auburn-, AL	80,826
334	Bismarck, ND	80,754
335	Pottsville, PA	80,397
336	Uniontown, PA	79,461
337	Napa, CA	79,326
338	Logan, UT	79,173
339	Middletown, NY	79,163
340	Cumberland, MD-WV	79,128
341	Hattiesburg, MS	78,776
342	Jackson, TN	78,432
343	Watsonville, CA	78,222
344	Salisbury, MD-DE	77,891
345	Valdosta, GA	77,590
346	Sherman-, TX	76,351
347	Longview, WA-OR	76,068
348	Danville, VA-NC	73,986
349	Dubuque, IA-WI-IL	73,570
350	Cheyenne, WY	72,857
351	Sharon, PA-OH	71,902
352	Owensboro, KY	71,502
353	Great Falls, MT	71,161
354	Paducah, KY-IL	70,799
355	Zanesville, OH	70,135
356	Porterville, CA	70,082
357	Jefferson City, MO	69,692
358	Hazleton, PA	68,670
359	Hot Springs, AR	67,794
360	Titusville, FL	67,439
361	Marion, IN	67,396
362	Pine Bluff, AR	67,137
363	Columbus, IN	66,969
364	Hanover, PA	66,826
365	Victoria, TX	66,604
366	Pottstown, PA	66,225
367	Pocatello, ID	65,692
368	Danville, IL	65,418
369	Watertown, NY	65,063
370	Butler, PA	65,046
371	Cape Girardeau, MO	65,017
372	Augusta, ME	64,589
373	De Kalb, IL	64,388
374	Farmington, NM	64,227
375	Lancaster, OH	63,954
376	Carlisle, PA	63,470
377	Fairbanks, AK	63,420
378	Lompoc, CA	63,316
379	Jamestown, NY	63,230
380	Newport, RI	63,197
381	Greenwood, SC	63,176
382	Portsmouth, OH-KY	63,075
383	Washington, PA	63,075
384	Brunswick, GA	62,815
385	Ames, IA	62,798
386	Meridian, MS	62,690
387	Lufkin, TX	62,376
388	Casper, WY	62,158
389	Richmond, IN-OH	61,141
390	Davis, CA	60,966
391	Monroe, MI	59,973
392	Hilo, HI	58,820
393	Jonesboro, AR	58,732
394	San Luis Obispo, CA	58,727
395	New Castle, PA	58,116
396	Brunswick-, ME	57,361
397	Fairmont, WV	56,699
398	Fond du Lac, WI	56,596
399	Lockport, NY	56,366
400	Grand Forks, ND-MN	55,642
401	Manitowoc, WI	55,553
402	Marion, OH	55,530
403	Latrobe, PA	55,327
404	Clarksburg, WV	54,529
405	Walla Walla, WA-OR	54,342
406	Columbus, MS	54,101
407	Roswell, NM	53,690
408	DeLand, FL	53,219
409	Quincy, IL	52,274
410	Alliance, OH	51,753
411	Lewiston, ID-WA	51,385
412	Muskogee, OK	50,853
413	Plattsburgh, NY	50,741
414	Mankato, MN	50,357
415	Enid, OK	49,931
416	Laurel, MS	49,532
417	Waterville, ME	49,192
418	Bowling Green, KY	48,992
419	Findlay, OH	48,737
420	Hutchinson, KS	48,601
421	Salina, KS	47,073
422	Grand Island, NE	46,175
423	Torrington, CT	46,151
424	Greenville, MS	44,961
425	Galesburg, IL	44,654
426	Manhattan, KS	44,482
427	Natchez, MS-LA	42,455
428	Leavenworth, KS	42,257
429	Ashtabula, OH	42,091
430	Vicksburg, MS-LA	41,403
431	Bartlesville, OK	40,774
432	Clovis, NM	39,060
433	East Liverpool, OH	38,759
434	Oil City-, PA	38,389
435	Clinton, IA-IL	37,644
436	Burlington, IA	35,380
437	Butte, MT	34,564
438	Hopkinsville, KY	34,486
439	Marshall, TX	30,254
440	Nogales, AZ-MEX.	25,220
441	Calexico, CA-MEX.	24,616
442	Sault Ste. Marie, MI-CAN.	18,601

Cities and Other Places of 35,000 or More

This table lists cities and other places of 35,000 or more, ranked according to 2000 Census population. In addition, the table presents the 1990 Census population and the 1990-2000 percent of population change. The Ranally City Rating classifies Principal Business Centers according to their relative business and economic importance; for a complete explanation, see the Introduction on pages 5-9. A list of all Principal Business Centers and other places with 30,000 or more, arranged in alphabetical order by state, appears on pages 74-87.

City Rank 2000	City, with Place Type	Ranally City Rating	Population: Census 4/1/00	Population: Census 4/1/90	Population: 1990-2000 % Change
1	New York, NY (Inc. Place)	1-AAAA	8,008,278	7,322,564	9.4
2	Los Angeles, CA (Inc. Place)	1-AAA	3,694,820	3,485,398	6.0
3	Chicago, IL (Inc. Place)	1-AAA	2,896,016	2,783,726	4.0
4	Houston, TX (Inc. Place)	1-AA	1,953,631	1,630,864	19.8
5	Philadelphia, PA (Inc. Place)	1-AA	1,517,550	1,585,577	-4.3
6	Phoenix, AZ (Inc. Place)	1-A	1,321,045	983,392	34.3
7	San Diego, CA (Inc. Place)	1-A	1,223,400	1,110,549	10.2
8	Dallas, TX (Inc. Place)	1-AA	1,188,580	1,006,877	18.0
9	San Antonio, TX (Inc. Place)	1-A	1,144,646	935,393	22.4
10	Detroit, MI (Inc. Place)	1-AA	951,270	1,027,974	-7.5
11	San Jose, CA (Inc. Place)	2-BB	894,943	782,248	14.4
12	Indianapolis, IN (Inc. Place)	1-A	781,870	731,327	6.9
13	San Francisco, CA (Inc. Place)	1-AA	776,733	723,959	7.3
14	Hempstead, NY (MCD-Town)		755,924	725,639	4.2
15	Jacksonville, FL (Inc. Place)	2-AA	735,617	635,230	15.8
16	Columbus, OH (Inc. Place)	1-A	711,470	632,910	12.4
17	Austin, TX (Inc. Place)	2-AA	656,562	465,648	41.0
18	Baltimore, MD (Independent City)	1-A	651,154	736,014	-11.5
19	Memphis, TN (Inc. Place)	2-AA	650,100	610,337	6.5
20	Milwaukee, WI (Inc. Place)	1-A	596,974	628,088	-5.0
21	Boston, MA (Inc. Place)	1-AA	589,141	574,283	2.6
22	Washington, DC (Inc. Place)	1-AA	572,059	606,900	-5.7
23	El Paso, TX (Inc. Place)	2-AA	563,662	515,342	9.4
24	Seattle, WA (Inc. Place)	1-A	563,374	516,259	9.1
25	Denver, CO (Inc. Place)	1-A	554,636	467,610	18.6
26	Nashville, TN (Inc. Place)	2-AA	545,524	488,374	11.7
27	Charlotte, NC (Inc. Place)	2-AA	540,828	395,934	36.6
28	Fort Worth, TX (Inc. Place)	2-BB	534,694	447,619	19.5
29	Portland, OR (Inc. Place)	1-A	529,121	437,319	21.0
30	Oklahoma City, OK (Inc. Place)	1-A	506,132	444,719	13.8
31	Tucson, AZ (Inc. Place)	2-AA	486,699	405,371	20.1
32	New Orleans, LA (Inc. Place)	1-A	484,674	496,938	-2.5
33	Las Vegas, NV (Inc. Place)	2-AA	478,434	258,295	85.2
34	Cleveland, OH (Inc. Place)	1-AA	478,403	505,616	-5.4
35	Long Beach, CA (Inc. Place)	2-S	461,522	429,433	7.5
36	Albuquerque, NM (Inc. Place)	2-AA	448,607	384,619	16.6
37	Brookhaven, NY (MCD-Town)		448,248	407,779	9.9
38	Kansas City, MO (Inc. Place)	1-A	441,545	435,146	1.5
39	Fresno, CA (Inc. Place)	2-A	427,652	354,202	20.7
40	Virginia Beach, VA (Independent City)	2-B	425,257	393,069	8.2
41	Atlanta, GA (Inc. Place)	1-AA	416,474	394,017	5.7
42	Sacramento, CA (Inc. Place)	2-AA	407,018	369,365	10.2
43	Oakland, CA (Inc. Place)	2-BB	399,484	372,242	7.3
44	Mesa, AZ (Inc. Place)	2-S	396,375	288,104	37.6
45	Tulsa, OK (Inc. Place)	2-AA	393,049	367,302	7.0
46	Omaha, NE (Inc. Place)	2-AA	390,007	335,719	16.2
47	Minneapolis, MN (Inc. Place)	1-AA	382,618	368,383	3.9
48	Honolulu, HI (CDP)	2-AA	371,657	365,272	1.7
49	Miami, FL (Inc. Place)	1-AA	362,470	358,548	1.1
50	Colorado Springs, CO (Inc. Place)	2-A	360,890	281,140	28.4
51	St. Louis, MO (Independent City)	1-AA	348,189	396,685	-12.2
52	Wichita, KS (Inc. Place)	2-AA	344,284	304,011	13.2
53	Santa Ana, CA (Inc. Place)	2-S	337,977	293,742	15.1
54	Pittsburgh, PA (Inc. Place)	1-AA	334,563	369,879	-9.5
55	Arlington, TX (Inc. Place)	2-S	332,969	261,721	27.2
56	Cincinnati, OH (Inc. Place)	1-A	331,285	364,040	-9.0
57	Anaheim, CA (Inc. Place)	2-S	328,014	266,406	23.1
58	Islip, NY (MCD-Town)		322,612	299,587	7.7
59	Toledo, OH (Inc. Place)	2-AA	313,619	332,943	-5.8
60	Tampa, FL (Inc. Place)	2-AA	303,447	280,015	8.4
61	Oyster Bay, NY (MCD-Town)		293,925	292,657	0.4
62	Buffalo, NY (Inc. Place)	2-AA	292,648	328,123	-10.8
63	St. Paul, MN (Inc. Place)	2-BB	287,151	272,235	5.5
64	Corpus Christi, TX (Inc. Place)	2-A	277,454	257,453	7.8
65	Aurora, CO (Inc. Place)	3-SS	276,393	222,103	24.4
66	Raleigh, NC (Inc. Place)	2-AA	276,093	207,951	32.8
67	Newark, NJ (Inc. Place)	2-CC	273,546	275,221	-0.6
68	Lexington, KY (Inc. Place)	2-AA	260,512	225,366	15.6
69	Anchorage, AK (Inc. Place)	2-A	260,283	226,338	15.0
70	Louisville, KY (Inc. Place)	2-AA	256,231	269,063	-4.8
71	Riverside, CA (Inc. Place)	2-C	255,166	226,505	12.7
72	Saint Petersburg, FL (Inc. Place)	2-BB	248,232	238,629	4.0
73	Bakersfield, CA (Inc. Place)	2-A	247,057	174,978	41.2
74	Stockton, CA (Inc. Place)	2-A	243,771	210,943	15.6
75	Birmingham, AL (Inc. Place)	2-AA	242,820	265,968	-8.7
76	Jersey City, NJ (Inc. Place)	3-SS	240,055	228,537	5.0
77	Norfolk, VA (Independent City)	2-AA	234,403	261,229	-10.3
78	Baton Rouge, LA (Inc. Place)	2-AA	227,818	219,531	3.8
79	Hialeah, FL (Inc. Place)	2-S	226,419	188,004	20.4
80	Lincoln, NE (Inc. Place)	3-AA	225,581	191,972	17.5
81	Greensboro, NC (Inc. Place)	2-A	223,891	183,521	22.0
82	North Hempstead, NY (MCD-Town)		222,611	211,393	5.3
83	Plano, TX (Inc. Place)	3-S	222,030	128,713	72.5
84	Rochester, NY (Inc. Place)	2-AA	219,773	231,636	-5.1
85	Glendale, AZ (Inc. Place)	3-S	218,812	147,864	48.0
86	Akron, OH (Inc. Place)	2-BB	217,074	223,019	-2.7
87	Garland, TX (Inc. Place)	3-S	215,768	180,650	19.4
88	Babylon, NY (MCD-Town)		211,792	202,889	4.4
89	Madison, WI (Inc. Place)	2-AA	208,054	191,262	8.8
90	Fort Wayne, IN (Inc. Place)	2-A	205,727	172,971	18.9
91	Fremont, CA (Inc. Place)	3-SS	203,413	173,339	17.3
92	Scottsdale, AZ (Inc. Place)	3-SS	202,705	130,075	55.8
93	Montgomery, AL (Inc. Place)	2-A	201,568	187,543	7.5
94	Shreveport, LA (Inc. Place)	2-AA	200,145	198,525	0.8
95	Lubbock, TX (Inc. Place)	2-A	199,564	186,206	7.2
96	Chesapeake, VA (Independent City)	3-S	199,184	151,976	31.1
97	Mobile, AL (Inc. Place)	2-A	198,915	196,263	1.4
98	Des Moines, IA (Inc. Place)	2-AA	198,682	193,187	2.8
99	Grand Rapids, MI (Inc. Place)	2-AA	197,800	189,126	4.6
100	Richmond, VA (Independent City)	2-AA	197,790	203,056	-2.6
101	Yonkers, NY (Inc. Place)	3-SS	196,086	188,082	4.3
102	Spokane, WA (Inc. Place)	2-AA	195,629	177,196	10.4
103	Huntington, NY (MCD-Town)		195,289	191,474	2.0
104	Augusta, GA (Inc. Place)	2-A	195,182	44,639	337.2
105	Glendale, CA (Inc. Place)	3-SS	194,973	180,038	8.3
106	Tacoma, WA (Inc. Place)	2-B	193,556	176,664	9.6
107	Irving, TX (Inc. Place)	3-S	191,615	155,037	23.6
108	Huntington Beach, CA (Inc. Place)	3-SS	189,594	181,519	4.4
109	Arlington, VA (CDP)	3-SS	189,453	170,936	10.8
110	Modesto, CA (Inc. Place)	2-A	188,856	164,730	14.6
111	Durham, NC (Inc. Place)	3-BB	187,035	136,612	36.9
112	Paradise, NV (CDP)		186,070	124,682	49.2
113	Orlando, FL (Inc. Place)	2-AA	185,951	164,693	12.9
114	Boise, ID (Inc. Place)	3-AA	185,787	125,551	48.0
115	Columbus, GA (Inc. Place)	3-AA	185,781	178,681	4.0
116	Winston Salem, NC (Inc. Place)	2-AA	185,776	143,485	29.5
117	San Bernardino, CA (Inc. Place)	2-C	185,401	164,676	12.6
118	Jackson, MS (Inc. Place)	2-AA	184,256	196,637	-6.3
119	Little Rock, AR (Inc. Place)	2-AA	183,133	175,795	4.2
120	Salt Lake City, UT (Inc. Place)	2-AA	181,743	159,936	13.6
121	Thornton, IL (MCD-Township)		180,802	175,896	2.8
122	Reno, NV (Inc. Place)	2-A	180,480	133,850	34.8
123	Newport News, VA (Independent City)	2-B	180,150	170,045	5.9
124	Rockford, IL (MCD-Township)		178,853	173,645	3.0
125	Chandler, AZ (Inc. Place)		176,581	90,533	95.0
126	Laredo, TX (Inc. Place)	3-AA	176,576	122,899	43.7
127	Henderson, NV (Inc. Place)		175,381	64,942	170.1
128	Knoxville, TN (Inc. Place)	2-AA	173,890	165,039	5.4
129	Amarillo, TX (Inc. Place)	2-A	173,627	157,615	10.2
130	Providence, RI (Inc. Place)	2-AA	173,618	160,728	8.0
131	Chula Vista, CA (Inc. Place)	3-S	173,556	135,163	28.4
132	Worcester, MA (Inc. Place)	2-A	172,648	169,759	1.7
133	Oxnard, CA (Inc. Place)	3-CC	170,358	142,216	19.8
134	Center, IN (MCD-Township)		167,055	182,140	-8.3
135	Dayton, OH (Inc. Place)	2-AA	166,179	182,044	-8.7
136	North, IN (MCD-Township)		165,656	166,928	-0.8
137	Garden Grove, CA (Inc. Place)	3-S	165,196	143,050	15.5
138	Oceanside, CA (Inc. Place)	3-C	161,029	128,398	25.4
139	Tempe, AZ (Inc. Place)	3-S	158,625	141,865	11.8
140	Huntsville, AL (Inc. Place)	3-AA	158,216	159,789	-1.0
141	Ontario, CA (Inc. Place)	3-S	158,007	133,179	18.6
142	Sunrise Manor, NV (CDP)		156,120	95,362	63.7
143	Wheeling, IL (MCD-Township)		155,834	148,641	4.8
144	Proviso, IL (MCD-Township)		155,831	152,443	2.2
145	Chattanooga, TN (Inc. Place)	2-A	155,554	152,466	2.0
146	Fort Lauderdale, FL (Inc. Place)	2-BB	152,397	149,377	2.0
147	Worth, IL (MCD-Township)		152,239	151,144	0.7
148	Springfield, MA (Inc. Place)	2-AA	152,082	156,983	-3.1
149	Springfield, MO (Inc. Place)	2-A	151,580	140,494	7.9
150	Santa Clarita, CA (Inc. Place)		151,088	110,690	36.5
151	Salinas, CA (Inc. Place)	3-AA	151,060	108,777	38.9
152	Tallahassee, FL (Inc. Place)	3-AA	150,624	124,773	20.7
153	Rockford, IL (Inc. Place)	2-A	150,115	140,003	7.2
154	Pomona, CA (Inc. Place)	3-SS	149,473	131,723	13.5
155	Paterson, NJ (Inc. Place)	3-S	149,222	140,891	5.9
156	Overland Park, KS (Inc. Place)	3-SSm	149,080	111,790	33.4
157	Downers Grove, IL (MCD-Township)		148,110	137,862	7.4
158	Santa Rosa, CA (Inc. Place)	3-CC	147,595	113,261	30.3
159	Syracuse, NY (Inc. Place)	2-AA	147,306	163,860	-10.1
160	Kansas City, KS (Inc. Place)	3-SS	146,866	149,800	-2.0
161	Hampton, VA (Independent City)	3-BB	146,437	133,793	9.5
162	Metairie, LA (CDP)		146,136	149,428	-2.2
163	Lakewood, CO (Inc. Place)	3-SS	144,126	126,481	14.0
164	Vancouver, WA (Inc. Place)	3-SS	143,560	46,380	209.5
165	Irvine, CA (Inc. Place)	4-Sr	143,072	110,330	29.7
166	Aurora, IL (Inc. Place)	3-SS	142,990	99,556	43.6
167	Moreno Valley, CA (Inc. Place)		142,381	118,779	19.9
168	Pasadena, TX (Inc. Place)	3-S	141,674	119,363	18.7
169	Hayward, CA (Inc. Place)	3-SS	140,030	111,343	25.8
170	Brownsville, TX (Inc. Place)	3-AA	139,722	98,962	41.2
171	Bridgeport, CT (Inc. Place)	2-C	139,529	141,686	-1.5
172	Bridgeport, CT (MCD-Town)		139,529	141,686	-1.5
173	Hollywood, FL (Inc. Place)	2-S	139,357	121,697	14.5
174	Warren, MI (Inc. Place)	3-SS	138,247	144,864	-4.6
175	Torrance, CA (Inc. Place)	2-S	137,946	133,107	3.6
176	Eugene, OR (Inc. Place)	2-A	137,893	112,669	22.4
177	Pembroke Pines, FL (Inc. Place)		137,427	65,452	110.0
178	Salem, OR (Inc. Place)	2-A	136,924	107,786	27.0
179	Maine, IL (MCD-Township)		135,623	128,837	5.3
180	Schaumburg, IL (MCD-Township)		134,114	127,625	5.1
181	Pasadena, CA (Inc. Place)	2-S	133,936	131,591	1.8
182	Escondido, CA (Inc. Place)	3-S	133,559	108,635	22.9
183	Wayne, IN (MCD-Township)		133,461	125,699	6.2
184	Washington, IN (MCD-Township)		132,927	133,969	-0.8
185	Sunnyvale, CA (Inc. Place)	3-S	131,760	117,229	12.4
186	Savannah, GA (Inc. Place)	2-A	131,510	137,560	-4.4
187	Fontana, CA (Inc. Place)	4-Sr	128,929	87,535	47.3
188	Orange, CA (Inc. Place)	3-SS	128,821	110,658	16.4
189	Naperville, IL (Inc. Place)	4-S	128,358	85,351	50.4
190	Alexandria, VA (Independent City)	3-SS	128,283	111,183	15.4
191	Calumet, IN (MCD-Township)		127,800	141,875	-9.9
192	Rancho Cucamonga, CA (Inc. Place)		127,743	101,409	26.0
193	Grand Prairie, TX (Inc. Place)	4-S	127,427	99,616	27.9
194	Fullerton, CA (Inc. Place)	3-SS	126,003	114,144	10.4
195	Corona, CA (Inc. Place)	4-S	124,966	76,095	64.2
196	Flint, MI (Inc. Place)	2-A	124,943	140,761	-11.2
197	York, IL (MCD-Township)		124,553	120,546	3.3
198	Mesquite, TX (Inc. Place)	3-Sm	124,523	101,484	22.7
199	Sterling Heights, MI (Inc. Place)	3-SSm	124,471	117,810	5.7
200	East Los Angeles, CA (CDP)		124,283	126,379	-1.7
201	Sioux Falls, SD (Inc. Place)	3-AA	123,975	100,814	23.0
202	New Haven, CT (Inc. Place)	2-AA	123,626	130,474	-5.2
203	New Haven, CT (MCD-Town)		123,626	130,474	-5.2
204	Topeka, KS (Inc. Place)	3-AA	122,377	119,883	2.1
205	Concord, CA (Inc. Place)	3-SS	121,780	111,348	9.4
206	Evansville, IN (Inc. Place)	2-A	121,582	126,272	-3.7
207	Hartford, CT (Inc. Place)	2-AA	121,578	139,739	-13.0
208	Hartford, CT (MCD-Town)		121,578	139,739	-13.0
209	Fayetteville, NC (Inc. Place)	2-A	121,015	75,695	59.9
210	Cedar Rapids, IA (Inc. Place)	3-AA	120,758	108,751	11.0
211	Elizabeth, NJ (Inc. Place)	3-S	120,568	110,002	9.6
212	Lansing, MI (Inc. Place)	2-A	119,128	127,321	-6.4
213	Lancaster, CA (Inc. Place)	3-C	118,718	97,291	22.0
214	Fort Collins, CO (Inc. Place)	3-A	118,652	87,758	35.2
215	Milton, IL (MCD-Township)		118,616	108,148	9.7
216	Lisle, IL (MCD-Township)		117,604	108,452	8.4
217	Coral Springs, FL (Inc. Place)		117,549	79,443	48.0
218	Spring Valley, NV (CDP)		117,390	51,726	126.9
219	Stamford, CT (Inc. Place)	2-S	117,083	108,056	8.4
220	Stamford, CT (MCD-Town)		117,083	108,056	8.4
221	Thousand Oaks, CA (Inc. Place)	3-S	117,005	104,352	12.1
222	Vallejo, CA (Inc. Place)	3-S	116,760	109,199	6.9
223	Palmdale, CA (Inc. Place)		116,670	68,946	69.2
224	Amherst, NY (MCD-Town)		116,510	111,711	4.3
225	Columbia, SC (Inc. Place)	2-AA	116,278	103,477	12.4
226	El Monte, CA (Inc. Place)	4-S	115,965	106,209	9.2
227	Abilene, TX (Inc. Place)	3-AA	115,930	106,654	8.7
228	Smithtown, NY (MCD-Town)		115,715	113,406	2.0
229	Aurora, IL (MCD-Township)		115,553	101,769	13.5
230	North Las Vegas, NV (Inc. Place)		115,488	47,707	142.1
231	Ann Arbor, MI (Inc. Place)	2-C	114,024	109,592	4.0
232	Beaumont, TX (Inc. Place)	2-A	113,866	114,323	-0.4
233	Waco, TX (Inc. Place)	3-AA	113,726	103,590	9.8
234	Independence, MO (Inc. Place)	3-S	113,288	112,301	0.9
235	Peoria, IL (Inc. Place)	2-AA	112,936	113,504	-0.5
236	Peoria City, IL (MCD-Township)		112,936	113,504	-0.5
237	Palatine, IL (MCD-Township)		112,740	103,273	9.2
238	Inglewood, CA (Inc. Place)	3-S	112,580	109,602	2.7
239	Lawrence, IN (MCD-Township)		111,961	94,548	18.4
240	Bloomingdale, IL (MCD-Township)		111,709	96,050	16.3
241	Capital, IL (MCD-Township)		111,471	104,126	7.1
242	Springfield, IL (Inc. Place)	2-A	111,454	105,417	5.7
243	Simi Valley, CA (Inc. Place)	3-S	111,351	100,217	11.1
244	Wayne, IN (MCD-Township)		111,117	116,005	-4.2
245	Lafayette, LA (Inc. Place)	2-A	110,257	94,421	16.8
246	Gilbert, AZ (Inc. Place)		109,697	29,122	276.7
247	Carrollton, TX (Inc. Place)	4-S	109,576	82,169	33.4
248	Bremen, IL (MCD-Township)		109,575	107,803	1.6
249	Bellevue, WA (Inc. Place)	3-SS	109,569	86,874	26.1
250	Lyons, IL (MCD-Township)		109,264	105,004	4.1
251	Ramapo, NY (MCD-Town)		108,905	93,861	16.0
252	West Valley, UT (Inc. Place)	3-S	108,896	86,976	25.2
253	Clearwater, FL (Inc. Place)	2-B	108,787	98,784	10.1
254	Costa Mesa, CA (Inc. Place)	2-S	108,724	96,357	12.8
255	Peoria, AZ (Inc. Place)		108,364	50,675	113.8
256	South Bend, IN (Inc. Place)	2-A	107,789	105,511	2.2
257	Downey, CA (Inc. Place)	3-S	107,323	91,444	17.4
258	Waterbury, CT (Inc. Place)	3-BB	107,271	108,961	-1.6
259	Waterbury, CT (MCD-Town)		107,271	108,961	-1.6
260	Manchester, NH (Inc. Place)	3-AA	107,006	99,567	7.5
261	Allentown, PA (Inc. Place)	2-AA	106,632	105,090	1.5
262	McAllen, TX (Inc. Place)	2-A	106,414	84,021	26.7
263	Joliet, IL (Inc. Place)	3-SS	106,221	76,836	38.2
264	Lowell, MA (Inc. Place)	3-SS	105,167	103,439	1.7
265	Provo, UT (Inc. Place)	3-AA	105,166	86,835	21.1
266	West Covina, CA (Inc. Place)	3-S	105,080	96,086	9.4
267	Wichita Falls, TX (Inc. Place)	3-AA	104,197	96,259	8.2
268	Erie, PA (Inc. Place)	2-A	103,717	108,718	-4.6
269	Daly City, CA (Inc. Place)	3-Sm	103,621	92,311	12.3
270	Clarksville, TN (Inc. Place)	3-A	103,455	75,494	37.0
271	Norwalk, CA (Inc. Place)	4-S	103,298	94,279	9.6
272	Gary, IN (Inc. Place)	3-S	102,746	116,646	-11.9
273	Berkeley, CA (Inc. Place)	3-S	102,743	102,724	0.0
274	Niles, IL (MCD-Township)		102,638	96,412	6.5
275	Santa Clara, CA (Inc. Place)	3-S	102,361	93,613	9.3
276	Green Bay, WI (Inc. Place)	2-A	102,313	96,466	6.1
277	Cape Coral, FL (Inc. Place)		102,286	74,991	36.4
278	Arvada, CO (Inc. Place)	4-S	102,153	89,218	14.5
279	Pueblo, CO (Inc. Place)	3-AA	102,121	98,640	3.5
280	Cambridge, MA (Inc. Place)	3-SS	101,355	95,802	5.8
281	Westminster, CO (Inc. Place)	4-S	100,940	74,625	35.3
282	Ventura, CA (Inc. Place)	3-CC	100,916	92,575	9.0
283	Portsmouth, VA (Independent City)	3-C	100,565	103,907	-3.2
284	Livonia, MI (Inc. Place)	3-SS	100,545	100,850	-0.3
285	Burbank, CA (Inc. Place)	3-S	100,316	93,643	7.1
286	Athens, GA (Inc. Place)	3-A	100,266	45,734	119.2
287	Richmond, CA (Inc. Place)	3-S	99,216	87,425	13.5
288	Davenport, IA (Inc. Place)	2-A	98,359	95,333	3.2
289	Dearborn, MI (Inc. Place)	2-S	97,775	89,286	9.5
290	Edison, NJ (CDP)		97,687	88,680	10.2
291	Edison, NJ (MCD-Township)	3-S	97,687	88,680	10.2
292	Macon, GA (Inc. Place)	3-AA	97,255	106,612	-8.8
293	Woodbridge, NJ (MCD-Township)	3-SSm	97,203	93,086	4.4
294	Charleston, SC (Inc. Place)	2-A	96,650	80,414	20.2
295	South Gate, CA (Inc. Place)	4-Sr	96,375	86,284	11.7
296	Fairfield, CA (Inc. Place)	3-C	96,178	77,211	24.6
297	Arden-Arcade, CA (CDP-Census Area Only)		96,025	92,040	4.3
298	Norman, OK (Inc. Place)	3-S	95,694	80,071	19.5
299	Albany, NY (Inc. Place)	2-AA	95,658	101,082	-5.4
300	Clinton, MI (MCD-Charter Township)		95,648	10,838	782.5
301	Clinton Township, MI (CDP)		95,648	85,866	11.4
302	Gainesville, FL (Inc. Place)	3-AA	95,447	84,770	12.6
303	Midland, TX (Inc. Place)	3-AA	94,996	89,443	6.2
304	Elk Grove, IL (MCD-Township)		94,969	87,857	8.1
305	Portage, IN (MCD-Township)		94,916	101,791	-6.8
306	Roanoke, VA (Independent City)	2-A	94,911	96,397	-1.5
307	El Cajon, CA (Inc. Place)	3-SS	94,869	88,693	7.0
308	Leyden, IL (MCD-Township)		94,685	89,142	6.2
309	Boulder, CO (Inc. Place)	3-CC	94,673	83,295	13.7
310	Cary, NC (Inc. Place)		94,536	43,858	115.6
311	Elgin, IL (Inc. Place)	3-S	94,487	77,010	22.7
312	Brockton, MA (Inc. Place)	3-SS	94,304	92,788	1.6
313	Greece, NY (MCD-Town)		94,141	90,106	4.5
314	Cheektowaga, NY (MCD-Town)		94,019	99,314	-5.3
315	Warren, IN (MCD-Township)		93,941	87,989	6.8
316	Bloom, IL (MCD-Township)		93,901	95,029	-1.2
317	New Bedford, MA (Inc. Place)	3-BB	93,768	99,922	-6.2
318	Compton, CA (Inc. Place)	4-Sr	93,493	90,454	3.4
319	Mission Viejo, CA (Inc. Place)		93,102	72,820	27.9
320	Olathe, KS (Inc. Place)	4-S	92,962	63,352	46.7
321	Perry, IN (MCD-Township)		92,838	85,060	9.1
322	Waukegan, IL (MCD-Township)		92,805	78,185	18.7
323	Lawton, OK (Inc. Place)	3-AA	92,757	80,561	15.1
324	San Mateo, CA (Inc. Place)	3-SS	92,482	85,486	8.2
325	Santa Barbara, CA (Inc. Place)	3-AA	92,325	85,571	7.9
326	Fall River, MA (Inc. Place)	3-BB	91,938	92,703	-0.8
327	Rialto, CA (Inc. Place)		91,873	72,388	26.9
328	Richardson, TX (Inc. Place)	3-S	91,802	74,840	22.7
329	Visalia, CA (Inc. Place)	3-AA	91,565	75,636	21.1
330	Everett, WA (Inc. Place)	3-CC	91,488	69,974	30.7
331	Orland, IL (MCD-Township)		91,418	69,542	31.5
332	Odessa, TX (Inc. Place)	3-AA	90,943	89,699	1.4
333	Fargo, ND (Inc. Place)	3-AA	90,599	74,111	22.2
334	Antioch, CA (Inc. Place)	3-S	90,532	62,195	45.6
335	Elgin, IL (MCD-Township)		90,384	72,355	24.9
336	Kenosha, WI (Inc. Place)	3-S	90,352	80,352	12.4
337	Gresham, OR (Inc. Place)	4-S	90,205	68,235	32.2
338	Vista, CA (Inc. Place)		89,857	71,872	25.0
339	Billings, MT (Inc. Place)	3-AA	89,847	81,151	10.7
340	Carson, CA (Inc. Place)	3-S	89,730	83,995	6.8
341	Dover, NJ (MCD-Township)	3-S	89,706	76,371	17.5
342	Lynn, MA (Inc. Place)	3-S	89,050	81,245	9.6
343	Addison, IL (MCD-Township)		88,900	82,727	7.5
344	Port Saint Lucie, FL (Inc. Place)		88,769	55,866	58.9
345	Vacaville, CA (Inc. Place)		88,625	71,479	24.0
346	San Angelo, TX (Inc. Place)	3-AA	88,439	84,474	4.7
347	Sandy, UT (Inc. Place)		88,418	75,058	17.8
348	Columbia, MD (CDP)		88,254	75,883	16.3
349	Westminster, CA (Inc. Place)	3-S	88,207	78,118	12.9
350	Quincy, MA (Inc. Place)	3-S	88,025	84,985	3.6
351	Miami Beach, FL (Inc. Place)	3-S	87,933	92,639	-5.1
352	Waukegan, IL (Inc. Place)	3-SS	87,901	69,392	26.7
353	Hamilton, NJ (MCD-Township)		87,109	86,553	0.6
354	Duluth, MN (Inc. Place)	3-AA	86,918	85,493	1.7
355	Killeen, TX (Inc. Place)	3-B	86,911	63,535	36.8
356	Greenburgh, NY (MCD-Town)		86,764	83,816	3.5
357	Nashua, NH (Inc. Place)	3-B	86,605	79,662	8.7
358	Westland, MI (Inc. Place)	3-S	86,602	84,724	2.2
359	Joliet, IL (MCD-Township)		86,468	84,243	2.6
360	Toms River, NJ (CDP)		86,327	7,524	1,047.4
361	Algonquin, IL (MCD-Township)		86,219	57,746	49.3
362	High Point, NC (Inc. Place)	3-B	85,839	69,496	23.5
363	Warwick, RI (Inc. Place)	3-CC	85,808	85,427	0.4
364	Rochester, MN (Inc. Place)	3-AA	85,806	70,745	21.3
365	Alhambra, CA (Inc. Place)	3-S	85,804	82,106	4.5
366	Sandy Springs, GA (CDP)		85,781	67,842	26.4
367	Sunrise, FL (Inc. Place)		85,779	64,407	33.2
368	Naperville, IL (MCD-Township)		85,736	49,533	73.1
369	Parma, OH (Inc. Place)	3-S	85,655	87,876	-2.5
370	Cicero, IL (Inc. Place)	4-Sr	85,616	67,436	27.0
371	Trenton, NJ (Inc. Place)	2-B	85,403	88,675	-3.7
372	Bloomington, MN (Inc. Place)	3-SS	85,172	86,335	-1.3
373	Citrus Heights, CA (Inc. Place)		85,071	82,045	3.7
374	Sioux City, IA (Inc. Place)	3-AA	85,013	80,505	5.6
375	Columbia, MO (Inc. Place)	3-A	84,531	69,101	22.3
376	Orem, UT (Inc. Place)	3-B	84,324	67,561	24.8
377	Hawthorne, CA (Inc. Place)	3-S	84,112	71,349	17.9
378	Santa Monica, CA (Inc. Place)	3-SS	84,084	86,905	-3.2
379	Newton, MA (Inc. Place)	3-SS	83,829	82,585	1.5
380	Whittier, CA (Inc. Place)	3-S	83,680	77,671	7.7
381	Tyler, TX (Inc. Place)	3-AA	83,650	75,450	10.9
382	Hanover, IL (MCD-Township)		83,471	62,308	34.0
383	Federal Way, WA (Inc. Place)		83,259	(d)	(d)
384	Hammond, IN (Inc. Place)	3-S	83,048	84,236	-1.4
385	Norwalk, CT (Inc. Place)	3-SS	82,951	78,331	5.9
386	Norwalk, CT (MCD-Town)		82,951	(d)	(d)
387	Plantation, FL (Inc. Place)	3-Sm	82,934	66,692	24.4
388	Northfield, IL (MCD-Township)		82,880	78,186	6.0
389	Thornton, CO (Inc. Place)	4-S	82,384	55,031	49.7
390	Farmington Hills, MI (Inc. Place)	4-S	82,111	74,652	10.0
391	West Palm Beach, FL (Inc. Place)	2-AA	82,103	67,643	21.4
392	Clarkstown, NY (MCD-Town)		82,082	79,346	3.4
393	Youngstown, OH (Inc. Place)	2-AA	82,026	95,732	-14.3
394	Decatur, IL (Inc. Place)	3-AA	81,860	83,885	-2.4
395	Racine, WI (Inc. Place)	3-CC	81,855	84,298	-2.9
396	Upper Darby, PA (MCD-Township)	3-S	81,821	81,177	0.8
397	Reading, PA (Inc. Place)	2-A	81,207	78,380	3.6
398	Troy, MI (Inc. Place)	2-Sm	80,959	72,884	11.1
399	Redding, CA (Inc. Place)	3-A	80,865	66,462	21.7
400	Canton, OH (Inc. Place)	2-A	80,806	84,161	-4.0
401	Denton, TX (Inc. Place)	3-S	80,537	66,270	21.5
402	Fort Smith, AR (Inc. Place)	3-AA	80,268	72,798	10.3
403	Lawrence, KS (Inc. Place)	3-A	80,098	65,608	22.1
404	Cheektowaga, NY (CDP)		79,988	84,387	-5.2
405	Roseville, CA (Inc. Place)	4-Sr	79,921	44,685	78.9
406	Camden, NJ (Inc. Place)	3-S	79,904	87,492	-8.7
407	North Charleston, SC (Inc. Place)	3-S	79,641	70,218	13.4
408	Kent, WA (Inc. Place)	4-S	79,524	37,960	109.5
409	San Leandro, CA (Inc. Place)	3-SS	79,452	68,223	16.5
410	Palm Bay, FL (Inc. Place)		79,413	62,632	26.8
411	Lakewood, CA (Inc. Place)	3-S	79,345	73,557	7.9
412	Roswell, GA (Inc. Place)	4-S	79,334	47,923	65.5
413	Cranston, RI (Inc. Place)	4-S	79,269	76,060	4.2
414	Colonie, NY (MCD-Town)		79,258	76,494	3.6
415	Clifton, NJ (Inc. Place)	4-S	78,672	71,742	9.7
416	Lakeland, FL (Inc. Place)	3-AA	78,452	70,576	11.2
417	Southfield, MI (Inc. Place)	2-S	78,296	75,728	3.4
418	Buena Park, CA (Inc. Place)	3-S	78,282	68,784	13.8
419	Carlsbad, CA (Inc. Place)	4-S	78,247	63,126	24.0
420	Pompano Beach, FL (Inc. Place)	3-S	78,191	72,411	8.0
421	Tonawanda, NY (MCD-Town)		78,155	82,464	-5.2
422	Tuscaloosa, AL (Inc. Place)	3-AA	77,906	77,759	0.2
423	Brandon, FL (CDP)		77,895	57,985	34.3
424	Lewisville, TX (Inc. Place)		77,737	46,521	67.1
425	Yuma, AZ (Inc. Place)	3-A	77,515	56,966	36.1
426	Somerville, MA (Inc. Place)	4-S	77,478	76,210	1.7
427	Santa Maria, CA (Inc. Place)	3-B	77,423	61,284	26.3
428	Ogden, UT (Inc. Place)	3-BB	77,226	63,909	20.8
429	Kalamazoo, MI (Inc. Place)	2-A	77,145	80,277	-3.9
430	Albany, GA (Inc. Place)	3-AA	76,939	78,122	-1.5
431	Greeley, CO (Inc. Place)	3-A	76,930	60,536	27.1
432	Silver Spring, MD (CDP)		76,540	76,046	0.6
433	Scranton, PA (Inc. Place)	2-A	76,415	81,805	-6.6
434	Canton, MI (CDP)		76,366	57,047	33.9
435	Canton, MI (MCD-Charter Township)		76,366	57,040	33.9
436	Beaverton, OR (Inc. Place)	3-S	76,129	53,310	42.8
437	Brick, NJ (MCD-Township)	4-S	76,119	66,473	14.5
438	Arlington Heights, IL (Inc. Place)	3-S	76,031	75,460	0.8
439	Wilmington, NC (Inc. Place)	3-AA	75,838	55,530	36.6
440	Baldwin Park, CA (Inc. Place)		75,837	69,330	9.4
441	Davie, FL (Inc. Place)		75,720	47,217	60.4
442	Redwood City, CA (Inc. Place)	3-S	75,402	66,072	14.1
443	Schaumburg, IL (Inc. Place)	3-SSm	75,386	68,586	9.9
444	Kendall, FL (CDP)		75,226	87,271	-13.8
445	Broken Arrow, OK (Inc. Place)	4-S	74,859	58,043	29.0
446	Danbury, CT (Inc. Place)	3-SS	74,848	65,585	14.1
447	Danbury, CT (MCD-Town)		74,848	65,585	14.1
448	Boca Raton, FL (Inc. Place)	3-B	74,764	61,492	21.6

Not classified as a Principal Business Center.
(d) Data not available.

Continued on next page

Cities and Other Places of 35,000 or More, *Continued*

City Rank 2000	City, with Place Type	Ranally City Rating	Population: Census 4/1/00	Population: Census 4/1/90	Population: 1990-2000 % Change
449	Las Cruces, NM (Inc. Place)	3-A	74,267	62,126	19.5
450	Evanston, IL (Inc. Place)	3-S	74,239	73,233	1.4
451	Evanston, IL (MCD-Township)		74,239	73,233	1.4
452	Saint Joseph, MO (Inc. Place)	3-AA	73,990	71,852	3.0
453	Livermore, CA (Inc. Place)	4-S	73,345	56,741	29.3
454	Longview, TX (Inc. Place)	3-AA	73,344	70,311	4.3
455	Waterford, MI (CDP)		73,150	66,692	9.7
456	Waterford, MI (MCD-Charter Township)		73,150	66,692	9.7
457	Pawtucket, RI (Inc. Place)	3-BB	72,958	72,644	0.4
458	Bellflower, CA (Inc. Place)	4-S	72,878	61,815	17.9
459	Miramar, FL (Inc. Place)		72,739	40,663	78.9
460	Wilmington, DE (Inc. Place)	2-BB	72,664	71,529	1.6
461	Napa, CA (Inc. Place)	3-S	72,585	61,842	17.4
462	Town 'n' Country, FL (CDP)		72,523	60,946	19.0
463	Alameda, CA (Inc. Place)	3-S	72,259	76,459	-5.5
464	New Rochelle, NY (Inc. Place)	3-S	72,182	67,265	7.3
465	Lawrence, MA (Inc. Place)	3-SS	72,043	70,207	2.6
466	Yakima, WA (Inc. Place)	3-AA	71,845	54,843	31.0
467	Lake Charles, LA (Inc. Place)	3-AA	71,757	70,580	1.7
468	Du Page, IL (MCD-Township)		71,745	55,444	29.4
469	New Britain, CT (Inc. Place)	3-C	71,538	75,491	-5.2
470	New Britain, CT (MCD-Town)		71,538	75,491	-5.2
471	Pike, IN (MCD-Township)		71,465	45,204	58.1
472	Melbourne, FL (Inc. Place)	2-A	71,382	59,646	19.7
473	Bethlehem, PA (Inc. Place)	3-B	71,329	71,428	-0.1
474	Gulfport, MS (Inc. Place)	3-B	71,127	40,775	74.4
475	Center, IN (MCD-Township)		71,120	74,656	-4.7
476	Longmont, CO (Inc. Place)	4-C	71,093	51,529	38.0
477	Highlands Ranch, CO (CDP)		70,931	10,181	596.7
478	Mountain View, CA (Inc. Place)	3-SS	70,708	67,460	4.8
479	Lees Summit, MO (Inc. Place)		70,700	46,418	52.3
480	Kenner, LA (Inc. Place)	4-S	70,517	72,033	-2.1
481	Hillsboro, OR (Inc. Place)	4-S	70,186	37,520	87.1
482	Appleton, WI (Inc. Place)	3-AA	70,087	65,695	6.7
483	Newport Beach, CA (Inc. Place)	3-SS	70,032	66,643	5.1
484	Cherry Hill, NJ (MCD-Township)	3-SS	69,965	69,319	0.9
485	Lynwood, CA (Inc. Place)	4-S	69,845	61,945	12.8
486	East Orange, NJ (Inc. Place)	4-Sr	69,824	73,552	-5.1
487	Deltona, FL (Inc. Place)		69,543	50,828	36.8
488	Largo, FL (Inc. Place)	4-S	69,371	65,674	5.6
489	Wyoming, MI (Inc. Place)	3-S	69,368	63,891	8.6
490	Bloomington, IN (Inc. Place)	3-A	69,291	60,633	14.3
491	Spring Hill, FL (CDP)		69,078	31,117	122.0
492	Asheville, NC (Inc. Place)	3-AA	68,889	61,855	11.4
493	Rochester Hills, MI (Inc. Place)		68,825	61,766	11.4
494	Murfreesboro, TN (Inc. Place)	3-C	68,816	44,922	53.2
495	Waterloo, IA (Inc. Place)	3-AA	68,747	66,467	3.4
496	Lorain, OH (Inc. Place)	3-S	68,652	71,245	-3.6
497	Clovis, CA (Inc. Place)	4-Sr	68,468	50,323	36.1
498	Upland, CA (Inc. Place)	3-S	68,393	63,374	7.9
499	Mount Vernon, NY (Inc. Place)	4-Sr	68,381	67,153	1.8
500	West Jordan, UT (Inc. Place)		68,336	42,892	59.3
501	Edmond, OK (Inc. Place)	4-S	68,315	52,315	30.6
502	St. Joseph, IN (MCD-Township)		68,276	61,167	11.6
503	College Station, TX (Inc. Place)	3-B	67,890	52,456	29.4
504	Passaic, NJ (Inc. Place)	4-S	67,861	58,041	16.9
505	Rich, IL (MCD-Township)		67,623	61,458	10.0
506	Champaign, IL (Inc. Place)	3-AA	67,518	63,502	6.3
507	Champaign City, IL (MCD-Township)		67,518	63,502	6.3
508	Tustin, CA (Inc. Place)	4-S	67,504	50,689	33.2
509	Knight, IN (MCD-Township)		67,491	65,522	3.0
510	Muncie, IN (Inc. Place)	3-AA	67,430	71,035	-5.1
511	Brooklyn Park, MN (Inc. Place)		67,388	56,381	19.5
512	Bellingham, WA (Inc. Place)	3-A	67,171	52,179	28.7
513	Chino, CA (Inc. Place)	4-Sr	67,168	59,682	12.5
514	Union City, NJ (Inc. Place)	3-S	67,088	58,012	15.6
515	Framingham, MA (CDP)		66,910	64,989	3.0
516	Framingham, MA (MCD-Town)	3-SS	66,910	64,989	3.0
517	Union City, CA (Inc. Place)		66,869	53,762	24.4
518	Chino Hills, CA (Inc. Place)		66,787	37,868	76.4
519	Jacksonville, NC (Inc. Place)	3-A	66,715	30,398	119.5
520	Baytown, TX (Inc. Place)	3-S	66,430	63,850	4.0
521	Sparks, NV (Inc. Place)	4-S	66,346	53,367	24.3
522	Pontiac, MI (Inc. Place)	3-SS	66,337	71,166	-6.8
523	Middletown, NJ (MCD-Township)		66,327	68,183	-2.7
524	Gastonia, NC (Inc. Place)	3-BB	66,277	54,732	21.1
525	Plymouth, MN (Inc. Place)		65,894	50,889	29.5
526	Taylor, MI (Inc. Place)	3-Sm	65,868	70,811	-7.0
527	Bryan, TX (Inc. Place)	3-A	65,660	55,002	19.4
528	Palatine, IL (Inc. Place)		65,479	38,894	68.4
529	Springfield, OH (Inc. Place)	3-BB	65,358	70,487	-7.3
530	Vernon, IL (MCD-Township)		65,355	51,141	27.8
531	Lynchburg, VA (Independent City)	3-AA	65,269	66,049	-1.2
532	Shelby, MI (MCD-Charter Township)		65,159	48,655	33.9
533	Shelby Township, MI (CDP)		65,159	48,655	33.9
534	West Bloomfield Township, MI (CDP)		64,862	54,843	18.3
535	West Bloomfield, MI (MCD-Charter Township)		64,860	54,843	18.3
536	Waukesha, WI (Inc. Place)	3-S	64,825	56,958	13.8
537	Bloomington, IL (Inc. Place)	3-AA	64,808	51,889	24.9
538	Bloomington City, IL (MCD-Township)		64,808	51,889	24.9
539	Clay, IN (MCD-Township)		64,709	43,007	50.5
540	Deerfield Beach, FL (Inc. Place)		64,583	46,325	39.4
541	Gloucester, NJ (MCD-Township)		64,350	53,797	19.6
542	Penn, IN (MCD-Township)		64,322	59,879	7.4
543	Walnut Creek, CA (Inc. Place)	3-SS	64,296	60,569	6.2
544	Portland, ME (Inc. Place)	2-A	64,249	64,358	-0.2
545	Daytona Beach, FL (Inc. Place)	2-A	64,112	61,921	3.5
546	Victorville, CA (Inc. Place)	4-C	64,029	40,674	57.4
547	Merced, CA (Inc. Place)	3-A	63,893	56,216	13.7
548	Wayne, IL (MCD-Township)		63,776	40,379	57.9
549	Suffolk, VA (Independent City)	4-S	63,677	52,141	22.1
550	Pleasanton, CA (Inc. Place)	4-S	63,654	50,553	25.9
551	Redlands, CA (Inc. Place)	3-S	63,591	60,394	5.3
552	West Hartford, CT (CDP)		63,589	60,110	5.8
553	West Hartford, CT (MCD-Town)	3-S	63,589	60,110	5.8
554	Eagan, MN (Inc. Place)		63,557	47,409	34.1
555	Pico Rivera, CA (Inc. Place)	4-S	63,428	59,177	7.2
556	Skokie, IL (Inc. Place)	3-SSm	63,348	59,432	6.6
557	Sugar Land, TX (Inc. Place)		63,328	24,549	158.0
558	Redondo Beach, CA (Inc. Place)	3-S	63,261	60,167	5.1
559	Medford, OR (Inc. Place)	3-AA	63,154	46,951	34.5
560	St. Clair Shores, MI (Inc. Place)	4-S	63,096	68,107	-7.4
561	Oshkosh, WI (Inc. Place)	3-B	62,916	55,006	14.4
562	Hoover, AL (Inc. Place)		62,742	39,788	57.7
563	Milpitas, CA (Inc. Place)		62,698	50,686	23.7
564	Hesperia, CA (Inc. Place)		62,582	50,418	24.1
565	Dundalk, MD (CDP)		62,306	65,800	-5.3
566	Iowa City, IA (Inc. Place)	3-A	62,220	59,738	4.2
567	Santa Fe, NM (Inc. Place)	3-A	62,203	55,859	11.4
568	Montebello, CA (Inc. Place)	4-S	62,150	59,564	4.3
569	Laguna Niguel, CA (Inc. Place)		61,891	44,400	39.4
570	Bayonne, NJ (Inc. Place)	4-S	61,842	61,444	0.6
571	Schenectady, NY (Inc. Place)	3-BB	61,821	65,566	-5.7
572	Saginaw, MI (Inc. Place)	2-A	61,799	69,512	-11.1
573	Tonawanda, NY (CDP)		61,729	65,284	-5.4
574	Eau Claire, WI (Inc. Place)	3-AA	61,704	56,856	8.5
575	Coon Rapids, MN (Inc. Place)	4-S	61,607	52,978	16.3
576	Huntington Park, CA (Inc. Place)	4-S	61,348	56,065	9.4
577	West Allis, WI (Inc. Place)	3-S	61,254	63,221	-3.1
578	Round Rock, TX (Inc. Place)		61,136	30,923	97.7
579	Greenwich, CT (MCD-Town)	3-S	61,101	58,441	4.6
580	Irvington, NJ (CDP)		60,695	59,774	1.5
581	Irvington, NJ (MCD-Township)	4-S	60,695	61,018	-0.5
582	Hamilton, OH (Inc. Place)	3-C	60,690	61,368	-1.1
583	Utica, NY (Inc. Place)	3-AA	60,651	68,637	-11.6
584	Victoria, TX (Inc. Place)	3-A	60,603	55,076	10.0
585	South San Francisco, CA (Inc. Place)	4-S	60,552	54,312	11.5
586	Greenville, NC (Inc. Place)	3-A	60,476	44,972	34.5
587	Old Bridge, NJ (MCD-Township)		60,456	56,475	7.0
588	North Little Rock, AR (Inc. Place)	3-S	60,433	61,741	-2.1
589	Boynton Beach, FL (Inc. Place)		60,389	46,194	30.7
590	Lakewood, NJ (MCD-Township)	4-Sr	60,352	45,048	34.0
591	Saint Charles, MO (Inc. Place)	3-S	60,321	54,555	10.6
592	Davis, CA (Inc. Place)		60,308	46,209	30.5
593	Burnsville, MN (Inc. Place)	3-Sm	60,220	51,288	17.4
594	Florence-Graham, CA (CDP-Census Area Only)		60,197	57,147	5.3
595	Colerain, OH (MCD-Township)		60,144	56,781	5.9
596	Bristol, CT (Inc. Place)	3-S	60,062	60,640	-1.0
597	Bristol, CT (MCD-Town)		60,062	60,640	-1.0
598	Royal Oak, MI (Inc. Place)	3-S	60,062	65,410	-8.2
599	Monterey Park, CA (Inc. Place)	4-S	60,051	60,738	-1.1
600	Anderson, IN (MCD-Township)		60,026	59,892	0.2
601	Delray Beach, FL (Inc. Place)	4-S	60,020	47,181	27.2
602	Elk Grove, CA (Inc. Place)		59,984	17,483	243.1
603	Chico, CA (Inc. Place)	3-A	59,954	40,079	49.6
604	North Miami, FL (Inc. Place)	4-Sr	59,880	49,998	19.8
605	Lower Merion, PA (MCD-Township)	3-S	59,850	58,003	3.2
606	Anderson, IN (Inc. Place)	3-A	59,734	59,459	0.5
607	Jackson, TN (Inc. Place)	3-A	59,643	48,949	21.8
608	Terre Haute, IN (Inc. Place)	3-AA	59,614	55,439	7.5
609	Rapid City, SD (Inc. Place)	3-A	59,607	54,523	9.3
610	Fountainbleau, FL (CDP)		59,549	(d)	(d)
611	Janesville, WI (Inc. Place)	3-A	59,498	52,133	14.1
612	Carol City, FL (CDP)		59,443	53,331	11.5
613	Warren, IL (MCD-Township)		59,424	34,785	70.8
614	Palm Harbor, FL (CDP)		59,248	50,256	17.9
615	Waltham, MA (Inc. Place)	3-S	59,226	57,878	2.3
616	St. Cloud, MN (Inc. Place)	3-A	59,107	48,812	21.1
617	La Habra, CA (Inc. Place)	4-S	58,974	51,266	15.0
618	Haverhill, MA (Inc. Place)	4-S	58,969	51,418	14.7
619	Yorba Linda, CA (Inc. Place)		58,918	52,422	12.4
620	Hemet, CA (Inc. Place)	3-C	58,812	36,094	62.9
621	Clay, NY (MCD-Town)		58,805	59,749	-1.6
622	Marietta, GA (Inc. Place)	3-S	58,748	44,129	33.1
623	Des Plaines, IL (Inc. Place)	3-S	58,720	53,223	10.3
624	El Toro, CA (Inc. Place)		58,707	56,065	4.7
625	Palo Alto, CA (Inc. Place)	3-SS	58,598	55,900	4.8
626	Layton, UT (Inc. Place)	4-S	58,474	41,784	39.9
627	Bensalem, PA (MCD-Township)	3-Sm	58,434	56,788	2.9
628	Decatur, IL (MCD-Township)		58,355	61,907	-5.7
629	Council Bluffs, IA (Inc. Place)	3-S	58,268	54,315	7.3
630	Dearborn Heights, MI (Inc. Place)	4-Sr	58,264	60,838	-4.2
631	Meriden, CT (Inc. Place)	3-B	58,244	59,479	-2.1
632	Meriden, CT (MCD-Town)		58,244	59,479	-2.1
633	Lakewood, WA (Inc. Place)		58,211	55,937	4.1
634	North Bergen, NJ (MCD-Township)	4-Sr	58,092	48,414	20.0
635	Fayetteville, AR (Inc. Place)	3-A	58,047	42,099	37.9
636	Encinitas, CA (Inc. Place)		58,014	55,386	4.7
637	Port Arthur, TX (Inc. Place)	3-B	57,755	58,724	-1.7
638	Gardena, CA (Inc. Place)	3-S	57,746	49,841	15.9
639	Burke, VA (CDP)		57,737	57,734	0.0
640	Dothan, AL (Inc. Place)	3-A	57,737	53,721	7.5
641	Temecula, CA (Inc. Place)		57,716	27,099	113.0
642	Wheaton-Glenmont, MD (CDP-Census Area Only)		57,694	53,720	7.4
643	Dubuque, IA (Inc. Place)	3-A	57,686	57,546	0.2
644	Lauderhill, FL (Inc. Place)	4-S	57,585	49,708	15.8
645	Harlingen, TX (Inc. Place)	3-B	57,564	48,735	18.1
646	Kettering, OH (Inc. Place)	3-S	57,502	60,569	-5.1
647	Taylorsville, UT (Inc. Place)		57,439	51,500	11.5
648	Fairfield, CT (MCD-Town)	4-S	57,340	53,418	7.3
649	Castro Valley, CA (CDP)		57,292	48,619	17.8
650	Galveston, TX (Inc. Place)	3-C	57,247	59,070	-3.1
651	Brookline, MA (CDP)		57,107	54,718	4.4
652	Brookline, MA (MCD-Town)	4-Sr	57,107	54,718	4.4
653	Camarillo, CA (Inc. Place)	4-Sr	57,077	52,303	9.1
654	Missoula, MT (Inc. Place)	3-A	57,053	42,918	32.9
655	Lodi, CA (Inc. Place)	4-C	56,999	51,874	9.9
656	Tracy, CA (Inc. Place)		56,929	33,558	69.6
657	Hamden, CT (MCD-Town)	4-S	56,913	52,434	8.5
658	Kendale Lakes, FL (CDP)		56,901	48,524	17.3
659	Pittsburg, CA (Inc. Place)	4-S	56,769	47,564	19.4
660	New Trier, IL (MCD-Township)		56,716	54,705	3.7
661	Jeffersonville, IN (MCD-Township)		56,695	53,449	6.1
662	Great Falls, MT (Inc. Place)	3-A	56,690	55,097	2.9
663	Lakewood, OH (Inc. Place)	4-Sr	56,646	59,718	-5.1
664	Hempstead, NY (Inc. Place)	3-S	56,554	49,453	14.4
665	Bossier City, LA (Inc. Place)	3-S	56,461	52,721	7.1
666	Reston, VA (CDP)		56,407	48,556	16.2
667	Ellicott City, MD (CDP)		56,397	41,396	36.2
668	Lafayette, IN (Inc. Place)	3-AA	56,397	43,758	28.9
669	Lancaster, PA (Inc. Place)	2-A	56,348	55,551	1.4
670	Malden, MA (Inc. Place)	4-S	56,340	53,884	4.6
671	Bolingbrook, IL (Inc. Place)		56,321	40,843	37.9
672	Union, NY (MCD-Town)		56,298	59,786	-5.8
673	Diamond Bar, CA (Inc. Place)		56,287	53,672	4.9
674	Vineland, NJ (Inc. Place)	3-C	56,271	54,780	2.7
675	Mount Prospect, IL (Inc. Place)	3-S	56,265	53,170	5.8
676	Hamburg, NY (MCD-Town)		56,259	53,735	4.7
677	Pensacola, FL (Inc. Place)	2-A	56,255	58,165	-3.3
678	Abington, PA (MCD-Township)	3-S	56,103	56,322	-0.4
679	San Rafael, CA (Inc. Place)	3-S	56,063	48,404	15.8
680	Greenville, SC (Inc. Place)	2-A	56,002	58,282	-3.9
681	Concord, NC (Inc. Place)	4-C	55,977	27,347	104.7
682	Taunton, MA (Inc. Place)	4-C	55,976	49,832	12.3
683	Dale City, VA (CDP)		55,971	47,170	18.7
684	Elyria, OH (Inc. Place)	3-S	55,953	56,746	-1.4
685	Rocky Mount, NC (Inc. Place)	3-A	55,893	48,997	14.1
686	Turlock, CA (Inc. Place)	4-C	55,810	42,198	32.3
687	Medford, MA (Inc. Place)	3-S	55,765	57,407	-2.9
688	Green, OH (MCD-Township)		55,660	52,687	5.6
689	The Woodlands, TX (CDP)		55,649	29,205	90.5
690	North Richland Hills, TX (Inc. Place)	4-S	55,635	45,895	21.2
691	Niagara Falls, NY (Inc. Place)	3-BB	55,593	61,840	-10.1
692	Tamarac, FL (Inc. Place)		55,588	44,822	24.0
693	Bismarck, ND (Inc. Place)	3-A	55,532	49,256	12.7
694	Bristol, PA (MCD-Township)		55,521	57,129	-2.8
695	Jonesboro, AR (Inc. Place)	3-A	55,515	46,535	19.3
696	Johnson City, TN (Inc. Place)	3-B	55,469	49,479	12.1
697	Germantown, MD (CDP)		55,419	41,145	34.7
698	Wheaton, IL (Inc. Place)		55,416	51,464	7.7
699	Concord, IN (MCD-Township)		55,377	49,126	12.7
700	Bethesda, MD (CDP)		55,277	62,936	-12.2
701	Paramount, CA (Inc. Place)		55,266	47,669	15.9
702	Oak Lawn, IL (Inc. Place)	3-S	55,245	56,182	-1.7
703	Goleta, CA (Inc. Place)		55,204	(d)	(d)
704	South Whittier, CA (CDP)		55,193	49,524	11.4
705	Pine Bluff, AR (Inc. Place)	3-A	55,085	57,140	-3.6
706	Rancho Cordova, CA (CDP)		55,060	48,731	13.0
707	Annandale, VA (CDP)		54,994	50,975	7.9
708	Fountain Valley, CA (Inc. Place)	3-S	54,978	53,691	2.4
709	San Marcos, CA (Inc. Place)		54,977	38,974	41.1
710	Avon, IL (MCD-Township)		54,957	35,989	52.7
711	Eden Prairie, MN (Inc. Place)		54,901	39,311	39.7
712	Union, OH (MCD-Township)		54,895	39,703	38.3
713	Tamiami, FL (CDP)		54,788	33,845	61.9
714	La Mesa, CA (Inc. Place)	3-S	54,749	52,931	3.4
715	Manchester, CT (MCD-Town)	3-S	54,740	51,618	6.0
716	Southampton, NY (MCD-Town)		54,712	44,976	21.6
717	Kennewick, WA (Inc. Place)	3-A	54,693	42,155	29.7
718	Chicopee, MA (Inc. Place)	4-S	54,653	56,632	-3.5
719	Santa Cruz, CA (Inc. Place)	3-C	54,593	49,040	11.3
720	Petaluma, CA (Inc. Place)	4-S	54,548	43,184	26.3
721	Temple, TX (Inc. Place)	3-A	54,514	46,109	18.2
722	Union, NJ (CDP)		54,405	50,024	8.8
723	Union, NJ (MCD-Township)	4-S	54,405	50,024	8.8
724	McKinney, TX (Inc. Place)		54,369	21,283	155.5
725	National City, CA (Inc. Place)	3-S	54,260	54,249	0.0
726	Apple Valley, CA (Inc. Place)		54,239	46,079	17.7
727	Midwest City, OK (Inc. Place)	3-S	54,088	52,267	3.5
728	Wayne, NJ (CDP)		54,069	47,025	15.0
729	Wayne, NJ (MCD-Township)	3-SSm	54,069	47,025	15.0
730	Owensboro, KY (Inc. Place)	3-A	54,067	53,549	1.0
731	Berwyn, IL (Inc. Place)	4-S	54,016	45,426	18.9
732	Berwyn, IL (MCD-Township)		54,016	45,426	18.9
733	Casas Adobes, AZ (CDP)		54,011	(d)	(d)
734	Weymouth, MA (CDP)		53,988	54,063	-0.1
735	Weymouth, MA (MCD-Town)	4-S	53,988	54,063	-0.1
736	Levittown, PA (CDP)	4-Sr	53,966	55,362	-2.5
737	Decatur, AL (Inc. Place)	3-A	53,929	48,778	10.6
738	Brentwood, NY (CDP)		53,917	45,218	19.2
739	Margate, FL (Inc. Place)		53,909	42,985	25.4
740	Catalina Foothills, AZ (CDP)		53,794	(d)	(d)
741	St. John, IN (MCD-Township)		53,701	41,782	28.5
742	Rosemead, CA (Inc. Place)	4-S	53,505	51,638	3.6
743	Charleston, WV (Inc. Place)	2-A	53,421	57,287	-6.7
744	Palos, IL (MCD-Township)		53,419	50,916	4.9
745	Battle Creek, MI (Inc. Place)	3-A	53,364	53,540	-0.3
746	Dundee, IL (MCD-Township)		53,207	39,070	36.2
747	Hacienda Heights, CA (CDP)		53,122	52,354	1.5
748	Monroe, LA (Inc. Place)	3-AA	53,107	54,909	-3.3
749	White Plains, NY (Inc. Place)	2-S	53,077	48,718	8.9
750	Levittown, NY (CDP)		53,067	53,286	-0.4
751	Arcadia, CA (Inc. Place)	3-Sm	53,054	48,290	9.9
752	Shoreline, WA (Inc. Place)		53,025	46,979	12.9
753	Cheyenne, WY (Inc. Place)	3-A	53,011	50,008	6.0
754	Washington, OH (MCD-Township)		52,991	46,609	13.7
755	Santee, CA (Inc. Place)		52,975	52,902	0.1
756	Missouri City, TX (Inc. Place)		52,913	36,176	46.3
757	Flagstaff, AZ (Inc. Place)	3-A	52,894	45,857	15.3
758	Springfield, OR (Inc. Place)	3-B	52,864	44,683	18.3
759	Frederick, MD (Inc. Place)	3-C	52,767	40,148	31.4
760	Euclid, OH (Inc. Place)	3-S	52,717	54,875	-3.9
761	Sarasota, FL (Inc. Place)	2-A	52,715	50,961	3.4
762	Gaithersburg, MD (Inc. Place)	3-S	52,613	39,542	33.1
763	Oak Park, IL (Inc. Place)	4-S	52,524	53,648	-2.1
764	Oak Park, IL (MCD-Township)		52,524	53,648	-2.1
765	Carson City, NV (Independent City)	4-C	52,457	40,443	29.7
766	West Haven, CT (Inc. Place)	4-S	52,360	54,021	-3.1
767	West Haven, CT (MCD-Town)		52,360	54,021	-3.1
768	Irondequoit, NY (CDP)		52,354	52,322	0.1
769	Irondequoit, NY (MCD-Town)		52,354	52,322	0.1
770	Milford, CT (MCD-Town)		52,305	49,938	4.7
771	Millcreek, PA (MCD-Township)	4-Sm	52,129	46,820	11.3
772	Bend, OR (Inc. Place)	3-A	52,029	20,447	154.5
773	Plain, OH (MCD-Township)		51,997	49,181	5.7
774	Harrison, IN (MCD-Township)		51,898	53,810	-3.6
775	Folsom, CA (Inc. Place)		51,884	29,802	74.1
776	Elkhart, IN (Inc. Place)	3-A	51,874	43,627	18.9
777	Nampa, ID (Inc. Place)	3-B	51,867	28,365	82.9
778	La Crosse, WI (Inc. Place)	3-AA	51,818	51,003	1.6
779	Towson, MD (CDP)		51,793	49,445	4.7
780	Rio Rancho, NM (Inc. Place)		51,765	32,505	59.3
781	Plymouth, MA (MCD-Town)		51,701	45,608	13.4
782	Redford, MI (CDP)		51,622	(d)	(d)
783	Redford, MI (MCD-Charter Township)		51,622	54,387	-5.1
784	Middletown, OH (Inc. Place)	3-C	51,605	46,022	12.1
785	Cerritos, CA (Inc. Place)	3-Sm	51,488	53,240	-3.3
786	Huntington, WV (Inc. Place)	2-A	51,475	54,844	-6.1
787	Pocatello, ID (Inc. Place)	3-A	51,466	46,080	11.7
788	Saint Peters, MO (Inc. Place)		51,381	45,779	12.2
789	Minnetonka, MN (Inc. Place)	3-Sm	51,301	48,370	6.1
790	Wabash, IN (MCD-Township)		51,261	49,348	3.9
791	Orland Park, IL (Inc. Place)	3-Sm	51,077	35,720	43.0
792	Franklin, NJ (MCD-Township)		50,903	42,780	19.0
793	Sheboygan, WI (Inc. Place)	3-A	50,792	49,676	2.2
794	Ames, IA (Inc. Place)	3-C	50,731	47,198	7.5
795	Idaho Falls, ID (Inc. Place)	3-A	50,730	43,929	15.5
796	Flower Mound, TX (Inc. Place)		50,702	15,527	226.5
797	Parsippany-Troy Hills, NJ (MCD-Township)	4-S	50,649	48,478	4.5
798	Biloxi, MS (Inc. Place)	3-AA	50,644	46,319	9.3
799	Loveland, CO (Inc. Place)	4-B	50,608	37,352	35.5
800	Milford, CT (Inc. Place)	3-S	50,594	48,168	5.0
801	Cupertino, CA (Inc. Place)	3-Sm	50,546	40,263	25.5
802	Florissant, MO (Inc. Place)	4-S	50,497	51,206	-1.4
803	Piscataway, NJ (MCD-Township)		50,482	(d)	(d)
804	Macomb, MI (MCD-Township)		50,478	22,714	122.2
805	Maple Grove, MN (Inc. Place)		50,365	38,736	30.0
806	Mentor, OH (Inc. Place)	3-Sm	50,278	47,358	6.2
807	Bowie, MD (Inc. Place)		50,269	37,589	33.7
808	Aspen Hill, MD (CDP)		50,228	45,494	10.4
809	Renton, WA (Inc. Place)	3-S	50,052	41,688	20.1
810	Stratford, CT (CDP)		49,976	49,389	1.2
811	Stratford, CT (MCD-Town)	4-S	49,976	49,389	1.2
812	Fairfield, IN (MCD-Township)		49,970	46,166	8.2
813	Cleveland Heights, OH (Inc. Place)	4-S	49,958	54,052	-7.6
814	San Clemente, CA (Inc. Place)		49,936	41,100	21.5
815	Rock Hill, SC (Inc. Place)	3-C	49,765	41,610	19.6
816	Carmichael, CA (CDP)		49,742	48,702	2.1
817	St. George, UT (Inc. Place)	4-A	49,663	28,502	74.2
818	Casper, WY (Inc. Place)	3-A	49,644	46,742	6.2
819	East Hartford, CT (CDP)		49,575	50,452	-1.7
820	East Hartford, CT (MCD-Town)	4-S	49,575	50,452	-1.7
821	Altoona, PA (Inc. Place)	3-AA	49,523	51,881	-4.5
822	Bradenton, FL (Inc. Place)	3-B	49,504	43,779	13.1
823	Hoffman Estates, IL (Inc. Place)		49,495	46,561	6.3
824	Glendora, CA (Inc. Place)	4-S	49,415	47,828	3.3
825	Cuyahoga Falls, OH (Inc. Place)	4-S	49,374	48,950	0.9
826	Mansfield, OH (Inc. Place)	3-AA	49,346	50,627	-2.5
827	Corvallis, OR (Inc. Place)	3-B	49,322	44,757	10.2
828	Grand Forks, ND (Inc. Place)	3-A	49,321	49,425	-0.2
829	Bowling Green, KY (Inc. Place)	3-A	49,296	40,641	21.3
830	Weston, FL (Inc. Place)		49,286	(d)	(d)
831	Manteca, CA (Inc. Place)		49,258	40,773	20.8
832	Ypsilanti, MI (MCD-Charter Township)		49,182	45,307	8.6
833	Troy, NY (Inc. Place)	3-C	49,170	54,269	-9.4
834	Woodland, CA (Inc. Place)	4-C	49,151	39,802	23.5
835	Indio, CA (Inc. Place)	3-C	49,116	36,793	33.5
836	Harrisburg, PA (Inc. Place)	2-AA	48,950	52,376	-6.5
837	Libertyville, IL (MCD-Township)		48,904	42,436	15.2
838	Howell, NJ (MCD-Township)		48,903	38,987	25.4
839	Warner Robins, GA (Inc. Place)	4-B	48,804	43,726	11.6
840	Downers Grove, IL (Inc. Place)	4-S	48,724	46,858	4.0
841	Chapel Hill, NC (Inc. Place)	3-C	48,715	38,719	25.8
842	East Providence, RI (Inc. Place)	4-S	48,688	50,380	-3.4
843	Centreville, VA (CDP)		48,661	26,585	83.0
844	New Brunswick, NJ (Inc. Place)	3-S	48,573	41,711	16.5
845	Rowland Heights, CA (CDP)		48,553	42,647	13.8
846	Haverford, PA (MCD-Township)		48,498	49,848	-2.7
847	New Albany, IN (MCD-Township)		48,476	44,958	7.8
848	Edinburg, TX (Inc. Place)	4-C	48,465	29,885	62.2
849	Danville, VA (Independent City)	3-A	48,411	53,056	-8.8
850	Tinley Park, IL (Inc. Place)		48,401	37,121	30.4
851	Fort Myers, FL (Inc. Place)	2-A	48,208	45,206	6.6
852	Peabody, MA (Inc. Place)	3-Sm	48,129	47,039	2.3
853	Roseville, MI (Inc. Place)	3-S	48,129	51,412	-6.4
854	Blue Springs, MO (Inc. Place)	4-S	48,080	40,153	19.7
855	Poway, CA (Inc. Place)		48,044	43,516	10.4
856	Shawnee, KS (Inc. Place)		47,996	37,993	26.3
857	Plainfield, NJ (Inc. Place)	4-S	47,829	46,567	2.7
858	Barnstable, MA (Inc. Place)		47,821	40,949	16.8
859	Kissimmee, FL (Inc. Place)	4-C	47,814	30,050	59.1
860	Orangetown, NY (MCD-Town)		47,711	46,742	2.1
861	Bloomfield, NJ (CDP)		47,683	45,061	5.8
862	Bloomfield, NJ (MCD-Township)	4-S	47,683	45,061	5.8
863	Colton, CA (Inc. Place)		47,662	40,213	18.5
864	Novato, CA (Inc. Place)		47,630	47,585	0.1
865	Center, IN (MCD-Township)		47,619	47,354	0.6
866	Mount Pleasant, SC (Inc. Place)		47,609	30,108	58.1
867	Edina, MN (Inc. Place)	3-SSm	47,425	46,070	2.9
868	Rockville, MD (Inc. Place)	3-SS	47,388	44,835	5.7
869	Novi, MI (Inc. Place)	3-Sm	47,386	32,998	43.6
870	Binghamton, NY (Inc. Place)	3-AA	47,380	53,008	-10.6
871	The Hammocks, FL (CDP)		47,379	(d)	(d)
872	Perth Amboy, NJ (Inc. Place)	4-S	47,303	41,967	12.7
873	Revere, MA (Inc. Place)		47,283	42,786	10.5
874	Wauwatosa, WI (Inc. Place)	3-S	47,271	49,366	-4.2
875	Rancho Santa Margarita, CA (Inc. Place)		47,214	11,390	314.5
876	Bedford, TX (Inc. Place)		47,152	43,762	7.7
877	Washington, NJ (MCD-Township)		47,114	41,960	12.3
878	Enid, OK (Inc. Place)	3-A	47,045	45,309	3.8
879	Covina, CA (Inc. Place)	3-S	46,837	43,207	8.4
880	Warren, OH (Inc. Place)	3-B	46,832	50,793	-7.8
881	Penn Hills, PA (CDP)		46,809	51,430	-9.0
882	Penn Hills, PA (MCD-Township)		46,809	51,430	-9.0
883	Chesterfield, MO (Inc. Place)		46,802	38,630	21.2
884	La Mirada, CA (Inc. Place)	4-S	46,783	40,452	15.7
885	East Brunswick, NJ (CDP)		46,756	43,548	7.4
886	East Brunswick, NJ (MCD-Township)	3-S	46,756	43,548	7.4
887	Pharr, TX (Inc. Place)	4-S	46,660	32,921	41.7
888	Mishawaka, IN (Inc. Place)	3-B	46,557	42,608	9.3
889	East Lansing, MI (Inc. Place)	4-S	46,525	50,677	-8.2
890	Placentia, CA (Inc. Place)		46,488	41,259	12.7
891	Woodbury, MN (Inc. Place)		46,463	20,075	131.4
892	Port Charlotte, FL (CDP)		46,451	41,535	11.8
893	West Des Moines, IA (Inc. Place)	4-Sm	46,403	31,702	46.4
894	Alexandria, LA (Inc. Place)	3-AA	46,342	49,188	-5.8
895	Newark, OH (Inc. Place)	3-C	46,279	44,389	4.3
896	Cypress, CA (Inc. Place)		46,229	42,655	8.4
897	O'Fallon, MO (Inc. Place)		46,169	18,698	146.9
898	Kokomo, IN (Inc. Place)	3-A	46,113	44,962	2.6
899	Perinton, NY (MCD-Town)		46,090	43,015	7.1
900	Euless, TX (Inc. Place)		46,005	38,149	20.6
901	Ocala, FL (Inc. Place)	3-AA	45,943	42,045	9.3
902	West Seneca, NY (CDP)		45,943	47,866	-4.0
903	West Seneca, NY (MCD-Town)		45,920	47,866	-4.1
904	Port Orange, FL (Inc. Place)		45,823	35,317	29.7
905	Springdale, AR (Inc. Place)	4-B	45,798	29,941	53.0
906	Pittsfield, MA (Inc. Place)	3-A	45,793	48,622	-5.8

Not classified as a Principal Business Center.
(d) Data not available.

Cities and Other Places of 35,000 or More, *Continued*

City Rank 2000	City, with Place Type	Ranally City Rating	Population: Census 4/1/00	Population: Census 4/1/90	Population: 1990-2000 % Change
907	West New York, NJ (Inc. Place)	4-S	45,768	38,125	20.0
908	Plainfield, IL (MCD-Township)		45,691	15,392	196.8
909	Salina, KS (Inc. Place)	3-A	45,679	42,303	8.0
910	Pinellas Park, FL (Inc. Place)	4-S	45,658	43,426	5.1
911	Normal, IL (MCD-Township)		45,637	40,449	12.8
912	Miami, OH (MCD-Township)		45,593	40,700	12.0
913	Apple Valley, MN (Inc. Place)		45,527	34,598	31.6
914	Joplin, MO (Inc. Place)	3-A	45,504	40,961	11.1
915	League City, TX (Inc. Place)		45,444	30,159	50.7
916	Mission, TX (Inc. Place)		45,408	28,653	58.5
917	Normal, IL (Inc. Place)	4-S	45,386	40,023	13.4
918	Roswell, NM (Inc. Place)	3-A	45,293	44,654	1.4
919	Redmond, WA (Inc. Place)	4-S	45,256	35,800	26.4
920	Kentwood, MI (Inc. Place)	4-Sm	45,255	37,826	19.6
921	Enfield, CT (MCD-Town)	4-S	45,212	45,532	-0.7
922	Winfield, IL (MCD-Township)		45,155	37,969	18.9
923	Kirkland, WA (Inc. Place)	4-S	45,054	40,052	12.5
924	Charlottesville, VA (Independent City)	3-AA	45,049	40,341	11.7
925	West Orange, NJ (CDP)		44,943	39,103	14.9
926	West Orange, NJ (MCD-Township)	4-S	44,943	39,103	14.9
927	Blaine, MN (Inc. Place)	4-Sm	44,942	38,975	15.3
928	Burlington, NC (Inc. Place)	3-A	44,917	39,498	13.7
929	Marion, OH (MCD-Township)		44,908	43,564	3.1
930	Kingsport, TN (Inc. Place)	3-AA	44,905	36,353	23.5
931	Portage, MI (Inc. Place)	3-Sm	44,897	41,042	9.4
932	Manhattan, KS (Inc. Place)	3-A	44,831	37,737	18.8
933	Potomac, MD (CDP)		44,822	45,634	-1.8
934	Hattiesburg, MS (Inc. Place)	3-A	44,779	41,882	6.9
935	San Ramon, CA (Inc. Place)		44,722	35,303	26.7
936	Azusa, CA (Inc. Place)		44,712	41,333	8.2
937	Highland, CA (Inc. Place)		44,605	34,439	29.5
938	Rowlett, TX (Inc. Place)		44,503	23,260	91.3
939	Lower Paxton, PA (MCD-Township)		44,424	39,162	13.4
940	Wilson, NC (Inc. Place)	3-B	44,405	36,930	20.2
941	Bellevue, NE (Inc. Place)	4-Sm	44,382	30,928	43.5
942	Wheatland, IL (MCD-Township)		44,349	10,746	312.7
943	Murrieta, CA (Inc. Place)		44,282	18,557	138.6
944	Watsonville, CA (Inc. Place)	4-C	44,265	31,099	42.3
945	Sylvania, OH (MCD-Township)		44,253	39,983	10.7
946	North Highlands, CA (CDP)		44,187	42,105	4.9
947	San Luis Obispo, CA (Inc. Place)	3-A	44,174	41,958	5.3
948	Middletown, PA (MCD-Township)		44,141	43,063	2.5
949	St. Louis Park, MN (Inc. Place)	4-S	44,126	43,787	0.8
950	Bell Gardens, CA (Inc. Place)		44,054	42,355	4.0
951	Tulare, CA (Inc. Place)		43,994	33,249	32.3
952	Portage, IN (MCD-Township)		43,956	40,929	7.4
953	Rye, NY (MCD-Town)		43,880	39,524	11.0
954	Strongsville, OH (Inc. Place)		43,858	35,308	24.2
955	Anderson, OH (MCD-Township)		43,857	39,939	9.8
956	Methuen, MA (Inc. Place)	3-Sm	43,789	39,990	9.5
957	Freeport, NY (Inc. Place)	4-Sr	43,783	39,894	9.7
958	Moline, IL (Inc. Place)	3-B	43,768	43,202	1.3
959	Wayne, IN (MCD-Township)		43,742	44,743	-2.2
960	Valdosta, GA (Inc. Place)	3-A	43,724	39,806	9.8
961	Coconut Creek, FL (Inc. Place)		43,566	27,485	58.5
962	Allen, TX (Inc. Place)		43,554	18,309	137.9
963	Southglenn, CO (CDP)		43,520	43,087	1.0
964	West Babylon, NY (CDP)		43,452	42,410	2.5
965	Shields, IL (MCD-Township)		43,382	43,414	-0.1
966	Covington, KY (Inc. Place)	4-S	43,370	43,264	0.2
967	Tuckahoe, VA (CDP)		43,242	42,629	1.4
968	Woonsocket, RI (Inc. Place)	3-S	43,224	43,877	-1.5
969	Mount Pleasant, NY (MCD-Town)		43,221	40,590	6.5
970	Madera, CA (Inc. Place)		43,207	29,281	47.6
971	Conway, AR (Inc. Place)	4-C	43,167	26,481	63.0
972	Middletown, CT (Inc. Place)	3-S	43,167	42,762	0.9
973	Middletown, CT (MCD-Town)		43,167	42,762	0.9
974	Lakeville, MN (Inc. Place)		43,128	24,854	73.5
975	Wilkes Barre, PA (Inc. Place)	3-BB	43,123	47,523	-9.3
976	Wallingford, CT (MCD-Town)	4-S	43,026	40,822	5.4
977	Bloomfield, MI (MCD-Township)		43,023	42,137	2.1
978	Bloomfield Township, MI (CDP)		43,021	42,137	2.1
979	Auburn, AL (Inc. Place)	3-B	42,987	33,830	27.1
980	Bridgewater, NJ (MCD-Township)	4-S	42,940	32,509	32.1
981	Grand Island, NE (Inc. Place)	3-A	42,940	39,386	9.0
982	Buffalo Grove, IL (Inc. Place)		42,909	36,427	17.8
983	Jackson, NJ (MCD-Township)		42,816	33,233	28.8
984	Palm Springs, CA (Inc. Place)	3-C	42,807	40,181	6.5
985	Poughkeepsie, NY (MCD-Town)		42,777	40,143	6.6
986	Elmhurst, IL (Inc. Place)	4-Sr	42,762	42,029	1.7
987	Hackensack, NJ (Inc. Place)	3-SS	42,677	37,049	15.2
988	Logan, UT (Inc. Place)	4-A	42,670	32,762	30.2
989	Cathedral City, CA (Inc. Place)		42,647	30,085	41.8
990	Altadena, CA (CDP)		42,610	42,658	-0.1
991	Boardman, OH (MCD-Township)		42,518	41,796	1.7
992	Olympia, WA (Inc. Place)	3-A	42,514	33,840	25.6
993	Newark, CA (Inc. Place)		42,471	37,861	12.2
994	Arlington, MA (CDP)		42,389	44,630	-5.0
995	Arlington, MA (MCD-Town)		42,389	44,630	-5.0
996	Union, OH (MCD-Township)		42,332	33,368	26.9
997	Lombard, IL (Inc. Place)	3-Sm	42,322	39,408	7.4
998	Evesham, NJ (MCD-Township)		42,275	35,309	19.7
999	Coral Gables, FL (Inc. Place)	3-S	42,249	40,091	5.4
1000	Rohnert Park, CA (Inc. Place)		42,236	36,326	16.3
1001	Fond du Lac, WI (Inc. Place)	3-A	42,203	37,757	11.8
1002	DeKalb, IL (MCD-Township)		42,189	38,710	9.0
1003	Fairfield, OH (Inc. Place)	4-S	42,097	39,729	6.0
1004	Attleboro, MA (Inc. Place)	3-S	42,068	38,383	9.6
1005	Grapevine, TX (Inc. Place)		42,059	29,202	44.0
1006	St. Charles, IL (MCD-Township)		42,051	33,112	27.0
1007	Lockport, IL (MCD-Township)		42,048	32,336	30.0
1008	Grand Junction, CO (Inc. Place)	3-A	41,986	29,255	43.5
1009	Lake Havasu City, AZ (Inc. Place)		41,938	24,363	72.1
1010	Glenview, IL (Inc. Place)	4-Sr	41,847	37,052	12.9
1011	Franklin, TN (Inc. Place)		41,842	20,098	108.2
1012	Pine Hills, FL (CDP)		41,764	35,322	18.2
1013	Beavercreek, OH (MCD-Township)		41,745	35,536	17.5
1014	Aloha, OR (CDP)		41,741	34,284	21.8
1015	McHenry, IL (MCD-Township)		41,740	37,034	12.7
1016	Danville, CA (Inc. Place)		41,715	31,306	33.2
1017	Hanford, CA (Inc. Place)	4-B	41,686	30,897	34.9
1018	Midland, MI (Inc. Place)	3-C	41,685	38,053	9.5
1019	Georgetown, MI (MCD-Charter Township)		41,658	32,672	27.5
1020	Greenville, MS (Inc. Place)	3-A	41,633	45,226	-7.9
1021	Texas City, TX (Inc. Place)	3-C	41,521	40,822	1.7
1022	Gilroy, CA (Inc. Place)		41,464	31,487	31.7
1023	Belleville, IL (Inc. Place)	3-S	41,410	42,785	-3.2
1024	Belleville, IL (MCD-Township)		41,410	42,785	-3.2
1025	Leominster, MA (Inc. Place)	3-B	41,303	38,145	8.3
1026	Bountiful, UT (Inc. Place)	4-S	41,301	36,147	14.3
1027	Frankfort, IL (MCD-Township)		41,292	25,755	60.3
1028	Hicksville, NY (CDP)		41,260	40,174	2.7
1029	Tigard, OR (Inc. Place)		41,223	29,344	40.5
1030	Yucaipa, CA (Inc. Place)		41,207	32,824	25.5
1031	Altamonte Springs, FL (Inc. Place)	3-Sm	41,200	34,879	18.1
1032	Columbus, IN (MCD-Township)		41,194	37,466	10.0
1033	Palm Desert, CA (Inc. Place)		41,155	23,252	77.0
1034	Rancho Palos Verdes, CA (Inc. Place)		41,145	41,659	-1.2
1035	Moore, OK (Inc. Place)		41,138	40,318	2.0
1036	Lompoc, CA (Inc. Place)	4-C	41,103	37,649	9.2
1037	La Puente, CA (Inc. Place)		41,063	36,955	11.1
1038	Chantilly, VA (CDP)		41,041	29,337	39.9
1039	Bloomington, IN (MCD-Township)		41,032	42,156	-2.7
1040	Smyrna, GA (Inc. Place)	3-S	40,999	30,981	32.3
1041	York, PA (Inc. Place)	3-AA	40,862	42,192	-3.2
1042	Albany, OR (Inc. Place)	3-B	40,852	29,540	38.3
1043	Hutchinson, KS (Inc. Place)	3-A	40,787	39,308	3.8
1044	North Miami Beach, FL (Inc. Place)	3-S	40,786	35,359	15.3
1045	Hilo, HI (CDP)	3-A	40,759	37,808	7.8
1046	Hempfield, PA (MCD-Township)		40,721	42,609	-4.4
1047	Concord, NH (Inc. Place)	3-B	40,687	36,006	13.0
1048	Titusville, FL (Inc. Place)	4-B	40,670	39,394	3.2
1049	Hendersonville, TN (Inc. Place)		40,620	32,188	26.2
1050	Bartlett, TN (Inc. Place)		40,543	26,989	50.2
1051	Atlantic City, NJ (Inc. Place)	3-AA	40,517	37,986	6.7
1052	Kearny, NJ (Inc. Place)	4-S	40,513	34,874	16.2
1053	Perry, IN (MCD-Township)		40,508	31,985	26.6
1054	Harrisonburg, VA (Independent City)	3-A	40,468	30,707	31.8
1055	Carol Stream, IL (Inc. Place)		40,438	31,759	27.3
1056	Salem, MA (Inc. Place)	3-S	40,407	38,091	6.1
1057	Sayreville, NJ (Inc. Place)		40,377	34,986	15.4
1058	Quincy, IL (Inc. Place)	3-A	40,366	39,682	1.7
1059	Quincy, IL (MCD-Township)		40,366	39,682	1.7
1060	Littleton, CO (Inc. Place)	4-S	40,340	33,685	19.8
1061	Auburn, WA (Inc. Place)	4-S	40,314	33,102	21.8
1062	Lenexa, KS (Inc. Place)	4-Sr	40,238	34,034	18.2
1063	Bath, OH (MCD-Township)		40,231	38,277	5.1
1064	Mount Laurel, NJ (MCD-Township)		40,221	30,270	32.9
1065	North Fort Myers, FL (CDP)		40,214	30,027	33.9
1066	Aliso Viejo, CA (Inc. Place)		40,166	7,612	427.7
1067	San Bruno, CA (Inc. Place)	4-Sm	40,165	38,961	3.1
1068	Muskegon, MI (Inc. Place)	3-AA	40,105	40,283	-0.4
1069	Lima, OH (Inc. Place)	3-AA	40,081	45,549	-12.0
1070	Westfield, MA (Inc. Place)	4-S	40,072	38,372	4.4
1071	Lincoln Park, MI (Inc. Place)	4-S	40,008	41,832	-4.4
1072	Berkeley, NJ (MCD-Township)		39,991	37,319	7.2
1073	Meridian, MS (Inc. Place)	3-A	39,968	41,036	-2.6
1074	Groton, CT (MCD-Town)		39,907	45,144	-11.6
1075	Pleasant, IN (MCD-Township)		39,901	28,094	42.0
1076	Beverly, MA (Inc. Place)	4-S	39,862	38,195	4.4
1077	Holyoke, MA (Inc. Place)	3-B	39,838	43,704	-8.8
1078	Catonsville, MD (CDP)		39,820	35,233	13.0
1079	San Gabriel, CA (Inc. Place)	4-S	39,804	37,120	7.2
1080	Southington, CT (MCD-Town)	4-S	39,728	38,518	3.1
1081	Bel Air South, MD (CDP-Census Area Only)		39,711	26,421	50.3
1082	Ela, IL (MCD-Township)		39,688	32,433	22.4
1083	Rock Island, IL (Inc. Place)	3-C	39,684	40,552	-2.1
1084	Spartanburg, SC (Inc. Place)	3-BB	39,673	43,467	-8.7
1085	Saginaw, MI (MCD-Charter Township)		39,657	37,684	5.2
1086	Sumter, SC (Inc. Place)	3-A	39,643	40,977	-3.3
1087	Hobart, IN (MCD-Township)		39,636	38,942	1.8
1088	Jefferson City, MO (Inc. Place)	3-A	39,636	35,481	11.7
1089	Porterville, CA (Inc. Place)	4-B	39,615	29,563	34.0
1090	East Point, GA (Inc. Place)	4-Sr	39,595	34,402	15.1
1091	Blacksburg, VA (Inc. Place)		39,573	34,590	14.4
1092	Edmonds, WA (Inc. Place)		39,515	30,744	28.5
1093	Linden, NJ (Inc. Place)	4-S	39,394	36,701	7.3
1094	Northampton, PA (MCD-Township)		39,384	35,406	11.2
1095	Jupiter, FL (Inc. Place)		39,328	24,907	57.9
1096	Teaneck, NJ (CDP)		39,260	37,825	3.8
1097	Teaneck, NJ (MCD-Township)	4-Sr	39,260	6,233	529.9
1098	Clay, IN (MCD-Township)		39,145	31,033	26.1
1099	Richmond, IN (Inc. Place)	3-A	39,124	38,705	1.1
1100	Meridian, MI (MCD-Charter Township)		39,116	35,644	9.7
1101	Fitchburg, MA (Inc. Place)	3-B	39,102	41,194	-5.1
1102	Essex, MD (CDP)		39,078	40,872	-4.4
1103	Calumet City, IL (Inc. Place)	3-Sm	39,071	37,840	3.3
1104	Stillwater, OK (Inc. Place)	4-A	39,065	36,676	6.5
1105	South Valley, NM (CDP)		39,060	35,701	9.4
1106	Columbus, IN (Inc. Place)	3-A	39,059	31,802	22.8
1107	Goldsboro, NC (Inc. Place)	3-A	39,043	40,709	-4.1
1108	Henrietta, NY (MCD-Town)		39,028	36,376	7.3
1109	Lancaster, NY (MCD-Town)		39,019	32,181	21.2
1110	DeKalb, IL (Inc. Place)	4-C	39,018	34,925	11.7
1111	Haltom City, TX (Inc. Place)		39,018	32,856	18.8
1112	Billerica, MA (MCD-Town)		38,981	37,609	3.6
1113	Gadsden, AL (Inc. Place)	3-A	38,978	42,523	-8.3
1114	Montclair, NJ (CDP)		38,977	37,729	3.3
1115	Montclair, NJ (MCD-Township)	4-S	38,977	37,729	3.3
1116	Findlay, OH (Inc. Place)	3-A	38,967	35,703	9.1
1117	McLean, VA (CDP)		38,929	38,163	2.0
1118	Manchester, NJ (MCD-Township)		38,928	35,976	8.2
1119	Glen Burnie, MD (CDP)		38,922	37,305	4.3
1120	Lawrence, IN (Inc. Place)		38,915	26,849	44.9
1121	Burlington, VT (Inc. Place)	3-AA	38,889	39,127	-0.6
1122	Rogers, AR (Inc. Place)	4-B	38,829	24,692	57.3
1123	Delano, CA (Inc. Place)		38,824	22,762	70.6
1124	Culver City, CA (Inc. Place)	3-S	38,816	38,793	0.1
1125	Richland, WA (Inc. Place)	3-B	38,708	32,315	19.8
1126	Ross, IN (MCD-Township)		38,685	34,683	11.5
1127	Stickney, IL (MCD-Township)		38,673	37,297	3.7
1128	Brookfield, WI (Inc. Place)	3-Sm	38,649	35,184	9.8
1129	North Bethesda, MD (CDP)		38,610	29,656	30.2
1130	North Atlanta, GA (CDP)		38,579	27,812	38.7
1131	Hoboken, NJ (Inc. Place)	4-S	38,577	33,397	15.5
1132	Cortlandt, NY (MCD-Town)		38,467	37,357	3.0
1133	Wausau, WI (Inc. Place)	3-A	38,426	37,060	3.7
1134	State College, PA (Inc. Place)	3-A	38,420	38,923	-1.3
1135	Pacifica, CA (Inc. Place)		38,390	37,670	1.9
1136	Muskogee, OK (Inc. Place)	3-A	38,310	37,708	1.6
1137	Sun City, AZ (CDP)		38,309	38,126	0.5
1138	Sanford, FL (Inc. Place)	4-S	38,291	32,387	18.2
1139	Hanover Park, IL (Inc. Place)		38,278	32,918	16.3
1140	New Berlin, WI (Inc. Place)		38,220	33,592	13.8
1141	Wellington, FL (Inc. Place)		38,216	20,670	84.9
1142	Huber Heights, OH (Inc. Place)		38,212	38,696	-1.3
1143	Center, IN (MCD-Township)		38,186	32,603	17.1
1144	Campbell, CA (Inc. Place)	4-S	38,138	36,048	5.8
1145	Shelton, CT (Inc. Place)		38,101	35,418	7.6
1146	Shelton, CT (MCD-Town)		38,101	35,418	7.6
1147	Montgomery Village, MD (CDP)		38,051	32,315	17.8
1148	Everett, MA (Inc. Place)		38,037	35,701	6.5
1149	Kendall West, FL (CDP-Census Area Only)		38,034	(d)	(d)
1150	Austintown, OH (MCD-Township)		38,001	36,740	3.4
1151	Crystal Lake, IL (Inc. Place)	4-S	38,000	24,512	55.0
1152	Beavercreek, OH (Inc. Place)		37,984	33,626	13.0
1153	Webster, NY (MCD-Town)		37,926	31,639	19.9
1154	Farmington, NM (Inc. Place)	3-A	37,844	33,997	11.3
1155	El Centro, CA (Inc. Place)	3-A	37,835	31,384	20.6
1156	Fishers, IN (Inc. Place)		37,835	7,508	403.9
1157	Park Ridge, IL (Inc. Place)	4-S	37,775	36,175	4.4
1158	Sierra Vista, AZ (Inc. Place)	4-A	37,775	32,983	14.5
1159	Jackson, OH (MCD-Township)		37,744	32,071	17.7
1160	South Brunswick, NJ (MCD-Township)		37,734	25,792	46.3
1161	Carmel, IN (Inc. Place)		37,733	25,380	48.7
1162	Desoto, TX (Inc. Place)		37,646	30,544	23.3
1163	Pearland, TX (Inc. Place)		37,640	18,927	98.9
1164	New Albany, IN (Inc. Place)	4-S	37,603	36,322	3.5
1165	Springfield, OH (MCD-Township)		37,587	38,509	-2.4
1166	Fort Pierce, FL (Inc. Place)	3-A	37,516	36,830	1.9
1167	East Meadow, NY (CDP)		37,461	36,909	1.5
1168	University City, MO (Inc. Place)		37,428	40,087	-6.6
1169	Chesterfield, MI (MCD-Charter Township)		37,405	25,905	44.4
1170	Stanton, CA (Inc. Place)		37,403	30,491	22.7
1171	Germantown, TN (Inc. Place)		37,348	32,893	13.5
1172	Bremerton, WA (Inc. Place)	3-A	37,259	38,142	-2.3
1173	Woburn, MA (Inc. Place)	3-S	37,258	35,943	3.7
1174	Hickory, NC (Inc. Place)	3-A	37,222	28,301	31.5
1175	Boardman, OH (CDP)		37,215	38,596	-3.6
1176	Cleveland, TN (Inc. Place)	3-A	37,192	30,354	22.5
1177	Monrovia, CA (Inc. Place)	4-S	36,929	35,761	3.3
1178	Kannapolis, NC (Inc. Place)	3-C	36,910	29,709	24.2
1179	Cheltenham, PA (MCD-Township)	4-S	36,875	34,923	5.6
1180	Chester, PA (Inc. Place)	4-Sr	36,854	41,856	-12.0
1181	Bay City, MI (Inc. Place)	3-B	36,817	38,936	-5.4
1182	Conroe, TX (Inc. Place)	3-S	36,811	27,610	33.3
1183	Yuba City, CA (Inc. Place)	3-A	36,758	27,437	34.0
1184	Bartlett, IL (Inc. Place)		36,706	19,373	89.5
1185	Hagerstown, MD (Inc. Place)	3-A	36,687	35,445	3.5
1186	Bell, CA (Inc. Place)		36,664	34,365	6.7
1187	Hillsborough, NJ (MCD-Township)		36,634	28,808	27.2
1188	Miami, OH (MCD-Township)		36,632	28,199	29.9
1189	South Moline, IL (MCD-Township)		36,586	36,781	-0.5
1190	Minot, ND (Inc. Place)	3-A	36,567	34,544	5.9
1191	Ossining, NY (MCD-Town)		36,534	34,124	7.1
1192	Kailua, HI (CDP)	4-S	36,513	36,818	-0.8
1193	New Braunfels, TX (Inc. Place)		36,494	27,334	33.5
1194	Parkway-South Sacramento, CA (CDP-Census Area Only)		36,468	31,903	14.3
1195	Panama City, FL (Inc. Place)	3-A	36,417	34,378	5.9
1196	Streamwood, IL (Inc. Place)		36,407	30,987	17.5
1197	Marlboro, NJ (MCD-Township)		36,398	27,974	30.1
1198	Cunningham, IL (MCD-Township)		36,395	36,344	0.1
1199	Urbana, IL (Inc. Place)	4-B	36,395	36,344	0.1
1200	Spring, TX (CDP)		36,385	33,111	9.9
1201	Valley Stream, NY (Inc. Place)	4-S	36,368	33,946	7.1
1202	Commack, NY (CDP)		36,367	36,124	0.7
1203	Rocklin, CA (Inc. Place)		36,330	19,033	90.9
1204	Yorktown, NY (MCD-Town)		36,318	33,467	8.5
1205	Jackson, MI (Inc. Place)	3-AA	36,316	37,446	-3.0
1206	Country Club, FL (CDP)		36,310	(d)	(d)
1207	Ormond Beach, FL (Inc. Place)		36,301	29,721	22.1
1208	North Brunswick, NJ (CDP)		36,287	31,287	16.0
1209	North Brunswick, NJ (MCD-Township)		36,287	31,287	16.0
1210	Hurst, TX (Inc. Place)	3-Sm	36,273	33,574	8.0
1211	Florence, AL (Inc. Place)	3-AA	36,264	36,426	-0.4
1212	Marlborough, MA (Inc. Place)	4-S	36,255	31,813	14.0
1213	Perris, CA (Inc. Place)		36,189	21,460	68.6
1214	Harlem, IL (MCD-Township)		36,171	28,453	27.1
1215	Marrero, LA (CDP)		36,165	36,671	-1.4
1216	Cedar Falls, IA (Inc. Place)	4-B	36,145	34,298	5.4
1217	Norwich, CT (Inc. Place)	4-B	36,117	37,391	-3.4
1218	Norwich, CT (MCD-Town)		36,117	37,391	-3.4
1219	Merritt Island, FL (CDP)		36,090	32,886	9.7
1220	Duncanville, TX (Inc. Place)	4-Sr	36,081	35,748	0.9
1221	Woodlawn, MD (CDP)		36,079	32,907	9.6
1222	Lakewood, NJ (CDP)		36,065	26,095	38.2
1223	Greenwood, IN (Inc. Place)	4-Sm	36,037	26,265	37.2
1224	Coppell, TX (Inc. Place)		35,958	16,881	113.0
1225	Belleville, NJ (CDP)		35,928	34,213	5.0
1226	Belleville, NJ (MCD-Township)	4-Sr	35,928	34,213	5.0
1227	North Chicago, IL (Inc. Place)		35,918	34,978	2.7
1228	Addison, IL (Inc. Place)	4-S	35,914	32,058	12.0
1229	Avondale, AZ (Inc. Place)		35,883	16,169	121.9
1230	Martinez, CA (Inc. Place)		35,866	31,808	12.8
1231	Annapolis, MD (Inc. Place)	3-C	35,838	33,187	8.0
1232	Mifflin, OH (MCD-Township)		35,787	28,449	25.8
1233	Beloit, WI (Inc. Place)	3-B	35,775	35,573	0.6
1234	Atascocita, TX (CDP)		35,757	(d)	(d)
1235	Hot Springs, AR (Inc. Place)	3-A	35,750	32,462	10.1
1236	Pennsauken, NJ (CDP)		35,737	34,738	2.9
1237	Pennsauken, NJ (MCD-Township)	4-S	35,737	34,738	2.9
1238	West Hollywood, CA (Inc. Place)		35,716	36,118	-1.1
1239	Ewing, NJ (MCD-Township)		35,707	34,185	4.5
1240	Ewing, NJ (CDP)		35,707	34,185	4.5
1241	Dunedin, FL (Inc. Place)		35,691	34,012	4.9
1242	Lewiston, ME (Inc. Place)	3-A	35,690	39,757	-10.2
1243	Brighton, NY (MCD-Town)		35,588	34,455	3.3
1244	Brighton, NY (CDP)		35,584	34,455	3.3
1245	Alamogordo, NM (Inc. Place)	4-C	35,582	27,596	28.9
1246	White River, IN (MCD-Township)		35,539	28,232	25.9
1247	Greenfield, WI (Inc. Place)	4-S	35,476	33,403	6.2
1248	Long Beach, NY (Inc. Place)		35,462	33,510	5.8
1249	Fort Lee, NJ (Inc. Place)		35,461	31,997	10.8
1250	Leavenworth, KS (Inc. Place)	4-C	35,420	38,495	-8.0
1251	Brea, CA (Inc. Place)	3-Sm	35,410	32,873	7.7
1252	Oxon Hill-Glassmanor, MD (CDP)		35,355	35,794	-1.2
1253	Cape Girardeau, MO (Inc. Place)	3-A	35,349	34,438	2.6
1254	Lancaster, OH (Inc. Place)	3-C	35,335	34,507	2.4
1255	Marion, OH (Inc. Place)	3-A	35,318	34,075	3.6
1256	Westerville, OH (Inc. Place)		35,318	30,269	16.7
1257	Seattle Hill-Silver Firs, WA (CDP-Census Area Only)		35,311	(d)	(d)
1258	Oakville, MO (CDP)		35,309	31,750	11.2
1259	Lake Oswego, OR (Inc. Place)		35,278	30,576	15.4
1260	Torrington, CT (MCD-Town)		35,202	33,687	4.5
1261	Torrington, CT (Inc. Place)	4-C	35,202	33,687	4.5
1262	Manassas, VA (Independent City)	4-S	35,135	27,957	25.7
1263	Lake Worth, FL (Inc. Place)	4-S	35,133	28,564	23.0
1264	Dana Point, CA (Inc. Place)		35,110	31,896	10.1
1265	Nunda, IL (MCD-Township)		35,104	24,759	41.8
1266	Sherman, TX (Inc. Place)	3-A	35,082	31,601	11.0
1267	Chelsea, MA (Inc. Place)	4-S	35,080	28,710	22.2
1268	Huntsville, TX (Inc. Place)	4-C	35,078	27,925	25.6
1269	Severn, MD (CDP)		35,076	24,499	43.2
1270	Palm Beach Gardens, FL (Inc. Place)		35,058	22,990	52.5
1271	Holland, MI (Inc. Place)	3-C	35,048	30,745	14.0

Not classified as a Principal Business Center.
(d) Data not available.

U.S. Colleges and Universities: Enrollment

NOTE: This list includes accredited four year colleges and universities with 600 or more students. The colleges and universitites are arranged in alphabetical order, by state. The city or town in which the college or university is located, or is associated with, appears in italic type. The student enrollment for each school is the last item in each entry. These figures are based primarily on Fall, 2005 enrollment.

Alabama

- Alabama Agricultural and Mechanical University, *Normal* ... 6,323
- Alabama State University, *Montgomery* ... 5,653
- American College of Computer & Information Sciences, *Birmingham* ... 1,272
- Athens State University, *Athens* ... 2,575
- Auburn University, *Auburn University* ... 22,928
- Auburn University at Montgomery, *Montgomery* ... 5,123
- Columbia Southern University, *Orange Beach* ... 10,100
- Concordia College, *Selma* ... 902
- Faulkner University, *Montgomery* ... 2,641
- Herzing College, *Birmingham* ... 936
- Huntingdon College, *Montgomery* ... 731
- Jacksonville State University, *Jacksonville* ... 8,930
- Miles College, *Birmingham* ... 1,715
- Oakwood College, *Huntsville* ... 1,753
- Samford University, *Birmingham* ... 4,416
- Southern Christian University, *Montgomery* ... 706
- Spring Hill College, *Mobile* ... 1,427
- Stillman College, *Tuscaloosa* ... 1,200
- Troy University, *Troy* ... 27,149
- Tuskegee University, *Tuskegee* ... 2,869
- University of Alabama at Birmingham, *Birmingham* ... 16,693
- University of Alabama in Huntsville, *Huntsville* ... 7,036
- University of Alabama, The, *Tuscaloosa* ... 20,929
- University of Mobile, *Mobile* ... 1,827
- University of Montevallo, *Montevallo* ... 3,061
- University of North Alabama, *Florence* ... 5,971
- University of South Alabama, *Mobile* ... 13,538
- University of West Alabama, The, *Livingston* ... 2,667
- Virginia College, *Birmingham* ... 3,921
- Virginia College, *Huntsville* ... 725

Alaska

- Alaska Pacific University, *Anchorage* ... 805
- Charter College, *Anchorage* ... 900
- University of Alaska Anchorage, *Anchorage* ... 19,753
- University of Alaska Fairbanks, *Fairbanks* ... 9,683
- University of Alaska Southeast, *Juneau* ... 4,309

Arizona

- Arizona State University at the Polytechnic Campus, *Mesa* ... 3,983
- Arizona State University Main, *Tempe* ... 49,171
- Arizona State University West, *Phoenix* ... 7,348
- Art Institute of Phoenix, The, *Phoenix* ... 1,302
- Collins College, *Tempe* ... 2,078
- DeVry University, *Phoenix* ... 1,700
- Embry-Riddle Aeronautical University - Prescott Campus, *Prescott* ... 1,668
- Everest College, *Phoenix* ... 630
- Grand Canyon University, *Phoenix* ... 2,887
- High-Tech Institute, *Phoenix* ... 1,200
- International Institute of the Americas, *Glendale* ... 1,451
- Midwestern University, *Glendale* ... 1,284
- Northcentral University, *Prescott* ... 2,100
- Northern Arizona University, *Flagstaff* ... 19,147
- Prescott College, *Prescott* ... 1,002
- Scottsdale Culinary Institute, *Scottsdale* ... 730
- Thunderbird, The Garvin School of International Management, *Glendale* ... 1,245
- University of Advancing Technology, *Tempe* ... 1,383
- University of Arizona, *Tucson* ... 36,932
- University of Phoenix, *Phoenix* ... 232,808
- Western International University, *Phoenix* ... 4,748

Arkansas

- Arkansas State University, *Jonesboro* ... 10,508
- Arkansas Tech University, *Russellville* ... 6,483
- Harding University Main Campus, *Searcy* ... 5,602
- Henderson State University, *Arkadelphia* ... 3,569
- Hendrix College, *Conway* ... 1,027
- John Brown University, *Siloam Springs* ... 1,947
- Ouachita Baptist University, *Arkadelphia* ... 1,511
- Philander Smith College, *Little Rock* ... 946
- Southern Arkansas University, *Magnolia* ... 3,057
- University of Arkansas at Fort Smith, *Fort Smith* ... 6,631
- University of Arkansas at Little Rock, *Little Rock* ... 11,806
- University of Arkansas at Monticello, *Monticello* ... 2,942
- University of Arkansas at Pine Bluff, *Pine Bluff* ... 3,303
- University of Arkansas for Medical Sciences, *Little Rock* ... 2,226
- University of Arkansas Main Campus, *Fayetteville* ... 17,269
- University of Central Arkansas, *Conway* ... 10,069
- University of the Ozarks, *Clarksville* ... 628
- Williams Baptist College, *Walnut Ridge* ... 632

California

- Academy of Art University, *San Francisco* ... 7,784
- Alliant International University - Los Angeles, *Alhambra* ... 647
- Alliant International University - San Diego, *San Diego* ... 1,430
- Alliant International University - San Francisco Bay Area, *San Francisco* ... 736
- American Graduate University, *Covina* ... 650
- American InterContinental University, *Los Angeles* ... 2,100
- Antioch University Southern California, *Culver City* ... 988
- Argosy University/Orange County, *Santa Ana* ... 790
- Art Center College of Design, *Pasadena* ... 1,500
- Art Institute of California - Los Angeles, The, *Santa Monica* ... 2,100
- Art Institute of California - Orange County, The, *Santa Ana* ... 1,844
- Art Institute of California - San Diego, The, *San Diego* ... 1,670
- Art Institute of California - San Francisco, The, *San Francisco* ... 920
- Azusa Pacific University, *Azusa* ... 8,180
- Biola University, *La Mirada* ... 5,370
- Brooks Institute, *Santa Barbara* ... 2,310
- California Baptist University, *Riverside* ... 2,718
- California Coast University, *Santa Ana* ... 3,500
- California College of the Arts, *San Francisco* ... 1,560
- California Institute of Integral Studies, *San Francisco* ... 979
- California Institute of Technology, *Pasadena* ... 2,172
- California Institute of the Arts, *Valencia* ... 1,325
- California Lutheran University, *Thousand Oaks* ... 3,019
- California Maritime Academy, *Vallejo* ... 702
- California Polytechnic State University - San Luis Obispo, *San Luis Obispo* ... 17,582
- California State Polytechnic University - Pomona, *Pomona* ... 19,003
- California State University - Bakersfield, *Bakersfield* ... 7,755
- California State University - Channel Islands, *Camarillo* ... 1,956
- California State University - Chico, *Chico* ... 15,734
- California State University - Dominguez Hills, *Carson* ... 12,613
- California State University - East Bay, *Hayward* ... 13,061
- California State University - Fresno, *Fresno* ... 19,781
- California State University - Fullerton, *Fullerton* ... 32,744
- California State University - Long Beach, *Long Beach* ... 27,180
- California State University - Los Angeles, *Los Angeles* ... 19,514
- California State University - Monterey Bay, *Seaside* ... 3,945
- California State University - Northridge, *Northridge* ... 31,312
- California State University - Sacramento, *Sacramento* ... 27,972
- California State University - San Bernardino, *San Bernardino* ... 16,194
- California State University - San Marcos, *San Marcos* ... 7,365
- California State University - Stanislaus, *Turlock* ... 7,858
- California Western School of Law, *San Diego* ... 977
- Chapman University, *Orange* ... 5,850
- Charles R. Drew University of Medicine & Science, *Los Angeles* ... 682
- Claremont Graduate University, *Claremont* ... 2,038
- Claremont McKenna College, *Claremont* ... 1,066
- Concordia University, *Irvine* ... 1,834
- Concord Law School, *Los Angeles* ... 1,715
- DeVry University, *Pomona* ... 2,493
- DeVry University, *Long Beach* ... 1,832
- DeVry University, *West Hills* ... 1,131
- DeVry University, *Fremont* ... 1,910
- Dominican University of California, *San Rafael* ... 1,977
- Expression College for Digital Arts, *Emeryville* ... 600
- Fashion Institute of Design and Merchandising, *Los Angeles* ... 3,191
- Fielding Graduate Institute, *Santa Barbara* ... 1,275
- Fresno Pacific University, *Fresno* ... 2,094
- Fuller Theological Seminary, *Pasadena* ... 4,198
- Golden Gate Baptist Theological Seminary, *Mill Valley* ... 1,115
- Golden Gate University, *San Francisco* ... 4,069
- Harvey Mudd College, *Claremont* ... 702
- Holy Names University, *Oakland* ... 973
- Hope International University, *Fullerton* ... 1,255
- Humboldt State University, *Arcata* ... 7,550
- Humphreys College, *Stockton* ... 675
- John F. Kennedy University, *Pleasant Hill* ... 1,720
- King's College and Seminary, The, *Los Angeles* ... 671
- La Sierra University, *Riverside* ... 1,908
- Loma Linda University, *Loma Linda* ... 4,034
- Loyola Marymount University, *Los Angeles* ... 8,776
- Master's College and Seminary, The, *Santa Clarita* ... 1,523
- Menlo College, *Atherton* ... 749
- Mills College, *Oakland* ... 1,256
- Monterey Institute of International Studies, *Monterey* ... 782
- Mount Saint Mary's College, *Los Angeles* ... 2,257
- Mount Sierra College, *Monrovia* ... 850
- Musicians Institute, *Hollywood* ... 1,155
- National University, *La Jolla* ... 25,684
- Naval Postgraduate School, *Monterey* ... 1,833
- New College School of Law, *San Francisco* ... 1,775
- Notre Dame de Namur University, *Belmont* ... 1,654
- Occidental College, *Los Angeles* ... 1,866
- Otis College of Art and Design, *Westchester* ... 1,043
- Pacific Oaks College, *Pasadena* ... 935
- Pacific Union College, *Angwin* ... 1,586
- Patten University, *Oakland* ... 725
- Pepperdine University, *Malibu* ... 8,226
- Pitzer College, *Claremont* ... 927
- Point Loma Nazarene University, *San Diego* ... 3,209
- Pomona College, *Claremont* ... 1,549
- Remington College, *San Diego* ... 611
- Saint Mary's College of California, *Moraga* ... 4,859
- Samuel Merritt College, *Oakland* ... 1,000
- San Diego State University, *San Diego* ... 32,936
- San Francisco Art Institute, *San Francisco* ... 643
- San Francisco State University, *San Francisco* ... 28,804
- San Jose State University, *San Jose* ... 29,003
- Santa Clara University, *Santa Clara* ... 8,213
- Scripps College, *Claremont* ... 816
- Silicon Valley College, *Fremont* ... 2,110
- Silicon Valley College - San Jose, *San Jose* ... 657
- Simpson University, *Redding* ... 1,184
- Sonoma State University, *Rohnert Park* ... 7,960
- South Baylo University, *Anaheim* ... 700
- Southern California University of Health Sciences, *Whittier* ... 685
- Southwestern University School of Law, *Los Angeles* ... 967
- Stanford University, *Stanford* ... 14,846
- Thomas Jefferson School of Law, *San Diego* ... 842
- Touro University - California, *Vallejo* ... 624
- Touro University International, *Cypress* ... 6,772
- University of California - Berkeley, *Berkeley* ... 32,814
- University of California - Davis, *Davis* ... 30,065
- University of California - Hastings College of the Law, *San Francisco* ... 1,266
- University of California - Irvine, *Irvine* ... 23,793
- University of California - Los Angeles, *Los Angeles* ... 37,563
- University of California - Riverside, *Riverside* ... 17,104
- University of California - San Diego, *La Jolla* ... 25,278
- University of California - San Francisco, *San Francisco* ... 2,704
- University of California - Santa Barbara, *Santa Barbara* ... 21,026
- University of California - Santa Cruz, *Santa Cruz* ... 15,950
- University of LaVerne, *La Verne* ... 8,140
- University of Redlands, *Redlands* ... 4,519
- University of San Diego, *San Diego* ... 7,486
- University of San Francisco, *San Francisco* ... 8,331
- University of Southern California, *Los Angeles* ... 32,000
- University of the Pacific, *Stockton* ... 6,268
- Vanguard University of Southern California, *Costa Mesa* ... 2,155
- Western University of Health Sciences, *Pomona* ... 1,885
- Westmont College, *Santa Barbara* ... 1,365
- Westwood College, *Anaheim* ... 738
- Westwood College - Inland Empire, *Upland* ... 1,010
- Whittier College, *Whittier* ... 1,304
- Woodbury University, *Burbank* ... 1,450

Colorado

- Adams State College, *Alamosa* ... 3,751
- Art Institute of Colorado, The, *Denver* ... 2,270
- Aspen University, *Denver* ... 641
- College for Financial Planning, *Greenwood Village* ... 12,000
- Colorado Christian University, *Lakewood* ... 1,680
- Colorado College, *Colorado Springs* ... 1,994
- Colorado School of Mines, *Golden* ... 3,666
- Colorado State University, *Fort Collins* ... 25,382
- Colorado State University - Pueblo, *Pueblo* ... 5,741
- Colorado Technical University, *Colorado Springs* ... 2,030
- Denver Seminary, *Littleton* ... 917
- DeVry University, *Westminster* ... 768
- Fort Lewis College, *Durango* ... 4,190
- Johnson & Wales University, *Denver* ... 1,512
- Jones International University, *Contennial* ... 4,520
- Mesa State College, *Grand Junction* ... 5,736
- Metropolitan State College of Denver, *Denver* ... 20,761
- Naropa University, *Boulder* ... 1,206
- Regis University, *Denver* ... 11,801
- University of Colorado at Boulder, *Boulder* ... 29,258
- University of Colorado at Colorado Springs, *Colorado Springs* ... 7,650
- University of Colorado at Denver and Health Sciences Center, *Denver* ... 15,071
- University of Denver, *Denver* ... 9,808
- University of Northern Colorado, *Greeley* ... 13,156
- Western State College, *Gunnison* ... 2,154
- Westwood College of Technology, *Denver* ... 3,330

Connecticut

- Albertus Magnus College, *New Haven* ... 2,389
- Central Connecticut State University, *New Britain* ... 12,320
- Charter Oak State College, *New Britain* ... 1,495
- Connecticut College, *New London* ... 1,931
- Eastern Connecticut State University, *Willimantic* ... 5,156
- Fairfield University, *Fairfield* ... 5,060
- Mitchell College, *New London* ... 701
- Post University, *Waterbury* ... 1,198
- Quinnipiac University, *Hamden* ... 7,220
- Rensselaer at Hartford, *Hartford* ... 1,035
- Sacred Heart University, *Fairfield* ... 5,694
- Saint Joseph College, *West Hartford* ... 1,792
- Southern Connecticut State University, *New Haven* ... 12,177
- Trinity College, *Hartford* ... 1,948
- United States Coast Guard Academy, *New London* ... 980
- University of Bridgeport, *Bridgeport* ... 3,274
- University of Connecticut, *Storrs* ... 27,579
- University of Hartford, *West Hartford* ... 7,246
- University of New Haven, *West Haven* ... 4,173
- Wesleyan University, *Middletown* ... 3,229
- Western Connecticut State University, *Danbury* ... 5,884
- Yale University, *New Haven* ... 11,359

Delaware

- Delaware State University, *Dover* ... 3,270
- Goldey-Beacom College, *Wilmington* ... 1,296
- University of Delaware, *Newark* ... 21,238
- Wesley College, *Dover* ... 2,400
- Widener University School of Law, *Wilmington* ... 1,402
- Wilmington College, *New Castle* ... 7,150

District of Columbia

- American University, *Washington* ... 11,962
- Catholic University of America, The, *Washington* ... 5,981
- Gallaudet University, *Washington* ... 1,834
- Georgetown University, *Washington* ... 13,233
- George Washington University, *Washington* ... 24,092
- Howard University, *Washington* ... 10,623
- Joint Military Intelligence College, *Washington* ... 600
- Southeastern University, *Washington* ... 950
- Strayer University, *Washington* ... 23,539
- Trinity College, *Washington* ... 1,700
- University of the District of Columbia, *Washington* ... 5,165
- Wesley Theological Seminary, *Washington* ... 747

Florida

- American InterContinental University, *Weston* ... 1,505
- Argosy University/Sarasota, *Sarasota* ... 1,965
- Art Institute of Fort Lauderdale, The, *Fort Lauderdale* ... 3,642
- Baptist College of Florida, The, *Graceville* ... 652
- Barry University, *Miami Shores* ... 9,207
- Bethune Cookman College, *Daytona Beach* ... 2,895
- Carlos Albizu University Miami Campus, *Miami* ... 1,010
- Chipola College, *Marianna* ... 2,323
- City College, *Fort Lauderdale* ... 1,292
- Clearwater Christian College, *Clearwater* ... 628
- DeVry University, *Miramar* ... 1,320
- DeVry University, *Orlando* ... 1,515
- Eckerd College, *Saint Petersburg* ... 1,684
- Edward Waters College, *Jacksonville* ... 1,206
- Embry-Riddle Aeronautical University, *Daytona Beach* ... 4,788
- Embry-Riddle Aeronautical University - Extended Campus, *Daytona Beach* ... 14,676
- Everglades University, *Boca Raton* ... 600
- Flagler College, *Saint Augustine* ... 2,465
- Florida Agricultural and Mechanical University, *Tallahassee* ... 13,067
- Florida Atlantic University, *Boca Raton* ... 25,662
- Florida Coastal School of Law, *Jacksonville* ... 904
- Florida Gulf Coast University, *Fort Myers* ... 6,198
- Florida Hospital College of Health Sciences, *Orlando* ... 1,793
- Florida Institute of Technology, *Melbourne* ... 4,683
- Florida International University, *Miami* ... 34,865
- Florida Memorial University, *Miami* ... 2,009
- Florida Metropolitan University - Brandon Campus, *Tampa* ... 1,332
- Florida Metropolitan University - Lakeland Campus, *Lakeland* ... 657
- Florida Metropolitan University - Melbourne Campus, *Melbourne* ... 900
- Florida Metropolitan University - North Orlando Campus, *Orlando* ... 4,300
- Florida Metropolitan University - Pinellas Campus, *Clearwater* ... 1,159
- Florida Metropolitan University - Pompano Beach Campus, *Pompano Beach* ... 1,572
- Florida Metropolitan University - South Orlando Campus, *Orlando* ... 1,750
- Florida Metropolitan University - Tampa Campus, *Tampa* ... 1,903
- Florida Southern College, *Lakeland* ... 1,830
- Florida State University, *Tallahassee* ... 38,886
- Full Sail Real World Education, *Winter Park* ... 4,415
- International Academy of Design & Technology, *Tampa* ... 2,300
- International College, *Naples* ... 1,544
- Jacksonville University, *Jacksonville* ... 2,946
- Johnson & Wales University, *North Miami* ... 2,389
- Jones College, *Jacksonville* ... 777
- Keiser College, *Fort Lauderdale* ... 8,317
- Lynn University, *Boca Raton* ... 2,510
- Miami-Dade College, *Miami* ... 59,066
- Miami International University of Art & Design, *Miami* ... 1,321
- New College of Florida, *Sarasota* ... 691
- Nova Southeastern University, *Fort Lauderdale* ... 25,430
- Okaloosa-Walton College, *Niceville* ... 8,000
- Palm Beach Atlantic University, *West Palm Beach* ... 3,066
- Reformed Theological Seminary, *Oviedo* ... 817
- Remington College - Tampa Campus, *Tampa* ... 892
- Ringling School of Art and Design, *Sarasota* ... 1,008
- Rollins College, *Winter Park* ... 3,726
- Saint Leo University, *Saint Leo* ... 12,677
- St. Petersburg College, *Saint Petersburg* ... 24,247
- St. Thomas University, *Miami Gardens* ... 2,630
- Schiller International University, *Dunedin* ... 1,200
- Southeastern University, *Lakeland* ... 1,964
- Stetson University, *DeLand* ... 3,577
- Universidad FLET, *Miami* ... 1,390
- University of Central Florida, *Orlando* ... 42,837
- University of Florida, *Gainesville* ... 47,993
- University of Miami, *Coral Gables* ... 15,250
- University of North Florida, *Jacksonville* ... 14,641
- University of South Florida, *Tampa* ... 42,556
- University of Tampa, *Tampa* ... 4,856
- University of West Florida, *Pensacola* ... 9,611
- Warner Southern College, *Lake Wales* ... 1,026
- Webber International University, *Babson Park* ... 642

Georgia

- Agnes Scott College, *Atlanta/Decatur* ... 1,027
- Albany State University, *Albany* ... 3,668
- American InterContinental University, *Atlanta* ... 1,630
- Argosy University/Atlanta, *Atlanta* ... 1,503
- Armstrong Atlantic State University, *Savannah* ... 7,009
- Art Institute of Atlanta, The, *Atlanta* ... 2,700
- Augusta State University, *Augusta* ... 6,368
- Bauder College, *Atlanta* ... 647
- Berry College, *Mount Berry* ... 2,008
- Beulah Heights Bible College, *Atlanta* ... 686
- Brenau University, *Gainesville* ... 2,117
- Brewton-Parker College, *Mount Vernon* ... 1,136
- Clark Atlanta University, *Atlanta* ... 4,598
- Clayton State University, *Morrow* ... 5,954
- Columbus State University, *Columbus* ... 7,224
- Covenant College, *Lookout Mountain* ... 878
- Dalton State College, *Dalton* ... 4,252
- DeVry University, *Decatur* ... 3,107
- DeVry University, *Alpharetta* ... 1,245
- Emmanuel College, *Franklin Springs* ... 754
- Emory University, *Atlanta* ... 11,781
- Fort Valley State University, *Fort Valley* ... 2,558
- Georgia College & State University, *Milledgeville* ... 5,531
- Georgia Institute of Technology, *Atlanta* ... 16,841
- Georgia Southern University, *Statesboro* ... 16,100
- Georgia Southwestern State University, *Americus* ... 2,323
- Georgia State University, *Atlanta* ... 27,267
- Kennesaw State University, *Kennesaw* ... 17,961
- LaGrange College, *La Grange* ... 1,045
- Life University, *Marietta* ... 1,210
- Luther Rice Seminary, *Lithonia* ... 1,783
- Macon State College, *Macon* ... 5,733
- Medical College of Georgia, *Augusta* ... 2,115
- Mercer University, *Macon* ... 7,300
- Morehouse College, *Atlanta* ... 2,716
- North Georgia College & State University, *Dahlonega* ... 4,552
- Oglethorpe University, *Atlanta* ... 1,053
- Paine College, *Augusta* ... 871
- Piedmont College, *Demorest* ... 2,222
- Reinhardt College, *Waleska* ... 1,096
- Savannah College of Art and Design, *Savannah* ... 6,776
- Savannah State University, *Savannah* ... 2,800
- Shorter College, *Rome* ... 2,340
- Southern Polytechnic State University, *Marietta* ... 3,803
- South University, *Savannah* ... 2,033
- Spelman College, *Atlanta* ... 2,186
- Thomas University, *Thomasville* ... 780
- Toccoa Falls College, *Toccoa Falls* ... 829
- University of Georgia, *Athens* ... 33,405
- University of West Georgia, *Carrollton* ... 10,216
- Valdosta State University, *Valdosta* ... 10,400
- Wesleyan College, *Macon* ... 645

Hawaii

- Brigham Young University Hawaii Campus, *Laie Oahu* ... 2,486
- Chaminade University of Honolulu, *Honolulu* ... 2,873
- Hawaii Pacific University, *Honolulu* ... 7,800
- University of Hawaii at Hilo, *Hilo* ... 3,288
- University of Hawaii at Manoa, *Honolulu* ... 20,549
- University of Hawaii West Oahu, *Pearl City* ... 834

Idaho

- Albertson College, *Caldwell* ... 810
- Boise State University, *Boise* ... 18,456
- Brigham Young University - Idaho, *Rexburg* ... 11,555
- Idaho State University, *Pocatello* ... 13,802
- Lewis-Clark State College, *Lewiston* ... 3,325
- Northwest Nazarene University, *Nampa* ... 1,587
- University of Idaho, *Moscow* ... 12,824

Illinois

- Argosy University/Chicago, *Chicago* ... 847
- Augustana College, *Rock Island* ... 2,292
- Aurora University, *Aurora* ... 3,326
- Benedictine University, *Lisle* ... 3,232
- Blackburn College, *Carlinville* ... 608
- Bradley University, *Peoria* ... 6,069
- Chicago School of Professional Psychology, *Chicago* ... 846
- Chicago State University, *Chicago* ... 6,835
- Columbia College Chicago, *Chicago* ... 10,354
- Concordia University, *River Forest* ... 1,134
- DePaul University, *Chicago* ... 23,570
- DeVry University, *Addison* ... 1,998
- DeVry University, *Chicago* ... 814
- DeVry University, *Chicago* ... 2,533
- Dominican University, *River Forest* ... 3,188
- Eastern Illinois University, *Charleston* ... 11,651
- East-West University, *Chicago* ... 1,118
- Elmhurst College, *Elmhurst* ... 2,682
- Governors State University, *University Park* ... 5,652
- Greenville College, *Greenville* ... 1,315
- Harrington College of Design, *Chicago* ... 1,553
- Illinois College, *Jacksonville* ... 1,037
- Illinois Institute of Art, The, *Chicago* ... 2,463
- Illinois Institute of Art, The, *Schaumburg* ... 1,165
- Illinois Institute of Technology, *Chicago* ... 6,378
- Illinois State University, *Normal* ... 20,419
- Illinois Wesleyan University, *Bloomington* ... 2,118
- International Academy of Design and Technology, *Chicago* ... 2,780
- John Marshall Law School, *Chicago* ... 1,583
- Judson College, *Elgin* ... 1,200
- Keller Graduate School of Management of DeVry University, *Tinley Park* ... 1,613
- Kendall College, *Chicago* ... 600
- Knox College, *Galesburg* ... 1,167
- Lake Forest College, *Lake Forest* ... 1,380
- Lake Forest Graduate School of Management, *Lake Forest* ... 791
- Lewis University, *Romeoville* ... 4,826
- Lincoln Christian College, *Lincoln* ... 1,260
- Lincoln College, *Lincoln* ... 1,272
- Loyola University Chicago, *Chicago* ... 13,909
- MacMurray College, *Jacksonville* ... 635
- McKendree College, *Lebanon* ... 1,904
- Midwestern University, *Downers Grove* ... 1,791
- Millikin University, *Decatur* ... 2,588
- Monmouth College, *Monmouth* ... 1,248
- Moody Bible Institute, *Chicago* ... 3,824
- National-Louis University, *Chicago* ... 7,332
- North Central College, *Naperville* ... 2,377
- Northeastern Illinois University, *Chicago* ... 12,164
- Northern Illinois University, *De Kalb* ... 24,820
- North Park University, *Chicago* ... 2,972
- Northwestern University, *Evanston* ... 16,663
- Olivet Nazarene University, *Bourbonnais* ... 4,364
- Quincy University, *Quincy* ... 1,294
- Robert Morris College, *Chicago* ... 6,858
- Rockford College, *Rockford* ... 1,039
- Roosevelt University, *Chicago* ... 7,385
- Rosalind Franklin University of Medicine & Science, *North Chicago* ... 1,687
- Rush University, *Chicago* ... 1,363
- St. Augustine College, *Chicago* ... 1,582
- Saint Xavier University, *Chicago* ... 5,722
- School of the Art Institute of Chicago, *Chicago* ... 2,688
- Southern Illinois University Carbondale, *Carbondale* ... 21,589
- Southern Illinois University Edwardsville, *Edwardsville* ... 13,493
- Trinity Christian College, *Palos Heights* ... 1,234
- Trinity International University, *Deerfield* ... 2,851
- University of Chicago, *Chicago* ... 13,400
- University of Illinois at Chicago, *Chicago* ... 24,862
- University of Illinois at Springfield, *Springfield* ... 4,396
- University of Illinois at Urbana-Champaign, *Champaign* ... 40,687
- University of Saint Francis, *Joliet* ... 4,129
- Western Illinois University, *Macomb* ... 13,558
- Wheaton College, *Wheaton* ... 2,898

Indiana

- Anderson University, *Anderson* ... 2,677
- Ball State University, *Muncie* ... 18,043
- Bethel College, *Mishawaka* ... 1,988
- Butler University, *Indianapolis* ... 4,415
- Calumet College of Saint Joseph, *Whiting* ... 1,331
- DePauw University, *Greencastle* ... 2,391
- Earlham College and Earlham School of Religion, *Richmond* ... 1,190
- Franklin College of Indiana, *Franklin* ... 997
- Goshen College, *Goshen* ... 908
- Grace College and Seminary, *Winona Lake* ... 1,310
- Hanover College, *Hanover* ... 1,062
- Huntington College, *Huntington* ... 975
- Indiana Institute of Technology, *Fort Wayne* ... 3,189
- Indiana State University, *Terre Haute* ... 11,200
- Indiana University at Bloomington, *Bloomington* ... 37,821
- Indiana University East, *Richmond* ... 2,516
- Indiana University Kokomo, *Kokomo* ... 3,170
- Indiana University Northwest, *Gary* ... 5,138
- Indiana University - Purdue University Fort Wayne, *Fort Wayne* ... 11,810
- Indiana University - Purdue University Indianapolis, *Indianapolis* ... 29,953
- Indiana University South Bend, *South Bend* ... 7,501
- Indiana University Southeast, *New Albany* ... 6,238
- Indiana Wesleyan University, *Marion* ... 11,412
- International Business College, *Fort Wayne* ... 793
- Manchester College, *North Manchester* ... 1,075
- Marian College, *Indianapolis* ... 1,678
- Martin University, *Indianapolis* ... 629
- Oakland City University, *Oakland City* ... 1,928
- Purdue University Calumet, *Hammond* ... 9,222
- Purdue University Main Campus, *West Lafayette* ... 38,653
- Purdue University North Central Campus, *Westville* ... 3,441
- Rose-Hulman Institute of Technology, *Terre Haute* ... 1,899
- Saint Joseph's College, *Rensselaer* ... 799
- Saint Mary-of-the-Woods College, *St Mary-of-the-Woods* ... 1,703
- Saint Mary's College, *Notre Dame* ... 1,505
- Taylor University, *Upland* ... 1,894
- Taylor University, Fort Wayne, *Fort Wayne* ... 638
- Trinity College of the Bible and Trinity Theological Seminary, *Newburgh* ... 6,476
- Tri-State University, *Angola* ... 1,456
- University of Evansville, *Evansville* ... 2,704
- University of Indianapolis, *Indianapolis* ... 4,116
- University of Notre Dame, *Notre Dame* ... 11,479
- University of Saint Francis, *Fort Wayne* ... 1,935
- University of Southern Indiana, *Evansville* ... 10,050
- Valparaiso University, *Valparaiso* ... 3,970
- Vincennes University, *Vincennes* ... 9,020
- Wabash College, *Crawfordsville* ... 853

Iowa

- Briar Cliff University, *Sioux City* ... 1,116
- Buena Vista University, *Storm Lake* ... 1,276
- Central College, *Pella* ... 1,750
- Clarke College, *Dubuque* ... 1,180
- Coe College, *Cedar Rapids* ... 1,354
- Cornell College, *Mount Vernon* ... 1,148
- Des Moines University, *Des Moines* ... 1,208
- Dordt College, *Sioux Center* ... 1,285
- Drake University, *Des Moines* ... 5,221
- Graceland University, *Lamoni* ... 2,351
- Grand View College, *Des Moines* ... 1,759
- Grinnell College, *Grinnell* ... 1,529
- Hamilton College, *Cedar Rapids* ... 3,244
- Hamilton College, *Urbandale* ... 800
- Iowa State University, *Ames* ... 26,380
- Iowa Wesleyan College, *Mount Pleasant* ... 774
- Kaplan University, *Davenport* ... 9,195
- Loras College, *Dubuque* ... 1,743
- Luther College, *Decorah* ... 2,573
- Maharishi University of Management, *Fairfield* ... 695
- Mercy College of Health Sciences, *Des Moines* ... 659
- Morningside College, *Sioux City* ... 1,204
- Mount Mercy College, *Cedar Rapids* ... 1,486
- Northwestern College, *Orange City* ... 1,284
- Palmer College of Chiropractic, *Davenport* ... 1,669
- St. Ambrose University, *Davenport* ... 3,534
- Simpson College, *Indianola* ... 1,955
- University of Dubuque, *Dubuque* ... 1,267
- University of Iowa, *Iowa City* ... 29,745
- University of Northern Iowa, *Cedar Falls* ... 12,824
- Upper Iowa University, *Fayette* ... 5,799
- Waldorf College, *Forest City* ... 629
- Wartburg College, *Waverly* ... 1,804
- William Penn University, *Oskaloosa* ... 1,682

Kansas

- Baker University, *Baldwin City* ... 3,138
- Benedictine College, *Atchison* ... 1,441
- Emporia State University, *Emporia* ... 6,194
- Fort Hays State University, *Hays* ... 8,500
- Friends University, *Wichita* ... 2,749
- Haskell Indian Nations University, *Lawrence* ... 928
- Kansas State University, *Manhattan* ... 23,151
- Kansas State University - Salina, College of Technology and Aviation, *Salina* ... 914
- Kansas Wesleyan University, *Salina* ... 825
- MidAmerica Nazarene University, *Olathe* ... 1,985
- Newman University, *Wichita* ... 2,179
- Ottawa University, *Ottawa* ... 3,427
- Pittsburg State University, *Pittsburg* ... 6,537
- Southwestern College, *Winfield* ... 1,420
- Tabor College, *Hillsboro* ... 606
- United States Army Command and General Staff College, *Fort Leavenworth* ... 1,005
- University of Kansas Main Campus, *Lawrence* ... 29,590
- University of Kansas Medical Center, *Kansas City* ... 2,610
- University of Saint Mary, *Leavenworth* ... 826
- Washburn University, *Topeka* ... 7,251
- Wichita State University, *Wichita* ... 14,297

Kentucky

- Asbury College, *Wilmore* ... 1,219
- Asbury Theological Seminary, *Wilmore* ... 1,724
- Bellarmine University, *Louisville* ... 2,506
- Berea College, *Berea* ... 1,514
- Brescia University, *Owensboro* ... 709
- Campbellsville University, *Campbellsville* ... 2,052
- Centre College, *Danville* ... 1,066
- Eastern Kentucky University, *Richmond* ... 16,183
- Georgetown College, *Georgetown* ... 1,835
- Kentucky Christian University, *Grayson* ... 600
- Kentucky State University, *Frankfort* ... 2,335
- Kentucky Wesleyan College, *Owensboro* ... 671
- Lindsey Wilson College, *Columbia* ... 1,851
- Mid-Continent University, *Mayfield* ... 815
- Midway College, *Midway* ... 1,271
- Morehead State University, *Morehead* ... 9,293
- Murray State University, *Murray* ... 10,128
- National College of Business & Technology, *Louisville* ... 900
- Northern Kentucky University, *Highland Heights* ... 13,921
- Pikeville College, *Pikeville* ... 1,066
- St. Catharine College, *Saint Catharine* ... 608
- Southern Baptist Theological Seminary, The, *Louisville* ... 2,983
- Spalding University, *Louisville* ... 1,684
- Sullivan University, *Louisville* ... 4,821
- Thomas More College, *Crestview Hills* ... 1,465
- Transylvania University, *Lexington* ... 1,114
- Union College, *Barbourville* ... 1,047
- University of Kentucky, *Lexington* ... 25,686
- University of Louisville, *Louisville* ... 21,725

U.S. Colleges and Universities: Enrollment, *Continued*

University of the Cumberlands, *Williamsburg* 1,744
Western Kentucky University, *Bowling Green* 18,513

Louisiana

Centenary College of Louisiana, *Shreveport* 1,040
Dillard University, *New Orleans* 2,155
Grambling State University, *Grambling* 5,040
Grantham University, *Slidell* 7,049
Louisiana College, *Pineville* 1,085
Louisiana State University and Agricultural and Mechanical College, *Baton Rouge* 31,561
Louisiana State University at Alexandria, *Alexandria* 3,001
Louisiana State University Health Sciences Center - New Orleans, *New Orleans* 2,238
Louisiana State University in Shreveport, *Shreveport* 4,401
Louisiana Tech University, *Ruston* 11,710
Loyola University New Orleans, *New Orleans* 5,748
McNeese State University, *Lake Charles* 8,784
New Orleans Baptist Theological Seminary, *New Orleans* 2,745
Nicholls State University, *Thibodaux* 7,482
Northwestern State University, *Natchitoches* 10,546
Our Lady of Holy Cross College, *New Orleans* 1,507
Our Lady of the Lake College, *Baton Rouge* 1,990
Southeastern Louisiana University, *Hammond* 15,472
Southern University and Agricultural and Mechanical College at Baton Rouge, *Baton Rouge* 9,438
Southern University at New Orleans, *New Orleans* 3,647
Tulane University, *New Orleans* 12,693
University of Louisiana at Lafayette, *Lafayette* 16,561
University of Louisiana at Monroe, *Monroe* 8,831
University of New Orleans, *New Orleans* 17,350
Xavier University of Louisiana, *New Orleans* 4,121

Maine

Bates College, *Lewiston* 1,743
Bowdoin College, *Brunswick* 1,677
Colby College, *Waterville* 1,815
Husson College, *Bangor* 1,995
Maine Maritime Academy, *Castine* 816
Saint Joseph's College, *Standish* 2,497
Thomas College, *Waterville* 870
University of Maine, *Orono* 11,288
University of Maine at Augusta, The, *Augusta* 5,538
University of Maine at Farmington, *Farmington* 2,042
University of Maine at Fort Kent, *Fort Kent* 1,076
University of Maine at Machias, *Machias* 1,191
University of Maine at Presque Isle, *Presque Isle* 1,652
University of New England, *Biddeford* 3,327
University of Southern Maine, *Portland* 11,089

Maryland

Baltimore International College, *Baltimore* 744
Bowie State University, *Bowie* 5,415
Capitol College, *Laurel* 739
College of Notre Dame of Maryland, *Baltimore* 3,307
Columbia Union College, *Takoma Park* 1,116
Coppin State University, *Baltimore* 3,875
Frostburg State University, *Frostburg* 5,327
Goucher College, *Towson* 2,439
Hood College, *Frederick* 1,953
Johns Hopkins University, *Baltimore* 18,882
Loyola College in Maryland, *Baltimore* 6,156
Maryland Institute College of Art, *Baltimore* 2,047
McDaniel College, *Westminster* 3,304
Morgan State University, *Baltimore* 6,892
Mount St. Mary's University, *Emmitsburg* 2,125
Peabody Institute of Johns Hopkins University, *Baltimore* 647
St. Mary's College of Maryland, *Saint Mary's City* 1,935
Salisbury University, *Salisbury* 6,942
Sojourner-Douglass College, *Baltimore* 1,286
Towson University, *Baltimore* 17,667
United States Naval Academy, *Annapolis* 4,349
University of Baltimore, *Baltimore* 5,045
University of Maryland Baltimore, *Baltimore* 5,602
University of Maryland Baltimore County, *Baltimore* 11,852
University of Maryland College Park, *College Park* 34,933
University of Maryland Eastern Shore, *Princess Anne* 3,775
University of Maryland University College, *Adelphi* 28,374
Villa Julie College, *Stevenson* 2,740
Washington Bible College/Capital Bible Seminary, *Lanham* 668
Washington College, *Chestertown* 1,308

Massachusetts

American International College, *Springfield* 1,625
Amherst College, *Amherst* 1,648
Anna Maria College, *Paxton* 1,108
Assumption College, *Worcester* 2,836
Babson College, *Babson Park* 3,288
Bay Path College, *Longmeadow* 1,347
Bay State College, *Boston* 890
Becker College - Worcester, *Worcester* 1,676
Bentley College, *Waltham* 5,554
Berklee College of Music, *Boston* 3,882
Boston Architectural Center, *Boston* 881
Boston College, *Chestnut Hill* 14,528
Boston University, *Boston* 30,101
Brandeis University, *Waltham* 5,072
Bridgewater State College, *Bridgewater* 9,731
Cambridge College, *Cambridge* 3,153
Clark University, *Worcester* 3,115
College of Our Lady of the Elms, *Chicopee* 998
College of the Holy Cross, *Worcester* 2,718
Curry College, *Milton* 2,877
Dean College, *Franklin* 1,298
Eastern Nazarene College, *Quincy* 1,234
Emerson College, *Boston* 4,398
Emmanuel College, *Boston* 2,165
Endicott College, *Beverly* 3,266
Fisher College, *Boston* 914
Fitchburg State College, *Fitchburg* 5,201
Framingham State College, *Framingham* 6,015
Gordon College, *Wenham* 1,617
Gordon-Conwell Theological Seminary, *South Hamilton* 2,011
Hampshire College, *Amherst* 1,352
Harvard University, *Cambridge* 19,789
Hebrew College, *Newton Centre* 650
Lasell College, *Newton* 1,140
Lesley University, *Cambridge* 6,333
Massachusetts College of Art, *Boston* 1,637
Massachusetts College of Liberal Arts, *North Adams* 1,835
Massachusetts College of Pharmacy and Health Sciences, *Boston* 2,587
Massachusetts Institute of Technology, *Cambridge* 10,320
Massachusetts Maritime Academy, *Buzzards Bay* 950
Massachusetts School of Law at Andover, *Andover* 605
Merrimack College, *North Andover* 2,326
MGH Institute of Health Professions, *Boston* 673
Mount Holyoke College, *South Hadley* 2,143
Mount Ida College, *Newton Centre* 1,298
National Graduate School of Quality Systems Management, The, *Falmouth* 1,000
Newbury College, *Brookline* 1,250
New England Conservatory of Music, *Boston* 750
New England Institute of Art, The, *Brookline* 1,190
New England School of Law, *Boston* 1,052
Nichols College, *Dudley* 1,792
Northeastern University, *Boston* 23,556
Regis College, *Weston* 1,271
Salem State College, *Salem* 9,347
School of the Museum of Fine Arts - Boston, *Boston* 752
Simmons College, *Boston* 3,522
Smith College, *Northampton* 3,119
Springfield College, *Springfield* 5,062
Stonehill College, *Easton* 2,490
Suffolk University, *Boston* 8,332
Tufts University, *Medford* 9,602
University of Massachusetts, *Amherst* 24,646
University of Massachusetts at Worcester, *Worcester* 897
University of Massachusetts Boston, *Boston* 11,682
University of Massachusetts Dartmouth, *North Dartmouth* 8,299
University of Massachusetts Lowell, *Lowell* 11,809
Wellesley College, *Wellesley* 2,289
Wentworth Institute of Technology, *Boston* 3,597
Western New England College, *Springfield* 4,025
Westfield State College, *Westfield* 5,014
Wheaton College, *Norton* 1,519
Wheelock College, *Boston* 957
Williams College, *Williamstown* 2,050
Worcester Polytechnic Institute, *Worcester* 3,810
Worcester State College, *Worcester* 5,404

Michigan

Adrian College, *Adrian* 1,013
Albion College, *Albion* 1,867
Alma College, *Alma* 1,215
Andrews University, *Berrien Springs* 3,017
Aquinas College, *Grand Rapids* 2,235
Baker College of Auburn Hills, *Auburn Hills* 3,226
Baker College of Cadillac, *Cadillac* 1,546
Baker College of Clinton Township, *Clinton Township* 4,823
Baker College of Flint, *Flint* 5,510
Baker College of Jackson, *Jackson* 1,600
Baker College of Muskegon, *Muskegon* 4,433
Baker College of Owosso, *Owosso* 2,716
Baker College of Port Huron, *Port Huron* 1,505
Calvin College, *Grand Rapids* 4,186
Central Michigan University, *Mount Pleasant* 27,683
Cleary University, *Ann Arbor* 626
College for Creative Studies, *Detroit* 1,265
Cornerstone University, *Grand Rapids* 2,612
Davenport University, *Grand Rapids* 13,590
Eastern Michigan University, *Ypsilanti* 23,862
Ferris State University, *Big Rapids* 11,803
Grand Valley State University, *Allendale* 22,063
Hillsdale College, *Hillsdale* 1,242
Hope College, *Holland* 3,112
Kalamazoo College, *Kalamazoo* 1,234
Kettering University, *Flint* 2,992
Lake Superior State University, *Sault Sainte Marie* 2,888
Lawrence Technological University, *Southfield* 4,148
Madonna University, *Livonia* 4,349
Marygrove College, *Detroit* 4,610
Michigan State University, *East Lansing* 44,836
Michigan Technological University, *Houghton* 6,443
Northern Michigan University, *Marquette* 9,331
Northwood University, *Midland* 5,843
Oakland University, *Rochester* 16,902
Olivet College, *Olivet* 1,073
Rochester College, *Rochester Hills* 1,011
Saginaw Valley State University, *University Center* 9,448
Siena Heights University, *Adrian* 2,161
Spring Arbor University, *Spring Arbor* 3,511
Thomas M. Cooley Law School, *Lansing* 2,884
University of Detroit Mercy, *Detroit* 5,521
University of Michigan - Ann Arbor, *Ann Arbor* 39,533
University of Michigan - Dearborn, *Dearborn* 8,631
University of Michigan - Flint, *Flint* 6,188
Walsh College of Accountancy and Business Administration, *Troy* 3,105
Wayne State University, *Detroit* 33,314
Western Michigan University, *Kalamazoo* 27,829

Minnesota

Argosy University/Twin Cities, *Eagan* 1,582
Art Institutes International Minnesota, The, *Minneapolis* 1,393
Augsburg College, *Minneapolis* 3,375
Bemidji State University, *Bemidji* 4,833
Bethel University, *Saint Paul* 4,659
Brown College, *Mendota Heights* 1,800
Capella University, *Minneapolis* 12,599
Carleton College, *Northfield* 1,932
College of Saint Benedict, *Saint Joseph* 1,960
College of Saint Catherine, *Saint Paul* 4,809
College of Saint Scholastica, The, *Duluth* 3,015
Concordia College - Moorhead, *Moorhead* 2,814
Concordia University, St. Paul, *Saint Paul* 2,036
Crown College, *Saint Bonifacius* 1,047
Globe College, *Oakdale* 1,209
Gustavus Adolphus College, *Saint Peter* 2,577
Hamline University, *Saint Paul* 1,993
Luther Seminary, *Saint Paul* 804
Macalester College, *Saint Paul* 1,900
Martin Luther College, *New Ulm* 946
Mayo School of Health Sciences, *Rochester* 800
Metropolitan State University, *Saint Paul* 6,516
Minneapolis College of Art Design, *Minneapolis* 712
Minnesota School of Business, *Brooklyn Center* 893
Minnesota School of Business, *Richfield* 923
Minnesota State University, Mankato, *Mankato* 14,151
Minnesota State University Moorhead, *Moorhead* 7,642
Normandale Community College, *Bloomington* 8,600
North Central University, *Minneapolis* 1,239
Northwestern College, *Saint Paul* 2,734
Northwestern Health Sciences University, *Bloomington* 813
St. Cloud State University, *Saint Cloud* 15,608
Saint John's University, *Collegeville* 1,952
Saint Mary's University of Minnesota, *Winona* 4,861
Saint Olaf College, *Northfield* 2,976
Southwest Minnesota State University, *Marshall* 5,977
University of Minnesota - Crookston, *Crookston* 2,088
University of Minnesota - Duluth, *Duluth* 10,366
University of Minnesota - Morris, *Morris* 1,839
University of Minnesota - Twin Cities, *Minneapolis* 50,954
University of Saint Thomas, *Saint Paul* 10,474
Walden University, *Minneapolis* 13,553
William Mitchell College of Law, *Saint Paul* 1,096
Winona State University, *Winona* 7,431

Mississippi

Alcorn State University, *Alcorn State* 3,443
Belhaven College, *Jackson* 2,493
Delta State University, *Cleveland* 3,990
Jackson State University, *Jackson* 8,351
Millsaps College, *Jackson* 1,146
Mississippi College, *Clinton* 3,588
Mississippi State University, *Mississippi State* 15,934
Mississippi University for Women, *Columbus* 2,291
Mississippi Valley State University, *Itta Bena* 3,621
Reformed Theological Seminary, *Jackson* 670
Rust College, *Holly Springs* 1,001
Tougaloo College, *Tougaloo* 921
University of Mississippi, *Tupelo* 14,497
University of Mississippi Medical Center, *Jackson* 2,003
University of Southern Mississippi, *Hattiesburg* 16,385
William Carey College, *Hattiesburg* 2,723

Missouri

A. T. Still University of Health Sciences, *Kirksville* 1,842
Avila University, *Kansas City* 2,104
Baptist Bible College, *Springfield* 665
Barnes-Jewish College of Nursing and Allied Health, *Saint Louis* 916
Central Bible College, *Springfield* 778
Central Methodist University, *Fayette* 2,128
Central Missouri State University, *Warrensburg* 10,051
College of the Ozarks, *Point Lookout* 1,348
Colorado Technical University, Kansas City, *North Kansas City* 730
Columbia College, *Columbia* 1,092
Concordia Seminary, *Saint Louis* 827
Covenant Theological Seminary, *Saint Louis* 881
Culver-Stockton College, *Canton* 855
DeVry University, *Kansas City* 1,641
Drury University, *Springfield* 4,829
Evangel University, *Springfield* 1,967
Fontbonne University, *Saint Louis* 2,827
Global University, *Springfield* 1,750
Hannibal-La Grange College, *Hannibal* 1,074
Harris-Stowe State College, *Saint Louis* 1,800
Kansas City University of Medicine & Biosciences, *Kansas City* 926
Lincoln University, *Jefferson City* 3,275
Lindenwood University, *Saint Charles* 8,615
Logan College of Chiropractic, *Chesterfield* 958
Maryville University of Saint Louis, *Saint Louis* 3,140
Midwestern Baptist Theological Seminary, *Kansas City* 604
Missouri Baptist University, *Saint Louis* 4,058
Missouri College, *Saint Louis* 605
Missouri Southern State University, *Joplin* 5,256
Missouri Valley College, *Marshall* 1,415
Missouri Western State University, *Saint Joseph* 5,105
Northwest Missouri State University, *Maryville* 6,252
Ozark Christian College, *Joplin* 841
Park University, *Parkville* 12,548
Ranken Technical College, *Saint Louis* 1,733
Rockhurst University, *Kansas City* 2,764
Saint Louis College of Pharmacy, *Saint Louis* 991
Saint Louis University, *Saint Louis* 11,422
Sanford-Brown College, *Fenton* 2,520
Southeast Missouri State University, *Cape Girardeau* 9,618
Southwest Baptist University, *Bolivar* 3,445
Southwest Missouri State University, *Springfield* 19,114
Springfield College, *Springfield* 625
Stephens College, *Columbia* 705
Truman State University, *Kirksville* 5,862
University of Missouri - Columbia, *Columbia* 27,003
University of Missouri - Kansas City, *Kansas City* 14,256
University of Missouri - Rolla, *Rolla* 5,407
University of Missouri - Saint Louis, *Saint Louis* 15,498
Vatterott College, *Saint Ann* 710
Washington University in St. Louis, *Saint Louis* 13,380
Webster University, *Webster Groves* 21,094
Westminster College, *Fulton* 861
William Jewell College, *Liberty* 1,558
William Woods University, *Fulton* 2,432

Montana

Carroll College, *Helena* 1,486
Montana State University - Billings, *Billings* 4,702
Montana State University - Bozeman, *Bozeman* 12,003
Montana State University - Northern, *Havre* 1,421
Montana Tech of The University of Montana, *Butte* 2,188
Rocky Mountain College, *Billings* 988
Salish Kootenai College, *Pablo* 1,129
University of Great Falls, *Great Falls* 764
University of Montana - Missoula College of Technology, The, *Missoula* 1,069
University of Montana - Missoula, The, *Missoula* 13,558
University of Montana-Western, The, *Dillon* 1,146

Nebraska

Bellevue University, *Bellevue* 5,524
Chadron State College, *Chadron* 2,569
Clarkson College, *Omaha* 666
College of Saint Mary, *Omaha* 994
Concordia University, *Seward* 1,332
Creighton University, *Omaha* 6,723
Dana College, *Blair* 637
Doane College, *Crete* 2,429
Hamilton College - Lincoln Campus, *Lincoln* 750
Hastings College, *Hastings* 1,134
Midland Lutheran College, *Fremont* 955
Nebraska Wesleyan University, *Lincoln* 1,958
Peru State College, *Peru* 1,683
Union College, *Lincoln* 936
University of Nebraska at Kearney, *Kearney* 6,382
University of Nebraska at Omaha, *Omaha* 14,667
University of Nebraska - Lincoln, *Lincoln* 21,792
University of Nebraska Medical Center, *Omaha* 2,423
Wayne State College, *Wayne* 3,412

Nevada

Art Institute of Las Vegas, The, *Henderson* 900
Community College of Southern Nevada, *Las Vegas* 34,654
Great Basin College, *Elko* 2,577
University of Nevada - Las Vegas, *Las Vegas* 27,344
University of Nevada, Reno, *Reno* 15,950

New Hampshire

Antioch New England Graduate School, *Keene* 862
Colby-Sawyer College, *New London* 954
Daniel Webster College, *Nashua* 1,002
Dartmouth College, *Hanover* 5,704
Franklin Pierce College, *Rindge* 1,588
Granite State College, *Concord* 1,627
Hesser College, *Manchester* 3,296
Keene State College, *Keene* 5,200
New England College, *Henniker* 1,312
Plymouth State University, *Plymouth* 4,451
Rivier College, *Nashua* 1,180
Saint Anselm College, *Manchester* 1,987
Southern New Hampshire University, *Manchester* 6,352
University of New Hampshire, *Durham* 13,349
University of New Hampshire at Manchester, *Manchester* 1,600

New Jersey

Berkeley College, *West Paterson* 2,313
Beth Medrash Govoha, *Lakewood* 4,333
Bloomfield College, *Bloomfield* 2,166
Caldwell College, *Caldwell* 2,175
Centenary College, *Hackettstown* 2,339
College of New Jersey, The, *Ewing* 6,812
College of Saint Elizabeth, *Morristown* 1,972
DeVry College of Technology, *North Brunswick* 2,007
Drew University, *Madison* 2,675
Fairleigh Dickinson University, *Teaneck* 11,381
Felician College, *Lodi* 1,700
Georgian Court University, *Lakewood* 3,065
Kean University, *Union* 12,897
Monmouth University, *West Long Branch* 6,329
Montclair State University, *Montclair* 15,637
New Jersey City University, *Jersey City* 8,799
New Jersey Institute of Technology, *Newark* 8,249
Princeton Theological Seminary, *Princeton* 767
Princeton University, *Princeton* 4,678
Ramapo College of New Jersey, *Mahwah* 5,617
Richard Stockton College of New Jersey, The, *Pomona* 6,579
Rider University, *Lawrenceville* 5,348
Rowan University, *Glassboro* 9,688
Rutgers the State University of New Jersey Camden Campus, *Camden* 5,563
Rutgers the State University of New Jersey Newark Campus, *Newark* 10,293
Rutgers the State University of New Jersey New Brunswick Campus, *New Brunswick* 38,587
Saint Peter's College, *Jersey City* 3,152
Seton Hall University, *South Orange* 9,823
Seton Hall University School of Law, *Newark* 1,291
Stevens Institute of Technology, *Hoboken* 3,500
Thomas Edison State College, *Trenton* 11,000
UMDNJ - Graduate School of Biomedical Sciences, *Newark* 1,056
UMDNJ - New Jersey Medical School, *Newark* 699
UMDNJ - Robert Wood Johnson Medical School, *Piscataway* 632
UMDNJ - School of Health-Related Professions, *Newark* 1,139
UMDNJ - School of Nursing, *Newark* 754
William Paterson University of New Jersey, *Wayne* 11,409

New Mexico

College of Santa Fe, *Santa Fe* 1,850
College of the Southwest, *Hobbs* 741
Eastern New Mexico University Main Campus, *Portales* 3,959
New Mexico Highlands University, *Las Vegas* 3,633
New Mexico Institute of Mining and Technology, *Socorro* 1,851
New Mexico State University Main Campus, *Las Cruces* 16,428
Northern New Mexico College, *Espanola* 2,009
University of New Mexico Main Campus, *Albuquerque* 26,339
Western New Mexico University, *Silver City* 2,858

New York

Adelphi University, *Garden City* 7,797
Albany College of Pharmacy of Union University, *Albany* 1,080
Albany Law School of Union University, *Albany* 740
Albany Medical College, *Albany* 680
Alfred University, *Alfred* 2,355
Bank Street College of Education, *New York* 980
Bard College, *Annandale-On-Hudson* 1,796
Barnard College, *New York* 2,287
Berkeley College, *New York* 2,670
Boricua College, *New York* 1,169
Briarcliffe College, *Bethpage* 3,227
Brooklyn Law School, *Brooklyn* 1,518
Bryant & Stratton College, *Buffalo* 620
Canisius College, *Buffalo* 5,018
Cazenovia College, *Cazenovia* 898
City University of New York Bernard M. Baruch College, *New York* 15,537
City University of New York Brooklyn College, *Brooklyn* 15,384
City University of New York College of Staten Island, *Staten Island* 12,442
City University of New York Graduate Center, *New York* 4,234
City University of New York Herbert H. Lehman College, *Bronx* 10,281
City University of New York Hunter College, *New York* 20,243
City University of New York John Jay College of Criminal Justice, *New York* 14,104
City University of New York Medgar Evers College, *Brooklyn* 5,300
City University of New York Queens College, *Flushing* 17,395
City University of New York The City College, *New York* 12,108
City University of New York York College, *Jamaica* 5,743
Clarkson University, *Potsdam* 3,123
Colgate University, *Hamilton* 2,800
College of Mount Saint Vincent, *Riverdale* 1,684
College of New Rochelle, The, *New Rochelle* 7,099
College of Saint Rose, *Albany* 4,980
Columbia University in the City of New York, *New York* 23,813
Concordia College, *Bronxville* 727
Cooper Union, *New York* 990
Cornell University, *Ithaca* 19,518
Culinary Institute of America, *Hyde Park* 2,453
Daemen College, *Amherst* 2,186
DeVry Institute of Technology, *Long Island City* 1,576
Dominican College of Blauvelt, *Orangeburg* 1,443
Dowling College, *Oakdale Long Island* 6,232
D'Youville College, *Buffalo* 2,755
Elmira College, *Elmira* 1,755
Excelsior College, *Albany* 26,449
Farmingdale State University of New York, *Farmingdale* 6,250
Fashion Institute of Technology, *New York* 10,380
Five Towns College, *Dix Hills* 1,177
Fordham University, *Bronx* 15,897
Genesee Community College, *Batavia* 6,106
Globe Institute of Technology, *New York* 811
Hamilton College, *Clinton* 1,792
Hartwick College, *Oneonta* 1,479
Hilbert College, *Hamburg* 1,107
Hobart and William Smith Colleges, *Geneva* 1,841
Hofstra University, *Hempstead* 12,999
Houghton College, *Houghton* 1,468
Iona College, *New Rochelle* 4,329
Ithaca College, *Ithaca* 6,337
Jewish Theological Seminary of America, *New York* 668
Juilliard School, The, *New York* 833
Keuka College, *Keuka Park* 1,206
Laboratory Institute of Merchandising, *New York* 608
Le Moyne College, *Syracuse* 3,487
Long Island University Brentwood Campus, *Brentwood* 1,065
Long Island University Brooklyn Campus, *Brooklyn* 8,003
Long Island University C. W. Post Campus, *Brookville* 8,421
Long Island University Southampton College, *Southampton* 916
Manhattan College, *Bronx* 2,905
Manhattan School of Music, *New York* 885
Manhattanville College, *Purchase* 2,620
Marist College, *Poughkeepsie* 5,646
Marymount Manhattan College, *New York* 1,835
Medaille College, *Buffalo* 2,526
Mercy College, *Dobbs Ferry* 9,771
Metropolitan College of New York, *New York* 1,589
Molloy College, *Rockville Centre* 3,363
Monroe College, *Bronx* 5,861
Mount Saint Mary College, *Newburgh* 2,621
Nazareth College of Rochester, *Rochester* 3,140
New School University, *New York* 8,812
New York Chiropractic College, *Seneca Falls* 681
New York City College of Technology/City University of New York, *Brooklyn* 11,762
New York College of Health Professions, *Syosset* 919
New York Institute of Technology - Central Islip Campus, *Central Islip* 716
New York Institute of Technology Main Campus - Old Westbury, *Old Westbury* 7,428
New York Institute of Technology - Manhattan Campus, *New York* 2,624
New York Law School, *New York* 1,400
New York Medical College, *Valhalla* 1,479
New York School of Interior Design, *New York* 745
New York University, *New York* 39,408
Niagara University, *Niagara University* 3,689
Nyack College, *Nyack* 2,908
Pace University, *New York* 13,670
Paul Smith's College of Arts and Sciences, *Paul Smiths* 817
Polytechnic University, *Brooklyn* 2,819
Pratt Institute, *Brooklyn* 4,417
Purchase College, State University of New York, *Purchase* 3,839
Rensselaer Polytechnic Institute, *Troy* 4,876
Roberts Wesleyan College, *Rochester* 1,926
Rochester Institute of Technology, *Rochester* 15,338
Russell Sage College, *Troy* 846
Sage College of Albany, *Albany* 1,051
Sage Graduate School, *Troy* 994
St. Bonaventure University, *Saint Bonaventure* 2,720
St. Francis College, *Brooklyn* 2,326
St. John Fisher College, *Rochester* 3,376
St. John's University, *Queens* 19,813
Saint Joseph's College, New York, *Brooklyn* 1,336
Saint Joseph's College - Suffolk Campus, *Patchogue* 4,005
St. Lawrence University, *Canton* 2,133
St. Thomas Aquinas College, *Sparkill* 2,350
Sarah Lawrence College, *Bronxville* 1,574
School of Visual Arts, *New York* 3,359
Siena College, *Loudonville* 3,338
Skidmore College, *Saratoga Springs* 2,691
State University of New York at Albany, *Albany* 16,293
State University of New York at Binghamton, *Binghamton* 13,860
State University of New York at Buffalo, *Buffalo* 26,592
State University of New York at Fredonia, *Fredonia* 5,359
State University of New York at New Paltz, *New Paltz* 7,603
State University of New York at Stony Brook, *Stony Brook* 21,685
State University of New York College at Brockport, *Brockport* 6,980
State University of New York College at Buffalo, *Buffalo* 11,860
State University of New York College at Cortland, *Cortland* 7,408
State University of New York College at Geneseo, *Geneseo* 5,573
State University of New York College at Old Westbury, *Old Westbury* 3,359
State University of New York College at Oneonta, *Oneonta* 5,667
State University of New York College at Oswego, *Oswego* 8,289
State University of New York College at Plattsburgh, *Plattsburgh* 5,909
State University of New York College at Potsdam, *Potsdam* 4,311
State University of New York College of Agriculture and Technology at Cobleskill, *Cobleskill* 2,510
State University of New York College of Agriculture and Technology at Morrisville, *Morrisville* 3,383
State University of New York College of Environmental Science and Forestry, *Syracuse* 2,238
State University of New York College of Technology at Alfred, *Alfred* 3,600
State University of New York College of Technology at Delhi, *Delhi* 2,483
State University of New York Empire State College, *Saratoga Springs* 9,766
State University of New York Health Science Center at Brooklyn, *Brooklyn* 1,569
State University of New York Institute of Technology at Utica - Rome, *Utica* 2,432
State University of New York Maritime College, *Bronx* 1,230
State University of New York Upstate Medical University, *Syracuse* 1,136
SUNY Canton - College of Technology, *Canton* 2,518
Swedish Institute College of Health Sciences, *New York* 604
Syracuse University Main Campus, *Syracuse* 18,286
Teachers College, Columbia University, *New York* 5,359
Touro College, *New York* 16,691
Union College, *Schenectady* 2,140
United States Merchant Marine Academy, *Kings Point* 1,030
United States Military Academy, *West Point* 4,041
United Talmudical Seminary, *Brooklyn* 1,557
University of Rochester, *Rochester* 8,375
U.T.A. Mesivta of Kiryas Joel, *Monroe* 717
Utica College, *Utica* 2,652
Vassar College, *Poughkeepsie* 2,475
Vaughn College of Aeronautics and Technology, *Flushing* 1,214
Wagner College, *Staten Island* 2,262
Weill Medical College of Cornell University, *New York* 712
Yeshiva University, *New York* 6,467

North Carolina

Appalachian State University, *Boone* 14,653
Art Institute of Charlotte, The, *Charlotte* 716
Barton College, *Wilson* 1,231
Belmont Abbey College, *Belmont* 814
Campbell University, *Buies Creek* 6,982
Catawba College, *Salisbury* 1,395
Chowan College, *Murfreesboro* 687
Davidson College, *Davidson* 1,714
Duke University, *Durham* 12,557
East Carolina University, *Greenville* 22,767
Elizabeth City State University, *Elizabeth City* 2,470
Elon University, *Elon* 4,796
Fayetteville State University, *Fayetteville* 5,441
Gardner-Webb University, *Boiling Springs* 3,813
Greensboro College, *Greensboro* 1,226
Guilford College, *Greensboro* 2,511
High Point University, *High Point* 2,891
Johnson & Wales University - Charlotte, *Charlotte* 1,014
Johnson C. Smith University, *Charlotte* 1,415
Lees-McRae College, *Banner Elk* 907
Lenoir-Rhyne College, *Hickory* 1,600
Livingstone College, *Salisbury* 1,016
Mars Hill College, *Mars Hill* 1,384
Meredith College, *Raleigh* 2,169
Methodist College, *Fayetteville* 2,277
Miller-Motte Technical College, *Wilmington* 740
Montreat College, *Montreat* 990
Mount Olive College, *Mount Olive* 2,583
North Carolina Agricultural and Technical State University, *Greensboro* 10,383
North Carolina Central University, *Durham* 7,727
North Carolina School of the Arts, *Winston-Salem* 684
North Carolina State University, *Raleigh* 29,957
North Carolina Wesleyan College, *Rocky Mount* 1,639
Peace College, *Raleigh* 695
Pfeiffer University, *Misenheimer* 2,053
Queens University of Charlotte, *Charlotte* 2,093
St. Andrews Presbyterian College, *Laurinburg* 741
St. Augustine's College, *Raleigh* 1,689
Salem College, *Winston-Salem* 1,114
Shaw University, *Raleigh* 2,516
Southeastern Baptist Theological Seminary, *Wake Forest* 2,490
University of North Carolina at Asheville, *Asheville* 3,488
University of North Carolina at Chapel Hill, *Chapel Hill* 26,878
University of North Carolina at Charlotte, *Charlotte* 19,846
University of North Carolina at Greensboro, *Greensboro* 15,266
University of North Carolina at Pembroke, *Pembroke* 5,027
University of North Carolina at Wilmington, *Wilmington* 11,327
Wake Forest University, *Winston-Salem* 6,504
Warren Wilson College, *Asheville* 785
Western Carolina University, *Cullowhee* 8,396
Wingate University, *Wingate* 1,560
Winston-Salem State University, *Winston-Salem* 4,805

U.S. Colleges and Universities: Enrollment, *Continued*

North Dakota

Dickinson State University, *Dickinson*	2,479
Jamestown College, *Jamestown*	1,064
Mayville State University, *Mayville*	904
Minot State University, *Minot*	3,851
North Dakota State University Main Campus, *Fargo*	12,026
University of Mary, *Bismarck*	2,757
University of North Dakota Main Campus, *Grand Forks*	13,187
Valley City State University, *Valley City*	1,033
Williston State College, *Williston*	937

Ohio

Air Force Institute of Technology, *Wright Patterson AFB*	962
Antioch University, *Yellow Springs*	3,273
Antioch University McGregor, *Yellow Springs*	737
Ashland University, *Ashland*	6,922
Baldwin-Wallace College, *Berea*	4,600
Bluffton University, *Bluffton*	1,191
Bowling Green State University, *Bowling Green*	20,975
Brown Mackie College - North Canton, *North Canton*	725
Capital University, *Columbus*	3,894
Case Western Reserve University, *Cleveland*	9,423
Cedarville University, *Cedarville*	2,931
Central State University, *Wilberforce*	1,820
Cincinnati Christian University, *Cincinnati*	899
Cleveland Institute of Art, *Cleveland*	607
Cleveland State University, *Cleveland*	15,706
College of Mount Saint Joseph, *Cincinnati*	2,158
College of Wooster, The, *Wooster*	1,827
Columbus College of Art & Design, *Columbus*	1,450
Defiance College, The, *Defiance*	1,035
Denison University, *Granville*	2,126
DeVry University, *Columbus*	3,270
Franciscan University of Steubenville, *Steubenville*	2,374
Franklin University, *Columbus*	6,935
Heidelberg College, *Tiffin*	1,483
Hiram College, *Hiram*	1,036
John Carroll University, *Cleveland*	4,101
Kent State University Geauga Campus, *Burton Township*	925
Kent State University Main Campus, *Kent*	24,011
Kent State University Salem Campus, *Salem*	1,371
Kent State University Stark Campus, *Canton*	3,880
Kent State University Tuscarawas Campus, *New Philadelphia*	1,935
Kenyon College, *Gambier*	1,611
Kettering College of Medical Arts, *Kettering*	734
Lake Erie College, *Painesville*	914
Laura and Alvin Siegal College of Judaic Studies, *Beachwood*	1,000
Lourdes College, *Sylvania*	1,491
Malone College, *Canton*	2,250
Marietta College, *Marietta*	1,351
Medical University of Ohio, *Toledo*	1,143
Mercy College of Northwest Ohio, *Toledo*	688
Miami University, *Oxford*	17,151
Miami University Hamilton Campus, *Hamilton*	3,165
Miami University Middletown, *Middletown*	2,005
Mount Union College, *Alliance*	2,333
Mount Vernon Nazarene University, *Mount Vernon*	2,455
Muskingum College, *New Concord*	1,663
Myers University, *Cleveland*	1,004
Notre Dame College, *South Euclid*	1,377
Oberlin College, *Oberlin*	2,827
Ohio Dominican University, *Columbus*	2,592
Ohio Northern University, *Ada*	3,388
Ohio State University at Lima Campus, The, *Lima*	1,281
Ohio State University at Marion, The, *Marion*	1,608
Ohio State University Main Campus, The, *Columbus*	50,995
Ohio State University Mansfield Campus, The, *Mansfield*	1,634
Ohio State University Newark Campus, The, *Newark*	2,143
Ohio University Chillicothe Campus, *Chillicothe*	2,048
Ohio University Eastern Campus, *Saint Clairsville*	862
Ohio University Lancaster Campus, *Lancaster*	1,713
Ohio University Main Campus, *Athens*	19,704
Ohio University Zanesville Branch, *Zanesville*	1,877
Ohio Wesleyan University, *Delaware*	1,910
Otterbein College, *Westerville*	3,090
Shawnee State University, *Portsmouth*	3,798
Tiffin University, *Tiffin*	1,634
Union Institute & University, *Cincinnati*	2,537
University of Akron, Main Campus, The, *Akron*	23,240
University of Cincinnati Main Campus, *Cincinnati*	34,364
University of Dayton, *Dayton*	10,495
University of Findlay, The, *Findlay*	3,461
University of Northwestern Ohio, *Lima*	2,318
University of Rio Grande, *Rio Grande*	2,812
University of Toledo, *Toledo*	19,480
Urbana University, *Urbana*	1,560
Ursuline College, *Cleveland*	1,462
Walsh University, *North Canton*	1,951
Wilberforce University, *Wilberforce*	1,007
Wilmington College, *Wilmington*	1,566
Wittenberg University, *Springfield*	2,007
Wright State University Main Campus, *Dayton*	16,944
Xavier University, *Cincinnati*	6,668
Youngstown State University, *Youngstown*	13,101

Oklahoma

Bacone College, *Muskogee*	752
Cameron University, *Lawton*	5,933
East Central University, *Ada*	4,661
Langston University, *Langston*	2,509
Mid-America Christian University, *Oklahoma City*	698
Northeastern State University, *Tahlequah*	9,562
Northwestern Oklahoma State University, *Alva*	2,169
Oklahoma Baptist University, *Shawnee*	1,684
Oklahoma Christian University, *Oklahoma City*	1,947
Oklahoma City University, *Oklahoma City*	3,712
Oklahoma Panhandle State University, *Goodwell*	1,237
Oklahoma State University Main Campus, *Stillwater*	23,626
Oklahoma State University - Okmulgee, *Okmulgee*	2,661
Oklahoma Wesleyan University, *Bartlesville*	850
Oral Roberts University, *Tulsa*	4,240
Rogers State University, *Claremore*	3,778
Saint Gregory's University, *Shawnee*	782
Southeastern Oklahoma State University, *Durant*	4,070
Southern Nazarene University, *Bethany*	2,177
Southwestern Oklahoma State University, *Weatherford*	5,426
Spartan College of Aeronautics and Technology, *Tulsa*	1,000
University of Central Oklahoma, *Edmond*	15,574
University of Oklahoma Health Sciences Center, *Oklahoma City*	3,584
University of Oklahoma Norman Campus, *Norman*	27,807
University of Science and Arts of Oklahoma, *Chickasha*	1,449
University of Tulsa, *Tulsa*	4,174

Oregon

Art Institute of Portland, The, *Portland*	1,538
Concordia University, *Portland*	1,404
Corban College, *Salem*	754
Eastern Oregon University, *La Grande*	3,338
George Fox University, *Newberg*	3,034
Lewis and Clark College, *Portland*	3,259
Linfield College, *McMinnville*	2,606
Marylhurst University, *Marylhurst*	1,235
Multnomah Bible College and Biblical Seminary, *Portland*	767
Oregon Health and Science University, *Portland*	2,553
Oregon Institute of Technology, *Klamath Falls*	3,373
Oregon State University, *Corvallis*	19,162
Pacific University, *Forest Grove*	2,534
Pioneer Pacific College, *Wilsonville*	1,100
Portland State University, *Portland*	21,348
Reed College, *Portland*	1,341
Southern Oregon University, *Ashland*	5,162
University of Oregon, *Eugene*	20,720
University of Portland, *Portland*	3,343
Western Oregon University, *Monmouth*	4,772
Western Seminary, *Portland*	689
Willamette University, *Salem*	2,663

Pennsylvania

Albright College, *Reading*	2,080
Allegheny College, *Meadville*	1,955
Alvernia College, *Reading*	2,586
Arcadia University, *Glenside*	3,423
Art Institute of Philadelphia, *Philadelphia*	3,273
Art Institute of Pittsburgh, *Pittsburgh*	4,850
Baptist Bible College and Seminary, *Clarks Summit*	1,138
Bloomsburg University of Pennsylvania, *Bloomsburg*	8,304
Bryn Mawr College, *Bryn Mawr*	1,777
Bucknell University, *Lewisburg*	3,609
Cabrini College, *Radnor*	2,148
California University of Pennsylvania, *California*	6,640
Carlow University, *Pittsburgh*	2,106
Carnegie Mellon University, *Pittsburgh*	9,803
Cedar Crest College, *Allentown*	1,856
Central Pennsylvania College, *Summerdale*	915
Chatham College, *Pittsburgh*	1,249
Chestnut Hill College, *Philadelphia*	1,679
Cheyney University of Pennsylvania, *Cheyney*	1,136
Clarion University of Pennsylvania, *Clarion*	6,421
Clarion University - Venango Campus, *Oil City*	720
College Misericordia, *Dallas*	2,271
Delaware Valley College, *Doylestown*	1,509
DeSales University, *Center Valley*	2,927
DeVry University, *Fort Washington*	778
Dickinson College, *Carlisle*	2,321
Drexel University, *Philadelphia*	17,656
Duquesne University, *Pittsburgh*	9,722
Eastern University, *Saint Davids*	3,836
East Stroudsburg University of Pennsylvania, *East Stroudsburg*	6,553
Edinboro University of Pennsylvania, *Edinboro*	7,773
Elizabethtown College, *Elizabethtown*	2,082
Franklin & Marshall College, *Lancaster*	2,048
Gannon University, *Erie*	2,430
Geneva College, *Beaver Falls*	2,145
Gettysburg College, *Gettysburg*	2,582
Grove City College, *Grove City*	2,318
Gwynedd-Mercy College, *Gwynedd Valley*	2,751
Haverford College, *Haverford*	1,172
Holy Family University, *Philadelphia*	3,276
Immaculata University, *Immaculata*	3,811
Indiana University of Pennsylvania, *Indiana*	13,998
Juniata College, *Huntingdon*	1,427
Keystone College, *La Plume*	1,658
King's College, *Wilkes-Barre*	2,223
Kutztown University of Pennsylvania, *Kutztown*	8,923
Lafayette College, *Easton*	2,303
Lake Erie College of Osteopathic Medicine, *Erie*	1,190
Lancaster Bible College, *Lancaster*	718
La Roche College, *Pittsburgh*	1,681
La Salle University, *Philadelphia*	6,221
Lebanon Valley College, *Annville*	1,600
Lehigh University, *Bethlehem*	4,577
Lincoln University, *Lincoln University*	2,012
Lock Haven University of Pennsylvania, *Lock Haven*	5,126
Lycoming College, *Williamsport*	1,499
Mansfield University of Pennsylvania, *Mansfield*	3,565
Marywood University, *Scranton*	3,127
Mercyhurst College, *Erie*	4,035
Messiah College, *Grantham*	2,917
Millersville University of Pennsylvania, *Millersville*	7,998
Moravian College, *Bethlehem*	1,828
Mount Aloysius College, *Cresson*	1,468
Muhlenberg College, *Allentown*	2,113
Neumann College, *Aston*	2,682
Peirce College, *Philadelphia*	1,892
Penn State Abington, *Abington*	3,143
Penn State Altoona, *Altoona*	3,766
Penn State Beaver, *Monaca*	666
Penn State Berks, *Reading*	2,416
Penn State Delaware County, *Media*	2,416
Penn State Dickinson School of Law, The, *Carlisle*	638
Penn State DuBois, *DuBois*	1,636
Penn State Erie, The Behrend College, *Erie*	3,593
Penn State Fayette, The Eberly Campus, *Uniontown*	1,066
Penn State Great Valley School of Graduate Professional Studies, *Malvern*	1,305
Penn State Harrisburg, *Middletown*	3,729
Penn State Hazleton, *Hazleton*	1,114
Penn State Lehigh Valley, *Fogelsville*	680
Penn State McKeesport, *McKeesport*	798
Penn State Milton S. Hershey Medical Center College of Medicine, *Hershey*	748
Penn State Mont Alto, *Mont Alto*	1,028
Penn State New Kensington, *Upper Burrell*	990
Penn State Schuylkill, *Schuylkill Haven*	969
Penn State Shenango, *Sharon*	958
Penn State University Park, *University Park*	41,289
Penn State Wilkes-Barre, *Lehman*	779
Penn State Worthington - Scranton, *Dunmore*	1,354
Penn State York, *York*	1,793
Pennsylvania College of Optometry, *Elkins Park*	625
Pennsylvania College of Technology, *Williamsport*	6,358
Philadelphia Biblical University, *Langhorne Manor*	1,397
Philadelphia College of Osteopathic Medicine, *Philadelphia*	1,631
Philadelphia University, *Philadelphia*	3,211
Point Park University, *Pittsburgh*	3,292
Robert Morris University, *Moon Township*	4,971
Rosemont College, *Rosemont*	1,083
Saint Francis University, *Loretto*	1,847
Saint Joseph's University, *Philadelphia*	7,730
Saint Vincent College, *Latrobe*	1,490
Seton Hill University, *Greensburg*	1,730
Shippensburg University of Pennsylvania, *Shippensburg*	7,653
Slippery Rock University of Pennsylvania, *Slippery Rock*	7,928
Susquehanna University, *Selinsgrove*	2,067
Swarthmore College, *Swarthmore*	1,474
Temple University, *Philadelphia*	33,979
Thiel College, *Greenville*	1,245
Thomas Jefferson University, *Philadelphia*	2,457
University of Pennsylvania, *Philadelphia*	23,305
University of Pittsburgh at Bradford, *Bradford*	1,451
University of Pittsburgh at Johnstown, *Johnstown*	3,208
University of Pittsburgh Greensburg Campus, *Greensburg*	1,900
University of Pittsburgh, Pittsburgh Campus, *Pittsburgh*	26,731
University of Scranton, The, *Scranton*	4,795
University of the Arts, The, *Philadelphia*	2,196
University of the Sciences in Philadelphia, *Philadelphia*	2,824
Ursinus College, *Collegeville*	1,484
Valley Forge Christian College, *Phoenixville*	856
Villanova University, *Villanova*	10,481
Washington and Jefferson College, *Washington*	1,355
Waynesburg College, *Waynesburg*	2,102
West Chester University of Pennsylvania, *West Chester*	12,822
Westminster College, *New Wilmington*	1,606
Westminster Theological Seminary, *Philadelphia*	777
Widener University, *Chester*	4,726
Wilkes University, *Wilkes-Barre*	4,364
Wilson College, *Chambersburg*	776
York College of Pennsylvania, *York*	5,669

Rhode Island

Brown University, *Providence*	7,819
Bryant University, *Smithfield*	3,518
Johnson & Wales University, *Providence*	9,982
New England Institute of Technology, *Warwick*	3,011
Providence College, *Providence*	5,366
Rhode Island College, *Providence*	8,878
Rhode Island School of Design, *Providence*	2,282
Roger Williams University, *Bristol*	4,190
Salve Regina University, *Newport*	2,469
University of Rhode Island, *Kingston*	14,749

South Carolina

Allen University, *Columbia*	643
Anderson College, *Anderson*	1,666
Benedict College, *Columbia*	2,770
Bob Jones University, *Greenville*	4,100
Charleston Southern University, *Charleston*	2,875
Citadel, The Military College of South Carolina, The, *Charleston*	3,676
Claflin University, *Orangeburg*	1,814
Clemson University, *Clemson*	17,110
Coastal Carolina University, *Conway*	7,021
Coker College, *Hartsville*	1,151
College of Charleston, *Charleston*	11,607
Columbia College, *Columbia*	1,149
Columbia International University, *Columbia*	1,016
Converse College, *Spartanburg*	1,217
Erskine College, *Due West*	962
Francis Marion University, *Florence*	3,698
Furman University, *Greenville*	2,625
Lander University, *Greenwood*	2,733
Limestone College, *Gaffney*	3,024
Medical University of South Carolina, *Charleston*	2,428
Morris College, *Sumter*	897
Newberry College, *Newberry*	779
North Greenville College, *Tigerville*	1,759
Presbyterian College, *Clinton*	1,188
South Carolina State University, *Orangeburg*	4,479
Southern Wesleyan University, *Central*	2,549
University of South Carolina Aiken, *Aiken*	3,382
University of South Carolina Beaufort, *Beaufort*	1,277
University of South Carolina Columbia, *Columbia*	25,596
University of South Carolina Upstate, *Spartanburg*	4,370
Voorhees College, *Denmark*	902
Winthrop University, *Rock Hill*	6,447
Wofford College, *Spartanburg*	1,177

South Dakota

Augustana College, *Sioux Falls*	1,799
Black Hills State University, *Spearfish*	3,846
Colorado Technical University, *Sioux Falls*	936
Dakota State University, *Madison*	2,295
Dakota Wesleyan University, *Mitchell*	681
Mount Marty College, *Yankton*	1,163
National American University, *Rapid City*	4,022
Northern State University, *Aberdeen*	2,284
Oglala Lakota College, *Kyle*	1,438
Presentation College, *Aberdeen*	639
Sinte Gleska University, *Mission*	2,110
South Dakota School of Mines and Technology, *Rapid City*	2,347
South Dakota State University, *Brookings*	10,954
University of Sioux Falls, *Sioux Falls*	1,304
University of South Dakota, The, *Vermillion*	8,120

Tennessee

Aquinas College, *Nashville*	801
Austin Peay State University, *Clarksville*	8,650
Baptist Memorial College of Health Science, *Memphis*	803
Belmont University, *Nashville*	3,317
Bethel College, *McKenzie*	1,147
Bryan College, *Dayton*	636
Carson-Newman College, *Jefferson City*	2,053
Christian Brothers University, *Memphis*	1,847
Crichton College, *Memphis*	969
Cumberland University, *Lebanon*	1,493
East Tennessee State University, *Johnson City*	11,635
Fisk University, *Nashville*	902
Freed-Hardeman University, *Henderson*	1,942
Johnson Bible College, *Knoxville*	889
King College, *Bristol*	812
Lambuth University, *Jackson*	806
Lane College, *Jackson*	1,045
Lee University, *Cleveland*	3,849
LeMoyne-Owen College, *Memphis*	790
Lincoln Memorial University, *Harrogate*	2,579
Lipscomb University, *Nashville*	2,535
Martin Methodist College, *Pulaski*	714
Maryville College, *Maryville*	1,080
Meharry Medical College, *Nashville*	844
Middle Tennessee State University, *Murfreesboro*	22,322
Milligan College, *Milligan College*	916
Remington College, *Memphis*	700
Rhodes College, *Memphis*	1,633
South College, *Knoxville*	622
Southern Adventist University, *Collegedale*	2,391
Tennessee State University, *Nashville*	9,100
Tennessee Technological University, *Cookeville*	9,217
Tennessee Wesleyan College, *Athens*	814
Trevecca Nazarene University, *Nashville*	2,089
Tusculum College, *Greeneville*	2,290
Union University, *Jackson*	2,919
University of Memphis, The, *Memphis*	20,668
University of Tennessee, *Knoxville*	25,653
University of Tennessee at Chattanooga, *Chattanooga*	8,689
University of Tennessee at Martin, *Martin*	6,098
University of Tennessee Health Science Center, *Memphis*	2,139
University of the South, The, *Sewanee*	1,492
Vanderbilt University, *Nashville*	11,294

Texas

Abilene Christian University, *Abilene*	4,761
Amberton University, *Garland*	1,680
Angelo State University, *San Angelo*	6,137
Art Institute of Dallas, *Dallas*	1,418
Art Institute of Houston, The, *Houston*	1,644
Austin College, *Sherman*	1,370
Baptist University of the Americas, *San Antonio*	645
Baylor College of Medicine, *Houston*	1,290
Baylor University, *Waco*	13,799
Brazosport College, *Lake Jackson*	4,000
College of Biblical Studies - Houston, *Houston*	1,493
Concordia University at Austin, *Austin*	1,162
Dallas Baptist University, *Dallas*	4,714
Dallas Theological Seminary, *Dallas*	1,877
DeVry University, *Irving*	2,386
East Texas Baptist University, *Marshall*	1,412
Hardin-Simmons University, *Abilene*	2,392
Houston Baptist University, *Houston*	2,227
Howard Payne University, *Brownwood*	1,319
Huston-Tillotson University, *Austin*	685
Lamar University, *Beaumont*	10,804
LeTourneau University, *Longview*	3,758
Lubbock Christian University, *Lubbock*	1,974
McMurry University, *Abilene*	1,386
Midland College, *Midland*	5,531
Midwestern State University, *Wichita Falls*	6,348
Our Lady of the Lake University, *San Antonio*	3,025
Parker College of Chiropractic, *Dallas*	900
Paul Quinn College, *Dallas*	966
Prairie View A & M University, *Prairie View*	7,820
Rice University, *Houston*	4,855
St. Edward's University, *Austin*	4,651
St. Mary's University, *San Antonio*	2,531
Sam Houston State University, *Huntsville*	14,335
Schreiner University, *Kerrville*	842
Southern Methodist University, *Dallas*	10,901
South Texas College, *McAllen*	17,138
South Texas College of Law, *Houston*	1,254
Southwestern Adventist University, *Keene*	894
Southwestern Assemblies of God University, *Waxahachie*	1,702
Southwestern Baptist Theological Seminary, *Fort Worth*	3,520
Southwestern University, *Georgetown*	1,277
Stephen F. Austin State University, *Nacogdoches*	11,287
Sul Ross State University, *Alpine*	1,949
Tarleton State University, *Stephenville*	9,033
Texas A & M International University, *Laredo*	4,218
Texas A & M University, *College Station*	44,435
Texas A & M University at Galveston, *Galveston*	1,689
Texas A & M University - Commerce, *Commerce*	8,547
Texas A & M University - Corpus Christi, *Corpus Christi*	8,227
Texas A & M University - Kingsville, *Kingsville*	7,126
Texas A&M University - Texarkana, *Texarkana*	1,559
Texas Christian University, *Fort Worth*	8,632
Texas College, *Tyler*	757
Texas Lutheran University, *Seguin*	1,414
Texas Southern University, *Houston*	11,635
Texas Southmost College, *Brownsville*	7,997
Texas State University - San Marcos, *San Marcos*	26,783
Texas Tech University, *Lubbock*	28,325
Texas Tech University Health Sciences Center, *Lubbock*	2,350
Texas Wesleyan University, *Fort Worth*	1,146
Texas Woman's University, *Denton*	10,763
Trinity University, *San Antonio*	2,718
University of Dallas, *Irving*	3,005
University of Houston, *Houston*	35,180
University of Houston - Clear Lake, *Houston*	7,785
University of Houston - Downtown, *Houston*	10,952
University of Houston - Victoria, *Victoria*	2,418
University of Mary Hardin - Baylor, *Belton*	2,706
University of North Texas, *Denton*	31,155
University of North Texas Health Science Center at Fort Worth, *Fort Worth*	1,021
University of St. Thomas, *Houston*	3,648
University of Texas at Arlington, The, *Arlington*	25,297
University of Texas at Austin, *Austin*	50,377
University of Texas at Brownsville, The, *Brownsville*	11,560
University of Texas at Dallas, *Richardson*	14,092
University of Texas at El Paso, *El Paso*	18,918
University of Texas at San Antonio, *San Antonio*	26,175
University of Texas at Tyler, *Tyler*	5,303
University of Texas Health Science Center at Houston, *Houston*	3,399
University of Texas Health Science Center at San Antonio, *San Antonio*	2,837
University of Texas Medical Branch, *Galveston*	2,121
University of Texas of the Permian Basin, *Odessa*	3,291
University of Texas - Pan American, *Edinburg*	17,030
University of Texas Southwestern Medical Center at Dallas, *Dallas*	1,814
University of the Incarnate Word, *San Antonio*	4,800
Wayland Baptist University, *Plainview*	6,185
West Texas A&M University, *Canyon*	7,299
Wiley College, *Marshall*	791

Utah

Brigham Young University, *Provo*	33,427
California College for Health Sciences, *Salt Lake City*	3,500
Dixie State College of Utah, *Saint George*	8,634
Southern Utah University, *Cedar City*	6,672
University of Utah, *Salt Lake City*	28,933
Utah State University, *Logan*	23,908
Utah Valley State College, *Orem*	24,149
Weber State University, *Ogden*	18,498
Western Governors University, *Salt Lake City*	1,550
Westminster College, *Salt Lake City*	2,417

Vermont

Bennington College, *Bennington*	820
Castleton State College, *Castleton*	1,971
Champlain College, *Burlington*	2,555
Green Mountain College, *Poultney*	617
Johnson State College, *Johnson*	1,760
Lyndon State College, *Lyndonville*	1,350
Middlebury College, *Middlebury*	2,357
Norwich University, *Northfield*	2,537
Saint Michael's College, *Colchester*	2,176
School for International Training, *Brattleboro*	1,437
University of Vermont, *Burlington*	9,848
Vermont Law School, *South Royalton*	639
Vermont Technical College, *Randolph Center*	1,332

Virginia

Argosy University/Washington DC, *Arlington*	789
Averett University, *Danville*	2,719
Bluefield College, *Bluefield*	817
Bridgewater College, *Bridgewater*	1,525
Catholic Distance University, The, *Hamilton*	663
Christopher Newport University, *Newport News*	4,788
College of William and Mary, *Williamsburg*	7,575
DeVry University, *Arlington*	736
Eastern Mennonite University, *Harrisonburg*	1,511
Eastern Virginia Medical School, *Norfolk*	765
ECPI College of Technology, *Virginia Beach*	3,300
ECPI Technical College, *Richmond*	650
Emory & Henry College, *Emory*	930
Ferrum College, *Ferrum*	941
George Mason University, *Fairfax*	28,874
Hampden-Sydney College, *Hampden-Sydney*	1,082
Hampton University, *Hampton*	6,151
Hollins University, *Roanoke*	1,057
James Madison University, *Harrisonburg*	15,649
Jefferson College of Health Sciences (Formerly Community Hospital), *Roanoke*	840
Liberty University, *Lynchburg*	10,475
Longwood University, *Farmville*	4,289
Lynchburg College, *Lynchburg*	2,248
Mary Baldwin College, *Staunton*	2,200
Marymount University, *Arlington*	3,873
National College of Business & Technology, *Salem*	748
Norfolk State University, *Norfolk*	6,165
Old Dominion University, *Norfolk*	20,595
Radford University, *Radford*	9,329
Randolph-Macon College, *Ashland*	1,126
Randolph-Macon Woman's College, *Lynchburg*	732
Regent University, *Virginia Beach*	3,447
Roanoke College, *Salem*	1,850
Saint Paul's College, *Lawrenceville*	628
Shenandoah University, *Winchester*	3,000
Southern Virginia University, *Buena Vista*	700
Stratford University, *Falls Church*	1,022
Sweet Briar College, *Sweet Briar*	738
University of Management & Technology, *Arlington*	1,400
University of Mary Washington, *Fredericksburg*	3,910
University of Northern Virginia, *Manassas*	4,420
University of Richmond, *Richmond*	4,475
University of Virginia, *Charlottesville*	23,341
University of Virginia's College at Wise, The, *Wise*	1,836
Virginia Commonwealth University, *Richmond*	28,462
Virginia Intermont College, *Bristol*	1,152
Virginia Military Institute, *Lexington*	1,362
Virginia Polytechnic Institute and State University, *Blacksburg*	27,619
Virginia State University, *Petersburg*	4,815
Virginia Union University, *Richmond*	1,722
Virginia Wesleyan College, *Norfolk*	1,442
Washington and Lee University, *Lexington*	2,168

Washington

Antioch University Seattle, *Seattle*	932
Art Institute of Seattle, The, *Seattle*	2,500
Bastyr University, *Kenmore*	1,132
Central Washington University, *Ellensburg*	9,912
City University, *Bellevue*	6,840
Cornish College of the Arts, *Seattle*	728
DeVry University, *Federal Way*	1,179
DigiPen Institute of Technology, *Redmond*	658
Eastern Washington University, *Cheney*	10,707
Evergreen State College, The, *Olympia*	4,410
Gonzaga University, *Spokane*	6,169
Heritage University, *Toppenish*	1,355
Northwest University, *Kirkland*	1,180
Pacific Lutheran University, *Tacoma*	3,643
Saint Martin's University, *Lacey*	1,511
Seattle Pacific University, *Seattle*	3,779
Seattle University, *Seattle*	6,810
University of Puget Sound, *Tacoma*	2,793
University of Washington, *Seattle*	42,907
Walla Walla College, *College Place*	1,968
Washington State University, *Pullman*	23,241
Western Washington University, *Bellingham*	12,940
Whitman College, *Walla Walla*	1,450
Whitworth College, *Spokane*	2,382

West Virginia

Alderson Broaddus College, *Philippi*	800
American Public University System, *Charles Town*	3,945
Bethany College, *Bethany*	857
Bluefield State College, *Bluefield*	3,506
Concord University, *Athens*	2,993
Davis & Elkins College, *Elkins*	625
Fairmont State University, *Fairmont*	7,423
Glenville State College, *Glenville*	1,313
Marshall University, *Huntington*	13,925
Mountain State University, *Beckley*	4,418
Salem International University, *Salem*	660
Shepherd University, *Shepherdstown*	5,206
University of Charleston, *Charleston*	981
West Liberty State College, *West Liberty*	2,374
West Virginia State University, *Institute*	3,344
West Virginia University, *Morgantown*	25,255
West Virginia University at Parkersburg, *Parkersburg*	3,853
West Virginia University Institute of Technology, *Montgomery*	1,698
West Virginia Wesleyan College, *Buckhannon*	1,522
Wheeling Jesuit University, *Wheeling*	1,356

Wisconsin

Alverno College, *Milwaukee*	2,241
Beloit College, *Beloit*	1,321
Bryant & Stratton College, *Milwaukee*	670
Cardinal Stritch University, *Milwaukee*	6,672
Carroll College, *Waukesha*	3,014
Carthage College, *Kenosha*	2,679
Concordia University Wisconsin, *Mequon*	5,395
Edgewood College, *Madison*	1,474
Herzing College, *Madison*	715
Lakeland College, *Sheboygan*	4,118
Lawrence University, *Appleton*	1,390
Maranatha Baptist Bible College, *Watertown*	904
Marian College of Fond Du Lac, *Fond Du Lac*	2,918
Marquette University, *Milwaukee*	11,510
Medical College of Wisconsin, *Milwaukee*	805
Milwaukee Institute of Art & Design, *Milwaukee*	635
Milwaukee School of Engineering, *Milwaukee*	2,400
Mount Mary College, *Milwaukee*	1,651
Northland Baptist Bible College, *Dunbar*	725
Northland College, *Ashland*	717
Ripon College, *Ripon*	929
Saint Norbert College, *De Pere*	2,020
Silver Lake College, *Manitowoc*	1,034
University of Wisconsin - Eau Claire, *Eau Claire*	10,590
University of Wisconsin - Green Bay, *Green Bay*	5,706
University of Wisconsin - La Crosse, *La Crosse*	9,019
University of Wisconsin - Madison, *Madison*	41,169
University of Wisconsin - Milwaukee, *Milwaukee*	17,922
University of Wisconsin - Oshkosh, *Oshkosh*	11,059
University of Wisconsin - Parkside, *Kenosha*	5,072
University of Wisconsin - Platteville, *Platteville*	6,158
University of Wisconsin - River Falls, *River Falls*	5,950
University of Wisconsin - Stevens Point, *Stevens Point*	8,710
University of Wisconsin - Stout, *Menomonie*	7,547
University of Wisconsin - Superior, *Superior*	2,804
University of Wisconsin - Whitewater, *Whitewater*	10,938
Viterbo University, *La Crosse*	2,692
Wisconsin Lutheran College, *Milwaukee*	697

Wyoming

University of Wyoming, *Laramie*	13,207

Business/Manufactures, by State

The tables below rank the most rapidly growing RMAs, PMSAs, MSAs, and CBSAs from 1990 to 2000. Also ranked are the top RMAs, PMSAs, MSAs, and CBSAs losing population between 1990 and 2000. Both the numerical change and the percentage change are shown.

Counties with more than 50,000 population increase (decrease) between 1990 and 2000 are also ranked. Only the numerical increase or decrease is listed. (For metropolitan area definitions and additional information about RMAs and counties, see the Introduction on pages 5-9.)

Most Rapidly Growing RMAs, 1990-2000

		Population		Population Increase	
No.	RMA	2000 Census	1990 Census	1990-2000 No.	1990-2000 %
1	Las Vegas, NV	1,344,700	724,700	620,000	85.6
2	Naples, FL	216,400	133,700	82,700	61.9
3	Kissimmee, FL	155,500	97,700	57,800	59.2
4	Denton, TX	128,100	80,900	47,200	58.3
5	Murfreesboro, TN	96,900	63,100	33,800	53.6
6	Yuma, AZ-CA	148,600	99,700	48,900	49.0
7	McAllen, TX-MX	448,800	302,300	146,500	48.5
8	Raleigh, NC	734,000	497,200	236,800	47.6
9	Austin, TX	1,009,200	687,200	322,000	46.9
10	Boise, ID	350,000	239,400	110,600	46.2
11	Laredo, TX-MEX.	180,700	124,700	56,000	44.9
12	Phoenix, AZ	3,078,500	2,124,900	953,600	44.9
13	Fredericksburg, VA	121,800	84,900	36,900	43.5
14	Fayetteville-, AR	132,500	94,200	38,300	40.7
15	Provo-, UT	360,700	258,000	102,700	39.8
16	Atlanta, GA	3,623,100	2,621,100	1,002,000	38.2
17	Greeley, CO	102,500	74,700	27,800	37.2
18	Myrtle Beach, SC-NC	156,300	114,400	41,900	36.6
19	Fort Collins-, CO	235,200	174,100	61,100	35.1
20	Wilmington, NC	181,100	134,800	46,300	34.3
21	Reno, NV	331,300	248,500	82,800	33.3
22	Ocala, FL	211,400	159,100	52,300	32.9
23	Hemet, CA	126,000	95,400	30,600	32.1
24	Palm Springs-, CA	203,500	154,100	49,400	32.1
25	Auburn-, AL	80,800	61,200	19,600	32.0

RMAs Most Rapidly Losing Population, 1990-2000

		Population		Population Increase	
No.	RMA	2000 Census	1990 Census	1990-2000 No.	1990-2000 %
1	Carbondale-, IL	122,400	143,000	-20,600	-14.4
2	Lafayette, LA	268,100	294,700	-26,600	-9.0
3	Steubenville-, OH-WV	107,400	116,000	-8,600	-7.4
4	Greenville, MS	45,000	48,500	-3,500	-7.2
5	Plattsburgh, NY	50,700	54,600	-3,900	-7.1
6	Manhattan, KS	44,500	47,400	-2,900	-6.1
7	Utica-, NY	221,500	235,500	-14,000	-5.9
8	Grand Forks, ND-MN	55,700	59,200	-3,500	-5.9
9	Johnstown, PA	123,300	129,600	-6,300	-4.9
10	Danville, IL	65,400	68,800	-3,400	-4.9
11	Binghamton, NY-PA	223,700	234,600	-10,900	-4.6
12	Wheeling, WV-OH	138,500	144,900	-6,400	-4.4
13	Elmira, NY	82,000	85,700	-3,700	-4.3
14	Alexandria, LA	96,700	100,700	-4,000	-4.0
15	Pittsfield, MA	85,900	88,700	-2,800	-3.2
16	Oil City-, PA	38,400	39,600	-1,200	-3.0
17	Natchez, MS-LA	42,400	43,700	-1,300	-3.0
18	Danville, VA-NC	74,000	76,100	-2,100	-2.8
19	Pittsburgh, PA	2,010,400	2,062,000	-51,600	-2.5
20	Anniston, AL	98,600	101,100	-2,500	-2.5
21	Scranton-, PA	469,200	479,700	-10,500	-2.2
22	Decatur, IL	103,800	106,100	-2,300	-2.2
23	Hazleton, PA	68,600	70,100	-1,500	-2.1
24	Newport, RI	63,200	64,500	-1,300	-2.0
25	Youngstown-, OH-PA	448,400	457,200	-8,800	-1.9

Most Rapidly Growing PMSAs and MSAs, 1990-2000

		Population		Population Increase	
No.	PMSA & MSA	2000 Census	1990 Census	1990-2000 No.	1990-2000 %
1	Las Vegas, NV-AZ MSA	1,563,282	852,737	710,545	83.3
2	Naples, FL MSA	251,377	152,099	99,278	65.3
3	Yuma, AZ MSA	160,026	106,895	53,131	49.7
4	McAllen-Edinburg-Mission, TX MSA	569,463	383,545	185,918	48.5
5	Austin-San Marcos, TX MSA	1,249,763	846,227	403,536	47.7
6	Fayetteville-Springdale-Rogers, AR MSA	311,121	210,908	100,213	47.5
7	Boise City, ID MSA	432,345	295,851	136,494	46.1
8	Phoenix-Mesa, AZ MSA	3,251,876	2,238,480	1,013,396	45.3
9	Laredo, TX MSA	193,117	133,239	59,878	44.9
10	Provo-Orem, UT MSA	368,536	263,590	104,946	39.8
11	Atlanta, GA MSA	4,112,198	2,959,950	1,152,248	38.9
12	Raleigh-Durham-Chapel Hill, NC MSA	1,187,941	855,545	332,396	38.9
13	Greeley, CO PMSA	180,936	131,821	49,115	37.3
14	Myrtle Beach, SC MSA	196,629	144,053	52,576	36.5
15	Wilmington, NC MSA	233,450	171,269	62,181	36.3
16	Fort Collins-Loveland, CO MSA	251,494	186,136	65,358	35.1
17	Orlando, FL MSA	1,644,561	1,224,852	419,709	34.3
18	Reno, NV MSA	339,486	254,667	84,819	33.3
19	Ocala, FL MSA	258,916	194,833	64,083	32.9
20	Auburn-Opelika, AL MSA	115,092	87,146	27,946	32.1
21	Fort Myers-Cape Coral, FL MSA	440,888	335,113	105,775	31.6
22	Dallas, TX PMSA	3,519,176	2,676,248	842,928	31.5
23	West Palm Beach-Boca Raton, FL MSA	1,131,184	863,518	267,666	31.0
24	Bellingham, WA MSA	166,814	127,780	39,034	30.5
25	Colorado Springs, CO MSA	516,929	397,014	119,915	30.2

PMSAs and MSAs Most Rapidly Losing Population, 1990-2000

		Population		Population Increase	
No.	RMA	2000 Census	1990 Census	1990-2000 No.	1990-2000 %
1	Steubenville-Weirton, OH-WV MSA	132,008	142,523	-10,515	-7.4
2	Grand Forks, ND-MN MSA	97,478	103,181	-5,703	-5.5
3	Utica-Rome, NY MSA	299,896	316,633	-16,737	-5.3
4	Binghamton, NY MSA	252,320	264,497	-12,177	-4.6
5	Pittsfield, MA MSA	84,699	88,695	-3,996	-4.5
6	Elmira, NY MSA	91,070	95,195	-4,125	-4.3
7	Alexandria, LA MSA	126,337	131,556	-5,219	-4.0
8	Wheeling, WV-OH MSA	153,172	159,301	-6,129	-3.8
9	Johnstown, PA MSA	232,621	241,247	-8,626	-3.6
10	Anniston, AL MSA	112,249	116,034	-3,785	-3.3
11	Lewiston-Auburn, ME MSA	90,830	93,679	-2,849	-3.0
12	Scranton--Wilkes-Barre--Hazleton, PA MSA	624,776	638,466	-13,690	-2.1
13	Decatur, IL MSA	114,706	117,206	-2,500	-2.1
14	Buffalo-Niagara Falls, NY MSA	1,170,111	1,189,288	-19,177	-1.6
15	Pittsburgh, PA MSA	2,358,695	2,394,811	-36,116	-1.5
16	Jamestown, NY MSA	139,750	141,895	-2,145	-1.5
17	Syracuse, NY MSA	732,117	742,177	-10,060	-1.4
18	Pine Bluff, AR MSA	84,278	85,487	-1,209	-1.4
19	Altoona, PA MSA	129,144	130,542	-1,398	-1.1
20	Youngstown-Warren, OH MSA	594,746	600,895	-6,149	-1.0
21	Bangor, ME MSA	90,864	91,611	-747	-0.8
22	Muncie, IN MSA	118,769	119,659	-890	-0.7
23	Sharon, PA MSA	120,293	121,003	-710	-0.6
24	New Bedford, MA PMSA	175,198	175,641	-443	-0.3
25	Dayton-Springfield, OH MSA	950,558	951,270	-712	-0.1

Most Rapidly Growing CBSAs, 1990-2000

		Population		Population Increase	
No.	CBSA	2000 Census	1990 Census	1990-2000 No.	1990-2000 %
1	St. George, UT	90,354	48,560	41,794	86.1
2	Las Vegas-Paradise, NV	1,375,765	741,459	634,306	85.5
3	Naples-Marco Island, FL	251,377	152,099	99,278	65.3
4	Coeur d'Alene, ID	108,685	69,795	38,890	55.7
5	Prescott, AZ	167,517	107,714	59,803	55.5
6	Bend, OR	115,367	74,958	40,409	53.9
7	Yuma, AZ	160,026	106,895	53,131	49.7
8	McAllen-Edinburg-Pharr, TX	569,463	383,545	185,918	48.5
9	Austin-Round Rock, TX	1,249,763	846,227	403,536	47.7
10	Raleigh-Cary, NC	797,071	541,100	255,971	47.3
11	Gainesville, GA	139,277	95,428	43,849	45.9
12	Boise City-Nampa, ID	464,840	319,596	145,244	45.4
13	Phoenix-Mesa-Scottsdale, AZ	3,251,876	2,238,480	1,013,396	45.3
14	Laredo, TX	193,117	133,239	59,878	44.9
15	Fayetteville-Springdale-Rogers, AR-MO	347,045	239,464	107,581	44.9
16	Provo-Orem, UT	376,774	269,407	107,367	39.9
17	Madera, CA	123,109	88,090	35,019	39.8
18	Atlanta-Sandy Springs-Marietta, GA	4,247,981	3,069,425	1,178,556	38.4
19	Greeley, CO*	180,926	131,817	49,109	37.3
20	Wilmington, NC	274,532	200,124	74,408	37.2
21	Myrtle Beach-Conway-North Myrtle Beach, SC	196,629	144,053	52,576	36.5
22	Fort Collins-Loveland, CO	251,494	186,136	65,358	35.1
23	Orlando, FL	1,644,561	1,224,852	419,709	34.3
24	Reno-Sparks, NV	342,885	257,193	85,692	33.3
25	Ocala, FL	258,916	194,833	64,083	32.9

* For the purposes of this table, Broomfield city is treated as if it were a county at the time of the 1990 and 2000 censuses. Broomfield county was formed from parts of Adams, Boulder, Jefferson, and Weld counties in 2001, and is coextensive with Broomfield city.

CBSAs Most Rapidly Losing Population, 1990-2000

		Population		Population Increase	
No.	RMA	2000 Census	1990 Census	1990-2000 No.	1990-2000 %
1	Weirton-Steubenville, WV-OH	132,008	142,523	-10,515	-7.4
2	Johnstown, PA	152,598	163,029	-10,431	-6.4
3	Grand Forks, ND-MN	97,478	103,181	-5,703	-5.5
4	Utica-Rome, NY	299,896	316,633	-16,737	-5.3
5	Danville, IL	83,919	88,257	-4,338	-4.9
6	Binghamton, NY	252,320	264,497	-12,177	-4.6
7	Elmira, NY	91,070	95,195	-4,125	-4.3
8	Wheeling, WV-OH	153,172	159,301	-6,129	-3.8
9	Anniston-Oxford, AL	112,249	116,034	-3,785	-3.3
10	Pittsfield, MA	134,953	139,352	-4,399	-3.2
11	Alexandria, LA	145,035	149,082	-4,047	-2.7
12	Scranton—Wilkes-Barre, PA	560,625	575,264	-14,639	-2.5
13	Decatur, IL	114,706	117,206	-2,500	-2.1
14	Springfield, OH	144,742	147,548	-2,806	-1.9
15	Youngstown-Warren-Boardman, OH-PA	602,964	613,622	-10,658	-1.7
16	Buffalo-Niagara Falls, NY	1,170,111	1,189,288	-19,177	-1.6
17	Pittsburgh, PA	2,431,087	2,468,289	-37,202	-1.5
18	Syracuse, NY	650,154	659,864	-9,710	-1.5
19	Bay City, MI	110,157	111,723	-1,566	-1.4
20	Lewiston-Auburn, ME	103,793	105,259	-1,466	-1.4
21	Lima, OH	108,473	109,755	-1,282	-1.2
22	Bangor, ME	144,919	146,601	-1,682	-1.1
23	Altoona, PA	129,144	130,542	-1,398	-1.1
24	Saginaw-Saginaw Township North, MI	210,039	211,946	-1,907	-0.9
25	Muncie, IN	118,769	119,659	-890	-0.7

Counties With More Than 50,000 Population Increase, 1990-2000

		Population		Numerical Increase 1990-2000
No.	County (Chief Urban Center)	2000 Census	1990 Census	
1	Maricopa, AZ (Phoenix)	3,072,149	2,122,101	950,048
2	Los Angeles, CA (Los Angeles)	9,519,338	8,863,164	656,174
3	Clark, NV (Las Vegas)	1,375,765	741,459	634,306
4	Harris, TX (Houston)	3,400,578	2,818,199	582,379
5	Orange, CA (Anaheim)	2,846,289	2,410,556	435,733
6	Riverside, CA (Riverside)	1,545,387	1,170,413	374,974
7	Broward, FL (Fort Lauderdale)	1,623,018	1,255,488	367,530
8	Dallas, TX (Dallas)	2,218,899	1,852,810	366,089
9	Dade, FL (Miami)	2,253,362	1,937,094	316,268
10	San Diego, CA (San Diego)	2,813,833	2,498,016	315,817
11	San Bernardino, CA (Riverside)	1,709,434	1,418,380	291,054
12	Queens, NY (New York)	2,229,379	1,951,598	277,781
13	Tarrant, TX (Fort Worth)	1,446,219	1,170,103	276,116
14	Cook, IL (Chicago)	5,376,741	5,105,067	271,674
15	Palm Beach, FL (West Palm Beach)	1,131,184	863,518	267,666
16	Travis, TX (Austin)	812,280	576,407	235,873
17	Gwinnett, GA (Atlanta)	588,448	352,910	235,538
18	King, WA (Seattle)	1,737,034	1,507,319	229,715
19	Collin, TX (Dallas)	491,675	264,036	227,639
20	Orange, FL (Orlando)	896,344	677,491	218,853
21	Bexar, TX (San Antonio)	1,392,931	1,185,394	207,537
22	Wake, NC (Raleigh)	627,846	423,380	204,466
23	Hidalgo, TX (McAllen)	569,463	383,545	185,918
24	Santa Clara, CA (San Jose)	1,682,585	1,497,577	185,008
25	Mecklenburg, NC (Charlotte)	695,454	511,433	184,021
26	Sacramento, CA (Sacramento)	1,223,499	1,041,219	182,280
27	Pima, AZ (Tucson)	843,746	666,880	176,866
28	Salt Lake, UT (Salt Lake City)	898,387	725,956	172,431
29	Fulton, GA (Atlanta)	816,006	648,951	167,055
30	Hillsborough, FL (Tampa)	998,948	834,054	164,894
31	Kings, NY (New York)	2,465,326	2,300,664	164,662
32	Alameda, CA (Oakland)	1,443,741	1,279,182	164,559
33	Cobb, GA (Atlanta)	607,751	447,745	160,006
34	Denton, TX (Dallas)	432,976	273,525	159,451
35	Fairfax, VA (Washington)	969,749	818,584	151,165
36	Contra Costa, CA (Oakland)	948,816	803,732	145,084
37	Will, IL (Chicago)	502,266	357,313	144,953
38	Snohomish, WA (Seattle)	606,024	465,642	140,382
39	Washington, OR (Portland)	445,342	311,554	133,788
40	Fresno, CA (Fresno)	799,407	667,490	131,917
41	Fort Bend, TX (Houston)	354,452	225,421	129,031
42	Bronx, NY (New York)	1,332,650	1,203,789	128,861
43	Lake, IL (Chicago)	644,356	516,418	127,938
44	DuPage, IL (Chicago)	904,161	781,666	122,495
45	DeKalb, GA (Atlanta)	665,865	545,837	120,028
46	El Paso, CO (Colorado Springs)	516,929	397,014	119,915
47	Kern, CA (Bakersfield)	661,645	543,477	118,168
48	Montgomery, MD (Washington)	873,341	757,027	116,314
49	Douglas, CO (Denver)	175,766	60,391	115,375
50	Pierce, WA (Tacoma)	700,820	586,203	114,617
51	Montgomery, TX (Houston)	293,768	182,201	111,567
52	Oakland, MI (Detroit)	1,194,156	1,083,592	110,564
53	Williamson, TX (Austin)	249,967	139,551	110,416
54	Franklin, OH (Columbus)	1,068,978	961,437	107,541
55	Clark, WA (Portland)	345,238	238,053	107,185
56	Duval, FL (Jacksonville)	778,879	672,971	105,908
57	Lee, FL (Fort Myers)	440,888	335,113	105,775
58	Utah, UT (Provo)	368,536	263,590	104,946
59	Collier, FL (Naples)	251,377	152,099	99,278
60	Adams, CO (Denver)	363,857	265,038	98,819
61	Suffolk, NY (Nassau)	1,419,369	1,321,864	97,505
62	Arapahoe, CO (Denver)	487,967	391,511	96,456
63	Johnson, KS (Kansas City)	451,086	355,054	96,032
64	Ada, ID (Boise City)	300,904	205,775	95,129
65	Jefferson, CO (Denver)	527,056	438,430	88,626
66	El Paso, TX (El Paso)	679,622	591,610	88,012
67	Denver, CO (Denver)	554,636	467,610	87,026
68	Kane, IL (Chicago)	404,119	317,471	86,648
69	Washoe, NV (Reno)	339,486	254,667	84,819
70	Ventura, CA (Ventura)	753,197	669,016	84,181
71	Hennepin, MN (Minneapolis)	1,116,200	1,032,431	83,769
72	Loudoun, VA (Washington)	169,599	86,129	83,470
73	San Joaquin, CA (Stockton)	563,598	480,628	82,970
74	Dakota, MN (Minneapolis)	355,904	275,227	80,677
75	Polk, FL (Lakeland)	483,924	405,382	78,542
76	Middlesex, NJ (New Brunswick)	750,162	671,780	78,382
77	Ocean, NJ (Lakewood)	510,916	433,203	77,713
78	Seminole, FL (Orlando)	365,196	287,529	77,667
79	Brevard, FL (Melbourne)	476,230	398,978	77,252
80	McHenry, IL (Chicago)	260,077	183,241	76,836
81	Multnomah, OR (Portland)	660,486	583,887	76,599
82	Stanislaus, CA (Modesto)	446,997	370,522	76,475
83	Bernalillo, NM (Albuquerque)	556,678	480,577	76,101
84	Placer, CA (Sacramento)	248,399	172,796	75,603
85	Cameron, TX (Brownsville)	335,227	260,120	75,107
86	Hamilton, IN (Indianapolis)	182,740	108,936	73,804
87	Kent, MI (Grand Rapids)	574,335	500,631	73,704
88	Guilford, NC (Greensboro)	421,048	347,420	73,628
89	Volusia, FL (Daytona Beach)	443,343	370,712	72,631
90	Prince George's, MD (Washington)	801,515	729,268	72,247
91	Montgomery, PA (Philadelphia)	750,097	678,111	71,986
92	Shelby, TN (Memphis)	897,472	826,330	71,142
93	St. Charles, MO (St. Louis)	283,883	212,907	70,976
94	Macomb, MI (Detroit)	788,149	717,400	70,749
95	Sonoma, CA (Santa Rosa)	458,614	388,222	70,392
96	Pinellas, FL (St. Petersburg)	921,482	851,659	69,823
97	Middlesex, MA (Boston)	1,465,396	1,398,468	66,928
98	Boulder, CO (Boulder)	291,288	225,339	65,949
99	Larimer, CO (Fort Collins)	251,494	186,136	65,358
100	Prince William, VA (Washington)	280,813	215,686	65,127
101	Osceola, FL (Orlando)	172,493	107,728	64,765
102	Richmond, NY (New York)	443,728	378,977	64,751
103	Marion, FL (Ocala)	258,916	194,833	64,083
104	Pasco, FL (Tampa)	344,765	281,131	63,634
105	Rutherford, TN (Nashville)	182,023	118,570	63,453
106	Pinal, AZ (Phoenix)	179,727	116,379	63,348
107	Marion, IN (Indianapolis)	860,454	797,159	63,295
108	Anne Arundel, MD (Baltimore)	489,656	427,239	62,417
109	Monmouth, NJ (Monmouth)	615,301	553,124	62,177
110	Baltimore, MD (Baltimore)	754,292	692,134	62,158
111	Mohave, AZ (Las Vegas)	155,032	93,497	61,535
112	Oklahoma, OK (Oklahoma City)	660,448	599,611	60,837
113	Henry, GA (Atlanta)	119,341	58,741	60,600
114	Howard, MD (Baltimore)	247,842	187,328	60,514
115	Tulsa, OK (Tulsa)	563,299	503,341	59,958
116	Webb, TX (Laredo)	193,117	133,239	59,878
117	Yavapai, AZ (Prescott)	167,517	107,714	59,803
118	Clackamas, OR (Portland)	338,391	278,850	59,541
119	Greenville, SC (Greenville)	379,616	320,167	59,449
120	Dane, WI (Madison)	426,526	367,085	59,441
121	Davidson, TN (Nashville)	569,891	510,784	59,107
122	Bergen, NJ (Bergen)	884,118	825,380	58,738
123	Lake, FL (Orlando)	210,528	152,104	58,424
124	New Castle, DE (Wilmington)	500,265	441,946	58,319
125	San Mateo, CA (San Francisco)	707,161	649,623	57,538
126	Somerset, NJ (Middlesex)	297,490	240,279	57,211
127	Chester, PA (Philadelphia)	433,501	376,396	57,105
128	Spokane, WA (Spokane)	417,939	361,364	56,575
129	Bucks, PA (Philadelphia)	597,635	541,174	56,461
130	Marion, OR (Salem)	284,834	228,483	56,351
131	Tulare, CA (Visalia)	368,021	311,921	56,100
132	Waukesha, WI (Milwaukee)	360,767	304,715	56,052
133	Benton, AR (Fayetteville)	153,406	97,499	55,907
134	Hudson, NJ (Jersey City)	608,975	553,099	55,876
135	Washington, MN (Minneapolis)	201,130	145,896	55,234
136	Fairfield, CT (Bridgeport)	882,567	827,645	54,922
137	Clayton, GA (Atlanta)	236,517	182,052	54,465
138	Anoka, MN (Minneapolis)	298,084	243,641	54,443
139	Forsyth, GA (Atlanta)	98,407	44,083	54,324
140	Solano, CA (Vallejo)	394,542	340,421	54,121
141	Essex, MA (Boston)	723,419	670,080	53,339
142	Yuma, AZ (Yuma)	160,026	106,895	53,131
143	San Francisco, CA (San Francisco)	776,733	723,959	52,774
144	Horry, SC (Myrtle Beach)	196,629	144,053	52,576
145	Manatee, FL (Bradenton)	264,002	211,707	52,295
146	Cherokee, GA (Atlanta)	141,903	90,204	51,699
147	Davis, UT (Salt Lake City)	238,994	187,941	51,053
148	Chesterfield, VA (Richmond)	259,903	209,274	50,629
149	Ottawa, MI (Grand Rapids)	238,314	187,768	50,546
150	Brazoria, TX (Brazoria)	241,767	191,707	50,060

Counties with More Than 50,000 Population Decrease, 1990-2000

		Population		Numerical Increase 1990-2000
No.	County (Chief Urban Center)	2000 Census	1990 Census	
1	Philadelphia, PA (Philadelphia)	1,517,550	1,585,577	-68,027
2	Allegheny, PA (Pittsburgh)	1,281,666	1,336,449	-54,783
3	Wayne, MI (Detroit)	2,061,162	2,111,687	-50,525

U.S.: Population and Agriculture

State	Capital	Chief City other than Capital	FIPS State Code†	Land Area (Sq. Miles) 2000	Population					Agriculture		
					Total 4/1/2000	Total 4/1/1900	Percent Change 1990-2000	Total 4/1/1980	Percent Change 1980-1990	Number of Farms 2002	Land in Farms (1,000 Acres) 2002	Final Agricultural Output ($1,000) 2002
Alabama	Montgomery	•Birmingham	01	50,744	4,447,100	4,040,587	10.1	3,894,046	3.8	45,000	8,900	3,343,000
Alaska	Juneau	•Anchorage	02	571,951	626,932	550,043	14.0	401,851	36.9	1,000	900	48,000
Arizona	•Phoenix	Tucson	04	113,635	5,130,632	3,665,228	40.0	2,716,756	34.9	7,000	26,600	2,427,000
Arkansas	•Little Rock	Fort Smith	05	52,068	2,673,400	2,350,725	13.7	2,286,357	2.8	47,000	14,500	5,189,000
California	Sacramento	•Los Angeles	06	155,959	33,871,648	29,760,021	13.8	23,667,372	25.7	80,000	27,600	25,906,000
Colorado	•Denver	Colorado Springs	08	103,718	4,301,261	3,294,394	30.6	2,889,735	14.0	31,000	31,100	4,651,000
Connecticut	•Hartford	Bridgeport	09	4,845	3,405,565	3,287,116	3.6	3,107,576	5.8	4,000	400	474,000
Delaware	Dover	•Wilmington	10	1,954	783,600	666,168	17.6	594,317	12.1	2,000	500	627,000
District of Columbia	•Washington		11	61	572,059	606,900	-5.7	638,432	-4.9	(n.a.)	(n.a.)	(n.a.)
Florida	Tallahassee	•Miami	12	53,927	15,982,378	12,937,926	23.5	9,747,015	32.7	44,000	10,400	6,264,000
Georgia	•Atlanta	Augusta	13	57,906	8,186,453	6,478,216	26.4	5,462,982	18.6	49,000	10,700	5,030,000
Hawaii	•Honolulu	Hilo	15	6,423	1,211,537	1,108,229	9.3	964,691	14.9	5,000	1,300	534,000
Idaho	•Boise	Nampa	16	82,747	1,293,953	1,006,749	28.5	944,127	6.6	25,000	11,800	4,002,000
Illinois	Springfield	•Chicago	17	55,584	12,419,293	11,430,602	8.6	11,427,414	0.0	73,000	27,300	8,089,000
Indiana	•Indianapolis	Fort Wayne	18	35,867	6,080,485	5,544,159	9.7	5,490,212	1.0	60,000	15,100	5,008,000
Iowa	•Des Moines	Cedar Rapids	19	55,869	2,926,324	2,776,755	5.4	2,913,808	-4.7	91,000	31,700	12,813,000
Kansas	Topeka	•Wichita	20	81,815	2,688,418	2,477,574	8.5	2,364,236	4.8	64,000	47,200	9,074,000
Kentucky	Frankfort	•Louisville	21	39,728	4,041,769	3,685,296	9.7	3,660,324	0.7	87,000	13,800	3,174,000
Louisiana	Baton Rouge	•New Orleans	22	43,562	4,468,976	4,219,973	5.9	4,206,098	0.3	27,000	7,800	1,939,000
Maine	Augusta	•Portland	23	30,862	1,274,923	1,227,928	3.8	1,125,043	9.1	7,000	1,400	472,000
Maryland	Annapolis	•Baltimore	24	9,774	5,296,486	4,781,468	10.8	4,216,933	13.4	12,000	2,100	1,326,000
Massachusetts	•Boston	Worcester	25	7,840	6,349,097	6,016,425	5.5	5,737,093	4.9	6,000	500	389,000
Michigan	Lansing	•Detroit	26	56,804	9,938,444	9,295,297	6.9	9,262,044	0.4	53,000	10,100	3,917,000
Minnesota	St. Paul	•Minneapolis	27	79,610	4,919,479	4,375,099	12.4	4,075,970	7.3	81,000	27,500	8,926,000
Mississippi	•Jackson	Gulfport	28	46,907	2,844,658	2,573,216	10.5	2,520,698	2.1	42,000	11,100	3,262,000
Missouri	Jefferson City	•St. Louis	29	68,886	5,595,211	5,117,073	9.3	4,916,759	4.1	107,000	29,900	5,248,000
Montana	Helena	•Billings	30	145,552	902,195	799,065	12.9	786,624	1.6	28,000	59,600	2,093,000
Nebraska	Lincoln	•Omaha	31	76,872	1,711,263	1,578,385	8.4	1,569,825	0.5	49,000	45,900	10,051,000
Nevada	Carson City	•Las Vegas	32	109,826	1,998,257	1,201,833	66.3	800,508	50.1	3,000	6,300	451,000
New Hampshire	Concord	•Manchester	33	8,968	1,235,786	1,109,252	11.4	920,610	20.5	3,000	400	149,000
New Jersey	Trenton	•Newark	34	7,417	8,414,350	7,730,188	8.9	7,365,011	5.0	10,000	800	754,000
New Mexico	Santa Fe	•Albuquerque	35	121,356	1,819,046	1,515,069	20.1	1,303,542	16.2	15,000	44,800	1,750,000
New York	Albany	•New York	36	47,214	18,976,457	17,990,455	5.5	17,558,165	2.5	37,000	7,700	3,228,000
North Carolina	Raleigh	•Charlotte	37	48,711	8,049,313	6,628,637	21.4	5,880,415	12.7	54,000	9,100	7,059,000
North Dakota	Bismarck	•Fargo	38	68,976	642,200	638,800	0.5	652,717	-2.1	31,000	39,300	3,526,000
Ohio	Columbus	•Cleveland	39	40,948	11,353,140	10,847,115	4.7	10,797,603	0.5	78,000	14,600	4,461,000
Oklahoma	•Oklahoma City	Tulsa	40	68,667	3,450,654	3,145,585	9.7	3,025,487	4.0	83,000	33,700	4,606,000
Oregon	Salem	•Portland	41	95,997	3,421,399	2,842,321	20.4	2,633,156	7.9	40,000	17,100	3,248,000
Pennsylvania	Harrisburg	•Philadelphia	42	44,817	12,281,054	11,881,643	3.4	11,864,751	0.1	58,000	7,700	4,343,000
Rhode Island	•Providence	Warwick	44	1,045	1,048,319	1,003,464	4.5	947,154	5.9	1,000	100	56,000
South Carolina	•Columbia	Charleston	45	30,110	4,012,012	3,486,703	15.1	3,120,730	11.7	25,000	4,800	1,528,000
South Dakota	Pierre	•Sioux Falls	46	75,885	754,844	696,004	8.5	690,768	0.8	32,000	43,800	4,050,000
Tennessee	•Nashville	Memphis	47	41,217	5,689,283	4,877,185	16.7	4,591,023	6.2	88,000	11,700	2,259,000
Texas	Austin	•Dallas	48	261,797	20,851,820	16,986,510	22.8	14,225,288	19.4	229,000	129,900	14,664,000
Utah	•Salt Lake City	West Valley	49	82,144	2,233,169	1,722,850	29.6	1,461,037	17.9	15,000	11,700	1,143,000
Vermont	Montpelier	•Burlington	50	9,250	608,827	562,758	8.2	511,456	10.0	7,000	1,200	497,000
Virginia	Richmond	•Virginia Beach	51	39,594	7,078,515	6,187,358	14.4	5,346,797	15.7	48,000	8,600	2,416,000
Washington	Olympia	•Seattle	53	66,544	5,894,121	4,866,692	21.1	4,132,353	17.8	36,000	15,300	5,465,000
West Virginia	•Charleston	Huntington	54	24,078	1,808,344	1,793,477	0.8	1,950,186	-8.0	21,000	3,600	488,000
Wisconsin	Madison	•Milwaukee	55	54,310	5,363,675	4,891,769	9.6	4,705,642	4.0	77,000	15,700	5,871,000
Wyoming	•Cheyenne	Casper	56	97,100	493,782	453,588	8.9	469,557	-3.4	9,000	34,400	902,000
United States Total	**Washington D.C.**	**•New York**		**3,537,438**	**281,421,906**	**248,709,873**	**13.2**	**226,542,294**	**9.8**	**2,129,000**	**938,300**	**207,192,000**

• Largest city (metropolitan population) in the state.
(n.a.) Not applicable.
† Federal Information Processing Standards (FIPS) code for States, as published by the National Bureau of Standards, U.S. Department of Commerce.
* Source: Statistical Abstract of the Unites States: 2004-2005.

U.S.: Population Characteristics*

State	Households 2000	Population in Households 2000	Persons per Household 2000	Population in Group Quarters 2000	Total Population	Hispanic or Latino 2000	Total Not Hispanic or Latino 2000	One Race 2000	White 2000	Black or African American 2000	American Indian and Alaska Native 2000	Asian 2000	Native Hawaiian and Other Pacific Islander 2000	Some Other Race 2000	Two or more Races 2000
Alabama	1,737,080	4,332,380	2.49	114,720	4,447,100	75,830	4,371,270	4,332,184	3,125,819	1,150,076	21,618	30,989	1,059	2,623	39,086
Alaska	221,600	607,583	2.74	19,349	626,932	25,852	601,080	570,626	423,788	21,073	96,505	24,741	3,181	1,338	30,454
Arizona	1,901,327	5,020,782	2.64	109,850	5,130,632	1,295,617	3,835,015	3,758,643	3,274,258	149,941	233,370	89,315	5,639	6,120	76,372
Arkansas	1,042,696	2,599,492	2.49	73,908	2,673,400	86,866	2,586,534	2,556,170	2,100,135	416,615	16,702	19,892	1,494	1,332	30,364
California	11,502,870	33,051,894	2.87	819,754	33,871,648	10,966,556	22,905,092	22,001,977	15,816,790	2,181,926	178,984	3,648,860	103,736	71,681	903,115
Colorado	1,658,238	4,198,306	2.53	102,955	4,301,261	735,601	3,565,660	3,492,939	3,202,880	158,443	28,982	93,277	3,845	5,512	72,721
Connecticut	1,301,670	3,297,626	2.53	107,939	3,405,565	320,323	3,085,242	3,032,346	2,638,845	295,571	7,267	81,564	958	8,141	52,896
Delaware	298,736	759,017	2.54	24,583	783,600	37,277	746,323	736,101	567,973	148,435	2,324	16,110	234	1,025	10,222
District of Columbia	248,338	536,497	2.16	35,562	572,059	44,953	527,106	517,522	159,178	340,088	1,274	15,039	273	1,670	9,584
Florida	6,337,929	15,593,433	2.46	388,945	15,982,378	2,682,715	13,299,663	13,062,709	10,458,509	2,264,268	42,358	261,693	6,887	28,994	236,954
Georgia	3,006,369	7,952,631	2.65	233,822	8,186,453	435,227	7,751,226	7,663,862	5,128,661	2,331,465	17,670	171,513	3,278	11,275	87,364
Hawaii	403,240	1,175,755	2.92	35,782	1,211,537	87,699	1,123,838	905,138	277,091	20,829	2,539	494,149	108,441	2,089	218,700
Idaho	469,645	1,262,457	2.69	31,496	1,293,953	101,690	1,192,263	1,174,002	1,139,291	4,889	15,789	11,641	1,200	1,192	18,261
Illinois	4,591,779	12,097,512	2.63	321,781	12,419,293	1,530,262	10,889,031	10,735,035	8,424,140	1,856,152	18,232	419,916	3,116	13,479	153,996
Indiana	2,336,306	5,902,331	2.53	178,154	6,080,485	214,536	5,865,949	5,804,834	5,219,373	505,462	13,654	58,424	1,573	6,348	61,115
Iowa	1,149,276	2,822,155	2.46	104,169	2,926,324	82,473	2,843,851	2,818,379	2,710,344	60,744	7,955	36,345	888	2,103	25,472
Kansas	1,037,891	2,606,468	2.51	81,950	2,688,418	188,252	2,500,166	2,457,658	2,233,997	151,407	22,322	46,301	1,154	2,477	42,508
Kentucky	1,590,647	3,926,965	2.47	114,804	4,041,769	59,939	3,981,830	3,944,080	3,608,013	293,639	7,939	29,368	1,275	3,846	37,750
Louisiana	1,656,053	4,333,011	2.62	135,965	4,468,976	107,738	4,361,238	4,321,978	2,794,391	1,443,390	24,129	54,256	1,076	4,736	39,260
Maine	518,200	1,240,011	2.39	34,912	1,274,923	9,360	1,265,563	1,253,832	1,230,297	6,440	6,911	9,014	334	836	11,731
Maryland	1,980,859	5,162,430	2.61	134,056	5,296,486	227,916	5,068,570	4,985,624	3,286,547	1,464,735	13,312	209,738	1,913	9,379	82,946
Massachusetts	2,443,580	6,127,881	2.51	221,216	6,349,097	428,729	5,920,368	5,810,030	5,198,359	318,329	11,264	236,786	1,706	43,586	110,338
Michigan	3,785,661	9,688,555	2.56	249,889	9,938,444	323,877	9,614,567	9,451,080	7,806,691	1,402,047	53,421	175,311	2,145	11,465	163,487
Minnesota	1,895,127	4,783,596	2.52	135,883	4,919,479	143,382	4,776,097	4,705,793	4,337,143	168,813	52,009	141,083	1,714	5,031	70,304
Mississippi	1,046,434	2,749,244	2.63	95,414	2,844,658	39,569	2,805,089	2,787,817	1,727,908	1,028,473	11,224	18,349	569	1,294	17,272
Missouri	2,194,594	5,433,153	2.48	162,058	5,595,211	118,592	5,476,619	5,404,714	4,686,474	625,667	23,302	61,041	2,939	5,291	71,905
Montana	358,667	877,433	2.45	24,762	902,195	18,081	884,114	870,346	807,823	2,534	54,426	4,569	425	569	13,768
Nebraska	666,184	1,660,445	2.49	50,818	1,711,263	94,425	1,616,838	1,599,142	1,494,494	67,537	13,460	21,677	647	1,327	17,696
Nevada	751,165	1,964,582	2.62	33,675	1,998,257	393,970	1,604,287	1,555,056	1,303,001	131,509	21,397	88,593	7,769	2,787	49,231
New Hampshire	474,606	1,200,247	2.53	35,539	1,235,786	20,489	1,215,297	1,203,691	1,175,252	8,354	2,698	15,803	330	1,254	11,606
New Jersey	3,064,645	8,219,529	2.68	194,821	8,414,350	1,117,191	7,297,159	7,163,470	5,557,209	1,096,171	11,338	477,012	2,175	19,565	133,689
New Mexico	677,971	1,782,739	2.63	36,307	1,819,046	765,386	1,053,660	1,027,867	813,495	30,654	161,460	18,257	992	3,009	25,793
New York	7,056,860	18,395,996	2.61	580,461	18,976,457	2,867,583	16,108,874	15,742,758	11,760,981	2,812,623	52,499	1,035,926	5,230	75,499	366,116
North Carolina	3,132,013	7,795,432	2.49	253,881	8,049,313	378,963	7,670,350	7,590,385	5,647,155	1,723,301	95,333	112,416	3,165	9,015	79,965
North Dakota	257,152	618,569	2.41	23,631	642,200	7,786	634,414	627,748	589,149	3,761	30,772	3,566	218	282	6,666
Ohio	4,445,773	11,054,019	2.49	299,121	11,353,140	217,123	11,136,017	10,998,247	9,538,111	1,290,662	21,985	131,670	2,336	13,483	137,770
Oklahoma	1,342,293	3,338,279	2.49	112,375	3,450,654	179,304	3,271,350	3,131,101	2,556,368	257,981	266,158	46,172	2,100	2,322	140,249
Oregon	1,333,723	3,343,908	2.51	77,491	3,421,399	275,314	3,146,085	3,063,352	2,857,616	53,325	40,130	100,333	7,398	4,550	82,733
Pennsylvania	4,777,003	11,847,753	2.48	433,301	12,281,054	394,088	11,886,966	11,773,869	10,322,455	1,202,437	14,904	218,296	2,691	13,086	113,097
Rhode Island	408,424	1,009,503	2.47	38,816	1,048,319	90,820	957,499	936,683	858,433	41,922	4,181	23,416	320	8,411	20,816
South Carolina	1,533,854	3,876,975	2.53	135,037	4,012,012	95,076	3,916,936	3,883,646	2,652,291	1,178,486	12,765	35,568	1,270	3,266	33,290
South Dakota	290,245	726,426	2.50	28,418	754,844	10,903	743,941	734,981	664,585	4,563	60,988	4,316	219	310	8,960
Tennessee	2,232,905	5,541,337	2.48	147,946	5,689,283	123,838	5,565,445	5,510,621	4,505,930	928,204	13,820	56,077	1,810	4,780	54,824
Texas	7,393,354	20,290,711	2.74	561,109	20,851,820	6,669,666	14,182,154	13,951,587	10,933,313	2,364,255	68,859	554,445	10,757	19,958	230,567
Utah	701,281	2,192,689	3.13	40,480	2,233,169	201,559	2,031,610	2,000,302	1,904,265	16,137	26,663	36,483	14,806	1,948	31,308
Vermont	240,634	588,067	2.44	20,760	608,827	5,504	603,323	596,514	585,431	2,921	2,325	5,160	120	557	6,809
Virginia	2,699,173	6,847,117	2.54	231,398	7,078,515	329,540	6,748,975	6,634,953	4,965,637	1,376,378	18,596	259,277	3,380	11,685	114,022
Washington	2,271,398	5,757,739	2.53	136,382	5,894,121	441,509	5,452,612	5,276,686	4,652,490	184,631	85,396	319,401	22,779	11,989	175,926
West Virginia	736,481	1,765,197	2.40	43,147	1,808,344	12,279	1,796,065	1,781,082	1,709,966	56,825	3,456	9,356	335	1,144	14,983
Wisconsin	2,084,544	5,207,717	2.50	155,958	5,363,675	192,921	5,170,754	5,118,833	4,681,630	300,245	43,980	87,995	1,346	3,637	51,921
Wyoming	193,608	479,699	2.48	14,083	493,782	31,669	462,113	455,949	438,799	3,504	10,238	2,670	264	474	6,164
United States Total	**105,480,101**	**273,643,273**	**2.59**	**7,778,633**	**281,421,906**	**35,305,818**	**246,116,088**	**241,513,942**	**194,552,774**	**33,947,837**	**2,068,883**	**10,123,169**	**353,509**	**467,770**	**4,602,146**

* Total U.S. population of 281,421,906 comprises White, Black, American Indian, Alaska Native, Asian, Native Hawaiian, other Pacific Islander, some other race, and two or more races.
Source: 2000 U.S. Census of Population and Housing.

† "Hispanic or Latino" consists of persons classifying themselves as Mexican, Puerto Rican, Cuban, South or Central American, or of other Spanish/Hispanic culture or origin.
Persons of Hispanic or Latino origin may be of any race.

Map Introduction

This section of the *Commercial Atlas & Marketing Guide* presents a series of maps of the United States. The first map in this series is a United States road map, followed by a map that shows both the distance and the approximate driving time between hundreds of cities across North America. Next is a mileage chart that offers more than 5,300 mileages between 90 North American cities and National Parks.

Next are 113 pages of state reference maps that enable the user to see the geographic location of the counties and places appearing in the *Commercial Atlas* tables and index. These maps include populated places, Ranally Metropolitan Areas (RMAs), major transportation features, time zones, selected parks, and important physical features. Inset maps for major cities provide a greater level of detail for these special areas. Places listed in the *Commercial Atlas* state index in Volume 2 are linked to the state reference maps using letters and numbers along the map border. For example, a place in the index with a key of D-9 would be located at the intersection of row D and column 9 on the map. For more information about the state index see the Introduction beginning on page 5 in Volume 2. A detailed legend for the state reference maps appears at the bottom of this page.

Following the state reference maps are county subdivision maps for New England and other selected states. Maps are included for every state for which townships and other selected county subdivisions are included in the *Commercial Atlas* index and tables. For general information about county subdivisions see the Glossary of Terms beginning on page 5. For detailed information about county subdivisions in an individual state, see the Administrative Divisions section that precedes the state index in Volume 2.

Legend for State Reference Maps

Cities and towns

- Ranally Metropolitan Areas (RMA)
- National capital
- State capital
- County seat
- Other city or town

Administrative areas

- State boundaries
- County boundaries
- COOK County names

Roads and related symbols

- Limited access highway
- Limited access highway — under construction
- Other through highway
- Other road
- Unpaved road
- 90 190 80/90 Interstate highway
- ALT 17 183 18 U.S. highway
- 8 18 14/83 State highway
- 43 147 Secondary state or county highway

Points of interest and parks

- Park
- National Forest
- Campsite
- Indian reservation
- Point of interest, historic site or monument
- Golf course

Other symbols

- Area covered by inset map
- 52 Inset map page indicator
- Hospital, medical center
- Building
- Airport; military installation
- Major airport outside map area
- Cemetery
- Dam
- Mountain peak; highest point in state
- Port of entry
- Tourist information center
- Swamp
- Time zone boundary
- Continental divide

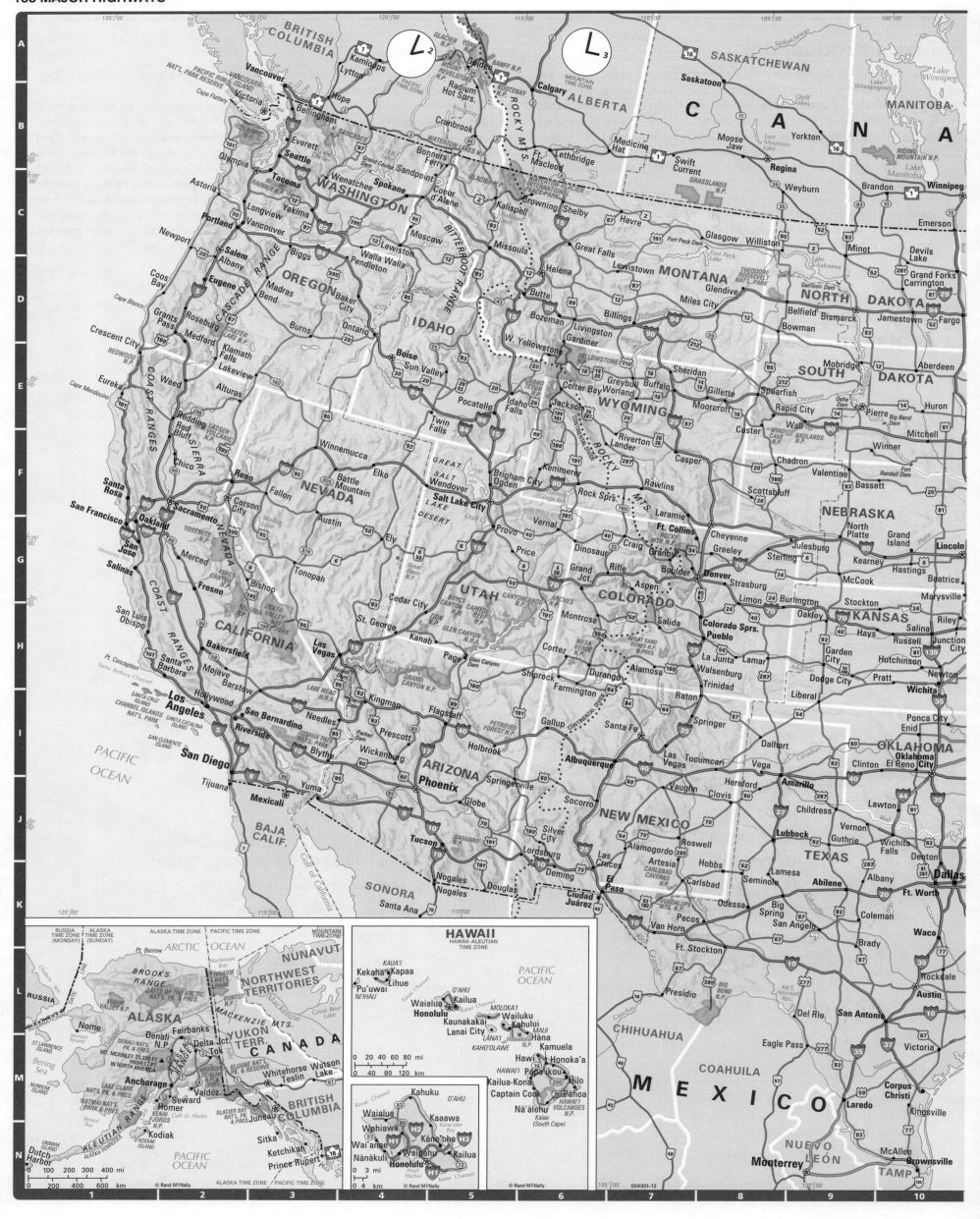

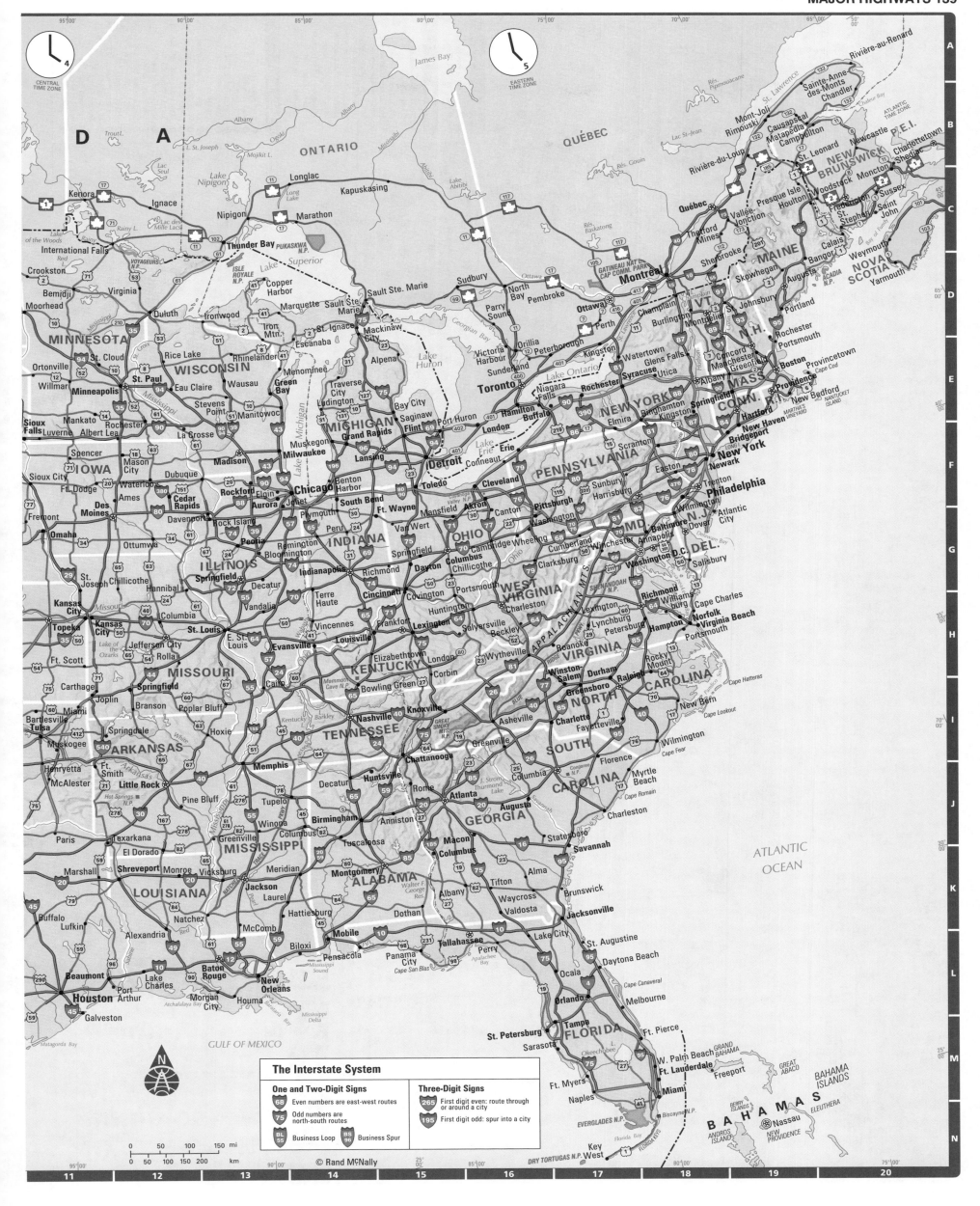

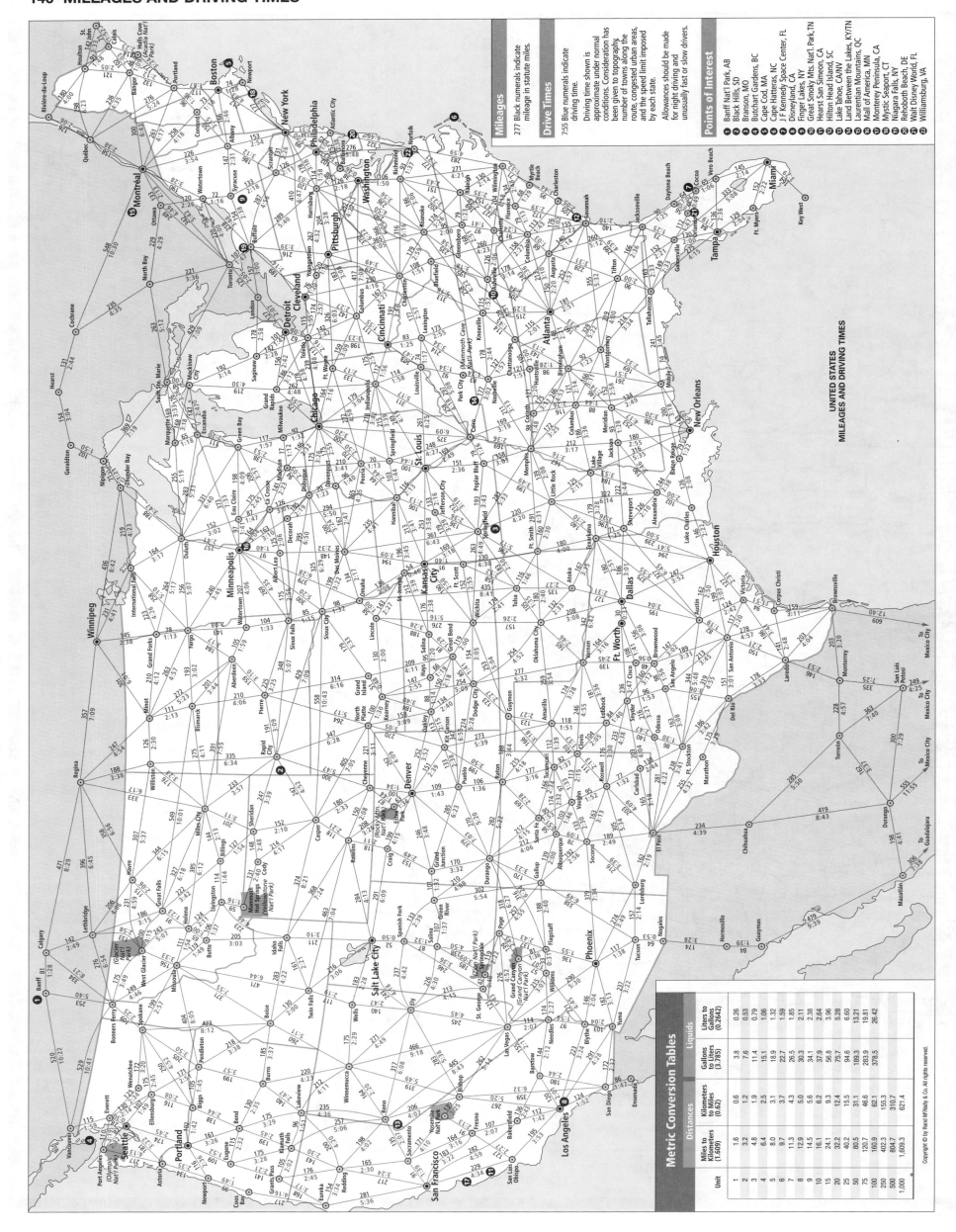

Copyright © by Rand McNally & Co. All rights reserved.

UNITED STATES
MILEAGES AND DRIVING TIMES

Mileages

277 Black numerals indicate mileage in statute miles.

755 Blue numerals indicate mileage in statute miles.

Drive Times

Driving time shown is approximate under normal conditions. Consideration has been given to topography, number of towns along the route, congested urban areas, and the speed limit imposed by each state.

Allowances should be made for night driving and unusually fast or slow drivers.

Points of Interest

1. Banff Nat'l Park, AB
2. Black Hills, SD
3. Branson, MO
4. Butchart Gardens, BC
5. Cape Cod, MA
6. Cape Hatteras, NC
7. J F Kennedy Space Center, FL
8. Disneyland, CA
9. Finger Lakes, NY
10. Great Smoky Mts. Nat'l Park, TN
11. Hearst San Simeon, CA
12. Hilton Head Island, SC
13. Lake Between the Lakes, KY/TN
14. Lake Tahoe, CA/NV
15. Laurentian Mountains, QC
16. Mall of America, MN
17. Monterey Peninsula, CA
18. Mystic Seaport, CT
19. Niagara Falls, NY
20. Rehoboth Beach, DE
21. Walt Disney World, FL
22. Williamsburg, VA

Metric Conversion Tables

	Distances		Liquids		
Unit	Miles to Kilometers (1.609)	Kilometers to Miles (0.62)	Gallons to Liters (3.785)	Liters to Gallons (0.2642)	
1	1.6	0.6	3.8	0.26	
2	3.2	1.2	7.6	0.53	
3	4.8	1.9	11.4	0.79	
4	6.4	2.5	15.1	1.06	
5	8.0	3.1	18.9	1.32	
6	9.7	3.7	22.7	1.59	
7	11.3	4.3	26.5	1.85	
8	12.9	5.0	30.3	2.11	
9	14.5	5.6	34.1	2.38	
10	16.1	6.2	37.9	2.64	
15	24.1	9.3	56.8	3.96	
25	40.2	15.5	94.6	6.60	
50	80.5	31.1	189.3	13.21	
100	160.9	62.1	283.9	19.81	
250	402.3	155.3	378.5	26.42	
500	804.7	310.7			
1,000	1,609.3	621.4			

Mileages in this chart are based upon the routes usually followed by motorists. Highway systems involved include interstate, U.S., and state highways.

Mileages ©Rand McNally

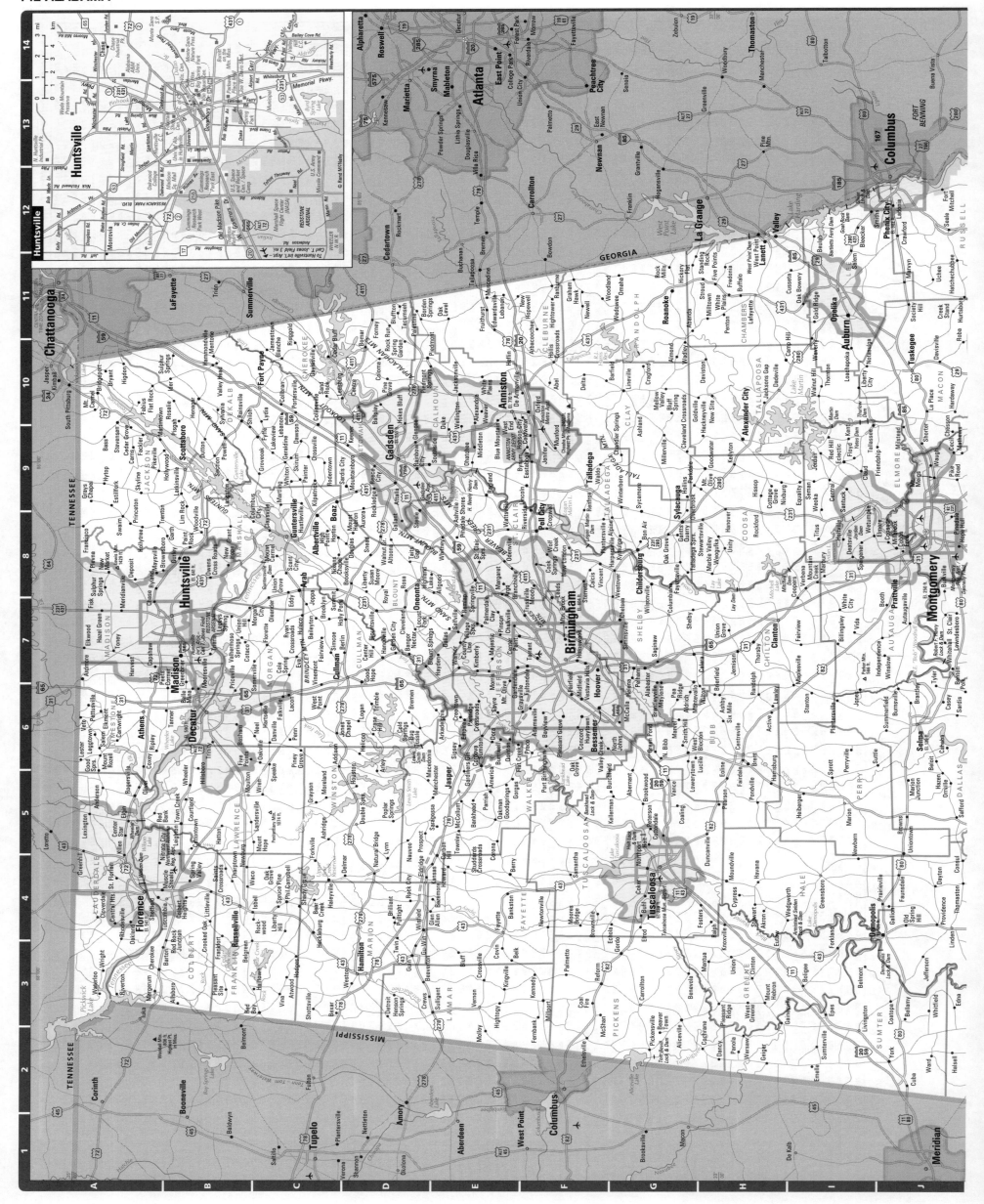

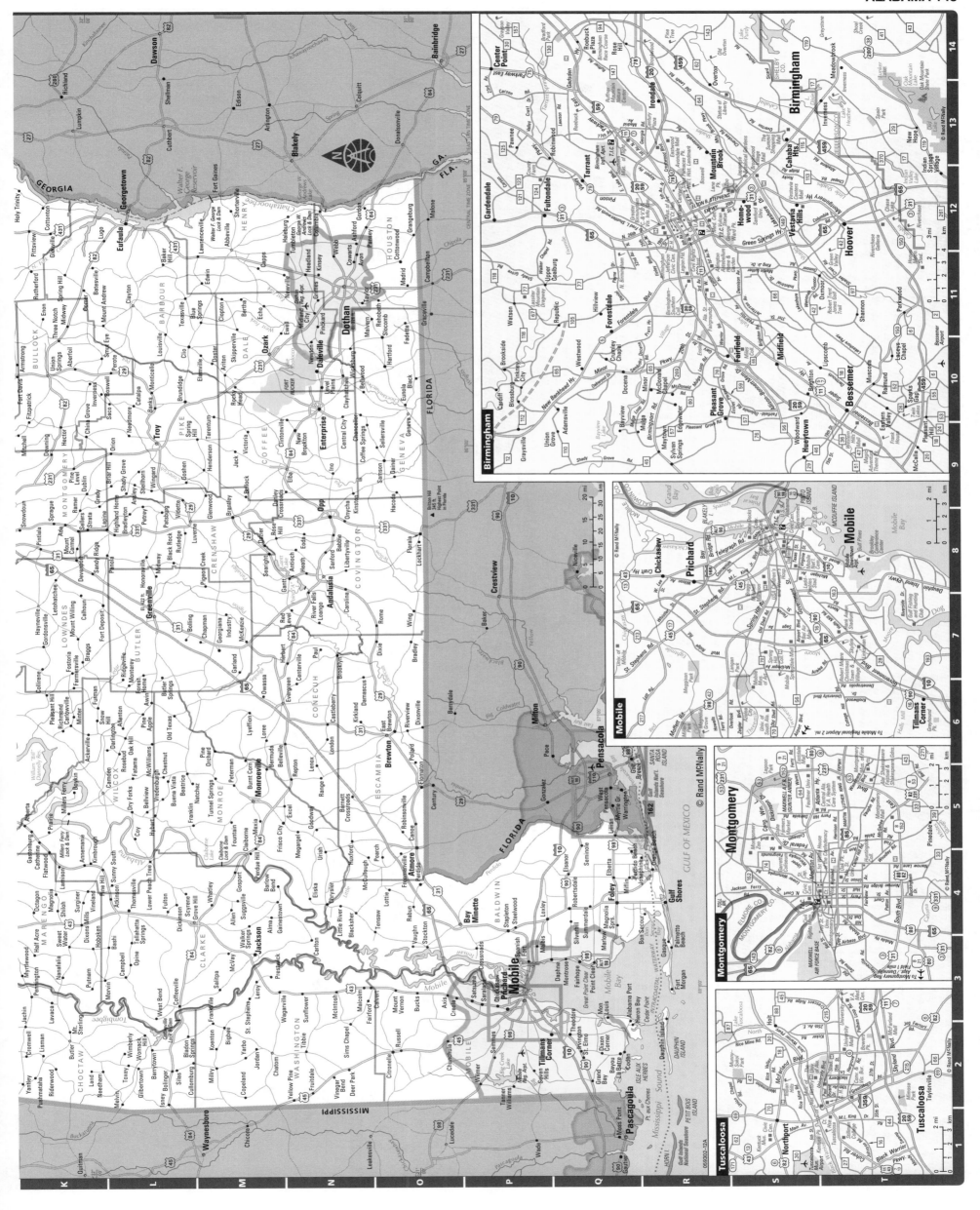

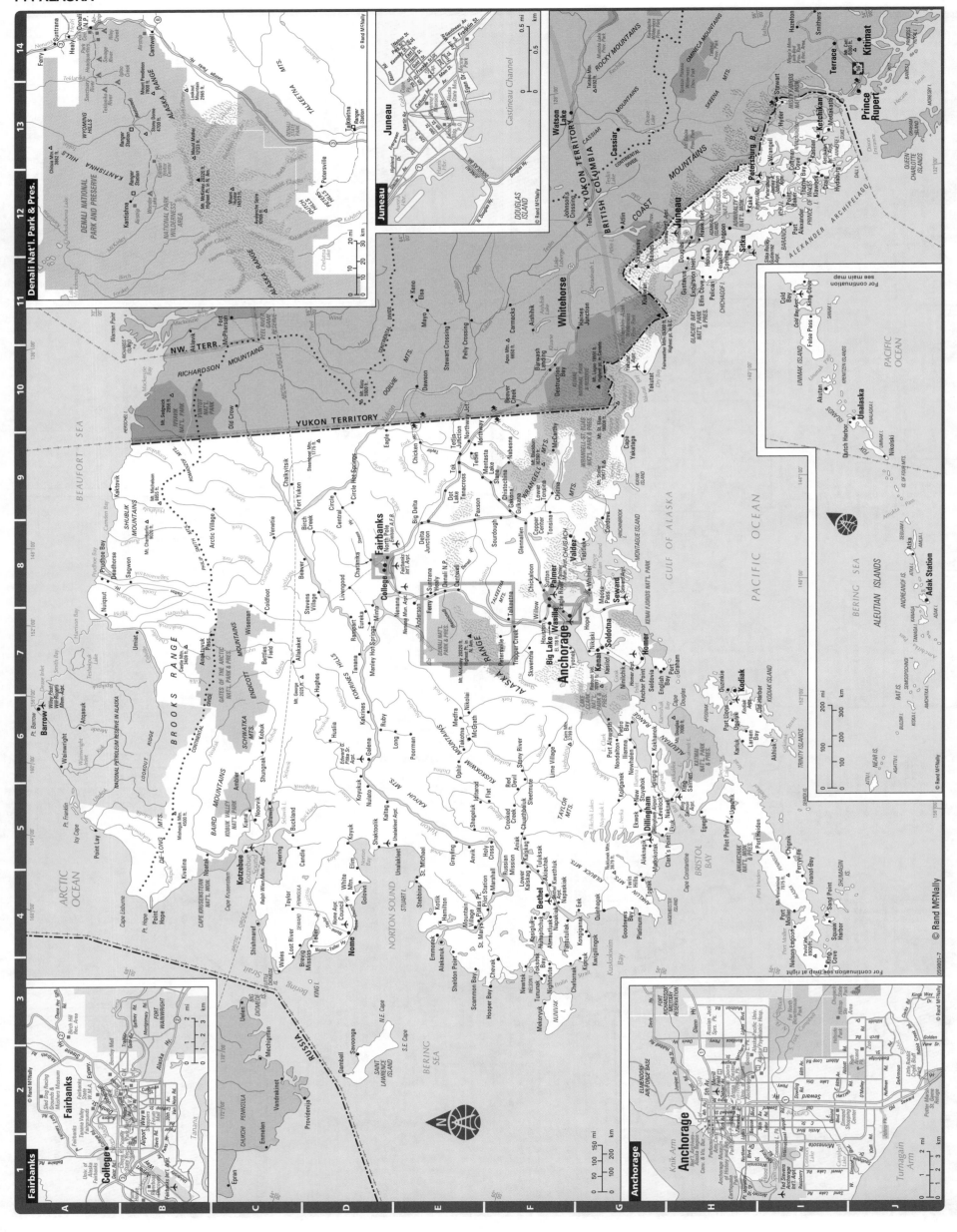

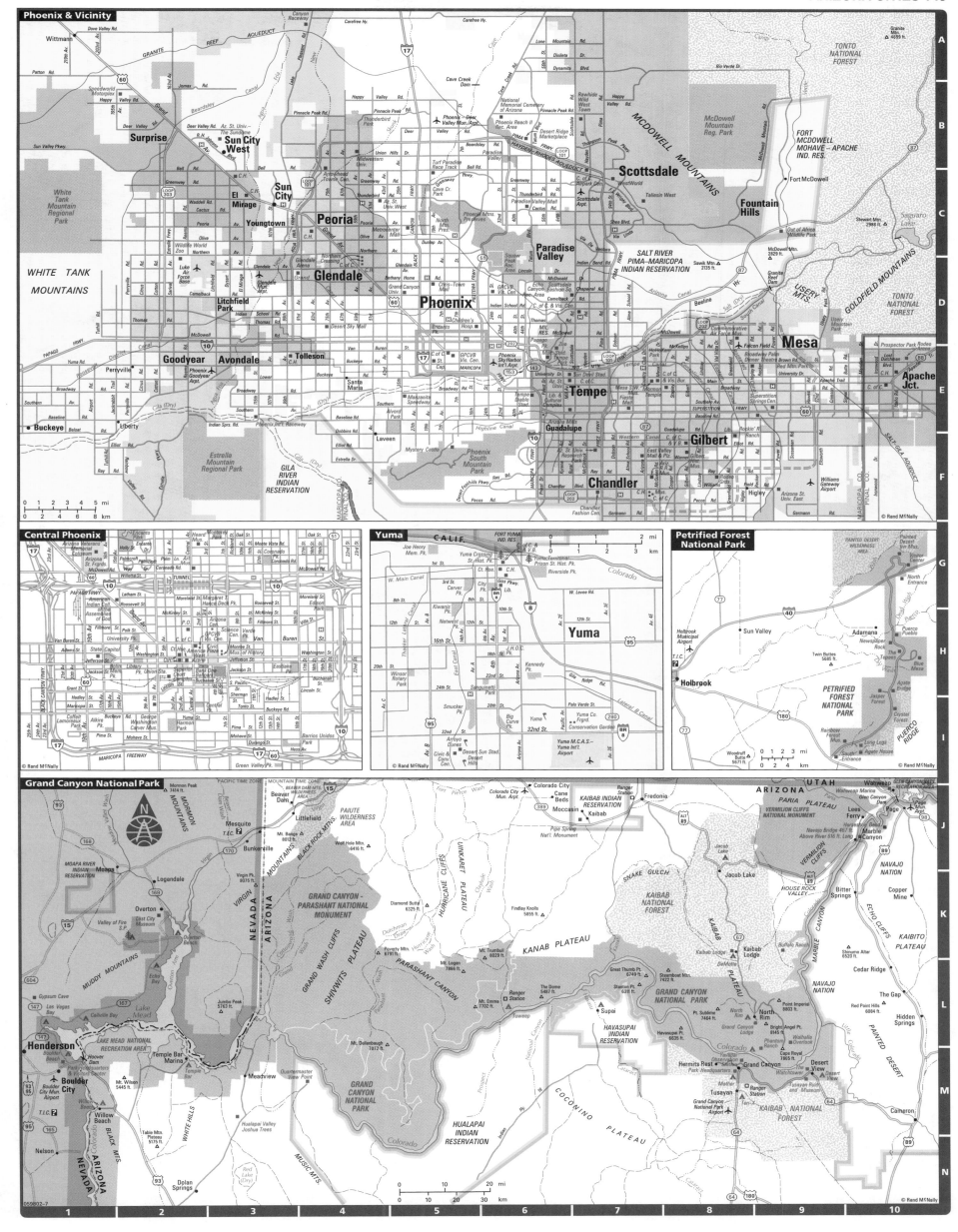

Phoenix & Vicinity

Central Phoenix

Yuma

Petrified Forest National Park

Grand Canyon National Park

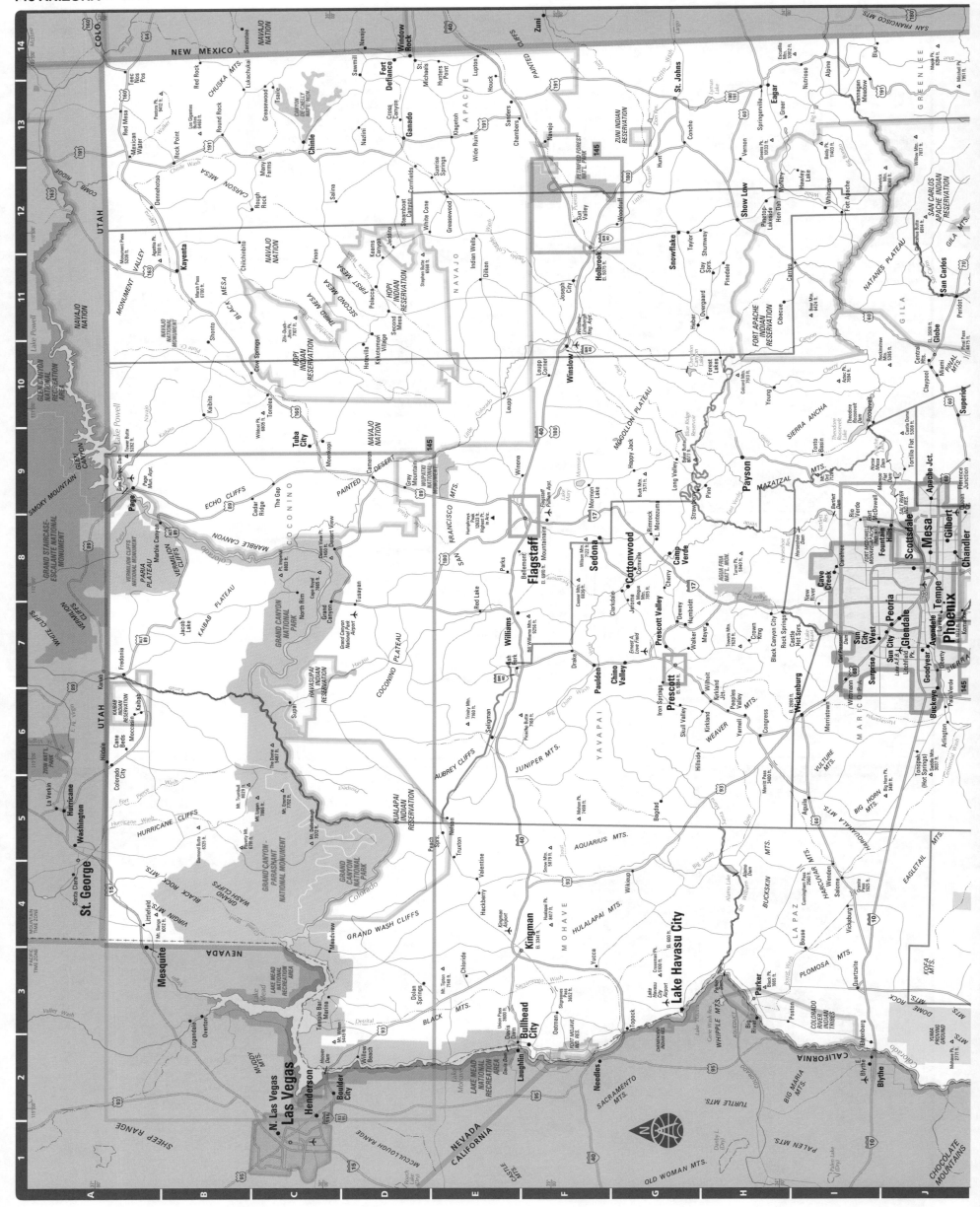

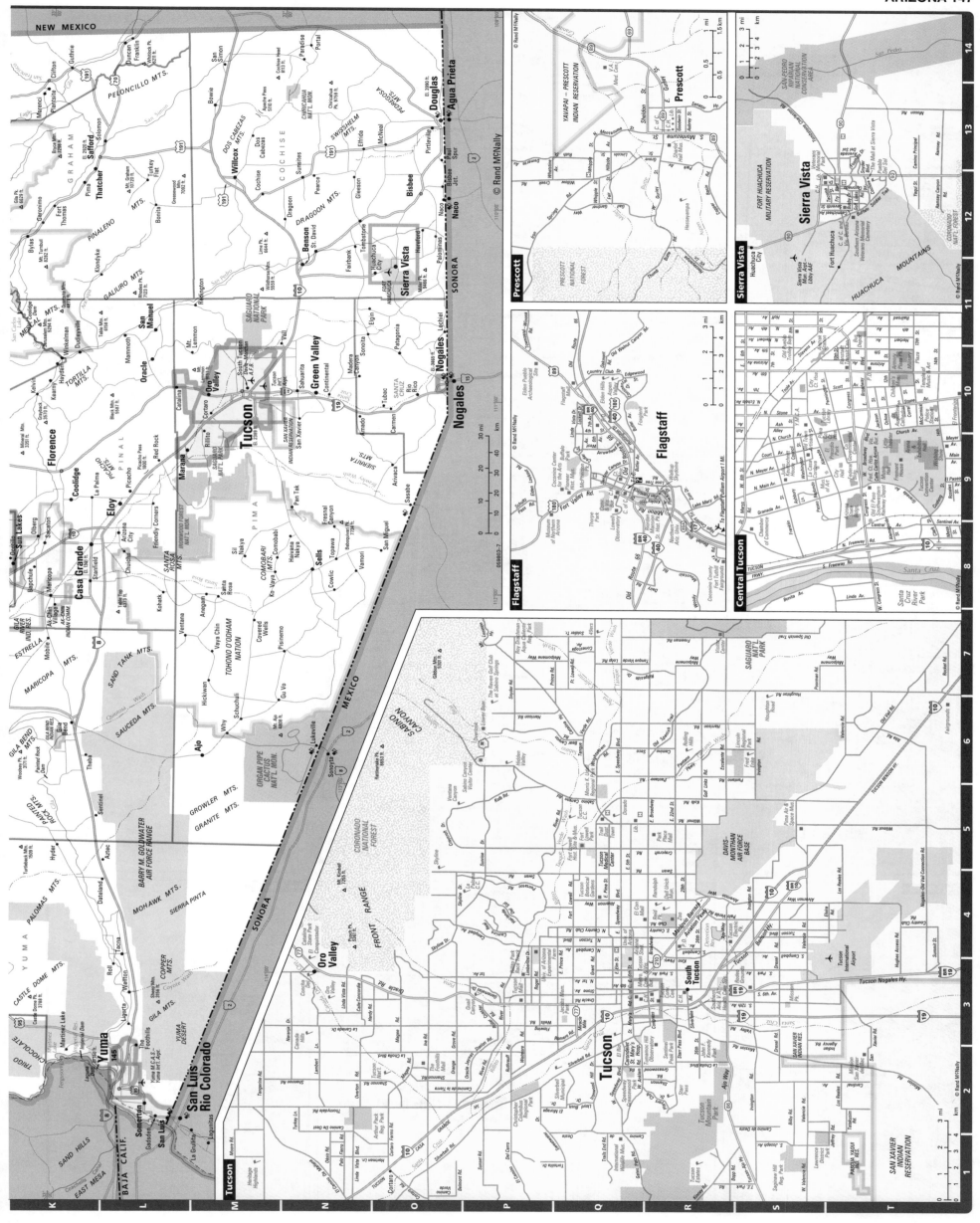

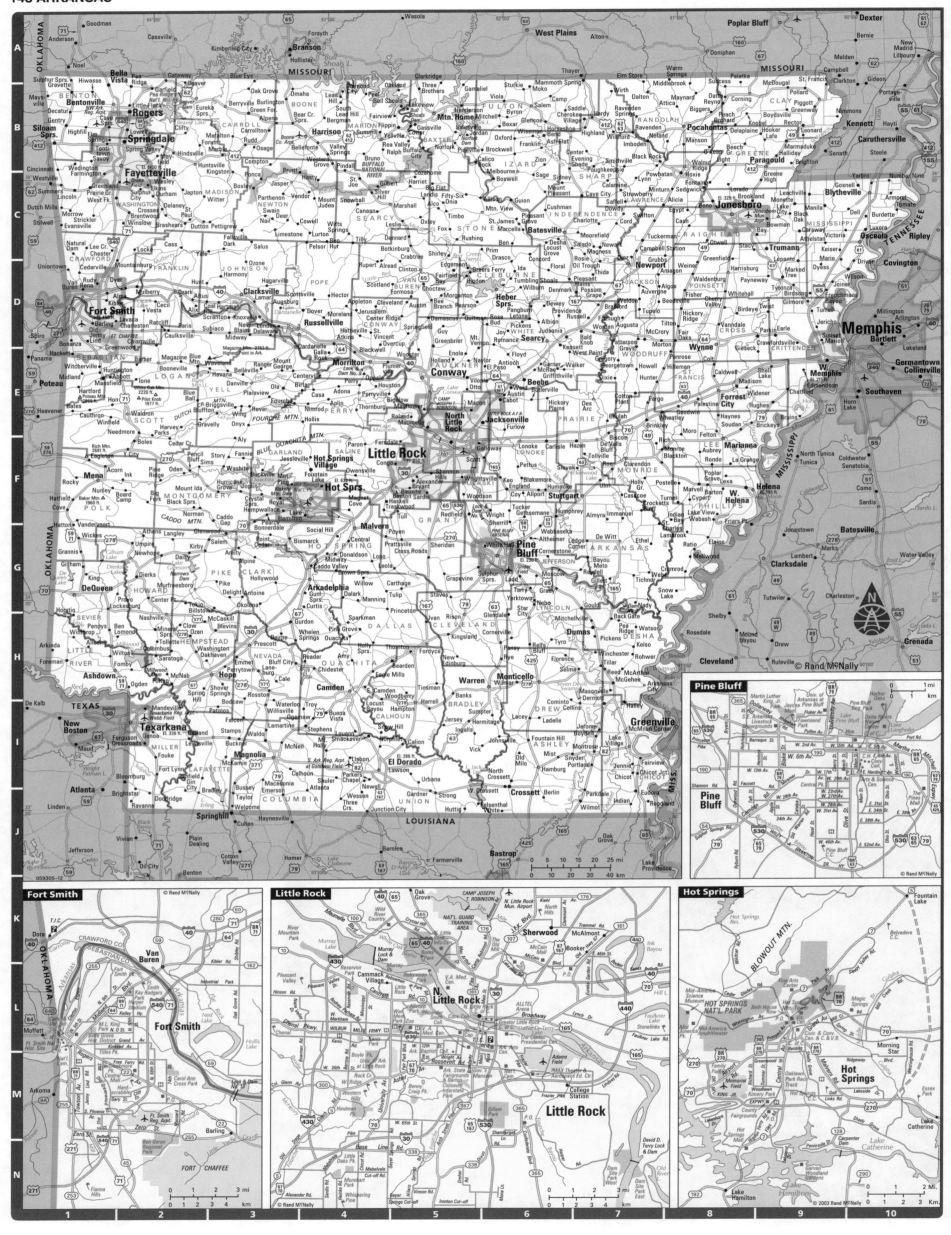

© Rand McNally

Pine Bluff

Fort Smith

Little Rock

Hot Springs

© Rand McNally

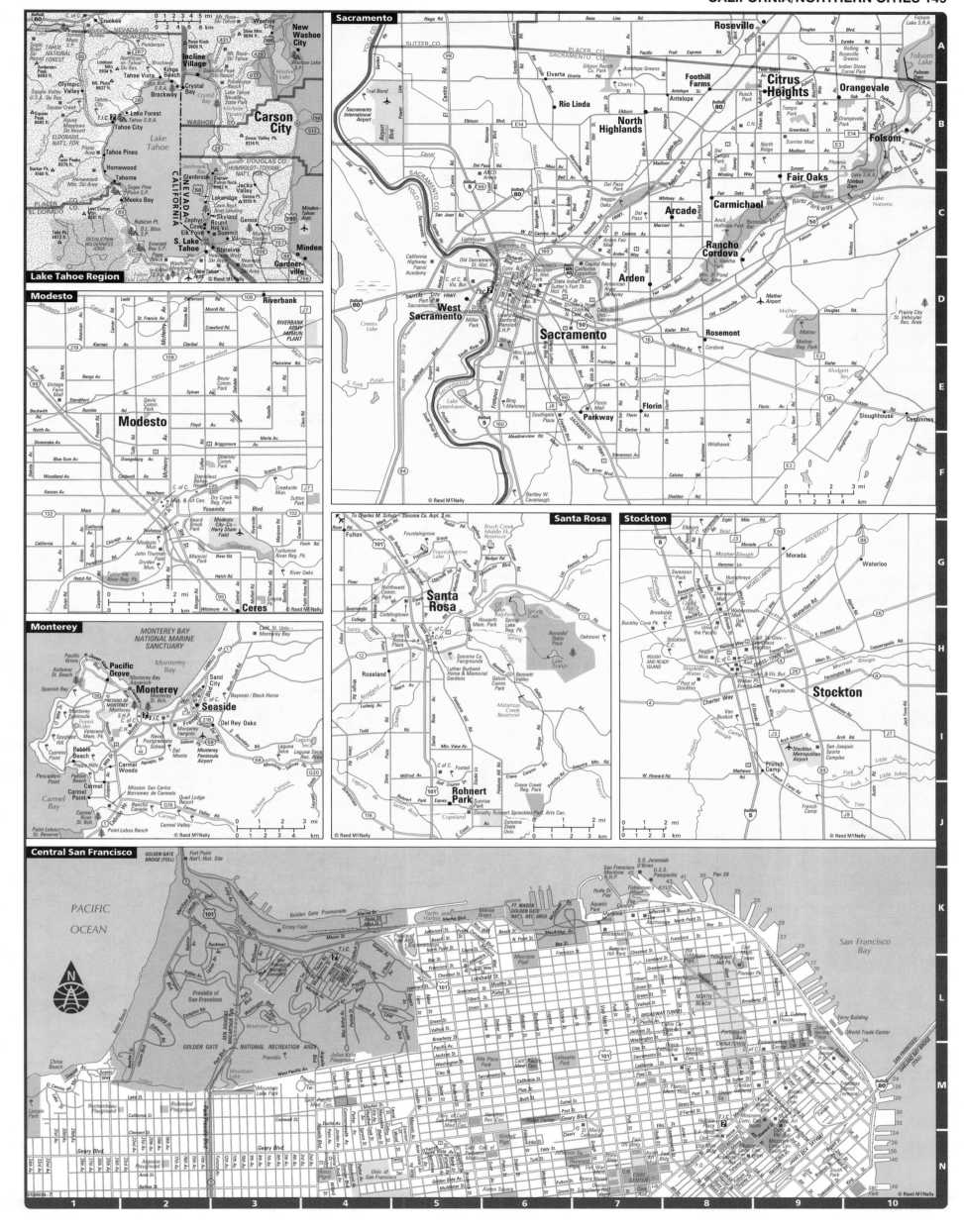

Lake Tahoe Region

Modesto

Monterey

Sacramento

Santa Rosa

Stockton

Central San Francisco

PACIFIC OCEAN

San Francisco Bay

© Rand McNally

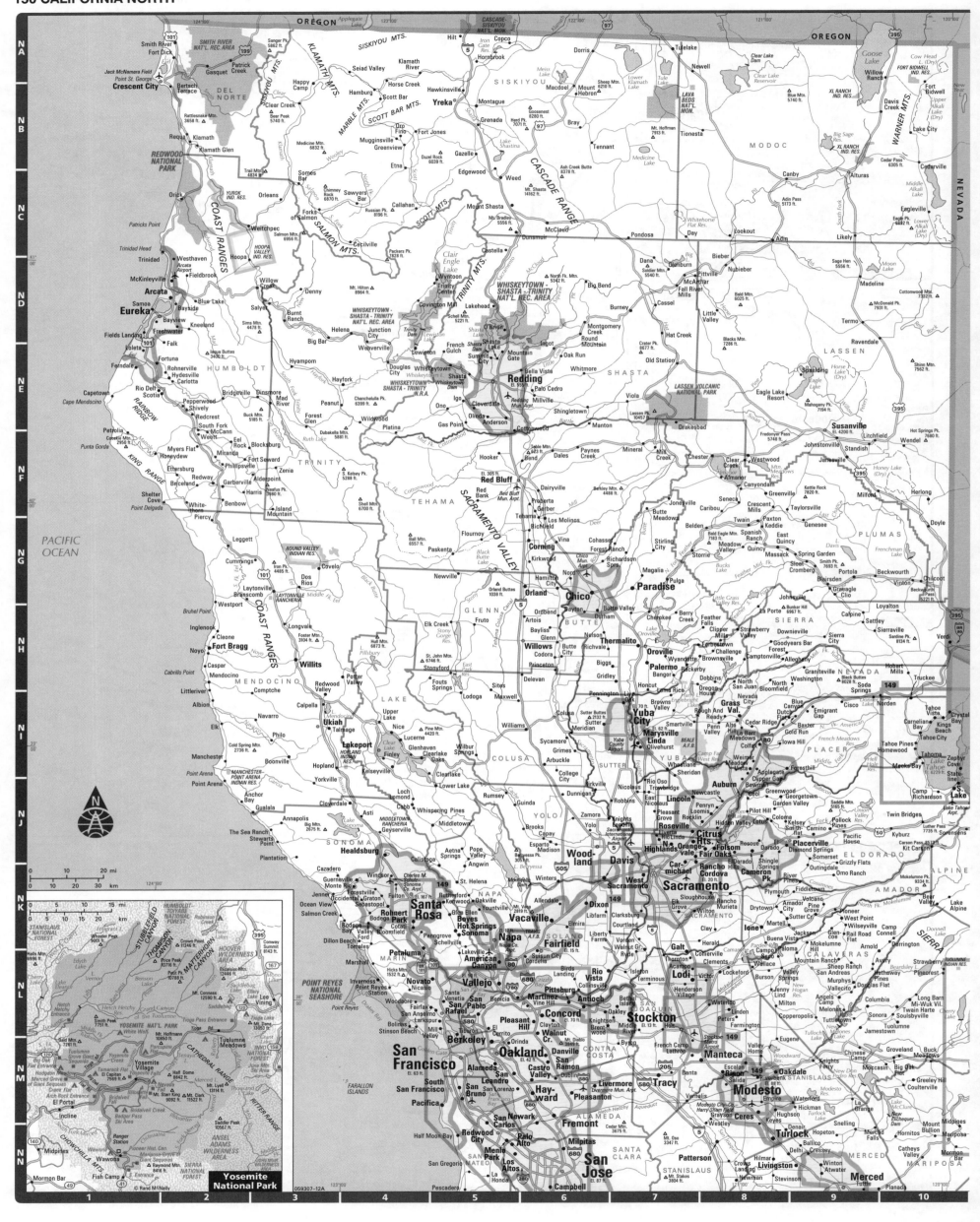

Yosemite
National Park

059307-12A

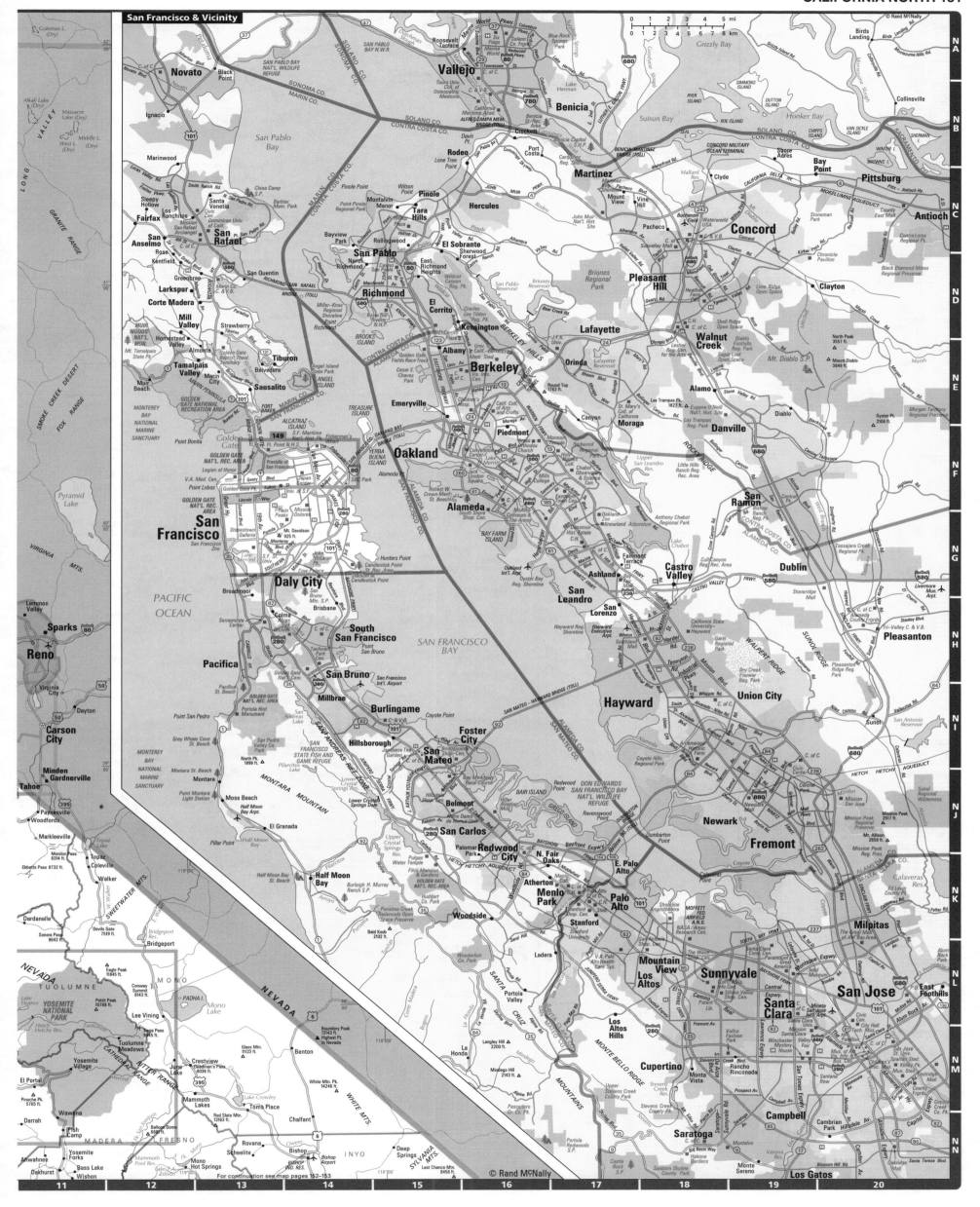

San Francisco & Vicinity

© Rand McNally

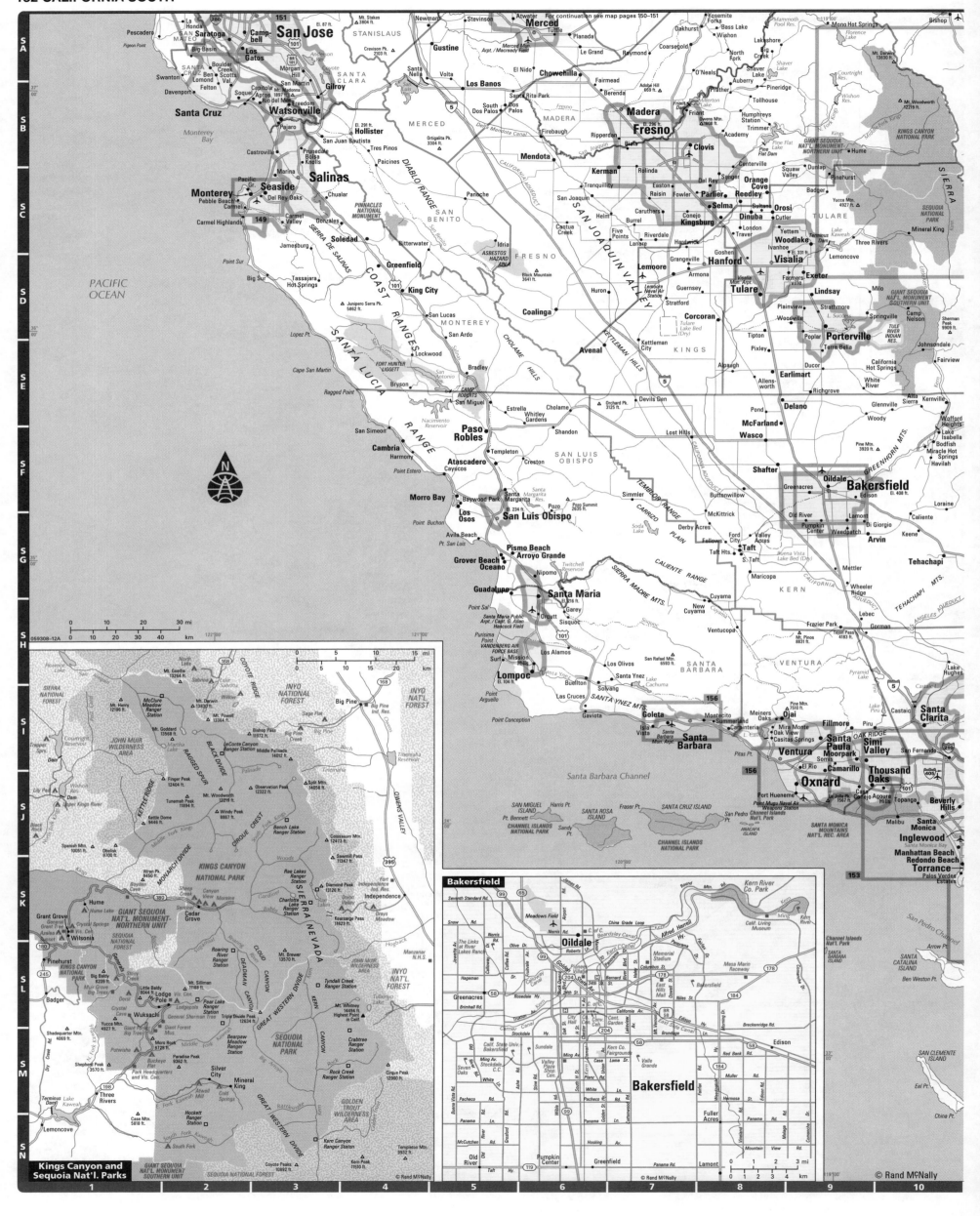

For continuation see map pages 150–151

PACIFIC
OCEAN

SANTA
CRUZ

SAN
MATEO

San Jose

Saratoga

Campbell

Los Gatos

Morgan Hill

SANTA
CLARA

STANISLAUS

Newman

Stevinson

Gustine

Merced

Santa Cruz

Watsonville

Hollister

SAN
BENITO

Los Banos

MERCED

Chowchilla

Madera

MADERA

Fresno

Clovis

Monterey

Seaside

Salinas

Soledad

Greenfield

King City

Coalinga

MONTEREY

FRESNO

SAN JOAQUIN VALLEY

Kerman

Hanford

KINGS

Tulare

Visalia

Porterville

TULARE

SEQUOIA
NATIONAL
PARK

SIERRA

Paso
Robles

Cambria

Atascadero

Morro Bay

San Luis Obispo

SAN LUIS
OBISPO

Avenal

Delano

McFarland

Wasco

Shafter

Bakersfield

Oildale

Pismo Beach
Arroyo Grande

Grover Beach
Oceano

Guadalupe

Santa Maria

KERN

Taft

Maricopa

Lompoc

SANTA
BARBARA

Goleta

Santa
Barbara

VENTURA

Ojai

Fillmore

Santa Clarita

Oxnard

Ventura

Santa Paula

Moorpark

Thousand
Oaks

Simi
Valley

Channel Islands
Nat'l. Park

SAN MIGUEL
ISLAND

SANTA ROSA
ISLAND

SANTA CRUZ ISLAND

Santa Barbara Channel

CHANNEL ISLANDS
NATIONAL PARK

ANACAPA
ISLAND

Beverly
Hills

Santa
Monica

Inglewood

Manhattan Beach
Redondo Beach
Torrance

SANTA CATALINA
ISLAND

SAN CLEMENTE
ISLAND

Kings Canyon and
Sequoia Nat'l. Parks

KINGS CANYON
NATIONAL PARK

SEQUOIA
NATIONAL
PARK

SEQUOIA
NATIONAL FOREST

INYO
NATIONAL
FOREST

SIERRA
NEVADA

OWENS VALLEY

Big Pine

Independence

Mt. Whitney
14494 ft.
Highest Point
in Calif.

GIANT SEQUOIA
NAT'L. MONUMENT-
NORTHERN UNIT

GIANT SEQUOIA
NAT'L. MONUMENT-
SOUTHERN UNIT

Bakersfield

Oildale

Greenacres

Bakersfield

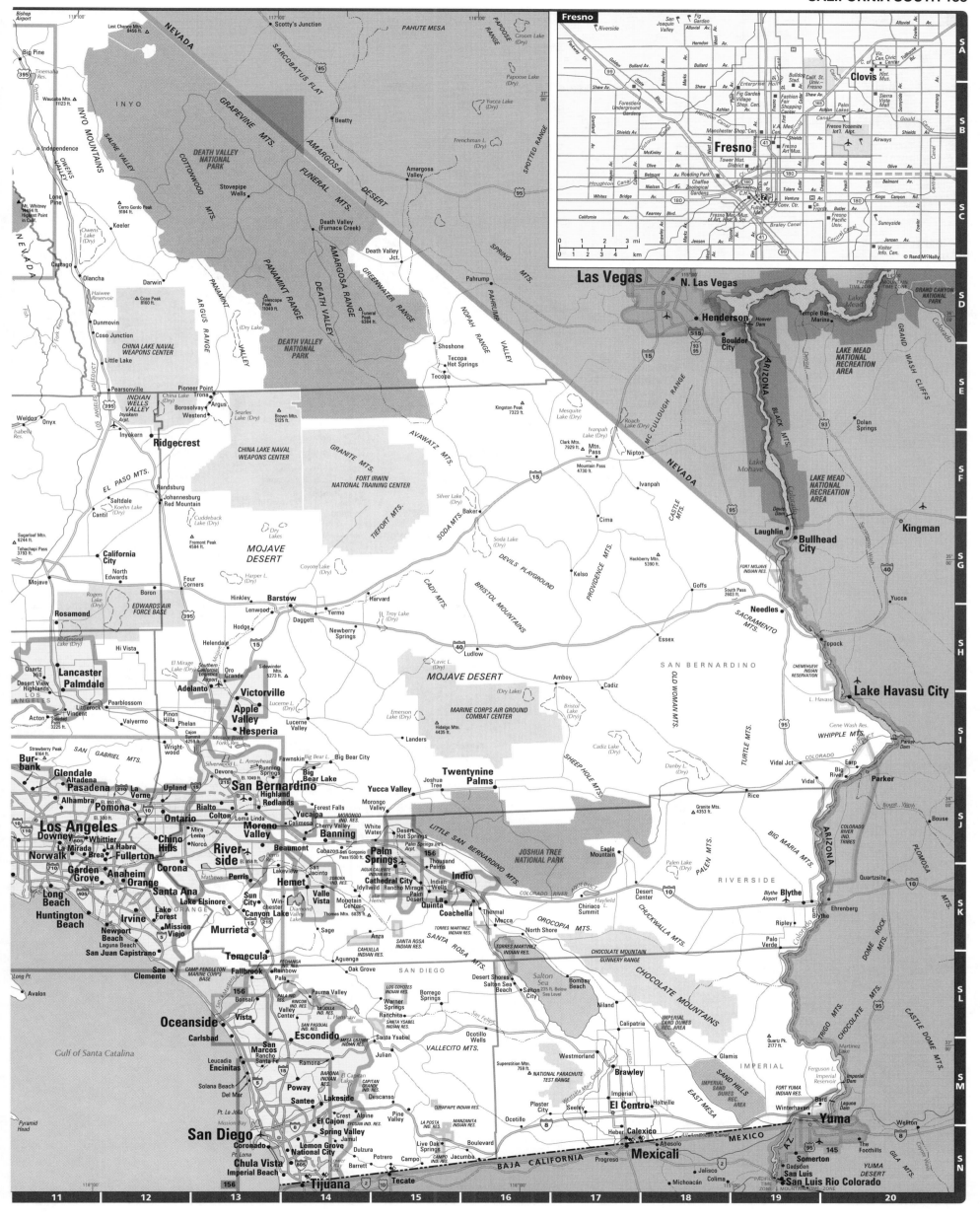

Fresno (inset map)

Clovis

Fresno

0 1 2 3 mi
0 1 2 3 4 km

© Rand McNally

Las Vegas
N. Las Vegas
Henderson
Boulder City
Hoover Dam

Laughlin
Bullhead City
Kingman

Needles

Lake Havasu City

Parker

Blythe

Yuma

Mexicali

Los Angeles
San Bernardino
Riverside
Palm Springs
Indio

San Diego
Tijuana
El Centro
Calexico

Ridgecrest
Barstow
Victorville
Lancaster
Palmdale

MOJAVE DESERT

DEATH VALLEY NATIONAL PARK

JOSHUA TREE NATIONAL PARK

NEVADA
ARIZONA
MEXICO
BAJA CALIFORNIA

11 12 13 14 15 16 17 18 19 20

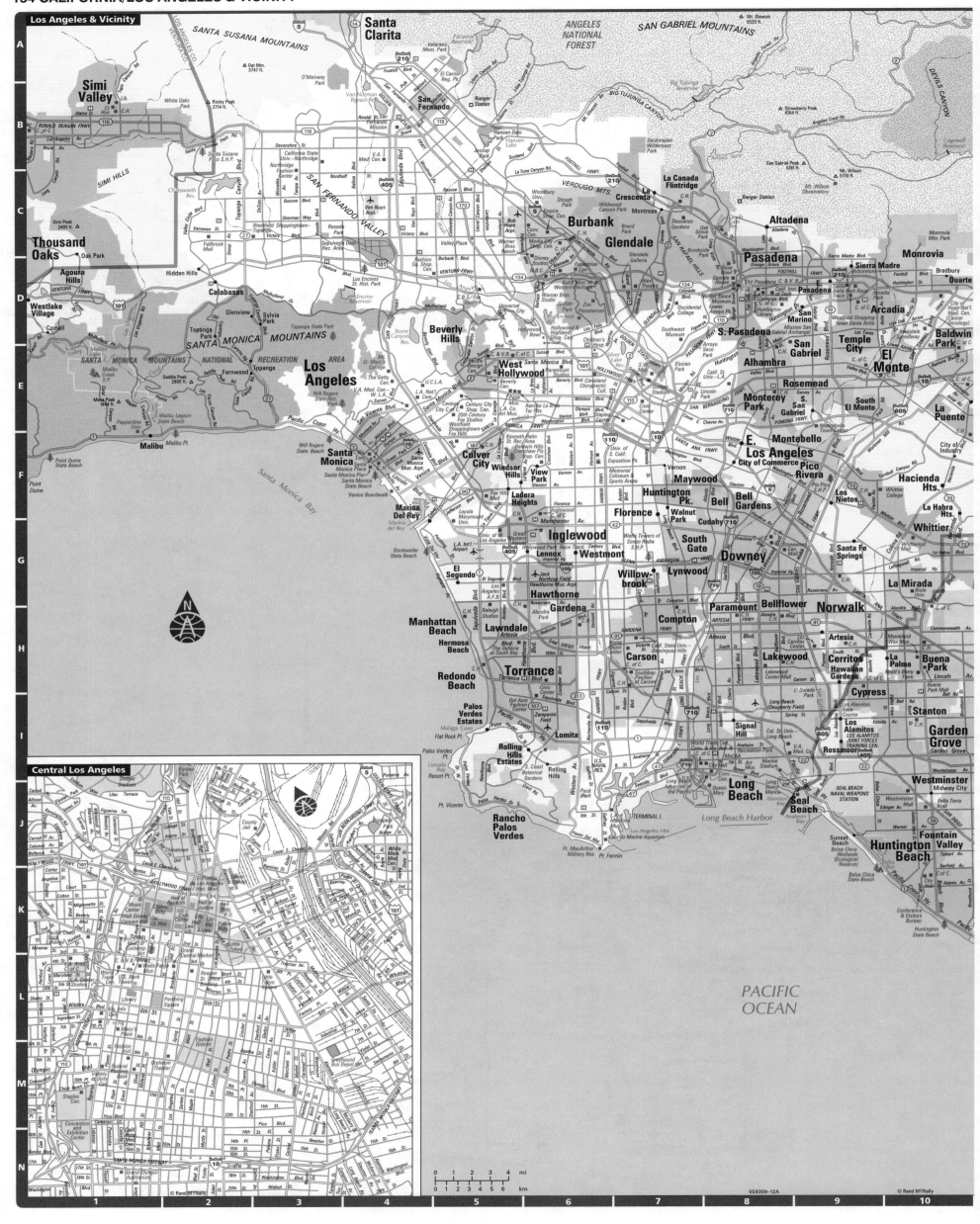

Los Angeles & Vicinity

Central Los Angeles

PACIFIC OCEAN

© Rand McNally

059309-12A   © Rand McNally

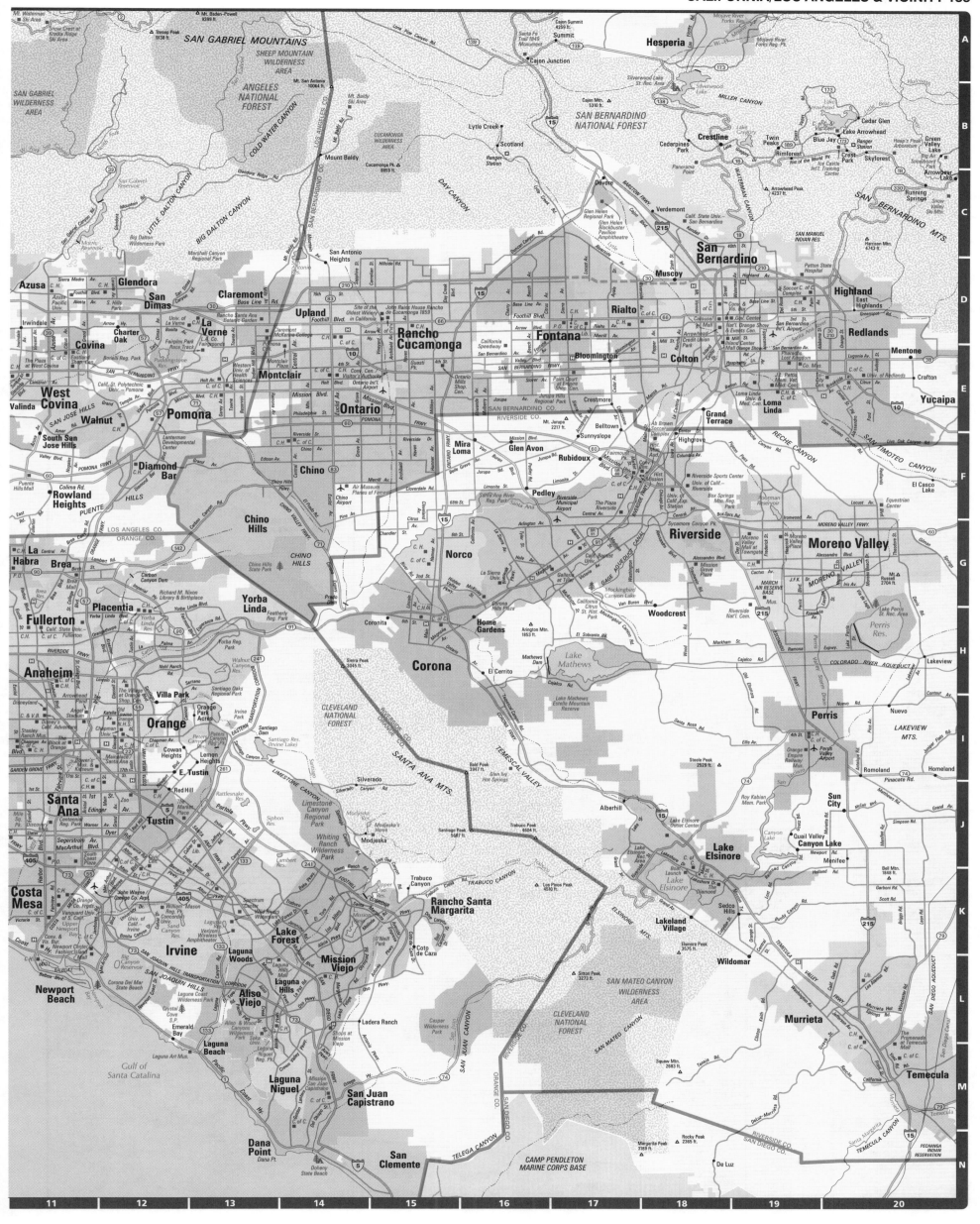

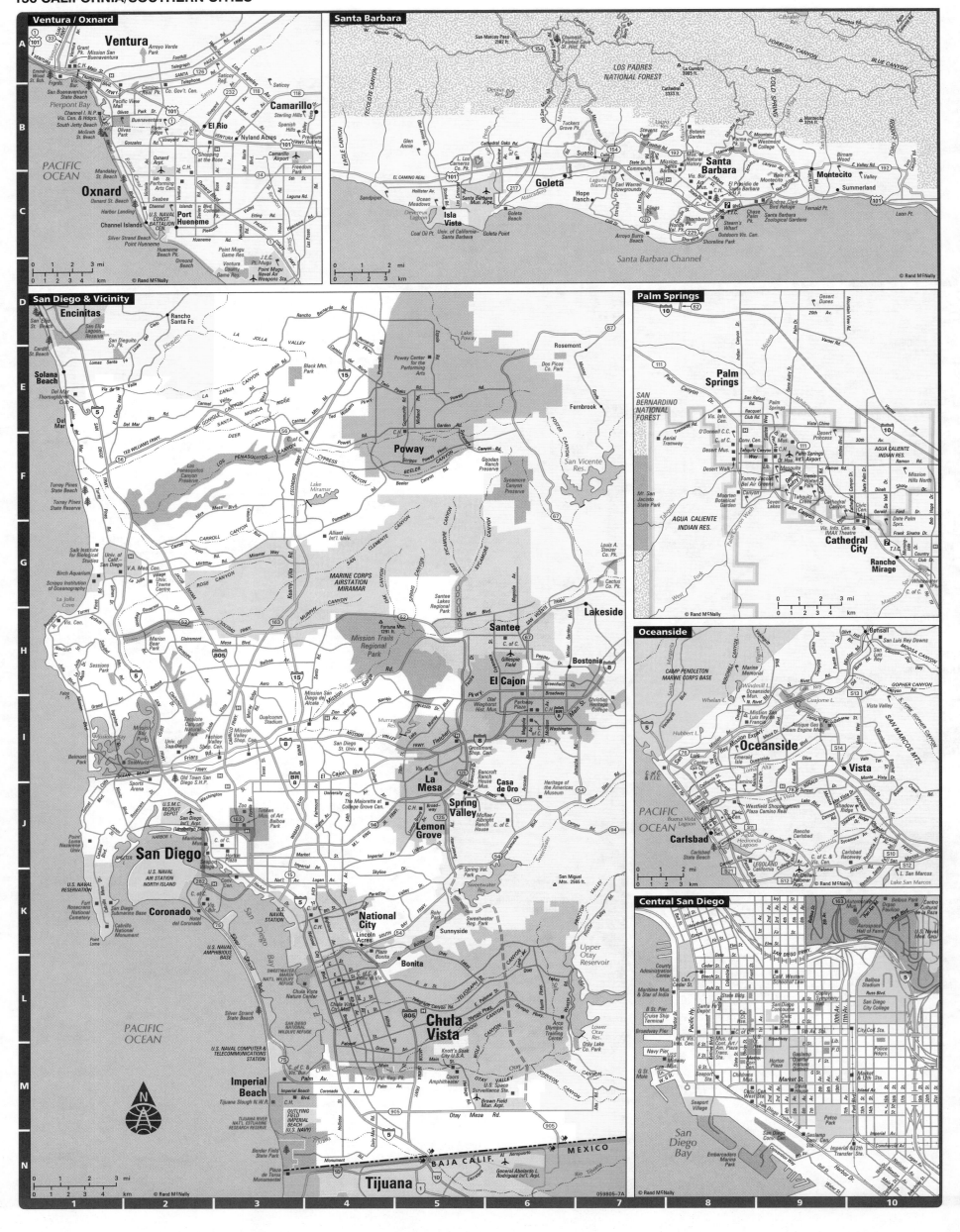

Ventura / Oxnard

Ventura

Oxnard

PACIFIC OCEAN

Port Hueneme

El Rio

Camarillo

Santa Barbara

LOS PADRES NATIONAL FOREST

Goleta

Santa Barbara

Montecito

Isla Vista

Santa Barbara Channel

San Diego & Vicinity

Encinitas

Solana Beach

Del Mar

Poway

Lakeside

Santee

El Cajon

Bostonia

La Mesa

Spring Valley

Lemon Grove

San Diego

Coronado

National City

Bonita

PACIFIC OCEAN

Chula Vista

Imperial Beach

Tijuana

BAJA CALIF.   MEXICO

Palm Springs

SAN BERNARDINO NATIONAL FOREST

Palm Springs

Cathedral City

Rancho Mirage

AGUA CALIENTE INDIAN RES.

Oceanside

CAMP PENDLETON MARINE CORPS BASE

Oceanside

Vista

Carlsbad

PACIFIC OCEAN

Central San Diego

San Diego Bay

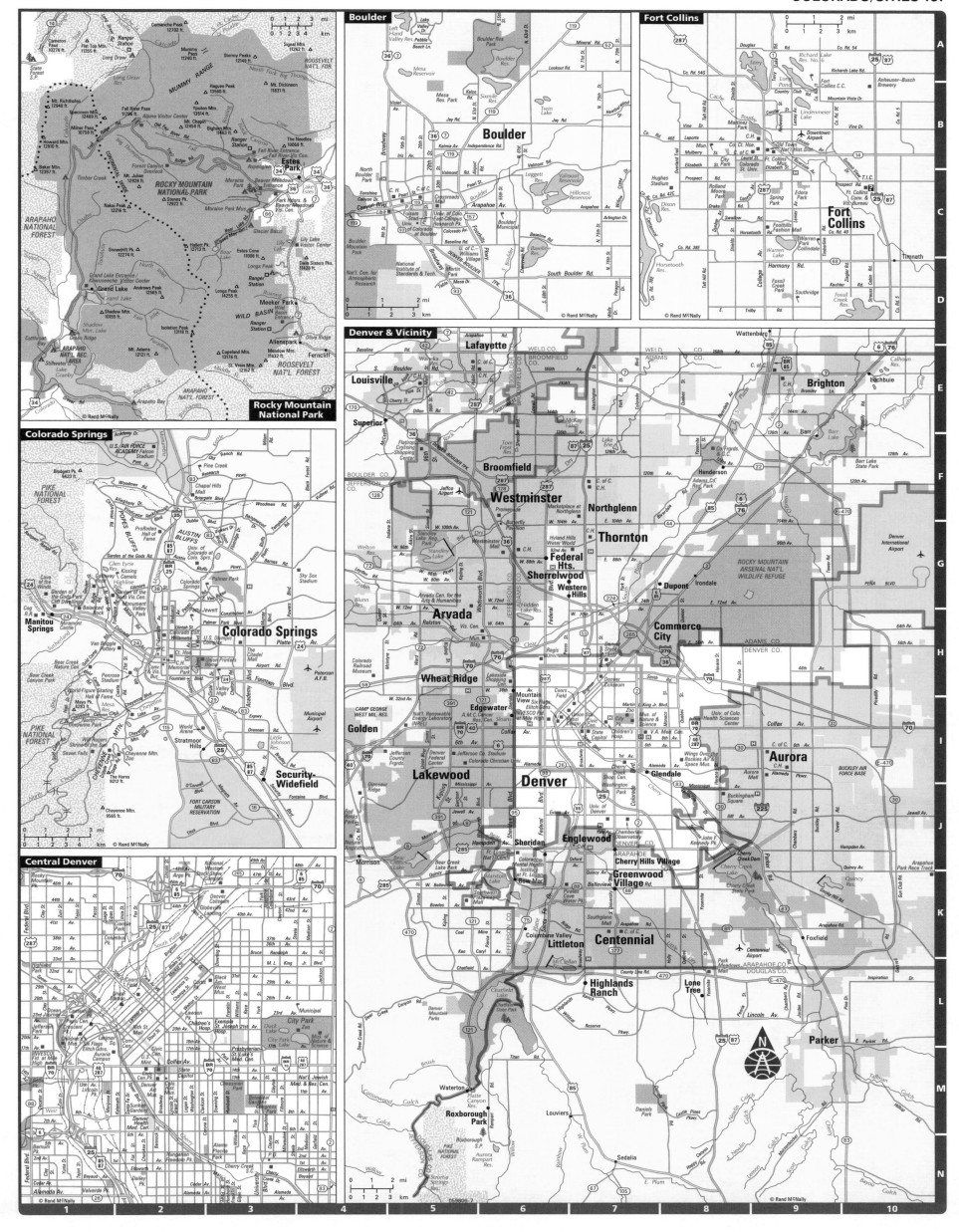

Rocky Mountain National Park

Boulder

Fort Collins

Colorado Springs

Central Denver

Denver & Vicinity

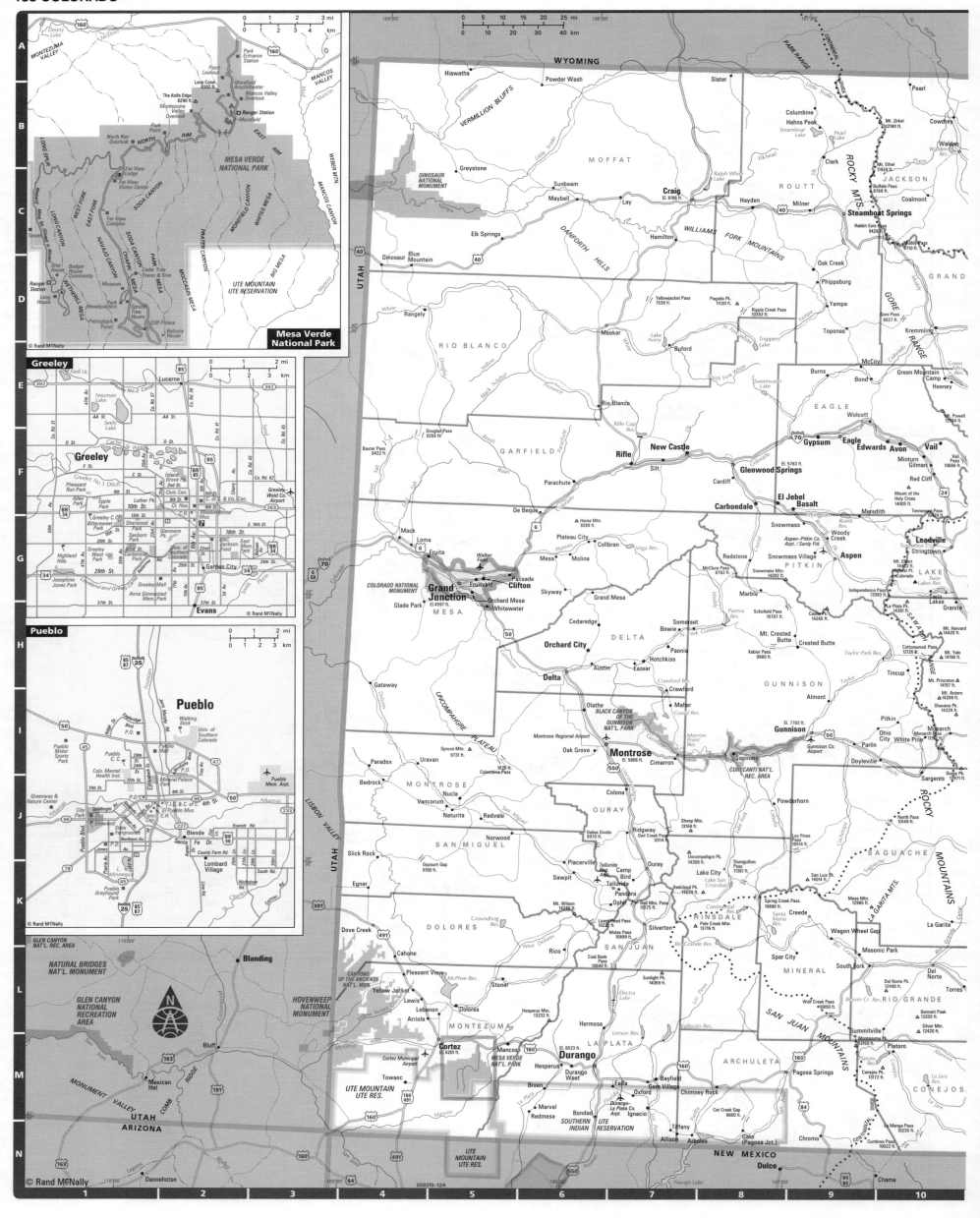

Mesa Verde National Park

Greeley

Pueblo

© Rand McNally

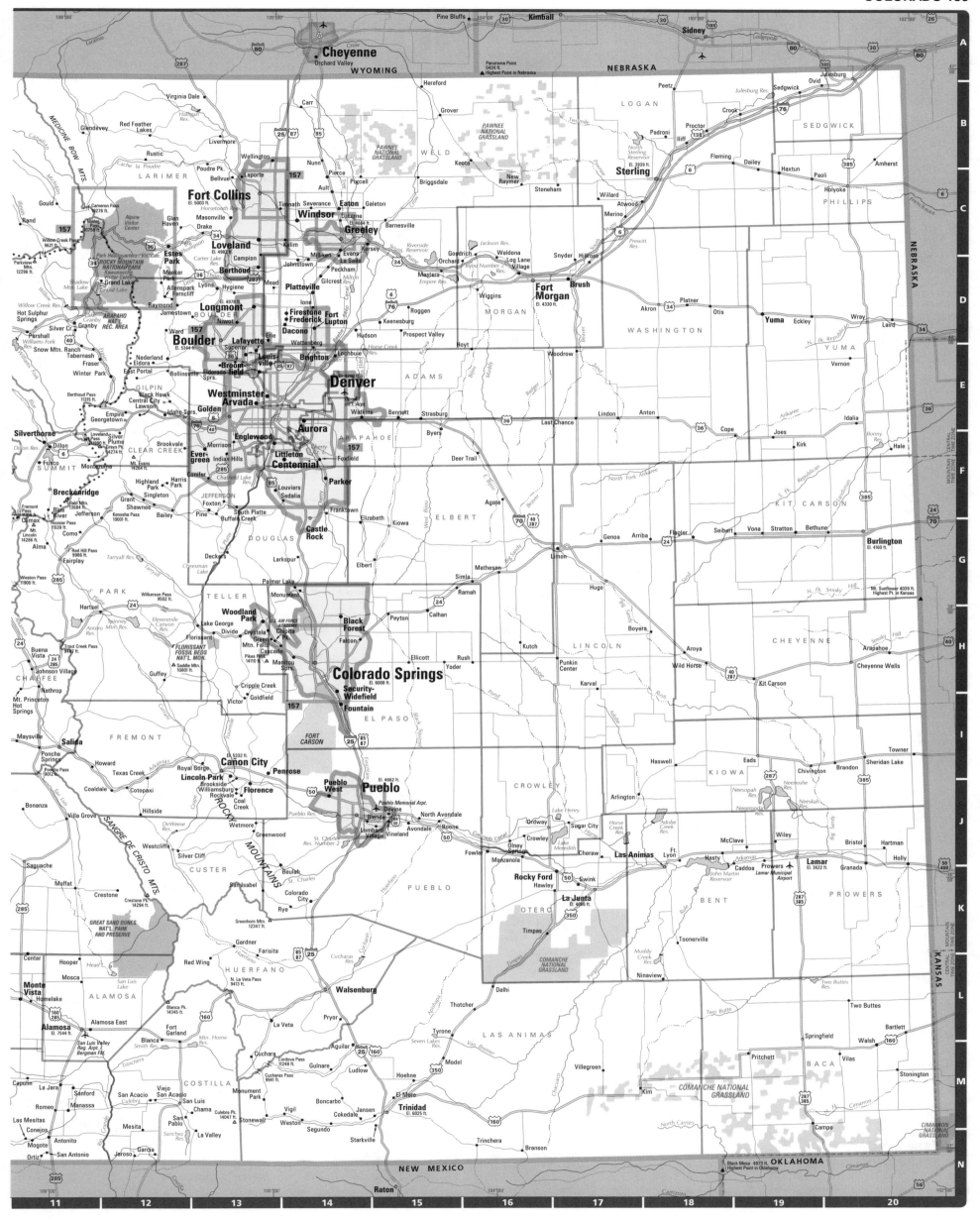

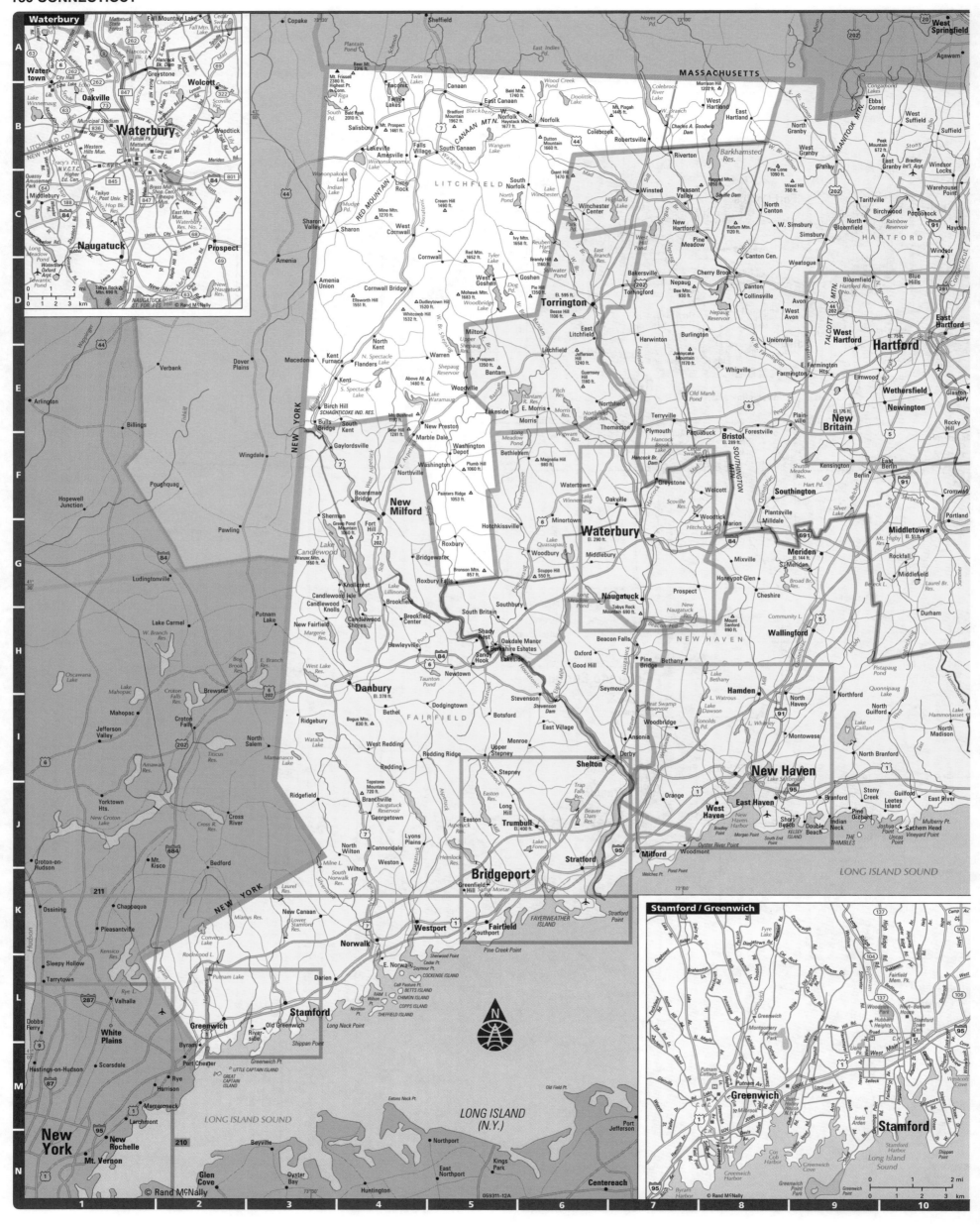

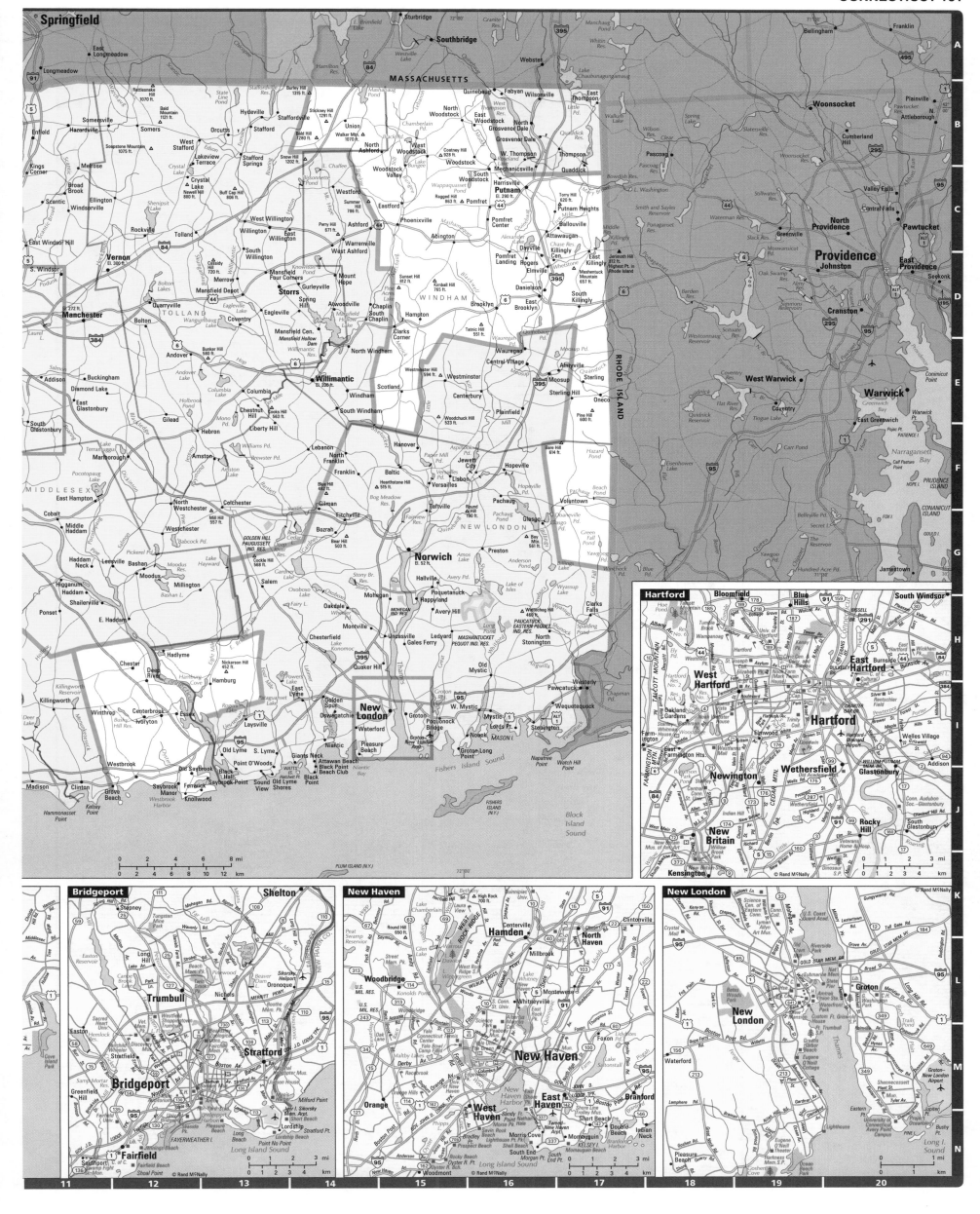

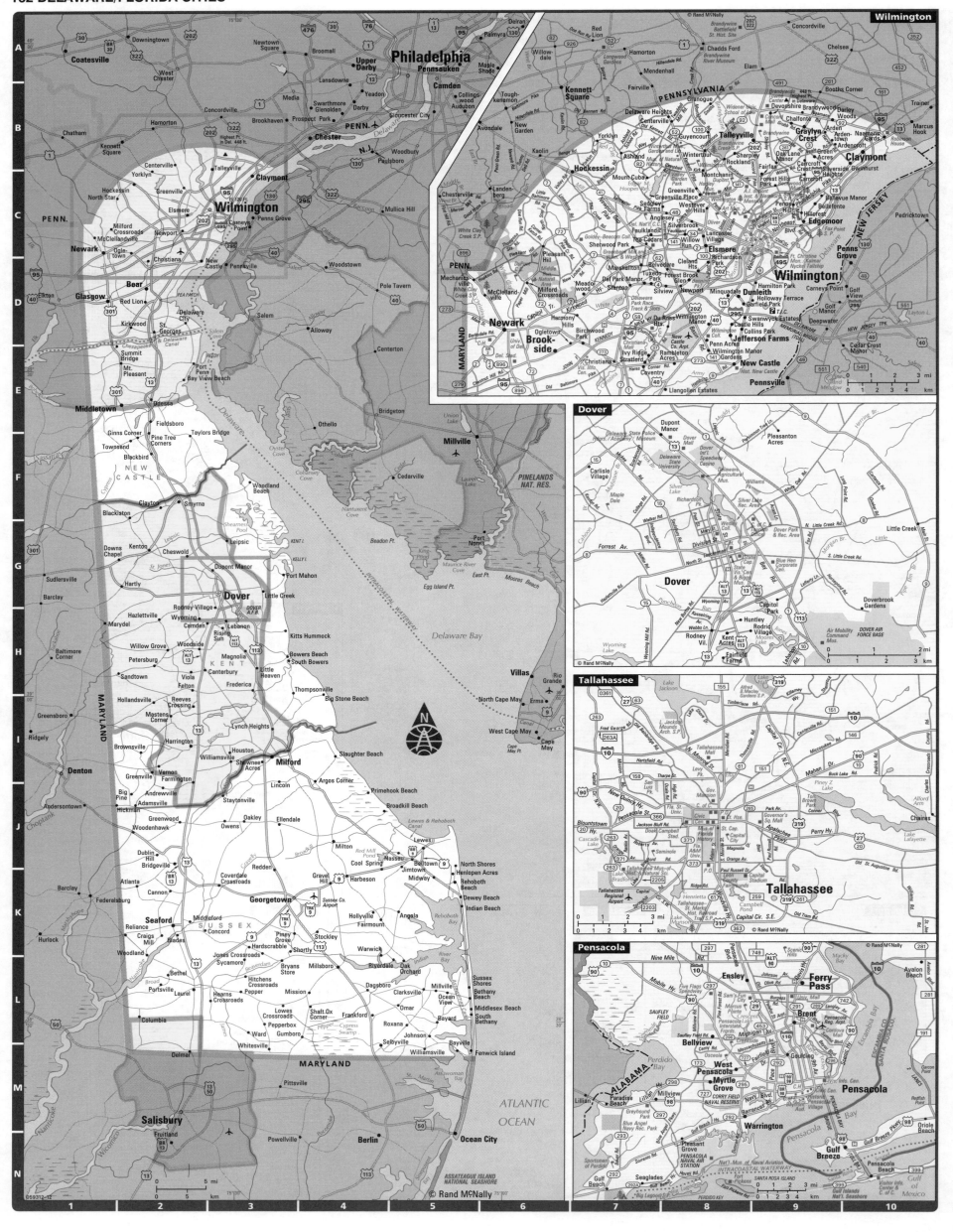

Dover

Tallahassee

Pensacola

© Rand McNally

ATLANTIC
OCEAN

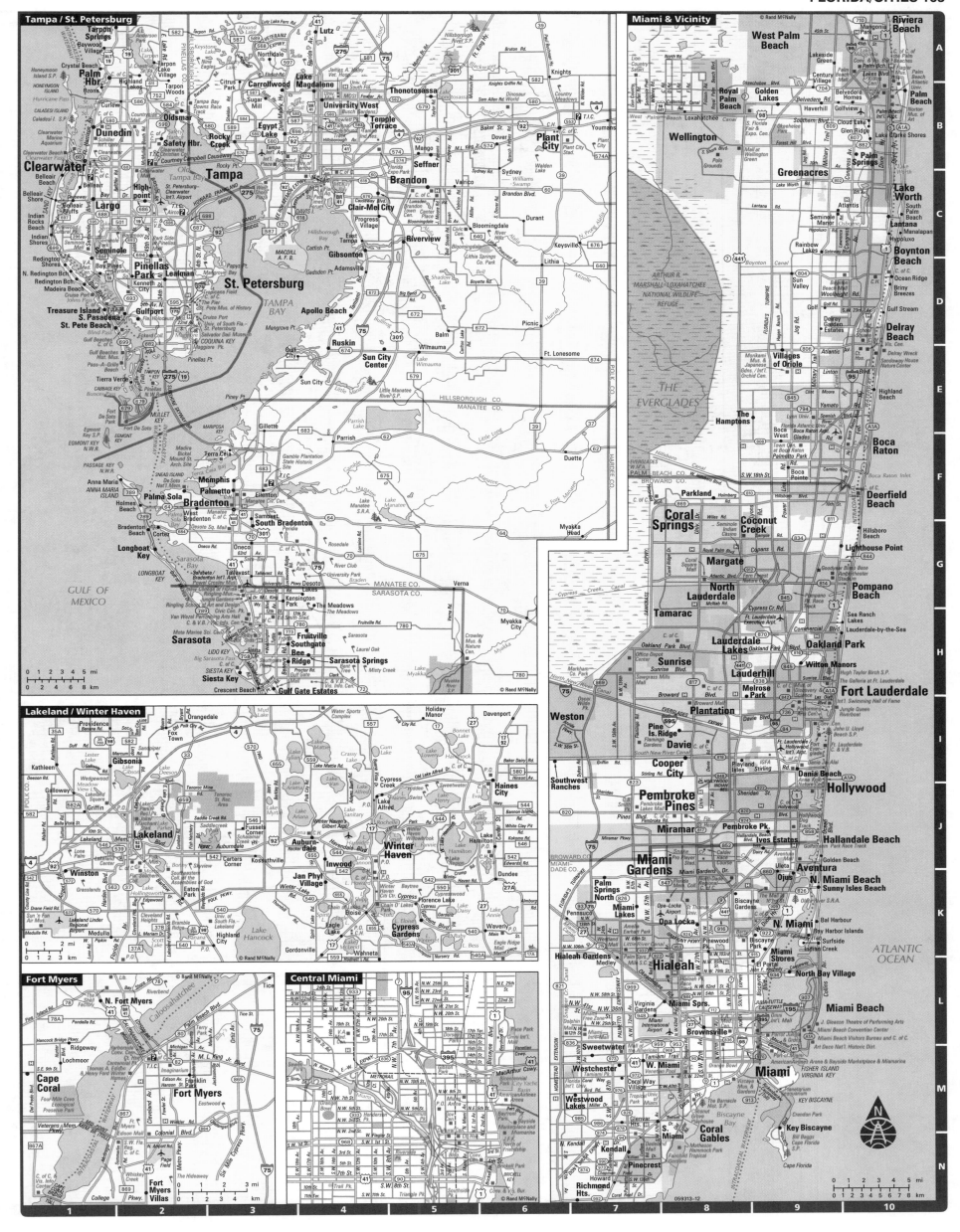

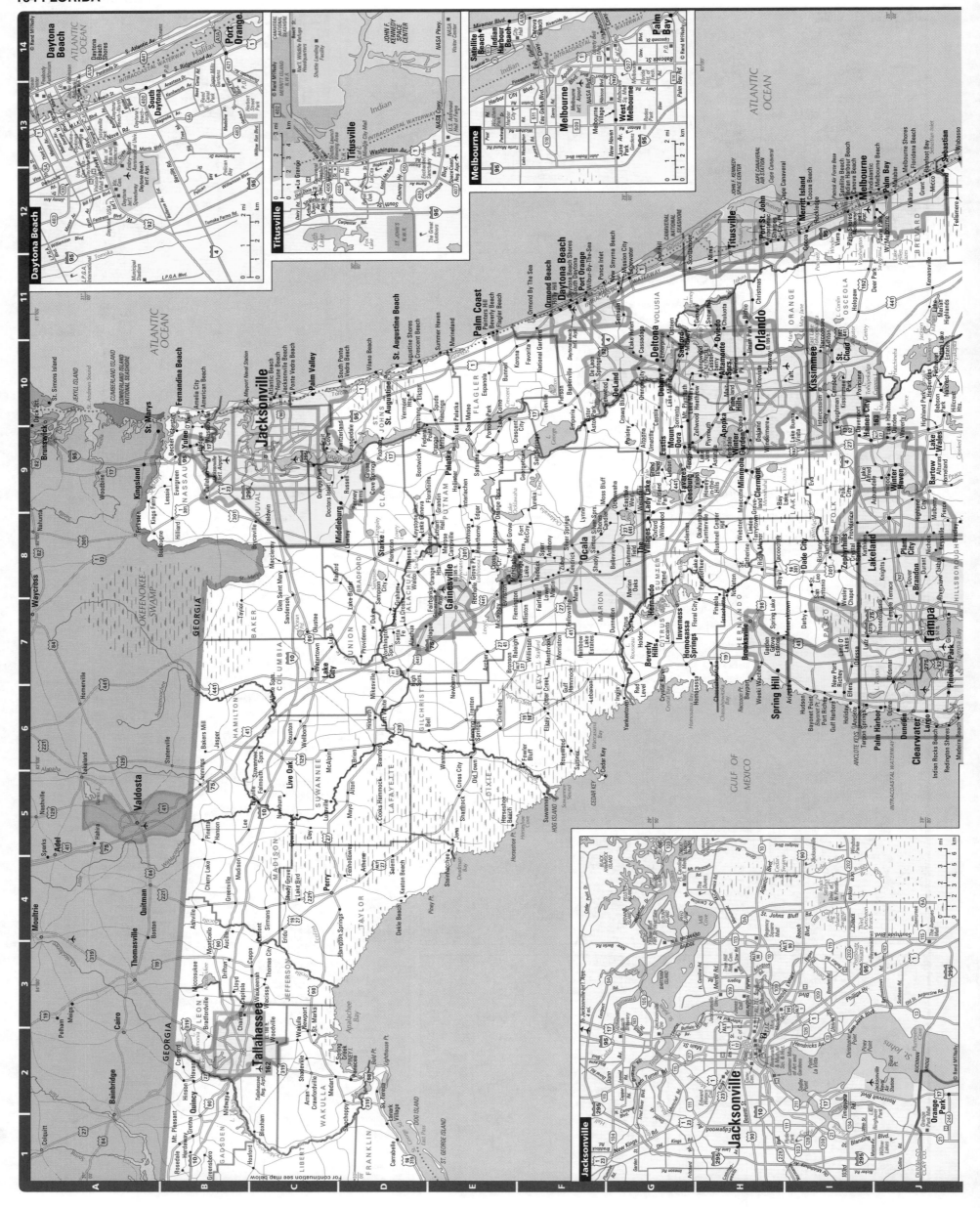

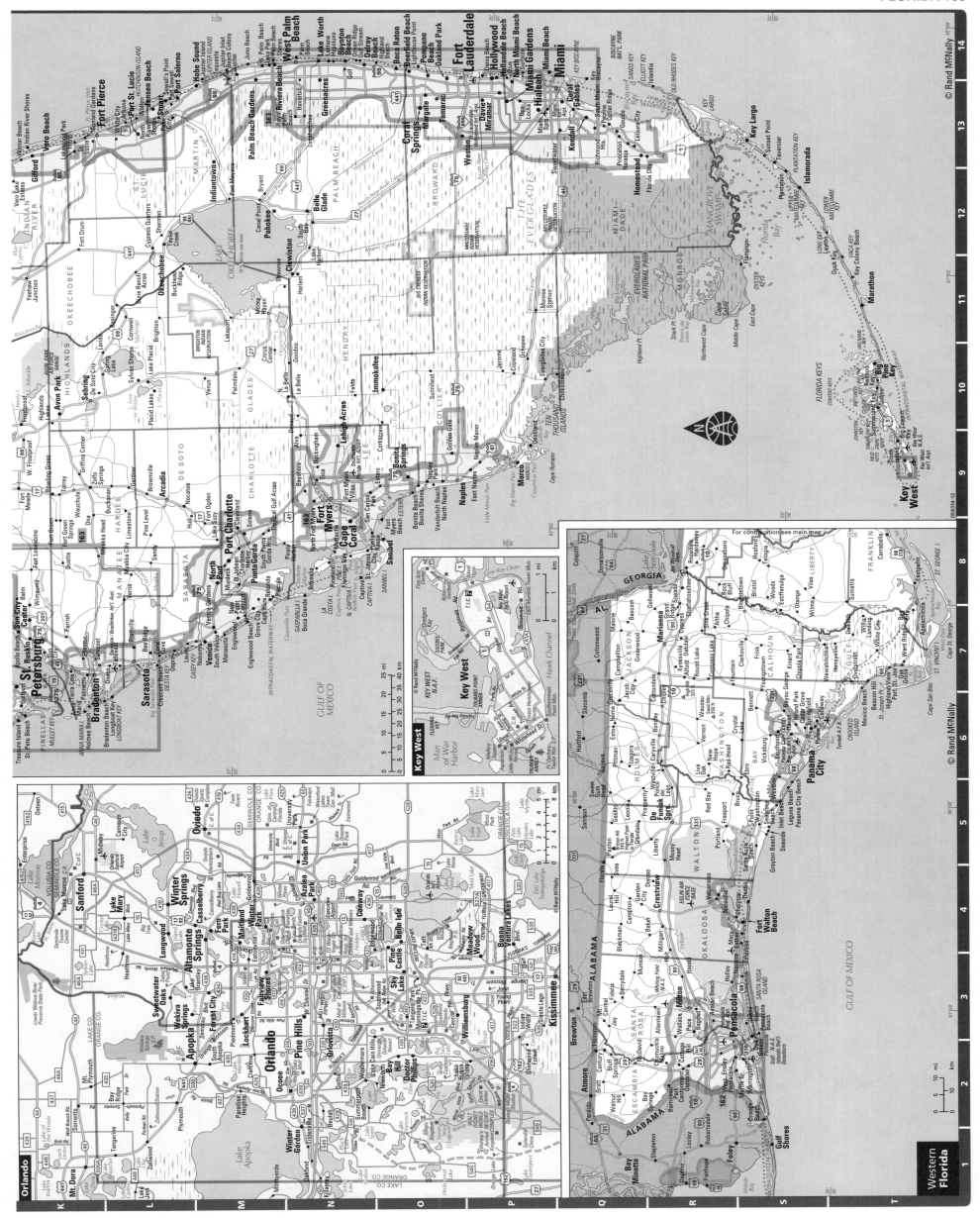

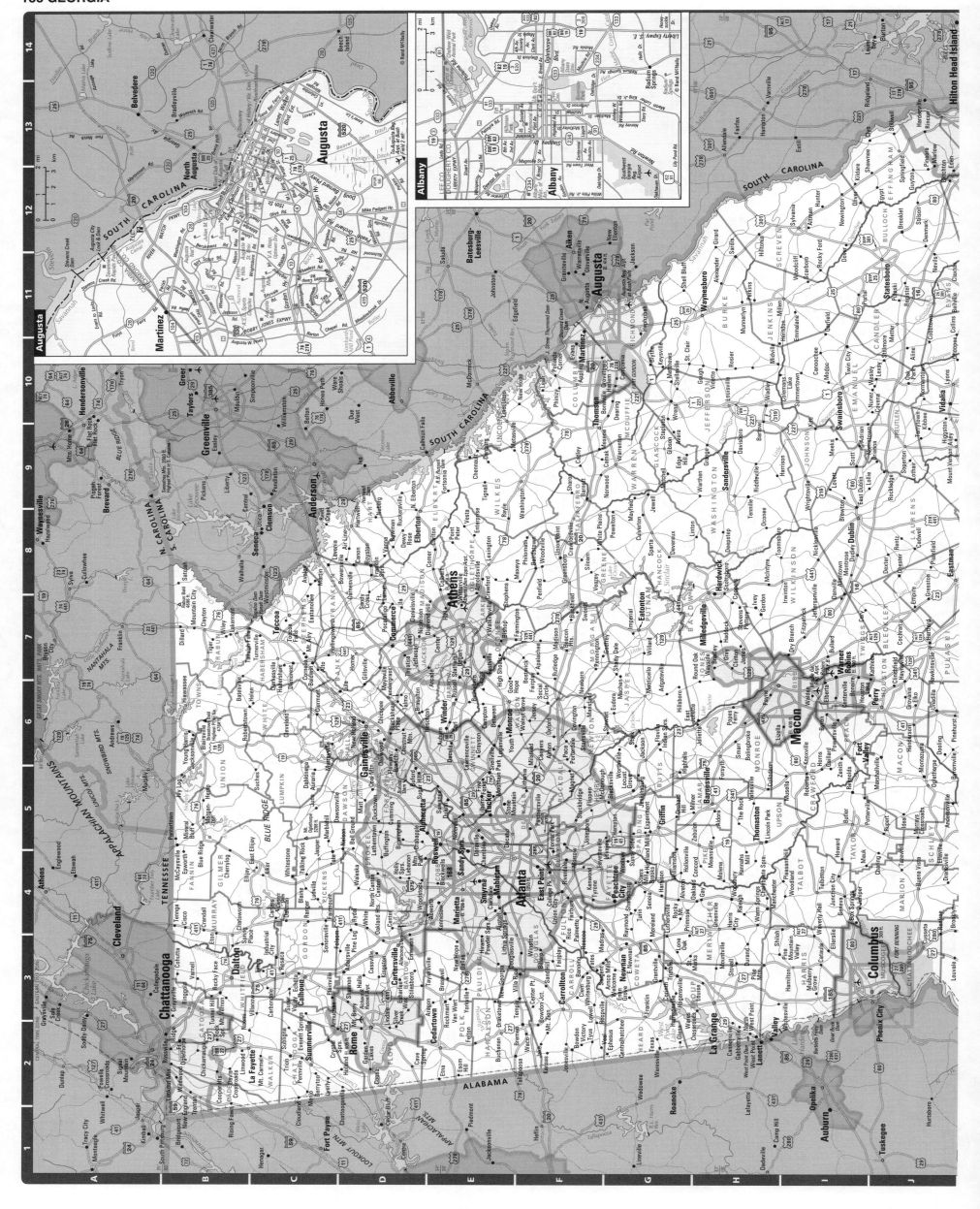

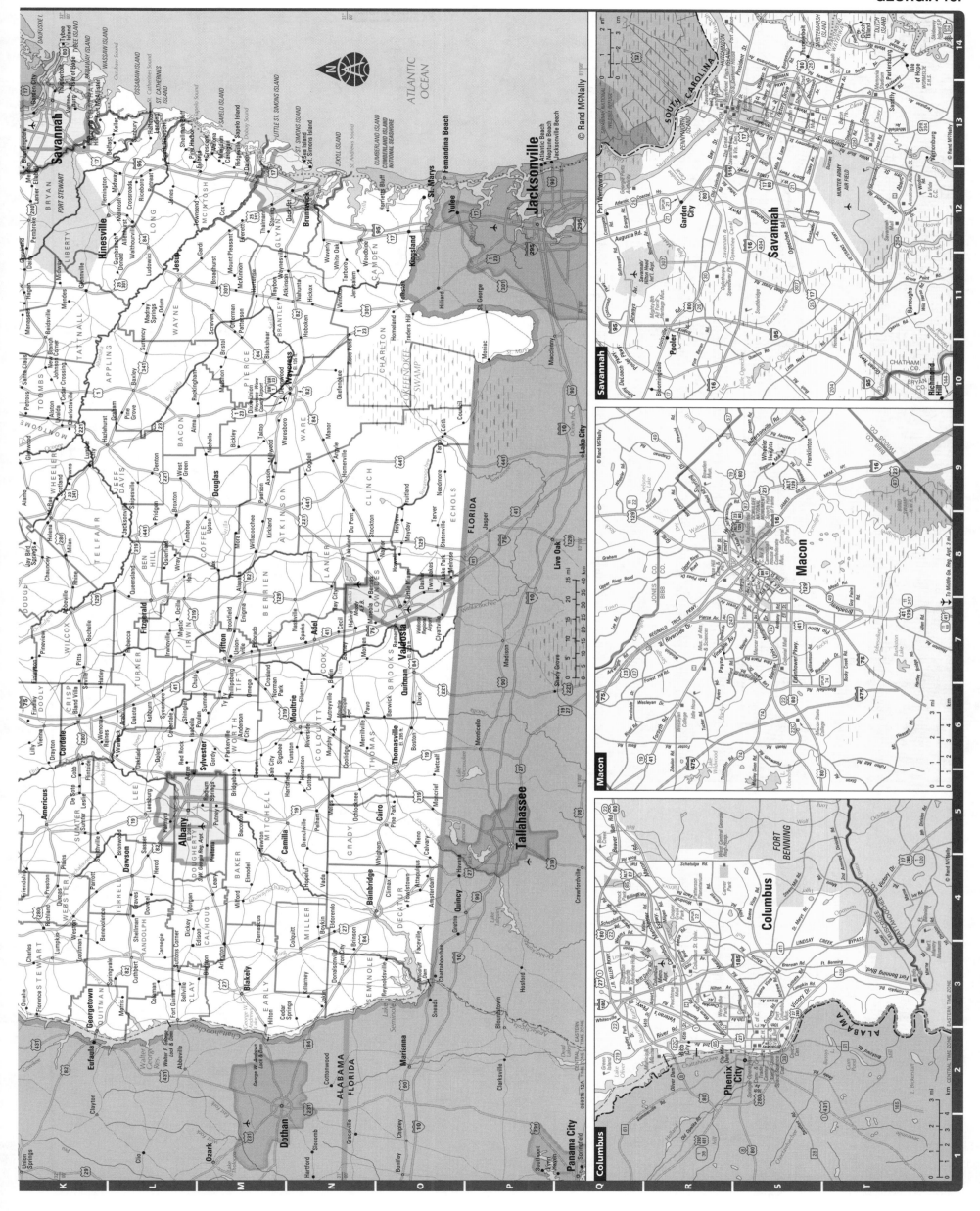

Savannah

Macon

Columbus

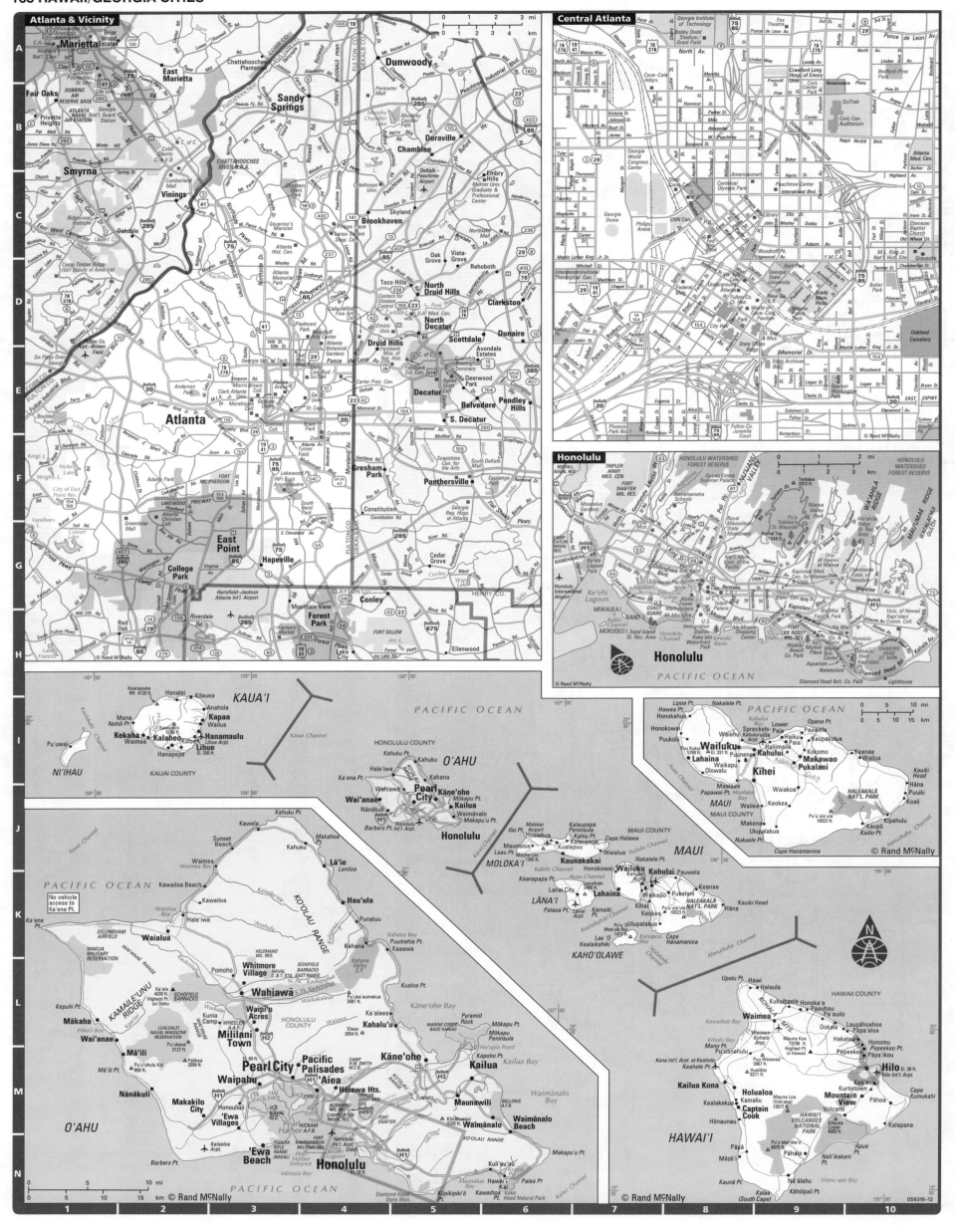

Atlanta & Vicinity

Central Atlanta

Honolulu

Honolulu

PACIFIC OCEAN

KAUA'I

NI'IHAU

KAUAI COUNTY

PACIFIC OCEAN

O'AHU

HONOLULU COUNTY

Honolulu

MOLOKA'I

MAUI COUNTY

MAUI

MAUI COUNTY

LĀNA'I

KAHO'OLAWE

PACIFIC OCEAN

HALEAKALĀ NAT'L PARK

PACIFIC OCEAN

O'AHU

HONOLULU COUNTY

Pearl City

Honolulu

HAWAI'I

HAWAII COUNTY

Hilo

HAWAI'I VOLCANOES NATIONAL PARK

© Rand McNally

059316-12

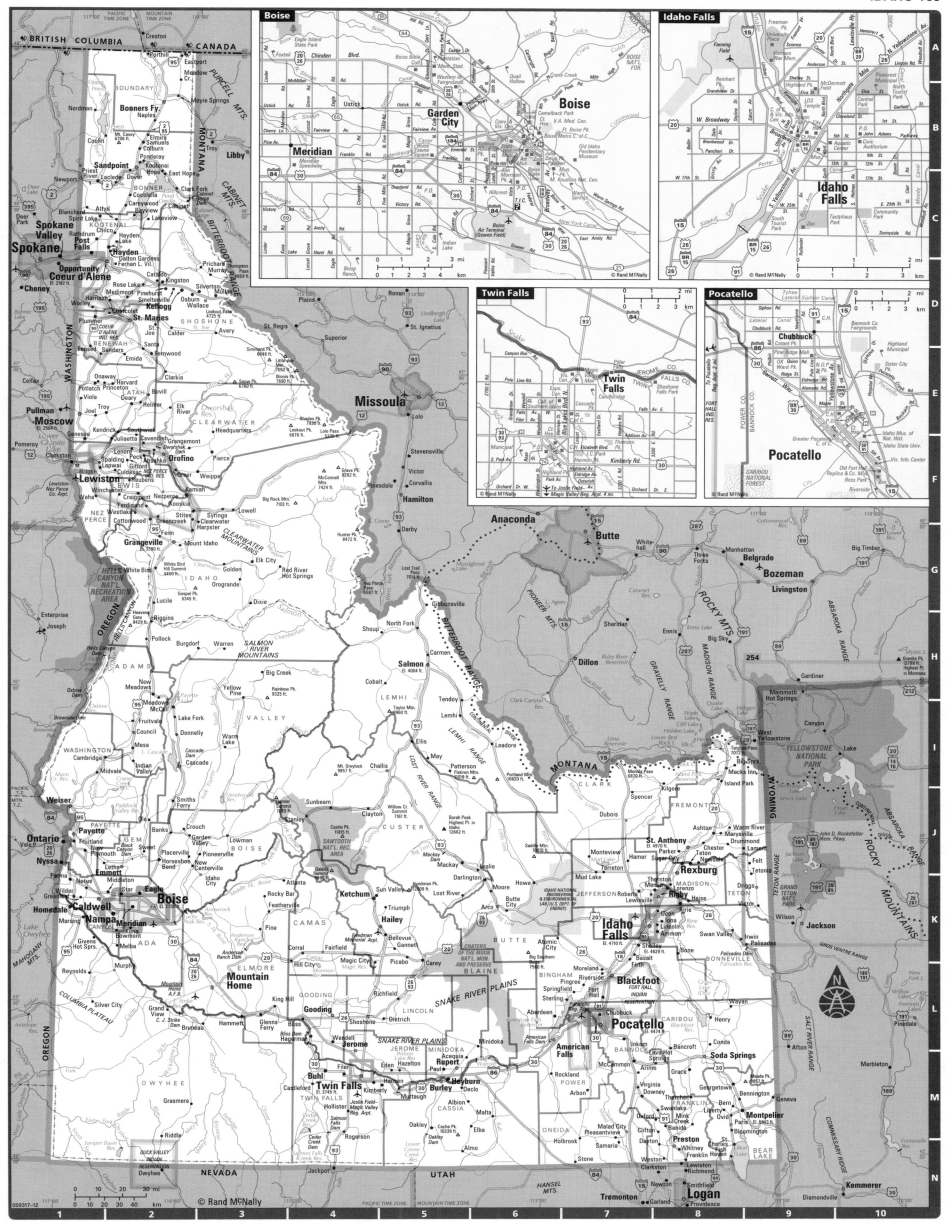

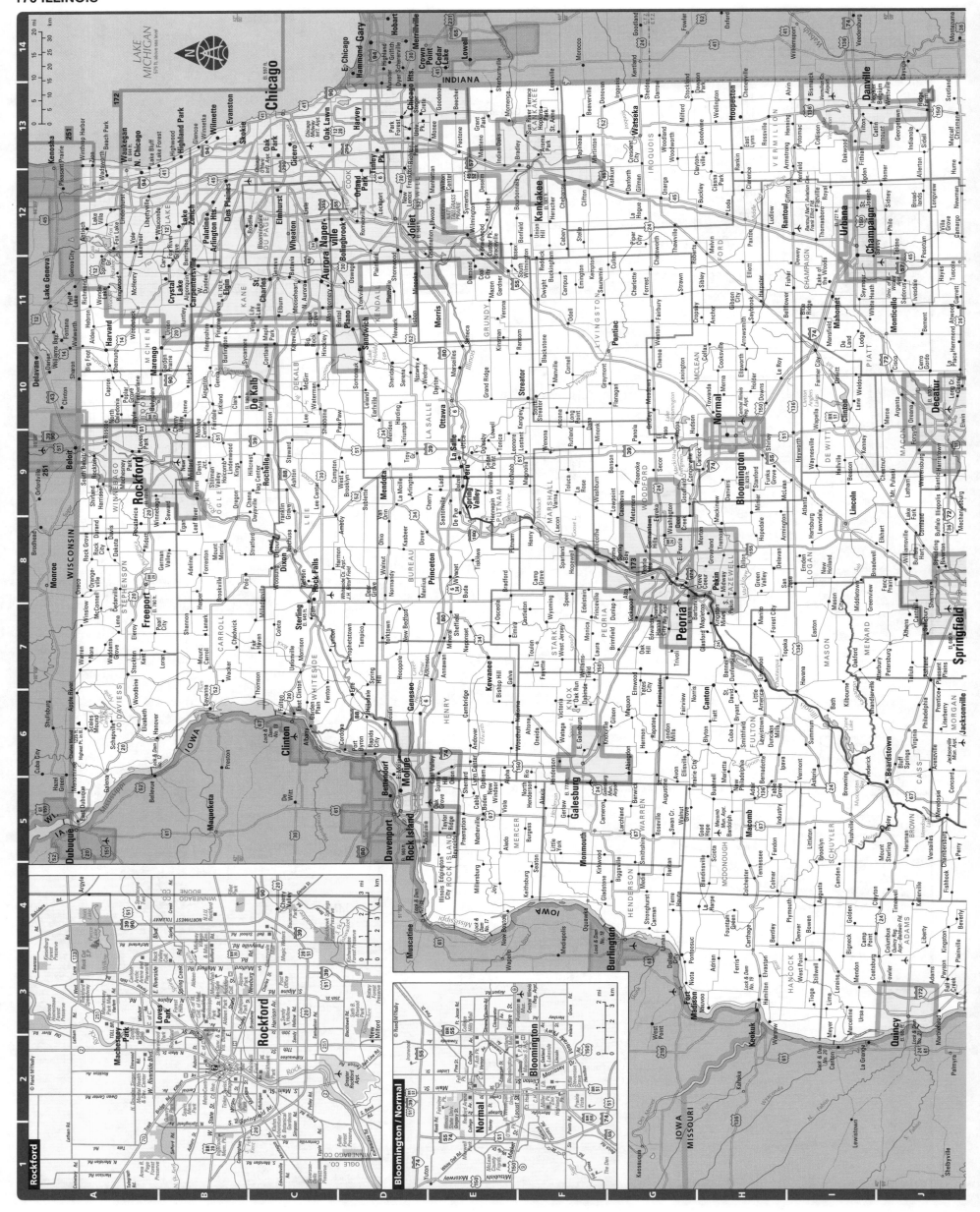

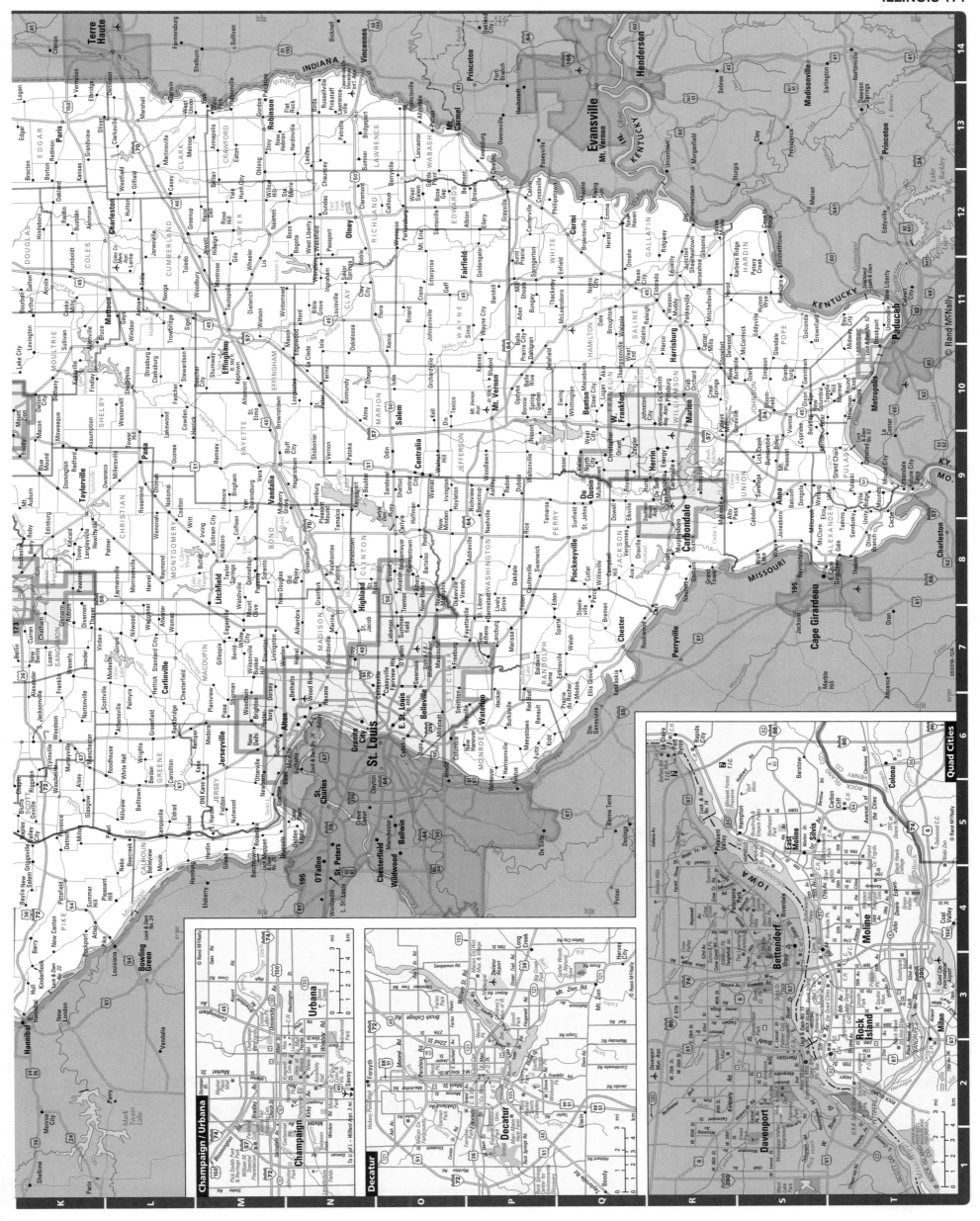

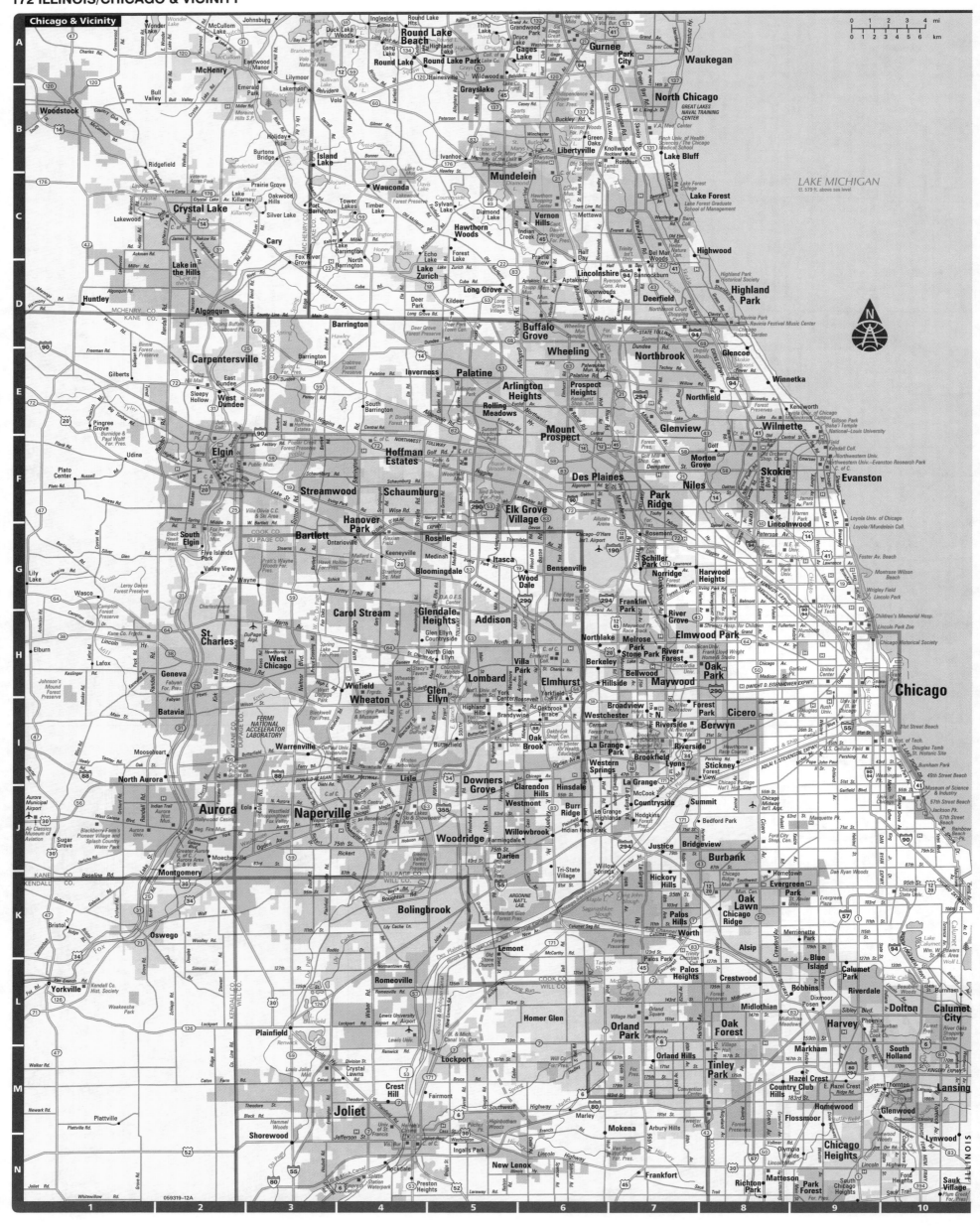

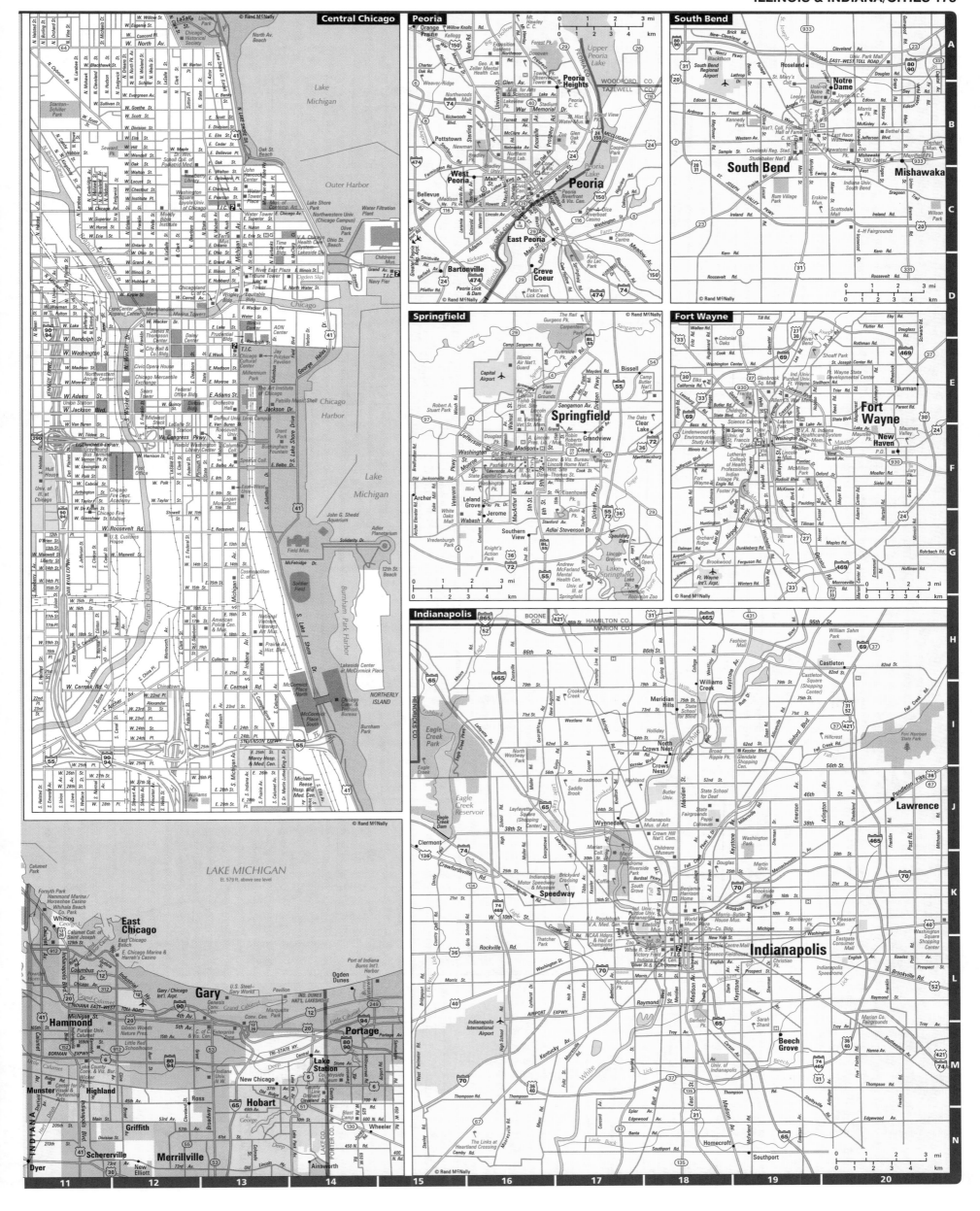

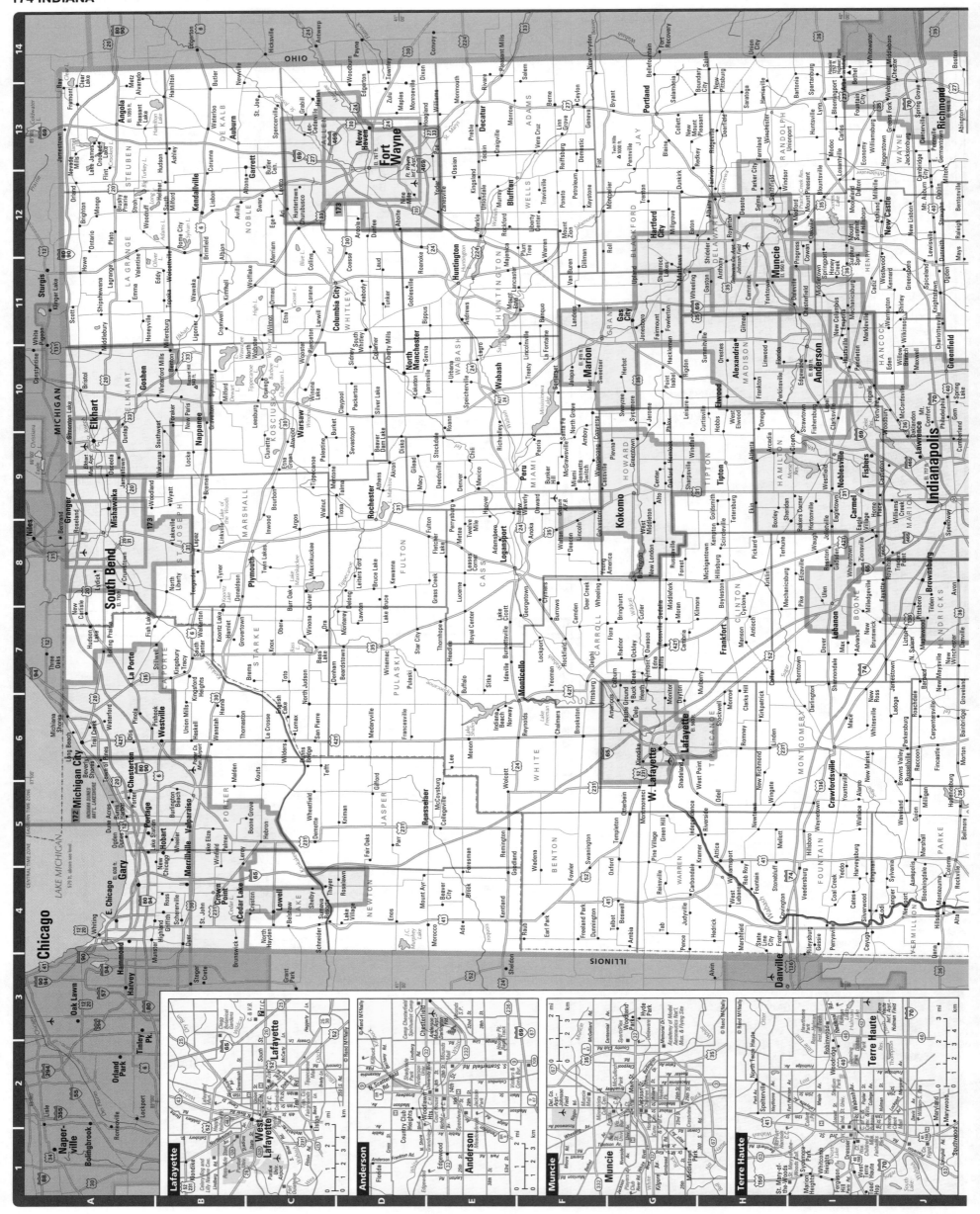

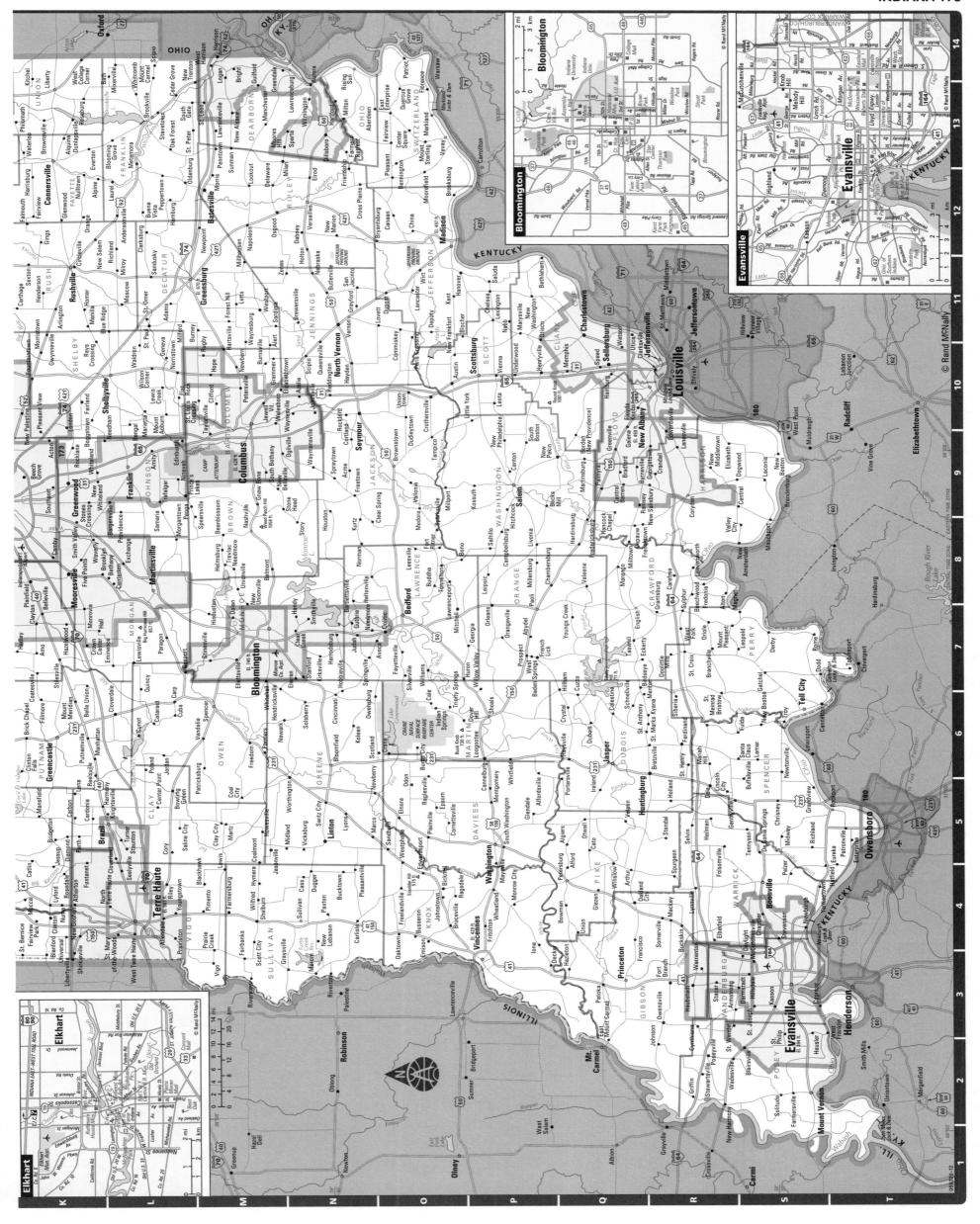

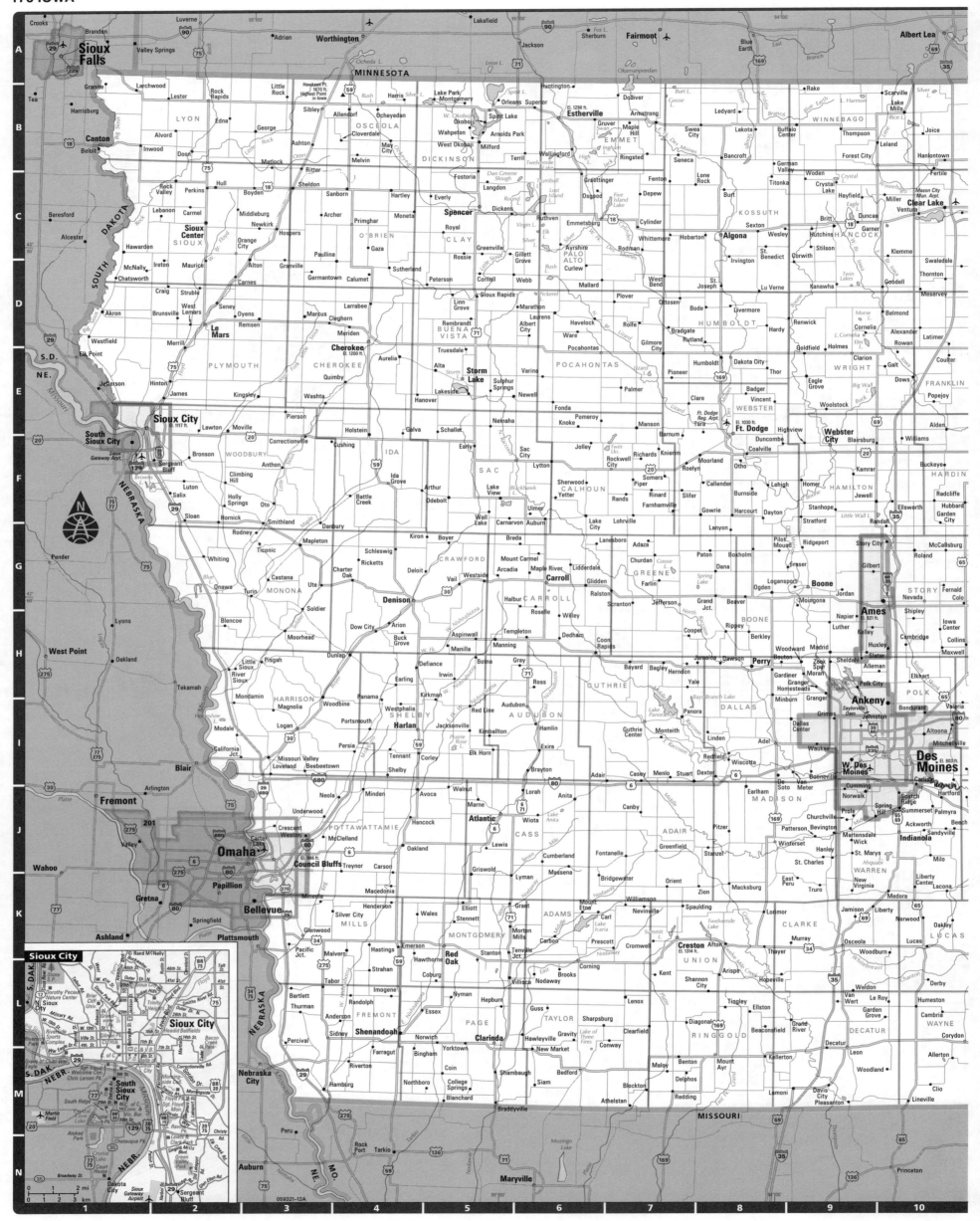

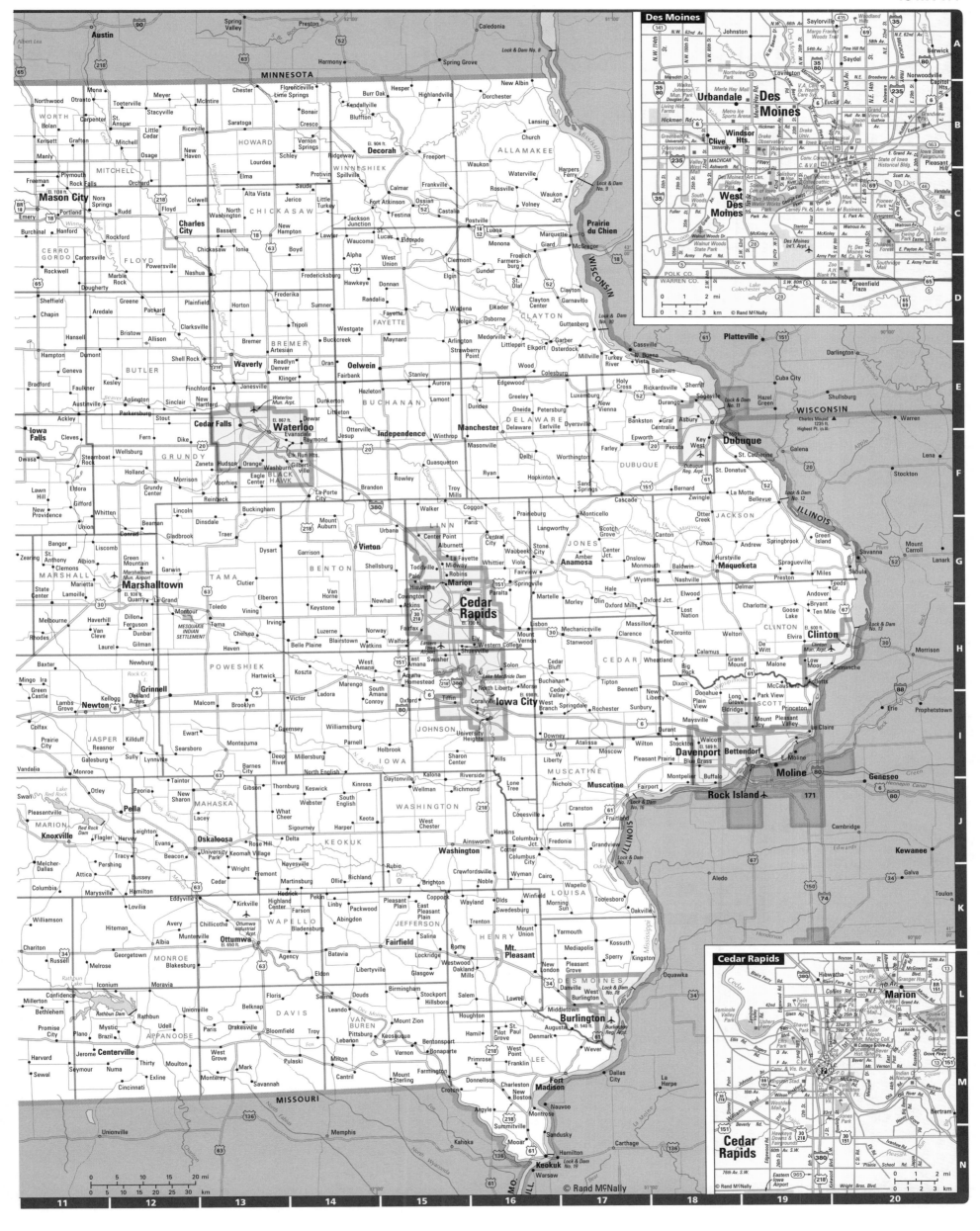

© Rand McNally

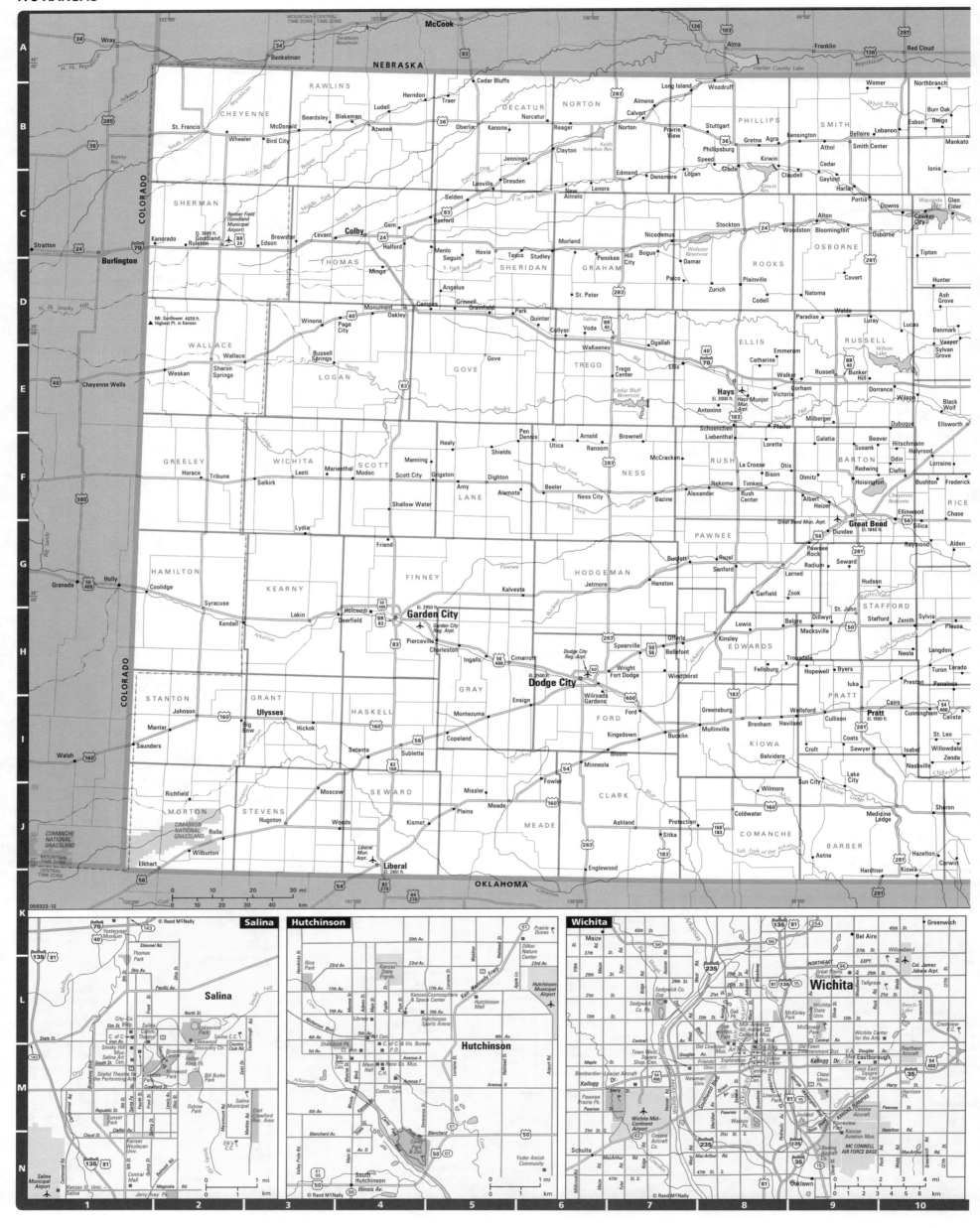

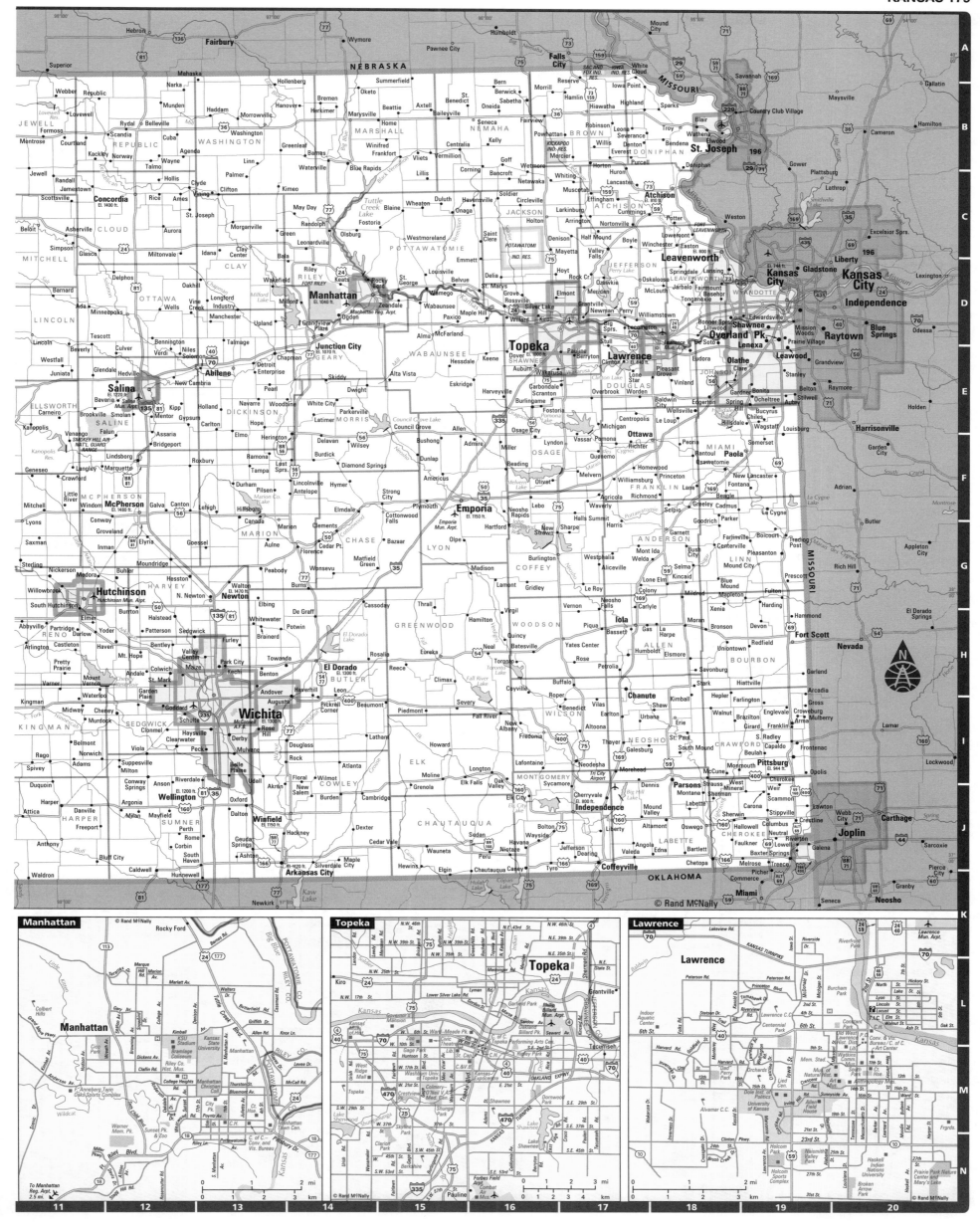

© Rand McNally

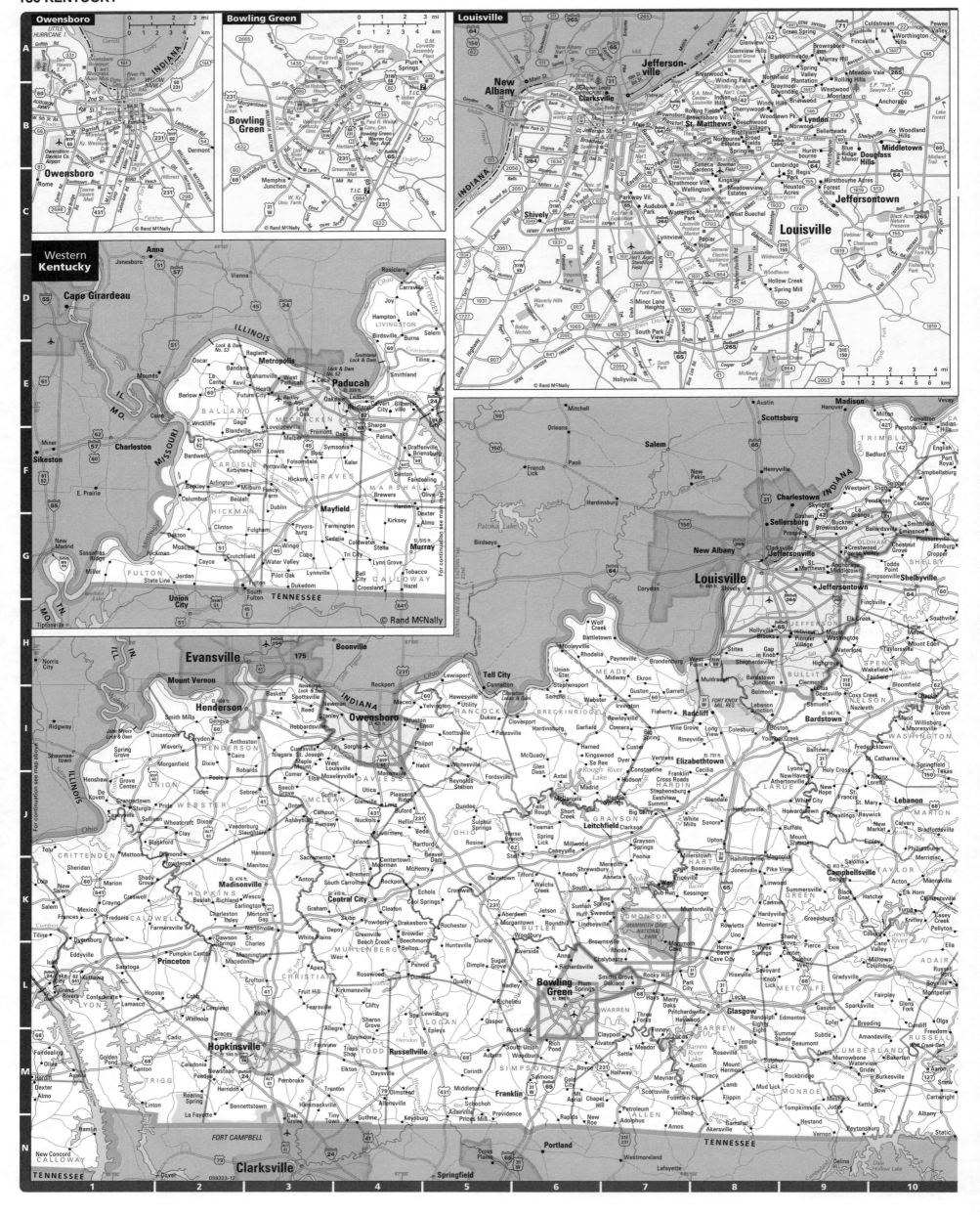

Owensboro

Bowling Green

Louisville

Western
Kentucky

© Rand McNally

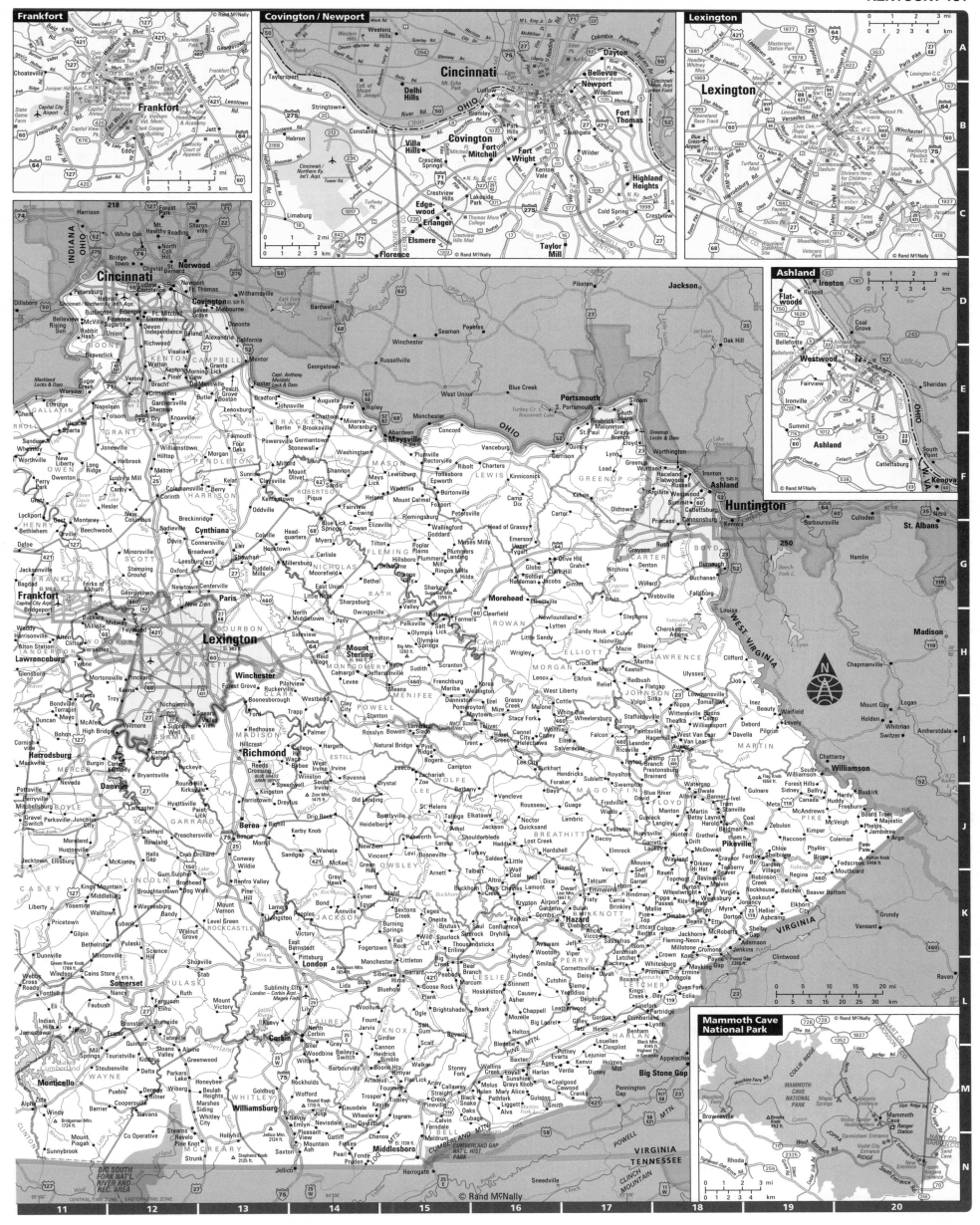

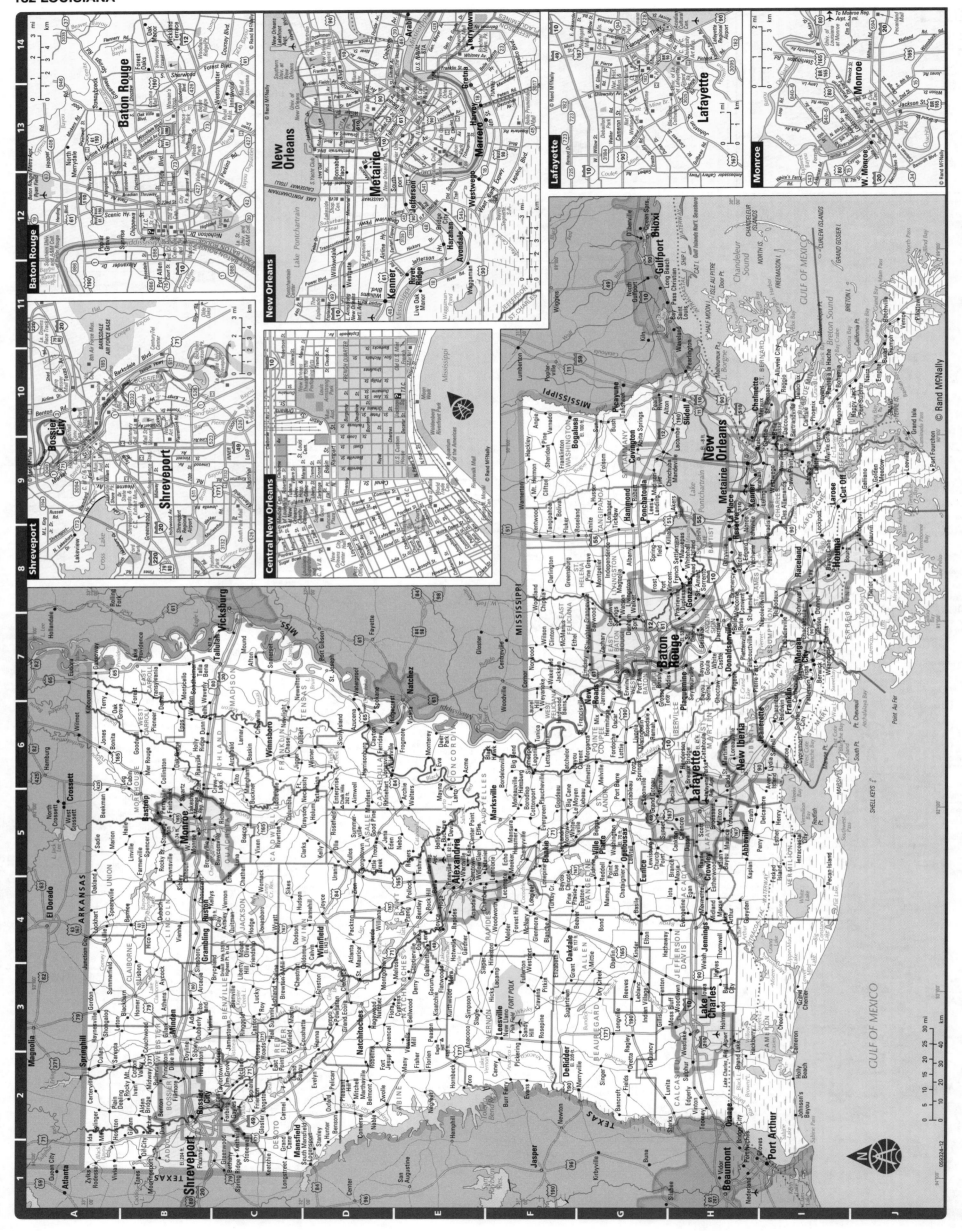

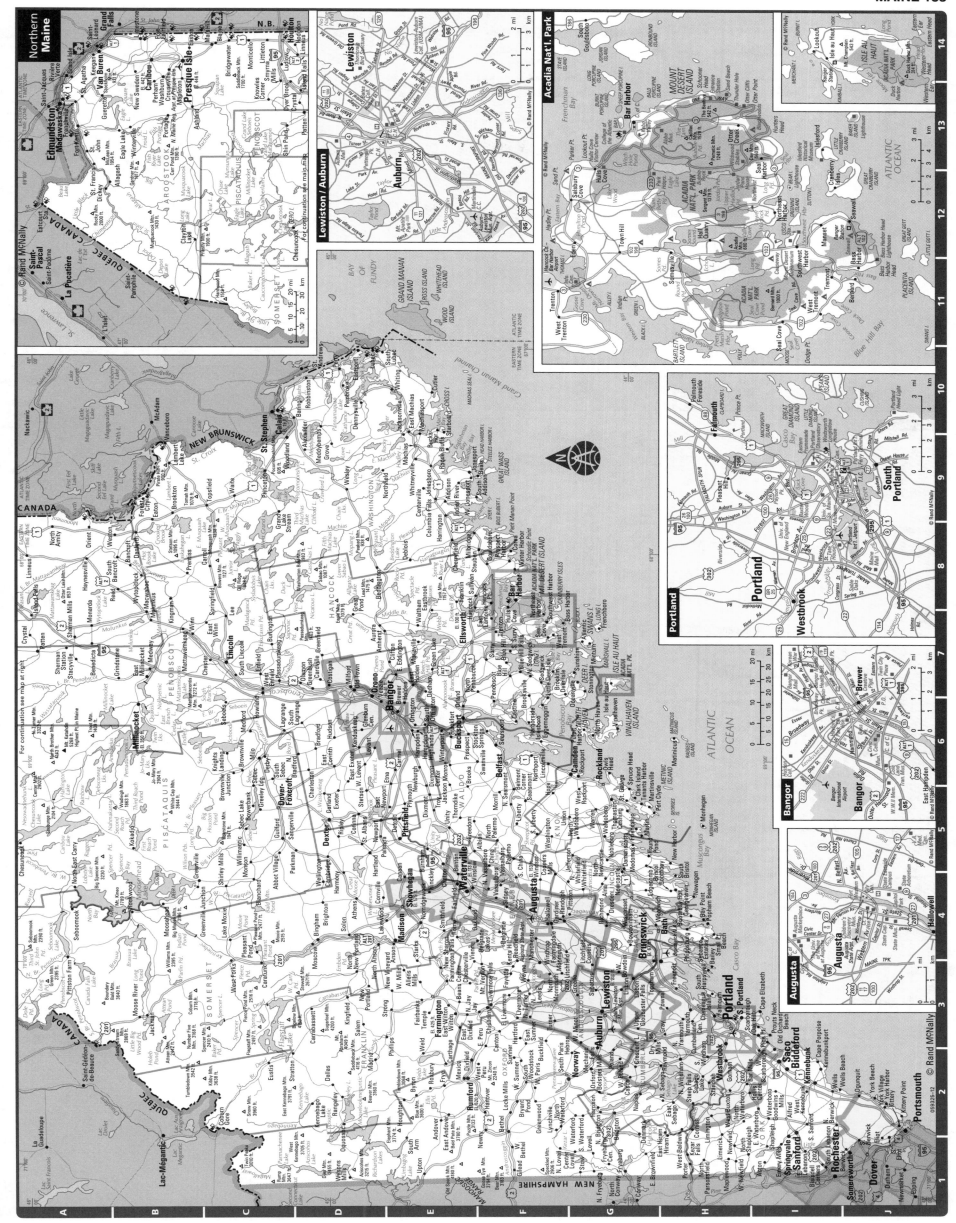

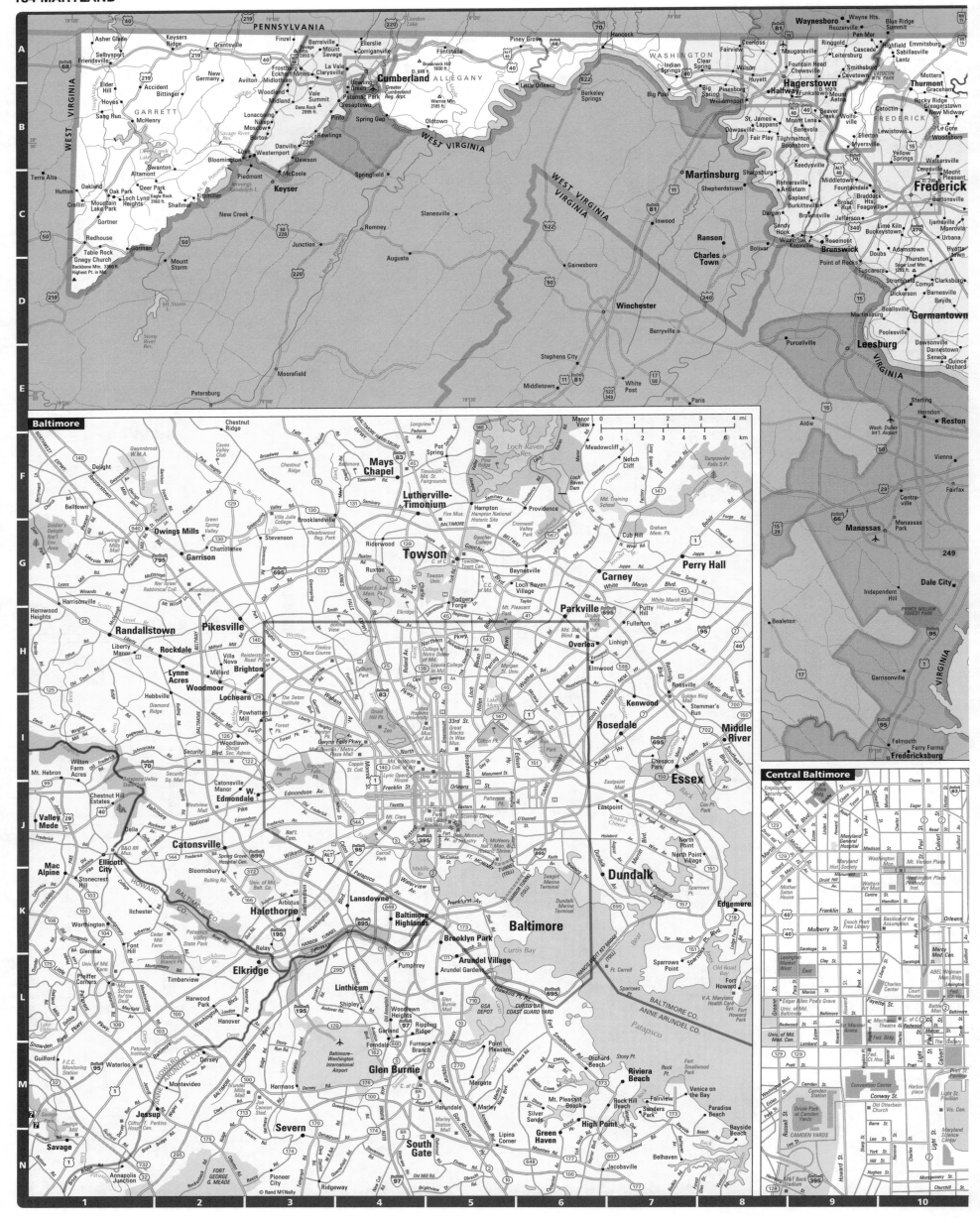

Baltimore

Central Baltimore

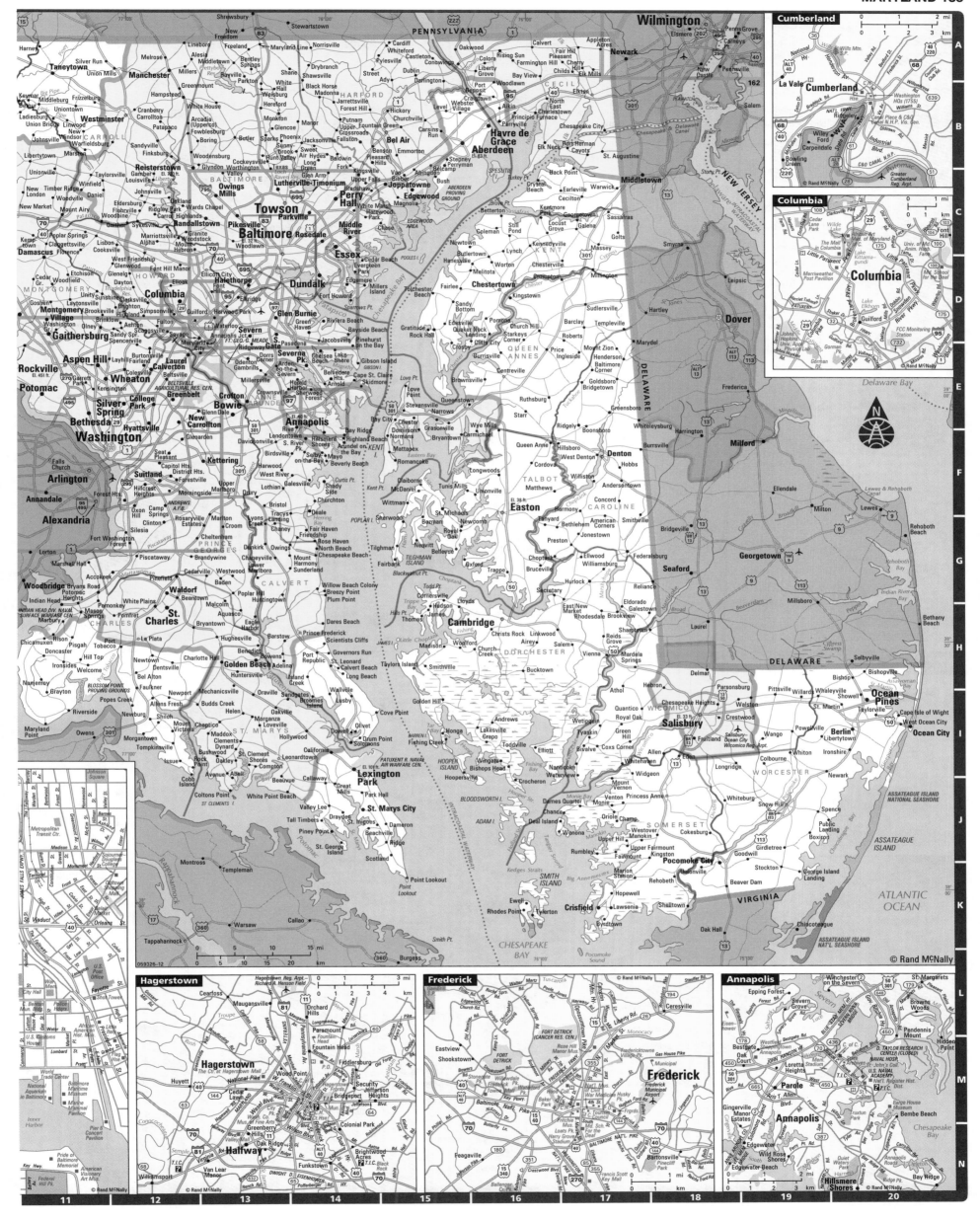

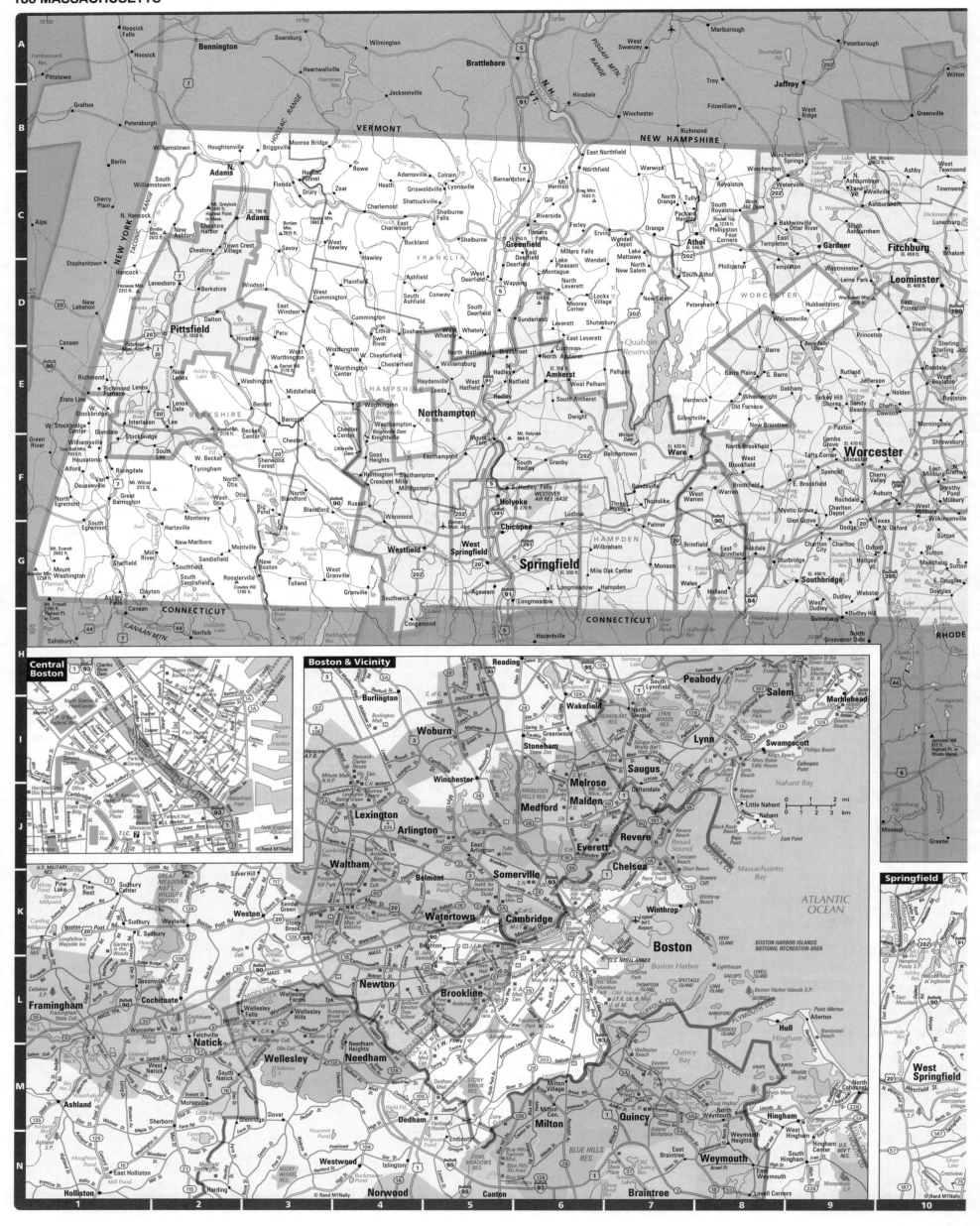

Central Boston

Boston & Vicinity

Springfield

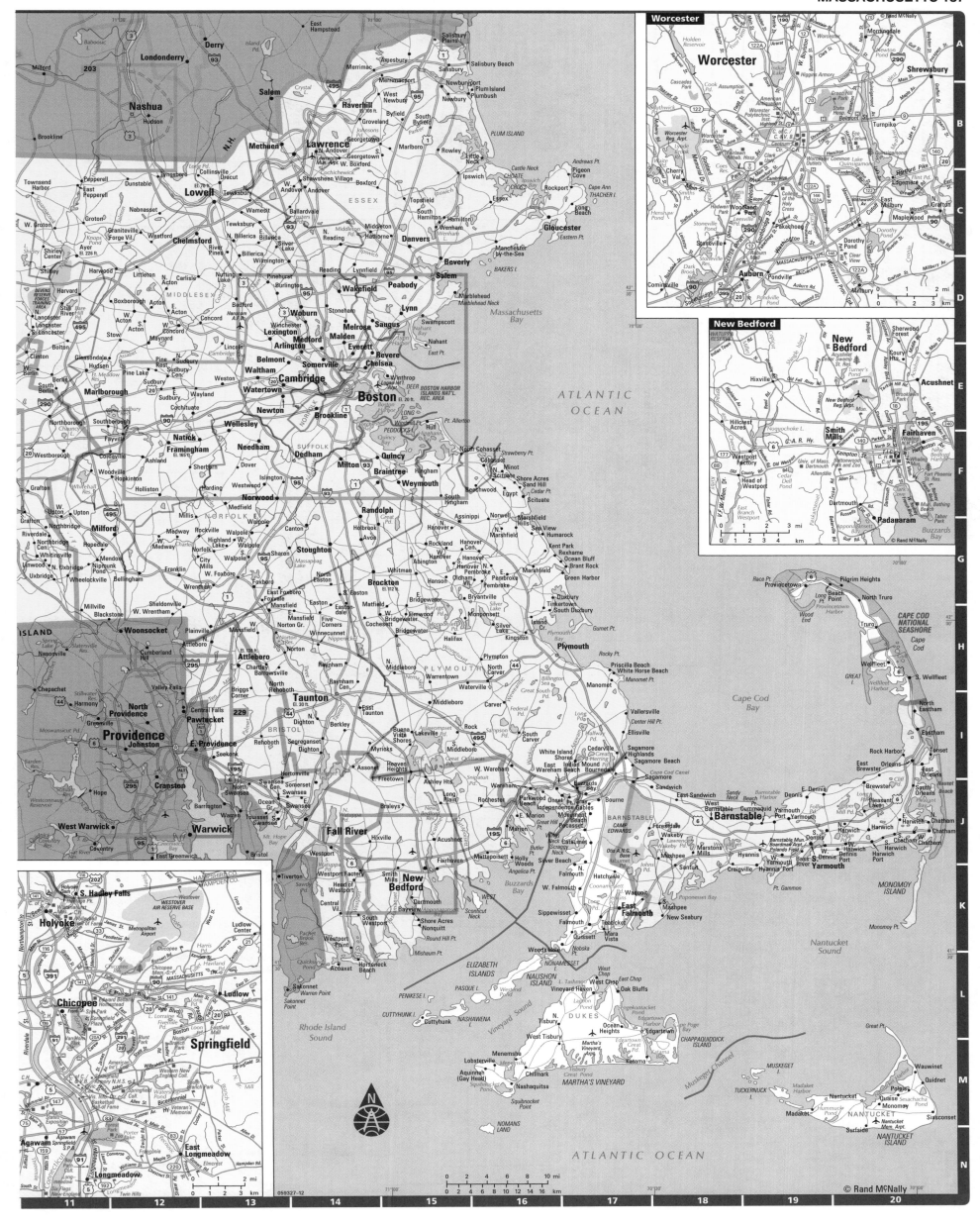

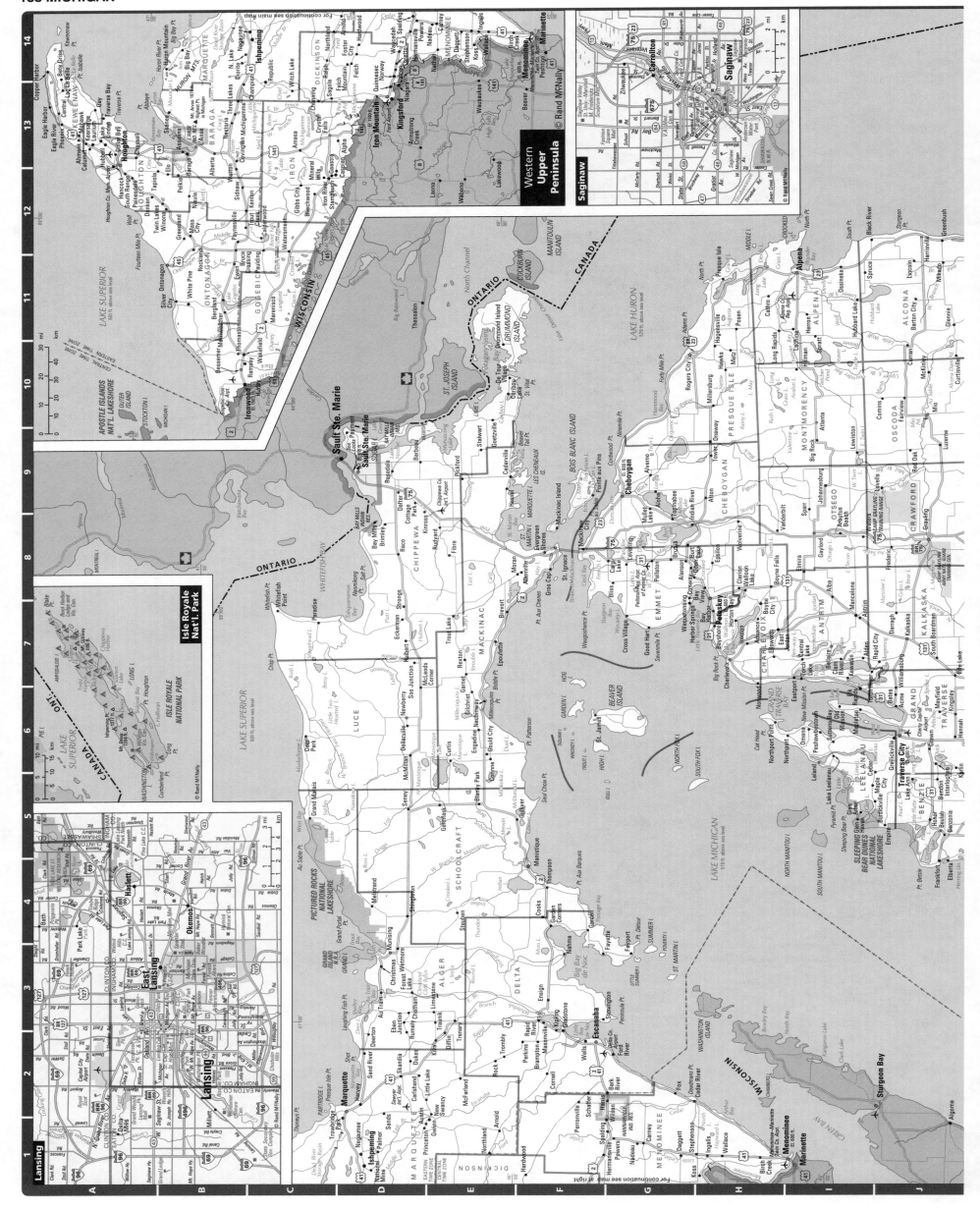

Western Upper Peninsula

Saginaw

Isle Royale Nat'l. Park

Lansing

© Rand McNally

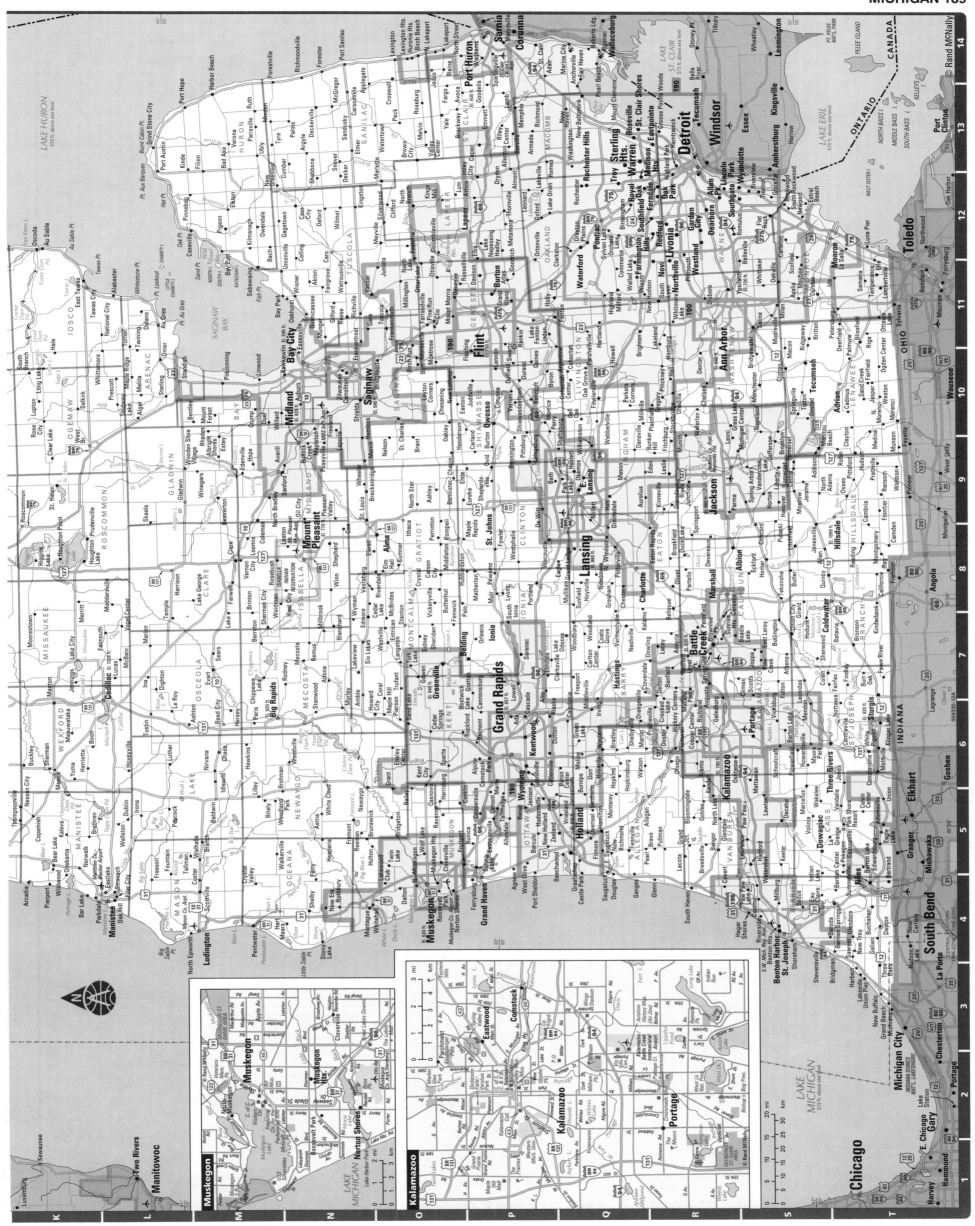

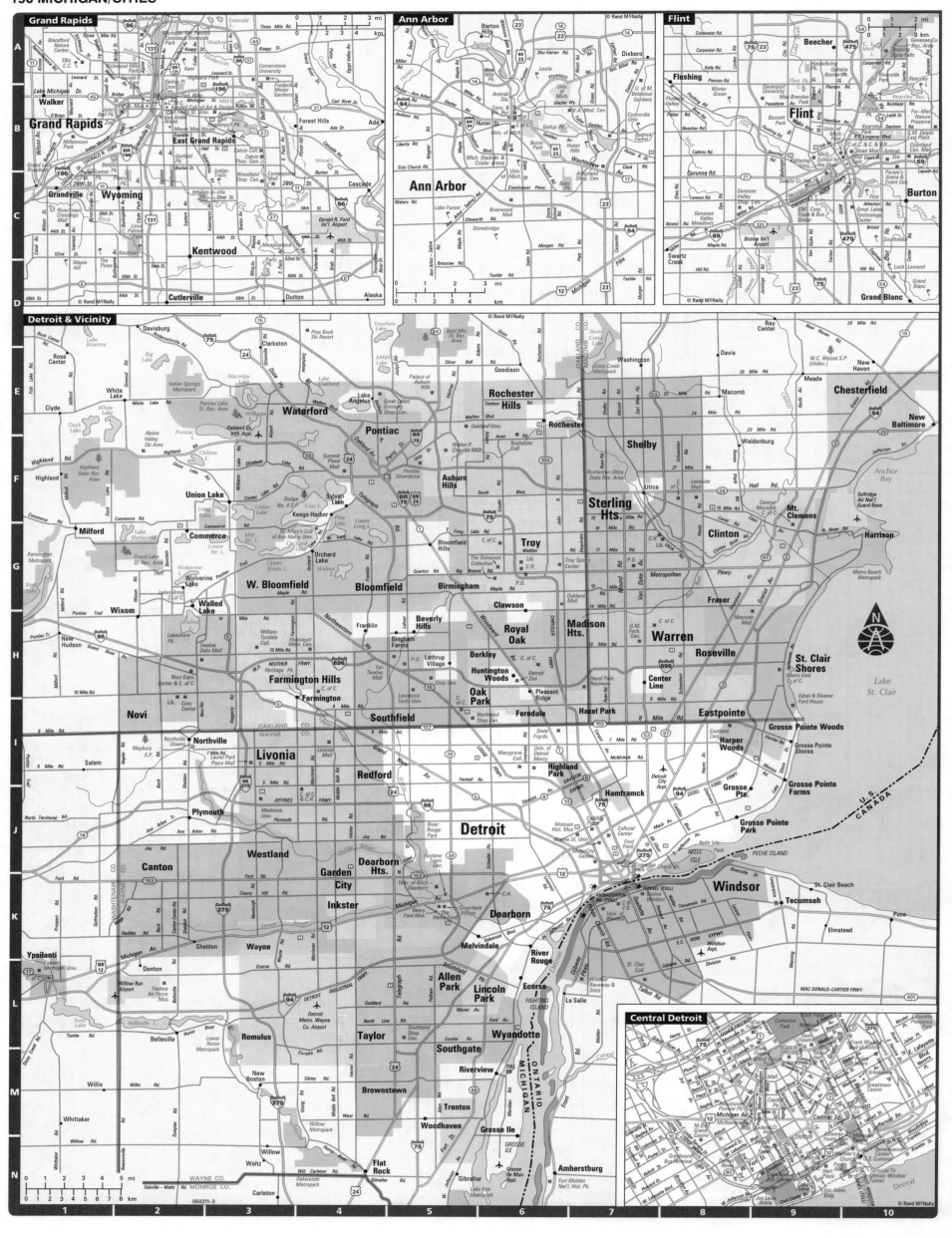

Grand Rapids

Ann Arbor

Flint

Detroit & Vicinity

Central Detroit

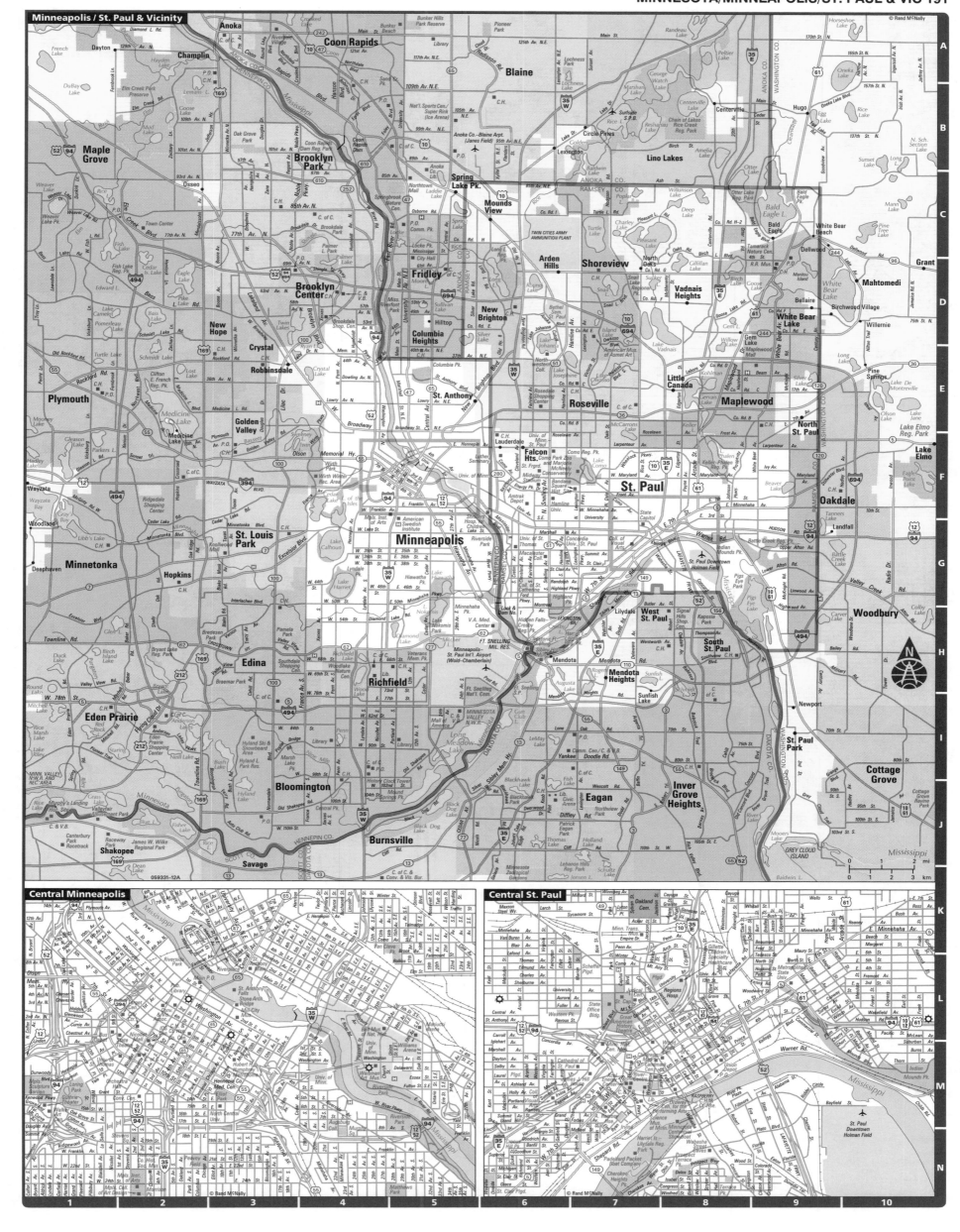

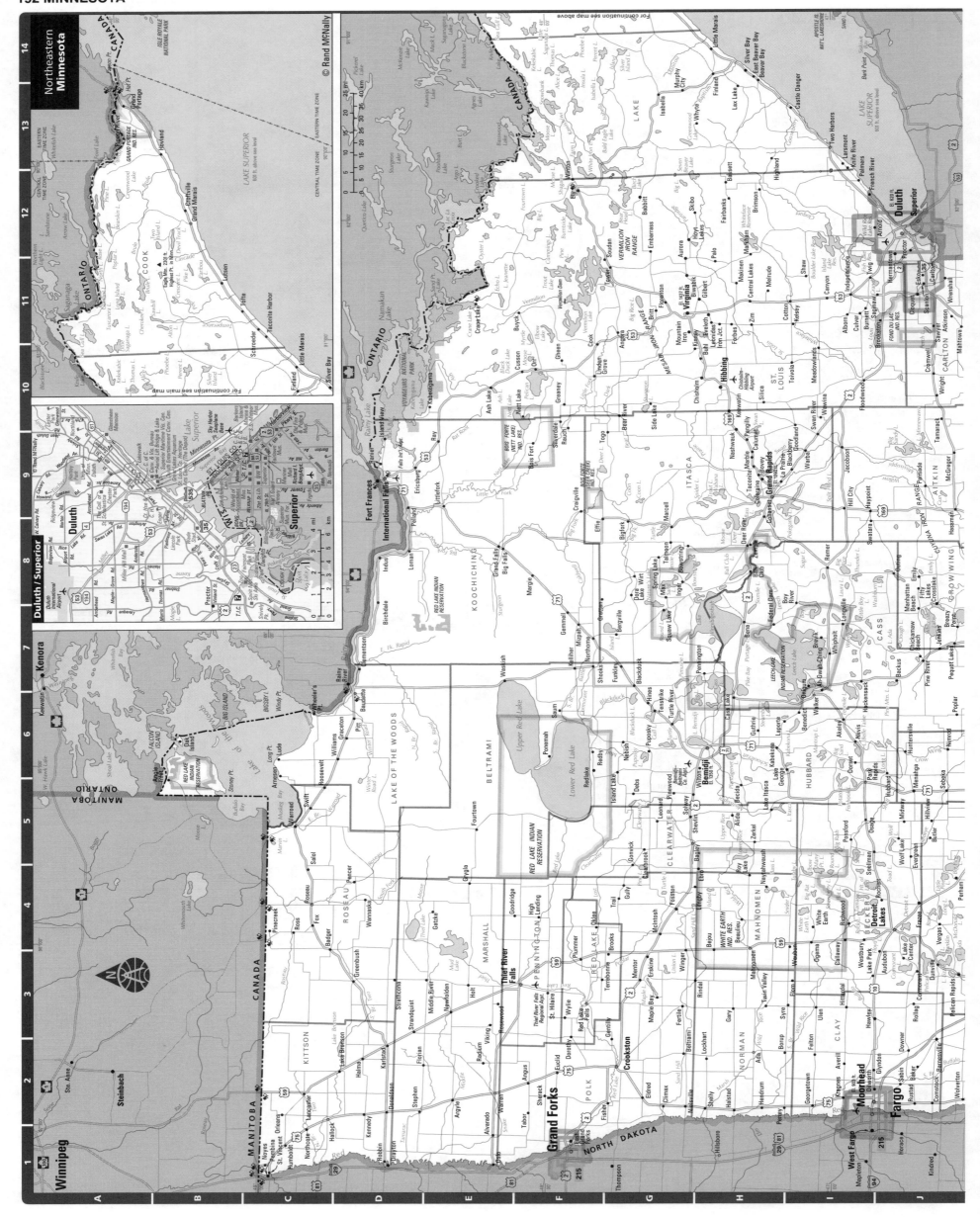

Northeastern Minnesota

Duluth / Superior

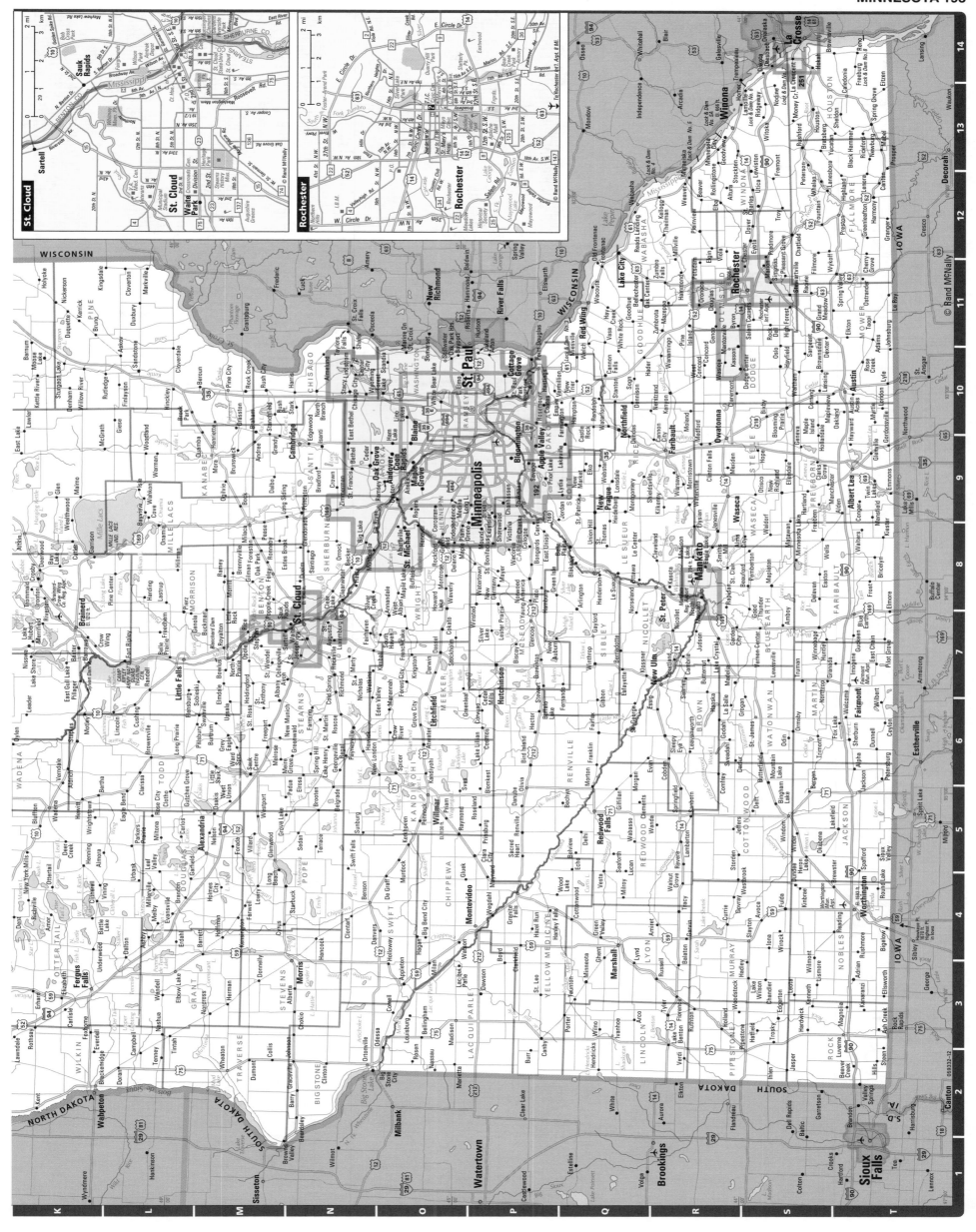

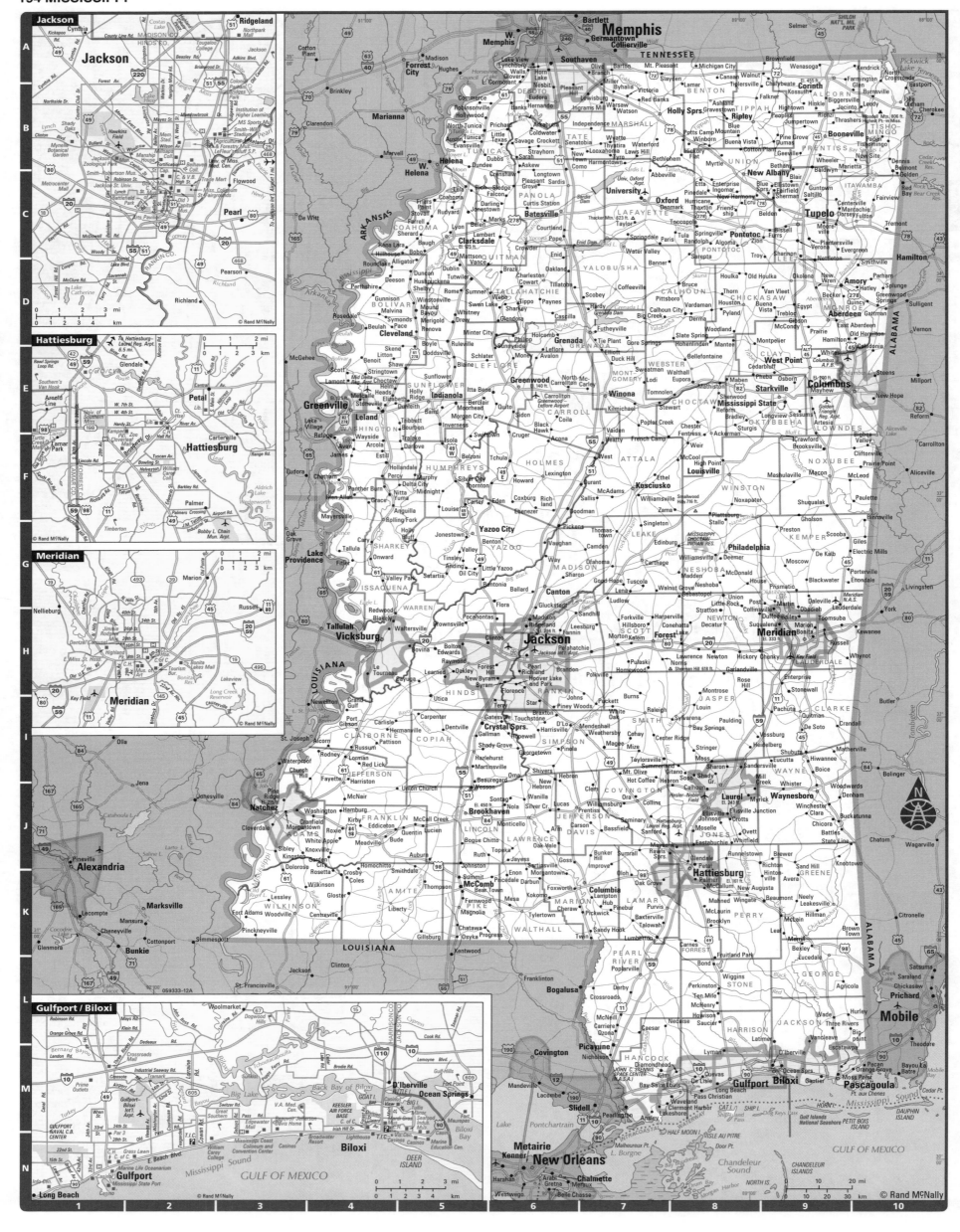

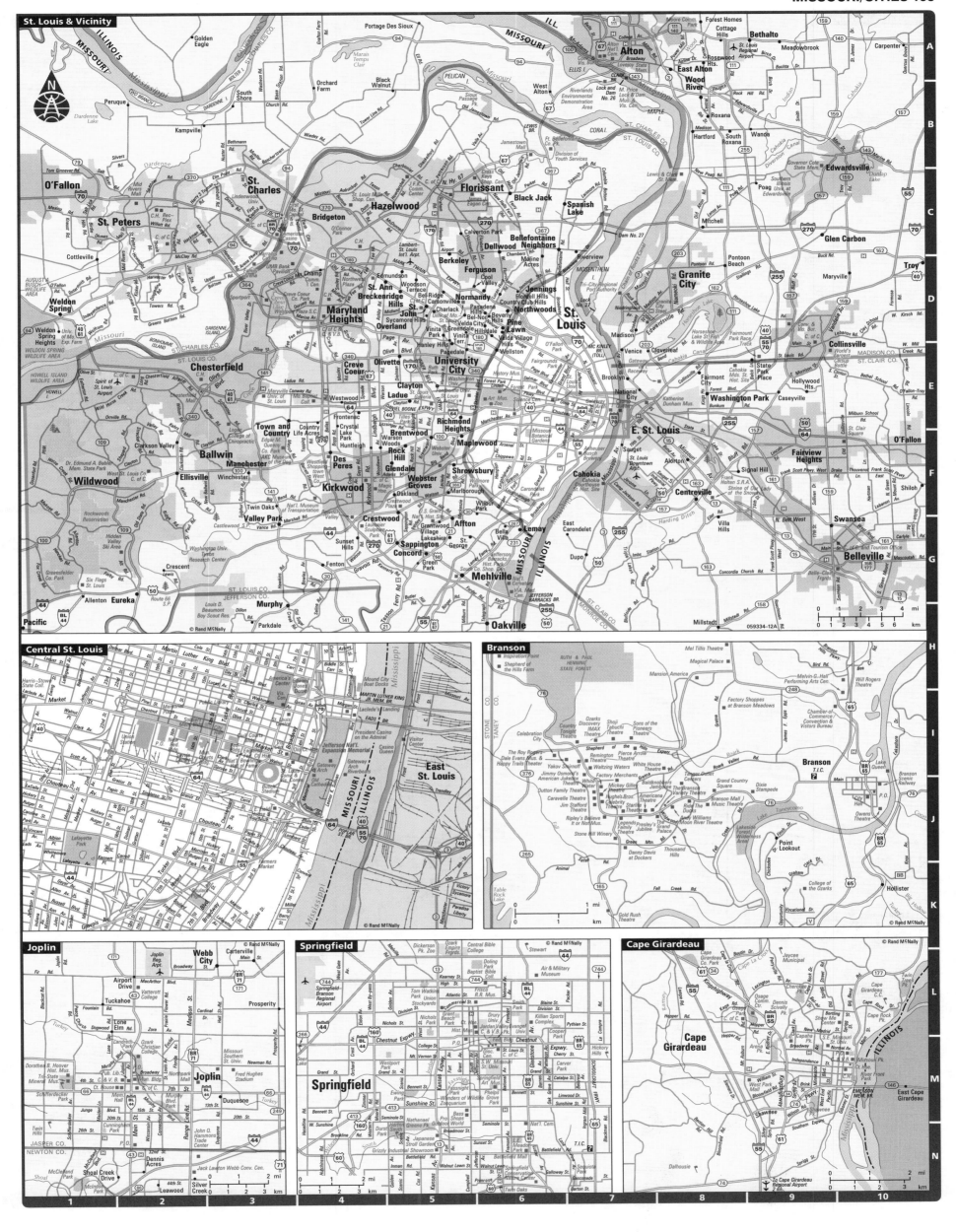

St. Louis & Vicinity

Central St. Louis

Branson

Joplin

Springfield

Cape Girardeau

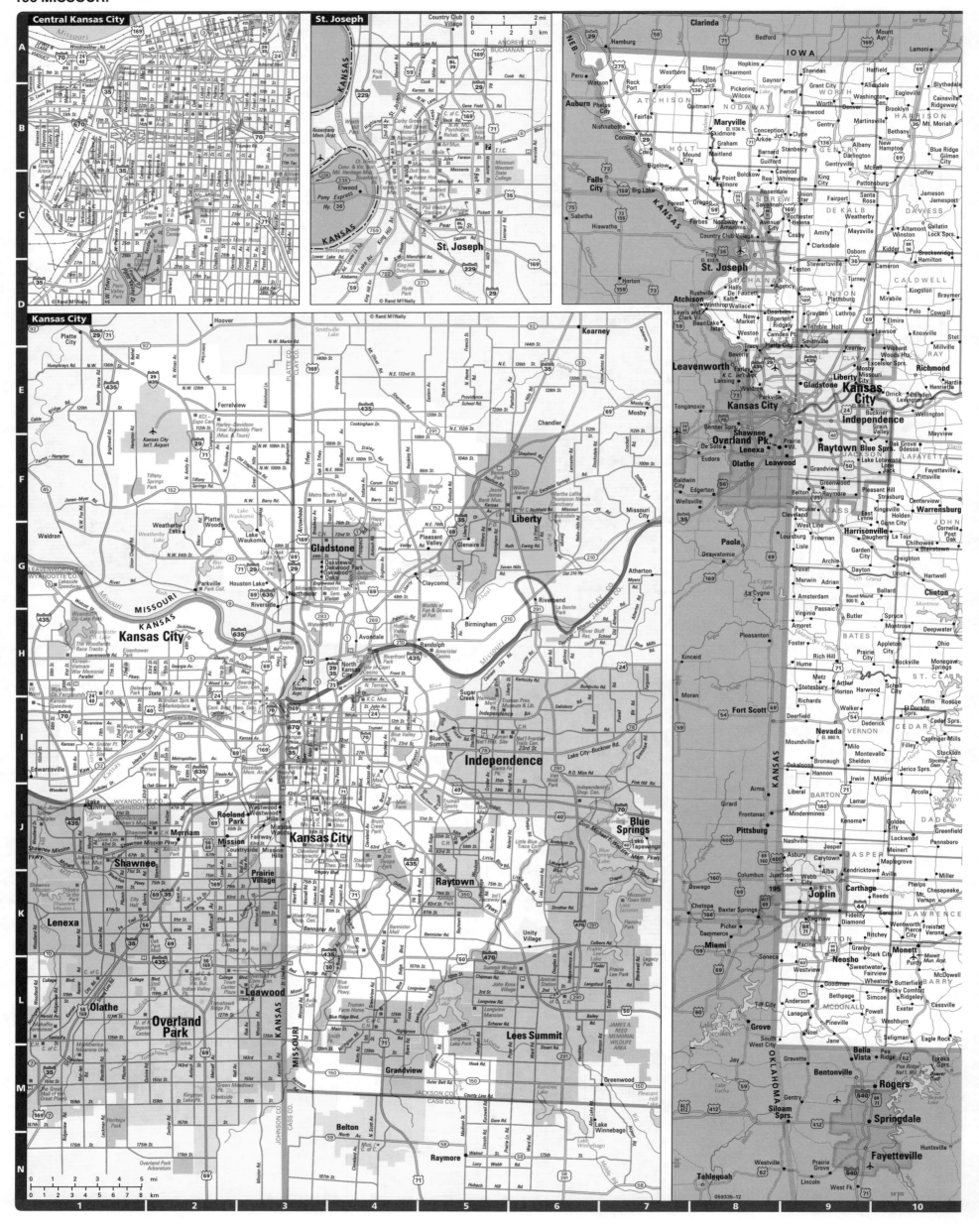

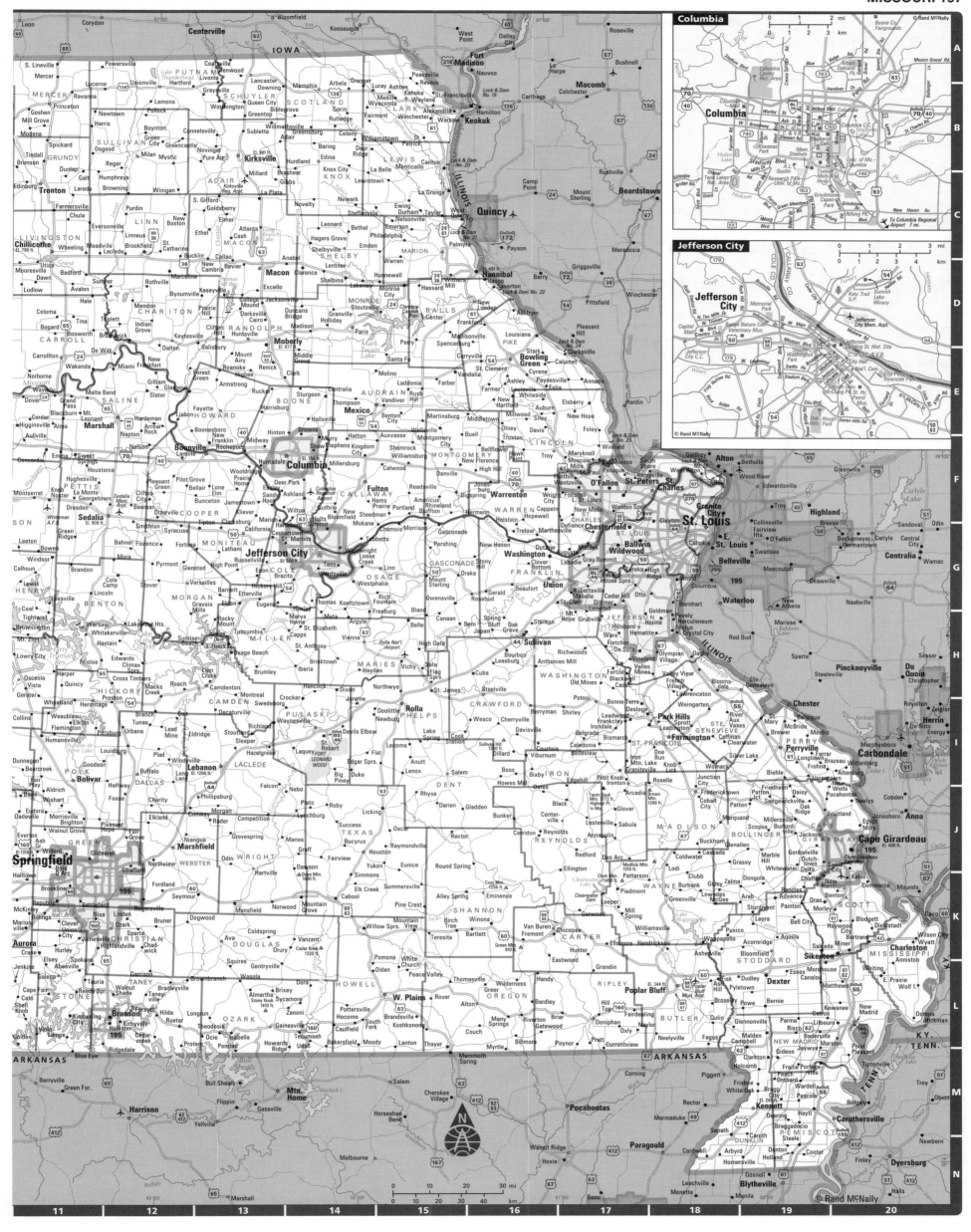

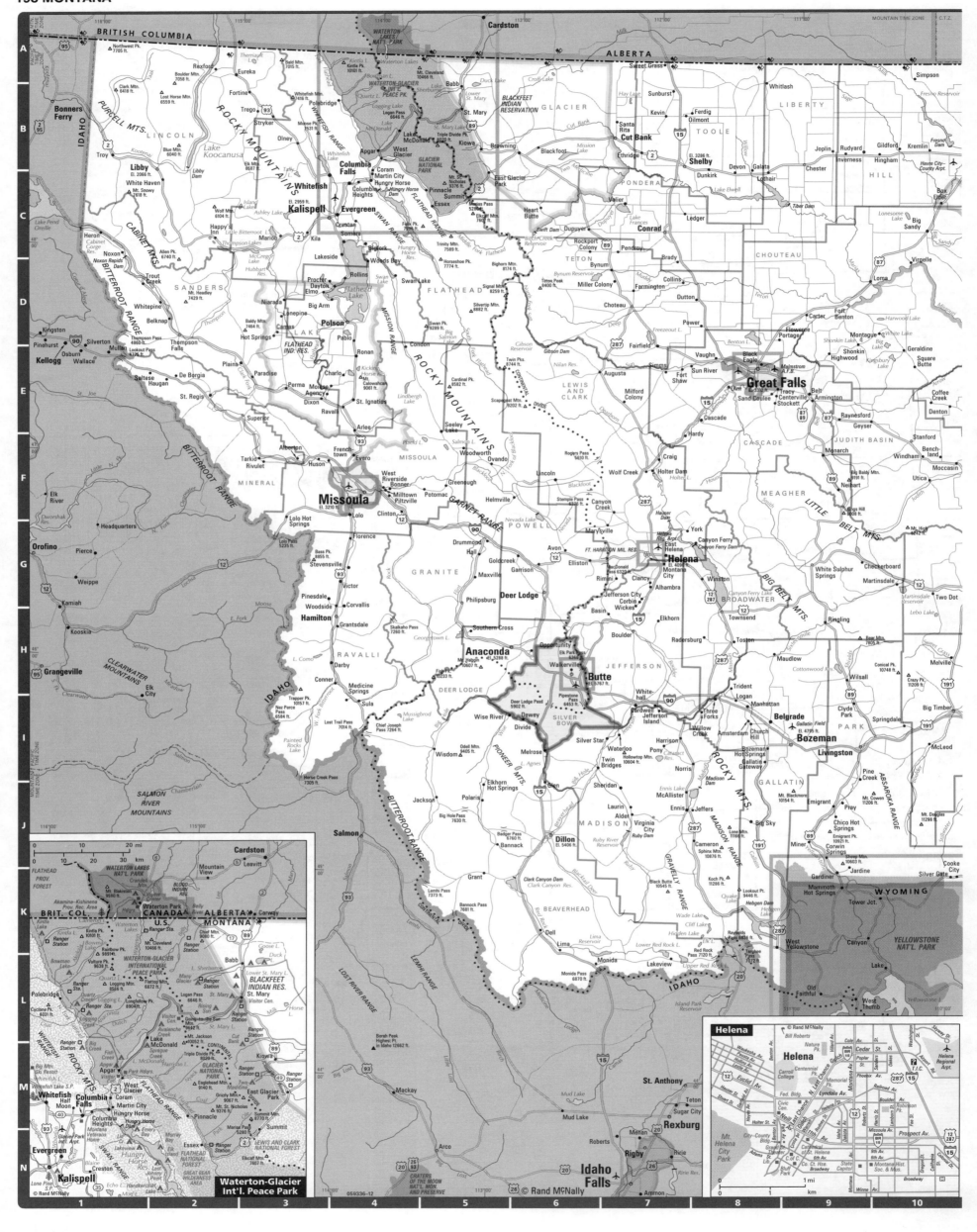

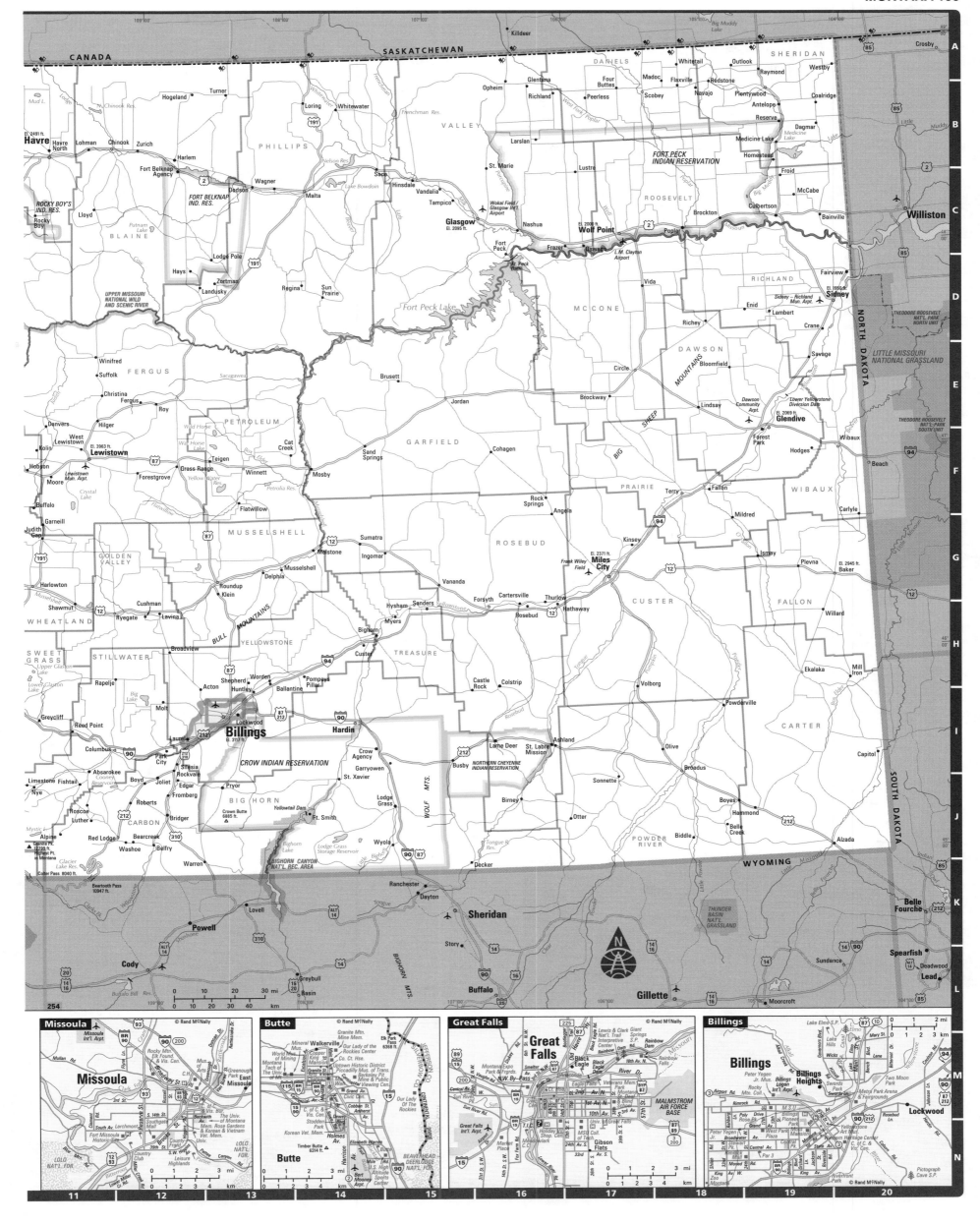

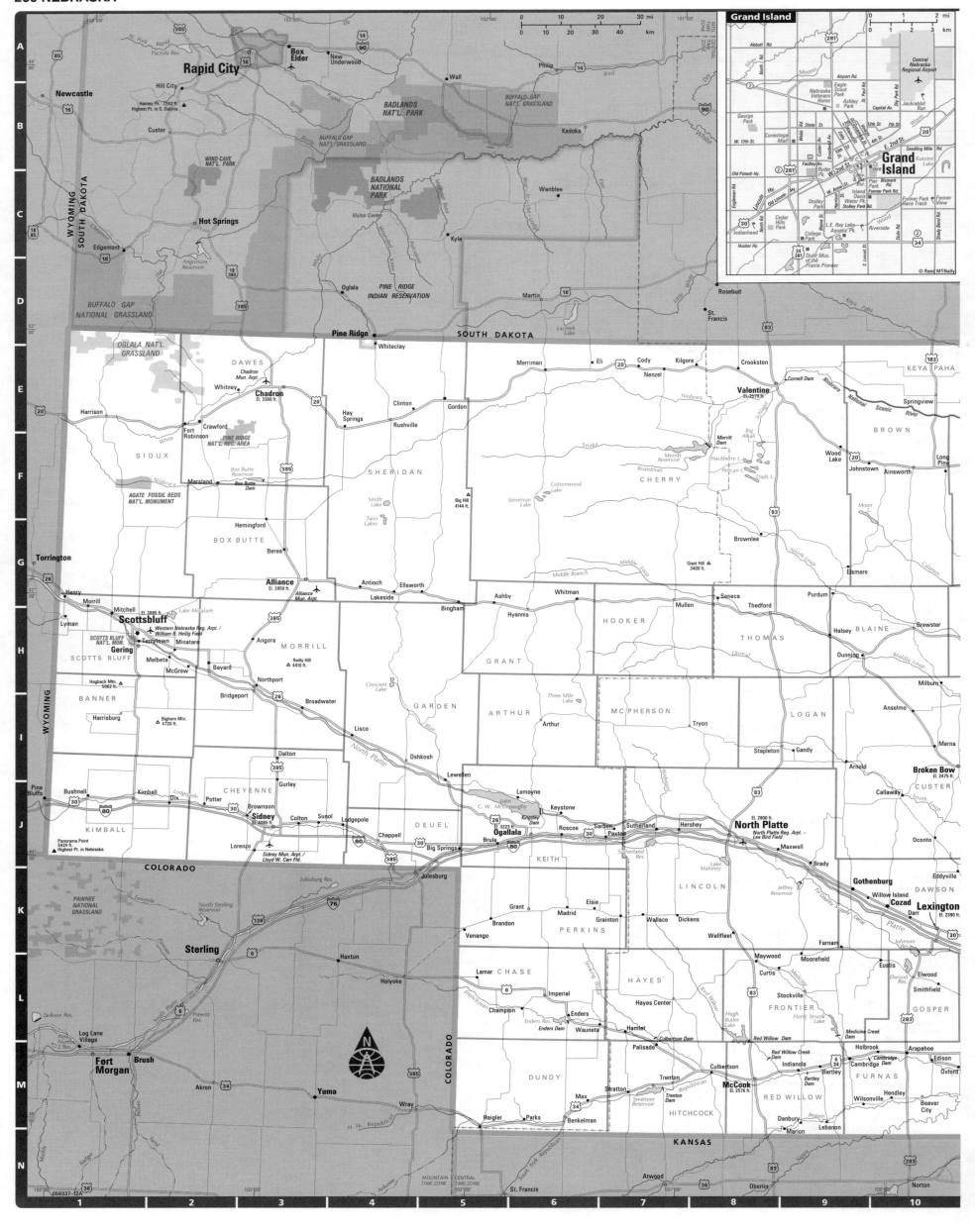

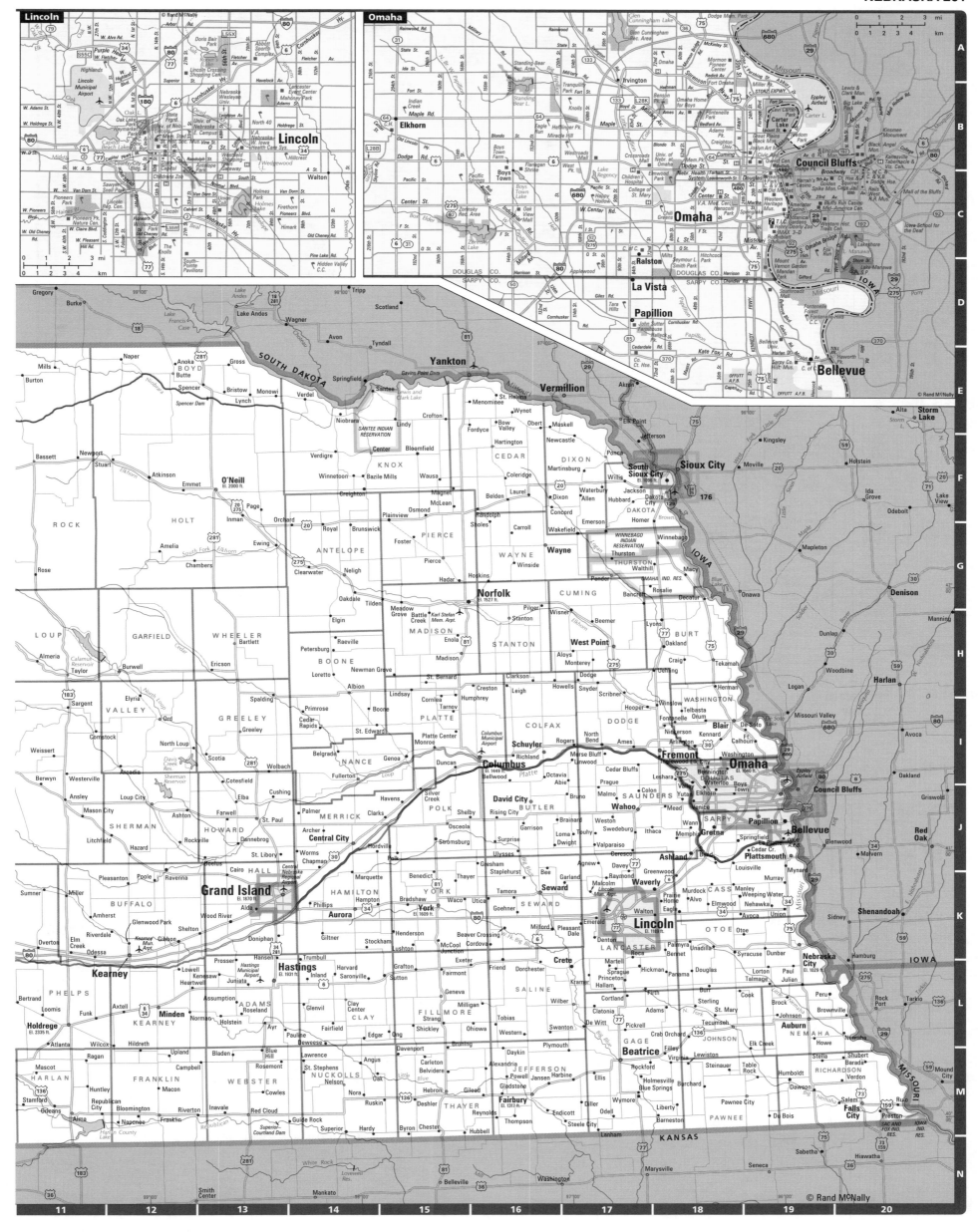

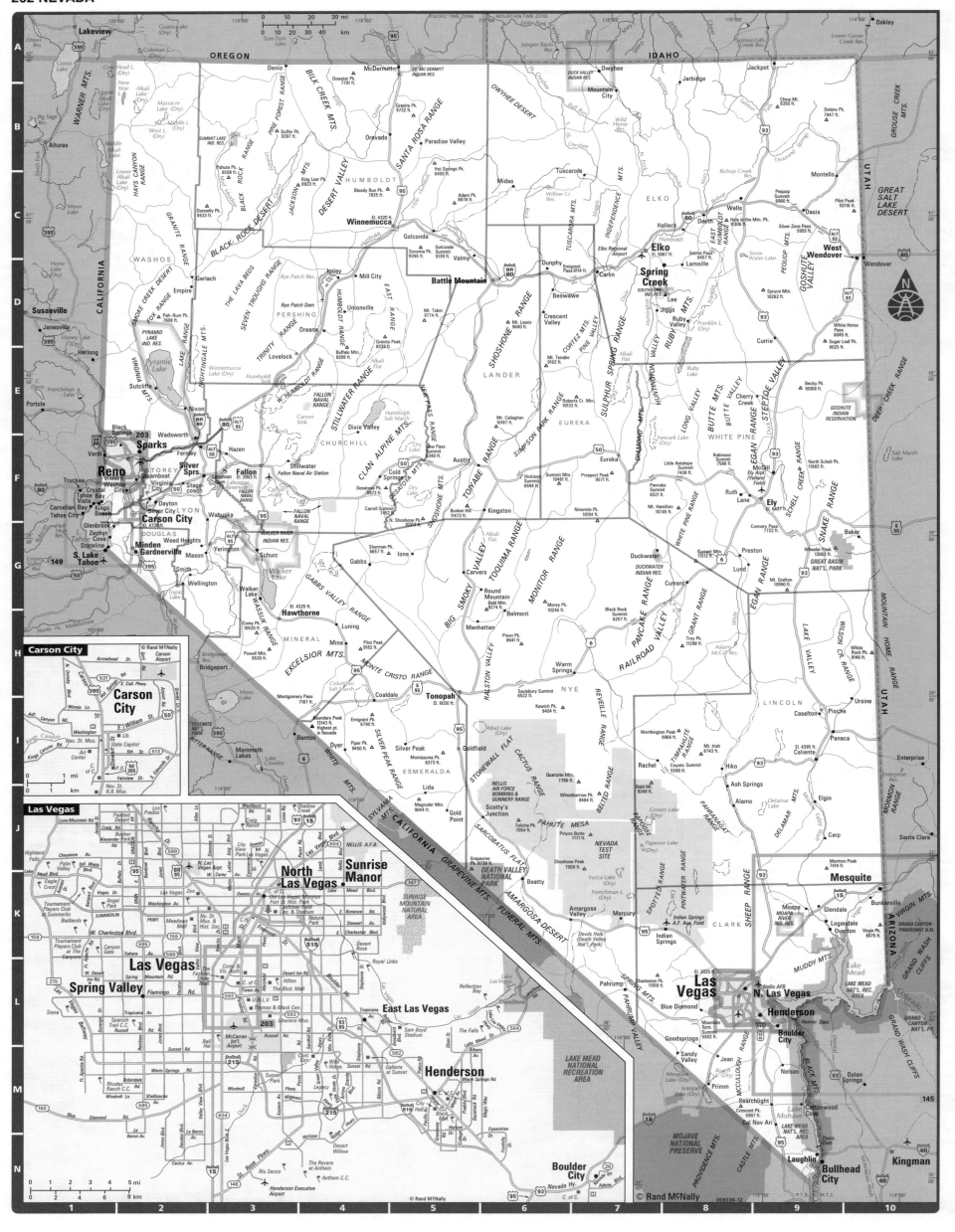

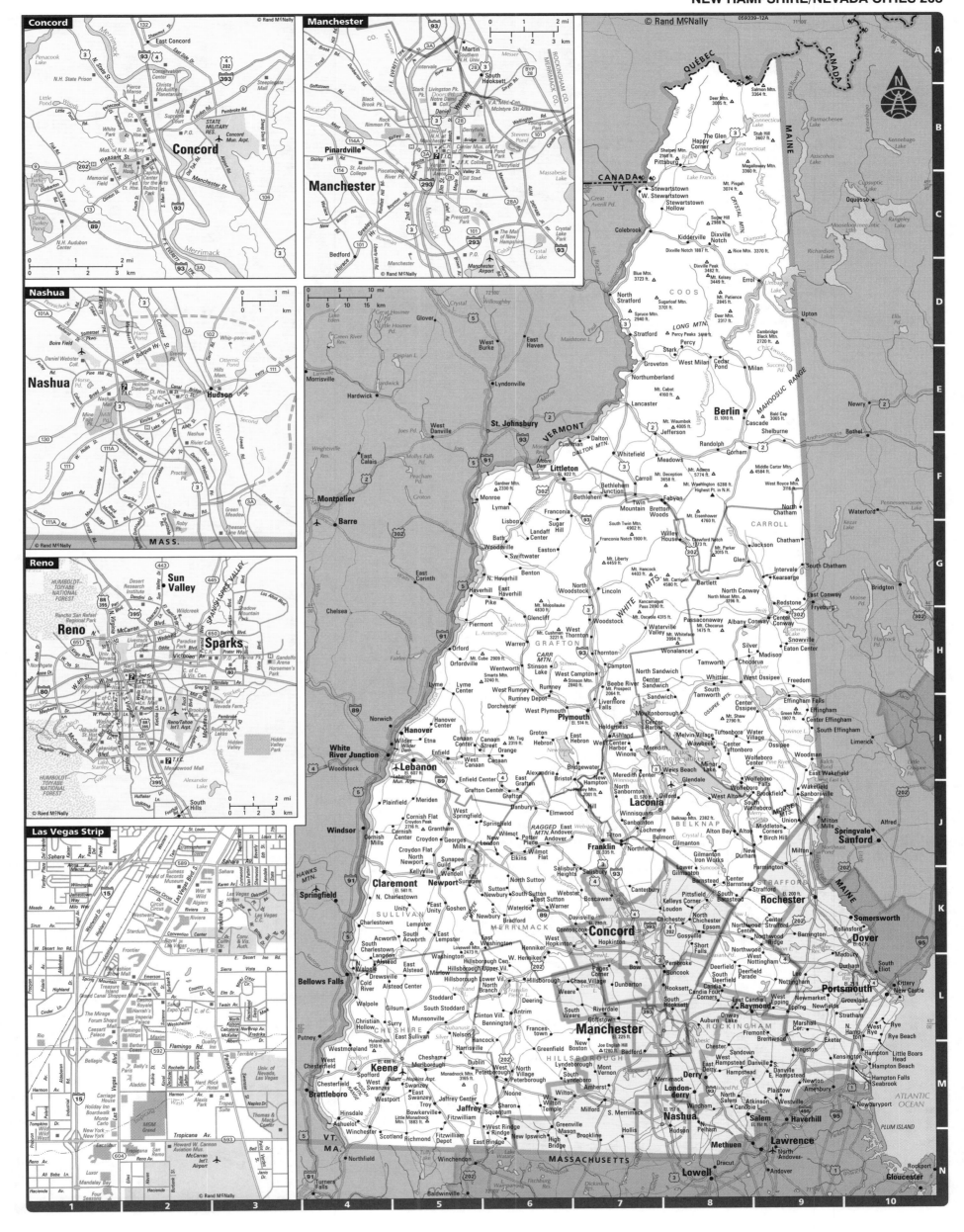

Concord

Manchester

Nashua

Reno

Las Vegas Strip

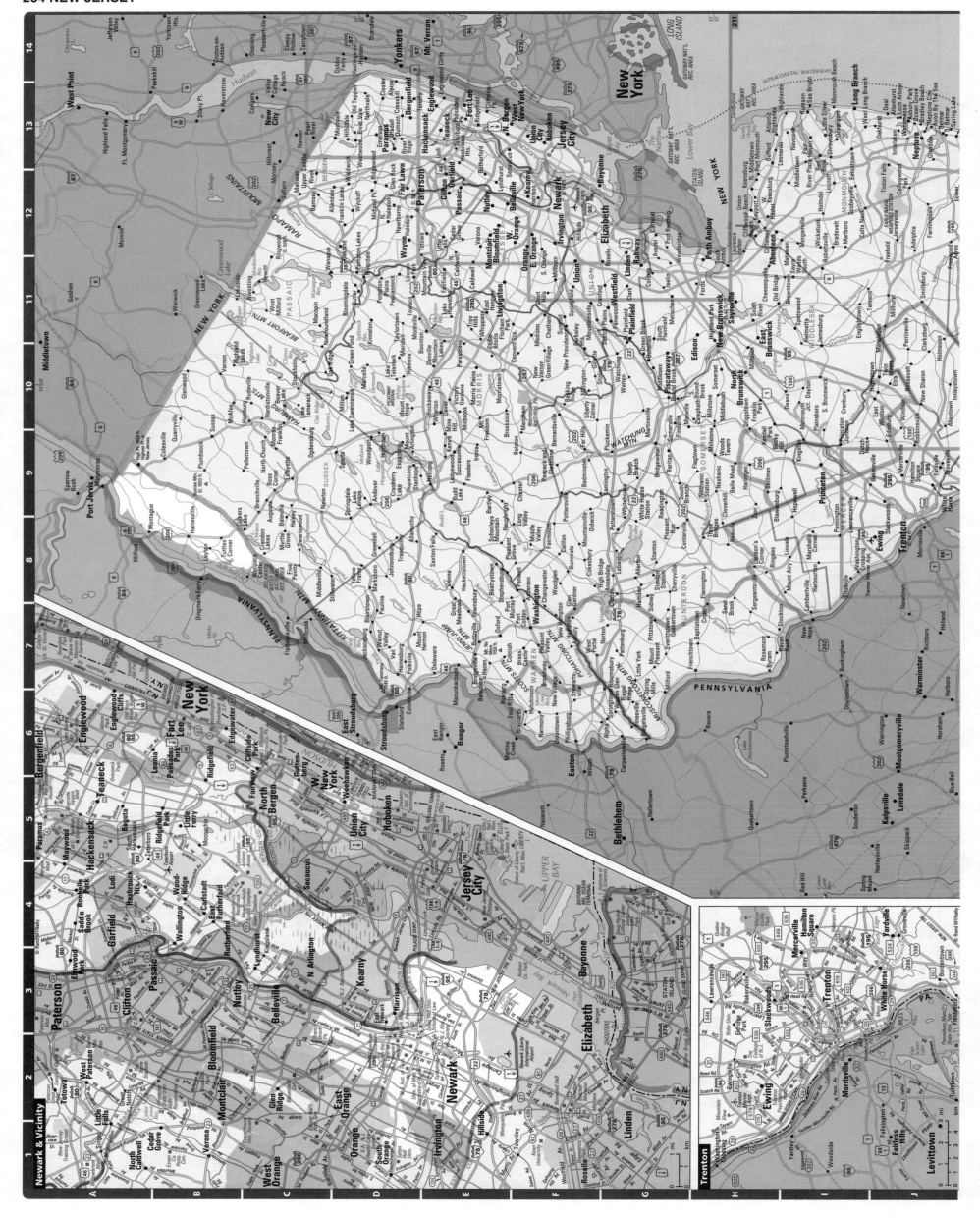

Newark & Vicinity

Trenton

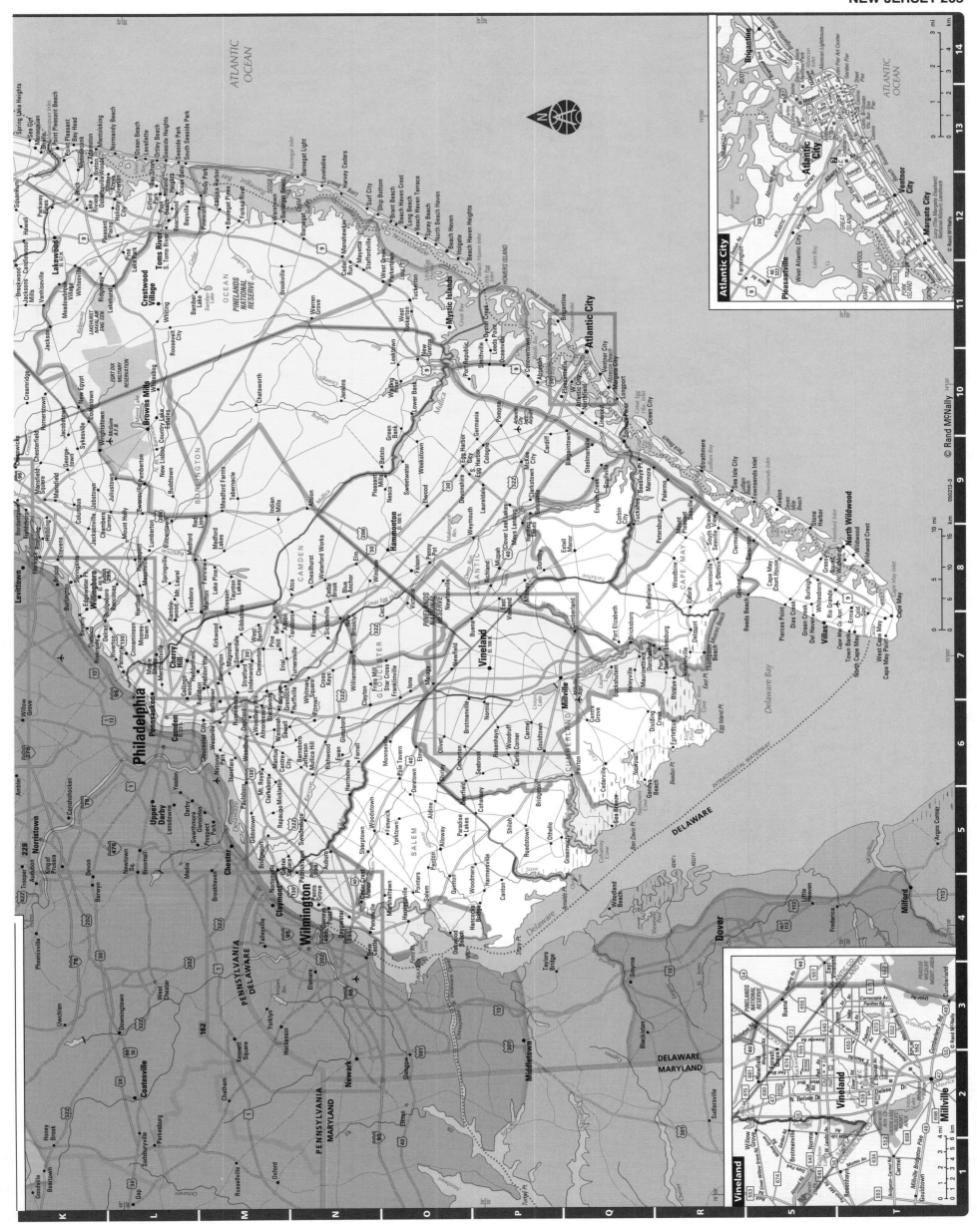

ATLANTIC OCEAN

Atlantic City

Ventnor City
Margate City

Atlantic City

PENNSYLVANIA
DELAWARE
MARYLAND

Philadelphia

Camden

Wilmington

Newark

Dover

Milford

Middletown

DELAWARE
MARYLAND

DELAWARE

Delaware Bay

ATLANTIC OCEAN

Lakewood

Toms River

Crestwood Village

PINELANDS NATIONAL RESERVE

Mystic Islands

Hammonton

Vineland

Millville

CAPE MAY

North Wildwood
Wildwood

Cape May

Vineland

Millville

© Rand McNally

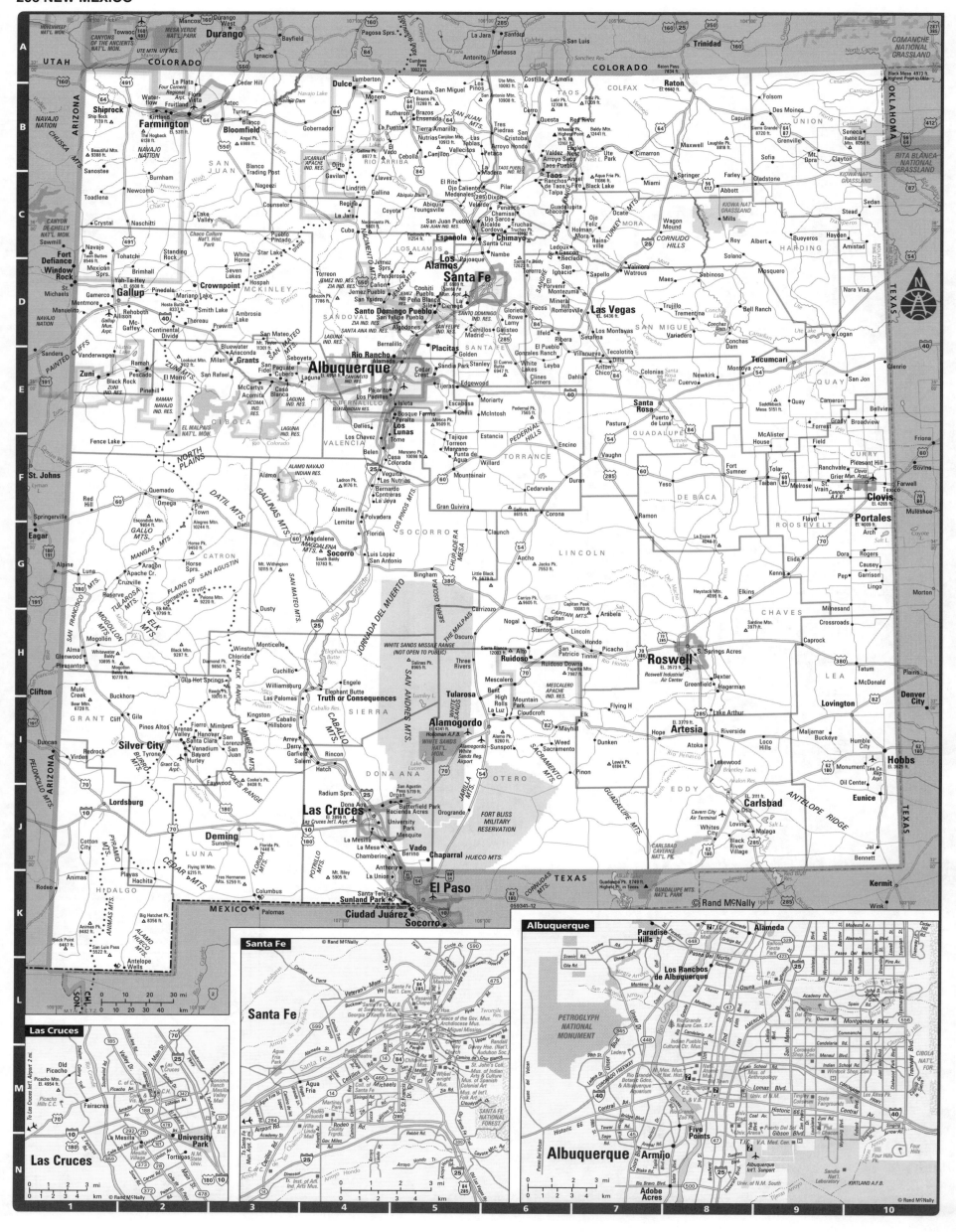

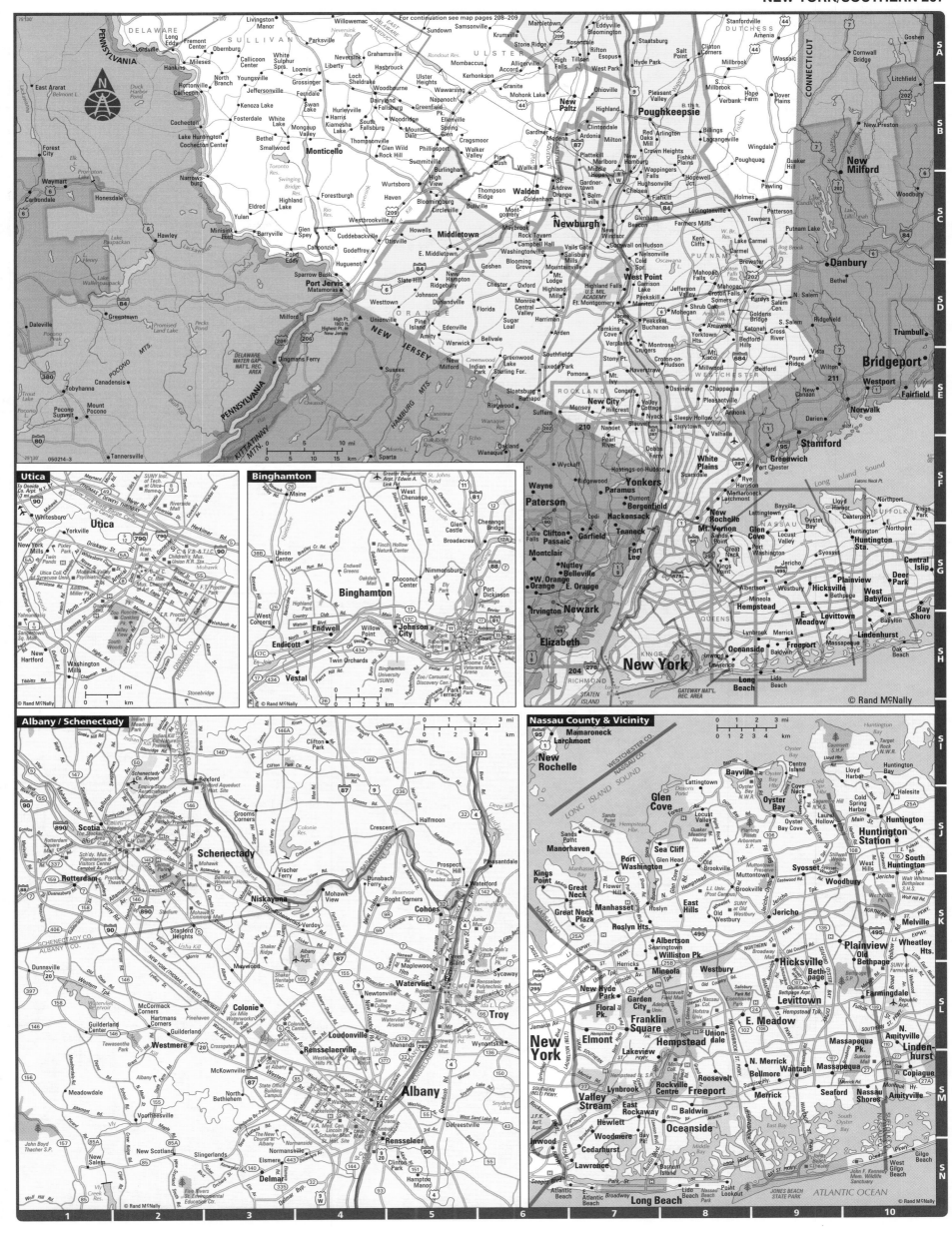

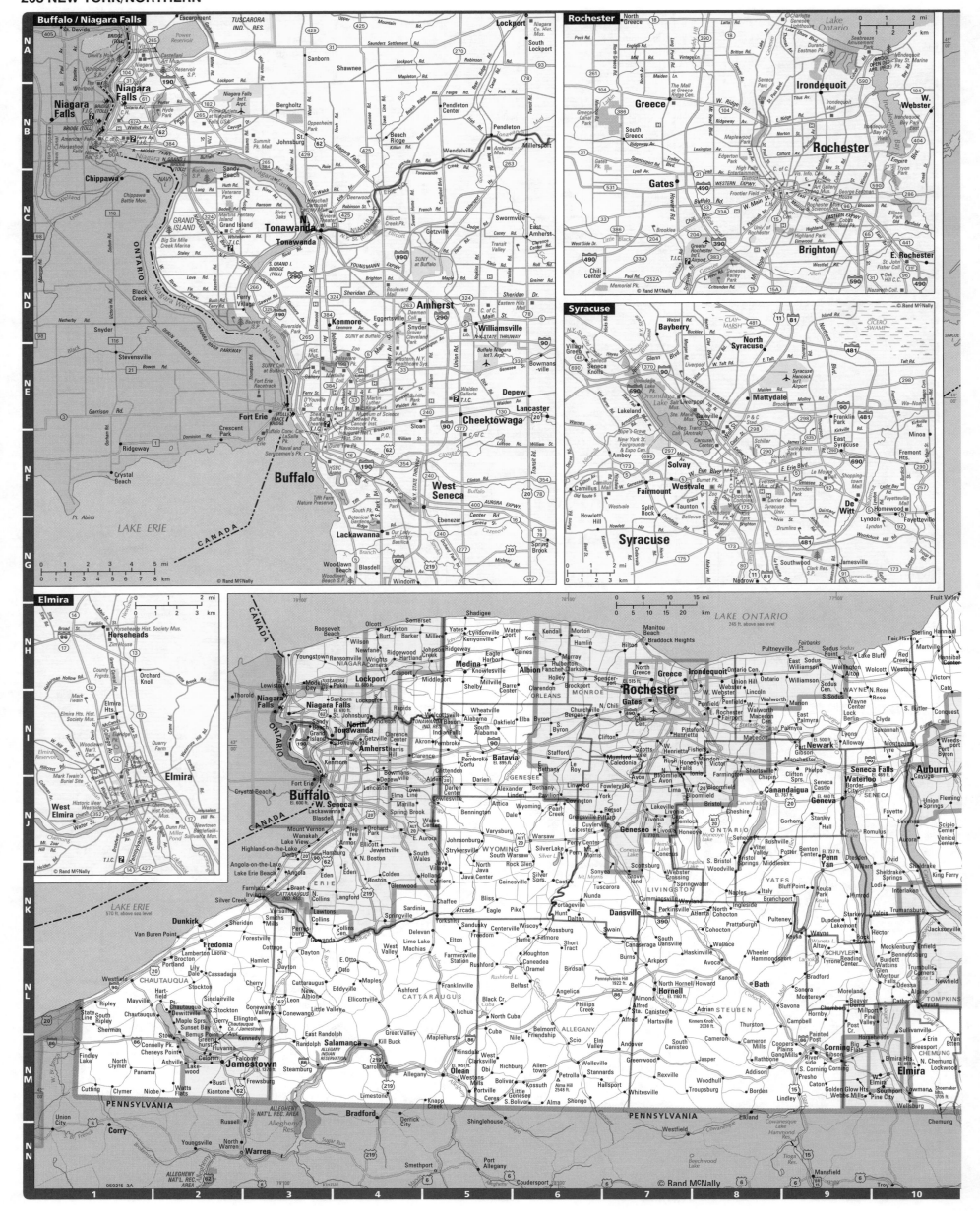

Buffalo / Niagara Falls

Rochester

Syracuse

Elmira

© Rand McNally

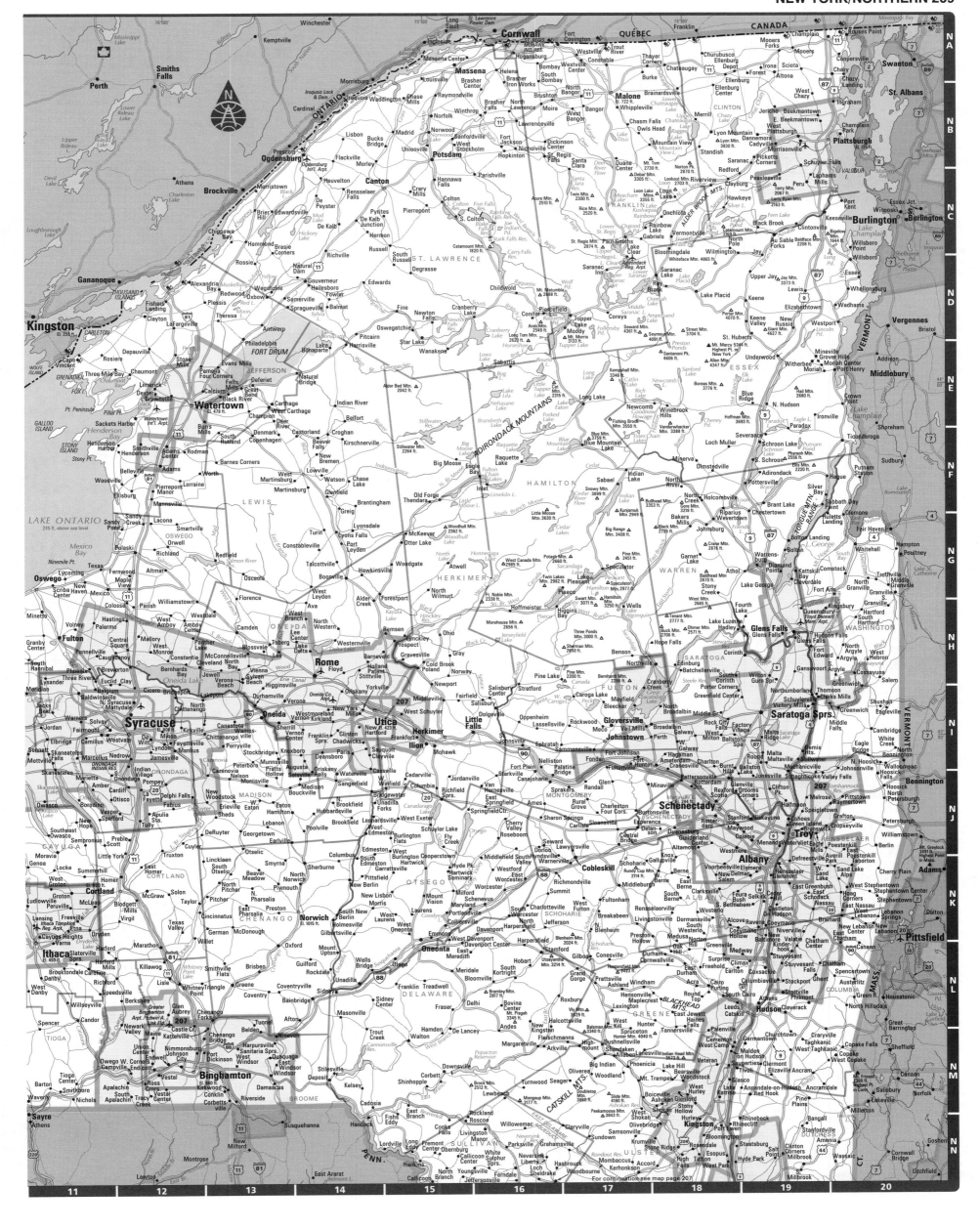

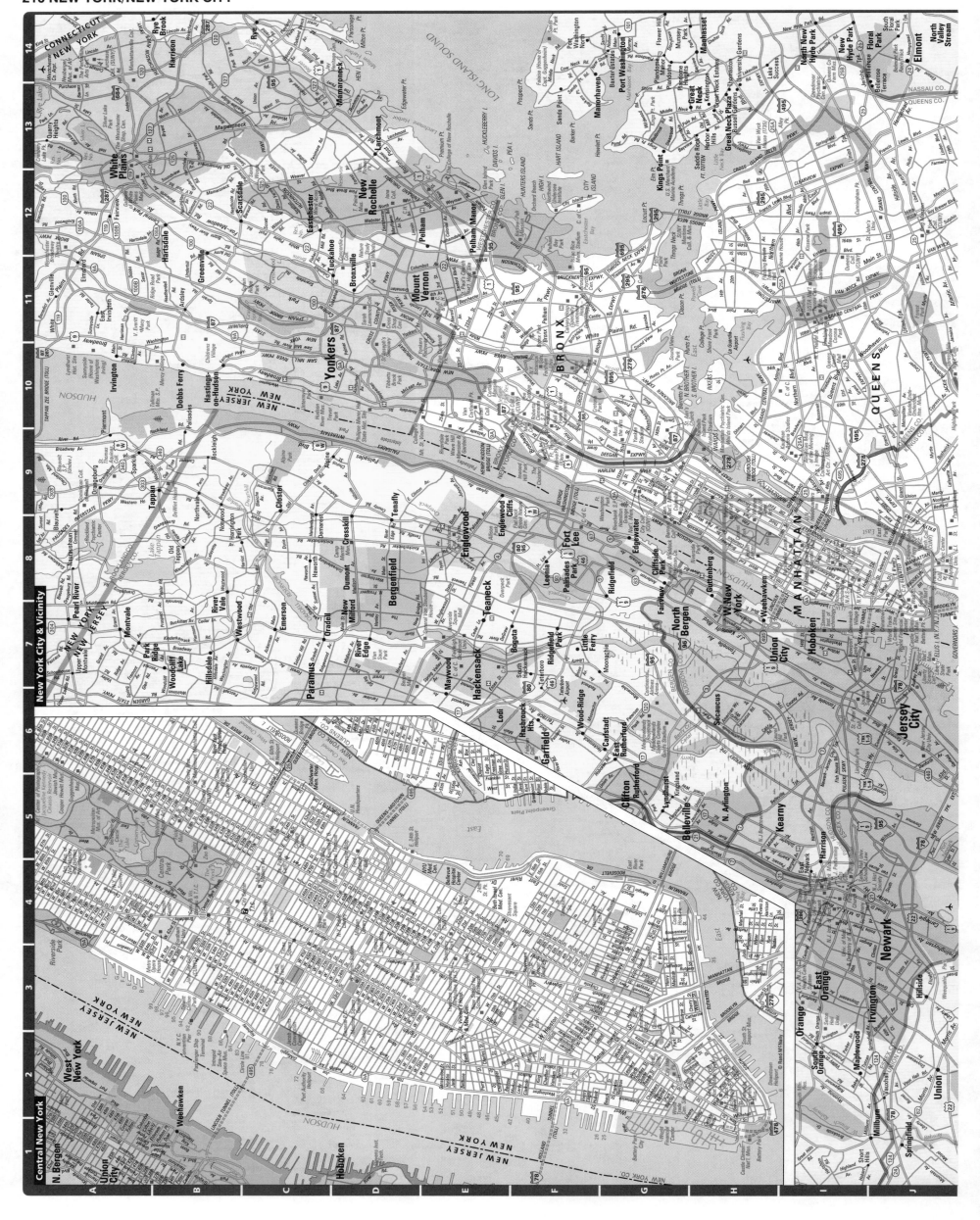

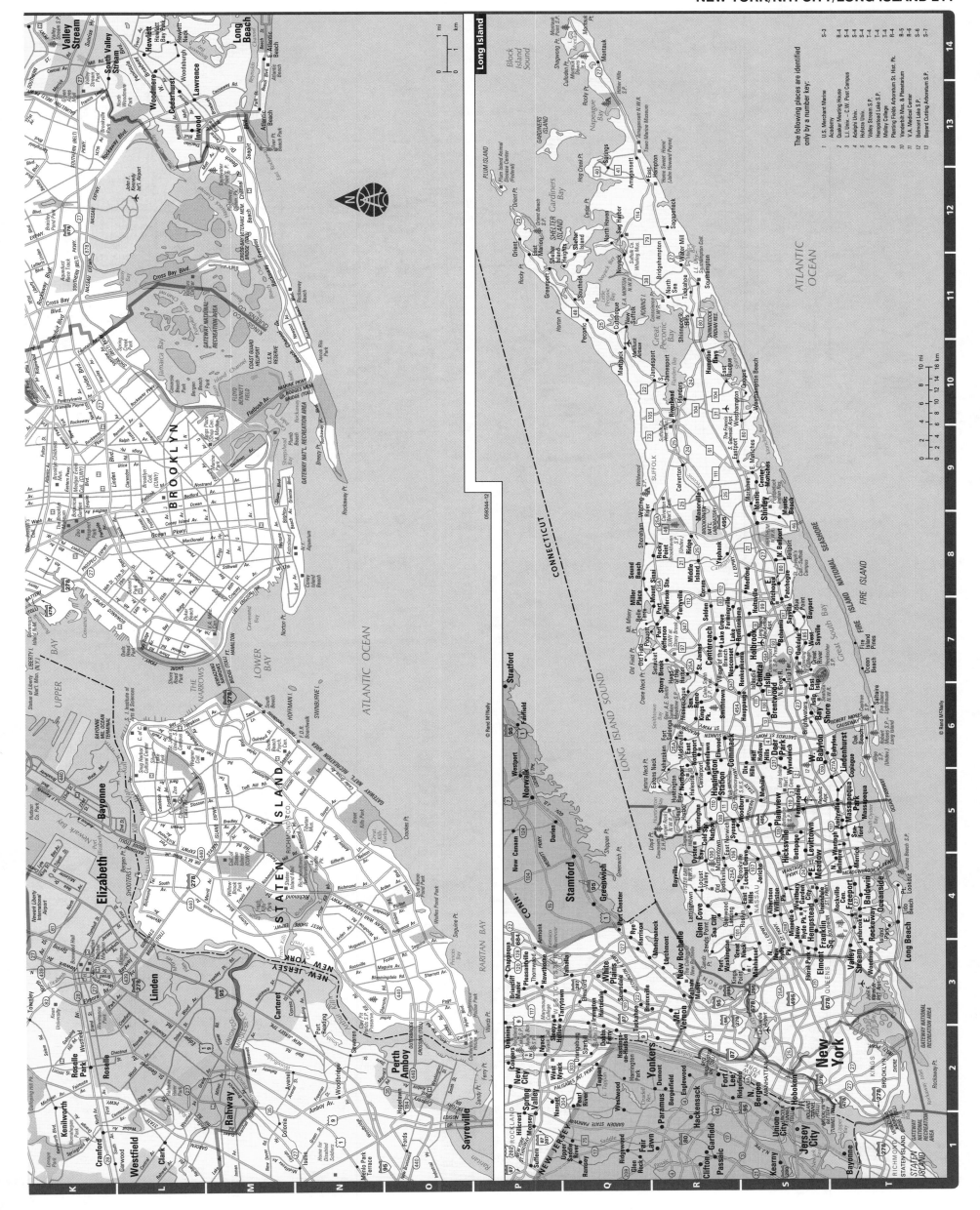

Long Island

The following places are identified
only by a number key:

1	U.S. Merchant Marine	S-3
2	Academy	R-4
3	Quaker Meeting House	S-4
4	L.I. Univ. – C.W. Post Campus	T-4
5	Adelphi Univ.	T-4
6	Hofstra Univ.	T-4
7	Valley Stream S.P.	T-4
8	Hempstead Lake S.P.	R-5
9	Molloy College	R-6
10	Planting Fields Arboretum St. Hist. Pk.	S-6
11	Vanderbilt Mus. & Planetarium	S-7
12	V.A. Medical Center	
13	Bayard Cutting Arboretum S.P.	

ATLANTIC OCEAN

LOWER BAY

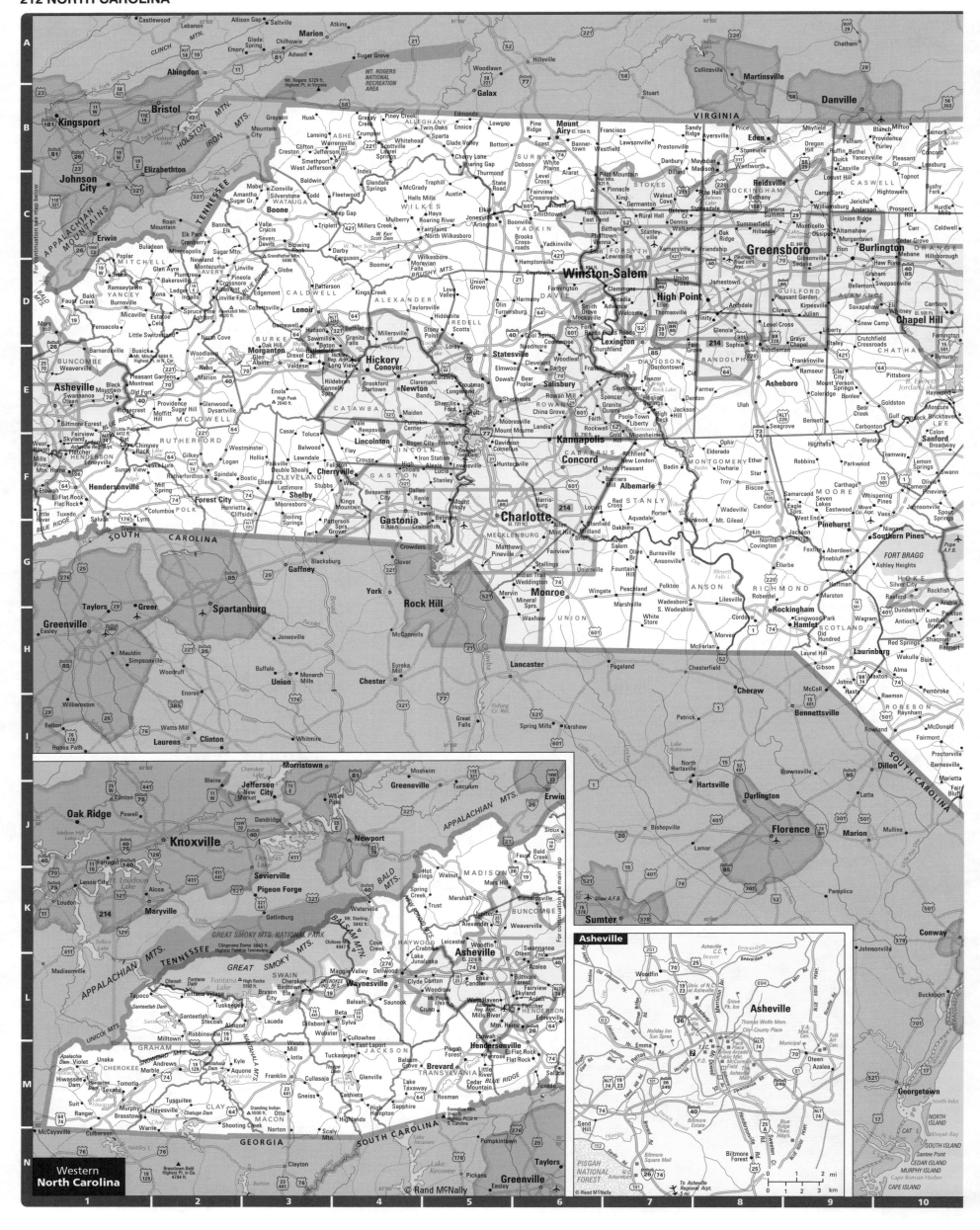

Western
North Carolina

Asheville

© Rand McNally

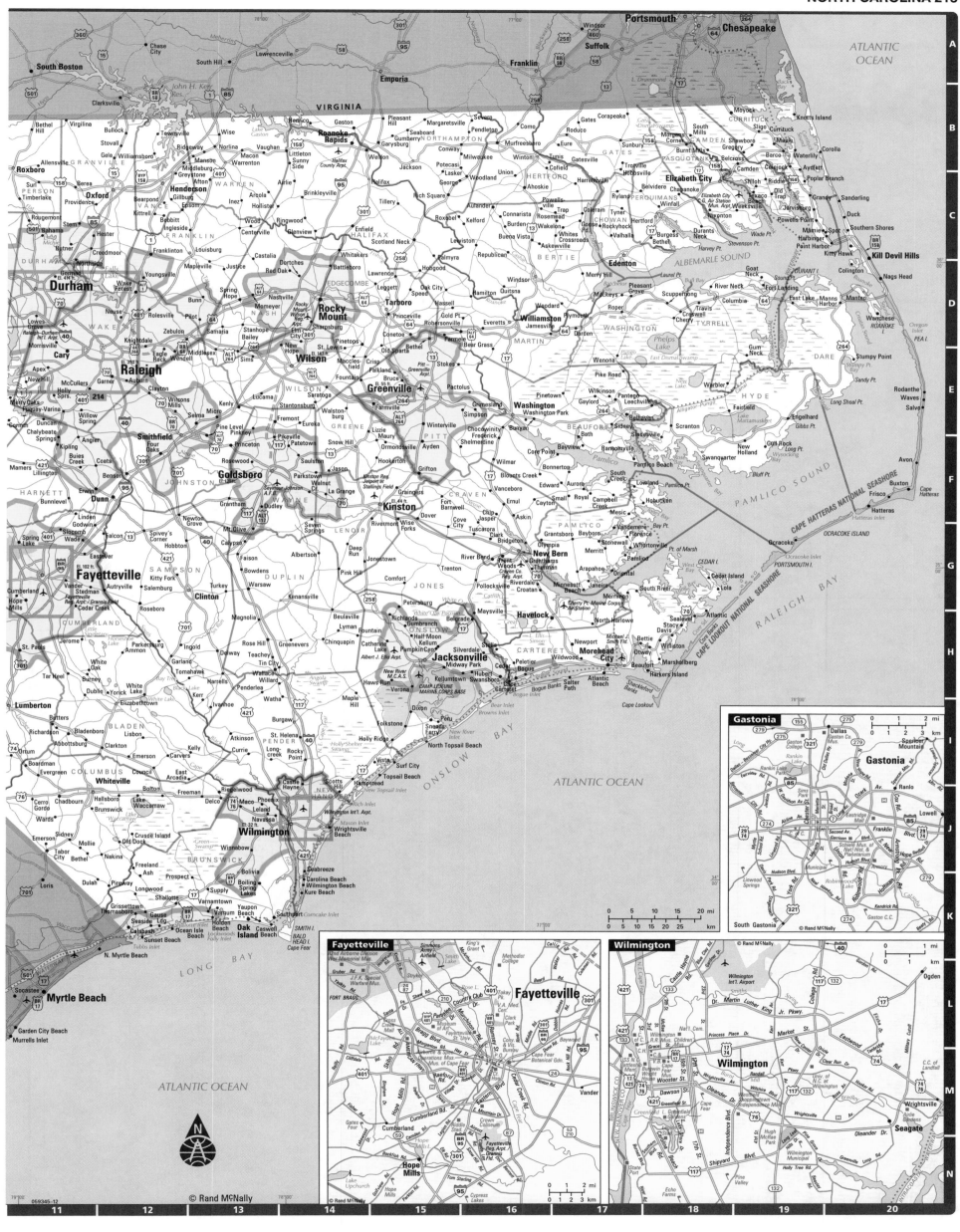

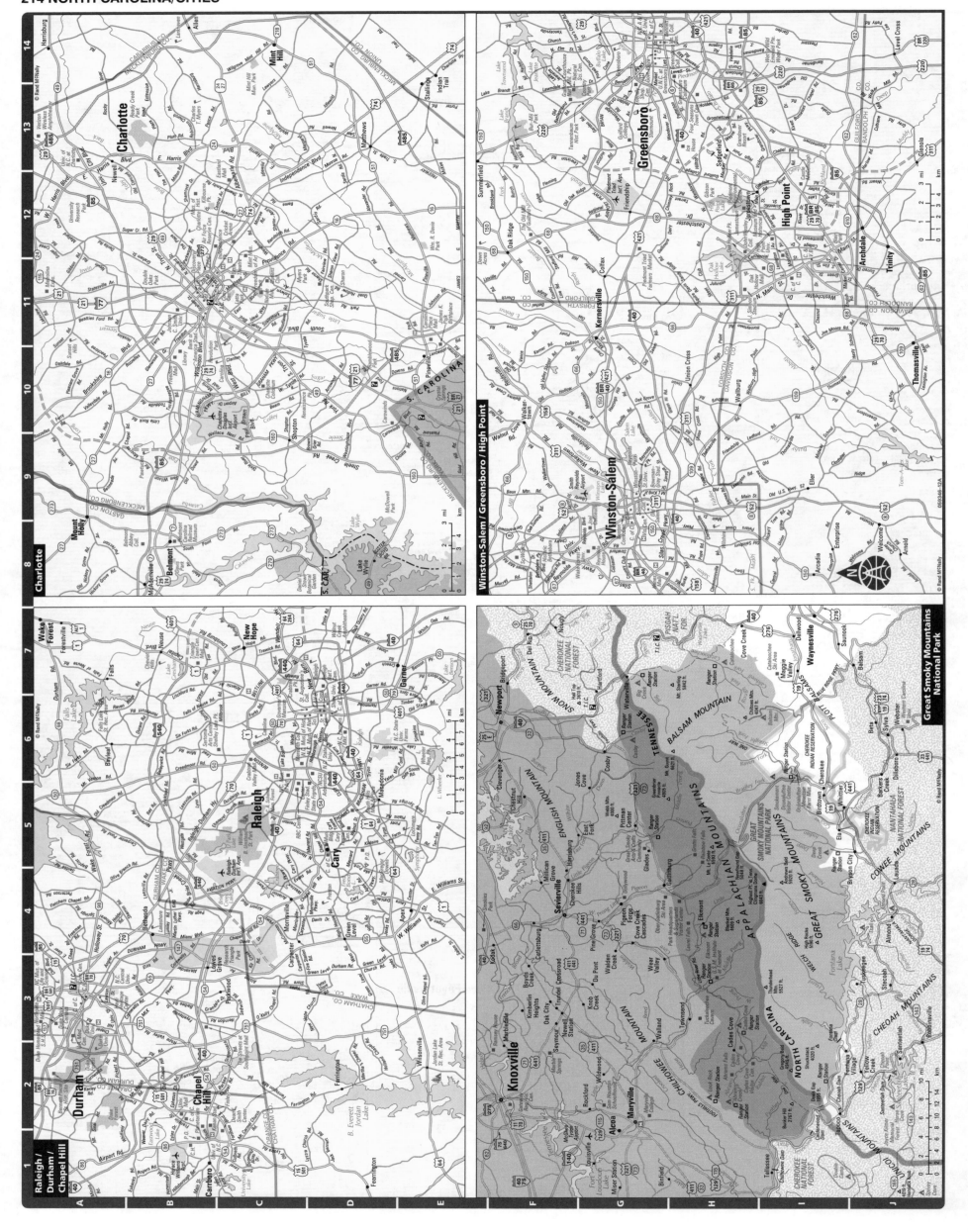

Charlotte

Winston-Salem / Greensboro / High Point

Raleigh / Durham / Chapel Hill

Great Smoky Mountains National Park

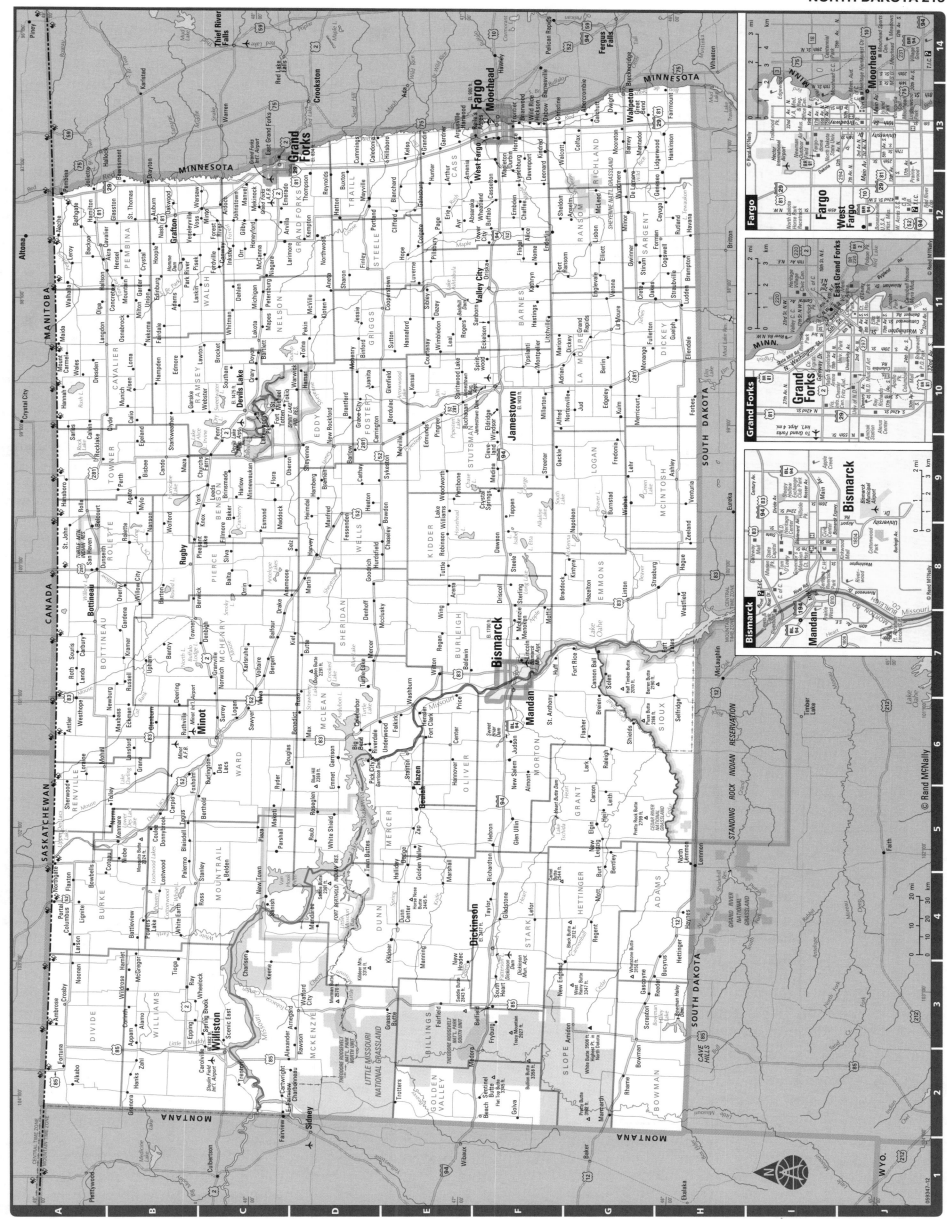

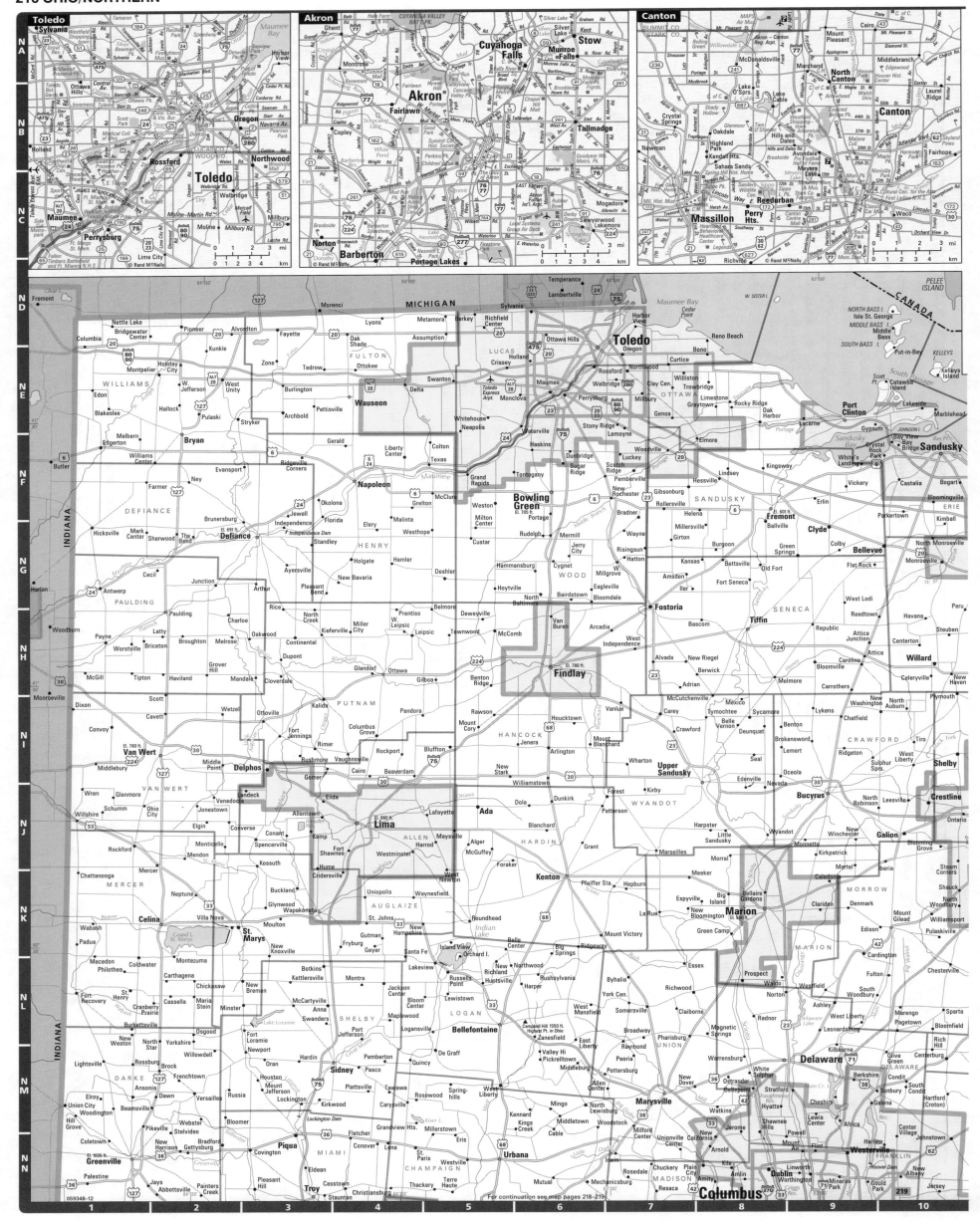

For continuation see map pages 218–219

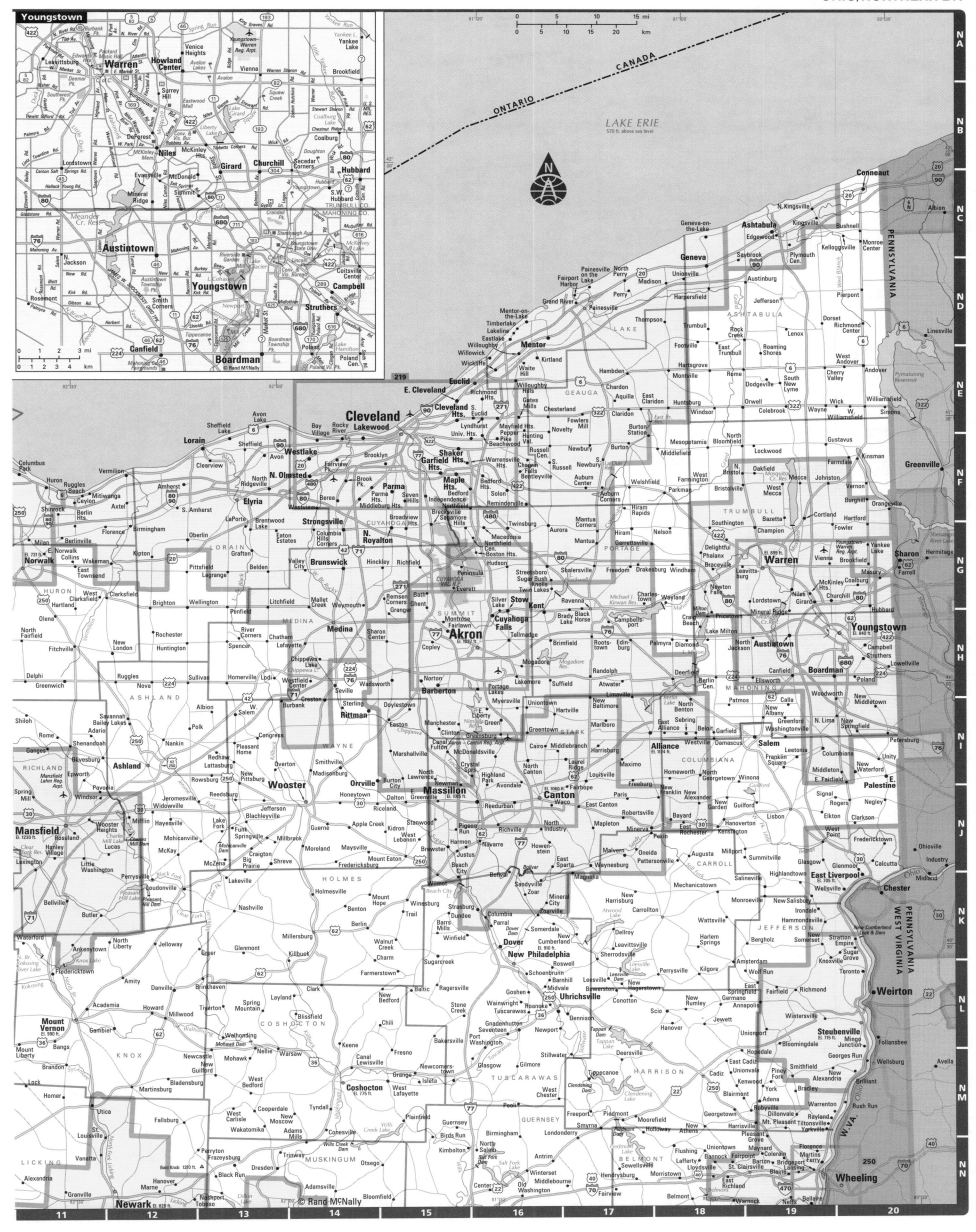

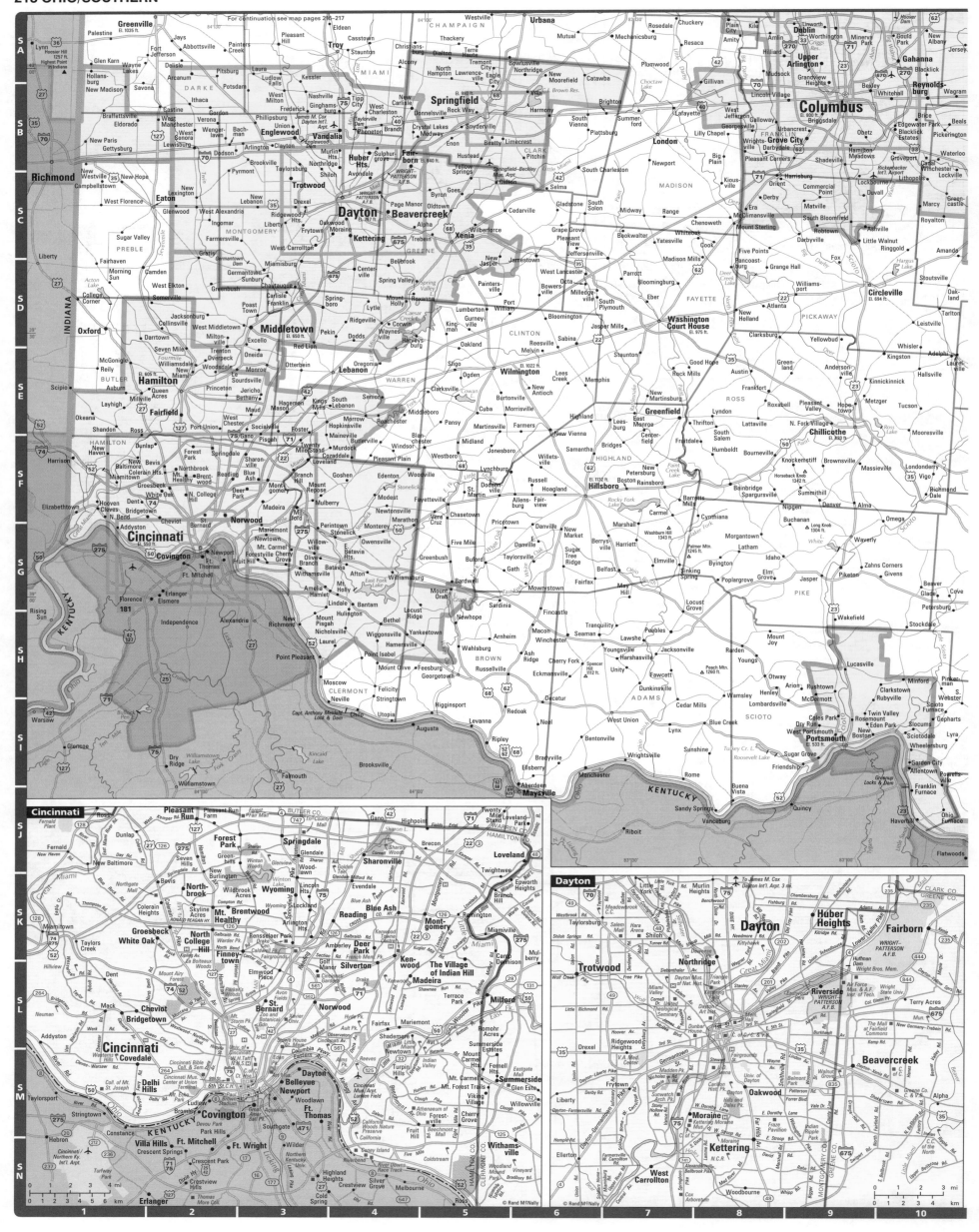

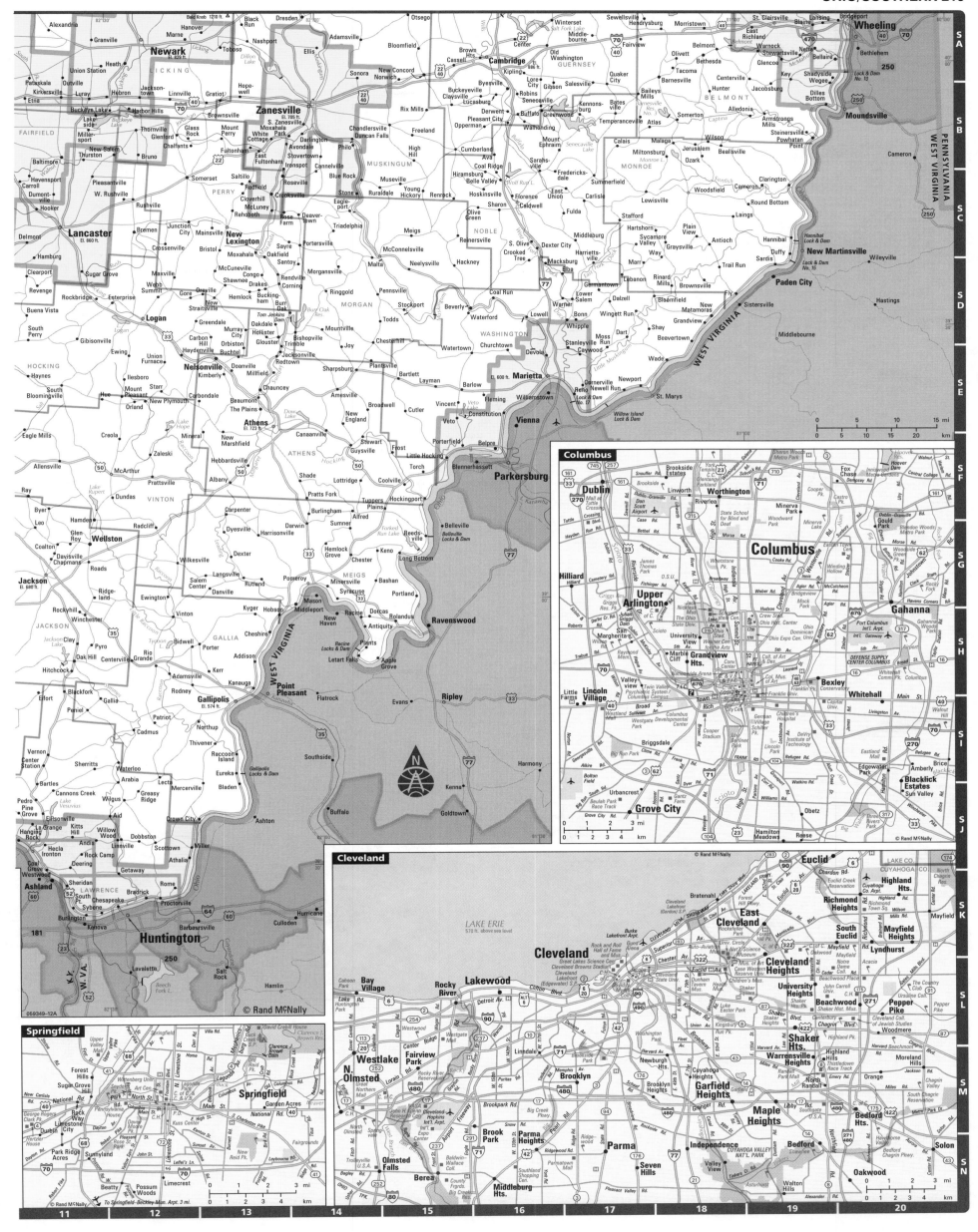

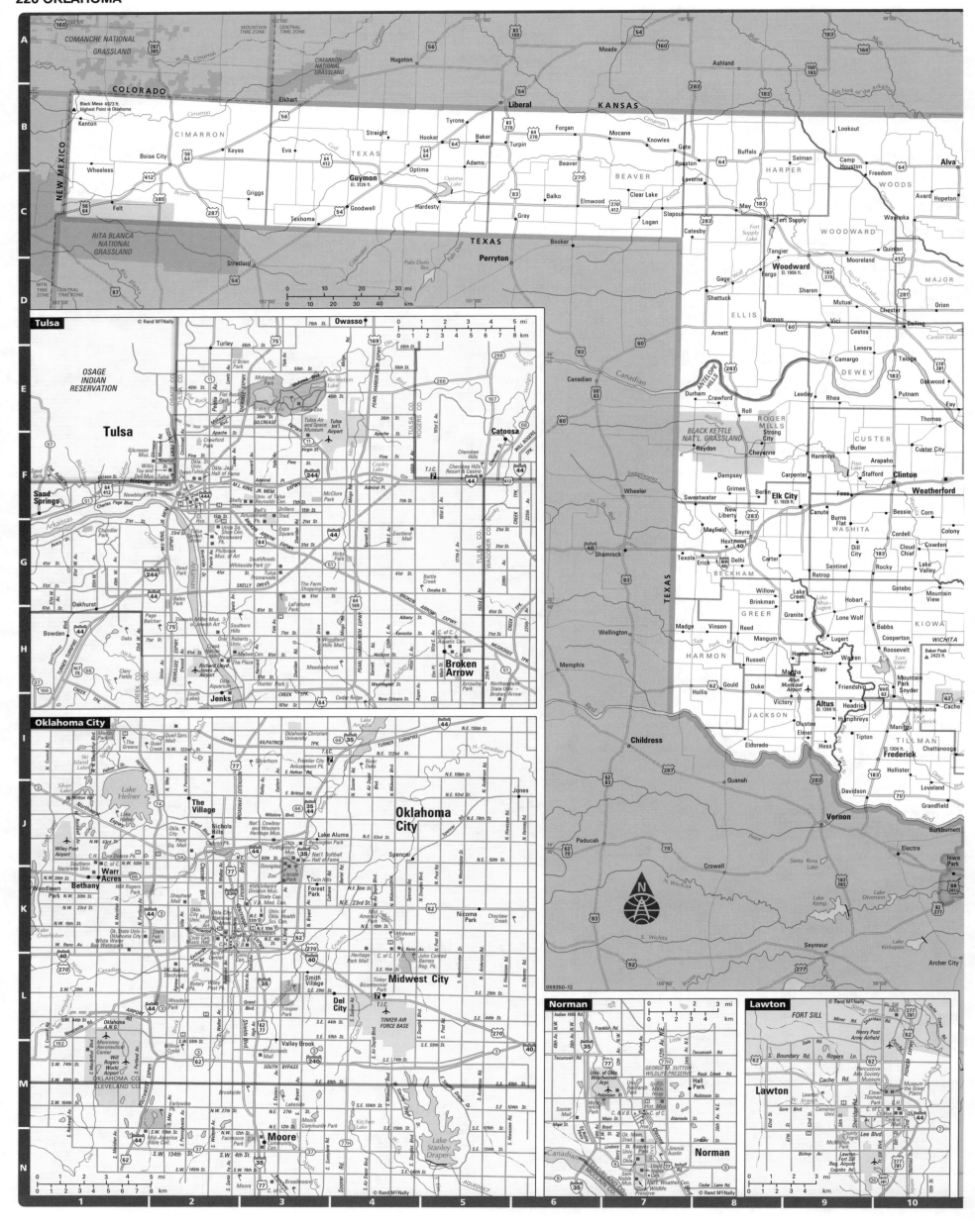

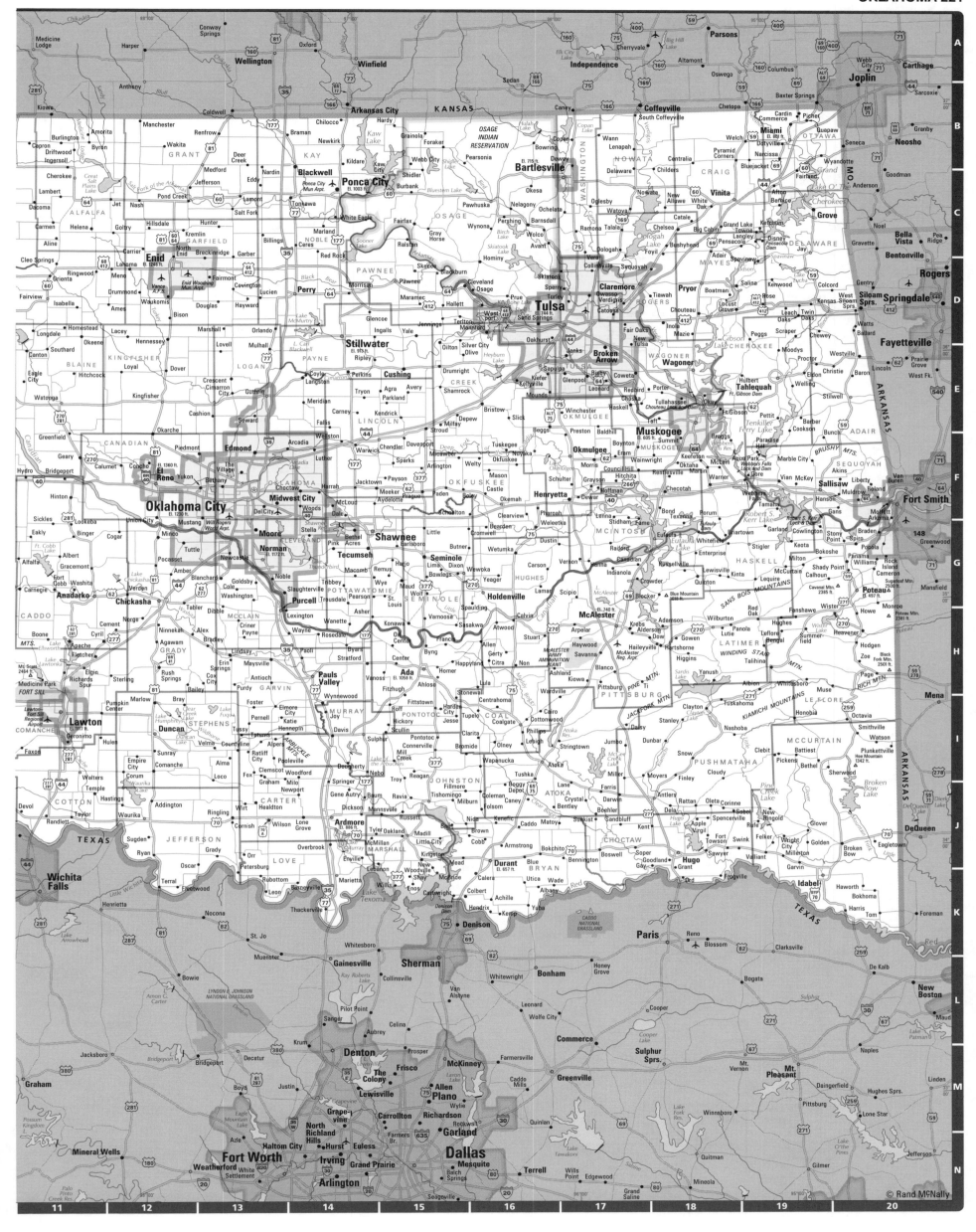

© Rand McNally

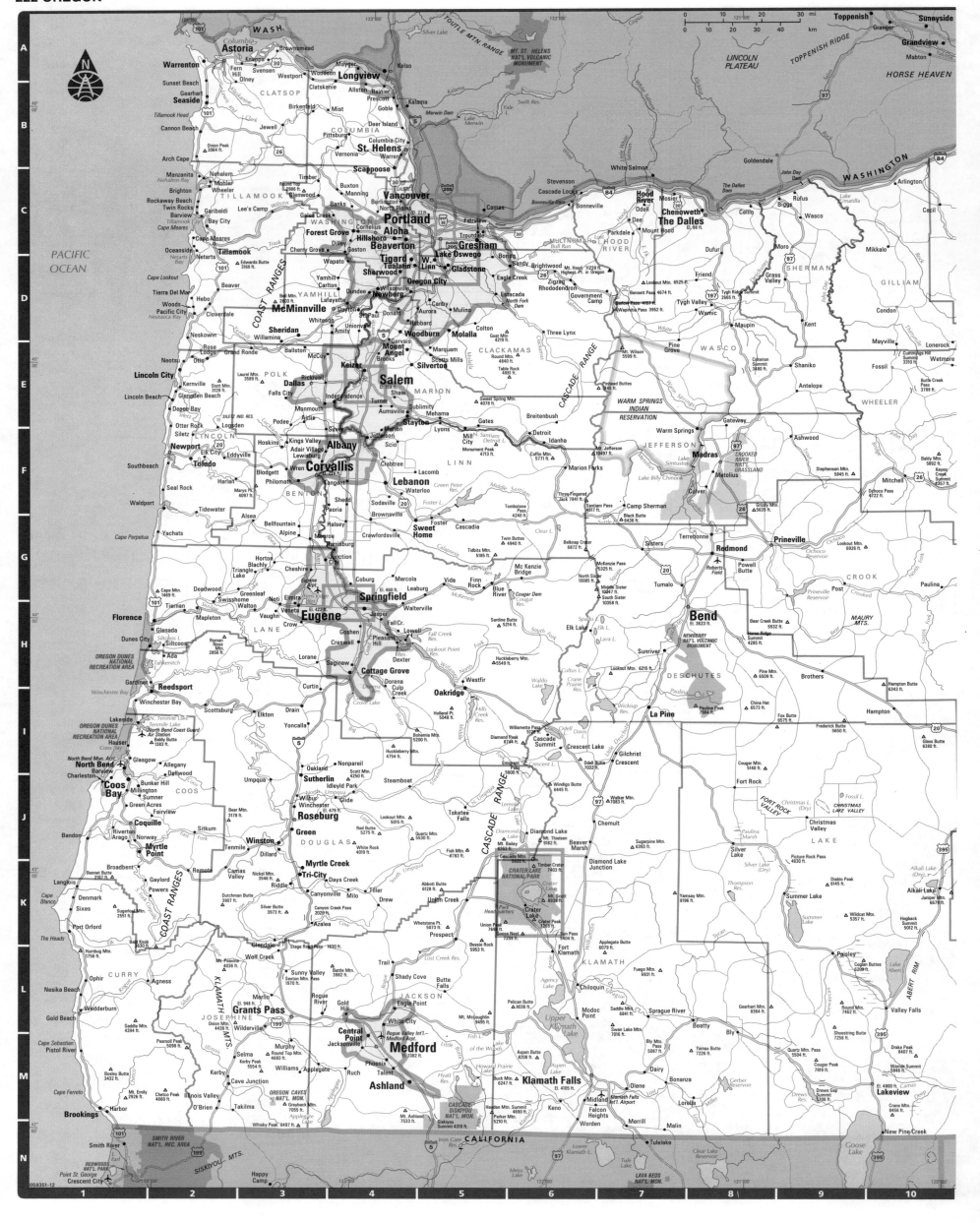

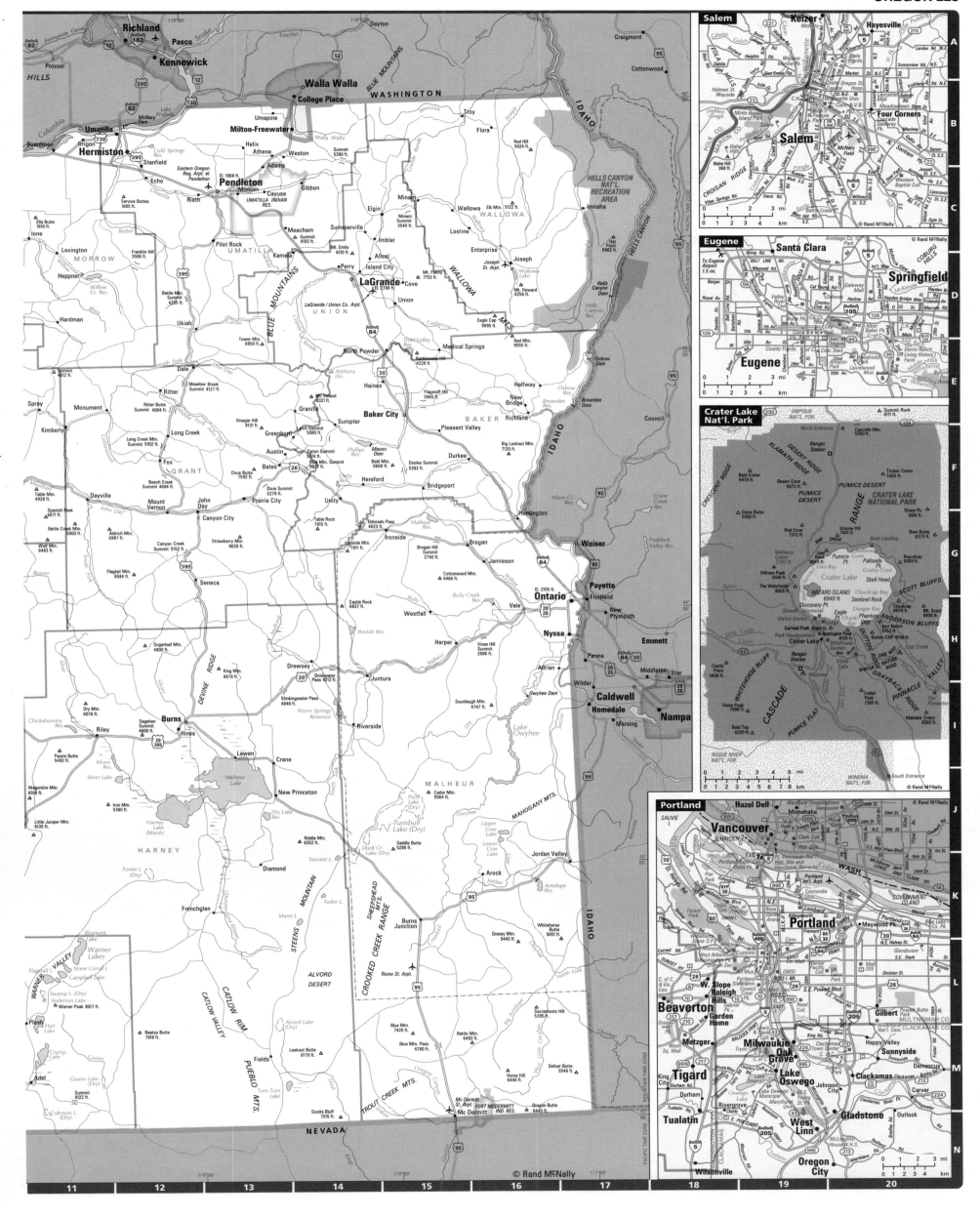

Salem

Eugene

Crater Lake Nat'l. Park

Portland

© Rand McNally

For continuation see map pages 226-227

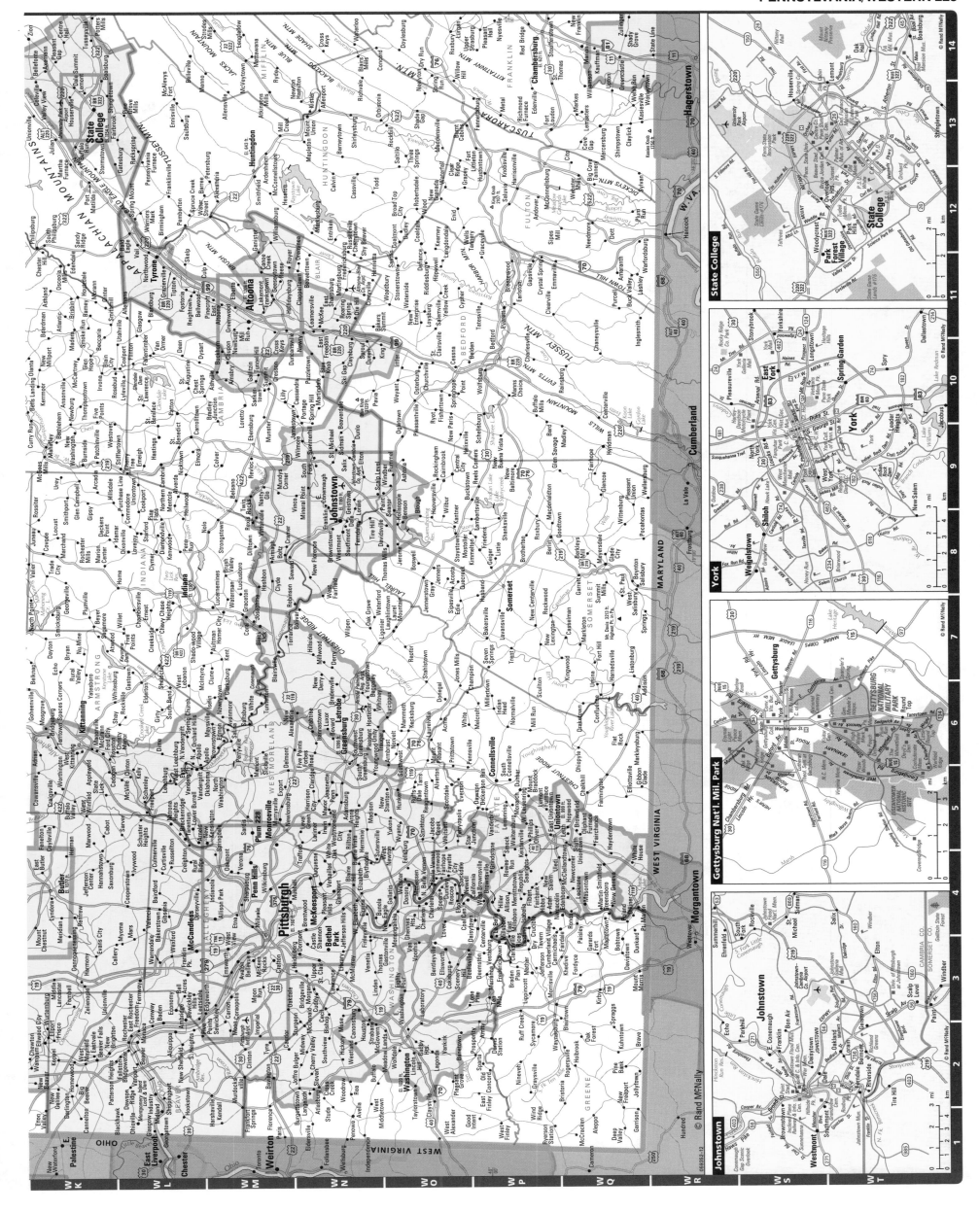

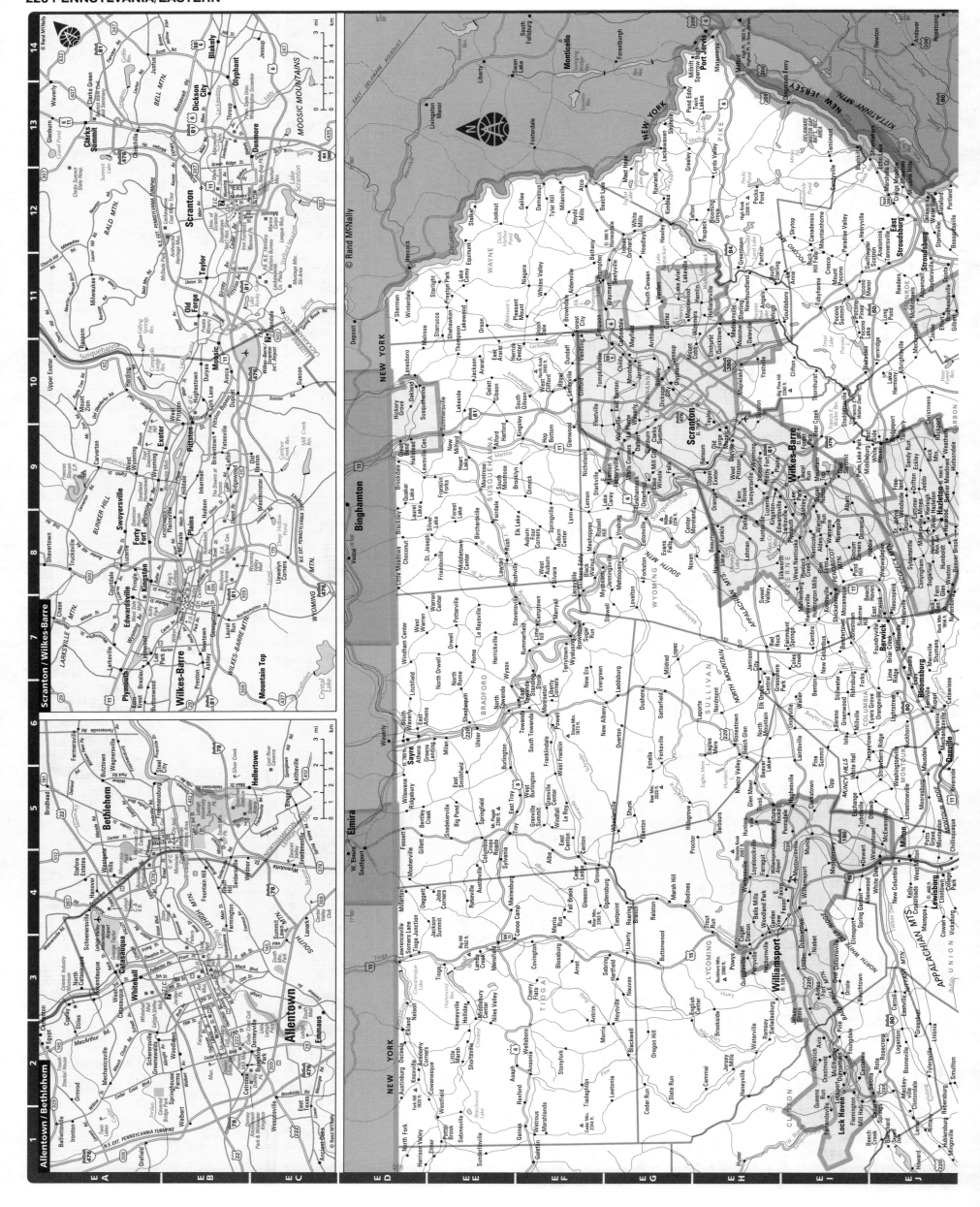

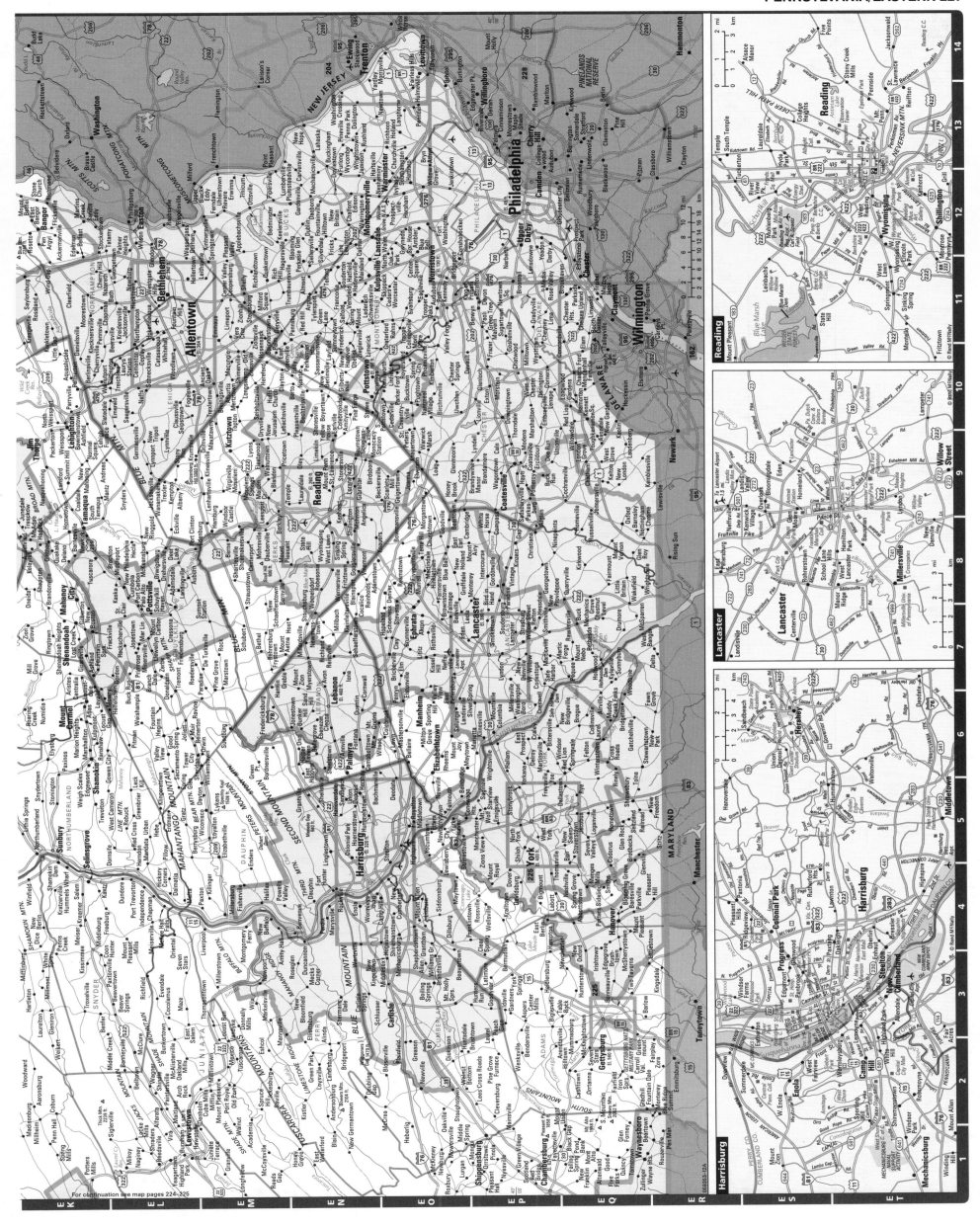

For continuation see map pages 224–225

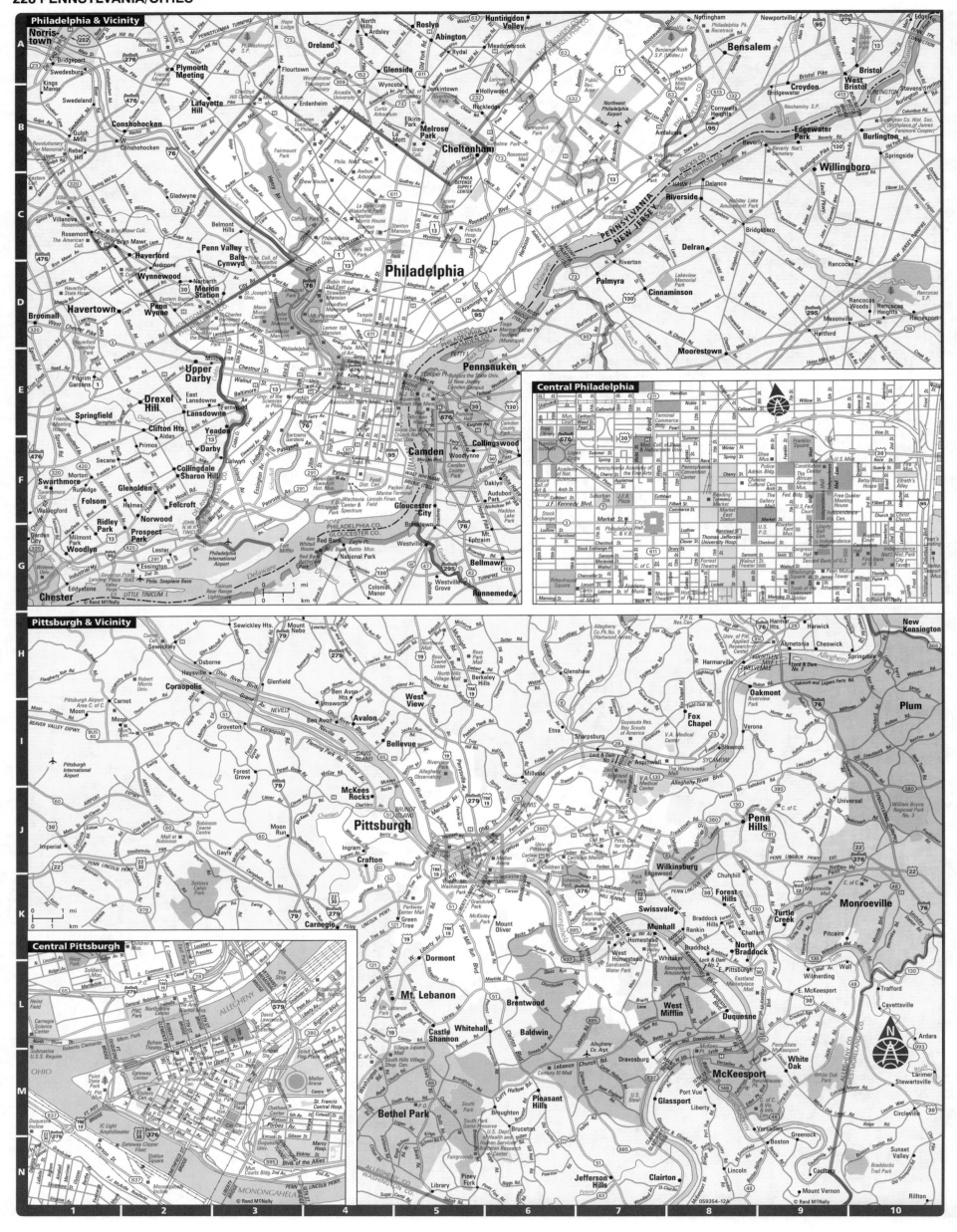

Philadelphia & Vicinity

Pittsburgh & Vicinity

Central Philadelphia

Central Pittsburgh

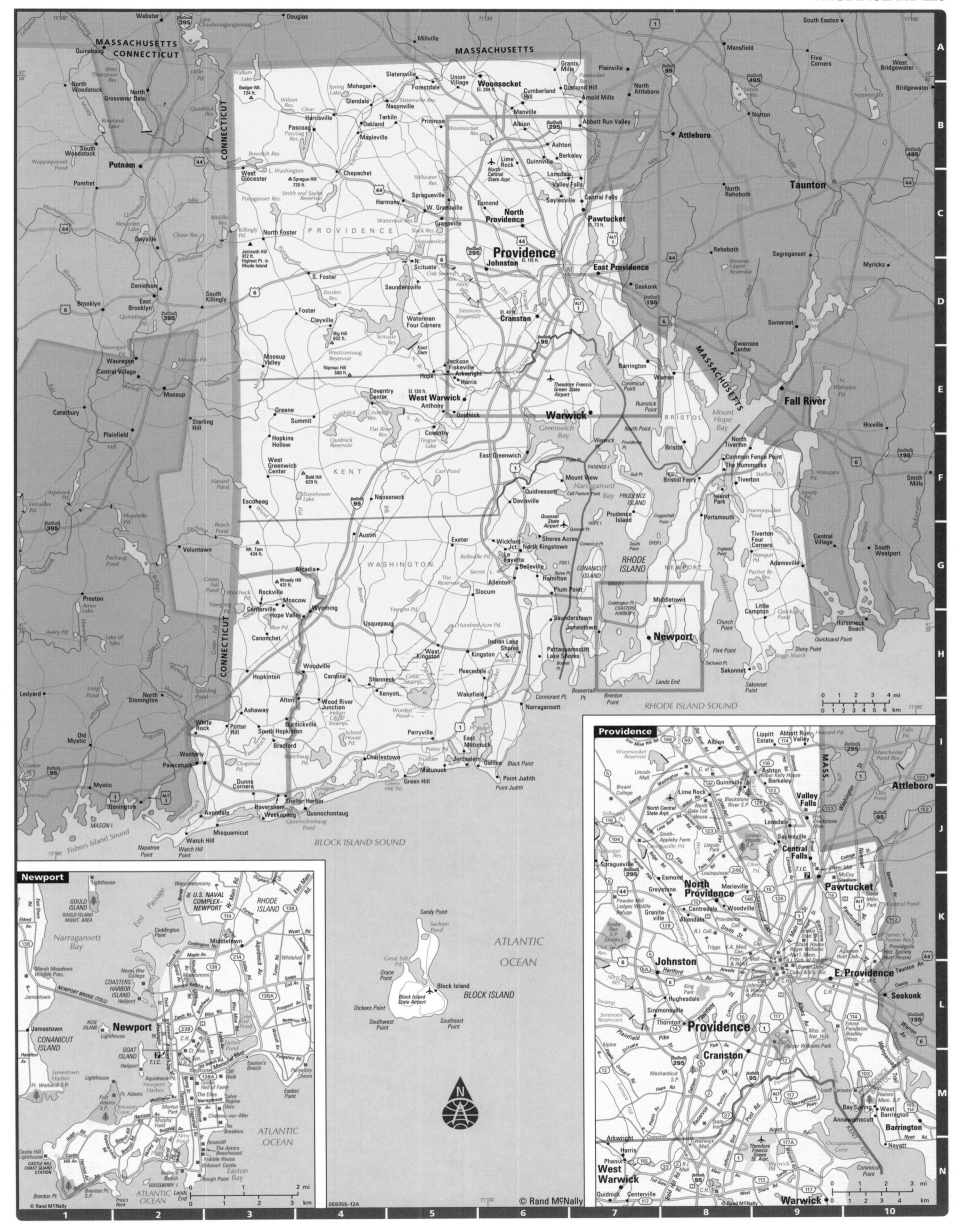

© Rand McNally

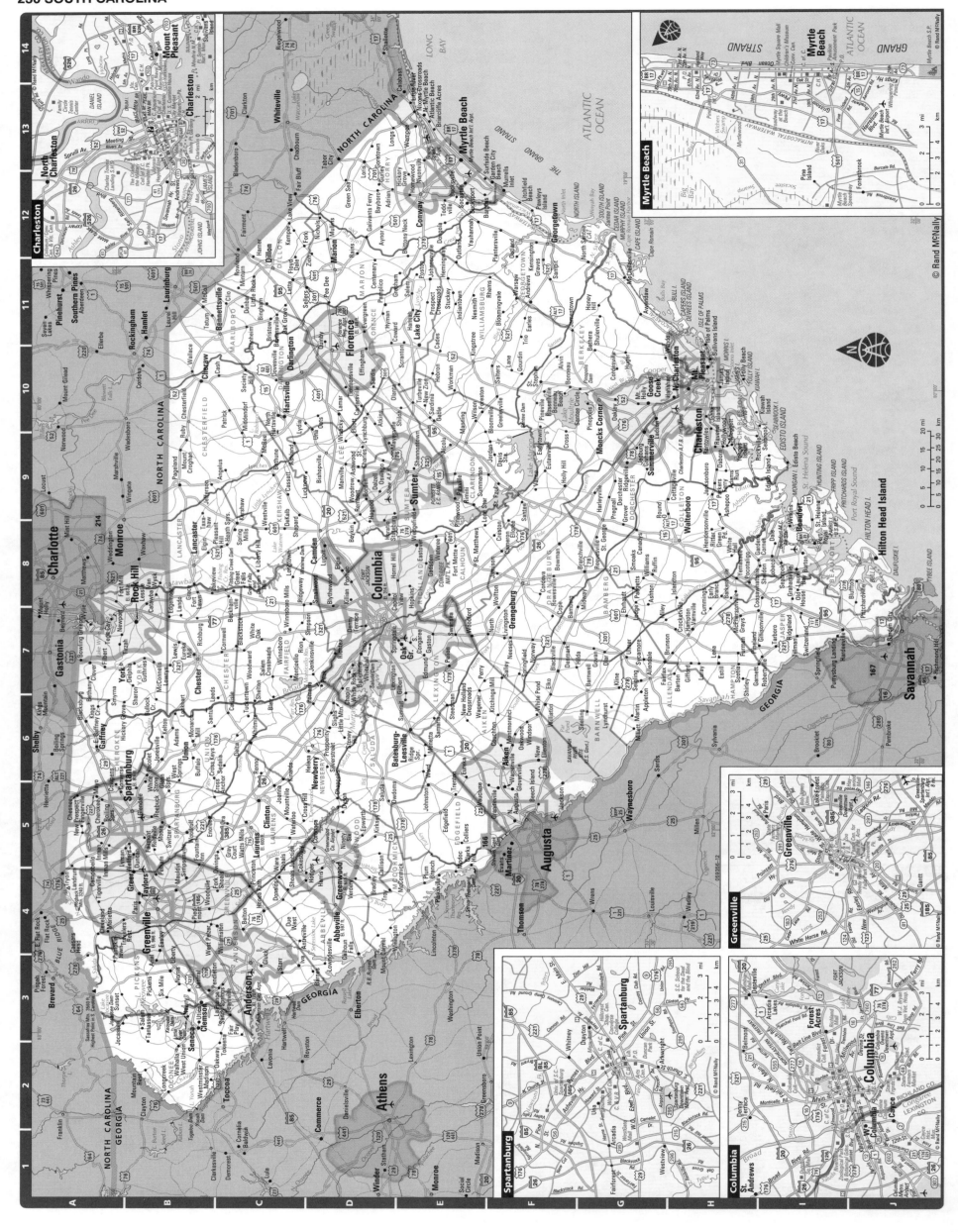

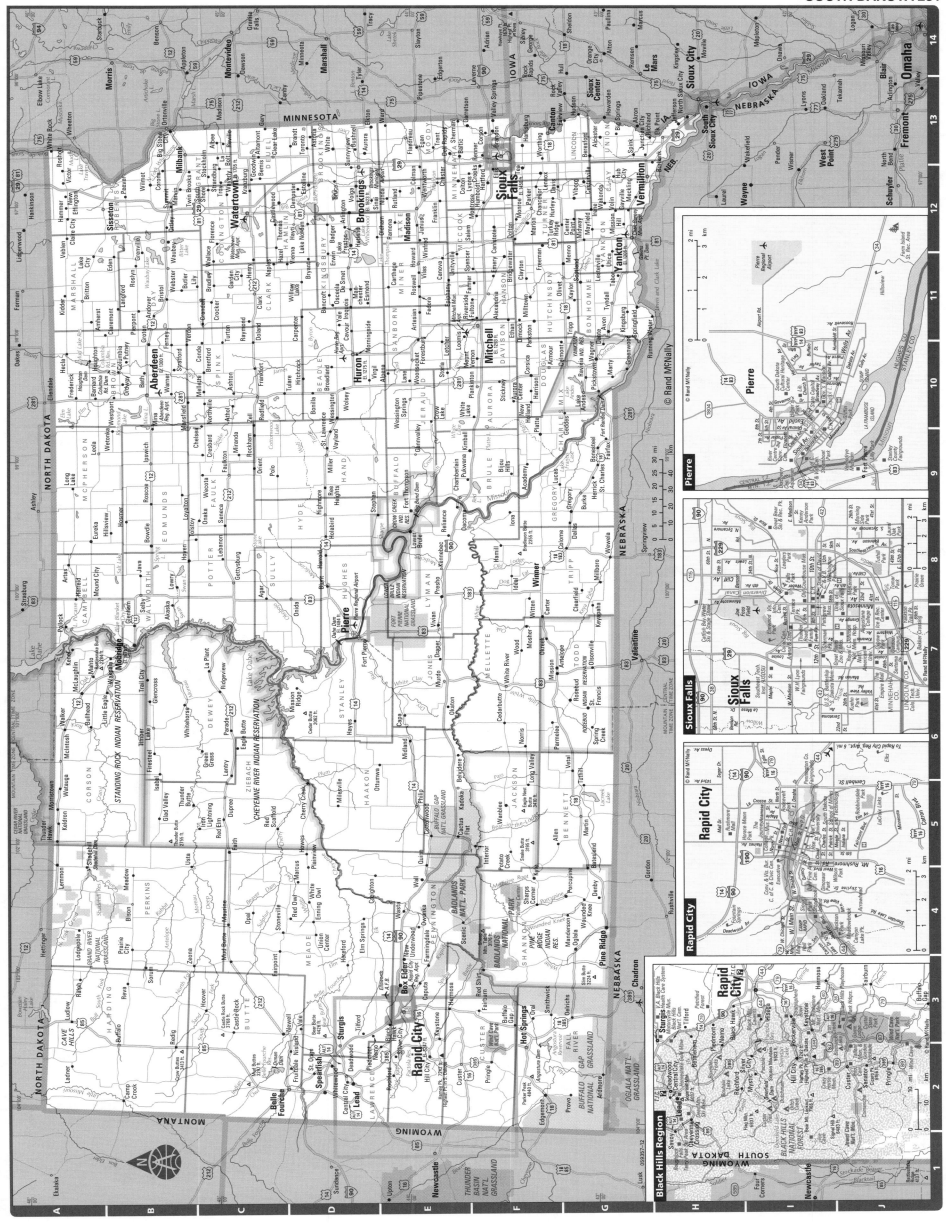

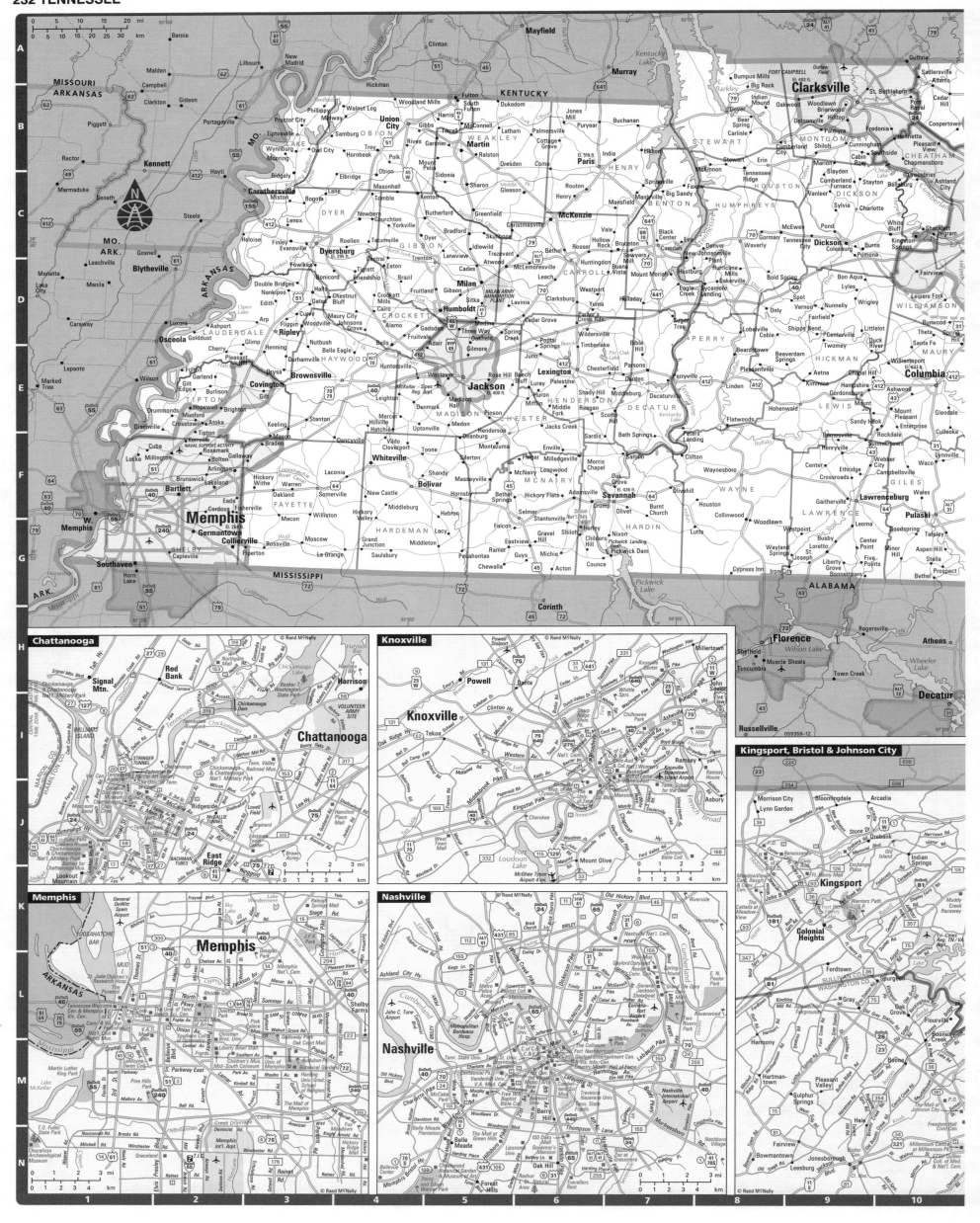

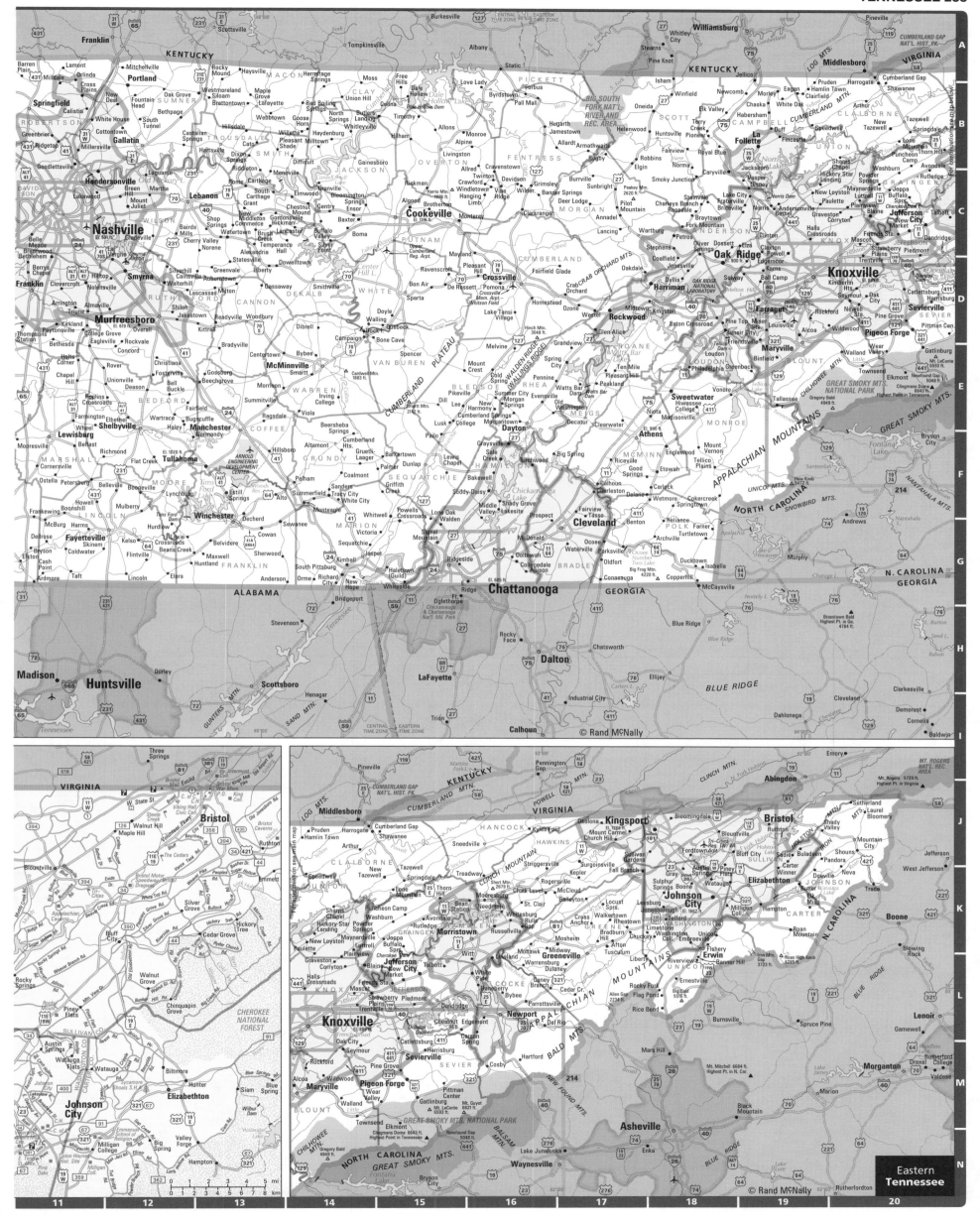

© Rand McNally

Eastern
Tennessee

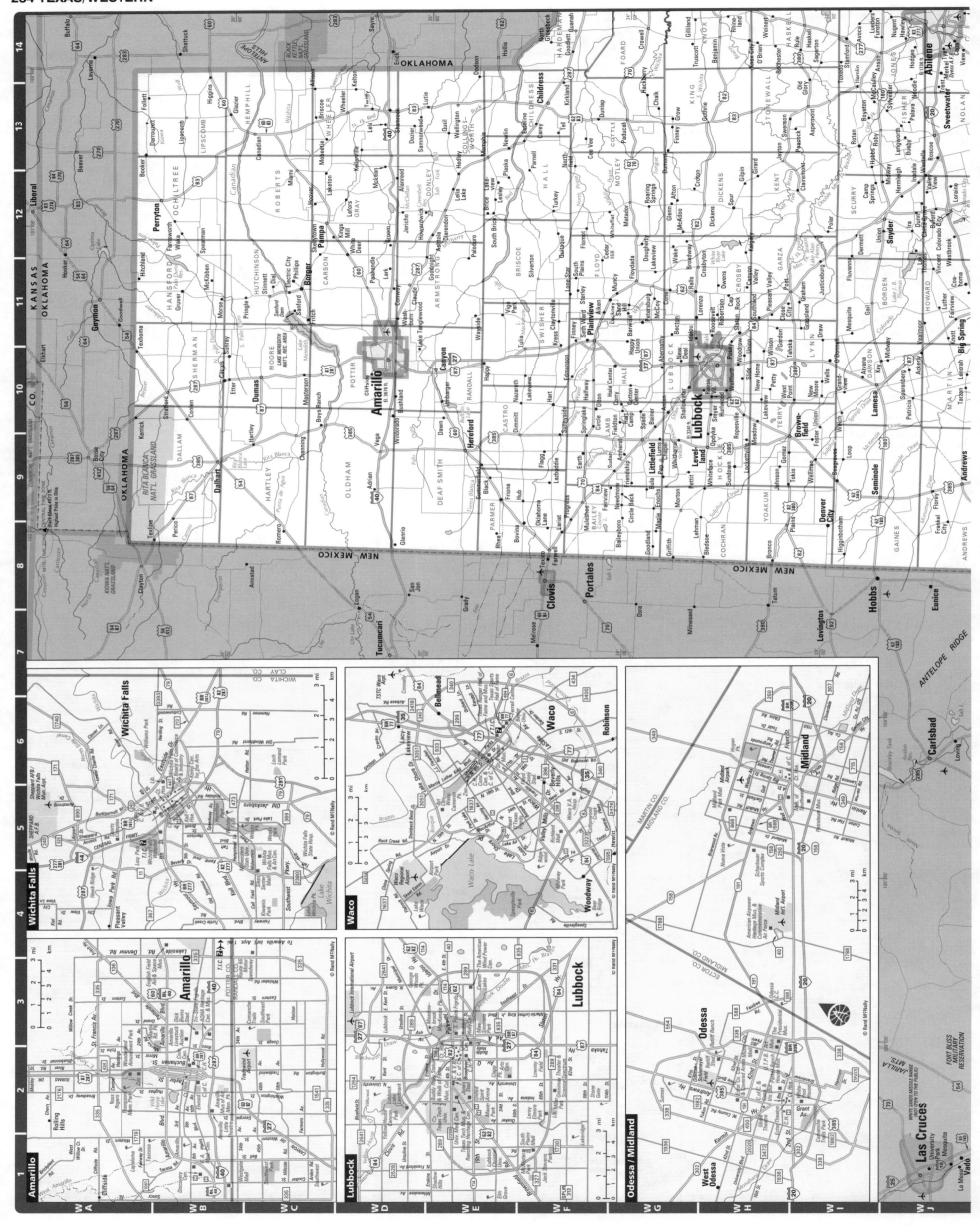

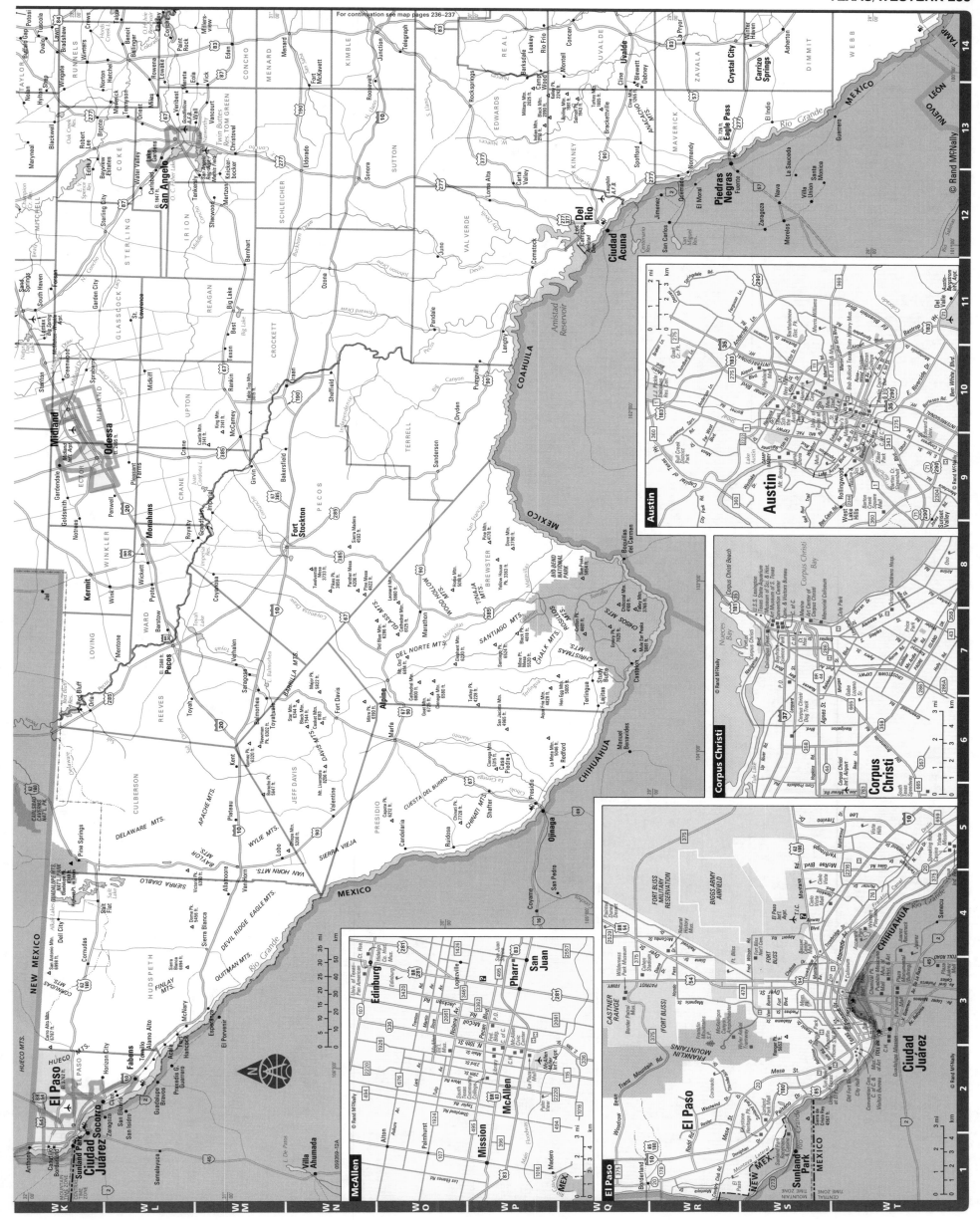

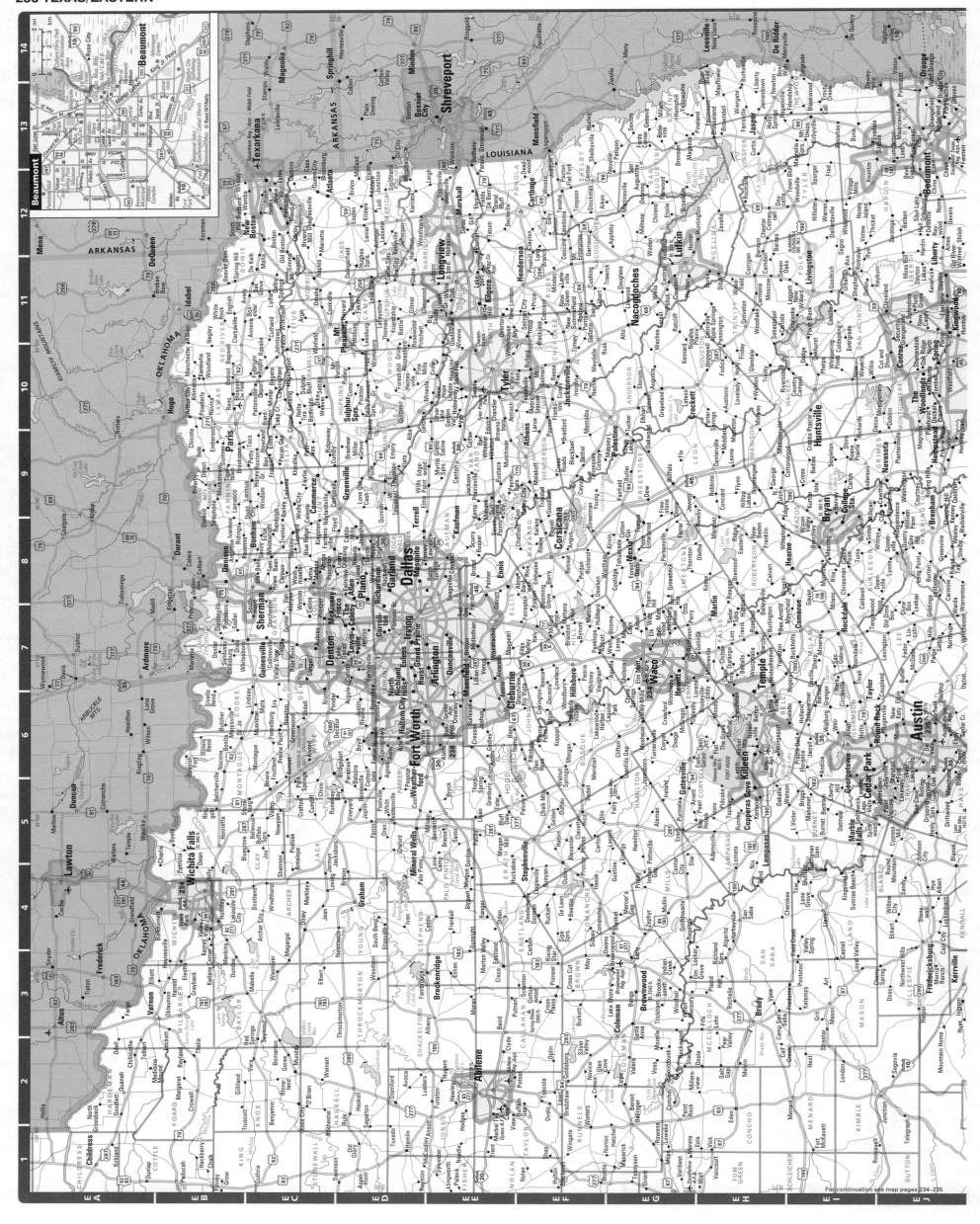

For continuation see map pages 234–235

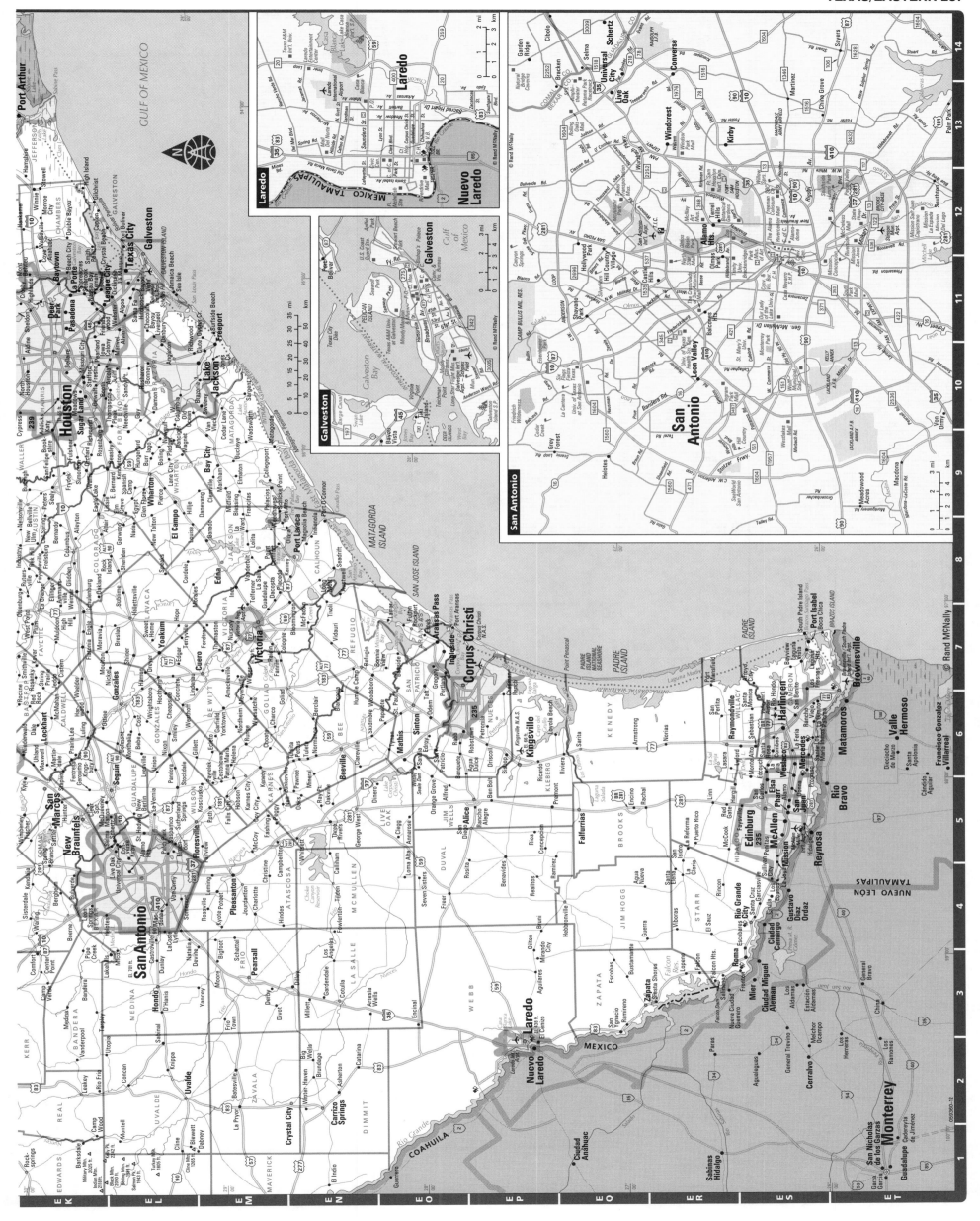

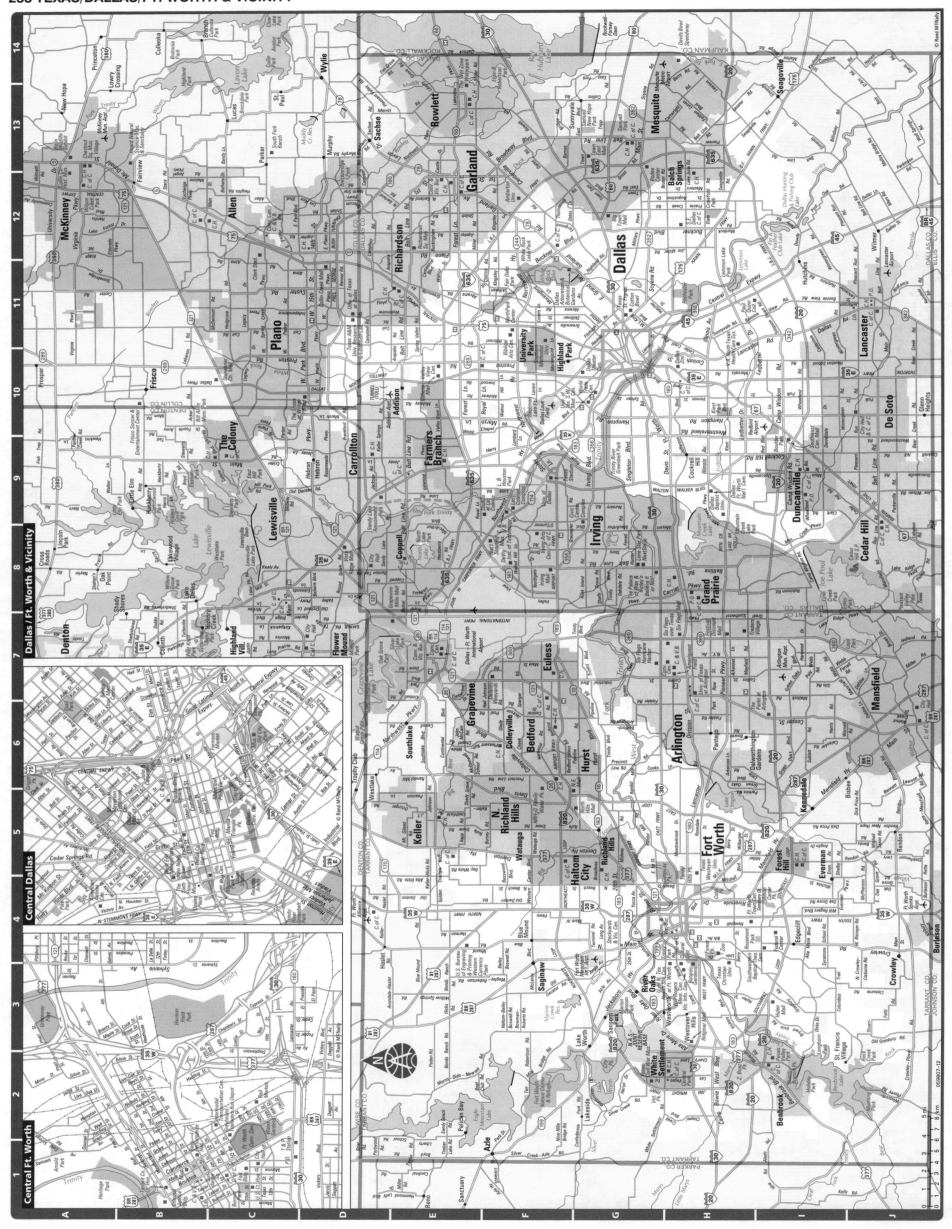

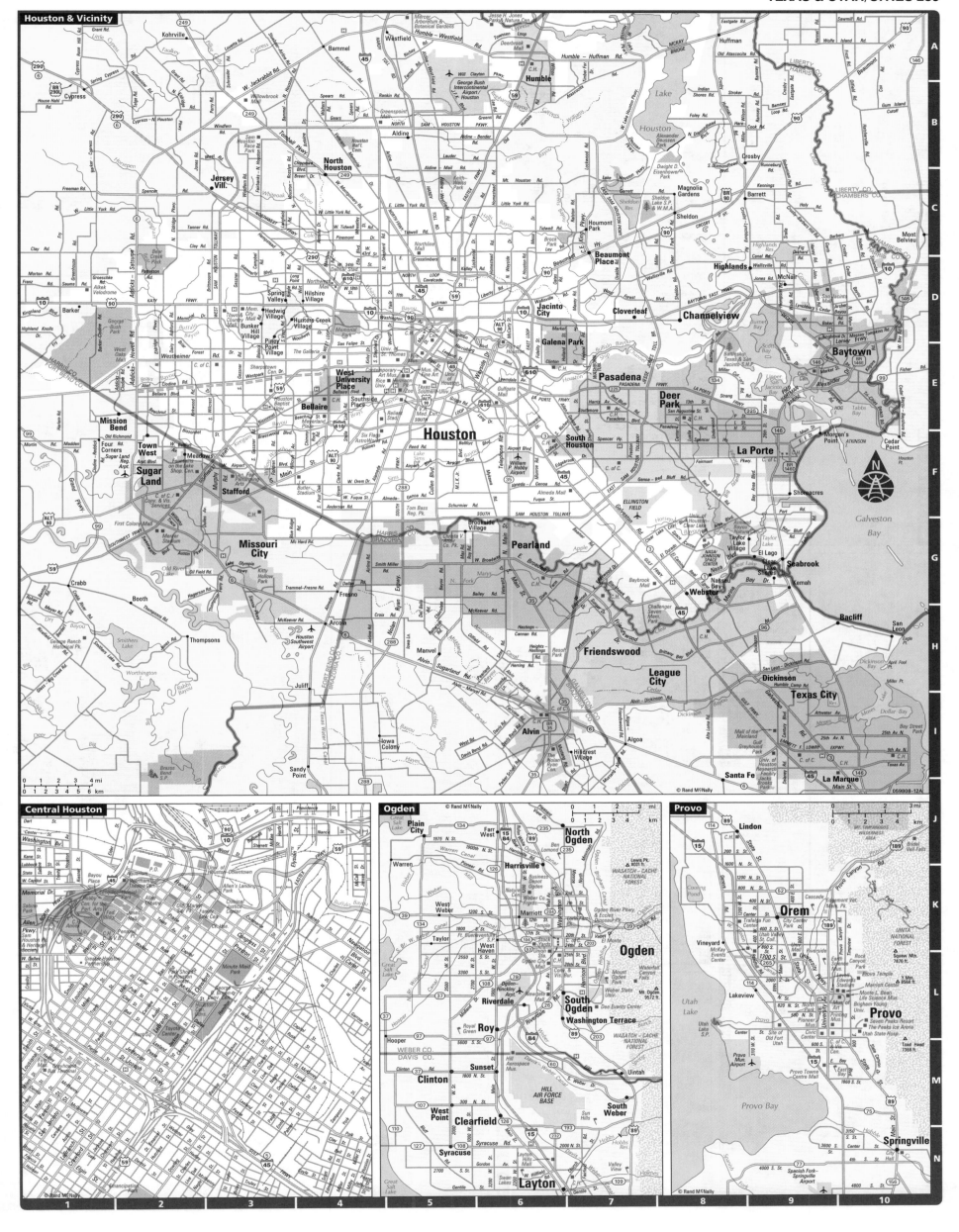

Houston & Vicinity

Central Houston

Ogden

Provo

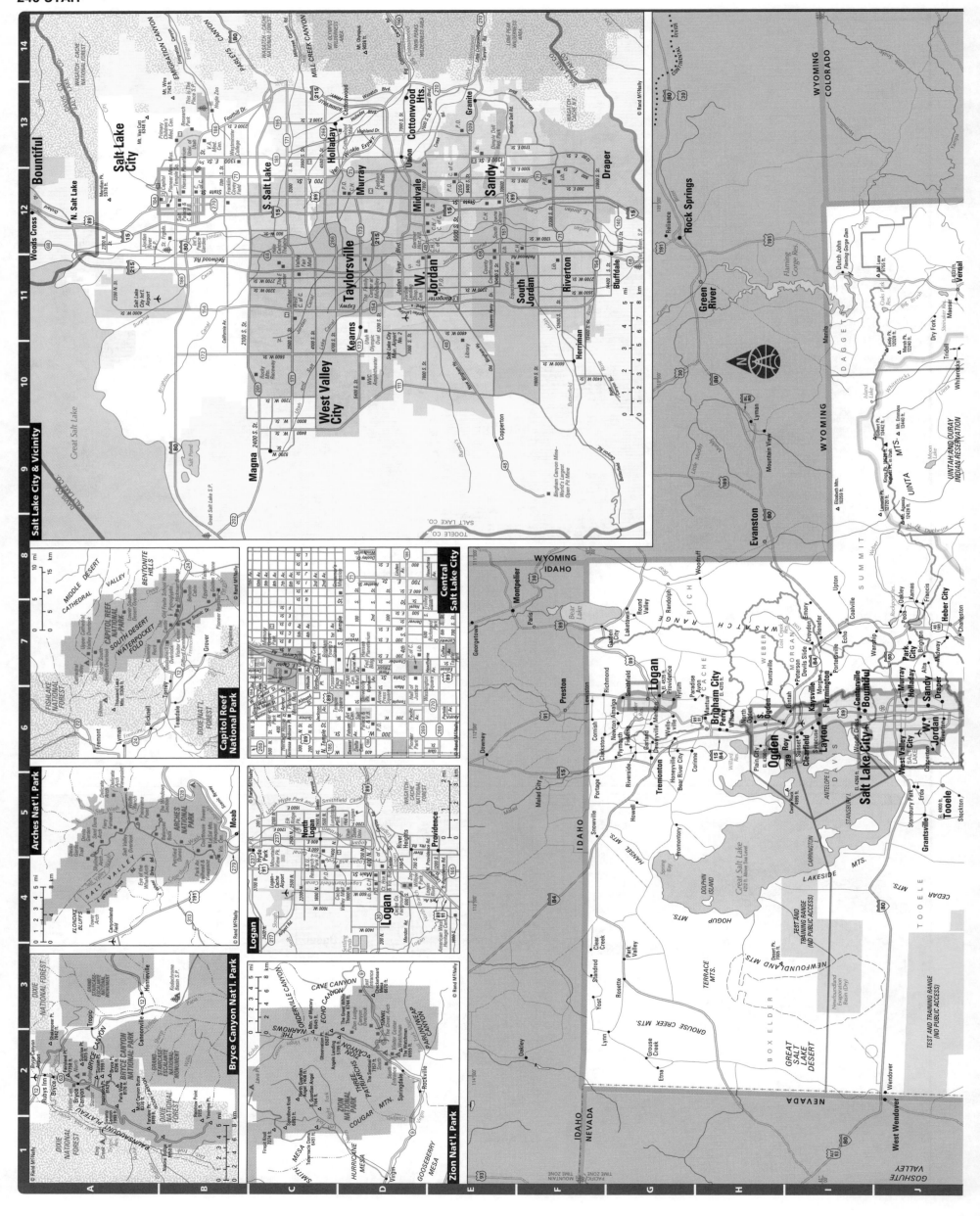

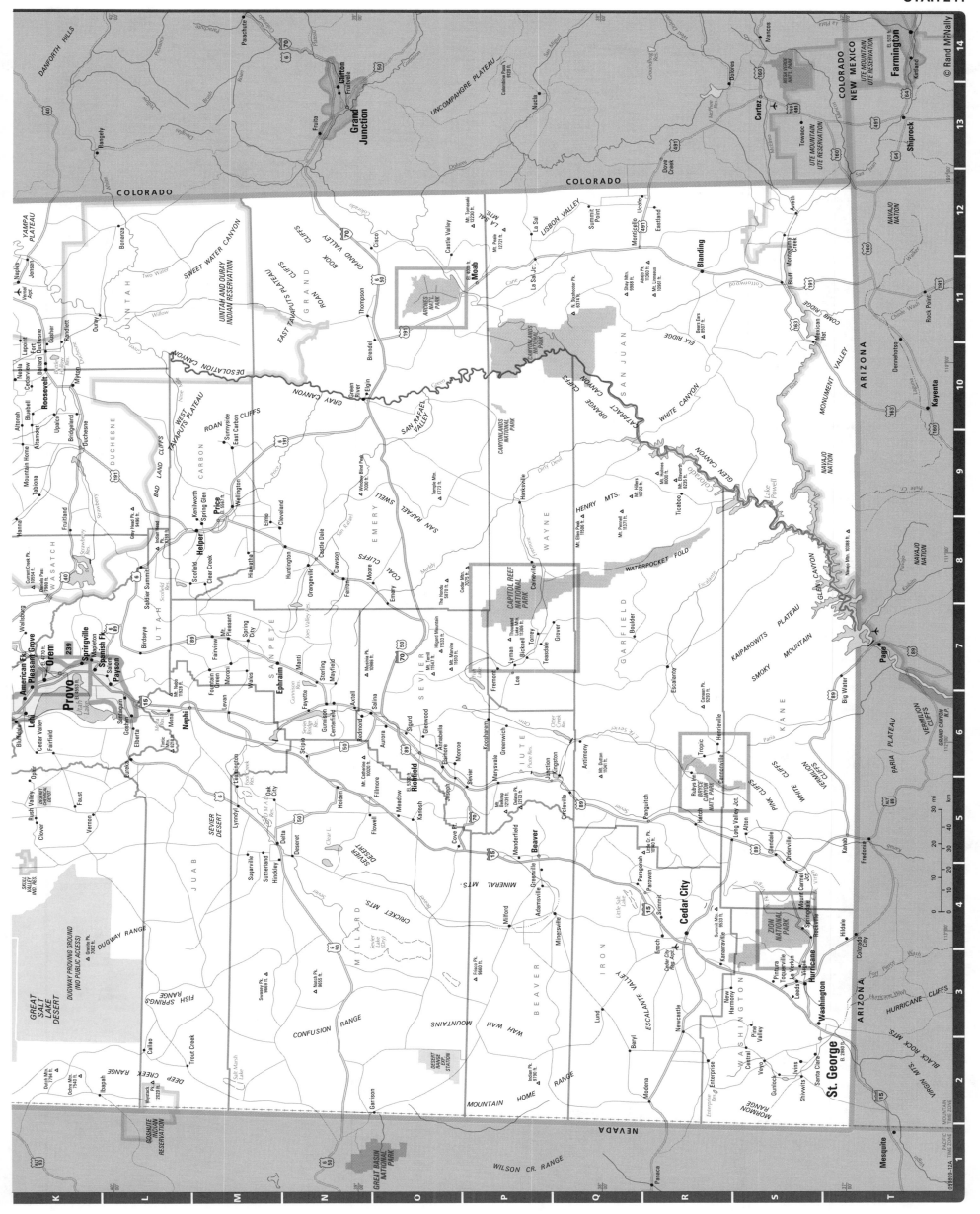

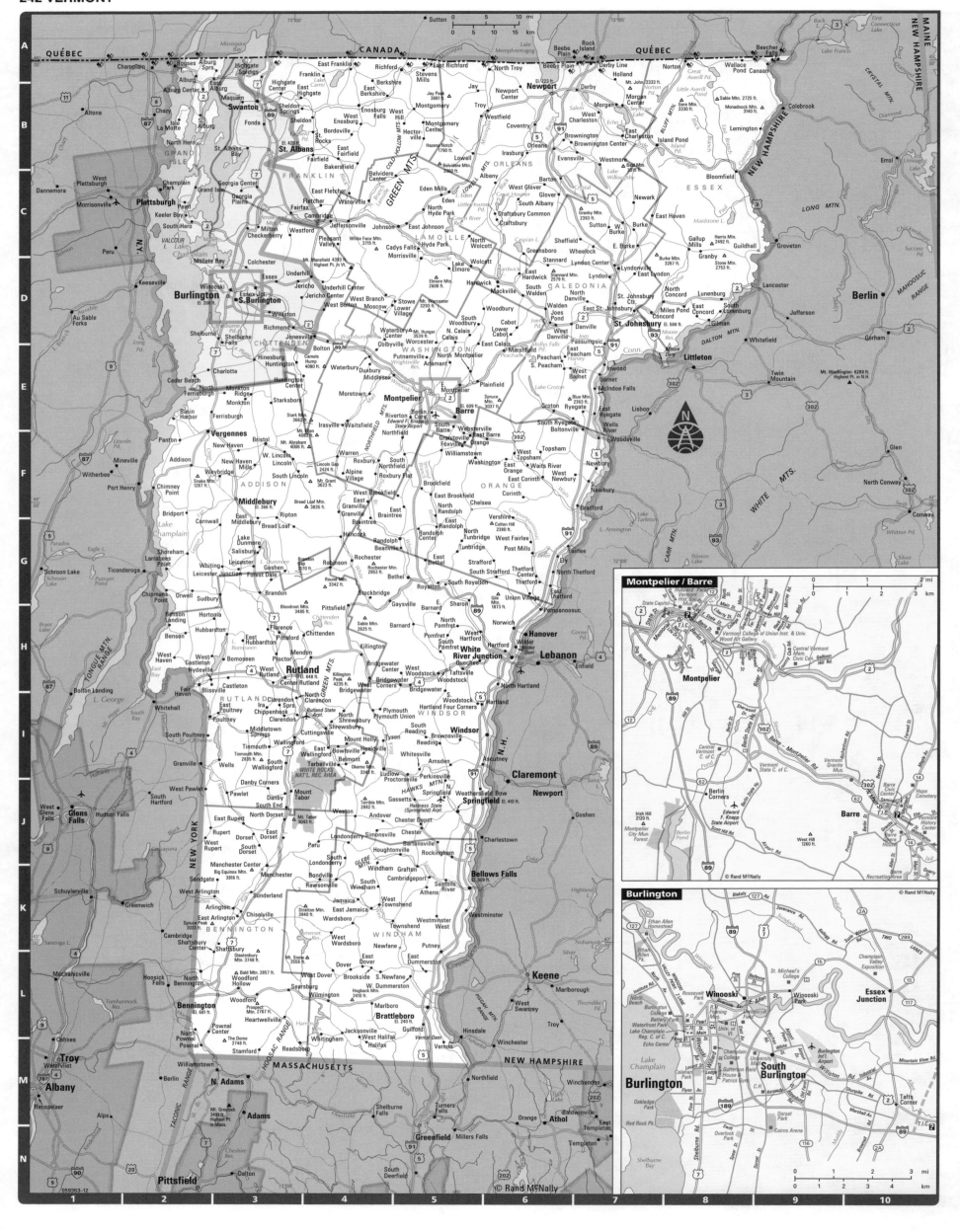

© Rand McNally

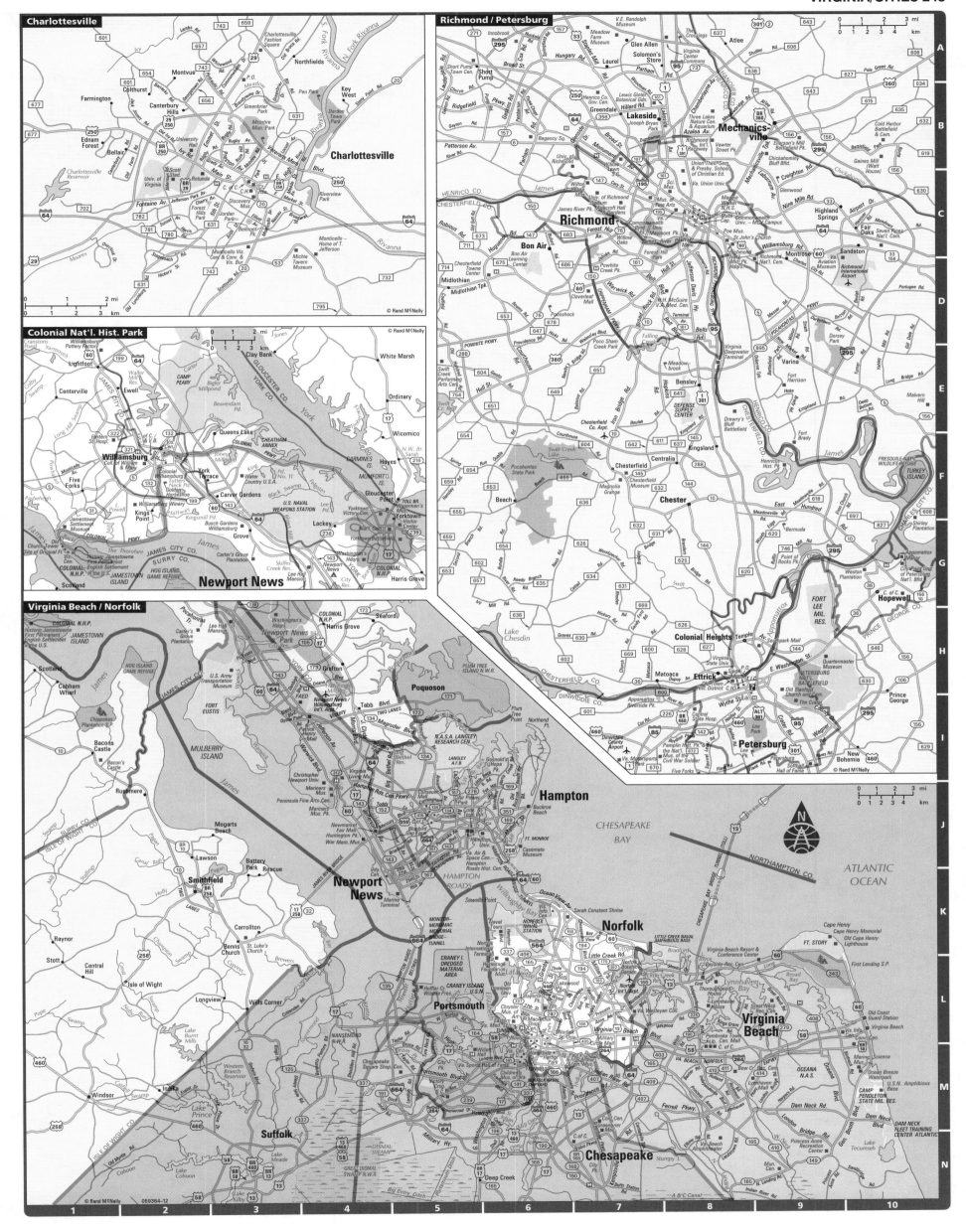

Charlottesville

Richmond / Petersburg

Colonial Nat'l. Hist. Park

Virginia Beach / Norfolk

© Rand McNally

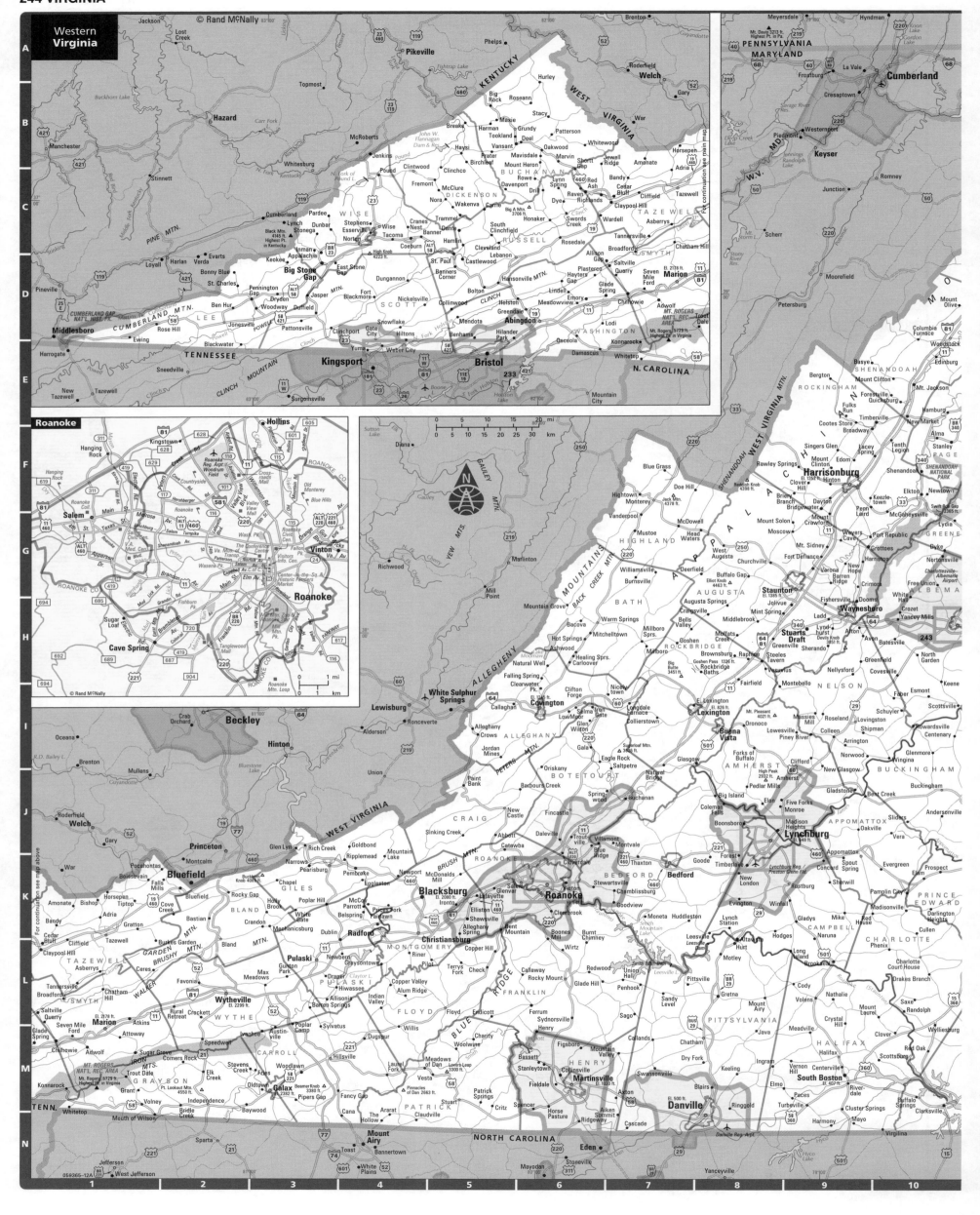

Western
Virginia

© RAND McNALLY

Roanoke

For continuation see main map

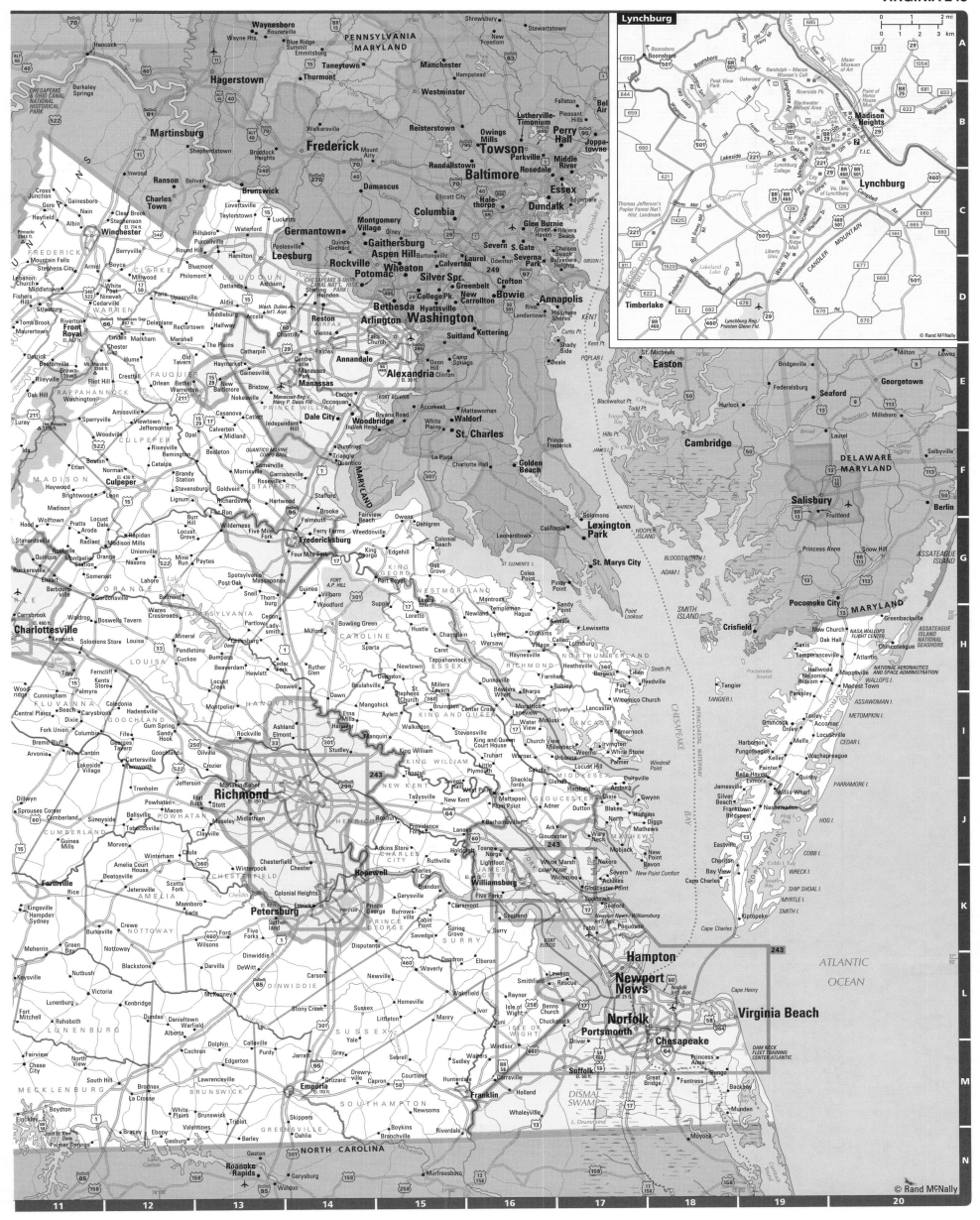

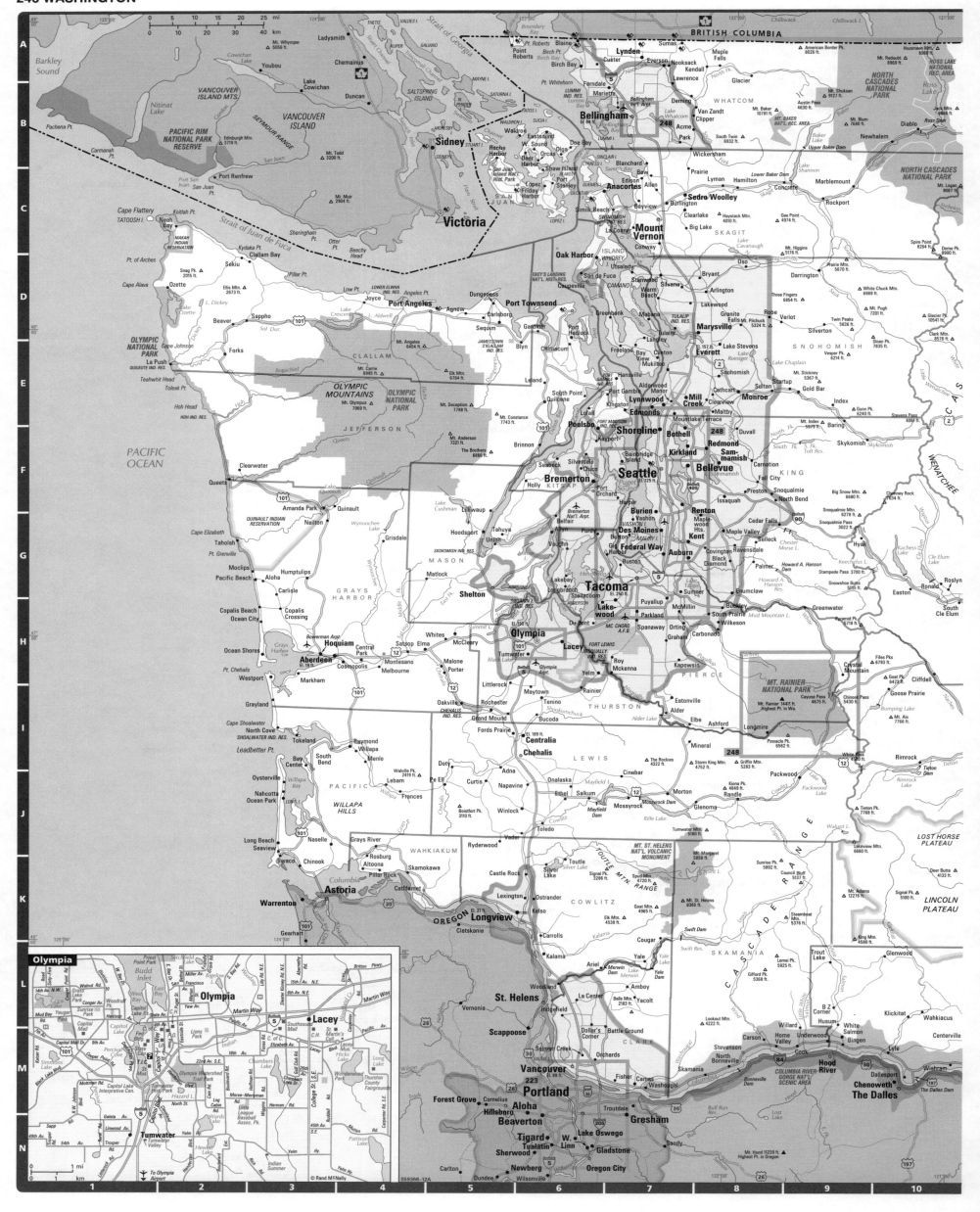

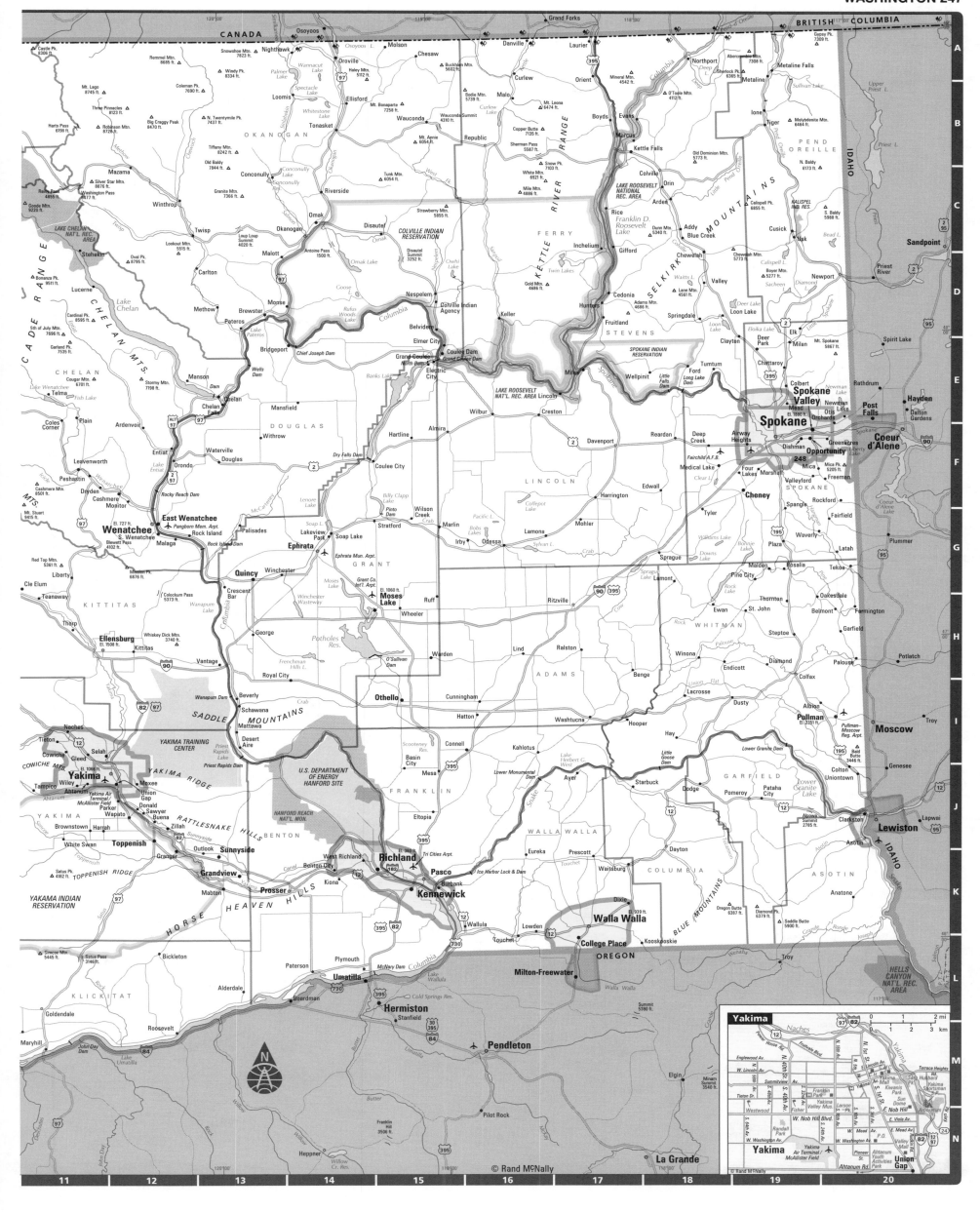

© Rand McNally

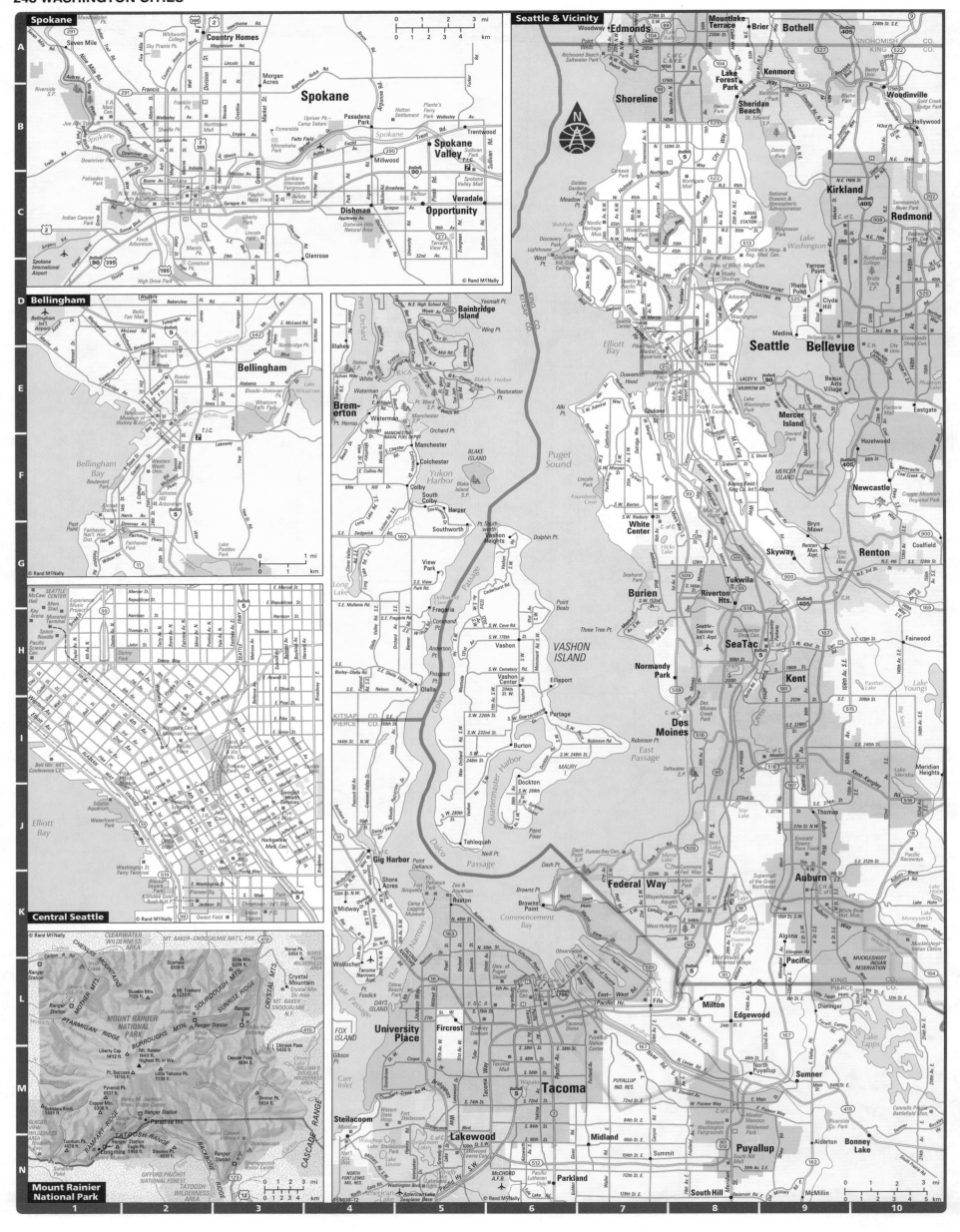

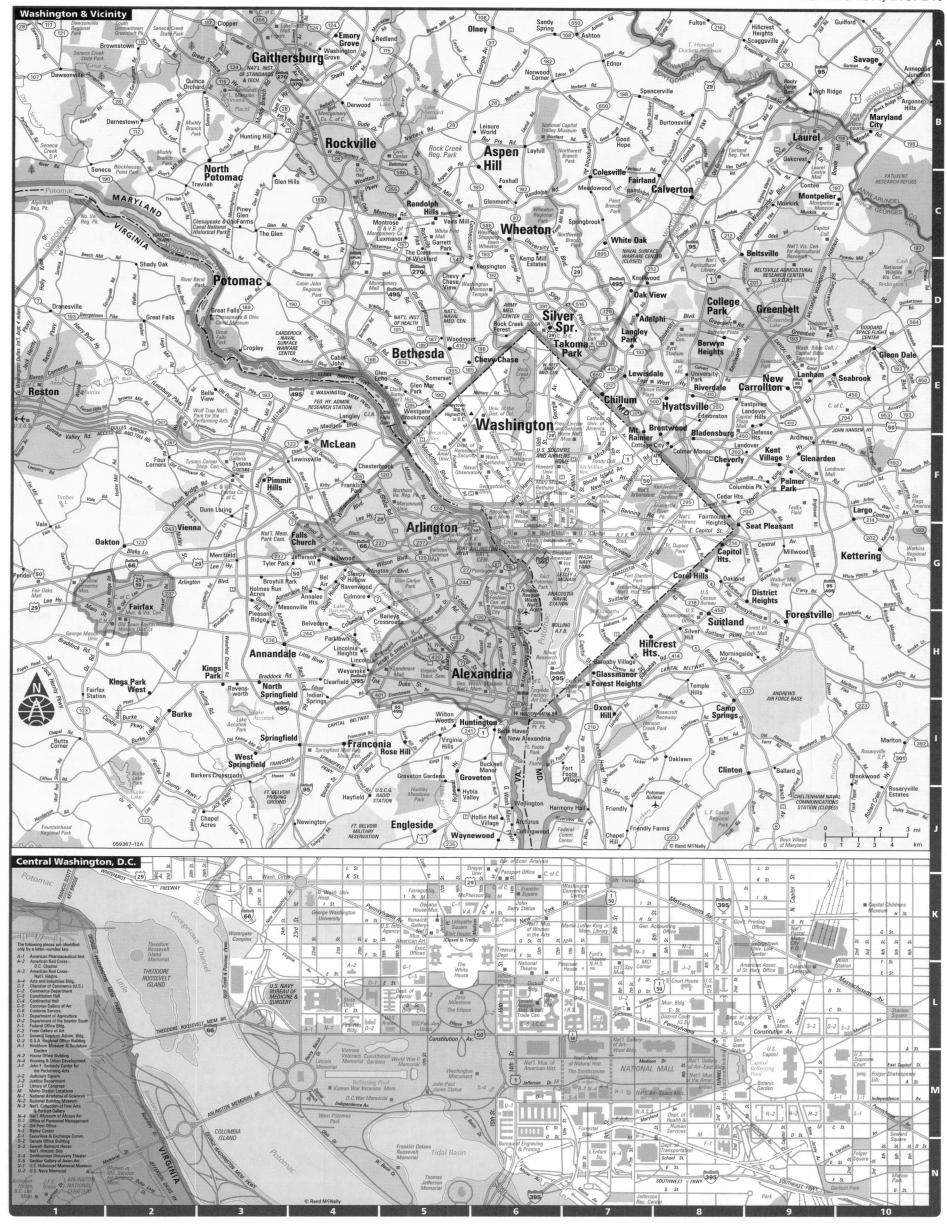

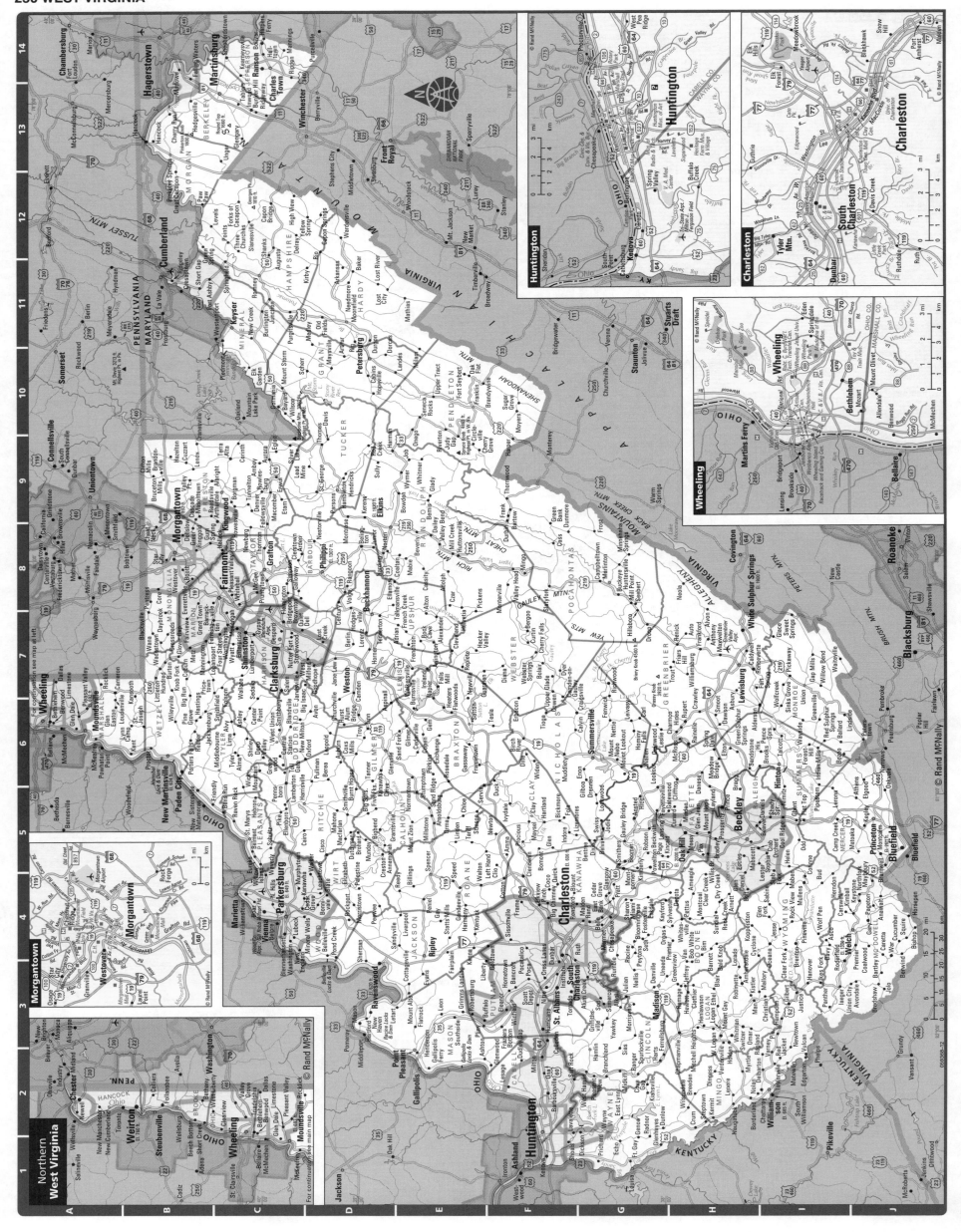

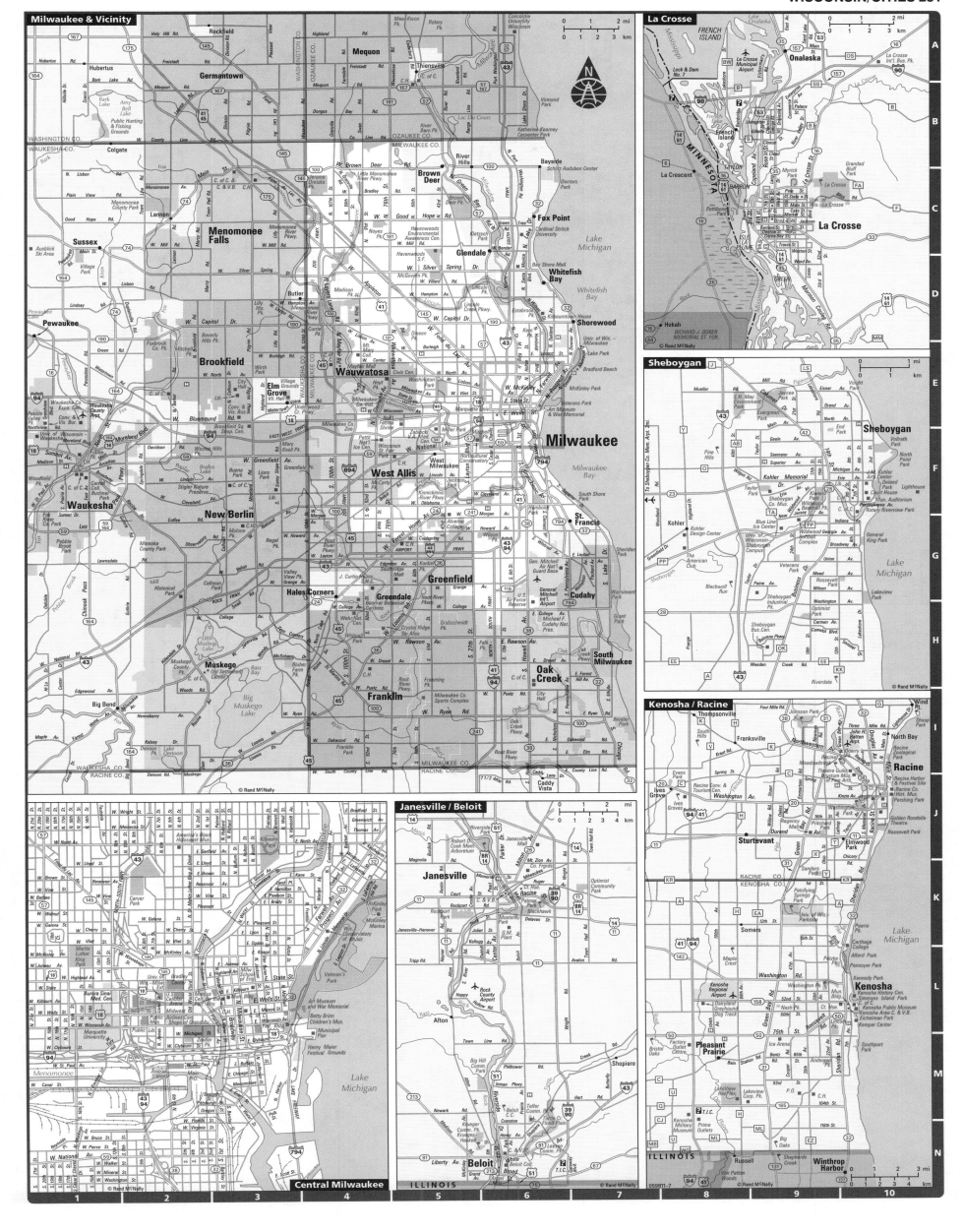

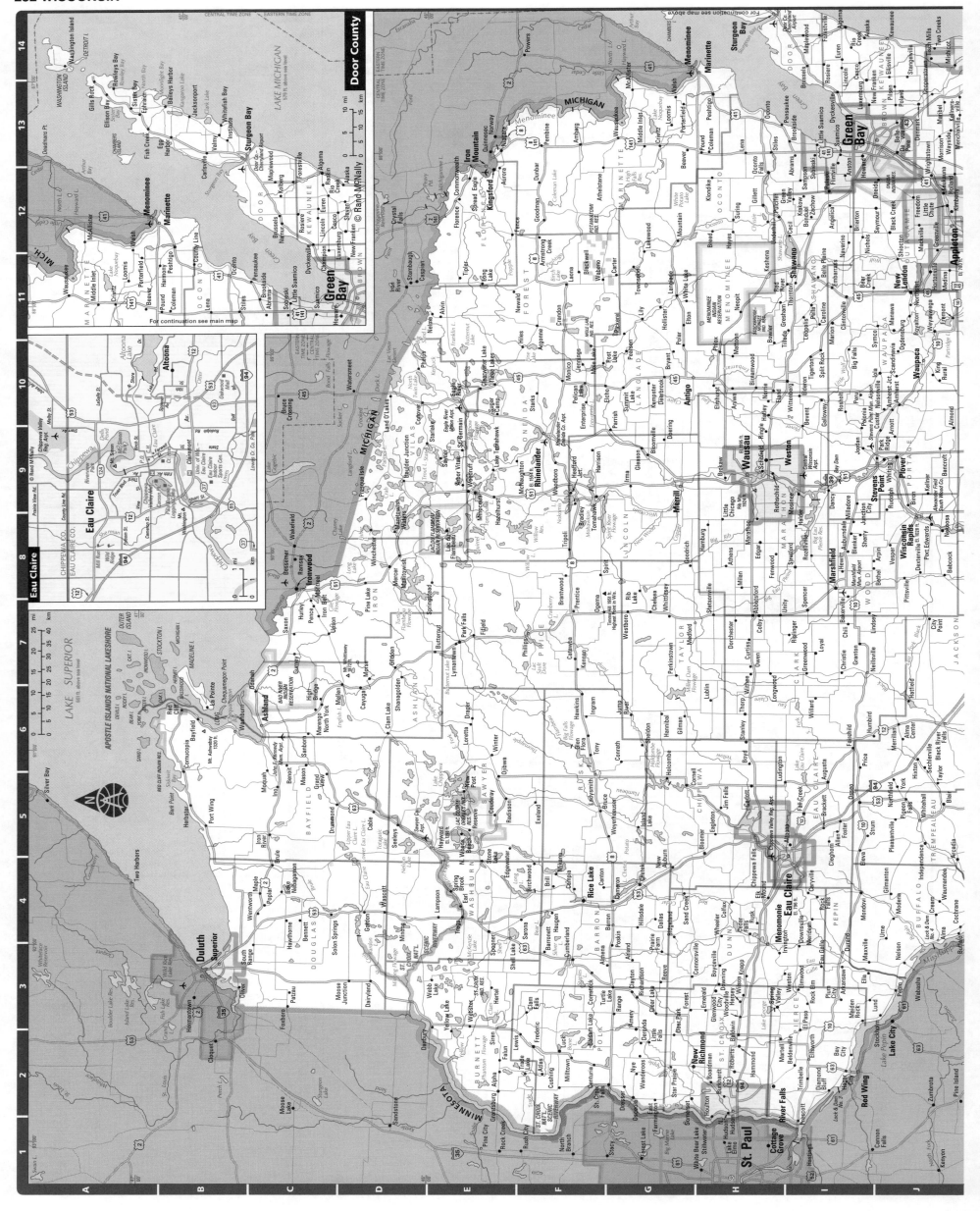

Door County

Eau Claire

APOSTLE ISLANDS NATIONAL LAKESHORE

LAKE SUPERIOR

LAKE MICHIGAN

MICHIGAN

MINNESOTA

Green Bay

Duluth
Superior

Eau Claire

St. Paul

Wausau

Appleton

Marinette
Menominee

© Rand McNally

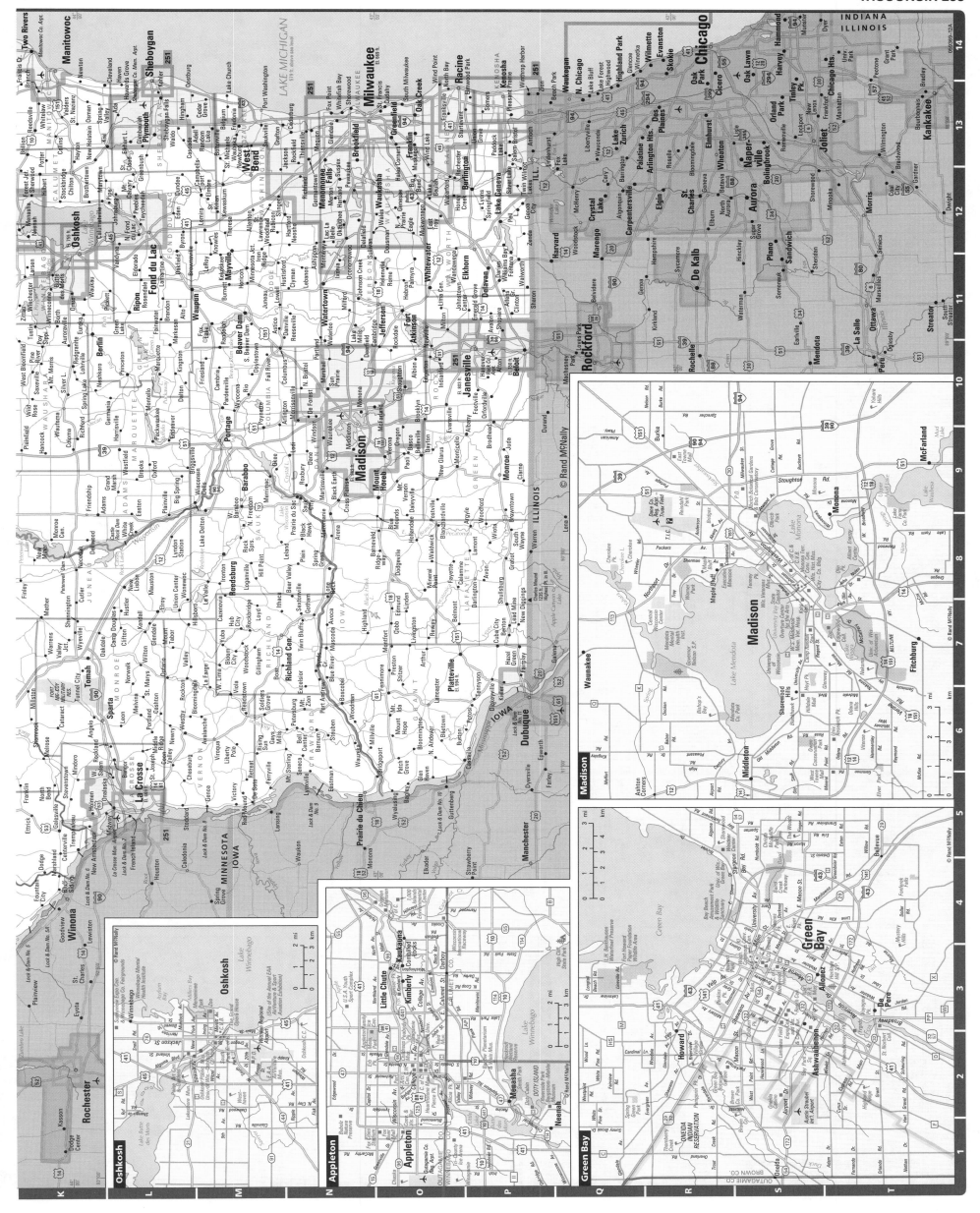

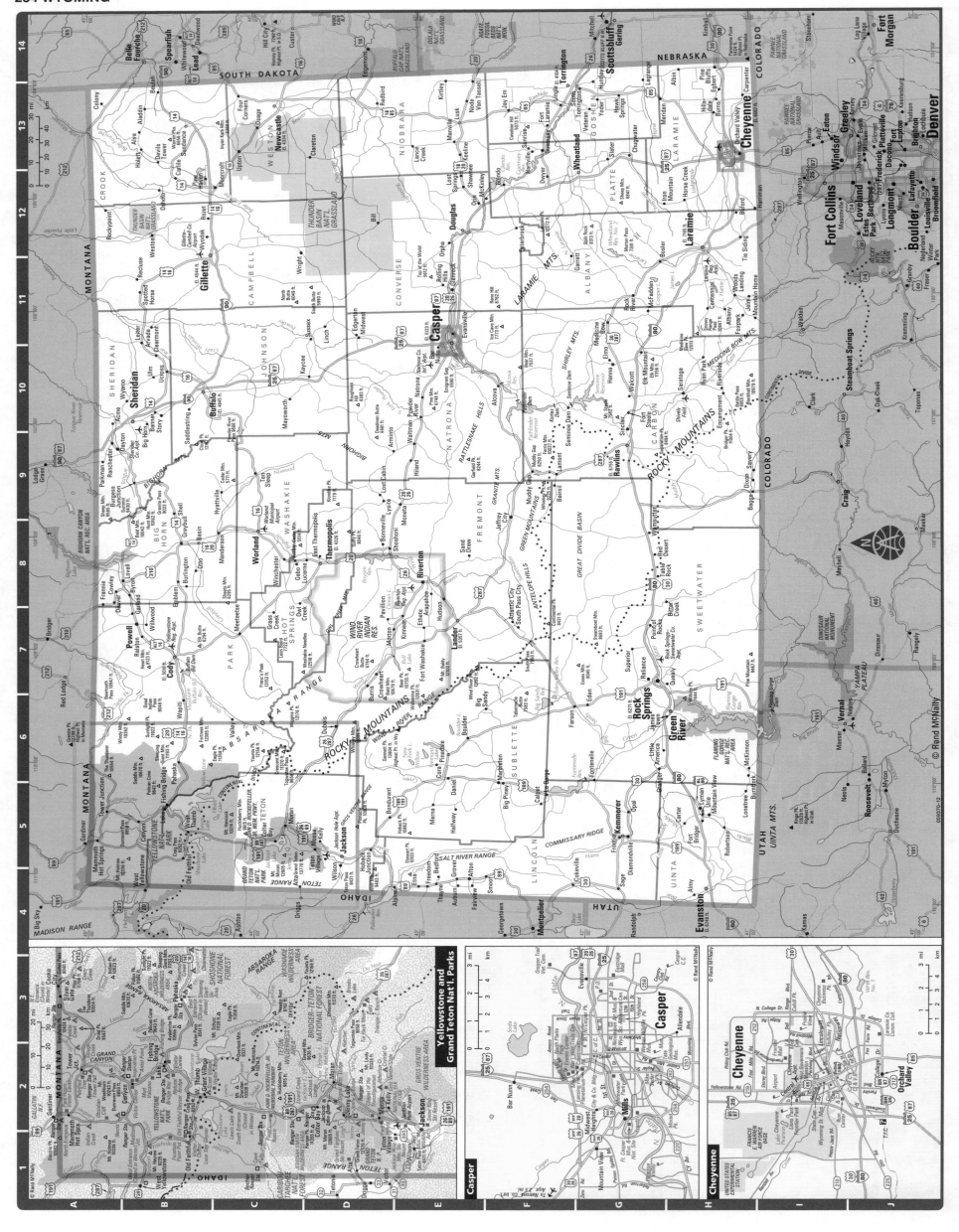

Casper

Cheyenne

Yellowstone and Grand Teton Nat'l. Parks

© Rand McNally

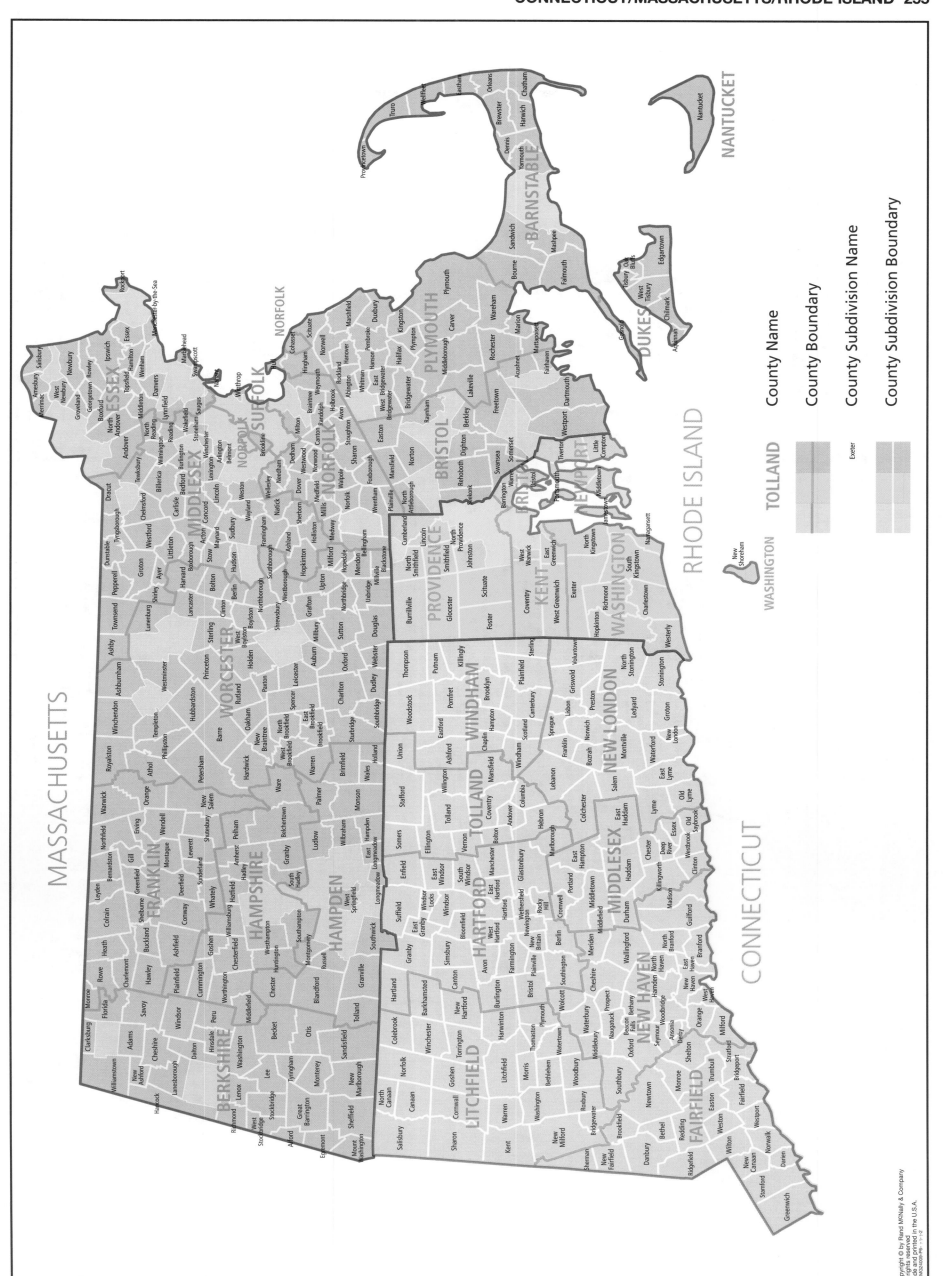

NANTUCKET

BARNSTABLE

DUKES

MASSACHUSETTS

ESSEX

SUFFOLK

NORFOLK

MIDDLESEX

WORCESTER

FRANKLIN

HAMPSHIRE

HAMPDEN

BERKSHIRE

PLYMOUTH

BRISTOL

NEWPORT

BRISTOL

PROVIDENCE

KENT

WASHINGTON

RHODE ISLAND

WINDHAM

TOLLAND

NEW-LONDON

HARTFORD

MIDDLESEX

NEW HAVEN

LITCHFIELD

FAIRFIELD

CONNECTICUT

County Name

County Boundary

County Subdivision Name

County Subdivision Boundary

TOLLAND

Exeter

WASHINGTON

New Shoreham

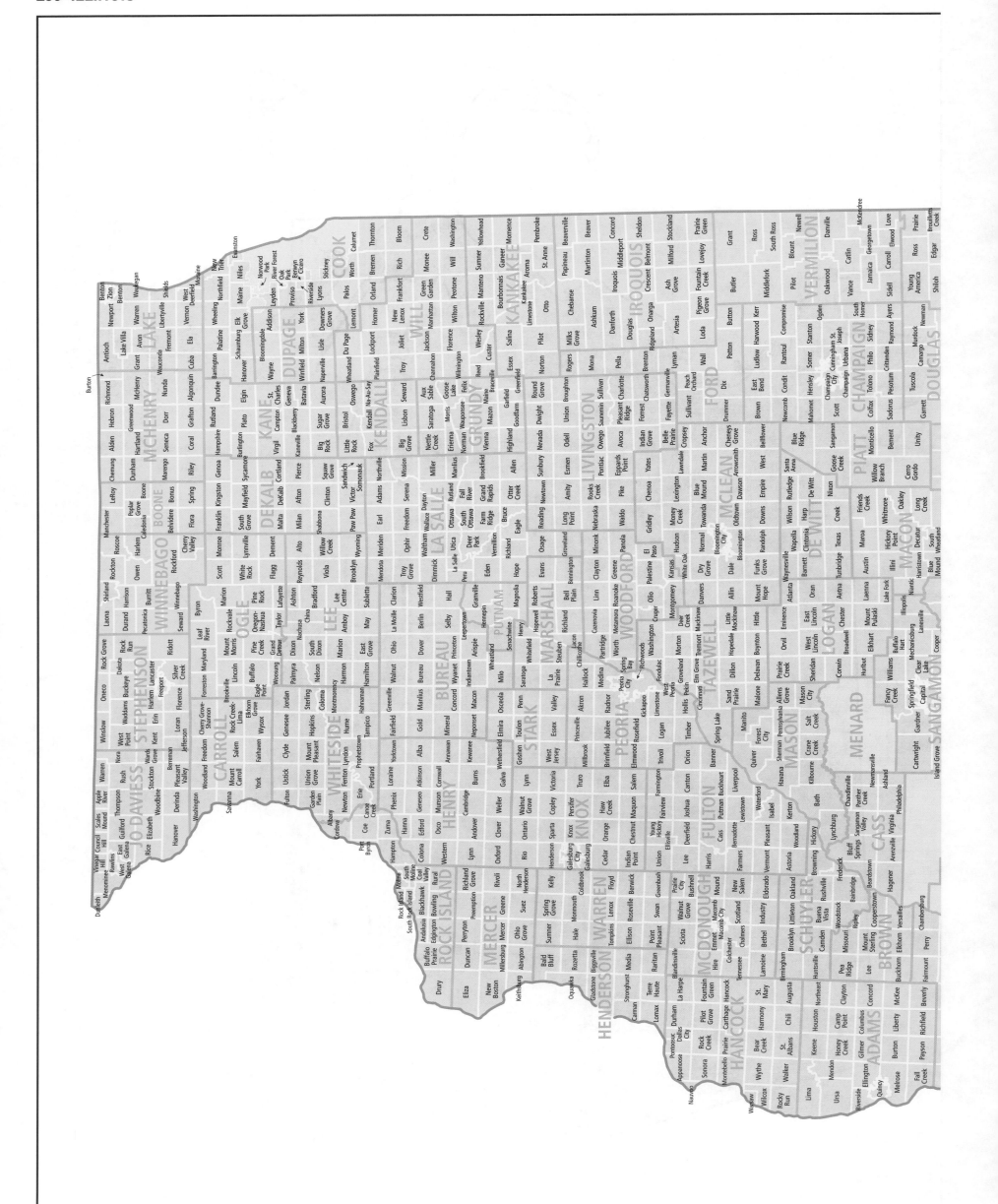

County Name

County Boundary

County Subdivision Name

County Subdivision Boundary

MARION

Oakdale

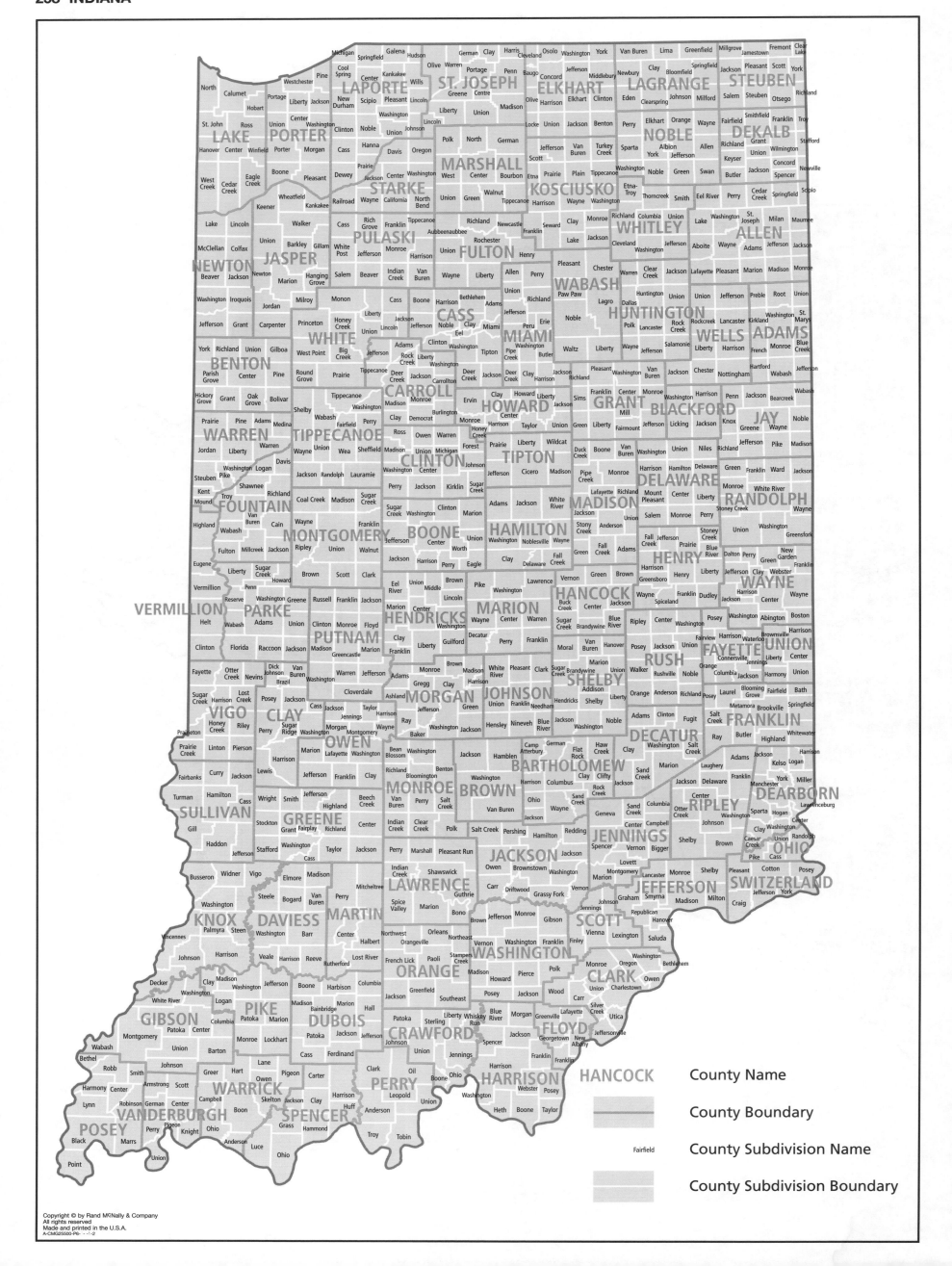

County Name

County Boundary

Fairfield   County Subdivision Name

County Subdivision Boundary

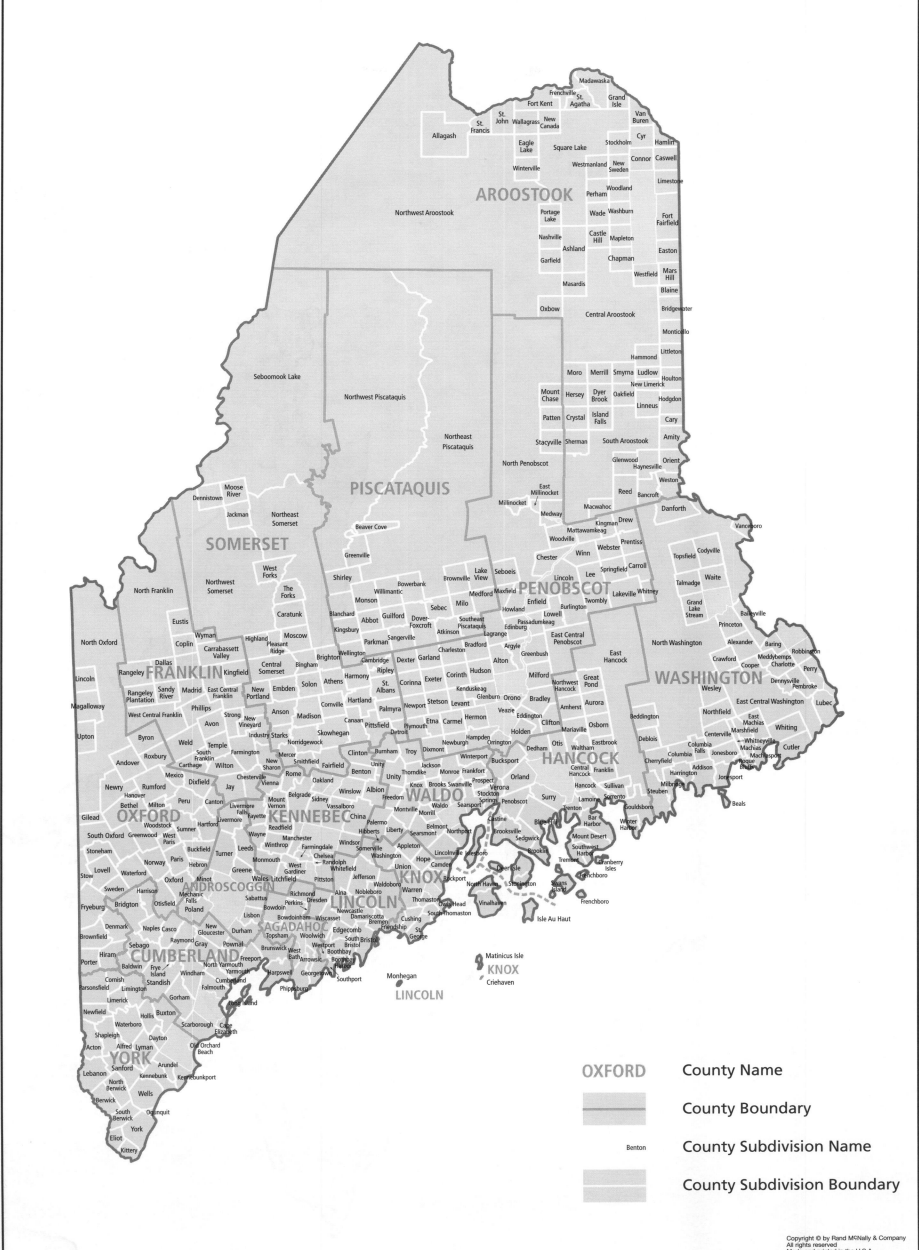

AROOSTOOK

Madawaska
Frenchville
Fort Kent
St. John
Wallagrass
New
Canada
St.
Agatha
Grand
Isle
Van
Buren

Allagash
St.
Francis

Eagle
Lake
Square Lake
Stockholm
Cyr
Hamlin

Winterville
Westmanland
New
Sweden
Connor
Caswell

Portage
Lake
Woodland
Perham
Wade
Washburn
Limestone

Nashville
Castle
Hill
Mapleton
Fort
Fairfield

Garfield
Ashland
Chapman
Easton

Masardis
Westfield
Mars
Hill
Blaine

Oxbow
Central Aroostook
Bridgewater

Monticello

Hammond
Littleton

Moro
Merrill
Smyrna
Ludlow
Houlton

Mount
Chase
Hersey
Dyer
Brook
Oakfield
New Limerick
Hodgdon

Patten
Crystal
Island
Falls
Linneus
Cary

Stacyville
Sherman
South Aroostook
Amity

North Penobscot
Glenwood
Haynesville
Orient

East
Millinocket
Macwahoc
Reed
Bancroft
Weston

Millinocket
Medway
Danforth

Northwest Aroostook

Seboomook Lake

Northwest Piscataquis

Northeast
Piscataquis

PISCATAQUIS

Kingman
Drew
Vanceboro

Mattawamkeag
Dennistown
Moose
River
Chester
Woodville
Prentiss

Jackman
Northeast
Somerset
Winn
Webster
Carroll

Beaver Cove
Lincoln
Lee
Springfield
Topsfield
Codyville

Greenville
Lakeville
Whitney
Talmadge
Waite

SOMERSET
Shirley
Lake
View
Seboeis

West
Forks
Bowerbank
Brownville
Medford
Maxfield
Enfield
Burlington
Twombly
Grand
Lake
Stream
Baileyville

The
Forks
Monson
Willimantic
Howland
Passadumkeag
Lowell

North Franklin
Caratunk
Blanchard
Sebec
Milo
Lagrange
East Central
Penobscot
Princeton
Alexander

Northwest
Somerset
Abbot
Guilford
Dover-
Foxcroft
Southeast
Piscataquis
Edinburg
Crawford
Meddybemps
Charlotte
Robbinston
Perry

Eustis
Moscow
Kingsbury
Sangerville
Atkinson
Argyle
Greenbush
North Washington
Cooper
Dennysville
Pembroke

Coplin
Wyman
Highland
Pleasant
Ridge
Brighton
Wellington
Cambridge
Parkman
Charleston
Bradford
Alton
Milford
Northwest
Hancock
Great
Pond
WASHINGTON
Wesley
East Central Washington
Lubec

North Oxford
Carrabassett
Valley
Kingfield
Central
Somerset
Bingham
Dexter
Garland
Corinth
Hudson
Bradley
Orono
Aurora
Northfield

Rangeley
Dallas
Madrid
East Central
Franklin
New
Portland
Solon
Athens
Ripley
Corinna
Exeter
Kenduskeag
Veazie
Amherst
Osborn
Beddington
East
Machias
Whiting

Lincoln
FRANKLIN
Embden
Harmony
St.
Albans
Stetson
Levant
Glenburn
Clifton
Mariaville
Centerville
Marshfield
Cutler

Magalloway
Rangeley
Plantation
Sandy
River
Phillips
Strong
New
Vineyard
Anson
Madison
Cornville
Palmyra
Newport
Etna
Carmel
Hermon
Eddington
Holden
Otis
Waltham
Eastbrook
Columbia
Falls
Jonesboro
Machiasport

West Central Franklin
Avon
Industry
Starks
Norridgewock
Skowhegan
Plymouth
Detroit
Dixmont
Newburgh
Hampden
Orrington
Dedham
Central
Hancock
Franklin
Cherryfield
Columbia
Addison
Rogue
Bluffs

Upton
Byron
Weld
Temple
Farmington
Mercer
Smithfield
Fairfield
Canaan
Pittsfield
Burnham
Troy
Jackson
Monroe
Winterport
Prospect
Bucksport
Orland
Hancock
Sullivan
Sorrento
Harrington
Steuben
Milbridge
Beals

Newry
Hanover
Roxbury
South
Franklin
Carthage
Dixfield
Jay
Wilton
Chesterville
Vienna
Rome
Oakland
Winslow
Albion
Knox
Brooks
Swanville
Searsport
Penobscot
Verona
Surry
Lamoine
Gouldsboro

Gilead
Bethel
Mexico
Peru
Canton
Livermore
Falls
Mount
Vernon
Belgrade
Sidney
Vassalboro
China
Unity
Thorndike
Montville
Morrill
Waldo
Stockton
Springs
Castine
Blue Hill
Trenton
Mount Desert
Winter
Harbor

OXFORD
Woodstock
Sumner
Hartford
Livermore
Fayette
Manchester
WALDO
Searsmont
Belmont
Northport
Brooksville
Sedgwick
Bar
Harbor

South Oxford
Greenwood
West
Paris
Buckfield
Turner
Leeds
Wayne
Winthrop
Farmingdale
Windsor
Somerville
Washington
Appleton
Hope
Lincolnville
Islesboro
Brooklin
Southwest
Harbor
Cranberry
Isles

Stoneham
Norway
Paris
Hebron
Greene
Monmouth
West
Gardiner
Chelsea
Randolph
Union
Camden
Deer
Isle
Tremont
Frenchboro

Lovell
Waterford
Oxford
Minot
Wales
Litchfield
Pittston
Jefferson
Waldoboro
KNOX
Rockport
North Haven
Stonington
Swans
Island
Frenchboro

Stow
Harrison
Mechanic
Falls
ANDROSCOGGIN
Sabattus
Richmond
Dresden
Newcastle
Alna
Nobleboro
Warren
Rockland
Owls
Head
Vinalhaven
Isle Au Haut

Fryeburg
Bridgton
Otisfield
Poland
Lisbon
Bowdoin
Bowdoinham
Wiscasset
Damariscotta
Jefferson
Thomaston
Cushing

Denmark
Naples
Casco
New
Gloucester
Durham
LINCOLN
Topsham
Woolwich
Edgecomb
Bremen
Friendship
St.
George
South Thomaston

Brownfield
Sebago
Raymond
Gray
Pownal
SAGADAHOC
Brunswick
West
Bath
Westport
South
Bristol
Bristol
Boothbay

Hiram
Baldwin
Frye
Island
North Yarmouth
Freeport
Harpswell
Arrowsic
Georgetown
Boothbay
Harbor

Porter
Cornish
Limington
Standish
Windham
Cumberland
Falmouth
CUMBERLAND
Southport
Matinicus Isle
KNOX

Parsonsfield
Limerick
Gorham
Chebeague Island
Phippsburg
Monhegan
Criehaven
LINCOLN

Newfield
Waterboro
Hollis
Buxton

Shapleigh
Dayton
Scarborough
Cape
Elizabeth
Old Orchard
Beach

Acton
Alfred
Lyman
Arundel

Lebanon
Sanford
YORK
Kennebunk
Kennebunkport

North
Berwick
Wells

Berwick
Ogunquit

South
Berwick
York

Eliot
Kittery

KENNEBEC
Gardiner
Pittston

HANCOCK

PENOBSCOT

OXFORD | County Name

County Boundary

Benton | County Subdivision Name

County Subdivision Boundary

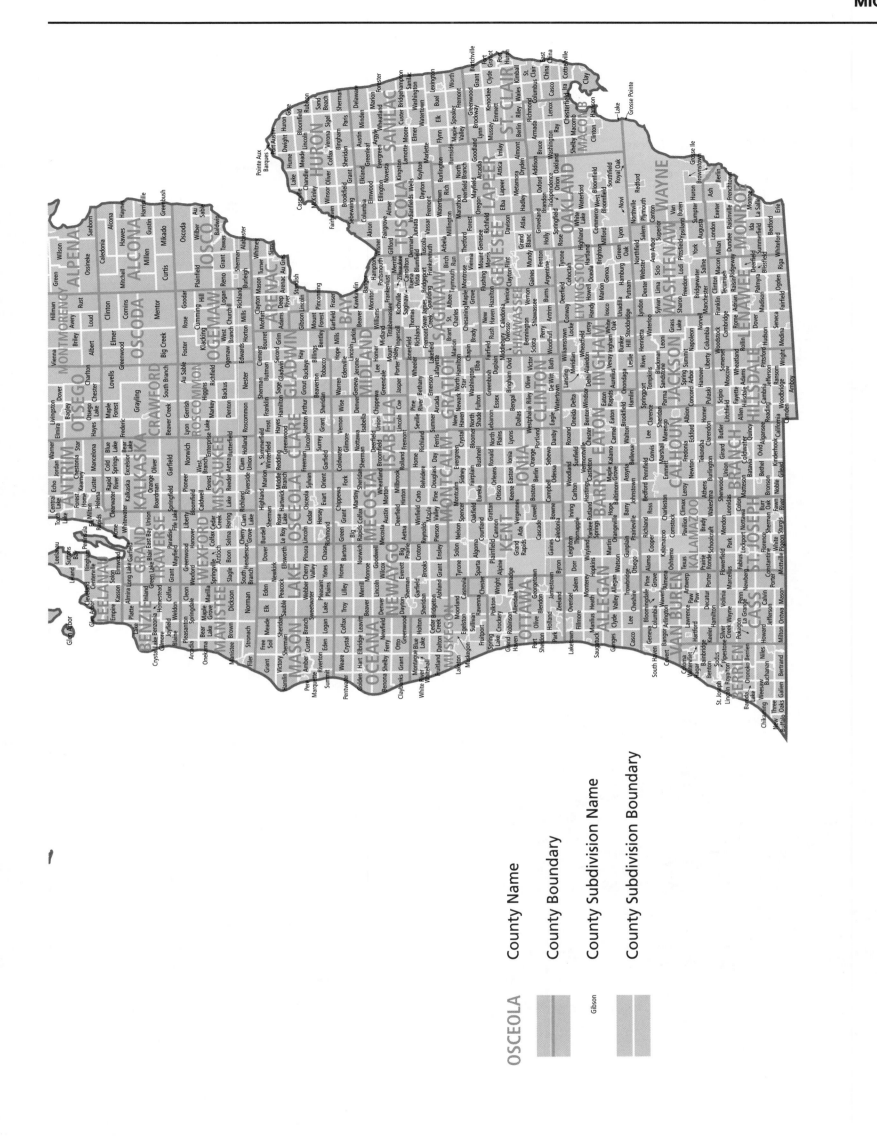

County Name   OSCEOLA

County Boundary

County Subdivision Name   Gibson

County Subdivision Boundary

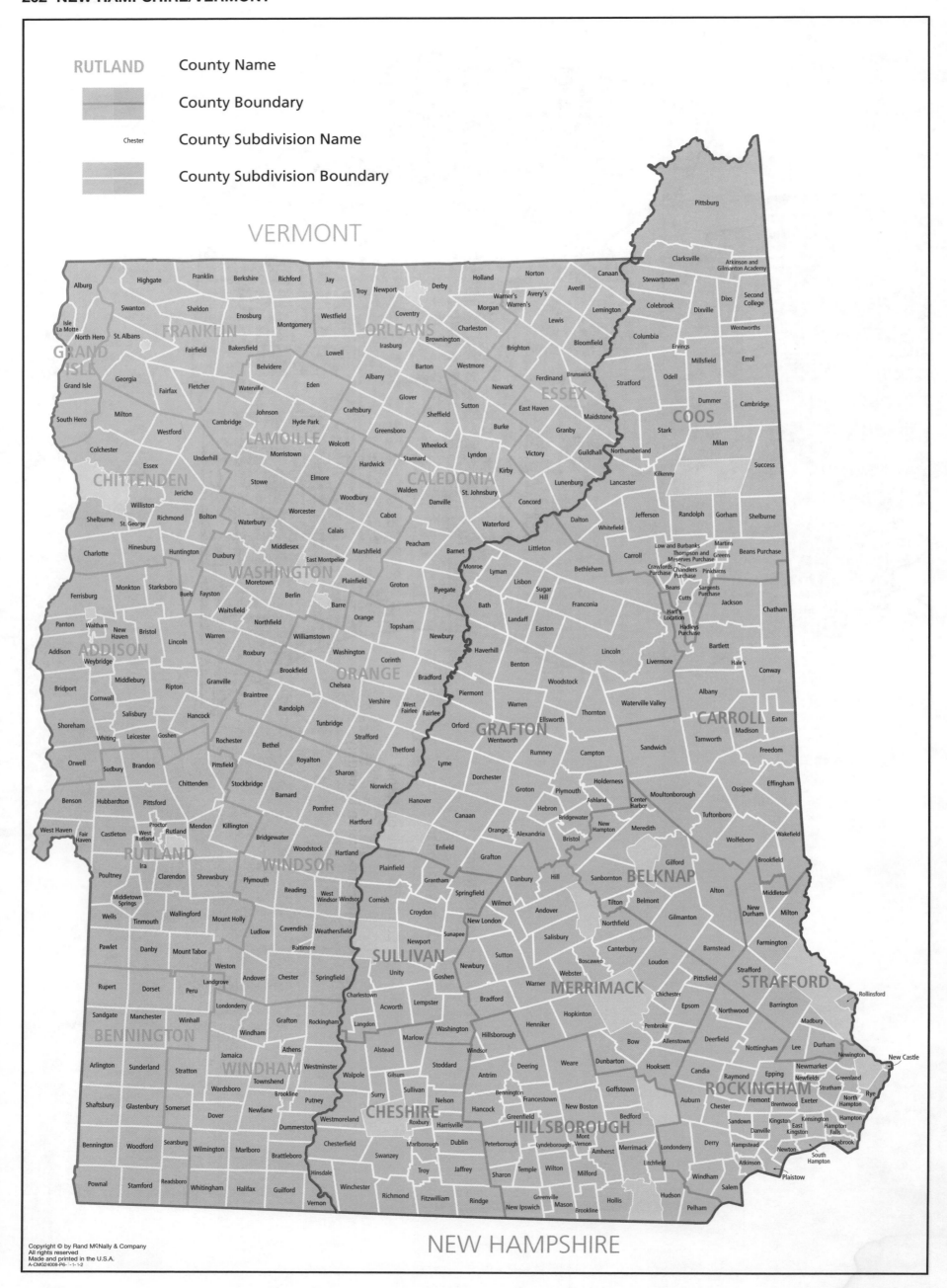

RUTLAND — County Name

County Boundary

Chester — County Subdivision Name

County Subdivision Boundary

VERMONT

NEW HAMPSHIRE

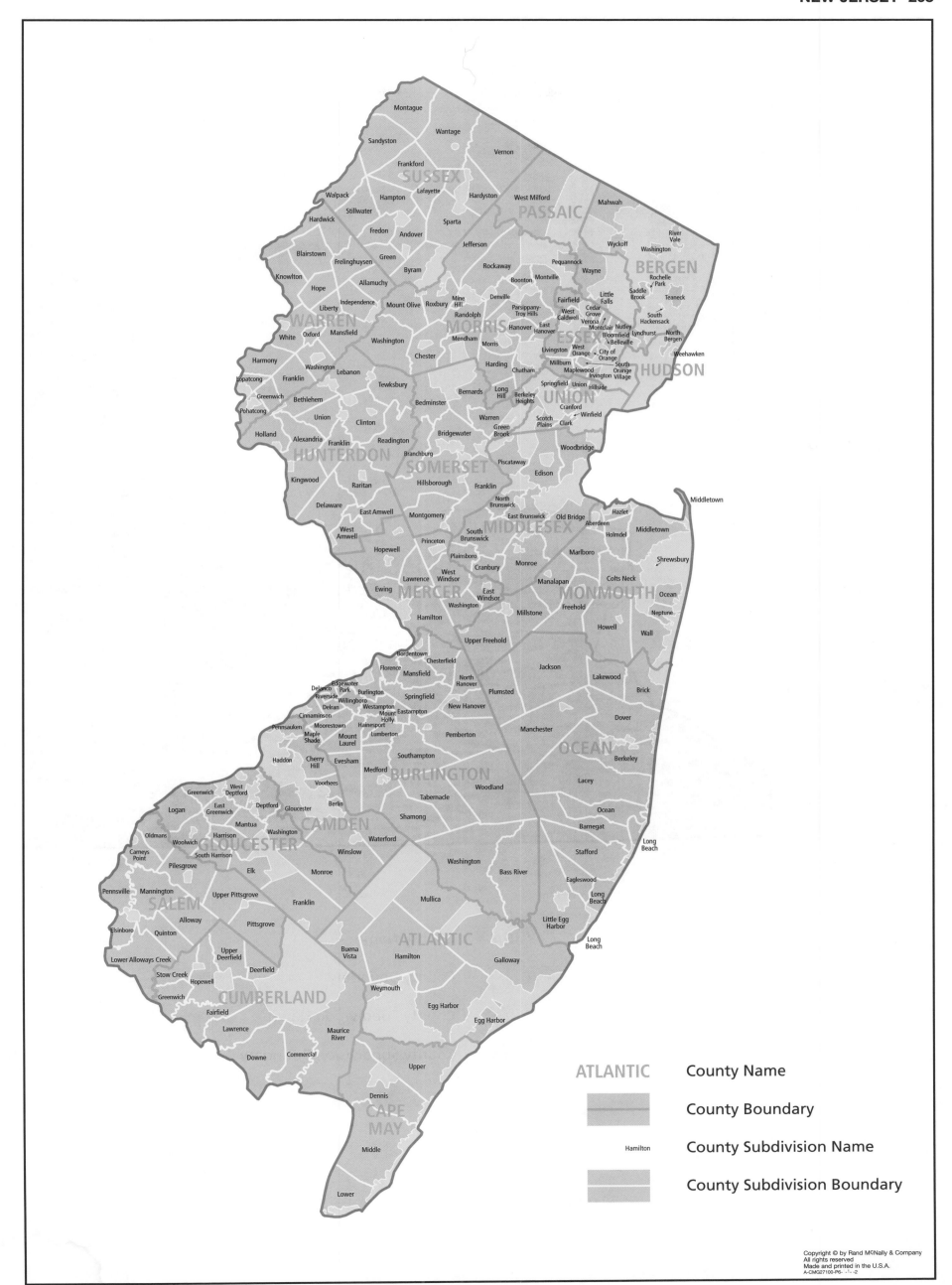

ATLANTIC County Name

County Boundary

Hamilton County Subdivision Name

County Subdivision Boundary

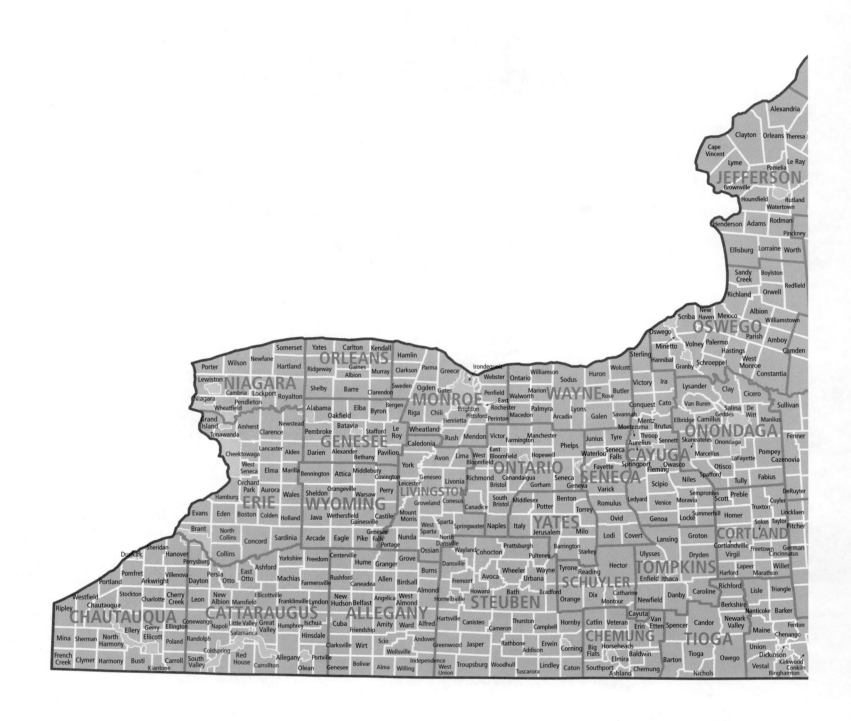

CAYUGA   County Name

County Boundary

Eaton   County Subdivision Name

County Subdivision Boundary

County names (large labels): OTTAWA, LUCAS, WILLIAMS, FULTON, OTTAWA, DEFIANCE, HENRY, WOOD, SANDUSKY, SENECA, PAULDING, PUTNAM, HANCOCK, WYANDOT, CRAWFORD, VAN WERT, ALLEN, HARDIN, MARION, MORROW, MERCER, AUGLAIZE, LOGAN, UNION, DELAWARE, SHELBY, DARKE, MIAMI, CHAMPAIGN, FRANKLIN, CLARK, MADISON, PREBLE, MONTGOMERY, GREENE, PICKAWAY, FAYETTE, CLINTON, ROSS, BUTLER, WARREN, HAMILTON, HIGHLAND, PIKE, CLERMONT, BROWN, ADAMS, SCIOTO

Put-in-Bay, Catawba Island, Danbury

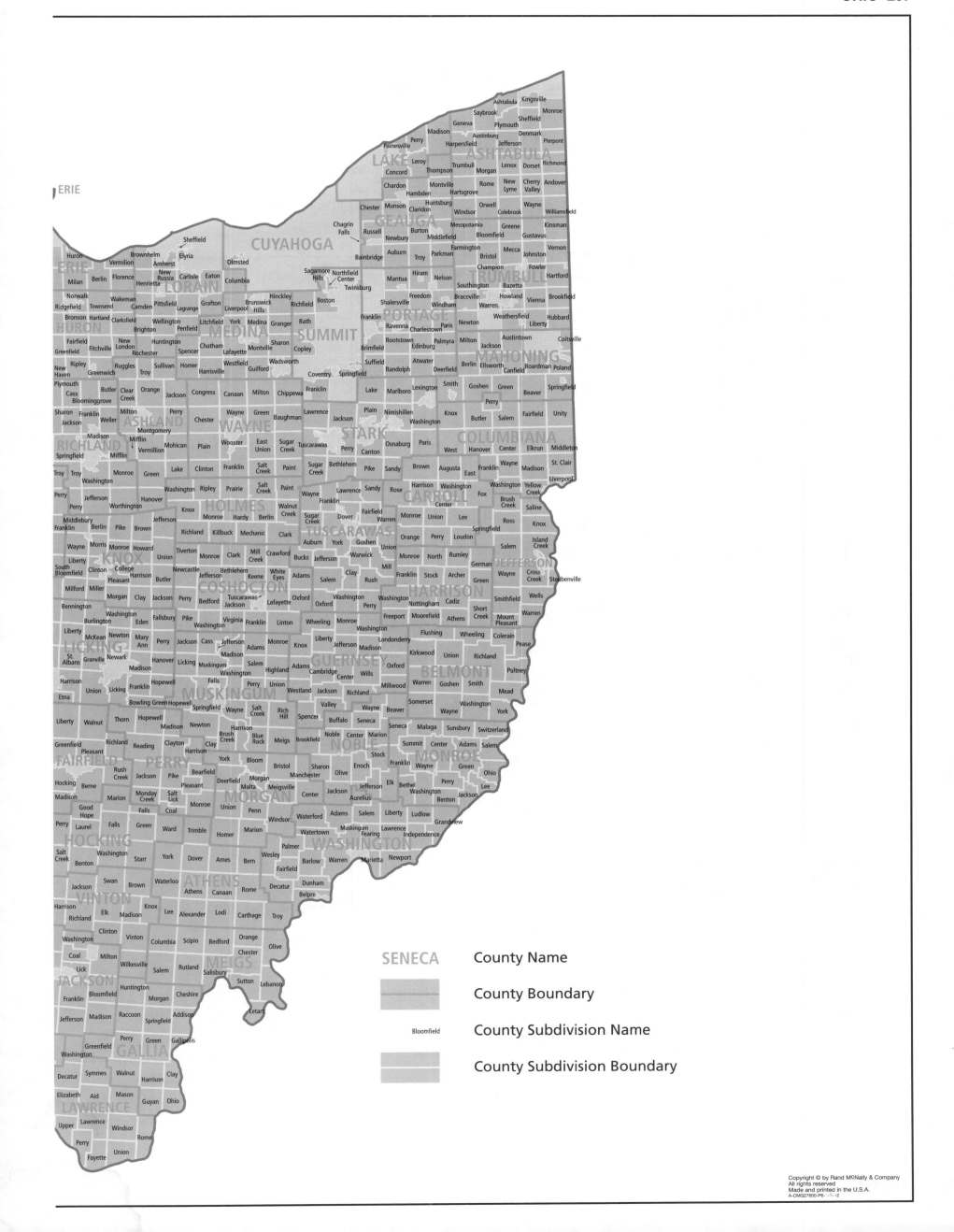

SENECA County Name

County Boundary

Bloomfield County Subdivision Name

County Subdivision Boundary

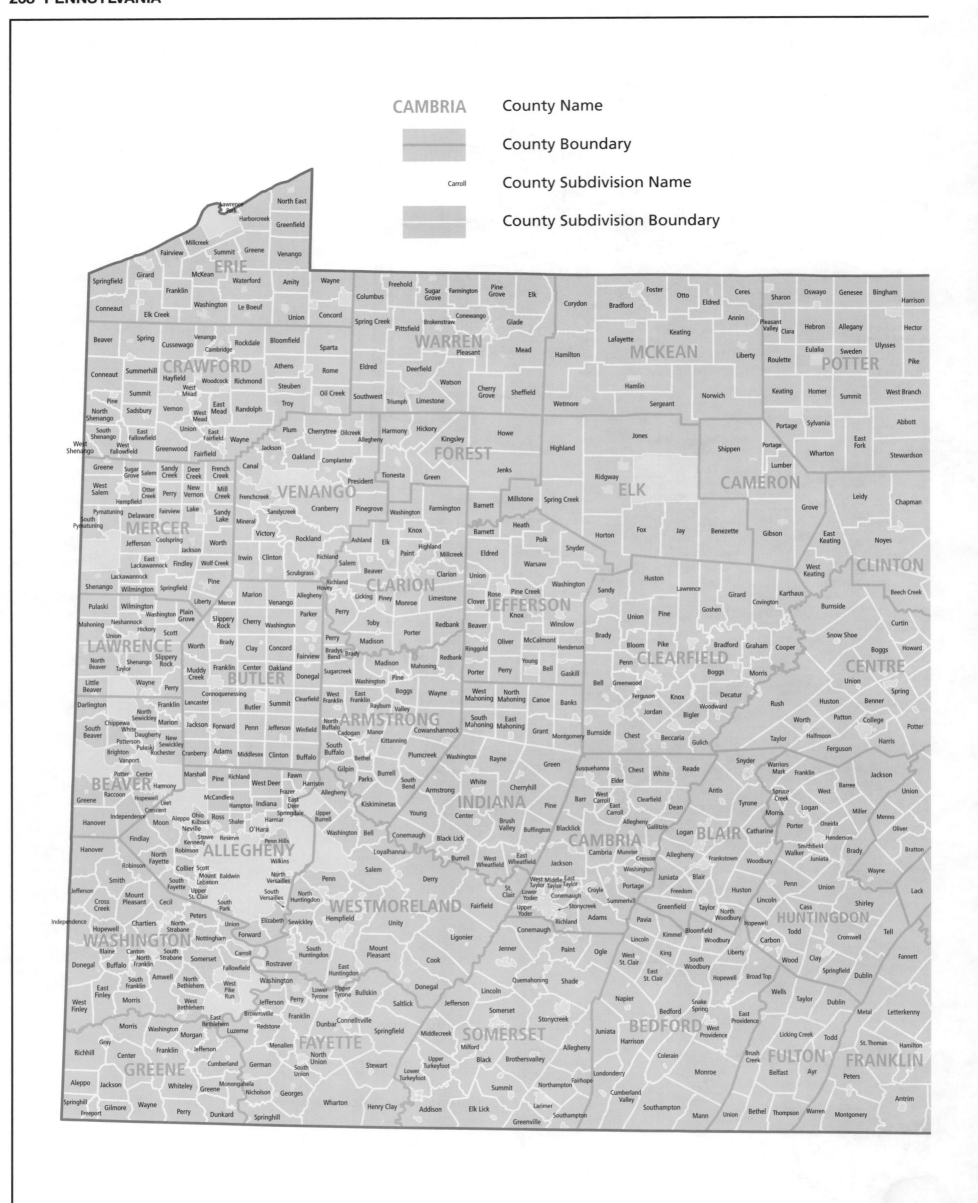

CAMBRIA — County Name

County Boundary

Carroll — County Subdivision Name

County Subdivision Boundary

CHESTER

1 North Coventry
2 East Coventry
3 East Vincent
4 East Pikeland
5 Schuylkill
6 Tredyffrin
7 Easttown
8 South Coventry
9 West Vincent
10 West Pikeland
11 Charlestown
12 East Whiteland
13 Willistown
14 Warwick
15 East Nantmeal
16 Upper Uwchlan
17 Uwchlan
18 West Whiteland
19 West Goshen
20 East Goshen
21 Westtown
22 Thornbury
23 West Nantmeal
24 Wallace
25 East Brandywine
26 East Caln
27 East Bradford
28 Birmingham
29 West Brandywine
30 Caln
31 West Bradford
32 Pocopson
33 Pennsbury
34 Honeybrook
35 West Caln
36 Valley
37 East Fallowfield
38 Newlin
39 East Marlborough
40 Kennett
41 Sadsbury
42 Highland
43 West Marlborough
44 London Grove
45 New Garden
46 West Sadsbury
47 West Fallowfield
48 Londonderry
49 Penn
50 New London
51 Franklin
52 London Britain
53 Upper Oxford
54 Lower Oxford
55 East Nottingham
56 West Nottingham
57 Elk

DELAWARE

1 Radnor
2 Haverford
3 Upper Darby
4 Newtown
5 Marple
6 Springfield
7 Darby
8 Upper Providence
9 Nether Providence
10 Ridley
11 Tinicum
12 Edgmont
13 Middletown
14 Aston
15 Chester
16 Thornbury
17 Concord
18 Bethel
19 Upper Chichester
20 Lower Chichester
21 Chadds Ford

MONTGOMERY

1 Upper Hanover
2 Marlborough
3 Salford
4 Franconia
5 Hatfield
6 Montgomery
7 Horsham
8 Upper Moreland
9 Lower Moreland
10 Douglass
11 New Hanover
12 Upper Frederick
13 Lower Frederick
14 Upper Salford
15 Lower Salford
16 Towamencin
17 Upper Gwynedd
18 Lower Gwynedd
19 Upper Dublin
20 Abington
21 Perkiomen
22 Skippack
23 Worcester
24 East Norriton
25 Whitpain
26 Whitemarsh
27 Springfield
28 Cheltenham
29 Upper Pottsgrove
30 West Pottsgrove
31 Lower Pottsgrove
32 Limerick
33 Upper Providence
34 Lower Providence
35 West Norriton
36 Upper Merion
37 Plymouth
38 Lower Merion

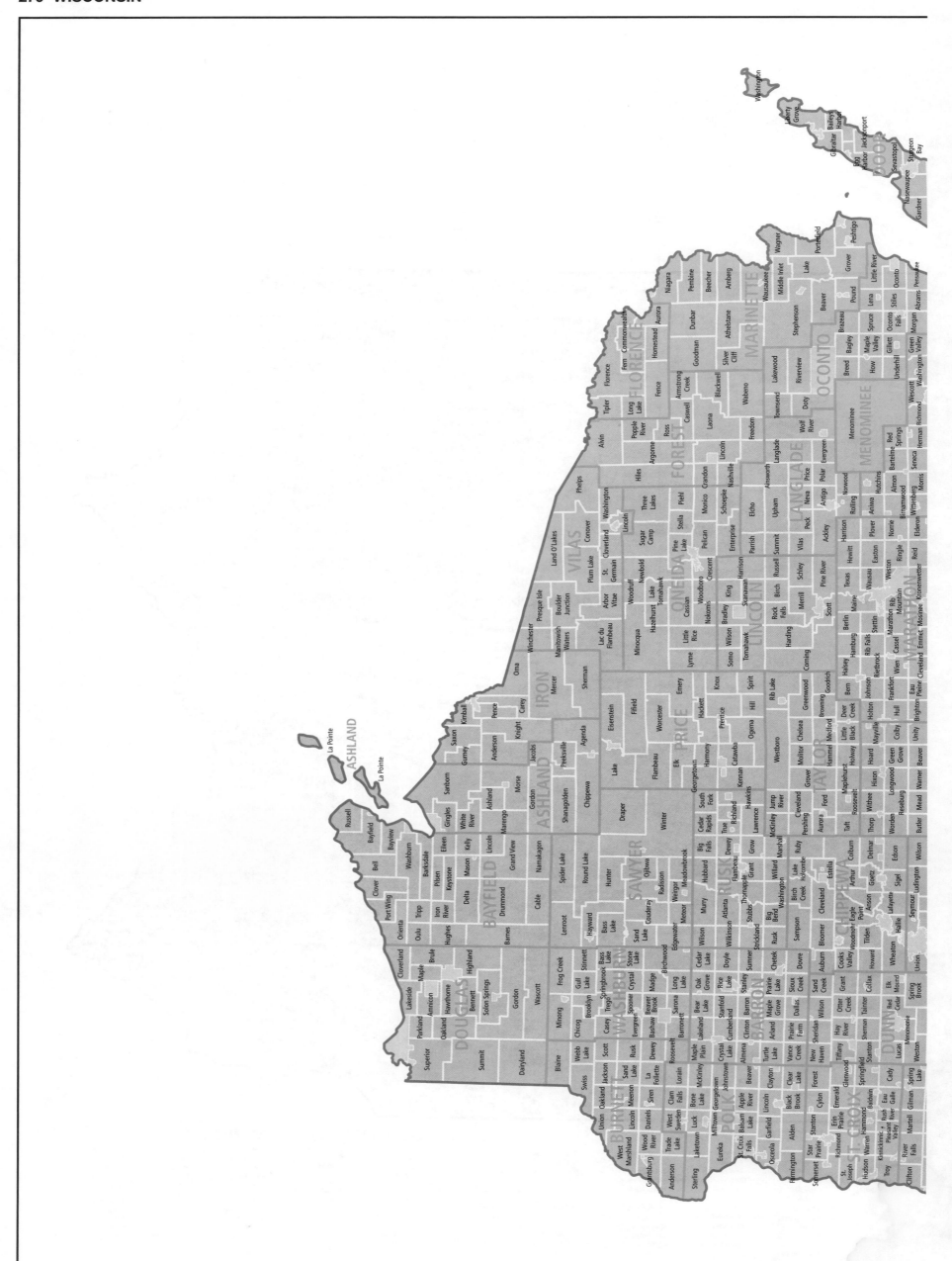

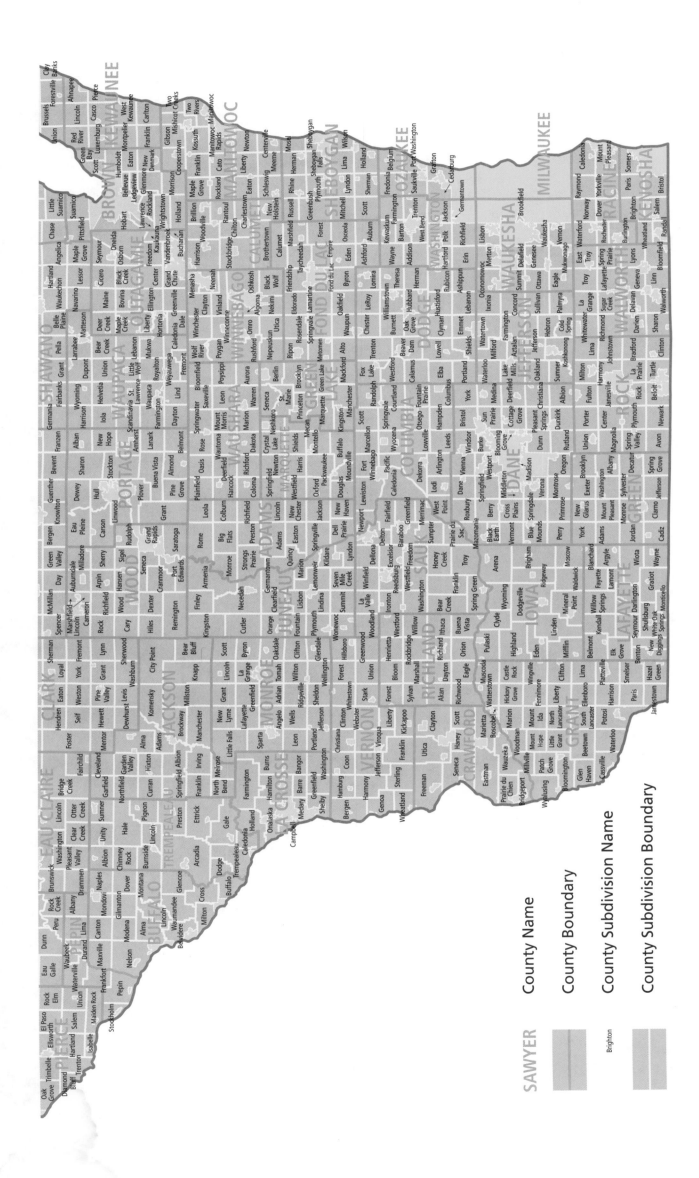

SAWYER — County Name

[——————] County Boundary

Brighton — County Subdivision Name

[——————] County Subdivision Boundary